Summa 365, Read the Summa in One Year
ST. THOMAS AQUINAS
SUMMA THEOLOGICA

SUMMA THEOLOGICA (Benziger Bros. edition, 1947)

Translated by Fathers of the English Dominican Province

Acknowledgment: This book was produced by T.J. Burdick through FreeTheology.com

Article. 1 - Whether Christ's Resurrection is the cause of the resurrection of our bodies?
Article. 2 - Whether Christ's Resurrection is the cause of the resurrection of souls?
Question. 57 - OF THE ASCENSION OF CHRIST (SIX ARTICLES)
Article. 1 - Whether it was fitting for Christ to ascend into heaven?
Article. 2 - Whether Christ's Ascension into heaven belonged to Him according to His Divine Nature?
Article. 3 - Whether Christ ascended by His own power?
Article. 4 - Whether Christ ascended above all the heavens?
Article. 5 - Whether Christ's body ascended above every spiritual creature?
Article. 6 - Whether Christ's Ascension is the cause of our salvation?

Question. 58 - OF CHRIST'S SITTING AT THE RIGHT HAND OF THE FATHER (FOUR ARTICLES)
Article. 1 - Whether it is fitting that Christ should sit at the right hand of God the Father?
Article. 2 - Whether it belongs to Christ as God to sit at the right hand of the Father?
Article. 3 - Whether it belongs to Christ as man to sit at the right hand of the Father?
Article. 4 - Whether it is proper to Christ to sit at the right hand of the Father?
Question. 59 - OF CHRIST'S JUDICIARY POWER (SIX ARTICLES)
Article. 1 - Whether judiciary power is to be specially attributed to Christ?
Article. 2 - Whether judiciary power belongs to Christ as man?
Article. 3 - Whether Christ acquired His judiciary power by His merits?
Article. 4 - Whether judiciary power belongs to Christ with respect to all human affairs?

Article. 5 - Whether after the Judgment that takes place in the present time, there remains yet another General Judgment?
Article. 6 - Whether Christ's judiciary power extends to the angels?
TREATISE ON THE SACRAMENTS (QQ[60]-90)
Question. 60 - WHAT IS A SACRAMENT? (EIGHT ARTICLES)
Article. 1 - Whether a sacrament is a kind of sign?
Article. 2 - Whether every sign of a holy thing is a sacrament?
Article. 3 - Whether a sacrament is a sign of one thing only?
Article. 4 - Whether a sacrament is always something sensible?
Article. 5 - Whether determinate things are required for a sacrament?
Article. 6 - Whether words are required for the signification of the sacraments?

Article. 7 - Whether determinate words are required in the sacraments?
Article. 8 - Whether it is lawful to add anything to the words in which the sacramental form consists?
Question. 61 - OF THE NECESSITY OF THE SACRAMENTS (FOUR ARTICLES)
Article. 1 - Whether sacraments are necessary for man's salvation?
Article. 2 - Whether before sin sacraments were necessary to man?
Article. 3 - Whether there should have been sacraments after sin, before Christ?
Article. 4 - Whether there was need for any sacraments after Christ came?
Question. 62 - OF THE SACRAMENTS' PRINCIPAL EFFECT, WHICH IS GRACE (SIX ARTICLES)
Article. 1 - Whether the sacraments are the cause of grace?
Article. 2 - Whether sacramental grace confers anything in addition to the grace of the virtues and gifts?

Article. 3 - Whether the sacraments of the New Law contain grace?
Article. 4 - Whether there be in the sacraments a power of causing grace?
Article. 5 - Whether the sacraments of the New Law derive their power from Christ's Passion?
Article. 6 - Whether the sacraments of the Old Law caused grace?
Question. 63 - OF THE OTHER EFFECT OF THE SACRAMENTS, WHICH IS A CHARACTER (SIX ARTICLES)
Article. 1 - Whether a sacrament imprints a character on the soul?
Article. 2 - Whether a character is a spiritual power?
Article. 3 - Whether the sacramental character is the character of Christ?
Article. 4 - Whether the character be subjected in the powers of the soul?

Article. 5 - Whether a character can be blotted out from the soul?
Article. 6 - Whether a character is imprinted by each sacrament of the New Law?
Question. 64 - OF THE CAUSES OF THE SACRAMENTS (TEN ARTICLES)
Article. 1 - Whether God alone, or the minister also, works inwardly unto the sacramental effect?
Article. 2 - Whether the sacraments are instituted by God alone?
Article. 3 - Whether Christ as man had the power of producing the inward sacramental effect?
Article. 4 - Whether Christ could communicate to ministers the power which He had in the sacraments?
Article. 5 - Whether the sacraments can be conferred by evil ministers?
Article. 6 - Whether wicked men sin in administering the sacraments?

Article. 7 - Whether angels can administer sacraments?
Article. 8 - Whether the minister's intention is required for the validity of a sacrament?
Article. 9 - Whether faith is required of necessity in the minister of a sacrament?
Article. 10 - Whether the validity of a sacrament requires a good intention in the minister?
Question. 65 - OF THE NUMBER OF THE SACRAMENTS (FOUR ARTICLES)
Article. 1 - Whether there should be seven sacraments?
Article. 2 - Whether the order of the sacraments, as given above, is becoming?
Article. 3 - Whether the Eucharist is the greatest of the sacraments?
Article. 4 - Whether all the sacraments are necessary for salvation?

Question. 66 - OF THE SACRAMENT OF BAPTISM (TWELVE ARTICLES)
Article. 1 - Whether Baptism is the mere washing?
Article. 2 - Whether Baptism was instituted after Christ's Passion?
Article. 3 - Whether water is the proper matter of Baptism?
Article. 4 - Whether plain water is necessary for Baptism?
Article. 5 - Whether this be a suitable form of Baptism: 'I baptize thee in the name of the Father, and of the Son, and of the Holy Ghost'?
Article. 6 - Whether Baptism can be conferred in the name of Christ?
Article. 7 - Whether immersion in water is necessary for Baptism?
Article. 8 - Whether trine immersion is essential to Baptism?

Article. 9 - Whether Baptism may be reiterated?
Article. 10 - Whether the Church observes a suitable rite in baptizing?
Article. 11 - Whether three kinds of Baptism are fittingly described----viz. Baptism of Water, of Blood, and of the Spirit?
Article. 12 - Whether the Baptism of Blood is the most excellent of these?
Question. 67 - OF THE MINISTERS BY WHOM THE SACRAMENT OF BAPTISM IS CONFERRED (EIGHT ARTICLES)
Article. 1 - Whether it is part of a deacon's duty to baptize?
Article. 2 - Whether to baptize is part of the priestly office, or proper to that of bishops?
Article. 3 - Whether a layman can baptize?
Article. 4 - Whether a woman can baptize?

Article. 5 - Whether one that is not baptized can confer the sacrament of Baptism?
Article. 6 - Whether several can baptize at the same time?
Article. 7 - Whether in Baptism it is necessary for someone to raise the baptized from the sacred font?
Article. 8 - Whether he who raises anyone from the sacred font is bound to instruct him?
Question. 68 - OF THOSE WHO RECEIVE BAPTISM (TWELVE ARTICLES)
Article. 1 - Whether all are bound to receive Baptism?
Article. 2 - Whether a man can be saved without Baptism?
Article. 3 - Whether Baptism should be deferred?
Article. 4 - Whether sinners should be baptized?

Article. 5 - Whether works of satisfaction should be enjoined on sinners that have been baptized?
Article. 6 - Whether sinners who are going to be baptized are bound to confess their sins?
Article. 7 - Whether the intention of receiving the sacrament of Baptism is required on the part of the one baptized?
Article. 8 - Whether faith is required on the part of the one baptized?
Article. 9 - Whether children should be baptized?
Article. 10 - Whether children of Jews or other unbelievers be baptized against the will of their parents?
Article. 11 - Whether a child can be baptized while yet in its mother's womb?
Article. 12 - Whether madmen and imbeciles should be baptized?

Question. 69 - OF THE EFFECTS OF BAPTISM (TEN ARTICLES)
Article. 1 - Whether all sins are taken away by Baptism?

Article. 2 - Whether man is freed by Baptism from all debt of punishment due to sin?
Article. 3 - Whether Baptism should take away the penalties of sin that belong to this life?
Article. 4 - Whether grace and virtues are bestowed on man by Baptism?
Article. 5 - Whether certain acts of the virtues are fittingly set down as effects of Baptism, to wit---incorporation in Christ, enlightenment, and fruitfulness?
Article. 6 - Whether children receive grace and virtue in Baptism?
Article. 7 - Whether the effect of Baptism is to open the gates of the heavenly kingdom?
Article. 8 - Whether Baptism has an equal effect in all?

Day 298

Article. 9 - Whether insincerity hinders the effect of Baptism?
Article. 10 - Whether Baptism produces its effect when the insincerity ceases?
Question. 70 - OF CIRCUMCISION (FOUR ARTICLES)
    Article. 1 - Whether circumcision was a preparation for, and a figure of Baptism?
    Article. 2 - Whether circumcision was instituted in a fitting manner?
    Article. 3 - Whether the rite of circumcision was fitting?
    Article. 4 - Whether circumcision bestowed sanctifying grace?
Question. 71 - OF THE PREPARATIONS THAT ACCOMPANY BAPTISM (FOUR ARTICLES)
    Article. 1 - Whether catechism should precede Baptism?
    Article. 2 - Whether exorcism should precede Baptism?

Day 299

Article. 3 - Whether what is done in the exorcism effects anything, or is a mere sign?
Article. 4 - Whether it belongs to a priest to catechize and exorcize the person to be baptized?
Question. 72 - CONFIRMATION (Q[72])
    Article. 1 - Whether confirmation is a sacrament?
    Article. 2 - Whether chrism is a fitting matter for this sacrament?
    Article. 3 - Whether it is essential to this sacrament that the chrism which is its matter be previously consecrated by a bishop?
    Article. 4 - Whether the proper form of this sacrament is: 'I sign thee with the sign of the cross,' etc.?
    Article. 5 - Whether the sacrament of Confirmation imprints a character?
    Article. 6 - Whether the character of Confirmation presupposes of necessity, the baptismal character?

Day 300

Article. 7 - Whether sanctifying grace is bestowed in this sacrament?
Article. 8 - Whether this sacrament should be given to all?
Article. 9 - Whether this sacrament should be given to man on the forehead?
Article. 10 - Whether he who is confirmed needs one to stand* for him? [*Literally, 'to hold him']
Article. 11 - Whether only a bishop can confer this sacrament?
Article. 12 - Whether the rite of this sacrament is appropriate?
Question. 73 - OF THE SACRAMENT OF THE EUCHARIST (SIX ARTICLES)
    Article. 1 - Whether the Eucharist is a sacrament?
    Article. 2 - Whether the Eucharist is one sacrament or several?

Day 301

Article. 3 - Whether the Eucharist is necessary for salvation?
Article. 4 - Whether this sacrament is suitably called by various names?
Article. 5 - Whether the institution of this sacrament was appropriate?
Article. 6 - Whether the Paschal Lamb was the chief figure of this sacrament?
Question. 74 - OF THE MATTER OF THIS SACRAMENT (EIGHT ARTICLES)
    Article. 1 - Whether the matter of this sacrament is bread and wine?
    Article. 2 - Whether a determinate quantity of bread and wine is required for the matter of this sacrament?
    Article. 3 - Whether wheaten bread is required for the matter of this sacrament?
    Article. 4 - Whether this sacrament ought to be made of unleavened bread?

Day 302

Article. 5 - Whether wine of the grape is the proper matter of this sacrament?
Article. 6 - Whether water should be mixed with the wine?
Article. 7 - Whether the mixing with water is essential to this sacrament?
Article. 8 - Whether water should be added in great quantity?
Question. 75 - OF THE CHANGE OF BREAD AND WINE INTO THE BODY AND BLOOD OF CHRIST (EIGHT ARTICLES)
    Article. 1 - Whether the body of Christ be in this sacrament in very truth, or merely as in a figure or sign?
    Article. 2 - Whether in this sacrament the substance of the bread and wine remains after the consecration?
    Article. 3 - Whether the substance of the bread or wine is annihilated after the consecration of this sacrament, or dissolved into their original matter?
    Article. 4 - Whether bread can be converted into the body of Christ?

Day 303

Article. 5 - Whether the accidents of the bread and wine remain in this sacrament after the change?
Article. 6 - Whether the substantial form of the bread remains in this sacrament after the consecration?
Article. 7 - Whether this change is wrought instantaneously?
Article. 8 - Whether this proposition is false: 'The body of Christ is made out of bread'?
Question. 76 - OF THE WAY IN WHICH CHRIST IS IN THIS SACRAMENT (EIGHT ARTICLES)
    Article. 1 - Whether the whole Christ is contained under this sacrament?
    Article. 2 - Whether the whole Christ is contained under each species of this sacrament?
    Article. 3 - Whether Christ is entire under every part of the species of the bread and wine?
    Article. 4 - Whether the whole dimensive quantity of Christ's body is in this sacrament?

Day 304

Article. 5 - Whether Christ's body is in this sacrament as in a place?
Article. 6 - Whether Christ's body is in this sacrament movably?
Article. 7 - Whether the body of Christ, as it is in this sacrament, can be seen by any eye, at least by a glorified one?
Article. 8 - Whether Christ's body is truly there when flesh or a child appears miraculously in this sacrament?
Question. 77 - OF THE ACCIDENTS WHICH REMAIN IN THIS SACRAMENT (EIGHT ARTICLES)
    Article. 1 - Whether the accidents remain in this sacrament without a subject?
    Article. 2 - Whether in this sacrament the dimensive quantity of the bread or wine is the subject of the other accidents?
    Article. 3 - Whether the species remaining in this sacrament can change external objects?
    Article. 4 - Whether the sacramental species can be corrupted?

Day 305

Article. 5 - Whether anything can be generated from the sacramental species?
Article. 6 - Whether the sacramental species can nourish?
Article. 7 - Whether the sacramental species are broken in this sacrament?
Article. 8 - Whether any liquid can be mingled with the consecrated wine?
Question. 78 - OF THE FORM OF THIS SACRAMENT (SIX ARTICLES)
    Article. 1 - Whether this is the form of this sacrament: 'This is My body,' and 'This is the chalice of My blood'?
    Article. 2 - Whether this is the proper form for the consecration of the bread: 'This is My body'?
    Article. 3 - Whether this is the proper form for the consecration of the wine: 'This is the chalice of My blood,' etc.?
    Article. 4 - Whether in the aforesaid words of the forms there be any created power which causes the consecration?

Day 306

Article. 5 - Whether the aforesaid expressions are true?
Article. 6 - Whether the form of the consecration of the bread accomplishes its effect before the form of the consecration of the wine be completed?
Question. 79 - OF THE EFFECTS OF THIS SACRAMENT (EIGHT ARTICLES)
    Article. 1 - Whether grace is bestowed through this sacrament?
    Article. 2 - Whether the attaining of glory is an effect of this sacrament?
    Article. 3 - Whether the forgiveness of mortal sin is an effect of this sacrament?
    Article. 4 - Whether venial sins are forgiven through this sacrament?
    Article. 5 - Whether the entire punishment due to sin is forgiven through this sacrament?
    Article. 6 - Whether man is preserved by this sacrament from future sins?

Day 307

Article. 7 - Whether this sacrament benefit others besides the recipients?
Article. 8 - Whether the effect of this sacrament is hindered by venial sin?
Question. 80 - OF THE USE OR RECEIVING OF THIS SACRAMENT IN GENERAL (TWELVE ARTICLES)
    Article. 1 - Whether there are two ways to be distinguished of eating Christ's body?
    Article. 2 - Whether it belongs to man alone to eat this sacrament spiritually?
    Article. 3 - Whether the just man alone may eat Christ sacramentally?
    Article. 4 - Whether the sinner sins in receiving Christ's body sacramentally?
    Article. 5 - Whether to approach this sacrament with consciousness of sin is the gravest of all sins?
    Article. 6 - Whether the priest ought to deny the body of Christ to the sinner seeking it?
    Article. 7 - Whether the seminal loss that occurs during sleep hinders anyone from receiving this sacrament?

Day 308

Article. 8 - Whether food or drink taken beforehand hinders the receiving of this sacrament?
Article. 9 - Whether those who have not the use of reason ought to receive this sacrament?
Article. 10 - Whether it is lawful to receive this sacrament daily?
Article. 11 - Whether it is lawful to abstain altogether from communion?

11

OF MARTYRDOM (FIVE ARTICLES)

We must now consider martyrdom, under which head there are five points of inquiry:

(1) Whether martyrdom is an act of virtue?

(2) Of what virtue is it the act?

(3) Concerning the perfection of this act;

(4) The pain of martyrdom;

(5) Its cause.

Whether martyrdom is an act of virtue?

Objection 1: It seems that martyrdom is not an act of virtue. For all acts of virtue are voluntary. But martyrdom is sometimes not voluntary, as in the case of the Innocents who were slain for Christ's sake, and of whom Hillary says (Super Matth. i) that "they attained the ripe age of eternity through the glory of martyrdom." Therefore martyrdom is not an act of virtue.

Objection 2: Further, nothing unlawful is an act of virtue. Now it is unlawful to kill oneself, as stated above ([3302]Q[64], A[5]), and yet martyrdom is achieved by so doing: for Augustine says (De Civ. Dei i) that "during persecution certain holy women, in order to escape from those who threatened their chastity, threw themselves into a river, and so ended their lives, and their martyrdom is honored in the Catholic Church with most solemn veneration." Therefore martyrdom is not an act of virtue.

Objection 3: Further, it is praiseworthy to offer oneself to do an act of virtue. But it is not praiseworthy to court martyrdom, rather would it seem to be presumptuous and rash. Therefore martyrdom is not an act of virtue.

On the contrary, The reward of beatitude is not due save to acts of virtue. Now it is due to martyrdom, since it is written (Mat. 5:10): "Blessed are they that suffer persecution for justice' sake, for theirs is the kingdom of heaven." Therefore martyrdom is an act of virtue.

I answer that, As stated above ([3303]Q[123], AA[1],3), it belongs to virtue to safeguard man in the good of reason. Now the good of reason consists in the truth as its proper object, and in justice as its proper effect, as shown above ([3304]Q[109], AA[1],2;[3305] Q[123], A[12]). And martyrdom consists essentially in standing firmly to truth and justice against the assaults of persecution. Hence it is evident that martyrdom is an act of virtue.

Reply to Objection 1: Some have said that in the case of the Innocents the use of their free will was miraculously accelerated, so that they suffered martyrdom even voluntarily. Since, however, Scripture contains no proof of this, it is better to say that these babes in being slain obtained by God's grace the glory of martyrdom which others acquire by their own will. For the shedding of one's blood for Christ's sake takes the place of Baptism. Wherefore just as in the case of baptized children the merit of Christ is conducive to the acquisition of glory through the baptismal grace, so in those who were slain for Christ's sake the merit of Christ's martyrdom is conducive to the acquisition of the martyr's palm. Hence Augustine says in a sermon on the Epiphany (De Diversis lxvi), as though he were addressing them: "A man that does not believe that children are benefited by the baptism of Christ will doubt of your being crowned in suffering for Christ. You were not old enough to believe in Christ's future sufferings, but you had a body wherein you could endure suffering of Christ Who was to suffer."

Reply to Objection 2: Augustine says (De Civ. Dei i) that "possibly the Church was induced by certain credible witnesses of Divine authority thus to honor the memory of those holy women [*Cf.[3306] Q[64], A[1], ad 2]."

Reply to Objection 3: The precepts of the Law are about acts of virtue. Now it has been stated ([3307]FS, Q[108], A[1], ad 4) that some of the precepts of the Divine Law are to be understood in reference to the preparation of the mind, in the sense that man ought to be prepared to do such and such a thing, whenever expedient. In the same way certain things belong to an act of virtue as regards the preparation of the mind, so that in such and such a case a man should act according to reason. And this observation would seem very much to the point in the case of martyrdom, which consists in the right endurance of sufferings unjustly inflicted. Nor ought a man to give another an occasion of acting unjustly: yet if anyone act unjustly, one ought to endure it in moderation.

Whether martyrdom is an act of fortitude?

Objection 1: It seems that martyrdom is not an act of fortitude. For the Greek {martyr} signifies a witness. Now witness is borne to the faith of Christ. according to Acts 1:8, "You shall be witnesses unto Me," etc. and Maximus says in a sermon: "The mother of martyrs is the Catholic faith which those glorious warriors have sealed with their blood." Therefore martyrdom is an act of faith rather than of fortitude.

Objection 2: Further, a praiseworthy act belongs chiefly to the virtue which inclines thereto, is manifested thereby, and without which the act avails nothing. Now charity is the chief incentive to martyrdom: Thus Maximus says in a sermon: "The charity of Christ is victorious in His martyrs." Again the greatest proof of charity lies in the act of martyrdom, according to Jn. 15:13, "Greater love than this no man hath, that a man lay down his life for his friends." Moreover without charity martyrdom avails nothing, according to 1 Cor. 13:3, "If I should deliver my body to be burned, and have not charity, it profiteth me nothing." Therefore martyrdom is an act of charity rather than of fortitude.

Objection 3: Further, Augustine says in a sermon on St. Cyprian: "It is easy to honor a martyr by singing his praises, but it is a great thing to imitate his faith and patience." Now that which calls chiefly for praise in a virtuous act, is the virtue of which it is the act. Therefore martyrdom is an act of patience rather than of fortitude.

On the contrary, Cyprian says (Ep. ad Mart. et Conf. ii): "Blessed martyrs, with what praise shall I extol you? Most valiant warriors, how shall I find words to proclaim the strength of your courage?" Now a person is praised on account of the virtue whose act he performs. Therefore martyrdom is an act of fortitude.

I answer that, As stated above ([3308]Q[123], A[1], seqq.), it belongs to fortitude to strengthen man in the good of virtue, especially against dangers, and chiefly against dangers of death, and most of all against those that occur in battle. Now it is evident that in martyrdom man is firmly strengthened in the good of virtue, since he cleaves to faith and justice notwithstanding the threatening danger of death, the imminence of which is moreover due to a kind of particular contest with his persecutors. Hence Cyprian says in a sermon (Ep. ad Mart. et Conf. ii): "The crowd of onlookers wondered to see an unearthly battle, and Christ's servants fighting erect, undaunted in speech, with souls unmoved, and strength divine." Wherefore it is evident that martyrdom is an act of fortitude; for which reason the Church reads in the office of Martyrs: They "became valiant in battle" [*Heb. 11:34].

Reply to Objection 1: Two things must be considered in the act of fortitude. one is the good wherein the brave man is strengthened, and this is the end of fortitude; the other is the firmness itself, whereby a man does not yield to the contraries that hinder him from achieving that good, and in this consists the essence of fortitude. Now just as civic fortitude strengthens a man's mind in human justice, for the safeguarding of which he braves the danger of death, so gratuitous fortitude strengthens man's soul in the good of Divine justice, which is "through faith in Christ Jesus," according to Rom. 3:22. Thus martyrdom is related to faith as the end in which one is strengthened, but to fortitude as the eliciting habit.

Reply to Objection 2: Charity inclines one to the act of martyrdom, as its first and chief motive cause, being the virtue commanding it, whereas fortitude inclines thereto as being its proper motive cause, being the virtue that elicits it. Hence martyrdom is an act of charity as commanding, and of fortitude as eliciting. For this reason also it manifests both virtues. It is due to charity that it is meritorious, like any other act of virtue: and for this reason it avails not without charity.

Reply to Objection 3: As stated above ([3309]Q[123], A[6]), the chief act of fortitude is endurance: to this and not to its secondary act, which is aggression, martyrdom belongs. And since patience serves fortitude on the part of its chief act, viz. endurance, hence it is that martyrs are also praised for their patience.

Whether martyrdom is an act of the greatest perfection?

Objection 1: It seems that martyrdom is not an act of the greatest perfection. For seemingly that which is a matter of counsel and not of precept pertains to perfection, because, to wit, it is not necessary for salvation. But it would seem that martyrdom is necessary for salvation, since the Apostle says (Rom. 10:10), "With the heart we believe unto justice, but with the mouth confession is made unto salvation," and it is written (1 Jn. 3:16), that "we ought to lay down our lives for the brethren." Therefore martyrdom does not pertain to perfection.

Objection 2: Further, it seems to point to greater perfection that a man give his soul to God, which is done by obedience, than that he give God his body, which is done by martyrdom: wherefore Gregory says (Moral. xxxv) that "obedience is preferable to all sacrifices." Therefore martyrdom is not an act of the greatest perfection.

Objection 3: Further, it would seem better to do good to others than to maintain oneself in good, since the "good of the nation is better than the good of the individual," according to the Philosopher (Ethic. i, 2). Now he that suffers martyrdom profits himself alone, whereas he that teaches does good to many. Therefore the act of teaching and guiding subjects is more perfect than the act of martyrdom.

On the contrary, Augustine (De Sanct. Virgin. xlvi) prefers martyrdom to virginity which pertains to perfection. Therefore martyrdom seems to belong to perfection in the highest degree.

I answer that, We may speak of an act of virtue in two ways. First, with regard to the species of that act, as compared to the virtue proximately eliciting it. In this way martyrdom, which consists in the due endurance of death, cannot be the most perfect of virtuous acts, because endurance of death is not praiseworthy in itself, but only in so far as it is directed to some good consisting in an act of virtue, such as faith or the love of God, so that this act of virtue being the end is better.

A virtuous act may be considered in another way, in comparison with its first motive cause, which is the love of charity, and it is in this respect that an act comes to belong to the perfection of life, since, as the Apostle says (Col. 3:14), that "charity . . . is the bond of perfection." Now, of all virtuous acts martyrdom is the greatest proof of the perfection of charity: since a man's love for a thing is proved to be so much the greater, according as that which he despises for its sake is more dear to him, or that which he chooses to suffer for its sake is more odious. But it is evident that of all the goods of the present life man loves life itself most, and on the other hand he hates death more than anything, especially when it is accompanied by the pains of bodily torment, "from fear of which even dumb animals refrain from the greatest pleasures," as Augustine observes (QQ[83], qu. 36). And from this point of view it is clear that martyrdom is the most perfect of human acts in respect of its genus, as being the sign of the greatest charity, according to Jn. 15:13: "Greater love than this no man hath, that a man lay down his life for his friends."

Reply to Objection 1: There is no act of perfection, which is a matter of counsel, but what in certain cases is a matter of precept, as being necessary for salvation. Thus Augustine declares (De Adult. Conjug. xiii) that a man is under the obligation of observing continency, through the absence or sickness of his wife. Hence it is not contrary to the perfection of martyrdom if in certain cases it be necessary for salvation, since there are cases when it is not necessary for salvation to suffer martyrdom; thus we read of many holy martyrs who through zeal for the faith or brotherly love gave themselves up to martyrdom of their own accord. As to these precepts, they are to be understood as referring to the preparation of the mind.

Reply to Objection 2: Martyrdom embraces the highest possible degree of obedience, namely obedience unto death; thus we read of Christ (Phil. 2:8) that He became "obedient unto death." Hence it is evident that martyrdom is of itself more perfect than obedience considered absolutely.

Reply to Objection 3: This argument considers martyrdom according to the proper species of its act, whence it derives no excellence over all other virtuous acts; thus neither is fortitude more excellent than all virtues.

Whether death is essential to martyrdom?

Objection 1: It seems that death is not essential to martyrdom. For Jerome says in a sermon on the Assumption (Epist. ad Paul. et Eustoch.): "I should say rightly that the Mother of God was both virgin and martyr, although she ended her days in peace": and Gregory says (Hom. iii in Evang.): "Although persecution has ceased to offer the opportunity, yet the peace we enjoy is not without its martyrdom, since even if we no longer yield the life of the body to the sword, yet do we slay fleshly desires in the soul with the sword of the spirit." Therefore there can be martyrdom without suffering death.

Objection 2: Further, we read of certain women as commended for despising life for the sake of safeguarding the integrity of the flesh: wherefore seemingly the integrity of chastity is preferable to the life of the body. Now sometimes the integrity of the flesh has been forfeited or has been threatened in confession of the Christian faith, as in the case of Agnes and Lucy. Therefore it seems that the name of martyr should be accorded to a woman who forfeits the integrity of the flesh for the sake of Christ's faith, rather than if she were to forfeit even the life of the body: wherefore also Lucy said: "If thou causest me to be violated against my will, my chastity will gain me a twofold crown."

Objection 3: Further, martyrdom is an act of fortitude. But it belongs to fortitude to brave not only death but also other hardships, as Augustine declares (Music. vi). Now there are many other hardships besides death, which one may suffer for Christ's faith, namely imprisonment, exile, being stripped of one's goods, as mentioned in Heb. 10:34, for which reason we celebrate the martyrdom of Pope Saint Marcellus, notwithstanding that he died in prison. Therefore it is not essential to martyrdom that one suffer the pain of death.

Objection 4: Further, martyrdom is a meritorious act, as stated above (A[2], ad 1; A[3]). Now it cannot be a meritorious act after death. Therefore it is before death; and consequently death is not essential to martyrdom.

On the contrary, Maximus says in a sermon on the martyrs that "in dying for the faith he conquers who would have been vanquished in living without faith."

I answer that As stated above [3310](A[2]), a martyr is so called as being a witness to the Christian faith, which teaches us to despise things visible for the sake of things invisible, as stated in Heb. 11. Accordingly it belongs to martyrdom that a man bear witness to the faith in showing by deed that he despises all things present, in order to obtain invisible goods to come. Now so long as a man retains the life of the body he does not show by deed that he despises all things relating to the body. For men are wont to despise both their kindred and all they possess, and even to suffer bodily pain, rather than lose life. Hence Satan testified against Job (Job 2:4): "Skin for skin, and all that a man hath he will give for his soul" [Douay: 'life'] i.e. for the life of his body. Therefore the perfect notion of martyrdom requires that a man suffer death for Christ's sake.

Reply to Objection 1: The authorities quoted, and the like that one may meet with, speak of martyrdom by way of similitude.

Reply to Objection 2: When a woman forfeits the integrity of the flesh, or is condemned to forfeit it under pretext of the Christian faith, it is not evident to men whether she suffers this for love of the Christian faith, or rather through contempt of chastity. Wherefore in the sight of men her testimony is not held to be sufficient, and consequently this is not martyrdom properly speaking. In the sight of God, however, Who searcheth the heart, this may be deemed worthy of a reward, as Lucy said.

Reply to Objection 3: As stated above ([3311]Q[123], AA[4],5), fortitude regards danger of death chiefly, and other dangers consequently; wherefore a person is not called a martyr merely for suffering imprisonment, or exile, or forfeiture of his wealth, except in so far as these result in death.

Reply to Objection 4: The merit of martyrdom is not after death, but in the voluntary endurance of death, namely in the fact that a person willingly suffers being put to death. It happens sometimes, however, that a man lives for some time after being mortally wounded for Christ's sake, or after suffering for the faith of Christ any other kind of hardship inflicted by persecution and continued until death ensues. The act of martyrdom is meritorious while a man is in this state, and at the very time that he is suffering these hardships.

Whether faith alone is the cause of martyrdom?

Objection 1: It seems that faith alone is the cause of martyrdom. For it is written (1 Pet. 4:15,16): "Let none of you suffer as a murderer, or a thief, or a railer, or a coveter of other men's things. But if as a Christian, let him not be ashamed, but let him glorify God in this name." Now a man is said to be a Christian because he holds the faith of Christ. Therefore only faith in Christ gives the glory of martyrdom to those who suffer.

Objection 2: Further, a martyr is a kind of witness. But witness is borne to the truth alone. Now one is not called a martyr for bearing witness to any truth, but only for witnessing to the Divine truth, otherwise a man would be a martyr if he were to die for confessing a truth of geometry or some other speculative science, which seems ridiculous. Therefore faith alone is the cause of martyrdom.

Objection 3: Further, those virtuous deeds would seem to be of most account which are directed to the common good, since "the good of the nation is better than the good of the individual," according to the Philosopher (Ethic. i, 2). If, then, some other good were the cause of martyrdom, it would seem that before all those would be martyrs who die for the defense of their country. Yet this is not consistent with Church observance, for we do not celebrate the martyrdom of those who die in a just war. Therefore faith alone is the cause of martyrdom.

On the contrary, It is written (Mat. 5:10): "Blessed are they that suffer persecution for justice' sake," which pertains to martyrdom, according to a gloss, as well as Jerome's commentary on this passage. Now not only faith but also the other virtues pertain to justice. Therefore other virtues can be the cause of martyrdom.

I answer that, As stated above [3312](A[4]), martyrs are so called as being witnesses, because by suffering in body unto death they bear witness to the truth; not indeed to any truth, but to the truth which is in accordance with godliness, and was made known to us by Christ: wherefore Christ's martyrs are His witnesses. Now this truth is the truth of faith. Wherefore the cause of all martyrdom is the truth of faith.

But the truth of faith includes not only inward belief, but also outward profession, which is expressed not only by words, whereby one confesses the faith, but also by deeds, whereby a person shows that he has faith, according to James 2:18, "I will show thee, by works, my faith." Hence it is written of certain people (Titus 1:16): "They profess that they know God but in their works they deny Him." Thus all virtuous deeds, inasmuch as they are referred to God, are professions of the faith whereby we come to know that God requires these works of us, and rewards us for them: and in this way they can be the cause of martyrdom. For this reason the Church celebrates the martyrdom of Blessed John the Baptist, who suffered death, not for refusing to deny the faith, but for reproving adultery.

Reply to Objection 1: A Christian is one who is Christ's. Now a person is said to be Christ's, not only through having faith in Christ, but also because he is actuated to virtuous deeds by the Spirit of Christ, according to Rom. 8:9, "If any man have not the Spirit of Christ, he is none of His"; and again because in imitation of Christ he is dead to sins, according to Gal. 5:24, "They that are Christ's have crucified their flesh with the vices and concupiscences." Hence to suffer as a Christian is not only to suffer in confession of the faith, which is done by words, but also to suffer for doing any good work, or for avoiding any sin, for Christ's sake, because this all comes under the head of witnessing to the faith.

Reply to Objection 2: The truth of other sciences has no connection with the worship of the Godhead: hence it is not called truth according to godliness, and consequently the confession thereof cannot be said to be the direct cause of martyrdom. Yet, since every lie is a sin, as stated above ([3313]Q[110], AA[3],4), avoidance of a lie, to whatever truth it may be contrary, may be the cause of martyrdom inasmuch as a lie is a sin against the Divine Law.

Reply to Objection 3: The good of one's country is paramount among human goods: yet the Divine good, which is the proper cause of martyrdom, is of more account than human good. Nevertheless, since human good may become Divine, for instance when it is referred to God, it follows that any human good in so far as it is referred to God, may be the cause of martyrdom.

OF FEAR* (FOUR ARTICLES) [*St. Thomas calls this vice indifferently 'fear' or
'timidity.' The translation requires one to adhere to these terms on account
of the connection with the passion of fear. Otherwise 'cowardice' would be a
better rendering.]
We must now consider the vices opposed to fortitude: (1) Fear; (2) Fearlessness; (3) Daring.
Under the first head there are four points of inquiry:
(1) Whether fear is a sin?
(2) Whether it is opposed to fortitude?
(3) Whether it is a mortal sin?
(4) Whether it excuses from sin, or diminishes it?

Whether fear is a sin?
Objection 1: It seems that fear is not a sin. For fear is a passion, as stated above ([3314]FS, Q[23], A[4]; Q[42]). Now we are neither praised nor blamed for passions, as stated in Ethic. ii. Since then every sin is blameworthy, it seems that fear is not a sin.

Objection 2: Further, nothing that is commanded in the Divine Law is a sin: since the "law of the Lord is unspotted" (Ps. 18:8). Yet fear is commanded in God's law, for it is written (Eph. 6:5): "Servants, be obedient to them that are your lords according to the flesh, with fear and trembling." Therefore fear is not a sin.

Objection 3: Further, nothing that is naturally in man is a sin, for sin is contrary to nature according to Damascene (De Fide Orth. iii). Now fear is natural to man: wherefore the Philosopher says (Ethic. iii, 7) that "a man would be insane or insensible to pain, if nothing, not even earthquakes nor deluges, inspired him with fear." Therefore fear is not a sin. .

On the contrary, our Lord said (Mat. 10:28): "Fear ye not them that kill the body," and it is written (Ezech. 2:6): "Fear not, neither be thou afraid of their words."

I answer that, A human act is said to be a sin on account of its being inordinate, because the good of a human act consists in order, as stated above ([3315]Q[109], A[2];[3316] Q[114], A[1]). Now this due order requires that the appetite be subject to the ruling of reason. And reason dictates that certain things should be shunned and some sought after. Among things to be shunned, it dictates that some are to be shunned more than others; and among things to be sought after, that some are to be sought after more than others. Moreover, the more a good is to be sought after, the more is the opposite evil to be shunned. The result is that reason dictates that certain goods are to be sought after more than certain evils are to be avoided. Accordingly when the appetite shuns what the reason dictates that we should endure rather than forfeit others that we should rather seek for, fear is inordinate and sinful. On the other hand, when the appetite fears so as to shun what reason requires to be shunned, the appetite is neither inordinate nor sinful.

Reply to Objection 1: Fear in its generic acceptation denotes avoidance in general. Hence in this way it does not include the notion of good or evil: and the same applies to every other passion. Wherefore the Philosopher says that passions call for neither praise nor blame, because, to wit, we neither praise nor blame those who are angry or afraid, but only those who behave thus in an ordinate or inordinate manner.

Reply to Objection 2: The fear which the Apostle inculcates is in accordance with reason, namely that servants should fear lest they be lacking in the service they owe their masters.

Reply to Objection 3: Reason dictates that we should shun the evils that we cannot withstand, and the endurance of which profits us nothing. Hence there is no sin in fearing them.

Whether the sin of fear is contrary to fortitude?

Objection 1: It seems that the sin of fear is not contrary to fortitude: because fortitude is about dangers of death, as stated above ([3317]Q[123], AA[4],5). But the sin of fear is not always connected with dangers of death, for a gloss on Ps. 127:1, "Blessed are all they that fear the Lord," says that "it is human fear whereby we dread to suffer carnal dangers, or to lose worldly goods." Again a gloss on Mat. 27:44, "He prayed the third time, saying the selfsame word," says that "evil fear is threefold, fear of death, fear of pain, and fear of contempt." Therefore the sin of fear is not contrary to fortitude.

Objection 2: Further, the chief reason why a man is commended for fortitude is that he exposes himself to the danger of death. Now sometimes a man exposes himself to death through fear of slavery or shame. Thus Augustine relates (De Civ. Dei i) that Cato, in order not to be Caesar's slave, gave himself up to death. Therefore the sin of fear bears a certain likeness to fortitude instead of being opposed thereto.

Objection 3: Further, all despair arises from fear. But despair is opposed not to fortitude but to hope, as stated above (Q[20], A[1]; [3318]FS, Q[40], A[4]). Neither therefore is the sin of fear opposed to fortitude.

On the contrary, The Philosopher (Ethic. ii, 7; iii, 7) states that timidity is opposed to fortitude.

I answer that, As stated above (Q[19], A[3]; [3319]FS, Q[43], A[1]), all fear arises from love; since no one fears save what is contrary to something he loves. Now love is not confined to any particular kind of virtue or vice: but ordinate love is included in every virtue, since every virtuous man loves the good proper to his virtue; while inordinate love is included in every sin, because inordinate love gives use to inordinate desire. Hence in like manner inordinate fear is included in every sin; thus the covetous man fears the loss of money, the intemperate man the loss of pleasure, and so on. But the greatest fear of all is that which has the danger of death for its object, as we find proved in Ethic. iii, 6. Wherefore the inordinateness of this fear is opposed to fortitude which regards dangers of death. For this reason timidity is said to be antonomastically* opposed to fortitude. [*Antonomasia is the figure of speech whereby we substitute the general for the individual term; e.g. The Philosopher for Aristotle: and so timidity, which is inordinate fear of any evil, is employed to denote inordinate fear of the danger of death.]

Reply to Objection 1: The passages quoted refer to inordinate fear in its generic acceptation, which can be opposed to various virtues.

Reply to Objection 2: Human acts are estimated chiefly with reference to the end, as stated above ([3320]FS, Q[1], A[3]; [3321]FS, Q[18], A[6]): and it belongs to a brave man to expose himself to danger of death for the sake of a good. But a man who exposes himself to danger of death in order to escape from slavery or hardships is overcome by fear, which is contrary to fortitude. Hence the Philosopher says (Ethic. iii, 7), that "to die in order to escape poverty, lust, or something disagreeable is an act not of fortitude but of cowardice: for to shun hardships is a mark of effeminacy."

Reply to Objection 3: As stated above ([3322]FS, Q[45], A[2]), fear is the beginning of despair even as hope is the beginning of daring. Wherefore, just as fortitude which employs daring in moderation presupposes hope, so on the other hand despair proceeds from some kind of fear. It does not follow, however, that any kind of despair results from any kind of fear, but that only from fear of the same kind. Now the despair that is opposed to hope is referred to another kind, namely to Divine things; whereas the fear that is opposed to fortitude regards dangers of death. Hence the argument does not prove.

Whether fear is a mortal sin?

Objection 1: It seems that fear is not a mortal sin. For, as stated above ([3323]FS, Q[23], A[1]), fear is in the irascible faculty which is a part of the sensuality. Now there is none but venial sin in the sensuality, as stated above ([3324]FS, Q[74], A[4]). Therefore fear is not a mortal sin.

Objection 2: Further, every mortal sin turns the heart wholly from God. But fear does not this, for a gloss on Judges 7:3, "Whosoever is fearful," etc., says that "a man is fearful when he trembles at the very thought of conflict; yet he is not so wholly terrified at heart, but that he can rally and take courage." Therefore fear is not a mortal sin.

Objection 3: Further, mortal sin is a lapse not only from perfection but also from a precept. But fear does not make one lapse from a precept, but only from perfection; for a gloss on Dt. 20:8, "What man is there that is fearful and fainthearted?" says: "We learn from this that no man can take up the profession of contemplation or spiritual warfare, if he still fears to be despoiled of earthly riches." Therefore fear is not a mortal sin.

On the contrary, For mortal sin alone is the pain of hell due: and yet this is due to the fearful, according to Apoc. 21:8, "But the fearful and unbelieving and the abominable," etc., "shall have their portion in the pool burning with fire and brimstone which is the second death." Therefore fear is a mortal sin.

I answer that, As stated above [3325](A[1]), fear is a sin through being inordinate, that is to say, through shunning what ought not to be shunned according to reason. Now sometimes this inordinateness of fear is confined to the sensitive appetites, without the accession of the rational appetite's consent: and then it cannot be a mortal, but only a venial sin. But sometimes this inordinateness of fear reaches to the rational appetite which is called the will, which deliberately shuns something against the dictate of reason: and this inordinateness of fear is sometimes a mortal, sometimes a venial sin. For if a man through fear of the danger of death or of any other temporal evil is so disposed as to do what is forbidden, or to omit what is commanded by the Divine law, such fear is a mortal sin: otherwise it is a venial sin.

Reply to Objection 1: This argument considers fear as confined to the sensuality.

Reply to Objection 2: This gloss also can be understood as referring to the fear that is confined within the sensuality. Or better still we may reply that a man is terrified with his whole heart when fear banishes his courage beyond remedy. Now even when fear is a mortal sin, it may happen nevertheless that one is not so wilfully terrified that one cannot be persuaded to put fear aside: thus sometimes a man sins mortally by consenting to concupiscence, and is turned aside from accomplishing what he purposed doing.

Reply to Objection 3: This gloss speaks of the fear that turns man aside from a good that is necessary, not for the fulfilment of a precept, but for the perfection of a counsel. Such like fear is not a mortal sin, but is sometimes venial: and sometimes it is not a sin, for instance when one has a reasonable cause for fear.

Whether fear excuses from sin?

Objection 1: It seems that fear does not excuse from sin. For fear is a sin, as stated above [3326](A[1]). But sin does not excuse from sin, rather does it aggravate it. Therefore fear does not excuse from sin.

Objection 2: Further, if any fear excuses from sin, most of all would this be true of the fear of death, to which, as the saying is, a courageous man is subject. Yet this fear, seemingly, is no excuse, because, since death comes, of necessity, to all, it does not seem to be an object of fear. Therefore fear does not excuse from sin.

Objection 3: Further, all fear is of evil, either temporal or spiritual. Now fear of spiritual evil cannot excuse sin, because instead of inducing one to sin, it withdraws one from sin: and fear of temporal evil does not excuse from sin, because according to the Philosopher (Ethic. iii, 6), "one should not fear poverty, nor sickness, nor anything that is not a result of one's own wickedness." Therefore it seems that in no sense does fear excuse from sin.

On the contrary, It is stated in the Decretals (I, Q[1], Cap. Constat.): "A man who has been forcibly and unwillingly ordained by heretics, has an ostensible excuse."

I answer that, As stated above [3327](A[3]), fear is sinful in so far as it runs counter to the order of reason. Now reason judges certain evils to be shunned rather than others. Wherefore it is no sin not to shun what is less to be shunned in order to avoid what reason judges to be more avoided: thus death of the body is more to be avoided than the loss of temporal goods. Hence a man would be excused from sin if through fear of death he were to promise or give something to a robber, and yet he would be guilty of sin were he to give to sinners, rather than to the good to whom he should give in preference. On the other hand, if through fear a man were to avoid evils which according to reason are less to be avoided, and so incur evils which according to reason are more to be avoided, he could not be wholly excused from sin, because such like fear would be inordinate. Now the evils of the soul are more to be feared than the evils of the body. and evils of the body more than evils of external things. Wherefore if one were to incur evils of the soul, namely sins, in order to avoid evils of the body, such as blows or death, or evils of external things, such as loss of money; or if one were to endure evils of the body in order to avoid loss of money, one would not be wholly excused from sin. Yet one's sin would be extenuated somewhat, for what is done through fear is less voluntary, because when fear lays hold of a man he is under a certain necessity of doing a certain thing. Hence the Philosopher (Ethic. iii, 1) says that these things that are done through fear are not simply voluntary, but a mixture of voluntary and involuntary.

Reply to Objection 1: Fear excuses, not in the point of its sinfulness, but in the point of its involuntariness.

Reply to Objection 2: Although death comes, of necessity, to all, yet the shortening of temporal life is an evil and consequently an object of fear.

Reply to Objection 3: According to the opinion of Stoics, who held temporal goods not to be man's goods, it follows in consequence that temporal evils are not man's evils, and that therefore they are nowise to be feared. But according to Augustine (De Lib. Arb. ii) these temporal things are goods of the least account, and this was also the opinion of the Peripatetics. Hence their contraries are indeed to be feared; but not so much that one ought for their sake to renounce that which is good according to virtue.

Day 216

OF FEARLESSNESS (TWO ARTICLES)
We must now consider the vice of fearlessness: under which head there are two points of inquiry:
(1) Whether it is a sin to be fearless?
(2) Whether it is opposed to fortitude?

Whether fearlessness is a sin?

Objection 1: It seems that fearlessness is not a sin. For that which is reckoned to the praise of a just man is not a sin. Now it is written in praise of the just man (Prov. 28:1): "The just, bold as a lion, shall be without dread." Therefore it is not a sin to be without fear.

Objection 2: Further, nothing is so fearful as death, according to the Philosopher (Ethic. iii, 6). Yet one ought not to fear even death, according to Mat. 10:28, "Fear ye not them that kill the body," etc., nor anything that can be inflicted by man, according to Is. 51:12, "Who art thou, that thou shouldst be afraid of a mortal man?" Therefore it is not a sin to be fearless.

Objection 3: Further, fear is born of love, as stated above ([3328]Q[125], A[2]). Now it belongs to the perfection of virtue to love nothing earthly, since according to Augustine (De Civ. Dei xiv), "the love of God to the abasement of self makes us citizens of the heavenly city." Therefore it is seemingly not a sin to fear nothing earthly.

On the contrary, It is said of the unjust judge (Lk. 18:2) that "he feared not God nor regarded man."

I answer that, Since fear is born of love, we must seemingly judge alike of love and fear. Now it is here a question of that fear whereby one dreads temporal evils, and which results from the love of temporal goods. And every man has it instilled in him by nature to love his own life and whatever is directed thereto; and to do so in due measure, that is, to love these things not as placing his end therein, but as things to be used for the sake of his last end. Hence it is contrary to the natural inclination, and therefore a sin, to fall short of loving them in due measure. Nevertheless, one never lapses entirely from this love: since what is natural cannot be wholly lost: for which reason the Apostle says (Eph. 5:29): "No man ever hated his own flesh." Wherefore even those that slay themselves do so from love of their own flesh, which they desire to free from present stress. Hence it may happen that a man fears death and other

17

temporal evils less than he ought, for the reason that he loves them* less than he ought. [*Viz. the contrary goods. One would expect 'se' instead of 'ea.' We should then read: For the reason that he loves himself less than he ought.] But that he fear none of these things cannot result from an entire lack of love, but only from the fact that he thinks it impossible for him to be afflicted by the evils contrary to the goods he loves. This is sometimes the result of pride of soul presuming on self and despising others, according to the saying of Job 41:24,25: "He [Vulg.: 'who'] was made to fear no one, he beholdeth every high thing": and sometimes it happens through a defect in the reason; thus the Philosopher says (Ethic. iii, 7) that the "Celts, through lack of intelligence, fear nothing." [*"A man would deserve to be called insane and senseless if there were nothing that he feared, not even an earthquake nor a storm at sea, as is said to be the case with the Celts."] It is therefore evident that fearlessness is a vice, whether it result from lack of love, pride of soul, or dullness of understanding: yet the latter is excused from sin if it be invincible.

Reply to Objection 1: The just man is praised for being without fear that withdraws him from good; not that he is altogether fearless, for it is written (Ecclus. 1:28): "He that is without fear cannot be justified."

Reply to Objection 2: Death and whatever else can be inflicted by mortal man are not to be feared so that they make us forsake justice: but they are to be feared as hindering man in acts of virtue, either as regards himself, or as regards the progress he may cause in others. Hence it is written (Prov. 14:16): "A wise man feareth and declineth from evil."

Reply to Objection 3: Temporal goods are to be despised as hindering us from loving and serving God, and on the same score they are not to be feared; wherefore it is written (Ecclus. 34:16): "He that feareth the Lord shall tremble at nothing." But temporal goods are not to be despised, in so far as they are helping us instrumentally to attain those things that pertain to Divine fear and love.

Whether fearlessness is opposed to fortitude?

Objection 1: It seems that fearlessness is not opposed to fortitude. For we judge of habits by their acts. Now no act of fortitude is hindered by a man being fearless: since if fear be removed, one is both brave to endure, and daring to attack. Therefore fearlessness is not opposed to fortitude.

Objection 2: Further, fearlessness is a vice, either through lack of due love, or on account of pride, or by reason of folly. Now lack of due love is opposed to charity, pride is contrary to humility, and folly to prudence or wisdom. Therefore the vice of fearlessness is not opposed to fortitude.

Objection 3: Further, vices are opposed to virtue and extremes to the mean. But one mean has only one extreme on the one side. Since then fortitude has fear opposed to it on the one side and daring on the other, it seems that fearlessness is not opposed thereto.

On the contrary, The Philosopher (Ethic. iii) reckons fearlessness to be opposed to fortitude.

I answer that, As stated above ([3329]Q[123], A[3]), fortitude is concerned about fear and daring. Now every moral virtue observes the rational mean in the matter about which it is concerned. Hence it belongs to fortitude that man should moderate his fear according to reason, namely that he should fear what he ought, and when he ought, and so forth. Now this mode of reason may be corrupted either by excess or by deficiency. Wherefore just as timidity is opposed to fortitude by excess of fear, in so far as a man fears what he ought not, and as he ought not, so too fearlessness is opposed thereto by deficiency of fear, in so far as a man fears not what he ought to fear.

Reply to Objection 1: The act of fortitude is to endure death without fear, and to be aggressive, not anyhow, but according to reason: this the fearless man does not do.

Reply to Objection 2: Fearlessness by its specific nature corrupts the mean of fortitude, wherefore it is opposed to fortitude directly. But in respect of its causes nothing hinders it from being opposed to other virtues.

Reply to Objection 3: The vice of daring is opposed to fortitude by excess of daring, and fearlessness by deficiency of fear. Fortitude imposes the mean on each passion. Hence there is nothing unreasonable in its having different extremes in different respects.

OF DARING [*Excessive daring or foolhardiness] (TWO ARTICLES)

We must now consider daring; and under this head there are two points of inquiry:

(1) Whether daring is a sin?
(2) Whether it is opposed to fortitude?

Whether daring is a sin?

Objection 1: It seems that daring is not a sin. For it is written (Job 39:21) concerning the horse, by which according to Gregory (Moral. xxxi) the godly preacher is denoted, that "he goeth forth boldly to meet armed men [*Vulg.: 'he pranceth boldly, he goeth forth to meet armed men']." But no vice redounds to a man's praise. Therefore it is not a sin to be daring.

Objection 2: Further, according to the Philosopher (Ethic. vi, 9), "one should take counsel in thought, and do quickly what has been counseled." But daring helps this quickness in doing. Therefore daring is not sinful but praiseworthy.

Objection 3: Further, daring is a passion caused by hope, as stated above ([3330]FS, Q[45], A[2]) when we were treating of the passions. But hope is accounted not a sin but a virtue. Neither therefore should daring be accounted a sin.

On the contrary, It is written (Ecclus. 8:18): "Go not on the way with a bold man, lest he burden thee with his evils." Now no man's fellowship is to be avoided save on account of sin. Therefore daring is a sin.

I answer that, Daring, as stated above ([3331]FS, Q[23], A[1]; Q[55]), is a passion. Now a passion is sometimes moderated according to reason, and sometimes it lacks moderation, either by excess or by deficiency, and on this account the passion is sinful. Again, the names of the passions are sometimes employed in the sense of excess, thus we speak of anger meaning not any but excessive anger, in which case it is sinful, and in the same way daring as implying excess is accounted a sin.

Reply to Objection 1: The daring spoken of there is that which is moderated by reason, for in that sense it belongs to the virtue of fortitude.

Reply to Objection 2: It is praiseworthy to act quickly after taking counsel, which is an act of reason. But to wish to act quickly before taking counsel is not praiseworthy but sinful; for this would be to act rashly, which is a vice contrary to prudence, as stated above ([3332]Q[58], A[3]). Wherefore daring which leads one to act quickly is so far praiseworthy as it is directed by reason.

Reply to Objection 3: Some vices are unnamed, and so also are some virtues, as the Philosopher remarks (Ethic. ii, 7; iv, 4,5,6). Hence the names of certain passions have to be applied to certain vices and virtues: and in order to designate vices we employ especially the names of those passions the object of which is an evil, as in the case of hatred, fear, anger and daring. But hope and love have a good for this object, and so we use them rather to designate virtues.

Whether daring is opposed to fortitude?

Objection 1: It seems that daring is not opposed to fortitude. For excess of daring seems to result from presumption of mind. But presumption pertains to pride which is opposed to humility. Therefore daring is opposed to humility rather than to fortitude.

Objection 2: Further, daring does not seem to call for blame, except in so far as it results in harm either to the daring person who puts himself in danger inordinately, or to others whom he attacks with daring, or exposes to danger. But this seemingly pertains to injustice. Therefore daring, as designating a sin, is opposed, not to fortitude but to justice.

Objection 3: Further, fortitude is concerned about fear and daring, as stated above ([3333]Q[123], A[3]). Now since timidity is opposed to fortitude in respect of an excess of fear, there is another vice opposed to timidity in respect of a lack of fear. If then, daring is opposed to fortitude, in the point of excessive daring, there will likewise be a vice opposed to it in the point of deficient daring. But there is no such vice. Therefore neither should daring be accounted a vice in opposition to fortitude.

On the contrary, The Philosopher in both the Second and Third Books of Ethics accounts daring to be opposed to fortitude.

I answer that, As stated above ([3334]Q[126], A[2]), it belongs to a moral virtue to observe the rational mean in the matter about which it is concerned. Wherefore every vice that denotes lack of moderation in the matter of a moral virtue is opposed to that virtue, as immoderate to moderate. Now daring, in so far as it denotes a vice, implies excess of passion, and this excess goes by the name of daring. Wherefore it is evident that it is opposed to the virtue of fortitude which is concerned about fear and daring, as stated above ([3335]Q[122], A[3]).

Reply to Objection 1: Opposition between vice and virtue does not depend chiefly on the cause of the vice but on the vice's very species. Wherefore it is not necessary that daring be opposed to the same virtue as presumption which is its cause.

Reply to Objection 2: Just as the direct opposition of a vice does not depend on its cause, so neither does it depend on its effect. Now the harm done by daring is its effect. Wherefore neither does the opposition of daring depend on this.

Reply to Objection 3: The movement of daring consists in a man taking the offensive against that which is in opposition to him: and nature inclines him to do this except in so far as such inclination is hindered by the fear of receiving harm from that source. Hence the vice which exceeds in daring has no contrary deficiency, save only timidity. Yet daring does not always accompany so great a lack of timidity, for as the Philosopher says (Ethic. iii, 7), "the daring are precipitate and eager to meet danger, yet fail when the danger is present," namely through fear.

OF THE PARTS OF FORTITUDE (ONE ARTICLE)

We must now consider the parts of fortitude; first we shall consider what are the parts of fortitude; and secondly we shall treat of each part.

Whether the parts of fortitude are suitably assigned?

Objection 1: It seems that the parts of fortitude are unsuitably assigned. For Tully (De Invent. Rhet. ii) assigns four parts to fortitude, namely "magnificence," "confidence," "patience," and "perseverance." Now magnificence seems to pertain to liberality; since both are concerned about money, and "a magnificent man must needs be liberal," as the Philosopher observes (Ethic. iv, 2). But liberality is a part of justice, as stated above ([3336]Q[117], A[5]). Therefore magnificence should not be reckoned a part of fortitude.

Objection 2: Further, confidence is apparently the same as hope. But hope does not seem to pertain to fortitude, but is rather a virtue by itself. Therefore confidence should not be reckoned a part of fortitude.

Objection 3: Further, fortitude makes a man behave aright in face of danger. But magnificence and confidence do not essentially imply any relation to danger. Therefore they are not suitably reckoned as parts of fortitude.

Objection 4: Further, according to Tully (De Invent. Rhet. ii) patience denotes endurance of hardships, and he ascribes the same to fortitude. Therefore patience is the same as fortitude and not a part thereof.

Objection 5: Further, that which is a requisite to every virtue should not be reckoned a part of a special virtue. But perseverance is required in every virtue: for it is written (Mat. 24:13): "He that shall persevere to the end he shall be saved." Therefore perseverance should not be accounted a part of fortitude.

Objection 6: Further, Macrobius (De Somn. Scip. i) reckons seven parts of fortitude, namely "magnanimity, confidence, security, magnificence, constancy, forbearance, stability." Andronicus also reckons seven virtues annexed to fortitude, and these are, "courage, strength of will, magnanimity, manliness, perseverance, magnificence." Therefore it seems that Tully's reckoning of the parts of fortitude is incomplete.

Objection 7: Further, Aristotle (Ethic. iii) reckons five parts of fortitude. The first is "civic" fortitude, which produces brave deeds through fear of dishonor or punishment; the second is "military" fortitude, which produces brave deeds as a result of warlike art or experience; the third is the fortitude which produces brave deeds resulting from passion, especially anger; the fourth is the fortitude which makes a man act bravely through being accustomed to overcome; the fifth is the fortitude which makes a man act bravely through being unaccustomed to danger. Now these kinds of fortitude are not comprised under any of the above enumerations. Therefore these enumerations of the parts of fortitude are unfitting.

I answer that, As stated above ([3337]Q[48]), a virtue can have three kinds of parts, subjective, integral, and potential. But fortitude, taken as a special virtue, cannot have subjective parts, since it is not divided into several specifically distinct virtues, for it is about a very special matter.

However, there are quasi-integral and potential parts assigned to it: integral parts, with regard to those things the concurrence of which is requisite for an act of fortitude; and potential parts, because what fortitude practices in face of the greatest hardships, namely dangers of death, certain other virtues practice in the matter of certain minor hardships and these virtues are annexed to fortitude as secondary virtues to the principal virtue. As stated above ([3338]Q[123], AA[3],6), the act of fortitude is twofold, aggression and endurance. Now two things are required for the act of aggression. The first regards preparation of the mind, and consists in one's having a mind ready for aggression. In this respect Tully mentions "confidence," of which he says (De Invent. Rhet. ii) that "with this the mind is much assured and firmly hopeful in great and honorable undertakings." The second regards the accomplishment of the deed, and consists in not failing to accomplish what one has confidently begun. In this respect Tully mentions "magnificence," which he describes as being "the discussion and administration," i.e. accomplishment "of great and lofty undertakings, with a certain broad and noble purpose of mind," so as to combine execution with greatness of purpose. Accordingly if these two be confined to the proper matter of fortitude, namely to dangers of death, they will be quasi-integral parts thereof, because without them there can be no fortitude; whereas if they be referred to other matters involving less hardship, they will be virtues specifically distinct from fortitude, but annexed thereto as secondary virtues to principal: thus "magnificence" is referred by the Philosopher (Ethic. iv) to great expenses, and "magnanimity," which seems to be the same as confidence, to great honors. Again, two things are requisite for the other act of fortitude, viz. endurance. The first is that the mind be not broken by sorrow, and fall away from its greatness, by reason of the stress of threatening evil. In this respect he mentions "patience," which he describes as "the voluntary and prolonged endurance of arduous and difficult things for the sake of virtue or profit." The other is that by the prolonged suffering of hardships man be not wearied so as to lose courage, according to Heb. 12:3, "That you be not wearied, fainting in your minds." In this respect he mentions "perseverance," which accordingly he describes as "the fixed and continued persistence in a well considered purpose." If these two be confined to the proper matter of fortitude, they will be quasi-integral parts thereof; but if they be referred to any kind of hardship they will be virtues distinct from fortitude, yet annexed thereto as secondary to principal.

Reply to Objection 1: Magnificence in the matter of liberality adds a certain greatness: this is connected with the notion of difficulty which is the object of the irascible faculty, that is perfected chiefly by fortitude: and to this virtue, in this respect, it belongs.

Reply to Objection 2: Hope whereby one confides in God is accounted a theological virtue, as stated above (Q[17], A[5]; [3339]FS, Q[62], A[3]). But by confidence which here is accounted a part of fortitude, man hopes in himself, yet under God withal.

Reply to Objection 3: To venture on anything great seems to involve danger, since to fail in such things is very disastrous. Wherefore although magnificence and confidence are referred to the accomplishment of or venturing on any other great things, they have a certain connection with fortitude by reason of the imminent danger.

Reply to Objection 4: Patience endures not only dangers of death, with which fortitude is concerned, without excessive sorrow, but also any other hardships or dangers. In this respect it is accounted a virtue annexed to fortitude: but as referred to dangers of death, it is an integral part thereof.

Reply to Objection 5: Perseverance as denoting persistence in a good deed unto the end, may be a circumstance of every virtue, but it is reckoned a part of fortitude in the sense stated in the body of the Article.

Reply to Objection 6: Macrobius reckons the four aforesaid mentioned by Tully, namely "confidence, magnificence, forbearance," which he puts in the place of patience, and "firmness," which he substitutes for perseverance. And he adds three, two of which, namely "magnanimity" and "security," are comprised by Tully under the head of confidence. But Macrobius is more specific in his enumeration. Because confidence denotes a man's hope for great things: and hope for anything presupposes an appetite stretching forth to great things by desire, and this belongs to magnanimity. For it has been stated above ([3340]FS, Q[40], A[2]) that hope presupposes love and desire of the thing hoped for.

A still better reply is that confidence pertains to the certitude of hope; while magnanimity refers to the magnitude of the thing hoped for. Now hope has no firmness unless its contrary be removed, for sometimes one, for one's own part, would hope for something, but hope is avoided on account of the obstacle of fear, since fear is somewhat contrary to hope, as stated above, ([3341]FS, Q[40], A[4], ad 1). Hence Macrobius adds security, which banishes fear. He adds a third, namely constancy, which may be comprised under magnificence. For in performing deeds of magnificence one needs to have a constant mind. For this reason Tully says that magnificence consists not only in accomplishing great things, but also in discussing them generously in the mind. Constancy may also pertain to perseverance, so that one may be called persevering through not desisting on account of delays, and constant through not desisting on account of any other obstacles.

Those that are mentioned by Andronicus seem to amount to the same as the above. For with Tully and Macrobius he mentions "perseverance" and "magnificence," and with Macrobius, "magnanimity." "Strength of will" is the same as patience or forbearance, for he says that "strength of will is a habit that makes one ready to attempt what ought to be attempted, and to endure what reason says should be endured"---i.e. good courage seems to be the same as assurance, for he defines it as "strength of soul in the accomplishment of its purpose." Manliness is apparently the same as confidence, for he says that "manliness is a habit of self-sufficiency in matters of virtue." Besides magnificence he mentions {andragathia}, i.e. manly goodness which we may render "strenuousness." For magnificence consists not only in being constant in the accomplishment of great deeds, which belongs to constancy, but also in bringing a certain manly prudence and solicitude to that accomplishment, and this belongs to {andragathia}, strenuousness: wherefore he says that {andragathia} is the virtue of a man, whereby he thinks out profitable works.

Accordingly it is evident that all these parts may be reduced to the four principal parts mentioned by Tully.

Reply to Objection 7: The five mentioned by Aristotle fall short of the true notion of virtue, for though they concur in the act of fortitude, they differ as to motive, as stated above ([3342]Q[123], A[1], ad 2); wherefore they are not reckoned parts but modes of fortitude.

OF MAGNANIMITY* (EIGHT ARTICLES) [*Not in the ordinary restricted sense but as explained by the author]

We must now consider each of the parts of fortitude, including, however, the other parts under those mentioned by Tully, with the exception of confidence, for which we shall substitute magnanimity, of which Aristotle treats. Accordingly we shall consider (1) Magnanimity; (2) Magnificence; (3) Patience; (4) Perseverance. As regards the first we shall treat (1) of magnanimity; (2) of its contrary vices. Under the first head there are eight points of inquiry:

(1) Whether magnanimity is about honors?
(2) Whether magnanimity is only about great honors?
(3) Whether it is a virtue?
(4) Whether it is a special virtue?
(5) Whether it is a part of fortitude?
(6) Of its relation to confidence;
(7) Of its relation to assurance;
(8) Of its relation to goods of fortune.

Whether magnanimity is about honors?

Objection 1: It seems that magnanimity is not about honors. For magnanimity is in the irascible faculty, as its very name shows, since "magnanimity" signifies greatness of mind, and "mind" denotes the irascible part, as appears from De Anima iii, 42, where the Philosopher says that "in the sensitive appetite are desire and mind," i.e. the concupiscible and irascible parts. But honor is a concupiscible good since it is the reward of virtue. Therefore it seems that magnanimity is not about honors.

Objection 2: Further, since magnanimity is a moral virtue, it must needs be about either passions or operations. Now it is not about operations, for then it would be a part of justice: whence it follows that it is about passions. But honor is not a passion. Therefore magnanimity is not about honors.

Objection 3: Further, the nature of magnanimity seems to regard pursuit rather than avoidance, for a man is said to be magnanimous because he tends to great things. But the virtuous are praised not for desiring honors, but for shunning them. Therefore magnanimity is not about honors.

On the contrary, The Philosopher says (Ethic. iv, 3) that "magnanimity is about honor and dishonor."

I answer that, Magnanimity by its very name denotes stretching forth of the mind to great things. Now virtue bears a relationship to two things, first to the matter about which is the field of its activity, secondly to its proper act, which consists in the right use of such matter. And since a virtuous habit is denominated chiefly from its act, a man is said to be magnanimous chiefly because he is minded to do some great act. Now an act may be called great in two ways: in one way proportionately, in another absolutely. An act may be called great proportionately, even if it consist in the use of some small or ordinary thing, if, for instance, one make a very good use of it: but an act is simply and absolutely great when it consists in the best use of the greatest thing.

The things which come into man's use are external things, and among these honor is the greatest simply, both because it is the most akin to virtue, since it is an attestation to a person's virtue, as stated above ([3343]Q[103], AA[1],2); and because it is offered to God and to the best; and again because, in order to obtain honor even as to avoid shame, men set aside all other things. Now a man is said to be magnanimous in respect of things that are great absolutely and simply, just as a man is said to be brave in respect of things that are difficult simply. It follows therefore that magnanimity is about honors.

Reply to Objection 1: Good and evil absolutely considered regard the concupiscible faculty, but in so far as the aspect of difficult is added, they belong to the irascible. Thus it is that magnanimity regards honor, inasmuch, to wit, as honor has the aspect of something great or difficult.

Reply to Objection 2: Although honor is neither a passion nor an operation, yet it is the object of a passion, namely hope, which tends to a difficult good. Wherefore magnanimity is immediately about the passions of hope, and mediately about honor as the object of hope: even so, we have stated ([3344]Q[123], AA[4],5) with regard to fortitude that it is about dangers of death in so far as they are the object of fear and daring.

Reply to Objection 3: Those are worthy of praise who despise riches in such a way as to do nothing unbecoming in order to obtain them, nor have too great a desire for them. If, however, one were to despise honors so as not to care to do what is worthy of honor, this would be deserving of blame. Accordingly magnanimity is about honors in the sense that a man strives to do what is deserving of honor, yet not so as to think much of the honor accorded by man.

Whether magnanimity is essentially about great honors?

Objection 1: It seems that magnanimity is not essentially about great honors. For the proper matter of magnanimity is honor, as stated above [3345](A[1]). But great and little are accidental to honor. Therefore it is not essential to magnanimity to be about great honors.

Objection 2: Further, just as magnanimity is about honor, so is meekness about anger. But it is not essential to meekness to be about either great or little anger. Therefore neither is it essential to magnanimity to be about great honor.

Objection 3: Further, small honor is less aloof from great honor than is dishonor. But magnanimity is well ordered in relation to dishonor, and consequently in relation to small honors also. Therefore it is not only about great honors.

On the contrary, The Philosopher says (Ethic. ii, 7) that magnanimity is about great honors.

I answer that According to the Philosopher (Phys. vii, 17, 18), virtue is a perfection, and by this we are to understand the perfection of a power, and that it regards the extreme limit of that power, as stated in De Coelo i, 116. Now the perfection of a power is not perceived in every operation of that power, but in such operations as are great or difficult: for every power, however imperfect, can extend to ordinary and trifling operations. Hence it is essential to a virtue to be about the difficult and the good, as stated in Ethic. ii, 3.

Now the difficult and the good (which amount to the same) in an act of virtue may be considered from two points of view. First, from the point of view of reason, in so far as it is difficult to find and establish the rational means in some particular matter: and this difficulty is found only in the act of intellectual virtues, and also of justice. The other difficulty is on the part of the matter, which may involve a certain opposition to the moderation of reason, which moderation has to be applied thereto: and this difficulty regards chiefly the other moral virtues, which are about the passions, because the passions resist reason as Dionysius states (Div. Nom. iv, 4).

Now as regards the passions it is to be observed that the greatness of this power of resistance to reason arises chiefly in some cases from the passions themselves, and in others from the things that are the objects of the passions. The passions themselves have no great power of resistance, unless they be violent, because the sensitive appetite, which is the seat of the passions, is naturally subject to reason. Hence the resisting virtues that are about these passions regard only that which is great in such passions: thus fortitude is about very great fear and daring; temperance about the concupiscence of the greatest pleasures, and likewise meekness about the greatest anger. On the other hand, some passions have great power of resistance to reason arising from the external things themselves that are the objects of those passions: such are the love or desire of money or of honor. And for these it is necessary to have a virtue not only regarding that which is greatest in those passions, but also about that which is ordinary or little: because things external, though they be little, are very desirable, as being necessary for human life. Hence with regard to the desire of money there are two virtues, one about ordinary or little sums of money, namely liberality, and another about large sums of money, namely "magnificence."

In like manner there are two virtues about honors, one about ordinary honors. This virtue has no name, but is denominated by its extremes, which are {philotimia}, i.e. love of honor, and {aphilotimia}, i.e. without love of honor: for sometimes a man is commended for loving honor, and sometimes for not caring about it, in so far, to wit, as both these things may be done in moderation. But with regard to great honors there is "magnanimity." Wherefore we must conclude that the proper matter of magnanimity is great honor, and that a magnanimous man tends to such things as are deserving of honor.

Reply to Objection 1: Great and little are accidental to honor considered in itself: but they make a great difference in their relation to reason, the mode of which has to be observed in the use of honor, for it is much more difficult to observe it in great than in little honors.

Reply to Objection 2: In anger and other matters only that which is greatest presents any notable difficulty, and about this alone is there any need of a virtue. It is different with riches and honors which are things existing outside the soul.

Reply to Objection 3: He that makes good use of great things is much more able to make good use of little things. Accordingly the magnanimous man looks upon great honors as a thing of which he is worthy, or even little honors as something he deserves, because, to wit, man cannot sufficiently honor virtue which deserves to be honored by God. Hence he is not uplifted by great honors, because he does not deem them above him; rather does he despise them, and much more such as are ordinary or little. In like manner he is not cast down by dishonor, but despises it, since he recognizes that he does not deserve it.

Whether magnanimity is a virtue?

Objection 1: It seems that magnanimity is not a virtue. For every moral virtue observes the mean. But magnanimity observes not the mean but the greater extreme: because the "magnanimous man deems himself worthy of the greatest things" (Ethic. iv, 3). Therefore magnanimity is not a virtue.

Objection 2: Further, he that has one virtue has them all, as stated above ([3346]FS, Q[65], A[1]). But one may have a virtue without having magnanimity: since the Philosopher says (Ethic. iv, 3) that "whosoever is worthy of little things and deems himself worthy of them, is temperate, but he is not magnanimous." Therefore magnanimity is not a virtue.

Objection 3: Further, "Virtue is a good quality of the mind," as stated above ([3347]FS, Q[55], A[4]). But magnanimity implies certain dispositions of the body: for the Philosopher says (Ethic. iv, 3) of "a magnanimous man that his gait is slow, his voice deep, and his utterance calm." Therefore magnanimity is not a virtue.

Objection 4: Further, no virtue is opposed to another virtue. But magnanimity is opposed to humility, since "the magnanimous deems himself worthy of great things, and despises others," according to Ethic. iv, 3. Therefore magnanimity is not a virtue.

Objection 5: Further, the properties of every virtue are praiseworthy. But magnanimity has certain properties that call for blame. For, in the first place, the magnanimous is unmindful of favors; secondly, he is remiss and slow of action; thirdly, he employs irony [*Cf. Q[113]] towards many; fourthly, he is unable to associate with others; fifthly, because he holds to the barren things rather than to those that are fruitful. Therefore magnanimity is not a virtue.

On the contrary, It is written in praise of certain men (2 Macc. 15:18): "Nicanor hearing of the valor of Judas' companions, and the greatness of courage [animi magnitudinem] with which they fought for their country, was afraid to try the matter by the sword." Now, only deeds of virtue are worthy of praise. Therefore magnanimity which consists in greatness of courage is a virtue.

I answer that, The essence of human virtue consists in safeguarding the good of reason in human affairs, for this is man's proper good. Now among external human things honors take precedence of all others, as stated above [3348](A[1]; [3349]FS, Q[11], A[2], OBJ[3]). Therefore magnanimity, which observes the mode of reason in great honors, is a virtue.

Reply to Objection 1: As the Philosopher again says (Ethic. iv, 3), "the magnanimous in point of quantity goes to extremes," in so far as he tends to what is greatest, "but in the matter of becomingness, he follows the mean," because he tends to the greatest things according to reason, for "he deems himself worthy in accordance with his worth" (Ethic. iv, 3), since his aims do not surpass his deserts.

Reply to Objection 2: The mutual connection of the virtues does not apply to their acts, as though every one were competent to practice the acts of all the virtues. Wherefore the act of magnanimity is not becoming to every virtuous man, but only to great men. on the other hand, as regards the principles of virtue, namely prudence and grace, all virtues are connected together, since their habits reside together in the soul, either in act or by way of a proximate disposition thereto. Thus it is possible for one to whom the act of magnanimity is not competent, to have the habit of magnanimity, whereby he is disposed to practice that act if it were competent to him according to his state.

Reply to Objection 3: The movements of the body are differentiated according to the different apprehensions and emotions of the soul. And so it happens that to magnanimity there accrue certain fixed accidents by way of bodily movements. For quickness of movement results from a man being intent on many things which he is in a hurry to accomplish, whereas the magnanimous is intent only on great things; these are few and require great attention, wherefore they call for slow movement. Likewise shrill and rapid speaking is chiefly competent to those who are quick to quarrel about anything, and this becomes not the magnanimous who are busy only about great things. And just as these dispositions of bodily movements are competent to the magnanimous man according to the mode of his emotions, so too in those who are naturally disposed to magnanimity these conditions are found naturally.

Reply to Objection 4: There is in man something great which he possesses through the gift of God; and something defective which accrues to him through the weakness of nature. Accordingly magnanimity makes a man deem himself worthy of great things in consideration of the gifts he holds from God: thus if his soul is endowed with great virtue, magnanimity makes him tend to perfect works of virtue; and the same is to be said of the use of any other good, such as science or external fortune. On the other hand, humility makes a man think little of himself in consideration of his own deficiency, and magnanimity makes him despise others in so far as they fall away from God's gifts: since he does not think so much of others as to do anything wrong for their sake. Yet humility makes us honor others and esteem them better than ourselves, in so far as we see some of God's gifts in them. Hence it is written of the just man (Ps. 14:4): "In his sight a vile person is contemned [*Douay: 'The malignant is brought to nothing, but he glorifieth,' etc.]," which indicates the contempt of magnanimity, "but he honoreth them that fear the Lord," which points to the reverential bearing of humility. It is therefore evident that magnanimity and humility are not contrary to one another, although they seem to tend in contrary directions, because they proceed according to different considerations.

Reply to Objection 5: These properties in so far as they belong to a magnanimous man call not for blame, but for very great praise. For in the first place, when it is said that the magnanimous is not mindful of those from whom he has received favors, this points to the fact that he takes no pleasure in accepting favors from others unless he repay them with yet greater favor; this belongs to the perfection of gratitude, in the act of which he wishes to excel, even as in the acts of other virtues. Again, in the second place, it is said that he is remiss and slow of action, not that he is lacking in doing what becomes him, but because he does not busy himself with all kinds of works, but only with great works, such as are becoming to him. He is also said, in the third place, to employ irony, not as opposed to truth, and so as either to say of himself vile things that are not true, or deny of himself great things that are true, but because he does not disclose all his greatness, especially to the large number of those who are beneath him, since, as also the Philosopher says (Ethic. iv, 3), "it belongs to a magnanimous man to be great towards persons of dignity and affluence, and unassuming towards the middle class." In the fourth place, it is said that he cannot associate with others: this means that he is not at home with others than his friends: because he altogether shuns flattery and hypocrisy, which belong to littleness of mind. But he associates with all, both great and little, according as he ought, as stated above (ad 1). It is also said, fifthly, that he prefers to have barren things, not indeed any, but good, i.e. virtuous; for in all things he prefers the virtuous to the useful, as being greater: since the useful is sought in order to supply a defect which is inconsistent with magnanimity.

Whether magnanimity is a special virtue?

Objection 1: It seems that magnanimity is not a special virtue. For no special virtue is operative in every virtue. But the Philosopher states (Ethic. iv, 3) that "whatever is great in each virtue belongs to the magnanimous." Therefore magnanimity is not a special virtue.

Objection 2: Further, the acts of different virtues are not ascribed to any special virtue. But the acts of different virtues are ascribed to the magnanimous man. For it is stated in Ethic. iv, 3 that "it belongs to the magnanimous not to avoid reproof" (which is an act of prudence), "nor to act unjustly" (which is an act of justice), "that he is ready to do favors" (which is an act of charity), "that he gives his services readily" (which is an act of liberality), that "he is truthful" (which is an act of truthfulness), and that "he is not given to complaining" (which is an act of patience). Therefore magnanimity is not a special virtue.

Objection 3: Further, every virtue is a special ornament of the soul, according to the saying of Is. 61:10, "He hath clothed me with the garments of salvation," and afterwards he adds, "and as a bride adorned with her jewels." But magnanimity is the ornament of all the virtues, as stated in Ethic. iv. Therefore magnanimity is a general virtue.

On the contrary, The Philosopher (Ethic. ii, 7) distinguishes it from the other virtues.

I answer that, As stated above (Q[123], A[2]), it belongs to a special virtue to establish the mode of reason in a determinate matter. Now magnanimity establishes the mode of reason in a determinate matter, namely honors, as stated above ([3350]AA[1],2): and honor, considered in itself, is a special good, and accordingly magnanimity considered in itself is a special virtue.

Since, however, honor is the reward of every virtue, as stated above ([3351]Q[103], A[1], ad 2), it follows that by reason of its matter it regards all the virtues.

Reply to Objection 1: Magnanimity is not about any kind of honor, but great honor. Now, as honor is due to virtue, so great honor is due to a great deed of virtue. Hence it is that the magnanimous is intent on doing great deeds in every virtue, in so far, to wit, as he tends to what is worthy of great honors.

Reply to Objection 2: Since the magnanimous tends to great things, it follows that he tends chiefly to things that involve a certain excellence, and shuns those that imply defect. Now it savors of excellence that a man is beneficent, generous and grateful. Wherefore he shows himself ready to perform actions of this kind, but not as acts of the other virtues. on the other hand, it is a proof of defect, that a man thinks so much of certain external goods or evils, that for their sake he abandons and gives up justice or any virtue whatever. Again, all concealment of the truth indicates a defect, since it seems to be the outcome of fear. Also that a man be given to complaining denotes a defect, because by so doing the mind seems to give way to external evils. Wherefore these and like things the magnanimous man avoids under a special aspect, inasmuch as they are contrary to his excellence or greatness.

Reply to Objection 3: Every virtue derives from its species a certain luster or adornment which is proper to each virtue: but further adornment results from the very greatness of a virtuous deed, through magnanimity which makes all virtues greater as stated in Ethic. iv, 3.

Day 217

Whether magnanimity is a part of fortitude?

Objection 1: It seems that magnanimity is not a part of fortitude. For a thing is not a part of itself. But magnanimity appears to be the same as fortitude. For Seneca says (De Quat. Virtut.): "If magnanimity, which is also called fortitude, be in thy soul, thou shalt live in great assurance": and Tully says (De Offic. i): "If a man is brave we expect him to be magnanimous, truth-loving, and far removed from deception." Therefore magnanimity is not a part of fortitude.

Objection 2: Further, the Philosopher (Ethic. iv, 3) says that a magnanimous man is not {philokindynos}, that is, a lover of danger. But it belongs to a brave man to expose himself to danger. Therefore magnanimity has nothing in common with fortitude so as to be called a part thereof.

Objection 3: Further, magnanimity regards the great in things to be hoped for, whereas fortitude regards the great in things to be feared or dared. But good is of more import than evil. Therefore magnanimity is a more important virtue than fortitude. Therefore it is not a part thereof.

On the contrary, Macrobius (De Somn. Scip. i) and Andronicus reckon magnanimity as a part of fortitude.

I answer that, As stated above ([3352]FS, Q[61], A[3]), a principal virtue is one to which it belongs to establish a general mode of virtue in a principal matter. Now one of the general modes of virtue is firmness of mind, because "a firm standing is necessary in every virtue," according to Ethic. ii. And this is chiefly commended in those virtues that tend to something difficult, in which it is most difficult to preserve firmness. Wherefore the more difficult it is to stand firm in some matter of difficulty, the more principal is the virtue which makes the mind firm in that matter.

Now it is more difficult to stand firm in dangers of death, wherein fortitude confirms the mind, than in hoping for or obtaining the greatest goods, wherein the mind is confirmed by magnanimity, for, as man loves his life above all things, so does he fly from dangers of death more than any others. Accordingly it is clear that magnanimity agrees with fortitude in confirming the mind about some difficult matter; but it falls short thereof, in that it confirms the mind about a matter wherein it is easier to stand firm. Hence magnanimity is reckoned a part of fortitude, because it is annexed thereto as secondary to principal.

Reply to Objection 1: As the Philosopher says (Ethic. v, 1,3), "to lack evil is looked upon as a good," wherefore not to be overcome by a grievous evil, such as the danger of death, is looked upon as though it were the obtaining of a great good, the former belonging to fortitude, and the latter to magnanimity: in this sense fortitude and magnanimity may be considered as identical. Since, however, there is a difference as regards the difficulty on the part of either of the aforesaid, it follows that properly speaking magnanimity, according to the Philosopher (Ethic. ii, 7), is a distinct virtue from fortitude.

Reply to Objection 2: A man is said to love danger when he exposes himself to all kinds of dangers, which seems to be the mark of one who thinks "many" the same as "great." This is contrary to the nature of a magnanimous man, for no one seemingly exposes himself to danger for the sake of a thing that he does not deem great. But for things that are truly great, a magnanimous man is most ready to expose himself to danger, since he does something great in the act of fortitude, even as in the acts of the other virtues. Hence the Philosopher says (Ethic. ii, 7) that the magnanimous man is not {mikrokindynos}, i.e. endangering himself for small things, but {megalokindynos}, i.e. endangering himself for great things. And Seneca says (De Quat. Virtut.): "Thou wilt be magnanimous if thou neither seekest dangers like a rash man, nor fearest them like a coward. For nothing makes the soul a coward save the consciousness of a wicked life."

Reply to Objection 3: Evil as such is to be avoided: and that one has to withstand it is accidental; in so far, to wit, as one has to suffer an evil in order to safeguard a good. But good as such is to be desired, and that one avoids it is only accidental, in so far, to wit, as it is deemed to surpass the ability of the one who desires it. Now that which is so essentially is always of more account than that which is so accidentally. Wherefore the difficult in evil things is always more opposed to firmness of mind than the difficult in good things. Hence the virtue of fortitude takes precedence of the virtue of magnanimity. For though good is simply of more import than evil, evil is of more import in this particular respect.

Whether confidence belongs to magnanimity?

Objection 1: It seems that confidence does not belong to magnanimity. For a man may have assurance not only in himself, but also in another, according to 2 Cor. 3:4,5, "Such confidence we have, through Christ towards God, not that we are sufficient to think anything of ourselves, as of ourselves." But this seems inconsistent with the idea of magnanimity. Therefore confidence does not belong to magnanimity.

Objection 2: Further, confidence seems to be opposed to fear, according to Is. 12:2, "I will deal confidently and will not fear." But to be without fear seems more akin to fortitude. Therefore confidence also belongs to fortitude rather than to magnanimity.

Objection 3: Further, reward is not due except to virtue. But a reward is due to confidence, according to Heb. 3:6, where it is said that we are the house of Christ, "if we hold fast the confidence and glory of hope unto the end." Therefore confidence is a virtue distinct from magnanimity: and this is confirmed by the fact that Macrobius enumerates it with magnanimity (In Somn. Scip. i).

On the contrary, Tully (De Suv. Rhet. ii) seems to substitute confidence for magnanimity, as stated above in the preceding Question (ad 6) and in the prologue to this.

I answer that, Confidence takes its name from "fides" [faith]: and it belongs to faith to believe something and in somebody. But confidence belongs to hope, according to Job 11:18, "Thou shalt have confidence, hope being set before thee." Wherefore confidence apparently denotes chiefly that a man derives hope through believing the word of one who promises to help him. Since, however, faith signifies also a strong opinion, and since one may come to have a strong opinion about something, not only on account of another's statement, but also on account of something we observe in another, it follows that confidence may denote the hope of having something, which hope we conceive through observing something either in oneself---for instance, through observing that he is healthy, a man is confident that he will live long. or in another, for instance, through observing that another is friendly to him and powerful, a man is confident that he will receive help from him.

Now it has been stated above (A[1], ad 2) that magnanimity is chiefly about the hope of something difficult. Wherefore, since confidence denotes a certain strength of hope arising from some observation which gives one a strong opinion that one will obtain a certain good, it follows that confidence belongs to magnanimity.

Reply to Objection 1: As the Philosopher says (Ethic. iv, 3), it belongs to the "magnanimous to need nothing," for need is a mark of the deficient. But this is to be understood according to the mode of a man, hence he adds "or scarcely anything." For it surpasses man to need nothing at all. For every man needs, first, the Divine assistance, secondly, even human assistance, since man is naturally a social animal, for he is sufficient by himself to provide for his own life. Accordingly, in so far as he needs others, it belongs to a magnanimous man to have confidence in others, for it is also a point of excellence in a man that he should have at hand those who are able to be of service to him. And in so far as his own ability goes, it belongs to a magnanimous man to be confident in himself.

Reply to Objection 2: As stated above ([3353]FS, Q[23], A[2]; [3354]FS, Q[40], A[4]), when we were treating of the passions, hope is directly opposed to despair, because the latter is about the same object, namely good. But as regards contrariety of objects it is opposed to fear, because the latter's object is evil. Now confidence denotes a certain strength of hope, wherefore it is opposed to fear even as hope is. Since, however, fortitude properly strengthens a man in respect of evil, and magnanimity in respect of the obtaining of good, it follows that confidence belongs more properly to magnanimity than to fortitude. Yet because hope causes daring, which belongs to fortitude, it follows in consequence that confidence pertains to fortitude.

Reply to Objection 3: Confidence, as stated above, denotes a certain mode of hope: for confidence is hope strengthened by a strong opinion. Now the mode applied to an affection may call for commendation of the act, so that it become meritorious, yet it is not this that draws it to a species of virtue, but its matter. Hence, properly speaking, confidence cannot denote a virtue, though it may denote the conditions of a virtue. For this reason it is reckoned among the parts of fortitude, not as an annexed virtue, except as identified with magnanimity by Tully (De Suv. Rhet. ii), but as an integral part, as stated in the preceding Question.

Whether security belongs to magnanimity?

Objection 1: It seems that security does not belong to magnanimity. For security, as stated above (Q[128], ad 6), denotes freedom from the disturbance of fear. But fortitude does this most effectively. Wherefore security is seemingly the same as fortitude. But fortitude does not belong to magnanimity; rather the reverse is the case. Neither therefore does security belong to magnanimity.

Objection 2: Further, Isidore says (Etym. x) that a man "is said to be secure because he is without care." But this seems to be contrary to virtue, which has a care for honorable things, according to 2 Tim. 2:15, "Carefully study to present thyself approved unto God." Therefore security does not belong to magnanimity, which does great things in all the virtues.

Objection 3: Further, virtue is not its own reward. But security is accounted the reward of virtue, according to Job 11:14,18, "If thou wilt put away from thee the iniquity that is in thy hand . . . being buried thou shalt sleep secure." Therefore security does not belong to magnanimity or to any other virtue, as a part thereof.

On the contrary, Tully says (De Offic. i) under the heading: "Magnanimity consists of two things," that "it belongs to magnanimity to give way neither to a troubled mind, nor to man, nor to fortune." But a man's security consists in this. Therefore security belongs to magnanimity.

I answer that, As the Philosopher says (Rhet. ii, 5), "fear makes a man take counsel," because, to wit he takes care to avoid what he fears. Now security takes its name from the removal of this care, of which fear is the cause: wherefore security denotes perfect freedom of the mind from fear, just as confidence denotes strength of hope. Now, as hope directly belongs to magnanimity, so fear directly regards fortitude. Wherefore as confidence belongs immediately to magnanimity, so security belongs immediately to fortitude.

It must be observed, however, that as hope is the cause of daring, so is fear the cause of despair, as stated above when we were treating of the passion ([3355]FS, Q[45], A[2]). Wherefore as confidence belongs indirectly to fortitude, in so far as it makes use of daring, so security belongs indirectly to magnanimity, in so far as it banishes despair.

Reply to Objection 1: Fortitude is chiefly commended, not because it banishes fear, which belongs to security, but because it denotes a firmness of mind in the matter of the passion. Wherefore security is not the same as fortitude, but is a condition thereof.

Reply to Objection 2: Not all security is worthy of praise but only when one puts care aside, as one ought, and in things when one should not fear: in this way it is a condition of fortitude and of magnanimity.

Reply to Objection 3: There is in the virtues a certain likeness to, and participation of, future happiness, as stated above ([3356]FS, Q[5], AA[3],7). Hence nothing hinders a certain security from being a condition of a virtue, although perfect security belongs to virtue's reward.

Whether goods of fortune conduce to magnanimity?

Objection 1: It seems that goods of fortune do not conduce to magnanimity. For according to Seneca (De Ira i: De vita beata xvi): "virtue suffices for itself." Now magnanimity takes every virtue great, as stated above (A[4], ad 3). Therefore goods of fortune do not conduce to magnanimity.

Objection 2: Further, no virtuous man despises what is helpful to him. But the magnanimous man despises whatever pertains to goods of fortune: for Tully says (De Offic. i) under the heading: "Magnanimity consists of two things," that "a great soul is commended for despising external things." Therefore a magnanimous man is not helped by goods of fortune.

Objection 3: Further, Tully adds (De Offic. i) that "it belongs to a great soul so to bear what seems troublesome, as nowise to depart from his natural estate, or from the dignity of a wise man." And Aristotle says (Ethic. iv, 3) that "a magnanimous man does not grieve at misfortune." Now troubles and misfortunes are opposed to goods of fortune, for every one grieves at the loss of what is helpful to him. Therefore external goods of fortune do not conduce to magnanimity.

On the contrary, The Philosopher says (Ethic. iv, 3) that "good fortune seems to conduce to magnanimity."

I answer that, As stated above [3357](A[1]), magnanimity regards two things: honor as its matter, and the accomplishment of something great as its end. Now goods of fortune conduce to both these things. For since honor is conferred on the virtuous, not only by the wise, but also by the multitude who hold these goods of fortune in the highest esteem, the result is that they show greater honor to those who possess goods of fortune. Likewise goods of fortune are useful organs or instruments of virtuous deeds: since we can easily accomplish things by means of riches, power and friends. Hence it is evident that goods of fortune conduce to magnanimity.

Reply to Objection 1: Virtue is said to be sufficient for itself, because it can be without even these external goods; yet it needs them in order to act more expeditiously.

Reply to Objection 2: The magnanimous man despises external goods, inasmuch as he does not think them so great as to be bound to do anything unbecoming for their sake. Yet he does not despise them, but that he esteems them useful for the accomplishment of virtuous deeds.

Reply to Objection 3: If a man does not think much of a thing, he is neither very joyful at obtaining it, nor very grieved at losing it. Wherefore, since the magnanimous man does not think much of external goods, that is goods of fortune, he is neither much uplifted by them if he has them, nor much cast down by their loss.

OF PRESUMPTION (TWO ARTICLES)

We must now consider the vices opposed to magnanimity; and in the first place, those that are opposed thereto by excess. These are three, namely, presumption, ambition, and vainglory. Secondly, we shall consider pusillanimity which is opposed to it by way of deficiency. Under the first head there are two points of inquiry:

(1) Whether presumption is a sin?
(2) Whether it is opposed to magnanimity by excess?

Whether presumption is a sin?

Objection 1: It seems that presumption is not a sin. For the Apostle says: "Forgetting the things that are behind, I stretch forth [Vulg.: 'and stretching forth'] myself to those that are before." But it seems to savor of presumption that one should tend to what is above oneself. Therefore presumption is not a sin.

Objection 2: Further, the Philosopher says (Ethic. i, 7) "we should not listen to those who would persuade us to relish human things because we are men, or mortal things because we are mortal, but we should relish those that make us immortal": and (Metaph. i) "that man should pursue divine things as far as possible." Now divine and immortal things are seemingly far above man. Since then presumption consists essentially in tending to what is above oneself, it seems that presumption is something praiseworthy, rather than a sin.

Objection 3: Further, the Apostle says (2 Cor. 3:5): "Not that we are sufficient to think anything of ourselves, as of ourselves." If then presumption, by which one strives at that for which one is not sufficient, be a sin, it seems that man cannot lawfully even think of anything good: which is absurd. Therefore presumption is not a sin.

On the contrary, It is written (Ecclus. 37:3): "O wicked presumption, whence camest thou?" and a gloss answers: "From a creature's evil will." Now all that comes of the root of an evil will is a sin. Therefore presumption is a sin.

I answer that, Since whatever is according to nature, is ordered by the Divine Reason, which human reason ought to imitate, whatever is done in accordance with human reason in opposition to the order established in general throughout natural things is vicious and sinful. Now it is established throughout all natural things, that every action is commensurate with the power of the agent, nor does any natural agent strive to do what exceeds its ability. Hence it is vicious and sinful, as being contrary to the natural order, that any one should assume to do what is above his power: and this is what is meant by presumption, as its very name shows. Wherefore it is evident that presumption is a sin.

Reply to Objection 1: Nothing hinders that which is above the active power of a natural thing, and yet not above the passive power of that same thing: thus the air is possessed of a passive power by reason of which it can be so changed as to obtain the action and movement of fire, which surpass the active power of air. Thus too it would be sinful and presumptuous for a man while in a state of imperfect virtue to attempt the immediate accomplishment of what belongs to perfect virtue. But it is not presumptuous or sinful for a man to endeavor to advance towards perfect virtue. In this way the Apostle stretched himself forth to the things that were before him, namely continually advancing forward.

Reply to Objection 2: Divine and immortal things surpass man according to the order of nature. Yet man is possessed of a natural power, namely the intellect, whereby he can be united to immortal and Divine things. In this respect the Philosopher says that "man ought to pursue immortal and divine things," not that he should do what it becomes God to do, but that he should be united to Him in intellect and will.

Reply to Objection 3: As the Philosopher says (Ethic. iii, 3), "what we can do by the help of others we can do by ourselves in a sense." Hence since we can think and do good by the help of God, this is not altogether above our ability. Hence it is not presumptuous for a man to attempt the accomplishment of a virtuous deed: but it would be presumptuous if one were to make the attempt without confidence in God's assistance.

Whether presumption is opposed to magnanimity by excess?

Objection 1: It seems that presumption is not opposed to magnanimity by excess. For presumption is accounted a species of the sin against the Holy Ghost, as stated above ([3358]Q[14], A[2];[3359] Q[21], A[1]). But the sin against the Holy Ghost is not opposed to magnanimity, but to charity. Neither therefore is presumption opposed to magnanimity.

Objection 2: Further, it belongs to magnanimity that one should deem oneself worthy of great things. But a man is said to be presumptuous even if he deem himself worthy of small things, if they surpass his ability. Therefore presumption is not directly opposed to magnanimity.

Objection 3: Further, the magnanimous man looks upon external goods as little things. Now according to the Philosopher (Ethic. iv, 3), "on account of external fortune the presumptuous disdain and wrong others, because they deem external goods as something great." Therefore presumption is opposed to magnanimity, not by excess, but only by deficiency.

On the contrary, The Philosopher says (Ethic. ii, 7; iv, 3) that the "vain man," i.e. a vaporer or a wind-bag, which with us denotes a presumptuous man, "is opposed to the magnanimous man by excess."

I answer that, As stated above ([3360]Q[129], A[3], ad 1), magnanimity observes the means, not as regards the quantity of that to which it tends, but in proportion to our own ability: for it does not tend to anything greater than is becoming to us.

Now the presumptuous man, as regards that to which he tends, does not exceed the magnanimous, but sometimes falls far short of him: but he does exceed in proportion to his own ability, whereas the magnanimous man does not exceed his. It is in this way that presumption is opposed to magnanimity by excess.

Reply to Objection 1: It is not every presumption that is accounted a sin against the Holy Ghost, but that by which one contemns the Divine justice through inordinate confidence in the Divine mercy. The latter kind of presumption, by reason of its matter, inasmuch, to wit, as it implies contempt of something Divine, is opposed to charity, or rather to the gift of fear, whereby we revere God. Nevertheless, in so far as this contempt exceeds the proportion to one's own ability, it can be opposed to magnanimity.

Reply to Objection 2: Presumption, like magnanimity, seems to tend to something great. For we are not, as a rule, wont to call a man presumptuous for going beyond his powers in something small. If, however, such a man be called presumptuous, this kind of presumption is not opposed to magnanimity, but to that virtue which is about ordinary honor, as stated above ([3361]Q[129], A[2]).

Reply to Objection 3: No one attempts what is above his ability, except in so far as he deems his ability greater than it is. In this one may err in two ways. First only as regards quantity, as when a man thinks he has greater virtue, or knowledge, or the like, than he has. Secondly, as regards the kind of thing, as when he thinks himself great, and worthy of great things, by reason of something that does not make him so, for instance by reason of riches or goods of fortune. For, as the Philosopher says (Ethic. iv, 3), "those who have these things without virtue, neither justly deem themselves worthy of great things, nor are rightly called magnanimous."

Again, the thing to which a man sometimes tends in excess of his ability, is sometimes in very truth something great, simply as in the case of Peter, whose intent was to suffer for Christ, which has exceeded his power; while sometimes it is something great, not simply, but only in the opinion of fools, such as wearing costly clothes, despising and wronging others. This savors of an excess of magnanimity, not in any truth, but in people's opinion. Hence Seneca says (De Quat. Virtut.) that "when magnanimity exceeds its measure, it makes a man high-handed, proud, haughty restless, and bent on excelling in all things, whether in words or in deeds, without any considerations of virtue." Thus it is evident that the presumptuous man sometimes falls short of the magnanimous in reality, although in appearance he surpasses him.

OF AMBITION (TWO ARTICLES)

We must now consider ambition: and under this head there are two points of inquiry:

(1) Whether it is a sin?

(2) Whether it is opposed to magnanimity by excess?

Whether ambition is a sin?

Objection 1: It seems that ambition is not a sin. For ambition denotes the desire of honor. Now honor is in itself a good thing, and the greatest of external goods: wherefore those who care not for honor are reproved. Therefore ambition is not a sin; rather is it something deserving of praise, in so far as a good is laudably desired.

Objection 2: Further, anyone may, without sin, desire what is due to him as a reward. Now honor is the reward of virtue, as the Philosopher states (Ethic. i, 12; iv, 3; viii, 14). Therefore ambition of honor is not a sin.

Objection 3: Further, that which heartens a man to do good and disheartens him from doing evil, is not a sin. Now honor heartens men to do good and to avoid evil; thus the Philosopher says (Ethic. iii, 8) that "with the bravest men, cowards are held in dishonor, and the brave in honor": and Tully says (De Tusc. Quaest. i) that "honor fosters the arts." Therefore ambition is not a sin.

On the contrary, It is written (1 Cor. 13:5) that "charity is not ambitious, seeketh not her own." Now nothing is contrary to charity, except sin. Therefore ambition is a sin.

I answer that, As stated above ([3362]Q[103], AA[1],2), honor denotes reverence shown to a person in witness of his excellence. Now two things have to be considered with regard to man's honor. The first is that a man has not from himself the thing in which he excels, for this is, as it were, something Divine in him, wherefore on this count honor is due principally, not to him but to God. The second point that calls for observation is that the thing in which man excels is given to him by God, that he may profit others thereby: wherefore a man ought so far to be pleased that others bear witness to his excellence, as this enables him to profit others.

Now the desire of honor may be inordinate in three ways. First, when a man desires recognition of an excellence which he has not: this is to desire more than his share of honor. Secondly, when a man desires honor for himself without referring it to God. Thirdly, when a man's appetite rests in honor itself, without referring it to the profit of others. Since then ambition denotes inordinate desire of honor, it is evident that it is always a sin.

Reply to Objection 1: The desire for good should be regulated according to reason, and if it exceed this rule it will be sinful. In this way it is sinful to desire honor in disaccord with the order of reason. Now those are reproved who care not for honor in accordance with reason's dictate that they should avoid what is contrary to honor.

Reply to Objection 2: Honor is not the reward of virtue, as regards the virtuous man, in this sense that he should seek for it as his reward: since the reward he seeks is happiness, which is the end of virtue. But it is said to be the reward of virtue as regards others, who have nothing greater than honor whereby to reward the virtuous; which honor derives greatness from the very fact that it bears witness to virtue. Hence it is evident that it is not an adequate reward, as stated in Ethic. iv, 3.

Reply to Objection 3: Just as some are heartened to do good and disheartened from doing evil, by the desire of honor, if this be desired in due measure; so, if it be desired inordinately, it may become to man an occasion of doing many evil things, as when a man cares not by what means he obtains honor. Wherefore Sallust says (Catilin.) that "the good as well as the wicked covet honors for themselves, but the one," i.e. the good, "go about it in the right way," whereas "the other," i.e. the wicked, "through lack of the good arts, make use of deceit and falsehood." Yet they who, merely for the sake of honor, either do good or avoid evil, are not virtuous, according to the Philosopher (Ethic. iii, 8), where he says that they who do brave things for the sake of honor are not truly brave.

Whether ambition is opposed to magnanimity by excess?

Objection 1: It seems that ambition is not opposed to magnanimity by excess. For one mean has only one extreme opposed to it on the one side. Now presumption is opposed to magnanimity by excess as stated above ([3363]Q[130], A[2]). Therefore ambition is not opposed to it by excess.

Objection 2: Further, magnanimity is about honors; whereas ambition seems to regard positions of dignity: for it is written (2 Macc. 4:7) that "Jason ambitiously sought the high priesthood." Therefore ambition is not opposed to magnanimity.

Objection 3: Further, ambition seems to regard outward show: for it is written (Acts 25:27) that "Agrippa and Berenice . . . with great pomp [ambitione]. . . had entered into the hall of audience" [*'Praetorium.' The Vulgate has 'auditorium,' but the meaning is the same], and (2 Para. 16:14) that when Asa died they "burned spices and . . . ointments over his body" with very great pomp [ambitione]. But magnanimity is not about outward show. Therefore ambition is not opposed to magnanimity.

On the contrary, Tully says (De Offic. i) that "the more a man exceeds in magnanimity, the more he desires himself alone to dominate others." But this pertains to ambition. Therefore ambition denotes an excess of magnanimity.

I answer that, As stated above [3364](A[1]), ambition signifies inordinate love of honor. Now magnanimity is about honors and makes use of them in a becoming manner. Wherefore it is evident that ambition is opposed to magnanimity as the inordinate to that which is well ordered.

Reply to Objection 1: Magnanimity regards two things. It regards one as its end, in so far as it is some great deed that the magnanimous man attempts in proportion to his ability. In this way presumption is opposed to magnanimity by excess: because the presumptuous man attempts great deeds beyond his ability. The other thing that magnanimity regards is its matter, viz. honor, of which it makes right use: and in this way ambition is opposed to magnanimity by excess. Nor is it impossible for one mean to be exceeded in various respects.

Reply to Objection 2: Honor is due to those who are in a position of dignity, on account of a certain excellence of their estate: and accordingly inordinate desire for positions of dignity pertains to ambition. For if a man were to have an inordinate desire for a position of dignity, not for the sake of honor, but for the sake of a right use of a dignity exceeding his ability, he would not be ambitious but presumptuous.

Reply to Objection 3: The very solemnity of outward worship is a kind of honor, wherefore in such cases honor is wont to be shown. This is signified by the words of James 2:2,3: "If there shall come into your assembly a man having a golden ring, in fine apparel . . . and you . . . shall say to him: Sit thou here well," etc. Wherefore ambition does not regard outward worship, except in so far as this is a kind of honor.

Day 218

OF VAINGLORY (FIVE ARTICLES)
We must now consider vainglory: under which head there are five points of inquiry:
(1) Whether desire of glory is a sin?
(2) Whether it is opposed to magnanimity?
(3) Whether it is a mortal sin?
(4) Whether it is a capital vice?
(5) Of its daughters.

Whether the desire of glory is a sin?

Objection 1: It seems that the desire of glory is not a sin. For no one sins in being likened to God: in fact we are commanded (Eph. 5:1): "Be ye . . . followers of God, as most dear children." Now by seeking glory man seems to imitate God, Who seeks glory from men: wherefore it is written (Is. 43:6,7): "Bring My sons from afar, and My daughters from the ends of the earth. And every one that calleth on My name, I have created him for My glory." Therefore the desire for glory is not a sin.

Objection 2: Further, that which incites a mar to do good is apparently not a sin. Now the desire of glory incites men to do good. For Tully says (De Tusc. Quaest. i) that "glory inflames every man to strive his utmost": and in Holy Writ glory is promised for good works, according to Rom. 2:7: "To them, indeed, who according to patience in good work . . . glory and honor" [*Vulg.: 'Who will render to every man according to his works, to them indeed who . . . seek glory and honor and incorruption, eternal life.']. Therefore the desire for glory is not a sin.

Objection 3: Further, Tully says (De Invent. Rhet. ii) that glory is "consistent good report about a person, together with praise": and this comes to the same as what Augustine says (Contra Maximin. iii), viz. that glory is, "as it were, clear knowledge with praise." Now it is no sin to desire praiseworthy renown: indeed, it seems itself to call for praise, according to Ecclus. 41:15, "Take care of a good name," and Rom. 12:17, "Providing good things not only in the sight of God, but also in the sight of all men." Therefore the desire of vainglory is not a sin.

On the contrary, Augustine says (De Civ. Dei v): "He is better advised who acknowledges that even the love of praise is sinful."

I answer that, Glory signifies a certain clarity, wherefore Augustine says (Tract. lxxxii, c, cxiv in Joan.) that to be "glorified is the same as to be clarified." Now clarity and comeliness imply a certain display: wherefore the word glory properly denotes the display of something as regards its seeming comely in the sight of men, whether it be a bodily or a spiritual good. Since, however, that which is clear simply can be seen by many, and by those who are far away, it follows that the word glory properly denotes that somebody's good is known and approved by many, according to the saying of Sallust (Catilin.) [*The quotation is from Livy: Hist., Lib. XXII C, 39]: "I must not boast while I am addressing one man."

But if we take the word glory in a broader sense, it not only consists in the knowledge of many, but also in the knowledge of few, or of one, or of oneself alone, as when one considers one's own good as being worthy of praise. Now it is not a sin to know and approve one's own good: for it is written (1 Cor. 2:12): "Now we have received not the spirit of this world, but the Spirit that is of God that we may know the things that are given us from God." Likewise it is not a sin to be willing to approve one's own good works: for it is written (Mat. 5:16): "Let your light shine before men." Hence the desire for glory does not, of itself, denote a sin: but the desire for empty or vain glory denotes a sin: for it is sinful to desire anything vain, according to Ps. 4:3, "Why do you love vanity, and seek after lying?"

Now glory may be called vain in three ways. First, on the part of the thing for which one seeks glory: as when a man seeks glory for that which is unworthy of glory, for instance when he seeks it for something frail and perishable: secondly, on the part of him from whom he seeks glory, for instance a man whose judgment is uncertain: thirdly, on the part of the man himself who seeks glory, for that he does not refer the desire of his own glory to a due end, such as God's honor, or the spiritual welfare of his neighbor.

Reply to Objection 1: As Augustine says on Jn. 13:13, "You call Me Master and Lord; and you say well" (Tract. lviii in Joan.): "Self-complacency is fraught with danger of one who has to beware of pride. But He Who is above all, however much He may praise Himself, does not uplift Himself. For knowledge of God is our need, not His: nor does any man know Him unless he be taught of Him Who knows." It is therefore evident that God seeks glory, not for His own sake, but for ours. In like manner a man may rightly seek his own glory for the good of others, according to Mat. 5:16, "That they may see your good works, and glorify your Father Who is in heaven."

Reply to Objection 2: That which we receive from God is not vain but true glory: it is this glory that is promised as a reward for good works, and of which it is written (2 Cor. 10:17,18): "He that glorieth let him glory in the Lord, for not he who commendeth himself is approved, but he whom God commendeth." It is true that some are heartened to do works of virtue, through desire for human glory, as also through the desire for other earthly goods. Yet he is not truly virtuous who does virtuous deeds for the sake of human glory, as Augustine proves (De Civ. Dei v).

Reply to Objection 3: It is requisite for man's perfection that he should know himself; but not that he should be known by others, wherefore it is not to be desired in itself. It may, however, be desired as being useful for something, either in order that God may be glorified by men, or that men may become better by reason of the good they know to be in another man, or in order that man, knowing by the testimony of others' praise the good which is in him, may himself strive to persevere therein and to become better. In this sense it is praiseworthy that a man should "take care of his good name," and that he should "provide good things in the sight of God and men": but not that he should take an empty pleasure in human praise.

Whether vainglory is opposed to magnanimity?

Objection 1: It seems that vainglory is not opposed to magnanimity. For, as stated above [3365](A[1]), vainglory consists in glorying in things that are not, which pertains to falsehood; or in earthly and perishable things, which pertains to covetousness; or in the testimony of men, whose judgment is uncertain, which pertains to imprudence. Now these vices are not contrary to magnanimity. Therefore vainglory is not opposed to magnanimity.

Objection 2: Further, vainglory is not, like pusillanimity, opposed to magnanimity by way of deficiency, for this seems inconsistent with vainglory. Nor is it opposed to it by way of excess, for in this way presumption and ambition are opposed to magnanimity, as stated above ([3366]Q[130], A[2];[3367] Q[131], A[2]): and these differ from vainglory. Therefore vainglory is not opposed to magnanimity.

Objection 3: Further, a gloss on Phil. 2:3, "Let nothing be done through contention, neither by vainglory," says: "Some among them were given to dissension and restlessness, contending with one another for the sake of vainglory." But contention [*Cf. Q[38]] is not opposed to magnanimity. Neither therefore is vainglory.

On the contrary, Tully says (De Offic. i) under the heading, "Magnanimity consists in two things: We should beware of the desire for glory, since it enslaves the mind, which a magnanimous man should ever strive to keep untrammeled." Therefore it is opposed to magnanimity.

I answer that, As stated above ([3368]Q[103], A[1], ad 3), glory is an effect of honor and praise: because from the fact that a man is praised, or shown any kind of reverence, he acquires charity in the knowledge of others. And since magnanimity is about honor, as stated above ([3369]Q[129], AA[1],2), it follows that it also is about glory: seeing that as a man uses honor moderately, so too does he use glory in moderation. Wherefore inordinate desire of glory is directly opposed to magnanimity.

Reply to Objection 1: To think so much of little things as to glory in them is itself opposed to magnanimity. Wherefore it is said of the magnanimous man (Ethic. iv) that honor is of little account to him. In like manner he thinks little of other things that are sought for honor's sake, such as power and wealth. Likewise it is inconsistent with magnanimity to glory in things that are not; wherefore it is said of the magnanimous man (Ethic. iv) that he cares more for truth than for opinion. Again it is incompatible with magnanimity for a man to glory in the testimony of human praise, as though he deemed this something great; wherefore it is said of the magnanimous man (Ethic. iv), that he cares not to be praised. And so, when a man looks upon little things as though they were great, nothing hinders this from being contrary to magnanimity, as well as to other virtues.

Reply to Objection 2: He that is desirous of vainglory does in truth fall short of being magnanimous, because he glories in what the magnanimous man thinks little of, as stated in the preceding Reply. But if we consider his estimate, he is opposed to the magnanimous man by way of excess, because the glory which he seeks is something great in his estimation, and he tends thereto in excess of his deserts.

Reply to Objection 3: As stated above ([3370]Q[127], A[2], ad 2), the opposition of vices does not depend on their effects. Nevertheless contention, if done intentionally, is opposed to magnanimity: since no one contends save for what he deems great. Wherefore the Philosopher says (Ethic. iv, 3) that the magnanimous man is not contentious, because nothing is great in his estimation.

Whether vainglory is a mortal sin?

Objection 1: It seems that vainglory is a mortal sin. For nothing precludes the eternal reward except a mortal sin. Now vainglory precludes the eternal reward: for it is written (Mat. 6:1): "Take heed, that you do not give justice before men, to be seen by them: otherwise you shall not have a reward of your Father Who is in heaven." Therefore vainglory is a mortal sin.

Objection 2: Further, whoever appropriates to himself that which is proper to God, sins mortally. Now by desiring vainglory, a man appropriates to himself that which is proper to God. For it is written (Is. 42:8): "I will not give My glory to another," and (1 Tim. 1:17): "To . . . the only God be honor and glory." Therefore vainglory is a mortal sin.

Objection 3: Further, apparently a sin is mortal if it be most dangerous and harmful. Now vainglory is a sin of this kind, because a gloss of Augustine on 1 Thess. 2:4, "God, Who proveth our hearts," says: "Unless a man war against the love of human glory he does not perceive its baneful power, for though it be easy for anyone not to desire praise as long as one does not get it, it is difficult not to take pleasure in it, when it is given." Chrysostom also says (Hom. xix in Matth.) that "vainglory enters secretly, and robs us insensibly of all our inward possessions." Therefore vainglory is a mortal sin.

On the contrary, Chrysostom says [*Hom. xiii in the Opus Imperfectum falsely ascribed to St. John Chrysostom] that "while other vices find their abode in the servants of the devil, vainglory finds a place even in the servants of Christ." Yet in the latter there is no mortal sin. Therefore vainglory is not a mortal sin.

I answer that, As stated above ([3371]Q[24], A[12];[3372] Q[110], A[4];[3373] Q[112], A[2]), a sin is mortal through being contrary to charity. Now the sin of vainglory, considered in itself, does not seem to be contrary to charity as regards the love of one's neighbor: yet as regards the love of God it may be contrary to charity in two ways. In one way, by reason of the matter about which one glories: for instance when one glories in something false that is opposed to the reverence we owe God, according to Ezech. 28:2, "Thy heart is lifted up, and Thou hast said: I am God," and 1 Cor. 4:7, "What hast thou that thou hast not received? And if thou hast received, why dost thou glory, as if thou hadst not received it?" Or again when a man prefers to God the temporal good in which he glories: for this is forbidden (Jer. 9:23,24): "Let not the wise man glory in his wisdom, and let not the strong man glory in his strength, and let not the rich man glory in his riches. But let him that glorieth glory in this, that he understandeth and knoweth Me." Or again when a man prefers the testimony of man to God's; thus it is written in reproval of certain people (Jn. 12:43): "For they loved the glory of men more than the glory of God."

In another way vainglory may be contrary to charity, on the part of the one who glories, in that he refers his intention to glory as his last end: so that he directs even virtuous deeds thereto, and, in order to obtain it, forbears not from doing even that which is against God. In this way it is a mortal sin. Wherefore Augustine says (De Civ. Dei v, 14) that "this vice," namely the love of human praise, "is so hostile to a godly faith, if the heart desires glory more than it fears or loves God, that our Lord said (Jn. 5:44): How can you believe, who receive glory one from another, and the glory which is from God alone, you do not seek?"

If, however, the love of human glory, though it be vain, be not inconsistent with charity, neither as regards the matter gloried in, nor as to the intention of him that seeks glory, it is not a mortal but a venial sin.

Reply to Objection 1: No man, by sinning, merits eternal life: wherefore a virtuous deed loses its power to merit eternal life, if it be done for the sake of vainglory, even though that vainglory be not a mortal sin. On the other hand when a man loses the eternal reward simply through vainglory, and not merely in respect of one act, vainglory is a mortal sin.

Reply to Objection 2: Not every man that is desirous of vainglory, desires the excellence which belongs to God alone. For the glory due to God alone differs from the glory due to a virtuous or rich man.

Reply to Objection 3: Vainglory is stated to be a dangerous sin, not only on account of its gravity, but also because it is a disposition to grave sins, in so far as it renders man presumptuous and too self-confident: and so it gradually disposes a man to lose his inward goods.

Whether vainglory is a capital vice?

Objection 1: It seems that vainglory is not a capital vice. For a vice that always arises from another vice is seemingly not capital. But vainglory always arises from pride. Therefore vainglory is not a capital vice.

Objection 2: Further, honor would seem to take precedence of glory, for this is its effect. Now ambition which is inordinate desire of honor is not a capital vice. Neither therefore is the desire of vainglory.

Objection 3: Further, a capital vice has a certain prominence. But vainglory seems to have no prominence, neither as a sin, because it is not always a mortal sin, nor considered as an appetible good, since human glory is apparently a frail thing, and is something outside man himself. Therefore vainglory is not a capital vice.

On the contrary, Gregory (Moral. xxxi) numbers vainglory among the seven capital vices.

I answer that, The capital vices are enumerated in two ways. For some reckon pride as one of their number: and these do not place vainglory among the capital vices. Gregory, however (Moral. xxxi), reckons pride to be the queen of all the vices, and vainglory, which is the immediate offspring of pride, he reckons to be a capital vice: and not without reason. For pride, as we shall state farther on ([3374]Q[152], AA[1],2), denotes inordinate desire of excellence. But whatever good one may desire, one desires a certain perfection and excellence therefrom: wherefore the end of every vice is directed to the end of pride, so that this vice seems to exercise a kind of causality over the other vices, and ought not to be reckoned among the special sources of vice, known as the capital vices. Now among the goods that are the means whereby man acquires honor, glory seems to be the most conducive to that effect, inasmuch as it denotes the manifestation of a man's goodness: since good is naturally loved and honored by all. Wherefore, just as by the glory which is in God's sight man acquires honor in Divine things, so too by the glory which is in the sight of man he acquires excellence in human things. Hence on account of its close connection with excellence, which men desire above all, it follows that it is most desirable. And since many vices arise from the inordinate desire thereof, it follows that vainglory is a capital vice.

Reply to Objection 1: It is not impossible for a capital vice to arise from pride, since as stated above (in the body of the Article and [3375]FS, Q[84], A[2]) pride is the queen and mother of all the vices.

Reply to Objection 2: Praise and honor, as stated above [3376](A[2]), stand in relation to glory as the causes from which it proceeds, so that glory is compared to them as their end. For the reason why a man loves to be honored and praised is that he thinks thereby to acquire a certain renown in the knowledge of others.

Reply to Objection 3: Vainglory stands prominent under the aspect of desirability, for the reason given above, and this suffices for it to be reckoned a capital vice. Nor is it always necessary for a capital vice to be a mortal sin; for mortal sin can arise from venial sin, inasmuch as venial sin can dispose man thereto.

Whether the daughters of vainglory are suitably reckoned to be disobedience, boastfulness, hypocrisy, contention, obstinacy, discord, and love of novelties?

Objection 1: It seems that the daughters of vainglory are unsuitably reckoned to be "disobedience, boastfulness, hypocrisy, contention, obstinacy, discord, and eccentricity [*Praesumptio novitatum, literally 'presumption of novelties']." For according to Gregory (Moral. xxiii) boastfulness is numbered among the species of pride. Now pride does not arise from vainglory, rather is it the other way about, as Gregory says (Moral. xxxi). Therefore boastfulness should not be reckoned among the daughters of vainglory.

Objection 2: Further, contention and discord seem to be the outcome chiefly of anger. But anger is a capital vice condivided with vainglory. Therefore it seems that they are not the daughters of vainglory.

Objection 3: Further, Chrysostom says (Hom. xix in Matth.) that vainglory is always evil, but especially in philanthropy, i.e. mercy. And yet this is nothing new, for it is an established custom among men. Therefore eccentricity should not be specially reckoned as a daughter of vainglory.

On the contrary, stands the authority of Gregory (Moral. xxxi), who there assigns the above daughters to vainglory.

I answer that, As stated above (Q[34], A[5]; Q[35], A[4]; [3377]FS, Q[84], AA[3],4), the vices which by their very nature are such as to be directed to the end of a certain capital vice, are called its daughters. Now the end of vainglory is the manifestation of one's own excellence, as stated above ([3378]AA[1],4): and to this end a man may tend in two ways. In one way directly, either by words, and this is boasting, or by deeds, and then if they be true and call for astonishment, it is love of novelties which men are wont to wonder at most; but if they be false, it is hypocrisy. In another way a man strives to make known his excellence by showing that he is not inferior to another, and this in four ways. First, as regards the intellect, and thus we have "obstinacy," by which a man is too much attached to his own opinion, being unwilling to believe one that is better. Secondly, as regards the will, and then we have "discord," whereby a man is unwilling to give up his own will, and agree with others. Thirdly, as regards "speech," and then we have "contention," whereby a man quarrels noisily with another. Fourthly as regards deeds, and this is "disobedience," whereby a man refuses to carry out the command of his superiors.

Reply to Objection 1: As stated above ([3379]Q[112], A[1], ad 2), boasting is reckoned a kind of pride, as regards its interior cause, which is arrogance: but outward boasting, according to Ethic. iv, is directed sometimes to gain, but more often to glory and honor, and thus it is the result of vainglory.

Reply to Objection 2: Anger is not the cause of discord and contention, except in conjunction with vainglory, in that a man thinks it a glorious thing for him not to yield to the will and words of others.

Reply to Objection 3: Vainglory is reproved in connection with almsdeeds on account of the lack of charity apparent in one who prefers vainglory to the good of his neighbor, seeing that he does the latter for the sake of the former. But a man is not reproved for presuming to give alms as though this were something novel.

OF PUSILLANIMITY (TWO ARTICLES)

We must now consider pusillanimity. Under this head there are two points of inquiry:

(1) Whether pusillanimity is a sin?

(2) To what virtue is it opposed?

Whether pusillanimity is a sin?

Objection 1: It seems that pusillanimity is not a sin. For every sin makes a man evil, just as every virtue makes a man good. But a fainthearted man is not evil, as the Philosopher says (Ethic. iv, 3). Therefore pusillanimity is not a sin.

Objection 2: Further, the Philosopher says (Ethic. iv, 3) that "a fainthearted man is especially one who is worthy of great goods, yet does not deem himself worthy of them." Now no one is worthy of great goods except the virtuous, since as the Philosopher again says (Ethic. iv, 3), "none but the virtuous are truly worthy of honor." Therefore the fainthearted are virtuous: and consequently pusillanimity is not a sin.

Objection 3: Further, "Pride is the beginning of all sin" (Ecclus. 10:15). But pusillanimity does not proceed from pride, since the proud man sets himself above what he is, while the fainthearted man withdraws from the things he is worthy of. Therefore pusillanimity is not a sin.

Objection 4: Further, the Philosopher says (Ethic. iv, 3) that "he who deems himself less worthy than he is, is said to be fainthearted." Now sometimes holy men deem themselves less worthy than they are; for instance, Moses and Jeremias, who were worthy of the office God chose them for, which they both humbly declined (Ex. 3:11; Jer. 1:6). Therefore pusillanimity is not a sin.

On the contrary, Nothing in human conduct is to be avoided save sin. Now pusillanimity is to be avoided: for it is written (Col. 3:21): "Fathers, provoke not your children to indignation, lest they be discouraged." Therefore pusillanimity is a sin.

I answer that, Whatever is contrary to a natural inclination is a sin, because it is contrary to a law of nature. Now everything has a natural inclination to accomplish an action that is commensurate with its power: as is evident in all natural things, whether animate or inanimate. Now just as presumption makes a man exceed what is proportionate to his power, by striving to do more than he can, so pusillanimity makes a man fall short of what is proportionate to his power, by refusing to tend to that which is commensurate thereto. Wherefore as presumption is a sin, so is pusillanimity. Hence it is that the servant who buried in the earth the money he had received from his master, and did not trade with it through fainthearted fear, was punished by his master (Mat. 25; Lk. 19).

Reply to Objection 1: The Philosopher calls those evil who injure their neighbor: and accordingly the fainthearted is said not to be evil, because he injures no one, save accidentally, by omitting to do what might be profitable to others. For Gregory says (Pastoral. i) that if "they who demur to do good to their neighbor in preaching be judged strictly, without doubt their guilt is proportionate to the good they might have done had they been less retiring."

Reply to Objection 2: Nothing hinders a person who has a virtuous habit from sinning venially and without losing the habit, or mortally and with loss of the habit of gratuitous virtue. Hence it is possible for a man, by reason of the virtue which he has, to be worthy of doing certain great things that are worthy of great honor, and yet through not trying to make use of his virtue, he sins sometimes venially, sometimes mortally.

Again it may be replied that the fainthearted is worthy of great things in proportion to his ability for virtue, ability which he derives either from a good natural disposition, or from science, or from external fortune, and if he fails to use those things for virtue, he becomes guilty of pusillanimity.

Reply to Objection 3: Even pusillanimity may in some way be the result of pride: when, to wit, a man clings too much to his own opinion, whereby he thinks himself incompetent for those things for which he is competent. Hence it is written (Prov. 26:16): "The sluggard is wiser in his own conceit than seven men that speak sentences." For nothing hinders him from depreciating himself in some things, and having a high opinion of himself in others. Wherefore Gregory says (Pastoral. i) of Moses that "perchance he would have been proud, had he undertaken the leadership of a numerous people without misgiving: and again he would have been proud, had he refused to obey the command of his Creator."

Reply to Objection 4: Moses and Jeremias were worthy of the office to which they were appointed by God, but their worthiness was of Divine grace: yet they, considering the insufficiency of their own weakness, demurred; though not obstinately lest they should fall into pride.

Whether pusillanimity is opposed to magnanimity?

Objection 1: It seems that pusillanimity is not opposed to magnanimity. For the Philosopher says (Ethic., 3) that "the fainthearted man knows not himself: for he would desire the good things, of which he is worthy, if he knew himself." Now ignorance of self seems opposed to prudence. Therefore pusillanimity is opposed to prudence.

Objection 2: Further our Lord calls the servant wicked and slothful who through pusillanimity refused to make use of the money. Moreover the Philosopher says (Ethic. iv, 3) that the fainthearted seem to be slothful. Now sloth is opposed to solicitude, which is an act of prudence, as stated above ([3380]Q[47], A[9]). Therefore pusillanimity is not opposed to magnanimity.

Objection 3: Further, pusillanimity seems to proceed from inordinate fear: hence it is written (Is. 35:4): "Say to the fainthearted: Take courage and fear not." It also seems to proceed from inordinate anger, according to Col. 3:21, "Fathers, provoke not your children to indignation, lest they be discouraged." Now inordinate fear is opposed to fortitude, and inordinate anger to meekness. Therefore pusillanimity is not opposed to magnanimity.

Objection 4: Further, the vice that is in opposition to a particular virtue is the more grievous according as it is more unlike that virtue. Now pusillanimity is more unlike magnanimity than presumption is. Therefore if pusillanimity is opposed to magnanimity, it follows that it is a more grievous sin than presumption: yet this is contrary to the saying of Ecclus. 37:3, "O wicked presumption, whence camest thou?" Therefore pusillanimity is not opposed to magnanimity.

On the contrary, Pusillanimity and magnanimity differ as greatness and littleness of soul, as their very names denote. Now great and little are opposites. Therefore pusillanimity is opposed to magnanimity.

I answer that, Pusillanimity may be considered in three ways. First, in itself; and thus it is evident that by its very nature it is opposed to magnanimity, from which it differs as great and little differ in connection with the same subject. For just as the magnanimous man tends to great things out of greatness of soul, so the pusillanimous man shrinks from great things out of littleness of soul. Secondly, it may be considered in reference to its cause, which on the part of the intellect is ignorance of one's own qualification, and on the part of the appetite is the fear of failure in what one falsely deems to exceed one's ability. Thirdly, it may be considered in reference to its effect, which is to shrink from the great things of which one is worthy. But, as stated above ([3381]Q[132], A[2], ad 3), opposition between vice and virtue depends rather on their respective species than on their cause or effect. Hence pusillanimity is directly opposed to magnanimity.

Reply to Objection 1: This argument considers pusillanimity as proceeding from a cause in the intellect. Yet it cannot be said properly that it is opposed to prudence, even in respect of its cause: because ignorance of this kind does not proceed from indiscretion but from laziness in considering one's own ability, according to Ethic. iv, 3, or in accomplishing what is within one's power.

Reply to Objection 2: This argument considers pusillanimity from the point of view of its effect.

Reply to Objection 3: This argument considers the point of view of cause. Nor is the fear that causes pusillanimity always a fear of the dangers of death: wherefore it does not follow from this standpoint that pusillanimity is opposed to fortitude. As regards anger, if we consider it under the aspect of its proper movement, whereby a man is roused to take vengeance, it does not cause pusillanimity, which disheartens the soul; on the contrary, it takes it away. If, however, we consider the causes of anger, which are injuries inflicted whereby the soul of the man who suffers them is disheartened, it conduces to pusillanimity.

Reply to Objection 4: According to its proper species pusillanimity is a graver sin than presumption, since thereby a man withdraws from good things, which is a very great evil according to Ethic. iv. Presumption, however, is stated to be "wicked" on account of pride whence it proceeds.

OF MAGNIFICENCE (FOUR ARTICLES)
We must now consider magnificence and the vices opposed to it. With regard to magnificence there are four points of inquiry:
(1) Whether magnificence is a virtue?
(2) Whether it is a special virtue?
(3) What is its matter?
(4) Whether it is a part of fortitude?

Whether magnificence is a virtue?
Objection 1: It seems that magnificence is not a virtue. For whoever has one virtue has all the virtues, as stated above ([3382]FS, Q[65], A[1]). But one may have the other virtues without having magnificence: because the Philosopher says (Ethic. iv, 2) that "not every liberal man is magnificent." Therefore magnificence is not a virtue.

Objection 2: Further, moral virtue observes the mean, according to Ethic. ii, 6. But magnificence does not seemingly observe the mean, for it exceeds liberality in greatness. Now "great" and "little" are opposed to one another as extremes, the mean of which is "equal," as stated in Metaph. x. Hence magnificence observes not the mean, but the extreme. Therefore it is not a virtue.

Objection 3: Further, no virtue is opposed to a natural inclination, but on the contrary perfects it, as stated above ([3383]Q[108], A[2];[3384] Q[117], A[1], OBJ[1]). Now according to the Philosopher (Ethic. iv, 2) the "magnificent man is not lavish towards himself": and this is opposed to the natural inclination one has to look after oneself. Therefore magnificence is not a virtue.

Objection 4: Further, according to the Philosopher (Ethic. vi, 4) "act is right reason about things to be made." Now magnificence is about things to be made, as its very name denotes [*Magnificence= magna facere---i.e. to make great things]. Therefore it is an act rather than a virtue.

On the contrary, Human virtue is a participation of Divine power. But magnificence [virtutis] belongs to Divine power, according to Ps. 47:35: "His magnificence and His power is in the clouds." Therefore magnificence is a virtue.

I answer that, According to De Coelo i, 16, "we speak of virtue in relation to the extreme limit of a thing's power," not as regards the limit of deficiency, but as regards the limit of excess, the very nature of which denotes something great. Wherefore to do something great, whence magnificence takes its name, belongs properly to the very notion of virtue. Hence magnificence denotes a virtue.

Reply to Objection 1: Not every liberal man is magnificent as regards his actions, because he lacks the wherewithal to perform magnificent deeds. Nevertheless every liberal man has the habit of magnificence, either actually or in respect of a proximate disposition thereto, as explained above (Q[129], A[3], ad 2), as also ([3385]FS, Q[65], A[1]) when we were treating of the connection of virtues.

Reply to Objection 2: It is true that magnificence observes the extreme, if we consider the quantity of the thing done: yet it observes the mean, if we consider the rule of reason, which it neither falls short of nor exceeds, as we have also said of magnanimity ([3386]Q[129], A[3], ad 1).

Reply to Objection 3: It belongs to magnificence to do something great. But that which regards a man's person is little in comparison with that which regards Divine things, or even the affairs of the community at large. Wherefore the magnificent man does not intend principally to be lavish towards himself, not that he does not seek his own good, but because to do so is not something great. Yet if anything regarding himself admits of greatness, the magnificent man accomplishes it magnificently: for instance, things that are done once, such as a wedding, or the like; or things that are of a lasting nature; thus it belongs to a magnificent man to provide himself with a suitable dwelling, as stated in Ethic. iv.

Reply to Objection 4: As the Philosopher says (Ethic. vi, 5) "there must needs be a virtue of act," i.e. a moral virtue, whereby the appetite is inclined to make good use of the rule of act: and this is what magnificence does. Hence it is not an act but a virtue.

Whether magnificence is a special virtue?
Objection 1: It seems that magnificence is not a special virtue. For magnificence would seem to consist in doing something great. But it may belong to any virtue to do something great, if the virtue be great: as in the case of one who has a great virtue of temperance, for he does a great work of temperance. Therefore, magnificence is not a special virtue, but denotes a perfect degree of any virtue.

Objection 2: Further, seemingly that which tends to a thing is the same as that which does it. But it belongs to magnanimity to tend to something great, as stated above ([3387]Q[129], AA[1],2). Therefore it belongs to magnanimity likewise to do something great. Therefore magnificence is not a special virtue distinct from magnanimity.

Objection 3: Further, magnificence seems to belong to holiness, for it is written (Ex. 15:11): "Magnificent [Douay: 'glorious'] in holiness," and (Ps. 95:6): "Holiness and magnificence [Douay: 'Majesty'] in His sanctuary." Now holiness is the same as religion, as stated above ([3388]Q[81], A[8]). Therefore magnificence is apparently the same as religion. Therefore it is not a special virtue, distinct from the others.

On the contrary, The Philosopher reckons it with other special virtues (Ethic. ii, 7; iv 2).

I answer that, It belongs to magnificence to do [facere] something great, as its name implies [magnificence= magna facere---i.e. to make great things]. Now "facere" may be taken in two ways, in a strict sense, and in a broad sense. Strictly "facere" means to work something in external matter, for instance to make a house, or something of the kind; in a broad sense "facere" is employed to denote any action, whether it passes into external matter, as to burn or cut, or remain in the agent, as to understand or will.

Accordingly if magnificence be taken to denote the doing of something great, the doing [factio] being understood in the strict sense, it is then a special virtue. For the work done is produced by act: in the use of which it is possible to consider a special aspect of goodness, namely that the work produced [factum] by the act is something great, namely in quantity, value, or dignity, and this is what magnificence does. In this way magnificence is a special virtue.

If, on the other hand, magnificence take its name from doing something great, the doing [facere] being understood in a broad sense, it is not a special virtue.

Reply to Objection 1: It belongs to every perfect virtue to do something great in the genus of that virtue, if "doing" [facere] be taken in the broad sense, but not if it be taken strictly, for this is proper to magnificence.

Reply to Objection 2: It belongs to magnanimity not only to tend to something great, but also to do great works in all the virtues, either by making [faciendo], or by any kind of action, as stated in Ethic. iv, 3: yet so that magnanimity, in this respect, regards the sole aspect of great, while the other virtues which, if they be perfect, do something great, direct their principal intention, not to something great, but to that which is proper to each virtue: and the greatness of the thing done is sometimes consequent upon the greatness of the virtue.

On the other hand, it belongs to magnificence not only to do something great, "doing" [facere] being taken in the strict sense, but also to tend with the mind to the doing of great things. Hence Tully says (De Invent. Rhet. ii) that "magnificence is the discussing and administering of great and lofty undertakings, with a certain broad and noble purpose of mind, discussion" referring to the inward intention, and "administration" to the outward accomplishment. Wherefore just as magnanimity intends something great in every matter, it follows that magnificence does the same in every work that can be produced in external matter [factibili].

Reply to Objection 3: The intention of magnificence is the production of a great work. Now works done by men are directed to an end: and no end of human works is so great as the honor of God: wherefore magnificence does a great work especially in reference to the Divine honor. Wherefore the Philosopher says (Ethic. iv, 2) that "the most commendable expenditure is that which is directed to Divine sacrifices": and this is the chief object of magnificence. For this reason magnificence is connected with holiness, since its chief effect is directed to religion or holiness.

Day 219

Whether the matter of magnificence is great expenditure?
Objection 1: It seems that the matter of magnificence is not great expenditure. For there are not two virtues about the same matter. But liberality is about expenditure, as stated above ([3389]Q[117], A[2]). Therefore magnificence is not about expenditure.

Objection 2: Further, "every magnificent man is liberal" (Ethic. iv, 2). But liberality is about gifts rather than about expenditure. Therefore magnificence also is not chiefly about expenditure, but about gifts.

Objection 3: Further, it belongs to magnificence to produce an external work. But not even great expenditure is always the means of producing an external work, for instance when one spends much in sending presents. Therefore expenditure is not the proper matter of magnificence.

Objection 4: Further, only the rich are capable of great expenditure. But the poor are able to possess all the virtues, since "the virtues do not necessarily require external fortune, but are sufficient for themselves," as Seneca says (De Ira i: De vita beata xvi). Therefore magnificence is not about great expenditure.

On the contrary, The Philosopher says (Ethic. iv, 2) that "magnificence does not extend, like liberality, to all transactions in money, but only to expensive ones, wherein it exceeds liberality in scale." Therefore it is only about great expenditure.

I answer that, As stated above [3390](A[2]), it belongs to magnificence to intend doing some great work. Now for the doing of a great work, proportionate expenditure is necessary, for great works cannot be produced without great expenditure. Hence it belongs to magnificence to spend much in order that some great work may be accomplished in becoming manner. Wherefore the Philosopher says (Ethic. iv, 2) that "a magnificent man will produce a more magnificent work with equal," i.e. proportionate, "expenditure." Now expenditure is the outlay of a sum of money; and a man may be hindered from making that outlay if he love money too much. Hence the matter of magnificence may be said to be both this expenditure itself, which the magnificent man uses to produce a great work, and also the very money which he employs in going to great expense, and as well as the love of money, which love the magnificent man moderates, lest he be hindered from spending much.

Reply to Objection 1: As stated above ([3391]Q[129], A[2]), those virtues that are about external things experience a certain difficulty arising from the genus itself of the thing about which the virtue is concerned, and another difficulty besides arising from the greatness of that same thing. Hence the need for two virtues, concerned about money and its use; namely, liberality, which regards the use of money in general, and magnificence, which regards that which is great in the use of money.

Reply to Objection 2: The use of money regards the liberal man in one way and the magnificent man in another. For it regards the liberal man, inasmuch as it proceeds from an ordinate affection in respect of money; wherefore all due use of money (such as gifts and expenditure), the obstacles to which are removed by a moderate love of money, belongs to liberality. But the use of money regards the magnificent man in relation to some great work which has to be produced, and this use is impossible without expenditure or outlay.

Reply to Objection 3: The magnificent man also makes gifts of presents, as stated in Ethic. iv, 2, but not under the aspect of gift, but rather under the aspect of expenditure directed to the production of some work, for instance in order to honor someone, or in order to do something which will reflect honor on the whole state: as when he brings to effect what the whole state is striving for.

Reply to Objection 4: The chief act of virtue is the inward choice, and a virtue may have this without outward fortune: so that even a poor man may be magnificent. But goods of fortune are requisite as instruments to the external acts of virtue: and in this way a poor man cannot accomplish the outward act of magnificence in things that are great simply. Perhaps, however, he may be able to do so in things that are great by comparison to some particular work; which, though little in itself, can nevertheless be done magnificently in proportion to its genus: for little and great are relative terms, as the Philosopher says (De Praedic. Cap. Ad aliquid.).

Whether magnificence is a part of fortitude?

Objection 1: It seems that magnificence is not a part of fortitude. For magnificence agrees in matter with liberality, as stated above [3392](A[3]). But liberality is a part, not of fortitude, but of justice. Therefore magnificence is not a part of fortitude.

Objection 2: Further, fortitude is about fear and darings. But magnificence seems to have nothing to do with fear, but only with expenditure, which is a kind of action. Therefore magnificence seems to pertain to justice, which is about actions, rather than to fortitude.

Objection 3: Further, the Philosopher says (Ethic. iv, 2) that "the magnificent man is like the man of science." Now science has more in common with prudence than with fortitude. Therefore magnificence should not be reckoned a part of fortitude.

On the contrary, Tully (De Invent. Rhet. ii) and Macrobius (De Somn. Scip. i) and Andronicus reckon magnificence to be a part of fortitude.

I answer that, Magnificence, in so far as it is a special virtue, cannot be reckoned a subjective part of fortitude, since it does not agree with this virtue in the point of matter: but it is reckoned a part thereof, as being annexed to it as secondary to principal virtue.

In order for a virtue to be annexed to a principal virtue, two things are necessary, as stated above ([3393]Q[80]). The one is that the secondary virtue agree with the principal, and the other is that in some respect it be exceeded thereby. Now magnificence agrees with fortitude in the point that as fortitude tends to something arduous and difficult, so also does magnificence: wherefore seemingly it is seated, like fortitude, in the irascible. Yet magnificence falls short of fortitude, in that the arduous thing to which fortitude tends derives its difficulty from a danger that threatens the person, whereas the arduous thing to which magnificence tends, derives its difficulty from the dispossession of one's property, which is of much less account than danger to one's person. Wherefore magnificence is accounted a part of fortitude.

Reply to Objection 1: Justice regards operations in themselves, as viewed under the aspect of something due: but liberality and magnificence regard sumptuary operations as related to the passions of the soul, albeit in different ways. For liberality regards expenditure in reference to the love and desire of money, which are passions of the concupiscible faculty, and do not hinder the liberal man from giving and spending: so that this virtue is in the concupiscible. On the other hand, magnificence regards expenditure in reference to hope, by attaining to the difficulty, not simply, as magnanimity does, but in a determinate matter, namely expenditure: wherefore magnificence, like magnanimity, is apparently in the irascible part.

Reply to Objection 2: Although magnificence does not agree with fortitude in matter, it agrees with it as the condition of its matter: since it tends to something difficult in the matter of expenditure, even as fortitude tends to something difficult in the matter of fear.

Reply to Objection 3: Magnificence directs the use of art to something great, as stated above and in the preceding Article. Now art is in the reason. Wherefore it belongs to the magnificent man to use his reason by observing proportion of expenditure to the work he has in hand. This is especially necessary on account of the greatness of both those things, since if he did not take careful thought, he would incur the risk of a great loss.

OF MEANNESS* (TWO ARTICLES) [*"Parvificentia," or doing mean things, just as "magnificentia" is doing great things.]

We must now consider the vices opposed to magnificence: under which head there are two points of inquiry:

(1) Whether meanness is a vice?

(2) Of the vice opposed to it.

Whether meanness is a vice?

Objection 1: It seems that meanness is not a vice. For just as vice moderates great things, so does it moderate little things: wherefore both the liberal and the magnificent do little things. But magnificence is a virtue. Therefore likewise meanness is a virtue rather than a vice.

Objection 2: Further, the Philosopher says (Ethic. iv, 2) that "careful reckoning is mean." But careful reckoning is apparently praiseworthy, since man's good is to be in accordance with reason, as Dionysius states (Div. Nom. iv, 4). Therefore meanness is not a vice.

Objection 3: Further, the Philosopher says (Ethic. iv, 2) that "a mean man is loth to spend money." But this belongs to covetousness or illiberality. Therefore meanness is not a distinct vice from the others.

On the contrary, The Philosopher (Ethic. ii) accounts meanness a special vice opposed to magnificence.

I answer that, As stated above ([3394]FS, Q[1], A[3]; [3395]FS, Q[18], A[6]), moral acts take their species from their end, wherefore in many cases they are denominated from that end. Accordingly a man is said to be mean [parvificus] because he intends to do something little [parvum]. Now according to the Philosopher (De Praedic. Cap. Ad aliquid.) great and little are relative terms: and when we say that a mean man intends to do something little, this must be understood in relation to the kind of work he does. This may be little or great in two ways: in one way as regards the work itself to be done, in another as regards the expense. Accordingly the magnificent man intends principally the greatness of his work, and secondarily he intends the greatness of the expense, which he does not shirk, so that he may produce a great work. Wherefore the Philosopher says (Ethic. iv, 4) that "the magnificent man with equal expenditure will produce a more magnificent result." On the other hand, the mean man intends principally to spend little, wherefore the Philosopher says (Ethic. iv, 2) that "he seeks how he may spend least." As a result of this he intends to produce a little work, that is, he does not shrink from producing a little work, so long as he spends little. Wherefore the Philosopher says that "the mean man after going to great expense forfeits the good" of the magnificent work, "for the trifle" that he is unwilling to spend. Therefore it is evident that the mean man fails to observe the proportion that reason demands between expenditure and work. Now the essence of vice is that it consists in failing to do what is in accordance with reason. Hence it is manifest that meanness is a vice.

Reply to Objection 1: Virtue moderates little things, according to the rule of reason: from which rule the mean man declines, as stated in the Article. For he is called mean, not for moderating little things, but for declining from the rule of reason in moderating great or little things: hence meanness is a vice.

Reply to Objection 2: As the Philosopher says (Rhet. ii, 5), "fear makes us take counsel": wherefore a mean man is careful in his reckonings, because he has an inordinate fear of spending his goods, even in things of the least account. Hence this is not praiseworthy, but sinful and reprehensible, because then a man does not regulate his affections according to reason, but, on the contrary, makes use of his reason in pursuance of his inordinate affections.

Reply to Objection 3: Just as the magnificent man has this in common with the liberal man, that he spends his money readily and with pleasure, so too the mean man in common with the illiberal or covetous man is loth and slow to spend. Yet they differ in this, that illiberality regards ordinary expenditure, while meanness regards great expenditure, which is a more difficult accomplishment: wherefore meanness is less sinful than illiberality. Hence the Philosopher says (Ethic. iv, 2) that "although meanness and its contrary vice are sinful, they do not bring shame on a man, since neither do they harm one's neighbor, nor are they very disgraceful."

Whether there is a vice opposed to meanness?

Objection 1: It seems that there is no vice opposed to meanness. For great is opposed to little. Now, magnificence is not a vice, but a virtue. Therefore no vice is opposed to meanness.

Objection 2: Further, since meanness is a vice by deficiency, as stated above [3396](A[1]), it seems that if any vice is opposed to meanness, it would merely consist in excessive spending. But those who spend much, where they ought to spend little, spend little where they ought to spend much, according to Ethic. iv, 2, and thus they have something of meanness. Therefore there is not a vice opposed to meanness.

Objection 3: Further, moral acts take their species from their end, as stated above [3397](A[1]). Now those who spend excessively, do so in order to make a show of their wealth, as stated in Ethic. iv, 2. But this belongs to vainglory, which is opposed to magnanimity, as stated above (Q[131], A[2]). Therefore no vice is opposed to meanness.

On the contrary, stands the authority of the Philosopher who (Ethic. ii, 8; iv, 2) places magnificence as a mean between two opposite vices.

I answer that, Great is opposed to little. Also little and great are relative terms, as stated above [3398](A[1]). Now just as expenditure may be little in comparison with the work, so may it be great in comparison with the work in that it exceeds the proportion which reason requires to exist between expenditure and work. Hence it is manifest that the vice of meanness, whereby a man intends to spend less than his work is worth, and thus fails to observe due proportion between his expenditure and his work, has a vice opposed to it, whereby a man exceeds this same proportion, by spending more than is proportionate to his work. This vice is called in Greek {banausia}, so called from the Greek {baunos}, because, like the fire in the furnace, it consumes everything. It is also called {apyrokalia}, i.e. lacking good fire, since like fire it consumes all, but not for a good purpose. Hence in Latin it may be called "consumptio" [waste].

Reply to Objection 1: Magnificence is so called from the great work done, but not from the expenditure being in excess of the work: for this belongs to the vice which is opposed to meanness.

Reply to Objection 2: To the one same vice there is opposed the virtue which observes the mean, and a contrary vice. Accordingly, then, the vice of waste is opposed to meanness in that it exceeds in expenditure the value of the work, by spending much where it behooved to spend little. But it is opposed to magnificence on the part of the great work, which the magnificent man intends principally, in so far as when it behooves to spend much, it spends little or nothing.

Reply to Objection 3: Wastefulness is opposed to meanness by the very species of its act, since it exceeds the rule of reason, whereas meanness falls short of it. Yet nothing hinders this from being directed to the end of another vice, such as vainglory or any other.

OF PATIENCE (FIVE ARTICLES)

We must now consider patience. Under this head there are five points of inquiry:

(1) Whether patience is a virtue?
(2) Whether it is the greatest of the virtues?
(3) Whether it can be had without grace?
(4) Whether it is a part of fortitude?
(5) Whether it is the same as longanimity?

Whether patience is a virtue?

Objection 1: It seems that patience is not a virtue. For the virtues are most perfect in heaven, as Augustine says (De Trin. xiv). Yet patience is not there, since no evils have to be borne there, according to Is. 49:10 and Apoc. 7:16, "They shall not hunger nor thirst, neither shall the heat nor the sun strike them." Therefore patience is not a virtue.

Objection 2: Further, no virtue can be found in the wicked, since virtue it is "that makes its possessor good." Yet patience is sometimes found in wicked men; for instance, in the covetous, who bear many evils patiently that they may amass money, according to Eccles. 5:16, "All the days of his life he eateth in darkness, and in many cares, and in misery and in sorrow." Therefore patience is not a virtue.

Objection 3: Further, the fruits differ from the virtues, as stated above ([3399]FS, Q[70], A[1], ad 3). But patience is reckoned among the fruits (Gal. 5:22). Therefore patience is not a virtue.

On the contrary, Augustine says (De Patientia i): "The virtue of the soul that is called patience, is so great a gift of God, that we even preach the patience of Him who bestows it upon us."

I answer that, As stated above ([3400]Q[123], A[1]), the moral virtues are directed to the good, inasmuch as they safeguard the good of reason against the impulse of the passions. Now among the passions sorrow is strong to hinder the good of reason, according to 2 Cor. 7:10, "The sorrow of the world worketh death," and Ecclus. 30:25, "Sadness hath killed many, and there is no profit in it." Hence the necessity for a virtue to safeguard the good of reason against sorrow, lest reason give way to sorrow: and this patience does. Wherefore Augustine says (De Patientia ii): "A man's patience it is whereby he bears evil with an equal mind," i.e. without being disturbed by sorrow, "lest he abandon with an unequal mind the goods whereby he may advance to better things." It is therefore evident that patience is a virtue.

Reply to Objection 1: The moral virtues do not remain in heaven as regards the same act that they have on the way, in relation, namely, to the goods of the present life, which will not remain in heaven: but they will remain in their relation to the end, which will be in heaven. Thus justice will not be in heaven in relation to buying and selling and other matters pertaining to the present life, but it will remain in the point of being subject to God. In like manner the act of patience, in heaven, will not consist in bearing things, but in enjoying the goods to which we had aspired by suffering. Hence Augustine says (De Civ. Dei xiv) that "patience itself will not be in heaven, since there is no need for it except where evils have to be borne: yet that which we shall obtain by patience will be eternal."

Reply to Objection 2: As Augustine says (De Patientia ii; v) "properly speaking those are patient who would rather bear evils without inflicting them, than inflict them without bearing them. As for those who bear evils that they may inflict evil, their patience is neither marvelous nor praiseworthy, for it is no patience at all: we may marvel at their hardness of heart, but we must refuse to call them patient."

Reply to Objection 3: As stated above ([3401]FS, Q[11], A[1]), the very notion of fruit denotes pleasure. And works of virtue afford pleasure in themselves, as stated in Ethic. i, 8. Now the names of the virtues are wont to be applied to their acts. Wherefore patience as a habit is a virtue. but as to the pleasure which its act affords, it is reckoned a fruit, especially in this, that patience safeguards the mind from being overcome by sorrow.

Whether patience is the greatest of the virtues?

Objection 1: It seems that patience is the greatest of the virtues. For in every genus that which is perfect is the greatest. Now "patience hath a perfect work" (James 1:4). Therefore patience is the greatest of the virtues.

Objection 2: Further, all the virtues are directed to the good of the soul. Now this seems to belong chiefly to patience; for it is written (Lk. 21:19): "In your patience you shall possess your souls." Therefore patience is the greatest of the virtues.

Objection 3: Further, seemingly that which is the safeguard and cause of other things is greater than they are. But according to Gregory (Hom. xxxv in Evang.) "patience is the root and safeguard of all the virtues." Therefore patience is the greatest of the virtues.

On the contrary, It is not reckoned among the four virtues which Gregory (Moral. xxii) and Augustine (De Morib. Eccl. xv) call principal.

I answer that, Virtues by their very nature are directed to good. For it is virtue that "makes its possessor good, and renders the latter's work good" (Ethic. ii, 6). Hence it follows that a virtue's superiority and preponderance over other virtues is the greater according as it inclines man to good more effectively and directly. Now those virtues which are effective of good, incline a man more directly to good than those which are a check on the things which lead man away from good: and just as among those that are effective of good, the greater is that which establishes man in a greater good (thus faith, hope, and charity /are greater than prudence and justice); so too among those that are a check on things that withdraw man from good, the greater virtue is the one which is a check on a greater obstacle to good. But dangers of death, about which is fortitude, and pleasures of touch, with which temperance is concerned, withdraw man from good more than any kind of hardship, which is the object of patience. Therefore patience is not the greatest of the virtues, but falls short, not only of the theological virtues, and of prudence and justice which directly establish man in good, but also of fortitude and temperance which withdraw him from greater obstacles to good.

Reply to Objection 1: Patience is said to have a perfect work in bearing hardships: for these give rise first to sorrow, which is moderated by patience; secondly, to anger, which is moderated by meekness; thirdly, to hatred, which charity removes; fourthly, to unjust injury, which justice forbids. Now that which removes the principle is the most perfect.

Yet it does not follow, if patience be more perfect in this respect, that it is more perfect simply.

Reply to Objection 2: Possession denotes undisturbed ownership; wherefore man is said to possess his soul by patience, in so far as it removes by the root the passions that are evoked by hardships and disturb the soul.

Reply to Objection 3: Patience is said to be the root and safeguard of all the virtues, not as though it caused and preserved them directly, but merely because it removes their obstacles.

Whether it is possible to have patience without grace?

Objection 1: It seems that it is possible to have patience without grace. For the more his reason inclines to a thing, the more is it possible for the rational creature to accomplish it. Now it is more reasonable to suffer evil for the sake of good than for the sake of evil. Yet some suffer evil for evil's sake, by their own virtue and without the help of grace; for Augustine says (De Patientia iii) that "men endure many toils and sorrows for the sake of the things they love sinfully." Much more, therefore, is it possible for man, without the help of grace, to bear evil for the sake of good, and this is to be truly patient.

Objection 2: Further, some who are not in a state of grace have more abhorrence for sinful evils than for bodily evils: hence some heathens are related to have endured many hardships rather than betray their country or commit some other misdeed. Now this is to be truly patient. Therefore it seems that it is possible to have patience without the help of grace.

Objection 3: Further, it is quite evident that some go through much trouble and pain in order to regain health of the body. Now the health of the soul is not less desirable than bodily health. Therefore in like manner one may, without the help of grace, endure many evils for the health of the soul, and this is to be truly patient.

On the contrary, It is written (Ps. 61:6): "From Him," i.e. from God, "is my patience."

I answer that, As Augustine says (De Patientia iv), "the strength of desire helps a man to bear toil and pain: and no one willingly undertakes to bear what is painful, save for the sake of that which gives pleasure." The reason of this is because sorrow and pain are of themselves displeasing to the soul, wherefore it would never choose to suffer them for their own sake, but only for the sake of an end. Hence it follows that the good for the sake of which one is willing to endure evils, is more desired and loved than the good the privation of which causes the sorrow that we bear patiently. Now the fact that a man prefers the good of grace to all natural goods, the loss of which may cause sorrow, is to be referred to charity, which loves God above all things. Hence it is evident that patience, as a virtue, is caused by charity, according to 1 Cor. 13:4, "Charity is patient."

But it is manifest that it is impossible to have charity save through grace, according to Rom. 5:5, "The charity of God is poured forth in our hearts by the Holy Ghost Who is given to us." Therefore it is clearly impossible to have patience without the help of grace.

Reply to Objection 1: The inclination of reason would prevail in human nature in the state of integrity. But in corrupt nature the inclination of concupiscence prevails, because it is dominant in man. Hence man is more prone to bear evils for the sake of goods in which the concupiscence delights here and now, than to endure evils for the sake of goods to come, which are desired in accordance with reason: and yet it is this that pertains to true patience.

Reply to Objection 2: The good of a social virtue [*Cf. [3402]FS, Q[61], A[5]] is commensurate with human nature; and consequently the human will can tend thereto without the help of sanctifying grace, yet not without the help of God's grace [*Cf. [3403]FS, Q[109], A[2]]. On the other hand, the good of grace is supernatural, wherefore man cannot tend thereto by a natural virtue. Hence the comparison fails.

Reply to Objection 3: Even the endurance of those evils which a man bears for the sake of his body's health, proceeds from the love a man naturally has for his own flesh. Hence there is no comparison between this endurance and patience which proceeds from a supernatural love.

Whether patience is a part of fortitude?

Objection 1: It seems that patience is not a part of fortitude. For a thing is not part of itself. Now patience is apparently the same as fortitude: because, as stated above ([3404]Q[123], A[6]), the proper act of fortitude is to endure; and this belongs also to patience. For it is stated in the Liber Sententiarum Prosperi [*The quotation is from St. Gregory, Hom. xxxv in Evang.] that "patience consists in enduring evils inflicted by others." Therefore patience is not a part of fortitude.

Objection 2: Further, fortitude is about fear and daring, as stated above ([3405]Q[123], A[3]), and thus it is in the irascible. But patience seems to be about sorrow, and consequently would seem to be in the concupiscible. Therefore patience is not a part of fortitude but of temperance.

Objection 3: Further, the whole cannot be without its part. Therefore if patience is a part of fortitude, there can be no fortitude without patience. Yet sometimes a brave man does not endure evils patiently, but even attacks the person who inflicts the evil. Therefore patience is not a part of fortitude.

On the contrary, Tully (De Invent. Rhet. ii) reckons it a part of fortitude.

I answer that, Patience is a quasi-potential part of fortitude, because it is annexed thereto as secondary to principal virtue. For it belongs to patience "to suffer with an equal mind the evils inflicted by others," as Gregory says in a homily (xxxv in Evang.). Now of those evils that are inflicted by others, foremost and most difficult to endure are those that are connected with the danger of death, and about these evils fortitude is concerned. Hence it is clear that in this matter fortitude has the principal place, and that it lays claim to that which is principal in this matter. Wherefore patience is annexed to fortitude as secondary to principal virtue, for which reason Prosper calls patience brave (Sent. 811).

Reply to Objection 1: It belongs to fortitude to endure, not anything indeed, but that which is most difficult to endure, namely dangers of death: whereas it may pertain to patience to endure any kind of evil.

Reply to Objection 2: The act of fortitude consists not only in holding fast to good against the fear of future dangers, but also in not failing through sorrow or pain occasioned by things present; and it is in the latter respect that patience is akin to fortitude. Yet fortitude is chiefly about fear, which of itself evokes flight which fortitude avoids; while patience is chiefly about sorrow, for a man is said to be patient, not because he does not fly, but because he behaves in a praiseworthy manner by suffering [patiendo] things which hurt him here and now, in such a way as not to be inordinately saddened by them. Hence fortitude is properly in the irascible, while patience is in the concupiscible faculty.

Nor does this hinder patience from being a part of fortitude, because the annexing of virtue to virtue does not regard the subject, but the matter or the form. Nevertheless patience is not to be reckoned a part of temperance, although both are in the concupiscible, because temperance is only about those sorrows that are opposed to pleasures of touch, such as arise through abstinence from pleasures of food and sex: whereas patience is chiefly about sorrows inflicted by other persons. Moreover it belongs to temperance to control these sorrows besides their contrary pleasures: whereas it belongs to patience that a man forsake not the good of virtue on account of such like sorrows, however great they be.

Reply to Objection 3: It may be granted that patience in a certain respect is an integral part of justice, if we consider the fact that a man may patiently endure evils pertaining to dangers of death; and it is from this point of view that the objection argues. Nor is it inconsistent with patience that a man should, when necessary, rise up against the man who inflicts evils on him; for Chrysostom [*Homily v. in the Opus Imperfectum, falsely ascribed to St. John Chrysostom] says on Mat. 4:10, "Begone Satan," that "it is praiseworthy to be patient under our own wrongs, but to endure God's wrongs patiently is most wicked": and Augustine says in a letter to Marcellinus (Ep. cxxxviii) that "the precepts of patience are not opposed to the good of the commonwealth, since in order to ensure that good we fight against our enemies." But in so far as patience regards all kinds of evils, it is annexed to fortitude as secondary to principal virtue.

Whether patience is the same as longanimity? [*Longsuffering. It is necessary to preserve the Latin word, on account of the comparison with magnanimity.]

Objection 1: It seems that patience is the same as longanimity. For Augustine says (De Patientia i) that "we speak of patience in God, not as though any evil made Him suffer, but because He awaits the wicked, that they may be converted." Wherefore it is written (Ecclus. 5:4): "The Most High is a patient rewarder." Therefore it seems that patience is the same as longanimity.

Objection 2: Further, the same thing is not contrary to two things. But impatience is contrary to longanimity, whereby one awaits a delay: for one is said to be impatient of delay, as of other evils. Therefore it seems that patience is the same as longanimity.

Objection 3: Further, just as time is a circumstance of wrongs endured, so is place. But no virtue is distinct from patience on the score of place. Therefore in like manner longanimity which takes count of time, in so far as a person waits for a long time, is not distinct from patience.

Objection 4: On the contrary, a gloss [*Origen, Comment. in Ep. ad Rom. ii] on Rom. 2:4, "Or despisest thou the riches of His goodness, and patience, and longsuffering?" says: "It seems that longanimity differs from patience, because those who offend from weakness rather than of set purpose are said to be borne with longanimity: while those who take a deliberate delight in their crimes are said to be borne patiently."

I answer that, Just as by magnanimity a man has a mind to tend to great things, so by longanimity a man has a mind to tend to something a long way off. Wherefore as magnanimity regards hope, which tends to good, rather than daring, fear, or sorrow, which have evil as their object, so also does longanimity. Hence longanimity has more in common with magnanimity than with patience.

Nevertheless it may have something in common with patience, for two reasons. First, because patience, like fortitude, endures certain evils for the sake of good, and if this good is awaited shortly, endurance is easier: whereas if it be delayed a long time, it is more difficult. Secondly, because the very delay of the good we hope for, is of a nature to cause sorrow, according to Prov. 13:12, "Hope that is deferred afflicteth the soul." Hence there may be patience in bearing this trial, as in enduring any other sorrows. Accordingly longanimity and constancy are both comprised under patience, in so far as both the delay of the hoped for good (which regards longanimity) and the toil which man endures in persistently accomplishing a good work (which regards constancy) may be considered under the one aspect of grievous evil.

For this reason Tully (De Invent. Rhet. ii) in defining patience, says that "patience is the voluntary and prolonged endurance of arduous and difficult things for the sake of virtue or profit." By saying "arduous" he refers to constancy in good; when he says "difficult" he refers to the grievousness of evil, which is the proper object of patience; and by adding "continued" or "long lasting," he refers to longanimity, in so far as it has something in common with patience.

This suffices for the Replies to the First and Second Objections.

Reply to Objection 3: That which is a long way off as to place, though distant from us, is not simply distant from things in nature, as that which is a long way off in point of time: hence the comparison fails. Moreover, what is remote as to place offers no difficulty save in the point of time, since what is placed a long way from us is a long time coming to us.

We grant the fourth argument. We must observe, however, that the reason for the difference assigned by this gloss is that it is hard to bear with those who sin through weakness, merely because they persist a long time in evil, wherefore it is said that they are borne with longanimity: whereas the very fact of sinning through pride seems to be unendurable; for which reason those who sin through pride are stated to be borne with patience.

Day 220

OF PERSEVERANCE (FOUR ARTICLES)
We must now consider perseverance and the vices opposed to it. Under the head of perseverance there are four points of inquiry:
(1) Whether perseverance is a virtue?
(2) Whether it is a part of fortitude?
(3) Of its relation to constancy;
(4) Whether it needs the help of grace?

Whether perseverance is a virtue?
Objection 1: It seems that perseverance is not a virtue. For, according to the Philosopher (Ethic. vii, 7), continency is greater than perseverance. But continency is not a virtue, as stated in Ethic. iv, 9. Therefore perseverance is not a virtue.

Objection 2: Further, "by virtue man lives aright," according to Augustine (De Lib. Arb. ii, 19). Now according to the same authority (De Persever. i), no one can be said to have perseverance while living, unless he persevere until death. Therefore perseverance is not a virtue.

Objection 3: Further, it is requisite of every virtue that one should persist unchangeably in the work of that virtue, as stated in Ethic. ii, 4. But this is what we understand by perseverance: for Tully says (De Invent. Rhet. ii) that "perseverance is the fixed and continued persistence in a well-considered purpose." Therefore perseverance is not a special virtue, but a condition of every virtue.

On the contrary, Andronicus [*Chrysippus: in De Affect.] says that "perseverance is a habit regarding things to which we ought to stand, and those to which we ought not to stand, as well as those that are indifferent." Now a habit that directs us to do something well, or to omit something, is a virtue. Therefore perseverance is a virtue.

I answer that, According to the Philosopher (Ethic. ii, 3), "virtue is about the difficult and the good"; and so where there is a special kind of difficulty or goodness, there is a special virtue. Now a virtuous deed may involve goodness or difficulty on two counts. First, from the act's very species, which is considered in respect of the proper object of that act: secondly, from the length of time, since to persist long in something difficult involves a special difficulty. Hence to persist long in something good until it is accomplished belongs to a special virtue.

Accordingly just as temperance and fortitude are special virtues, for the reason that the one moderates pleasures of touch (which is of itself a difficult thing), while the other moderates fear and daring in connection with dangers of death (which also is something difficult in itself), so perseverance is a special virtue, since it consists in enduring delays in the above or other virtuous deeds, so far as necessity requires.

Reply to Objection 1: The Philosopher is taking perseverance there, as it is found in one who bears those things which are most difficult to endure long. Now it is difficult to endure, not good, but evil. And evils that involve danger of death, for the most part are not endured for a long time, because often they soon pass away: wherefore it is not on this account that perseverance has its chief title to praise. Among other evils foremost are those which are opposed to pleasures of touch, because evils of this kind affect the necessaries of life: such are the lack of food and the like, which at times call for long endurance. Now it is not difficult to endure these things for a long time for one who grieves not much at them, nor delights much in the contrary goods; as in the case of the temperate man, in whom these passions are not violent. But they are most difficult to bear for one who is strongly affected by such things, through lacking the perfect virtue that moderates these passions. Wherefore if perseverance be taken in this sense it is not a perfect virtue, but something imperfect in the genus of virtue. On the other hand, if we take perseverance as denoting long persistence in any kind of difficult good, it is consistent in one who has even perfect virtue: for even if it is less difficult for him to persist, yet he persists in the more perfect good. Wherefore such like perseverance may be a virtue, because virtue derives perfection from the aspect of good rather than from the aspect of difficulty.

Reply to Objection 2: Sometimes a virtue and its act go by the same name: thus Augustine says (Tract. in Joan. lxxix): "Faith is to believe without seeing." Yet it is possible to have a habit of virtue without performing the act: thus a poor man has the habit of magnificence without exercising the act. Sometimes, however, a person who has the habit, begins to perform the act, yet does not accomplish it, for instance a builder begins to build a house, but does not complete it. Accordingly we must reply that the term "perseverance" is sometimes used to denote the habit whereby one chooses to persevere, sometimes for the act of persevering: and sometimes one who has the habit of perseverance chooses to persevere and begins to carry out his choice by persisting for a time, yet completes not the act, through not persisting to the end. Now the end is twofold: one is the end of the work, the other is the end of human life. Properly speaking it belongs to perseverance to persevere to the end of the virtuous work, for instance that a soldier persevere to the end of the fight, and the magnificent man until his work be accomplished. There are, however, some virtues whose acts must endure throughout the whole of life, such as faith, hope, and charity, since they regard the last end of the entire life of man. Wherefore as regards these which are the principal virtues, the act of perseverance is not accomplished until the end of life. It is in this sense that Augustine speaks of perseverance as denoting the consummate act of perseverance.

Reply to Objection 3: Unchangeable persistence may belong to a virtue in two ways. First, on account of the intended end that is proper to that virtue; and thus to persist in good for a long time until the end, belongs to a special virtue called perseverance, which intends this as its special end. Secondly, by reason of the relation of the habit to its subject: and thus unchangeable persistence is consequent upon every virtue, inasmuch as virtue is a "quality difficult to change."

Whether perseverance is a part of fortitude?

Objection 1: It seems that perseverance is not a part of fortitude. For, according to the Philosopher (Ethic. viii, 7), "perseverance is about pains of touch." But these belong to temperance. Therefore perseverance is a part of temperance rather than of fortitude.

Objection 2: Further, every part of a moral virtue is about certain passions which that virtue moderates. Now perseverance does not imply moderation of the passions: since the more violent the passions, the more praiseworthy is it to persevere in accordance with reason. Therefore it seems that perseverance is a part not of a moral virtue, but rather of prudence which perfects the reason.

Objection 3: Further, Augustine says (De Persev. i) that no one can lose perseverance; whereas one can lose the other virtues. Therefore perseverance is greater than all the other virtues. Now a principal virtue is greater than its part. Therefore perseverance is not a part of a virtue, but is itself a principal virtue.

On the contrary, Tully (De Invent. Rhet. ii) reckons perseverance as a part of fortitude.

I answer that, As stated above (Q[123], A[2]; [3406]FS, Q[61], AA[3],4), a principal virtue is one to which is principally ascribed something that lays claim to the praise of virtue, inasmuch as it practices it in connection with its own matter, wherein it is most difficult of accomplishment. In accordance with this it has been stated (Q[123], A[2]) that fortitude is a principal virtue, because it observes firmness in matters wherein it is most difficult to stand firm, namely in dangers of death. Wherefore it follows of necessity that every virtue which has a title to praise for the firm endurance of something difficult must be annexed to fortitude as secondary to principal virtue. Now the endurance of difficulty arising from delay in accomplishing a good work gives perseverance its claim to praise: nor is this so difficult as to endure dangers of death. Therefore perseverance is annexed to fortitude, as secondary to principal virtue.

Reply to Objection 1: The annexing of secondary to principal virtues depends not only on the matter [*Cf.[3407] Q[136], A[4], ad 2], but also on the mode, because in everything form is of more account than matter. Wherefore although, as to matter, perseverance seems to have more in common with temperance than with fortitude, yet, in mode, it has more in common with fortitude, in the point of standing firm against the difficulty arising from length of time.

Reply to Objection 2: The perseverance of which the Philosopher speaks (Ethic. vii, 4,7) does not moderate any passions, but consists merely in a certain firmness of reason and will. But perseverance, considered as a virtue, moderates certain passions, namely fear of weariness or failure on account of the delay. Hence this virtue, like fortitude, is in the irascible.

Reply to Objection 3: Augustine speaks there of perseverance, as denoting, not a virtuous habit, but a virtuous act sustained to the end, according to Mat. 24:13, "He that shall persevere to the end, he shall be saved." Hence it is incompatible with such like perseverance for it to be lost, since it would no longer endure to the end.

Whether constancy pertains to perseverance?

Objection 1: It seems that constancy does not pertain to perseverance. For constancy pertains to patience, as stated above (Q[137], A[5]): and patience differs from perseverance. Therefore constancy does not pertain to perseverance.

Objection 2: Further, "virtue is about the difficult and the good." Now it does not seem difficult to be constant in little works, but only in great deeds, which pertain to magnificence. Therefore constancy pertains to magnificence rather than to perseverance.

Objection 3: Further, if constancy pertained to perseverance, it would seem nowise to differ from it, since both denote a kind of unchangeableness. Yet they differ: for Macrobius (In Somn. Scip. i) condivides constancy with firmness by which he indicates perseverance, as stated above (Q[128], A[6]). Therefore constancy does not pertain to perseverance.

On the contrary, One is said to be constant because one stands to a thing. Now it belongs to perseverance to stand to certain things, as appears from the definition given by Andronicus. Therefore constancy belongs to perseverance.

I answer that, Perseverance and constancy agree as to end, since it belongs to both to persist firmly in some good: but they differ as to those things which make it difficult to persist in good. Because the virtue of perseverance properly makes man persist firmly in good, against the difficulty that arises from the very continuance of the act: whereas constancy makes him persist firmly in good against difficulties arising from any other external hindrances. Hence perseverance takes precedence of constancy as a part of fortitude, because the difficulty arising from continuance of action is more intrinsic to the act of virtue than that which arises from external obstacles.

Reply to Objection 1: External obstacles to persistence in good are especially those which cause sorrow. Now patience is about sorrow, as stated above ([3408]Q[136], A[1]). Hence constancy agrees with perseverance as to end: while it agrees with patience as to those things which occasion difficulty. Now the end is of most account: wherefore constancy pertains to perseverance rather than to patience.

Reply to Objection 2: It is more difficult to persist in great deeds: yet in little or ordinary deeds, it is difficult to persist for any length of time, if not on account of the greatness of the deed which magnificence considers, yet from its very continuance which perseverance regards. Hence constancy may pertain to both.

Reply to Objection 3: Constancy pertains to perseverance in so far as it has something in common with it: but it is not the same thing in the point of their difference, as stated in the Article.

Whether perseverance needs the help of grace? [*Cf. FS, Q[109], A[10]]

Objection 1: It seems that perseverance does not need the help of grace. For perseverance is a virtue, as stated above [3409](A[1]). Now according to Tully (De Invent. Rhet. ii) virtue acts after the manner of nature. Therefore the sole inclination of virtue suffices for perseverance. Therefore this does not need the help of grace.

Objection 2: Further, the gift of Christ's grace is greater than the harm brought upon us by Adam, as appears from Rom. 5:15, seqq. Now "before sin man was so framed that he could persevere by means of what he had received," as Augustine says (De Correp. et Grat. xi). Much more therefore can man, after being repaired by the grace of Christ, persevere without the help of a further grace.

Objection 3: Further, sinful deeds are sometimes more difficult than deeds of virtue: hence it is said in the person of the wicked (Wis. 5:7): "We . . . have walked through hard ways." Now some persevere in sinful deeds without the help of another. Therefore man can also persevere in deeds of virtue without the help of grace.

On the contrary, Augustine says (De Persev. i): "We hold that perseverance is a gift of God, whereby we persevere unto the end, in Christ."

I answer that, As stated above (A[1], ad 2; A[2], ad 3), perseverance has a twofold signification. First, it denotes the habit of perseverance, considered as a virtue. In this way it needs the gift of habitual grace, even as the other infused virtues. Secondly, it may be taken to denote the act of perseverance enduring until death: and in this sense it needs not only habitual grace, but also the gratuitous help of God sustaining man in good until the end of life, as stated above ([3410]FS, Q[109], A[10]), when we were treating of grace. Because, since the free-will is changeable by its very nature, which changeableness is not taken away from it by the habitual grace bestowed in the present life, it is not in the power of the free-will, albeit repaired by grace, to abide unchangeably in good, though it is in its power to choose this: for it is often in our power to choose yet not to accomplish.

Reply to Objection 1: The virtue of perseverance, so far as it is concerned, inclines one to persevere: yet since it is a habit, and a habit is a thing one uses at will, it does not follow that a person who has the habit of virtue uses it unchangeably until death.

Reply to Objection 2: As Augustine says (De Correp. et Grat. xi), "it was given to the first man, not to persevere, but to be able to persevere of his free-will: because then no corruption was in human nature to make perseverance difficult. Now, however, by the grace of Christ, the predestined receive not only the possibility of persevering, but perseverance itself. Wherefore the first man whom no man threatened, of his own free-will rebelling against a threatening God, forfeited so great a happiness and so great a facility of avoiding sin: whereas these, although the world rage against their constancy, have persevered in faith."

Reply to Objection 3: Man is able by himself to fall into sin, but he cannot by himself arise from sin without the help of grace. Hence by falling into sin, so far as he is concerned man makes himself to be persevering in sin, unless he be delivered by God's grace. On the other hand, by doing good he does not make himself to be persevering in good, because he is able, by himself, to sin: wherefore he needs the help of grace for that end.

OF THE VICES OPPOSED TO PERSEVERANCE (TWO ARTICLES)

We must now consider the vices opposed to perseverance; under which head there are two points of inquiry:

(1) Of effeminacy;

(2) Of pertinacity.

Whether effeminacy* is opposed to perseverance? [*Mollities, literally 'softness']

Objection 1: It seems that effeminacy is not opposed to perseverance. For a gloss on 1 Cor. 6:9,10, "Nor adulterers, nor the effeminate, nor liers with mankind," expounds the text thus: "Effeminate---i.e. obscene, given to unnatural vice." But this is opposed to chastity. Therefore effeminacy is not a vice opposed to perseverance.

Objection 2: Further, the Philosopher says (Ethic. vii, 7) that "delicacy is a kind of effeminacy." But to be delicate seems akin to intemperance. Therefore effeminacy is not opposed to perseverance but to temperance.

Objection 3: Further, the Philosopher says (Ethic. vii, 7) that "the man who is fond of amusement is effeminate." Now immoderate fondness of amusement is opposed to {eutrapelia}, which is the virtue about pleasures of play, as stated in Ethic. iv, 8. Therefore effeminacy is not opposed to perseverance.

On the contrary, The Philosopher says (Ethic. vii, 7) that "the persevering man is opposed to the effeminate."

I answer that, As stated above ([3411]Q[137], AA[1],2), perseverance is deserving of praise because thereby a man does not forsake a good on account of long endurance of difficulties and toils: and it is directly opposed to this, seemingly, for a man to be ready to forsake a good on account of difficulties which he cannot endure. This is what we understand by effeminacy, because a thing is said to be "soft" if it readily yields to the touch. Now a thing is not declared to be soft through yielding to a heavy blow, for walls yield to the battering-ram. Wherefore a man is not said to be effeminate if he yields to heavy blows. Hence the Philosopher says (Ethic. vii, 7) that "it is no wonder, if a person is overcome by strong and overwhelming pleasures or sorrows; but he is to be pardoned if he struggles against them." Now it is evident that fear of danger is more impelling than the desire of pleasure: wherefore Tully says (De Offic. i) under the heading "True magnanimity consists of two things: It is inconsistent for one who is not cast down by fear, to be defeated by lust, or who has proved himself unbeaten by toil, to yield to pleasure." Moreover, pleasure itself is a stronger motive of attraction than sorrow, for the lack of pleasure is a motive of withdrawal, since lack of pleasure is a pure privation. Wherefore, according to the Philosopher (Ethic. vii, 7), properly speaking an effeminate man is one who withdraws from good on account of sorrow caused by lack of pleasure, yielding as it were to a weak motion.

Reply to Objection 1: This effeminacy is caused in two ways. In one way, by custom: for where a man is accustomed to enjoy pleasures, it is more difficult for him to endure the lack of them. In another way, by natural disposition, because, to wit, his mind is less persevering through the frailty of his temperament. This is how women are compared to men, as the Philosopher says (Ethic. vii, 7): wherefore those who are passively sodomitical are said to be effeminate, being womanish themselves, as it were.

Reply to Objection 2: Toil is opposed to bodily pleasure: wherefore it is only toilsome things that are a hindrance to pleasures. Now the delicate are those who cannot endure toils, nor anything that diminishes pleasure. Hence it is written (Dt. 28:56): "The tender and delicate woman, that could not go upon the ground, nor set down her foot for . . . softness [Douay: 'niceness']." Thus delicacy is a kind of effeminacy. But properly speaking effeminacy regards lack of pleasures, while delicacy regards the cause that hinders pleasure, for instance toil or the like.

Reply to Objection 3: In play two things may be considered. In the first place there is the pleasure, and thus inordinate fondness of play is opposed to {eutrapelia}. Secondly, we may consider the relaxation or rest which is opposed to toil. Accordingly just as it belongs to effeminacy to be unable to endure toilsome things, so too it belongs thereto to desire play or any other relaxation inordinately.

Whether pertinacity is opposed to perseverance?

Objection 1: It seems that pertinacity is not opposed to perseverance. For Gregory says (Moral. xxxi) that pertinacity arises from vainglory. But vainglory is not opposed to perseverance but to magnanimity, as stated above ([3412]Q[132], A[2]). Therefore pertinacity is not opposed to perseverance.

Objection 2: Further, if it is opposed to perseverance, this is so either by excess or by deficiency. Now it is not opposed by excess: because the pertinacious also yield to certain pleasure and sorrow, since according to the Philosopher (Ethic. vii, 9) "they rejoice when they prevail, and grieve when their opinions are rejected." And if it be opposed by deficiency, it will be the same as effeminacy, which is clearly false. Therefore pertinacity is nowise opposed to perseverance.

Objection 3: Further, just as the persevering man persists in good against sorrow, so too do the continent and the temperate against pleasures, the brave against fear, and the meek against anger. But pertinacity is over-persistence in something. Therefore pertinacity is not opposed to perseverance more than to other virtues.

On the contrary, Tully says (De Invent. Rhet. ii) that pertinacity is to perseverance as superstition is to religion. But superstition is opposed to religion, as stated above ([3413]Q[92], A[1]). Therefore pertinacity is opposed to perseverance.

I answer that, As Isidore says (Etym. x) "a person is said to be pertinacious who holds on impudently, as being utterly tenacious." "Pervicacious" has the same meaning, for it signifies that a man "perseveres in his purpose until he is victorious: for the ancients called 'vicia' what we call victory." These the Philosopher (Ethic. vii, 9) calls {ischyrognomones}, that is "head-strong," or {idiognomones}, that is "self-opinionated," because they abide by their opinions more than they should; whereas the effeminate man does so less than he ought, and the persevering man, as he ought. Hence it is clear that perseverance is commended for observing the mean, while pertinacity is reproved for exceeding the mean, and effeminacy for falling short of it.

Reply to Objection 1: The reason why a man is too persistent in his own opinion, is that he wishes by this means to make a show of his own excellence: wherefore this is the result of vainglory as its cause. Now it has been stated above ([3414]Q[127], A[2], ad 1; [3415] Q[133], A[2]), that opposition of vices to virtues depends, not on their cause, but on their species.

Reply to Objection 2: The pertinacious man exceeds by persisting inordinately in something against many difficulties: yet he takes a certain pleasure in the end, just as the brave and the persevering man. Since, however, this pleasure is sinful, seeing that he desires it too much, and shuns the contrary pain, he is like the incontinent or effeminate man.

Reply to Objection 3: Although the other virtues persist against the onslaught of the passions, they are not commended for persisting in the same way as perseverance is. As to continence, its claim to praise seems to lie rather in overcoming pleasures. Hence pertinacity is directly opposed to perseverance.

OF THE GIFT OF FORTITUDE (TWO ARTICLES)

We must next consider the gift corresponding to fortitude, and this is the gift of fortitude. Under this head there are two points of inquiry:

(1) Whether fortitude is a gift?
(2) Which among the beatitudes and fruits correspond to it?

Whether fortitude is a gift?

Objection 1: It seems that fortitude is not a gift. For the virtues differ from the gifts: and fortitude is a virtue. Therefore it should not be reckoned a gift.

Objection 2: Further, the acts of the gift remain in heaven, as stated above ([3416]FS, Q[68], A[6]). But the act of fortitude does not remain in heaven: for Gregory says (Moral. i) that "fortitude encourages the fainthearted against hardships, which will be altogether absent from heaven." Therefore fortitude is not a gift.

Objection 3: Further, Augustine says (De Doctr. Christ. ii) that "it is a sign of fortitude to cut oneself adrift from all the deadly pleasures of the passing show." Now noisome pleasures and delights are the concern of temperance rather than of fortitude. Therefore it seems that fortitude is not the gift corresponding to the virtue of fortitude.

On the contrary, Fortitude is reckoned among the other gifts of the Holy Ghost (Is. 11:2).

I answer that, Fortitude denotes a certain firmness of mind, as stated above (Q[123], A[2]; [3417]FS, Q[61], A[3]): and this firmness of mind is required both in doing good and in enduring evil, especially with regard to goods or evils that are difficult. Now man, according to his proper and connatural mode, is able to have this firmness in both these respects, so as not to forsake the good on account of difficulties, whether in accomplishing an arduous work, or in enduring grievous evil. In this sense fortitude denotes a special or general virtue, as stated above (Q[123], A[2]).

Yet furthermore man's mind is moved by the Holy Ghost, in order that he may attain the end of each work begun, and avoid whatever perils may threaten. This surpasses human nature: for sometimes it is not in a man's power to attain the end of his work, or to avoid evils or dangers, since these may happen to overwhelm him in death. But the Holy Ghost works this in man, by bringing him to everlasting life, which is the end of all good deeds, and the release from all perils. A certain confidence of this is infused into the mind by the Holy Ghost Who expels any fear of the contrary. It is in this sense that fortitude is reckoned a gift of the Holy Ghost. For it has been stated above ([3418]FS, Q[68], AA[1],2) that the gifts regard the motion of the mind by the Holy Ghost.

Reply to Objection 1: Fortitude, as a virtue, perfects the mind in the endurance of all perils whatever; but it does not go so far as to give confidence of overcoming all dangers: this belongs to the fortitude that is a gift of the Holy Ghost.

Reply to Objection 2: The gifts have not the same acts in heaven as on the way: for they exercise acts in connection with the enjoyment of the end. Hence the act of fortitude there is to enjoy full security from toil and evil.

Reply to Objection 3: The gift of fortitude regards the virtue of fortitude not only because it consists in enduring dangers, but also inasmuch as it consists in accomplishing any difficult work. Wherefore the gift of fortitude is directed by the gift of counsel, which seems to be concerned chiefly with the greater goods.

Whether the fourth beatitude: "Blessed are they that hunger and thirst after justice," corresponds to the gift of fortitude?

Objection 1: It seems that the fourth beatitude, "Blessed are they that hunger and thirst after justice," does not correspond to the gift of fortitude. For the gift of piety and not the gift of fortitude corresponds to the virtue of justice. Now hungering and thirsting after justice pertain to the act of justice. Therefore this beatitude corresponds to the gift of piety rather than to the gift of fortitude.

Objection 2: Further, hunger and thirst after justice imply a desire for good. Now this belongs properly to charity, to which the gift of wisdom, and not the gift of fortitude, corresponds, as stated above ([3419]Q[45]). Therefore this beatitude corresponds, not to the gift of fortitude, but to the gift of wisdom.

Objection 3: Further, the fruits are consequent upon the beatitudes, since delight is essential to beatitude, according to Ethic. i, 8. Now the fruits, apparently, include none pertaining to fortitude. Therefore neither does any beatitude correspond to it.

On the contrary, Augustine says (De Serm. Dom. in Monte i): "Fortitude becomes the hungry and thirsty: since those who desire to enjoy true goods, and wish to avoid loving earthly and material things, must toil."

I answer that, As stated above ([3420]Q[121], A[2]), Augustine makes the beatitudes correspond to the gifts according to the order in which they are set forth, observing at the same time a certain fittingness between them. Wherefore he ascribes the fourth beatitude, concerning the hunger and thirst for justice, to the fourth gift, namely fortitude.

Yet there is a certain congruity between them, because, as stated (A[1]), fortitude is about difficult things. Now it is very difficult, not merely to do virtuous deeds, which receive the common designation of works of justice, but furthermore to do them with an unsatiable desire, which may be signified by hunger and thirst for justice.

Reply to Objection 1: As Chrysostom says (Hom. xv in Matth.), we may understand here not only particular, but also universal justice, which is related to all virtuous deeds according to Ethic. v, 1, wherein whatever is hard is the object of that fortitude which is a gift.

Reply to Objection 2: Charity is the root of all the virtues and gifts, as stated above (Q[23], A[8], ad 3; [3421]FS, Q[68], A[4], ad 3). Hence whatever pertains to fortitude may also be referred to charity.

Reply to Objection 3: There are two of the fruits which correspond sufficiently to the gift of fortitude: namely, patience, which regards the enduring of evils: and longanimity, which may regard the long delay and accomplishment of goods.

Day 221

OF THE PRECEPTS OF FORTITUDE (TWO ARTICLES)
We must next consider the precepts of fortitude:
(1) The precepts of fortitude itself;
(2) The precepts of its parts.

Whether the precepts of fortitude are suitably given in the Divine Law?

Objection 1: It seems that the precepts of fortitude are not suitably given in the Divine Law. For the New Law is more perfect than the Old Law. Yet the Old Law contains precepts of fortitude (Dt. 20). Therefore precepts of fortitude should have been given in the New Law also.

Objection 2: Further, affirmative precepts are of greater import than negative precepts, since the affirmative include the negative, but not vice versa. Therefore it is unsuitable for the Divine Law to contain none but negative precepts in prohibition of fear.

Objection 3: Further, fortitude is one of the principal virtues, as stated above (Q[123], A[2]; [3422]FS, Q[61], A[2]). Now the precepts are directed to the virtues as to their end: wherefore they should be proportionate to them. Therefore the precepts of fortitude should have been placed among the precepts of the decalogue, which are the chief precepts of the Law.

On the contrary, stands Holy Writ which contains these precepts.

I answer that, Precepts of law are directed to the end intended by the lawgiver. Wherefore precepts of law must needs be framed in various ways according to the various ends intended by lawgivers, so that even in human affairs there are laws of democracies, others of kingdoms, and others again of tyrannical governments. Now the end of the Divine Law is that man may adhere to God: wherefore the Divine Law contains precepts both of fortitude and of the other virtues, with a view to directing the mind to God. For this reason it is written (Dt. 20:3,4): "Fear ye them not: because the Lord your God is in the midst of you, and will fight for you against your enemies."

As to human laws, they are directed to certain earthly goods, and among them we find precepts of fortitude according to the requirements of those goods.

Reply to Objection 1: The Old Testament contained temporal promises, while the promises of the New Testament are spiritual and eternal, according to Augustine (Contra Faust. iv). Hence in the Old Law there was need for the people to be taught how to fight, even in a bodily contest, in order to obtain an earthly possession. But in the New Testament men were to be taught how to come to the possession of eternal life by fighting spiritually, according to Mat. 11:12, "The kingdom of heaven suffereth violence, and the violent bear it away." Hence Peter commands (1 Pet. 5:8,9): "Your adversary the devil, as a roaring lion, goeth about, seeking whom he may devour: whom resist ye, strong in faith," as also James 4:7: "Resist the devil, and he will fly from you." Since, however, men while tending to spiritual goods may be withdrawn from them by corporal dangers, precepts of fortitude had to be given even in the New Law, that they might bravely endure temporal evils, according to Mat. 10:28, "Fear ye not them that kill the body."

Reply to Objection 2: The law gives general directions in its precepts. But the things that have to be done in cases of danger are not, like the things to be avoided, reducible to some common thing. Hence the precepts of fortitude are negative rather than affirmative.

Reply to Objection 3: As stated above ([3423]Q[122], A[1]), the precepts of the decalogue are placed in the Law, as first principles, which need to be known to all from the outset. Wherefore the precepts of the decalogue had to be chiefly about those acts of justice in which the notion of duty is manifest, and not about acts of fortitude, because it is not so evident that it is a duty for a person not to fear dangers of death.

Whether the precepts of the parts of fortitude are suitably given in the Divine Law?

Objection 1: It seems that the precept of the parts of fortitude are unsuitably given in the Divine Law. For just as patience and perseverance are parts of fortitude, so also are magnificence, magnanimity, and confidence, as stated above ([3424]Q[128]). Now we find precepts of patience in the Divine Law, as also of perseverance. Therefore there should also have been precepts of magnificence and magnanimity.

Objection 2: Further, patience is a very necessary virtue, since it is the guardian of the other virtues, as Gregory says (Hom. in Evang. xxxv). Now the other virtues are commanded absolutely. Therefore patience should not have been commanded merely, as Augustine says (De Serm. Dom. in Monte i), as to the preparedness of the mind.

Objection 3: Further, patience and perseverance are parts of fortitude, as stated above ([3425]Q[128];[3426] Q[136], A[4];[3427] Q[137], A[2]). Now the precepts of fortitude are not affirmative but only negative, as stated above (A[1], ad 2). Therefore the precepts of patience and perseverance should have been negative and not affirmative.

The contrary, however, follows from the way in which they are given by Holy Writ.

I answer that, The Divine Law instructs man perfectly about such things as are necessary for right living. Now in order to live aright man needs not only the principal virtues, but also the secondary and annexed virtues. Wherefore the Divine Law contains precepts not only about the acts of the principal virtues, but also about the acts of the secondary and annexed virtues.

Reply to Objection 1: Magnificence and magnanimity do not belong to the genus of fortitude, except by reason of a certain excellence of greatness which they regard in their respective matters. Now things pertaining to excellence come under the counsels of perfection rather than under precepts of obligation. Wherefore, there was need of counsels, rather than of precepts about magnificence and magnanimity. On the other hand, the hardships and toils of the present life pertain to patience and perseverance, not by reason of any greatness observable in them, but on account of the very nature of those virtues. Hence the need of precepts of patience and perseverance.

Reply to Objection 2: As stated above ([3428]Q[3], A[2]), although affirmative precepts are always binding, they are not binding for always, but according to place and time. Wherefore just as the affirmative precepts about the other virtues are to be understood as to the preparedness of the mind, in the sense that man be prepared to fulfil them when necessary, so too are the precepts of patience to be understood in the same way.

Reply to Objection 3: Fortitude, as distinct from patience and perseverance, is about the greatest dangers wherein one must proceed with caution; nor is it necessary to determine what is to be done in particular. On the other hand, patience and perseverance are about minor hardships and toils, wherefore there is less danger in determining, especially in general, what is to be done in such cases.

OF TEMPERANCE (EIGHT ARTICLES)

In the next place we must consider temperance: (1) Temperance itself; (2) its parts; (3) its precepts. With regard to temperance we must consider (1) temperance itself; (2) the contrary vices.

Under the first head there are eight points of inquiry:

(1) Whether temperance is a virtue?

(2) Whether it is a special virtue?

(3) Whether it is only about desires and pleasures?

(4) Whether it is only about pleasures of touch?

(5) Whether it is about pleasures of taste, as such, or only as a kind of touch?

(6) What is the rule of temperance?

(7) Whether it is a cardinal, or principal, virtue?

(8) Whether it is the greatest of virtues ?

Whether temperance is a virtue?

Objection 1: It seems that temperance is not a virtue. For no virtue goes against the inclination of nature, since "there is in us a natural aptitude for virtue," as stated in Ethic. ii, 1. Now temperance withdraws us from pleasures to which nature inclines, according to Ethic. ii, 3,8. Therefore temperance is not a virtue.

Objection 2: Further, virtues are connected with one another, as stated above ([3429]FS, Q[65], A[1]). But some people have temperance without having the other virtues: for we find many who are temperate, and yet covetous or timid. Therefore temperance is not a virtue.

Objection 3: Further, to every virtue there is a corresponding gift, as appears from what we have said above ([3430]FS, Q[68], A[4]). But seemingly no gift corresponds to temperance, since all the gifts have been already ascribed to the other virtues (QQ[8], 9,19,45,52, 71,139). Therefore temperance is not a virtue.

On the contrary, Augustine says (Music. vi, 15): "Temperance is the name of a virtue."

I answer that, As stated above ([3431]FS, Q[55], A[3]), it is essential to virtue to incline man to good. Now the good of man is to be in accordance with reason, as Dionysius states (Div. Nom. iv). Hence human virtue is that which inclines man to something in accordance with reason. Now temperance evidently inclines man to this, since its very name implies moderation or temperateness, which reason causes. Therefore temperance is a virtue.

Reply to Objection 1: Nature inclines everything to whatever is becoming to it. Wherefore man naturally desires pleasures that are becoming to him. Since, however, man as such is a rational being, it follows that those pleasures are becoming to man which are in accordance with reason. From such pleasures temperance does not withdraw him, but from those which are contrary to reason. Wherefore it is clear that temperance is not contrary to the inclination of human nature, but is in accord with it. It is, however, contrary to the inclination of the animal nature that is not subject to reason.

Reply to Objection 2: The temperance which fulfils the conditions of perfect virtue is not without prudence, while this is lacking to all who are in sin. Hence those who lack other virtues, through being subject to the opposite vices, have not the temperance which is a virtue, though they do acts of temperance from a certain natural disposition, in so far as certain imperfect virtues are either natural to man, as stated above ([3432]FS, Q[63], A[1]), or acquired by habituation, which virtues, through lack of prudence, are not perfected by reason, as stated above ([3433]FS, Q[65], A[1]).

Reply to Objection 3: Temperance also has a corresponding gift, namely, fear, whereby man is withheld from the pleasures of the flesh, according to Ps. 118:120: "Pierce Thou my flesh with Thy fear." The gift of fear has for its principal object God, Whom it avoids offending, and in this respect it corresponds to the virtue of hope, as stated above ([3434]Q[19], A[9], ad 1). But it may have for its secondary object whatever a man shuns in order to avoid offending God. Now man stands in the greatest need of the fear of God in order to shun those things which are most seductive, and these are the matter of temperance: wherefore the gift of fear corresponds to temperance also.

Whether temperance is a special virtue?

Objection 1: It would seem that temperance is not a special virtue. For Augustine says (De Morib. Eccl. xv) that "it belongs to temperance to preserve one's integrity and freedom from corruption for God's sake." But this is common to every virtue. Therefore temperance is not a special virtue.

Objection 2: Further, Ambrose says (De Offic. i, 42) that "what we observe and seek most in temperance is tranquillity of soul." But this is common to every virtue. Therefore temperance is not a special virtue.

Objection 3: Further, Tully says (De Offic. i, 27) that "we cannot separate the beautiful from the virtuous," and that "whatever is just is beautiful." Now the beautiful is considered as proper to temperance, according to the same authority (Tully, De Offic. i, 27). Therefore temperance is not a special virtue.

On the contrary, The Philosopher (Ethic. ii, 7; iii, 10) reckons it a special virtue.

I answer that, It is customary in human speech to employ a common term in a restricted sense in order to designate the principal things to which that common term is applicable: thus the word "city" is used antonomastically* to designate Rome. [*Antonomasia is the figure of speech whereby we substitute the general for the individual term; e.g. The Philosopher for Aristotle]. Accordingly the word "temperance" has a twofold acceptation. First, in accordance with its common signification: and thus temperance is not a special but a general virtue, because the word "temperance" signifies a certain temperateness or moderation, which reason appoints to human operations and passions: and this is common to every moral virtue. Yet there is a logical difference between temperance and fortitude, even if we take them both as general virtues: since temperance withdraws man from things which seduce the appetite from obeying reason, while fortitude incites him to endure or withstand those things on account of which he forsakes the good of reason.

On the other hand, if we take temperance antonomastically, as withholding the appetite from those things which are most seductive to man, it is a special virtue, for thus it has, like fortitude, a special matter.

Reply to Objection 1: Man's appetite is corrupted chiefly by those things which seduce him into forsaking the rule of reason and Divine law. Wherefore integrity, which Augustine ascribes to temperance, can, like the latter, be taken in two ways: first, in a general sense, and secondly in a sense of excellence.

Reply to Objection 2: The things about which temperance is concerned have a most disturbing effect on the soul, for the reason that they are natural to man, as we shall state further on ([3435]AA[4],5). Hence tranquillity of soul is ascribed to temperance by way of excellence, although it is a common property of all the virtues.

Reply to Objection 3: Although beauty is becoming to every virtue, it is ascribed to temperance, by way of excellence, for two reasons. First, in respect of the generic notion of temperance, which consists in a certain moderate and fitting proportion, and this is what we understand by beauty, as attested by Dionysius (Div. Nom. iv). Secondly, because the things from which temperance withholds us, hold the lowest place in man, and are becoming to him by reason of his animal nature, as we shall state further on ([3436]AA[4],5; Q[142], A[4]), wherefore it is natural that such things should defile him. In consequence beauty is a foremost attribute of temperance which above all hinders man from being defiled. In like manner honesty [*Honesty must be taken here in its broad sense as synonymous with moral goodness, from the point of view of decorum] is a special attribute of temperance: for Isidore says (Etym. x): "An honest man is one who has no defilement, for honesty means an honorable state." This is most applicable to temperance, which withstands the vices that bring most dishonor on man, as we shall state further on (Q[142], A[4]).

Whether temperance is only about desires and pleasures?

Objection 1: It would seem that temperance is not only about desires and pleasures. For Tully says (De Invent. Rhet. ii, 54) that "temperance is reason's firm and moderate mastery of lust and other wanton emotions of the mind." Now all the passions of the soul are called emotions of the mind. Therefore it seems that temperance is not only about desires and pleasures.

Objection 2: Further, "Virtue is about the difficult and the good" [*Ethic. ii, 3]. Now it seems more difficult to temper fear, especially with regard to dangers of death, than to moderate desires and pleasures, which are despised on account of deadly pains and dangers, according to Augustine (QQ[83], qu. 36). Therefore it seems that the virtue of temperance is not chiefly about desires and pleasures.

Objection 3: Further, according to Ambrose (De Offic. i, 43) "the grace of moderation belongs to temperance": and Tully says (De Offic. ii, 27) that "it is the concern of temperance to calm all disturbances of the mind and to enforce moderation." Now moderation is needed, not only in desires and pleasures, but also in external acts and whatever pertains to the exterior. Therefore temperance is not only about desires and pleasures.

On the contrary, Isidore says (Etym.) [*The words quoted do not occur in the work referred to; Cf. his De Summo Bono xxxvii, xlii, and De Different. ii, 39]: that "it is temperance whereby lust and desire are kept under control."

I answer that, As stated above (Q[123], A[12]; Q[136], A[1]), it belongs to moral virtue to safeguard the good of reason against the passions that rebel against reason. Now the movement of the soul's passions is twofold, as stated above ([3437]FS, Q[23], A[2]), when we were treating of the passions: the one, whereby the sensitive appetite pursues sensible and bodily goods, the other whereby it flies from sensible and bodily evils.

The first of these movements of the sensitive appetite rebels against reason chiefly by lack of moderation. Because sensible and bodily goods, considered in their species, are not in opposition to reason, but are subject to it as instruments which reason employs in order to attain its proper end: and that they are opposed to reason is owing to the fact that the sensitive appetite fails to tend towards them in accord with the mode of reason. Hence it belongs properly to moral virtue to moderate those passions which denote a pursuit of the good.

On the other hand, the movement of the sensitive appetite in flying from sensible evil is mostly in opposition to reason, not through being immoderate, but chiefly in respect of its flight: because, when a man flies from sensible and bodily evils, which sometimes accompany the good of reason, the result is that he flies from the good of reason. Hence it belongs to moral virtue to make man while flying from evil to remain firm in the good of reason.

Accordingly, just as the virtue of fortitude, which by its very nature bestows firmness, is chiefly concerned with the passion, viz. fear, which regards flight from bodily evils, and consequently with daring, which attacks the objects of fear in the hope of attaining some good, so, too, temperance, which denotes a kind of moderation, is chiefly concerned with those passions that tend towards sensible goods, viz. desire and pleasure, and consequently with the sorrows that arise from the absence of those pleasures. For just as daring presupposes objects of fear, so too such like sorrow arises from the absence of the aforesaid pleasures.

Reply to Objection 1: As stated above ([3438]FS, Q[23], AA[1],2; [3439]FS, Q[25], A[1]), when we were treating of the passions, those passions which pertain to avoidance of evil, presuppose the passions pertaining to the pursuit of good; and the passions of the irascible presuppose the passions of the concupiscible. Hence, while temperance directly moderates the passions of the concupiscible which tend towards good, as a consequence, it moderates all the other passions, inasmuch as moderation of the passions that precede results in moderation of the passions that follow: since he that is not immoderate in desire is moderate in hope, and grieves moderately for the absence of the things he desires.

Reply to Objection 2: Desire denotes an impulse of the appetite towards the object of pleasure and this impulse needs control, which belongs to temperance. on the other hand fear denotes a withdrawal of the mind from certain evils, against which man needs firmness of mind, which fortitude bestows. Hence temperance is properly about desires, and fortitude about fears.

Reply to Objection 3: External acts proceed from the internal passions of the soul: wherefore their moderation depends on the moderation of the internal passions.

Whether temperance is only about desires and pleasures of touch?

Objection 1: It would seem that temperance is not only about desires and pleasures of touch. For Augustine says (De Morib. Eccl. xix) that "the function of temperance is to control and quell the desires which draw us to the things which withdraw us from the laws of God and from the fruit of His goodness"; and a little further on he adds that "it is the duty of temperance to spurn all bodily allurements and popular praise." Now we are withdrawn from God's laws not only by the desire for pleasures of touch, but also by the desire for pleasures of the other senses, for these, too, belong to the bodily allurements, and again by the desire for riches or for worldly glory: wherefore it is written (1 Tim. 6:10). "Desire [*'Cupiditas,' which is the Douay version following the Greek {philargyria} renders 'desire of money'] is the root of all evils." Therefore temperance is not only about desires of pleasures of touch.

Objection 2: Further, the Philosopher says (Ethic. iv, 3) that "one who is worthy of small things and deems himself worthy of them is temperate, but he is not magnificent." Now honors, whether small or great, of which he is speaking there, are an object of pleasure, not of touch, but in the soul's apprehension. Therefore temperance is not only about desires for pleasures of touch.

Objection 3: Further, things that are of the same genus would seem to pertain to the matter of a particular virtue under one same aspect. Now all pleasures of sense are apparently of the same genus. Therefore they all equally belong to the matter of temperance.

Objection 4: Further, spiritual pleasures are greater than the pleasures of the body, as stated above ([3440]FS, Q[31], A[5]) in the treatise on the passions. Now sometimes men forsake God's laws and the state of virtue through desire for spiritual pleasures, for instance, through curiosity in matters of knowledge: wherefore the devil promised man knowledge, saying (Gn. 3:5): "Ye shall be as Gods, knowing good and evil." Therefore temperance is not only about pleasures of touch.

Objection 5: Further, if pleasures of touch were the proper matter of temperance, it would follow that temperance is about all pleasures of touch. But it is not about all, for instance, about those which occur in games. Therefore pleasures of touch are not the proper matter of temperance.

On the contrary, The Philosopher says (Ethic. iii, 10) that "temperance is properly about desires of pleasures of touch."

I answer that, As stated above [3441](A[3]), temperance is about desires and pleasures in the same way as fortitude is about fear and daring. Now fortitude is about fear and daring with respect to the greatest evils whereby nature itself is dissolved; and such are dangers of death. Wherefore in like manner temperance must needs be about desires for the greatest pleasures. And since pleasure results from a natural operation, it is so much the greater according as it results from a more natural operation. Now to animals the most natural operations are those which preserve the nature of the individual by means of meat and drink, and the nature of the species by the union of the sexes. Hence temperance is properly about pleasures of meat and drink and sexual pleasures. Now these pleasures result from the sense of touch. Wherefore it follows that temperance is about pleasures of touch.

Reply to Objection 1: In the passage quoted Augustine apparently takes temperance, not as a special virtue having a determinate matter, but as concerned with the moderation of reason, in any matter whatever: and this is a general condition of every virtue. However, we may also reply that if a man can control the greatest pleasures, much more can he control lesser ones. Wherefore it belongs chiefly and properly to temperance to moderate desires and pleasures of touch, and secondarily other pleasures.

Reply to Objection 2: The Philosopher takes temperance as denoting moderation in external things, when, to wit, a man tends to that which is proportionate to him, but not as denoting moderation in the soul's emotions, which pertains to the virtue of temperance.

Reply to Objection 3: The pleasures of the other senses play a different part in man and in other animals. For in other animals pleasures do not result from the other senses save in relation to sensibles of touch: thus the lion is pleased to see the stag, or to hear its voice, in relation to his food. On the other hand man derives pleasure from the other senses, not only for this reason, but also on account of the becomingness of the sensible object. Wherefore temperance is about the pleasures of the other senses, in relation to pleasures of touch, not principally but consequently: while in so far as the sensible objects of the other senses are pleasant on account of their becomingness, as when a man is pleased at a well-harmonized sound, this pleasure has nothing to do with the preservation of nature. Hence these passions are not of such importance that temperance can be referred to them antonomastically.

Reply to Objection 4: Although spiritual pleasures are by their nature greater than bodily pleasures, they are not so perceptible to the senses, and consequently they do not so strongly affect the sensitive appetite, against whose impulse the good of reason is safeguarded by moral virtue. We may also reply that spiritual pleasures, strictly speaking, are in accordance with reason, wherefore they need no control, save accidentally, in so far as one spiritual pleasure is a hindrance to another greater and more binding.

Reply to Objection 5: Not all pleasures of touch regard the preservation of nature, and consequently it does not follow that temperance is about all pleasures of touch.

Whether temperance is about the pleasures proper to the taste?

Objection 1: It would seem that temperance is about pleasures proper to the taste. For pleasures of the taste result from food and drink, which are more necessary to man's life than sexual pleasures, which regard the touch. But according to what has been said [3442](A[4]), temperance is about pleasures in things that are necessary to human life. Therefore temperance is about pleasures proper to the taste rather than about those proper to the touch.

Objection 2: Further, temperance is about the passions rather than about things themselves. Now, according to De Anima ii, 3, "the touch is the sense of food," as regards the very substance of the food, whereas "savor" which is the proper object of the taste, is "the pleasing quality of the food." Therefore temperance is about the taste rather than about the touch.

Objection 3: Further, according to Ethic. vii, 4,7: "temperance and intemperance are about the same things, and so are continence and incontinence, perseverance, and effeminacy," to which delicacy pertains. Now delicacy seems to regard the delight taken in savors which are the object of the taste. Therefore temperance is about pleasures proper to the taste.

On the contrary, The Philosopher says (Ethic. iii, 10) that "seemingly temperance and intemperance have little if anything to do with the taste."

I answer that, As stated above [3443](A[4]), temperance is about the greatest pleasures, which chiefly regard the preservation of human life either in the species or in the individual. In these matters certain things are to be considered as principal and others as secondary. The principal thing is the use itself of the necessary means, of the woman who is necessary for the preservation of the species, or of food and drink which are necessary for the preservation of the individual: while the very use of these necessary things has a certain essential pleasure annexed thereto.

In regard to either use we consider as secondary whatever makes the use more pleasurable, such as beauty and adornment in woman, and a pleasing savor and likewise odor in food. Hence temperance is chiefly about the pleasure of touch, that results essentially from the use of these necessary things, which use is in all cases attained by the touch. Secondarily, however, temperance and intemperance are about pleasures of the taste, smell, or sight, inasmuch as the sensible objects of these senses conduce to the pleasurable use of the necessary things that have relation to the touch. But since the taste is more akin to the touch than the other senses are, it follows that temperance is more about the taste than about the other senses.

Reply to Objection 1: The use of food and the pleasure that essentially results therefrom pertain to the touch. Hence the Philosopher says (De Anima ii, 3) that "touch is the sense of food, for food is hot or cold, wet or dry." To the taste belongs the discernment of savors, which make the food pleasant to eat, in so far as they are signs of its being suitable for nourishment.

Reply to Objection 2: The pleasure resulting from savor is additional, so to speak, whereas the pleasure of touch results essentially from the use of food and drink.

Reply to Objection 3: Delicacy regards principally the substance of the food, but secondarily it regards its delicious savor and the way in which it is served.

Whether the rule of temperance depends on the need of the present life?

Objection 1: It would seem that the rule of temperance does not depend on the needs of the present life. For higher things are not regulated according to lower. Now, as temperance is a virtue of the soul, it is above the needs of the body. Therefore the rule of temperance does not depend on the needs of the body.

Objection 2: Further, whoever exceeds a rule sins. Therefore if the needs of the body were the rule of temperance, it would be a sin against temperance to indulge in any other pleasure than those required by nature, which is content with very little. But this would seem unreasonable.

Objection 3: Further, no one sins in observing a rule. Therefore if the need of the body were the rule of temperance, there would be no sin in using any pleasure for the needs of the body, for instance, for the sake of health. But this is apparently false. Therefore the need of the body is not the rule of temperance.

On the contrary, Augustine says (De Morib. Eccl. xxi): "In both Testaments the temperate man finds confirmation of the rule forbidding him to love the things of this life, or to deem any of them desirable for its own sake, and commanding him to avail himself of those things with the moderation of a user not the attachment of a lover, in so far as they are requisite for the needs of this life and of his station."

I answer that, As stated above [3444](A[1]; Q[109], A[2]; Q[123], A[12]), the good of moral virtue consists chiefly in the order of reason: because "man's good is to be in accord with reason," as Dionysius asserts (Div. Nom. iv). Now the principal order of reason is that by which it directs certain things towards their end, and the good of reason consists chiefly in this order; since good has the aspect of end, and the end is the rule of whatever is directed to the end. Now all the pleasurable objects that are at man's disposal, are directed to some necessity of this life as to their end. Wherefore temperance takes the need of this life, as the rule of the pleasurable objects of which it makes use, and uses them only for as much as the need of this life requires.

Reply to Objection 1: As stated above, the need of this life is regarded as a rule in so far as it is an end. Now it must be observed that sometimes the end of the worker differs from the end of the work, thus it is clear that the end of building is a house, whereas sometimes the end of the builder is profit. Accordingly the end and rule of temperance itself is happiness; while the end and rule of the thing it makes use of is the need of human life, to which whatever is useful for life is subordinate.

Reply to Objection 2: The need of human life may be taken in two ways. First, it may be taken in the sense in which we apply the term "necessary" to that without which a thing cannot be at all; thus food is necessary to an animal. Secondly, it may be taken for something without which a thing cannot be becomingly. Now temperance regards not only the former of these needs, but also the latter. Wherefore the Philosopher says (Ethic. iii, 11) that "the temperate man desires pleasant things for the sake of health, or for the sake of a sound condition of body." Other things that are not necessary for this purpose may be divided into two classes. For some are a hindrance to health and a sound condition of body; and these temperance makes not use of whatever, for this would be a sin against temperance. But others are not a hindrance to those things, and these temperance uses moderately, according to the demands of place and time, and in keeping with those among whom one dwells. Hence the Philosopher (Ethic. iii, 11) says that the "temperate man also desires other pleasant things," those namely that are not necessary for health or a sound condition of body, "so long as they are not prejudicial to these things."

Reply to Objection 3: As stated (ad 2), temperance regards need according to the requirements of life, and this depends not only on the requirements of the body, but also on the requirements of external things, such as riches and station, and more still on the requirements of good conduct. Hence the Philosopher adds (Ethic. iii, 11) that "the temperate man makes use of pleasant things provided that not only they be not prejudicial to health and a sound bodily condition, but also that they be not inconsistent with good," i.e. good conduct, nor "beyond his substance," i.e. his means. And Augustine says (De Morib. Eccl. xxi) that the "temperate man considers the need" not only "of this life" but also "of his station."

Day 222

Whether temperance is a cardinal virtue?

Objection 1: It would seem that temperance is not a cardinal virtue. For the good of moral virtue depends on reason. But temperance is about those things that are furthest removed from reason, namely about pleasures common to us and the lower animals, as stated in Ethic. iii, 10. Therefore temperance, seemingly, is not a principal virtue.

Objection 2: Further, the greater the impetus the more difficult is it to control. Now anger, which is controlled by meekness, seems to be more impetuous than desire, which is controlled by temperance. For it is written (Prov. 27:4): "Anger hath no mercy, nor fury when it breaketh forth; and who can bear the violence [impetum] of one provoked?" Therefore meekness is a principal virtue rather than temperance.

Objection 3: Further, hope as a movement of the soul takes precedence of desire and concupiscence, as stated above ([3445]FS, Q[25], A[4]). But humility controls the presumption of immoderate hope. Therefore, seemingly, humility is a principal virtue rather than temperance which controls concupiscence.

On the contrary, Gregory reckons temperance among the principal virtues (Moral. ii, 49).

I answer that, As stated above (Q[123], A[11]; Q[61], A[3]), a principal or cardinal virtue is so called because it has a foremost claim to praise on account of one of those things that are requisite for the notion of virtue in general. Now moderation, which is requisite in every virtue, deserves praise principally in pleasures of touch, with which temperance is concerned, both because these pleasures are most natural to us, so that it is more difficult to abstain from them, and to control the desire for them, and because their objects are more necessary to the present life, as stated above [3446](A[4]). For this reason temperance is reckoned a principal or cardinal virtue.

Reply to Objection 1: The longer the range of its operation, the greater is the agent's power [virtus] shown to be: wherefore the very fact that the reason is able to moderate desires and pleasures that are furthest removed from it, proves the greatness of reason's power. This is how temperance comes to be a principal virtue.

Reply to Objection 2: The impetuousness of anger is caused by an accident, for instance, a painful hurt; wherefore it soon passes, although its impetus be great. On the other hand, the impetuousness of the desire for pleasures of touch proceeds from a natural cause, wherefore it is more lasting and more general, and consequently its control regards a more principal virtue.

Reply to Objection 3: The object of hope is higher than the object of desire, wherefore hope is accounted the principal passion in the irascible. But the objects of desires and pleasures of touch move the appetite with greater force, since they are more natural. Therefore temperance, which appoints the mean in such things, is a principal virtue.

Whether temperance is the greatest of the virtues?

Objection 1: It would seem that temperance is the greatest of the virtues. For Ambrose says (De Offic. i, 43) that "what we observe and seek most in temperance is the safeguarding of what is honorable, and the regard for what is beautiful." Now virtue deserves praise for being honorable and beautiful. Therefore temperance is the greatest of the virtues.

Objection 2: Further, the more difficult the deed the greater the virtue. Now it is more difficult to control desires and pleasures of touch than to regulate external actions, the former pertaining to temperance and the latter to justice. Therefore temperance is a greater virtue than justice.

Objection 3: Further, seemingly the more general a thing is, the more necessary and the better it is. Now fortitude is about dangers of death which occur less frequently than pleasures of touch, for these occur every day; so that temperance is in more general use than fortitude. Therefore temperance is a more excellent virtue than fortitude.

On the contrary, The Philosopher says (Rhet. i, 9) that the "greatest virtues are those which are most profitable to others, for which reason we give the greatest honor to the brave and the just."

I answer that, As the Philosopher declares (Ethic. i, 2) "the good of the many is more of the godlike than the good of the individual," wherefore the more a virtue regards the good of the many, the better it is. Now justice and fortitude regard the good of the many more than temperance does, since justice regards the relations between one man and another, while fortitude regards dangers of battle which are endured for the common weal: whereas temperance moderates only the desires and pleasures which affect man himself. Hence it is evident that justice and fortitude are more excellent virtues than temperance: while prudence and the theological virtues are more excellent still.

Reply to Objection 1: Honor and beauty are especially ascribed to temperance, not on account of the excellence of the good proper to temperance, but on account of the disgrace of the contrary evil from which it withdraws us, by moderating the pleasures common to us and the lower animals.

Reply to Objection 2: Since virtue is about the difficult and the good, the excellence of a virtue is considered more under the aspect of good, wherein justice excels, than under the aspect of difficult, wherein temperance excels.

Reply to Objection 3: That which is general because it regards the many conduces more to the excellence of goodness than that which is general because it occurs frequently: fortitude excels in the former way, temperance in the latter. Hence fortitude is greater simply, although in some respects temperance may be described as greater not only than fortitude but also than justice.

OF THE VICES OPPOSED TO TEMPERANCE (FOUR ARTICLES)

We must now consider the vices opposed to temperance. Under this head there are four points of inquiry:

(1) Whether insensibility is a sin?
(2) Whether intemperance is a childish sin?
(3) Of the comparison between intemperance and timidity;
(4) Whether intemperance is the most disgraceful of vices?

Whether insensibility is a vice?

Objection 1: It would seem that insensibility is not a vice. For those are called insensible who are deficient with regard to pleasures of touch. Now seemingly it is praiseworthy and virtuous to be altogether deficient in such matters: for it is written (Dan. 10:2,3): "In those days Daniel mourned the days of three weeks, I ate no desirable bread, and neither flesh nor wine entered my mouth, neither was I anointed with ointment." Therefore insensibility is not a sin.

Objection 2: Further, "man's good is to be in accord with reason," according to Dionysius (Div. Nom. iv). Now abstinence from all pleasures of touch is most conducive to man's progress in the good of reason: for it is written (Dan. 1:17) that "to the children" who took pulse for their food (Dan. 1:12), "God gave knowledge, and understanding in every book and wisdom." Therefore insensibility, which rejects these pleasures altogether, is not sinful.

Objection 3: Further, that which is a very effective means of avoiding sin would seem not to be sinful. Now the most effective remedy in avoiding sin is to shun pleasures, and this pertains to insensibility. For the Philosopher says (Ethic. ii, 9) that "if we deny ourselves pleasures we are less liable to sin." Therefore there is nothing vicious in insensibility.

On the contrary, Nothing save vice is opposed to virtue. Now insensibility is opposed to the virtue of temperance according to the Philosopher (Ethic. ii, 7; iii, 11). Therefore insensibility is a vice.

I answer that, Whatever is contrary to the natural order is vicious. Now nature has introduced pleasure into the operations that are necessary for man's life. Wherefore the natural order requires that man should make use of these pleasures, in so far as they are necessary for man's well-being, as regards the preservation either of the individual or of the species. Accordingly, if anyone were to reject pleasure to the extent of omitting things that are necessary for nature's preservation, he would sin, as acting counter to the order of nature. And this pertains to the vice of insensibility.

It must, however, be observed that it is sometimes praiseworthy, and even necessary for the sake of an end, to abstain from such pleasures as result from these operations. Thus, for the sake of the body's health, certain persons refrain from pleasures of meat, drink, and sex; as also for the fulfilment of certain engagements: thus athletes and soldiers have to deny themselves many pleasures, in order to fulfil their respective duties. In like manner penitents, in order to recover health of soul, have recourse to abstinence from pleasures, as a kind of diet, and those who are desirous of giving themselves up to contemplation and Divine things need much to refrain from carnal things. Nor do any of these things pertain to the vice of insensibility, because they are in accord with right reason.

Reply to Objection 1: Daniel abstained thus from pleasures, not through any horror of pleasure as though it were evil in itself, but for some praiseworthy end, in order, namely, to adapt himself to the heights of contemplation by abstaining from pleasures of the body. Hence the text goes on to tell of the revelation that he received immediately afterwards.

Reply to Objection 2: Since man cannot use his reason without his sensitive powers. which need a bodily organ. as stated in the [3447]FP, Q[84], AA[7],8, man needs to sustain his body in order that he may use his reason. Now the body is sustained by means of operations that afford pleasure: wherefore the good of reason cannot be in a man if he abstain from all pleasures. Yet this need for using pleasures of the body will be greater or less, according as man needs more or less the powers of his body in accomplishing the act of reason. Wherefore it is commendable for those who undertake the duty of giving themselves to contemplation, and of imparting to others a spiritual good, by a kind of spiritual procreation, as it were, to abstain from many pleasures, but not for those who are in duty bound to bodily occupations and carnal procreation.

Reply to Objection 3: In order to avoid sin, pleasure must be shunned, not altogether, but so that it is not sought more than necessity requires.

Whether intemperance is a childish sin?
Objection 1: It would seem that intemperance is not a childish sin. For Jerome in commenting on Mat. 18:3, "Unless you be converted, and become as little children," says that "a child persists not in anger, is unmindful of injuries, takes no pleasure in seeing a beautiful woman," all of which is contrary to intemperance. Therefore intemperance is not a childish sin.

Objection 2: Further, children have none but natural desires. Now "in respect of natural desires few sin by intemperance," according to the Philosopher (Ethic. iii, 11). Therefore intemperance is not a childish sin.

Objection 3: Further, children should be fostered and nourished: whereas concupiscence and pleasure, about which intemperance is concerned, are always to be thwarted and uprooted, according to Col. 3:5, "Mortify . . . your members upon the earth, which are . . . concupiscence" [*Vulg.: 'your members which are upon the earth, fornication . . . concupiscence'], etc. Therefore intemperance is not a childish sin.

On the contrary, The Philosopher says (Ethic. iii, 12) that "we apply the term intemperance* to childish faults." [*{Akolasia} which Aristotle refers to {kolazo} to punish, so that its original sense would be 'impunity' or 'unrestraint.']

I answer that, A thing is said to be childish for two reasons. First, because it is becoming to children, and the Philosopher does not mean that the sin of intemperance is childish in this sense. Secondly. by way of likeness, and it is in this sense that sins of intemperance are said to be childish. For the sin of intemperance is one of unchecked concupiscence, which is likened to a child in three ways. First, as rewards that which they both desire, for like a child concupiscence desires something disgraceful. This is because in human affairs a thing is beautiful according as it harmonizes with reason. Wherefore Tully says (De Offic. i, 27) under the heading "Comeliness is twofold," that "the beautiful is that which is in keeping with man's excellence in so far as his nature differs from other animals." Now a child does not attend to the order of reason; and in like manner "concupiscence does not listen to reason," according to Ethic. vii, 6. Secondly, they are alike as to the result. For a child, if left to his own will, becomes more self-willed: hence it is written (Ecclus. 30:8): "A horse not broken becometh stubborn, and a child left to himself will become headstrong." So, too, concupiscence, if indulged, gathers strength: wherefore Augustine says (Confess. viii, 5): "Lust served became a custom, and custom not resisted became necessity." Thirdly, as to the remedy which is applied to both. For a child is corrected by being restrained; hence it is written (Prov. 23:13,14): "Withhold not correction from a child . . . Thou shalt beat him with a rod, and deliver his soul from Hell." In like manner by resisting concupiscence we moderate it according to the demands of virtue. Augustine indicates this when he says (Music. vi, 11) that if the mind be lifted up to spiritual things, and remain fixed "thereon, the impulse of custom," i.e. carnal concupiscence, "is broken, and being suppressed is gradually weakened: for it was stronger when we followed it, and though not wholly destroyed, it is certainly less strong when we curb it." Hence the Philosopher says (Ethic. iii, 12) that "as a child ought to live according to the direction of his tutor, so ought the concupiscible to accord with reason."

Reply to Objection 1: This argument takes the term "childish" as denoting what is observed in children. It is not in this sense that the sin of intemperance is said to be childish, but by way of likeness, as stated above.

Reply to Objection 2: A desire may be said to be natural in two ways. First, with regard to its genus, and thus temperance and intemperance are about natural desires, since they are about desires of food and sex, which are directed to the preservation of nature.

Secondly, a desire may be called natural with regard to the species of the thing that nature requires for its own preservation; and in this way it does not happen often that one sins in the matter of natural desires, for nature requires only that which supplies its need, and there is no sin in desiring this, save only where it is desired in excess as to quantity. This is the only way in which sin can occur with regard to natural desires, according to the Philosopher (Ethic. iii, 11).

There are other things in respect of which sins frequently occur, and these are certain incentives to desire devised by human curiosity [*Cf. Q[167]], such as the nice [curiosa] preparation of food, or the adornment of women. And though children do not affect these things much, yet intemperance is called a childish sin for the reason given above.

Reply to Objection 3: That which regards nature should be nourished and fostered in children, but that which pertains to the lack of reason in them should not be fostered, but corrected, as stated above.

Whether cowardice* is a greater vice than intemperance? [*Cf. Q[125]]

Objection 1: It would seem that cowardice is a greater vice than intemperance. For a vice deserves reproach through being opposed to the good of virtue. Now cowardice is opposed to fortitude, which is a more excellent virtue than temperance, as stated above [3448] (A[2]; Q[141], A[8]). Therefore cowardice is a greater vice than intemperance.

Objection 2: Further, the greater the difficulty to be surmounted, the less is a man to be reproached for failure, wherefore the Philosopher says (Ethic. vii, 7) that "it is no wonder, in fact it is pardonable, if a man is mastered by strong and overwhelming pleasures or pains." Now seemingly it is more difficult to control pleasures than other passions; hence it is stated in Ethic. ii, 3, that "it is more difficult to contend against pleasure than against anger, which would seem to be stronger than fear." Therefore intemperance, which is overcome by pleasure, is a less grievous sin than cowardice, which is overcome by fear.

Objection 3: Further, it is essential to sin that it be voluntary. Now cowardice is more voluntary than intemperance, since no man desires to be intemperate, whereas some desire to avoid dangers of death, which pertains to cowardice. Therefore cowardice is a more grievous sin than intemperance.

On the contrary, The Philosopher says (Ethic. iii, 12) that "intemperance seems more akin to voluntary action than cowardice." Therefore it is more sinful.

I answer that, one may be compared with another in two ways. First, with regard to the matter or object; secondly, on the part of the man who sins: and in both ways intemperance is a more grievous sin than cowardice.

First, as regards the matter. For cowardice shuns dangers of death, to avoid which the principal motive is the necessity of preserving life. On the other hand, intemperance is about pleasures, the desire of which is not so necessary for the preservation of life, because, as stated above (A[2], ad 2), intemperance is more about certain annexed pleasures or desires than about natural desires or pleasures. Now the more necessary the motive of sin the less grievous the sin. Wherefore intemperance is a more grievous vice than cowardice, on the part of the object or motive matter.

In like manner again, on the part of the man who sins, and this for three reasons. First, because the more sound-minded a man is, the more grievous his sin, wherefore sins are not imputed to those who are demented. Now grave fear and sorrow, especially in dangers of death, stun the human mind, but not so pleasure which is the motive of intemperance. Secondly, because the more voluntary a sin the graver it is. Now intemperance has more of the voluntary in it than cowardice has, and this for two reasons. The first is because actions done through fear have their origin in the compulsion of an external agent, so that they are not simply voluntary but mixed, as stated in Ethic. iii, 1, whereas actions done for the sake of pleasure are simply voluntary. The second reason is because the actions of an intemperate man are more voluntary individually and less voluntary generically. For no one would wish to be intemperate, yet man is enticed by individual pleasures which make of him an intemperate man. Hence the most effective remedy against intemperance is not to dwell on the consideration of singulars. It is the other way about in matters relating to cowardice: because the particular action that imposes itself on a man is less voluntary, for instance to cast aside his shield, and the like, whereas the general purpose is more voluntary, for instance to save himself by flight. Now that which is more voluntary in the particular circumstances in which the act takes place, is simply more voluntary. Wherefore intemperance, being simply more voluntary than cowardice, is a greater vice. Thirdly, because it is easier to find a remedy for intemperance than for cowardice, since pleasures of food and sex, which are the matter of intemperance, are of everyday occurrence, and it is possible for man without danger by frequent practice in their regard to become temperate; whereas dangers of death are of rare occurrence, and it is more dangerous for man to encounter them frequently in order to cease being a coward.

Reply to Objection 1: The excellence of fortitude in comparison with temperance may be considered from two standpoints. First, with regard to the end, which has the aspect of good: because fortitude is directed to the common good more than temperance is. And from this point of view cowardice has a certain precedence over intemperance, since by cowardice some people forsake the defense of the common good. Secondly, with regard to the difficulty, because it is more difficult to endure dangers of death than to refrain from any pleasures whatever: and from this point of view there is no need for cowardice to take precedence of intemperance. For just as it is a greater strength that does not succumb to a stronger force, so on the other hand to be overcome by a stronger force is proof of a lesser vice, and to succumb to a weaker force, is the proof of a greater vice.

Reply to Objection 2: Love of self-preservation, for the sake of which one shuns perils of death, is much more connatural than any pleasures whatever of food and sex which are directed to the preservation of life. Hence it is more difficult to overcome the fear of dangers of death, than the desire of pleasure in matters of food and sex: although the latter is more difficult to resist than anger, sorrow, and fear, occasioned by certain other evils.

Reply to Objection 3: The voluntary, in cowardice, depends rather on a general than on a particular consideration: wherefore in such cases we have the voluntary not simply but in a restricted sense.

Whether intemperance is the most disgraceful of sins?

Objection 1: It would seem that intemperance is not the most disgraceful of sins. As honor is due to virtue so is disgrace due to sin. Now some sins are more grievous than intemperance: for instance murder, blasphemy, and the like. Therefore intemperance is not the most disgraceful of sins.

Objection 2: Further, those sins which are the more common are seemingly less disgraceful, since men are less ashamed of them. Now sins of intemperance are most common, because they are about things connected with the common use of human life, and in which many happen to sin. Therefore sins of intemperance do not seem to be most disgraceful.

Objection 3: Further, the Philosopher says (Ethic. vii, 6) temperance and intemperance are about human desires and pleasures. Now certain desires and pleasures are more shameful than human desires and pleasures; such are brutal pleasures and those caused by disease as the Philosopher states (Ethic. vii, 5). Therefore intemperance is not the most disgraceful of sins.

On the contrary, The Philosopher says (Ethic. iii, 10) that "intemperance is justly more deserving of reproach than other vices."

I answer that, Disgrace is seemingly opposed to honor and glory. Now honor is due to excellence, as stated above ([3449]Q[103], A[1]), and glory denotes clarity ([3450]Q[103], A[1], ad 3). Accordingly intemperance is most disgraceful for two reasons. First, because it is most repugnant to human excellence, since it is about pleasures common to us and the lower animals, as stated above ([3451]Q[141], AA[2],3). Wherefore it is written (Ps. 48:21): "Man, when he was in honor, did not understand: he hath been compared to senseless beasts, and made like to them." Secondly, because it is most repugnant to man's clarity or beauty; inasmuch as the pleasures which are the matter of intemperance dim the light of reason from which all the clarity and beauty of virtue arises: wherefore these pleasures are described as being most slavish.

Reply to Objection 1: As Gregory says [*Moral. xxxiii. 12], "the sins of the flesh," which are comprised under the head of intemperance, although less culpable, are more disgraceful. The reason is that culpability is measured by inordinateness in respect of the end, while disgrace regards shamefulness, which depends chiefly on the unbecomingness of the sin in respect of the sinner.

Reply to Objection 2: The commonness of a sin diminishes the shamefulness and disgrace of a sin in the opinion of men, but not as regards the nature of the vices themselves.

Reply to Objection 3: When we say that intemperance is most disgraceful, we mean in comparison with human vices, those, namely, that are connected with human passions which to a certain extent are in conformity with human nature. But those vices which exceed the mode of human nature are still more disgraceful. Nevertheless such vices are apparently reducible to the genus of intemperance, by way of excess: for instance, if a man delight in eating human flesh, or in committing the unnatural vice.

OF THE PARTS OF TEMPERANCE, IN GENERAL (ONE ARTICLE)
We must now consider the parts of temperance: we shall consider these same parts (1) in general; (2) each of them in particular.

Whether the parts of temperance are rightly assigned?

Objection 1: It would seem that Tully (De Invent. Rhet. ii, 54) unbecomingly assigns the parts of temperance, when he asserts them to be "continence, mildness, and modesty." For continence is reckoned to be distinct from virtue (Ethic. vii, 1): whereas temperance is comprised under virtue. Therefore continence is not a part of temperance.

Objection 2: Further, mildness seemingly softens hatred or anger. But temperance is not about these things, but about pleasures of touch, as stated above ([3452]Q[141], A[4]). Therefore mildness is not a part of temperance.

Objection 3: Further, modesty concerns external action, wherefore the Apostle says (Phil. 4:5): "Let your modesty be known to all men." Now external actions are the matter of justice, as stated above ([3453]Q[58], A[8]). Therefore modesty is a part of justice rather than of temperance.

Objection 4: Further, Macrobius (In Somn. Scip. i, 8) reckons many more parts of temperance: for he says that "temperance results in modesty, shamefacedness, abstinence, chastity, honesty, moderation, lowliness, sobriety, purity." Andronicus also says [*De Affectibus] that "the companions of temperance are gravity, continence, humility, simplicity, refinement, method, contentment." [*'Per-se-sufficientiam' which could be rendered 'self-sufficiency,' but for the fact that this is taken in a bad sense. See[3454] Q[169], A[1].] Therefore it seems that Tully insufficiently reckoned the parts of temperance.

I answer that, As stated above (QQ[48],128), a cardinal virtue may have three kinds of parts, namely integral, subjective, and potential. The integral parts of a virtue are the conditions the concurrence of which are necessary for virtue: and in this respect there are two integral parts of temperance, "shamefacedness," whereby one recoils from the disgrace that is contrary to temperance, and "honesty," whereby one loves the beauty of temperance. For, as stated above ([3455]Q[141], A[2], ad 3), temperance more than any other virtue lays claim to a certain comeliness, and the vices of intemperance excel others in disgrace.

The subjective parts of a virtue are its species: and the species of a virtue have to be differentiated according to the difference of matter or object. Now temperance is about pleasures of touch, which are of two kinds. For some are directed to nourishment: and in these as regards meat, there is "abstinence," and as regards drink properly there is "sobriety." Other pleasures are directed to the power of procreation, and in these as regards the principal pleasure of the act itself of procreation, there is "chastity," and as to the pleasures incidental to the act, resulting, for instance, from kissing, touching, or fondling, we have "purity."

The potential parts of a principal virtue are called secondary virtues: for while the principal virtue observes the mode in some principal matter, these observe the mode in some other matter wherein moderation is not so difficult. Now it belongs to temperance to moderate pleasures of touch, which are most difficult to moderate. Wherefore any virtue that is effective of moderation in some matter or other, and restrains the appetite in its impulse towards something, may be reckoned a part of temperance, as a virtue annexed thereto.

This happens in three ways: first, in the inward movements of the soul; secondly, in the outward movements and actions of the body; thirdly, in outward things. Now besides the movement of concupiscence, which temperance moderates and restrains, we find in the soul three movements towards a particular object. In the first place there is the movement of the will when stirred by the impulse of passion: and this movement is restrained by "continence," the effect of which is that, although a man suffer immoderate concupiscences, his will does not succumb to them. Another inward movement towards something is the movement of hope, and of the resultant daring, and this is moderated or restrained by "humility." The third movement is that of anger, which tends towards revenge, and this is restrained by "meekness" or "mildness."

With regard to bodily movements and actions, moderation and restraint is the effect of "modesty," which, according to Andronicus, has three parts. The first of these enables one to discern what to do and what not to do, and to observe the right order, and to persevere in what we do: this he assigns to "method." The second is that a man observe decorum in what he does, and this he ascribes to "refinement." The third has to do with the conversation or any other intercourse between a man and his friends, and this is called "gravity."

With regard to external things, a twofold moderation has to be observed. First, we must not desire too many, and to this Macrobius assigns "lowliness," and Andronicus "contentment"; secondly, we must not be too nice in our requirements, and to this Macrobius ascribes "moderation," Andronicus "simplicity."

Reply to Objection 1: It is true that continence differs from virtue, just as imperfect differs from perfect, as we shall state further on ([3456]Q[165], A[1]); and in this sense it is condivided with virtue. Yet it has something in common with temperance both as to matter, since it is about pleasures of touch, and as to mode, since it is a kind of restraint. Hence it is suitably assigned as a part of temperance.

Reply to Objection 2: Mildness or meekness is reckoned a part of temperance not because of a likeness of matter, but because they agree as to the mode of restraint and moderation as stated above.

Reply to Objection 3: In the matter of external action justice considers what is due to another. Modesty does not consider this, but only a certain moderation. Hence it is reckoned a part not of justice but of temperance.

Reply to Objection 4: Under modesty Tully includes whatever pertains to the moderation of bodily movements and external things, as well as the moderation of hope which we reckoned as pertaining to humility.

OF SHAMEFACEDNESS (FOUR ARTICLES)

We must now consider the parts of temperance in particular: and in the first place the integral parts, which are shamefacedness and honesty. With regard to shamefacedness there are four points of inquiry:

(1) Whether shamefacedness is a virtue?
(2) What is its object?
(3) Who are the cause of a man being ashamed?
(4) What kind of people are ashamed?

Whether shamefacedness is a virtue?

Objection 1: It seems that shamefacedness is a virtue. For it is proper to a virtue "to observe the mean as fixed by reason": this is clear from the definition of virtue given in Ethic. ii, 6. Now shamefacedness observes the mean in this way, as the Philosopher observes (Ethic. ii, 7). Therefore shamefacedness is a virtue.

Objection 2: Further, whatever is praiseworthy is either a virtue or something connected with virtue. Now shamefacedness is praiseworthy. But it is not part of a virtue. For it is not a part of prudence, since it is not in the reason but in the appetite; nor is it a part of justice. since shamefacedness implies a certain passion, whereas justice is not about the passions; nor again is it a part of fortitude, because it belongs to fortitude to be persistent and aggressive, while it belongs to shamefacedness to recoil from something; nor lastly is it a part of temperance, since the latter is about desires, whereas shamefacedness is a kind of fear according as the Philosopher states (Ethic. iv, 9) and Damascene (De Fide Orth. ii, 15). Hence it follows that shamefacedness is a virtue.

Objection 3: Further, the honest and the virtuous are convertible according to Tully (De Offic. i, 27). Now shamefacedness is a part of honesty: for Ambrose says (De Offic. i, 43) that "shamefacedness is the companion and familiar of the restful mind, averse to wantonness, a stranger to any kind of excess, the friend of sobriety and the support of what is honest, a seeker after the beautiful." Therefore shamefacedness is a virtue.

Objection 4: Further, every vice is opposed to a virtue. Now certain vices are opposed to shamefacedness, namely shamelessness and inordinate prudery. Therefore shamefacedness is a virtue.

Objection 5: Further, "like acts beget like habits," according to Ethic. ii, 1. Now shamefacedness implies a praiseworthy act; wherefore from many such acts a habit results. But a habit of praiseworthy deeds is a virtue, according to the Philosopher (Ethic. i, 12). Therefore shamefacedness is a virtue.

On the contrary, The Philosopher says (Ethic. ii, 7; iv, 9) that shamefacedness is not a virtue.

I answer that, Virtue is taken in two ways, in a strict sense and in a broad sense. Taken strictly virtue is a perfection, as stated in Phys. vii, 17,18. Wherefore anything that is inconsistent with perfection, though it be good, falls short of the notion of virtue. Now shamefacedness is inconsistent with perfection, because it is the fear of something base, namely of that which is disgraceful. Hence Damascene says (De Fide Orth. ii, 15) that "shamefacedness is fear of a base action." Now just as hope is about a possible and difficult good, so is fear about a possible and arduous evil, as stated above ([3457]FS, Q[40], A[1]; [3458]FS, Q[41], A[2]; [3459]FS, Q[42], A[3]), when we were treating of the passions. But one who is perfect as to a virtuous habit, does not apprehend that which would be disgraceful and base to do, as being possible and arduous, that is to say difficult for him to avoid; nor does he actually do anything base, so as to be in fear of disgrace. Therefore shamefacedness, properly speaking, is not a virtue, since it falls short of the perfection of virtue.

Taken, however, in a broad sense virtue denotes whatever is good and praiseworthy in human acts or passions; and in this way / shamefacedness is sometimes called a virtue, since it is a praiseworthy passion.

Reply to Objection 1: Observing the mean is not sufficient for the notion of virtue, although it is one of the conditions included in virtue's definition: but it is requisite, in addition to this, that it be "an elective habit," that is to say, operating from choice. Now shamefacedness denotes, not a habit but a passion, nor does its movement result from choice, but from an impulse of passion. Hence it falls short of the notion of virtue.

Reply to Objection 2: As stated above, shamefacedness is fear of baseness and disgrace. Now it has been stated ([3460]Q[142], A[4]) that the vice of intemperance is most base and disgraceful. Wherefore shamefacedness pertains more to temperance than to any other virtue, by reason of its motive cause, which is a base action though not according to the species of the passion, namely fear. Nevertheless in so far as the vices opposed to other virtues are base and disgraceful, shamefacedness may also pertain to other virtues.

Reply to Objection 3: Shamefacedness fosters honesty, by removing that which is contrary thereto, but not so as to attain to the perfection of honesty.

Reply to Objection 4: Every defect causes a vice, but not every good is sufficient for the notion of virtue. Consequently it does not follow that whatever is directly opposed to vice is a virtue, although every vice is opposed to a virtue, as regards its origin. Hence shamelessness, in so far as it results from excessive love of disgraceful things, is opposed to temperance.

Reply to Objection 5: Being frequently ashamed causes the habit of an acquired virtue whereby one avoids disgraceful things which are the object of shamefacedness, without continuing to be ashamed in their regard: although as a consequence of this acquired virtue, a man would be more ashamed, if confronted with the matter of shamefacedness.

Whether shamefacedness is about a disgraceful action?

Objection 1: It would seem that shamefacedness is not about a disgraceful action. For the Philosopher says (Ethic. iv, 9) that "shamefacedness is fear of disgrace." Now sometimes those who do nothing wrong suffer ignominy, according to Ps. 67:8, "For thy sake I have borne reproach, shame hath covered my face." Therefore shamefacedness is not properly about a disgraceful action.

Objection 2: Further, nothing apparently is disgraceful but what is sinful. Yet man is ashamed of things that are not sins, for instance when he performs a menial occupation. Therefore it seems that shamefacedness is not properly about a disgraceful action.

Objection 3: Further, virtuous deeds are not disgraceful but most beautiful according to Ethic. i, 8. Yet sometimes people are ashamed to do virtuous deeds, according to Lk. 9:26, "He that shall be ashamed of Me and My words, of him the Son of man shall be ashamed," etc. Therefore shamefacedness is not about a disgraceful action.

Objection 4: Further, if shamefacedness were properly about a disgraceful action, it would follow that the more disgraceful the action the more ashamed would one be. Yet sometimes a man is more ashamed of lesser sins, while he glories in those which are most grievous, according to Ps. 51:3, "Why dost thou glory in malice?" Therefore shamefacedness is not properly about a disgraceful action.

On the contrary, Damascene (De Fide Orth. ii, 15) and Gregory of Nyssa [*Nemesius, (De Nat. Hom. xx)] say that "shamefacedness is fear of doing a disgraceful deed or of a disgraceful deed done."

I answer that, As stated above ([3461]FS, Q[41], A[2]; [3462]FS, Q[42], A[3]), when we were treating of the passions, fear is properly about an arduous evil, one, namely, that is difficult to avoid. Now disgrace is twofold. There is the disgrace inherent to vice, which consists in the deformity of a voluntary act: and this, properly speaking, has not the character of an arduous evil. For that which depends on the will alone does not appear to be arduous and above man's ability: wherefore it is not apprehended as fearful, and for this reason the Philosopher says (Rhet. ii, 5) that such evils are not a matter of fear.

The other kind of disgrace is penal so to speak, and it consists in the reproach that attaches to a person, just as the clarity of glory consists in a person being honored. And since this reproach has the character of an arduous evil, just as honor has the character of an arduous good, shamefacedness, which is fear of disgrace, regards first and foremost reproach or ignominy. And since reproach is properly due to vice, as honor is due to virtue, it follows that shamefacedness regards also the disgrace inherent to vice. Hence the Philosopher says (Rhet. ii, 5) that "a man is less ashamed of those defects which are not the result of any fault of his own."

Now shamefacedness regards fault in two ways. In one way a man refrains from vicious acts through fear of reproach: in another way a man while doing a disgraceful deed avoids the public eye through fear of reproach. In the former case, according to Gregory of Nyssa (Nemesius, De Nat. Hom. xx), we speak of a person "blushing," in the latter we say that he is "ashamed." Hence he says that "the man who is ashamed acts in secret, but he who blushes fears to be disgraced."

Reply to Objection 1: Shamefacedness properly regards disgrace as due to sin which is a voluntary defect. Hence the Philosopher says (Rhet. ii, 6) that "a man is more ashamed of those things of which he is the cause." Now the virtuous man despises the disgrace to which he is subject on account of virtue, because he does not deserve it; as the Philosopher says of the magnanimous (Ethic. iv, 3). Thus we find it said of the apostles (Acts 5:41) that "they (the apostles) went from the presence of the council, rejoicing that they were accounted worthy to suffer reproach for the name of Jesus." It is owing to imperfection of virtue that a man is sometimes ashamed of the reproaches which he suffers on account of virtue, since the more virtuous a man is, the more he despises external things, whether good or evil. Wherefore it is written (Is. 51:7): "Fear ye not the reproach of men."

Reply to Objection 2: As stated above ([3463]Q[63], A[3]), though honor is not really due save to virtue alone, yet it regards a certain excellence: and the same applies to reproach, for though it is properly due to sin alone, yet, at least in man's opinion, it regards any kind of defect. Hence a man is ashamed of poverty, disrepute, servitude, and the like.

Reply to Objection 3: Shamefacedness does not regard virtuous deeds as such. Yet it happens accidentally that a man is ashamed of them either because he looks upon them as vicious according to human opinion, or because he is afraid of being marked as presumptuous or hypocritical for doing virtuous deeds.

Reply to Objection 4: Sometimes more grievous sins are less shameful, either because they are less disgraceful, as spiritual sins in comparison with sins of the flesh, or because they connote a certain abundance of some temporal good; thus a man is more ashamed of cowardice than of daring, of theft than of robbery, on account of a semblance of power. The same applies to other sins.

Day 223

Whether man is more shamefaced of those who are more closely connected with him?

Objection 1: It would seem that man is not more shamefaced of those who are more closely connected with him. For it is stated in Rhet. ii, 6 that "men are more shamefaced of those from whom they desire approbation." Now men desire this especially from people of the better sort who are sometimes not connected with them. Therefore man is not more shamefaced of those who are more closely connected with him.

Objection 2: Further, seemingly those are more closely connected who perform like deeds. Now man is not made ashamed of his sin by those whom he knows to be guilty of the same sin, because according to Rhet. ii, 6, "a man does not forbid his neighbor what he does himself." Therefore he is not more shamefaced of those who are most closely connected with him.

Objection 3: Further, the Philosopher says (Rhet. ii, 6) that "men take more shame from those who retail their information to many, such as jokers and fable-tellers." But those who are more closely connected with a man do not retail his vices. Therefore one should not take shame chiefly from them.

Objection 4: Further, the Philosopher says (Rhet. ii, 6) that "men are most liable to be made ashamed by those among whom they have done nothing amiss; by those of whom they ask something for the first time; by those whose friends they wish to become." Now these are less closely connected with us. Therefore man is not made most ashamed by those who are more closely united to him.

On the contrary, It is stated in Rhet. ii, 6 that "man is made most ashamed by those who are to be continually with him."

I answer that, Since reproach is opposed to honor, just as honor denotes attestation to someone's excellence, especially the excellence which is according to virtue, so too reproach, the fear of which is shamefacedness, denotes attestation to a person's defect, especially that which results from sin. Hence the more weighty a person's attestation is considered to be, the more does he make another person ashamed. Now a person's attestation may be considered as being more weighty, either because he is certain of the truth or because of its effect. Certitude of the truth attaches to a person's attestations for two reasons. First on account of the rectitude of his judgement, as in the case of wise and virtuous men, by whom man is more desirous of being honored and by whom he is brought to a greater sense of shame. Hence children and the lower animals inspire no one with shame, by reason of their lack of judgment. Secondly, on account of his knowledge of the matter attested, because "everyone judges well of what is known to him" [*Ethic. i, 3]. In this way we are more liable to be made ashamed by persons connected with us, since they are better acquainted with our deeds: whereas strangers and persons entirely unknown to us, who are ignorant of what we do, inspire us with no shame at all.

An attestation receives weight from its effect by reason of some advantage or harm resulting therefrom; wherefore men are more desirous of being honored by those who can be of use to them, and are more liable to be made ashamed by those who are able to do them some harm. And for this reason again, in a certain respect, persons connected with us make us more ashamed, since we are to be continually in their society, as though this entailed a continual harm to us: whereas the harm that comes from strangers and passersby ceases almost at once.

Reply to Objection 1: People of the better sort make us ashamed for the same reason as those who are more closely connected with us; because just as the attestation of the better men carries more weight since they have a more universal knowledge of things, and in their judgments hold fast to the truth: so, too, the attestation of those among whom we live is more cogent since they know more about our concerns in detail.

Reply to Objection 2: We fear not the attestation of those who are connected with us in the likeness of sin, because we do not think that they look upon our defect as disgraceful.

Reply to Objection 3: Tale-bearers make us ashamed on account of the harm they do by making many think ill of us.

Reply to Objection 4: Even those among whom we have done no wrong, make us more ashamed, on account of the harm that would follow, because, to wit, we should forfeit the good opinion they had of us: and again because when contraries are put in juxtaposition their opposition seems greater, so that when a man notices something disgraceful in one whom he esteemed good, he apprehends it as being the more disgraceful. The reason why we are made more ashamed by those of whom we ask something for the first time, or whose friends we wish to be, is that we fear to suffer some injury, by being disappointed in our request, or by failing to become their friends.

Whether even virtuous men can be ashamed?

Objection 1: It would seem that even virtuous men can be ashamed. For contraries have contrary effects. Now those who excel in wickedness are not ashamed, according to Jer. 3:3, "Thou hadst a harlot's forehead, thou wouldst not blush." Therefore those who are virtuous are more inclined to be ashamed.

Objection 2: Further, the Philosopher says (Rhet. ii, 6) that "men are ashamed not only of vice, but also of the signs of evil": and this happens also in the virtuous. Therefore virtuous men can be ashamed.

Objection 3: Further, shamefacedness is "fear of disgrace" [*Ethic. iv, 9]. Now virtuous people may happen to be ignominious, for instance if they are slandered, or if they suffer reproach undeservedly. Therefore a virtuous man can be ashamed.

Objection 4: Further, shamefacedness is a part of temperance, as stated above ([3464]Q[143]). Now a part is not separated from its whole. Since then temperance is in a virtuous man, it means that shamefacedness is also.

On the contrary, The Philosopher says (Ethic. iv, 9) that a "virtuous man is not shamefaced."

56

I answer that, As stated above ([3465]AA[1],2) shamefacedness is fear of some disgrace. Now it may happen in two ways that an evil is not feared: first, because it is not reckoned an evil; secondly because one reckons it impossible with regard to oneself, or as not difficult to avoid.

Accordingly shame may be lacking in a person in two ways. First, because the things that should make him ashamed are not deemed by him to be disgraceful; and in this way those who are steeped in sin are without shame, for instead of disapproving of their sins, they boast of them. Secondly, because they apprehend disgrace as impossible to themselves, or as easy to avoid. In this way the old and the virtuous are not shamefaced. Yet they are so disposed, that if there were anything disgraceful in them they would be ashamed of it. Wherefore the Philosopher says (Ethic. iv, 9) that "shame is in the virtuous hypothetically."

Reply to Objection 1: Lack of shame occurs in the best and in the worst men through different causes, as stated in the Article. In the average men it is found, in so far as they have a certain love of good, and yet are not altogether free from evil.

Reply to Objection 2: It belongs to the virtuous man to avoid not only vice, but also whatever has the semblance of vice, according to 1 Thess. 5:22, "From all appearance of evil refrain yourselves." The Philosopher, too, says (Ethic. iv, 9) that the virtuous man should avoid "not only what is really evil, but also those things that are regarded as evil."

Reply to Objection 3: As stated above (A[1], ad 1) the virtuous man despises ignominy and reproach, as being things he does not deserve, wherefore he is not much ashamed of them. Nevertheless, to a certain extent, shame, like the other passions, may forestall reason.

Reply to Objection 4: Shamefacedness is a part of temperance, not as though it entered into its essence, but as a disposition to it: wherefore Ambrose says (De Offic. i, 43) that "shamefacedness lays the first foundation of temperance," by inspiring man with the horror of whatever is disgraceful.

OF HONESTY* (FOUR ARTICLES) [*Honesty must be taken here in its broad sense as synonymous with moral goodness, from the point of view of decorum.]
We must now consider honesty, under which head there are four points of inquiry:
(1) The relation between the honest and the virtuous;
(2) Its relation with the beautiful [*As honesty here denotes moral goodness, so beauty stands for moral beauty];
(3) Its relation with the useful and the pleasant;
(4) Whether honesty is a part of temperance?

Whether honesty is the same as virtue?
Objection 1: It would seem that honesty is not the same as virtue. For Tully says (De Invent. Rhet. ii, 53) that "the honest is what is desired for its own sake." Now virtue is desired, not for its own sake, but for the sake of happiness, for the Philosopher says (Ethic. i, 9) that "happiness is the reward and the end of virtue." Therefore honesty is not the same as virtue.

Objection 2: Further, according to Isidore (Etym. x) "honesty means an honorable state." Now honor is due to many things besides virtue, since "it is praise that is the proper due of virtue" (Ethic. i, 12). Therefore honesty is not the same as virtue.

Objection 3: Further, the "principal part of virtue is the interior choice," as the Philosopher says (Ethic. viii, 13). But honesty seems to pertain rather to exterior conduct, according to 1 Cor. 14:40, "Let all things be done decently [honeste] and according to order" among you. Therefore honesty is not the same as virtue.

Objection 4: Further, honesty apparently consists in external wealth. According to Ecclus. 11:14, "good things and evil, life and death [poverty and riches] are from God" [*The words in brackets are omitted in the Leonine edition. For riches the Vulgate has 'honestas']. But virtue does not consist in external wealth. Therefore honesty is not the same as virtue.

On the contrary, Tully (De Offic. i, 5; Rhet. ii, 53) divides honesty into the four principal virtues, into which virtue is also divided. Therefore honesty is the same as virtue.

I answer that, As Isidore says (Etym. x) "honesty means an honorable state," wherefore a thing may be said to be honest through being worthy of honor. Now honor, as stated above ([3466]Q[144], A[2], ad 2), is due to excellence: and the excellence of a man is gauged chiefly according to his virtue, as stated in Phys. vii, 17. Therefore, properly speaking, honesty refers to the same thing as virtue.

Reply to Objection 1: According to the Philosopher (Ethic. i, 7), of those things that are desired for their own sake, some are desired for their own sake alone, and never for the sake of something else, such as happiness which is the last end; while some are desired, not only for their own sake, inasmuch as they have an aspect of goodness in themselves, even if no further good accrued to us through them, but also for the sake of something else, inasmuch as they are conducive to some more perfect good. It is thus that the virtues are desirable for their own sake: wherefore Tully says (De Invent. Rhet. ii, 52) that "some things allure us by their own force, and attract us by their own worth, such as virtue, truth, knowledge." And this suffices to give a thing the character of honest.

Reply to Objection 2: Some of the things which are honored besides virtue are more excellent than virtue, namely God and happiness, and such like things are not so well known to us by experience as virtue which we practice day by day. Hence virtue has a greater claim to the name of honesty. Other things which are beneath virtue are honored, in so far as they are a help to the practice of virtue, such as rank, power, and riches [*Ethic. i, 8]. For as the Philosopher says (Ethic. iv, 3) that these things "are honored by some people, but in truth it is only the good man who is worthy of honor." Now a man is good in respect of virtue. Wherefore praise is due to virtue in so far as the latter is desirable for the sake of something else, while honor is due to virtue for its own sake: and it is thus that virtue has the character of honesty.

Reply to Objection 3: As we have stated honest denotes that to which honor is due. Now honor is an attestation to someone's excellence, as stated above ([3467]Q[103], AA[1],2). But one attests only to what one knows; and the internal choice is not made known save by external actions. Wherefore external conduct has the character of honesty, in so far as it reflects internal rectitude. For this reason honesty consists radically in the internal choice, but its expression lies in the external conduct.

Reply to Objection 4: It is because the excellence of wealth is commonly regarded as making a man deserving of honor, that sometimes the name of honesty is given to external prosperity.

Whether the honest is the same as the beautiful?

Objection 1: It would seem that the honest is not the same as the beautiful. For the aspect of honest is derived from the appetite, since the honest is "what is desirable for its own sake" [*Cicero, De Invent. Rhet. ii, 53]. But the beautiful regards rather the faculty of vision to which it is pleasing. Therefore the beautiful is not the same as the honest.

Objection 2: Further, beauty requires a certain clarity, which is characteristic of glory: whereas the honest regards honor. Since then honor and glory differ, as stated above ([3468]Q[103], A[1], ad 3), it seems also that the honest and the beautiful differ.

Objection 3: Further, honesty is the same as virtue, as stated above [3469](A[1]). But a certain beauty is contrary to virtue, wherefore it is written (Ezech. 16:15): "Trusting in thy beauty thou playest the harlot because of thy renown." Therefore the honest is not the same as the beautiful.

On the contrary, The Apostle says (1 Cor. 12:23,24): "Those that are our uncomely [inhonesta] parts, have more abundant comeliness [honestatem], but our comely [honesta] parts have no need." Now by uncomely parts he means the baser members, and by comely parts the beautiful members. Therefore the honest and the beautiful are apparently the same.

I answer that, As may be gathered from the words of Dionysius (Div. Nom. iv), beauty or comeliness results from the concurrence of clarity and due proportion. For he states that God is said to be beautiful, as being "the cause of the harmony and clarity of the universe." Hence the beauty of the body consists in a man having his bodily limbs well proportioned, together with a certain clarity of color. In like manner spiritual beauty consists in a man's conduct or actions being well proportioned in respect of the spiritual clarity of reason. Now this is what is meant by honesty, which we have stated [3470](A[1]) to be the same as virtue; and it is virtue that moderates according to reason all that is connected with man. Wherefore "honesty is the same as spiritual beauty." Hence Augustine says (QQ[83], qu. 30): "By honesty I mean intelligible beauty, which we properly designate as spiritual," and further on he adds that "many things are beautiful to the eye, which it would be hardly proper to call honest."

Reply to Objection 1: The object that moves the appetite is an apprehended good. Now if a thing is perceived to be beautiful as soon as it is apprehended, it is taken to be something becoming and good. Hence Dionysius says (Div. Nom. iv) that "the beautiful and the good are beloved by all." Wherefore the honest, inasmuch as it implies spiritual beauty, is an object of desire, and for this reason Tully says (De Offic. i, 5): "Thou perceivest the form and the features, so to speak, of honesty; and were it to be seen with the eye, would, as Plato declares, arouse a wondrous love of wisdom."

Reply to Objection 2: As stated above ([3471]Q[103], A[1], ad 3), glory is the effect of honor: because through being honored or praised, a person acquires clarity in the eyes of others. Wherefore, just as the same thing makes a man honorable and glorious, so is the same thing honest and beautiful.

Reply to Objection 3: This argument applies to the beauty of the body: although it might be replied that to be proud of one's honesty is to play the harlot because of one's spiritual beauty, according to Ezech. 28:17, "Thy heart was lifted up with thy beauty, thou hast lost thy wisdom in thy beauty."

Whether the honest differs from the useful and the pleasant?

Objection 1: It would seem that the honest does not differ from the useful and the pleasant. For the honest is "what is desirable for its own sake" [*Cicero, De Invent. Rhet. ii, 53]. Now pleasure is desired for its own sake, for "it seems ridiculous to ask a man why he wishes to be pleased," as the Philosopher remarks (Ethic. x, 2). Therefore the honest does not differ from the pleasant.

Objection 2: Further, riches are comprised under the head of useful good: for Tully says (De Invent. Rhet. ii, 52): "There is a thing that attracts the desire not by any force of its own, nor by its very nature, but on account of its fruitfulness and utility": and "that is money." Now riches come under the head of honesty, for it is written (Ecclus. 11:14): "Poverty and riches [honestas] are from God," and (Ecclus. 13:2): "He shall take a burden upon him that hath fellowship with one more honorable," i.e. richer, "than himself." Therefore the honest differs not from the useful.

Objection 3: Further, Tully proves (De Offic. ii, 3) that nothing can be useful unless it be honest: and Ambrose makes the same statement (De Offic. ii, 6). Therefore the useful differs not from the honest.

On the contrary, Augustine says (Q[83], qu. 30): "The honest is that which is desirable for its own sake: the useful implies reference to something else."

I answer that, The honest concurs in the same subject with the useful and the pleasant, but it differs from them in aspect. For, as stated above [3472](A[2]), a thing is said to be honest, in so far as it has a certain beauty through being regulated by reason. Now whatever is regulated in accordance with reason is naturally becoming to man. Again, it is natural for a thing to take pleasure in that which is becoming to it. Wherefore an honest thing is naturally pleasing to man: and the Philosopher proves this with regard to acts of virtue (Ethic. i, 8). Yet not all that is pleasing is honest, since a thing may be becoming according to the senses, but not according to reason. A pleasing thing of this kind is beside man's reason which perfects his nature. Even virtue itself, which is essentially honest, is referred to something else as its end namely happiness. Accordingly the honest the useful, and the pleasant concur in the one subject.

Nevertheless they differ in aspect. For a thing is said to be honest as having a certain excellence deserving of honor on account of its spiritual beauty: while it is said to be pleasing, as bringing rest to desire, and useful, as referred to something else. The pleasant, however, extends to more things than the useful and the honest: since whatever is useful and honest is pleasing in some respect, whereas the converse does not hold (Ethic. ii, 3).

Reply to Objection 1: A thing is said to be honest, if it is desired for its own sake by the rational appetite. which tends to that which is in accordance with reason: while a thing is said to be pleasant if it is desired for its own sake by the sensitive appetite.

Reply to Objection 2: Riches are denominated honesty according of the opinion of the many who honor wealth: or because they are intended to be the instruments of virtuous deeds, as stated above (A[1], ad 2).

Reply to Objection 3: Tully and Ambrose mean to say that nothing incompatible with honesty can be simply and truly useful, since it follows that it is contrary to man's last end, which is a good in accordance with reason; although it may perhaps be useful in some respect, with regard to a particular end. But they do not mean to say that every useful thing as such may be classed among those that are honest.

Whether honesty should be reckoned a part of temperance?

Objection 1: It would seem that honesty should not be reckoned a part of temperance. For it is not possible for a thing to be part and whole in respect of one same thing. Now "temperance is a part of honesty," according to Tully (De Invent. Rhet. ii, 53). Therefore honesty is not a part of temperance.

Objection 2: Further, it is stated (3 Esdra 3:21) that "wine . . . makes all thoughts honest." But the use of wine, especially in excess, in which sense the passage quoted should seemingly be taken, pertains to intemperance rather than to temperance. Therefore honesty is not a part of temperance.

Objection 3: Further, the honest is that which is deserving of honor. Now "it is the just and the brave who receive most honor," according to the Philosopher (Rhet. i, 9). Therefore honesty pertains, not to temperance, but rather to justice and fortitude: wherefore Eleazar said as related in 2 Macc. 6:28: "I suffer an honorable [honesta] death, for the most venerable and most holy laws."

On the contrary, Macrobius [*In Somn. Scip. i] reckons honesty a part of temperance, and Ambrose (De Offic. i, 43) ascribes honesty as pertaining especially to temperance.

I answer that, As stated above [3473](A[2]), honesty is a kind of spiritual beauty. Now the disgraceful is opposed to the beautiful: and opposites are most manifest of one another. Wherefore seemingly honesty belongs especially to temperance, since the latter repels that which is most disgraceful and unbecoming to man, namely animal lusts. Hence by its very name temperance is most significative of the good of reason to which it belongs to moderate and temper evil desires. Accordingly honesty, as being ascribed for a special reason to temperance, is reckoned as a part thereof, not as a subjective part, nor as an annexed virtue, but as an integral part or condition attaching thereto.

Reply to Objection 1: Temperance is accounted a subjective part of honesty taken in a wide sense: it is not thus that the latter is reckoned a part of temperance.

Reply to Objection 2: When a man is intoxicated, "the wine makes his thoughts honest" according to his own reckoning because he deems himself great and deserving of honor [*Cf.[3474] Q[148], A[6]].

Reply to Objection 3: Greater honor is due to justice and fortitude than to temperance, because they excel in the point of a greater good: yet greater honor is due to temperance, because the vices which it holds in check are the most deserving of reproach, as stated above. Thus honesty is more to be ascribed to temperance according to the rule given by the Apostle (1 Cor. 12:23) when he says that "our uncomely parts have more abundant comeliness," which, namely, destroys whatever is uncomely.

OF ABSTINENCE (TWO ARTICLES)

We must now consider the subjective parts of temperance: first, those which are about pleasures of food; secondly, those which are about pleasures of sex. The first consideration will include abstinence, which is about meat and drink, and sobriety, which is specifically about drink.

With regard to abstinence three points have to be considered: (1) Abstinence itself; (2) its act which is fasting; (3) its opposite vice which is gluttony. Under the first head there are two points of inquiry:

(1) Whether abstinence is a virtue?

(2) Whether it is a special virtue?

Whether abstinence is a virtue?

Objection 1: It seems that abstinence is not a virtue. For the Apostle says (1 Cor. 4:20): "The kingdom of God is not in speech but in power [virtute]." Now the kingdom of God does not consist in abstinence, for the Apostle says (Rom. 14:17): "The kingdom of God is not meat and drink," where a gloss [*Cf. St. Augustine, QQ. Evang. ii, qu. 11] observes that "justice consists neither in abstaining nor in eating." Therefore abstinence is not a virtue.

Objection 2: Further, Augustine says (Confess. x, 11) addressing himself to God: "This hast Thou taught me, that I should set myself to take food as physic." Now it belongs not to virtue, but to the medical art to regulate medicine. Therefore, in like manner, to regulate one's food, which belongs to abstinence, is an act not of virtue but of art.

Objection 3: Further, every virtue "observes the mean," as stated in Ethic. ii, 6,7. But abstinence seemingly inclines not to the mean but to deficiency, since it denotes retrenchment. Therefore abstinence is not a virtue.

Objection 4: Further, no virtue excludes another virtue. But abstinence excludes patience: for Gregory says (Pastor. iii, 19) that "impatience not unfrequently dislodges the abstainer's mind from its peaceful seclusion." Likewise he says (Pastor. iii, 19) that "sometimes the sin of pride pierces the thoughts of the abstainer," so that abstinence excludes humility. Therefore abstinence is not a virtue.

On the contrary, It is written (2 Pet. 1:5,6): "Join with your faith virtue, and with virtue knowledge, and with knowledge abstinence"; where abstinence is numbered among other virtues. Therefore abstinence is a virtue.

I answer that, Abstinence by its very name denotes retrenchment of food. Hence the term abstinence may be taken in two ways. First, as denoting retrenchment of food absolutely, and in this way it signifies neither a virtue nor a virtuous act, but something indifferent. Secondly, it may be taken as regulated by reason, and then it signifies either a virtuous habit or a virtuous act. This is the meaning of Peter's words quoted above, where he says that we ought "to join abstinence with knowledge," namely that in abstaining from food a man should act with due regard for those among whom he lives, for his own person, and for the requirements of health.

Reply to Objection 1: The use of and abstinence from food, considered in themselves, do not pertain to the kingdom of God, since the Apostle says (1 Cor. 8:8): "Meat doth not commend us to God. For neither, if we eat not [*Vulg.: 'Neither if we eat . . . nor if we eat not'], shall we have the less, nor if we eat, shall we have the more," i.e. spiritually. Nevertheless they both belong to the kingdom of God, in so far as they are done reasonably through faith and love of God.

Reply to Objection 2: The regulation of food, in the point of quantity and quality, belongs to the art of medicine as regards the health of the body: but in the point of internal affections with regard to the good of reason, it belongs to abstinence. Hence Augustine says (QQ. Evang. ii, qu. 11): "It makes no difference whatever to virtue what or how much food a man takes, so long as he does it with due regard for the people among whom he lives, for his own person, and for the requirements of his health: but it matters how readily and uncomplainingly he does without food when bound by duty or necessity to abstain."

Reply to Objection 3: It belongs to temperance to bridle the pleasures which are too alluring to the soul, just as it belongs to fortitude to strengthen the soul against fears that deter it from the good of reason. Wherefore, just as fortitude is commended on account of a certain excess, from which all the parts of fortitude take their name, so temperance is commended for a kind of deficiency, from which all its parts are denominated. Hence abstinence, since it is a part of temperance, is named from deficiency, and yet it observes the mean, in so far as it is in accord with right reason.

Reply to Objection 4: Those vices result from abstinence in so far as it is not in accord with right reason. For right reason makes one abstain as one ought, i.e. with gladness of heart, and for the due end, i.e. for God's glory and not one's own.

Whether abstinence is a special virtue?

Objection 1: It would seem that abstinence is not a special virtue. For every virtue is praiseworthy by itself. But abstinence is not praiseworthy by itself; for Gregory says (Pastor. iii, 19) that "the virtue of abstinence is praised only on account of the other virtues." Therefore abstinence is not a special virtue.

Objection 2: Further, Augustine [*Fulgentius] says (De Fide ad Pet. xlii) that "the saints abstain from meat and drink, not that any creature of God is evil, but merely in order to chastise the body." Now this belongs to chastity, as its very name denotes. Therefore abstinence is not a special virtue distinct from chastity.

Objection 3: Further, as man should be content with moderate meat, so should he be satisfied with moderate clothes, according to 1 Tim. 6:8, "Having food, and wherewith to be covered, with these we should be [Vulg.: 'are'] content." Now there is no special virtue in being content with moderate clothes. Neither, therefore, is there in abstinence which moderates food.

On the contrary, Macrobius [*In Somn. Scip. i, 8] reckons abstinence as a special part of temperance.

I answer that, As stated above ([3475]Q[136], A[1];[3476] Q[141], A[3]) moral virtue maintains the good of reason against the onslaught of the passions: hence whenever we find a special motive why a passion departs from the good of reason, there is need of a special virtue. Now pleasures of the table are of a nature to withdraw man from the good of reason, both because they are so great, and because food is necessary to man who needs it for the maintenance of life, which he desires above all other things. Therefore abstinence is a special virtue.

Reply to Objection 1: Virtues are of necessity connected together, as stated above ([3477]FS, Q[65], A[1]). Wherefore one virtue receives help and commendation from another, as justice from fortitude. Accordingly in this way the virtue of abstinence receives commendation on account of the other virtues.

Reply to Objection 2: The body is chastised by means of abstinence, not only against the allurements of lust, but also against those of gluttony: since by abstaining a man gains strength for overcoming the onslaughts of gluttony, which increase in force the more he yields to them. Yet abstinence is not prevented from being a special virtue through being a help to chastity, since one virtue helps another.

Reply to Objection 3: The use of clothing was devised by art, whereas the use of food is from nature. Hence it is more necessary to have a special virtue for the moderation of food than for the moderation of clothing.

Day 224

OF FASTING (EIGHT ARTICLES)
We must now consider fasting: under which head there are eight points of inquiry:
(1) Whether fasting is an act of virtue?
(2) Of what virtue is it the act?
(3) Whether it is a matter of precept?
(4) Whether anyone is excused from fulfilling this precept?
(5) The time of fasting;
(6) Whether it is requisite for fasting to eat but once?
(7) The hour of eating for those who fast;
(8) The meats from which it is necessary to abstain.

Whether fasting is an act of virtue?

Objection 1: It would seem that fasting is not an act of virtue. For every act of virtue is acceptable to God. But fasting is not always acceptable to God, according to Is. 58:3, "Why have we fasted and Thou hast not regarded?" Therefore fasting is not an act of virtue.

Objection 2: Further, no act of virtue forsakes the mean of virtue. Now fasting forsakes the mean of virtue, which in the virtue of abstinence takes account of the necessity of supplying the needs of nature, whereas by fasting something is retrenched therefrom: else those who do not fast would not have the virtue of abstinence. Therefore fasting is not an act of virtue.

Objection 3: Further, that which is competent to all, both good and evil, is not an act of virtue. Now such is fasting, since every one is fasting before eating. Therefore fasting is not an act of virtue.

On the contrary, It is reckoned together with other virtuous acts (2 Cor. 6:5,6) where the Apostle says: "In fasting, in knowledge, in chastity, etc. [Vulg.: 'in chastity, in knowledge']."

I answer that, An act is virtuous through being directed by reason to some virtuous [honestum] [*Cf.[3478] Q[145], A[1]] good. Now this is consistent with fasting, because fasting is practiced for a threefold purpose. First, in order to bridle the lusts of the flesh, wherefore the Apostle says (2 Cor. 6:5,6): "In fasting, in chastity," since fasting is the guardian of chastity. For, according to Jerome [*Contra Jov. ii.] "Venus is cold when Ceres and Bacchus are not there," that is to say, lust is cooled by abstinence in meat and drink. Secondly, we have recourse to fasting in order that the mind may arise more freely to the contemplation of heavenly things: hence it is related (Dan. 10) of Daniel that he received a revelation from God after fasting for three weeks. Thirdly, in order to satisfy for sins: wherefore it is written (Joel 2:12): "Be converted to Me with all your heart, in fasting and in weeping and in mourning." The same is declared by Augustine in a sermon (De orat. et Jejun. [*Serm. lxxii (ccxxx, de Tempore)]): "Fasting cleanses the soul, raises the mind, subjects one's flesh to the spirit, renders the heart contrite and humble, scatters the clouds of concupiscence, quenches the fire of lust, kindles the true light of chastity."

Reply to Objection 1: An act that is virtuous generically may be rendered vicious by its connection with certain circumstances. Hence the text goes on to say: "Behold in the day of your fast your own will is founded," and a little further on (Is. 58:4): "You fast for debates and strife and strike with the fist wickedly." These words are expounded by Gregory (Pastor. iii, 19) as follows: "The will indicates joy and the fist anger. In vain then is the flesh restrained if the mind allowed to drift to inordinate movements be wrecked by vice." And Augustine says (in the same sermon) that "fasting loves not many words, deems wealth superfluous, scorns pride, commends humility, helps man to perceive what is frail and paltry."

Reply to Objection 2: The mean of virtue is measured not according to quantity but according to right reason, as stated in Ethic. ii, 6. Now reason judges it expedient, on account of some special motive, for a man to take less food than would be becoming to him under ordinary circumstances, for instance in order to avoid sickness, or in order to perform certain bodily works with greater ease: and much more does reason direct this to the avoidance of spiritual evils and the pursuit of spiritual goods. Yet reason does not retrench so much from one's food as to refuse nature its necessary support: thus Jerome says:* "It matters not whether thou art a long or a short time in destroying thyself, since to afflict the body immoderately, whether by excessive lack of nourishment, or by eating or sleeping too little, is to offer a sacrifice of stolen goods." [*The quotation is from the Corpus of Canon Law (Cap. Non mediocriter, De Consecrationibus, dist. 5). Gratian there ascribes the quotation to St. Jerome, but it is not to be found in the saint's works.] In like manner right reason does not retrench so much from a man's food as to render him incapable of fulfilling his duty. Hence Jerome says (in the same reference) "Rational man forfeits his dignity, if he sets fasting before chastity, or night-watchings before the well-being of his senses."

Reply to Objection 3: The fasting of nature, in respect of which a man is said to be fasting until he partakes of food, consists in a pure negation, wherefore it cannot be reckoned a virtuous act. Such is only the fasting of one who abstains in some measure from food for a reasonable purpose. Hence the former is called natural fasting [jejunium jejunii] [*Literally the 'fast of fasting']: while the latter is called the faster's fast, because he fasts for a purpose.

Whether fasting is an act of abstinence?

Objection 1: It would seem that fasting is not an act of abstinence. For Jerome [*The quotation is from the Ordinary Gloss, where the reference is lacking] commenting on Mat. 17:20, "This kind of devil" says: "To fast is to abstain not only from food but also from all manner of lusts." Now this belongs to every virtue. Therefore fasting is not exclusively an act of abstinence.

Objection 2: Further, Gregory says in a Lenten Homily (xvi in Evang.) that "the Lenten fast is a tithe of the whole year." Now paying tithes is an act of religion, as stated above ([3479]Q[87], A[1]). Therefore fasting is an act of religion and not of abstinence.

Objection 3: Further, abstinence is a part of temperance, as stated above (QQ[143],146, A[1], ad 3). Now temperance is condivided with fortitude, to which it belongs to endure hardships, and this seems very applicable to fasting. Therefore fasting is not an act of abstinence.

On the contrary, Isidore says (Etym. vi, 19) that "fasting is frugality of fare and abstinence from food."

I answer that, Habit and act have the same matter. Wherefore every virtuous act about some particular matter belongs to the virtue that appoints the mean in that matter. Now fasting is concerned with food, wherein the mean is appointed by abstinence. Wherefore it is evident that fasting is an act of abstinence.

Reply to Objection 1: Properly speaking fasting consists in abstaining from food, but speaking metaphorically it denotes abstinence from anything harmful, and such especially is sin.

We may also reply that even properly speaking fasting is abstinence from all manner of lust, since, as stated above (A[1], ad 1), an act ceases to be virtuous by the conjunction of any vice.

Reply to Objection 2: Nothing prevents the act of one virtue belonging to another virtue, in so far as it is directed to the end of that virtue, as explained above ([3480]Q[32], A[1], ad 2;[3481] Q[85], A[3]). Accordingly there is no reason why fasting should not be an act of religion, or of chastity, or of any other virtue.

Reply to Objection 3: It belongs to fortitude as a special virtue, to endure, not any kind of hardship, but only those connected with the danger of death. To endure hardships resulting from privation of pleasure of touch, belongs to temperance and its parts: and such are the hardships of fasting.

Whether fasting is a matter of precept?

Objection 1: It would seem that fasting is not a matter of precept. For precepts are not given about works of supererogation which are a matter of counsel. Now fasting is a work of supererogation: else it would have to be equally observed at all places and times. Therefore fasting is not a matter of precept.

Objection 2: Further, whoever infringes a precept commits a mortal sin. Therefore if fasting were a matter of precept, all who do not fast would sin mortally, and a widespreading snare would be laid for men.

Objection 3: Further, Augustine says (De Vera Relig. 17) that "the Wisdom of God having taken human nature, and called us to a state of freedom, instituted a few most salutary sacraments whereby the community of the Christian people, that is, of the free multitude, should be bound together in subjection to one God." Now the liberty of the Christian people seems to be hindered by a great number of observances no less than by a great number of sacraments. For Augustine says (Ad inquis. Januar., Ep. lv) that "whereas God in His mercy wished our religion to be distinguished by its freedom and the evidence and small number of its solemn sacraments, some people render it oppressive with slavish burdens." Therefore it seems that the Church should not have made fasting a matter of precept.

On the contrary, Jerome (Ad Lucin., Ep. lxxi) speaking of fasting says: "Let each province keep to its own practice, and look upon the commands of the elders as though they were laws of the apostles." Therefore fasting is a matter of precept.

I answer that, Just as it belongs to the secular authority to make legal precepts which apply the natural law to matters of common weal in temporal affairs, so it belongs to ecclesiastical superiors to prescribe by statute those things that concern the common weal of the faithful in spiritual goods.

Now it has been stated above [3482](A[1]) that fasting is useful as atoning for and preventing sin, and as raising the mind to spiritual things. And everyone is bound by the natural dictate of reason to practice fasting as far as it is necessary for these purposes. Wherefore fasting in general is a matter of precept of the natural law, while the fixing of the time and manner of fasting as becoming and profitable to the Christian people, is a matter of precept of positive law established by ecclesiastical authority: the latter is the Church fast, the former is the fast prescribed by nature.

Reply to Objection 1: Fasting considered in itself denotes something not eligible but penal: yet it becomes eligible in so far as it is useful to some end. Wherefore considered absolutely it is not binding under precept, but it is binding under precept to each one that stands in need of such a remedy. And since men, for the most part, need this remedy, both because "in many things we all offend" (James 3:2), and because "the flesh lusteth against the spirit" (Gal. 5:17), it was fitting that the Church should appoint certain fasts to be kept by all in common. In doing this the Church does not make a precept of a matter of supererogation, but particularizes in detail that which is of general obligation.

Reply to Objection 2: Those commandments which are given under the form of a general precept, do not bind all persons in the same way, but subject to the requirements of the end intended by the lawgiver. It will be a mortal sin to disobey a commandment through contempt of the lawgiver's authority, or to disobey it in such a way as to frustrate the end intended by him: but it is not a mortal sin if one fails to keep a commandment, when there is a reasonable motive, and especially if the lawgiver would not insist on its observance if he were present. Hence it is that not all, who do not keep the fasts of the Church, sin mortally.

Reply to Objection 3: Augustine is speaking there of those things "that are neither contained in the authorities of Holy Scripture, nor found among the ordinances of bishops in council, nor sanctioned by the custom of the universal Church." On the other hand, the fasts that are of obligation are appointed by the councils of bishops and are sanctioned by the custom of the universal Church. Nor are they opposed to the freedom of the faithful, rather are they of use in hindering the slavery of sin, which is opposed to spiritual freedom, of which it is written (Gal. 5:13): "You, brethren, have been called unto liberty; only make not liberty an occasion to the flesh."

Whether all are bound to keep the fasts of the Church?

Objection 1: It would seem that all are bound to keep the fasts of the Church. For the commandments of the Church are binding even as the commandments of God, according to Lk. 10:16, "He that heareth you heareth Me." Now all are bound to keep the commandments of God. Therefore in like manner all are bound to keep the fasts appointed by the Church.

Objection 2: Further, children especially are seemingly not exempt from fasting, on account of their age: for it is written (Joel 2:15): "Sanctify a fast," and further on (Joel 2:16): "Gather together the little ones, and them that suck the breasts." Much more therefore are all others bound to keep the fasts.

Objection 3: Further, spiritual things should be preferred to temporal, and necessary things to those that are not necessary. Now bodily works are directed to temporal gain; and pilgrimages, though directed to spiritual things, are not a matter of necessity. Therefore, since fasting is directed to a spiritual gain, and is made a necessary thing by the commandment of the Church, it seems that the fasts of the Church ought not to be omitted on account of a pilgrimage, or bodily works.

Objection 4: Further, it is better to do a thing willingly than through necessity, as stated in 2 Cor. 9:7. Now the poor are wont to fast through necessity, owing to lack of food. Much more therefore ought they to fast willingly.

On the contrary, It seems that no righteous man is bound to fast. For the commandments of the Church are not binding in opposition to Christ's teaching. But our Lord said (Lk. 5:34) that "the children of the bridegroom cannot fast whilst the bridegroom is with them [*Vulg.: 'Can you make the children of the bridegroom fast, whilst the bridegroom is with them?'].". Now He is with all the righteous by dwelling in them in a special manner [*Cf. [3483]FP, Q[8], A[3]], wherefore our Lord said (Mat. 28:20): "Behold I am with you . . . even to the consummation of the world." Therefore the righteous are not bound by the commandment of the Church to fast.

I answer that, As stated above ([3484]FS, Q[90], A[2]; [3485]FS, Q[98], AA[2],6), general precepts are framed according to the requirements of the many. Wherefore in making such precepts the lawgiver considers what happens generally and for the most part, and he does not intend the precept to be binding on a person in whom for some special reason there is something incompatible with observance of the precept. Yet discretion must be brought to bear on the point. For if the reason be evident, it is lawful for a man to use his own judgment in omitting to fulfil the precept, especially if custom be in his favor, or if it be difficult for him to have recourse to superior authority. on the other hand, if the reason be doubtful, one should have recourse to the superior who has power to grant a dispensation in such cases. And this must be done in the fasts appointed by the Church, to which all are bound in general, unless there be some special obstacle to this observance.

Reply to Objection 1: The commandments of God are precepts of the natural law, which are, of themselves, necessary for salvation. But the commandments of the Church are about matters which are necessary for salvation, not of themselves, but only through the ordinance of the Church. Hence there may be certain obstacles on account of which certain persons are not bound to keep the fasts in question.

Reply to Objection 2: In children there is a most evident reason for not fasting, both on account of their natural weakness, owing to which they need to take food frequently, and not much at a time, and because they need much nourishment owing to the demands of growth, which results from the residuum of nourishment. Wherefore as long as the stage of growth lasts, which as a rule lasts until they have completed the third period of seven years, they are not bound to keep the Church fasts: and yet it is fitting that even during that time they should exercise themselves in fasting, more or less, in accordance with their age. Nevertheless when some great calamity threatens, even children are commanded to fast, in sign of more severe penance, according to Jonah 3:7, "Let neither men nor beasts . . . taste anything . . . nor drink water."

Reply to Objection 3: Apparently a distinction should be made with regard to pilgrims and working people. For if the pilgrimage or laborious work can be conveniently deferred or lessened without detriment to the bodily health and such external conditions as are necessary for the upkeep of bodily or spiritual life, there is no reason for omitting the fasts of the Church. But if one be under the necessity of starting on the pilgrimage at once, and of making long stages, or of doing much work, either for one's bodily livelihood, or for some need of the spiritual life, and it be impossible at the same time to keep the fasts of the Church, one is not bound to fast: because in ordering fasts the Church would not seem to have intended to prevent other pious and more necessary undertakings. Nevertheless, in such cases one ought seemingly, to seek the superior's dispensation; except perhaps when the above course is recognized by custom, since when superiors are silent they would seem to consent.

Reply to Objection 4: Those poor who can provide themselves with sufficient for one meal are not excused, on account of poverty, from keeping the fasts of the Church. On the other hand, those would seem to be exempt who beg their food piecemeal, since they are unable at any one time to have a sufficiency of food.

Reply to Objection 5: This saying of our Lord may be expounded in three ways. First, according to Chrysostom (Hom. xxx in Matth.), who says that "the disciples, who are called children of the bridegroom, were as yet of a weakly disposition, wherefore they are compared to an old garment." Hence while Christ was with them in body they were to be fostered with kindness rather than drilled with the harshness of fasting. According to this interpretation, it is fitting that dispensations should be granted to the imperfect and to beginners, rather than to the elders and the perfect, according to a gloss on Ps. 130:2, "As a child that is weaned is towards his mother." Secondly, we may say with Jerome [*Bede, Comment. in Luc. v] that our Lord is speaking here of the fasts of the observances of the Old Law. Wherefore our Lord means to say that the apostles were not to be held back by the old observances, since they were to be filled with the newness of grace. Thirdly, according to Augustine (De Consensu Evang. ii, 27), who states that fasting is of two kinds. one pertains to those who are humbled by disquietude, and this is not befitting perfect men, for they are called "children of the bridegroom"; hence when we read in Luke: "The children of the bridegroom cannot fast [*Hom. xiii, in Matth.]," we read in Mat. 9:15: "The children of the bridegroom cannot mourn [*Vulg.: 'Can the children of the bridegroom mourn?']." The other pertains to the mind that rejoices in adhering to spiritual things: and this fasting is befitting the perfect.

Whether the times for the Church fast are fittingly ascribed?

Objection 1: It would seem that the times for the Church fast are unfittingly appointed. For we read (Mat. 4) that Christ began to fast immediately after being baptized. Now we ought to imitate Christ, according to 1 Cor. 4:16, "Be ye followers of me, as I also am of Christ." Therefore we ought to fast immediately after the Epiphany when Christ's baptism is celebrated.

Objection 2: Further, it is unlawful in the New Law to observe the ceremonies of the Old Law. Now it belongs to the solemnities of the Old Law to fast in certain particular months: for it is written (Zech. 8:19): "The fast of the fourth month and the fast of the fifth, and the fast of the seventh, and the fast of the tenth shall be to the house of Judah, joy and gladness and great solemnities." Therefore the fast of certain months, which are called Ember days, are unfittingly kept in the Church.

Objection 3: Further, according to Augustine (De Consensu Evang. ii, 27), just as there is a fast "of sorrow," so is there a fast "of joy." Now it is most becoming that the faithful should rejoice spiritually in Christ's Resurrection. Therefore during the five weeks which the Church solemnizes on account of Christ's Resurrection, and on Sundays which commemorate the Resurrection, fasts ought to be appointed.

On the contrary, stands the general custom of the Church.

I answer that, As stated above ([3486]AA[1],3), fasting is directed to two things, the deletion of sin, and the raising of the mind to heavenly things. Wherefore fasting ought to be appointed specially for those times, when it behooves man to be cleansed from sin, and the minds of the faithful to be raised to God by devotion: and these things are particularly requisite before the feast of Easter, when sins are loosed by baptism, which is solemnly conferred on Easter-eve, on which day our Lord's burial is commemorated, because "we are buried together with Christ by baptism unto death" (Rom. 6:4). Moreover at the Easter festival the mind of man ought to be devoutly raised to the glory of eternity, which Christ restored by rising from the dead, and so the Church ordered a fast to be observed immediately before the Paschal feast; and for the same reason, on the eve of the chief festivals, because it is then that one ought to make ready to keep the coming feast devoutly. Again it is the custom in the Church for Holy orders to be conferred every quarter of the year (in sign whereof our Lord fed four thousand men with seven loaves, which signify the New Testament year as Jerome says [*Comment. in Marc. viii]): and then both the ordainer, and the candidates for ordination, and even the whole people, for whose good they are ordained, need to fast in order to make themselves ready for the ordination. Hence it is related (Lk. 6:12) that before choosing His disciples our Lord "went out into a mountain to pray": and Ambrose [*Exposit. in Luc.] commenting on these words says: "What shouldst thou do, when thou desirest to undertake some pious work, since Christ prayed before sending His apostles?"

With regard to the forty day's fast, according to Gregory (Hom. xvi in Evang.) there are three reasons for the number. First, "because the power of the Decalogue is accomplished in the four books of the Holy Gospels: since forty is the product of ten multiplied by four." Or "because we are composed of four elements in this mortal body through whose lusts we transgress the Lord's commandments which are delivered to us in the Decalogue. Wherefore it is fitting we should punish that same body forty times. or, because, just as under the Law it was commanded that tithes should be paid of things, so we strive to pay God a tithe of days, for since a year is composed of three hundred and sixty-six days, by punishing ourselves for thirty-six days" (namely, the fasting days during the six weeks of Lent) "we pay God a tithe of our year." According to Augustine (De Doctr. Christ. ii, 16) a fourth reason may be added. For the Creator is the "Trinity," Father, Son, and Holy Ghost: while the number "three" refers to the invisible creature, since we are commanded to love God, with our whole heart, with our whole soul, and with our whole mind: and the number "four" refers to the visible creature, by reason of heat, cold, wet and dry. Thus the number "ten" [*Ten is the sum of three, three, and four] signifies all things, and if this be multiplied by four which refers to the body whereby we make use of things, we have the number forty.

Each fast of the Ember days is composed of three days, on account of the number of months in each season: or on account of the number of Holy orders which are conferred at these times.

Reply to Objection 1: Christ needed not baptism for His own sake, but in order to commend baptism to us. Wherefore it was competent for Him to fast, not before, but after His baptism, in order to invite us to fast before our baptism.

Reply to Objection 2: The Church keeps the Ember fasts, neither at the very same time as the Jews, nor for the same reasons. For they fasted in July, which is the fourth month from April (which they count as the first), because it was then that Moses coming down from Mount Sinai broke the tables of the Law (Ex. 32), and that, according to Jer. 39:2, "the walls of the city were first broken through." In the fifth month, which we call August, they fasted because they were commanded not to go up on to the mountain, when the people had rebelled on account of the spies (Num. 14): also in this month the temple of Jerusalem was burnt down by Nabuchodonosor (Jer. 52) and afterwards by Titus. In the seventh month which we call October, Godolias was slain, and the remnants of the people were dispersed (Jer. 51). In the tenth month, which we call January, the people who were with Ezechiel in captivity heard of the destruction of the temple (Ezech. 4).

Reply to Objection 3: The "fasting of joy" proceeds from the instigation of the Holy Ghost Who is the Spirit of liberty, wherefore this fasting should not be a matter of precept. Accordingly the fasts appointed by the commandment of the Church are rather "fasts of sorrow" which are inconsistent with days of joy. For this reason fasting is not ordered by the Church during the whole of the Paschal season, nor on Sundays: and if anyone were to fast at these times in contradiction to the custom of Christian people, which as Augustine declares (Ep. xxxvi) "is to be considered as law," or even through some erroneous opinion (thus the Manichees fast, because they deem such fasting to be of obligation)---he would not be free from sin. Nevertheless fasting considered in itself is commendable at all times; thus Jerome wrote (Ad Lucin., Ep. lxxi): "Would that we might fast always."

Whether it is requisite for fasting that one eat but once?

Objection 1: It would seem that it is not requisite for fasting that one eat but once. For, as stated above [3487](A[2]), fasting is an act of the virtue of abstinence, which observes due quantity of food not less than the number of meals. Now the quantity of food is not limited for those who fast. Therefore neither should the number of meals be limited.

Objection 2: Further, Just as man is nourished by meat, so is he by drink: wherefore drink breaks the fast, and for this reason we cannot receive the Eucharist after drinking. Now we are not forbidden to drink at various hours of the day. Therefore those who fast should not be forbidden to eat several times.

Objection 3: Further, digestives are a kind of food: and yet many take them on fasting days after eating. Therefore it is not essential to fasting to take only one meal.

On the contrary, stands the common custom of the Christian people.

I answer that, Fasting is instituted by the Church in order to bridle concupiscence, yet so as to safeguard nature. Now only one meal is seemingly sufficient for this purpose, since thereby man is able to satisfy nature; and yet he withdraws something from concupiscence by minimizing the number of meals. Therefore it is appointed by the Church, in her moderation, that those who fast should take one meal in the day.

Reply to Objection 1: It was not possible to fix the same quantity of food for all, on account of the various bodily temperaments, the result being that one person needs more, and another less food: whereas, for the most part, all are able to satisfy nature by only one meal.

Reply to Objection 2: Fasting is of two kinds [*Cf. A[1], ad 3]. One is the natural fast, which is requisite for receiving the Eucharist. This is broken by any kind of drink, even of water, after which it is not lawful to receive the Eucharist. The fast of the Church is another kind and is called the "fasting of the faster," and this is not broken save by such things as the Church intended to forbid in instituting the fast. Now the Church does not intend to command abstinence from drink, for this is taken more for bodily refreshment, and digestion of the food consumed, although it nourishes somewhat. It is, however, possible to sin and lose the merit of fasting, by partaking of too much drink: as also by eating immoderately at one meal.

Reply to Objection 3: Although digestives nourish somewhat they are not taken chiefly for nourishment, but for digestion. Hence one does not break one's fast by taking them or any other medicines, unless one were to take digestives, with a fraudulent intention, in great quantity and by way of food.

Whether the ninth hour is suitably fixed for the faster's meal?

Objection 1: It would seem that the ninth hour is not suitably fixed for the faster's meal. For the state of the New Law is more perfect than the state of the Old Law. Now in the Old Testament they fasted until evening, for it is written (Lev. 23:32): "It is a sabbath . . . you shall afflict your souls," and then the text continues: "From evening until evening you shall celebrate your sabbaths." Much more therefore under the New Testament should the fast be ordered until the evening.

Objection 2: Further, the fast ordered by the Church is binding on all. But all are not able to know exactly the ninth hour. Therefore it seems that the fixing of the ninth hour should not form part of the commandment to fast.

Objection 3: Further, fasting is an act of the virtue of abstinence, as stated above [3488](A[2]). Now the mean of moral virtue does not apply in the same way to all, since what is much for one is little for another, as stated in Ethic. ii, 6. Therefore the ninth hour should not be fixed for those who fast.

On the contrary, The Council of Chalons [*The quotation is from the Capitularies (Cap. 39) of Theodulf, bishop of Orleans (760-821) and is said to be found in the Corpus Juris, Cap. Solent, dist. 1, De Consecratione] says: "During Lent those are by no means to be credited with fasting who eat before the celebration of the office of Vespers," which in the Lenten season is said after the ninth hour. Therefore we ought to fast until the ninth hour.

I answer that, As stated above ([3489]AA[1],3,5), fasting is directed to the deletion and prevention of sin. Hence it ought to add something to the common custom, yet so as not to be a heavy burden to nature. Now the right and common custom is for men to eat about the sixth hour: both because digestion is seemingly finished (the natural heat being withdrawn inwardly at night-time on account of the surrounding cold of the night), and the humor spread about through the limbs (to which result the heat of the day conduces until the sun has reached its zenith), and again because it is then chiefly that the nature of the human body needs assistance against the external heat that is in the air, lest the humors be parched within. Hence, in order that those who fast may feel some pain in satisfaction for their sins, the ninth hour is suitably fixed for their meal.

Moreover, this hour agrees with the mystery of Christ's Passion, which was brought to a close at the ninth hour, when "bowing His head, He gave up the ghost" (Jn. 19:30): because those who fast by punishing their flesh, are conformed to the Passion of Christ, according to Gal. 5:24, "They that are Christ's, have crucified their flesh with the vices and concupiscences."

Reply to Objection 1: The state of the Old Testament is compared to the night, while the state of the New Testament is compared to the day, according to Rom. 13:12, "The night is passed and the day is at hand." Therefore in the Old Testament they fasted until night, but not in the New Testament.

Reply to Objection 2: Fasting requires a fixed hour based, not on a strict calculation, but on a rough estimate: for it suffices that it be about the ninth hour, and this is easy for anyone to ascertain.

Reply to Objection 3: A little more or a little less cannot do much harm. Now it is not a long space of time from the sixth hour at which men for the most part are wont to eat, until the ninth hour, which is fixed for those who fast. Wherefore the fixing of such a time cannot do much harm to anyone, whatever his circumstances may be. If however this were to prove a heavy burden to a man on account of sickness, age, or some similar reason, he should be dispensed from fasting, or be allowed to forestall the hour by a little.

Whether it is fitting that those who fast should be bidden to abstain from flesh meat, eggs, and milk foods?

Objection 1: It would seem unfitting that those who fast should be bidden to abstain from flesh meat, eggs, and milk foods. For it has been stated above [3490](A[6]) that fasting was instituted as a curb on the concupiscence of the flesh. Now concupiscence is kindled by drinking wine more than by eating flesh; according to Prov. 20:1, "Wine is a luxurious thing," and Eph. 5:18, "Be not drunk with wine, wherein is luxury." Since then those who fast are not forbidden to drink wine, it seems that they should not be forbidden to eat flesh meat.

Objection 2: Further, some fish are as delectable to eat as the flesh of certain animals. Now "concupiscence is desire of the delectable," as stated above ([3491]FS, Q[30], A[1]). Therefore since fasting which was instituted in order to bridle concupiscence does not exclude the eating of fish, neither should it exclude the eating of flesh meat.

Objection 3: Further, on certain fasting days people make use of eggs and cheese. Therefore one can likewise make use of them during the Lenten fast.

On the contrary, stands the common custom of the faithful.

I answer that, As stated above [3492](A[6]), fasting was instituted by the Church in order to bridle the concupiscences of the flesh, which regard pleasures of touch in connection with food and sex. Wherefore the Church forbade those who fast to partake of those foods which both afford most pleasure to the palate, and besides are a very great incentive to lust. Such are the flesh of animals that take their rest on the earth, and of those that breathe the air and their products, such as milk from those that walk on the earth, and eggs from birds. For, since such like animals are more like man in body, they afford greater pleasure as food, and greater nourishment to the human body, so that from their consumption there results a greater surplus available for seminal matter, which when abundant becomes a great incentive to lust. Hence the Church has bidden those who fast to abstain especially from these foods.

Reply to Objection 1: Three things concur in the act of procreation, namely, heat, spirit [*Cf. P. I., Q. 118, A[1], ad 3], and humor. Wine and other things that heat the body conduce especially to heat: flatulent foods seemingly cooperate in the production of the vital spirit: but it is chiefly the use of flesh meat which is most productive of nourishment, that conduces to the production of humor. Now the alteration occasioned by heat, and the increase in vital spirits are of short duration, whereas the substance of the humor remains a long time. Hence those who fast are forbidden the use of flesh meat rather than of wine or vegetables which are flatulent foods.

Reply to Objection 2: In the institution of fasting, the Church takes account of the more common occurrences. Now, generally speaking, eating flesh meat affords more pleasure than eating fish, although this is not always the case. Hence the Church forbade those who fast to eat flesh meat, rather than to eat fish.

Reply to Objection 3: Eggs and milk foods are forbidden to those who fast, for as much as they originate from animals that provide us with flesh: wherefore the prohibition of flesh meat takes precedence of the prohibition of eggs and milk foods. Again the Lenten fast is the most solemn of all, both because it is kept in imitation of Christ, and because it disposes us to celebrate devoutly the mysteries of our redemption. For this reason the eating of flesh meat is forbidden in every fast, while the Lenten fast lays a general prohibition even on eggs and milk foods. As to the use of the latter things in other fasts the custom varies among different people, and each person is bound to conform to that custom which is in vogue with those among whom he is dwelling. Hence Jerome says [*Augustine, De Lib. Arb. iii, 18; cf. De Nat. et Grat. lxvii]: "Let each province keep to its own practice, and look upon the commands of the elders as though they were the laws of the apostles."

OF GLUTTONY (SIX ARTICLES)
We must now consider gluttony. Under this head there are six points of inquiry:
(1) Whether gluttony is a sin?
(2) Whether it is a mortal sin?
(3) Whether it is the greatest of sins?
(4) Its species;
(5) Whether it is a capital sin?
(6) Its daughters.

Whether gluttony is a sin?
Objection 1: It would seem that gluttony is not a sin. For our Lord said (Mat. 15:11): "Not that which goeth into the mouth defileth a man." Now gluttony regards food which goes into a man. Therefore, since every sin defiles a man, it seems that gluttony is not a sin.

Objection 2: Further, "No man sins in what he cannot avoid" [*Ep. lxxi, ad Lucin.]. Now gluttony is immoderation in food; and man cannot avoid this, for Gregory says (Moral. xxx, 18): "Since in eating pleasure and necessity go together, we fail to discern between the call of necessity and the seduction of pleasure," and Augustine says (Confess. x, 31): "Who is it, Lord, that does not eat a little more than necessary?" Therefore gluttony is not a sin.

Objection 3: Further, in every kind of sin the first movement is a sin. But the first movement in taking food is not a sin, else hunger and thirst would be sinful. Therefore gluttony is not a sin.

On the contrary, Gregory says (Moral. xxx, 18) that "unless we first tame the enemy dwelling within us, namely our gluttonous appetite, we have not even stood up to engage in the spiritual combat." But man's inward enemy is sin. Therefore gluttony is a sin.

I answer that, Gluttony denotes, not any desire of eating and drinking, but an inordinate desire. Now desire is said to be inordinate through leaving the order of reason, wherein the good of moral virtue consists: and a thing is said to be a sin through being contrary to virtue. Wherefore it is evident that gluttony is a sin.

Reply to Objection 1: That which goes into man by way of food, by reason of its substance and nature, does not defile a man spiritually. But the Jews, against whom our Lord is speaking, and the Manichees deemed certain foods to make a man unclean, not on account of their signification, but by reason of their nature [*Cf. [3493]FS, Q[102], A[6], ad 1]. It is the inordinate desire of food that defiles a man spiritually.

Reply to Objection 2: As stated above, the vice of gluttony does not regard the substance of food, but in the desire thereof not being regulated by reason. Wherefore if a man exceed in quantity of food, not from desire of food, but through deeming it necessary to him, this pertains, not to gluttony, but to some kind of inexperience. It is a case of gluttony only when a man knowingly exceeds the measure in eating, from a desire for the pleasures of the palate.

Reply to Objection 3: The appetite is twofold. There is the natural appetite, which belongs to the powers of the vegetal soul. In these powers virtue and vice are impossible, since they cannot be subject to reason; wherefore the appetitive power is differentiated from the powers of secretion, digestion, and excretion, and to it hunger and thirst are to be referred. Besides this there is another, the sensitive appetite, and it is in the concupiscence of this appetite that the vice of gluttony consists. Hence the first movement of gluttony denotes inordinateness in the sensitive appetite, and this is not without sin.

Day 225

Whether gluttony is a mortal sin?
Objection 1: It would seem that gluttony is not a mortal sin. For every mortal sin is contrary to a precept of the Decalogue: and this, apparently, does not apply to gluttony. Therefore gluttony is not a mortal sin.

Objection 2: Further, every mortal sin is contrary to charity, as stated above ([3494]Q[132], A[3]). But gluttony is not opposed to charity, neither as regards the love of God, nor as regards the love of one's neighbor. Therefore gluttony is never a mortal sin.

Objection 3: Further, Augustine says in a sermon on Purgatory [*Cf. Append. to St. Augustine's works: Serm. civ (xli, de sanctis)]: "Whenever a man takes more meat and drink than is necessary, he should know that this is one of the lesser sins." But this pertains to gluttony. Therefore gluttony is accounted among the lesser, that is to say venial, sins.

Objection 4: On the contrary, Gregory says (Moral. xxx, 18): "As long as the vice of gluttony has a hold on a man, all that he has done valiantly is forfeited by him: and as long as the belly is unrestrained, all virtue comes to naught." But virtue is not done away save by mortal sin. Therefore gluttony is a mortal sin.

I answer that, As stated above [3495](A[1]), the vice of gluttony properly consists in inordinate concupiscence. Now the order of reason in regulating the concupiscence may be considered from two points of view. First, with regard to things directed to the end, inasmuch as they may be incommensurate and consequently improportionate to the end; secondly, with regard to the end itself, inasmuch as concupiscence turns man away from his due end. Accordingly, if the inordinate concupiscence in gluttony be found to turn man away from the last end, gluttony will be a mortal sin. This is the case when he adheres to the pleasure of gluttony as his end, for the sake of which he contemns God, being ready to disobey God's commandments, in order to obtain those pleasures. On the other hand, if the inordinate concupiscence in the vice of gluttony be found to affect only such things as are directed to the end, for instance when a man has too great a desire for the pleasures of the palate, yet would not for their sake do anything contrary to God's law, it is a venial sin.

Reply to Objection 1: The vice of gluttony becomes a mortal sin by turning man away from his last end: and accordingly, by a kind of reduction, it is opposed to the precept of hallowing the sabbath, which commands us to rest in our last end. For mortal sins are not all directly opposed to the precepts of the Decalogue, but only those which contain injustice: because the precepts of the Decalogue pertain specially to justice and its parts, as stated above ([3496]Q[122], A[1]).

Reply to Objection 2: In so far as it turns man away from his last end, gluttony is opposed to the love of God, who is to be loved, as our last end, above all things: and only in this respect is gluttony a mortal sin.

Reply to Objection 3: This saying of Augustine refers to gluttony as denoting inordinate concupiscence merely in regard of things directed to the end.

Reply to Objection 4: Gluttony is said to bring virtue to naught, not so much on its own account, as on account of the vices which arise from it. For Gregory says (Pastor. iii, 19): "When the belly is distended by gluttony, the virtues of the soul are destroyed by lust."

Whether gluttony is the greatest of sins?

Objection 1: It would seem that gluttony is the greatest of sins. For the grievousness of a sin is measured by the grievousness of the punishment. Now the sin of gluttony is most grievously punished, for Chrysostom says [*Hom. xiii in Matth.]: "Gluttony turned Adam out of Paradise, gluttony it was that drew down the deluge at the time of Noah." According to Ezech. 16:49, "This was the iniquity of Sodom, thy sister . . . fulness of bread," etc. Therefore the sin of gluttony is the greatest of all.

Objection 2: Further, in every genus the cause is the most powerful. Now gluttony is apparently the cause of other sins, for a gloss on Ps. 135:10, "Who smote Egypt with their first-born," says: "Lust, concupiscence, pride are the first-born of gluttony." Therefore gluttony is the greatest of sins.

Objection 3: Further, man should love himself in the first place after God, as stated above ([3497]Q[25], A[4]). Now man, by the vice of gluttony, inflicts an injury on himself: for it is written (Ecclus. 37:34): "By surfeiting many have perished." Therefore gluttony is the greatest of sins, at least excepting those that are against God.

On the contrary, The sins of the flesh, among which gluttony is reckoned, are less culpable according to Gregory (Moral. xxxiii).

I answer that, The gravity of a sin may be measured in three ways. First and foremost it depends on the matter in which the sin is committed: and in this way sins committed in connection with Divine things are the greatest. From this point of view gluttony is not the greatest sin, for it is about matters connected with the nourishment of the body. Secondly, the gravity of a sin depends on the person who sins, and from this point of view the sin of gluttony is diminished rather than aggravated, both on account of the necessity of taking food, and on account of the difficulty of proper discretion and moderation in such matters. Thirdly, from the point of view of the result that follows, and in this way gluttony has a certain gravity, inasmuch as certain sins are occasioned thereby.

Reply to Objection 1: These punishments are to be referred to the vices that resulted from gluttony, or to the root from which gluttony sprang, rather than to gluttony itself. For the first man was expelled from Paradise on account of pride, from which he went on to an act of gluttony: while the deluge and the punishment of the people of Sodom were inflicted for sins occasioned by gluttony.

Reply to Objection 2: This objection argues from the standpoint of the sins that result from gluttony. Nor is a cause necessarily more powerful, unless it be a direct cause: and gluttony is not the direct cause but the accidental cause, as it were, and the occasion of other vices.

Reply to Objection 3: The glutton intends, not the harm to his body, but the pleasure of eating: and if injury results to his body, this is accidental. Hence this does not directly affect the gravity of gluttony, the guilt of which is nevertheless aggravated, if a man incur some bodily injury through taking too much food.

Whether the species of gluttony are fittingly distinguished?

Objection 1: It seems that the species of gluttony are unfittingly distinguished by Gregory who says (Moral. xxx, 18): "The vice of gluttony tempts us in five ways. Sometimes it forestalls the hour of need; sometimes it seeks costly meats; sometimes it requires the food to be daintily cooked; sometimes it exceeds the measure of refreshment by taking too much; sometimes we sin by the very heat of an immoderate appetite"---which are contained in the following verse: "Hastily, sumptuously, too much, greedily, daintily."

For the above are distinguished according to diversity of circumstance. Now circumstances, being the accidents of an act, do not differentiate its species. Therefore the species of gluttony are not distinguished according to the aforesaid.

Objection 2: Further, as time is a circumstance, so is place. If then gluttony admits of one species in respect of time, it seems that there should likewise be others in respect of place and other circumstances.

Objection 3: Further, just as temperance observes due circumstances, so do the other moral virtues. Now the species of the vices opposed to the other moral virtues are not distinguished according to various circumstances. Neither, therefore, are the species of gluttony distinguished thus.

On the contrary, stands the authority of Gregory quoted above.

I answer that, As stated above [3498](A[1]), gluttony denotes inordinate concupiscence in eating. Now two things are to be considered in eating, namely the food we eat, and the eating thereof. Accordingly, the inordinate concupiscence may be considered in two ways. First, with regard to the food consumed: and thus, as regards the substance or species of food a man seeks "sumptuous"---i.e. costly food; as regards its quality, he seeks food prepared too nicely---i.e. "daintily"; and as regards quantity, he exceeds by eating "too much."

Secondly, the inordinate concupiscence is considered as to the consumption of food: either because one forestalls the proper time for eating, which is to eat "hastily," or one fails to observe the due manner of eating, by eating "greedily."

Isidore [*De Summo Bon. ii, 42] comprises the first and second under one heading, when he says that the glutton exceeds in "what" he eats, or in "how much," "how" or "when he eats."

Reply to Objection 1: The corruption of various circumstances causes the various species of gluttony, on account of the various motives, by reason of which the species of moral things are differentiated. For in him that seeks sumptuous food, concupiscence is aroused by the very species of the food; in him that forestalls the time concupiscence is disordered through impatience of delay, and so forth.

Reply to Objection 2: Place and other circumstances include no special motive connected with eating, that can cause a different species of gluttony.

Reply to Objection 3: In all other vices, whenever different circumstances correspond to different motives, the difference of circumstances argues a specific difference of vice: but this does not apply to all circumstances, as stated above ([3499]FS, Q[72], A[9]).

Whether gluttony is a capital vice?

Objection 1: It would seem that gluttony is not a capital vice. For capital vices denote those whence, under the aspect of final cause, other vices originate. Now food, which is the matter of gluttony, has not the aspect of end, since it is sought, not for its own sake, but for the body's nourishment. Therefore gluttony is not a capital vice.

Objection 2: Further, a capital vice would seem to have a certain pre-eminence in sinfulness. But this does not apply to gluttony, which, in respect of its genus, is apparently the least of sins, seeing that it is most akin to what is in respect of its genus, is apparently the least gluttony is not a capital vice.

Objection 3: Further, sin results from a man forsaking the food of virtue on account of something useful to the present life, or pleasing to the senses. Now as regards goods having the aspect of utility, there is but one capital vice, namely covetousness. Therefore, seemingly, there would be but one capital vice in respect of pleasures: and this is lust, which is a greater vice than gluttony, and is about greater pleasures. Therefore gluttony is not a capital vice.

On the contrary, Gregory (Moral. xxxi, 45) reckons gluttony among the capital vices.

I answer that, As stated above ([3500]FS, Q[84], A[3]), a capital vice denotes one from which, considered as final cause, i.e. as having a most desirable end, other vices originate: wherefore through desiring that end men are incited to sin in many ways. Now an end is rendered most desirable through having one of the conditions of happiness which is desirable by its very nature: and pleasure is essential to happiness, according to Ethic. i, 8; x, 3,7,8. Therefore the vice of gluttony, being about pleasures of touch which stand foremost among other pleasures, is fittingly reckoned among the capital vices.

Reply to Objection 1: It is true that food itself is directed to something as its end: but since that end, namely the sustaining of life, is most desirable and whereas life cannot be sustained without food, it follows that food too is most desirable: indeed, nearly all the toil of man's life is directed thereto, according to Eccles. 6:7, "All the labor of man is for his mouth." Yet gluttony seems to be about pleasures of food rather than about food itself; wherefore, as Augustine says (De Vera Relig. liii), "with such food as is good for the worthless body, men desire to be fed," wherein namely the pleasure consists, "rather than to be filled: since the whole end of that desire is this---not to thirst and not to hunger."

Reply to Objection 2: In sin the end is ascertained with respect to the conversion, while the gravity of sin is determined with regard to the aversion. Wherefore it does not follow that the capital sin which has the most desirable end surpasses the others in gravity.

Reply to Objection 3: That which gives pleasure is desirable in itself: and consequently corresponding to its diversity there are two capital vices, namely gluttony and lust. On the other hand, that which is useful is desirable, not in itself, but as directed to something else: wherefore seemingly in all useful things there is one aspect of desirability. Hence there is but one capital vice, in respect of such things.

Whether six daughters are fittingly assigned to gluttony?

Objection 1: It would seem that six daughters are unfittingly assigned to gluttony, to wit, "unseemly joy, scurrility, uncleanness, loquaciousness, and dullness of mind as regards the understanding." For unseemly joy results from every sin, according to Prov. 2:14, "Who are glad when they have done evil, and rejoice in most wicked things." Likewise dullness of mind is associated with every sin, according to Prov. 14:22, "They err that work evil." Therefore they are unfittingly reckoned to be daughters of gluttony.

Objection 2: Further, the uncleanness which is particularly the result of gluttony would seem to be connected with vomiting, according to Is. 28:8, "All tables were full of vomit and filth." But this seems to be not a sin but a punishment; or even a useful thing that is a matter of counsel, according to Ecclus. 31:25, "If thou hast been forced to eat much, arise, go out, and vomit; and it shall refresh thee." Therefore it should not be reckoned among the daughters of gluttony.

Objection 3: Further, Isidore (QQ. in Deut. xvi) reckons scurrility as a daughter of lust. Therefore it should not be reckoned among the daughters of gluttony.

On the contrary, Gregory (Moral. xxxi, 45) assigns these daughters to gluttony.

I answer that, As stated above ([3501]AA[1],2,3), gluttony consists properly in an immoderate pleasure in eating and drinking. Wherefore those vices are reckoned among the daughters of gluttony, which are the results of eating and drinking immoderately. These may be accounted for either on the part of the soul or on the part of the body. on the part of the soul these results are of four kinds. First, as regards the reason, whose keenness is dulled by immoderate meat and drink, and in this respect we reckon as a daughter of gluttony, "dullness of sense in the understanding," on account of the fumes of food disturbing the brain. Even so, on the other hand, abstinence conduces to the penetrating power of wisdom, according to Eccles. 2:3, "I thought in my heart to withdraw my flesh from wine, that I might turn my mind in wisdom." Secondly, as regards the. appetite, which is disordered in many ways by immoderation in eating and drinking, as though reason were fast asleep at the helm, and in this respect "unseemly joy" is reckoned, because all the other inordinate passions are directed to joy or sorrow, as stated in Ethic. ii, 5. To this we must refer the saying of 3 Esdra 3:20, that "wine . . . gives every one a confident and joyful mind." Thirdly, as regards inordinate words, and thus we have "loquaciousness," because as Gregory says (Pastor. iii, 19), "unless gluttons were carried away by immoderate speech, that rich man who is stated to have feasted sumptuously every day would not have been so tortured in his tongue." Fourthly, as regards inordinate action, and in this way we have "scurrility," i.e. a kind of levity resulting from lack of reason, which is unable not only to bridle the speech, but also to restrain outward behavior. Hence a gloss on Eph. 5:4, "Or foolish talking or scurrility," says that "fools call this geniality---i.e. jocularity, because it is wont to raise a laugh." Both of these, however, may be referred to the words which may happen to be sinful, either by reason of excess which belongs to "loquaciousness," or by reason of unbecomingness, which belongs to "scurrility."

On the part of the body, mention is made of "uncleanness," which may refer either to the inordinate emission of any kind of superfluities, or especially to the emission of the semen. Hence a gloss on Eph. 5:3, "But fornication and all uncleanness," says: "That is, any kind of incontinence that has reference to lust."

Reply to Objection 1: Joy in the act or end of sin results from every sin, especially the sin that proceeds from habit, but the random riotous joy which is described as "unseemly" arises chiefly from immoderate partaking of meat or drink. In like manner, we reply that dullness of sense as regards matters of choice is common to all sin, whereas dullness of sense in speculative matters arises chiefly from gluttony, for the reason given above.

Reply to Objection 2: Although it does one good to vomit after eating too much, yet it is sinful to expose oneself to its necessity by immoderate meat or drink. However, it is no sin to procure vomiting as a remedy for sickness if the physician prescribes it.

Reply to Objection 3: Scurrility proceeds from the act of gluttony, and not from the lustful act, but from the lustful will: wherefore it may be referred to either vice.

OF SOBRIETY (FOUR ARTICLES)

We must now consider sobriety and the contrary vice, namely drunkenness. As regards sobriety there are four points of inquiry:

(1) What is the matter of sobriety?
(2) Whether it is a special virtue?
(3) Whether the use of wine is lawful?
(4) To whom especially is sobriety becoming?

Whether drink is the matter of sobriety?

Objection 1: It would seem that drink is not the matter proper to sobriety. For it is written (Rom. 12:3): "Not to be more wise than it behooveth to be wise, but to be wise unto sobriety." Therefore sobriety is also about wisdom, and not only about drink.

Objection 2: Further, concerning the wisdom of God, it is written (Wis. 8:7) that "she teacheth sobriety [Douay: 'temperance'], and prudence, and justice, and fortitude," where sobriety stands for temperance. Now temperance is not only about drink, but also about meat and sexual matters. Therefore sobriety is not only about drink.

Objection 3: Further, sobriety would seem to take its name from "measure" [*'Bria,' a measure, a cup; Cf. Facciolati and Forcellini's Lexicon]. Now we ought to be guided by the measure in all things appertaining to us: for it is written (Titus 2:12): "We should live soberly and justly and godly," where a gloss remarks: "Soberly, in ourselves"; and (1 Tim. 2:9): "Women . . . in decent apparel, adorning themselves with modesty and sobriety." Consequently it would seem that sobriety regards not only the interior man, but also things appertaining to external apparel. Therefore drink is not the matter proper to sobriety.

On the contrary, It is written (Ecclus. 31:32): "Wine taken with sobriety is equal life to men; if thou drink it moderately, thou shalt be sober."

I answer that, When a virtue is denominated from some condition common to the virtues, the matter specially belonging to it is that in which it is most difficult and most commendable to satisfy that condition of virtue: thus fortitude is about dangers of death, and temperance about pleasures of touch. Now sobriety takes its name from "measure," for a man is said to be sober because he observes the "bria," i.e. the measure. Wherefore sobriety lays a special claim to that matter wherein /the observance of the measure is most deserving of praise. Such matter is the drinking of intoxicants, because the measured use thereof is most profitable, while immoderate excess therein is most harmful, since it hinders the use of reason even more than excessive eating. Hence it is written (Ecclus. 31:37,38): "Sober drinking is health to soul and body; wine drunken with excess raiseth quarrels, and wrath and many ruins." For this reason sobriety is especially concerned with drink, not any kind of drink, but that which by reason of its volatility is liable to disturb the brain, such as wine and all intoxicants. Nevertheless, sobriety may be employed in a general sense so as to apply to any matter, as stated above ([3502]Q[123], A[2];[3503] Q[141], A[2]) with regard to fortitude and temperance.

Reply to Objection 1: Just as the material wine intoxicates a man as to his body, so too, speaking figuratively, the consideration of wisdom is said to be an inebriating draught, because it allures the mind by its delight, according to Ps. 22:5, "My chalice which inebriateth me, how goodly is it!" Hence sobriety is applied by a kind of metaphor in speaking of the contemplation of wisdom.

Reply to Objection 2: All the things that belong properly to temperance are necessary to the present life, and their excess is harmful. Wherefore it behooves one to apply a measure in all such things. This is the business of sobriety: and for this reason sobriety is used to designate temperance. Yet slight excess is more harmful in drink than in other things, wherefore sobriety is especially concerned with drink.

Reply to Objection 3: Although a measure is needful in all things, sobriety is not properly employed in connection with all things, but only in those wherein there is most need for a measure.

Whether sobriety is by itself a special virtue?

Objection 1: It would seem that sobriety is not by itself a special virtue. For abstinence is concerned with both meat and drink. Now there is no special virtue about meat. Therefore neither is sobriety, which is about drink, a special virtue.

Objection 2: Further, abstinence and gluttony are about pleasures of touch as sensitive to food. Now meat and drink combine together to make food, since an animal needs a combination of wet and dry nourishment. Therefore sobriety, which is about drink, is not a. special virtue.

Objection 3: Further, just as in things pertaining to nourishment, drink is distinguished from meat, so are there various kinds of meats and of drinks. Therefore if sobriety is by itself a special virtue, seemingly there will be a special virtue corresponding to each different kind of meat or drink, which is unreasonable. Therefore it would seem that sobriety is not a special virtue.

On the contrary, Macrobius [*In Somno Scip. i, 8] reckons sobriety to be a special part of temperance.

I answer that, As stated above ([3504]Q[146], A[2]), it belongs to moral virtue to safeguard the good of reason against those things which may hinder it. Hence wherever we find a special hindrance to reason, there must needs be a special virtue to remove it. Now intoxicating drink is a special kind of hindrance to the use of reason, inasmuch as it disturbs the brain by its fumes. Wherefore in order to remove this hindrance to reason a special virtue, which is sobriety, is requisite.

Reply to Objection 1: Meat and drink are alike capable of hindering the good of reason, by embroiling the reason with immoderate pleasure: and in this respect abstinence is about both meat and drink alike. But intoxicating drink is a special kind of hindrance, as stated above, wherefore it requires a special virtue.

Reply to Objection 2: The virtue of abstinence is about meat and drink, considered, not as food but as a hindrance to reason. Hence it does not follow that special kinds of virtue correspond to different kinds of food.

Reply to Objection 3: In all intoxicating drinks there is one kind of hindrance to the use of reason: so that the difference of drinks bears an accidental relation to virtue. Hence this difference does not call for a difference of virtue. The same applies to the difference of meats.

Whether the use of wine is altogether unlawful?

Objection 1: It would seem that the use of wine is altogether unlawful. For without wisdom, a man cannot be in the state of salvation: since it is written (Wis. 7:28): "God loveth none but him that dwelleth with wisdom," and further on (Wis. 9:19): "By wisdom they were healed, whosoever have pleased Thee, O Lord, from the beginning." Now the use of wine is a hindrance to wisdom, for it is written (Eccles. 2:3): "I thought in my heart to withdraw my flesh from wine, that I might turn my mind to wisdom." Therefore wine-drinking is altogether unlawful.

Objection 2: Further, the Apostle says (Rom. 14:21): "It is good not to eat flesh, and not to drink wine, nor anything whereby thy brother is offended or scandalized, or made weak." Now it is sinful to forsake the good of virtue, as likewise to scandalize one's brethren. Therefore it is unlawful to make use of wine.

Objection 3: Further, Jerome says [*Contra Jovin. i] that "after the deluge wine and flesh were sanctioned: but Christ came in the last of the ages and brought back the end into line with the beginning." Therefore it seems unlawful to use wine under the Christian law.

On the contrary, The Apostle says (1 Tim. 5:23): "Do not still drink water, but use a little wine for thy stomach's sake, and thy frequent infirmities"; and it is written (Ecclus. 31:36): "Wine drunken with moderation is the joy of the soul and the heart."

I answer that, No meat or drink, considered in itself, is unlawful, according to Mat. 15:11, "Not that which goeth into the mouth defileth a man." Wherefore it is not unlawful to drink wine as such. Yet it may become unlawful accidentally. This is sometimes owing to a circumstance on the part of the drinker, either because he is easily the worse for taking wine, or because he is bound by a vow not to drink wine: sometimes it results from the mode of drinking, because to wit he exceeds the measure in drinking: and sometimes it is on account of others who would be scandalized thereby.

Reply to Objection 1: A man may have wisdom in two ways. First, in a general way, according as it is sufficient for salvation: and in this way it is required, in order to have wisdom, not that a man abstain altogether from wine, but that he abstain from its immoderate use. Secondly, a man may have wisdom in some degree of perfection: and in this way, in order to receive wisdom perfectly, it is requisite for certain persons that they abstain altogether from wine, and this depends on circumstances of certain persons and places.

Reply to Objection 2: The Apostle does not declare simply that it is good to abstain from wine, but that it is good in the case where this would give scandal to certain people.

Reply to Objection 3: Christ withdraws us from some things as being altogether unlawful, and from others as being obstacles to perfection. It is in the latter way that he withdraws some from the use of wine, that they may aim at perfection, even as from riches and the like.

Whether sobriety is more requisite in persons of greater standing?

Objection 1: It would seem that sobriety is more requisite in persons of greater standing. For old age gives a man a certain standing; wherefore honor and reverence are due to the old, according to Lev. 19:32, "Rise up before the hoary head, and honor the person of the aged man." Now the Apostle declares that old men especially should be exhorted to sobriety, according to Titus 2:2, "That the aged man be sober." Therefore sobriety is most requisite in persons of standing.

Objection 2: Further, a bishop has the highest degree in the Church: and the Apostle commands him to be sober, according to 1 Tim. 3:2, "It behooveth . . . a bishop to be blameless, the husband of one wife, sober, prudent," etc. Therefore sobriety is chiefly required in persons of high standing.

Objection 3: Further, sobriety denotes abstinence from wine. Now wine is forbidden to kings, who hold the highest place in human affairs: while it is allowed to those who are in a state of affliction, according to Prov. 31:4, "Give not wine to kings," and further on (Prov. 31:6), "Give strong drink to them that are sad, and wine to them that are grieved in mind." Therefore sobriety is more requisite in persons of standing.

On the contrary, The Apostle says (1 Tim. 3:11): "The women in like manner, chaste . . . sober," etc., and (Titus 2:6) "Young men in like manner exhort that they be sober."

I answer that, Virtue includes relationship to two things, to the contrary vices which it removes, and to the end to which it leads. Accordingly a particular virtue is more requisite in certain persons for two reasons. First, because they are more prone to the concupiscences which need to be restrained by virtue, and to the vices which are removed by virtue. In this respect, sobriety is most requisite in the young and in women, because concupiscence of pleasure thrives in the young on account of the heat of youth, while in women there is not sufficient strength of mind to resist concupiscence. Hence, according to Valerius Maximus [*Dict. Fact. Memor. ii, 1] among the ancient Romans women drank no wine. Secondly, sobriety is more requisite in certain persons, as being more necessary for the operations proper to them. Now immoderate use of wine is a notable obstacle to the use of reason: wherefore sobriety is specially prescribed to the old, in whom reason should be vigorous in instructing others: to bishops and all ministers of the Church, who should fulfil their spiritual duties with a devout mind; and to kings, who should rule their subjects with wisdom.

This suffices for the Replies to the Objections.

Day 226

OF DRUNKENNESS (FOUR ARTICLES)

We must now consider drunkenness. Under this head there are four points of inquiry:

(1) Whether drunkenness is a sin?

(2) Whether it is a mortal sin?

(3) Whether it is the most grievous sin?

(4) Whether it excuses from sin?

Whether drunkenness is a sin?

Objection 1: It would seem that drunkenness is not a sin. For every sin has a corresponding contrary sin, thus timidity is opposed to daring, and presumption to pusillanimity. But no sin is opposed to drunkenness. Therefore drunkenness is not a sin.

Objection 2: Further, every sin is voluntary [*Augustine, De Vera Relig. xiv]. But no man wishes to be drunk, since no man wishes to be deprived of the use of reason. Therefore drunkenness is not a sin.

Objection 3: Further, whoever causes another to sin, sins himself. Therefore, if drunkenness were a sin, it would follow that it is a sin to ask a man to drink that which makes him drunk, which would seem very hard.

Objection 4: Further, every sin calls for correction. But correction is not applied to drunkards: for Gregory [*Cf. Canon Denique, dist. 4 where Gratian refers to a letter of St. Gregory to St. Augustine of Canterbury] says that "we must forbear with their ways, lest they become worse if they be compelled to give up the habit." Therefore drunkenness is not a sin.

On the contrary, The Apostle says (Rom. 13:13): "Not in rioting and drunkenness."

I answer that, Drunkenness may be understood in two ways. First, it may signify the defect itself of a man resulting from his drinking much wine, the consequence being that he loses the use of reason. In this sense drunkenness denotes not a sin, but a penal defect resulting from a fault. Secondly, drunkenness may denote the act by which a man incurs this defect. This act may cause drunkenness in two ways. In one way, through the wine being too strong, without the drinker being cognizant of this: and in this way too, drunkenness may occur without sin, especially if it is not through his negligence, and thus we believe that Noah was made drunk as related in Gn. 9. In another way drunkenness may result from inordinate concupiscence and use of wine: in this way it is accounted a sin, and is comprised under gluttony as a species under its genus. For gluttony is divided into "surfeiting [Douay:,'rioting'] and drunkenness," which are forbidden by the Apostle (Rom. 13:13).

Reply to Objection 1: As the Philosopher says (Ethic. iii, 11), insensibility which is opposed to temperance "is not very common," so that like its species which are opposed to the species of intemperance it has no name. Hence the vice opposed to drunkenness is unnamed; and yet if a man were knowingly to abstain from wine to the extent of molesting nature grievously, he would not be free from sin.

Reply to Objection 2: This objection regards the resulting defect which is involuntary: whereas immoderate use of wine is voluntary, and it is in this that the sin consists.

Reply to Objection 3: Even as he that is drunk is excused if he knows not the strength of the wine, so too is he that invites another to drink excused from sin, if he be unaware that the drinker is the kind of person to be made drunk by the drink offered. But if ignorance be lacking neither is excused from sin.

Reply to Objection 4: Sometimes the correction of a sinner is to be foregone, as stated above ([3505]Q[33], A[6]). Hence Augustine says in a letter (Ad Aurel. Episc. Ep. xxii), "Meseems, such things are cured not by bitterness, severity, harshness, but by teaching rather than commanding, by advice rather than threats. Such is the course to be followed with the majority of sinners: few are they whose sins should be treated with severity."

Whether drunkenness is a mortal sin?

Objection 1: It would seem that drunkenness is not a mortal sin. For Augustine says in a sermon on Purgatory [*Serm. civ in the Appendix to St. Augustine's works] that "drunkenness if indulged in assiduously, is a mortal sin." Now assiduity denotes a circumstance which does not change the species of a sin; so that it cannot aggravate a sin infinitely, and make a mortal sin of a venial sin, as shown above ([3506]FS, Q[88], A[5]). Therefore if drunkenness /is not a mortal sin for some other reason, neither is it for this.

Objection 2: Further, Augustine says [*Serm. civ in the Appendix to St. Augustine's works]: "Whenever a man takes more meat and drink than is necessary, he should know that this is one of the lesser sins." Now the lesser sins are called venial. Therefore drunkenness, which is caused by immoderate drink, is a venial sin.

Objection 3: Further, no mortal sin should be committed on the score of medicine. Now some drink too much at the advice of the physician, that they may be purged by vomiting; and from this excessive drink drunkenness ensues. Therefore drunkenness is not a mortal sin.

On the contrary, We read in the Canons of the apostles (Can. xli, xlii): "A bishop, priest or deacon who is given to drunkenness or gambling, or incites others thereto, must either cease or be deposed; a subdeacon, reader or precentor who does these things must either give them up or be excommunicated; the same applies to the laity." Now such punishments are not inflicted save for mortal sins. Therefore drunkenness is a mortal sin.

I answer that, The sin of drunkenness, as stated in the foregoing Article, consists in the immoderate use and concupiscence of wine. Now this may happen to a man in three ways. First, so that he knows not the drink to be immoderate and intoxicating: and then drunkenness may be without sin, as stated above [3507](A[1]). Secondly, so that he perceives the drink to be immoderate, but without knowing it to be intoxicating, and then drunkenness may involve a venial sin. Thirdly, it may happen that a man is well aware that the drink is immoderate and intoxicating, and yet he would rather be drunk than abstain from drink. Such a man is a drunkard properly speaking, because morals take their species not from things that occur accidentally and beside the intention, but from that which is directly intended. In this way drunkenness is a mortal sin, because then a man willingly and knowingly deprives himself of the use of reason, whereby he performs virtuous deeds and avoids sin, and thus he sins mortally by running the risk of falling into sin. For Ambrose says (De Patriarch. [*De Abraham i.]): "We learn that we should shun drunkenness, which prevents us from avoiding grievous sins. For the things we avoid when sober, we unknowingly commit through drunkenness." Therefore drunkenness, properly speaking, is a mortal sin.

Reply to Objection 1: Assiduity makes drunkenness a mortal sin, not on account of the mere repetition of the act, but because it is impossible for a man to become drunk assiduously, without exposing himself to drunkenness knowingly and willingly, since he has many times experienced the strength of wine and his own liability to drunkenness.

Reply to Objection 2: To take more meat or drink than is necessary belongs to the vice of gluttony, which is not always a mortal sin: but knowingly to take too much drink to the point of being drunk, is a mortal sin. Hence Augustine says (Confess. x, 31): "Drunkenness is far from me: Thou wilt have mercy, that it come not near me. But full feeding sometimes hath crept upon Thy servant."

Reply to Objection 3: As stated above ([3508]Q[141], A[6]), meat and drink should be moderate in accordance with the demands of the body's health. Wherefore, just as it happens sometimes that the meat and drink which are moderate for a healthy man are immoderate for a sick man, so too it may happen conversely, that what is excessive for a healthy man is moderate for one that is ailing. In this way when a man eats or drinks much at the physician's advice in order to provoke vomiting, he is not to be deemed to have taken excessive meat or drink. There is, however, no need for intoxicating drink in order to procure vomiting, since this is caused by drinking lukewarm water: wherefore this is no sufficient cause for excusing a man from drunkenness.

Whether drunkenness is the gravest of sins?

Objection 1: It would seem that drunkenness is the gravest of sins. For Chrysostom says (Hom. lviii in Matth.) that "nothing gains the devil's favor so much as drunkenness and lust, the mother of all the vices." And it is written in the Decretals (Dist. xxxv, can. Ante omnia): "Drunkenness, more than anything else, is to be avoided by the clergy, for it foments and fosters all the vices."

Objection 2: Further, from the very fact that a thing excludes the good of reason, it is a sin. Now this is especially the effect of drunkenness. Therefore drunkenness is the greatest of sins.

Objection 3: Further, the gravity of a sin is shown by the gravity of its punishment. Now seemingly drunkenness is punished most severely; for Ambrose says [*De Elia et de Jejunio v] that "there would be no slavery, were there no drunkards." Therefore drunkenness is the greatest of sins.

On the contrary, According to Gregory (Moral. xxxiii, 12), spiritual vices are greater than carnal vices. Now drunkenness is one of the carnal vices. Therefore it is not the greatest of sins.

I answer that, A thing is said to be evil because it removes a good. Wherefore the greater the good removed by an evil, the graver the evil. Now it is evident that a Divine good is greater than a human good. Wherefore the sins that are directly against God are graver than the sin of drunkenness, which is directly opposed to the good of human reason.

Reply to Objection 1: Man is most prone to sins of intemperance, because such like concupiscences and pleasures are connatural to us, and for this reason these sins are said to find greatest favor with the devil, not for being graver than other sins, but because they occur more frequently among men.

Reply to Objection 2: The good of reason is hindered in two ways: in one way by that which is contrary to reason, in another by that which takes away the use of reason. Now that which is contrary to reason has more the character of an evil, than that which takes away the use of reason for a time, since the use of reason, which is taken away by drunkenness, may be either good or evil, whereas the goods of virtue, which are taken away by things that are contrary to reason, are always good.

Reply to Objection 3: Drunkenness was the occasional cause of slavery, in so far as Cham brought the curse of slavery on to his descendants, for having laughed at his father when the latter was made drunk. But slavery was not the direct punishment of drunkenness.

Whether drunkenness excuses from sin?

Objection 1: It would seem that drunkenness does not excuse from sin. For the Philosopher says (Ethic. iii, 5) that "the drunkard deserves double punishment." Therefore drunkenness aggravates a sin instead of excusing from it.

Objection 2: Further, one sin does not excuse another, but increases it. Now drunkenness is a sin. Therefore it is not an excuse for sin.

Objection 3: Further, the Philosopher says (Ethic. vii, 3) that just as man's reason is tied by drunkenness, so is it by concupiscence. But concupiscence is not an excuse for sin: neither therefore is drunkenness.

On the contrary, According to Augustine (Contra Faust. xxii, 43), Lot was to be excused from incest on account of drunkenness.

I answer that, Two things are to be observed in drunkenness, as stated above [3509](A[1]), namely the resulting defect and the preceding act. on the part of the resulting defect whereby the use of reason is fettered, drunkenness may be an excuse for sin, in so far as it causes an act to be involuntary through ignorance. But on the part of the preceding act, a distinction would seem necessary; because, if the drunkenness that results from that act be without sin, the subsequent sin is entirely excused from fault, as perhaps in the case of Lot. If, however, the preceding act was sinful, the person is not altogether excused from the subsequent sin, because the latter is rendered voluntary through the voluntariness of the preceding act, inasmuch as it was through doing something unlawful that he fell into the subsequent sin. Nevertheless, the resulting sin is diminished, even as the character of voluntariness is diminished. Wherefore Augustine says (Contra Faust. xxii, 44) that "Lot's guilt is to be measured, not by the incest, but by his drunkenness."

Reply to Objection 1: The Philosopher does not say that the drunkard deserves more severe punishment, but that he deserves double punishment for his twofold sin. Or we may reply that he is speaking in view of the law of a certain Pittacus, who, as stated in Polit. ii, 9, ordered "those guilty of assault while drunk to be more severely punished than if they had been sober, because they do wrong in more ways than one." In this, as Aristotle observes (Polit. ii, 9), "he seems to have considered the advantage," namely of the prevention of wrong, "rather than the leniency which one should have for drunkards," seeing that they are not in possession of their faculties.

Reply to Objection 2: Drunkenness may be an excuse for sin, not in the point of its being itself a sin, but in the point of the defect that results from it, as stated above.

Reply to Objection 3: Concupiscence does not altogether fetter the reason, as drunkenness does, unless perchance it be so vehement as to make a man insane. Yet the passion of concupiscence diminishes sin, because it is less grievous to sin through weakness than through malice.

OF CHASTITY (FOUR ARTICLES)

We must next consider chastity: (1) The virtue itself of chastity: (2) virginity, which is a part of chastity: (3) lust, which is the contrary vice. Under the first head there are four points of inquiry:

(1) Whether chastity is a virtue?
(2) Whether it is a general virtue?
(3) Whether it is a virtue distinct from abstinence?
(4) Of its relation to purity.

Whether chastity is a virtue?

Objection 1: It would seem that chastity is not a virtue. For here we are treating of virtues of the soul. But chastity, seemingly, belongs to the body: for a person is said to be chaste because he behaves in a certain way as regards the use of certain parts of the body. Therefore chastity is not a virtue.

Objection 2: Further, virtue is "a voluntary habit," as stated in Ethic. ii, 6. But chastity, apparently, is not voluntary, since it can be taken away by force from a woman to whom violence is done. Therefore it seems that chastity is not a virtue.

Objection 3: Further, there is no virtue in unbelievers. Yet some unbelievers are chaste. Therefore chastity is not a virtue.

Objection 4: Further, the fruits are distinct from the virtues. But chastity is reckoned among the fruits (Gal. 5:23). Therefore chastity is not a virtue.

On the contrary, Augustine says (De Decem Chord. [*Serm. ix de Tempore]): "Whereas thou shouldst excel thy wife in virtue, since chastity is a virtue, thou yieldest to the first onslaught of lust, while thou wishest thy wife to be victorious."

I answer that, Chastity takes its name from the fact that reason "chastises" concupiscence, which, like a child, needs curbing, as the Philosopher states (Ethic. iii, 12). Now the essence of human virtue consists in being something moderated by reason, as shown above ([3510]FS, Q[64], A[1]). Therefore it is evident that chastity is a virtue.

Reply to Objection 1: Chastity does indeed reside in the soul as its subject, though its matter is in the body. For it belongs to chastity that a man make moderate use of bodily members in accordance with the judgment of his reason and the choice of his will.

Reply to Objection 2: As Augustine says (De Civ. Dei i, 18), "so long as her mind holds to its purpose, whereby she has merited to be holy even in body, not even the violence of another's lust can deprive her body of its holiness, which is safeguarded by her persevering continency." He also says (De Civ. Dei i, 18) that "in the mind there is a virtue which is the companion of fortitude, whereby it is resolved to suffer any evil whatsoever rather than consent to evil."

Reply to Objection 3: As Augustine says (Contra Julian. iv, 3), "it is impossible to have any true virtue unless one be truly just; nor is it possible to be just unless one live by faith." Whence he argues that in unbelievers there is neither true chastity, nor any other virtue, because, to wit, they are not referred to the due end, and as he adds (Contra Julian. iv, 3) "virtues are distinguished from vices not by their functions," i.e. their acts, "but by their ends."

Reply to Objection 4: Chastity is a virtue in so far as it works in accordance with reason, but in so far as it delights in its act, it is reckoned among the fruits.

Whether chastity is a general virtue?

Objection 1: It would seem that chastity is a general virtue. For Augustine says (De Mendacio xx) that "chastity of the mind is the well-ordered movement of the mind that does not prefer the lesser to the greater things." But this belongs to every virtue. Therefore chastity is a general virtue.

Objection 2: Further, "Chastity" takes its name from "chastisement" [*Cf. A[1]]. Now every movement of the appetitive part should be chastised by reason. Since, then, every moral virtue curbs some movement of the appetite, it seems that every moral virtue is chastity.

Objection 3: Further, chastity is opposed to fornication. But fornication seems to belong to every kind of sin: for it is written (Ps. 72:27): "Thou shalt destroy [Vulg.: 'hast destroyed'] all them that go awhoring from [Douay: 'are disloyal to'] Thee." Therefore chastity is a general virtue.

On the contrary, Macrobius [*In Somn. Scip. i, 8] reckons it to be a part of temperance.

I answer that, The word "chastity" is employed in two ways. First, properly; and thus it is a special virtue having a special matter, namely the concupiscences relating to venereal pleasures. Secondly, the word "chastity" is employed metaphorically: for just as a mingling of bodies conduces to venereal pleasure which is the proper matter of chastity and of lust its contrary vice, so too the spiritual union of the mind with certain things conduces to a pleasure which is the matter of a spiritual chastity metaphorically speaking, as well as of a spiritual fornication likewise metaphorically so called. For if the human mind delight in the spiritual union with that to which it behooves it to be united, namely God, and refrains from delighting in union with other things against the requirements of the order established by God, this may be called a spiritual chastity, according to 2 Cor. 11:2, "I have espoused you to one husband, that I may present you as a chaste virgin to Christ." If, on the other hand, the mind be united to any other things whatsoever, against the prescription of the Divine order, it will be called spiritual fornication, according to Jer. 3:1, "But thou hast prostituted thyself to many lovers." Taking chastity in this sense, it is a general virtue, because every virtue withdraws the human mind from delighting in a union with unlawful things. Nevertheless, the essence of this chastity consists principally in charity and the other theological virtues, whereby the human mind is united to God.

Reply to Objection 1: This argument takes chastity in the metaphorical sense.

Reply to Objection 2: As stated above [3511](A[1]; Q[142], A[2]), the concupiscence of that which gives pleasure is especially likened to a child, because the desire of pleasure is connatural to us, especially of pleasures of touch which are directed to the maintenance of nature. Hence it is that if the concupiscence of such pleasures be fostered by consenting to it, it will wax very strong, as in the case of a child left to his own will. Wherefore the concupiscence of these pleasures stands in very great need of being chastised: and consequently chastity is applied antonomastically to such like concupiscences, even as fortitude is about those matters wherein we stand in the greatest need of strength of mind.

Reply to Objection 3: This argument considers spiritual fornication metaphorically so called, which is opposed to spiritual chastity, as stated.

Whether chastity is a distinct virtue from abstinence?

Objection 1: It would seem that chastity is not a distinct virtue from abstinence. Because where the matter is generically the same, one virtue suffices. Now it would seem that things pertaining to the same sense are of one genus. Therefore, since pleasures of the palate which are the matter of abstinence, and venereal pleasures which are the matter of chastity, pertain to the touch, it seems that chastity is not a distinct virtue from abstinence.

Objection 2: Further, the Philosopher (Ethic. iii, 12) likens all vices of intemperance to childish sins, which need chastising. Now "chastity" takes its name from "chastisement" of the contrary vices. Since then certain vices are bridled by abstinence, it seems that abstinence is chastity.

Objection 3: Further, the pleasures of the other senses are the concern of temperance in so far as they refer to pleasures of touch; which are the matter of temperance. Now pleasures of the palate, which are the matter of abstinence, are directed to venereal pleasures, which are the matter of chastity: wherefore Jerome says [*Ep. cxlvii ad Amand. Cf. Gratian, Dist. xliv.], commenting on Titus 1:7, "Not given to wine, no striker," etc.: "The belly and the organs of generation are neighbors, that the neighborhood of the organs may indicate their complicity in vice." Therefore abstinence and chastity are not distinct virtues.

On the contrary, The Apostle (2 Cor. 6:5,6) reckons "chastity" together with "fastings" which pertain to abstinence.

I answer that, As stated above ([3512]Q[141], A[4]), temperance is properly about the concupiscences of the pleasures of touch: so that where there are different kinds of pleasure, there are different virtues comprised under temperance. Now pleasures are proportionate to the actions whose perfections they are, as stated in Ethic. ix, 4,5: and it is evident that actions connected with the use of food whereby the nature of the individual is maintained differ generically from actions connected with the use of matters venereal, whereby the nature of the species is preserved. Therefore chastity, which is about venereal pleasures, is a distinct virtue from abstinence, which is about pleasures of the palate.

Reply to Objection 1: Temperance is chiefly about pleasures of touch, not as regards the sense's judgment concerning the objects of touch. which judgment is of uniform character concerning all such objects, but as regards the use itself of those objects, as stated in Ethic. iii, 10. Now the uses of meats, drinks, and venereal matters differ in character. Wherefore there must needs be different virtues, though they regard the one sense.

Reply to Objection 2: Venereal pleasures are more impetuous, and are more oppressive on the reason than the pleasures of the palate: and therefore they are in greater need of chastisement and restraint, since if one consent to them this increases the force of concupiscence and weakens the strength of the mind. Hence Augustine says (Soliloq. i, 10): "I consider that nothing so casts down the manly mind from its heights as the fondling of women, and those bodily contacts which belong to the married state."

Reply to Objection 3: The pleasures of the other senses do not pertain to the maintenance of man's nature, except in so far as they are directed to pleasures of touch. Wherefore in the matter of such pleasures there is no other virtue comprised under temperance. But the pleasures of the palate, though directed somewhat to venereal pleasures, are essentially directed to the preservation of man's life: wherefore by their very nature they have a special virtue, although this virtue which is called abstinence directs its act to chastity as its end.

Whether purity belongs especially to chastity?

Objection 1: It would seem that purity does not belong especially to chastity. For Augustine says (De Civ. Dei i, 18) that "purity is a virtue of the soul." Therefore it is not something belonging to chastity, but is of itself a virtue distinct from chastity.

Objection 2: Further, "pudicitia" [purity] is derived from "pudor," which is equivalent to shame. Now shame, according to Damascene [*De Fide Orth. ii, 15], is about a disgraceful act, and this is common to all sinful acts. Therefore purity belongs no more to chastity than to the other virtues.

Objection 3: Further, the Philosopher says (Ethic. iii, 12) that "every kind of intemperance is most deserving of reproach." Now it would seem to belong to purity to avoid all that is deserving of reproach. Therefore purity belongs to all the parts of temperance, and not especially to chastity.

On the contrary, Augustine says (De Perseverantia xx): "We must give praise to purity, that he who has ears to hear, may put to none but a lawful use the organs intended for procreation." Now the use of these organs is the proper matter of chastity. Therefore purity belongs properly to chastity.

I answer that, As stated above (OBJ[2]), "pudicitia" [purity] takes its name from "pudor," which signifies shame. Hence purity must needs be properly about the things of which man is most ashamed. Now men are most ashamed of venereal acts, as Augustine remarks (De Civ. Dei xiv, 18), so much so that even the conjugal act, which is adorned by the honesty [*Cf. Q[145]] of marriage, is not devoid of shame: and this because the movement of the organs of generation is not subject to the command of reason, as are the movements of the other external members. Now man is ashamed not only of this sexual union but also of all the signs thereof, as the Philosopher observes (Rhet. ii, 6). Consequently purity regards venereal matters properly, and especially the signs thereof, such as impure looks, kisses, and touches. And since the latter are more wont to be observed, purity regards rather these external signs, while chastity regards rather sexual union. Therefore purity is directed to chastity, not as a virtue distinct therefrom, but as expressing a circumstance of chastity. Nevertheless the one is sometimes used to designate the other.

Reply to Objection 1: Augustine is here speaking of purity as designating chastity.

Reply to Objection 2: Although every vice has a certain disgrace, the vices of intemperance are especially disgraceful, as stated above ([3513]Q[142], A[4]).

Reply to Objection 3: Among the vices of intemperance, venereal sins are most deserving of reproach, both on account of the insubordination of the genital organs, and because by these sins especially, the reason is absorbed.

Day 227

OF VIRGINITY (FIVE ARTICLES)
We must now consider virginity: and under this head there are five points of inquiry:
(1) In what does virginity consist?
(2) Whether it is lawful?
(3) Whether it is a virtue?
(4) Of its excellence in comparison with marriage;
(5) Of its excellence in comparison with the other virtues.

Whether virginity consists in integrity of the flesh?

Objection 1: It would seem that virginity does not consist in integrity of the flesh. For Augustine says (De Nup. et Concup.) [*The quotation is from De Sancta Virgin. xiii] that "virginity is the continual meditation on incorruption in a corruptible flesh." But meditation does not concern the flesh. Therefore virginity is not situated in the flesh.

Objection 2: Further, virginity denotes a kind of purity. Now Augustine says (De Civ. Dei i, 18) that "purity dwells in the soul." Therefore virginity is not incorruption of the flesh.

Objection 3: Further, the integrity of the flesh would seem to consist in the seal of virginal purity. Yet sometimes the seal is broken without loss of virginity. For Augustine says (De Civ. Dei i, 18) that "those organs may be injured through being wounded by mischance. Physicians, too, sometimes do for the sake of health that which makes one shudder to see: and a midwife has been known to destroy by touch the proof of virginity that she sought." And he adds: "Nobody, I think, would be so foolish as to deem this maiden to have forfeited even bodily sanctity, though she lost the integrity of that organ." Therefore virginity does not consist in incorruption of the flesh.

Objection 4: Further, corruption of the flesh consists chiefly in resolution of the semen: and this may take place without copulation, whether one be asleep or awake. Yet seemingly virginity is not lost without copulation: for Augustine says (De Virgin. xiii) that "virginal integrity and holy continency that refrains from all sexual intercourse is the portion of angels." Therefore virginity does not consist in incorruption of the flesh.

On the contrary, Augustine says (De Virgin. viii) that "virginity is continence whereby integrity of the flesh is vowed, consecrated and observed in honor of the Creator of both soul and flesh."

I answer that, Virginity takes its name apparently from "viror" [freshness], and just as a thing is described as fresh and retaining its freshness, so long as it is not parched by excessive heat, so too, virginity denotes that the person possessed thereof is unseared by the heat of concupiscence which is experienced in achieving the greatest bodily pleasure which is that of sexual intercourse. Hence, Ambrose says (De Virgin. i, 5) that "virginal chastity is integrity free of pollution."

Now venereal pleasures offer three points for consideration. The first is on the part of the body, viz. the violation of the seal of virginity. The second is the link between that which concerns the soul and that which concerns the body, and this is the resolution of the semen, causing sensible pleasure. The third is entirely on the part of the soul, namely the purpose of attaining this pleasure. Of these three the first is accidental to the moral act, which as such must be considered in reference to the soul. The second stands in the relation of matter to the moral act, since the sensible passions are the matters of moral acts. But the third stands in the position of form and complement, because the essence of morality is perfected in that which concerns the reason. Since then virginity consists in freedom from the aforesaid corruption, it follows that the integrity of the bodily organ is accidental to virginity; while freedom from pleasure in resolution of the semen is related thereto materially; and the purpose of perpetually abstaining from this pleasure is the formal and completive element in virginity.

Reply to Objection 1: This definition of Augustine's expresses directly that which is formal in virginity. For "meditation" denotes reason's purpose; and the addition "perpetual" does not imply that a virgin must always retain this meditation actually, but that she should bear in mind the purpose of always persevering therein. The material element is expressed indirectly by the words "on incorruption in a corruptible body." This is added to show the difficulty of virginity: for if the flesh were incorruptible, it would not be difficult to maintain a perpetual meditation on incorruption.

Reply to Objection 2: It is true that purity, as to its essence, is in the soul; but as to its matter, it is in the body: and it is the same with virginity. Wherefore Augustine says (De Virgin. viii) that "although virginity resides in the flesh," and for this reason is a bodily quality, "yet it is a spiritual thing, which a holy continency fosters and preserves."

Reply to Objection 3: As stated above, the integrity of a bodily organ is accidental to virginity, in so far as a person, through purposely abstaining from venereal pleasure, retains the integrity of a bodily organ. Hence if the organ lose its integrity by chance in some other way, this is no more prejudicial to virginity than being deprived of a hand or foot.

Reply to Objection 4: Pleasure resulting from resolution of semen may arise in two ways. If this be the result of the mind's purpose, it destroys virginity, whether copulation takes place or not. Augustine, however, mentions copulation, because such like resolution is the ordinary and natural result thereof. In another way this may happen beside the purpose of the mind, either during sleep, or through violence and without the mind's consent, although the flesh derives pleasure from it, or again through weakness of nature, as in the case of those who are subject to a flow of semen. In such cases virginity is not forfeit, because such like pollution is not the result of impurity which excludes virginity.

Whether virginity is unlawful?

Objection 1: It would seem that virginity is unlawful. For whatever is contrary to a precept of the natural law is unlawful. Now just as the words of Gn. 2:16, "Of every tree" that is in "paradise, thou shalt eat," indicate a precept of the natural law, in reference to the preservation of the individual, so also the words of Gn. 1:28, "Increase and multiply, and fill the earth," express a precept of the natural law, in reference to the preservation of the species. Therefore just as it would be a sin to abstain from all food, as this would be to act counter to the good of the individual, so too it is a sin to abstain altogether from the act of procreation, for this is to act against the good of the species.

Objection 2: Further, whatever declines from the mean of virtue is apparently sinful. Now virginity declines from the mean of virtue, since it abstains from all venereal pleasures: for the Philosopher says (Ethic. ii, 2), that "he who revels in every pleasure, and abstains from not even one, is intemperate: but he who refrains from all is loutish and insensible." Therefore virginity is something sinful.

Objection 3: Further, punishment is not due save for a vice. Now in olden times those were punished who led a celibate life, as Valerius Maximus asserts [*Dict. Fact. Mem. ii, 9]. Hence according to Augustine (De Vera Relig. iii) Plato "is said to have sacrificed to nature, in order that he might atone for his perpetual continency as though it were a sin." Therefore virginity is a sin.

On the contrary, No sin is a matter of direct counsel. But virginity is a matter of direct counsel: for it is written (1 Cor. 7:25): "Concerning virgins I have no commandment of the Lord: but I give counsel." Therefore virginity is not an unlawful thing.

I answer that, In human acts, those are sinful which are against right reason. Now right reason requires that things directed to an end should be used in a measure proportionate to that end. Again, man's good is threefold as stated in Ethic. i, 8; one consisting in external things, for instance riches; another, consisting in bodily goods; the third, consisting in the goods of the soul among which the goods of the contemplative life take precedence of the goods of the active life, as the Philosopher shows (Ethic. x, 7), and as our Lord declared (Lk. 10:42), "Mary hath chosen the better part." Of these goods those that are external are directed to those which belong to the body, and those which belong to the body are directed to those which belong to the soul; and furthermore those which belong to the active life are directed to those which belong to the life of contemplation. Accordingly, right reason dictates that one use external goods in a measure proportionate to the body, and in like manner as regards the rest. Wherefore if a man refrain from possessing certain things (which otherwise it were good for him to possess), for the sake of his body's good, or of the contemplation of truth, this is not sinful, but in accord /with right reason. In like manner if a man abstain from bodily pleasures, in order more freely to give himself to the contemplation of truth, this is in accordance with the rectitude of reason. Now holy virginity refrains from all venereal pleasure in order more freely to have leisure for Divine contemplation: for the Apostle says (1 Cor. 7:34): "The unmarried woman and the virgin thinketh on the things of the Lord: that she may be holy in both body and in spirit. But she that is married thinketh on the things of the world, how she may please her husband." Therefore it follows that virginity instead of being sinful is worthy of praise.

Reply to Objection 1: A precept implies a duty, as stated above ([3514]Q[122], A[1]). Now there are two kinds of duty. There is the duty that has to be fulfilled by one person; and a duty of this kind cannot be set aside without sin. The other duty has to be fulfilled by the multitude, and the fulfilment of this kind of duty is not binding on each one of the multitude. For the multitude has many obligations which cannot be discharged by the individual; but are fulfilled by one person doing this, and another doing that. Accordingly the precept of natural law which binds man to eat must needs be fulfilled by each individual, otherwise the individual cannot be sustained. On the other hand, the precept of procreation regards the whole multitude of men, which needs not only to multiply in body, but also to advance spiritually. Wherefore sufficient provision is made for the human multitude, if some betake themselves to carnal procreation, while others abstaining from this betake themselves to the contemplation of Divine things, for the beauty and welfare of the whole human race. Thus too in an army, some take sentry duty, others are standard-bearers, and others fight with the sword: yet all these things are necessary for the multitude, although they cannot be done by one person.

Reply to Objection 2: The person who, beside the dictate of right reason, abstains from all pleasures through aversion, as it were, for pleasure as such, is insensible as a country lout. But a virgin does not refrain from every pleasure, but only from that which is venereal: and abstains therefrom according to right reason, as stated above. Now the mean of virtue is fixed with reference, not to quantity but to right reason, as stated in Ethic. ii, 6: wherefore it is said of the magnanimous (Ethic. iv, 3) that "in point of quantity he goes to the extreme, but in point of becomingness he follows the mean."

Reply to Objection 3: Laws are framed according to what occurs more frequently. Now it seldom happened in olden times that anyone refrained from all venereal pleasure through love of the contemplation of truth: as Plato alone is related to have done. Hence it was not through thinking this a sin, that he offered sacrifice, but "because he yielded to the false opinion of his fellow countrymen," as Augustine remarks (De Vera Relig. iii).

Whether virginity is a virtue?

Objection 1: It would seem that virginity is not a virtue. For "no virtue is in us by nature," as the Philosopher says (Ethic. ii, 1). Now virginity is in us by nature, since all are virgins when born. Therefore virginity is not a virtue.

Objection 2: Further, whoever has one virtue has all virtues, as stated above ([3515]FS, Q[65], A[1]). Yet some have other virtues without having virginity: else, since none can go to the heavenly kingdom without virtue, no one could go there without virginity, which would involve the condemnation of marriage. Therefore virginity is not a virtue.

Objection 3: Further, every virtue is recovered by penance. But virginity is not recovered by penance: wherefore Jerome says [*Ep. xxii ad Eustoch.]: "Other things God can do, but He cannot restore the virgin after her downfall." Therefore seemingly virginity is not a virtue.

Objection 4: Further, no virtue is lost without sin. Yet virginity is lost without sin, namely by marriage. Therefore virginity is not a virtue.

Objection 5: Further, virginity is condivided with widowhood and conjugal purity. But neither of these is a virtue. Therefore virginity is not a virtue.

On the contrary, Ambrose says (De Virgin. i, 3): "Love of virginity moves us to say something about virginity, lest by passing it over we should seem to cast a slight on what is a virtue of high degree."

I answer that, As stated above [3516](A[1]), the formal and completive element in virginity is the purpose of abstaining from venereal pleasure, which purpose is rendered praiseworthy by its end, in so far, to wit, as this is done in order to have leisure for Divine things: while the material element in virginity is integrity of the flesh free of all experience of venereal pleasure. Now it is manifest that where a good action has a special matter through having a special excellence, there is a special kind of virtue: for example, magnificence which is about great expenditure is for this reason a special virtue distinct from liberality, which is about all uses of money in general. Now to keep oneself free from the experience of venereal pleasure has an excellence of its own deserving of greater praise than keeping oneself free from inordinate venereal pleasure. Wherefore virginity is a special virtue being related to chastity as magnificence to liberality.

Reply to Objection 1: Men have from their birth that which is material in virginity, namely integrity of the flesh and freedom from venereal experience. But they have not that which is formal in virginity, namely the purpose of safeguarding this integrity for God's sake, which purpose gives virginity its character of virtue. Hence Augustine says (De Virgin. xi): "Nor do we praise virgins for being virgins, but, because their virginity is consecrated to God by holy continency."

Reply to Objection 2: Virtues are connected together by reason of that which is formal in them, namely charity, or by reason of prudence, as stated above ([3517]Q[129], A[3], ad 2), but not by reason of that which is material in them. For nothing hinders a virtuous man from providing the matter of one virtue, and not the matter of another virtue: thus a poor man has the matter of temperance, but not that of magnificence. It is in this way that one who has the other virtues lacks the matter of virginity, namely the aforesaid integrity of the flesh: nevertheless he can have that which is formal in virginity, his mind being so prepared that he has the purpose of safeguarding this same integrity of the flesh, should it be fitting for him to do so: even as a poor man may be so prepared in mind as to have the purpose of being magnificent in his expenditure, were he in a position to do so: or again as a prosperous man is so prepared in mind as to purpose bearing misfortune with equanimity: without which preparedness of the mind no man can be virtuous.

Reply to Objection 3: Virtue can be recovered by penance as regards that which is formal in virtue, but not as to that which is material therein. For if a magnificent man has squandered all his wealth he does not recover his riches by repenting of his sin. In like manner a person who has lost virginity by sin, recovers by repenting, not the matter of virginity but the purpose of virginity.

As regards the matter of virginity there is that which can be miraculously restored by God, namely the integrity of the organ, which we hold to be accidental to virginity: while there is something else which cannot be restored even by miracle, to wit, that one who has experienced venereal lust should cease to have had that experience. For God cannot make that which is done not to have been done, as stated in the [3518]FP, Q[25] , A[4].

Reply to Objection 4: Virginity as a virtue denotes the purpose, confirmed by vow, of observing perpetual integrity. For Augustine says (De Virgin. viii) that "by virginity, integrity of the flesh is vowed, consecrated and observed in honor of the Creator of both soul and flesh." Hence virginity, as a virtue, is never lost without sin.

Reply to Objection 5: Conjugal chastity is deserving of praise merely because it abstains from unlawful pleasures: hence no excellence attaches to it above that of chastity in general. Widowhood, however, adds something to chastity in general; but it does not attain to that which is perfect in this matter, namely to entire freedom from venereal pleasure; virginity alone achieves this. Wherefore virginity alone is accounted a virtue above chastity, even as magnificence is reckoned above liberality.

Whether virginity is more excellent than marriage?

Objection 1: It would seem that virginity is not more excellent than marriage. For Augustine says (De Bono Conjug. xxi): "Continence was equally meritorious in John who remained unmarried and Abraham who begot children." Now a greater virtue has greater merit. Therefore virginity is not a greater virtue than conjugal chastity.

Objection 2: Further, the praise accorded a virtuous man depends on his virtue. If, then, virginity were preferable to conjugal continence, it would seem to follow that every virgin is to be praised more than any married woman. But this is untrue. Therefore virginity is not preferable to marriage.

Objection 3: Further, the common good takes precedence of the private good, according to the Philosopher (Ethic. i, 2). Now marriage is directed to the common good: for Augustine says (De Bono Conjug. xvi): "What food is to a man's wellbeing, such is sexual intercourse to the welfare of the human race." On the other hand, virginity is ordered to the individual good, namely in order to avoid what the Apostle calls the "tribulation of the flesh," to which married people are subject (1 Cor. 7:28). Therefore virginity is not greater than conjugal continence.

On the contrary, Augustine says (De Virgin. xix): "Both solid reason and the authority of Holy Writ show that neither is marriage sinful, nor is it to be equaled to the good of virginal continence or even to that of widowhood."

I answer that, According to Jerome (Contra Jovin. i) the error of Jovinian consisted in holding virginity not to be preferable to marriage. This error is refuted above all by the example of Christ Who both chose a virgin for His mother, and remained Himself a virgin, and by the teaching of the Apostle who (1 Cor. 7) counsels virginity as the greater good. It is also refuted by reason, both because a Divine good takes precedence of a human good, and because the good of the soul is preferable to the good of the body, and again because the good of the contemplative life is better than that of the active life. Now virginity is directed to the good of the soul in respect of the contemplative life, which consists in thinking "on the things of God" [Vulg.: 'the Lord'], whereas marriage is directed to the good of the body, namely the bodily increase of the human race, and belongs to the active life, since the man and woman who embrace the married life have to think "on the things of the world," as the Apostle says (1 Cor. 7:34). Without doubt therefore virginity is preferable to conjugal continence.

Reply to Objection 1: Merit is measured not only by the kind of action, but still more by the mind of the agent. Now Abraham had a mind so disposed, that he was prepared to observe virginity, if it were in keeping with the times for him to do so. Wherefore in him conjugal continence was equally meritorious with the virginal continence of John, as regards the essential reward, but not as regards the accidental reward. Hence Augustine says (De Bono Conjug. xxi) that both "the celibacy of John and the marriage of Abraham fought Christ's battle in keeping with the difference of the times: but John was continent even in deed, whereas Abraham was continent only in habit."

Reply to Objection 2: Though virginity is better than conjugal continence, a married person may be better than a virgin for two reasons. First, on the part of chastity itself; if to wit, the married person is more prepared in mind to observe virginity, if it should be expedient, than the one who is actually a virgin. Hence Augustine (De Bono Conjug. xxii) charges the virgin to say: "I am no better than Abraham, although the chastity of celibacy is better than the chastity of marriage." Further on he gives the reason for this: "For what I do now, he would have done better, if it were fitting for him to do it then; and what they did I would even do now if it behooved me now to do it." Secondly, because perhaps the person who is not a virgin has some more excellent virtue. Wherefore Augustine says (De Virgin. xliv): "Whence does a virgin know the things that belong to the Lord, however solicitous she be about them, if perchance on account of some mental fault she be not yet ripe for martyrdom, whereas this woman to whom she delighted in preferring herself is already able to drink the chalice of the Lord?"

Reply to Objection 3: The common good takes precedence of the private good, if it be of the same genus: but it may be that the private good is better generically. It is thus that the virginity that is consecrated to God is preferable to carnal fruitfulness. Hence Augustine says (De Virgin. ix): "It must be confessed that the fruitfulness of the flesh, even of those women who in these times seek naught else from marriage but children in order to make them servants of Christ, cannot compensate for lost virginity."

Whether virginity is the greatest of virtues?

Objection 1: It would seem that virginity is the greatest of virtues. For Cyprian says (De Virgin. [*De Habitu Virg.]): "We address ourselves now to the virgins. Sublime is their glory, but no less exalted is their vocation. They are a flower of the Church's sowing, the pride and ornament of spiritual grace, the most honored portion of Christ's flock."

Objection 2: Further, a greater reward is due to the greater virtue. Now the greatest reward is due to virginity, namely the hundredfold fruit, according to a gloss on Mat. 13:23. Therefore virginity is the greatest of the virtues.

Objection 3: Further, the more a virtue conforms us to Christ, the greater it is. Now virginity above all conforms us to Christ; for it is declared in the Apocalypse 14:4 that virgins "follow the Lamb whithersoever He goeth," and (Apoc. 14:3) that they sing "a new canticle," which "no" other "man" could say. Therefore virginity is the greatest of the virtues.

On the contrary, Augustine says (De Virgin. xlvi): "No one, methinks, would dare prefer virginity to martyrdom," and (De Virgin. xlv): "The authority of the Church informs the faithful in no uncertain manner, so that they know in what place the martyrs and the holy virgins who have departed this life are commemorated in the Sacrament of the Altar." By this we are given to understand that martyrdom, and also the monastic state, are preferable to virginity.

I answer that, A thing may excel all others in two ways. First, in some particular genus: and thus virginity is most excellent, namely in the genus of chastity, since it surpasses the chastity both of widowhood and of marriage. And because comeliness is ascribed to chastity antonomastically, it follows that surpassing beauty is ascribed to chastity. Wherefore Ambrose says (De Virgin. i, 7): "Can anyone esteem any beauty greater than a virgin's, since she is beloved of her King, approved by her Judge, dedicated to her Lord, consecrated to her God?" Secondly, a thing may be most excellent simply, and in this way virginity is not the most excellent of the virtues. Because the end always excels that which is directed to the end; and the more effectively a thing is directed to the end, the better it is. Now the end which renders virginity praiseworthy is that one may have leisure for Divine things, as stated above [3519] (A[4]). Wherefore the theological virtues as well as the virtue of religion, the acts of which consist in being occupied about Divine things, are preferable to virginity. Moreover, martyrs work more mightily in order to cleave to God---since for this end they hold their own life in contempt; and those who dwell in monasteries---since for this end they give up their own will and all that they may possess---than virgins who renounce venereal pleasure for that same purpose. Therefore virginity is not simply the greatest of virtues.

Reply to Objection 1: Virgins are "the more honored portion of Christ's flock," and "their glory more sublime" in comparison with widows and married women.

Reply to Objection 2: The hundredfold fruit is ascribed to virginity, according to Jerome [*Ep. cxxiii ad Ageruch.], on account of its superiority to widowhood, to which the sixtyfold fruit is ascribed, and to marriage, to which is ascribed the thirtyfold fruit. But according to Augustine (De QQ. Evang. i, 9), "the hundredfold fruit is given to martyrs, the sixtyfold to virgins, and the thirtyfold to married persons." Wherefore it does not follow that virginity is simply the greatest of virtues, but only in comparison with other degrees of chastity.

Reply to Objection 3: Virgins "follow the Lamb whithersoever He goeth," because they imitate Christ, by integrity not only of the mind but also of the flesh, as Augustine says (De Virgin. xxvii). Wherefore they follow the Lamb in more ways, but this does not imply that they follow more closely, because other virtues make us cleave to God more closely by imitation of the mind. The "new hymn" which virgins alone sing, is their joy at having preserved integrity of the flesh.

OF LUST (FIVE ARTICLES)

We must next consider the vice of lust which is opposed to chastity: (1) Lust in general; (2) its species. Under the first head there are five points of inquiry:

(1) What is the matter of lust?
(2) Whether all copulation is unlawful?
(3) Whether lust is a mortal sin?
(4) Whether lust is a capital vice?
(5) Concerning its daughters.

Whether the matter of lust is only venereal desires and pleasures?

Objection 1: It would seem that the matter of lust is not only venereal desires and pleasures. For Augustine says (Confess. ii, 6) that "lust affects to be called surfeit and abundance." But surfeit regards meat and drink, while abundance refers to riches. Therefore lust is not properly about venereal desires and pleasures.

Objection 2: Further, it is written (Prov. 20:1): "Wine is a lustful [Douay: 'luxurious'] thing." Now wine is connected with pleasure of meat and drink. Therefore these would seem to be the matter of lust.

Objection 3: Further, lust is defined "as the desire of wanton pleasure" [*Alexander of Hales, Summ. Theol. ii, cxvlii]. But wanton pleasure regards not only venereal matters but also many others. Therefore lust is not only about venereal desires and pleasures.

On the contrary, To the lustful it is said (De Vera Relig. iii [*Written by St. Augustine]): "He that soweth in the flesh, of the flesh shall reap corruption." Now the sowing of the flesh refers to venereal pleasures. Therefore these belong to lust.

I answer that, As Isidore says (Etym. x), "a lustful man is one who is debauched with pleasures." Now venereal pleasures above all debauch a man's mind. Therefore lust is especially concerned with such like pleasures.

Reply to Objection 1: Even as temperance chiefly and properly applies to pleasures of touch, yet consequently and by a kind of likeness is referred to other matters, so too, lust applies chiefly to venereal pleasures, which more than anything else work the greatest havoc in a man's mind, yet secondarily it applies to any other matters pertaining to excess. Hence a gloss on Gal. 5:19 says "lust is any kind of surfeit."

Reply to Objection 2: Wine is said to be a lustful thing, either in the sense in which surfeit in any matter is ascribed to lust, or because the use of too much wine affords an incentive to venereal pleasure.

Reply to Objection 3: Although wanton pleasure applies to other matters, the name of lust has a special application to venereal pleasures, to which also wantonness is specially applicable, as Augustine remarks (De Civ. xiv, 15,16).

Whether no venereal act can be without sin?

Objection 1: It would seem that no venereal act can be without sin. For nothing but sin would seem to hinder virtue. Now every venereal act is a great hindrance to virtue. For Augustine says (Soliloq. i, 10): "I consider that nothing so casts down the manly mind from its height as the fondling of a woman, and those bodily contacts." Therefore, seemingly, no venereal act is without sin.

Objection 2: Further, any excess that makes one forsake the good of reason is sinful, because virtue is corrupted by "excess" and "deficiency" as stated in Ethic. ii, 2. Now in every venereal act there is excess of pleasure, since it so absorbs the mind, that "it is incompatible with the act of understanding," as the Philosopher observes (Ethic. vii, 11); and as Jerome [*Origen, Hom. vi in Num.; Cf. Jerome, Ep. cxxiii ad Ageruch.] states, rendered the hearts of the prophets, for the moment, insensible to the spirit of prophecy. Therefore no venereal act can be without sin.

Objection 3: Further, the cause is more powerful than its effect. Now original sin is transmitted to children by concupiscence, without which no venereal act is possible, as Augustine declares (De Nup. et Concup. i, 24). Therefore no venereal act can be without sin.

On the contrary, Augustine says (De Bono Conjug. xxv): "This is a sufficient answer to heretics, if only they will understand that no sin is committed in that which is against neither nature, nor morals, nor a commandment": and he refers to the act of sexual intercourse between the patriarchs of old and their several wives. Therefore not every venereal act is a sin.

I answer that, A sin, in human acts, is that which is against the order of reason. Now the order of reason consists in its ordering everything to its end in a fitting manner. Wherefore it is no sin if one, by the dictate of reason, makes use of certain things in a fitting manner and order for the end to which they are adapted, provided this end be something truly good. Now just as the preservation of the bodily nature of one individual is a true good, so, too, is the preservation of the nature of the human species a very great good. And just as the use of food is directed to the preservation of life in the individual, so is the use of venereal acts directed to the preservation of the whole human race. Hence Augustine says (De Bono Conjug. xvi): "What food is to a man's well being, such is sexual intercourse to the welfare of the whole human race." Wherefore just as the use of food can be without sin, if it be taken in due manner and order, as required for the welfare of the body, so also the use of venereal acts can be without sin, provided they be performed in due manner and order, in keeping with the end of human procreation.

Reply to Objection 1: A thing may be a hindrance to virtue in two ways. First, as regards the ordinary degree of virtue, and as to this nothing but sin is an obstacle to virtue. Secondly, as regards the perfect degree of virtue, and as to this virtue may be hindered by that which is not a sin, but a lesser good. In this way sexual intercourse casts down the mind not from virtue, but from the height, i.e. the perfection of virtue. Hence Augustine says (De Bono Conjug. viii): "Just as that was good which Martha did when busy about serving holy men, yet better still that which Mary did in hearing the word of God: so, too, we praise the good of Susanna's conjugal chastity, yet we prefer the good of the widow Anna, and much more that of the Virgin Mary."

Reply to Objection 2: As stated above (Q[152], A[2], ad 2; [3520]FS, Q[64], A[2]), the mean of virtue depends not on quantity but on conformity with right reason: and consequently the exceeding pleasure attaching to a venereal act directed according to reason, is not opposed to the mean of virtue. Moreover, virtue is not concerned with the amount of pleasure experienced by the external sense, as this depends on the disposition of the body; what matters is how much the interior appetite is affected by that pleasure. Nor does it follow that the act in question is contrary to virtue, from the fact that the free act of reason in considering spiritual things is incompatible with the aforesaid pleasure. For it is not contrary to virtue, if the act of reason be sometimes interrupted for something that is done in accordance with reason, else it would be against virtue for a person to set himself to sleep. That venereal concupiscence and pleasure are not subject to the command and moderation of reason, is due to the punishment of the first sin, inasmuch as the reason, for rebelling against God, deserved that its body should rebel against it, as Augustine says (De Civ. Dei xiii, 13).

Reply to Objection 3: As Augustine says (De Civ. Dei xiii, 13), "the child, shackled with original sin, is born of fleshly concupiscence (which is not imputed as sin to the regenerate) as of a daughter of sin." Hence it does not follow that the act in question is a sin, but that it contains something penal resulting from the first sin.

Whether the lust that is about venereal acts can be a sin?

Objection 1: It would seem that lust about venereal acts cannot be a sin. For the venereal act consists in the emission of semen which is the surplus from food, according to the Philosopher (De Gener. Anim. i, 18). But there is no sin attaching to the emission of other superfluities. Therefore neither can there be any sin in venereal acts.

Objection 2: Further, everyone can lawfully make what use he pleases of what is his. But in the venereal act a man uses only what is his own, except perhaps in adultery or rape. Therefore there can be no sin in venereal acts, and consequently lust is no sin.

Objection 3: Further, every sin has an opposite vice. But, seemingly, no vice is opposed to lust. Therefore lust is not a sin.

On the contrary, The cause is more powerful than its effect. Now wine is forbidden on account of lust, according to the saying of the Apostle (Eph. 5:18), "Be not drunk with wine wherein is lust [Douay: 'luxury']." Therefore lust is forbidden.

Further, it is numbered among the works of the flesh: Gal. 5:19 [Douay: 'luxury'].

I answer that, The more necessary a thing is, the more it behooves one to observe the order of reason in its regard; wherefore the more sinful it becomes if the order of reason be forsaken. Now the use of venereal acts, as stated in the foregoing Article, is most necessary for the common good, namely the preservation of the human race. Wherefore there is the greatest necessity for observing the order of reason in this matter: so that if anything be done in this connection against the dictate of reason's ordering, it will be a sin.

Now lust consists essentially in exceeding the order and mode of reason in the matter of venereal acts. Wherefore without any doubt lust is a sin.

Reply to Objection 1: As the Philosopher says in the same book (De Gener. Anim. i, 18), "the semen is a surplus that is needed." For it is said to be superfluous, because it is the residue from the action of the nutritive power, yet it is needed for the work of the generative power. But the other superfluities of the human body are such as not to be needed, so that it matters not how they are emitted, provided one observe the decencies of social life. It is different with the emission of semen, which should be accomplished in a manner befitting the end for which it is needed.

Reply to Objection 2: As the Apostle says (1 Cor. 6:20) in speaking against lust, "You are bought with a great price: glorify and bear God in your body." Wherefore by inordinately using the body through lust a man wrongs God Who is the Supreme Lord of our body. Hence Augustine says (De Decem. Chord. 10 [*Serm. ix (xcvi de Temp.)]): "God Who thus governs His servants for their good, not for His, made this order and commandment, lest unlawful pleasures should destroy His temple which thou hast begun to be."

Reply to Objection 3: The opposite of lust is not found in many, since men are more inclined to pleasure. Yet the contrary vice is comprised under insensibility, and occurs in one who has such a dislike for sexual intercourse as not to pay the marriage debt.

Whether lust is a capital vice?

Objection 1: It seems that lust is not a capital vice. For lust is apparently the same as "uncleanness," according to a gloss on Eph. 5:3 (Cf. 2 Cor. 12:21). But uncleanness is a daughter of gluttony, according to Gregory (Moral. xxxi, 45). Therefore lust is not a capital vice.

Objection 2: Further, Isidore says (De Summo Bono ii, 39) that "as pride of mind leads to the depravity of lust, so does humility of mind safeguard the chastity of the flesh." Now it is seemingly contrary to the nature of a capital vice to arise from another vice. Therefore lust is not a capital vice.

Objection 3: Further, lust is caused by despair, according to Eph. 4:19, "Who despairing, have given themselves up to lasciviousness." But despair is not a capital vice; indeed, it is accounted a daughter of sloth, as stated above ([3521]Q[35], A[4], ad 2). Much less, therefore, is lust a capital vice.

On the contrary, Gregory (Moral. xxxi, 45) places lust among the capital vices.

I answer that, As stated above (Q[148], A[5]; [3522]FS, Q[84], AA[3],4), a capital vice is one that has a very desirable end, so that through desire for that end, a man proceeds to commit many sins, all of which are said to arise from that vice as from a principal vice. Now the end of lust is venereal pleasure, which is very great. Wherefore this pleasure is very desirable as regards the sensitive appetite, both on account of the intensity of the pleasure, and because such like concupiscence is connatural to man. Therefore it is evident that lust is a capital vice.

Reply to Objection 1: As stated above ([3523]Q[148], A[6]), according to some, the uncleanness which is reckoned a daughter of gluttony is a certain uncleanness of the body, and thus the objection is not to the point. If, however, it denote the uncleanness of lust, we must reply that it is caused by gluttony materially---in so far as gluttony provides the bodily matter of lust---and not under the aspect of final cause, in which respect chiefly the capital vices are said to be the cause of others.

Reply to Objection 2: As stated above ([3524]Q[132], A[4], ad 1), when we were treating of vainglory, pride is accounted the common mother of all sins, so that even the capital vices originate therefrom.

Reply to Objection 3: Certain persons refrain from lustful pleasures chiefly through hope of the glory to come, which hope is removed by despair, so that the latter is a cause of lust, as removing an obstacle thereto, not as its direct cause; whereas this is seemingly necessary for a capital vice.

Whether the daughters of lust are fittingly described?

Objection 1: It would seem that the daughters of lust are unfittingly reckoned to be "blindness of mind, thoughtlessness, inconstancy, rashness, self-love, hatred of God, love of this world and abhorrence or despair of a future world." For mental blindness, thoughtlessness and rashness pertain to imprudence, which is to be found in every sin, even as prudence is in every virtue. Therefore they should not be reckoned especially as daughters of lust.

Objection 2: Further, constancy is reckoned a part of fortitude, as stated above (Q[128], ad 6;[3525] Q[137], A[3]). But lust is contrary, not to fortitude but to temperance. Therefore inconstancy is not a daughter of lust.

Objection 3: Further, "Self-love extending to the contempt of God" is the origin of every sin, as Augustine says (De Civ. Dei xiv, 28). Therefore it should not be accounted a daughter of lust.

Objection 4: Further, Isidore [*QQ. in Deut., qu. xvi] mentions four, namely, "obscene," "scurrilous," "wanton" and "foolish talking." There the aforesaid enumeration would seem to be superfluous.

On the contrary, stands the authority of Gregory (Moral. xxxi, 45).

I answer that, When the lower powers are strongly moved towards their objects, the result is that the higher powers are hindered and disordered in their acts. Now the effect of the vice of lust is that the lower appetite, namely the concupiscible, is most vehemently intent on its object, to wit, the object of pleasure, on account of the vehemence of the pleasure. Consequently the higher powers, namely the reason and the will, are most grievously disordered by lust.

Now the reason has four acts in matters of action. First there is simple understanding, which apprehends some end as good, and this act is hindered by lust, according to Dan. 13:56, "Beauty hath deceived thee, and lust hath perverted thy heart." In this respect we have "blindness of mind." The second act is counsel about what is to be done for the sake of the end: and this is also hindered by the concupiscence of lust. Hence Terence says (Eunuch., act 1, sc. 1), speaking of lecherous love: "This thing admits of neither counsel nor moderation, thou canst not control it by counseling." In this respect there is "rashness," which denotes absence of counsel, as stated above ([3526]Q[53], A[3]). The third act is judgment about the things to be done, and this again is hindered by lust. For it is said of the lustful old men (Dan. 13:9): "They perverted their own mind . . . that they might not . . . remember just judgments." In this respect there is "thoughtlessness." The fourth act is the reason's command about the thing to be done, and this also is impeded by lust, in so far as through being carried away by concupiscence, a man is hindered from doing what his reason ordered to be done. [To this "inconstancy" must be referred.] [*The sentence in brackets is omitted in the Leonine edition.] Hence Terence says (Eunuch., act 1, sc. 1) of a man who declared that he would leave his mistress: "One little false tear will undo those words."

On the part of the will there results a twofold inordinate act. One is the desire for the end, to which we refer "self-love," which regards the pleasure which a man desires inordinately, while on the other hand there is "hatred of God," by reason of His forbidding the desired pleasure. The other act is the desire for the things directed to the end. With regard to this there is "love of this world," whose pleasures a man desires to enjoy, while on the other hand there is "despair of a future world," because through being held back by carnal pleasures he cares not to obtain spiritual pleasures, since they are distasteful to him.

Reply to Objection 1: According to the Philosopher (Ethic. vi, 5), intemperance is the chief corruptive of prudence: wherefore the vices opposed to prudence arise chiefly from lust, which is the principal species of intemperance.

Reply to Objection 2: The constancy which is a part of fortitude regards hardships and objects of fear; but constancy in refraining from pleasures pertains to continence which is a part of temperance, as stated above ([3527]Q[143]). Hence the inconstancy which is opposed thereto is to be reckoned a daughter of lust. Nevertheless even the first named inconstancy arises from lust, inasmuch as the latter enfeebles a man's heart and renders it effeminate, according to Osee 4:11, "Fornication and wine and drunkenness take away the heart [Douay: 'understanding']." Vegetius, too, says (De Re Milit. iii) that "the less a man knows of the pleasures of life, the less he fears death." Nor is there any need, as we have repeatedly stated, for the daughters of a capital vice to agree with it in matter (cf.[3528] Q[35], A[4], ad 2;[3529] Q[118], A[8], ad 1;[3530] Q[148], A[6]).

Reply to Objection 3: Self-love in respect of any goods that a man desires for himself is the common origin of all sins; but in the special point of desiring carnal pleasures for oneself, it is reckoned a daughter of lust.

Reply to Objection 4: The sins mentioned by Isidore are inordinate external acts, pertaining in the main to speech; wherein there is a fourfold inordinateness. First, on account of the matter, and to this we refer "obscene words": for since "out of the abundance of the heart the mouth speaketh" (Mat. 12:34), the lustful man, whose heart is full of lewd concupiscences, readily breaks out into lewd words. Secondly, on account of the cause: for, since lust causes thoughtlessness and rashness, the result is that it makes a man speak without weighing or giving a thought to his words. which are described as "scurrilous." Thirdly, on account of the end: for since the lustful man seeks pleasure, he directs his speech thereto, and so gives utterance to "wanton words." Fourthly, on account of the sentiments expressed by his words, for through causing blindness of mind, lust perverts a man's sentiments, and so he gives way "to foolish talking," for instance, by expressing a preference for the pleasures he desires to anything else.

Day 228

OF THE PARTS OF LUST (TWELVE ARTICLES)
We must now consider the parts of lust, under which head there are twelve points of inquiry:
(1) Into what parts is lust divided?
(2) Whether simple fornication is a mortal sin?
(3) Whether it is the greatest of sins?
(4) Whether there is mortal sin in touches, kisses and such like seduction?
(5) Whether nocturnal pollution is a mortal sin?
(6) Of seduction;
(7) Of rape;
(8) Of adultery;
(9) Of incest;
(10) Of sacrilege;
(11) Of the sin against nature;
(12) Of the order of gravity in the aforesaid sins.

Whether six species are fittingly assigned to lust?
Objection 1: It would seem that six species are unfittingly assigned to lust, namely, "simple fornication, adultery, incest, seduction, rape, and the unnatural vice." For diversity of matter does not diversify the species. Now the aforesaid division is made with regard to diversity of matter, according as the woman with whom a man has intercourse is married or a virgin, or of some other condition. Therefore it seems that the species of lust are diversified in this way.

Objection 2: Further, seemingly the species of one vice are not differentiated by things that belong to another vice. Now adultery does not differ from simple fornication, save in the point of a man having intercourse with one who is another's, so that he commits an injustice. Therefore it seems that adultery should not be reckoned a species of lust.

Objection 3: Further, just as a man may happen to have intercourse with a woman who is bound to another man by marriage, so may it happen that a man has intercourse with a woman who is bound to God by vow. Therefore sacrilege should be reckoned a species of lust, even as adultery is.

Objection 4: Further, a married man sins not only if he be with another woman, but also if he use his own wife inordinately. But the latter sin is comprised under lust. Therefore it should be reckoned among the species thereof.

Objection 5: Further, the Apostle says (2 Cor. 12:21): "Lest again, when I come, God humble me among you, and I mourn many of them /that sinned before, and have not done penance for the uncleanness and fornication and lasciviousness that they have committed." Therefore it seems that also uncleanness and lasciviousness should be reckoned species of lust, as well as fornication.

Objection 6: Further, the thing divided is not to be reckoned among its parts. But lust is reckoned together with the aforesaid: for it is written (Gal. 5:19): "The works of the flesh are manifest, which are fornication, uncleanness, immodesty, lust [Douay: 'luxury']." Therefore it seems that fornication is unfittingly reckoned a species of lust.

On the contrary, The aforesaid division is given in the Decretals 36, qu. i [*Append. Grat. ad can. Lex illa].

I answer that As stated above ([3531]Q[153], A[3]), the sin of lust consists in seeking venereal pleasure not in accordance with right reason. This may happen in two ways. First, in respect of the matter wherein this pleasure is sought; secondly, when, whereas there is due matter, other due circumstances are not observed. And since a circumstance, as such, does not specify a moral act, whose species is derived from its object which is also its matter, it follows that the species of lust must be assigned with respect to its matter or object.

Now this same matter may be discordant with right reason in two ways. First, because it is inconsistent with the end of the venereal act. In this way, as hindering the begetting of children, there is the "vice against nature," which attaches to every venereal act from which generation cannot follow; and, as hindering the due upbringing and advancement of the child when born, there is "simple fornication," which is the union of an unmarried man with an unmarried woman. Secondly, the matter wherein the venereal act is consummated may be discordant with right reason in relation to other persons; and this in two ways. First, with regard to the woman, with whom a man has connection, by reason of due honor not being paid to her; and thus there is "incest," which consists in the misuse of a woman who is related by consanguinity or affinity. Secondly, with regard to the person under whose authority the woman is placed: and if she be under the authority of a husband, it is "adultery," if under the authority of her father, it is "seduction," in the absence of violence, and "rape" if violence be employed.

These species are differentiated on the part of the woman rather than of the man, because in the venereal act the woman is passive and is by way of matter, whereas the man is by way of agent; and it has been stated above (OBJ[1]) that the aforesaid species are assigned with regard to a difference of matter.

Reply to Objection 1: The aforesaid diversity of matter is connected with a formal difference of object, which difference results from different modes of opposition to right reason, as stated above.

Reply to Objection 2: As stated above ([3532]FS, Q[18], A[7]), nothing hinders the deformities of different vices concurring in the one act, and in this way adultery is comprised under lust and injustice. Nor is this deformity of injustice altogether accidental to lust: since the lust that obeys concupiscence so far as to lead to injustice, is thereby shown to be more grievous.

Reply to Objection 3: Since a woman, by vowing continence, contracts a spiritual marriage with God, the sacrilege that is committed in the violation of such a woman is a spiritual adultery. In like manner, the other kinds of sacrilege pertaining to lustful matter are reduced to other species of lust.

Reply to Objection 4: The sin of a husband with his wife is not connected with undue matter, but with other circumstances, which do not constitute the species of a moral act, as stated above ([3533]FS, Q[18], A[2]).

Reply to Objection 5: As a gloss says on this passage, "uncleanness" stands for lust against nature, while "lasciviousness" is a man's abuse of boys, wherefore it would appear to pertain to seduction. We may also reply that "lasciviousness" relates to certain acts circumstantial to the venereal act, for instance kisses, touches, and so forth.

Reply to Objection 6: According to a gloss on this passage "lust" there signifies any kind of excess.

Whether simple fornication is a mortal sin?

Objection 1: It would seem that simple fornication is not a mortal sin. For things that come under the same head would seem to be on a par with one another. Now fornication comes under the same head as things that are not mortal sins: for it is written (Acts 15:29): "That you abstain from things sacrificed to idols, and from blood, and from things strangled, and from fornication." But there is not mortal sin in these observances, according to 1 Tim. 4:4, "Nothing is rejected that is received with thanksgiving." Therefore fornication is not a mortal sin.

Objection 2: Further, no mortal sin is the matter of a Divine precept. But the Lord commanded (Osee 1:2): "Go take thee a wife of fornications, and have of her children of fornications." Therefore fornication is not a mortal sin.

Objection 3: Further, no mortal sin is mentioned in Holy Writ without disapprobation. Yet simple fornication is mentioned without disapprobation by Holy Writ in connection with the patriarchs. Thus we read (Gn. 16:4) that Abraham went in to his handmaid Agar; and further on (Gn. 30:5, 9) that Jacob went in to Bala and Zelpha the handmaids of his wives; and again (Gn. 38:18) that Juda was with Thamar whom he thought to be a harlot. Therefore simple fornication is not a mortal sin.

Objection 4: Further, every mortal sin is contrary to charity. But simple fornication is not contrary to charity, neither as regards the love of God, since it is not a sin directly against. God, nor as regards the love of our neighbor, since thereby no one is injured. Therefore simple fornication is not a mortal sin.

Objection 5: Further, every mortal sin leads to eternal perdition. But simple fornication has not this result: because a gloss of Ambrose [*The quotation is from the Gloss of Peter Lombard, who refers it to St. Ambrose: whereas it is from Hilary the deacon] on 1 Tim. 4:8, "Godliness is profitable to all things," says: "The whole of Christian teaching is summed up in mercy and godliness: if a man conforms to this, even though he gives way to the inconstancy of the flesh, doubtless he will be punished, but he will not perish." Therefore simple fornication is not a mortal sin.

Objection 6: Further, Augustine says (De Bono Conjug. xvi) that "what food is to the well-being of the body, such is sexual intercourse to the welfare of the human race." But inordinate use of food is not always a mortal sin. Therefore neither is all inordinate sexual intercourse; and this would seem to apply especially to simple fornication, which is the least grievous of the aforesaid species.

On the contrary, It is written (Tob. 4:13): "Take heed to keep thyself . . . from all fornication, and beside thy wife never endure to know a crime." Now crime denotes a mortal sin. Therefore fornication and all intercourse with other than one's wife is a mortal sin.

Further, nothing but mortal sin debars a man from God's kingdom. But fornication debars him, as shown by the words of the Apostle (Gal. 5:21), who after mentioning fornication and certain other vices, adds: "They who do such things shall not obtain the kingdom of God." Therefore simple fornication is a mortal sin.

Further, it is written in the Decretals (XXII, qu. i, can. Praedicandum): "They should know that the same penance is to be enjoined for perjury as for adultery, fornication, and wilful murder and other criminal offenses." Therefore simple fornication is a criminal or mortal sin.

I answer that, Without any doubt we must hold simple fornication to be a mortal sin, notwithstanding that a gloss [*St. Augustine, QQ. in Deut., qu. 37] on Dt. 23:17, says: "This is a prohibition against going with whores, whose vileness is venial." For instead of "venial" it should be "venal," since such is the wanton's trade. In order to make this evident, we must take note that every sin committed directly against human life is a mortal sin. Now simple fornication implies an inordinateness that tends to injure the life of the offspring to be born of this union. For we find in all animals where the upbringing of the offspring needs care of both male and female, that these come together not indeterminately, but the male with a certain female, whether one or several; such is the case with all birds: while, on the other hand, among those animals, where the female alone suffices for the offspring's upbringing, the union is indeterminate, as in the case of dogs and like animals. Now it is evident that the upbringing of a human child requires not only the mother's care for his nourishment, but much more the care of his father as guide and guardian, and under whom he progresses in goods both internal and external. Hence human nature rebels against an indeterminate union of the sexes and demands that a man should be united to a determinate woman and should abide with her a long time or even for a whole lifetime. Hence it is that in the human race the male has a natural solicitude for the certainty of offspring, because on him devolves the upbringing of the child: and this certainly would cease if the union of sexes were indeterminate.

This union with a certain definite woman is called matrimony; which for the above reason is said to belong to the natural law. Since, however, the union of the sexes is directed to the common good of the whole human race, and common goods depend on the law for their determination, as stated above ([3534]FS, Q[90], A[2]), it follows that this union of man and woman, which is called matrimony, is determined by some law. What this determination is for us will be stated in the Third Part of this work (XP, Q[50], seqq.), where we shall treat of the sacrament of matrimony. Wherefore, since fornication is an indeterminate union of the sexes, as something incompatible with matrimony, it is opposed to the good of the child's upbringing, and consequently it is a mortal sin.

Nor does it matter if a man having knowledge of a woman by fornication, make sufficient provision for the upbringing of the child: because a matter that comes under the determination of the law is judged according to what happens in general, and not according to what may happen in a particular case.

Reply to Objection 1: Fornication is reckoned in conjunction with these things, not as being on a par with them in sinfulness, but because the matters mentioned there were equally liable to cause dispute between Jews and Gentiles, and thus prevent them from agreeing unanimously. For among the Gentiles, fornication was not deemed unlawful, on account of the corruption of natural reason: whereas the Jews, taught by the Divine law, considered it to be unlawful. The other things mentioned were loathsome to the Jews through custom introduced by the law into their daily life. Hence the Apostles forbade these things to the Gentiles, not as though they were unlawful in themselves, but because they were loathsome to the Jews, as stated above ([3535]FS, Q[103], A[4], ad 3).

Reply to Objection 2: Fornication is said to be a sin, because it is contrary to right reason. Now man's reason is right, in so far as it is ruled by the Divine Will, the first and supreme rule. Wherefore that which a man does by God's will and in obedience to His command, is not contrary to right reason, though it may seem contrary to the general order of reason: even so, that which is done miraculously by the Divine power is not contrary to nature, though it be contrary to the usual course of nature. Therefore just as Abraham did not sin in being willing to slay his innocent son, because he obeyed God, although considered in itself it was contrary to right human reason in general, so, too, Osee sinned not in committing fornication by God's command. Nor should such a copulation be strictly called fornication, though it be so called in reference to the general course of things. Hence Augustine says (Confess. iii, 8): "When God commands a thing to be done against the customs or agreement of any people, though it were never done by them heretofore, it is to be done"; and afterwards he adds: "For as among the powers of human society, the greater authority is obeyed in preference to the lesser, so must God in preference to all."

Reply to Objection 3: Abraham and Jacob went in to their handmaidens with no purpose of fornication, as we shall show further on when we treat of matrimony ([3536]XP, Q[65], A[5], ad 2). As to Juda there is no need to excuse him, for he also caused Joseph to be sold.

Reply to Objection 4: Simple fornication is contrary to the love of our neighbor, because it is opposed to the good of the child to be born, as we have shown, since it is an act of generation accomplished in a manner disadvantageous to the future child.

Reply to Objection 5: A person, who, while given to works of piety, yields to the inconstancy of the flesh, is freed from eternal loss, in so far as these works dispose him to receive the grace to repent, and because by such works he makes satisfaction for his past inconstancy; but not so as to be freed by pious works, if he persist in carnal inconstancy impenitent until death.

Reply to Objection 6: One copulation may result in the begetting of a man, wherefore inordinate copulation, which hinders the good of the future child, is a mortal sin as to the very genus of the act, and not only as to the inordinateness of concupiscence. On the other hand, one meal does not hinder the good of a man's whole life, wherefore the act of gluttony is not a mortal sin by reason of its genus. It would, however, be a mortal sin, if a man were knowingly to partake of a food which would alter the whole condition of his life, as was the case with Adam.

Nor is it true that fornication is the least of the sins comprised under lust, for the marriage act that is done out of sensuous pleasure is a lesser sin.

Whether fornication is the most grievous of sins?

Objection 1: It would seem that fornication is the most grievous of sins. For seemingly a sin is the more grievous according as it proceeds from a greater sensuous pleasure. Now the greatest sensuous pleasure is in fornication, for a gloss on 1 Cor. 7:9 says that the "flame of sensuous pleasure is most fierce in lust." Therefore it seems that fornication is the gravest of sins.

Objection 2: Further, a sin is the more grievous that is committed against a person more closely united to the sinner: thus he sins more grievously who strikes his father than one who strikes a stranger. Now according to 1 Cor. 6:18, "He that committeth fornication sinneth against his own body," which is most intimately connected with a man. Therefore it seems that fornication is the most grievous of sins.

Objection 3: Further, the greater a good is, the graver would seem to be the sin committed against it. Now the sin of fornication is seemingly opposed to the good of the whole human race, as appears from what was said in the foregoing Article. It is also against Christ, according to 1 Cor. 6:15, "Shall I . . . take the members of Christ, and make them the members of a harlot?" Therefore fornication is the most grievous of sins.

On the contrary, Gregory says (Moral. xxxiii, 12) that the sins of the flesh are less grievous than spiritual sins.

I answer that, The gravity of a sin may be measured in two ways, first with regard to the sin in itself, secondly with regard to some accident. The gravity of a sin is measured with regard to the sin itself, by reason of its species, which is determined according to the good to which that sin is opposed. Now fornication is contrary to the good of the child to be born. Wherefore it is a graver sin, as to its species, than those sins which are contrary to external goods, such as theft and the like; while it is less grievous than those which are directly against God, and sins that are injurious to the life of one already born, such as murder.

Reply to Objection 1: The sensual pleasure that aggravates a sin is that which is in the inclination of the will. But the sensual pleasure that is in the sensitive appetite, lessens sin, because a sin is the less grievous according as it is committed under the impulse of a greater passion. It is in this way that the greatest sensual pleasure is in fornication. Hence Augustine says (De Agone Christiano [*Serm. ccxciii; ccl de Temp.; see Appendix to St. Augustine's works]) that of all a Christian's conflicts, the most difficult combats are those of chastity; wherein the fight is a daily one, but victory rare: and Isidore declares (De Summo Bono ii, 39) that "mankind is subjected to the devil by carnal lust more than by anything else," because, to wit, the vehemence of this passion is more difficult to overcome.

Reply to Objection 2: The fornicator is said to sin against his own body, not merely because the pleasure of fornication is consummated in the flesh, which is also the case in gluttony, but also because he acts against the good of his own body by an undue resolution and defilement thereof, and an undue association with another. Nor does it follow from this that fornication is the most grievous sin, because in man reason is of greater value than the body, wherefore if there be a sin more opposed to reason, it will be more grievous.

Reply to Objection 3: The sin of fornication is contrary to the good of the human race, in so far as it is prejudicial to the individual begetting of the one man that may be born. Now one who is already an actual member of the human species attains to the perfection of the species more than one who is a man potentially, and from this point of view murder is a more grievous sin than fornication and every kind of lust, through being more opposed to the good of the human species. Again, a Divine good is greater than the good of the human race: and therefore those sins also that are against God are more grievous. Moreover, fornication is a sin against God, not directly as though the fornicator intended to offend God, but consequently, in the same way as all mortal sins. And just as the members of our body are Christ's members, so too, our spirit is one with Christ, according to 1 Cor. 6:17, "He who is joined to the Lord is one spirit." Wherefore also spiritual sins are more against Christ than fornication is.

Whether there can be mortal sin in touches and kisses?

Objection 1: It would seem that there is no mortal sin in touches and kisses. For the Apostle says (Eph. 5:3): "Fornication and all uncleanness, or covetousness, let it not so much as be named among you, as becometh saints," then he adds: "Or obscenity" (which a gloss refers to "kissing and fondling"), "or foolish talking" (as "soft speeches"), "or scurrility" (which "fools call geniality---i.e. jocularity"), and afterwards he continues (Eph. 5:5): "For know ye this and understand that no fornicator, or unclean, or covetous person (which is the serving of idols), hath inheritance in the kingdom of Christ and of God," thus making no further mention of obscenity, as neither of foolish talking or scurrility. Therefore these are not mortal sins.

Objection 2: Further, fornication is stated to be a mortal sin as being prejudicial to the good of the future child's begetting and upbringing. But these are not affected by kisses and touches or blandishments. Therefore there is no mortal sin in these.

Objection 3: Further, things that are mortal sins in themselves can never be good actions. Yet kisses, touches, and the like can be done sometimes without sin. Therefore they are not mortal sins in themselves.

On the contrary, A lustful look is less than a touch, a caress or a kiss. But according to Mat. 5:28, "Whosoever shall look on a woman to lust after her hath already committed adultery with her in his heart." Much more therefore are lustful kisses and other like things mortal sins.

Further, Cyprian says (Ad Pompon, de Virgin., Ep. lxii), "By their very intercourse, their blandishments, their converse, their embraces, those who are associated in a sleep that knows neither honor nor shame, acknowledge their disgrace and crime." Therefore by doing these things a man is guilty of a crime, that is, of mortal sin.

I answer that, A thing is said to be a mortal works. /sin in two ways. First, by reason of its species, and in this way a kiss, caress, or touch does not, of its very nature, imply a mortal sin, for it is possible to do such things without lustful pleasure, either as being the custom of one's country, or on account of some obligation or reasonable cause. Secondly, a thing is said to be a mortal sin by reason of its cause: thus he who gives an alms, in order to lead someone into heresy, sins mortally on account of his corrupt intention. Now it has been stated above ([3537]FS, Q[74], A[8]), that it is a mortal sin not only to consent to the act, but also to the delectation of a mortal sin. Wherefore since fornication is a mortal sin, and much more so the other kinds of lust, it follows that in such like sins not only consent to the act but also consent to the pleasure is a mortal sin. Consequently, when these kisses and caresses are done for this delectation, it follows that they are mortal sins, and only in this way are they said to be lustful. Therefore in so far as they are lustful, they are mortal sins.

Reply to Objection 1: The Apostle makes no further mention of these three because they are not sinful except as directed to those that he had mentioned before.

Reply to Objection 2: Although kisses and touches do not by their very nature hinder the good of the human offspring, they proceed from lust, which is the source of this hindrance: and on this account they are mortally sinful.

Reply to Objection 3: This argument proves that such things are not mortal sins in their species.

Whether nocturnal pollution is a mortal sin?

Objection 1: It would seem that nocturnal pollution is a sin. For the same things are the matter of merit and demerit. Now a man may merit while he sleeps, as was the case with Solomon, who while asleep obtained the gift of wisdom from the Lord (3 Kings 3:2, Par. 1). Therefore a man may demerit while asleep; and thus nocturnal pollution would seem to be a sin.

Objection 2: Further, whoever has the use of reason can sin. Now a man has the use of reason while asleep, since in our sleep we frequently discuss matters, choose this rather than that, consenting to one thing, or dissenting to another. Therefore one may sin while asleep, so that nocturnal pollution is not prevented by sleep from being a sin, seeing that it is a sin according to its genus.

Objection 3: Further, it is useless to reprove and instruct one who cannot act according to or against reason. Now man, while asleep, is instructed and reproved by God, according to Job 33:15,16, "By a dream in a vision by night, when deep sleep is wont to lay hold of men [*Vulg.: 'When deep sleep falleth upon men.' St. Thomas is apparently quoting from memory, as the passage is given correctly above[3538], Q[95], A[6], OBJ[1]] . . . Then He openeth the ears of men, and teaching instructeth them in what they are to learn." Therefore a man, while asleep, can act according to or against his reason, and this is to do good or sinful actions, and thus it seems that nocturnal pollution is a sin.

On the contrary, Augustine says (Gen. ad lit. xii, 15): "When the same image that comes into the mind of a speaker presents itself to the mind of the sleeper, so that the latter is unable to distinguish the imaginary from the real union of bodies, the flesh is at once moved, with the result that usually follows such motions; and yet there is as little sin in this as there is in speaking and therefore thinking about such things while one is awake."

I answer that, Nocturnal pollution may be considered in two ways. First, in itself; and thus it has not the character of a sin. For every sin depends on the judgment of reason, since even the first movement of the sensuality has nothing sinful in it, except in so far as it can be suppressed by reason; wherefore in the absence of reason's judgment, there is no sin in it. Now during sleep reason has not a free judgment. For there is no one who while sleeping does not regard some of the images formed by his imagination as though they were real, as stated above in the [3539]FP, Q[84], A[8], ad 2. Wherefore what a man does while he sleeps and is deprived of reason's judgment, is not imputed to him as a sin, as neither are the actions of a maniac or an imbecile.

Secondly, nocturnal pollution may be considered with reference to its cause. This may be threefold. One is a bodily cause. For when there is excess of seminal humor in the body, or when the humor is disintegrated either through overheating of the body or some other disturbance, the sleeper dreams things that are connected with the discharge of this excessive or disintegrated humor: the same thing happens when nature is cumbered with other superfluities, so that phantasms relating to the discharge of those superfluities are formed in the imagination. Accordingly if this excess of humor be due to a sinful cause (for instance excessive eating or drinking), nocturnal pollution has the character of sin from its cause: whereas if the excess or disintegration of these superfluities be not due to a sinful cause, nocturnal pollution is not sinful, neither in itself nor in its cause.

A second cause of nocturnal pollution is on the part of the soul and the inner man: for instance when it happens to the sleeper on account of some previous thought. For the thought which preceded while he was awake, is sometimes purely speculative, for instance when one thinks about the sins of the flesh for the purpose of discussion; while sometimes it is accompanied by a certain emotion either of concupiscence or of abhorrence. Now nocturnal pollution is more apt to arise from thinking about carnal sins with concupiscence for such pleasures, because this leaves its trace and inclination in the soul, so that the sleeper is more easily led in his imagination to consent to acts productive of pollution. In this sense the Philosopher says (Ethic. i, 13) that "in so far as certain movements in some degree pass" from the waking state to the state of sleep, "the dreams of good men are better than those of any other people": and Augustine says (Gen. ad lit. xii, 15) that "even during sleep, the soul may have conspicuous merit on account of its good disposition." Thus it is evident that nocturnal pollution may be sinful on the part of its cause. on the other hand, it may happen that nocturnal pollution ensues after thoughts about carnal acts, though they were speculative, or accompanied by abhorrence, and then it is not sinful, neither in itself nor in its cause.

The third cause is spiritual and external; for instance when by the work of a devil the sleeper's phantasms are disturbed so as to induce the aforesaid result. Sometimes this is associated with a previous sin, namely the neglect to guard against the wiles of the devil. Hence the words of the hymn at even: "Our enemy repress, that so our bodies no uncleanness know" [*Translation W. K. Blount].

On the other hand, this may occur without any fault on man's part, and through the wickedness of the devil alone. Thus we read in the Collationes Patrum (Coll. xxii, 6) of a man who was ever wont to suffer from nocturnal pollution on festivals, and that the devil brought this about in order to prevent him from receiving Holy Communion. Hence it is manifest that nocturnal pollution is never a sin, but is sometimes the result of a previous sin.

Reply to Objection 1: Solomon did not merit to receive wisdom from God while he was asleep. He received it in token of his previous desire. It is for this reason that his petition is stated to have been pleasing to God (3 Kings 3:10), as Augustine observes (Gen. ad lit. xii, 15).

Reply to Objection 2: The use of reason is more or less hindered in sleep, according as the inner sensitive powers are more or less overcome by sleep, on account of the violence or attenuation of the evaporations. Nevertheless it is always hindered somewhat, so as to be unable to elicit a judgment altogether free, as stated in the [3540]FP, Q[84], A[8], ad 2. Therefore what it does then is not imputed to it as a sin.

Reply to Objection 3: Reason's apprehension is not hindered during sleep to the same extent as its judgment, for this is accomplished by reason turning to sensible objects, which are the first principles of human thought. Hence nothing hinders man's reason during sleep from apprehending anew something arising out of the traces left by his previous thoughts and phantasms presented to him, or again through Divine revelation, or the interference of a good or bad angel.

Whether seduction should be reckoned a species of lust?

Objection 1: It would seem that seduction should not be reckoned a species of lust. For seduction denotes the unlawful violation of a virgin, according to the Decretals (XXXVI, qu. 1) [*Append. Grat. ad can. Lex illa]. But this may occur between an unmarried man and an unmarried woman, which pertains to fornication. Therefore seduction should not be reckoned a species of lust, distinct from fornication.

Objection 2: Further, Ambrose says (De Patriarch. [*De Abraham i, 4]): "Let no man be deluded by human laws: all seduction is adultery." Now a species is not contained under another that is differentiated in opposition to it. Therefore since adultery is a species of lust, it seems that seduction should not be reckoned a species of lust.

Objection 3: Further, to do a person an injury would seem to pertain to injustice rather than to lust. Now the seducer does an injury to another, namely the violated maiden's father, who "can take the injury as personal to himself" [*Gratian, ad can. Lex illa], and sue the seducer for damages. Therefore seduction should not be reckoned a species of lust.

On the contrary, Seduction consists properly in the venereal act whereby a virgin is violated. Therefore, since lust is properly about venereal actions, it would seem that seduction is a species of lust.

I answer that, When the matter of a vice has a special deformity, we must reckon it to be a determinate species of that vice. Now lust is a sin concerned with venereal matter, as stated above ([3541]Q[153], A[1]). And a special deformity attaches to the violation of a virgin who is under her father's care: both on the part of the maid, who through being violated without any previous compact of marriage is both hindered from contracting a lawful marriage and is put on the road to a wanton life from which she was withheld lest she should lose the seal of virginity: and on the part of the father, who is her guardian, according to Ecclus. 42:11, "Keep a sure watch over a shameless daughter, lest at any time she make thee become a laughing-stock to thy enemies." Therefore it is evident that seduction which denotes the unlawful violation of a virgin, while still under the guardianship of her parents, is a determinate species of lust.

Reply to Objection 1: Although a virgin is free from the bond of marriage, she is not free from her father's power. Moreover, the seal of virginity is a special obstacle to the intercourse of fornication, in that it should be removed by marriage only. Hence seduction is not simple fornication, since the latter is intercourse with harlots, women, namely, who are no longer virgins, as a gloss observes on 2 Cor. 12:, "And have not done penance for the uncleanness and fornication," etc.

Reply to Objection 2: Ambrose here takes seduction in another sense, as applicable in a general way to any sin of lust. Wherefore seduction, in the words quoted, signifies the intercourse between a married man and any woman other than his wife. This is clear from his adding: "Nor is it lawful for the husband to do what the wife may not." In this sense, too, we are to understand the words of Num. 5:13: "If [Vulg.: 'But'] the adultery is secret, and cannot be provided by witnesses, because she was not found in adultery [stupro]."

Reply to Objection 3: Nothing prevents a sin from having a greater deformity through being united to another sin. Now the sin of lust obtains a greater deformity from the sin of injustice, because the concupiscence would seem to be more inordinate, seeing that it refrains not from the pleasurable object so that it may avoid an injustice. In fact a twofold injustice attaches to it. One is on the part of the virgin, who, though not violated by force, is nevertheless seduced, and thus the seducer is bound to compensation. Hence it is written (Ex. 22:16,17): "If a man seduce a virgin not yet espoused, and lie with her, he shall endow her and have her to wife. If the maid's father will not give her to him, he shall give money according to the dowry, which virgins are wont to receive." The other injury is done to the maid's father: wherefore the seducer is bound by the Law to a penalty in his regard. For it is written (Dt. 22:28,29): "If a man find a damsel that is a virgin, who is not espoused, and taking her, lie with her, and the matter come to judgment: he that lay with her shall give to the father of the maid fifty sicles of silver, and shall have her to wife, and because he hath humbled her, he may not put her away all the days of his life": and this, lest he should prove to have married her in mockery, as Augustine observes. [*QQ. in Dt., qu. xxxiv.]

Whether rape is a species of lust, distinct from seduction?

Objection 1: It would seem that rape is not a species of lust, distinct from seduction. For Isidore says (Etym. v, 26) that "seduction [stuprum], or rape, properly speaking, is unlawful intercourse, and takes its name from its causing corruption: wherefore he that is guilty of rape is a seducer." Therefore it seems that rape should not be reckoned a species of lust distinct from seduction.

Objection 2: Further, rape, apparently, implies violence. For it is stated in the Decretals (XXXVI, qu. 1 [*Append. Grat. ad can. Lex illa]) that "rape is committed when a maid is taken away by force from her father's house that after being violated she may be taken to wife." But the employment of force is accidental to lust, for this essentially regards the pleasure of intercourse. Therefore it seems that rape should not be reckoned a determinate species of lust.

Objection 3: Further, the sin of lust is curbed by marriage: for it is written (1 Cor. 7:2): "For fear of fornication, let every man have his own wife." Now rape is an obstacle to subsequent marriage, for it was enacted in the council of Meaux: "We decree that those who are guilty of rape, or of abducting or seducing women, should not have those women in marriage, although they should have subsequently married them with the consent of their parents." Therefore rape is not a determinate species of lust distinct from seduction.

Objection 4: Further, a man may have knowledge of his newly married wife without committing a sin of lust. Yet he may commit rape if he take her away by force from her parents' house, and have carnal knowledge of her. Therefore rape should not be reckoned a determinate species of lust.

On the contrary, Rape is unlawful sexual intercourse, as Isidore states (Etym. v, 26). But this pertains to the sin of lust. Therefore rape is a species of lust.

I answer that, Rape, in the sense in which we speak of it now, is a species of lust: and sometimes it coincides with seduction; sometimes there is rape without seduction, and sometimes seduction without rape.

They coincide when a man employs force in order unlawfully to violate a virgin. This force is employed sometimes both towards the virgin and towards her father; and sometimes towards the father and not to the virgin, for instance if she allows herself to be taken away by force from her father's house. Again, the force employed in rape differs in another way, because sometimes a maid is taken away by force from her parents' house, and is forcibly violated: while sometimes, though taken away by force, she is not forcibly violated, but of her own consent, whether by act of fornication or by the act of marriage: for the conditions of rape remain no matter how force is employed. There is rape without seduction if a man abduct a widow or one who is not a virgin. Hence Pope Symmachus says [*Ep. v ad Caesarium; Cf. can. Raptores xxxvi, qu. 2], "We abhor abductors whether of widows or of virgins on account of the heinousness of their crime."

There is seduction without rape when a man, without employing force, violates a virgin unlawfully.

Reply to Objection 1: Since rape frequently coincides with seduction, the one is sometimes used to signify the other.

Reply to Objection 2: The employment of force would seem to arise from the greatness of concupiscence, the result being that a man does not fear to endanger himself by offering violence.

Reply to Objection 3: The rape of a maiden who is promised in marriage is to be judged differently from that of one who is not so promised. For one who is promised in marriage must be restored to her betrothed, who has a right to her in virtue of their betrothal: whereas one that is not promised to another must first of all be restored to her father's care, and then the abductor may lawfully marry her with her parents' consent. Otherwise the marriage is unlawful, since whosoever steals a thing he is bound to restore it. Nevertheless rape does not dissolve a marriage already contracted, although it is an impediment to its being contracted. As to the decree of the council in question, it was made in abhorrence of this crime, and has been abrogated. Wherefore Jerome [*The quotation is from Can. Tria. xxxvi, qu. 2] declares the contrary: "Three kinds of lawful marriage," says he, "are mentioned in Holy Writ. The first is that of a chaste maiden given away lawfully in her maidenhood to a man. The second is when a man finds a maiden in the city, and by force has carnal knowledge of her. If the father be willing, the man shall endow her according to the father's estimate, and shall pay the price of her purity [*Cf. Dt. 22:23-29]. The third is, when the maiden is taken away from such a man, and is given to another at the father's will."

We may also take this decree to refer to those who are promised to others in marriage, especially if the betrothal be expressed by words in the present tense.

Reply to Objection 4: The man who is just married has, in virtue of the betrothal, a certain right in her: wherefore, although he sins by using violence, he is not guilty of the crime of rape. Hence Pope Gelasius says [*Can. Lex illa, xxvii, qu. 2; xxxvi, qu. 1]: "This law of bygone rulers stated that rape was committed when a maiden, with regard to whose marriage nothing had so far been decided, was taken away by force."

Whether adultery is determinate species of lust, distinct from the other species?

Objection 1: It would seem that adultery is not a determinate species of lust, distinct from the other species. For adultery takes its name from a man having intercourse "with a woman who is not his own [ad alteram]," according to a gloss [*St. Augustine: Serm. li, 13 de Divers. lxiii] on Ex. 20:14. Now a woman who is not one's own may be of various conditions, namely either a virgin, or under her father's care, or a harlot, or of any other description. Therefore it seems that adultery is not a species of lust distinct from the others.

Objection 2: Further, Jerome says [*Contra Jovin. i]: "It matters not for what reason a man behaves as one demented. Hence Sixtus the Pythagorean says in his Maxims: He that is insatiable of his wife is an adulterer," and in like manner one who is over enamored of any woman. Now every kind of lust includes a too ardent love. Therefore adultery is in every kind of lust: and consequently it should not be reckoned a species of lust.

Objection 3: Further, where there is the same kind of deformity, there would seem to be the same species of sin. Now, apparently, there is the same kind of deformity in seduction and adultery: since in either case a woman is violated who is under another person's authority. Therefore adultery is not a determinate species of lust, distinct from the others.

On the contrary, Pope Leo [*St. Augustine, De Bono Conjug. iv; Cf. Append. Grat. ad can. Ille autem. xxxii, qu. 5] says that "adultery is sexual intercourse with another man or woman in contravention of the marriage compact, whether through the impulse of one's own lust, or with the consent of the other party." Now this implies a special deformity of lust. Therefore adultery is a determinate species of lust.

I answer that, Adultery, as its name implies, "is access to another's marriage-bed [ad alienum torum]" [*Cf. Append. Gratian, ad can. Ille autem. xxxii, qu. 1]. By so doing a man is guilty of a twofold offense against chastity and the good of human procreation. First, by accession to a woman who is not joined to him in marriage, which is contrary to the good of the upbringing of his own children. Secondly, by accession to a woman who is united to another in marriage, and thus he hinders the good of another's children. The same applies to the married woman who is corrupted by adultery. Wherefore it is written (Ecclus. 23:32,33): "Every woman . . . that leaveth her husband . . . shall be guilty of sin. For first she hath been unfaithful to the law of the Most High" (since there it is commanded: "Thou shalt not commit adultery"); "and secondly, she hath offended against her husband," by making it uncertain that the children are his: "thirdly, she hath fornicated in adultery, and hath gotten children of another man," which is contrary to the good of her offspring. The first of these, however, is common to all mortal sins, while the two others belong especially to the deformity of adultery. Hence it is manifest that adultery is a determinate species of lust, through having a special deformity in venereal acts.

Reply to Objection 1: If a married man has intercourse with another woman, his sin may be denominated either with regard to him, and thus it is always adultery, since his action is contrary to the fidelity of marriage, or with regard to the woman with whom he has intercourse; and thus sometimes it is adultery, as when a married man has intercourse with another's wife; and sometimes it has the character of seduction, or of some other sin, according to various conditions affecting the woman with whom he has intercourse: and it has been stated above [3542](A[1]) that the species of lust correspond to the various conditions of women.

Reply to Objection 2: Matrimony is specially ordained for the good of human offspring, as stated above [3543](A[2]). But adultery is specially opposed to matrimony, in the point of breaking the marriage faith which is due between husband and wife. And since the man who is too ardent a lover of his wife acts counter to the good of marriage if he use her indecently, although he be not unfaithful, he may in a sense be called an adulterer; and even more so than he that is too ardent a lover of another woman.

Reply to Objection 3: The wife is under her husband's authority, as united to him in marriage: whereas the maid is under her father's authority, as one who is to be married by that authority. Hence the sin of adultery is contrary to the good of marriage in one way, and the sin of seduction in another; wherefore they are reckoned to differ specifically. Of other matters concerning adultery we shall speak in the Third Part [*[3544]XP, Q[59], A[3] ; XP, QQ[60],62], when we treat of matrimony.

Day 229

Whether incest is a determinate species of lust?

Objection 1: It would seem that incest is not a determinate species of lust. For incest [*'Incestus' is equivalent to 'in-castus = 'unchaste'] takes its name from being a privation of chastity. But all kinds of lust are opposed to chastity. Therefore it seems that incest is not a species of lust, but is lust itself in general.

Objection 2: Further, it is stated in the Decretals (XXXVI, qu. 1 [*Cf. Append. Grat. ad can. Lex illa]) that "incest is intercourse between a man and a woman related by consanguinity or affinity." Now affinity differs from consanguinity. Therefore it is not one but several species of lust.

Objection 3: Further, that which does not, of itself, imply a deformity, does not constitute a determinate species of vice. But intercourse between those who are related by consanguinity or affinity does not, of itself, contain any deformity, else it would never have been lawful. Therefore incest is not a determinate species of lust.

On the contrary, The species of lust are distinguished according to the various conditions of women with whom a man has unlawful intercourse. Now incest implies a special condition on the part of the woman, because it is unlawful intercourse with a woman related by consanguinity or affinity as stated (OBJ[2]). Therefore incest is a determinate species of lust.

I answer that, As stated above ([3545]AA[1],6) wherever we find something incompatible with the right use of venereal actions, there must needs be a determinate species of lust. Now sexual intercourse with women related by consanguinity or affinity is unbecoming to venereal union on three counts. First, because man naturally owes a certain respect to his parents and therefore to his other blood relations, who are descended in near degree from the same parents: so much so indeed that among the ancients, as Valerius Maximus relates [*Dict. Fact. Memor. ii, 1], it was not deemed right for a son to bathe with his father, lest they should see one another naked. Now from what has been said (Q[142], A[4]: Q[151], A[4]), it is evident that in venereal acts there is a certain shamefulness inconsistent with respect, wherefore men are ashamed of them. Wherefore it is unseemly that such persons should be united in venereal intercourse. This reason seems to be indicated (Lev. 18:7) where we read: "She is thy mother, thou shalt not uncover her nakedness," and the same is expressed further on with regard to others.

The second reason is because blood relations must needs live in close touch with one another. Wherefore if they were not debarred from venereal union, opportunities of venereal intercourse would be very frequent and thus men's minds would be enervated by lust. Hence in the Old Law [*Lev. 18] the prohibition was apparently directed specially to those persons who must needs live together.

The third reason is, because this would hinder a man from having many friends: since through a man taking a stranger to wife, all his wife's relations are united to him by a special kind of friendship, as though they were of the same blood as himself. Wherefore Augustine says (De Civ. Dei xv, 16): "The demands of charity are most perfectly satisfied by men uniting together in the bonds that the various ties of friendship require, so that they may live together in a useful and becoming amity; nor should one man have many relationships in one, but each should have one."

Aristotle adds another reason (2 Polit. ii): for since it is natural that a man should have a liking for a woman of his kindred, if to this be added the love that has its origin in venereal intercourse, his love would be too ardent and would become a very great incentive to lust: and this is contrary to chastity. Hence it is evident that incest is a determinate species of lust.

Reply to Objection 1: Unlawful intercourse between persons related to one another would be most prejudicial to chastity, both on account of the opportunities it affords, and because of the excessive ardor of love, as stated in the Article. Wherefore the unlawful intercourse between such persons is called "incest" antonomastically.

Reply to Objection 2: Persons are related by affinity through one who is related by consanguinity: and therefore since the one depends on the other, consanguinity and affinity entail the same kind of unbecomingness.

Reply to Objection 3: There is something essentially unbecoming and contrary to natural reason in sexual intercourse between persons related by blood, for instance between parents and children who are directly and immediately related to one another, since children naturally owe their parents honor. Hence the Philosopher instances a horse (De Animal. ix, 47) which covered its own mother by mistake and threw itself over a precipice as though horrified at what it had done, because some animals even have a natural respect for those that have begotten them. There is not the same essential unbecomingness attaching to other persons who are related to one another not directly but through their parents: and, as to this, becomingness or unbecomingness varies according to custom, and human or Divine law: because, as stated above [3546](A[2]), sexual intercourse, being directed to the common good, is subject to law. Wherefore, as Augustine says (De Civ. Dei xv, 16), whereas the union of brothers and sisters goes back to olden times, it became all the more worthy of condemnation when religion forbade it.

Whether sacrilege can be a species of lust?

Objection 1: It would seem that sacrilege cannot be a species of lust. For the same species is not contained under different genera that are not subalternated to one another. Now sacrilege is a species of irreligion, as stated above ([3547]Q[99], A[2]). Therefore sacrilege cannot be reckoned a species of lust.

Objection 2: Further, the Decretals (XXXVI, qu. 1 [*Append. Grat. ad can. Lex illa]), do not place sacrilege among other sins which are reckoned species of lust. Therefore it would seem not to be a species of lust.

Objection 3: Further, something derogatory to a sacred thing may be done by the other kinds of vice, as well as by lust. But sacrilege is not reckoned a species of gluttony, or of any other similar vice. Therefore neither should it be reckoned a species of lust.

On the contrary, Augustine says (De Civ. Dei xv, 16) that "if it is wicked, through covetousness, to go beyond one's earthly bounds, how much more wicked is it through venereal lust to transgress the bounds of morals!" Now to go beyond one's earthly bounds in sacred matters is a sin of sacrilege. Therefore it is likewise a sin of sacrilege to overthrow the bounds of morals through venereal desire in sacred matters. But venereal desire pertains to lust. Therefore sacrilege is a species of lust.

I answer that, As stated above ([3548]FS, Q[18], AA[6],7), the act of a virtue or vice, that is directed to the end of another virtue or vice, assumes the latter's species: thus, theft committed for the sake of adultery, passes into the species of adultery. Now it is evident that as Augustine states (De Virgin. 8), the observance of chastity, by being directed to the worship of God, becomes an act of religion, as in the case of those who vow and keep chastity. Wherefore it is manifest that lust also, by violating something pertaining to the worship of God, belongs to the species of sacrilege: and in this way sacrilege may be accounted a species of lust.

Reply to Objection 1: Lust, by being directed to another vice as its end, becomes a species of that vice: and so a species of lust may be also a species of irreligion, as of a higher genus.

Reply to Objection 2: The enumeration referred to, includes those sins which are species of lust by their very nature: whereas sacrilege is a species of lust in so far as it is directed to another vice as its end, and may coincide with the various species of lust. For unlawful intercourse between persons mutually united by spiritual relationship, is a sacrilege after the manner of incest. Intercourse with a virgin consecrated to God, inasmuch as she is the spouse of Christ, is sacrilege resembling adultery. If the maiden be under her father's authority, it will be spiritual seduction; and if force be employed it will be spiritual rape, which kind of rape even the civil law punishes more severely than others. Thus the Emperor Justinian says [*Cod. i, iii de Episc. et Cler. 5]: "If any man dare, I will not say to rape, but even to tempt a consecrated virgin with a view to marriage, he shall be liable to capital punishment."

Reply to Objection 3: Sacrilege is committed on a consecrated thing. Now a consecrated thing is either a consecrated person, who is desired for sexual intercourse, and thus it is a kind of lust, or it is desired for possession, and thus it is a kind of injustice. Sacrilege may also come under the head of anger, for instance, if through anger an injury be done to a consecrated person. Again, one may commit a sacrilege by partaking gluttonously of sacred food. Nevertheless, sacrilege is ascribed more specially to lust which is opposed to chastity for the observance of which certain persons are specially consecrated.

Whether the unnatural vice is a species of lust?

Objection 1: It would seem that the unnatural vice is not a species of lust. For no mention of the vice against nature is made in the enumeration given above (A[1], OBJ[1]). Therefore it is not a species of lust.

Objection 2: Further, lust is contrary to virtue; and so it is comprised under vice. But the unnatural vice is comprised not under vice, but under bestiality, according to the Philosopher (Ethic. vii, 5). Therefore the unnatural vice is not a species of lust.

Objection 3: Further, lust regards acts directed to human generation, as stated above ([3549]Q[153], A[2]): Whereas the unnatural vice concerns acts from which generation cannot follow. Therefore the unnatural vice is not a species of lust.

On the contrary, It is reckoned together with the other species of lust (2 Cor. 12:21) where we read: "And have not done penance for the uncleanness, and fornication, and lasciviousness," where a gloss says: "Lasciviousness, i.e., unnatural lust."

I answer that, As stated above ([3550]AA[6],9) wherever there occurs a special kind of deformity whereby the venereal act is rendered unbecoming, there is a determinate species of lust. This may occur in two ways: First, through being contrary to right reason, and this is common to all lustful vices; secondly, because, in addition, it is contrary to the natural order of the venereal act as becoming to the human race: and this is called "the unnatural vice." This may happen in several ways. First, by procuring pollution, without any copulation, for the sake of venereal pleasure: this pertains to the sin of "uncleanness" which some call "effeminacy." Secondly, by copulation with a thing of undue species, and this is called "bestiality." Thirdly, by copulation with an undue sex, male with male, or female with female, as the Apostle states (Rom. 1:27): and this is called the "vice of sodomy." Fourthly, by not observing the natural manner of copulation, either as to undue means, or as to other monstrous and bestial manners of copulation.

Reply to Objection 1: There we enumerated the species of lust that are not contrary to human nature: wherefore the unnatural vice was omitted.

Reply to Objection 2: Bestiality differs from vice, for the latter is opposed to human virtue by a certain excess in the same matter as the virtue, and therefore is reducible to the same genus.

Reply to Objection 3: The lustful man intends not human generation but venereal pleasures. It is possible to have this without those acts from which human generation follows: and it is that which is sought in the unnatural vice.

Whether the unnatural vice is the greatest sin among the species of lust?

Objection 1: It would seem that the unnatural vice is not the greatest sin among the species of lust. For the more a sin is contrary to charity the graver it is. Now adultery, seduction and rape which are injurious to our neighbor are seemingly more contrary to the love of our neighbor, than unnatural sins, by which no other person is injured. Therefore the unnatural sin is not the greatest among the species of lust.

Objection 2: Further, sins committed against God would seem to be the most grievous. Now sacrilege is committed directly against God, since it is injurious to the Divine worship. Therefore sacrilege is a graver sin than the unnatural vice.

Objection 3: Further, seemingly, a sin is all the more grievous according as we owe a greater love to the person against whom that sin is committed. Now the order of charity requires that a man love more those persons who are united to him---and such are those whom he defiles by incest---than persons who are not connected with him, and whom in certain cases he defiles by the unnatural vice. Therefore incest is a graver sin than the unnatural vice.

Objection 4: Further, if the unnatural vice is most grievous, the more it is against nature the graver it would seem to be. Now the sin of uncleanness or effeminacy would seem to be most contrary to nature, since it would seem especially in accord with nature that agent and patient should be distinct from one another. Hence it would follow that uncleanness is the gravest of unnatural vices. But this is not true. Therefore unnatural vices are not the most grievous among sins of lust.

On the contrary, Augustine says (De adult. conjug. [*The quotation is from Cap. Adulterii xxxii, qu. 7. Cf. Augustine, De Bono Conjugali, viii.]) that "of all these," namely the sins belonging to lust, "that which is against nature is the worst."

I answer that, In every genus, worst of all is the corruption of the principle on which the rest depend. Now the principles of reason are those things that are according to nature, because reason presupposes things as determined by nature, before disposing of other things according as it is fitting. This may be observed both in speculative and in practical matters. Wherefore just as in speculative matters the most grievous and shameful error is that which is about things the knowledge of which is naturally bestowed on man, so in matters of action it is most grave and shameful to act against things as determined by nature. Therefore, since by the unnatural vices man transgresses that which has been determined by nature with regard to the use of venereal actions, it follows that in this matter this sin is gravest of all. After it comes incest, which, as stated above [3551](A[9]), is contrary to the natural respect which we owe persons related to us.

With regard to the other species of lust they imply a transgression merely of that which is determined by right reason, on the presupposition, however, of natural principles. Now it is more against reason to make use of the venereal act not only with prejudice to the future offspring, but also so as to injure another person besides. Wherefore simple fornication, which is committed without injustice to another person, is the least grave among the species of lust. Then, it is a greater injustice to have intercourse with a woman who is subject to another's authority as regards the act of generation, than as regards merely her guardianship. Wherefore adultery is more grievous than seduction. And both of these are aggravated by the use of violence. Hence rape of a virgin is graver than seduction, and rape of a wife than adultery. And all these are aggravated by coming under the head of sacrilege, as stated above (A[10], ad 2).

Reply to Objection 1: Just as the ordering of right reason proceeds from man, so the order of nature is from God Himself: wherefore in sins contrary to nature, whereby the very order of nature is violated, an injury is done to God, the Author of nature. Hence Augustine says (Confess. iii, 8): "Those foul offenses that are against nature should be everywhere and at all times detested and punished, such as were those of the people of Sodom, which should all nations commit, they should all stand guilty of the same crime, by the law of God which hath not so made men that they should so abuse one another. For even that very intercourse which should be between God and us is violated, when that same nature, of which He is the Author, is polluted by the perversity of lust."

Reply to Objection 2: Vices against nature are also against God, as stated above (ad 1), and are so much more grievous than the depravity of sacrilege, as the order impressed on human nature is prior to and more firm than any subsequently established order.

Reply to Objection 3: The nature of the species is more intimately united to each individual, than any other individual is. Wherefore sins against the specific nature are more grievous.

Reply to Objection 4: Gravity of a sin depends more on the abuse of a thing than on the omission of the right use. Wherefore among sins against nature, the lowest place belongs to the sin of uncleanness, which consists in the mere omission of copulation with another. While the most grievous is the sin of bestiality, because use of the due species is not observed. Hence a gloss on Gn. 37:2, "He accused his brethren of a most wicked crime," says that "they copulated with cattle." After this comes the sin of sodomy, because use of the right sex is not observed. Lastly comes the sin of not observing the right manner of copulation, which is more grievous if the abuse regards the "vas" than if it affects the manner of copulation in respect of other circumstances.

OF CONTINENCE (FOUR ARTICLES)

We must next consider the potential parts of temperance: (1) continence; (2) clemency; (3) modesty. Under the first head we must consider continence and incontinence. With regard to continence there are four points of inquiry:

(1) Whether continence is a virtue?
(2) What is its matter?
(3) What is its subject?
(4) Of its comparison with temperance.

Whether continence is a virtue?

Objection 1: It would seem that continence is not a virtue. For species and genus are not co-ordinate members of the same division. But continence is co-ordinated with virtue, according to the Philosopher (Ethic. vii, 1,9). Therefore continence is not a virtue.

Objection 2: Further, no one sins by using a virtue, since, according to Augustine (De Lib. Arb. ii, 18,19), "a virtue is a thing that no one makes ill use of." Yet one may sin by containing oneself: for instance, if one desire to do a good, and contain oneself from doing it. Therefore continence is not a virtue.

Objection 3: Further, no virtue withdraws man from that which is lawful, but only from unlawful things: for a gloss on Gal. 5:23, "Faith, modesty," etc., says that by continence a man refrains even from things that are lawful. Therefore continence is not a virtue.

On the contrary, Every praiseworthy habit would seem to be a virtue. Now such is continence, for Andronicus says [*De Affectibus] that "continence is a habit unconquered by pleasure." Therefore continence is a virtue.

I answer that, The word "continence" is taken by various people in two ways. For some understand continence to denote abstention from all venereal pleasure: thus the Apostle joins continence to chastity (Gal. 5:23). In this sense perfect continence is virginity in the first place, and widowhood in the second. Wherefore the same applies to continence understood thus, as to virginity which we have stated above ([3552]Q[152], A[3]) to be a virtue. Others, however, understand continence as signifying that whereby a man resists evil desires, which in him are vehement. In this sense the Philosopher takes continence (Ethic. vii, 7), and thus also it is used in the Conferences of the Fathers (Collat. xii, 10,11). In this way continence has something of the nature of a virtue, in so far, to wit, as the reason stands firm in opposition to the passions, lest it be led astray by them: yet it does not attain to the perfect nature of a moral virtue, by which even the sensitive appetite is subject to reason so that vehement passions contrary to reason do not arise in the sensitive appetite. Hence the Philosopher says (Ethic. iv, 9) that "continence is not a virtue but a mixture," inasmuch as it has something of virtue, and somewhat falls short of virtue.

If, however, we take virtue in a broad sense, for any principle of commendable actions, we may say that continence is a virtue.

Reply to Objection 1: The Philosopher includes continence in the same division with virtue in so far as the former falls short of virtue.

Reply to Objection 2: Properly speaking, man is that which is according to reason. Wherefore from the very fact that a man holds [tenet se] to that which is in accord with reason, he is said to contain himself. Now whatever pertains to perversion of reason is not according to reason. Hence he alone is truly said to be continent who stands to that which is in accord with right reason, and not to that which is in accord with perverse reason. Now evil desires are opposed to right reason, even as good desires are opposed to perverse reason. Wherefore he is properly and truly continent who holds to right reason, by abstaining from evil desires, and not he who holds to perverse reason, by abstaining from good desires: indeed, the latter should rather be said to be obstinate in evil.

Reply to Objection 3: The gloss quoted takes continence in the first sense, as denoting a perfect virtue, which refrains not merely from unlawful goods, but also from certain lawful things that are lesser goods, in order to give its whole attention to the more perfect goods.

Whether desires for pleasures of touch are the matter of continence?

Objection 1: It would seem that desires for pleasures of touch are not the matter of continence. For Ambrose says (De Offic. i, 46): "General decorum by its consistent form and the perfection of what is virtuous is restrained* in its every action." [*"Continentem" according to St. Thomas' reading; St. Ambrose wrote "concinentem = harmonious"].

Objection 2: Further, continence takes its name from a man standing for the good of right reason, as stated above (A[1], ad 2). Now other passions lead men astray from right reason with greater vehemence than the desire for pleasures of touch: for instance, the fear of mortal dangers, which stupefies a man, and anger which makes him behave like a madman, as Seneca remarks [*De Ira i, 1]. Therefore continence does not properly regard the desires for pleasures of touch.

Objection 3: Further, Tully says (De Invent. Rhet. ii, 54): "It is continence that restrains cupidity with the guiding hand of counsel." Now cupidity is generally used to denote the desire for riches rather than the desire for pleasures of touch, according to 1 Tim. 6:10, "Cupidity [Douay: 'The desire of money'] ({philargyria}), is the root of all evils." Therefore continence is not properly about the desires for pleasures of touch

Objection 4: Further, there are pleasures of touch not only in venereal matters but also in eating. But continence is wont to be applied only to the use of venereal matters. Therefore the desire for pleasures of touch is not its proper matter.

Objection 5: Further, among pleasures of touch some are not human but bestial, both as regards food---for instance, the pleasure of eating human flesh; and as regards venereal matters---for instance the abuse of animals or boys. But continence is not about such like things, as stated in Ethic. vii, 5. Therefore desires for pleasures of touch are not the proper matter of continence.

On the contrary, The Philosopher says (Ethic. vii, 4) that "continence and incontinence are about the same things as temperance and intemperance." Now temperance and intemperance are about the desires for pleasures of touch, as stated above ([3553]Q[141], A[4]). Therefore continence and incontinence are also about that same matter.

I answer that, Continence denotes, by its very name, a certain curbing, in so far as a man contains himself from following his passions. Hence continence is properly said in reference to those passions which urge a man towards the pursuit of something, wherein it is praiseworthy that reason should withhold man from pursuing: whereas it is not properly about those passions, such as fear and the like, which denote some kind of withdrawal: since in these it is praiseworthy to remain firm in pursuing what reason dictates, as stated above (Q[123], AA[3],4). Now it is to be observed that natural inclinations are the principles of all supervening inclinations, as stated above ([3554]FP, Q[60], A[2]). Wherefore the more they follow the inclination of nature, the more strongly do the passions urge to the pursuance of an object. Now nature inclines chiefly to those things that are necessary to it, whether for the maintenance of the individual, such as food, or for the maintenance of the species, such as venereal acts, the pleasures of which pertain to the touch. Therefore continence and incontinence refer properly to desires for pleasures of touch.

Reply to Objection 1: Just as temperance may be used in a general sense in connection with any matter; but is properly applied to that matter wherein it is best for man to be curbed: so, too, continence properly speaking regards that matter wherein it is best and most difficult to contain oneself, namely desires for pleasures of touch, and yet in a general sense and relatively may be applied to any other matter: and in this sense Ambrose speaks of continence.

Reply to Objection 2: Properly speaking we do not speak of continence in relation to fear, but rather of firmness of mind which fortitude implies. As to anger, it is true that it begets an impulse to the pursuit of something, but this impulse follows an apprehension of the soul---in so far as a man apprehends that someone has injured him---rather than an inclination of nature. Wherefore a man may be said to be continent of anger, relatively but not simply.

Reply to Objection 3: External goods, such as honors, riches and the like, as the Philosopher says (Ethic. vii, 4), seem to be objects of choice in themselves indeed, but not as being necessary for the maintenance of nature. Wherefore in reference to such things we speak of a person as being continent or incontinent, not simply, but relatively, by adding that they are continent or incontinent in regard to wealth, or honor and so forth. Hence Tully either understood continence in a general sense, as including relative continence, or understood cupidity in a restricted sense as denoting desire for pleasures of touch.

Reply to Objection 4: Venereal pleasures are more vehement than pleasures of the palate: wherefore we are wont to speak of continence and incontinence in reference to venereal matters rather than in reference to food; although according to the Philosopher they are applicable to both.

Reply to Objection 5: Continence is a good of the human reason: wherefore it regards those passions which can be connatural to man. Hence the Philosopher says (Ethic. vii, 5) that "if a man were to lay hold of a child with desire of eating him or of satisfying an unnatural passion whether he follow up his desire or not, he is said to be continent [*See A[4]], not absolutely, but relatively."

Whether the subject of continence is the concupiscible power?

Objection 1: It would seem that the subject of continence is the concupiscible power. For the subject of a virtue should be proportionate to the virtue's matter. Now the matter of continence, as stated [3555](A[2]), is desires for the pleasures of touch, which pertain to the concupiscible power. Therefore continence is in the concupiscible power.

Objection 2: Further, "Opposites are referred to one same thing" [*Categ. viii]. But incontinence is in the concupiscible, whose passions overcome reason, for Andronicus says [*De Affectibus] that "incontinence is the evil inclination of the concupiscible, by following which it chooses wicked pleasures in disobedience to reason." Therefore continence is likewise in the concupiscible.

Objection 3: Further, the subject of a human virtue is either the reason, or the appetitive power, which is divided into the will, the concupiscible and the irascible. Now continence is not in the reason, for then it would be an intellectual virtue; nor is it in the will, since continence is about the passions which are not in the will; nor again is it in the irascible, because it is not properly about the passions of the irascible, as stated above (A[2], ad 2). Therefore it follows that it is in the concupiscible.

On the contrary, Every virtue residing in a certain power removes the evil act of that power. But continence does not remove the evil act of the concupiscible: since "the continent man has evil desires," according to the Philosopher (Ethic. vii, 9). Therefore continence is not in the concupiscible power.

I answer that, Every virtue while residing in a subject, makes that subject have a different disposition from that which it has while subjected to the opposite vice. Now the concupiscible has the same disposition in one who is continent and in one who is incontinent, since in both of them it breaks out into vehement evil desires. Wherefore it is manifest that continence is not in the concupiscible as its subject. Again the reason has the same disposition in both, since both the continent and the incontinent have right reason, and each of them, while undisturbed by passion, purposes not to follow his unlawful desires. Now the primary difference between them is to be found in their choice: since the continent man, though subject to vehement desires, chooses not to follow them, because of his reason; whereas the incontinent man chooses to follow them, although his reason forbids. Hence continence must needs reside in that power of the soul, whose act it is to choose; and that is the will, as stated above ([3556]FS, Q[13], A[1]).

Reply to Objection 1: Continence has for its matter the desires for pleasures of touch, not as moderating them (this belongs to temperance which is in the concupiscible), but its business with them is to resist them. For this reason it must be in another power, since resistance is of one thing against another.

Reply to Objection 2: The will stands between reason and the concupiscible, and may be moved by either. In the continent man it is moved by the reason, in the incontinent man it is moved by the concupiscible. Hence continence may be ascribed to the reason as to its first mover, and incontinence to the concupiscible power: though both belong immediately to the will as their proper subject.

Reply to Objection 3: Although the passions are not in the will as their subject, yet it is in the power of the will to resist them: thus it is that the will of the continent man resists desires.

Whether continence is better than temperance?

Objection 1: It would seem that continence is better than temperance. For it is written (Ecclus. 26:20): "No price is worthy of a continent soul." Therefore no virtue can be equalled to continence.

Objection 2: Further, the greater the reward a virtue merits, the greater the virtue. Now continence apparently merits the greater reward; for it is written (2 Tim. 2:5): "He . . . is not crowned, except he strive lawfully," and the continent man, since he is subject to vehement evil desires, strives more than the temperate man, in whom these things are not vehement. Therefore continence is a greater virtue than temperance.

Objection 3: Further, the will is a more excellent power than the concupiscible. But continence is in the will, whereas temperance is in the concupiscible, as stated above [3557](A[3]). Therefore continence is a greater virtue than temperance.

On the contrary, Tully (De Invent. Rhet. ii, 54) and Andronicus [*De Affectibus] reckon continence to be annexed to temperance, as to a principal virtue.

I answer that, As stated above [3558](A[1]), continence has a twofold signification. In one way it denotes cessation from all venereal pleasures; and if continence be taken in this sense, it is greater than temperance considered absolutely, as may be gathered from what we said above (Q[152], A[5]) concerning the preeminence of virginity over chastity considered absolutely. In another way continence may be taken as denoting the resistance of the reason to evil desires when they are vehement in a man: and in this sense temperance is far greater than continence, because the good of a virtue derives its praise from that which is in accord with reason. Now the good of reason flourishes more in the temperate man than in the continent man, because in the former even the sensitive appetite is obedient to reason, being tamed by reason so to speak, whereas in the continent man the sensitive appetite strongly resists reason by its evil desires. Hence continence is compared to temperance, as the imperfect to the perfect.

Reply to Objection 1: The passage quoted may be understood in two ways. First in reference to the sense in which continence denotes abstinence from all things venereal: and thus it means that "no price is worthy of a continent soul," in the genus of chastity the fruitfulness of the flesh is the purpose of marriage is equalled to the continence of virginity or of widowhood, as stated above ([3559]Q[152], AA[4],5). Secondly it may be understood in reference to the general sense in which continence denotes any abstinence from things unlawful: and thus it means that "no price is worthy of a continent soul," because its value is not measured with gold or silver, which are appreciable according to weight.

Reply to Objection 2: The strength or weakness of concupiscence may proceed from two causes. For sometimes it is owing to a bodily cause: because some people by their natural temperament are more prone to concupiscence than others; and again opportunities for pleasure which inflame the concupiscence are nearer to hand for some people than for others. Such like weakness of concupiscence diminishes merit, whereas strength of concupiscence increases it. on the other hand, weakness or strength of concupiscence arises from a praiseworthy spiritual cause, for instance the vehemence of charity, or the strength of reason, as in the case of a temperate man. In this way weakness of concupiscence, by reason of its cause, increases merit, whereas strength of concupiscence diminishes it.

Reply to Objection 3: The will is more akin to the reason than the concupiscible power is. Wherefore the good of reason---on account of which virtue is praised by the very fact that it reaches not only to the will but also to the concupiscible power, as happens in the temperate man---is shown to be greater than if it reach only to the will, as in the case of one who is continent.

Day 230

OF INCONTINENCE (FOUR ARTICLES)
We must now consider incontinence: and under this head there are four points of inquiry:
(1) Whether incontinence pertains to the soul or to the body?
(2) Whether incontinence is a sin?
(3) The comparison between incontinence and intemperance;
(4) Which is the worse, incontinence in anger, or incontinence in desire?

Whether incontinence pertains to the soul or to the body?
Objection 1: It would seem that incontinence pertains not to the soul but to the body. For sexual diversity comes not from the soul but from the body. Now sexual diversity causes diversity of incontinence: for the Philosopher says (Ethic. vii, 5) that women are not described either as continent or as incontinent. Therefore incontinence pertains not to the soul but to the body.

Objection 2: Further, that which pertains to the soul does not result from the temperament of the body. But incontinence results from the bodily temperament: for the Philosopher says (Ethic. vii, 7) that "it is especially people of a quick or choleric and atrabilious temper whose incontinence is one of unbridled desire." Therefore incontinence regards the body.

Objection 3: Further, victory concerns the victor rather than the vanquished. Now a man is said to be incontinent, because "the flesh lusteth against the spirit," and overcomes it. Therefore incontinence pertains to the flesh rather than to the soul.

On the contrary, Man differs from beast chiefly as regards the soul. Now they differ in respect of continence and incontinence, for we ascribe neither continence nor incontinence to the beasts, as the Philosopher states (Ethic. vii, 3). Therefore incontinence is chiefly on the part of the soul.

I answer that, Things are ascribed to their direct causes rather than to those which merely occasion them. Now that which is on the part of the body is merely an occasional cause of incontinence; since it is owing to a bodily disposition that vehement passions can arise in the sensitive appetite which is a power of the organic body. Yet these passions, however vehement they be, are not the sufficient cause of incontinence, but are merely the occasion thereof, since, so long as the use of reason remains, man is always able to resist his passions. If, however, the passions gain such strength as to take away the use of reason altogether---as in the case of those who become insane through the vehemence of their passions---the essential conditions of continence or incontinence cease, because such people do not retain the judgment of reason, which the continent man follows and the incontinent forsakes. From this it follows that the direct cause of incontinence is on the part of the soul, which fails to resist a passion by the reason. This happens in two ways, according to the Philosopher (Ethic. vii, 7): first, when the soul yields to the passions, before the reason has given its counsel; and this is called "unbridled incontinence" or "impetuosity": secondly, when a man does not stand to what has been counselled, through holding weakly to reason's judgment; wherefore this kind of incontinence is called "weakness." Hence it is manifest that incontinence pertains chiefly to the soul.

Reply to Objection 1: The human soul is the form of the body, and has certain powers which make use of bodily organs. The operations of these organs conduce somewhat to those operations of the soul which are accomplished without bodily instruments, namely to the acts of the intellect and of the will, in so far as the intellect receives from the senses, and the will is urged by passions of the sensitive appetite. Accordingly, since woman, as regards the body, has a weak temperament, the result is that for the most part, whatever she holds to, she holds to it weakly; although in /rare cases the opposite occurs, according to Prov. 31:10, "Who shall find a valiant woman?" And since small and weak things "are accounted as though they were not" [*Aristotle, Phys. ii, 5] the Philosopher speaks of women as though they had not the firm judgment of reason, although the contrary happens in some women. Hence he states that "we do not describe women as being continent, because they are vacillating" through being unstable of reason, and "are easily led" so that they follow their passions readily.

Reply to Objection 2: It is owing to the impulse of passion that a man at once follows his passion before his reason counsels him. Now the impulse of passion may arise either from its quickness, as in bilious persons [*Cf. [3560]FS, Q[46], A[5]], or from its vehemence, as in the melancholic, who on account of their earthy temperament are most vehemently aroused. Even so, on the other hand, a man fails to stand to that which is counselled, because he holds to it in weakly fashion by reason of the softness of his temperament, as we have stated with regard to woman (ad 1). This is also the case with phlegmatic temperaments, for the same reason as in women. And these results are due to the fact that the bodily temperament is an occasional but not a sufficient cause of incontinence, as stated above.

Reply to Objection 3: In the incontinent man concupiscence of the flesh overcomes the spirit, not necessarily, but through a certain negligence of the spirit in not resisting strongly.

Whether incontinence is a sin?

Objection 1: It would seem that incontinence is not a sin. For as Augustine says (De Lib. Arb. iii, 18): "No man sins in what he cannot avoid." Now no man can by himself avoid incontinence, according to Wis. 8:21, "I know [Vulg.: 'knew'] that I could not . . . be continent, except God gave it." Therefore incontinence is not a sin.

Objection 2: Further, apparently every sin originates in the reason. But the judgment of reason is overcome in the incontinent man. Therefore incontinence is not a sin.

Objection 3: Further, no one sins in loving God vehemently. Now a man becomes incontinent through the vehemence of divine love: for Dionysius says (Div. Nom. iv) that "Paul, through incontinence of divine love, exclaimed: I live, now not I" (Gal. 2:20). Therefore incontinence is not a sin.

On the contrary, It is numbered together with other sins (2 Tim. 3:3) where it is written: "Slanderers, incontinent, unmerciful," etc. Therefore incontinence is a sin.

I answer that, Incontinence about a matter may be considered in two ways. First it may be considered properly and simply: and thus incontinence is about concupiscences of pleasures of touch, even as intemperance is, as we have said in reference to continence ([3561]Q[155], A[2]). In this way incontinence is a sin for two reasons: first, because the incontinent man goes astray from that which is in accord with reason; secondly, because he plunges into shameful pleasures. Hence the Philosopher says (Ethic. vii, 4) that "incontinence is censurable not only because it is wrong"---that is, by straying from reason---"but also because it is wicked"---that is, by following evil desires. Secondly, incontinence about a matter is considered, properly---inasmuch as it is a straying from reason---but not simply; for instance when a man does not observe the mode of reason in his desire for honor, riches, and so forth, which seem to be good in themselves. About such things there is incontinence, not simply but relatively, even as we have said above in reference to continence ([3562]Q[155], A[2], ad 3). In this way incontinence is a sin, not from the fact that one gives way to wicked desires, but because one fails to observe the mode of reason even in the desire for things that are of themselves desirable.

Thirdly, incontinence is said to be about a matter, not properly, but metaphorically. for instance about the desires for things of which one cannot make an evil use, such as the desire for virtue. A man may be said to be incontinent in these matters metaphorically, because just as the incontinent man is entirely led by his evil desire, even so is a man entirely led by his good desire which is in accord with reason. Such like incontinence is no sin, but pertains to the perfection of virtue.

Reply to Objection 1: Man can avoid sin and do good, yet not without God's help, according to Jn. 15:5: "Without Me you can do nothing." Wherefore the fact that man needs God's help in order to be continent, does not show incontinence to be no sin, for, as stated in Ethic. iii, 3, "what we can do by means of a friend we do, in a way, ourselves."

Reply to Objection 2: The judgment of reason is overcome in the incontinent man, not necessarily, for then he would commit no sin, but through a certain negligence on account of his not standing firm in resisting the passion by holding to the judgment formed by his reason.

Reply to Objection 3: This argument takes incontinence metaphorically and not properly.

Whether the incontinent man sins more gravely than the intemperate?

Objection 1: It would seem that the incontinent man sins more gravely than the intemperate. For, seemingly, the more a man acts against his conscience, the more gravely he sins, according to Lk. 12:47, "That servant who knew the will of his lord . . . and did not . . . shall be beaten with many stripes." Now the incontinent man would seem to act against his conscience more than the intemperate because, according to Ethic. vii, 3, the incontinent man, though knowing how wicked are the things he desires, nevertheless acts through passion, whereas the intemperate man judges what he desires to be good. Therefore the incontinent man sins more gravely than the intemperate.

Objection 2: Further, apparently, the graver a sin is, the more incurable it is: wherefore the sins against the Holy Ghost, being most grave, are declared to be unpardonable. Now the sin of incontinence would appear to be more incurable than the sin of intemperance. For a person's sin is cured by admonishment and correction, which seemingly are no good to the incontinent man, since he knows he is doing wrong, and does wrong notwithstanding: whereas it seems to the intemperate man that he is doing well, so that it were good for him to be admonished. Therefore it would appear that the incontinent man sins more gravely than the intemperate.

Objection 3: Further, the more eagerly man sins, the more grievous his sin. Now the incontinent sins more eagerly than the intemperate, since the incontinent man has vehement passions and desires, which the intemperate man does not always have. Therefore the incontinent man sins more gravely than the intemperate.

On the contrary, Impenitence aggravates every sin: wherefore Augustine says (De Verb. Dom. serm. xi, 12,13) that "impenitence is a sin against the Holy Ghost." Now according to the Philosopher (Ethic. vii, 8) "the intemperate man is not inclined to be penitent, for he holds on to his choice: but every incontinent man is inclined to repentance." Therefore the intemperate man sins more gravely than the incontinent.

I answer that, According to Augustine [*De Duab. Anim. x, xi] sin is chiefly an act of the will, because "by the will we sin and live aright" [*Retract. i, 9]. Consequently where there is a greater inclination of the will to sin, there is a graver sin. Now in the intemperate man, the will is inclined to sin in virtue of its own choice, which proceeds from a habit acquired through custom: whereas in the incontinent man, the will is inclined to sin through a passion. And since passion soon passes, whereas a habit is "a disposition difficult to remove," the result is that the incontinent man repents at once, as soon as the passion has passed; but not so the intemperate man; in fact he rejoices in having sinned, because the sinful act has become connatural to him by reason of his habit. Wherefore in reference to such persons it is written (Prov. 2:14) that "they are glad when they have done evil, and rejoice in most wicked things." Hence it follows that "the intemperate man is much worse than the incontinent," as also the Philosopher declares (Ethic. vii, 7).

Reply to Objection 1: Ignorance in the intellect sometimes precedes the inclination of the appetite and causes it, and then the greater the ignorance, the more does it diminish or entirely excuse the sin, in so far as it renders it involuntary. On the other hand, ignorance in the reason sometimes follows the inclination of the appetite, and then such like ignorance, the greater it is, the graver the sin, because the inclination of the appetite is shown thereby to be greater. Now in both the incontinent and the intemperate man, ignorance arises from the appetite being inclined to something, either by passion, as in the incontinent, or by habit, as in the intemperate. Nevertheless greater ignorance results thus in the intemperate than in the incontinent. In one respect as regards duration, since in the incontinent man this ignorance lasts only while the passion endures, just as an attack of intermittent fever lasts as long as the humor is disturbed: whereas the ignorance of the intemperate man endures without ceasing, on account of the endurance of the habit, wherefore it is likened to phthisis or any chronic disease, as the Philosopher says (Ethic. vii, 8). In another respect the ignorance of the intemperate man is greater as regards the thing ignored. For the ignorance of the incontinent man regards some particular detail of choice (in so far as he deems that he must choose this particular thing now): whereas the intemperate man's ignorance is about the end itself, inasmuch as he judges this thing good, in order that he may follow his desires without being curbed. Hence the Philosopher says (Ethic. vii, 7,8) that "the incontinent man is better than the intemperate, because he retains the best principle [*{To beltiston, e arche}, 'the best thing, i.e. the principle']," to wit, the right estimate of the end.

Reply to Objection 2: Mere knowledge does not suffice to cure the incontinent man, for he needs the inward assistance of grace which quenches concupiscence, besides the application of the external remedy of admonishment and correction, which induce him to begin to resist his desires, so that concupiscence is weakened, as stated above ([3563]Q[142], A[2]). By these same means the intemperate man can be cured. But his curing is more difficult, for two reasons. The first is on the part of reason, which is corrupt as regards the estimate of the last end, which holds the same position as the principle in demonstrations. Now it is more difficult to bring back to the truth one who errs as to the principle; and it is the same in practical matters with one who errs in regard to the end. The other reason is on the part of the inclination of the appetite: for in the intemperate man this proceeds from a habit, which is difficult to remove, whereas the inclination of the incontinent man proceeds from a passion, which is more easily suppressed.

Reply to Objection 3: The eagerness of the will, which increases a sin, is greater in the intemperate man than in the incontinent, as explained above. But the eagerness of concupiscence in the sensitive appetite is sometimes greater in the incontinent man, because he does not sin except through vehement concupiscence, whereas the intemperate man sins even through slight concupiscence and sometimes forestalls it. Hence the Philosopher says (Ethic. vii, 7) that we blame more the intemperate man, "because he pursues pleasure without desiring it or with calm," i.e. slight desire. "For what would he have done if he had desired it with passion?"

Whether the incontinent in anger is worse than the incontinent in desire?

Objection 1: It would seem that the incontinent in anger is worse than the incontinent in desire. For the more difficult it is to resist the passion, the less grievous, apparently is incontinence: wherefore the Philosopher says (Ethic. vii, 7): "It is not wonderful, indeed it is pardonable if a person is overcome by strong and overwhelming pleasures or pains." Now, "as Heraclitus says, it is more difficult to resist desire than anger" [*Ethic. ii. 3]. Therefore incontinence of desire is less grievous than incontinence of anger.

Objection 2: Further, one is altogether excused from sin if the passion be so vehement as to deprive one of the judgment of reason, as in the case of one who becomes demented through passion. Now he that is incontinent in anger retains more of the judgment of reason, than one who is incontinent in desire: since "anger listens to reason somewhat, but desire does not" as the Philosopher states (Ethic. vii, 6). Therefore the incontinent in anger is worse than the incontinent in desire.

Objection 3: Further, the more dangerous a sin the more grievous it is. Now incontinence of anger would seem to be more dangerous, since it leads a man to a greater sin, namely murder, for this is a more grievous sin than adultery, to which incontinence of desire leads. Therefore incontinence of anger is graver than incontinence of desire.

On the contrary, The Philosopher says (Ethic. vii, 6) that "incontinence of anger is less disgraceful than incontinence of desire."

I answer that, The sin of incontinence may be considered in two ways. First, on the part of the passion which occasions the downfall of reason. In this way incontinence of desire is worse than incontinence of anger, because the movement of desire is more inordinate than the movement of anger. There are four reasons for this, and the Philosopher indicates them, Ethic. vii, 6: First, because the movement of anger partakes somewhat of reason, since the angry man tends to avenge the injury done to him, and reason dictates this in a certain degree. Yet he does not tend thereto perfectly, because he does not intend the due mode of vengeance. on the other hand, the movement of desire is altogether in accord with sense and nowise in accord with reason. Secondly, because the movement of anger results more from the bodily temperament owing to the quickness of the movement of the bile which tends to anger. Hence one who by bodily temperament is disposed to anger is more readily angry than one who is disposed to concupiscence is liable to be concupiscent: wherefore also it happens more often that the children of those who are disposed to anger are themselves disposed to anger, than that the children of those who are disposed to concupiscence are also disposed to concupiscence. Now that which results from the natural disposition of the body is deemed more deserving of pardon. Thirdly, because anger seeks to work openly, whereas concupiscence is fain to disguise itself and creeps in by stealth. Fourthly, because he who is subject to concupiscence works with pleasure, whereas the angry man works as though forced by a certain previous displeasure.

Secondly, the sin of incontinence may be considered with regard to the evil into which one falls through forsaking reason; and thus incontinence of anger is, for the most part, more grievous, because it leads to things that are harmful to one's neighbor.

Reply to Objection 1: It is more difficult to resist pleasure perseveringly than anger, because concupiscence is enduring. But for the moment it is more difficult to resist anger, on account of its impetuousness.

Reply to Objection 2: Concupiscence is stated to be without reason, not as though it destroyed altogether the judgment of reason, but because nowise does it follow the judgment of reason: and for this reason it is more disgraceful.

Reply to Objection 3: This argument considers incontinence with regard to its result.

OF CLEMENCY AND MEEKNESS (FOUR ARTICLES)
We must next consider clemency and meekness, and the contrary vices. Concerning the virtues themselves there are four points of inquiry:
(1) Whether clemency and meekness are altogether identical?
(2) Whether each of them is a virtue?
(3) Whether each is a part of temperance?
(4) Of their comparison with the other virtues.

Whether clemency and meekness are absolutely the same?
Objection 1: It would seem that clemency and meekness are absolutely the same. For meekness moderates anger, according to the Philosopher (Ethic. iv, 5). Now anger is "desire of vengeance" [*Aristotle, Rhet. ii, 2]. Since, then, clemency "is leniency of a superior in inflicting punishment on an inferior," as Seneca states (De Clementia ii, 3), and vengeance is taken by means of punishment, it would seem that clemency and meekness are the same.

Objection 2: Further, Tully says (De Invent. Rhet. ii, 54) that "clemency is a virtue whereby the mind is restrained by kindness when unreasonably provoked to hatred of a person," so that apparently clemency moderates hatred. Now, according to Augustine [*Ep. ccxi], hatred is caused by anger; and this is the matter of meekness and clemency. Therefore seemingly clemency and meekness are absolutely the same.

Objection 3: Further, the same vice is not opposed to different virtues. But the same vice, namely cruelty, is opposed to meekness and clemency. Therefore it seems that meekness and clemency are absolutely the same.

On the contrary, According to the aforesaid definition of Seneca (OBJ[1]) "clemency is leniency of a superior towards an inferior": whereas meekness is not merely of superior to inferior, but of each to everyone. Therefore meekness and clemency are not absolutely the same.

I answer that, As stated in Ethic. ii, 3, a moral virtue is "about passions and actions." Now internal passions are principles of external actions, and are likewise obstacles thereto. Wherefore virtues that moderate passions, to a certain extent, concur towards the same effect as virtues that moderate actions, although they differ specifically. Thus it belongs properly to justice to restrain man from theft, whereunto he is inclined by immoderate love or desire of money, which is restrained by liberality; so that liberality concurs with justice towards the effect, which is abstention from theft. This applies to the case in point; because through the passion of anger a man is provoked to inflict a too severe punishment, while it belongs directly to clemency to mitigate punishment, and this might be prevented by excessive anger.

Consequently meekness, in so far as it restrains the onslaught of anger, concurs with clemency towards the same effect; yet they differ from one another, inasmuch as clemency moderates external punishment, while meekness properly mitigates the passion of anger.

Reply to Objection 1: Meekness regards properly the desire itself of vengeance; whereas clemency regards the punishment itself which is applied externally for the purpose of vengeance.

Reply to Objection 2: Man's affections incline to the moderation of things that are unpleasant to him in themselves. Now it results from one man loving another that he takes no pleasure in the latter's punishment in itself, but only as directed to something else, for instance justice, or the correction of the person punished. Hence love makes one quick to mitigate punishment ---and this pertains to clemency---while hatred is an obstacle to such mitigation. For this reason Tully says that "the mind provoked to hatred" that is to punish too severely, "is restrained by clemency," from inflicting too severe a punishment, so that clemency directly moderates not hatred but punishment.

Reply to Objection 3: The vice of anger, which denotes excess in the passion of anger, is properly opposed to meekness, which is directly concerned with the passion of anger; while cruelty denotes excess in punishing. Wherefore Seneca says (De Clementia ii, 4) that "those are called cruel who have reason for punishing, but lack moderation in punishing." Those who delight in a man's punishment for its own sake may be called savage or brutal, as though lacking the human feeling that leads one man to love another.

Whether both clemency and meekness are virtues?
Objection 1: It would seem that neither clemency nor meekness is a virtue. For no virtue is opposed to another virtue. Yet both of these are apparently opposed to severity, which is a virtue. Therefore neither clemency nor meekness is a virtue.

Objection 2: Further, "Virtue is destroyed by excess and defect" [*Ethic. ii, 2]. But both clemency and meekness consist in a certain decrease; for clemency decreases punishment, and meekness decreases anger. Therefore neither clemency nor meekness is a virtue.

Objection 3: Further, meekness or mildness is included (Mat. 5:4) among the beatitudes, and (Gal. 5:23) among the fruits. Now the virtues differ from the beatitudes and fruits. Therefore they are not comprised under virtue.

On the contrary, Seneca says (De Clementia ii, 5): "Every good man is conspicuous for his clemency and meekness." Now it is virtue properly that belongs to a good man, since "virtue it is that makes its possessor good, and renders his works good also" (Ethic. ii, 6). Therefore clemency and meekness are virtues.

I answer that, The nature of moral virtue consists in the subjection of appetite to reason, as the Philosopher declares (Ethic. i, 13). Now this is verified both in clemency and in meekness. For clemency, in mitigating punishment, "is guided by reason," according to Seneca (De Clementia ii, 5), and meekness, likewise, moderates anger according to right reason, as stated in Ethic. iv, 5. Wherefore it is manifest that both clemency and meekness are virtues.

Reply to Objection 1: Meekness is not directly opposed to severity; for meekness is about anger. On the other hand, severity regards the external infliction of punishment, so that accordingly it would seem rather to be opposed to clemency, which also regards external punishing, as stated above [3564](A[1]). Yet they are not really opposed to one another, since they are both according to right reason. For severity is inflexible in the infliction of punishment when right reason requires it; while clemency mitigates punishment also according to right reason, when and where this is requisite. Wherefore they are not opposed to one another as they are not about the same thing.

Reply to Objection 2: According to the Philosopher (Ethic. iv, 5), "the habit that observes the mean in anger is unnamed; so that the virtue is denominated from the diminution of anger, and is designated by the name of meekness." For the virtue is more akin to diminution than to excess, because it is more natural to man to desire vengeance for injuries done to him, than to be lacking in that desire, since "scarcely anyone belittles an injury done to himself," as Sallust observes [*Cf. Q[120]]. As to clemency, it mitigates punishment, not in respect of that which is according to right reason, but as regards that which is according to common law, which is the object of legal justice: yet on account of some particular consideration, it mitigates the punishment, deciding, as it were, that a man is not to be punished any further. Hence Seneca says (De Clementia ii, 1): "Clemency grants this, in the first place, that those whom she sets free are declared immune from all further punishment; and remission of punishment due amounts to a pardon." Wherefore it is clear that clemency is related to severity as equity [the Greek 'epieikeia' [*Cf. Q[120]]] to legal justice, whereof severity is a part, as regards the infliction of punishment in accordance with the law. Yet clemency differs from equity, as we shall state further on (A[3], ad 1).

Reply to Objection 3: The beatitudes are acts of virtue: while the fruits are delights in virtuous acts. Wherefore nothing hinders meekness being reckoned both virtue, and beatitude and fruit.

Whether the aforesaid virtues are parts of temperance?

Objection 1: It would seem that the aforesaid virtues are not parts of temperance. For clemency mitigates punishment, as stated above [3565](A[2]). But the Philosopher (Ethic. v, 10) ascribes this to equity, which pertains to justice, as stated above (Q[120], A[2]). Therefore seemingly clemency is not a part of temperance.

Objection 2: Further, temperance is concerned with concupiscences; whereas meekness and clemency regard, not concupiscences, but anger and vengeance. Therefore they should not be reckoned parts of temperance.

Objection 3: Further, Seneca says (De Clementia ii, 4): "A man may be said to be of unsound mind when he takes pleasure in cruelty." Now this is opposed to clemency and meekness. Since then an unsound mind is opposed to prudence, it seems that clemency and meekness are parts of prudence rather than of temperance.

On the contrary, Seneca says (De Clementia ii, 3) that "clemency is temperance of the soul in exercising the power of taking revenge." Tully also (De Invent. Rhet. ii, 54) reckons clemency a part of temperance.

I answer that, Parts are assigned to the principal virtues, in so far as they imitate them in some secondary matter as to the mode whence the virtue derives its praise and likewise its name. Thus the mode and name of justice consist in a certain "equality," those of fortitude in a certain "strength of mind," those of temperance in a certain "restraint," inasmuch as it restrains the most vehement concupiscences of the pleasures of touch. Now clemency and meekness likewise consist in a certain restraint, since clemency mitigates punishment, while meekness represses anger, as stated above ([3566]AA[1],2). Therefore both clemency and meekness are annexed to temperance as principal virtue, and accordingly are reckoned to be parts thereof.

Reply to Objection 1: Two points must be considered in the mitigation of punishment. one is that punishment should be mitigated in accordance with the lawgiver's intention, although not according to the letter of the law; and in this respect it pertains to equity. The other point is a certain moderation of a man's inward disposition, so that he does not exercise his power of inflicting punishment. This belongs properly to clemency, wherefore Seneca says (De Clementia ii, 3) that "it is temperance of the soul in exercising the power of taking revenge." This moderation of soul comes from a certain sweetness of disposition, whereby a man recoils from anything that may be painful to another. Wherefore Seneca says (De Clementia ii, 3) that "clemency is a certain smoothness of the soul"; for, on the other hand, there would seem to be a certain roughness of soul in one who fears not to pain others.

Reply to Objection 2: The annexation of secondary to principal virtues depends on the mode of virtue, which is, so to speak, a kind of form of the virtue, rather than on the matter. Now meekness and clemency agree with temperance in mode, as stated above, though they agree not in matter.

Reply to Objection 3: "Unsoundness" is corruption of "soundness." Now just as soundness of body is corrupted by the body lapsing from the condition due to the human species, so unsoundness of mind is due to the mind lapsing from the disposition due to the human species. This occurs both in respect of the reason, as when a man loses the use of reason, and in respect of the appetitive power, as when a man loses that humane feeling whereby "every man is naturally friendly towards all other men" (Ethic. viii, 1). The unsoundness of mind that excludes the use of reason is opposed to prudence. But that a man who takes pleasure in the punishment of others is said to be of unsound mind, is because he seems on this account to be devoid of the humane feeling which gives rise to clemency.

Whether clemency and meekness are the greatest virtues?

Objection 1: It would seem that clemency and meekness are the greatest virtues. For virtue is deserving of praise chiefly because it directs man to happiness that consists in the knowledge of God. Now meekness above all directs man to the knowledge of God: for it is written (James 1:21): "With meekness receive the ingrafted word," and (Ecclus. 5:13): "Be meek to hear the word" of God. Again, Dionysius says (Ep. viii ad Demophil.) that "Moses was deemed worthy of the Divine apparition on account of his great meekness." Therefore meekness is the greatest of virtues.

Objection 2: Further, seemingly a virtue is all the greater according as it is more acceptable to God and men. Now meekness would appear to be most acceptable to God. For it is written (Ecclus. 1:34,35): "That which is agreeable" to God is "faith and meekness"; wherefore Christ expressly invites us to be meek like unto Himself (Mat. 11:29), where He says: "Learn of Me, because I am meek and humble of heart"; and Hilary declares [*Comment. in Matth. iv, 3] that "Christ dwells in us by our meekness of soul." Again, it is most acceptable to men; wherefore it is written (Ecclus. 3:19): "My son, do thy works in meekness, and thou shalt be beloved above the glory of men": for which reason it is also declared (Prov. 20:28) that the King's "throne is strengthened by clemency." Therefore meekness and clemency are the greatest of virtues.

Objection 3: Further, Augustine says (De Serm. Dom. in Monte i, 2) that "the meek are they who yield to reproaches, and resist not evil, but overcome evil by good." Now this seems to pertain to mercy or piety which would seem to be the greatest of virtues: because a gloss of Ambrose [*Hilary the deacon] on 1 Tim. 4:8, "Piety [Douay: 'Godliness'] is profitable to all things," observes that "piety is the sum total of the Christian religion." Therefore meekness and clemency are the greatest virtues.

On the contrary, They are not reckoned as principal virtues, but are annexed to another, as to a principal, virtue.

I answer that, Nothing prevents certain virtues from being greatest, not indeed simply, nor in every respect, but in a particular genus. It is impossible for clemency or meekness to be absolutely the greatest virtues, since they owe their praise to the fact that they withdraw a man from evil, by mitigating anger or punishment. Now it is more perfect to obtain good than to lack evil. Wherefore those virtues like faith, hope, charity, and likewise prudence and justice, which direct one to good simply, are absolutely greater virtues than clemency and meekness.

Yet nothing prevents clemency and meekness from having a certain restricted excellence among the virtues which resist evil inclinations. For anger, which is mitigated by meekness, is, on account of its impetuousness, a very great obstacle to man's free judgment of truth: wherefore meekness above all makes a man self-possessed. Hence it is written (Ecclus. 10:31): "My son, keep thy soul in meekness." Yet the concupiscences of the pleasures of touch are more shameful, and harass more incessantly, for which reason temperance is more rightly reckoned as a principal virtue. as stated above ([3567]Q[141], A[7], ad 2). As to clemency, inasmuch as it mitigates punishment, it would seem to approach nearest to charity, the greatest of the virtues, since thereby we do good towards our neighbor, and hinder his evil.

Reply to Objection 1: Meekness disposes man to the knowledge of God, by removing an obstacle; and this in two ways. First, because it makes man self-possessed by mitigating his anger, as stated above; secondly, because it pertains to meekness that a man does not contradict the words of truth, which many do through being disturbed by anger. Wherefore Augustine says (De Doctr. Christ. ii, 7): "To be meek is not to contradict Holy Writ, whether we understand it, if it condemn our evil ways, or understand it not, as though we might know better and have a clearer insight of the truth."

Reply to Objection 2: Meekness and clemency make us acceptable to God and men, in so far as they concur with charity, the greatest of the virtues, towards the same effect, namely the mitigation of our neighbor's evils.

Reply to Objection 3: Mercy and piety agree indeed with meekness and clemency by concurring towards the same effect, namely the mitigation of our neighbor's evils. Nevertheless they differ as to motive. For piety relieves a neighbor's evil through reverence for a superior, for instance God or one's parents: mercy relieves a neighbor's evil, because this evil is displeasing to one, in so far as one looks upon it as affecting oneself, as stated above ([3568]Q[30], A[2]): and this results from friendship which makes friends rejoice and grieve for the same things: meekness does this, by removing anger that urges to vengeance, and clemency does this through leniency of soul, in so far as it judges equitable that a person be no further punished.

Day 231

OF ANGER (EIGHT ARTICLES)

We must next consider the contrary vices: (1) Anger that is opposed to meekness; (2) Cruelty that is opposed to clemency. Concerning anger there are eight points of inquiry:

(1) Whether it is lawful to be angry?

(2) Whether anger is a sin?

(3) Whether it is a mortal sin?

(4) Whether it is the most grievous of sins?

(5) Of its species;

(6) Whether anger is a capital vice?

(7) Of its daughters;

(8) Whether it has a contrary vice?

Whether it is lawful to be angry?

Objection 1: It would seem that it cannot be lawful to be angry. For Jerome in his exposition on Mat. 5:22, "Whosoever is angry with his brother," etc. says: "Some codices add 'without cause.' However, in the genuine codices the sentence is unqualified, and anger is forbidden altogether." Therefore it is nowise lawful to be angry.

Objection 2: Further, according to Dionysius (Div. Nom. iv) "The soul's evil is to be without reason." Now anger is always without reason: for the Philosopher says (Ethic. vii, 6) that "anger does not listen perfectly to reason"; and Gregory says (Moral. v, 45) that "when anger sunders the tranquil surface of the soul, it mangles and rends it by its riot"; and Cassian says (De Inst. Caenob. viii, 6): "From whatever cause it arises, the angry passion boils over and blinds the eye of the mind." Therefore it is always evil to be angry.

Objection 3: Further, anger is "desire for vengeance" [*Aristotle, Rhet. ii, 2] according to a gloss on Lev. 19:17, "Thou shalt not hate thy brother in thy heart." Now it would seem unlawful to desire vengeance, since this should be left to God, according to Dt. 32:35, "Revenge is Mine." Therefore it would seem that to be angry is always an evil.

Objection 4: Further, all that makes us depart from likeness to God is evil. Now anger always makes us depart from likeness to God, since God judges with tranquillity according to Wis. 12:18. Therefore to be angry is always an evil.

On the contrary, Chrysostom [*Hom. xi in the Opus Imperfectum, falsely ascribed to St. John Chrysostom] says: "He that is angry without cause, shall be in danger; but he that is angry with cause, shall not be in danger: for without anger, teaching will be useless, judgments unstable, crimes unchecked." Therefore to be angry is not always an evil.

I answer that, Properly speaking anger is a passion of the sensitive appetite, and gives its name to the irascible power, as stated above ([3569]FS, Q[46], A[1]) when we were treating of the passions. Now with regard to the passions of the soul, it is to be observed that evil may be found in them in two ways. First by reason of the passion's very species, which is derived from the passion's object. Thus envy, in respect of its species, denotes an evil, since it is displeasure at another's good, and such displeasure is in itself contrary to reason: wherefore, as the Philosopher remarks (Ethic. ii, 6), "the very mention of envy denotes something evil." Now this does not apply to anger, which is the desire for revenge, since revenge may be desired both well and ill. Secondly, evil is found in a passion in respect of the passion's quantity, that is in respect of its excess or deficiency; and thus evil may be found in anger, when, to wit, one is angry, more or less than right reason demands. But if one is angry in accordance with right reason, one's anger is deserving of praise.

Reply to Objection 1: The Stoics designated anger and all the other passions as emotions opposed to the order of reason; and accordingly they deemed anger and all other passions to be evil, as stated above ([3570]FS, Q[24], A[2]) when we were treating of the passions. It is in this sense that Jerome considers anger; for he speaks of the anger whereby one is angry with one's neighbor, with the intent of doing him a wrong.---But, according to the Peripatetics, to whose opinion Augustine inclines (De Civ. Dei ix, 4), anger and the other passions of the soul are movements of the sensitive appetite, whether they be moderated or not, according to reason: and in this sense anger is not always evil.

Reply to Objection 2: Anger may stand in a twofold relation to reason. First, antecedently; in this way it withdraws reason from its rectitude, and has therefore the character of evil. Secondly, consequently, inasmuch as the movement of the sensitive appetite is directed against vice and in accordance with reason, this anger is good, and is called "zealous anger." Wherefore Gregory says (Moral. v, 45): "We must beware lest, when we use anger as an instrument of virtue, it overrule the mind, and go before it as its mistress, instead of following in reason's train, ever ready, as its handmaid, to obey." This latter anger, although it hinder somewhat the judgment of reason in the execution of the act, does not destroy the rectitude of reason. Hence Gregory says (Moral. v, 45) that "zealous anger troubles the eye of reason, whereas sinful anger blinds it." Nor is it incompatible with virtue that the deliberation of reason be interrupted in the execution of what reason has deliberated: since art also would be hindered in its act, if it were to deliberate about what has to be done, while having to act.

Reply to Objection 3: It is unlawful to desire vengeance considered as evil to the man who is to be punished, but it is praiseworthy to desire vengeance as a corrective of vice and for the good of justice; and to this the sensitive appetite can tend, in so far as it is moved thereto by the reason: and when revenge is taken in accordance with the order of judgment, it is God's work, since he who has power to punish "is God's minister," as stated in Rom. 13:4.

Reply to Objection 4: We can and ought to be like to God in the desire for good; but we cannot be altogether likened to Him in the mode of our desire, since in God there is no sensitive appetite, as in us, the movement of which has to obey reason. Wherefore Gregory says (Moral. v, 45) that "anger is more firmly erect in withstanding vice, when it bows to the command of reason."

Whether anger is a sin?

Objection 1: It would seem that anger is not a sin. For we demerit by sinning. But "we do not demerit by the passions, even as neither do we incur blame thereby," as stated in Ethic. ii, 5. Consequently no passion is a sin. Now anger is a passion as stated above ([3571]FS, Q[46], A[1]) in the treatise on the passions. Therefore anger is not a sin.

Objection 2: Further, in every sin there is conversion to some mutable good. But in anger there is conversion not to a mutable good, but to a person's evil. Therefore anger is not a sin.

Objection 3: Further, "No man sins in what he cannot avoid," as Augustine asserts [*De Lib. Arb. iii, 18]. But man cannot avoid anger, for a gloss on Ps. 4:5, "Be ye angry and sin not," says: "The movement of anger is not in our power." Again, the Philosopher asserts (Ethic. vii, 6) that "the angry man acts with displeasure." Now displeasure is contrary to the will. Therefore anger is not a sin.

Objection 4: Further, sin is contrary to nature, according to Damascene [*De Fide Orth. ii, 4,30]. But it is not contrary to man's nature to be angry, and it is the natural act of a power, namely the irascible; wherefore Jerome says in a letter [*Ep. xii ad Anton. Monach.] that "to be angry is the property of man." Therefore it is not a sin to be angry.

On the contrary, The Apostle says (Eph. 4:31): "Let all indignation and anger [*Vulg.: 'Anger and indignation'] . . . be put away from you."

I answer that, Anger, as stated above [3572](A[1]), is properly the name of a passion. A passion of the sensitive appetite is good in so far as it is regulated by reason, whereas it is evil if it set the order of reason aside. Now the order of reason, in regard to anger, may be considered in relation to two things. First, in relation to the appetible object to which anger tends, and that is revenge. Wherefore if one desire revenge to be taken in accordance with the order of reason, the desire of anger is praiseworthy, and is called "zealous anger" [*Cf. Greg., Moral. v, 45]. On the other hand, if one desire the taking of vengeance in any way whatever contrary to the order of reason, for instance if he desire the punishment of one who has not deserved it, or beyond his deserts, or again contrary to the order prescribed by law, or not for the due end, namely the maintaining of justice and the correction of defaults, then the desire of anger will be sinful, and this is called sinful anger.

Secondly, the order of reason in regard to anger may be considered in relation to the mode of being angry, namely that the movement of anger should not be immoderately fierce, neither internally nor externally; and if this condition be disregarded, anger will not lack sin, even though just vengeance be desired.

Reply to Objection 1: Since passion may be either regulated or not regulated by reason, it follows that a passion considered absolutely does not include the notion of merit or demerit, of praise or blame. But as regulated by reason, it may be something meritorious and deserving of praise; while on the other hand, as not regulated by reason, it may be demeritorious and blameworthy. Wherefore the Philosopher says (Ethic. ii, 5) that "it is he who is angry in a certain way, that is praised or blamed."

Reply to Objection 2: The angry man desires the evil of another, not for its own sake but for the sake of revenge, towards which his appetite turns as to a mutable good.

Reply to Objection 3: Man is master of his actions through the judgment of his reason, wherefore as to the movements that forestall that judgment, it is not in man's power to prevent them as a whole, i.e. so that none of them arise, although his reason is able to check each one, if it arise. Accordingly it is stated that the movement of anger is not in man's power, to the extent namely that no such movement arise. Yet since this movement is somewhat in his power, it is not entirely sinless if it be inordinate. The statement of the Philosopher that "the angry man acts with displeasure," means that he is displeased, not with his being angry, but with the injury which he deems done to himself: and through this displeasure he is moved to seek vengeance.

Reply to Objection 4: The irascible power in man is naturally subject to his reason, wherefore its act is natural to man, in so far as it is in accord with reason, and in so far as it is against reason, it is contrary to man's nature.

Whether all anger is a mortal sin?

Objection 1: It would seem that all anger is a mortal sin. For it is written (Job 5:2): "Anger killeth the foolish man [*Vulg.: 'Anger indeed killeth the foolish']," and he speaks of the spiritual killing, whence mortal sin takes its name. Therefore all anger is a mortal sin.

Objection 2: Further, nothing save mortal sin is deserving of eternal condemnation. Now anger deserves eternal condemnation; for our Lord said (Mat. 5:22): "Whosoever is angry with his brother shall be in danger of the judgment": and a gloss on this passage says that "the three things mentioned there, namely judgment, council, and hell-fire, signify in a pointed manner different abodes in the state of eternal damnation corresponding to various sins." Therefore anger is a mortal sin.

Objection 3: Further, whatsoever is contrary to charity is a mortal sin. Now anger is of itself contrary to charity, as Jerome declares in his commentary on Mat. 5:22, "Whosoever is angry with his brother," etc. where he says that this is contrary to the love of your neighbor. Therefore anger is a mortal sin.

On the contrary, A gloss on Ps. 4:5, "Be ye angry and sin not," says: "Anger is venial if it does not proceed to action."

I answer that, The movement of anger may be inordinate and sinful in two ways, as stated above [3573](A[2]). First, on the part of the appetible object, as when one desires unjust revenge; and thus anger is a mortal sin in the point of its genus, because it is contrary to charity and justice. Nevertheless such like anger may happen to be a venial sin by reason of the imperfection of the act. This imperfection is considered either in relation to the subject desirous of vengeance, as when the movement of anger forestalls the judgment of his reason; or in relation to the desired object, as when one desires to be avenged in a trifling matter, which should be deemed of no account, so that even if one proceeded to action, it would not be a mortal sin, for instance by pulling a child slightly by the hair, or by some other like action. Secondly, the movement of anger may be inordinate in the mode of being angry, for instance, if one be too fiercely angry inwardly, or if one exceed in the outward signs of anger. In this way anger is not a mortal sin in the point of its genus; yet it may happen to be a mortal sin, for instance if through the fierceness of his anger a man fall away from the love of God and his neighbor.

Reply to Objection 1: It does not follow from the passage quoted that all anger is a mortal sin, but that the foolish are killed spiritually by anger, because, through not checking the movement of anger by their reason, they fall into mortal sins, for instance by blaspheming God or by doing injury to their neighbor.

Reply to Objection 2: Our Lord said this of anger, by way of addition to the words of the Law: "Whosoever shall kill shall be in danger of the judgment" (Mat. 5:21). Consequently our Lord is speaking here of the movement of anger wherein a man desires the killing or any grave injury of his neighbor: and should the consent of reason be given to this desire, without doubt it will be a mortal sin.

Reply to Objection 3: In the case where anger is contrary to charity, it is a mortal sin, but it is not always so, as appears from what we have said.

Whether anger is the most grievous sin?

Objection 1: It would seem that anger is the most grievous sin. For Chrysostom says [*Hom. xlviii in Joan.] that "nothing is more repulsive than the look of an angry man, and nothing uglier than a ruthless* face, and most of all than a cruel soul." [*'Severo'. The correct text is 'Si vero.' The translation would then run thus . . . 'and nothing uglier.' And if his 'face is ugly, how much uglier is his soul!']. Therefore anger is the most grievous sin.

Objection 2: Further, the more hurtful a sin is, the worse it would seem to be; since, according to Augustine (Enchiridion xii), "a thing is said to be evil because it hurts." Now anger is most hurtful, because it deprives man of his reason, whereby he is master of himself; for Chrysostom says (Hom. xlviii in Joan.) that "anger differs in no way from madness; it is a demon while it lasts, indeed more troublesome than one harassed by a demon." Therefore anger is the most grievous sin.

Objection 3: Further, inward movements are judged according to their outward effects. Now the effect of anger is murder, which is a most grievous sin. Therefore anger is a most grievous sin.

On the contrary, Anger is compared to hatred as the mote to the beam; for Augustine says in his Rule (Ep. ccxi): "Lest anger grow into hatred and a mote become a beam." Therefore anger is not the most grievous sin.

I answer that, As stated above ([3574]AA[1],2), the inordinateness of anger is considered in a twofold respect, namely with regard to an undue object, and with regard to an undue mode of being angry. As to the appetible object which it desires, anger would seem to be the least of sins, for anger desires the evil of punishment for some person, under the aspect of a good that is vengeance. Hence on the part of the evil which it desires the sin of anger agrees with those sins which desire the evil of our neighbor, such as envy and hatred; but while hatred desires absolutely another's evil as such, and the envious man desires another's evil through desire of his own glory, the angry man desires another's evil under the aspect of just revenge. Wherefore it is evident that hatred is more grievous than envy, and envy than anger: since it is worse to desire evil as an evil, than as a good; and to desire evil as an external good such as honor or glory, than under the aspect of the rectitude of justice. On the part of the good, under the aspect of which the angry man desires an evil, anger concurs with the sin of concupiscence that tends to a good. In this respect again, absolutely speaking. the sin of anger is apparently less grievous than that of concupiscence, according as the good of justice, which the angry man desires, is better than the pleasurable or useful good which is desired by the subject of concupiscence. Wherefore the Philosopher says (Ethic. vii, 4) that "the incontinent in desire is more disgraceful than the incontinent in anger."

On the other hand, as to the inordinateness which regards the mode of being angry, anger would seem to have a certain pre-eminence on account of the strength and quickness of its movement, according to Prov. 27:4, "Anger hath no mercy, nor fury when it breaketh forth: and who can bear the violence of one provoked?" Hence Gregory says (Moral. v, 45): "The heart goaded by the pricks of anger is convulsed, the body trembles, the tongue entangles itself, the face is inflamed, the eyes are enraged and fail utterly to recognize those whom we know: the tongue makes sounds indeed, but there is no sense in its utterance."

Reply to Objection 1: Chrysostom is alluding to the repulsiveness of the outward gestures which result from the impetuousness of anger.

Reply to Objection 2: This argument considers the inordinate movement of anger, that results from its impetuousness, as stated above.

Reply to Objection 3: Murder results from hatred and envy no less than from anger: yet anger is less grievous, inasmuch as it considers the aspect of justice, as stated above.

Whether the Philosopher suitably assigns the species of anger?

Objection 1: It would seem that the species of anger are unsuitably assigned by the Philosopher (Ethic. iv, 5) where he says that some angry persons are "choleric," some "sullen," and some "ill-tempered" or "stern." According to him, a person is said to be "sullen" whose anger "is appeased with difficulty and endures a long time." But this apparently pertains to the circumstance of time. Therefore it seems that anger can be differentiated specifically in respect also of the other circumstances.

Objection 2: Further, he says (Ethic. iv, 5) that "ill-tempered" or "stern" persons "are those whose anger is not appeased without revenge, or punishment." Now this also pertains to the unquenchableness of anger. Therefore seemingly the ill-tempered is the same as bitterness.

Objection 3: Further, our Lord mentions three degrees of anger, when He says (Mat. 5:22): "Whosoever is angry with his brother, shall be in danger of the judgment: and whosoever shall say to his brother, Raca, shall be in danger of the council, and whosoever shall say" to his brother, "Thou fool." But these degrees are not referable to the aforesaid species. Therefore it seems that the above division of anger is not fitting.

On the contrary, Gregory of Nyssa [*Nemesius, De Nat. Hom. xxi] says "there are three species of irascibility," namely, "the anger which is called wrath [*'Fellea,' i.e. like gall. But in [3575]FS, Q[46], A[8], St. Thomas quoting the same authority has {Cholos} which we render 'wrath'],", and "ill-will" which is a disease of the mind, and "rancour." Now these three seem to coincide with the three aforesaid. For "wrath" he describes as "having beginning and movement," and the Philosopher (Ethic. iv, 5) ascribes this to "choleric" persons: "ill-will" he describes as "an anger that endures and grows old," and this the Philosopher ascribes to "sullenness"; while he describes "rancour" as "reckoning the time for vengeance," which tallies with the Philosopher's description of the "ill-tempered." The same division is given by Damascene (De Fide Orth. ii, 16). Therefore the aforesaid division assigned by the Philosopher is not unfitting.

I answer that, The aforesaid distinction may be referred either to the passion, or to the sin itself of anger. We have already stated when treating of the passions ([3576]FS, Q[46], A[8]) how it is to be applied to the passion of anger. And it would seem that this is chiefly what Gregory of Nyssa and Damascene had in view. Here, however, we have to take the distinction of these species in its application to the sin of anger, and as set down by the Philosopher.

For the inordinateness of anger may be considered in relation to two things. First, in relation to the origin of anger, and this regards "choleric" persons, who are angry too quickly and for any slight cause. Secondly, in relation to the duration of anger, for that anger endures too long; and this may happen in two ways. In one way, because the cause of anger, to wit, the inflicted injury, remains too long in a man's memory, the result being that it gives rise to a lasting displeasure, wherefore he is "grievous" and "sullen" to himself. In another way, it happens on the part of vengeance, which a man seeks with a stubborn desire: this applies to "ill-tempered" or "stern" people, who do not put aside their anger until they have inflicted punishment.

Reply to Objection 1: It is not time, but a man's propensity to anger, or his pertinacity in anger, that is the chief point of consideration in the aforesaid species.

Reply to Objection 2: Both "sullen" and "ill-tempered" people have a long-lasting anger, but for different reasons. For a "sullen" person has an abiding anger on account of an abiding displeasure, which he holds locked in his breast; and as he does not break forth into the outward signs of anger, others cannot reason him out of it, nor does he of his own accord lay aside his anger, except his displeasure wear away with time and thus his anger cease. On the other hand, the anger of "ill-tempered" persons is long-lasting on account of their intense desire for revenge, so that it does not wear out with time, and can be quelled only by revenge.

Reply to Objection 3: The degrees of anger mentioned by our Lord do not refer to the different species of anger, but correspond to the course of the human act [*Cf. [3577]FS, Q[46], A[8], OBJ[3]]. For the first degree is an inward conception, and in reference to this He says: "Whosoever is angry with his brother." The second degree is when the anger is manifested by outward signs, even before it breaks out into effect; and in reference to this He says: "Whosoever shall say to his brother, Raca!" which is an angry exclamation. The third degree is when the sin conceived inwardly breaks out into effect. Now the effect of anger is another's hurt under the aspect of revenge; and the least of hurts is that which is done by a mere word; wherefore in reference to this He says: "Whosoever shall say to his brother Thou fool!" Consequently it is clear that the second adds to the first, and the third to both the others; so that, if the first is a mortal sin, in the case referred to by our Lord, as stated above (A[3], ad 2), much more so are the others. Wherefore some kind of condemnation is assigned as corresponding to each one of them. In the first case "judgment" is assigned, and this is the least severe, for as Augustine says [*Serm. Dom. in Monte i, 9], "where judgment is to be delivered, there is an opportunity for defense": in the second case "council" is assigned, "whereby the judges deliberate together on the punishment to be inflicted": to the third case is assigned "hell-fire," i.e. "decisive condemnation."

Whether anger should be reckoned among the capital vices?

Objection 1: It would seem that anger should not be reckoned among the capital sins. For anger is born of sorrow which is a capital vice known by the name of sloth. Therefore anger should not be reckoned a capital vice.

Objection 2: Further, hatred is a graver sin than anger. Therefore it should be reckoned a capital vice rather than anger.

Objection 3: Further, a gloss on Prov. 29:22, "An angry [Douay: 'passionate'] man provoketh quarrels," says: "Anger is the door to all vices: if it be closed, peace is ensured within to all the virtues; if it be opened, the soul is armed for every crime." Now no capital vice is the origin of all sins, but only of certain definite ones. Therefore anger should not be reckoned among the capital vices.

On the contrary, Gregory (Moral. xxxi, 45) places anger among the capital vices.

I answer that, As stated above ([3578]FS, Q[84], A[3],4), a capital vice is defined as one from which many vices arise. Now there are two reasons for which many vices can arise from anger. The first is on the part of its object which has much of the aspect of desirability, in so far as revenge is desired under the aspect of just or honest*, which is attractive by its excellence, as stated above [3579](A[4]). [*Honesty must be taken here in its broad sense as synonymous with moral goodness, from the point of view of decorum; Cf. Q[145], A[1]]. The second is on the part of its impetuosity, whereby it precipitates the mind into all kinds of inordinate action. Therefore it is evident that anger is a capital vice.

Reply to Objection 1: The sorrow whence anger arises is not, for the most part, the vice of sloth, but the passion of sorrow, which results from an injury inflicted.

Reply to Objection 2: As stated above (Q[118], A[7]; Q[148], A[5]; Q[153], A[4]; [3580]FS, Q[84], A[4]), it belongs to the notion of a capital vice to have a most desirable end, so that many sins are committed through the desire thereof. Now anger, which desires evil under the aspect of good, has a more desirable end than hatred has, since the latter desires evil under the aspect of evil: wherefore anger is more a capital vice than hatred is.

Reply to Objection 3: Anger is stated to be the door to the vices accidentally, that is by removing obstacles, to wit by hindering the judgment of reason, whereby man is withdrawn from evil. It is, however, directly the cause of certain special sins, which are called its daughters.

Whether six daughters are fittingly assigned to anger?

Objection 1: It would seem that six daughters are unfittingly assigned to anger, namely "quarreling, swelling of the mind, contumely, clamor, indignation and blasphemy." For blasphemy is reckoned by Isidore [*QQ. in Deut., qu. xvi] to be a daughter of pride. Therefore it should not be accounted a daughter of anger.

Objection 2: Further, hatred is born of anger, as Augustine says in his rule (Ep. ccxi). Therefore it should be placed among the daughters of anger.

Objection 3: Further, "a swollen mind" would seem to be the same as pride. Now pride is not the daughter of a vice, but "the mother of all vices," as Gregory states (Moral. xxxi, 45). Therefore swelling of the mind should not be reckoned among the daughters of anger.

On the contrary, Gregory (Moral. xxxi, 45) assigns these daughters to anger.

I answer that, Anger may be considered in three ways. First, as consisting in thought, and thus two vices arise from anger. one is on the part of the person with whom a man is angry, and whom he deems unworthy [indignum] of acting thus towards him, and this is called "indignation." The other vice is on the part of the man himself, in so far as he devises various means of vengeance, and with such like thoughts fills his mind, according to Job 15:2, "Will a wise man . . . fill his stomach with burning heat?" And thus we have "swelling of the mind."

Secondly, anger may be considered, as expressed in words: and thus a twofold disorder arises from anger. One is when a man manifests his anger in his manner of speech, as stated above (A[5], ad 3) of the man who says to his brother, "Raca": and this refers to "clamor," which denotes disorderly and confused speech. The other disorder is when a man breaks out into injurious words, and if these be against God, it is "blasphemy," if against one's neighbor, it is "contumely."

Thirdly, anger may be considered as proceeding to deeds; and thus anger gives rise to "quarrels," by which we are to understand all manner of injuries inflicted on one's neighbor through anger.

Reply to Objection 1: The blasphemy into which a man breaks out deliberately proceeds from pride, whereby a man lifts himself up against God: since, according to Ecclus. 10:14, "the beginning of the pride of man is to fall off from God," i.e. to fall away from reverence for Him is the first part of pride [*Cf.[3581] Q[162], A[7], ad 2]; and this gives rise to blasphemy. But the blasphemy into which a man breaks out through a disturbance of the mind, proceeds from anger.

Reply to Objection 2: Although hatred sometimes arises from anger, it has a previous cause, from which it arises more directly, namely displeasure, even as, on the other hand, love is born of pleasure. Now through displeasure, a man is moved sometimes to anger, sometimes to hatred. Wherefore it was fitting to reckon that hatred arises from sloth rather than from anger.

Reply to Objection 3: Swelling of the mind is not taken here as identical with pride, but for a certain effort or daring attempt to take vengeance; and daring is a vice opposed to fortitude.

Whether there is a vice opposed to anger resulting from lack of anger?

Objection 1: It would seem that there. is not a vice opposed to anger, resulting from lack of anger. For no vice makes us like to God. Now by being entirely without anger, a man becomes like to God, Who judges "with tranquillity" (Wis. 12:18). Therefore seemingly it is not a vice to be altogether without anger.

Objection 2: Further, it is not a vice to lack what is altogether useless. But the movement of anger is useful for no purpose, as Seneca proves in the book he wrote on anger (De Ira i, 9, seqq.). Therefore it seems that lack of anger is not a vice.

Objection 3: Further, according to Dionysius (Div. Nom. iv), "man's evil is to be without reason." Now the judgment of reason remains unimpaired, if all movement of anger be done away. Therefore no lack of anger amounts to a vice.

On the contrary, Chrysostom [*Hom. xi in Matth. in the Opus Imperfectum, falsely ascribed to St. John Chrysostom] says: "He who is not angry, whereas he has cause to be, sins. For unreasonable patience is the hotbed of many vices, it fosters negligence, and incites not only the wicked but even the good to do wrong."

I answer that, Anger may be understood in two ways. In one way, as a simple movement of the will, whereby one inflicts punishment, not through passion, but in virtue of a judgment of the reason: and thus without doubt lack of anger is a sin. This is the sense in which anger is taken in the saying of Chrysostom, for he says (Hom. xi in Matth., in the Opus Imperfectum, falsely ascribed to St. John Chrysostom): "Anger, when it has a cause, is not anger but judgment. For anger, properly speaking, denotes a movement of passion": and when a man is angry with reason, his anger is no longer from passion: wherefore he is said to judge, not to be angry. In another way anger is taken for a movement of the sensitive appetite, which is with passion resulting from a bodily transmutation. This movement is a necessary sequel, in man, to the movement of his will, since the lower appetite necessarily follows the movement of the higher appetite, unless there be an obstacle. Hence the movement of anger in the sensitive appetite cannot be lacking altogether, unless the movement of the will be altogether lacking or weak. Consequently lack of the passion of anger is also a vice, even as the lack of movement in the will directed to punishment by the judgment of reason.

Reply to Objection 1: He that is entirely without anger when he ought to be angry, imitates God as to lack of passion, but not as to God's punishing by judgment.

Reply to Objection 2: The passion of anger, like all other movements of the sensitive appetite, is useful, as being conducive to the more prompt execution [*Cf. [3582]FS, Q[24], A[3]] of reason's dictate: else, the sensitive appetite in man would be to no purpose, whereas "nature does nothing without purpose" [*Aristotle, De Coelo i, 4].

Reply to Objection 3: When a man acts inordinately, the judgment of his reason is cause not only of the simple movement of the will but also of the passion in the sensitive appetite, as stated above. Wherefore just as the removal of the effect is a sign that the cause is removed, so the lack of anger is a sign that the judgment of reason is lacking.

Day 232

OF CRUELTY (TWO ARTICLES)
We must now consider cruelty, under which head there are two points of inquiry:
(1) Whether cruelty is opposed to clemency?
(2) Of its comparison with savagery or brutality.

Whether cruelty is opposed to clemency?

Objection 1: It would seem that cruelty is not opposed to clemency. For Seneca says (De Clementia ii, 4) that "those are said to be cruel who exceed in punishing," which is contrary to justice. Now clemency is reckoned a part, not of justice but of temperance. Therefore apparently cruelty is not opposed to clemency.

Objection 2: Further, it is written (Jer. 6:23): "They are cruel, and will have no mercy"; so that cruelty would seem opposed to mercy. Now mercy is not the same as clemency, as stated above ([3583]Q[157], A[4], ad 3). Therefore cruelty is not opposed to clemency.

Objection 3: Further, clemency is concerned with the infliction of punishment, as stated above ([3584]Q[157], A[1]): whereas cruelty applies to the withdrawal of beneficence, according to Prov. 11:17, "But he that is cruel casteth off even his own kindred." Therefore cruelty is not opposed to clemency.

On the contrary, Seneca says (De Clementia ii, 4) that "the opposite of clemency is cruelty, which is nothing else but hardness of heart in exacting punishment."

I answer that, Cruelty apparently takes its name from "cruditas" [rawness]. Now just as things when cooked and prepared are wont to have an agreeable and sweet savor, so when raw they have a disagreeable and bitter taste. Now it has been stated above ([3585]Q[157], A[3], ad 1; A[4], ad 3) that clemency denotes a certain smoothness or sweetness of soul, whereby one is inclined to mitigate punishment. Hence cruelty is directly opposed to clemency.

Reply to Objection 1: Just as it belongs to equity to mitigate punishment according to reason, while the sweetness of soul which inclines one to this belongs to clemency: so too, excess in punishing, as regards the external action, belongs to injustice; but as regards the hardness of heart, which makes one ready to increase punishment, belongs to cruelty.

Reply to Objection 2: Mercy and clemency concur in this, that both shun and recoil from another's unhappiness, but in different ways. For it belongs to mercy [*Cf.[3586] Q[30], A[1]] to relieve another's unhappiness by a beneficent action, while it belongs to clemency to mitigate another's unhappiness by the cessation of punishment. And since cruelty denotes excess in exacting punishment, it is more directly opposed to clemency than to mercy; yet on account of the mutual likeness of these virtues, cruelty is sometimes taken for mercilessness.

Reply to Objection 3: Cruelty is there taken for mercilessness, which is lack of beneficence. We may also reply that withdrawal of beneficence is in itself a punishment.

Whether cruelty differs from savagery or brutality?

Objection 1: It would seem that cruelty differs not from savagery or brutality. For seemingly one vice is opposed in one way to one virtue. Now both savagery and cruelty are opposed to clemency by way of excess. Therefore it would seem that savagery and cruelty are the same.

Objection 2: Further, Isidore says (Etym. x) that "severity is as it were savagery with verity, because it holds to justice without attending to piety": so that savagery would seem to exclude that mitigation of punishment in delivering judgment which is demanded by piety. Now this has been stated to belong to cruelty (A[1], ad 1). Therefore cruelty is the same as savagery.

Objection 3: Further, just as there is a vice opposed to a virtue by way of excess, so is there a vice opposed to it by way of deficiency, which latter is opposed both to the virtue which is the mean, and to the vice which is in excess. Now the same vice pertaining to deficiency is opposed to both cruelty and savagery, namely remission or laxity. For Gregory says (Moral. xx, 5): "Let there be love, but not that which enervates, let there be severity, but without fury, let there be zeal without unseemly savagery, let there be piety without undue clemency." Therefore savagery is the same as cruelty.

On the contrary, Seneca says (De Clementia ii, 4) that "a man who is angry without being hurt, or with one who has not offended him, is not said to be cruel, but to be brutal or savage."

I answer that, "Savagery" and "brutality" take their names from a likeness to wild beasts which are also described as savage. For animals of this kind attack man that they may feed on his body, and not for some motive of justice the consideration of which belongs to reason alone. Wherefore, properly speaking, brutality or savagery applies to those who in inflicting punishment have not in view a default of the person punished, but merely the pleasure they derive from a man's torture. Consequently it is evident that it is comprised under bestiality: for such like pleasure is not human but bestial, and resulting as it does either from evil custom, or from a corrupt nature, as do other bestial emotions. On the other hand, cruelty not only regards the default of the person punished, but exceeds in the mode of punishing: wherefore cruelty differs from savagery or brutality, as human wickedness differs from bestiality, as stated in Ethic. vii, 5.

Reply to Objection 1: Clemency is a human virtue; wherefore directly opposed to it is cruelty which is a form of human wickedness. But savagery or brutality is comprised under bestiality, wherefore it is directly opposed not to clemency, but to a more excellent virtue, which the Philosopher (Ethic. vii, 5) calls "heroic" or "god-like," which according to us, would seem to pertain to the gifts of the Holy Ghost. Consequently we may say that savagery is directly opposed to the gift of piety.

Reply to Objection 2: A severe man is not said to be simply savage, because this implies a vice; but he is said to be "savage as regards the truth," on account of some likeness to savagery which is not inclined to mitigate punishment.

Reply to Objection 3: Remission of punishment is not a vice, except it disregard the order of justice, which requires a man to be punished on account of his offense, and which cruelty exceeds. On the other hand, cruelty disregards this order altogether. Wherefore remission of punishment is opposed to cruelty, but not to savagery.

OF MODESTY (TWO ARTICLES)

We must now consider modesty: and (1) Modesty in general; (2) Each of its species. Under the first head there are two points of inquiry:

(1) Whether modesty is a part of temperance?
(2) What is the matter of modesty?

Whether modesty is a part of temperance?

Objection 1: It would seem that modesty is not a part of temperance. For modesty is denominated from mode. Now mode is requisite in every virtue: since virtue is directed to good; and "good," according to Augustine (De Nat. Boni 3), "consists in mode, species, and order." Therefore modesty is a general virtue, and consequently should not be reckoned a part of temperance.

Objection 2: Further, temperance would seem to be deserving of praise chiefly on account of its moderation. Now this gives modesty its name. Therefore modesty is the same as temperance, and not one of its parts.

Objection 3: Further, modesty would seem to regard the correction of our neighbor, according to 2 Tim. 2:24,25, "The servant of the Lord must not wrangle, but be mild towards all men . . . with modesty admonishing them that resist the truth." Now admonishing wrong-doers is an act of justice or of charity, as stated above ([3587]Q[33], A[1]). Therefore seemingly modesty is a part of justice rather than of temperance.

On the contrary, Tully (De Invent. Rhet. ii, 54) reckons modesty as a part of temperance.

I answer that, As stated above ([3588]Q[141], A[4];[3589] Q[157], A[3]), temperance brings moderation into those things wherein it is most difficult to be moderate, namely the concupiscences of pleasures of touch. Now whenever there is a special virtue about some matter of very great moment, there must needs be another virtue about matters of lesser import: because the life of man requires to be regulated by the virtues with regard to everything: thus it was stated above ([3590]Q[134], A[3], ad 1), that while magnificence is about great expenditure, there is need in addition for liberality, which is concerned with ordinary expenditure. Hence there is need for a virtue to moderate other lesser matters where moderation is not so difficult. This virtue is called modesty, and is annexed to temperance as its principal.

Reply to Objection 1: When a name is common to many it is sometimes appropriated to those of the lowest rank; thus the common name of angel is appropriated to the lowest order of angels. In the same way, mode which is observed by all virtues in common, is specially appropriated to the virtue which prescribes the mode in the slightest things.

Reply to Objection 2: Some things need tempering on account of their strength, thus we temper strong wine. But moderation is necessary in all things: wherefore temperance is more concerned with strong passions, and modesty about weaker passions.

Reply to Objection 3: Modesty is to be taken there for the general moderation which is necessary in all virtues.

Whether modesty is only about outward actions?

Objection 1: It would seem that modesty is only about outward actions. For the inward movements of the passions cannot be known to other persons. Yet the Apostle enjoins (Phil. 4:5): "Let your modesty be known to all men." Therefore modesty is only about outward actions.

Objection 2: Further, the virtues that are about the passions are distinguished from justice which is about operations. Now modesty is seemingly one virtue. Therefore, if it be about outward works, it will not be concerned with inward passions.

Objection 3: Further, no one same virtue is both about things pertaining to the appetite---which is proper to the moral virtues---and about things pertaining to knowledge---which is proper to the intellectual virtues---and again about things pertaining to the irascible and concupiscible faculties. Therefore, if modesty be one virtue, it cannot be about all these things.

On the contrary, In all these things it is necessary to observe the "mode" whence modesty takes its name. Therefore modesty is about all of them.

I answer that, As stated above [3591](A[1]), modesty differs from temperance, in that temperance moderates those matters where restraint is most difficult, while modesty moderates those that present less difficulty. Authorities seem to have had various opinions about modesty. For wherever they found a special kind of good or a special difficulty of moderation, they withdrew it from the province of modesty, which they confined to lesser matters. Now it is clear to all that the restraint of pleasures of touch presents a special difficulty: wherefore all distinguished temperance from modesty.

In addition to this, moreover, Tully (De Invent. Rhet. ii, 54) considered that there was a special kind of good in the moderation of punishment; wherefore he severed clemency also from modesty, and held modesty to be about the remaining ordinary matters that require moderation. These seemingly are of four kinds. one is the movement of the mind towards some excellence, and this is moderated by "humility." The second is the desire of things pertaining to knowledge, and this is moderated by "studiousness" which is opposed to curiosity. The third regards bodily movements and actions, which require to be done becomingly and honestly [*Cf.[3592] Q[145], A[1]], whether we act seriously or in play. The fourth regards outward show, for instance in dress and the like.

To some of these matters, however, other authorities appointed certain special virtues: thus Andronicus [*De Affectibus] mentions "meekness, simplicity, humility," and other kindred virtues, of which we have spoken above (Q[143]); while Aristotle (Ethic. ii, 7) assigned {eutrapelia} to pleasures in games, as stated above ([3593]FS, Q[60], A[5]). All these are comprised under modesty as understood by Tully; and in this way modesty regards not only outward but also inward actions.

Reply to Objection 1: The Apostle speaks of modesty as regarding externals. Nevertheless the moderation of the inner man may be shown by certain outward signs.

Reply to Objection 2: Various virtues assigned by various authorities are comprised under modesty. Wherefore nothing prevents modesty from regarding matters which require different virtues. Yet there is not so great a difference between the various parts of modesty, as there is between justice, which is about operations, and temperance, which is about passions, because in actions and passions that present no great difficulty on the part of the matter, but only on the part of moderation, there is but one virtue, one namely for each kind of moderation.

Wherefore the Reply to the Third Objection also is clear.

OF HUMILITY (SIX ARTICLES)

We must consider next the species of modesty: (1) Humility, and pride which is opposed to it; (2) Studiousness, and its opposite, Curiosity; (3) Modesty as affecting words or deeds; (4) Modesty as affecting outward attire.

Concerning humility there are six points of inquiry:

(1) Whether humility is a virtue?
(2) Whether it resides in the appetite, or in the judgment of reason?
(3) Whether by humility one ought to subject oneself to all men?

(4) Whether it is a part of modesty or temperance?
(5) Of its comparison with the other virtues;
(6) Of the degrees of humility.

Whether humility is a virtue?

Objection 1: It would seem that humility is not a virtue. For virtue conveys the notion of a penal evil, according to Ps. 104:18, "They humbled his feet in fetters." Therefore humility is not a virtue.

Objection 2: Further, virtue and vice are mutually opposed. Now humility seemingly denotes a vice, for it is written (Ecclus. 19:23): "There is one that humbleth himself wickedly." Therefore humility is not a virtue.

Objection 3: Further, no virtue is opposed to another virtue. But humility is apparently opposed to the virtue of magnanimity, which aims at great things, whereas humility shuns them. Therefore it would seem that humility is not a virtue.

Objection 4: Further, virtue is "the disposition of that which is perfect" (Phys. vii, text. 17). But humility seemingly belongs to the imperfect: wherefore it becomes not God to be humble, since He can be subject to none. Therefore it seems that humility is not a virtue.

Objection 5: Further, every moral virtue is about actions and passions, according to Ethic. ii, 3. But humility is not reckoned by the Philosopher among the virtues that are about passions, nor is it comprised under justice which is about actions. Therefore it would seem not to be a virtue.

On the contrary, Origen commenting on Lk. 1:48, "He hath regarded the humility of His handmaid," says (Hom. viii in Luc.): "One of the virtues, humility, is particularly commended in Holy Writ; for our Saviour said: 'Learn of Me, because I am meek, and humble of heart.'"

I answer that, As stated above ([3594]FS, Q[23], A[2]) when we were treating of the passions, the difficult good has something attractive to the appetite, namely the aspect of good, and likewise something repulsive to the appetite, namely the difficulty of obtaining it. In respect of the former there arises the movement of hope, and in respect of the latter, the movement of despair. Now it has been stated above ([3595]FS, Q[61], A[2]) that for those appetitive movements which are a kind of impulse towards an object, there is need of a moderating and restraining moral virtue, while for those which are a kind of recoil, there is need, on the part of the appetite, of a moral virtue to strengthen it and urge it on. Wherefore a twofold virtue is necessary with regard to the difficult good: one, to temper and restrain the mind, lest it tend to high things immoderately; and this belongs to the virtue of humility: and another to strengthen the mind against despair, and urge it on to the pursuit of great things according to right reason; and this is magnanimity. Therefore it is evident that humility is a virtue.

Reply to Objection 1: As Isidore observes (Etym. x), "a humble man is so called because he is, as it were, 'humo acclinis'" [*Literally, 'bent to the ground'], i.e. inclined to the lowest place. This may happen in two ways. First, through an extrinsic principle, for instance when one is cast down by another, and thus humility is a punishment. Secondly, through an intrinsic principle: and this may be done sometimes well, for instance when a man, considering his own failings, assumes the lowest place according to his mode: thus Abraham said to the Lord (Gn. 18:27), "I will speak to my Lord, whereas I am dust and ashes." In this way humility is a virtue. Sometimes, however, this may be ill-done, for instance when man, "not understanding his honor, compares himself to senseless beasts, and becomes like to them" (Ps. 48:13).

Reply to Objection 2: As stated (ad 1), humility, in so far as it is a virtue, conveys the notion of a praiseworthy self-abasement to the lowest place. Now this is sometimes done merely as to outward signs and pretense: wherefore this is "false humility," of which Augustine says in a letter (Ep. cxlix) that it is "grievous pride," since to wit, it would seem to aim at excellence of glory. Sometimes, however, this is done by an inward movement of the soul, and in this way, properly speaking, humility is reckoned a virtue, because virtue does not consist externals, but chiefly in the inward choice of the mind, as the Philosopher states (Ethic. ii, 5).

Reply to Objection 3: Humility restrains the appetite from aiming at great things against right reason: while magnanimity urges the mind to great things in accord with right reason. Hence it is clear that magnanimity is not opposed to humility: indeed they concur in this, that each is according to right reason.

Reply to Objection 4: A thing is said to be perfect in two ways. First absolutely; such a thing contains no defect, neither in its nature nor in respect of anything else, and thus God alone is perfect. To Him humility is fitting, not as regards His Divine nature, but only as regards His assumed nature. Secondly, a thing may be said to be perfect in a restricted sense, for instance in respect of its nature or state or time. Thus a virtuous man is perfect: although in comparison with God his perfection is found wanting, according to the word of Is. 40:17, "All nations are before Him as if they had no being at all." In this way humility may be competent to every man.

Reply to Objection 5: The Philosopher intended to treat of virtues as directed to civic life, wherein the subjection of one man to another is defined according to the ordinance of the law, and consequently is a matter of legal justice. But humility, considered as a special virtue, regards chiefly the subjection of man to God, for Whose sake he humbles himself by subjecting himself to others.

Whether humility has to do with the appetite?

Objection 1: It would seem that humility concerns, not the appetite but the judgment of reason. Because humility is opposed to pride. Now pride concerns things pertaining to knowledge: for Gregory says (Moral. xxxiv, 22) that "pride, when it extends outwardly to the body, is first of all shown in the eyes": wherefore it is written (Ps. 130:1), "Lord, my heart is not exalted, nor are my eyes lofty." Now eyes are the chief aids to knowledge. Therefore it would seem that humility is chiefly concerned with knowledge, whereby one thinks little of oneself.

Objection 2: Further, Augustine says (De Virginit. xxxi) that "almost the whole of Christian teaching is humility." Consequently nothing contained in Christian teaching is incompatible with humility. Now Christian teaching admonishes us to seek the better things, according to 1 Cor. 12:31, "Be zealous for the better gifts." Therefore it belongs to humility to restrain not the desire of difficult things but the estimate thereof.

Objection 3: Further, it belongs to the same virtue both to restrain excessive movement, and to strengthen the soul against excessive withdrawal: thus fortitude both curbs daring and fortifies the soul against fear. Now it is magnanimity that strengthens the soul against the difficulties that occur in the pursuit of great things. Therefore if humility were to curb the desire of great things, it would follow that humility is not a distinct virtue from magnanimity, which is evidently false. Therefore humility is concerned, not with the desire but with the estimate of great things.

Objection 4: Further, Andronicus [*De Affectibus] assigns humility to outward show; for he says that humility is "the habit of avoiding excessive expenditure and parade." Therefore it is not concerned with the movement of the appetite.

On the contrary, Augustine says (De Poenit. [*Serm. cccli]) that "the humble man is one who chooses to be an abject in the house of the Lord, rather than to dwell in the tents of sinners." But choice concerns the appetite. Therefore humility has to do with the appetite rather than with the estimative power.

I answer that, As stated above [3596](A[1]), it belongs properly to humility, that a man restrain himself from being borne towards that which is above him. For this purpose he must know his disproportion to that which surpasses his capacity. Hence knowledge of one's own deficiency belongs to humility, as a rule guiding the appetite. Nevertheless humility is essentially in the appetite itself; and consequently it must be said that humility, properly speaking, moderates the movement of the appetite.

Reply to Objection 1: Lofty eyes are a sign of pride, inasmuch as it excludes respect and fear: for fearing and respectful persons are especially wont to lower the eyes, as though not daring to compare themselves with others. But it does not follow from this that humility is essentially concerned with knowledge.

Reply to Objection 2: It is contrary to humility to aim at greater things through confiding in one's own powers: but to aim at greater things through confidence in God's help, is not contrary to humility; especially since the more one subjects oneself to God, the more is one exalted in God's sight. Hence Augustine says (De Virginit. xxxi): "It is one thing to raise oneself to God, and another to raise oneself up against God. He that abases himself before Him, him He raiseth up; he that raises himself up against Him, him He casteth down."

Reply to Objection 3: In fortitude there is the same reason for restraining daring and for strengthening the soul against fear: since the reason in both cases is that man should set the good of reason before dangers of death. But the reason for restraining presumptuous hope which pertains to humility is not the same as the reason for strengthening the soul against despair. Because the reason for strengthening the soul against despair is the acquisition of one's proper good lest man, by despair, render himself unworthy of a good which was competent to him; while the chief reason for suppressing presumptuous hope is based on divine reverence, which shows that man ought not to ascribe to himself more than is competent to him according to the position in which God has placed him. Wherefore humility would seem to denote in the first place man's subjection to God; and for this reason Augustine (De Serm. Dom. in Monte i, 4) ascribes humility, which he understands by poverty of spirit, to the gift of fear whereby man reveres God. Hence it follows that the relation of fortitude to daring differs from that of humility to hope. Because fortitude uses daring more than it suppresses it: so that excess of daring is more like fortitude than lack of daring is. On the other hand, humility suppresses hope or confidence in self more than it uses it; wherefore excessive self-confidence is more opposed to humility than lack of confidence is.

Reply to Objection 4: Excess in outward expenditure and parade is wont to be done with a view of boasting, which is suppressed by humility. Accordingly humility has to do, in a secondary way, with externals, as signs of the inward movement of the appetite.

Whether one ought, by humility, to subject oneself to all men?

Objection 1: It would seem that one ought not, by humility, to subject oneself to all men. For, as stated above (A[2], ad 3), humility consists chiefly in man's subjection to God. Now one ought not to offer to a man that which is due to God, as is the case with all acts of religious worship. Therefore, by humility, one ought not to subject oneself to man.

Objection 2: Further, Augustine says (De Nat. et Gratia xxxiv): "Humility should take the part of truth, not of falsehood." Now some men are of the highest rank, who cannot, without falsehood, subject themselves to their inferiors. Therefore one ought not, by humility, to subject oneself to all men.

Objection 3: Further no one ought to do that which conduces to the detriment of another's spiritual welfare. But if a man subject himself to another by humility, this is detrimental to the person to whom he subjects himself; for the latter might wax proud, or despise the other. Hence Augustine says in his Rule (Ep. ccxi): "Lest through excessive humility the superior lose his authority." Therefore a man ought not, by humility, to subject himself to all.

On the contrary, It is written (Phil. 2:3): "In humility, let each esteem others better than themselves."

I answer that, We may consider two things in man, namely that which is God's, and that which is man's. Whatever pertains to defect is man's: but whatever pertains to man's welfare and perfection is God's, according to the saying of Osee 13:9, "Destruction is thy own, O Israel; thy help is only in Me." Now humility, as stated above (A[1], ad 5; A[2], ad 3), properly regards the reverence whereby man is subject to God. Wherefore every man, in respect of that which is his own, ought to subject himself to every neighbor, in respect of that which the latter has of God's: but humility does not require a man to subject what he has of God's to that which may seem to be God's in another. For those who have a share of God's gifts know that they have them, according to 1 Cor. 2:12: "That we may know the things that are given us from God." Wherefore without prejudice to humility they may set the gifts they have received from God above those that others appear to have received from Him; thus the Apostle says (Eph. 3:5): "(The mystery of Christ) was not known to the sons of men as it is now revealed to His holy apostles." In like manner. humility does not require a man to subject that which he has of his own to that which his neighbor has of man's: otherwise each one would have to esteem himself a greater sinner than anyone else: whereas the Apostle says without prejudice to humility (Gal. 2:15): "We by nature are Jews, and not of the Gentiles, sinners."

Nevertheless a man may esteem his neighbor to have some good which he lacks himself, or himself to have some evil which another has not: by reason of which, he may subject himself to him with humility.

Reply to Objection 1: We must not only revere God in Himself, but also that which is His in each one, although not with the same measure of reverence as we revere God. Wherefore we should subject ourselves with humility to all our neighbors for God's sake, according to 1 Pet. 2:13, "Be ye subject . . . to every human creature for God's sake"; but to God alone do we owe the worship of latria.

Reply to Objection 2: If we set what our neighbor has of God's above that which we have of our own, we cannot incur falsehood. Wherefore a gloss [*St. Augustine, QQ. lxxxiii, qu. 71] on Phil. 2:3, "Esteem others better than themselves," says: "We must not esteem by pretending to esteem; but we should in truth think it possible for another person to have something that is hidden to us and whereby he is better than we are, although our own good whereby we are apparently better than he, be not hidden."

Reply to Objection 3: Humility, like other virtues, resides chiefly inwardly in the soul. Consequently a man, by an inward act of the soul, may subject himself to another, without giving the other man an occasion of detriment to his spiritual welfare. This is what Augustine means in his Rule (Ep. ccxi): "With fear, the superior should prostrate himself at your feet in the sight of God." On the other hand, due moderation must be observed in the outward acts of humility even as of other virtues, lest they conduce to the detriment of others. If, however, a man does as he ought, and others take therefrom an occasion of sin, this is not imputed to the man who acts with humility; since he does not give scandal, although others take it.

Whether humility is a part of modesty or temperance?

Objection 1: It would seem that humility is not a part of modesty or temperance. For humility regards chiefly the reverence whereby one is subject to God, as stated above [3597](A[3]). Now it belongs to a theological virtue to have God for its object. Therefore humility should be reckoned a theological virtue rather than a part of temperance or modesty.

Objection 2: Further, temperance is in the concupiscible, whereas humility would seem to be in the irascible, just as pride which is opposed to it, and whose object is something difficult. Therefore apparently humility is not a part of temperance or modesty.

Objection 3: Further, humility and magnanimity are about the same object, as stated above (A[1], ad 3). But magnanimity is reckoned a part, not of temperance but of fortitude, as stated above ([3598]Q[129], A[5]). Therefore it would seem that humility is not a part of temperance or modesty.

On the contrary, Origen says (Hom. viii super Luc.): "If thou wilt hear the name of this virtue, and what it was called by the philosophers, know that humility which God regards is the same as what they called {metriotes}, i.e. measure or moderation." Now this evidently pertains to modesty or temperance. Therefore humility is a part of modesty or temperance.

I answer that, As stated above ([3599]Q[137], A[2], ad 1;[3600] Q[157], A[3], ad 2), in assigning parts to a virtue we consider chiefly the likeness that results from the mode of the virtue. Now the mode of temperance, whence it chiefly derives its praise, is the restraint or suppression of the impetuosity of a passion. Hence whatever virtues restrain or suppress, and the actions which moderate the impetuosity of the emotions, are reckoned parts of temperance. Now just as meekness suppresses the movement of anger, so does humility suppress the movement of hope, which is the movement of a spirit aiming at great things. Wherefore, like meekness, humility is accounted a part of temperance. For this reason the Philosopher (Ethic. iv, 3) says that a man who aims at small things in proportion to his mode is not magnanimous but "temperate," and such a man we may call humble. Moreover, for the reason given above ([3601]Q[160], A[2]), among the various parts of temperance, the one under which humility is comprised is modesty as understood by Tully (De Invent. Rhet. ii, 54), inasmuch as humility is nothing else than a moderation of spirit: wherefore it is written (1 Pet. 3:4): "In the incorruptibility of a quiet and meek spirit."

Reply to Objection 1: The theological virtues, whose object is our last end, which is the first principle in matters of appetite, are the causes of all the other virtues. Hence the fact that humility is caused by reverence for God does not prevent it from being a part of modesty or temperance.

Reply to Objection 2: Parts are assigned to a principal virtue by reason of a sameness, not of subject or matter, but of formal mode, as stated above ([3602]Q[137], A[2], ad 1;[3603] Q[157], A[3], ad 2). Consequently, although humility is in the irascible as its subject, it is assigned as a part of modesty or temperance by reason of its mode.

Reply to Objection 3: Although humility and magnanimity agree as to matter, they differ as to mode, by reason of which magnanimity is reckoned a part of fortitude, and humility a part of temperance.

Day 233

Whether humility is the greatest of the virtues?

Objection 1: It would seem that humility is the greatest of the virtues. For Chrysostom, expounding the story of the Pharisee and the publican (Lk. 18), says [*Eclog. hom. vii de Humil. Animi.] that "if humility is such a fleet runner even when hampered by sin that it overtakes the justice that is the companion of pride, whither will it not reach if you couple it with justice? It will stand among the angels by the judgment seat of God." Hence it is clear that humility is set above justice. Now justice is either the most exalted of all the virtues, or includes all virtues, according to the Philosopher (Ethic. v, 1). Therefore humility is the greatest of the virtues.

Objection 2: Further, Augustine says (De Verb. Dom., Serm. [*S. 10, C[1]]): "Are you thinking of raising the great fabric of spirituality? Attend first of all to the foundation of humility." Now this would seem to imply that humility is the foundation of all virtue. Therefore apparently it is greater than the other virtues.

Objection 3: Further, the greater virtue deserves the greater reward. Now the greatest reward is due to humility, since "he that humbleth himself shall be exalted" (Lk. 14:11). Therefore humility is the greatest of virtues.

Objection 4: Further, according to Augustine (De Vera Relig. 16), "Christ's whole life on earth was a lesson in moral conduct through the human nature which He assumed." Now He especially proposed His humility for our example, saying (Mat. 11:29): "Learn of Me, because I am meek and humble of heart." Moreover, Gregory says (Pastor. iii, 1) that the "lesson proposed to us in the mystery of our redemption is the humility of God." Therefore humility would seem to be the greatest of virtues.

On the contrary, Charity is set above all the virtues, according to Col. 3:14, "Above all . . . things have charity." Therefore humility is not the greatest of virtues.

I answer that, The good of human virtue pertains to the order of reason: which order is considered chiefly in reference to the end: wherefore the theological virtues are the greatest because they have the last end for their object. Secondarily, however, it is considered in reference to the ordering of the means to the end. This ordinance, as to its essence, is in the reason itself from which it issues, but by participation it is in the appetite ordered by the reason; and this ordinance is the effect of justice, especially of legal justice. Now humility makes a man a good subject to ordinance of all kinds and in all matters; while every other virtue has this effect in some special matter. Therefore after the theological virtues, after the intellectual virtues which regard the reason itself, and after justice, especially legal justice, humility stands before all others.

Reply to Objection 1: Humility is not set before justice, but before that justice which is coupled with pride, and is no longer a virtue; even so, on the other hand, sin is pardoned through humility: for it is said of the publican (Lk. 18:14) that through the merit of his humility "he went down into his house justified." Hence Chrysostom says [*De incompr. Nat. Dei, Hom. v]: "Bring me a pair of two-horse chariots: in the one harness pride with justice, in the other sin with humility: and you will see that sin outrunning justice wins not by its own strength, but by that of humility: while you will see the other pair beaten, not by the weakness of justice, but by the weight and size of pride."

Reply to Objection 2: Just as the orderly assembly of virtues is, by reason of a certain likeness, compared to a building, so again that which is the first step in the acquisition of virtue is likened to the foundation, which is first laid before the rest of the building. Now the virtues are in truth infused by God. Wherefore the first step in the acquisition of virtue may be understood in two ways. First by way of removing obstacles: and thus humility holds the first place, inasmuch as it expels pride, which "God resisteth," and makes man submissive and ever open to receive the influx of Divine grace. Hence it is written (James 4:6): "God resisteth the proud, and giveth grace to the humble." In this sense humility is said to be the foundation of the spiritual edifice. Secondly, a thing is first among virtues directly, because it is the first step towards God. Now the first step towards God is by faith, according to Heb. 11:6, "He that cometh to God must believe." In this sense faith is the foundation in a more excellent way than humility.

Reply to Objection 3: To him that despises earthly things, heavenly things are promised: thus heavenly treasures are promised to those who despise earthly riches, according to Mat. 6:19,20, "Lay not up to yourselves treasures on earth . . . but lay up to yourselves treasures in heaven." Likewise heavenly consolations are promised to those who despise worldly joys, according to Mat. 4:5, "Blessed are they that mourn, for they shall be comforted." In the same way spiritual uplifting is promised to humility, not that humility alone merits it, but because it is proper to it to despise earthly uplifting. Wherefore Augustine says (De Poenit. [*Serm. cccli]): "Think not that he who humbles himself remains for ever abased, for it is written: 'He shall be exalted.' And do not imagine that his exaltation in men's eyes is effected by bodily uplifting."

Reply to Objection 4: The reason why Christ chiefly proposed humility to us, was because it especially removes the obstacle to man's spiritual welfare consisting in man's aiming at heavenly and spiritual things, in which he is hindered by striving to become great in earthly things. Hence our Lord, in order to remove an obstacle to our spiritual welfare, showed by giving an example of humility, that outward exaltation is to be despised. Thus humility is, as it were, a disposition to man's untrammeled access to spiritual and divine goods. Accordingly as perfection is greater than disposition, so charity, and other virtues whereby man approaches God directly, are greater than humility.

Whether twelve degrees of humility are fittingly distinguished in the Rule of the Blessed Benedict?

Objection 1: It would seem that the twelve degrees of humility that are set down in the Rule of the Blessed Benedict [*St. Thomas gives these degrees in the reverse order to that followed by St. Benedict] are unfittingly distinguished. The first is to be "humble not only in heart, but also to show it in one's very person, one's eyes fixed on the ground"; the second is "to speak few and sensible words, and not to be loud of voice"; the third is "not to be easily moved, and disposed to laughter"; the fourth is "to maintain silence until one is asked"; the fifth is "to do nothing but to what one is exhorted by the common rule of the monastery"; the sixth is "to believe and acknowledge oneself viler than all"; the seventh is "to think oneself worthless and unprofitable for all purposes"; the eighth is "to confess one's sin"; the ninth is "to embrace patience by obeying under difficult and contrary circumstances"; the tenth is "to subject oneself to a superior"; the eleventh is "not to delight in fulfilling one's own desires"; the twelfth is "to fear God and to be always mindful of everything that God has commanded." For among these there are some things pertaining to the other virtues, such as obedience and patience. Again there are some that seem to involve a false opinion---and this is inconsistent with any virtue---namely to declare oneself more despicable than all men, and to confess and believe oneself to be in all ways worthless and unprofitable. Therefore these are unfittingly placed among the degrees of humility.

Objection 2: Further, humility proceeds from within to externals, as do other virtues. Therefore in the aforesaid degrees, those which concern outward actions are unfittingly placed before those which pertain to inward actions.

Objection 3: Further, Anselm (De Simil. ci, seqq.) gives seven degrees of humility, the first of which is "to acknowledge oneself contemptible"; the second, "to grieve for this"; the third, "to confess it"; the fourth, "to convince others of this, that is to wish them to believe it"; the fifth, "to bear patiently that this be said of us"; the sixth, "to suffer oneself to be treated with contempt"; the seventh, "to love being thus treated." Therefore the aforesaid degrees would seem to be too numerous.

Objection 4: Further, a gloss on Mat. 3:15 says: "Perfect humility has three degrees. The first is to subject ourselves to those who are above us, and not to set ourselves above our equals: this is sufficient. The second is to submit to our equals, and not to set ourselves before our inferiors; this is called abundant humility. The third degree is to subject ourselves to inferiors, and in this is perfect righteousness." Therefore the aforesaid degrees would seem to be too numerous.

Objection 5: Further, Augustine says (De Virginit. xxxi): "The measure of humility is apportioned to each one according to his rank. It is imperiled by pride, for the greater a man is the more liable is he to be entrapped." Now the measure of a man's greatness cannot be fixed according to a definite number of degrees. Therefore it would seem that it is not possible to assign the aforesaid degrees to humility.

I answer that, As stated above [3604](A[2]) humility has essentially to do with the appetite, in so far as a man restrains the impetuosity of his soul, from tending inordinately to great things: yet its rule is in the cognitive faculty, in that we should not deem ourselves to be above what we are. Also, the principle and origin of both these things is the reverence we bear to God. Now the inward disposition of humility leads to certain outward signs in words, deeds, and gestures, which manifest that which is hidden within, as happens also with the other virtues. For "a man is known by his look, and a wise man, when thou meetest him, by his countenance" (Ecclus. 19:26). Wherefore the aforesaid degrees of humility include something regarding the root of humility, namely the twelfth degree, "that a man fear God and bear all His commandments in mind."

Again, they include certain things with regard to the appetite, lest one aim inordinately at one's own excellence. This is done in three ways. First, by not following one's own will, and this pertains to the eleventh degree; secondly, by regulating it according to one's superior judgment, and this applies to the tenth degree; thirdly, by not being deterred from this on account of the difficulties and hardships that come in our way, and this belongs to the ninth degree.

Certain things also are included referring to the estimate a man forms in acknowledging his own deficiency, and this in three ways. First by acknowledging and avowing his own shortcomings; this belongs to the eighth degree: secondly, by deeming oneself incapable of great things, and this pertains to the seventh degree: thirdly, that in this respect one should put others before oneself, and this belongs to the sixth degree.

Again, some things are included that refer to outward signs. One of these regards deeds, namely that in one's work one should not depart from the ordinary way; this applies to the fifth degree. Two others have reference to words, namely that one should not be in a hurry to speak, which pertains to the fourth degree, and that one be not immoderate in speech, which refers to the second. The others have to do with outward gestures, for instance in restraining haughty looks, which regards the first, and in outwardly checking laughter and other signs of senseless mirth, and this belongs to the third degree.

Reply to Objection 1: It is possible, without falsehood, to deem and avow oneself the most despicable of men, as regards the hidden faults which we acknowledge in ourselves, and the hidden gifts of God which others have. Hence Augustine says (De Virginit. lii): "Bethink you that some persons are in some hidden way better than you, although outwardly you are better than they." Again, without falsehood one may avow and believe oneself in all ways unprofitable and useless in respect of one's own capability, so as to refer all one's sufficiency to God, according to 2 Cor. 3:5, "Not that we are sufficient to think anything of ourselves as of ourselves: but our sufficiency is from God." And there is nothing unbecoming in ascribing to humility those things that pertain to other virtues, since, just as one vice arises from another, so, by a natural sequence, the act of one virtue proceeds from the act of another.

Reply to Objection 2: Man arrives at humility in two ways. First and chiefly by a gift of grace, and in this way the inner man precedes the outward man. The other way is by human effort, whereby he first of all restrains the outward man, and afterwards succeeds in plucking out the inward root. It is according to this order that the degrees of humility are here enumerated.

Reply to Objection 3: All the degrees mentioned by Anselm are reducible to knowledge, avowal, and desire of one's own abasement. For the first degree belongs to the knowledge of one's own deficiency; but since it would be wrong for one to love one's own failings, this is excluded by the second degree. The third and fourth degrees regard the avowal of one's own deficiency; namely that not merely one simply assert one's failing, but that one convince another of it. The other three degrees have to do with the appetite, which seeks, not outward excellence, but outward abasement, or bears it with equanimity, whether it consist of words or deeds. For as Gregory says (Regist. ii, 10, Ep. 36), "there is nothing great in being humble towards those who treat us with regard, for even worldly people do this: but we should especially be humble towards those who make us suffer," and this belongs to the fifth and sixth degrees: or the appetite may even go so far as lovingly to embrace external abasement, and this pertains to the seventh degree; so that all these degrees are comprised under the sixth and seventh mentioned above.

Reply to Objection 4: These degrees refer, not to the thing itself, namely the nature of humility, but to the degrees among men, who are either of higher or lower or of equal degree.

Reply to Objection 5: This argument also considers the degrees of humility not according to the nature of the thing, in respect of which the aforesaid degrees are assigned, but according to the various conditions of men.

OF PRIDE (EIGHT ARTICLES)

We must next consider pride, and (1) pride in general; (2) the first man's sin, which we hold to have been pride. Under the first head there are eight points of inquiry:

(1) Whether pride is a sin?
(2) Whether it is a special vice?
(3) Wherein does it reside as in its subject?
(4) Of its species;
(5) Whether it is a mortal sin?
(6) Whether it is the most grievous of all sins?
(7) Of its relation to other sins;
(8) Whether it should be reckoned a capital vice?

Whether pride is a sin?

Objection 1: It would seem that pride is not a sin. For no sin is the object of God's promise. For God's promises refer to what He will do; and He is not the author of sin. Now pride is numbered among the Divine promises: for it is written (Is. 60:15): "I will make thee to be an everlasting pride [Douay: 'glory'], a joy unto generation and generation." Therefore pride is not a sin.

Objection 2: Further, it is not a sin to wish to be like unto God: for every creature has a natural desire for this; and especially does this become the rational creature which is made to God's image and likeness. Now it is said in Prosper's Lib. Sent. 294, that "pride is love of one's own excellence, whereby one is likened to God who is supremely excellent." Hence Augustine says (Confess. ii, 6): "Pride imitates exaltedness; whereas Thou alone art God exalted over all." Therefore pride is not a sin.

Objection 3: Further, a sin is opposed not only to a virtue but also to a contrary vice, as the Philosopher states (Ethic. ii, 8). But no vice is found to be opposed to pride. Therefore pride is not a sin.

On the contrary, It is written (Tob. 4:14): "Never suffer pride to reign in thy mind or in thy words."

I answer that, Pride [superbia] is so called because a man thereby aims higher [supra] than he is; wherefore Isidore says (Etym. x): "A man is said to be proud, because he wishes to appear above (super) what he really is"; for he who wishes to overstep beyond what he is, is proud. Now right reason requires that every man's will should tend to that which is proportionate to him. Therefore it is evident that pride denotes something opposed to right reason, and this shows it to have the character of sin, because according to Dionysius (Div. Nom. iv, 4), "the soul's evil is to be opposed to reason." Therefore it is evident that pride is a sin.

Reply to Objection 1: Pride [superbia] may be understood in two ways. First, as overpassing [supergreditur] the rule of reason, and in this sense we say that it is a sin. Secondly, it may simply denominate "super-abundance"; in which sense any super-abundant thing may be called pride: and it is thus that God promises pride as significant of super-abundant good. Hence a gloss of Jerome on the same passage (Is. 61:6) says that "there is a good and an evil pride"; or "a sinful pride which God resists, and a pride that denotes the glory which He bestows."

It may also be replied that pride there signifies abundance of those things in which men may take pride.

Reply to Objection 2: Reason has the direction of those things for which man has a natural appetite; so that if the appetite wander from the rule of reason, whether by excess or by default, it will be sinful, as is the case with the appetite for food which man desires naturally. Now pride is the appetite for excellence in excess of right reason. Wherefore Augustine says (De Civ. Dei xiv, 13) that pride is the "desire for inordinate exaltation": and hence it is that, as he asserts (De Civ. Dei xiv, 13; xix, 12), "pride imitates God inordinately: for it hath equality of fellowship under Him, and wishes to usurp Hi. dominion over our fellow-creatures."

Reply to Objection 3: Pride is directly opposed to the virtue of humility, which, in a way, is concerned about the same matter as magnanimity, as stated above ([3605]Q[161], A[1], ad 3). Hence the vice opposed to pride by default is akin to the vice of pusillanimity, which is opposed by default to magnanimity. For just as it belongs to magnanimity to urge the mind to great things against despair, so it belongs to humility to withdraw the mind from the inordinate desire of great things against presumption. Now pusillanimity, if we take it for a deficiency in pursuing great things, is properly opposed to magnanimity by default; but if we take it for the mind's attachment to things beneath what is becoming to a man, it is opposed to humility by default; since each proceeds from a smallness of mind. In the same way, on the other hand, pride may be opposed by excess, both to magnanimity and humility, from different points of view: to humility, inasmuch as it scorns subjection, to magnanimity, inasmuch as it tends to great things inordinately. Since, however, pride implies a certain elation, it is more directly opposed to humility, even as pusillanimity, which denotes littleness of soul in tending towards great things, is more directly opposed to magnanimity.

Whether pride is a special sin?

Objection 1: It would seem that pride is not a special sin. For Augustine says (De Nat. et Grat. xxix) that "you will find no sin that is not labelled pride"; and Prosper says (De Vita Contempl. iii, 2) that "without pride no sin is, or was, or ever will be possible." Therefore pride is a general sin.

Objection 2: Further, a gloss on Job 33:17, "That He may withdraw man from wickedness [*Vulg.: 'From the things that he is doing, and may deliver him from pride']," says that "a man prides himself when he transgresses His commandments by sin." Now according to Ambrose [*De Parad. viii], "every sin is a transgression of the Divine law, and a disobedience of the heavenly commandments." Therefore every sin is pride.

Objection 3: Further, every special sin is opposed to a special virtue. But pride is opposed to all the virtues, for Gregory says (Moral. xxxiv, 23): "Pride is by no means content with the destruction of one virtue; it raises itself up against all the powers of the soul, and like an all-pervading and poisonous disease corrupts the whole body"; and Isidore says (Etym. [*De Summo Bono ii, 38]) that it is "the downfall of all virtues." Therefore pride is not a special sin.

Objection 4: Further, every special sin has a special matter. Now pride has a general matter, for Gregory says (Moral. xxxiv, 23) that "one man is proud of his gold, another of his eloquence: one is elated by mean and earthly things, another by sublime and heavenly virtues." Therefore pride is not a special but a general sin.

On the contrary, Augustine says (De Nat. et Grat. xxix): "If he look into the question carefully, he will find that, according to God's law, pride is a very different sin from other vices." Now the genus is not different from its species. Therefore pride is not a general but a special sin.

I answer that, The sin of pride may be considered in two ways. First with regard to its proper species, which it has under the aspect of its proper object. In this way pride is a special sin, because it has a special object: for it is inordinate desire of one's own excellence, as stated (A[1], ad 2). Secondly, it may be considered as having a certain influence towards other sins. In this way it has somewhat of a generic character, inasmuch as all sins may arise from pride, in two ways. First directly, through other sins being directed to the end of pride which is one's own excellence, to which may be directed anything that is inordinately desired. Secondly, indirectly and accidentally as it were, that is by removing an obstacle, since pride makes a man despise the Divine law which hinders him from sinning, according to Jer. 2:20, "Thou hast broken My yoke, thou hast burst My bands, and thou saidst: I will not serve."

It must, however, be observed that this generic character of pride admits of the possibility of all vices arising from pride sometimes, but it does not imply that all vices originate from pride always. For though one may break the commandments of the Law by any kind of sin, through contempt which pertains to pride, yet one does not always break the Divine commandments through contempt, but sometimes through ignorance. and sometimes through weakness: and for this reason Augustine says (De Nat. et Grat. xxix) that "many things are done amiss which are not done through pride."

Reply to Objection 1: These words are introduced by Augustine into his book De Nat. et Grat., not as being his own, but as those of someone with whom he is arguing. Hence he subsequently disproves the assertion, and shows that not all sins are committed through pride. We might, however, reply that these authorities must be understood as referring to the outward effect of pride, namely the breaking of the commandments, which applies to every sin, and not to the inward act of pride, namely contempt of the commandment. For sin is committed, not always through contempt, but sometimes through ignorance, sometimes through weakness, as stated above.

Reply to Objection 2: A man may sometimes commit a sin effectively, but not affectively; thus he who, in ignorance, slays his father, is a parricide effectively, but not affectively, since he did not intend it. Accordingly he who breaks God's commandment is said to pride himself against God, effectively always, but not always affectively.

Reply to Objection 3: A sin may destroy a virtue in two ways. In one way by direct contrariety to a virtue, and thus pride does not corrupt every virtue, but only humility; even as every special sin destroys the special virtue opposed to it, by acting counter thereto. In another way a sin destroys a virtue, by making ill use of that virtue: and thus pride destroys every virtue, in so far as it finds an occasion of pride in every virtue, just as in everything else pertaining to excellence. Hence it does not follow that it is a general sin.

Reply to Objection 4: Pride regards a special aspect in its object, which aspect may be found in various matters: for it is inordinate love of one's excellence, and excellence may be found in various things.

Whether the subject of pride is the irascible faculty?

Objection 1: It would seem that the subject of pride is not the irascible faculty. For Gregory says (Moral. xxiii, 17): "A swollen mind is an obstacle to truth, for the swelling shuts out the light." Now the knowledge of truth pertains, not to the irascible but to the rational faculty. Therefore pride is not in the irascible.

Objection 2: Further, Gregory says (Moral. xxiv, 8) that "the proud observe other people's conduct not so as to set themselves beneath them with humility, but so as to set themselves above them with pride": wherefore it would seem that pride originates in undue observation. Now observation pertains not to the irascible but to the rational faculty.

Objection 3: Further. pride seeks pre-eminence not only in sensible things, but also in spiritual and intelligible things: while it consists essentially in the contempt of God, according to Ecclus. 10:14, "The beginning of the pride of man is to fall off from God." Now the irascible, since it is a part of the sensitive appetite, cannot extend to God and things intelligible. Therefore pride cannot be in the irascible.

Objection 4: Further, as stated in Prosper's Liber Sententiarum, sent. 294, "Pride is love of one's own excellence." But love is not in the irascible, but in the concupiscible. Therefore pride is not in the irascible.

On the contrary, Gregory (Moral. ii, 49) opposes pride to the gift of fear. Now fear belongs to the irascible. Therefore pride is in the irascible.

I answer that, The subject of any virtue or vice is to be ascertained from its proper object: for the object of a habit or act cannot be other than the object of the power, which is the subject of both. Now the proper object of pride is something difficult, for pride is the desire of one's own excellence, as stated above ([3606]AA[1],2). Wherefore pride must needs pertain in some way to the irascible faculty. Now the irascible may be taken in two ways. First in a strict sense, and thus it is a part of the sensitive appetite, even as anger, strictly speaking, is a passion of the sensitive appetite. Secondly, the irascible may be taken in a broader sense, so as to belong also to the intellective appetite, to which also anger is sometimes ascribed. It is thus that we attribute anger to God and the angels, not as a passion, but as denoting the sentence of justice pronouncing judgment. Nevertheless the irascible understood in this broad sense is not distinct from the concupiscible power, as stated above in the [3607]FP, Q[59], A[4]; FS, Q[82], A[5], ad 1 and 2.

Consequently if the difficult thing which is the object of pride, were merely some sensible object, whereto the sensitive appetite might tend, pride would have to be in the irascible which is part of the sensitive appetite. But since the difficult thing which pride has in view is common both to sensible and to spiritual things, we must needs say that the subject of pride is the irascible not only strictly so called, as a part of the sensitive appetite, but also in its wider acceptation, as applicable to the intellective appetite. Wherefore pride is ascribed also to the demons.

Reply to Objection 1: Knowledge of truth is twofold. One is purely speculative, and pride hinders this indirectly by removing its cause. For the proud man subjects not his intellect to God, that he may receive the knowledge of truth from Him, according to Mat. 11:25, "Thou hast hid these things from the wise and the prudent," i.e. from the proud, who are wise and prudent in their own eyes, "and hast revealed them to little ones," i.e. to the humble.

Nor does he deign to learn anything from man, whereas it is written (Ecclus. 6:34): "If thou wilt incline thy ear, thou shalt receive instruction." The other knowledge of truth is affective, and this is directly hindered by pride, because the proud, through delighting in their own excellence, disdain the excellence of truth; thus Gregory says (Moral. xxiii, 17) that "the proud, although certain hidden truths be conveyed to their understanding, cannot realize their sweetness: and if they know of them they cannot relish them." Hence it is written (Prov. 11:2): "Where humility is there also is wisdom."

Reply to Objection 2: As stated above ([3608]Q[161], AA[2], 6), humility observes the rule of right reason whereby a man has true self-esteem. Now pride does not observe this rule of right reason, for he esteems himself greater than he is: and this is the outcome of an inordinate desire for his own excellence, since a man is ready to believe what he desires very much, the result being that his appetite is borne towards things higher than what become him. Consequently whatsoever things lead a man to inordinate self-esteem lead him to pride: and one of those is the observing of other people's failings, just as, on the other hand, in the words of Gregory (Moral. xxiii, 17), "holy men, by a like observation of other people's virtues, set others above themselves." Accordingly the conclusion is not that pride is in the rational faculty, but that one of its causes is in the reason.

Reply to Objection 3: Pride is in the irascible, not only as a part of the sensitive appetite, but also as having a more general signification, as stated above.

Reply to Objection 4: According to Augustine (De Civ. Dei xiv, 7,9), "love precedes all other emotions of the soul, and is their cause," wherefore it may be employed to denote any of the other emotions. It is in this sense that pride is said to be "love of one's own excellence," inasmuch as love makes a man presume inordinately on his superiority over others, and this belongs properly to pride.

Whether the four species of pride are fittingly assigned by Gregory?

Objection 1: It seems that the four species of pride are unfittingly assigned by Gregory, who says (Moral. xxiii, 6): "There are four marks by which every kind of pride of the arrogant betrays itself; either when they think that their good is from themselves, or if they believe it to be from above, yet they think that it is due to their own merits; or when they boast of having what they have not, or despise others and wish to appear the exclusive possessors of what they have." For pride is a vice distinct from unbelief, just as humility is a distinct virtue from faith. Now it pertains to unbelief, if a man deem that he has not received his good from God, or that he has the good of grace through his own merits. Therefore this should not be reckoned a species of pride.

Objection 2: Further, the same thing should not be reckoned a species of different genera. Now boasting is reckoned a species of lying, as stated above ([3609]Q[110], A[2];[3610] Q[112]). Therefore it should not be accounted a species of pride.

Objection 3: Further, some other things apparently pertain to pride, which are not mentioned here. For Jerome [*Reference unknown] says that "nothing is so indicative of pride as to show oneself ungrateful": and Augustine says (De Civ. Dei xiv, 14) that "it belongs to pride to excuse oneself of a sin one has committed." Again, presumption whereby one aims at having what is above one, would seem to have much to do with pride. Therefore the aforesaid division does not sufficiently account for the different species of pride.

Objection 4: Further, we find other divisions of pride. For Anselm [*Eadmer, De Similit. xxii, seqq.] divides the uplifting of pride, saying that there is "pride of will, pride of speech, end pride of deed." Bernard [*De Grad. Humil. et Superb. x, seqq.] also reckons twelve degrees of pride, namely "curiosity, frivolity of mind, senseless mirth, boasting, singularity, arrogance, presumption, defense of one's sins, deceitful confession, rebelliousness, license, sinful habit." Now these apparently are not comprised under the species mentioned by Gregory. Therefore the latter would seem to be assigned unfittingly.

On the contrary, The authority of Gregory suffices.

I answer that, As stated above ([3611]AA[1],2,3), pride denotes immoderate desire of one's own excellence, a desire, to wit, that is not in accord with right reason. Now it must be observed that all excellence results from a good possessed. Such a good may be considered in three ways. First, in itself. For it is evident that the greater the good that one has, the greater the excellence that one derives from it. Hence when a man ascribes to himself a good greater than what he has, it follows that his appetite tends to his own excellence in a measure exceeding his competency: and thus we have the third species of pride, namely "boasting of having what one has not."

Secondly, it may be considered with regard to its cause, in so far as to have a thing of oneself is more excellent than to have it of another. Hence when a man esteems the good he has received of another as though he had it of himself, the result is that his appetite is borne towards his own excellence immoderately. Now one is cause of one's own good in two ways, efficiently and meritoriously: and thus we have the first two species of pride, namely "when a man thinks he has from himself that which he has from God," or "when he believes that which he has received from above to be due to his own merits."

Thirdly, it may be considered with regard to the manner of having it, in so far as a man obtains greater excellence through possessing some good more excellently than other men; the result again being that his appetite is borne inordinately towards his own excellence: and thus we have the fourth species of pride, which is "when a man despises others and wishes to be singularly conspicuous."

Reply to Objection 1: A true judgment may be destroyed in two ways. First, universally: and thus in matters of faith, a true judgment is destroyed by unbelief. Secondly, in some particular matter of choice, and unbelief does not do this. Thus a man who commits fornication, judges that for the time being it is good for him to commit fornication; yet he is not an unbeliever, as he would be, were he to say that universally fornication is good. It is thus in the question in point: for it pertains to unbelief to assert universally that there is a good which is not from God, or that grace is given to men for their merits, whereas, properly speaking, it belongs to pride and not to unbelief, through inordinate desire of one's own excellence, to boast of one's goods as though one had them of oneself, or of one's own merits.

Reply to Objection 2: Boasting is reckoned a species of lying, as regards the outward act whereby a man falsely ascribes to himself what he has not: but as regards the inward arrogance of the heart it is reckoned by Gregory to be a species of pride.

Reply to Objection 3: The ungrateful man ascribes to himself what he has from another: wherefore the first two species of pride pertain to ingratitude. To excuse oneself of a sin one has committed, belongs to the third species, since by so doing a man ascribes to himself the good of innocence which he has not. To aim presumptuously at what is above one, would seem to belong chiefly to the fourth species, which consists in wishing to be preferred to others.

Reply to Objection 4: The three mentioned by Anselm correspond to the progress of any particular sin: for it begins by being conceived in thought, then is uttered in word, and thirdly is accomplished in deed.

The twelve degrees mentioned by Bernard are reckoned by way of opposition to the twelve degrees of humility, of which we have spoken above ([3612]Q[161], A[6]). For the first degree of humility is to "be humble in heart, and to show it in one's very person, one's eyes fixed on the ground": and to this is opposed "curiosity," which consists in looking around in all directions curiously and inordinately. The second degree of humility is "to speak few and sensible words, and not to be loud of voice": to this is opposed "frivolity of mind," by which a man is proud of speech. The third degree of humility is "not to be easily moved and disposed to laughter," to which is opposed "senseless mirth." The fourth degree of humility is "to maintain silence until one is asked," to which is opposed "boasting". The fifth degree of humility is "to do nothing but to what one is exhorted by the common rule of the monastery," to which is opposed "singularity," whereby a man wishes to seem more holy than others. The sixth degree of humility is "to believe and acknowledge oneself viler than all," to which is opposed "arrogance," whereby a man sets himself above others. The seventh degree of humility is "to think oneself worthless and unprofitable for all purposes," to which is opposed "presumption," whereby a man thinks himself capable of things that are above him. The eighth degree of humility is "to confess one's sins," to which is opposed "defense of one's sins." The ninth degree is "to embrace patience by obeying under difficult and contrary circumstances," to which is opposed "deceitful confession," whereby a man being unwilling to be punished for his sins confesses them deceitfully. The tenth degree of humility is "obedience," to which is opposed "rebelliousness." The eleventh degree of humility is "not to delight in fulfilling one's own desires"; to this is opposed "license," whereby a man delights in doing freely whatever he will. The last degree of humility is "fear of God": to this is opposed "the habit of sinning," which implies contempt of God.

In these twelve degrees not only are the species of pride indicated, but also certain things that precede and follow them, as we have stated above with regard to humility ([3613]Q[161], A[6]).

Whether pride is a mortal sin?

Objection 1: It would seem that pride is not a mortal sin. For a gloss on Ps. 7:4, "O Lord my God, if I have done this thing," says: "Namely, the universal sin which is pride." Therefore if pride were a mortal sin, so would every sin be.

Objection 2: Further, every mortal sin is contrary to charity. But pride is apparently not contrary to charity, neither as to the love of God, nor as to the love of one's neighbor, because the excellence which, by pride, one desires inordinately, is not always opposed to God's honor, or our neighbor's good. Therefore pride is not a mortal sin.

Objection 3: Further, every mortal sin is opposed to virtue. But pride is not opposed to virtue; on the contrary, it arises therefrom, for as Gregory says (Moral. xxxiv, 23), "sometimes a man is elated by sublime and heavenly virtues." Therefore pride is not a mortal sin.

On the contrary, Gregory says (Moral. xxxiv, 23) that "pride is a most evident sign of the reprobate, and contrariwise, humility of the elect." But men do not become reprobate on account of venial sins. Therefore pride is not a venial but a mortal sin.

I answer that, Pride is opposed to humility. Now humility properly regards the subjection of man to God, as stated above ([3614]Q[161], A[1], ad 5). Hence pride properly regards lack of this subjection, in so far as a man raises himself above that which is appointed to him according to the Divine rule or measure, against the saying of the Apostle (2 Cor. 10:13), "But we will not glory beyond our measure; but according to the measure of the rule which God hath measured to us." Wherefore it is written (Ecclus. 10:14): "The beginning of the pride of man is to fall off from God" because, to wit, the root of pride is found to consist in man not being, in some way, subject to God and His rule. Now it is evident that not to be subject to God is of its very nature a mortal sin, for this consists in turning away from God: and consequently pride is, of its genus, a mortal sin. Nevertheless just as in other sins which are mortal by their genus (for instance fornication and adultery) there are certain motions that are venial by reason of their imperfection (through forestalling the judgment of reason, and being without its consent), so too in the matter of pride it happens that certain motions of pride are venial sins, when reason does not consent to them.

Reply to Objection 1: As stated above [3615](A[2]) pride is a general sin, not by its essence but by a kind of influence, in so far as all sins may have their origin in pride. Hence it does not follow that all sins are mortal, but only such as arise from perfect pride, which we have stated to be a mortal sin.

Reply to Objection 2: Pride is always contrary to the love of God, inasmuch as the proud man does not subject himself to the Divine rule as he ought. Sometimes it is also contrary to the love of our neighbor; when, namely, a man sets himself inordinately above his neighbor: and this again is a transgression of the Divine rule, which has established order among men, so that one ought to be subject to another.

Reply to Objection 3: Pride arises from virtue, not as from its direct cause, but as from an accidental cause, in so far as a man makes a virtue an occasion for pride. And nothing prevents one contrary from being the accidental cause of another, as stated in Phys. viii, 1. Hence some are even proud of their humility.

Whether pride is the most grievous of sins?

Objection 1: It would seem that pride is not the most grievous of sins. For the more difficult a sin is to avoid, the less grievous it would seem to be. Now pride is most difficult to avoid; for Augustine says in his Rule (Ep. ccxi), "Other sins find their vent in the accomplishment of evil deeds, whereas pride lies in wait for good deeds to destroy them." Therefore pride is not the most grievous of sins.

Objection 2: Further, "The greater evil is opposed to the greater good," as the Philosopher asserts (Ethic. viii, 10). Now humility to which pride is opposed is not the greatest of virtues, as stated above (Q[61], A[5]). Therefore the vices that are opposed to greater virtues, such as unbelief, despair, hatred of God, murder, and so forth, are more grievous sins than pride.

Objection 3: Further, the greater evil is not punished by a lesser evil. But pride is sometimes punished by other sins according to Rom. 1:28, where it is stated that on account of their pride of heart, men of science were delivered "to a reprobate sense, to do those things which are not convenient." Therefore pride is not the most grievous of sins.

On the contrary, A gloss on Ps. 118:51, "The proud did iniquitously," says: "The greatest sin in man is pride."

I answer that, Two things are to be observed in sin, conversion to a mutable good, and this is the material part of sin; and aversion from the immutable good, and this gives sin its formal aspect and complement. Now on the part of the conversion, there is no reason for pride being the greatest of sins, because uplifting which pride covets inordinately, is not essentially most incompatible with the good of virtue. But on the part of the aversion, pride has extreme gravity, because in other sins man turns away from God, either through ignorance or through weakness, or through desire for any other good whatever; whereas pride denotes aversion from God simply through being unwilling to be subject to God and His rule. Hence Boethius [*Cf. Cassian, de Caenob. Inst. xii, 7] says that "while all vices flee from God, pride alone withstands God"; for which reason it is specially stated (James 4:6) that "God resisteth the proud." Wherefore aversion from God and His commandments, which is a consequence as it were in other sins, belongs to pride by its very nature, for its act is the contempt of God. And since that which belongs to a thing by its nature is always of greater weight than that which belongs to it through something else, it follows that pride is the most grievous of sins by its genus, because it exceeds in aversion which is the formal complement of sin.

Reply to Objection 1: A sin is difficult to avoid in two ways. First, on account of the violence of its onslaught; thus anger is violent in its onslaught on account of its impetuosity; and "still more difficult is it to resist concupiscence, on account of its connaturality," as stated in Ethic. ii, 3,9. A difficulty of this kind in avoiding sin diminishes the gravity of the sin; because a man sins the more grievously, according as he yields to a less impetuous temptation, as Augustine says (De Civ. Dei xiv, 12,15).

Secondly, it is difficult to avoid a sin, on account of its being hidden. In this way it is difficult to avoid pride, since it takes occasion even from good deeds, as stated (A[5], ad 3). Hence Augustine says pointedly that it "lies in wait for good deeds"; and it is written (Ps. 141:4): "In the way wherein I walked, the proud [*Cf. Ps. 139:6, 'The proud have hidden a net for me.'] [Vulg.: 'they'] have hidden a snare for me." Hence no very great gravity attaches to the movement of pride while creeping in secretly, and before it is discovered by the judgment of reason: but once discovered by reason, it is easily avoided, both by considering one's own infirmity, according to Ecclus. 10:9, "Why is earth and ashes proud?" and by considering God's greatness, according to Job 15:13, "Why doth thy spirit swell against God?" as well as by considering the imperfection of the goods on which man prides himself, according to Is. 40:6, "All flesh is grass, and all the glory thereof as the flower of the field"; and farther on (Is. 64:6), "all our justices" are become "like the rag of a menstruous woman."

Reply to Objection 2: Opposition between a vice and a virtue is inferred from the object, which is considered on the part of conversion. In this way pride has no claim to be the greatest of sins, as neither has humility to be the greatest of virtues. But it is the greatest on the part of aversion, since it brings greatness upon other sins. For unbelief, by the very fact of its arising out of proud contempt, is rendered more grievous than if it be the outcome of ignorance or weakness. The same applies to despair and the like.

Reply to Objection 3: Just as in syllogisms that lead to an impossible conclusion one is sometimes convinced by being faced with a more evident absurdity, so too, in order to overcome their pride, God punishes certain men by allowing them to fall into sins of the flesh, which though they be less grievous are more evidently shameful. Hence Isidore says (De Summo Bono ii, 38) that "pride is the worst of all vices; whether because it is appropriate to those who are of highest and foremost rank, or because it originates from just and virtuous deeds, so that its guilt is less perceptible. on the other hand, carnal lust is apparent to all, because from the outset it is of a shameful nature: and yet, under God's dispensation, it is less grievous than pride. For he who is in the clutches of pride and feels it not, falls into the lusts of the flesh, that being thus humbled he may rise from his abasement."

From this indeed the gravity of pride is made manifest. For just as a wise physician, in order to cure a worse disease, allows the patient to contract one that is less dangerous, so the sin of pride is shown to be more grievous by the very fact that, as a remedy, God allows men to fall into other sins.

Day 234

Whether pride is the first sin of all?

Objection 1: It would seem that pride is not the first sin of all. For the first is maintained in all that follows. Now pride does not accompany all sins, nor is it the origin of all: for Augustine says (De Nat. et Grat. xx) that many things are done "amiss which are not done with pride." Therefore pride is not the first sin of all.

Objection 2: Further, it is written (Ecclus. 10:14) that the "beginning of . . . pride is to fall off from God." Therefore falling away from God precedes pride.

Objection 3: Further, the order of sins would seem to be according to the order of virtues. Now, not humility but faith is the first of all virtues. Therefore pride is not the first sin of all.

Objection 4: Further, it is written (2 Tim. 3:13): "Evil men and seducers shall grow worse and worse"; so that apparently man's beginning of wickedness is not the greatest of sins. But pride is the greatest of sins as stated in the foregoing Article. Therefore pride is not the first sin.

Objection 5: Further, resemblance and pretense come after the reality. Now the Philosopher says (Ethic. iii, 7) that "pride apes fortitude and daring." Therefore the vice of daring precedes the vice of pride.

On the contrary, It is written (Ecclus. 10:15): "Pride is the beginning of all sin."

I answer that, The first thing in every genus is that which is essential. Now it has been stated above [3616](A[6]) that aversion from God, which is the formal complement of sin, belongs to pride essentially, and to other sins, consequently. Hence it is that pride fulfils the conditions of a first thing, and is "the beginning of all sins," as stated above ([3617]FS, Q[84], A[2]), when we were treating of the causes of sin on the part of the aversion which is the chief part of sin.

Reply to Objection 1: Pride is said to be "the beginning of all sin," not as though every sin originated from pride, but because any kind of sin is naturally liable to arise from pride.

Reply to Objection 2: To fall off from God is said to be the beginning of pride, not as though it were a distinct sin from pride, but as being the first part of pride. For it has been said above [3618](A[5]) that pride regards chiefly subjection to God which it scorns, and in consequence it scorns to be subject to a creature for God's sake.

Reply to Objection 3: There is no need for the order of virtues to be the same as that of vices. For vice is corruptive of virtue. Now that which is first to be generated is the last to be corrupted. Wherefore as faith is the first of virtues, so unbelief is the last of sins, to which sometimes man is led by other sins. Hence a gloss on Ps. 136:7, "Rase it, rase it, even to the foundation thereof," says that "by heaping vice upon vice a man will lapse into unbelief," and the Apostle says (1 Tim. 1:19) that "some rejecting a good conscience have made shipwreck concerning the faith."

Reply to Objection 4: Pride is said to be the most grievous of sins because that which gives sin its gravity is essential to pride. Hence pride is the cause of gravity in other sins. Accordingly previous to pride there may be certain less grievous sins that are committed through ignorance or weakness. But among the grievous sins the first is pride, as the cause whereby other sins are rendered more grievous. And as that which is the first in causing sins is the last in the withdrawal from sin, a gloss on Ps. 18:13, "I shall be cleansed from the greatest sin," says: "Namely from the sin of pride, which is the last in those who return to God, and the first in those who withdraw from God."

Reply to Objection 5: The Philosopher associates pride with feigned fortitude, not that it consists precisely in this, but because man thinks he is more likely to be uplifted before men, if he seem to be daring or brave.

Whether pride should be reckoned a capital vice?

Objection 1: It would seem that pride should be reckoned a capital vice, since Isidore [*Comment. in Deut. xvi] and Cassian [*De Inst. Caenob. v, 1: Collat. v, 2] number pride among the capital vices.

Objection 2: Further, pride is apparently the same as vainglory, since both covet excellence. Now vainglory is reckoned a capital vice. Therefore pride also should be reckoned a capital vice.

Objection 3: Further, Augustine says (De Virginit. xxxi) that "pride begets envy, nor is it ever without this companion." Now envy is reckoned a capital vice, as stated above ([3619]Q[36], A[4]). Much more therefore is pride a capital vice.

On the contrary, Gregory (Moral. xxxi, 45) does not include pride among the capital vices.

I answer that, As stated above ([3620]AA[2],5, ad 1) pride may be considered in two ways; first in itself, as being a special sin; secondly, as having a general influence towards all sins. Now the capital vices are said to be certain special sins from which many kinds of sin arise. Wherefore some, considering pride in the light of a special sin, numbered it together with the other capital vices. But Gregory, taking into consideration its general influence towards all vices, as explained above (A[2], OBJ[3]), did not place it among the capital vices, but held it to be the "queen and mother of all the vices." Hence he says (Moral. xxxi, 45): "Pride, the queen of vices, when it has vanquished and captured the heart, forthwith delivers it into the hands of its lieutenants the seven principal vices, that they may despoil it and produce vices of all kinds."

This suffices for the Reply to the First Objection.

Reply to Objection 2: Pride is not the same as vainglory, but is the cause thereof: for pride covets excellence inordinately: while vainglory covets the outward show of excellence.

Reply to Objection 3: The fact that envy, which is a capital vice, arises from pride, does not prove that pride is a capital vice, but that it is still more principal than the capital vices themselves.

OF THE FIRST MAN'S SIN (FOUR ARTICLES)

We must now consider the first man's sin which was pride: and (1) his sin; (2) its punishment; (3) the temptation whereby he was led to sin.

Under the first head there are four points of inquiry:

(1) Whether pride was the first man's first sin?

(2) What the first man coveted by sinning?

(3) Whether his sin was more grievous than all other sins?

(4) Which sinned more grievously, the man or the woman?

Whether pride was the first man's first sin?

Objection 1: It would seem that pride was not the first man's first sin. For the Apostle says (Rom. 5:19) that "by the disobedience of one man many were made sinners." Now the first man's first sin is the one by which all men were made sinners in the point of original sin. Therefore disobedience, and not pride, was the first man's first sin.

Objection 2: Further, Ambrose says, commenting on Lk. 4:3, "And the devil said to Him," that the devil in tempting Christ observed the same order as in overcoming the first man. Now Christ was first tempted to gluttony, as appears from Mat. 4:3, where it was said to Him: "If thou be the Son of God, command that these stones be made bread." Therefore the first man's first sin was not pride but gluttony.

Objection 3: Further, man sinned at the devil's suggestion. Now the devil in tempting man promised him knowledge (Gn. 3:5). Therefore inordinateness in man was through the desire of knowledge, which pertains to curiosity. Therefore curiosity, and not pride, was the first sin.

Objection 4: Further, a gloss [*St. Augustine, Gen. ad lit. xi] on 1 Tim. 2:14, "The woman being seduced was in the transgression," says: "The Apostle rightly calls this seduction, for they were persuaded to accept a falsehood as being true; namely that God had forbidden them to touch that tree, because He knew that if they touched it, they would be like gods, as though He who made them men, begrudged them the godhead . . ." Now it pertains to unbelief to believe such a thing. Therefore man's first sin was unbelief and not pride.

On the contrary, It is written (Ecclus. 10:15): "Pride is the beginning of all sin." Now man's first sin is the beginning of all sin, according to Rom. 5:12, "By one man sin entered into this world." Therefore man's first sin was pride.

I answer that, Many movements may concur towards one sin, and the character of sin attaches to that one in which inordinateness is first found. And it is evident that inordinateness is in the inward movement of the soul before being in the outward act of the body; since, as Augustine says (De Civ. Dei i, 18), the sanctity of the body is not forfeited so long as the sanctity of the soul remains. Also, among the inward movements, the appetite is moved towards the end before being moved towards that which is desired for the sake of the end; and consequently man's first sin was where it was possible for his appetite to be directed to an inordinate end. Now man was so appointed in the state of innocence, that there was no rebellion of the flesh against the spirit. Wherefore it was not possible for the first inordinateness in the human appetite to result from his coveting a sensible good, to which the concupiscence of the flesh tends against the order of reason. It remains therefore that the first inordinateness of the human appetite resulted from his coveting inordinately some spiritual good. Now he would not have coveted it inordinately, by desiring it according to his measure as established by the Divine rule. Hence it follows that man's first sin consisted in his coveting some spiritual good above his measure: and this pertains to pride. Therefore it is evident that man's first sin was pride.

Reply to Objection 1: Man's disobedience to the Divine command was not willed by man for his own sake, for this could not happen unless one presuppose inordinateness in his will. It remains therefore that he willed it for the sake of something else. Now the first thing he coveted inordinately was his own excellence; and consequently his disobedience was the result of his pride. This agrees with the statement of Augustine, who says (Ad Oros [*Dial. QQ. lxv, qu. 4]) that "man puffed up with pride obeyed the serpent's prompting, and scorned God's commands."

Reply to Objection 2: Gluttony also had a place in the sin of our first parents. For it is written (Gn. 3:6): "The woman saw that the tree was good to eat, and fair to the eyes, and delightful to behold, and she took of the fruit thereof, and did eat." Yet the very goodness and beauty of the fruit was not their first motive for sinning, but the persuasive words of the serpent, who said (Gn. 3:5): "Your eyes shall be opened and you shall be as Gods": and it was by coveting this that the woman fell into pride. Hence the sin of gluttony resulted from the sin of pride.

Reply to Objection 3: The desire for knowledge resulted in our first parents from their inordinate desire for excellence. Hence the serpent began by saying: "You shall be as Gods," and added: "Knowing good and evil."

Reply to Objection 4: According to Augustine (Gen. ad lit. xi, 30), "the woman had not believed the serpent's statement that they were debarred by God from a good and useful thing, were her mind not already filled with the love of her own power, and a certain proud self-presumption." This does not mean that pride preceded the promptings of the serpent, but that as soon as the serpent had spoken his words of persuasion, her mind was puffed up, the result being that she believed the demon to have spoken truly.

Whether the first man's pride consisted in his coveting God's likeness?

Objection 1: It would seem that the first man's pride did not consist in his coveting the Divine likeness. For no one sins by coveting that which is competent to him according to his nature. Now God's likeness is competent to man according to his nature: for it is written (Gn. 1:26): "Let us make man to our image and likeness." Therefore he did not sin by coveting God's likeness.

Objection 2: Further, it would seem that man coveted God's likeness in order that he might obtain knowledge of good and evil: for this was the serpent's suggestion: "You shall be as Gods knowing good and evil." Now the desire of knowledge is natural to man, according to the saying of the Philosopher at the beginning of his Metaphysics i, 1: "All men naturally desire knowledge." Therefore he did not sin by coveting God's likeness.

Objection 3: Further, no wise man chooses the impossible. Now the first man was endowed with wisdom, according to Ecclus. 17:5, "He filled them with the knowledge of understanding." Since then every sin consists in a deliberate act of the appetite, namely choice, it would seem that the first man did not sin by coveting something impossible. But it is impossible for man to be like God, according to the saying of Ex. 15:11, "Who is like to Thee among the strong, O Lord?" Therefore the first man did not sin by coveting God's likeness.

On the contrary, Augustine commenting on Ps. 68:5 [*Enarr. in Ps. 68], "Then did I restore [Douay: 'pay'] that which I took not away," says: "Adam and Eve wished to rob the Godhead and they lost happiness."

I answer that, likeness is twofold. One is a likeness of absolute equality [*Cf. [3621]FP, Q[93], A[1]]: and such a likeness to God our first parents did not covet, since such a likeness to God is not conceivable to the mind, especially of a wise man.

The other is a likeness of imitation, such as is possible for a creature in reference to God, in so far as the creature participates somewhat of God's likeness according to its measure. For Dionysius says (Div. Nom. ix): "The same things are like and unlike to God; like, according as they imitate Him, as far as He can be imitated; unlike, according as an effect falls short of its cause." Now every good existing in a creature is a participated likeness of the first good.

Wherefore from the very fact that man coveted a spiritual good above his measure, as stated in the foregoing Article, it follows that he coveted God's likeness inordinately.

It must, however, be observed that the proper object of the appetite is a thing not possessed. Now spiritual good, in so far as the rational creature participates in the Divine likeness, may be considered in reference to three things. First, as to natural being: and this likeness was imprinted from the very outset of their creation, both on man---of whom it is written (Gn. 1:26) that God made man "to His image and likeness"---and on the angel, of whom it is written (Ezech. 28:12): "Thou wast the seal of resemblance." Secondly, as to knowledge: and this likeness was bestowed on the angel at his creation, wherefore immediately after the words just quoted, "Thou wast the seal of resemblance," we read: "Full of wisdom." But the first man, at his creation, had not yet received this likeness actually but only in potentiality. Thirdly, as to the power of operation: and neither angel nor man received this likeness actually at the very outset of his creation, because to each there remained something to be done whereby to obtain happiness.

Accordingly, while both (namely the devil and the first man) coveted God's likeness inordinately, neither of them sinned by coveting a likeness of nature. But the first man sinned chiefly by coveting God's likeness as regards "knowledge of good and evil," according to the serpent's instigation, namely that by his own natural power he might decide what was good, and what was evil for him to do; or again that he should of himself foreknow what good and what evil would befall him. Secondarily he sinned by coveting God's likeness as regards his own power of operation, namely that by his own natural power he might act so as to obtain happiness. Hence Augustine says (Gen. ad lit. xi, 30) that "the woman's mind was filled with love of her own power." On the other hand, the devil sinned by coveting God's likeness, as regards power. Wherefore Augustine says (De Vera Relig. 13) that "he wished to enjoy his own power rather than God's." Nevertheless both coveted somewhat to be equal to God, in so far as each wished to rely on himself in contempt of the order of the Divine rule.

Reply to Objection 1: This argument considers the likeness of nature: and man did not sin by coveting this, as stated.

Reply to Objection 2: It is not a sin to covet God's likeness as to knowledge, absolutely; but to covet this likeness inordinately, that is, above one's measure, this is a sin. Hence Augustine commenting on Ps. 70:18, "O God, who is like Thee?" says: "He who desires to be of himself, even as God is of no one, wishes wickedly to be like God. Thus did the devil, who was unwilling to be subject to Him, and man who refused to be, as a servant, bound by His command."

Reply to Objection 3: This argument considers the likeness of equality.

Whether the sin of our first parents was more grievous than other sins?

Objection 1: It would seem that the sin of our first parents was more grievous than other sins. For Augustine says (De Civ. Dei xiv, 15): "Great was the wickedness in sinning, when it was so easy to avoid sin." Now it was very easy for our first parents to avoid sin, because they had nothing within them urging them to sin. Therefore the sin of our first parents was more grievous than other sins.

Objection 2: Further, punishment is proportionate to guilt. Now the sin of our first parents was most severely punished, since by it "death entered into this world," as the Apostle says (Rom. 5:12). Therefore that sin was more grievous than other sins.

Objection 3: Further, the first in every genus is seemingly the greatest (Metaph. ii, 4 [*Ed. Diel. i, 1]). Now the sin of our first parents was the first among sins of men. Therefore it was the greatest.

On the contrary, Origen says [*Peri Archon i, 3]: "I think that a man who stands on the highest step of perfection cannot fail or fall suddenly: this can happen only by degrees and little by little." Now our first parents were established on the highest and perfect grade. Therefore their first sin was not the greatest of all sins.

I answer that, There is a twofold gravity to be observed in sin. one results from the very species of the sin: thus we say that adultery is a graver sin than simple fornication. The other gravity of sin results from some circumstance of place, person, or time. The former gravity is more essential to sin and is of greater moment: hence a sin is said to be grave in respect of this gravity rather than of the other. Accordingly we must say that the first man's sin was not graver than all other sins of men, as regards the species of the sin. For though pride, of its genus, has a certain pre-eminence over other sins, yet the pride whereby one denies or blasphemes God is greater than the pride whereby one covets God's likeness inordinately, such as the pride of our first parents, as stated [3622](A[2]).

But if we consider the circumstances of the persons who sinned, that sin was most grave on account of the perfection of their state. We must accordingly conclude that this sin was most grievous relatively but not simply.

Reply to Objection 1: This argument considers the gravity of sin as resulting from the person of the sinner.

Reply to Objection 2: The severity of the punishment awarded to that first sin corresponds to the magnitude of the sin, not as regards its species but as regards its being the first sin: because it destroyed the innocence of our original state, and by robbing it of innocence brought disorder upon the whole human nature.

Reply to Objection 3: Where things are directly subordinate, the first must needs be the greatest. Such is not the order among sins, for one follows from another accidentally. And thus it does not follow that the first sin is the greatest.

Whether Adam's sin was more grievous than Eve's?

Objection 1: It would seem that Adam's sin was more grievous than Eve's. For it is written (1 Tim. 2:14): "Adam was not seduced, but the woman being seduced was in the transgression": and so it would seem that the woman sinned through ignorance, but the man through assured knowledge. Now the latter is the graver sin, according to Lk. 12:47,48, "That servant who knew the will of his lord . . . and did not according to his will, shall be beaten with many stripes: but he that knew not, and did things worthy of stripes, shall be beaten with few stripes." Therefore Adam's sin was more grievous than Eve's.

Objection 2: Further, Augustine says (De Decem Chordis 3 [*Serm. ix; xcvi de Temp.]): "If the man is the head, he should live better, and give an example of good deeds to his wife, that she may imitate him." Now he who ought to do better, sins more grievously, if he commit a sin. Therefore Adam sinned more grievously than Eve.

Objection 3: Further, the sin against the Holy Ghost would seem to be the most grievous. Now Adam, apparently, sinned against the Holy Ghost, because while sinning he relied on God's mercy [*Cf.[3623] Q[21], A[2], OBJ[3]. St. Thomas is evidently alluding to the words of Peter Lombard quoted there], and this pertains to the sin of presumption. Therefore it seems that Adam sinned more grievously than Eve.

On the contrary, Punishment corresponds to guilt. Now the woman was more grievously punished than the man, as appears from Gn. 3. Therefore she sinned more grievously than the man.

I answer that, As stated [3624](A[3]), the gravity of a sin depends on the species rather than on a circumstance of that sin. Accordingly we must assert that, if we consider the condition attaching to these persons, the man's sin is the more grievous, because he was more perfect than the woman.

As regards the genus itself of the sin, the sin of each is considered to be equal, for each sinned by pride. Hence Augustine says (Gen. ad lit. xi, 35): "Eve in excusing herself betrays disparity of sex, though parity of pride."

But as regards the species of pride, the woman sinned more grievously, for three reasons. First, because she was more puffed up than the man. For the woman believed in the serpent's persuasive words, namely that God had forbidden them to eat of the tree, lest they should become like to Him; so that in wishing to attain to God's likeness by eating of the forbidden fruit, her pride rose to the height of desiring to obtain something against God's will. On the other hand, the man did not believe this to be true; wherefore he did not wish to attain to God's likeness against God's will: but his pride consisted in wishing to attain thereto by his own power. Secondly, the woman not only herself sinned, but suggested sin to the man; wherefore she sinned against both God and her neighbor. Thirdly, the man's sin was diminished by the fact that, as Augustine says (Gen. ad lit. xi, 42), "he consented to the sin out of a certain friendly good-will, on account of which a man sometimes will offend God rather than make an enemy of his friend. That he ought not to have done so is shown by the just issue of the Divine sentence."

It is therefore evident that the woman's sin was more grievous than the man's.

Reply to Objection 1: The woman was deceived because she was first of all puffed up with pride. Wherefore her ignorance did not excuse, but aggravated her sin, in so far as it was the cause of her being puffed up with still greater pride.

Reply to Objection 2: This argument considers the circumstance of personal condition, on account of which the man's sin was more grievous than the woman's.

Reply to Objection 3: The man's reliance on God's mercy did not reach to contempt of God's justice, wherein consists the sin against the Holy Ghost, but as Augustine says (Gen. ad lit. xi [*De Civ. Dei xiv, 11]), it was due to the fact that, "having had no experience of God's severity, he thought the sin to be venial," i.e. easily forgiven [*Cf. [3625]FS, Q[89], A[3], ad 1].

OF THE PUNISHMENTS OF THE FIRST MAN'S SIN (TWO ARTICLES)

We must now consider the punishments of the first sin; and under this head there are two points of inquiry: (1) Death, which is the common punishment; (2) the other particular punishments mentioned in Genesis.

Whether death is the punishment of our first parents' sin?

Objection 1: It would seem that death is not the punishment of our first parents' sin. For that which is natural to man cannot be called a punishment of sin, because sin does not perfect nature but vitiates it. Now death is natural to man: and this is evident both from the fact that his body is composed of contraries, and because "mortal" is included in the definition of man. Therefore death is not a punishment of our first parents' sin.

Objection 2: Further, death and other bodily defects are similarly found in man as well as in other animals, according to Eccles. 3:19, "The death of man and of beasts is one, and the condition of them both equal." But in dumb animals death is not a punishment of sin. Therefore neither is it so in men.

Objection 3: Further, the sin of our first parents was the sin of particular individuals: whereas death affects the entire human nature. Therefore it would seem that it is not a punishment of our first parents' sin.

Objection 4: Further, all are equally descended from our first parents. Therefore if death were the punishment of our first parents' sin, it would follow that all men would suffer death in equal measure. But this is clearly untrue, since some die sooner, and some more painfully, than others. Therefore death is not the punishment of the first sin.

Objection 5: Further, the evil of punishment is from God, as stated above ([3626]FP, Q[48], A[6]; [3627]FP, Q[49], A[2]). But death, apparently, is not from God: for it is written (Wis. 1:13): "God made not death." Therefore death is not the punishment of the first sin.

Objection 6: Further, seemingly, punishments are not meritorious, since merit is comprised under good, and punishment under evil. Now death is sometimes meritorious, as in the case of a martyr's death. Therefore it would seem that death is not a punishment.

Objection 7: Further, punishment would seem to be painful. But death apparently cannot be painful, since man does not feel it when he is dead, and he cannot feel it when he is not dying. Therefore death is not a punishment of sin.

Objection 8: Further, if death were a punishment of sin, it would have followed sin immediately. But this is not true, for our first parents lived a long time after their sin (Gn. 5:5). Therefore, seemingly, death is not a punishment of sin.

On the contrary, The Apostle says (Rom. 5:12): "By one man sin entered into this world, and by sin death."

I answer that, If any one, on account of his fault, be deprived of a favor bestowed on him the privation of that favor is a punishment of that fault. Now as we stated in the [3628]FP, Q[95], A[1]; [3629]FP, Q[97], A[1], God bestowed this favor on man, in his primitive state, that as long as his mind was subject to God, the lower powers of his soul would be subject to his rational mind, and his body to his soul. But inasmuch as through sin man's mind withdrew from subjection to God, the result was that neither were his lower powers wholly subject to his reason, whence there followed so great a rebellion of the carnal appetite against the reason: nor was the body wholly subject to the soul; whence arose death and other bodily defects. For life and soundness of body depend on the body being subject to the soul, as the perfectible is subject to its perfection. Consequently, on the other hand, death, sickness, and all defects of the body are due to the lack of the body's subjection to the soul.

It is therefore evident that as the rebellion of the carnal appetite against the spirit is a punishment of our first parents' sin, so also are death and all defects of the body.

Reply to Objection 1: A thing is said to be natural if it proceeds from the principles of nature. Now the essential principles of nature are form and matter. The form of man is his rational soul, which is, of itself, immortal: wherefore death is not natural to man on the part of his form. The matter of man is a body such as is composed of contraries, of which corruptibility is a necessary consequence, and in this respect death is natural to man. Now this condition attached to the nature of the human body results from a natural necessity, since it was necessary for the human body to be the organ of touch, and consequently a mean between objects of touch: and this was impossible, were it not composed of contraries, as the Philosopher states (De Anima ii, 11). On the other hand, this condition is not attached to the adaptability of matter to form because, if it were possible, since the form is incorruptible, its matter should rather be incorruptible. In the same way a saw needs to be of iron, this being suitable to its form and action, so that its hardness may make it fit for cutting. But that it be liable to rust is a necessary result of such a matter and is not according to the agent's choice; for, if the craftsman were able, of the iron he would make a saw that would not rust. Now God Who is the author of man is all-powerful, wherefore when He first made man, He conferred on him the favor of being exempt from the necessity resulting from such a matter: which favor, however, was withdrawn through the sin of our first parents. Accordingly death is both natural on account of a condition attaching to matter, and penal on account of the loss of the Divine favor preserving man from death [*Cf. [3630]FS, Q[85], A[6]].

Reply to Objection 2: This likeness of man to other animals regards a condition attaching to matter, namely the body being composed of contraries. But it does not regard the form, for man's soul is immortal, whereas the souls of dumb animals are mortal.

Reply to Objection 3: Our first parents were made by God not only as particular individuals, but also as principles of the whole human nature to be transmitted by them to their posterity, together with the Divine favor preserving them from death. Hence through their sin the entire human nature, being deprived of that favor in their posterity, incurred death.

Reply to Objection 4: A twofold defect arises from sin. One is by way of a punishment appointed by a judge: and such a defect should be equal in those to whom the sin pertains equally. The other defect is that which results accidentally from this punishment; for instance, that one who has been deprived of his sight for a sin he has committed, should fall down in the road. Such a defect is not proportionate to the sin, nor does a human judge take it into account, since he cannot foresee chance happenings. Accordingly, the punishment appointed for the first sin and proportionately corresponding thereto, was the withdrawal of the Divine favor whereby the rectitude and integrity of human nature was maintained. But the defects resulting from this withdrawal are death and other penalties of the present life. Wherefore these punishments need not be equal in those to whom the first sin equally appertains. Nevertheless, since God foreknows all future events, Divine providence has so disposed that these penalties are apportioned in different ways to various people. This is not on account of any merits or demerits previous to this life, as Origen held [*Peri Archon ii, 9]: for this is contrary to the words of Rom. 9:11, "When they . . . had not done any good or evil"; and also contrary to statements made in the [3631]FP, Q[90], A[4]; [3632]FP, Q[118], A[3], namely that the soul is not created before the body: but either in punishment of their parents' sins, inasmuch as the child is something belonging to the father, wherefore parents are often punished in their children; or again it is for a remedy intended for the spiritual welfare of the person who suffers these penalties, to wit that he may thus be turned away from his sins, or lest he take pride in his virtues, and that he may be crowned for his patience.

Reply to Objection 5: Death may be considered in two ways. First, as an evil of human nature, and thus it is not of God, but is a defect befalling man through his fault. Secondly, as having an aspect of good, namely as being a just punishment, and thus it is from God. Wherefore Augustine says (Retract. i, 21) that God is not the author of death, except in so far as it is a punishment.

Reply to Objection 6: As Augustine says (De Civ. Dei xiii, 5), "just as the wicked abuse not only evil but also good things, so do the righteous make good use not only of good but also of evil things. Hence it is that both evil men make evil use of the law, though the law is good, while good men die well, although death is an evil." Wherefore inasmuch as holy men make good use of death, their death is to them meritorious.

Reply to Objection 7: Death may be considered in two ways. First, as the privation of life, and thus death cannot be felt, since it is the privation of sense and life. In this way it involves not pain of sense but pain of loss. Secondly, it may be considered as denoting the corruption which ends in the aforesaid privation. Now we may speak of corruption even as of generation in two ways: in one way as being the term of alteration, and thus in the first instant in which life departs, death is said to be present. In this way also death has no pain of sense. In another way corruption may be taken as including the previous alteration: thus a person is said to die, when he is in motion towards death; just as a thing is said to be engendered, while in motion towards the state of having been engendered: and thus death may be painful.

Reply to Objection 8: According to Augustine (Gen. ad lit. [*De Pecc. Mer. et Rem. i, 16. Cf. Gen. ad lit. ii. 32]), "although our first parents lived thereafter many years, they began to die on the day when they heard the death-decree, condemning them to decline to old age."

Whether the particular punishments of our first parents are suitably appointed in Scripture?

Objection 1: It would seem that the particular punishments of our first parents are unsuitably appointed in Scripture. For that which would have occurred even without sin should not be described as a punishment for sin. Now seemingly there would have been "pain in child-bearing," even had there been no sin: for the disposition of the female sex is such that offspring cannot be born without pain to the bearer. Likewise the "subjection of woman to man" results from the perfection of the male, and the imperfection of the female sex. Again it belongs to the nature of the earth "to bring forth thorns and thistles," and this would have occurred even had there been no sin. Therefore these are unsuitable punishments of the first sin.

Objection 2: Further, that which pertains to a person's dignity does not, seemingly, pertain to his punishment. But the "multiplying of conceptions" pertains to a woman's dignity. Therefore it should not be described as the woman's punishment.

Objection 3: Further, the punishment of our first parents' sin is transmitted to all, as we have stated with regard to death [3633] (A[1]). But all "women's conceptions" are not "multiplied," nor does "every man eat bread in the sweat of his face." Therefore these are not suitable punishments of the first sin.

Objection 4: Further, the place of paradise was made for man. Now nothing in the order of things should be without purpose. Therefore it would seem that the exclusion of man from paradise was not a suitable punishment of man.

Objection 5: Further, this place of the earthly paradise is said to be naturally inaccessible. Therefore it was useless to put other obstacles in the way lest man should return thither, to wit the cherubim, and the "flaming sword turning every way."

Objection 6: Further, immediately after his sin man was subject to the necessity of dying, so that he could not be restored to immortality by the beneficial tree of life. Therefore it was useless to forbid him to eat of the tree of life, as instanced by the words of Gn. 3:22: "See, lest perhaps he . . . take . . . of the tree of life . . . and live for ever."

Objection 7: Further, to mock the unhappy seems inconsistent with mercy and clemency, which are most of all ascribed to God in Scripture, according to Ps. 144:9, "His tender mercies are over all His works." Therefore God is unbecomingly described as mocking our first parents, already reduced through sin to unhappy straits, in the words of Gn. 3:22, "Behold Adam is become as one of Us, knowing good and evil."

Objection 8: Further, clothes are necessary to man, like food, according to 1 Tim. 6:8, "Having food, and wherewith to be covered, with these we are content." Therefore just as food was appointed to our first parents before their sin, so also should clothing have been ascribed to them. Therefore after their sin it was unsuitable to say that God made for them garments of skin.

Objection 9: Further, the punishment inflicted for a sin should outweigh in evil the gain realized through the sin: else the punishment would not deter one from sinning. Now through sin our first parents gained in this, that their eyes were opened, according to Gn. 3:7. But this outweighs in good all the penal evils which are stated to have resulted from sin. Therefore the punishments resulting from our first parents' sin are unsuitably described.

On the contrary, These punishments were appointed by God, Who does all things, "in number, weight, and measure [*Vulg.: 'Thou hast ordered all things in measure, and number, and weight.']" (Wis. 11:21).

I answer that, As stated in the foregoing Article, on account of their sin, our first parents were deprived of the Divine favor, whereby the integrity of human nature was maintained in them, and by the withdrawal of this favor human nature incurred penal defects. Hence they were punished in two ways. In the first place by being deprived of that which was befitting the state of integrity, namely the place of the earthly paradise: and this is indicated (Gn. 3:23) where it is stated that "God sent him out of the paradise of pleasure." And since he was unable, of himself, to return to that state of original innocence, it was fitting that obstacles should be placed against his recovering those things that were befitting his original state, namely food (lest he should take of the tree of life) and place; for "God placed before . . . paradise . . . Cherubim, and a flaming sword." Secondly, they were punished by having appointed to them things befitting a nature bereft of the aforesaid favor: and this as regards both the body and the soul. With regard to the body, to which pertains the distinction of sex, one punishment was appointed to the woman and another to the man. To the woman punishment was appointed in respect of two things on account of which she is united to the man; and these are the begetting of children, and community of works pertaining to family life. As regards the begetting of children, she was punished in two ways: first in the weariness to which she is subject while carrying the child after conception, and this is indicated in the words (Gn. 3:16), "I will multiply thy sorrows, and thy conceptions"; secondly, in the pain which she suffers in giving birth, and this is indicated by the words (Gn. 3:16), "In sorrow shalt thou bring forth." As regards family life she was punished by being subjected to her husband's authority, and this is conveyed in the words (Gn. 3:16), "Thou shalt be under thy husband's power."

Now, just as it belongs to the woman to be subject to her husband in matters relating to the family life, so it belongs to the husband to provide the necessaries of that life. In this respect he was punished in three ways. First, by the barrenness of the earth, in the words (Gn. 3:17), "Cursed is the earth in thy work." Secondly, by the cares of his toil, without which he does not win the fruits of the earth; hence the words (Gn. 3:17), "With labor and toil shalt thou eat thereof all the days of thy life." Thirdly, by the obstacles encountered by the tillers of the soil, wherefore it is written (Gn. 3:18), "Thorns and thistles shall it bring forth to thee."

Likewise a triple punishment is ascribed to them on the part of the soul. First, by reason of the confusion they experienced at the rebellion of the flesh against the spirit; hence it is written (Gn. 3:7): "The eyes of them both were opened; and . . . they perceived themselves to be naked." Secondly, by the reproach for their sin, indicated by the words (Gn. 3:22), "Behold Adam is become as one of Us." Thirdly, by the reminder of their coming death, when it was said to him (Gn. 3:19): "Dust thou art and into dust thou shalt return." To this also pertains that God made them garments of skin, as a sign of their mortality.

Reply to Objection 1: In the state of innocence child-bearing would have been painless: for Augustine says (De Civ. Dei xiv, 26): "Just as, in giving birth, the mother would then be relieved not by groans of pain, but by the instigations of maturity, so in bearing and conceiving the union of both sexes would be one not of lustful desire but of deliberate action" [*Cf. [3634]FP, Q[98], A[2]].

The subjection of the woman to her husband is to be understood as inflicted in punishment of the woman, not as to his headship (since even before sin the man was the "head" and governor "of the woman"), but as to her having now to obey her husband's will even against her own.

If man had not sinned, the earth would have brought forth thorns and thistles to be the food of animals, but not to punish man, because their growth would bring no labor or punishment for the tiller of the soil, as Augustine says (Gen. ad lit. iii, 18). Alcuin [*Interrog. et Resp. in Gen. lxxix], however, holds that, before sin, the earth brought forth no thorns and thistles, whatever: but the former opinion is the better.

Reply to Objection 2: The multiplying of her conceptions was appointed as a punishment to the woman, not on account of the begetting of children, for this would have been the same even before sin, but on account of the numerous sufferings to which the woman is subject, through carrying her offspring after conception. Hence it is expressly stated: "I will multiply thy sorrows, and thy conceptions."

Reply to Objection 3: These punishments affect all somewhat. For any woman who conceives must needs suffer sorrows and bring forth her child with pain: except the Blessed Virgin, who "conceived without corruption, and bore without pain" [*St. Bernard, Serm. in Dom. inf. oct. Assum. B. V. M.], because her conceiving was not according to the law of nature, transmitted from our first parents. And if a woman neither conceives nor bears, she suffers from the defect of barrenness, which outweighs the aforesaid punishments. Likewise whoever tills the soil must needs eat his bread in the sweat of his brow: while those who do not themselves work on the land, are busied with other labors, for "man is born to labor" (Job 5:7): and thus they eat the bread for which others have labored in the sweat of their brow.

Reply to Objection 4: Although the place of the earthly paradise avails not man for his use, it avails him for a lesson; because he knows himself deprived of that place on account of sin, and because by the things that have a bodily existence in that paradise, he is instructed in things pertaining to the heavenly paradise, the way to which is prepared for man by Christ.

Reply to Objection 5: Apart from the mysteries of the spiritual interpretation, this place would seem to be inaccessible, chiefly on account of the extreme heat in the middle zone by reason of the nighness of the sun. This is denoted by the "flaming sword," which is described as "turning every way," as being appropriate to the circular movement that causes this heat. And since the movements of corporal creatures are set in order through the ministry of the angels, according to Augustine (De Trin. iii, 4), it was fitting that, besides the sword turning every way, there should be cherubim "to keep the way of the tree of life." Hence Augustine says (Gen. ad lit. xi, 40): "It is to be believed that even in the visible paradise this was done by heavenly powers indeed, so that there was a fiery guard set there by the ministry of angels."

Reply to Objection 6: After sin, if man had ate of the tree of life, he would not thereby have recovered immortality, but by means of that beneficial food he might have prolonged his life. Hence in the words "And live for ever," "for ever" signifies "for a long time." For it was not expedient for man to remain longer in the unhappiness of this life.

Reply to Objection 7: According to Augustine (Gen. ad lit. xi, 39), "these words of God are not so much a mockery of our first parents as a deterrent to others, for whose benefit these things are written, lest they be proud likewise, because Adam not only failed to become that which he coveted to be, but did not keep that to which he was made."

Reply to Objection 8: Clothing is necessary to man in his present state of unhappiness for two reasons. First, to supply a deficiency in respect of external harm caused by, for instance, extreme heat or cold. Secondly, to hide his ignominy and to cover the shame of those members wherein the rebellion of the flesh against the spirit is most manifest. Now these two motives do not apply to the primitive state. because then man's body could not be hurt by any outward thing, as stated in the [3635]FP, Q[97], A[2], nor was there in man's body anything shameful that would bring confusion on him. Hence it is written (Gn. 2:23): "And they were both naked, to wit Adam and his wife, and were not ashamed." The same cannot be said of food, which is necessary to entertain the natural heat, and to sustain the body.

Reply to Objection 9: As Augustine says (Gen. ad lit. xi, 31), "We must not imagine that our first parents were created with their eyes closed, especially since it is stated that the woman saw that the tree was fair, and good to eat. Accordingly the eyes of both were opened so that they saw and thought on things which had not occurred to their minds before, this was a mutual concupiscence such as they had not hitherto."

Day 235

OF OUR FIRST PARENTS' TEMPTATION (TWO ARTICLES)
We must now consider our first parents' temptation, concerning which there are two points of inquiry:
(1) Whether it was fitting for man to be tempted by the devil?
(2) Of the manner and order of that temptation.

Whether it was fitting for man to be tempted by the devil?
Objection 1: It would seem that it was not fitting for man to be tempted by the devil. For the same final punishment is appointed to the angels' sin and to man's, according to Mat. 25:41, "Go [Vulg.: 'Depart from Me'] you cursed into everlasting fire, which was prepared for the devil and his angels." Now the angels' first sin did not follow a temptation from without. Therefore neither should man's first sin have resulted from an outward temptation.

Objection 2: Further, God, Who foreknows the future, knew that through the demon's temptation man would fall into sin, and thus He knew full well that it was not expedient for man to be tempted. Therefore it would seem unfitting for God to allow him to be tempted.

Objection 3: Further, it seems to savor of punishment that anyone should have an assailant, just as on the other hand the cessation of an assault is akin to a reward. Now punishment should not precede fault. Therefore it was unfitting for man to be tempted before he sinned.

On the contrary, It is written (Ecclus. 34:11): "He that hath not been tempted [Douay: 'tried'], what manner of things doth he know?"

I answer that, God's wisdom "orders all things sweetly" (Wis. 8:1), inasmuch as His providence appoints to each one that which is befitting it according to its nature. For as Dionysius says (Div. Nom. iv), "it belongs to providence not to destroy, but to maintain, nature." Now it is a condition attaching to human nature that one creature can be helped or impeded by another. Wherefore it was fitting that God should both allow man in the state of innocence to be tempted by evil angels, and should cause him to be helped by good angels. And by a special favor of grace, it was granted him that no creature outside himself could harm him against his own will, whereby he was able even to resist the temptation of the demon.

Reply to Objection 1: Above the human nature there is another that admits of the possibility of the evil of fault: but there is not above the angelic nature. Now only one that is already become evil through sin can tempt by leading another into evil. Hence it was fitting that by an evil angel man should be tempted to sin, even as according to the order of nature he is moved forward to perfection by means of a good angel. An angel could be perfected in good by something above him, namely by God, but he could not thus be led into sin, because according to James 1:13, "God is not a tempter of evils."

Reply to Objection 2: Just as God knew that man, through being tempted, would fall into sin, so too He knew that man was able, by his free will, to resist the tempter. Now the condition attaching to man's nature required that he should be left to his own will, according to Ecclus. 15:14, "God left" man "in the hand of his own counsel." Hence Augustine says (Gen. ad lit. xi, 4): "It seems to me that man would have had no prospect of any special praise, if he were able to lead a good life simply because there was none to persuade him to lead an evil life; since both by nature he had the power, and in his power he had the will, not to consent to the persuader."

Reply to Objection 3: An assault is penal if it be difficult to resist it: but, in the state of innocence, man was able, without any difficulty, to resist temptation. Consequently the tempter's assault was not a punishment to man.

Whether the manner and order of the first temptation was fitting?

Objection 1: It would seem that the manner and order of the first temptation was not fitting. For just as in the order of nature the angel was above man, so was the man above the woman. Now sin came upon man through an angel: therefore in like manner it should have come upon the woman through the man; in other words the woman should have been tempted by the man, and not the other way about.

Objection 2: Further, the temptation of our first parents was by suggestion. Now the devil is able to make suggestions to man without making use of an outward sensible creature. Since then our first parents were endowed with a spiritual mind, and adhered less to sensible than to intelligible things, it would have been more fitting for man to be tempted with a merely spiritual, instead of an outward, temptation.

Objection 3: Further, one cannot fittingly suggest an evil except through some apparent good. But many other animals have a greater appearance of good than the serpent has. Therefore man was unfittingly tempted by the devil through a serpent.

Objection 4: Further, the serpent is an irrational animal. Now wisdom, speech, and punishment are not befitting an irrational animal. Therefore the serpent is unfittingly described (Gn. 3:1) as "more subtle than any of the beasts of the earth," or as "the most prudent of all beasts" according to another version [*The Septuagint]: and likewise is unfittingly stated to have spoken to the woman, and to have been punished by God.

On the contrary, That which is first in any genus should be proportionate to all that follow it in that genus. Now in every kind of sin we find the same order as in the first temptation. For, according to Augustine (De Trin. xii, 12), it begins with the concupiscence of sin in the sensuality, signified by the serpent; extends to the lower reason, by pleasure, signified by the woman; and reaches to the higher reason by consent in the sin, signified by the man. Therefore the order of the first temptation was fitting.

I answer that, Man is composed of a twofold nature, intellective and sensitive. Hence the devil, in tempting man, made use of a twofold incentive to sin: one on the part of the intellect, by promising the Divine likeness through the acquisition of knowledge which man naturally desires to have; the other on the part of sense. This he did by having recourse to those sensible things, which are most akin to man, partly by tempting the man through the woman who was akin to him in the same species; partly by tempting the woman through the serpent, who was akin to them in the same genus; partly by suggesting to them to eat of the forbidden fruit, which was akin to them in the proximate genus.

Reply to Objection 1: In the act of tempting the devil was by way of principal agent; whereas the woman was employed as an instrument of temptation in bringing about the downfall of the man, both because the woman was weaker than the man, and consequently more liable to be deceived, and because, on account of her union with man, the devil was able to deceive the man especially through her. Now there is no parity between principal agent and instrument, because the principal agent must exceed in power, which is not requisite in the instrumental agent.

Reply to Objection 2: A suggestion whereby the devil suggests something to man spiritually, shows the devil to have more power against man than outward suggestion has, since by an inward suggestion, at least, man's imagination is changed by the devil [*Cf. [3636]FP, Q[91], A[3]]; whereas by an outward suggestion, a change is wrought merely on an outward creature. Now the devil had a minimum of power against man before sin, wherefore he was unable to tempt him by inward suggestion, but only by outward suggestion.

Reply to Objection 3: According to Augustine (Gen. ad lit. xi, 3), "we are not to suppose that the devil chose the serpent as his means of temptation; but as he was possessed of the lust of deceit, he could only do so by the animal he was allowed to use for that purpose."

Reply to Objection 4: According to Augustine (Gen. ad lit. xi, 29), "the serpent is described as most prudent or subtle, on account of the cunning of the devil, who wrought his wiles in it: thus, we speak of a prudent or cunning tongue, because it is the instrument of a prudent or cunning man in advising something prudently or cunningly. Nor indeed (Gen. ad lit. xi, 28) did the serpent understand the sounds which were conveyed through it to the woman; nor again are we to believe that its soul was changed into a rational nature, since not even men, who are rational by nature, know what they say when a demon speaks in them. Accordingly (Gen. ad lit. xi, 29) the serpent spoke to man, even as the ass on which Balaam sat spoke to him, except that the former was the work of a devil, whereas the latter was the work of an angel. Hence (Gen. ad lit. xi, 36) the serpent was not asked why it had done this, because it had not done this in its own nature, but the devil in it, who was already condemned to everlasting fire on account of his sin: and the words addressed to the serpent were directed to him who wrought through the serpent."

Moreover, as again Augustine says (Super Gen. contra Manich. ii, 17,18), "his, that is, the devil's, punishment mentioned here is that for which we must be on our guard against him, not that which is reserved till the last judgment. For when it was said to him: 'Thou art cursed among all cattle and beasts of the earth,' the cattle are set above him, not in power, but in the preservation of their nature, since the cattle lost no heavenly bliss, seeing that they never had it, but they continue to live in the nature which they received." It is also said to him: "'Upon thy breast and belly shalt thou creep,'" according to another version [*The Septuagint] "Here the breast signifies pride, because it is there that the impulse of the soul dominates, while the belly denotes carnal desire, because this part of the body is softest to the touch: and on these he creeps to those whom he wishes to deceive." The words, "'Earth shalt thou eat all the days of thy life' may be understood in two ways. Either 'Those shall belong to thee, whom thou shalt deceive by earthly lust,' namely sinners who are signified under the name of earth, or a third kind of temptation, namely curiosity, is signified by these words:

for to eat earth is to look into things deep and dark." The putting of enmities between him and the woman "means that we cannot be tempted by the devil, except through that part of the soul which bears or reflects the likeness of a woman. The seed of the devil is the temptation to evil, the seed of the woman is the fruit of good works, whereby the temptation to evil is resisted. Wherefore the serpent lies in wait for the woman's heel, that if at any time she fall away towards what is unlawful, pleasure may seize hold of her: and she watches his head that she may shut him out at the very outset of the evil temptation."

OF STUDIOUSNESS (TWO ARTICLES)
We must next consider studiousness and its opposite, curiosity. Concerning studiousness there are two points of inquiry:
(1) What is the matter of studiousness?
(2) Whether it is a part of temperance?

Whether the proper matter of studiousness is knowledge?
Objection 1: It would seem that knowledge is not the proper matter of studiousness. For a person is said to be studious because he applies study to certain things. Now a man ought to apply study to every matter, in order to do aright what has to be done. Therefore seemingly knowledge is not the special matter of studiousness.

Objection 2: Further, studiousness is opposed to curiosity. Now curiosity, which is derived from "cura" [care], may also refer to elegance of apparel and other such things, which regard the body; wherefore the Apostle says (Rom. 13:14): "Make not provision [curam] for the flesh in its concupiscences."

Objection 3: Further it is written (Jer. 6:13): "From the least of them even to the greatest, all study [Douay: 'are given to'] covetousness." Now covetousness is not properly about knowledge, but rather about the possession of wealth, as stated above ([3637]Q[118], A[2]). Therefore studiousness, which is derived from "study," is not properly about knowledge.

On the contrary, It is written (Prov. 27:11): "Study wisdom, my son, and make my heart joyful, that thou mayest give an answer to him that reproacheth." Now study, which is commended as a virtue, is the same as that to which the Law urges. Therefore studiousness is properly about "knowledge."

I answer that, Properly speaking, study denotes keen application of the mind to something. Now the mind is not applied to a thing except by knowing that thing. Wherefore the mind's application to knowledge precedes its application to those things to which man is directed by his knowledge. Hence study regards knowledge in the first place, and as a result it regards any other things the working of which requires to be directed by knowledge. Now the virtues lay claim to that matter about which they are first and foremost; thus fortitude is concerned about dangers of death, and temperance about pleasures of touch. Therefore studiousness is properly ascribed to knowledge.

Reply to Objection 1: Nothing can be done aright as regards other matters, except in so far as is previously directed by the knowing reason. Hence studiousness, to whatever matter it be applied, has a prior regard for knowledge.

Reply to Objection 2: Man's mind is drawn, on account of his affections, towards the things for which he has an affection, according to Mat. 6:21, "Where thy treasure is, there is thy heart also." And since man has special affection for those things which foster the flesh, it follows that man's thoughts are concerned about things that foster his flesh, so that man seeks to know how he may best sustain his body. Accordingly curiosity is accounted to be about things pertaining to the body by reason of things pertaining to knowledge.

Reply to Objection 3: Covetousness craves the acquisition of gain, and for this it is very necessary to be skilled in earthly things. Accordingly studiousness is ascribed to things pertaining to covetousness.

Whether studiousness is a part of temperance?
Objection 1: It would seem that studiousness is not a part of temperance. For a man is said to be studious by reason of his studiousness. Now all virtuous persons without exception are called studious according to the Philosopher, who frequently employs the term "studious" ({spoudaios}) in this sense (Ethic. ix, 4,8,9). [*In the same sense Aristotle says in Ethic. iii, 2, that "every vicious person is ignorant of what he ought to do."] Therefore studiousness is a general virtue, and not a part of temperance.

Objection 2: Further, studiousness, as stated [3638](A[1]), pertains to knowledge. But knowledge has no connection with the moral virtues which are in the appetitive part of the soul, and pertains rather to the intellectual virtues which are in the cognitive part: wherefore solicitude is an act of prudence as stated above (Q[47], A[9]). Therefore studiousness is not a part of temperance.

Objection 3: Further, a virtue that is ascribed as part of a principal virtue resembles the latter as to mode. Now studiousness does not resemble temperance as to mode, because temperance takes its name from being a kind of restraint, wherefore it is more opposed to the vice that is in excess: whereas studiousness is denominated from being the application of the mind to something, so that it would seem to be opposed to the vice that is in default, namely, neglect of study, rather than to the vice which is in excess, namely curiosity. wherefore, on account of its resemblance to the latter, Isidore says (Etym. x) that "a studious man is one who is curious to study." Therefore studiousness is not a part of temperance.

On the contrary, Augustine says (De Morib. Eccl. 21): "We are forbidden to be curious: and this is a great gift that temperance bestows." Now curiosity is prevented by moderate studiousness. Therefore studiousness is a part of temperance.

I answer that, As stated above ([3639]Q[141], AA[3],4,5), it belongs to temperance to moderate the movement of the appetite, lest it tend excessively to that which is desired naturally. Now just as in respect of his corporeal nature man naturally desires the pleasures of food and sex, so, in respect of his soul, he naturally desires to know something; thus the Philosopher observes at the beginning of his Metaphysics i, 1: "All men have a natural desire for knowledge."

The moderation of this desire pertains to the virtue of studiousness; wherefore it follows that studiousness is a potential part of temperance, as a subordinate virtue annexed to a principal virtue. Moreover, it is comprised under modesty for the reason given above ([3640]Q[160], A[2]).

Reply to Objection 1: Prudence is the complement of all the moral virtues, as stated in Ethic. vi, 13. Consequently, in so far as the knowledge of prudence pertains to all the virtues, the term "studiousness," which properly regards knowledge, is applied to all the virtues.

Reply to Objection 2: The act of a cognitive power is commanded by the appetitive power, which moves all the powers, as stated above ([3641]FS, Q[9], A[1]). Wherefore knowledge regards a twofold good. One is connected with the act of knowledge itself; and this good pertains to the intellectual virtues, and consists in man having a true estimate about each thing. The other good pertains to the act of the appetitive power, and consists in man's appetite being directed aright in applying the cognitive power in this or that way to this or that thing. And this belongs to the virtue of seriousness. Wherefore it is reckoned among the moral virtues.

Reply to Objection 3: As the Philosopher says (Ethic. ii, 93) in order to be virtuous we must avoid those things to which we are most naturally inclined. Hence it is that, since nature inclines us. chiefly to fear dangers of death, and to seek pleasures of the flesh, fortitude is chiefly commended for a certain steadfast perseverance against such dangers, and temperance for a certain restraint from pleasures of the flesh. But as regards knowledge, man has contrary inclinations. For on the part of the soul, he is inclined to desire knowledge of things; and so it behooves him to exercise a praiseworthy restraint on this desire, lest he seek knowledge immoderately: whereas on the part of his bodily nature, man is inclined to avoid the trouble of seeking knowledge. Accordingly, as regards the first inclination studiousness is a kind of restraint, and it is in this sense that it is reckoned a part of temperance. But as to the second inclination, this virtue derives its praise from a certain keenness of interest in seeking knowledge of things; and from this it takes its name. The former is more essential to this virtue than the latter: since the desire to know directly regards knowledge, to which studiousness is directed, whereas the trouble of learning is an obstacle to knowledge, wherefore it is regarded by this virtue indirectly, as by that which removes an obstacle.

OF CURIOSITY (TWO ARTICLES)
We must next consider curiosity, under which head there are two points of inquiry:
(1) Whether the vice of curiosity can regard intellective knowledge?
(2) Whether it is about sensitive knowledge?

Whether curiosity can be about intellective knowledge?
Objection 1: It would seem that curiosity cannot be about intellective knowledge. Because, according to the Philosopher (Ethic. ii, 6), there can be no mean and extremes in things which are essentially good. Now intellective knowledge is essentially good: because man's perfection would seem to consist in his intellect being reduced from potentiality to act, and this is done by the knowledge of truth. For Dionysius says (Div. Nom. iv) that "the good of the human soul is to be in accordance with reason," whose perfection consists in knowing the truth. Therefore the vice of curiosity cannot be about intellective knowledge.

Objection 2: Further, that which makes man like to God, and which he receives from God, cannot be an evil. Now all abundance of knowledge is from God, according to Ecclus. 1:1, "All wisdom is from the Lord God," and Wis. 7:17, "He hath given me the true knowledge of things that are, to know the disposition of the whole world, and the virtues of the elements," etc. Again, by knowing the truth man is likened to God, since "all things are naked and open to His eyes" (Heb. 4:13), and "the Lord is a God of all knowledge" (1 Kings 2:3). Therefore however abundant knowledge of truth may be, it is not evil but good. Now the desire of good is not sinful. Therefore the vice of curiosity cannot be about the intellective knowledge of truth.

Objection 3: Further, if the vice of curiosity can be about any kind of intellective knowledge, it would be chiefly about the philosophical sciences. But, seemingly, there is no sin in being intent on them: for Jerome says (Super Daniel 1:8): "Those who refused to partake of the king's meat and wine, lest they should be defiled, if they had considered the wisdom and teaching of the Babylonians to be sinful, would never have consented to learn that which was unlawful": and Augustine says (De Doctr. Christ. ii, 40) that "if the philosophers made any true statements, we must claim them for our own use, as from unjust possessors." Therefore curiosity about intellective knowledge cannot be sinful.

On the contrary, Jerome [*Comment. in Ep. ad Ephes. iv, 17] says: "Is it not evident that a man who day and night wrestles with the dialectic art, the student of natural science whose gaze pierces the heavens, walks in vanity of understanding and darkness of mind?" Now vanity of understanding and darkness of mind are sinful. Therefore curiosity about intellective sciences may be sinful.

I answer that, As stated above ([3642]Q[166], A[2], ad 2) studiousness is directly, not about knowledge itself, but about the desire and study in the pursuit of knowledge. Now we must judge differently of the knowledge itself of truth, and of the desire and study in the pursuit of the knowledge of truth. For the knowledge of truth, strictly speaking, is good, but it may be evil accidentally, by reason of some result, either because one takes pride in knowing the truth, according to 1 Cor. 8:1, "Knowledge puffeth up," or because one uses the knowledge of truth in order to sin.

On the other hand, the desire or study in pursuing the knowledge of truth may be right or wrong. First, when one tends by his study to the knowledge of truth as having evil accidentally annexed to it, for instance those who study to know the truth that they may take pride in their knowledge. Hence Augustine says (De Morib. Eccl. 21): "Some there are who forsaking virtue, and ignorant of what God is, and of the majesty of that nature which ever remains the same, imagine they are doing something great, if with surpassing curiosity and keenness they explore the whole mass of this body which we call the world. So great a pride is thus begotten, that one would think they dwelt in the very heavens about which they argue." In like manner, those who study to learn something in order to sin are engaged in a sinful study, according to the saying of Jer. 9:5, "They have taught their tongue to speak lies, they have labored to commit iniquity."

Secondly, there may be sin by reason of the appetite or study directed to the learning of truth being itself inordinate; and this in four ways. First, when a man is withdrawn by a less profitable study from a study that is an obligation incumbent on him; hence Jerome says [*Epist. xxi ad Damas]: "We see priests forsaking the gospels and the prophets, reading stage-plays, and singing the love songs of pastoral idylls." Secondly, when a man studies to learn of one, by whom it is unlawful to be taught, as in the case of those who seek to know the future through the demons. This is superstitious curiosity, of which Augustine says (De Vera Relig. 4): "Maybe, the philosophers were debarred from the faith by their sinful curiosity in seeking knowledge from the demons."

Thirdly, when a man desires to know the truth about creatures, without referring his knowledge to its due end, namely, the knowledge of God. Hence Augustine says (De Vera Relig. 29) that "in studying creatures, we must not be moved by empty and perishable curiosity; but we should ever mount towards immortal and abiding things."

Fourthly, when a man studies to know the truth above the capacity of his own intelligence, since by so doing men easily fall into error: wherefore it is written (Ecclus. 3:22): "Seek not the things that are too high for thee, and search not into things above thy ability . . . and in many of His works be not curious," and further on (Ecclus. 3:26), "For . . . the suspicion of them hath deceived many, and hath detained their minds in vanity."

Reply to Objection 1: Man's good consists in the knowledge of truth; yet man's sovereign good consists, not in the knowledge of any truth, but in the perfect knowledge of the sovereign truth, as the Philosopher states (Ethic. x, 7,8). Hence there may be sin in the knowledge of certain truths, in so far as the desire of such knowledge is not directed in due manner to the knowledge of the sovereign truth, wherein supreme happiness consists.

Reply to Objection 2: Although this argument shows that the knowledge of truth is good in itself, this does not prevent a man from misusing the knowledge of truth for an evil purpose, or from desiring the knowledge of truth inordinately, since even the desire for good should be regulated in due manner.

Reply to Objection 3: The study of philosophy is in itself lawful and commendable, on account of the truth which the philosophers acquired through God revealing it to them, as stated in Rom. 1:19. Since, however, certain philosophers misuse the truth in order to assail the faith, the Apostle says (Col. 2:8): "Beware lest any man cheat you by philosophy and vain deceit, according to the tradition of men . . . and not according to Christ": and Dionysius says (Ep. vii ad Polycarp.) of certain philosophers that "they make an unholy use of divine things against that which is divine, and by divine wisdom strive to destroy the worship of God."

Whether the vice of curiosity is about sensitive knowledge?

Objection 1: It would seem that the vice of curiosity is not about sensitive knowledge. For just as some things are known by the sense of sight, so too are some things known by the senses of touch and taste. Now the vice concerned about objects of touch and taste is not curiosity but lust or gluttony. Therefore seemingly neither is the vice of curiosity about things known by the sight.

Objection 2: Further, curiosity would seem to refer to watching games; wherefore Augustine says (Confess. vi, 8) that when "a fall occurred in the fight, a mighty cry of the whole people struck him strongly, and overcome by curiosity Alypius opened his eyes." But it does not seem to be sinful to watch games, because it gives pleasure on account of the representation, wherein man takes a natural delight, as the Philosopher states (Poet. vi). Therefore the vice of curiosity is not about the knowledge of sensible objects.

Objection 3: Further, it would seem to pertain to curiosity to inquire into our neighbor's actions, as Bede observes [*Comment. in 1 Jn. 2:16]. Now, seemingly, it is not a sin to inquire into the actions of others, because according to Ecclus. 17:12, God "gave to every one of them commandment concerning his neighbor." Therefore the vice of curiosity does not regard the knowledge of such like particular sensible objects.

On the contrary, Augustine says (De Vera Relig. 38) that "concupiscence of the eyes makes men curious." Now according to Bede (Comment. in 1 Jn. 2:16) "concupiscence of the eyes refers not only to the learning of magic arts, but also to sight-seeing, and to the discovery and dispraise of our neighbor's faults," and all these are particular objects of sense. Therefore since concupiscence of the eyes is a sin, even as concupiscence of the flesh and pride of life, which are members of the same division (1 Jn. 2:16), it seems that the vice of curiosity is about the knowledge of sensible things.

I answer that, The knowledge of sensible things is directed to two things. For in the first place, both in man and in other animals, it is directed to the upkeep of the body, because by knowledge of this kind, man and other animals avoid what is harmful to them, and seek those things that are necessary for the body's sustenance. In the second place, it is directed in a manner special to man, to intellective knowledge, whether speculative or practical. Accordingly to employ study for the purpose of knowing sensible things may be sinful in two ways. First, when the sensitive knowledge is not directed to something useful, but turns man away from some useful consideration. Hence Augustine says (Confess. x, 35), "I go no more to see a dog coursing a hare in the circus; but in the open country, if I happen to be passing, that coursing haply will distract me from some weighty thought, and draw me after it . . . and unless Thou, having made me see my weakness, didst speedily admonish me, I become foolishly dull." Secondly, when the knowledge of sensible things is directed to something harmful, as looking on a woman is directed to lust: even so the busy inquiry into other people's actions is directed to detraction. on the other hand, if one be ordinately intent on the knowledge of sensible things by reason of the necessity of sustaining nature, or for the sake of the study of intelligible truth, this studiousness about the knowledge of sensible things is virtuous.

Reply to Objection 1: Lust and gluttony are about pleasures arising from the use of objects of touch, whereas curiosity is about pleasures arising from the knowledge acquired through all the senses. According to Augustine (Confess. x, 35) "it is called concupiscence of the eyes" because "the sight is the sense chiefly used for obtaining knowledge, so that all sensible things are said to be seen," and as he says further on: "By this it may more evidently be discerned wherein pleasure and wherein curiosity is the object of the senses; for pleasure seeketh objects beautiful, melodious, fragrant, savory, soft; but curiosity, for trial's sake, seeketh even the contraries of these, not for the sake of suffering annoyance, but out of the lust of experiment and knowledge."

Reply to Objection 2: Sight-seeing becomes sinful, when it renders a man prone to the vices of lust and cruelty on account of things he sees represented. Hence Chrysostom says [*Hom. vi in Matth.] that such sights make men adulterers and shameless.

Reply to Objection 3: One may watch other people's actions or inquire into them, with a good intent, either for one's own good---that is in order to be encouraged to better deeds by the deeds of our neighbor---or for our neighbor's good---that is in order to correct him, if he do anything wrong, according to the rule of charity and the duty of one's position. This is praiseworthy, according to Heb. 10:24, "Consider one another to provoke unto charity and to good works." But to observe our neighbor's faults with the intention of looking down upon them, or of detracting them, or even with no further purpose than that of disturbing them, is sinful: hence it is written (Prov. 24:15), "Lie not in wait, nor seek after wickedness in the house of the just, nor spoil his rest."

OF MODESTY AS CONSISTING IN THE OUTWARD MOVEMENTS OF THE BODY (FOUR ARTICLES)

We must next consider modesty as consisting in the outward movements of the body, and under this head there are four points of inquiry:

(1) Whether there can be virtue and vice in the outward movements of the body that are done seriously?

(2) Whether there can be a virtue about playful actions?

(3) Of the sin consisting in excess of play;

(4) Of the sin consisting in lack of play.

Whether any virtue regards the outward movements of the body?

Objection 1: It would seem that no virtue regards the outward movements of the body. For every virtue pertains to the spiritual beauty of the soul, according to Ps. 44:14, "All the glory of the king's daughter is within," and a gloss adds, "namely, in the conscience." Now the movements of the body are not within, but without. Therefore there can be no virtue about them.

Objection 2: Further, "Virtues are not in us by nature," as the Philosopher states (Ethic. ii, 1). But outward bodily movements are in man by nature, since it is by nature that some are quick, and some slow of movement, and the same applies to other differences of outward movements. Therefore there is no virtue about movements of this kind.

Objection 3: Further, every moral virtue is either about actions directed to another person, as justice, or about passions, as temperance and fortitude. Now outward bodily movements are not directed to another person, nor are they passions. Therefore no virtue is connected with them.

Objection 4: Further, study should be applied to all works of virtue, as stated above ([3643]Q[166], A[1], OBJ[1]; A[2], ad 1). Now it is censurable to apply study to the ordering of one's outward movements: for Ambrose says (De Offic. i, 18): "A becoming gait is one that reflects the carriage of authority, has the tread of gravity, and the foot-print of tranquillity: yet so that there be neither study nor affectation, but natural and artless movement." Therefore seemingly there is no virtue about the style of outward movements.

On the contrary, The beauty of honesty [*Cf.[3644] Q[145], A[1]] pertains to virtue. Now the style of outward movements pertains to the beauty of honesty. For Ambrose says (De Offic. i, 18): "The sound of the voice and the gesture of the body are distasteful to me, whether they be unduly soft and nerveless, or coarse and boorish. Let nature be our model; her reflection is gracefulness of conduct and beauty of honesty." Therefore there is a virtue about the style of outward movement.

I answer that, Moral virtue consists in the things pertaining to man being directed by his reason. Now it is manifest that the outward movements of man are dirigible by reason, since the outward members are set in motion at the command of reason. Hence it is evident that there is a moral virtue concerned with the direction of these movements.

Now the direction of these movements may be considered from a twofold standpoint. First, in respect of fittingness to the person; secondly, in respect of fittingness to externals, whether persons, business, or place. Hence Ambrose says (De Offic. i, 18): "Beauty of conduct consists in becoming behavior towards others, according to their sex and person," and this regards the first. As to the second, he adds: "This is the best way to order our behavior, this is the polish becoming to every action."

Hence Andronicus [*De Affectibus] ascribes two things to these outward movements: namely "taste" [ornatus] which regards what is becoming to the person, wherefore he says that it is the knowledge of what is becoming in movement and behavior; and "methodicalness" [bona ordinatio] which regards what is becoming to the business in hand, and to one's surroundings, wherefore he calls it "the practical knowledge of separation," i.e. of the distinction of "acts."

Reply to Objection 1: Outward movements are signs of the inward disposition, according to Ecclus. 19:27, "The attire of the body, and the laughter of the teeth, and the gait of the man, show what he is"; and Ambrose says (De Offic. i, 18) that "the habit of mind is seen in the gesture of the body," and that "the body's movement is an index of the soul."

Reply to Objection 2: Although it is from natural disposition that a man is inclined to this or that style of outward movement, nevertheless what is lacking to nature can be supplied by the efforts of reason. Hence Ambrose says (De Offic. i, 18): "Let nature guide the movement: and if nature fail in any respect, surely effort will supply the defect."

Reply to Objection 3: As stated (ad 1) outward movements are indications of the inward disposition, and this regards chiefly the passions of the soul. Wherefore Ambrose says (De Offic. i, 18) that "from these things," i.e. the outward movements, "the man that lies hidden in our hearts is esteemed to be either frivolous, or boastful, or impure, or on the other hand sedate, steady, pure, and free from blemish." It is moreover from our outward movements that other men form their judgment about us, according to Ecclus. 19:26, "A man is known by his look, and a wise man, when thou meetest him, is known by his countenance." Hence moderation of outward movements is directed somewhat to other persons, according to the saying of Augustine in his Rule (Ep. ccxi), "In all your movements, let nothing be done to offend the eye of another, but only that which is becoming to the holiness of your state." Wherefore the moderation of outward movements may be reduced to two virtues, which the Philosopher mentions in Ethic. iv, 6,7. For, in so far as by outward movements we are directed to other persons, the moderation of our outward movements belongs to "friendliness or affability" [*Cf.[3645] Q[114], A[1]]. This regards pleasure or pain which may arise from words or deeds in reference to others with whom a man comes in contact. And, in so far as outward movements are signs of our inward disposition, their moderation belongs to the virtue of truthfulness [*Cf. Q[9]], whereby a man, by word and deed, shows himself to be such as he is inwardly.

Reply to Objection 4: It is censurable to study the style of one's outward movements, by having recourse to pretense in them, so that they do not agree with one's inward disposition. Nevertheless it behooves one to study them, so that if they be in any way inordinate, this may be corrected. Hence Ambrose says (De Offic. i, 18): "Let them be without artifice, but not without correction."

Whether there can be a virtue about games?

Objection 1: It would seem that there cannot be a virtue about games. For Ambrose says (De Offic. i, 23): "Our Lord said: 'Woe to you who laugh, for you shall weep.' Wherefore I consider that all, and not only excessive, games should be avoided." Now that which can be done virtuously is not to be avoided altogether. Therefore there cannot be a virtue about games.

Objection 2: Further, "Virtue is that which God forms in us, without us," as stated above ([3646]FS, Q[55], A[4]). Now Chrysostom says [*Hom. vi in Matth.]: "It is not God, but the devil, that is the author of fun. Listen to what happened to those who played: 'The people sat down to eat and drink, and they rose up to play.'" Therefore there can be no virtue about games.

Objection 3: Further, the Philosopher says (Ethic. x, 6) that "playful actions are not directed to something else." But it is a requisite of virtue that the agent in choosing should "direct his action to something else," as the Philosopher states (Ethic. ii, 4). Therefore there can be no virtue about games.

On the contrary, Augustine says (Music. ii, 15): "I pray thee, spare thyself at times: for it becomes a wise man sometimes to relax the high pressure of his attention to work." Now this relaxation of the mind from work consists in playful words or deeds. Therefore it becomes a wise and virtuous man to have recourse to such things at times. Moreover the Philosopher [*Ethic. ii, 7; iv, 8] assigns to games the virtue of {eutrapelia}, which we may call "pleasantness."

I answer that, Just as man needs bodily rest for the body's refreshment, because he cannot always be at work, since his power is finite and equal to a certain fixed amount of labor, so too is it with his soul, whose power is also finite and equal to a fixed amount of work. Consequently when he goes beyond his measure in a certain work, he is oppressed and becomes weary, and all the more since when the soul works, the body is at work likewise, in so far as the intellective soul employs forces that operate through bodily organs. Now sensible goods are connatural to man, and therefore, when the soul arises above sensibles, through being intent on the operations of reason, there results in consequence a certain weariness of soul, whether the operations with which it is occupied be those of the practical or of the speculative reason. Yet this weariness is greater if the soul be occupied with the work of contemplation, since thereby it is raised higher above sensible things; although perhaps certain outward works of the practical reason entail a greater bodily labor. In either case, however, one man is more soul-wearied than another, according as he is more intensely occupied with works of reason. Now just as weariness of the body is dispelled by resting the body, so weariness of the soul must needs be remedied by resting the soul: and the soul's rest is pleasure, as stated above ([3647]FS, Q[25], A[2]; [3648]FS, Q[31], A[1], ad 2). Consequently, the remedy for weariness of soul must needs consist in the application of some pleasure, by slackening the tension of the reason's study. Thus in the Conferences of the Fathers xxiv, 21, it is related of Blessed John the Evangelist, that when some people were scandalized on finding him playing together with his disciples, he is said to have told one of them who carried a bow to shoot an arrow. And when the latter had done this several times, he asked him whether he could do it indefinitely, and the man answered that if he continued doing it, the bow would break. Whence the Blessed John drew the inference that in like manner man's mind would break if its tension were never relaxed.

Now such like words or deeds wherein nothing further is sought than the soul's delight, are called playful or humorous. Hence it is necessary at times to make use of them, in order to give rest, as it were, to the soul. This is in agreement with the statement of the Philosopher (Ethic. iv, 8) that "in the intercourse of this life there is a kind of rest that is associated with games": and consequently it is sometimes necessary to make use of such things.

Nevertheless it would seem that in this matter there are three points which require especial caution. The first and chief is that the pleasure in question should not be sought in indecent or injurious deeds or words. Wherefore Tully says (De Offic. i, 29) that "one kind of joke is discourteous, insolent, scandalous, obscene." Another thing to be observed is that one lose not the balance of one's mind altogether. Hence Ambrose says (De Offic. i, 20): "We should beware lest, when we seek relaxation of mind, we destroy all that harmony which is the concord of good works": and Tully says (De Offic. i, 29), that, "just as we do not allow children to enjoy absolute freedom in their games, but only that which is consistent with good behavior, so our very fun should reflect something of an upright mind." Thirdly, we must be careful, as in all other human actions, to conform ourselves to persons, time, and place, and take due account of other circumstances, so that our fun "befit the hour and the man," as Tully says (De Offic. i, 29).

Now these things are directed according to the rule of reason: and a habit that operates according to reason is virtue. Therefore there can be a virtue about games. The Philosopher gives it the name of wittiness ({eutrapelia}), and a man is said to be pleasant through having a happy turn* of mind, whereby he gives his words and deeds a cheerful turn: and inasmuch as this virtue restrains a man from immoderate fun, it is comprised under modesty. [*{Eutrapelia} is derived from {trepein} = 'to turn'].

Reply to Objection 1: As stated above, fun should fit with business and persons; wherefore Tully says (De Invent. Rhet. i, 17) that "when the audience is weary, it will be useful for the speaker to try something novel or amusing, provided that joking be not incompatible with the gravity of the subject." Now the sacred doctrine is concerned with things of the greatest moment, according to Prov. 8:6, "Hear, for I will speak of great things." Wherefore Ambrose does not altogether exclude fun from human speech, but from the sacred doctrine; hence he begins by saying: "Although jokes are at times fitting and pleasant, nevertheless they are incompatible with the ecclesiastical rule; since how can we have recourse to things which are not to be found in Holy Writ?"

Reply to Objection 2: This saying of Chrysostom refers to the inordinate use of fun, especially by those who make the pleasure of games their end; of whom it is written (Wis. 15:12): "They have accounted our life a pastime." Against these Tully says (De Offic. i,

29): "We are so begotten by nature that we appear to be made not for play and fun, but rather for hardships, and for occupations of greater gravity and moment."

Reply to Objection 3: Playful actions themselves considered in their species are not directed to an end: but the pleasure derived from such actions is directed to the recreation and rest of the soul, and accordingly if this be done with moderation, it is lawful to make use of fun. Hence Tully says (De Offic. i, 29): "It is indeed lawful to make use of play and fun, but in the same way as we have recourse to sleep and other kinds of rest, then only when we have done our duty by grave and serious matters."

Whether there can be sin in the excess of play?

Objection 1: It would seem that there cannot be sin in the excess of play. For that which is an excuse for sin is not held to be sinful. Now play is sometimes an excuse for sin, for many things would be grave sins if they were done seriously, whereas if they be done in fun, are either no sin or but slightly sinful. Therefore it seems that there is no sin in excessive play.

Objection 2: Further, all other vices are reducible to the seven capital vices, as Gregory states (Moral. xxxi, 17). But excess of play does not seem reducible to any of the capital vices. Therefore it would seem not to be a sin.

Objection 3: Further, comedians especially would seem to exceed in play, since they direct their whole life to playing. Therefore if excess of play were a sin, all actors would be in a state of sin; moreover all those who employ them, as well as those who make them any payment, would sin as accomplices of their sin. But this would seem untrue; for it is related in the Lives of the Fathers (ii. 16; viii. 63) that is was revealed to the Blessed Paphnutius that a certain jester would be with him in the life to come.

On the contrary, A gloss on Prov. 14:13, "Laughter shall be mingled with sorrow and mourning taketh hold of the end of joy," remarks: "A mourning that will last for ever." Now there is inordinate laughter and inordinate joy in excessive play. Therefore there is mortal sin therein, since mortal sin alone is deserving of everlasting mourning.

I answer that, In all things dirigible according to reason, the excessive is that which goes beyond, and the deficient is that which falls short of the rule of reason. Now it has been stated [3649](A[2]) that playful or jesting words or deeds are dirigible according to reason. Wherefore excessive play is that which goes beyond the rule of reason: and this happens in two ways. First, on account of the very species of the acts employed for the purpose of fun, and this kind of jesting, according to Tully (De Offic. i, 29), is stated to be "discourteous, insolent, scandalous, and obscene," when to wit a man, for the purpose of jesting, employs indecent words or deeds, or such as are injurious to his neighbor, these being of themselves mortal sins. And thus it is evident that excessive play is a mortal sin.

Secondly, there may be excess in play, through lack of due circumstances: for instance when people make use of fun at undue times or places, or out of keeping with the matter in hand, or persons. This may be sometimes a mortal sin on account of the strong attachment to play, when a man prefers the pleasure he derives therefrom to the love of God, so as to be willing to disobey a commandment of God or of the Church rather than forego, such like amusements. Sometimes, however, it is a venial sin, for instance where a man is not so attached to amusement as to be willing for its sake to do anything in disobedience to God.

Reply to Objection 1: Certain things are sinful on account of the intention alone, because they are done in order to injure someone. Such an intention is excluded by their being done in fun, the intention of which is to please, not to injure: in these cases fun excuses from sin, or diminishes it. Other things, however, are sins according to their species, such as murder, fornication, and the like: and fun is no excuse for these; in fact they make fun scandalous and obscene.

Reply to Objection 2: Excessive play pertains to senseless mirth, which Gregory (Moral. xxxi, 17) calls a daughter of gluttony. Wherefore it is written (Ex. 32:6): "The people sat down to eat and drink, and they rose up to play."

Reply to Objection 3: As stated [3650](A[2]), play is necessary for the intercourse of human life. Now whatever is useful to human intercourse may have a lawful employment ascribed to it. Wherefore the occupation of play-actors, the object of which is to cheer the heart of man, is not unlawful in itself; nor are they in a state of sin provided that their playing be moderated, namely that they use no unlawful words or deeds in order to amuse, and that they do not introduce play into undue matters and seasons. And although in human affairs, they have no other occupation in reference to other men, nevertheless in reference to themselves, and to God, they perform other actions both serious and virtuous, such as prayer and the moderation of their own passions and operations, while sometimes they give alms to the poor. Wherefore those who maintain them in moderation do not sin but act justly, by rewarding them for their services. on the other hand, if a man spends too much on such persons, or maintains those comedians who practice unlawful mirth, he sins as encouraging them in their sin. Hence Augustine says (Tract. c. in Joan.) that "to give one's property to comedians is a great sin, not a virtue"; unless by chance some play-actor were in extreme need, in which case one would have to assist him, for Ambrose says (De Offic. [*Quoted in Canon Pasce, dist. 86]): "Feed him that dies of hunger; for whenever thou canst save a man by feeding him, if thou hast not fed him, thou hast slain him."

Whether there is a sin in lack of mirth?

Objection 1: It would seem that there is no sin in lack of mirth. For no sin is prescribed to a penitent. But Augustine speaking of a penitent says (De Vera et Falsa Poenit. 15) [*Spurious]: "Let him refrain from games and the sights of the world, if he wishes to obtain the grace of a full pardon." Therefore there is no sin in lack of mirth.

Objection 2: Further, no sin is included in the praise given to holy men. But some persons are praised for having refrained from mirth; for it is written (Jer. 15:17): "I sat not in the assembly of jesters," and (Tobias 3:17): "Never have I joined myself with them that play; neither have I made myself partaker with them that walk in lightness." Therefore there can be no sin in the lack of mirth.

Objection 3: Further, Andronicus counts austerity to be one of the virtues, and he describes it as a habit whereby a man neither gives nor receives the pleasures of conversation. Now this pertains to the lack of mirth. Therefore the lack of mirth is virtuous rather than sinful.

On the contrary, The Philosopher (Ethic. ii, 7; iv, 8) reckons the lack of mirth to be a vice.

I answer that, In human affairs whatever is against reason is a sin. Now it is against reason for a man to be burdensome to others, by offering no pleasure to others, and by hindering their enjoyment. Wherefore Seneca [*Martin of Braga, Formula Vitae Honestae: cap. De Continentia] says (De Quat. Virt., cap. De Continentia): "Let your conduct be guided by wisdom so that no one will think you rude, or despise you as a cad." Now a man who is without mirth, not only is lacking in playful speech, but is also burdensome to others, since he is deaf to the moderate mirth of others. Consequently they are vicious, and are said to be boorish or rude, as the Philosopher states (Ethic. iv, 8).

Since, however, mirth is useful for the sake of the rest and pleasures it affords; and since, in human life, pleasure and rest are not in quest for their own sake, but for the sake of operation, as stated in Ethic. x, 6, it follows that "lack of mirth is less sinful than excess thereof." Hence the Philosopher says (Ethic. ix, 10): "We should make few friends for the sake of pleasure, since but little sweetness suffices to season life, just as little salt suffices for our meat."

Reply to Objection 1: Mirth is forbidden the penitent because he is called upon to mourn for his sins. Nor does this imply a vice in default, because this very diminishment of mirth in them is in accordance with reason.

Reply to Objection 2: Jeremias speaks there in accordance with the times, the state of which required that man should mourn; wherefore he adds: "I sat alone, because Thou hast filled me with threats." The words of Tobias 3 refer to excessive mirth; and this is evident from his adding: "Neither have I made myself partaker with them that walk in lightness."

Reply to Objection 3: Austerity, as a virtue, does not exclude all pleasures, but only such as are excessive and inordinate; wherefore it would seem to pertain to affability, which the Philosopher (Ethic. iv, 6) calls "friendliness," or {eutrapelia}, otherwise wittiness. Nevertheless he names and defines it thus in respect of its agreement with temperance, to which it belongs to restrain pleasure.

Day 236

OF MODESTY IN THE OUTWARD APPAREL (TWO ARTICLES)
We must now consider modesty as connected with the outward apparel, and under this head there are two points of inquiry:
(1) Whether there can be virtue and vice in connection with outward apparel?
(2) Whether women sin mortally by excessive adornment?

Whether there can be virtue and vice in connection with outward apparel?
Objection 1: It would seem that there cannot be virtue and vice in connection with outward apparel. For outward adornment does not belong to us by nature, wherefore it varies according to different times and places. Hence Augustine says (De Doctr. Christ. iii, 12) that "among the ancient Romans it was scandalous for one to wear a cloak with sleeves and reaching to the ankles, whereas now it is scandalous for anyone hailing from a reputable place to be without them." Now according to the Philosopher (Ethic. ii, 1) there is in us a natural aptitude for the virtues. Therefore there is no virtue or vice about such things.

Objection 2: Further, if there were virtue and vice in connection with outward attire, excess in this matter would be sinful. Now excess in outward attire is not apparently sinful, since even the ministers of the altar use most precious vestments in the sacred ministry. Likewise it would seem not to be sinful to be lacking in this, for it is said in praise of certain people (Heb. 11:37): "They wandered about in sheepskins and in goatskins." Therefore it seems that there cannot be virtue and vice in this matter.

Objection 3: Further, every virtue is either theological, or moral, or intellectual. Now an intellectual virtue is not conversant with matter of this kind, since it is a perfection regarding the knowledge of truth. Nor is there a theological virtue connected therewith, since that has God for its object; nor are any of the moral virtues enumerated by the Philosopher (Ethic. ii, 7), connected with it. Therefore it seems that there cannot be virtue and vice in connection with this kind of attire.

On the contrary, Honesty [*Cf. Q[145]] pertains to virtue. Now a certain honesty is observed in the outward apparel; for Ambrose says (De Offic. i, 19): "The body should be bedecked naturally and without affectation, with simplicity, with negligence rather than nicety, not with costly and dazzling apparel, but with ordinary clothes, so that nothing be lacking to honesty and necessity, yet nothing be added to increase its beauty." Therefore there can be virtue and vice in the outward attire.

I answer that, It is not in the outward things themselves which man uses, that there is vice, but on the part of man who uses them immoderately. This lack of moderation occurs in two ways. First, in comparison with the customs of those among whom one lives; wherefore Augustine says (Confess. iii, 8): "Those offenses which are contrary to the customs of men, are to be avoided according to the customs generally prevailing, so that a thing agreed upon and confirmed by custom or law of any city or nation may not be violated at the lawless pleasure of any, whether citizen or foreigner. For any part, which harmonizeth not with its whole, is offensive." Secondly, the lack of moderation in the use of these things may arise from the inordinate attachment of the user, the result being that a man sometimes takes too much pleasure in using them, either in accordance with the custom of those among whom he dwells or contrary to such custom. Hence Augustine says (De Doctr. Christ. iii, 12): "We must avoid excessive pleasure in the use of things, for it leads not only wickedly to abuse the customs of those among whom we dwell, but frequently to exceed their bounds, so that, whereas it lay hidden, while under the restraint of established morality, it displays its deformity in a most lawless outbreak."

In point of excess, this inordinate attachment occurs in three ways. First when a man seeks glory from excessive attention to dress; in so far as dress and such like things are a kind of ornament. Hence Gregory says (Hom. xl in Ev.): "There are some who think that attention to finery and costly dress is no sin. Surely, if this were no fault, the word of God would not say so expressly that the rich man who was tortured in hell had been clothed in purple and fine linen. No one, forsooth, seeks costly apparel" (such, namely, as exceeds his estate) "save for vainglory." Secondly, when a man seeks sensuous pleasure from excessive attention to dress, in so far as dress is directed to the body's comfort. Thirdly, when a man is too solicitous [*Cf.[3651] Q[55], A[6]] in his attention to outward apparel.

Accordingly Andronicus [*De Affectibus] reckons three virtues in connection with outward attire; namely "humility," which excludes the seeking of glory, wherefore he says that humility is "the habit of avoiding excessive expenditure and parade";

"contentment" [*Cf. Q[143], OBJ[4]], which excludes the seeking of sensuous pleasure, wherefore he says that "contentedness is the habit that makes a man satisfied with what is suitable, and enables him to determine what is becoming in his manner of life" (according to the saying of the Apostle, 1 Tim. 6:8): "Having food and wherewith to be covered, with these let us be content;"---and "simplicity," which excludes excessive solicitude about such things, wherefore he says that "simplicity is a habit that makes a man contented with what he has."

In the point of deficiency there may be inordinate attachment in two ways. First, through a man's neglect to give the requisite study or trouble to the use of outward apparel. Wherefore the Philosopher says (Ethic. vii, 7) that "it is a mark of effeminacy to let one's cloak trail on the ground to avoid the trouble of lifting it up." Secondly, by seeking glory from the very lack of attention to outward attire. Hence Augustine says (De Serm. Dom. in Monte ii, 12) that "not only the glare and pomp of outward things, but even dirt and the weeds of mourning may be a subject of ostentation, all the more dangerous as being a decoy under the guise of God's service"; and the Philosopher says (Ethic. iv, 7) that "both excess and inordinate defect are a subject of ostentation."

Reply to Objection 1: Although outward attire does not come from nature, it belongs to natural reason to moderate it; so that we are naturally inclined to be the recipients of the virtue that moderates outward raiment.

Reply to Objection 2: Those who are placed in a position of dignity, or again the ministers of the altar, are attired in more costly apparel than others, not for the sake of their own glory, but to indicate the excellence of their office or of the Divine worship: wherefore this is not sinful in them. Hence Augustine says (De Doctr. Christ. iii, 12): "Whoever uses outward things in such a way as to exceed the bounds observed by the good people among whom he dwells, either signifies something by so doing, or is guilty of sin, inasmuch as he uses these things for sensual pleasure or ostentation."

Likewise there may be sin on the part of deficiency: although it is not always a sin to wear coarser clothes than other people. For, if this be done through ostentation or pride, in order to set oneself above others, it is a sin of superstition; whereas, if this be done to tame the flesh, or to humble the spirit, it belongs to the virtue of temperance. Hence Augustine says (De Doctr. Christ. iii, 12): "Whoever uses transitory things with greater restraint than is customary with those among whom he dwells, is either temperate or superstitious." Especially, however, is the use of coarse raiment befitting to those who by word and example urge others to repentance, as did the prophets of whom the Apostle is speaking in the passage quoted. Wherefore a gloss on Mat. 3:4, says: "He who preaches penance, wears the garb of penance."

Reply to Objection 3: This outward apparel is an indication of man's estate; wherefore excess, deficiency, and mean therein, are referable to the virtue of truthfulness, which the Philosopher (Ethic. ii, 7) assigns to deeds and words, which are indications of something connected with man's estate.

Whether the adornment of women is devoid of mortal sin?

Objection 1: It would seem that the adornment of women is not devoid of mortal sin. For whatever is contrary to a precept of the Divine law is a mortal sin. Now the adornment of women is contrary to a precept of the Divine law; for it is written (1 Pet. 3:3): "Whose," namely women's, "adorning, let it not be the outward plaiting of the hair, or the wearing of gold, or the putting on of apparel." Wherefore a gloss of Cyprian says: "Those who are clothed in silk and purple cannot sincerely put on Christ: those who are bedecked with gold and pearls and trinkets have forfeited the adornments of mind and body." Now this is not done without a mortal sin. Therefore the adornment of women cannot be devoid of mortal sin.

Objection 2: Further, Cyprian says (De Habit. Virg.): "I hold that not only virgins and widows, but also wives and all women without exception, should be admonished that nowise should they deface God's work and fabric, the clay that He has fashioned, with the aid of yellow pigments, black powders or rouge, or by applying any dye that alters the natural features." And afterwards he adds: "They lay hands on God, when they strive to reform what He has formed. This is an assault on the Divine handiwork, a distortion of the truth. Thou shalt not be able to see God, having no longer the eyes that God made, but those the devil has unmade; with him shalt thou burn on whose account thou art bedecked." But this is not due except to mortal sin. Therefore the adornment of women is not devoid of mortal sin.

Objection 3: Further, just as it is unbecoming for a woman to wear man's clothes, so is it unbecoming for her to adorn herself inordinately. Now the former is a sin, for it is written (Dt. 22:5): "A woman shall not be clothed with man's apparel, neither shall a man use woman's apparel." Therefore it seems that also the excessive adornment of women is a mortal sin.

Objection 4: On the contrary, If this were true it would seem that the makers of these means of adornment sin mortally.

I answer that, As regards the adornment of women, we must bear in mind the general statements made above [3652](A[1]) concerning outward apparel, and also something special, namely that a woman's apparel may incite men to lust, according to Prov. 7:10, "Behold a woman meeteth him in harlot's attire, prepared to deceive souls."

Nevertheless a woman may use means to please her husband, lest through despising her he fall into adultery. Hence it is written (1 Cor. 7:34) that the woman "that is married thinketh on the things of the world, how she may please her husband." Wherefore if a married woman adorn herself in order to please her husband she can do this without sin.

But those women who have no husband nor wish to have one, or who are in a state of life inconsistent with marriage, cannot without sin desire to give lustful pleasure to those men who see them, because this is to incite them to sin. And if indeed they adorn themselves with this intention of provoking others to lust, they sin mortally; whereas if they do so from frivolity, or from vanity for the sake of ostentation, it is not always mortal, but sometimes venial. And the same applies to men in this respect. Hence Augustine says (Ep. ccxlv ad Possid.): "I do not wish you to be hasty in forbidding the wearing of gold or costly attire except in the case of those who being neither married nor wishful to marry, should think how they may please God: whereas the others think on the things of the world, either husbands how they may please their wives, or wives how they may please their husbands, except that it is unbecoming for women though married to uncover their hair, since the Apostle commands them to cover the head." Yet in this case some might be excused from sin, when they do this not through vanity but on account of some contrary custom: although such a custom is not to be commended.

Reply to Objection 1: As a gloss says on this passage, "The wives of those who were in distress despised their husbands, and decked themselves that they might please other men": and the Apostle forbids this. Cyprian is speaking in the same sense; yet he does not forbid married women to adorn themselves in order to please their husbands, lest the latter be afforded an occasion of sin with other women. Hence the Apostle says (1 Tim. 2:9): "Women . . . in ornate [Douay: 'decent'] apparel, adorning themselves with modesty and sobriety, not with plaited hair, or gold, or pearls, or costly attire": whence we are given to understand that women are not forbidden to adorn themselves soberly and moderately but to do so excessively, shamelessly, and immodestly.

Reply to Objection 2: Cyprian is speaking of women painting themselves: this is a kind of falsification, which cannot be devoid of sin. Wherefore Augustine says (Ep. ccxlv ad Possid.): "To dye oneself with paints in order to have a rosier or a paler complexion is a lying counterfeit. I doubt whether even their husbands are willing to be deceived by it, by whom alone" (i.e. the husbands) "are they to be permitted, but not ordered, to adorn themselves." However, such painting does not always involve a mortal sin, but only when it is done for the sake of sensuous pleasure or in contempt of God, and it is to like cases that Cyprian refers.

It must, however, be observed that it is one thing to counterfeit a beauty one has not, and another to hide a disfigurement arising from some cause such as sickness or the like. For this is lawful, since according to the Apostle (1 Cor. 12:23), "such as we think to be the less honorable members of the body, about these we put more abundant honor."

Reply to Objection 3: As stated in the foregoing Article, outward apparel should be consistent with the estate of the person, according to the general custom. Hence it is in itself sinful for a woman to wear man's clothes, or vice versa; especially since this may be a cause of sensuous pleasure; and it is expressly forbidden in the Law (Dt. 22) because the Gentiles used to practice this change of attire for the purpose of idolatrous superstition. Nevertheless this may be done sometimes without sin on account of some necessity, either in order to hide oneself from enemies, or through lack of other clothes, or for some similar motive.

Reply to Objection 4: In the case of an art directed to the production of goods which men cannot use without sin, it follows that the workmen sin in making such things, as directly affording others an occasion of sin; for instance, if a man were to make idols or anything pertaining to idolatrous worship. But in the case of an art the products of which may be employed by man either for a good or for an evil use, such as swords, arrows, and the like, the practice of such an art is not sinful. These alone should be called arts; wherefore Chrysostom says [*Hom. xlix super Matth.]: "The name of art should be applied to those only which contribute towards and produce necessaries and mainstays of life." In the case of an art that produces things which for the most part some people put to an evil use, although such arts are not unlawful in themselves, nevertheless, according to the teaching of Plato, they should be extirpated from the State by the governing authority. Accordingly, since women may lawfully adorn themselves, whether to maintain the fitness of their estate, or even by adding something thereto, in order to please their husbands, it follows that those who make such means of adornment do not sin in the practice of their art, except perhaps by inventing means that are superfluous and fantastic. Hence Chrysostom says (Super Matth.) that "even the shoemakers' and clothiers' arts stand in need of restraint, for they have lent their art to lust, by abusing its needs, and debasing art by art."

OF THE PRECEPTS OF TEMPERANCE (TWO ARTICLES)
We must next consider the precepts of temperance:
(1) The precepts of temperance itself;
(2) The precepts of its parts.

Whether the precepts of temperance are suitably given in the Divine law?
Objection 1: It would seem that the precepts of temperance are unsuitably given in the Divine law. Because fortitude is a greater virtue than temperance, as stated above (Q[123], A[12]; Q[141], A[8]; [3653]FS, Q[66], A[4]). Now there is no precept of fortitude among the precepts of the decalogue, which are the most important among the precepts of the Law. Therefore it was unfitting to include among the precepts of the decalogue the prohibition of adultery, which is contrary to temperance, as stated above (Q[154], AA[1],8).

Objection 2: Further, temperance is not only about venereal matters, but also about pleasures of meat and drink. Now the precepts of the decalogue include no prohibition of a vice pertaining to pleasures of meat and drink, or to any other species of lust. Neither, therefore, should they include a precept prohibiting adultery, which pertains to venereal pleasure.

Objection 3: Further, in the lawgiver's intention inducement to virtue precedes the prohibition of vice, since vices are forbidden in order that obstacles to virtue may be removed. Now the precepts of the decalogue are the most important in the Divine law. Therefore the precepts of the decalogue should have included an affirmative precept directly prescribing the virtue of temperance, rather than a negative precept forbidding adultery which is directly opposed thereto.

On the contrary, stands the authority of Scripture in the decalogue (Ex. 20:14, 17).

I answer that, As the Apostle says (1 Tim. 1:5), "the end of the commandment is charity," which is enjoined upon us in the two precepts concerning the love of God and of our neighbor. Wherefore the decalogue contains those precepts which tend more directly to the love of God and of our neighbor. Now among the vices opposed to temperance, adultery would seem most of all opposed to the love of our neighbor, since thereby a man lays hold of another's property for his own use, by abusing his neighbor's wife. Wherefore the precepts of the decalogue include a special prohibition of adultery, not only as committed in deed, but also as desired in thought.

Reply to Objection 1: Among the species of vices opposed to fortitude there is not one that is so directly opposed to the love of our neighbor as adultery, which is a species of lust that is opposed to temperance. And yet the vice of daring, which is opposed to

133

fortitude, is wont to be sometimes the cause of murder, which is forbidden by one of the precepts of the decalogue: for it is written (Ecclus. 8:18): "Go not on the way with a bold man lest he burden thee with his evils."

Reply to Objection 2: Gluttony is not directly opposed to the love of our neighbor, as adultery is. Nor indeed is any other species of lust, for a father is not so wronged by the seduction of the virgin over whom he has no connubial right, as is the husband by the adultery of his wife, for he, not the wife herself, has power over her body [*1 Cor. 7:4].

Reply to Objection 3: As stated above ([3654]Q[122], AA[1],4) the precepts of the decalogue are universal principles of the Divine law; hence they need to be common precepts. Now it was not possible to give any common affirmative precepts of temperance, because the practice of temperance varies according to different times, as Augustine remarks (De Bono Conjug. xv, 7), and according to different human laws and customs.

Whether the precepts of the virtues annexed to temperance are suitably given in the Divine law?

Objection 1: It would seem that the precepts of the virtues annexed to temperance are unsuitably given in the Divine law. For the precepts of the Decalogue, as stated above (A[1], ad 3), are certain universal principles of the whole Divine law. Now "pride is the beginning of all sin," according to Ecclus. 10:15. Therefore among the precepts of the Decalogue there should have been one forbidding pride.

Objection 2: Further, a place before all should have been given in the decalogue to those precepts by which men are especially induced to fulfil the Law, because these would seem to be the most important. Now since humility subjects man to God, it would seem most of all to dispose man to the fulfilment of the Divine law; wherefore obedience is accounted one of the degrees of humility, as stated above ([3655]Q[161], A[6]); and the same apparently applies to meekness, the effect of which is that a man does not contradict the Divine Scriptures, as Augustine observes (De Doctr. Christ. ii, 7). Therefore it seems that the Decalogue should have contained precepts of humility and meekness.

Objection 3: Further, it was stated in the foregoing Article that adultery is forbidden in the decalogue, because it is contrary to the love of our neighbor. But inordinateness of outward movements, which is contrary to modesty, is opposed to neighborly love: wherefore Augustine says in his Rule (Ep. ccxii): "In all your movements let nothing be done to offend the eye of any person whatever." Therefore it seems that this kind of inordinateness should also have been forbidden by a precept of the Decalogue.

On the contrary, suffices the authority of Scripture.

I answer that, The virtues annexed to temperance may be considered in two ways: first, in themselves; secondly, in their effects. Considered in themselves they have no direct connection with the love of God or of our neighbor; rather do they regard a certain moderation of things pertaining to man himself. But considered in their effects, they may regard the love of God or of our neighbor: and in this respect the decalogue contains precepts that relate to the prohibition of the effects of the vices opposed to the parts of temperance. Thus the effect of anger, which is opposed to meekness, is sometimes that a man goes on to commit murder (and this is forbidden in the Decalogue), and sometimes that he refuses due honor to his parents, which may also be the result of pride, which leads many to transgress the precepts of the first table.

Reply to Objection 1: Pride is the beginning of sin, but it lies hidden in the heart; and its inordinateness is not perceived by all in common. Hence there was no place for its prohibition among the precepts of the Decalogue, which are like first self-evident principles.

Reply to Objection 2: Those precepts which are essentially an inducement to the observance of the Law presuppose the Law to be already given, wherefore they cannot be first precepts of the Law so as to have a place in the Decalogue.

Reply to Objection 3: Inordinate outward movement is not injurious to one's neighbor, if we consider the species of the act, as are murder, adultery, and theft, which are forbidden in the decalogue; but only as being signs of an inward inordinateness, as stated above ([3656]Q[168], A[1], ad 1,3).

TREATISE ON GRATUITOUS GRACES (QQ[171]-182)

OF PROPHECY (SIX ARTICLES)

After treating individually of all the virtues and vices that pertain to men of all conditions and estates, we must now consider those things which pertain especially to certain men. Now there is a triple difference between men as regards things connected with the soul's habits and acts. First, in reference to the various gratuitous graces, according to 1 Cor. 12:4, 7: "There are diversities of graces . . . and to one . . . by the Spirit is given the word of wisdom, to another the word of knowledge," etc. Another difference arises from the diversities of life, namely the active and the contemplative life, which correspond to diverse purposes of operation, wherefore it is stated (1 Cor. 12:4, 7) that "there are diversities of operations." For the purpose of operation in Martha, who "was busy about much serving," which pertains to the active life, differed from the purpose of operation in Mary, "who sitting . . . at the Lord's feet, heard His word" (Lk. 10:39,40), which pertains to the contemplative life. A third difference corresponds to the various duties and states of life, as expressed in Eph. 4:11, "And He gave some apostles; and some prophets; and other some evangelists; and other some pastors and doctors": and this pertains to diversity of ministries, of which it is written (1 Cor. 12:5): "There are diversities of ministries."

With regard to gratuitous graces, which are the first object to be considered, it must be observed that some of them pertain to knowledge, some to speech, and some to operation. Now all things pertaining to knowledge may be comprised under "prophecy," since prophetic revelation extends not only to future events relating to man, but also to things relating to God, both as to those which are to be believed by all and are matters of "faith," and as to yet higher mysteries, which concern the perfect and belong to "wisdom."

Again, prophetic revelation is about things pertaining to spiritual substances, by whom we are urged to good or evil; this pertains to the "discernment of spirits." Moreover it extends to the direction of human acts, and this pertains to "knowledge," as we shall explain further on ([3657]Q[177]). Accordingly we must first of all consider prophecy, and rapture which is a degree of prophecy.

Prophecy admits of four heads of consideration: (1) its essence; (2) its cause; (3) the mode of prophetic knowledge; (4) the division of prophecy.

Under the first head there are six points of inquiry:

(1) Whether prophecy pertains to knowledge?

(2) Whether it is a habit?

(3) Whether it is only about future contingencies?

(4) Whether a prophet knows all possible matters of prophecy?

(5) Whether a prophet distinguishes that which he perceives by the gift of God, from that which he perceives by his own spirit?

(6) Whether anything false can be the matter of prophecy?

Whether prophecy pertains to knowledge?

Objection 1: It would seem that prophecy does not pertain to knowledge. For it is written (Ecclus. 48:14) that after death the body of Eliseus prophesied, and further on (Ecclus. 49:18) it is said of Joseph that "his bones were visited, and after death they prophesied." Now no knowledge remains in the body or in the bones after death. Therefore prophecy does not pertain to knowledge.

Objection 2: Further, it is written (1 Cor. 14:3): "He that prophesieth, speaketh to men unto edification." Now speech is not knowledge itself, but its effect. Therefore it would seem that prophecy does not pertain to knowledge.

Objection 3: Further, every cognitive perfection excludes folly and madness. Yet both of these are consistent with prophecy; for it is written (Osee 9:7): "Know ye, O Israel, that the prophet was foolish and mad [*Vulg.: 'the spiritual man was mad']." Therefore prophecy is not a cognitive perfection.

Objection 4: Further, just as revelation regards the intellect, so inspiration regards, apparently, the affections, since it denotes a kind of motion. Now prophecy is described as "inspiration" or "revelation," according to Cassiodorus [*Prolog. super Psalt. i]. Therefore it would seem that prophecy does not pertain to the intellect more than to the affections.

On the contrary, It is written (1 Kings 9:9): "For he that is now called a prophet, in time past was called a seer." Now sight pertains to knowledge. Therefore prophecy pertains to knowledge.

I answer that, Prophecy first and chiefly consists in knowledge, because, to wit, prophets know things that are far [procul] removed from man's knowledge. Wherefore they may be said to take their name from {phanos}, "apparition," because things appear to them from afar. Wherefore, as Isidore states (Etym. vii, 8), "in the Old Testament, they were called Seers, because they saw what others saw not, and surveyed things hidden in mystery." Hence among heathen nations they were known as "vates, on account of their power of mind [vi mentis]," [*The Latin 'vates' is from the Greek {phates}, and may be rendered 'soothsayer'] (Etym. viii, 7).

Since, however, it is written (1 Cor. 12:7): "The manifestation of the Spirit is given to every man unto profit," and further on (1 Cor. 14:12): "Seek to abound unto the edification of the Church," it follows that prophecy consists secondarily in speech, in so far as the prophets declare for the instruction of others, the things they know through being taught of God, according to the saying of Is. 21:10, "That which I have heard of the Lord of hosts, the God of Israel, I have declared unto you." Accordingly, as Isidore says (Etym. viii, 7), "prophets" may be described as "proefatores [foretellers], because they tell from afar [porro fantur]," that is, speak from a distance, "and foretell the truth about things to come."

Now those things above human ken which are revealed by God cannot be confirmed by human reason, which they surpass as regards the operation of the Divine power, according to Mk. 16:20, "They . . . preached everywhere, the Lord working withal and confirming the word with signs that followed." Hence, thirdly, prophecy is concerned with the working of miracles, as a kind of confirmation of the prophetic utterances. Wherefore it is written (Dt. 34:10,11): "There arose no more a prophet in Israel like unto Moses, whom the Lord knew face to face, in all the signs and wonders."

Reply to Objection 1: These passages speak of prophecy in reference to the third point just mentioned, which regards the proof of prophecy.

Reply to Objection 2: The Apostle is speaking there of the prophetic utterances.

Reply to Objection 3: Those prophets who are described as foolish and mad are not true but false prophets, of whom it is said (Jer. 3:16): "Hearken not to the words of the prophets that prophesy to you, and deceive you; they speak a vision of their own heart, and not out of the mouth of the Lord," and (Ezech. 13:3): "Woe to the foolish prophets, that follow their own spirit, and see nothing."

Reply to Objection 4: It is requisite to prophecy that the intention of the mind be raised to the perception of Divine things: wherefore it is written (Ezech. 2:1): "Son of man, stand upon thy feet, and I will speak to thee." This raising of the intention is brought about by the motion of the Holy Ghost, wherefore the text goes on to say: "And the Spirit entered into me . . . and He set me upon my feet." After the mind's intention has been raised to heavenly things, it perceives the things of God; hence the text continues: "And I heard Him speaking to me." Accordingly inspiration is requisite for prophecy, as regards the raising of the mind, according to Job 32:8, "The inspiration of the Almighty giveth understanding": while revelation is necessary, as regards the very perception of Divine things, whereby prophecy is completed; by its means the veil of darkness and ignorance is removed, according to Job 12:22, "He discovereth great things out of darkness."

Whether prophecy is a habit?

Objection 1: It would seem that prophecy is a habit. For according to Ethic. ii, 5, "there are three things in the soul, power, passion, and habit." Now prophecy is not a power, for then it would be in all men, since the powers of the soul are common to them. Again it is not a passion, since the passions belong to the appetitive faculty, as stated above ([3658]FS, Q[22] , A[2]); whereas prophecy pertains principally to knowledge, as stated in the foregoing Article. Therefore prophecy is a habit.

Objection 2: Further, every perfection of the soul, which is not always in act, is a habit. Now prophecy is a perfection of the soul; and it is not always in act, else a prophet could not be described as asleep. Therefore seemingly prophecy is a habit.

Objection 3: Further, prophecy is reckoned among the gratuitous graces. Now grace is something in the soul, after the manner of a habit, as stated above ([3659]FS, Q[110], A[2]). Therefore prophecy is a habit.

On the contrary, A habit is something "whereby we act when we will," as the Commentator [*Averroes or Ibn Roshd, 1120-1198] says (De Anima iii). But a man cannot make use of prophecy when he will, as appears in the case of Eliseus (4 Kings 3:15), "who on Josaphat inquiring of him concerning the future, and the spirit of prophecy failing him, caused a minstrel to be brought to him, that the spirit of prophecy might come down upon him through the praise of psalmody, and fill his mind with things to come," as Gregory observes (Hom. i super Ezech.). Therefore prophecy is not a habit.

I answer that, As the Apostle says (Eph. 5:13), "all that is made manifest is light," because, to wit, just as the manifestation of the material sight takes place through material light, so too the manifestation of intellectual sight takes place through intellectual light. Accordingly manifestation must be proportionate to the light by means of which it takes place, even as an effect is proportionate to its cause. Since then prophecy pertains to a knowledge that surpasses natural reason, as stated above [3660](A[1]), it follows that prophecy requires an intellectual light surpassing the light of natural reason. Hence the saying of Micah 7:8: "When I sit in darkness, the Lord is my light." Now light may be in a subject in two ways: first, by way of an abiding form, as material light is in the sun, and in fire; secondly, by way of a passion, or passing impression, as light is in the air. Now the prophetic light is not in the prophet's intellect by way of an abiding form, else a prophet would always be able to prophesy, which is clearly false. For Gregory says (Hom. i super Ezech.): "Sometimes the spirit of prophecy is lacking to the prophet, nor is it always within the call of his mind, yet so that in its absence he knows that its presence is due to a gift." Hence Eliseus said of the Sunamite woman (4 Kings 4:27): "Her soul is in anguish, and the Lord hath hid it from me, and hath not told me." The reason for this is that the intellectual light that is in a subject by way of an abiding and complete form, perfects the intellect chiefly to the effect of knowing the principle of the things manifested by that light; thus by the light of the active intellect the intellect knows chiefly the first principles of all things known naturally. Now the principle of things pertaining to supernatural knowledge, which are manifested by prophecy, is God Himself, Whom the prophets do not see in His essence, although He is seen by the blessed in heaven, in whom this light is by way of an abiding and complete form, according to Ps. 35:10, "In Thy light we shall see light."

It follows therefore that the prophetic light is in the prophet's soul by way of a passion or transitory impression. This is indicated Ex. 33:22: "When my glory shall pass, I will set thee in a hole of the rock," etc., and 3 Kings 19:11: "Go forth and stand upon the mount before the Lord; and behold the Lord passeth," etc. Hence it is that even as the air is ever in need of a fresh enlightening, so too the prophet's mind is always in need of a fresh revelation; thus a disciple who has not yet acquired the principles of an art needs to have every detail explained to him. Wherefore it is written (Is. 1:4): "In the morning He wakeneth my ear, so that I may hear Him as a master." This is also indicated by the very manner in which prophecies are uttered: thus it is stated that "the Lord spake to such and such a prophet," or that "the word of the Lord," or "the hand of the Lord was made upon him."

But a habit is an abiding form. Wherefore it is evident that, properly speaking, prophecy is not a habit.

Reply to Objection 1: This division of the Philosopher's does not comprise absolutely all that is in the soul, but only such as can be principles of moral actions, which are done sometimes from passion, sometimes from habit, sometimes from mere power, as in the case of those who perform an action from the judgment of their reason before having the habit of that action.

However, prophecy may be reduced to a passion, provided we understand passion to denote any kind of receiving, in which sense the Philosopher says (De Anima iii, 4) that "to understand is, in a way, to be passive." For just as, in natural knowledge, the possible intellect is passive to the light of the active intellect, so too in prophetic knowledge the human intellect is passive to the enlightening of the Divine light.

Reply to Objection 2: Just as in corporeal things, when a passion ceases, there remains a certain aptitude to a repetition of the passion---thus wood once ignited is more easily ignited again, so too in the prophet's intellect, after the actual enlightenment has ceased, there remains an aptitude to be enlightened anew---thus when the mind has once been aroused to devotion, it is more easily recalled to its former devotion. Hence Augustine says (De orando Deum. Ep. cxxx, 9) that our prayers need to be frequent, "lest devotion be extinguished as soon as it is kindled."

We might, however, reply that a person is called a prophet, even while his prophetic enlightenment ceases to be actual, on account of his being deputed by God, according to Jer. 1:5, "And I made thee a prophet unto the nations."

Reply to Objection 3: Every gift of grace raises man to something above human nature, and this may happen in two ways. First, as to the substance of the act---for instance, the working of miracles, and the knowledge of the uncertain and hidden things of Divine wisdom---and for such acts man is not granted a habitual gift of grace. Secondly, a thing is above human nature as to the mode but not the substance of the act---for instance to love God and to know Him in the mirror of His creatures---and for this a habitual gift of grace is bestowed.

Whether prophecy is only about future contingencies?

Objection 1: It would seem that prophecy is only about future contingencies. For Cassiodorus says [*Prol. super Psalt. i] that "prophecy is a Divine inspiration or revelation, announcing the issue of things with unchangeable truth." Now issues pertain to future contingencies. Therefore the prophetic revelation is about future contingencies alone.

Objection 2: Further, according to 1 Cor. 12, the grace of prophecy is differentiated from wisdom and faith, which are about Divine things; and from the discernment of spirits, which is about created spirits; and from knowledge, which is about human things. Now habits and acts are differentiated by their objects, as stated above ([3661]FS, Q[54], A[2]). Therefore it seems that the object of prophecy is not connected with any of the above. Therefore it follows that it is about future contingencies alone.

Objection 3: Further, difference of object causes difference of species, as stated above ([3662]FS, Q[54], A[2]). Therefore, if one prophecy is about future contingencies, and another about other things, it would seem to follow that these are different species of prophecy.

On the contrary, Gregory says (Hom. i super Ezech.) that some prophecies are "about the future, for instance (Is. 7:14), 'Behold a virgin shall conceive, and bear a son'"; some are "about the past, as (Gn. 1:1), 'In the beginning God created heaven and earth'"; some are "about the present," as (1 Cor. 14:24,25), "If all prophesy, and there come in one that believeth not . . . the secrets of his heart are made manifest." Therefore prophecy is not about future contingencies alone.

I answer that, A manifestation made by means of a certain light can extend to all those things that are subject to that light: thus the body's sight extends to all colors, and the soul's natural knowledge extends to whatever is subject to the light of the active intellect. Now prophetic knowledge comes through a Divine light, whereby it is possible to know all things both Divine and human, both spiritual and corporeal; and consequently the prophetic revelation extends to them all. Thus by the ministry of spirits a prophetic revelation concerning the perfections of God and the angels was made to Is. 6:1, where it is written, "I saw the Lord sitting upon a throne high and elevated." Moreover his prophecy contains matters referring to natural bodies, according to the words of Is. 40:12, "Who hath measured the waters in the hollow of His hand," etc. It also contains matters relating to human conduct, according to Is. 58:1, "Deal thy bread to the hungry," etc.; and besides this it contains things pertaining to future events, according to Is. 47:9, "Two things shall come upon thee suddenly in one day, barrenness and widowhood."

Since, however, prophecy is about things remote from our knowledge, it must be observed that the more remote things are from our knowledge the more pertinent they are to prophecy. Of such things there are three degrees. One degree comprises things remote from the knowledge, either sensitive or intellective, of some particular man, but not from the knowledge of all men; thus a particular man knows by sense things present to him locally, which another man does not know by human sense, since they are removed from him. Thus Eliseus knew prophetically what his disciple Giezi had done in his absence (4 Kings 5:26), and in like manner the secret thoughts of one man are manifested prophetically to another, according to 1 Cor. 14:25; and again in this way what one man knows by demonstration may be revealed to another prophetically.

The second degree comprises those things which surpass the knowledge of all men without exception, not that they are in themselves unknowable, but on account of a defect in human knowledge; such as the mystery of the Trinity, which was revealed by the Seraphim saying: "Holy, Holy, Holy," etc. (Is. 6:3).

The last degree comprises things remote from the knowledge of all men, through being in themselves unknowable; such are future contingencies, the truth of which is indeterminate. And since that which is predicated universally and by its very nature, takes precedence of that which is predicated in a limited and relative sense, it follows that revelation of future events belongs most properly to prophecy, and from this prophecy apparently takes its name. Hence Gregory says (Hom. i super Ezech.): "And since a prophet is so called because he foretells the future, his name loses its significance when he speaks of the past or present."

Reply to Objection 1: Prophecy is there defined according to its proper signification; and it is in this sense that it is differentiated from the other gratuitous graces.

Reply to Objection 2: This is evident from what has just been said. We might also reply that all those things that are the matter of prophecy have the common aspect of being unknowable to man except by Divine revelation; whereas those that are the matter of "wisdom," "knowledge," and the "interpretation of speeches," can be known by man through natural reason, but are manifested in a higher way through the enlightening of the Divine light. As to "faith," although it is about things invisible to man, it is not concerned with the knowledge of the things believed, but with a man's certitude of assent to things known by others.

Reply to Objection 3: The formal element in prophetic knowledge is the Divine light, which being one, gives unity of species to prophecy, although the things prophetically manifested by the Divine light are diverse.

Whether by the Divine revelation a prophet knows all that can be known prophetically?

Objection 1: It would seem that by the Divine revelation a prophet knows all that can be known prophetically. For it is written (Amos 3:7): "The Lord God doth nothing without revealing His secret to His servants the prophets." Now whatever is revealed prophetically is something done by God. Therefore there is not one of them but what is revealed to the prophet.

Objection 2: Further, "God's works are perfect" (Dt. 32:4). Now prophecy is a "Divine revelation," as stated above [3663](A[3]). Therefore it is perfect; and this would not be so unless all possible matters of prophecy were revealed prophetically, since "the perfect is that which lacks nothing" (Phys. iii, 6). Therefore all possible matters of prophecy are revealed to the prophet.

Objection 3: Further, the Divine light which causes prophecy is more powerful than the right of natural reason which is the cause of human science. Now a man who has acquired a science knows whatever pertains to that science; thus a grammarian knows all matters of grammar. Therefore it would seem that a prophet knows all matters of prophecy.

On the contrary, Gregory says (Hom. i super Ezech.) that "sometimes the spirit of prophecy indicates the present to the prophet's mind and nowise the future; and sometimes it points not to the present but to the future." Therefore the prophet does not know all matters of prophecy.

I answer that, Things which differ from one another need not exist simultaneously, save by reason of some one thing in which they are connected and on which they depend: thus it has been stated above ([3664]FS, Q[65], AA[1],2) that all the virtues must needs exist simultaneously on account of prudence and charity. Now all the things that are known through some principle are connected in that principle and depend thereon. Hence he who knows a principle perfectly, as regards all to which its virtue extends, knows at the same time all that can be known through that principle; whereas if the common principle is unknown, or known only in a general way, it does not follow that one knows all those things at the same time, but each of them has to be manifested by itself, so that consequently some of them may be known, and some not.

Now the principle of those things that are prophetically manifested by the Divine light is the first truth, which the prophets do not see in itself. Wherefore there is no need for their knowing all possible matters of prophecy; but each one knows some of them according to the special revelation of this or that matter.

Reply to Objection 1: The Lord reveals to the prophets all things that are necessary for the instruction of the faithful; yet not all to every one, but some to one, and some to another.

Reply to Objection 2: Prophecy is by way of being something imperfect in the genus of Divine revelation: hence it is written (1 Cor. 13:8) that "prophecies shall be made void," and that "we prophesy in part," i.e. imperfectly. The Divine revelation will be brought to its perfection in heaven; wherefore the same text continues (1 Cor. 113:10): "When that which is perfect is come, that which is in part shall be done away." Consequently it does not follow that nothing is lacking to prophetic revelation, but that it lacks none of those things to which prophecy is directed.

Reply to Objection 3: He who has a science knows the principles of that science, whence whatever is pertinent to that science depends; wherefore to have the habit of a science perfectly, is to know whatever is pertinent to that science. But God Who is the principle of prophetic knowledge is not known in Himself through prophecy; wherefore the comparison fails.

Day 237

Whether the prophet always distinguishes what he says by his own spirit from what he says by the prophetic spirit?

Objection 1: It would seem that the prophet always distinguishes what he says by his own spirit from what he says by the prophetic spirit. For Augustine states (Confess. vi, 13) that his mother said "she could, through a certain feeling, which in words she could not express, discern betwixt Divine revelations, and the dreams of her own soul." Now prophecy is a Divine revelation, as stated above [3665](A[3]). Therefore the prophet always distinguishes what he says by the spirit of prophecy, from what he says by his own spirit.

Objection 2: Further, God commands nothing impossible, as Jerome [*Pelagius. Ep. xvi, among the supposititious works of St. Jerome] says. Now the prophets were commanded (Jer. 23:28): "The prophet that hath a dream, let him tell a dream; and he that hath My word, let him speak My word with truth." Therefore the prophet can distinguish what he has through the spirit of prophecy from what he sees otherwise.

Objection 3: Further, the certitude resulting from a Divine light is greater than that which results from the light of natural reason. Now he that has science, by the light of natural reason knows for certain that he has it. Therefore he that has prophecy by a Divine light is much more certain that he has it.

On the contrary, Gregory says (Hom. i super Ezech.): "It must be observed that sometimes the holy prophets, when consulted, utter certain things by their own spirit, through being much accustomed to prophesying, and think they are speaking by the prophetic spirit."

I answer that, The prophet's mind is instructed by God in two ways: in one way by an express revelation, in another way by a most mysterious instinct to "which the human mind is subjected without knowing it," as Augustine says (Gen. ad lit. ii, 17). Accordingly the prophet has the greatest certitude about those things which he knows by an express revelation, and he has it for certain that they are revealed to him by God; wherefore it is written (Jer. 26:15): "In truth the Lord sent me to you, to speak all these words in your hearing." Else, were he not certain about this, the faith which relies on the utterances of the prophet would not be certain. A sign of the prophet's certitude may be gathered from the fact that Abraham being admonished in a prophetic vision, prepared to sacrifice his only-begotten son, which he nowise would have done had he not been most certain of the Divine revelation.

On the other hand, his position with regard to the things he knows by instinct is sometimes such that he is unable to distinguish fully whether his thoughts are conceived of Divine instinct or of his own spirit. And those things which we know by Divine instinct are not all manifested with prophetic certitude, for this instinct is something imperfect in the genus of prophecy. It is thus that we are to understand the saying of Gregory. Lest, however, this should lead to error, "they are very soon set aright by the Holy Ghost [*For instance, cf. 2 Kings 7:3 seqq.], and from Him they hear the truth, so that they reproach themselves for having said what was untrue," as Gregory adds (Hom. i super Ezech.).

The arguments set down in the first place consider the revelation that is made by the prophetic spirit; wherefore the answer to all the objections is clear.

Whether things known or declared prophetically can be false?

Objection 1: It would seem that things known or declared prophetically can be false. For prophecy is about future contingencies, as stated above (A[3]). Now future contingencies may possibly not happen; else they would happen of necessity. Therefore the matter of prophecy can be false.

Objection 2: Further, Isaias prophesied to Ezechias saying (Is. 38:1): "Take order with thy house, for thou shalt surely die, and shalt not live," and yet fifteen years were added to his life (4 Kings 20:6). Again the Lord said (Jer. 18:7,8): "I will suddenly speak against a nation and against a kingdom, to root out and to pull down and to destroy it. If that nation against which I have spoken shall repent of their evil, I also will repent of the evil that I have thought to do them." This is instanced in the example of the Ninevites, according to Jn. 3:10: "The Lord [Vulg.: 'God'] had mercy with regard to the evil which He had said that He would do to them, and He did it not." Therefore the matter of prophecy can be false.

Objection 3: Further, in a conditional proposition, whenever the antecedent is absolutely necessary, the consequent is absolutely necessary, because the consequent of a conditional proposition stands in the same relation to the antecedent, as the conclusion to the premises in a syllogism, and a syllogism whose premises are necessary always leads to a necessary conclusion, as we find proved in I Poster. 6. But if the matter of a prophecy cannot be false, the following conditional proposition must needs be true: "If a thing has been

138

prophesied, it will be." Now the antecedent of this conditional proposition is absolutely necessary, since it is about the past. Therefore the consequent is also necessary absolutely; yet this is unfitting, for then prophecy would not be about contingencies. Therefore it is untrue that the matter of prophecy cannot be false.

On the contrary, Cassiodorus says [*Prol. in Psalt. i] that "prophecy is a Divine inspiration or revelation, announcing the issue of things with invariable truth." Now the truth of prophecy would not be invariable, if its matter could be false. Therefore nothing false can come under prophecy.

I answer that, As may be gathered from what has been said ([3666]AA[1],3,5), prophecy is a kind of knowledge impressed under the form of teaching on the prophet's intellect, by Divine revelation. Now the truth of knowledge is the same in disciple and teacher since the knowledge of the disciple is a likeness of the knowledge of the teacher, even as in natural things the form of the thing generated is a likeness of the form of the generator. Jerome speaks in this sense when he says [*Comment. in Daniel ii, 10] that "prophecy is the seal of the Divine foreknowledge." Consequently the same truth must needs be in prophetic knowledge and utterances, as in the Divine knowledge, under which nothing false can possibly come, as stated in the [3667]FP, Q[16], A[8]. Therefore nothing false can come under prophecy.

Reply to Objection 1: As stated in the [3668]FP, Q[14], A[13] the certitude of the Divine foreknowledge does not exclude the contingency of future singular events, because that knowledge regards the future as present and already determinate to one thing. Wherefore prophecy also, which is an "impressed likeness" or "seal of the Divine foreknowledge," does not by its unchangeable truth exclude the contingency of future things.

Reply to Objection 2: The Divine foreknowledge regards future things in two ways. First, as they are in themselves, in so far, to wit, as it sees them in their presentiality: secondly, as in their causes, inasmuch as it sees the order of causes in relation to their effects. And though future contingencies, considered as in themselves, are determinate to one thing, yet, considered as in their causes, they are not so determined but that they can happen otherwise. Again, though this twofold knowledge is always united in the Divine intellect, it is not always united in the prophetic revelation, because an imprint made by an active cause is not always on a par with the virtue of that cause. Hence sometimes the prophetic revelation is an imprinted likeness of the Divine foreknowledge, in so far as the latter regards future contingencies in themselves: and such things happen in the same way as foretold, for example this saying of Is. 7:14: "Behold a virgin shall conceive." Sometimes, however, the prophetic revelation is an imprinted likeness of the Divine foreknowledge as knowing the order of causes to effects; and then at times the event is otherwise than foretold. Yet the prophecy does not cover a falsehood, for the meaning of the prophecy is that inferior causes, whether they be natural causes or human acts, are so disposed as to lead to such a result. In this way we are to understand the saying of Is. 38:1: "Thou shalt die, and not live"; in other words, "The disposition of thy body has a tendency to death": and the saying of Jonah 3:4, "Yet forty days, and Nineveh shall be destroyed," that is to say, "Its merits demand that it should be destroyed." God is said "to repent," metaphorically, inasmuch as He bears Himself after the manner of one who repents, by "changing His sentence, although He changes not His counsel" [*Cf. [3669]FP, Q[19], A[7], ad 2].

Reply to Objection 3: Since the same truth of prophecy is the same as the truth of Divine foreknowledge, as stated above, the conditional proposition: "If this was prophesied, it will be," is true in the same way as the proposition: "If this was foreknown, it will be": for in both cases it is impossible for the antecedent not to be. Hence the consequent is necessary, considered, not as something future in our regard, but as being present to the Divine foreknowledge, as stated in the [3670]FP, Q[14], A[13], ad 2.

OF THE CAUSE OF PROPHECY (SIX ARTICLES)
We must now consider the cause of prophecy. Under this head there are six points of inquiry:
(1) Whether prophecy is natural?
(2) Whether it is from God by means of the angels?
(3) Whether a natural disposition is requisite for prophecy?
(4) Whether a good life is requisite?
(5) Whether any prophecy is from the demons?
(6) Whether prophets of the demons ever tell what is true?

Whether prophecy can be natural?
Objection 1: It would seem that prophecy can be natural. For Gregory says (Dial. iv, 26) that "sometimes the mere strength of the soul is sufficiently cunning to foresee certain things": and Augustine says (Gen. ad lit. xii, 13) that the human soul, according as it is withdrawn from the sense of the body, is able to foresee the future [*Cf. [3671]FP, Q[86], A[4], ad 2]. Now this pertains to prophecy. Therefore the soul can acquire prophecy naturally.

Objection 2: Further, the human soul's knowledge is more alert while one wakes than while one sleeps. Now some, during sleep, naturally foresee the future, as the Philosopher asserts (De Somn. et Vigil. [*De Divinat. per Somn. ii, which is annexed to the work quoted]). Much more therefore can a man naturally foreknow the future.

Objection 3: Further, man, by his nature, is more perfect than dumb animals. Yet some dumb animals have foreknowledge of future things that concern them. Thus ants foreknow the coming rains, which is evident from their gathering grain into their nest before the rain commences; and in like manner fish foreknow a coming storm, as may be gathered from their movements in avoiding places exposed to storm. Much more therefore can men foreknow the future that concerns themselves, and of such things is prophecy. Therefore prophecy comes from nature.

Objection 4: Further, it is written (Prov. 29:18): "When prophecy shall fail, the people shall be scattered abroad"; wherefore it is evident that prophecy is necessary for the stability of the human race. Now "nature does not fail in necessaries" [*Aristotle, de Anima iii, 9]. Therefore it seems that prophecy is from nature.

On the contrary, It is written (2 Pet. 1:21): "For prophecy came not by the will of man at any time, but the holy men of God spoke, inspired by the Holy Ghost." Therefore prophecy comes not from nature, but through the gift of the Holy Ghost.

I answer that, As stated above (Q[171], A[6], ad 2) prophetic foreknowledge may regard future things in two ways: in one way, as they are in themselves; in another way, as they are in their causes. Now, to foreknow future things, as they are in themselves, is proper to the Divine intellect, to Whose eternity all things are present, as stated in the [3672]FP, Q[14], A[13]. Wherefore such like foreknowledge of the future cannot come from nature, but from Divine revelation alone. On the other hand, future things can be foreknown in their causes with a natural knowledge even by man: thus a physician foreknows future health or death in certain causes, through previous experimental knowledge of the order of those causes to such effects. Such like knowledge of the future may be understood to be in a man by nature in two ways. In one way that the soul, from that which it holds, is able to foreknow the future, and thus Augustine says (Gen. ad lit. xii, 13): "Some have deemed the human soul to contain a certain power of divination." This seems to be in accord with the opinion of Plato [*Phaed. xxvii; Civit. vi], who held that our souls have knowledge of all things by participating in the ideas; but that this knowledge is obscured in them by union with the body; yet in some more, in others less, according to a difference in bodily purity. According to this it might be said that men, whose souls are not much obscured through union with the body, are able to foreknow such like future things by their own knowledge. Against this opinion Augustine says (Gen. ad lit. xii, 13): "How is it that the soul cannot always have this power of divination, since it always wishes to have it?"

Since, however, it seems truer, according to the opinion of Aristotle, that the soul acquires knowledge from sensibles, as stated in the [3673]FP, Q[84], A[6], it is better to have recourse to another explanation, and to hold that men have no such foreknowledge of the future, but that they can acquire it by means of experience, wherein they are helped by their natural disposition, which depends on the perfection of a man's imaginative power, and the clarity of his understanding.

Nevertheless this latter foreknowledge of the future differs in two ways from the former, which comes through Divine revelation. First, because the former can be about any events whatever, and this infallibly; whereas the latter foreknowledge, which can be had naturally, is about certain effects, to which human experience may extend. Secondly, because the former prophecy is "according to the unchangeable truth" [*[3674]Q[171], A[3], OBJ[1]], while the latter is not, and can cover a falsehood. Now the former foreknowledge, and not the latter, properly belongs to prophecy, because, as stated above ([3675]Q[171], A[3]), prophetic knowledge is of things which naturally surpass human knowledge. Consequently we must say that prophecy strictly so called cannot be from nature, but only from Divine revelation.

Reply to Objection 1: When the soul is withdrawn from corporeal things, it becomes more adapted to receive the influence of spiritual substances [*Cf. FP, Q[88], A[4], ad 2], and also is more inclined to receive the subtle motions which take place in the human imagination through the impression of natural causes, whereas it is hindered from receiving them while occupied with sensible things. Hence Gregory says (Dial. iv, 26) that "the soul, at the approach of death, foresees certain future things, by reason of the subtlety of its nature," inasmuch as it is receptive even of slight impressions. Or again, it knows future things by a revelation of the angels; but not by its own power, because according to Augustine (Gen. ad lit. xii, 13), "if this were so, it would be able to foreknow the future whenever it willed," which is clearly false.

Objection 2: Knowledge of the future by means of dreams, comes either from the revelation of spiritual substances, or from a corporeal cause, as stated above ([3676]Q[95], A[6]), when we were treating of divination. Now both these causes are more applicable to a person while asleep than while awake, because, while awake, the soul is occupied with external sensibles, so that it is less receptive of the subtle impressions either of spiritual substances, or even of natural causes; although as regards the perfection of judgment, the reason is more alert in waking than in sleeping.

Reply to Objection 3: Even dumb animals have no foreknowledge of future events, except as these are foreknown in their causes, whereby their imagination is moved more than man's, because man's imagination, especially in waking, is more disposed according to reason than according to the impression of natural causes. Yet reason effects much more amply in man, that which the impression of natural causes effects in dumb animals; and Divine grace by inspiring the prophecy assists man still more.

Reply to Objection 4: The prophetic light extends even to the direction of human acts; and in this way prophecy is requisite for the government of a people, especially in relation to Divine worship; since for this nature is not sufficient, and grace is necessary.

Whether prophetic revelation comes through the angels?

Objection 1: It would seem that prophetic revelation does not come through the angels. For it is written (Wis. 7:27) that Divine wisdom "conveyeth herself into holy souls," and "maketh the friends of God, and the prophets." Now wisdom makes the friends of God immediately. Therefore it also makes the prophets immediately, and not through the medium of the angels.

Objection 2: Further, prophecy is reckoned among the gratuitous graces. But the gratuitous graces are from the Holy Ghost, according to 1 Cor. 12:4, "There are diversities of graces, but the same Spirit." Therefore the prophetic revelation is not made by means of an angel.

Objection 3: Further, Cassiodorus [*Prol. in Psalt. i] says that prophecy is a "Divine revelation": whereas if it were conveyed by the angels, it would be called an angelic revelation. Therefore prophecy is not bestowed by means of the angels.

On the contrary, Dionysius says (Coel. Hier. iv): "Our glorious fathers received Divine visions by means of the heavenly powers"; and he is speaking there of prophetic visions. Therefore prophetic revelation is conveyed by means of the angels.

I answer that, As the Apostle says (Rom. 13:1), "Things that are of God are well ordered [*Vulg.: 'Those that are, are ordained of God.']." Now the Divine ordering, according to Dionysius [*Coel. Hier. iv; Eccl. Hier. v], is such that the lowest things are directed by middle things. Now the angels hold a middle position between God and men, in that they have a greater share in the perfection of the Divine goodness than men have. Wherefore the Divine enlightenments and revelations are conveyed from God to men by the angels. Now prophetic knowledge is bestowed by Divine enlightenment and revelation. Therefore it is evident that it is conveyed by the angels.

Reply to Objection 1: Charity which makes man a friend of God, is a perfection of the will, in which God alone can form an impression; whereas prophecy is a perfection of the intellect, in which an angel also can form an impression, as stated in the [3677]FP, Q[111], A[1], wherefore the comparison fails between the two.

Reply to Objection 2: The gratuitous graces are ascribed to the Holy Ghost as their first principle: yet He works grace of this kind in men by means of the angels.

Reply to Objection 3: The work of the instrument is ascribed to the principal agent by whose power the instrument acts. And since a minister is like an instrument, prophetic revelation, which is conveyed by the ministry of the angels, is said to be Divine.

Whether a natural disposition is requisite for prophecy?

Objection 1: It would seem that a natural disposition is requisite for prophecy. For prophecy is received by the prophet according to the disposition of the recipient, since a gloss of Jerome on Amos 1:2, "The Lord will roar from Sion," says: "Anyone who wishes to make a comparison naturally turns to those things of which he has experience, and among which his life is spent. For example, sailors compare their enemies to the winds, and their losses to a shipwreck. In like manner Amos, who was a shepherd, likens the fear of God to that which is inspired by the lion's roar." Now that which is received by a thing according to the mode of the recipient requires a natural disposition. Therefore prophecy requires a natural disposition.

Objection 2: Further, the considerations of prophecy are more lofty than those of acquired science. Now natural indisposition hinders the considerations of acquired science, since many are prevented by natural indisposition from succeeding to grasp the speculations of science. Much more therefore is a natural disposition requisite for the contemplation of prophecy.

Objection 3: Further, natural indisposition is a much greater obstacle than an accidental impediment. Now the considerations of prophecy are hindered by an accidental occurrence. For Jerome says in his commentary on Matthew [*The quotation is from Origen, Hom. vi in Num.] that "at the time of the marriage act, the presence of the Holy Ghost will not be vouchsafed, even though it be a prophet that fulfils the duty of procreation." Much more therefore does a natural indisposition hinder prophecy; and thus it would seem that a good natural disposition is requisite for prophecy.

On the contrary, Gregory says in a homily for Pentecost (xxx in Ev.): "He," namely the Holy Ghost, "fills the boy harpist and makes him a Psalmist; He fills the herdsman plucking wild figs, and makes him a prophet." Therefore prophecy requires no previous disposition, but depends on the will alone of the Holy Ghost, of Whom it is written (1 Cor. 12:2): "All these things, one and the same Spirit worketh, dividing to every one according as He will."

I answer that, As stated above [3678](A[1]), prophecy in its true and exact sense comes from Divine inspiration; while that which comes from a natural cause is not called prophecy except in a relative sense. Now we must observe that as God Who is the universal efficient cause requires neither previous matter nor previous disposition of matter in His corporeal effects, for He is able at the same instant to bring into being matter and disposition and form, so neither does He require a previous disposition in His spiritual effects, but is able to produce both the spiritual effect and at the same time the fitting disposition as requisite according to the order of nature. More than this, He is able at the same time, by creation, to produce the subject, so as to dispose a soul for prophecy and give it the prophetic grace, at the very instant of its creation.

Reply to Objection 1: It matters not to prophecy by what comparisons the thing prophesied is expressed; and so the Divine operation makes no change in a prophet in this respect. Yet if there be anything in him incompatible with prophecy, it is removed by the Divine power.

Reply to Objection 2: The considerations of science proceed from a natural cause, and nature cannot work without a previous disposition in matter. This cannot be said of God Who is the cause of prophecy.

Reply to Objection 3: A natural indisposition, if not removed, might be an obstacle to prophetic revelation, for instance if a man were altogether deprived of the natural senses. In the same way a man might be hindered from the act of prophesying by some very strong passion, whether of anger, or of concupiscence as in coition, or by any other passion. But such a natural indisposition as this is removed by the Divine power, which is the cause of prophecy.

Whether a good life is requisite for prophecy?

Objection 1: It would seem that a good life is requisite for prophecy. For it is written (Wis. 7:27) that the wisdom of God "through nations conveyeth herself into holy souls," and "maketh the friends of God, and prophets." Now there can be no holiness without a good life and sanctifying grace. Therefore prophecy cannot be without a good life and sanctifying grace.

Objection 2: Further, secrets are not revealed save to a friend, according to Jn. 15:15, "But I have called you friends, because all things whatsoever I have heard of My Father, I have made known to you." Now God reveals His secrets to the prophets (Amos 3:7). Therefore it would seem that the prophets are the friends of God; which is impossible without charity. Therefore seemingly prophecy cannot be without charity; and charity is impossible without sanctifying grace.

Objection 3: Further, it is written (Mat. 7:15): "Beware of false prophets, who come to you in the clothing of sheep, but inwardly they are ravening wolves." Now all who are without grace are likened inwardly to a ravening wolf, and consequently all such are false prophets. Therefore no man is a true prophet except he be good by grace.

Objection 4: Further, the Philosopher says (De Somn. et Vigil. [*Cf. De Divinat. per Somn. i, which is annexed to the work quoted]) that "if interpretation of dreams is from God, it is unfitting for it to be bestowed on any but the best." Now it is evident that the gift of prophecy is from God. Therefore the gift of prophecy is vouchsafed only to the best men.

On the contrary, To those who had said, "Lord, have we not prophesied in Thy name?" this reply is made: "I never knew you" (Mat. 7:22,23). Now "the Lord knoweth who are His" (2 Tim. 2:19). Therefore prophecy can be in those who are not God's by grace.

I answer that, A good life may be considered from two points of view. First, with regard to its inward root, which is sanctifying grace. Secondly, with regard to the inward passions of the soul and the outward actions. Now sanctifying grace is given chiefly in order that man's soul may be united to God by charity. Wherefore Augustine says (De Trin. xv, 18): "A man is not transferred from the left side to the right, unless he receive the Holy Ghost, by Whom he is made a lover of God and of his neighbor." Hence whatever can be without charity can be without sanctifying grace, and consequently without goodness of life. Now prophecy can be without charity; and this is clear on two counts. First, on account of their respective acts: for prophecy pertains to the intellect, whose act precedes the act of the will, which power is perfected by charity. For this reason the Apostle (1 Cor. 13) reckons prophecy with other things pertinent to the intellect, that can be had without charity. Secondly, on account of their respective ends. For prophecy like other gratuitous graces is given for the good of the Church, according to 1 Cor. 12:7, "The manifestation of the Spirit is given to every man unto profit"; and is not directly intended to unite man's affections to God, which is the purpose of charity. Therefore prophecy can be without a good life, as regards the first root of this goodness.

If, however, we consider a good life, with regard to the passions of the soul, and external actions, from this point of view an evil life is an obstacle to prophecy. For prophecy requires the mind to be raised very high in order to contemplate spiritual things, and this is hindered by strong passions, and the inordinate pursuit of external things. Hence we read of the sons of the prophets (4 Kings 4:38) that they "dwelt together with [Vulg.: 'before']" Eliseus, leading a solitary life, as it were, lest worldly employment should be a hindrance to the gift of prophecy.

Reply to Objection 1: Sometimes the gift of prophecy is given to a man both for the good of others, and in order to enlighten his own mind; and such are those whom Divine wisdom, "conveying itself" by sanctifying grace to their minds, "maketh the friends of God, and prophets." Others, however, receive the gift of prophecy merely for the good of others. Hence Jerome commenting on Mat. 7:22, says: "Sometimes prophesying, the working of miracles, and the casting out of demons are accorded not to the merit of those who do these things, but either to the invoking the name of Christ, or to the condemnation of those who invoke, and for the good of those who see and hear."

Reply to Objection 2: Gregory [*Hom. xxvii in Ev.] expounding this passage [*Jn. 15:15] says: "Since we love the lofty things of heaven as soon as we hear them, we know them as soon as we love them, for to love is to know. Accordingly He had made all things known to them, because having renounced earthly desires they were kindled by the torches of perfect love." In this way the Divine secrets are not always revealed to prophets.

Reply to Objection 3: Not all wicked men are ravening wolves, but only those whose purpose is to injure others. For Chrysostom says [*Opus Imperf. in Matth., Hom. xix, among the works of St. John Chrysostom, and falsely ascribed to him] that "Catholic teachers, though they be sinners, are called slaves of the flesh, but never ravening wolves, because they do not purpose the destruction of Christians." And since prophecy is directed to the good of others, it is manifest that such are false prophets, because they are not sent for this purpose by God.

Reply to Objection 4: God's gifts are not always bestowed on those who are simply the best, but sometimes are vouchsafed to those who are best as regards the receiving of this or that gift. Accordingly God grants the gift of prophecy to those whom He judges best to give it to.

Whether any prophecy comes from the demons?

Objection 1: It would seem that no prophecy comes from the demons. For prophecy is "a Divine revelation," according to Cassiodorus [*Prol. in Psalt. i]. But that which is done by a demon is not Divine. Therefore no prophecy can be from a demon.

Objection 2: Further, some kind of enlightenment is requisite for prophetic knowledge, as stated above (Q[171], AA[2],3). Now the demons do not enlighten the human intellect, as stated above in the FP, Q[119], A[3]. Therefore no prophecy can come from the demons.

Objection 3: Further, a sign is worthless if it betokens contraries. Now prophecy is a sign in confirmation of faith; wherefore a gloss on Rom. 12:6, "Either prophecy to be used according to the rule of faith," says: "Observe that in reckoning the graces, he begins with prophecy, which is the first proof of the reasonableness of our faith; since believers, after receiving the Spirit, prophesied." Therefore prophecy cannot be bestowed by the demons.

On the contrary, It is written (3 Kings 18:19): "Gather unto me all Israel unto mount Carmel, and the prophets of Baal four hundred and fifty, and the prophets of the grove four hundred, who eat at Jezebel's table." Now these were worshippers of demons. Therefore it would seem that there is also a prophecy from the demons.

I answer that, As stated above ([3679]Q[171], A[1]), prophecy denotes knowledge far removed from human knowledge. Now it is evident that an intellect of a higher order can know some things that are far removed from the knowledge of an inferior intellect. Again, above the human intellect there is not only the Divine intellect, but also the intellects of good and bad angels according to the order of nature. Hence the demons, even by their natural knowledge, know certain things remote from men's knowledge, which they can reveal to men: although those things which God alone knows are remote simply and most of all.

Accordingly prophecy, properly and simply, is conveyed by Divine revelations alone; yet the revelation which is made by the demons may be called prophecy in a restricted sense. Wherefore those men to whom something is revealed by the demons are styled in the Scriptures as prophets, not simply, but with an addition, for instance as "false prophets," or "prophets of idols." Hence Augustine says (Gen. ad lit. xii, 19): "When the evil spirit lays hold of a man for such purposes as these," namely visions, "he makes him either devilish, or possessed, or a false prophet."

Reply to Objection 1: Cassiodorus is here defining prophecy in its proper and simple acceptation.

Reply to Objection 2: The demons reveal what they know to men, not by enlightening the intellect, but by an imaginary vision, or even by audible speech; and in this way this prophecy differs from true prophecy.

Reply to Objection 3: The prophecy of the demons can be distinguished from Divine prophecy by certain, and even outward, signs. Hence Chrysostom says [*Opus Imperf. in Matth., Hom. xix, falsely ascribed to St. John Chrysostom] that "some prophesy by the spirit of the devil, such as diviners, but they may be discerned by the fact that the devil sometimes utters what is false, the Holy Ghost never." Wherefore it is written (Dt. 18:21,22): "If in silent thought thou answer: How shall I know the word that the Lord hath spoken? Thou shalt have this sign: Whatsoever that same prophet foretelleth in the name of the Lord, and it come not to pass, that thing the Lord hath not spoken."

Whether the prophets of the demons ever foretell the truth?

Objection 1: It would seem that the prophets of the demons never foretell the truth. For Ambrose [*Hilary the Deacon (Ambrosiaster) on 1 Cor. 12:3] says that "Every truth, by whomsoever spoken, is from the Holy Ghost." Now the prophets of the demons do not speak from the Holy Ghost, because "there is no concord between Christ and Belial [*'What concord hath Christ with Belial?']" (2 Cor. 6:15). Therefore it would seem that they never foretell the truth.

Objection 2: Further, just as true prophets are inspired by the Spirit of truth, so the prophets of the demons are inspired by the spirit of untruth, according to 3 Kings 22:22, "I will go forth, and be a lying spirit in the mouth of all his prophets." Now the prophets inspired by the Holy Ghost never speak false, as stated above (Q[111], A[6]). Therefore the prophets of the demons never speak truth.

Objection 3: Further, it is said of the devil (Jn. 8:44) that "when he speaketh a lie, he speaketh of his own, for the devil is a liar, and the father thereof," i.e. of lying. Now by inspiring his prophets, the devil speaks only of his own, for he is not appointed God's minister to declare the truth, since "light hath no fellowship with darkness [*Vulg.: 'What fellowship hath light with darkness?']" (2 Cor. 6:14). Therefore the prophets of the demons never foretell the truth.

On the contrary, A gloss on Num. 22:14, says that "Balaam was a diviner, for he sometimes foreknew the future by help of the demons and the magic art." Now he foretold many true things, for instance that which is to be found in Num. 24:17: "A star shall rise out of Jacob, and a scepter shall spring up from Israel." Therefore even the prophets of the demons foretell the truth.

I answer that, As the good is in relation to things, so is the true in relation to knowledge. Now in things it is impossible to find one that is wholly devoid of good. Wherefore it is also impossible for any knowledge to be wholly false, without some mixture of truth. Hence Bede says [*Comment. in Luc. xvii, 12; Cf. Augustine, QQ. Evang. ii, 40] that "no teaching is so false that it never mingles truth with falsehood." Hence the teaching of the demons, with which they instruct their prophets, contains some truths whereby it is rendered acceptable. For the intellect is led astray to falsehood by the semblance of truth, even as the will is seduced to evil by the semblance of goodness. Wherefore Chrysostom says [*Opus Imperf. in Matth., Hom. xix, falsely ascribed to St. John Chrysostom]: "The devil is allowed sometimes to speak true things, in order that his unwonted truthfulness may gain credit for his lie."

Reply to Objection 1: The prophets of the demons do not always speak from the demons' revelation, but sometimes by Divine inspiration. This was evidently the case with Balaam, of whom we read that the Lord spoke to him (Num. 22:12), though he was a prophet of the demons, because God makes use even of the wicked for the profit of the good. Hence He foretells certain truths even by the demons' prophets, both that the truth may be rendered more credible, since even its foes bear witness to it, and also in order that men, by believing such men, may be more easily led on to truth. Wherefore also the Sibyls foretold many true things about Christ.

Yet even when the demons' prophets are instructed by the demons, they foretell the truth, sometimes by virtue of their own nature, the author of which is the Holy Ghost, and sometimes by revelation of the good spirits, as Augustine declares (Gen. ad lit. xii, 19): so that even then this truth which the demons proclaim is from the Holy Ghost.

Reply to Objection 2: A true prophet is always inspired by the Spirit of truth, in Whom there is no falsehood, wherefore He never says what is not true; whereas a false prophet is not always instructed by the spirit of untruth, but sometimes even by the Spirit of truth. Even the very spirit of untruth sometimes declares true things, sometimes false, as stated above.

Reply to Objection 3: Those things are called the demons' own, which they have of themselves, namely lies and sins; while they have, not of themselves but of God, those things which belong to them by nature: and it is by virtue of their own nature that they sometimes foretell the truth, as stated above (ad 1). Moreover God makes use of them to make known the truth which is to be accomplished through them, by revealing Divine mysteries to them through the angels, as already stated (Gen. ad lit. xii, 19; [3680]FP, Q[109], A[4], ad 1).

Day 238

OF THE MANNER IN WHICH PROPHETIC KNOWLEDGE IS CONVEYED (FOUR ARTICLES)

We must now consider the manner in which prophetic knowledge is conveyed, and under this head there are four points of inquiry:
(1) Whether the prophets see God's very essence?
(2) Whether the prophetic revelation is effected by the infusion of certain species, or by the infusion of Divine light alone?
(3) Whether prophetic revelation is always accompanied by abstraction from the sense?
(4) Whether prophecy is always accompanied by knowledge of the things prophesied?

Whether the prophets see the very essence of God?

Objection 1: It would seem that the prophets see the very essence of God, for a gloss on Is. 38:1, "Take order with thy house, for thou shalt die and not live," says: "Prophets can read in the book of God's foreknowledge in which all things are written." Now God's foreknowledge is His very essence. Therefore prophets see God's very essence.

Objection 2: Further, Augustine says (De Trin. ix, 7) that "in that eternal truth from which all temporal things are made, we see with the mind's eye the type both of our being and of our actions." Now, of all men, prophets have the highest knowledge of Divine things. Therefore they, especially, see the Divine essence.

Objection 3: Further, future contingencies are foreknown by the prophets "with unchangeable truth." Now future contingencies exist thus in God alone. Therefore the prophets see God Himself.

143

On the contrary, The vision of the Divine essence is not made void in heaven; whereas "prophecy is made void" (1 Cor. 13:8). Therefore prophecy is not conveyed by a vision of the Divine essence.

I answer that, Prophecy denotes Divine knowledge as existing afar off. Wherefore it is said of the prophets (Heb. 11:13) that "they were beholding . . . afar off." But those who are in heaven and in the state of bliss see, not as from afar off, but rather, as it were, from near at hand, according to Ps. 139:14, "The upright shall dwell with Thy countenance." Hence it is evident that prophetic knowledge differs from the perfect knowledge, which we shall have in heaven, so that it is distinguished therefrom as the imperfect from the perfect, and when the latter comes the former is made void, as appears from the words of the Apostle (1 Cor. 13:10).

Some, however, wishing to discriminate between prophetic knowledge and the knowledge of the blessed, have maintained that the prophets see the very essence of God (which they call the "mirror of eternity") [*Cf. De Veritate, xii, 6; Sent. II, D, XI, part 2, art. 2, ad 4], not, however, in the way in which it is the object of the blessed, but as containing the types [*Cf. FP, Q[15]] of future events. But this is altogether impossible. For God is the object of bliss in His very essence, according to the saying of Augustine (Confess. v, 4): "Happy whoso knoweth Thee, though he know not these," i.e. creatures. Now it is not possible to see the types of creatures in the very essence of God without seeing It, both because the Divine essence is Itself the type of all things that are made---the ideal type adding nothing to the Divine essence save only a relationship to the creature---and because knowledge of a thing in itself---and such is the knowledge of God as the object of heavenly bliss---precedes knowledge of that thing in its relation to something else---and such is the knowledge of God as containing the types of things. Consequently it is impossible for prophets to see God as containing the types of creatures, and yet not as the object of bliss. Therefore we must conclude that the prophetic vision is not the vision of the very essence of God, and that the prophets do not see in the Divine essence Itself the things they do see, but that they see them in certain images, according as they are enlightened by the Divine light.

Wherefore Dionysius (Coel. Hier. iv), in speaking of prophetic visions, says that "the wise theologian calls that vision divine which is effected by images of things lacking a bodily form through the seer being rapt in divine things." And these images illumined by the Divine light have more of the nature of a mirror than the Divine essence: since in a mirror images are formed from other things, and this cannot be said of God. Yet the prophet's mind thus enlightened may be called a mirror, in so far as a likeness of the truth of the Divine foreknowledge is formed therein, for which reason it is called the "mirror of eternity," as representing God's foreknowledge, for God in His eternity sees all things as present before Him, as stated above ([3681]Q[172], A[1]).

Reply to Objection 1: The prophets are said to read the book of God's foreknowledge, inasmuch as the truth is reflected from God's foreknowledge on the prophet's mind.

Reply to Objection 2: Man is said to see in the First Truth the type of his existence, in so far as the image of the First Truth shines forth on man's mind, so that he is able to know himself.

Reply to Objection 3: From the very fact that future contingencies are in God according to unalterable truth, it follows that God can impress a like knowledge on the prophet's mind without the prophet seeing God in His essence.

Whether, in prophetic revelation, new species of things are impressed on the prophet's mind, or merely a new light?

Objection 1: It would seem that in prophetic revelation no new species of things are impressed on the prophet's mind, but only a new light. For a gloss of Jerome on Amos 1:2 says that "prophets draw comparisons from things with which they are conversant." But if prophetic vision were effected by means of species newly impressed, the prophet's previous experience of things would be inoperative. Therefore no new species are impressed on the prophet's soul, but only the prophetic light.

Objection 2: Further, according to Augustine (Gen. ad lit. xii, 9), "it is not imaginative but intellective vision that makes the prophet"; wherefore it is declared (Dan. 10:1) that "there is need of understanding in a vision." Now intellective vision, as stated in the same book (Gen. ad lit. xii, 6) is not effected by means of images, but by the very truth of things. Therefore it would seem that prophetic revelation is not effected by impressing species on the soul.

Objection 3: Further, by the gift of prophecy the Holy Ghost endows man with something that surpasses the faculty of nature. Now man can by his natural faculties form all kinds of species of things. Therefore it would seem that in prophetic revelation no new species of things are impressed, but merely an intellectual light.

On the contrary, It is written (Osee 12:10): "I have multiplied" their "visions, and I have used similitudes, by the ministry of the prophets." Now multiplicity of visions results, not from a diversity of intellectual light, which is common to every prophetic vision, but from a diversity of species, whence similitudes also result. Therefore it seems that in prophetic revelation new species of things are impressed, and not merely an intellectual light.

I answer that, As Augustine says (Gen. ad lit. xii, 9), "prophetic knowledge pertains most of all to the intellect." Now two things have to be considered in connection with the knowledge possessed by the human mind, namely the acceptance or representation of things, and the judgment of the things represented. Now things are represented to the human mind under the form of species: and according to the order of nature, they must be represented first to the senses, secondly to the imagination, thirdly to the passive intellect, and these are changed by the species derived from the phantasms, which change results from the enlightening action of the active intellect. Now in the imagination there are the forms of sensible things not only as received from the senses, but also transformed in various ways, either on account of some bodily transformation (as in the case of people who are asleep or out of their senses), or through the coordination of the phantasms, at the command of reason, for the purpose of understanding something. For just as the various arrangements of the letters of the alphabet convey various ideas to the understanding, so the various coordinations of the phantasms produce various intelligible species of the intellect.

As to the judgment formed by the human mind, it depends on the power of the intellectual light.

Now the gift of prophecy confers on the human mind something which surpasses the natural faculty in both these respects, namely as to the judgment which depends on the inflow of intellectual light, and as to the acceptance or representation of things, which is

144

effected by means of certain species. Human teaching may be likened to prophetic revelation in the second of these respects, but not in the first. For a man represents certain things to his disciple by signs of speech, but he cannot enlighten him inwardly as God does.

But it is the first of these two that holds the chief place in prophecy, since judgment is the complement of knowledge. Wherefore if certain things are divinely represented to any man by means of imaginary likenesses, as happened to Pharaoh (Gn. 41:1-7) and to Nabuchodonosor (Dan. 4:1-2), or even by bodily likenesses, as happened to Balthasar (Dan. 5:5), such a man is not to be considered a prophet, unless his mind be enlightened for the purpose of judgment; and such an apparition is something imperfect in the genus of prophecy. Wherefore some [*Rabbi Moyses, Doct. Perplex. II, xxxvi] have called this "prophetic ecstasy," and such is divination by dreams. And yet a man will be a prophet, if his intellect be enlightened merely for the purpose of judging of things seen in imagination by others, as in the case of Joseph who interpreted Pharaoh's dream. But, as Augustine says (Gen. ad lit. xii, 9), "especially is he a prophet who excels in both respects, so," to wit, "as to see in spirit likenesses significant of things corporeal, and understand them by the quickness of his intellect."

Now sensible forms are divinely presented to the prophet's mind, sometimes externally by means of the senses---thus Daniel saw the writing on the wall (Dan. 5:25)---sometimes by means of imaginary forms, either of exclusively Divine origin and not received through the senses (for instance, if images of colors were imprinted on the imagination of one blind from birth), or divinely coordinated from those derived from the senses---thus Jeremiah saw the "boiling caldron . . . from the face of the north" (Jer. 1:13)---or by the direct impression of intelligible species on the mind, as in the case of those who receive infused scientific knowledge or wisdom, such as Solomon or the apostles.

But intellectual light is divinely imprinted on the human mind---sometimes for the purpose of judging of things seen by others, as in the case of Joseph, quoted above, and of the apostles whose understanding our Lord opened "that they might understand the scriptures" (Lk. 24:45); and to this pertains the "interpretation of speeches"---sometimes for the purpose of judging according to Divine truth, of the things which a man apprehends in the ordinary course of nature---sometimes for the purpose of discerning truthfully and efficaciously what is to be done, according to Is. 63:14, "The Spirit of the Lord was their leader."

Hence it is evident that prophetic revelation is conveyed sometimes by the mere infusion of light, sometimes by imprinting species anew, or by a new coordination of species.

Reply to Objection 1: As stated above, sometimes in prophetic revelation imaginary species previously derived from the senses are divinely coordinated so as to accord with the truth to be revealed, and then previous experience is operative in the production of the images, but not when they are impressed on the mind wholly from without.

Reply to Objection 2: Intellectual vision is not effected by means of bodily and individual images, but by an intelligible image. Hence Augustine says (De Trin. ix, 11) that "the soul possesses a certain likeness of the species known to it." Sometimes this intelligible image is, in prophetic revelation, imprinted immediately by God, sometimes it results from pictures in the imagination, by the aid of the prophetic light, since a deeper truth is gathered from these pictures in the imagination by means of the enlightenment of the higher light.

Reply to Objection 3: It is true that man is able by his natural powers to form all kinds of pictures in the imagination, by simply considering these pictures, but not so that they be directed to the representation of intelligible truths that surpass his intellect, since for this purpose he needs the assistance of a supernatural light.

Whether the prophetic vision is always accompanied by abstraction from the senses?

Objection 1: It would seem that the prophetic vision is always accompanied by abstraction from the senses. For it is written (Num. 12:6): "If there be among you a prophet of the Lord, I will appear to him in a vision, or I will speak to him in a dream." Now a gloss says at the beginning of the Psalter, "a vision that takes place by dreams and apparitions consists of things which seem to be said or done." But when things seem to be said or done, which are neither said nor done, there is abstraction from the senses. Therefore prophecy is always accompanied by abstraction from the senses.

Objection 2: Further, when one power is very intent on its own operation, other powers are drawn away from theirs; thus men who are very intent on hearing something fail to see what takes place before them. Now in the prophetic vision the intellect is very much uplifted, and intent on its act. Therefore it seems that the prophetic vision is always accompanied by abstraction from the senses.

Objection 3: Further, the same thing cannot, at the same time, tend in opposite directions. Now in the prophetic vision the mind tends to the acceptance of things from above, and consequently it cannot at the same time tend to sensible objects. Therefore it would seem necessary for prophetic revelation to be always accompanied by abstraction from the senses.

Objection 4: On the contrary, It is written (1 Cor. 14:32): "The spirits of the prophets are subject to the prophets." Now this were impossible if the prophet were not in possession of his faculties, but abstracted from his senses. Therefore it would seem that prophetic vision is not accompanied by abstraction from the senses.

I answer that, As stated in the foregoing Article, the prophetic revelation takes place in four ways: namely, by the infusion of an intelligible light, by the infusion of intelligible species, by impression or coordination of pictures in the imagination, and by the outward presentation of sensible images. Now it is evident that there is no abstraction from the senses, when something is presented to the prophet's mind by means of sensible species---whether these be divinely formed for this special purpose, as the bush shown to Moses (Ex. 3:2), and the writing shown to Daniel (Dan. 5:)---or whether they be produced by other causes; yet so that they are ordained by Divine providence to be prophetically significant of something, as, for instance, the Church was signified by the ark of Noah.

Again, abstraction from the external senses is not rendered necessary when the prophet's mind is enlightened by an intellectual light, or impressed with intelligible species, since in us the perfect judgment of the intellect is effected by its turning to sensible objects, which are the first principles of our knowledge, as stated in the [3682]FP, Q[84], A[6].

When, however, prophetic revelation is conveyed by images in the imagination, abstraction from the senses is necessary lest the things thus seen in imagination be taken for objects of external sensation. Yet this abstraction from the senses is sometimes complete, so that a man perceives nothing with his senses; and sometimes it is incomplete, so that he perceives something with his senses, yet does not fully discern the things he perceives outwardly from those he sees in imagination. Hence Augustine says (Gen. ad lit. xii, 12): "Those images of bodies which are formed in the soul are seen just as bodily things themselves are seen by the body, so that we see with our eyes one who is present, and at the same time we see with the soul one who is absent, as though we saw him with our eyes."

Yet this abstraction from the senses takes place in the prophets without subverting the order of nature, as is the case with those who are possessed or out of their senses; but is due to some well-ordered cause. This cause may be natural---for instance, sleep---or spiritual---for instance, the intenseness of the prophets' contemplation; thus we read of Peter (Acts 10:9) that while he was praying in the supper-room [*Vulg.: 'the house-top' or 'upper-chamber'] "he fell into an ecstasy"---or he may be carried away by the Divine power, according to the saying of Ezechiel 1:3: "The hand of the Lord was upon him."

Reply to Objection 1: The passage quoted refers to prophets in whom imaginary pictures were formed or coordinated, either while asleep, which is denoted by the word "dream," or while awake, which is signified by the word "vision."

Reply to Objection 2: When the mind is intent, in its act, upon distant things which are far removed from the senses, the intensity of its application leads to abstraction from the senses; but when it is intent, in its act, upon the coordination of or judgment concerning objects of sense, there is no need for abstraction from the senses.

Reply to Objection 3: The movement of the prophetic mind results not from its own power, but from a power acting on it from above. Hence there is no abstraction from the senses when the prophet's mind is led to judge or coordinate matters relating to objects of sense, but only when the mind is raised to the contemplation of certain more lofty things.

Reply to Objection 4: The spirit of the prophets is said to be subject to the prophets as regards the prophetic utterances to which the Apostle refers in the words quoted; because, to wit, the prophets in declaring what they have seen speak their own mind, and are not thrown off their mental balance, like persons who are possessed, as Priscilla and Montanus maintained. But as regards the prophetic revelation itself, it would be more correct to say that the prophets are subject to the. spirit of prophecy, i.e. to the prophetic gift.

Whether prophets always know the things which they prophesy?

Objection 1: It would seem that the prophets always know the things which they prophesy. For, as Augustine says (Gen. ad lit. xii, 9), "those to whom signs were shown in spirit by means of the likenesses of bodily things, had not the gift of prophecy, unless the mind was brought into action, so that those signs were also understood by them." Now what is understood cannot be unknown. Therefore the prophet is not ignorant of what he prophesies.

Objection 2: Further, the light of prophecy surpasses the light of natural reason. Now one who possesses a science by his natural light, is not ignorant of his scientific acquirements. Therefore he who utters things by the prophetic light cannot ignore them.

Objection 3: Further, prophecy is directed for man's enlightenment; wherefore it is written (2 Pet. 1:19): "We have the more firm prophetical word, whereunto you do well to attend, as to a light that shineth in a dark place." Now nothing can enlighten others unless it be lightsome in itself. Therefore it would seem that the prophet is first enlightened so as to know what he declares to others.

On the contrary, It is written (Jn. 11:51): "And this he" (Caiphas) "spoke, not of himself, but being the High Priest of that year, he prophesied that Jesus should die for the nation," etc. Now Caiphas knew this not. Therefore not every prophet knows what he prophesies.

I answer that, In prophetic revelation the prophet's mind is moved by the Holy Ghost, as an instrument that is deficient in regard to the principal agent. Now the prophet's mind is moved not only to apprehend something, but also to speak or to do something; sometimes indeed to all these three together, sometimes to two, sometimes to one only, and in each case there may be a defect in the prophet's knowledge. For when the prophet's mind is moved to think or apprehend a thing, sometimes he is led merely to apprehend that thing, and sometimes he is further led to know that it is divinely revealed to him.

Again, sometimes the prophet's mind is moved to speak something, so that he understands what the Holy Ghost means by the words he utters; like David who said (2 Kings 23:2): "The Spirit of the Lord hath spoken by me"; while, on the other hand, sometimes the person whose mind is moved to utter certain words knows not what the Holy Ghost means by them, as was the case with Caiphas (Jn. 11:51).

Again, when the Holy Ghost moves a man's mind to do something, sometimes the latter understands the meaning of it, like Jeremias who hid his loin-cloth in the Euphrates (Jer. 13:1-11); while sometimes he does not understand it---thus the soldiers, who divided Christ's garments, understood not the meaning of what they did.

Accordingly, when a man knows that he is being moved by the Holy Ghost to think something, or signify something by word or deed, this belongs properly to prophecy; whereas when he is moved, without his knowing it, this is not perfect prophecy, but a prophetic instinct. Nevertheless it must be observed that since the prophet's mind is a defective instrument, as stated above, even true prophets know not all that the Holy Ghost means by the things they see, or speak, or even do.

And this suffices for the Replies to the Objections, since the arguments given at the beginning refer to true prophets whose minds are perfectly enlightened from above.

OF THE DIVISION OF PROPHECY (SIX ARTICLES)

We must now consider the division of prophecy, and under this head there are six points of inquiry:

(1) The division of prophecy into its species;
(2) Whether the more excellent prophecy is that which is without imaginative vision?
(3) The various degrees of prophecy;

(4) Whether Moses was the greatest of the prophets?

(5) Whether a comprehensor can be a prophet?

(6) Whether prophecy advanced in perfection as time went on?

Whether prophecy is fittingly divided into the prophecy of divine predestination, of foreknowledge, and of denunciation?

Objection 1: It would seem that prophecy is unfittingly divided according to a gloss on Mat. 1:23, "Behold a virgin shall be with child," where it is stated that "one kind of prophecy proceeds from the Divine predestination, and must in all respects be accomplished so that its fulfillment is independent of our will, for instance the one in question. Another prophecy proceeds from God's foreknowledge: and into this our will enters. And another prophecy is called denunciation, which is significative of God's disapproval." For that which results from every prophecy should not be reckoned a part of prophecy. Now all prophecy is according to the Divine foreknowledge, since the prophets "read in the book of foreknowledge," as a gloss says on Is. 38:1. Therefore it would seem that prophecy according to foreknowledge should not be reckoned a species of prophecy.

Objection 2: Further, just as something is foretold in denunciation, so is something foretold in promise, and both of these are subject to alteration. For it is written (Jer. 18:7,8): "I will suddenly speak against a nation and against a kingdom, to root out, and to pull down, and to destroy it. If that nation against which I have spoken shall repent of their evil, I also will repent"---and this pertains to the prophecy of denunciation, and afterwards the text continues in reference to the prophecy of promise (Jer. 18:9,10): "I will suddenly speak of a nation and of a kingdom, to build up and plant it. If it shall do evil in My sight . . . I will repent of the good that I have spoken to do unto it." Therefore as there is reckoned to be a prophecy of denunciation, so should there be a prophecy of promise.

Objection 3: Further, Isidore says (Etym. vii, 8): "There are seven kinds of prophecy. The first is an ecstasy, which is the transport of the mind: thus Peter saw a vessel descending from heaven with all manner of beasts therein. The second kind is a vision, as we read in Isaias, who says (Is. 6:1): 'I saw the Lord sitting,' etc. The third kind is a dream: thus Jacob in a dream, saw a ladder. The fourth kind is from the midst of a cloud: thus God spake to Moses. The fifth kind is a voice from heaven, as that which called to Abraham saying (Gn. 22:11): 'Lay not thy hand upon the boy.' The sixth kind is taking up a parable, as in the example of Balaam (Num. 23:7; 24:15). The seventh kind is the fullness of the Holy Ghost, as in the case of nearly all the prophets." Further, he mentions three kinds of vision; "one by the eyes of the body, another by the soul's imagination, a third by the eyes of the mind." Now these are not included in the aforesaid division. Therefore it is insufficient.

On the contrary, stands the authority of Jerome to whom the gloss above quoted is ascribed.

I answer that, The species of moral habits and acts are distinguished according to their objects. Now the object of prophecy is something known by God and surpassing the faculty of man. Wherefore, according to the difference of such things, prophecy is divided into various species, as assigned above. Now it has been stated above (Q[71], A[6], ad 2) that the future is contained in the Divine knowledge in two ways. First, as in its cause: and thus we have the prophecy of "denunciation," which is not always fulfilled. but it foretells the relation of cause to effect, which is sometimes hindered by some other occurrence supervening. Secondly, God foreknows certain things in themselves---either as to be accomplished by Himself, and of such things is the prophecy of "predestination," since, according to Damascene (De Fide Orth. ii, 30), "God predestines things which are not in our power"---or as to be accomplished through man's free-will, and of such is the prophecy of "foreknowledge." This may regard either good or evil, which does not apply to the prophecy of predestination, since the latter regards good alone. And since predestination is comprised under foreknowledge, the gloss in the beginning of the Psalter assigns only two species to prophecy, namely of "foreknowledge," and of "denunciation."

Reply to Objection 1: Foreknowledge, properly speaking, denotes precognition of future events in themselves, and in this sense it is reckoned a species of prophecy. But in so far as it is used in connection with future events, whether as in themselves, or as in their causes, it is common to every species of prophecy.

Reply to Objection 2: The prophecy of promise is included in the prophecy of denunciation, because the aspect of truth is the same in both. But it is denominated in preference from denunciation, because God is more inclined to remit punishment than to withdraw promised blessings.

Reply to Objection 3: Isidore divides prophecy according to the manner of prophesying. Now we may distinguish the manner of prophesying---either according to man's cognitive powers, which are sense, imagination, and intellect, and then we have the three kinds of vision mentioned both by him and by Augustine (Gen. ad lit. xii, 6,7)---or according to the different ways in which the prophetic current is received. Thus as regards the enlightening of the intellect there is the "fullness of the Holy Ghost" which he mentions in the seventh place. As to the imprinting of pictures on the imagination he mentions three, namely "dreams," to which he gives the third place; "vision," which occurs to the prophet while awake and regards any kind of ordinary object, and this he puts in the second place; and "ecstasy," which results from the mind being uplifted to certain lofty things, and to this he assigns the first place. As regards sensible signs he reckons three kinds of prophecy, because a sensible sign is---either a corporeal thing offered externally to the sight, such as "a cloud," which he mentions in the fourth place---or a "voice" sounding from without and conveyed to man's hearing---this he puts in the fifth place---or a voice proceeding from a man, conveying something under a similitude, and this pertains to the "parable" to which he assigns the sixth place.

Whether the prophecy which is accompanied by intellective and imaginative vision is more excellent than that which is accompanied by intellective vision alone?

Objection 1: It would seem that the prophecy which has intellective and imaginative vision is more excellent than that which is accompanied by intellective vision alone. For Augustine says (Gen. ad lit. xii, 9): "He is less a prophet, who sees in spirit nothing but the signs representative of things, by means of the images of things corporeal: he is more a prophet, who is merely endowed with the understanding of these signs; but most of all is he a prophet, who excels in both ways," and this refers to the prophet who has intellective together with imaginative vision. Therefore this kind of prophecy is more excellent.

Objection 2: Further, the greater a thing's power is, the greater the distance to which it extends. Now the prophetic light pertains chiefly to the mind, as stated above ([3683]Q[173], A[2]). Therefore apparently the prophecy that extends to the imagination is greater than that which is confined to the intellect.

Objection 3: Further, Jerome (Prol. in Lib. Reg.) distinguishes the "prophets" from the "sacred writers." Now all those whom he calls prophets (such as Isaias, Jeremias, and the like) had intellective together with imaginative vision: but not those whom he calls sacred writers, as writing by the inspiration of the Holy Ghost (such as Job, David, Solomon, and the like). Therefore it would seem more proper to call prophets those who had intellective together with imaginative vision, than those who had intellective vision alone.

Objection 4: Further, Dionysius says (Coel. Hier. i) that "it is impossible for the Divine ray to shine on us, except as screened round about by the many-colored sacred veils." Now the prophetic revelation is conveyed by the infusion of the divine ray. Therefore it seems that it cannot be without the veils of phantasms.

On the contrary, A gloss says at the beginning of the Psalter that "the most excellent manner of prophecy is when a man prophesies by the mere inspiration of the Holy Ghost, apart from any outward assistance of deed, word, vision, or dream."

I answer that, The excellence of the means is measured chiefly by the end. Now the end of prophecy is the manifestation of a truth that surpasses the faculty of man. Wherefore the more effective this manifestation is, the more excellent the prophecy. But it is evident that the manifestation of divine truth by means of the bare contemplation of the truth itself, is more effective than that which is conveyed under the similitude of corporeal things, for it approaches nearer to the heavenly vision whereby the truth is seen in God's essence. Hence it follows that the prophecy whereby a supernatural truth is seen by intellectual vision, is more excellent than that in which a supernatural truth is manifested by means of the similitudes of corporeal things in the vision of the imagination.

Moreover the prophet's mind is shown thereby to be more lofty: even as in human teaching the hearer, who is able to grasp the bare intelligible truth the master propounds, is shown to have a better understanding than one who needs to be taken by the hand and helped by means of examples taken from objects of sense. Hence it is said in commendation of David's prophecy (2 Kings 23:3): "The strong one of Israel spoke to me," and further on (2 Kings 23:4): "As the light of the morning, when the sun riseth, shineth in the morning without clouds."

Reply to Objection 1: When a particular supernatural truth has to be revealed by means of corporeal images, he that has both, namely the intellectual light and the imaginary vision, is more a prophet than he that has only one, because his prophecy is more perfect; and it is in this sense that Augustine speaks as quoted above. Nevertheless the prophecy in which the bare intelligible truth is revealed is greater than all.

Reply to Objection 2: The same judgment does not apply to things that are sought for their own sake, as to things sought for the sake of something else. For in things sought for their own sake, the agent's power is the more effective according as it extends to more numerous and more remote objects; even so a physician is thought more of, if he is able to heal more people, and those who are further removed from health. on the other hand, in things sought only for the sake of something else, that agent would seem to have greater power, who is able to achieve his purpose with fewer means and those nearest to hand: thus more praise is awarded the physician who is able to heal a sick person by means of fewer and more gentle remedies. Now, in the prophetic knowledge, imaginary vision is required, not for its own sake, but on account of the manifestation of the intelligible truth. Wherefore prophecy is all the more excellent according as it needs it less.

Reply to Objection 3: The fact that a particular predicate is applicable to one thing and less properly to another, does not prevent this latter from being simply better than the former: thus the knowledge of the blessed is more excellent than the knowledge of the wayfarer, although faith is more properly predicated of the latter knowledge, because faith implies an imperfection of knowledge. In like manner prophecy implies a certain obscurity, and remoteness from the intelligible truth; wherefore the name of prophet is more properly applied to those who see by imaginary vision. And yet the more excellent prophecy is that which is conveyed by intellectual vision, provided the same truth be revealed in either case. If, however, the intellectual light be divinely infused in a person, not that he may know some supernatural things, but that he may be able to judge, with the certitude of divine truth, of things that can be known by human reason, such intellectual prophecy is beneath that which is conveyed by an imaginary vision leading to a supernatural truth. It was this kind of prophecy that all those had who are included in the ranks of the prophets, who moreover were called prophets for the special reason that they exercised the prophetic calling officially. Hence they spoke as God's representatives, saying to the people: "Thus saith the Lord": but not so the authors of the "sacred writings," several of whom treated more frequently of things that can be known by human reason, not in God's name, but in their own, yet with the assistance of the Divine light withal.

Reply to Objection 4: In the present life the enlightenment by the divine ray is not altogether without any veil of phantasms, because according to his present state of life it is unnatural to man not to understand without a phantasm. Sometimes, however, it is sufficient to have phantasms abstracted in the usual way from the senses without any imaginary vision divinely vouchsafed, and thus prophetic vision is said to be without imaginary vision.

Whether the degrees of prophecy can be distinguished according to the imaginary vision?

Objection 1: It would seem that the degrees of prophecy cannot be distinguished according to the imaginary vision. For the degrees of a thing bear relation to something that is on its own account, not on account of something else. Now, in prophecy, intellectual vision is sought on its own account, and imaginary vision on account of something else, as stated above (A[2], ad 2). Therefore it would seem that the degrees of prophecy are distinguished not according to imaginary, but only according to intellectual, vision.

Objection 2: Further, seemingly for one prophet there is one degree of prophecy. Now one prophet receives revelation through various imaginary visions. Therefore a difference of imaginary visions does not entail a difference of prophecy.

Objection 3: Further, according to a gloss [*Cassiodorus, super Prolog. Hieron. in Psalt.], prophecy consists of words, deeds, dreams, and visions. Therefore the degrees of prophecy should not be distinguished according to imaginary vision, to which vision and dreams pertain, rather than according to words and deeds.

On the contrary, The medium differentiates the degrees of knowledge: thus science based on direct [*"Propter quid"] proofs is more excellent than science based on indirect [*"Quia"] premises or than opinion, because it comes through a more excellent medium. Now imaginary vision is a kind of medium in prophetic knowledge. Therefore the degrees of prophecy should be distinguished according to imaginary vision.

I answer that, As stated above ([3684]Q[173], A[2]), the prophecy wherein, by the intelligible light, a supernatural truth is revealed through an imaginary vision, holds the mean between the prophecy wherein a supernatural truth is revealed without imaginary vision, and that wherein through the intelligible light and without an imaginary vision, man is directed to know or do things pertaining to human conduct. Now knowledge is more proper to prophecy than is action; wherefore the lowest degree of prophecy is when a man, by an inward instinct, is moved to perform some outward action. Thus it is related of Samson (Judges 15:14) that "the Spirit of the Lord came strongly upon him, and as the flax [*'Lina.' St. Thomas apparently read 'ligna' ('wood')] is wont to be consumed at the approach of fire, so the bands with which he was bound were broken and loosed." The second degree of prophecy is when a man is enlightened by an inward light so as to know certain things, which, however, do not go beyond the bounds of natural knowledge: thus it is related of Solomon (3 Kings 4:32,33) that "he spoke . . . parables . . . and he treated about trees from the cedar that is in Libanus unto the hyssop that cometh out of the wall, and he discoursed of beasts and of fowls, and of creeping things and of fishes": and all of this came from divine inspiration, for it was stated previously (3 Kings 4:29): "God gave to Solomon wisdom and understanding exceeding much."

Nevertheless these two degrees are beneath prophecy properly so called, because they do not attain to supernatural truth. The prophecy wherein supernatural truth is manifested through imaginary vision is differentiated first according to the difference between dreams which occur during sleep, and vision which occurs while one is awake. The latter belongs to a higher degree of prophecy, since the prophetic light that draws the soul away to supernatural things while it is awake and occupied with sensible things would seem to be stronger than that which finds a man's soul asleep and withdrawn from objects of sense. Secondly the degrees of this prophecy are differentiated according to the expressiveness of the imaginary signs whereby the intelligible truth is conveyed. And since words are the most expressive signs of intelligible truth, it would seem to be a higher degree of prophecy when the prophet, whether awake or asleep, hears words expressive of an intelligible truth, than when he sees things significative of truth, for instance "the seven full ears of corn" signified "seven years of plenty" (Gn. 41:22, 26). In such like signs prophecy would seem to be the more excellent, according as the signs are more expressive, for instance when Jeremias saw the burning of the city under the figure of a boiling cauldron (Jer. 1:13). Thirdly, it is evidently a still higher degree of prophecy when a prophet not only sees signs of words or deeds, but also, either awake or asleep, sees someone speaking or showing something to him, since this proves the prophet's mind to have approached nearer to the cause of the revelation. Fourthly, the height of a degree of prophecy may be measured according to the appearance of the person seen: for it is a higher degree of prophecy, if he who speaks or shows something to the waking or sleeping prophet be seen by him under the form of an angel, than if he be seen by him under the form of man: and higher still is it, if he be seen by the prophet whether asleep or awake, under the appearance of God, according to Is. 6:1, "I saw the Lord sitting."

But above all these degrees there is a third kind of prophecy, wherein an intelligible and supernatural truth is shown without any imaginary vision. However, this goes beyond the bounds of prophecy properly so called, as stated above (A[2], ad 3); and consequently the degrees of prophecy are properly distinguished according to imaginary vision.

Reply to Objection 1: We are unable to know how to distinguish the intellectual light, except by means of imaginary or sensible signs. Hence the difference in the intellectual light is gathered from the difference in the things presented to the imagination.

Reply to Objection 2: As stated above ([3685]Q[171], A[2]), prophecy is by way, not of an abiding habit, but of a transitory passion; wherefore there is nothing inconsistent if one and the same prophet, at different times, receive various degrees of prophetic revelation.

Reply to Objection 3: The words and deeds mentioned there do not pertain to the prophetic revelation, but to the announcement, which is made according to the disposition of those to whom that which is revealed to the prophet is announced; and this is done sometimes by words, sometimes by deeds. Now this announcement, and the working of miracles, are something consequent upon prophecy, as stated above ([3686]Q[171], A[1]).

Whether Moses was the greatest of the prophets?

Objection 1: It would seem that Moses was not the greatest of the prophets. For a gloss at the beginning of the Psalter says that "David is called the prophet by way of excellence." Therefore Moses was not the greatest of all.

Objection 2: Further, greater miracles were wrought by Josue, who made the sun and moon to stand still (Josh. 10:12-14), and by Isaias, who made the sun to turn back (Is. 38:8), than by Moses, who divided the Red Sea (Ex. 14:21). In like manner greater miracles were wrought by Elias, of whom it is written (Ecclus. 48:4,5): "Who can glory like to thee? Who raisedst up a dead man from below." Therefore Moses was not the greatest of the prophets.

Objection 3: Further, it is written (Mat. 11:11) that "there hath not risen, among them that are born of women, a greater than John the Baptist." Therefore Moses was not greater than all the prophets.

On the contrary, It is written (Dt. 34:10): "There arose no more a prophet in Israel like unto Moses."

I answer that, Although in some respect one or other of the prophets was greater than Moses, yet Moses was simply the greatest of all. For, as stated above [3687](A[3]; Q[171], A[1]), in prophecy we may consider not only the knowledge, whether by intellectual or by imaginary vision, but also the announcement and the confirmation by miracles. Accordingly Moses was greater than the other prophets. First, as regards the intellectual vision, since he saw God's very essence, even as Paul in his rapture did, according to

Augustine (Gen. ad lit. xii, 27). Hence it is written (Num. 12:8) that he saw God "plainly and not by riddles." Secondly, as regards the imaginary vision, which he had at his call, as it were, for not only did he hear words, but also saw one speaking to him under the form of God, and this not only while asleep, but even when he was awake. Hence it is written (Ex. 33:11) that "the Lord spoke to Moses face to face, as a man is wont to speak to his friend." Thirdly, as regards the working of miracles which he wrought on a whole nation of unbelievers. Wherefore it is written (Dt. 34:10,11): "There arose no more a prophet in Israel like unto Moses, whom the Lord knew face to face: in all the signs and wonders, which He sent by him, to do in the land of Egypt to Pharaoh, and to all his servants, and to his whole land."

Reply to Objection 1: The prophecy of David approaches near to the vision of Moses, as regards the intellectual vision, because both received a revelation of intelligible and supernatural truth, without any imaginary vision. Yet the vision of Moses was more excellent as regards the knowledge of the Godhead; while David more fully knew and expressed the mysteries of Christ's incarnation.

Reply to Objection 2: These signs of the prophets mentioned were greater as to the substance of the thing done; yet the miracles of Moses were greater as regards the way in which they were done, since they were wrought on a whole people.

Reply to Objection 3: John belongs to the New Testament, whose ministers take precedence even of Moses, since they are spectators of a fuller revelation, as stated in 2 Cor. 3.

Day 239

Whether there is a degree of prophecy in the blessed?

Objection 1: It would seem that there is a degree of prophecy in the blessed. For, as stated above [3688](A[4]), Moses saw the Divine essence, and yet he is called a prophet. Therefore in like manner the blessed can be called prophets.

Objection 2: Further, prophecy is a "divine revelation." Now divine revelations are made even to the blessed angels. Therefore even blessed angels can be prophets.

Objection 3: Further, Christ was a comprehensor from the moment of His conception; and yet He calls Himself a prophet (Mat. 13:57), when He says: "A prophet is not without honor, save in his own country." Therefore even comprehensors and the blessed can be called prophets.

Objection 4: Further, it is written of Samuel (Ecclus. 46:23): "He lifted up his voice from the earth in prophecy to blot out the wickedness of the nation." Therefore other saints can likewise be called prophets after they have died.

On the contrary, The prophetic word is compared (2 Pet. 1:19) to a "light that shineth in a dark place." Now there is no darkness in the blessed. Therefore they cannot be called prophets.

I answer that, Prophecy denotes vision of some supernatural truth as being far remote from us. This happens in two ways. First, on the part of the knowledge itself, because, to wit, the supernatural truth is not known in itself, but in some of its effects; and this truth will be more remote if it be known by means of images of corporeal things, than if it be known in its intelligible effects; and such most of all is the prophetic vision, which is conveyed by images and likenesses of corporeal things. Secondly, vision is remote on the part of the seer, because, to wit, he has not yet attained completely to his ultimate perfection, according to 2 Cor. 5:6, "While we are in the body, we are absent from the Lord."

Now in neither of these ways are the blessed remote; wherefore they cannot be called prophets.

Reply to Objection 1: This vision of Moses was interrupted after the manner of a passion, and was not permanent like the beatific vision, wherefore he was as yet a seer from afar. For this reason his vision did not entirely lose the character of prophecy.

Reply to Objection 2: The divine revelation is made to the angels, not as being far distant, but as already wholly united to God; wherefore their revelation has not the character of prophecy.

Reply to Objection 3: Christ was at the same time comprehensor and wayfarer [*Cf. TP, QQ[9], seqq.]. Consequently the notion of prophecy is not applicable to Him as a comprehensor, but only as a wayfarer.

Reply to Objection 4: Samuel had not yet attained to the state of blessedness. Wherefore although by God's will the soul itself of Samuel foretold to Saul the issue of the war as revealed to him by God, this pertains to the nature of prophecy. It is not the same with the saints who are now in heaven. Nor does it make any difference that this is stated to have been brought about by the demons' art, because although the demons are unable to evoke the soul of a saint, or to force it to do any particular thing, this can be done by the power of God, so that when the demon is consulted, God Himself declares the truth by His messenger: even as He gave a true answer by Elias to the King's messengers who were sent to consult the god of Accaron (4 Kings 1).

It might also be replied [*The Book of Ecclesiasticus was not as yet declared by the Church to be Canonical Scripture; Cf. [3689]FP, Q[89], A[8], ad 2] that it was not the soul of Samuel, but a demon impersonating him; and that the wise man calls him Samuel, and describes his prediction as prophetic, in accordance with the thoughts of Saul and the bystanders who were of this opinion.

Whether the degrees of prophecy change as time goes on?

Objection 1: It would seem that the degrees of prophecy change as time goes on. For prophecy is directed to the knowledge of Divine things, as stated above [3690](A[2]). Now according to Gregory (Hom. in Ezech.), "knowledge of God went on increasing as time went on." Therefore degrees of prophecy should be distinguished according to the process of time.

Objection 2: Further, prophetic revelation is conveyed by God speaking to man; while the prophets declared both in words and in writing the things revealed to them. Now it is written (1 Kings 3:1) that before the time of Samuel "the word of the Lord was precious," i.e. rare; and yet afterwards it was delivered to many. In like manner the books of the prophets do not appear to have been written before the time of Isaias, to whom it was said (Is. 8:1): "Take thee a great book and write in it with a man's pen," after which many prophets wrote their prophecies. Therefore it would seem that in course of time the degree of prophecy made progress.

Objection 3: Further, our Lord said (Mat. 11:13): "The prophets and the law prophesied until John"; and afterwards the gift of prophecy was in Christ's disciples in a much more excellent manner than in the prophets of old, according to Eph. 3:5, "In other generations" the mystery of Christ "was not known to the sons of men, as it is now revealed to His holy apostles and prophets in the Spirit." Therefore it would seem that in course of time the degree of prophecy advanced.

On the contrary, As stated above [3691](A[4]), Moses was the greatest of the prophets, and yet he preceded the other prophets. Therefore prophecy did not advance in degree as time went on.

I answer that, As stated above [3692](A[2]), prophecy is directed to the knowledge of Divine truth, by the contemplation of which we are not only instructed in faith, but also guided in our actions, according to Ps. 42:3, "Send forth Thy light and Thy truth: they have conducted me." Now our faith consists chiefly in two things: first, in the true knowledge of God, according to Heb. 11:6, "He that cometh to God must believe that He is"; secondly, in the mystery of Christ's incarnation, according to Jn. 14:1, "You believe in God, believe also in Me." Accordingly, if we speak of prophecy as directed to the Godhead as its end, it progressed according to three divisions of time, namely before the law, under the law, and under grace. For before the law, Abraham and the other patriarchs were prophetically taught things pertinent to faith in the Godhead. Hence they are called prophets, according to Ps. 104:15, "Do no evil to My prophets," which words are said especially on behalf of Abraham and Isaac. Under the Law prophetic revelation of things pertinent to faith in the Godhead was made in a yet more excellent way than hitherto, because then not only certain special persons or families but the whole people had to be instructed in these matters. Hence the Lord said to Moses (Ex. 6:2,3): "I am the Lord that appeared to Abraham, to Isaac, and to Jacob, by the name of God almighty, and My name Adonai I did not show to them"; because previously the patriarchs had been taught to believe in a general way in God, one and Almighty, while Moses was more fully instructed in the simplicity of the Divine essence, when it was said to him (Ex. 3:14): "I am Who am"; and this name is signified by Jews in the word "Adonai" on account of their veneration for that unspeakable name. Afterwards in the time of grace the mystery of the Trinity was revealed by the Son of God Himself, according to Mat. 28:19: "Going . . . teach ye all nations, baptizing them in the name of the Father, and of the Son, and of the Holy Ghost."

In each state, however, the most excellent revelation was that which was given first. Now the first revelation, before the Law, was given to Abraham, for it was at that time that men began to stray from faith in one God by turning aside to idolatry, whereas hitherto no such revelation was necessary while all persevered in the worship of one God. A less excellent revelation was made to Isaac, being founded on that which was made to Abraham. Wherefore it was said to him (Gn. 26:24): "I am the God of Abraham thy father," and in like manner to Jacob (Gn. 28:13): "I am the God of Abraham thy father, and the God of Isaac." Again in the state of the Law the first revelation which was given to Moses was more excellent, and on this revelation all the other revelations to the prophets were founded. And so, too, in the time of grace the entire faith of the Church is founded on the revelation vouchsafed to the apostles, concerning the faith in one God and three Persons, according to Mat. 16:18, "On this rock," i.e. of thy confession, "I will build My Church."

As to the faith in Christ's incarnation, it is evident that the nearer men were to Christ, whether before or after Him, the more fully, for the most part, were they instructed on this point, and after Him more fully than before, as the Apostle declares (Eph. 3:5).

As regards the guidance of human acts, the prophetic revelation varied not according to the course of time, but according as circumstances required, because as it is written (Prov. 29:18), "When prophecy shall fail, the people shall be scattered abroad." Wherefore at all times men were divinely instructed about what they were to do, according as it was expedient for the spiritual welfare of the elect.

Reply to Objection 1: The saying of Gregory is to be referred to the time before Christ's incarnation, as regards the knowledge of this mystery.

Reply to Objection 2: As Augustine says (De Civ. Dei xviii, 27), "just as in the early days of the Assyrian kingdom promises were made most explicitly to Abraham, so at the outset of the western Babylon," which is Rome, "and under its sway Christ was to come, in Whom were to be fulfilled the promises made through the prophetic oracles testifying in word and writing to that great event to come," the promises, namely, which were made to Abraham. "For while prophets were scarcely ever lacking to the people of Israel from the time that they began to have kings, it was exclusively for their benefit, not for that of the nations. But when those prophetic writings were being set up with greater publicity, which at some future time were to benefit the nations, it was fitting to begin when this city," Rome to wit, "was being built, which was to govern the nations."

The reason why it behooved that nation to have a number of prophets especially at the time of the kings, was that then it was not over-ridden by other nations, but had its own king; wherefore it behooved the people, as enjoying liberty, to have prophets to teach them what to do.

Reply to Objection 3: The prophets who foretold the coming of Christ could not continue further than John, who with his finger pointed to Christ actually present. Nevertheless as Jerome says on this passage, "This does not mean that there were no more prophets after John. For we read in the Acts of the apostles that Agabus and the four maidens, daughters of Philip, prophesied." John, too, wrote a prophetic book about the end of the Church; and at all times there have not been lacking persons having the spirit of prophecy, not indeed for the declaration of any new doctrine of faith, but for the direction of human acts. Thus Augustine says (De Civ. Dei v, 26) that "the emperor Theodosius sent to John who dwelt in the Egyptian desert, and whom he knew by his ever-increasing fame to be endowed with the prophetic spirit: and from him he received a message assuring him of victory."

OF RAPTURE (SIX ARTICLES)

We must now consider rapture. Under this head there are six points of inquiry:

(1) Whether the soul of man is carried away to things divine?

(2) Whether rapture pertains to the cognitive or to the appetitive power?

(3) Whether Paul when in rapture saw the essence of God?

(4) Whether he was withdrawn from his senses?
(5) Whether, when in that state, his soul was wholly separated from his body?
(6) What did he know, and what did he not know about this matter?

Whether the soul of man is carried away to things divine?

Objection 1: It would seem that the soul of man is not carried away to things divine. For some define rapture as "an uplifting by the power of a higher nature, from that which is according to nature to that which is above nature" [*Reference unknown; Cf. De Veritate xiii, 1]. Now it is in accordance with man's nature that he be uplifted to things divine; for Augustine says at the beginning of his Confessions: "Thou madest us, Lord, for Thyself, and our heart is restless, till it rest in Thee." Therefore man's soul is not carried away to things divine.

Objection 2: Further, Dionysius says (Div. Nom. viii) that "God's justice is seen in this that He treats all things according to their mode and dignity." But it is not in accordance with man's mode and worth that he be raised above what he is according to nature. Therefore it would seem that man's soul is not carried away to things divine.

Objection 3: Further, rapture denotes violence of some kind. But God rules us not by violence or force, as Damascene says [*De Fide Orth. ii, 30]. Therefore man's soul is not carried away to things divine.

On the contrary, The Apostle says (2 Cor. 12:2): "I know a man in Christ . . . rapt even to the third heaven." On which words a gloss says: "Rapt, that is to say, uplifted contrary to nature."

I answer that, Rapture denotes violence of a kind as stated above (OBJ[3]); and "the violent is that which has its principle without, and in which he that suffers violence concurs not at all" (Ethic. iii, 1). Now everything concurs in that to which it tends in accordance with its proper inclination, whether voluntary or natural. Wherefore he who is carried away by some external agent, must be carried to something different from that to which its inclination tends. This difference arises in two ways: in one way from the end of the inclination---for instance a stone, which is naturally inclined to be borne downwards, may be thrown upwards; in another way from the manner of tending---for instance a stone may be thrown downwards with greater velocity than consistent with its natural movement.

Accordingly man's soul also is said to be carried away, in a twofold manner, to that which is contrary to its nature: in one way, as regards the term of transport---as when it is carried away to punishment, according to Ps. 49:22, "Lest He snatch you away, and there be none to deliver you"; in another way, as regards the manner connatural to man, which is that he should understand the truth through sensible things. Hence when he is withdrawn from the apprehension of sensibles, he is said to be carried away, even though he be uplifted to things whereunto he is directed naturally: provided this be not done intentionally, as when a man betakes himself to sleep which is in accordance with nature, wherefore sleep cannot be called rapture, properly speaking.

This withdrawal, whatever its term may be, may arise from a threefold cause. First, from a bodily cause, as happens to those who suffer abstraction from the senses through weakness: secondly, by the power of the demons, as in those who are possessed: thirdly, by the power of God. In this last sense we are now speaking of rapture, whereby a man is uplifted by the spirit of God to things supernatural, and withdrawn from his senses, according to Ezech. 8:3, "The spirit lifted me up between the earth and the heaven, and brought me in the vision of God into Jerusalem."

It must be observed, however, that sometimes a person is said to be carried away, not only through being withdrawn from his senses, but also through being withdrawn from the things to which he was attending, as when a person's mind wanders contrary to his purpose. But this is to use the expression in a less proper signification.

Reply to Objection 1: It is natural to man to tend to divine things through the apprehension of things sensible, according to Rom. 1:20, "The invisible things of God . . . are clearly seen, being understood by the things that are made." But the mode, whereby a man is uplifted to divine things and withdrawn from his senses, is not natural to man.

Reply to Objection 2: It belongs to man's mode and dignity that he be uplifted to divine things, from the very fact that he is made to God's image. And since a divine good infinitely surpasses the faculty of man in order to attain that good, he needs the divine assistance which is bestowed on him in every gift of grace. Hence it is not contrary to nature, but above the faculty of nature that man's mind be thus uplifted in rapture by God.

Reply to Objection 3: The saying of Damascene refers to those things which a man does by himself. But as to those things which are beyond the scope of the free-will, man needs to be uplifted by a stronger operation, which in a certain respect may be called force if we consider the mode of operation, but not if we consider its term to which man is directed both by nature and by his intention.

Whether rapture pertains to the cognitive rather than to the appetitive power?

Objection 1: It would seem that rapture pertains to the appetitive rather than to the cognitive power. For Dionysius says (Div. Nom. iv): "The Divine love causes ecstasy." Now love pertains to the appetitive power. Therefore so does ecstasy or rapture.

Objection 2: Further, Gregory says (Dial. ii, 3) that "he who fed the swine debased himself by a dissipated mind and an unclean life; whereas Peter, when the angel delivered him and carried him into ecstasy, was not beside himself, but above himself." Now the prodigal son sank into the depths by his appetite. Therefore in those also who are carried up into the heights it is the appetite that is affected.

Objection 3: Further, a gloss on Ps. 30:1, "In Thee, O Lord, have I hoped, let me never be confounded," says in explaining the title [*Unto the end, a psalm for David, in an ecstasy]: "{Ekstasis} in Greek signifies in Latin 'excessus mentis,' an aberration of the mind. This happens in two ways, either through dread of earthly things or through the mind being rapt in heavenly things and forgetful of this lower world." Now dread of earthly things pertains to the appetite. Therefore rapture of the mind in heavenly things, being placed in opposition to this dread, also pertains to the appetite.

On the contrary, A gloss on Ps. 115:2, "I said in my excess: Every man is a liar," says: "We speak of ecstasy, not when the mind wanders through fear, but when it is carried aloft on the wings of revelation." Now revelation pertains to the intellective power. Therefore ecstasy or rapture does also.

I answer that, We can speak of rapture in two ways. First, with regard to the term of rapture, and thus, properly speaking, rapture cannot pertain to the appetitive, but only to the cognitive power. For it was stated [3693](A[1]) that rapture is outside the inclination of the person who is rapt; whereas the movement of the appetitive power is an inclination to an appetible good. Wherefore, properly speaking, in desiring something, a man is not rapt, but is moved by himself.

Secondly, rapture may be considered with regard to its cause, and thus it may have a cause on the part of the appetitive power. For from the very fact that the appetite is strongly affected towards something, it may happen, owing to the violence of his affection, that a man is carried away from everything else. Moreover, it has an effect on the appetitive power, when for instance a man delights in the things to which he is rapt. Hence the Apostle said that he was rapt, not only "to the third heaven"---which pertains to the contemplation of the intellect---but also into "paradise," which pertains to the appetite.

Reply to Objection 1: Rapture adds something to ecstasy. For ecstasy means simply a going out of oneself by being placed outside one's proper order [*Cf. [3694]FS, Q[28], A[3]]; while rapture denotes a certain violence in addition. Accordingly ecstasy may pertain to the appetitive power, as when a man's appetite tends to something outside him, and in this sense Dionysius says that "the Divine love causes ecstasy," inasmuch as it makes man's appetite tend to the object loved. Hence he says afterwards that "even God Himself, the cause of all things, through the overflow of His loving goodness, goes outside Himself in His providence for all beings." But even if this were said expressly of rapture, it would merely signify that love is the cause of rapture.

Reply to Objection 2: There is a twofold appetite in man; to wit, the intellective appetite which is called the will, and the sensitive appetite known as the sensuality. Now it is proper to man that his lower appetite be subject to the higher appetite, and that the higher move the lower. Hence man may become outside himself as regards the appetite, in two ways. In one way, when a man's intellective appetite tends wholly to divine things, and takes no account of those things whereto the sensitive appetite inclines him; thus Dionysius says (Div. Nom. iv) that "Paul being in ecstasy through the vehemence of Divine love" exclaimed: "I live, now not I, but Christ liveth in me."

In another way, when a man tends wholly to things pertaining to the lower appetite, and takes no account of his higher appetite. It is thus that "he who fed the swine debased himself"; and this latter kind of going out of oneself, or being beside oneself, is more akin than the former to the nature of rapture because the higher appetite is more proper to man. Hence when through the violence of his lower appetite a man is withdrawn from the movement of his higher appetite, it is more a case of being withdrawn from that which is proper to him. Yet, because there is no violence therein, since the will is able to resist the passion, it falls short of the true nature of rapture, unless perchance the passion be so strong that it takes away entirely the use of reason, as happens to those who are mad with anger or love.

It must be observed. however, that both these excesses affecting the appetite may cause an excess in the cognitive power, either because the mind is carried away to certain intelligible objects, through being drawn away from objects of sense, or because it is caught up into some imaginary vision or fanciful apparition.

Reply to Objection 3: Just as love is a movement of the appetite with regard to good, so fear is a movement of the appetite with regard to evil. Wherefore either of them may equally cause an aberration of mind; and all the more since fear arises from love, as Augustine says (De Civ. Dei xiv, 7,9).

Whether Paul, when in rapture, saw the essence of God?

Objection 1: It would seem that Paul, when in rapture, did not see the essence of God. For just as we read of Paul that he was rapt to the third heaven, so we read of Peter (Acts 10:10) that "there came upon him an ecstasy of mind." Now Peter, in his ecstasy, saw not God's essence but an imaginary vision. Therefore it would seem that neither did Paul see the essence of God.

Objection 2: Further, the vision of God is beatific. But Paul, in his rapture, was not beatified; else he would never have returned to the unhappiness of this life, but his body would have been glorified by the overflow from his soul, as will happen to the saints after the resurrection, and this clearly was not the case. Therefore Paul when in rapture saw not the essence of God.

Objection 3: Further, according to 1 Cor. 13:10-12, faith and hope are incompatible with the vision of the Divine essence. But Paul when in this state had faith and hope. Therefore he saw not the essence of God.

Objection 4: Further, as Augustine states (Gen. ad lit. xii, 6,7), "pictures of bodies are seen in the imaginary vision." Now Paul is stated (2 Cor. 12:2, 4) to have seen certain pictures in his rapture, for instance of the "third heaven" and of "paradise." Therefore he would seem to have been rapt to an imaginary vision rather than to the vision of the Divine essence.

On the contrary, Augustine (Ep. CXLVII, 13; ad Paulin., de videndo Deum) concludes that "possibly God's very substance was seen by some while yet in this life: for instance by Moses, and by Paul who in rapture heard unspeakable words, which it is not granted unto man to utter."

I answer that, Some have said that Paul, when in rapture, saw "not the very essence of God, but a certain reflection of His clarity." But Augustine clearly comes to an opposite decision, not only in his book (De videndo Deum), but also in Gen. ad lit. xii, 28 (quoted in a gloss on 2 Cor. 12:2). Indeed the words themselves of the Apostle indicate this. For he says that "he heard secret words, which it is not granted unto man to utter": and such would seem to be words pertaining to the vision of the blessed, which transcends the state of the wayfarer, according to Is. 64:4, "Eye hath not seen, O God, besides Thee, what things Thou hast prepared for them that love [Vulg.: 'wait for'] Thee" [*1 Cor. 2:9]. Therefore it is more becoming to hold that he saw God in His essence.

Reply to Objection 1: Man's mind is rapt by God to the contemplation of divine truth in three ways. First, so that he contemplates it through certain imaginary pictures, and such was the ecstasy that came upon Peter. Secondly, so that he contemplates the divine truth through its intelligible effects; such was the ecstasy of David, who said (Ps. 115:11): "I said in my excess: Every man is a liar."

Thirdly, so that he contemplates it in its essence. Such was the rapture of Paul, as also of Moses [*Cf. Q[174], A[4]]; and not without reason, since as Moses was the first Teacher of the Jews, so was Paul the first "Teacher of the gentiles" [*Cf. [3695]FP, Q[68], A[4]].

Reply to Objection 2: The Divine essence cannot be seen by a created intellect save through the light of glory, of which it is written (Ps. 35:10): "In Thy light we shall see light." But this light can be shared in two ways. First by way of an abiding form, and thus it beatifies the saints in heaven. Secondly, by way of a transitory passion, as stated above ([3696]Q[171] , A[2]) of the light of prophecy; and in this way that light was in Paul when he was in rapture. Hence this vision did not beatify him simply, so as to overflow into his body, but only in a restricted sense. Consequently this rapture pertains somewhat to prophecy.

Reply to Objection 3: Since, in his rapture, Paul was beatified not as to the habit, but only as to the act of the blessed, it follows that he had not the act of faith at the same time, although he had the habit.

Reply to Objection 4: In one way by the third heaven we may understand something corporeal, and thus the third heaven denotes the empyrean [*1 Tim. 2:7; Cf. [3697]FP, Q[12], A[11], ad 2], which is described as the "third," in relation to the aerial and starry heavens, or better still, in relation to the aqueous and crystalline heavens. Moreover Paul is stated to be rapt to the "third heaven," not as though his rapture consisted in the vision of something corporeal, but because this place is appointed for the contemplation of the blessed. Hence the gloss on 2 Cor. 12 says that the "third heaven is a spiritual heaven, where the angels and the holy souls enjoy the contemplation of God: and when Paul says that he was rapt to this heaven he means that God showed him the life wherein He is to be seen forevermore."

In another way the third heaven may signify a supra-mundane vision. Such a vision may be called the third heaven in three ways. First, according to the order of the cognitive powers. In this way the first heaven would indicate a supramundane bodily vision, conveyed through the senses; thus was seen the hand of one writing on the wall (Dan. 5:5); the second heaven would be an imaginary vision such as Isaias saw, and John in the Apocalypse; and the third heaven would denote an intellectual vision according to Augustine's explanation (Gen. ad lit. xii, 26,28,34). Secondly, the third heaven may be taken according to the order of things knowable, the first heaven being "the knowledge of heavenly bodies, the second the knowledge of heavenly spirits, the third the knowledge of God Himself." Thirdly, the third heaven may denote the contemplation of God according to the degrees of knowledge whereby God is seen. The first of these degrees belongs to the angels of the lowest hierarchy [*Cf. [3698]FP, Q[108], A[1]], the second to the angels of the middle hierarchy, the third to the angels of the highest hierarchy, according to the gloss on 2 Cor. 12.

And since the vision of God cannot be without delight, he says that he was not only "rapt to the third heaven" by reason of his contemplation, but also into "Paradise" by reason of the consequent delight.

Whether Paul, when in rapture, was withdrawn from his senses?

Objection 1: It would seem that Paul, when in rapture, was not withdrawn from his senses. For Augustine says (Gen. ad lit. xii, 28): "Why should we not believe that when so great an apostle, the teacher of the gentiles, was rapt to this most sublime vision, God was willing to vouchsafe him a glimpse of that eternal life which is to take the place of the present life?" Now in that future life after the resurrection the saints will see the Divine essence without being withdrawn from the senses of the body. Therefore neither did such a withdrawal take place in Paul.

Objection 2: Further, Christ was truly a wayfarer, and also enjoyed an uninterrupted vision of the Divine essence, without, however, being withdrawn from His senses. Therefore there was no need for Paul to be withdrawn from his senses in order for him to see the essence of God.

Objection 3: Further, after seeing God in His essence, Paul remembered what he had seen in that vision; hence he said (2 Cor. 12:4): "He heard secret words, which it is not granted to man to utter." Now the memory belongs to the sensitive faculty according to the Philosopher (De Mem. et Remin. i). Therefore it seems that Paul, while seeing the essence of God, was not withdrawn from his senses.

On the contrary, Augustine says (Gen. ad lit. xii, 27): "Unless a man in some way depart this life, whether by going altogether out of his body or by turning away and withdrawing from his carnal senses, so that he truly knows not as the Apostle said, whether he be in the body or out of the body, he is not rapt and caught up into that vision.*" [*The text of St. Augustine reads: "when he is rapt," etc.]

I answer that, The Divine essence cannot be seen by man through any cognitive power other than the intellect. Now the human intellect does not turn to intelligible objects except by means of the phantasms [*Cf. [3699]FP, Q[84], A[7]] which it takes from the senses through the intelligible species; and it is in considering these phantasms that the intellect judges of and coordinates sensible objects. Hence in any operation that requires abstraction of the intellect from phantasms, there must be also withdrawal of the intellect from the senses. Now in the state of the wayfarer it is necessary for man's intellect, if it see God's essence, to be withdrawn from phantasms. For God's essence cannot be seen by means of a phantasm, nor indeed by any created intelligible species [*Cf. [3700]FP, Q[12], A[2]], since God's essence infinitely transcends not only all bodies, which are represented by phantasms, but also all intelligible creatures. Now when man's intellect is uplifted to the sublime vision of God's essence, it is necessary that his mind's whole attention should be summoned to that purpose in such a way that he understand naught else by phantasms, and be absorbed entirely in God. Therefore it is impossible for man while a wayfarer to see God in His essence without being withdrawn from his senses.

Reply to Objection 1: As stated above (A[3], OBJ[2]), after the resurrection, in the blessed who see God in His essence, there will be an overflow from the intellect to the lower powers and even to the body. Hence it is in keeping with the rule itself of the divine vision that the soul will turn towards phantasms and sensible objects. But there is no such overflow in those who are raptured, as stated (A[3], OBJ[2], ad 2), and consequently the comparison fails.

Reply to Objection 2: The intellect of Christ's soul was glorified by the habit of the light of glory, whereby He saw the Divine essence much more fully than an angel or a man. He was, however, a wayfarer on account of the possibility of His body, in respect of which He was "made a little lower than the angels" (Heb. 2:9), by dispensation, and not on account of any defect on the part of His intellect. Hence there is no comparison between Him and other wayfarers.

Reply to Objection 3: Paul, after seeing God in His essence, remembered what he had known in that vision, by means of certain intelligible species that remained in his intellect by way of habit; even as in the absence of the sensible object, certain impressions remain in the soul which it recollects when it turns to the phantasms. And so this was the knowledge that he was unable wholly to think over or express in words.

Whether, while in this state, Paul's soul was wholly separated from his body?

Objection 1: It would seem that, while in this state, Paul's soul was wholly separated from his body. For the Apostle says (2 Cor. 5:6,7): "While we are in the body we are absent from the Lord. For we walk by faith, and not by sight" [*'Per speciem,' i.e. by an intelligible species]. Now, while in that state, Paul was not absent from the Lord, for he saw Him by a species, as stated above [3701] (A[3]). Therefore he was not in the body.

Objection 2: Further, a power of the soul cannot be uplifted above the soul's essence wherein it is rooted. Now in this rapture the intellect, which is a power of the soul, was withdrawn from its bodily surroundings through being uplifted to divine contemplation. Much more therefore was the essence of the soul separated from the body.

Objection 3: Further, the forces of the vegetative soul are more material than those of the sensitive soul. Now in order for him to be rapt to the vision of God, it was necessary for him to be withdrawn from the forces of the sensitive soul, as stated above [3702](A[4]). Much more, therefore, was it necessary for him to be withdrawn from the forces of the vegetative soul. Now when these forces cease to operate, the soul is no longer in any way united to the body. Therefore it would seem that in Paul's rapture it was necessary for the soul to be wholly separated from the body.

On the contrary, Augustine says (Ep. CXLVII, 13, ad Paulin.; de videndo Deum): "It is not incredible that this sublime revelation" (namely, that they should see God in His essence) "was vouchsafed certain saints, without their departing this life so completely as to leave nothing but a corpse for burial." Therefore it was not necessary for Paul's soul, when in rapture, to be wholly separated from his body.

I answer that, As stated above (A[1], OBJ[1]), in the rapture of which we are speaking now, man is uplifted by God's power, "from that which is according to nature to that which is above nature." Wherefore two things have to be considered: first, what pertains to man according to nature; secondly, what has to be done by God in man above his nature. Now, since the soul is united to the body as its natural form, it belongs to the soul to have a natural disposition to understand by turning to phantasms; and this is not withdrawn by the divine power from the soul in rapture, since its state undergoes no change, as stated above (A[3], ad 2,3). Yet, this state remaining, actual conversion to phantasms and sensible objects is withdrawn from the soul, lest it be hindered from being uplifted to that which transcends all phantasms, as stated above [3703](A[4]). Therefore it was not necessary that his soul in rapture should be so separated from the body as to cease to be united thereto as its form; and yet it was necessary for his intellect to be withdrawn from phantasms and the perception of sensible objects.

Reply to Objection 1: In this rapture Paul was absent from the Lord as regards his state, since he was still in the state of a wayfarer, but not as regards the act by which he saw God by a species, as stated above (A[3], ad 2,3).

Reply to Objection 2: A faculty of the soul is not uplifted by the natural power above the mode becoming the essence of the soul; but it can be uplifted by the divine power to something higher, even as a body by the violence of a stronger power is lifted up above the place befitting it according to its specific nature.

Reply to Objection 3: The forces of the vegetative soul do not operate through the soul being intent thereon, as do the sensitive forces, but by way of nature. Hence in the case of rapture there is no need for withdrawal from them, as from the sensitive powers, whose operations would lessen the intentness of the soul on intellective knowledge.

Did Paul know whether his soul were separated from his body?

Objection 1: It would seem that Paul was not ignorant whether his soul were separated from his body. For he says (2 Cor. 12:2): "I know a man in Christ rapt even to the third heaven." Now man denotes something composed of soul and body; and rapture differs from death. Seemingly therefore he knew that his soul was not separated from his body by death, which is the more probable seeing that this is the common opinion of the Doctors.

Objection 2: Further, it appears from the same words of the Apostle that he knew whither he was rapt, since it was "to the third heaven." Now this shows that he knew whether he was in the body or not, for if he knew the third heaven to be something corporeal, he must have known that his soul was not separated from his body, since a corporeal thing cannot be an object of sight save through the body. Therefore it would seem that he was not ignorant whether his soul were separated from his body.

Objection 3: Further, Augustine says (Gen. ad lit. xii, 28) that "when in rapture, he saw God with the same vision as the saints see Him in heaven." Now from the very fact that the saints see God, they know whether their soul is separated from their body. Therefore Paul too knew this.

On the contrary, It is written (2 Cor. 12:3): "Whether in the body, or out of the body, I know not, God knoweth."

I answer that, The true answer to this question must be gathered from the Apostle's very words, whereby he says he knew something, namely that he was "rapt even to the third heaven," and that something he knew not, namely "whether" he were "in the body or out of the body." This may be understood in two ways. First, the words "whether in the body or out of the body" may refer not to the very being of the man who was rapt (as though he knew not whether his soul were in his body or not), but to the mode of rapture, so that he ignored whether his body besides his soul, or, on the other hand, his soul alone, were rapt to the third heaven. Thus Ezechiel is stated (Ezech. 8:3) to have been "brought in the vision of God into Jerusalem." This was the explanation of a certain Jew according to Jerome (Prolog. super Daniel.), where he says that "lastly our Apostle" (thus said the Jew) "durst not assert that he was rapt in his body, but said: 'Whether in the body or out of the body, I know not.'"

Augustine, however, disapproves of this explanation (Gen. ad lit. xii, 3 seqq.) for this reason that the Apostle states that he knew he was rapt even to the third heaven. Wherefore he knew it to be really the third heaven to which he was rapt, and not an imaginary likeness of the third heaven: otherwise if he gave the name of third heaven to an imaginary third heaven, in the same way he might state that he was rapt in the body, meaning, by body, an image of his body, such as appears in one's dreams. Now if he knew it to be really the third heaven, it follows that either he knew it to be something spiritual and incorporeal, and then his body could not be rapt thither; or he knew it to be something corporeal, and then his soul could not be rapt thither without his body, unless it were separated from his body. Consequently we must explain the matter otherwise, by saying that the Apostle knew himself to be rapt both in soul and body, but that he ignored how his soul stood in relation to his body, to wit, whether it were accompanied by his body or not.

Here we find a diversity of opinions. For some say that the Apostle knew his soul to be united to his body as its form, but ignored whether it were abstracted from its senses, or again whether it were abstracted from the operations of the vegetative soul. But he could not but know that it was abstracted from the senses, seeing that he knew himself to be rapt; and as to his being abstracted from the operation of the vegetative soul, this was not of such importance as to require him to be so careful in mentioning it. It follows, then, that the Apostle ignored whether his soul were united to his body as its form, or separated from it by death. Some, however, granting this say that the Apostle did not consider the matter while he was in rapture, because he was wholly intent upon God, but that afterwards he questioned the point, when taking cognizance of what he had seen. But this also is contrary to the Apostle's words, for he there distinguishes between the past and what happened subsequently, since he states that at the present time he knows that he was rapt "fourteen years ago," and that at the present time he knows not "whether he was in the body or out of the body."

Consequently we must assert that both before and after he ignored whether his soul were separated from his body. Wherefore Augustine (Gen. ad lit. xii, 5), after discussing the question at length, concludes: "Perhaps then we must infer that he ignored whether, when he was rapt to the third heaven, his soul was in his body (in the same way as the soul is in the body, when we speak of a living body either of a waking or of a sleeping man, or of one that is withdrawn from his bodily senses during ecstasy), or whether his soul went out of his body altogether, so that his body lay dead."

Reply to Objection 1: Sometimes by the figure of synecdoche a part of man, especially the soul which is the principal part, denotes a man. or again we might take this to mean that he whom he states to have been rapt was a man not at the time of his rapture, but fourteen years afterwards: for he says "I know a man," not "I know a rapt man." Again nothing hinders death brought about by God being called rapture; and thus Augustine says (Gen. ad lit. xii, 3): "If the Apostle doubted the matter, who of us will dare to be certain about it?" Wherefore those who have something to say on this subject speak with more conjecture than certainty.

Reply to Objection 2: The Apostle knew that either the heaven in question was something incorporeal, or that he saw something incorporeal in that heaven; yet this could be done by his intellect, even without his soul being separated from his body.

Reply to Objection 3: Paul's vision, while he was in rapture, was like the vision of the blessed in one respect, namely as to the thing seen; and, unlike, in another respect, namely as to the mode of seeing, because he saw not so perfectly as do the saints in heaven. Hence Augustine says (Gen. ad lit. xii, 36): "Although, when the Apostle was rapt from his carnal senses to the third heaven, he lacked that full and perfect knowledge of things which is in the angels, in that he knew not whether he was in the body, or out of the body, this will surely not be lacking after reunion with the body in the resurrection of the dead, when this corruptible will put on incorruption."

Day 240

OF THE GRACE OF TONGUES (TWO ARTICLES)
We must now consider those gratuitous graces that pertain to speech, and (1) the grace of tongues; (2) the grace of the word of wisdom and knowledge. Under the first head there are two points of inquiry:
(1) Whether by the grace of tongues a man acquires the knowledge of all languages?
(2) Of the comparison between this gift and the grace of prophecy.

Whether those who received the gift of tongues spoke in every language?
Objection 1: It seems that those who received the gift of tongues did not speak in every language. For that which is granted to certain persons by the divine power is the best of its kind: thus our Lord turned the water into good wine, as stated in Jn. 2:10. Now those who had the gift of tongues spoke better in their own language; since a gloss on Heb. 1, says that "it is not surprising that the epistle to the Hebrews is more graceful in style than the other epistles, since it is natural for a man to have more command over his own than over a strange language. For the Apostle wrote the other epistles in a foreign, namely the Greek, idiom; whereas he wrote this in the Hebrew tongue." Therefore the apostles did not receive the knowledge of all languages by a gratuitous grace.

Objection 2: Further, nature does not employ many means where one is sufficient; and much less does God Whose work is more orderly than nature's. Now God could make His disciples to be understood by all, while speaking one tongue: hence a gloss on Acts 2:6, "Every man heard them speak in his own tongue," says that "they spoke in every tongue, or speaking in their own, namely the Hebrew language, were understood by all, as though they spoke the language proper to each." Therefore it would seem that they had not the knowledge to speak in all languages.

Objection 3: Further, all graces flow from Christ to His body, which is the Church, according to Jn. 1:16, "Of His fullness we all have received." Now we do not read that Christ spoke more than one language, nor does each one of the faithful now speak save in one tongue. Therefore it would seem that Christ's disciples did not receive the grace to the extent of speaking in all languages.

On the contrary, It is written (Acts 2:4) that "they were all filled with the Holy Ghost, and they began to speak with divers tongues, according as the Holy Ghost gave them to speak"; on which passage a gloss of Gregory [*Hom. xxx in Ev.] says that "the Holy Ghost appeared over the disciples under the form of fiery tongues, and gave them the knowledge of all tongues."

I answer that, Christ's first disciples were chosen by Him in order that they might disperse throughout the whole world, and preach His faith everywhere, according to Mat. 28:19, "Going . . . teach ye all nations." Now it was not fitting that they who were being sent to teach others should need to be taught by others, either as to how they should speak to other people, or as to how they were to understand those who spoke to them; and all the more seeing that those who were being sent were of one nation, that of Judea, according to Is. 27:6, "When they shall rush out from Jacob [*Vulg.: 'When they shall rush in unto Jacob,' etc.] . . . they shall fill the face of the world with seed." Moreover those who were being sent were poor and powerless; nor at the outset could they have easily found someone to interpret their words faithfully to others, or to explain what others said to them, especially as they were sent to unbelievers. Consequently it was necessary, in this respect, that God should provide them with the gift of tongues; in order that, as the diversity of tongues was brought upon the nations when they fell away to idolatry, according to Gn. 11, so when the nations were to be recalled to the worship of one God a remedy to this diversity might be applied by the gift of tongues.

Reply to Objection 1: As it is written (1 Cor. 12:7), "the manifestation of the Spirit is given to every man unto profit"; and consequently both Paul and the other apostles were divinely instructed in the languages of all nations sufficiently for the requirements of the teaching of the faith. But as regards the grace and elegance of style which human art adds to a language, the Apostle was instructed in his own, but not in a foreign tongue. Even so they were sufficiently instructed in wisdom and scientific knowledge, as required for teaching the faith, but not as to all things known by acquired science, for instance the conclusions of arithmetic and geometry.

Reply to Objection 2: Although either was possible, namely that, while speaking in one tongue they should be understood by all, or that they should speak in all tongues, it was more fitting that they should speak in all tongues, because this pertained to the perfection of their knowledge, whereby they were able not only to speak, but also to understand what was said by others. Whereas if their one language were intelligible to all, this would either have been due to the knowledge of those who understood their speech, or it would have amounted to an illusion, since a man's words would have had a different sound in another's ears, from that with which they were uttered. Hence a gloss says on Acts 2:6 that "it was a greater miracle that they should speak all kinds of tongues"; and Paul says (1 Cor. 14:18): "I thank my God I speak with all your tongues."

Reply to Objection 3: Christ in His own person purposed preaching to only one nation, namely the Jews. Consequently, although without any doubt He possessed most perfectly the knowledge of all languages, there was no need for Him to speak in every tongue. And therefore, as Augustine says (Tract. xxxii in Joan.), "whereas even now the Holy Ghost is received, yet no one speaks in the tongues of all nations, because the Church herself already speaks the languages of all nations: since whoever is not in the Church, receives not the Holy Ghost."

Whether the gift of tongues is more excellent than the grace of prophecy?

Objection 1: It would seem that the gift of tongues is more excellent than the grace of prophecy. For, seemingly, better things are proper to better persons, according to the Philosopher (Topic. iii, 1). Now the gift of tongues is proper to the New Testament, hence we sing in the sequence of Pentecost [*The sequence: 'Sancti Spiritus adsit nobis gratia' ascribed to King Robert of France, the reputed author of the 'Veni Sancte Spiritus.' Cf. Migne, Patr. Lat. tom. CXLI]: "On this day Thou gavest Christ's apostles an unwonted gift, a marvel to all time": whereas prophecy is more pertinent to the Old Testament, according to Heb. 1:1, "God Who at sundry times and in divers manners spoke in times past to the fathers by the prophets." Therefore it would seem that the gift of tongues is more excellent than the gift of prophecy.

Objection 2: Further, that whereby we are directed to God is seemingly more excellent than that whereby we are directed to men. Now, by the gift of tongues, man is directed to God, whereas by prophecy he is directed to man; for it is written (1 Cor. 14:2,3): "He that speaketh in a tongue, speaketh not unto men, but unto God . . . but he that prophesieth, speaketh unto men unto edification." Therefore it would seem that the gift of tongues is more excellent than the gift of prophecy.

Objection 3: Further, the gift of tongues abides like a habit in the person who has it, and "he can use it when he will"; wherefore it is written (1 Cor. 14:18): "I thank my God I speak with all your tongues." But it is not so with the gift of prophecy, as stated above ([3704]Q[171], A[2]). Therefore the gift of tongues would seem to be more excellent than the gift of prophecy.

Objection 4: Further, the "interpretation of speeches" would seem to be contained under prophecy, because the Scriptures are expounded by the same Spirit from Whom they originated. Now the interpretation of speeches is placed after "divers kinds of tongues" (1 Cor. 12:10). Therefore it seems that the gift of tongues is more excellent than the gift of prophecy, particularly as regards a part of the latter.

On the contrary, The Apostle says (1 Cor. 14:5): "Greater is he that prophesieth than he that speaketh with tongues."

I answer that, The gift of prophecy surpasses the gift of tongues, in three ways. First, because the gift of tongues regards the utterance of certain words, which signify an intelligible truth, and this again is signified by the phantasms which appear in an imaginary vision; wherefore Augustine compares (Gen. ad lit. xii, 8) the gift of tongues to an imaginary vision. On the other hand, it has been stated above ([3705]Q[173], A[2]) that the gift of prophecy consists in the mind itself being enlightened so as to know an intelligible truth. Wherefore, as the prophetic enlightenment is more excellent than the imaginary vision, as stated above ([3706]Q[174], A[2]), so also is prophecy more excellent than the gift of tongues considered in itself. Secondly, because the gift of prophecy regards the knowledge of things, which is more excellent than the knowledge of words, to which the gift of tongues pertains.

Thirdly, because the gift of prophecy is more profitable. The Apostle proves this in three ways (1 Cor. 14); first, because prophecy is more profitable to the edification of the Church, for which purpose he that speaketh in tongues profiteth nothing, unless interpretation follow (1 Cor. 14:4,5). Secondly, as regards the speaker himself, for if he be enabled to speak in divers tongues without understanding them, which pertains to the gift of prophecy, his own mind would not be edified (1 Cor. 14:7-14). Thirdly, as to unbelievers for whose especial benefit the gift of tongues seems to have been given; since perchance they might think those who speak

157

in tongues to be mad (1 Cor. 14:23), for instance the Jews deemed the apostles drunk when the latter spoke in various tongues (Acts 2:13): whereas by prophecies the unbeliever is convinced, because the secrets of his heart are made manifest (Acts 2:25).

Reply to Objection 1: As stated above ([3707]Q[174], A[3], ad 1), it belongs to the excellence of prophecy that a man is not only enlightened by an intelligible light, but also that he should perceive an imaginary vision: and so again it belongs to the perfection of the Holy Ghost's operation, not only to fill the mind with the prophetic light, and the imagination with the imaginary vision, as happened in the Old Testament, but also to endow the tongue with external erudition, in the utterance of various signs of speech. All this is done in the New Testament, according to 1 Cor. 14:26, "Every one of you hath a psalm, hath a doctrine, hath a tongue, hath a revelation," i.e. a prophetic revelation.

Reply to Objection 2: By the gift of prophecy man is directed to God in his mind, which is more excellent than being directed to Him in his tongue. "He that speaketh in a tongue "is said to speak "not unto men," i.e. to men's understanding or profit, but unto God's understanding and praise. On the other hand, by prophecy a man is directed both to God and to man; wherefore it is the more perfect gift.

Reply to Objection 3: Prophetic revelation extends to the knowledge of all things supernatural; wherefore from its very perfection it results that in this imperfect state of life it cannot be had perfectly by way of habit, but only imperfectly by way of passion. on the other hand, the gift of tongues is confined to a certain particular knowledge, namely of human words; wherefore it is not inconsistent with the imperfection of this life, that it should be had perfectly and by way of habit.

Reply to Objection 4: The interpretation of speeches is reducible to the gift of prophecy, inasmuch as the mind is enlightened so as to understand and explain any obscurities of speech arising either from a difficulty in the things signified, or from the words uttered being unknown, or from the figures of speech employed, according to Dan. 5:16, "I have heard of thee, that thou canst interpret obscure things, and resolve difficult things." Hence the interpretation of speeches is more excellent than the gift of tongues, as appears from the saying of the Apostle (1 Cor. 14:5), "Greater is he that prophesieth than he that speaketh with tongues; unless perhaps he interpret." Yet the interpretation of speeches is placed after the gift of tongues, because the interpretation of speeches extends even to the interpretation of divers kinds of tongues.

OF THE GRATUITOUS GRACE CONSISTING IN WORDS (TWO ARTICLES)

We must now consider the gratuitous grace that attaches to words; of which the Apostle says (1 Cor. 12:8): "To one . . . by the Spirit is given the word of wisdom, and to another the word of knowledge." Under this head there are two points of inquiry:

(1) Whether any gratuitous grace attaches to words?

(2) To whom is the grace becoming?

Whether any gratuitous grace attaches to words?

Objection 1: It would seem that a gratuitous grace does not attach to words. For grace is given for that which surpasses the faculty of nature. But natural reason has devised the art of rhetoric whereby a man is able to speak so as to teach, please, and persuade, as Augustine says (De Doctr. Christ. iv, 12). Now this belongs to the grace of words. Therefore it would seem that the grace of words is not a gratuitous grace.

Objection 2: Further, all grace pertains to the kingdom of God. But the Apostle says (1 Cor. 4:20): "The kingdom of God is not in speech, but in power." Therefore there is no gratuitous grace connected with words.

Objection 3: Further, no grace is given through merit, since "if by grace, it is not now of works" (Rom. 11:6). But the word is sometimes given to a man on his merits. For Gregory says (Moral. xi, 15) in explanation of Ps. 118:43, "Take not Thou the word of truth utterly out of my mouth" that "the word of truth is that which Almighty God gives to them that do it, and takes away from them that do it not." Therefore it would seem that the gift of the word is not a gratuitous grace.

Objection 4: Further, it behooves man to declare in words things pertaining to the virtue of faith, no less than those pertaining to the gift of wisdom or of knowledge. Therefore if the word of wisdom and the word of knowledge are reckoned gratuitous graces, the word of faith should likewise be placed among the gratuitous graces.

On the contrary, It is written (Ecclus. 6:5): "A gracious tongue in a good man shall abound [Vulg.: 'aboundeth']." Now man's goodness is by grace. Therefore graciousness in words is also by grace.

I answer that, The gratuitous graces are given for the profit of others, as stated above ([3708]FS, Q[111], AA[1],4). Now the knowledge a man receives from God cannot be turned to another's profit, except by means of speech. And since the Holy Ghost does not fail in anything that pertains to the profit of the Church, He provides also the members of the Church with speech; to the effect that a man not only speaks so as to be understood by different people, which pertains to the gift of tongues, but also speaks with effect, and this pertains to the grace "of the word."

This happens in three ways. First, in order to instruct the intellect, and this is the case when a man speaks so as "to teach." Secondly, in order to move the affections, so that a man willingly hearkens to the word of God. This is the case when a man speaks so as "to please" his hearers, not indeed with a view to his own favor, but in order to draw them to listen to God's word. Thirdly, in order that men may love that which is signified by the word, and desire to fulfill it, and this is the case when a man so speaks as "to sway" his hearers. In order to effect this the Holy Ghost makes use of the human tongue as of an instrument; but He it is Who perfects the work within. Hence Gregory says in a homily for Pentecost (Hom. xxx in Ev.): "Unless the Holy Ghost fill the hearts of the hearers, in vain does the voice of the teacher resound in the ears of the body."

Reply to Objection 1: Even as by a miracle God sometimes works in a more excellent way those things which nature also can work, so too the Holy Ghost effects more excellently by the grace of words that which art can effect in a less efficient manner.

Reply to Objection 2: The Apostle is speaking there of the word that relies on human eloquence without the power of the Holy Ghost. Wherefore he says just before (1 Cor. 4:19): "I . . . will know, not the speech of them that are puffed up, but the power": and of himself he had already said (1 Cor. 2:4): "My speech and my preaching was not in the persuasive words of human wisdom, but in the showing of the spirit and power."

Reply to Objection 3: As stated above, the grace of the word is given to a man for the profit of others. Hence it is withdrawn sometimes through the fault of the hearer, and sometimes through the fault of the speaker. The good works of either of them do not merit this grace directly, but only remove the obstacles thereto. For sanctifying grace also is withdrawn on account of a person's fault, and yet he does not merit it by his good works, which, however, remove the obstacles to grace.

Reply to Objection 4: As stated above, the grace of the word is directed to the profit of others. Now if a man communicates his faith to others this is by the word of knowledge or of wisdom. Hence Augustine says (De Trin. xiv, 1) that "to know how faith may profit the godly and be defended against the ungodly, is apparently what the Apostle means by knowledge." Hence it was not necessary for him to mention the word of faith, but it was sufficient for him to mention the word of knowledge and of wisdom.

Whether the grace of the word of wisdom and knowledge is becoming to women?

Objection 1: It would seem that the grace of the word of wisdom and knowledge is becoming even to women. For teaching is pertinent to this grace, as stated in the foregoing Article. Now it is becoming to a woman to teach; for it is written (Prov. 4:3,4): "I was an only son in the sight of my mother, and she taught me [*Vulg.: 'I was my father's son, tender, and as an only son in the sight of my mother. And he taught me.'].'" Therefore this grace is becoming to women.

Objection 2: Further, the grace of prophecy is greater than the grace of the word, even as the contemplation of truth is greater than its utterance. But prophecy is granted to women, as we read of Deborah (Judges 4:4), and of Holda the prophetess, the wife of Sellum (4 Kings 22:14), and of the four daughters of Philip (Acts 21:9). Moreover the Apostle says (1 Cor. 11:5): "Every woman praying or prophesying," etc. Much more therefore would it seem that the grace of the word is becoming to a woman.

Objection 3: Further, it is written (1 Pet. 4:10): "As every man hath received grace ministering the same one to another." Now some women receive the grace of wisdom and knowledge, which they cannot minister to others except by the grace of the word. Therefore the grace of the word is becoming to women.

On the contrary, The Apostle says (1 Cor. 14:34): "Let women keep silence in the churches," and (1 Tim. 2:12): "I suffer not a woman to teach." Now this pertains especially to the grace of the word. Therefore the grace of the word is not becoming to women.

I answer that, Speech may be employed in two ways: in one way privately, to one or a few, in familiar conversation, and in this respect the grace of the word may be becoming to women; in another way, publicly, addressing oneself to the whole church, and this is not permitted to women. First and chiefly, on account of the condition attaching to the female sex, whereby woman should be subject to man, as appears from Gn. 3:16. Now teaching and persuading publicly in the church belong not to subjects but to the prelates (although men who are subjects may do these things if they be so commissioned, because their subjection is not a result of their natural sex, as it is with women, but of some thing supervening by accident). Secondly, lest men's minds be enticed to lust, for it is written (Ecclus. 9:11): "Her conversation burneth as fire." Thirdly, because as a rule women are not perfected in wisdom, so as to be fit to be intrusted with public teaching.

Reply to Objection 1: The passage quoted speaks of private teaching whereby a father instructs his son.

Reply to Objection 2: The grace of prophecy consists in God enlightening the mind, on the part of which there is no difference of sex among men, according to Col. 3:10,11, "Putting on the new" man, "him who is renewed unto knowledge, according to the image of Him that created him, where there is neither male nor female [*Vulg.: 'Neither Gentile nor Jew, circumcision nor uncircumcision, Barbarian nor Scythian, bond nor free.' Cf. [3709]FP, Q[93], A[6], ad 2 footnote].'" Now the grace of the word pertains to the instruction of men among whom the difference of sex is found. Hence the comparison fails.

Reply to Objection 3: The recipients of a divinely conferred grace administer it in different ways according to their various conditions. Hence women, if they have the grace of wisdom or of knowledge, can administer it by teaching privately but not publicly.

OF THE GRACE OF MIRACLES (TWO ARTICLES)
We must next consider the grace of miracles, under which head there are two points of inquiry:
(1) Whether there is a gratuitous grace of working miracles?
(2) To whom is it becoming?

Whether there is a gratuitous grace of working miracles?

Objection 1: It would seem that no gratuitous grace is directed to the working of miracles. For every grace puts something in the one to whom it is given (Cf. [3710]FS, Q[90], A[1]). Now the working of miracles puts nothing in the soul of the man who receives it since miracles are wrought at the touch even of a dead body. Thus we read (4 Kings 13:21) that "some . . . cast the body into the sepulchre of Eliseus. And when it had touched the bones of Eliseus, the man came to life, and stood upon his feet." Therefore the working of miracles does not belong to a gratuitous grace.

Objection 2: Further, the gratuitous graces are from the Holy Ghost, according to 1 Cor. 12:4, "There are diversities of graces, but the same Spirit." Now the working of miracles is effected even by the unclean spirit, according to Mat. 24:24, "There shall arise false Christs and false prophets, and shall show great signs and wonders." Therefore it would seem that the working of miracles does not belong to a gratuitous grace.

Objection 3: Further, miracles are divided into "signs," "wonders" or "portents," and "virtues." [*Cf. 2 Thess. 2:9, where the Douay version renders 'virtus' by 'power.' The use of the word 'virtue' in the sense of a miracle is now obsolete, and the generic term 'miracle' is elsewhere used in its stead: Cf. 1 Cor. 12:10, 28; Heb. 2:4; Acts 2:22]. Therefore it is unreasonable to reckon the "working of miracles" a gratuitous grace, any more than the "working of signs" and "wonders."

Objection 4: Further, the miraculous restoring to health is done by the power of God. Therefore the grace of healing should not be distinguished from the working of miracles.

Objection 5: Further, the working of miracles results from faith---either of the worker, according to 1 Cor. 13:2, "If I should have all faith, so that I could remove mountains," or of other persons for whose sake miracles are wrought, according to Mat. 13:58, "And He wrought not many miracles there, because of their unbelief." Therefore, if faith be reckoned a gratuitous grace, it is superfluous to reckon in addition the working of signs as another gratuitous grace.

On the contrary, The Apostle (1 Cor. 12:9,10) says that among other gratuitous graces, "to another" is given "the grace of healing . . . to another, the working of miracles."

I answer that, As stated above ([3711]Q[177], A[1]), the Holy Ghost provides sufficiently for the Church in matters profitable unto salvation, to which purpose the gratuitous graces are directed. Now just as the knowledge which a man receives from God needs to be brought to the knowledge of others through the gift of tongues and the grace of the word, so too the word uttered needs to be confirmed in order that it be rendered credible. This is done by the working of miracles, according to Mk. 16:20, "And confirming the word with signs that followed": and reasonably so. For it is natural to man to arrive at the intelligible truth through its sensible effects. Wherefore just as man led by his natural reason is able to arrive at some knowledge of God through His natural effects, so is he brought to a certain degree of supernatural knowledge of the objects of faith by certain supernatural effects which are called miracles. Therefore the working of miracles belongs to a gratuitous grace.

Reply to Objection 1: Just as prophecy extends to whatever can be known supernaturally, so the working of miracles extends to all things that can be done supernaturally; the cause whereof is the divine omnipotence which cannot be communicated to any creature. Hence it is impossible for the principle of working miracles to be a quality abiding as a habit in the soul. On the other hand, just as the prophet's mind is moved by divine inspiration to know something supernaturally, so too is it possible for the mind of the miracle worker to be moved to do something resulting in the miraculous effect which God causes by His power. Sometimes this takes place after prayer, as when Peter raised to life the dead Tabitha (Acts 9:40): sometimes without any previous prayer being expressed, as when Peter by upbraiding the lying Ananias and Saphira delivered them to death (Acts 5:4, 9). Hence Gregory says (Dial. ii, 30) that "the saints work miracles, sometimes by authority, sometimes by prayer." In either case, however, God is the principal worker, for He uses instrumentally either man's inward movement, or his speech, or some outward action, or again the bodily contact of even a dead body. Thus when Josue had said as though authoritatively (Josh. 10:12): "Move not, O sun, toward Gabaon," it is said afterwards (Josh. 10:14): "There was not before or after so long a day, the Lord obeying the voice of a man."

Reply to Objection 2: Our Lord is speaking there of the miracles to be wrought at the time of Antichrist, of which the Apostle says (2 Thess. 2:9) that the coming of Antichrist will be "according to the working of Satan, in all power, and signs, and lying wonders." To quote the words of Augustine (De Civ. Dei xx, 19), "it is a matter of debate whether they are called signs and lying wonders, because he will deceive the senses of mortals by imaginary visions, in that he will seem to do what he does not, or because, though they be real wonders, they will seduce into falsehood them that believe." They are said to be real, because the things themselves will be real, just as Pharaoh's magicians made real frogs and real serpents; but they will not be real miracles, because they will be done by the power of natural causes, as stated in the [3712]FP, Q[114], A[4]; whereas the working of miracles which is ascribed to a gratuitous grace, is done by God's power for man's profit.

Reply to Objection 3: Two things may be considered in miracles. One is that which is done: this is something surpassing the faculty of nature, and in this respect miracles are called "virtues." The other thing is the purpose for which miracles are wrought, namely the manifestation of something supernatural, and in this respect they are commonly called "signs": but on account of some excellence they receive the name of "wonder" or "prodigy," as showing something from afar [procul].

Reply to Objection 4: The "grace of healing" is mentioned separately, because by its means a benefit, namely bodily health, is conferred on man in addition to the common benefit bestowed in all miracles, namely the bringing of men to the knowledge of God.

Reply to Objection 5: The working of miracles is ascribed to faith for two reasons. First, because it is directed to the confirmation of faith, secondly, because it proceeds from God's omnipotence on which faith relies. Nevertheless, just as besides the grace of faith, the grace of the word is necessary that people may be instructed in the faith, so too is the grace of miracles necessary that people may be confirmed in their faith.

Whether the wicked can work miracles?

Objection 1: It would seem that the wicked cannot work miracles. For miracles are wrought through prayer, as stated above (A[1], ad 1). Now the prayer of a sinner is not granted, according to Jn. 9:31, "We know that God doth not hear sinners," and Prov. 28:9, "He that turneth away his ear from hearing the law, his prayer shall be an abomination." Therefore it would seem that the wicked cannot work miracles.

Objection 2: Further, miracles are ascribed to faith, according to Mat. 17:19, "If you have faith as a grain of mustard seed you shall say to this mountain: Remove from hence hither, and it shall remove." Now "faith without works is dead," according to James 2:20, so that, seemingly, it is devoid of its proper operation. Therefore it would seem that the wicked, since they do not good works, cannot work miracles.

Objection 3: Further, miracles are divine attestations, according to Heb. 2:4, "God also bearing them witness by signs and wonders and divers miracles": wherefore in the Church the canonization of certain persons is based on the attestation of miracles. Now God cannot bear witness to a falsehood. Therefore it would seem that wicked men cannot work miracles.

Objection 4: Further, the good are more closely united to God than the wicked. But the good do not all work miracles. Much less therefore do the wicked.

On the contrary, The Apostle says (1 Cor. 13:2): "If I should have all faith, so that I could remove mountains, and have not charity, I am nothing." Now whosoever has not charity is wicked, because "this gift alone of the Holy Ghost distinguishes the children of the kingdom from the children of perdition," as Augustine says (De Trin. xv, 18). Therefore it would seem that even the wicked can work miracles.

I answer that, Some miracles are not true but imaginary deeds, because they delude man by the appearance of that which is not; while others are true deeds, yet they have not the character of a true miracle, because they are done by the power of some natural cause. Both of these can be done by the demons, as stated above (A[1], ad 2).

True miracles cannot be wrought save by the power of God, because God works them for man's benefit, and this in two ways: in one way for the confirmation of truth declared, in another way in proof of a person's holiness, which God desires to propose as an example of virtue. In the first way miracles can be wrought by any one who preaches the true faith and calls upon Christ's name, as even the wicked do sometimes. In this way even the wicked can work miracles. Hence Jerome commenting on Mat. 7:22, "Have not we prophesied in Thy name?" says: "Sometimes prophesying, the working of miracles, and the casting out of demons are accorded not to the merit of those who do these things, but to the invoking of Christ's name, that men may honor God, by invoking Whom such great miracles are wrought."

In the second way miracles are not wrought except by the saints, since it is in proof of their holiness that miracles are wrought during their lifetime or after death, either by themselves or by others. For we read (Acts 19:11,12) that "God wrought by the hand of Paul . . . miracles" and "even there were brought from his body to the sick, handkerchiefs . . . and the diseases departed from them." In this way indeed there is nothing to prevent a sinner from working miracles by invoking a saint; but the miracle is ascribed not to him, but to the one in proof of whose holiness such things are done.

Reply to Objection 1: As stated above ([3713]Q[83], A[16]) when we were treating of prayer, the prayer of impetration relies not on merit but on God's mercy, which extends even to the wicked, wherefore the prayers even of sinners are sometimes granted by God. Hence Augustine says (Tract. xliv in Joan.) that "the blind man spoke these words before he was anointed," that is, before he was perfectly enlightened; "since God does hear sinners." When it is said that the prayer of one who hears not the law is an abomination, this must be understood so far as the sinner's merit is concerned; yet it is sometimes granted, either for the spiritual welfare of the one who prays---as the publican was heard (Lk. 18:14)---or for the good of others and for God's glory.

Reply to Objection 2: Faith without works is said to be dead, as regards the believer, who lives not, by faith, with the life of grace. But nothing hinders a living thing from working through a dead instrument, as a man through a stick. It is thus that God works while employing instrumentally the faith of a sinner.

Reply to Objection 3: Miracles are always true witnesses to the purpose for which they are wrought. Hence wicked men who teach a false doctrine never work true miracles in confirmation of their teaching, although sometimes they may do so in praise of Christ's name which they invoke, and by the power of the sacraments which they administer. If they teach a true doctrine, sometimes they work true miracles as confirming their teaching, but not as an attestation of holiness. Hence Augustine says (QQ. lxxxiii, qu. 79): "Magicians work miracles in one way, good Christians in another, wicked Christians in another. Magicians by private compact with the demons, good Christians by their manifest righteousness, evil Christians by the outward signs of righteousness."

Reply to Objection 4: As Augustine says (QQ. lxxxiii, qu. 79), "the reason why these are not granted to all holy men is lest by a most baneful error the weak be deceived into thinking such deeds to imply greater gifts than the deeds of righteousness whereby eternal life is obtained."

OF THE DIVISION OF LIFE INTO ACTIVE AND CONTEMPLATIVE (TWO ARTICLES)

We must next consider active and contemplative life. This consideration will be fourfold: (1) Of the division of life into active and contemplative; (2) Of the contemplative life; (3) Of the active life; (4) Of the comparison between the active and the contemplative life.

Under the first head there are two points of inquiry:
(1) Whether life is fittingly divided into active and contemplative?
(2) Whether this is an adequate division?

Whether life is fittingly divided into active and contemplative?

Objection 1: It would seem that life is not fittingly divided into active and contemplative. For the soul is the principle of life by its essence: since the Philosopher says (De Anima ii, 4) that "in living things to live is to be." Now the soul is the principle of action and contemplation by its powers. Therefore it would seem that life is not fittingly divided into active and contemplative.

Objection 2: Further, the division of that which comes afterwards is unfittingly applied to that which comes first. Now active and contemplative, or "speculative" and "practical," are differences of the intellect (De Anima iii, 10); while "to live" comes before "to understand," since "to live" comes first to living things through the vegetative soul, as the Philosopher states (De Anima ii, 4). Therefore life is unfittingly divided into active and contemplative.

Objection 3: Further, the word "life" implies movement, according to Dionysius (Div. Nom. vi): whereas contemplation consists rather in rest, according to Wis. 8:16: "When I enter into my house, I shall repose myself with her." Therefore it would seem that life is unfittingly divided into active and contemplative.

On the contrary, Gregory says (Hom. xiv super Ezech.): "There is a twofold life wherein Almighty God instructs us by His holy word, the active life and the contemplative."

I answer that, Properly speaking, those things are said to live whose movement or operation is from within themselves. Now that which is proper to a thing and to which it is most inclined is that which is most becoming to it from itself; wherefore every living thing gives proof of its life by that operation which is most proper to it, and to which it is most inclined. Thus the life of plants is said to consist in nourishment and generation; the life of animals in sensation and movement; and the life of men in their understanding and acting according to reason. Wherefore also in men the life of every man would seem to be that wherein he delights most, and on which he is most intent; thus especially does he wish "to associate with his friends" (Ethic. ix, 12).

Accordingly since certain men are especially intent on the contemplation of truth, while others are especially intent on external actions, it follows that man's life is fittingly divided into active and contemplative.

Reply to Objection 1: Each thing's proper form that makes it actually "to be" is properly that thing's principle of operation. Hence "to live" is, in living things, "to be," because living things through having "being" from their form, act in such and such a way.

Reply to Objection 2: Life in general is not divided into active and contemplative, but the life of man, who derives his species from having an intellect, wherefore the same division applies to intellect and human life.

Reply to Objection 3: It is true that contemplation enjoys rest from external movements. Nevertheless to contemplate is itself a movement of the intellect, in so far as every operation is described as a movement; in which sense the Philosopher says (De Anima iii, 7) that sensation and understanding are movements of a kind, in so far as movement is defined "the act of a perfect thing." In this way Dionysius (Div. Nom. iv) ascribes three movements to the soul in contemplation, namely, "straight," "circular," and "oblique" [*Cf. [3714] Q[180], A[6]].

Whether life is adequately divided into active and contemplative?

Objection 1: It would seem that life is not adequately divided into active and contemplative. For the Philosopher says (Ethic. i, 5) that there are three most prominent kinds of life, the life of "pleasure," the "civil" which would seem to be the same as the active, and the "contemplative" life. Therefore the division of life into active and contemplative would seem to be inadequate.

Objection 2: Further, Augustine (De Civ. Dei xix, 1,2,3,19) mentions three kinds of life, namely the life of "leisure" which pertains to the contemplative, the "busy" life which pertains to the active, and a third "composed of both." Therefore it would seem that life is inadequately divided into active and contemplative.

Objection 3: Further, man's life is diversified according to the divers actions in which men are occupied. Now there are more than two occupations of human actions. Therefore it would seem that life should be divided into more kinds than the active and the contemplative.

On the contrary, These two lives are signified by the two wives of Jacob; the active by Lia, and the contemplative by Rachel: and by the two hostesses of our Lord; the contemplative life by Mary, and the active life by Martha, as Gregory declares (Moral. vi, 37 [*Hom. xiv in Ezech.]). Now this signification would not be fitting if there were more than two lives. Therefore life is adequately divided into active and contemplative.

I answer that, As stated above (A[1], ad 2), this division applies to the human life as derived from the intellect. Now the intellect is divided into active and contemplative, since the end of intellective knowledge is either the knowledge itself of truth, which pertains to the contemplative intellect, or some external action, which pertains to the practical or active intellect. Therefore life too is adequately divided into active and contemplative.

Reply to Objection 1: The life of pleasure places its end in pleasures of the body, which are common to us and dumb animals; wherefore as the Philosopher says (Ethic. Ethic. i, 5), it is the life "of a beast." Hence it is not included in this division of the life of a man into active and contemplative.

Reply to Objection 2: A mean is a combination of extremes, wherefore it is virtually contained in them, as tepid in hot and cold, and pale in white and black. In like manner active and contemplative comprise that which is composed of both. Nevertheless as in every mixture one of the simples predominates, so too in the mean state of life sometimes the contemplative, sometimes the active element, abounds.

Reply to Objection 3: All the occupations of human actions, if directed to the requirements of the present life in accord with right reason, belong to the active life which provides for the necessities of the present life by means of well-ordered activity. If, on the other hand, they minister to any concupiscence whatever, they belong to the life of pleasure, which is not comprised under the active life. Those human occupations that are directed to the consideration of truth belong to the contemplative life.

Day 241

OF THE CONTEMPLATIVE LIFE (EIGHT ARTICLES)
We must now consider the contemplative life, under which head there are eight points of inquiry:
(1) Whether the contemplative life pertains to the intellect only, or also to the affections?
(2) Whether the moral virtues pertain to the contemplative life?
(3) Whether the contemplative life consists in one action or in several?
(4) Whether the consideration of any truth whatever pertains to the contemplative life?
(5) Whether the contemplative life of man in this state can arise to the vision of God?
(6) Of the movements of contemplation assigned by Dionysius (Div. Nom. iv);
(7) Of the pleasure of contemplation;
(8) Of the duration of contemplation.

Whether the contemplative life has nothing to do with the affections, and pertains wholly to the intellect?

Objection 1: It would seem that the contemplative life has nothing to do with the affections and pertains wholly to the intellect. For the Philosopher says (Metaph. ii, text. 3 [*Ed Did. ia, 1]) that "the end of contemplation is truth." Now truth pertains wholly to the intellect. Therefore it would seem that the contemplative life wholly regards the intellect.

Objection 2: Further, Gregory says (Moral. vi, 37; Hom. xix in Ezech.) that "Rachel, which is interpreted 'vision of the principle' [*Or rather, 'One seeing the principle,' if derived from {rah} and {irzn}; Cf. Jerome, De Nom. Hebr.], signifies the contemplative life." Now the vision of a principle belongs properly to the intellect. Therefore the contemplative life belongs properly to the intellect.

Objection 3: Further, Gregory says (Hom. xiv in Ezech.) that it belongs to the contemplative life, "to rest from external action." Now the affective or appetitive power inclines to external actions. Therefore it would seem that the contemplative life has nothing to do with the appetitive power.

On the contrary, Gregory says (Hom. xiv in Ezech.) that "the contemplative life is to cling with our whole mind to the love of God and our neighbor, and to desire nothing beside our Creator." Now desire and love pertain to the affective or appetitive power, as stated above ([3715]FS, Q[25], A[2]; [3716]FS, Q[26], A[2]). Therefore the contemplative life has also something to do with the affective or appetitive power.

I answer that, As stated above (Q[179], A[1]) theirs is said to be the contemplative who are chiefly intent on the contemplation of truth. Now intention is an act of the will, as stated above ([3717]FS, Q[12], A[1]), because intention is of the end which is the object of the will. Consequently the contemplative life, as regards the essence of the action, pertains to the intellect, but as regards the motive cause of the exercise of that action it belongs to the will, which moves all the other powers, even the intellect, to their actions, as stated above ([3718]FP, Q[82], A[4]; [3719]FS, Q[9], A[1]).

Now the appetitive power moves one to observe things either with the senses or with the intellect, sometimes for love of the thing seen because, as it is written (Mat. 6:21), "where thy treasure is, there is thy heart also," sometimes for love of the very knowledge that one acquires by observation. Wherefore Gregory makes the contemplative life to consist in the "love of God," inasmuch as through loving God we are aflame to gaze on His beauty. And since everyone delights when he obtains what he loves, it follows that the contemplative life terminates in delight, which is seated in the affective power, the result being that love also becomes more intense.

Reply to Objection 1: From the very fact that truth is the end of contemplation, it has the aspect of an appetible good, both lovable and delightful, and in this respect it pertains to the appetitive power.

Reply to Objection 2: We are urged to the vision of the first principle, namely God, by the love thereof; wherefore Gregory says (Hom. xiv in Ezech.) that "the contemplative life tramples on all cares and longs to see the face of its Creator."

Reply to Objection 3: The appetitive power moves not only the bodily members to perform external actions, but also the intellect to practice the act of contemplation, as stated above.

Whether the moral virtues pertain to the contemplative life?

Objection 1: It would seem that the moral virtues pertain to the contemplative life. For Gregory says (Hom. xiv in Ezech.) that "the contemplative life is to cling to the love of God and our neighbor with the whole mind." Now all the moral virtues, since their acts are prescribed by the precepts of the Law, are reducible to the love of God and of our neighbor, for "love . . . is the fulfilling of the Law" (Rom. 13:10). Therefore it would seem that the moral virtues belong to the contemplative life.

Objection 2: Further, the contemplative life is chiefly directed to the contemplation of God; for Gregory says (Hom. xiv in Ezech.) that "the mind tramples on all cares and longs to gaze on the face of its Creator." Now no one can accomplish this without cleanness of heart, which is a result of moral virtue [*Cf.[3720] Q[8], A[7]]. For it is written (Mat. 5:8): "Blessed are the clean of heart, for they shall see God": and (Heb. 12:14): "Follow peace with all men, and holiness, without which no man shall see God." Therefore it would seem that the moral virtues pertain to the contemplative life.

Objection 3: Further, Gregory says (Hom. xiv in Ezech.) that "the contemplative life gives beauty to the soul," wherefore it is signified by Rachel, of whom it is said (Gn. 29:17) that she was "of a beautiful countenance." Now the beauty of the soul consists in the moral virtues, especially temperance, as Ambrose says (De Offic. i, 43,45,46). Therefore it seems that the moral virtues pertain to the contemplative life.

On the contrary, The moral virtues are directed to external actions. Now Gregory says (Moral. vi [*Hom. xiv in Ezech.; Cf. A[1], OBJ[3]]) that it belongs to the contemplative life "to rest from external action." Therefore the moral virtues do not pertain to the contemplative life.

I answer that, A thing may belong to the contemplative life in two ways, essentially or dispositively. The moral virtues do not belong to the contemplative life essentially, because the end of the contemplative life is the consideration of truth: and as the Philosopher states (Ethic. ii, 4), "knowledge," which pertains to the consideration of truth, "has little influence on the moral virtues": wherefore he declares (Ethic. x, 8) that the moral virtues pertain to active but not to contemplative happiness.

On the other hand, the moral virtues belong to the contemplative life dispositively. For the act of contemplation, wherein the contemplative life essentially consists, is hindered both by the impetuosity of the passions which withdraw the soul's intention from intelligible to sensible things, and by outward disturbances. Now the moral virtues curb the impetuosity of the passions, and quell the disturbance of outward occupations. Hence moral virtues belong dispositively to the contemplative life.

Reply to Objection 1: As stated above [3721](A[1]), the contemplative life has its motive cause on the part of the affections, and in this respect the love of God and our neighbor is requisite to the contemplative life. Now motive causes do not enter into the essence of a thing, but dispose and perfect it. Wherefore it does not follow that the moral virtues belong essentially to the contemplative life.

Reply to Objection 2: Holiness or cleanness of heart is caused by the virtues that are concerned with the passions which hinder the purity of the reason; and peace is caused by justice which is about operations, according to Is. 32:17, "The work of justice shall be peace": since he who refrains from wronging others lessens the occasions of quarrels and disturbances. Hence the moral virtues dispose one to the contemplative life by causing peace and cleanness of heart.

Reply to Objection 3: Beauty, as stated above ([3722]Q[145], A[2]), consists in a certain clarity and due proportion. Now each of these is found radically in the reason; because both the light that makes beauty seen, and the establishing of due proportion among things belong to reason. Hence since the contemplative life consists in an act of the reason, there is beauty in it by its very nature and essence; wherefore it is written (Wis. 8:2) of the contemplation of wisdom: "I became a lover of her beauty."

On the other hand, beauty is in the moral virtues by participation, in so far as they participate in the order of reason; and especially is it in temperance, which restrains the concupiscences which especially darken the light of reason. Hence it is that the virtue of chastity most of all makes man apt for contemplation, since venereal pleasures most of all weigh the mind down to sensible objects, as Augustine says (Soliloq. i, 10).

Whether there are various actions pertaining to the contemplative life?

Objection 1: It would seem that there are various actions pertaining to the contemplative life. For Richard of St. Victor [*De Grat. Contempl. i, 3,4] distinguishes between "contemplation," "meditation," and "cogitation." Yet all these apparently pertain to contemplation. Therefore it would seem that there are various actions pertaining to the contemplative life.

Objection 2: Further, the Apostle says (2 Cor. 3:18): "But we . . . beholding [speculantes] the glory of the Lord with open face, are transformed into the same clarity [*Vulg.: 'into the same image from glory to glory.']." Now this belongs to the contemplative life. Therefore in addition to the three aforesaid, vision [speculatio] belongs to the contemplative life.

Objection 3: Further, Bernard says (De Consid. v, 14) that "the first and greatest contemplation is admiration of the Majesty." Now according to Damascene (De Fide Orth. ii, 15) admiration is a kind of fear. Therefore it would seem that several acts are requisite for the contemplative life.

Objection 4: Further, "Prayer," "reading," and "meditation" [*Hugh of St. Victor, Alleg. in N.T. iii, 4] are said to belong to the contemplative life. Again, "hearing" belongs to the contemplative life: since it is stated that Mary (by whom the contemplative life is signified) "sitting . . . at the Lord's feet, heard His word" (Lk. 10:39). Therefore it would seem that several acts are requisite for the contemplative life.

On the contrary, Life signifies here the operation on which a man is chiefly intent. Wherefore if there are several operations of the contemplative life, there will be, not one, but several contemplative lives.

I answer that, We are now speaking of the contemplative life as applicable to man. Now according to Dionysius (Div. Nom. vii) between man and angel there is this difference, that an angel perceives the truth by simple apprehension, whereas man arrives at the perception of a simple truth by a process from several premises. Accordingly, then, the contemplative life has one act wherein it is finally completed, namely the contemplation of truth, and from this act it derives its unity. Yet it has many acts whereby it arrives at this final act. Some of these pertain to the reception of principles, from which it proceeds to the contemplation of truth; others are concerned with deducing from the principles, the truth, the knowledge of which is sought; and the last and crowning act is the contemplation itself of the truth.

Reply to Objection 1: According to Richard of St. Victor "cogitation" would seem to regard the consideration of the many things from which a person intends to gather one simple truth. Hence cogitation may comprise not only the perceptions of the senses in taking cognizance of certain effects, but also the imaginations. and again the reason's discussion of the various signs or of anything that conduces to the truth in view: although, according to Augustine (De Trin. xiv, 7), cogitation may signify any actual operation of the intellect. "Meditation" would seem to be the process of reason from certain principles that lead to the contemplation of some truth: and "consideration" has the same meaning, according to Bernard (De Consid. ii, 2), although, according to the Philosopher (De Anima ii, 1), every operation of the intellect may be called "consideration." But "contemplation" regards the simple act of gazing on the truth; wherefore Richard says again (De Grat. Contempl. i, 4) that "contemplation is the soul's clear and free dwelling upon the object of its gaze; meditation is the survey of the mind while occupied in searching for the truth: and cogitation is the mind's glance which is prone to wander."

Reply to Objection 2: According to a gloss [*Cf. De Trin. xv, 8] of Augustine on this passage, "beholding" [speculatio] denotes "seeing in a mirror [speculo], not from a watch-tower [specula]." Now to see a thing in a mirror is to see a cause in its effect wherein its likeness is reflected. Hence "beholding" would seem to be reducible to meditation.

Reply to Objection 3: Admiration is a kind of fear resulting from the apprehension of a thing that surpasses our faculties: hence it results from the contemplation of the sublime truth. For it was stated above [3723](A[1]) that contemplation terminates in the affections.

Reply to Objection 4: Man reaches the knowledge of truth in two ways. First, by means of things received from another. In this way, as regards the things he receives from God, he needs "prayer," according to Wis. 7:7, "I called upon" God, "and the spirit of wisdom came upon me": while as regards the things he receives from man, he needs "hearing," in so far as he receives from the spoken word, and "reading," in so far as he receives from the tradition of Holy Writ. Secondly, he needs to apply himself by his personal study, and thus he requires "meditation."

Whether the contemplative life consists in the mere contemplation of God, or also in the consideration of any truth whatever?

Objection 1: It would seem that the contemplative life consists not only in the contemplation of God, but also in the consideration of any truth. For it is written (Ps. 138:14): "Wonderful are Thy works, and my soul knoweth right well." Now the knowledge of God's works is effected by any contemplation of the truth. Therefore it would seem that it pertains to the contemplative life to contemplate not only the divine truth, but also any other.

Objection 2: Further, Bernard says (De Consid. v, 14) that "contemplation consists in admiration first of God's majesty, secondly of His judgments, thirdly of His benefits, fourthly of His promises." Now of these four the first alone regards the divine truth, and the other three pertain to His effects. Therefore the contemplative life consists not only in the contemplation of the divine truth, but also in the consideration of truth regarding the divine effects.

Objection 3: Further, Richard of St. Victor [*De Grat. Contempl. i, 6] distinguishes six species of contemplation. The first belongs to "the imagination alone," and consists in thinking of corporeal things. The second is in "the imagination guided by reason," and consists in considering the order and disposition of sensible objects. The third is in "the reason based on the imagination"; when, to wit, from the consideration of the visible we rise to the invisible. The fourth is in "the reason and conducted by the reason," when the mind is intent on things invisible of which the imagination has no cognizance. The fifth is "above the reason," but not contrary to reason, when by divine revelation we become cognizant of things that cannot be comprehended by the human reason. The sixth is "above reason and contrary to reason"; when, to wit, by the divine enlightening we know things that seem contrary to human reason, such as the doctrine of the mystery of the Trinity. Now only the last of these would seem to pertain to the divine truth. Therefore the contemplation of truth regards not only the divine truth, but also that which is considered in creatures.

Objection 4: Further, in the contemplative life the contemplation of truth is sought as being the perfection of man. Now any truth is a perfection of the human intellect. Therefore the contemplative life consists in the contemplation of any truth.

On the contrary, Gregory says (Moral. vi, 37) that "in contemplation we seek the principle which is God."

I answer that, As stated above [3724](A[2]), a thing may belong to the contemplative life in two ways: principally, and secondarily, or dispositively. That which belongs principally to the contemplative life is the contemplation of the divine truth, because this contemplation is the end of the whole human life. Hence Augustine says (De Trin. i, 8) that "the contemplation of God is promised us as being the goal of all our actions and the everlasting perfection of our joys." This contemplation will be perfect in the life to come, when we shall see God face to face, wherefore it will make us perfectly happy: whereas now the contemplation of the divine truth is competent to us imperfectly, namely "through a glass" and "in a dark manner" (1 Cor. 13:12). Hence it bestows on us a certain inchoate beatitude, which begins now and will be continued in the life to come; wherefore the Philosopher (Ethic. x, 7) places man's ultimate happiness in the contemplation of the supreme intelligible good.

Since, however, God's effects show us the way to the contemplation of God Himself, according to Rom. 1:20, "The invisible things of God . . . are clearly seen, being understood by the things that are made," it follows that the contemplation of the divine effects also belongs to the contemplative life, inasmuch as man is guided thereby to the knowledge of God. Hence Augustine says (De Vera Relig. xxix) that "in the study of creatures we must not exercise an empty and futile curiosity, but should make them the stepping-stone to things unperishable and everlasting."

Accordingly it is clear from what has been said ([3725]AA[1],2,3) that four things pertain, in a certain order, to the contemplative life; first, the moral virtues; secondly, other acts exclusive of contemplation; thirdly, contemplation of the divine effects; fourthly, the complement of all which is the contemplation of the divine truth itself.

Reply to Objection 1: David sought the knowledge of God's works, so that he might be led by them to God; wherefore he says elsewhere (Ps. 142:5,6): "I meditated on all Thy works: I meditated upon the works of Thy hands: I stretched forth my hands to Thee."

Reply to Objection 2: By considering the divine judgments man is guided to the consideration of the divine justice; and by considering the divine benefits and promises, man is led to the knowledge of God's mercy or goodness, as by effects already manifested or yet to be vouchsafed.

Reply to Objection 3: These six denote the steps whereby we ascend by means of creatures to the contemplation of God. For the first step consists in the mere consideration of sensible objects; the second step consists in going forward from sensible to intelligible objects; the third step is to judge of sensible objects according to intelligible things; the fourth is the absolute consideration of the intelligible objects to which one has attained by means of sensibles; the fifth is the contemplation of those intelligible objects that are unattainable by means of sensibles, but which the reason is able to grasp; the sixth step is the consideration of such intelligible things as the reason can neither discover nor grasp, which pertain to the sublime contemplation of divine truth, wherein contemplation is ultimately perfected.

Reply to Objection 4: The ultimate perfection of the human intellect is the divine truth: and other truths perfect the intellect in relation to the divine truth.

Whether in the present state of life the contemplative life can reach to the vision of the Divine essence?

Objection 1: It would seem that in the present state of life the contemplative life can reach to the vision of the Divine essence. For, as stated in Gn. 32:30, Jacob said: "I have seen God face to face, and my soul has been saved." Now the vision of God's face is the vision of the Divine essence. Therefore it would seem that in the present life one may come, by means of contemplation, to see God in His essence.

Objection 2: Further, Gregory says (Moral. vi, 37) that "contemplative men withdraw within themselves in order to explore spiritual things, nor do they ever carry with them the shadows of things corporeal, or if these follow them they prudently drive them away: but being desirous of seeing the incomprehensible light, they suppress all the images of their limited comprehension, and through longing to reach what is above them, they overcome that which they are." Now man is not hindered from seeing the Divine essence, which is the incomprehensible light, save by the necessity of turning to corporeal phantasms. Therefore it would seem that the contemplation of the present life can extend to the vision of the incomprehensible light in its essence.

Objection 3: Further, Gregory says (Dial. ii, 35): "All creatures are small to the soul that sees its Creator: wherefore when the man of God," the blessed Benedict, to wit, "saw a fiery globe in the tower and angels returning to heaven, without doubt he could only see such things by the light of God." Now the blessed Benedict was still in this life. Therefore the contemplation of the present life can extend to the vision of the essence of God.

On the contrary, Gregory says (Hom. xiv in Ezech.): "As long as we live in this mortal flesh, no one reaches such a height of contemplation as to fix the eyes of his mind on the ray itself of incomprehensible light."

I answer that, As Augustine says (Gen. ad lit. xii, 27), "no one seeing God lives this mortal life wherein the bodily senses have their play: and unless in some way he depart this life, whether by going altogether out of his body, or by withdrawing from his carnal senses, he is not caught up into that vision." This has been carefully discussed above (Q[175], AA[4],5), where we spoke of rapture, and in the [3726]FP, Q[12], A[2], where we treated of the vision of God.

Accordingly we must state that one may be in this life in two ways. First, with regard to act, that is to say by actually making use of the bodily senses, and thus contemplation in the present life can nowise attain to the vision of God's essence. Secondly, one may be in this life potentially and not with regard to act, that is to say, when the soul is united to the mortal body as its form, yet so as to make use neither of the bodily senses, nor even of the imagination, as happens in rapture; and in this way the contemplation of the present life can attain to the vision of the Divine essence. Consequently the highest degree of contemplation in the present life is that which Paul had in rapture, whereby he was in a middle state between the present life and the life to come.

Reply to Objection 1: As Dionysius says (Ep. i ad Caium. Monach.), "if anyone seeing God, understood what he saw, he saw not God Himself, but something belonging to God." And Gregory says (Hom. xiv in Ezech.): "By no means is God seen now in His glory; but the soul sees something of lower degree, and is thereby refreshed so that afterwards it may attain to the glory of vision." Accordingly the words of Jacob, "I saw God face to face" do not imply that he saw God's essence, but that he saw some shape [*Cf. [3727]FP, Q[12], A[11], ad 1], imaginary of course, wherein God spoke to him. Or, "since we know a man by his face, by the face of God he signified his knowledge of Him," according to a gloss of Gregory on the same passage.

Reply to Objection 2: In the present state of life human contemplation is impossible without phantasms, because it is connatural to man to see the intelligible species in the phantasms, as the Philosopher states (De Anima iii, 7). Yet intellectual knowledge does not consist in the phantasms themselves, but in our contemplating in them the purity of the intelligible truth: and this not only in natural knowledge, but also in that which we obtain by revelation. For Dionysius says (Coel. Hier. i) that "the Divine glory shows us the angelic hierarchies under certain symbolic figures, and by its power we are brought back to the single ray of light," i.e. to the simple knowledge of the intelligible truth. It is in this sense that we must understand the statement of Gregory that "contemplatives do not carry along with them the shadows of things corporeal," since their contemplation is not fixed on them, but on the consideration of the intelligible truth.

Reply to Objection 3: By these words Gregory does not imply that the blessed Benedict, in that vision, saw God in His essence, but he wishes to show that because "all creatures are small to him that sees God," it follows that all things can easily be seen through the enlightenment of the Divine light. Wherefore he adds: "For however little he may see of the Creator's light, all created things become petty to him."

Whether the operation of contemplation is fittingly divided into a threefold movement, circular, straight and oblique?

Objection 1: It would seem that the operation of contemplation is unfittingly divided into a threefold movement, "circular," "straight," and "oblique" (Div. Nom. iv). For contemplation pertains exclusively to rest, according to Wis. 8:16, "When I go into my house, I shall repose myself with her." Now movement is opposed to rest. Therefore the operations of the contemplative life should not be described as movements.

Objection 2: Further, the action of the contemplative life pertains to the intellect, whereby man is like the angels. Now Dionysius describes these movements as being different in the angels from what they are in the soul. For he says (Div. Nom. iv) that the "circular" movement in the angel is "according to his enlightenment by the beautiful and the good." On the other hand, he assigns the circular movement of the soul to several things: the first of which is the "withdrawal of the soul into itself from externals"; the second is "a certain concentration of its powers, whereby it is rendered free of error and of outward occupation"; and the third is "union with those things that are above it." Again, he describes differently their respective straight movements. For he says that the straight movement of the angel is that by which he proceeds to the care of those things that are beneath him. On the other hand, he describes the straight movement of the soul as being twofold: first, "its progress towards things that are near it"; secondly, "its uplifting from external things to simple contemplation." Further, he assigns a different oblique movement to each. For he assigns the oblique movement of the angels to the fact that "while providing for those who have less they remain unchanged in relation to God": whereas he assigns the oblique movement of the soul to the fact that "the soul is enlightened in Divine knowledge by reasoning and discoursing." Therefore it would seem that the operations of contemplation are unfittingly assigned according to the ways mentioned above.

Objection 3: Further, Richard of St. Victor (De Contempl. i, 5) mentions many other different movements in likeness to the birds of the air. "For some of these rise at one time to a great height, at another swoop down to earth, and they do so repeatedly; others fly now to the right, now to the left again and again; others go forwards or lag behind many times; others fly in a circle now more now less extended; and others remain suspended almost immovably in one place." Therefore it would seem that there are only three movements of contemplation.

On the contrary, stands the authority of Dionysius (Div. Nom. iv).

I answer that, As stated above ([3728]Q[119], A[1], ad 3), the operation of the intellect, wherein contemplation essentially consists, is called a movement, in so far as movement is the act of a perfect thing, according to the Philosopher (De Anima iii, 1). Since, however, it is through sensible objects that we come to the knowledge of intelligible things, and since sensible operations do not take place without movement, the result is that even intelligible operations are described as movements, and are differentiated in likeness to various movements. Now of bodily movements, local movements are the most perfect and come first, as proved in Phys. viii, 7; wherefore the foremost among intelligible operations are described by being likened to them. These movements are of three kinds; for there is the "circular" movement, by which a thing moves uniformly round one point as center, another is the "straight" movement, by which a thing goes from one point to another; the third is "oblique," being composed as it were of both the others. Consequently, in intelligible operations, that which is simply uniform is compared to circular movement; the intelligible operation by which one proceeds from one point to another is compared to the straight movement; while the intelligible operation which unites something of uniformity with progress to various points is compared to the oblique movement.

Reply to Objection 1: External bodily movements are opposed to the quiet of contemplation, which consists in rest from outward occupations: but the movements of intellectual operations belong to the quiet of contemplation.

Reply to Objection 2: Man is like the angels in intellect generically, but the intellective power is much higher in the angel than in man. Consequently these movements must be ascribed to souls and angels in different ways, according as they are differently related to uniformity. For the angelic intellect has uniform knowledge in two respects. First, because it does not acquire intelligible truth from the variety of composite objects; secondly, because it understands the truth of intelligible objects not discursively, but by simple intuition. On the other hand, the intellect of the soul acquires intelligible truth from sensible objects, and understands it by a certain discoursing of the reason.

Wherefore Dionysius assigns the "circular" movement of the angels to the fact that their intuition of God is uniform and unceasing, having neither beginning nor end: even as a circular movement having neither beginning nor end is uniformly around the one same center. But on the part of the soul, ere it arrive at this uniformity, its twofold lack of uniformity needs to be removed. First, that which arises from the variety of external things: this is removed by the soul withdrawing from externals, and so the first thing he mentions regarding the circular movement of the soul is "the soul's withdrawal into itself from external objects." Secondly, another lack of uniformity requires to be removed from the soul, and this is owing to the discoursing of reason. This is done by directing all the soul's operations to the simple contemplation of the intelligible truth, and this is indicated by his saying in the second place that "the soul's intellectual powers must be uniformly concentrated," in other words that discoursing must be laid aside and the soul's gaze fixed on the contemplation of the one simple truth. In this operation of the soul there is no error, even as there is clearly no error in the understanding of first principles which we know by simple intuition. Afterwards these two things being done, he mentions thirdly the uniformity which is like that of the angels, for then all things being laid aside, the soul continues in the contemplation of God alone. This he expresses by saying: "Then being thus made uniform unitedly," i.e. conformably, "by the union of its powers, it is conducted to the good and the beautiful." The "straight" movement of the angel cannot apply to his proceeding from one thing to another by considering them, but only to the order of his providence, namely to the fact that the higher angel enlightens the lower angels through the angels that are intermediate. He indicates this when he says: "The angel's movement takes a straight line when he proceeds to the care of things subject to him, taking in his course whatever things are direct," i.e. in keeping with the dispositions of the direct order. Whereas he ascribes the "straight" movement in the soul to the soul's proceeding from exterior sensibles to the knowledge of intelligible objects. The "oblique" movement in the angels he describes as being composed of the straight and circular movements, inasmuch as their care for those beneath them is in accordance with their contemplation of God: while the "oblique" movement in the soul he also declares to be partly straight and partly circular, in so far as in reasoning it makes use of the light received from God.

Reply to Objection 3: These varieties of movement that are taken from the distinction between above and below, right and left, forwards and backwards, and from varying circles, are all comprised under either straight and oblique movement, because they all denote discursions of reason. For if the reason pass from the genus to the species, or from the part to the whole, it will be, as he explains, from above to below: if from one opposite to another, it will be from right to left; if from the cause to the effect, it will be backwards and forwards; if it be about accidents that surround a thing near at hand or far remote, the movement will be circular. The discoursing of reason from sensible to intelligible objects, if it be according to the order of natural reason, belongs to the straight movement; but if it be according to the Divine enlightenment, it will belong to the oblique movement as explained above (ad 2). That alone which he describes as immobility belongs to the circular movement.

Wherefore it is evident that Dionysius describes the movement of contemplation with much greater fulness and depth.

Whether there is delight in contemplation?

Objection 1: It would seem that there is no delight in contemplation. For delight belongs to the appetitive power; whereas contemplation resides chiefly in the intellect. Therefore it would seem that there is no delight in contemplation.

Objection 2: Further, all strife and struggle is a hindrance to delight. Now there is strife and struggle in contemplation. For Gregory says (Hom. xiv in Ezech.) that "when the soul strives to contemplate God, it is in a state of struggle; at one time it almost overcomes, because by understanding and feeling it tastes something of the incomprehensible light, and at another time it almost succumbs, because even while tasting, it fails." Therefore there is no delight in contemplation.

Objection 3: Further, delight is the result of a perfect operation, as stated in Ethic. x, 4. Now the contemplation of wayfarers is imperfect, according to 1 Cor. 13:12, "We see now through a glass in a dark manner." Therefore seemingly there is no delight in the contemplative life.

Objection 4: Further, a lesion of the body is an obstacle to delight. Now contemplation causes a lesion of the body; wherefore it is stated (Gn. 32) that after Jacob had said (Gn. 32:30), "'I have seen God face to face' . . . he halted on his foot (Gn. 32:31) . . . because he touched the sinew of his thigh and it shrank" (Gn. 32:32). Therefore seemingly there is no delight in contemplation.

On the contrary, It is written of the contemplation of wisdom (Wis. 8:16): "Her conversation hath no bitterness, nor her company any tediousness, but joy and gladness": and Gregory says (Hom. xiv in Ezech.) that "the contemplative life is sweetness exceedingly lovable."

I answer that, There may be delight in any particular contemplation in two ways. First by reason of the operation itself [*Cf. [3729]FS, Q[3], A[5]], because each individual delights in the operation which befits him according to his own nature or habit. Now contemplation of the truth befits a man according to his nature as a rational animal: the result being that "all men naturally desire to know," so that consequently they delight in the knowledge of truth. And more delightful still does this become to one who has the habit of wisdom and knowledge, the result of which is that he contemplates without difficulty. Secondly, contemplation may be delightful on the part of its object, in so far as one contemplates that which one loves; even as bodily vision gives pleasure, not only because to see is pleasurable in itself, but because one sees a person whom one loves. Since, then, the contemplative life consists chiefly in the contemplation of God, of which charity is the motive, as stated above ([3730]AA[1],2, ad 1), it follows that there is delight in the contemplative life, not only by reason of the contemplation itself, but also by reason of the Divine love.

In both respects the delight thereof surpasses all human delight, both because spiritual delight is greater than carnal pleasure, as stated above ([3731]FS, Q[31], A[5]), when we were treating of the passions, and because the love whereby God is loved out of charity surpasses all love. Hence it is written (Ps. 33:9): "O taste and see that the Lord is sweet."

Reply to Objection 1: Although the contemplative life consists chiefly in an act of the intellect, it has its beginning in the appetite, since it is through charity that one is urged to the contemplation of God. And since the end corresponds to the beginning, it follows that the term also and the end of the contemplative life has its being in the appetite, since one delights in seeing the object loved, and the very delight in the object seen arouses a yet greater love. Wherefore Gregory says (Hom. xiv in Ezech.) that "when we see one whom we love, we are so aflame as to love him more." And this is the ultimate perfection of the contemplative life, namely that the Divine truth be not only seen but also loved.

Reply to Objection 2: Strife or struggle arising from the opposition of an external thing, hinders delight in that thing. For a man delights not in a thing against which he strives: but in that for which he strives; when he has obtained it, other things being equal, he delights yet more: wherefore Augustine says (Confess. viii, 3) that "the more peril there was in the battle, the greater the joy in the triumph." But there is no strife or struggle in contemplation on the part of the truth which we contemplate, though there is on the part of our defective understanding and our corruptible body which drags us down to lower things, according to Wis. 9:15, "The corruptible body ss a load upon the soul, and the earthly habitation presseth down the mind that museth upon many things." Hence it is that when man attains to the contemplation of truth, he loves it yet more, while he hates the more his own deficiency and the weight of his corruptible body, so as to say with the Apostle (Rom. 7:24): "Unhappy man that I am, who shall deliver me from the body of this death?" Wherefore Gregory say (Hom. xiv in Ezech.): "When God is once known by desire and understanding, He withers all carnal pleasure in us."

Reply to Objection 3: The contemplation of God in this life is imperfect in comparison with the contemplation in heaven; and in like manner the delight of the wayfarer's contemplation is imperfect as compared with the delight of contemplation in heaven, of which it is written (Ps. 35:9): "Thou shalt make them drink of the torrent of Thy pleasure." Yet, though the contemplation of Divine things which is to be had by wayfarers is imperfect, it is more delightful than all other contemplation however perfect, on account of the excellence of that which is contemplated. Hence the Philosopher says (De Part. Animal. i, 5): "We may happen to have our own little theories about those sublime beings and godlike substances, and though we grasp them but feebly, nevertheless so elevating is the knowledge that they give us more delight than any of those things that are round about us": and Gregory says in the same sense (Hom. xiv in Ezech.): "The contemplative life is sweetness exceedingly lovable; for it carries the soul away above itself, it opens heaven and discovers the spiritual world to the eyes of the mind."

Reply to Objection 4: After contemplation Jacob halted with one foot, "because we need to grow weak in the love of the world ere we wax strong in the love of God," as Gregory says (Hom. xiv in Ezech.). "Thus when we have known the sweetness of God, we have one foot sound while the other halts; since every one who halts on one foot leans only on that foot which is sound."

Whether the contemplative life is continuous?

Objection 1: It would seem that the contemplative life is not continuous. For the contemplative life consists essentially in things pertaining to the intellect. Now all the intellectual perfections of this life will be made void, according to 1 Cor. 13:8, "Whether prophecies shall be made void, or tongues shall cease, or knowledge shall be destroyed." Therefore the contemplative life is made void.

Objection 2: Further, a man tastes the sweetness of contemplation by snatches and for a short time only: wherefore Augustine says (Confess. x, 40), "Thou admittest me to a most unwonted affection in my inmost soul, to a strange sweetness . . . yet through my grievous weight I sink down again." Again, Gregory commenting on the words of Job 4:15, "When a spirit passed before me," says (Moral. v, 33): "The mind does not remain long at rest in the sweetness of inward contemplation, for it is recalled to itself and beaten back by the very immensity of the light." Therefore the contemplative life is not continuous.

Objection 3: Further, that which is not connatural to man cannot be continuous. Now the contemplative life, according to the Philosopher (Ethic. x, 7), "is better than the life which is according to man." Therefore seemingly the contemplative life is not continuous.

On the contrary, our Lord said (Lk. 10:42): "Mary hath chosen the best part, which shall not be taken away from her," since as Gregory says (Hom. xiv in Ezech.), "the contemplative life begins here so that it may be perfected in our heavenly home."

I answer that, A thing may be described as continuous in two ways: first, in regard to its nature; secondly, in regard to us. It is evident that in regard to itself contemplative life is continuous for two reasons: first, because it is about incorruptible and unchangeable things; secondly, because it has no contrary, for there is nothing contrary to the pleasure of contemplation, as stated in Topic. i, 13. But even in our regard contemplative life is continuous---both because it is competent to us in respect of the incorruptible part of the soul, namely the intellect, wherefore it can endure after this life---and because in the works of the contemplative life we work not with our bodies, so that we are the more able to persevere in the works thereof, as the Philosopher observes (Ethic. x, 7).

Reply to Objection 1: The manner of contemplation is not the same here as in heaven: yet the contemplative life is said to remain by reason of charity, wherein it has both its beginning and its end. Gregory speaks in this sense (Hom. xiv in Ezech.): "The contemplative life begins here, so as to be perfected in our heavenly home, because the fire of love which begins to burn here is aflame with a yet greater love when we see Him Whom we love."

Reply to Objection 2: No action can last long at its highest pitch. Now the highest point of contemplation is to reach the uniformity of Divine contemplation, according to Dionysius [*Cf. Coel. Hier. iii], and as we have stated above (A[6], ad 2). Hence although contemplation cannot last long in this respect, it can be of long duration as regards the other contemplative acts.

Reply to Objection 3: The Philosopher declares the contemplative life to be above man, because it befits us "so far as there is in us something divine" (Ethic. x, 7), namely the intellect, which is incorruptible and impassible in itself, wherefore its act can endure longer.

Day 242

OF THE ACTIVE LIFE (FOUR ARTICLES)
We must now consider the active life, under which head there are four points of inquiry:
(1) Whether all the works of the moral virtues pertain to the active life?
(2) Whether prudence pertains to the active life?
(3) Whether teaching pertains to the active life?
(4) Of the duration of the active life.

Whether all the actions of the moral virtues pertain to the active life?
Objection 1: It would seem that the acts of the moral virtues do not all pertain to the active life. For seemingly the active life regards only our relations with other persons: hence Gregory says (Hom. xiv in Ezech.) that "the active life is to give bread to the hungry," and after mentioning many things that regard our relations with other people he adds finally, "and to give to each and every one whatever he needs." Now we are directed in our relations to others, not by all the acts of moral virtues, but only by those of justice and its parts, as stated above (Q[58], AA[2],8; [3732]FS, Q[60], AA[2],3). Therefore the acts of the moral virtues do not all pertain to the active life.

Objection 2: Further, Gregory says (Hom. xiv in Ezech.) that Lia who was blear-eyed but fruitful signifies the active life: which "being occupied with work, sees less, and yet since it urges one's neighbor both by word and example to its imitation it begets a numerous offspring of good deeds." Now this would seem to belong to charity, whereby we love our neighbor, rather than to the moral virtues. Therefore seemingly the acts of moral virtue do not pertain to the active life.

Objection 3: Further, as stated above ([3733]Q[180], A[2]), the moral virtues dispose one to the contemplative life. Now disposition and perfection belong to the same thing. Therefore it would seem that the moral virtues do not pertain to the active life.

On the contrary, Isidore says (De Summo Bono iii, 15): "In the active life all vices must first of all be extirpated by the practice of good works, in order that in the contemplative life the mind's eye being purified one may advance to the contemplation of the Divine light." Now all vices are not extirpated save by acts of the moral virtues. Therefore the acts of the moral virtues pertain to the active life.

I answer that, As stated above ([3734]Q[179], A[1]) the active and the contemplative life differ according to the different occupations of men intent on different ends: one of which occupations is the consideration of the truth; and this is the end of the contemplative life, while the other is external work to which the active life is directed.

Now it is evident that the moral virtues are directed chiefly, not to the contemplation of truth but to operation. Wherefore the Philosopher says (Ethic. ii, 4) that "for virtue knowledge is of little or no avail." Hence it is clear that the moral virtues belong essentially to the active life; for which reason the Philosopher (Ethic. x, 8) subordinates the moral virtues to active happiness.

Reply to Objection 1: The chief of the moral virtues is justice by which one man is directed in his relations towards another, as the Philosopher proves (Ethic. v, 1). Hence the active life is described with reference to our relations with other people, because it consists in these things, not exclusively, but principally.

Reply to Objection 2: It is possible, by the acts of all the moral virtues, for one to direct one's neighbor to good by example: and this is what Gregory here ascribes to the active life.

Reply to Objection 3: Even as the virtue that is directed to the end of another virtue passes, as it were, into the species of the latter virtue, so again when a man makes use of things pertaining to the active life, merely as dispositions to contemplation, such things are comprised under the contemplative life. On the other hand, when we practice the works of the moral virtues, as being good in themselves, and not as dispositions to the contemplative life, the moral virtues belong to the active life.

It may also be replied, however, that the active life is a disposition to the contemplative life.

Whether prudence pertains to the active life?
Objection 1: It would seem that prudence does not pertain to the active life. For just as the contemplative life belongs to the cognitive power, so the active life belongs to the appetitive power. Now prudence belongs not to the appetitive but to the cognitive power. Therefore prudence does not belong to the active life.

Objection 2: Further, Gregory says (Hom. xiv in Ezech.) that the "active life being occupied with work, sees less," wherefore it is signified by Lia who was blear-eyed. But prudence requires clear eyes, so that one may judge aright of what has to be done. Therefore it seems that prudence does not pertain to the active life.

Objection 3: Further, prudence stands between the moral and the intellectual virtues. Now just as the moral virtues belong to the active life, as stated above [3735](A[1]), so do the intellectual virtues pertain to the contemplative life. Therefore it would seem that prudence pertains neither to the active nor to the contemplative life, but to an intermediate kind of life, of which Augustine makes mention (De Civ. Dei xix, 2,3,19).

On the contrary, The Philosopher says (Ethic. x, 8) that prudence pertains to active happiness, to which the moral virtues belong.

169

I answer that, As stated above (A[1], ad 3; [3736]FS, Q[18], A[6]), if one thing be directed to another as its end, it is drawn, especially in moral matters, to the species of the thing to which it is directed: for instance "he who commits adultery that he may steal, is a thief rather than an adulterer," according to the Philosopher (Ethic. v, 2). Now it is evident that the knowledge of prudence is directed to the works of the moral virtues as its end, since it is "right reason applied to action" (Ethic. vi, 5); so that the ends of the moral virtues are the principles of prudence, as the Philosopher says in the same book. Accordingly, as it was stated above (A[1], ad 3) that the moral virtues in one who directs them to the quiet of contemplation belong to the contemplative life, so the knowledge of prudence, which is of itself directed to the works of the moral virtues, belongs directly to the active life, provided we take prudence in its proper sense as the Philosopher speaks of it.

If, however, we take it in a more general sense, as comprising any kind of human knowledge, then prudence, as regards a certain part thereof, belongs to the contemplative life. In this sense Tully (De Offic. i, 5) says that "the man who is able most clearly and quickly to grasp the truth and to unfold his reasons, is wont to be considered most prudent and wise."

Reply to Objection 1: Moral works take their species from their end, as stated above ([3737]FS, Q[18], AA[4],6), wherefore the knowledge pertaining to the contemplative life is that which has its end in the very knowledge of truth; whereas the knowledge of prudence, through having its end in an act of the appetitive power, belongs to the active life.

Reply to Objection 2: External occupation makes a man see less in intelligible things, which are separated from sensible objects with which the works of the active life are concerned. Nevertheless the external occupation of the active life enables a man to see more clearly in judging of what is to be done, which belongs to prudence, both on account of experience, and on account of the mind's attention, since "brains avail when the mind is attentive" as Sallust observes [*Bell. Catilin., LI].

Reply to Objection 3: Prudence is said to be intermediate between the intellectual and the moral virtues because it resides in the same subject as the intellectual virtues, and has absolutely the same matter as the moral virtues. But this third kind of life is intermediate between the active and the contemplative life as regards the things about which it is occupied, because it is occupied sometimes with the contemplation of the truth, sometimes with eternal things.

Whether teaching is a work of the active or of the contemplative life?

Objection 1: It would seem that teaching is a work not of the active but of the contemplative life. For Gregory says (Hom. v in Ezech.) that "the perfect who have been able to contemplate heavenly goods, at least through a glass, proclaim them to their brethren, whose minds they inflame with love for their hidden beauty." But this pertains to teaching. Therefore teaching is a work of the contemplative life.

Objection 2: Further, act and habit would seem to be referable to the same kind of life. Now teaching is an act of wisdom: for the Philosopher says (Metaph. i, 1) that "to be able to teach is an indication of knowledge." Therefore since wisdom or knowledge pertain to the contemplative life, it would seem that teaching also belongs to the contemplative life.

Objection 3: Further, prayer, no less than contemplation, is an act of the contemplative life. Now prayer, even when one prays for another, belongs to the contemplative life. Therefore it would seem that it belongs also to the contemplative life to acquaint another, by teaching him, of the truth we have meditated.

On the contrary, Gregory says (Hom. xiv in Ezech.): "The active life is to give bread to the hungry, to teach the ignorant the words of wisdom."

I answer that, The act of teaching has a twofold object. For teaching is conveyed by speech, and speech is the audible sign of the interior concept. Accordingly one object of teaching is the matter or object of the interior concept; and as to this object teaching belongs sometimes to the active, sometimes to the contemplative life. It belongs to the active life, when a man conceives a truth inwardly, so as to be directed thereby in his outward action; but it belongs to the contemplative life when a man conceives an intelligible truth, in the consideration and love whereof he delights. Hence Augustine says (De Verb. Dom. Serm. civ, 1): "Let them choose for themselves the better part," namely the contemplative life, "let them be busy with the word, long for the sweetness of teaching, occupy themselves with salutary knowledge," thus stating clearly that teaching belongs to the contemplative life.

The other object of teaching is on the part of the speech heard, and thus the object of teaching is the hearer. As to this object all doctrine belongs to the active life to which external actions pertain.

Reply to Objection 1: The authority quoted speaks expressly of doctrine as to its matter, in so far as it is concerned with the consideration and love of truth.

Reply to Objection 2: Habit and act have a common object. Hence this argument clearly considers the matter of the interior concept. For it pertains to the man having wisdom and knowledge to be able to teach, in so far as he is able to express his interior concept in words, so as to bring another man to understand the truth.

Reply to Objection 3: He who prays for another does nothing towards the man for whom he prays, but only towards God Who is the intelligible truth; whereas he who teaches another does something in his regard by external action. Hence the comparison fails.

Whether the active life remains after this life?

Objection 1: It would seem that the active life remains after this life. For the acts of the moral virtues belong to the active life, as stated above [3738](A[1]). But the moral virtues endure after this life according to Augustine (De Trin. xiv, 9). Therefore the active life remains after this life.

Objection 2: Further, teaching others belongs to the active life, as stated above [3739](A[3]). But in the life to come when "we shall be like the angels," teaching will be possible: even as apparently it is in the angels of whom one "enlightens, cleanses, and perfects" [*Coel. Hier. iii, viii] another, which refers to the "receiving of knowledge," according to Dionysius (Coel. Hier. vii). Therefore it would seem that the active life remains after this life.

Objection 3: Further, the more lasting a thing is in itself, the more is it able to endure after this life. But the active life is seemingly more lasting in itself: for Gregory says (Hom. v in Ezech.) that "we can remain fixed in the active life, whereas we are nowise able to maintain an attentive mind in the contemplative life." Therefore the active life is much more able than the contemplative to endure after this life.

On the contrary, Gregory says (Hom. xiv in Ezech.): "The active life ends with this world, but the contemplative life begins here, to be perfected in our heavenly home."

I answer that, As stated above [3740](A[1]), the active life has its end in external actions: and if these be referred to the quiet of contemplation, for that very reason they belong to the contemplative life. But in the future life of the blessed the occupation of external actions will cease, and if there be any external actions at all, these will be referred to contemplation as their end. For, as Augustine says at the end of De Civitate Dei xxii, 30, "there we shall rest and we shall see, we shall see and love, we shall love and praise." And he had said before (De Civ. Dei xxii, 30) that "there God will be seen without end, loved without wearying, praised without tiring: such will be the occupation of all, the common love, the universal activity."

Reply to Objection 1: As stated above ([3741]Q[136], A[1], ad 1), the moral virtues will remain not as to those actions which are about the means, but as to the actions which are about the end. Such acts are those that conduce to the quiet of contemplation, which in the words quoted above Augustine denotes by "rest," and this rest excludes not only outward disturbances but also the inward disturbance of the passions.

Reply to Objection 2: The contemplative life, as stated above ([3742]Q[180], A[4]), consists chiefly in the contemplation of God, and as to this, one angel does not teach another, since according to Mat. 18:10, "the little ones' angels," who belong to the lower order, "always see the face of the Father"; and so, in the life to come, no man will teach another of God, but "we shall" all "see Him as He is" (1 Jn. 3:2). This is in keeping with the saying of Jeremiah 31:34: "They shall teach no more every man his neighbor . . . saying: Know the Lord: for all shall know me, from the least of them even to the greatest."

But as regards things pertaining to the "dispensation of the mysteries of God," one angel teaches another by cleansing, enlightening, and perfecting him: and thus they have something of the active life so long as the world lasts, from the fact that they are occupied in administering to the creatures below them. This is signified by the fact that Jacob saw angels "ascending" the ladder---which refers to contemplation---and "descending" ---which refers to action. Nevertheless, as Gregory remarks (Moral. ii, 3), "they do not wander abroad from the Divine vision, so as to be deprived of the joys of inward contemplation." Hence in them the active life does not differ from the contemplative life as it does in us for whom the works of the active life are a hindrance to contemplation.

Nor is the likeness to the angels promised to us as regards the administering to lower creatures, for this is competent to us not by reason of our natural order, as it is to the angels, but by reason of our seeing God.

Reply to Objection 3: That the durability of the active life in the present state surpasses the durability of the contemplative life arises not from any property of either life considered in itself, but from our own deficiency, since we are withheld from the heights of contemplation by the weight of the body. Hence Gregory adds (Moral. ii, 3) that "the mind through its very weakness being repelled from that immense height recoils on itself."

OF THE ACTIVE LIFE IN COMPARISON WITH THE CONTEMPLATIVE LIFE (FOUR ARTICLES)

We must now consider the active life in comparison with the contemplative life, under which head there are four points of inquiry:
(1) Which of them is of greater import or excellence?
(2) Which of them has the greater merit?
(3) Whether the contemplative life is hindered by the active life?
(4) Of their order.

Whether the active life is more excellent than the contemplative?

Objection 1: It would seem that the active life is more excellent than the contemplative. For "that which belongs to better men would seem to be worthier and better," as the Philosopher says (Top. iii, 1). Now the active life belongs to persons of higher rank, namely prelates, who are placed in a position of honor and power; wherefore Augustine says (De Civ. Dei xix, 19) that "in our actions we must not love honor or power in this life." Therefore it would seem that the active life is more excellent than the contemplative.

Objection 2: Further, in all habits and acts, direction belongs to the more important; thus the military art, being the more important, directs the art of the bridle-maker [*Ethic. i, 1]. Now it belongs to the active life to direct and command the contemplative, as appears from the words addressed to Moses (Ex. 19:21), "Go down and charge the people, lest they should have a mind to pass the" fixed "limits to see the Lord." Therefore the active life is more excellent than the contemplative.

Objection 3: Further, no man should be taken away from a greater thing in order to be occupied with lesser things: for the Apostle says (1 Cor. 12:31): "Be zealous for the better gifts." Now some are taken away from the state of the contemplative life to the occupations of the active life, as in the case of those who are transferred to the state of prelacy. Therefore it would seem that the active life is more excellent than the contemplative.

On the contrary, Our Lord said (Lk. 10:42): "Mary hath chosen the best part, which shall not be taken away from her." Now Mary figures the contemplative life. Therefore the contemplative life is more excellent than the active.

I answer that, Nothing prevents certain things being more excellent in themselves, whereas they are surpassed by another in some respect. Accordingly we must reply that the contemplative life is simply more excellent than the active: and the Philosopher proves this by eight reasons (Ethic. x, 7,8). The first is, because the contemplative life becomes man according to that which is best in him, namely the intellect, and according to its proper objects, namely things intelligible; whereas the active life is occupied with externals. Hence Rachael, by whom the contemplative life is signified, is interpreted "the vision of the principle," [*Or rather, 'One seeing the principle,' if derived from {rah} and {irzn}; Cf. Jerome, De Nom. Hebr.] whereas as Gregory says (Moral. vi, 37) the active life is signified by Lia who was blear-eyed. The second reason is because the contemplative life can be more continuous, although not as regards the highest degree of contemplation, as stated above ([3743]Q[180], A[8], ad 2;[3744] Q[181], A[4], ad 3), wherefore Mary, by whom the contemplative life is signified, is described as "sitting" all the time "at the Lord's feet." Thirdly, because the contemplative life is more delightful than the active; wherefore Augustine says (De Verb. Dom. Serm. ciii) that "Martha was troubled, but Mary feasted." Fourthly, because in the contemplative life man is more self-sufficient, since he needs fewer things for that purpose; wherefore it was said (Lk. 10:41): "Martha, Martha, thou art careful and art troubled about many things." Fifthly, because the contemplative life is loved more for its own sake, while the active life is directed to something else. Hence it is written (Ps. 36:4): "One thing I have asked of the Lord, this will I seek after, that I may dwell in the house of the Lord all the days of my life, that I may see the delight of the Lord." Sixthly, because the contemplative life consists in leisure and rest, according to Ps. 45:11, "Be still and see that I am God." Seventhly, because the contemplative life is according to Divine things, whereas active life is according to human things; wherefore Augustine says (De Verb. Dom. Serm. civ): "'In the beginning was the Word': to Him was Mary hearkening: 'The Word was made flesh': Him was Martha serving." Eighthly, because the contemplative life is according to that which is most proper to man, namely his intellect; whereas in the works of the active life the lower powers also, which are common to us and brutes, have their part; wherefore (Ps. 35:7) after the words, "Men and beasts Thou wilt preserve, O Lord," that which is special to man is added (Ps. 35:10): "In Thy light we shall see light."

Our Lord adds a ninth reason (Lk. 10:42) when He says: "Mary hath chosen the best part, which shall not be taken away from her," which words Augustine (De Verb. Dom. Serm. ciii) expounds thus: "Not---Thou hast chosen badly but---She has chosen better. Why better? Listen---because it shall not be taken away from her. But the burden of necessity shall at length be taken from thee: whereas the sweetness of truth is eternal."

Yet in a restricted sense and in a particular case one should prefer the active life on account of the needs of the present life. Thus too the Philosopher says (Topic. iii, 2): "It is better to be wise than to be rich, yet for one who is in need, it is better to be rich . . ."

Reply to Objection 1: Not only the active life concerns prelates, they should also excel in the contemplative life; hence Gregory says (Pastor. ii, 1): "A prelate should be foremost in action, more uplifted than others in contemplation."

Reply to Objection 2: The contemplative life consists in a certain liberty of mind. For Gregory says (Hom. iii in Ezech.) that "the contemplative life obtains a certain freedom of mind, for it thinks not of temporal but of eternal things." And Boethius says (De Consol. v, 2): "The soul of man must needs be more free while it continues to gaze on the Divine mind, and less so when it stoops to bodily things." Wherefore it is evident that the active life does not directly command the contemplative life, but prescribes certain works of the active life as dispositions to the contemplative life; which it accordingly serves rather than commands. Gregory refers to this when he says (Hom. iii in Ezech.) that "the active life is bondage, whereas the contemplative life is freedom."

Reply to Objection 3: Sometimes a man is called away from the contemplative life to the works of the active life, on account of some necessity of the present life, yet not so as to be compelled to forsake contemplation altogether. Hence Augustine says (De Civ. Dei xix, 19): "The love of truth seeks a holy leisure, the demands of charity undertake an honest toil," the work namely of the active life. "If no one imposes this burden upon us we must devote ourselves to the research and contemplation of truth, but if it be imposed on us, we must bear it because charity demands it of us. Yet even then we must not altogether forsake the delights of truth, lest we deprive ourselves of its sweetness, and this burden overwhelm us." Hence it is clear that when a person is called from the contemplative life to the active life, this is done by way not of subtraction but of addition.

Whether the active life is of greater merit than the contemplative?

Objection 1: It would seem that the active life is of greater merit than the contemplative. For merit implies relation to meed; and meed is due to labor, according to 1 Cor. 3:8, "Every man shall receive his own reward according to his own labor." Now labor is ascribed to the active life, and rest to the contemplative life; for Gregory says (Hom. xiv in Ezech.): "Whosoever is converted to God must first of all sweat from labor, i.e. he must take Lia, that afterwards he may rest in the embraces of Rachel so as to see the principle." Therefore the active life is of greater merit than the contemplative.

Objection 2: Further, the contemplative life is a beginning of the happiness to come; wherefore Augustine commenting on Jn. 21:22, "So I will have him to remain till I come," says (Tract. cxxiv in Joan.): "This may be expressed more clearly: Let perfect works follow Me conformed to the example of My passion, and let contemplation begun here remain until I come, that it may be perfected when I shall come." And Gregory says (Hom. xiv in Ezech.) that "contemplation begins here, so as to be perfected in our heavenly home." Now the life to come will be a state not of meriting but of receiving the reward of our merits. Therefore the contemplative life would seem to have less of the character of merit than the active, but more of the character of reward.

Objection 3: Further, Gregory says (Hom. xii in Ezech.) that "no sacrifice is more acceptable to God than zeal for souls." Now by the zeal for souls a man turns to the occupations of the active life. Therefore it would seem that the contemplative life is not of greater merit than the active.

On the contrary, Gregory says (Moral. vi, 37): "Great are the merits of the active life, but greater still those of the contemplative."

I answer that, As stated above ([3745]FS, Q[114], A[4]), the root of merit is charity; and, while, as stated above (Q[25], A[1]), charity consists in the love of God and our neighbor, the love of God is by itself more meritorious than the love of our neighbor, as stated above (Q[27], A[8]). Wherefore that which pertains more directly to the love of God is generically more meritorious than that which pertains directly to the love of our neighbor for God's sake. Now the contemplative life pertains directly and immediately to the love of God; for Augustine says (De Civ. Dei xix, 19) that "the love of" the Divine "truth seeks a holy leisure," namely of the contemplative life, for it is that truth above all which the contemplative life seeks, as stated above (Q[181], A[4], ad 2). On the other hand, the active life is more directly concerned with the love of our neighbor, because it is "busy about much serving" (Lk. 10:40). Wherefore the contemplative life is generically of greater merit than the active life. This is moreover asserted by Gregory (Hom. iii in

Ezech.): "The contemplative life surpasses in merit the active life, because the latter labors under the stress of present work," by reason of the necessity of assisting our neighbor, "while the former with heartfelt relish has a foretaste of the coming rest," i.e. the contemplation of God.

Nevertheless it may happen that one man merits more by the works of the active life than another by the works of the contemplative life. For instance through excess of Divine love a man may now and then suffer separation from the sweetness of Divine contemplation for the time being, that God's will may be done and for His glory's sake. Thus the Apostle says (Rom. 9:3): "I wished myself to be an anathema from Christ, for my brethren"; which words Chrysostom expounds as follows (De Compunct. i, 7 [*Ad Demetr. de Compunct. Cordis.]): "His mind was so steeped in the love of Christ that, although he desired above all to be with Christ, he despised even this, because thus he pleased Christ."

Reply to Objection 1: External labor conduces to the increase of the accidental reward; but the increase of merit with regard to the essential reward consists chiefly in charity, whereof external labor borne for Christ's sake is a sign. Yet a much more expressive sign thereof is shown when a man, renouncing whatsoever pertains to this life, delights to occupy himself entirely with Divine contemplation.

Reply to Objection 2: In the state of future happiness man has arrived at perfection, wherefore there is no room for advancement by merit; and if there were, the merit would be more efficacious by reason of the greater charity. But in the present life contemplation is not without some imperfection, and can always become more perfect; wherefore it does not remove the idea of merit, but causes a yet greater merit on account of the practice of greater Divine charity.

Reply to Objection 3: A sacrifice is rendered to God spiritually when something is offered to Him; and of all man's goods, God specially accepts that of the human soul when it is offered to Him in sacrifice. Now a man ought to offer to God, in the first place, his soul, according to Ecclus. 30:24, "Have pity on thy own soul, pleasing God"; in the second place, the souls of others, according to Apoc. 22:17, "He that heareth, let him say: Come." And the more closely a man unites his own or another's soul to God, the more acceptable is his sacrifice to God; wherefore it is more acceptable to God that one apply one's own soul and the souls of others to contemplation than to action. Consequently the statement that "no sacrifice is more acceptable to God than zeal for souls," does not mean that the merit of the active life is preferable to the merit of the contemplative life, but that it is more meritorious to offer to God one's own soul and the souls of others, than any other external gifts.

Whether the contemplative life is hindered by the active life?

Objection 1: It would seem that the contemplative life is hindered by the active life. For the contemplative life requires a certain stillness of mind, according to Ps. 45:11, "Be still, and see that I am God"; whereas the active life involves restlessness, according to Lk. 10:41, "Martha, Martha, thou art careful and troubled about many things." Therefore the active life hinders the contemplative.

Objection 2: Further, clearness of vision is a requisite for the contemplative life. Now active life is a hindrance to clear vision; for Gregory says (Hom. xiv in Ezech.) that it "is blear-eyed and fruitful, because the active life, being occupied with work, sees less." Therefore the active life hinders the contemplative.

Objection 3: Further, one contrary hinders the other. Now the active and the contemplative life are apparently contrary to one another, since the active life is busy about many things, while the contemplative life attends to the contemplation of one; wherefore they differ in opposition to one another. Therefore it would seem that the contemplative life is hindered by the active.

On the contrary, Gregory says (Moral. vi, 37): "Those who wish to hold the fortress of contemplation, must first of all train in the camp of action."

I answer that, The active life may be considered from two points of view. First, as regards the attention to and practice of external works: and thus it is evident that the active life hinders the contemplative, in so far as it is impossible for one to be busy with external action, and at the same time give oneself to Divine contemplation. Secondly, active life may be considered as quieting and directing the internal passions of the soul; and from this point of view the active life is a help to the contemplative, since the latter is hindered by the inordinateness of the internal passions. Hence Gregory says (Moral. vi, 37): "Those who wish to hold the fortress of contemplation must first of all train in the camp of action. Thus after careful study they will learn whether they no longer wrong their neighbor, whether they bear with equanimity the wrongs their neighbors do to them, whether their soul is neither overcome with joy in the presence of temporal goods, nor cast down with too great a sorrow when those goods are withdrawn. In this way they will known when they withdraw within themselves, in order to explore spiritual things, whether they no longer carry with them the shadows of the things corporeal, or, if these follow them, whether they prudently drive them away." Hence the work of the active life conduces to the contemplative, by quelling the interior passions which give rise to the phantasms whereby contemplation is hindered.

This suffices for the Replies to the Objections; for these arguments consider the occupation itself of external actions, and not the effect which is the quelling of the passions.

Whether the active life precedes the contemplative?

Objection 1: It would seem that the active life does not precede the contemplative. For the contemplative life pertains directly to the love of God; while the active life pertains to the love of our neighbor. Now the love of God precedes the love of our neighbor, since we love our neighbor for God's sake. Seemingly therefore the contemplative life also precedes the active life.

Objection 2: Further, Gregory says (Hom. xiv in Ezech.): "It should be observed that while a well-ordered life proceeds from action to contemplation, sometimes it is useful for the soul to turn from the contemplative to the active life." Therefore the active is not simply prior to the contemplative.

Objection 3: Further, it would seem that there is not necessarily any order between things that are suitable to different subjects. Now the active and the contemplative life are suitable to different subjects; for Gregory says (Moral. vi, 37): "Often those who were able to contemplate God so long as they were undisturbed have fallen when pressed with occupation; and frequently they who might live advantageously occupied with the service of their fellow-creatures are killed by the sword of their inaction."

I answer that, A thing is said to precede in two ways. First, with regard to its nature; and in this way the contemplative life precedes the active, inasmuch as it applies itself to things which precede and are better than others, wherefore it moves and directs the active life. For the higher reason which is assigned to contemplation is compared to the lower reason which is assigned to action, and the husband is compared to his wife, who should be ruled by her husband, as Augustine says (De Trin. xii, 3,7,12).

Secondly, a thing precedes with regard to us, because it comes first in the order of generation. In this way the active precedes the contemplative life, because it disposes one to it, as stated above [3746](A[1]; Q[181], A[1], ad 3); and, in the order of generation, disposition precedes form, although the latter precedes simply and according to its nature.

Reply to Objection 1: The contemplative life is directed to the love of God, not of any degree, but to that which is perfect; whereas the active life is necessary for any degree of the love of our neighbor. Hence Gregory says (Hom. iii in Ezech.): "Without the contemplative life it is possible to enter the heavenly kingdom, provided one omit not the good actions we are able to do; but we cannot enter therein without the active life, if we neglect to do the good we can do."

From this it is also evident that the active precedes the contemplative life, as that which is common to all precedes, in the order of generation, that which is proper to the perfect.

Reply to Objection 2: Progress from the active to the contemplative life is according to the order of generation; whereas the return from the contemplative life to the active is according to the order of direction, in so far as the active life is directed by the contemplative. Even thus habit is acquired by acts, and by the acquired habit one acts yet more perfectly, as stated in Ethic. ii, 7.

Reply to Objection 3: He that is prone to yield to his passions on account of his impulse to action is simply more apt for the active life by reason of his restless spirit. Hence Gregory says (Moral. vi, 37) that "there be some so restless that when they are free from labor they labor all the more, because the more leisure they have for thought, the worse interior turmoil they have to bear." Others, on the contrary, have the mind naturally pure and restful, so that they are apt for contemplation, and if they were to apply themselves wholly to action, this would be detrimental to them. Wherefore Gregory says (Moral. vi, 37) that "some are so slothful of mind that if they chance to have any hard work to do they give way at the very outset." Yet, as he adds further on, "often . . . love stimulates slothful souls to work, and fear restrains souls that are disturbed in contemplation." Consequently those who are more adapted to the active life can prepare themselves for the contemplative by the practice of the active life; while none the less, those who are more adapted to the contemplative life can take upon themselves the works of the active life, so as to become yet more apt for contemplation.

Day 243

TREATISE ON THE STATES OF LIFE (QQ[183]-189)

OF MAN'S VARIOUS DUTIES AND STATES IN GENERAL (FOUR ARTICLES)
We must next consider man's various states and duties. We shall consider (1) man's duties and states in general; (2) the state of the perfect in particular.

Under the first head there are four points of inquiry:
(1) What constitutes a state among men?
(2) Whether among men there should be various states and duties?
(3) Of the diversity of duties;
(4) Of the diversity of states.

Whether the notion of a state denotes a condition of freedom or servitude?
Objection 1: It would seem that the notion of a state does not denote a condition of freedom or servitude. For "state" takes its name from "standing." Now a person is said to stand on account of his being upright; and Gregory says (Moral. vii, 17): "To fall by speaking harmful words is to forfeit entirely the state of righteousness." But a man acquires spiritual uprightness by submitting his will to God; wherefore a gloss on Ps. 32:1, "Praise becometh the upright," says: "The upright are those who direct their heart according to God's will." Therefore it would seem that obedience to the Divine commandments suffices alone for the notion of a state.

Objection 2: Further, the word "state" seems to denote immobility according to 1 Cor. 15:48, "Be ye steadfast [stabiles] and immovable"; wherefore Gregory says (Hom. xxi in Ezech.): "The stone is foursquare, and is stable on all sides, if no disturbance will make it fall." Now it is virtue that enables us "to act with immobility," according to Ethic. ii, 4. Therefore it would seem that a state is acquired by every virtuous action.

Objection 3: Further, the word "state" seems to indicate height of a kind; because to stand is to be raised upwards. Now one man is made higher than another by various duties; and in like manner men are raised upwards in various ways by various grades and orders. Therefore the mere difference of grades, orders, or duties suffices for a difference of states.

On the contrary, It is thus laid down in the Decretals (II, qu. vi, can. Si Quando): "Whenever anyone intervene in a cause where life or state is at stake he must do so, not by a proxy, but in his own person"; and "state" here has reference to freedom or servitude. Therefore it would seem that nothing differentiates a man's state, except that which refers to freedom or servitude.

I answer that, "State," properly speaking, denotes a kind of position, whereby a thing is disposed with a certain immobility in a manner according with its nature. For it is natural to man that his head should be directed upwards, his feet set firmly on the ground, and his other intermediate members disposed in becoming order; and this is not the case if he lie down, sit, or recline, but only when he stands upright: nor again is he said to stand, if he move, but only when he is still. Hence it is again that even in human acts, a matter is said to have stability [statum] in reference to its own disposition in the point of a certain immobility or restfulness. Consequently matters which easily change and are extrinsic to them do not constitute a state among men, for instance that a man be rich or poor, of high or low rank, and so forth. Wherefore in the civil law [*Dig. I, IX, De Senatoribus] (Lib. Cassius ff. De Senatoribus) it is said that if a man be removed from the senate, he is deprived of his dignity rather than of his state. But that alone seemingly pertains to a man's state, which regards an obligation binding his person, in so far, to wit, as a man is his own master or subject to another, not indeed from any slight or unstable cause, but from one that is firmly established; and this is something pertaining to the nature of freedom or servitude. Therefore state properly regards freedom or servitude whether in spiritual or in civil matters.

Reply to Objection 1: Uprightness as such does not pertain to the notion of state, except in so far as it is connatural to man with the addition of a certain restfulness. Hence other animals are said to stand without its being required that they should be upright; nor again are men said to stand, however upright their position be, unless they be still.

Reply to Objection 2: Immobility does not suffice for the notion of state; since even one who sits or lies down is still, and yet he is not said to stand.

Reply to Objection 3: Duty implies relation to act; while grades denote an order of superiority and inferiority. But state requires immobility in that which regards a condition of the person himself.

Whether there should be different duties or states in the Church?

Objection 1: It would seem that there should not be different duties or states in the Church. For distinction is opposed to unity. Now the faithful of Christ are called to unity according to Jn. 17:21,22: "That they . . . may be one in Us . . . as We also are one." Therefore there should not be a distinction of duties and states in the Church.

Objection 2: Further, nature does not employ many means where one suffices. But the working of grace is much more orderly than the working of nature. Therefore it were more fitting for things pertaining to the operations of grace to be administered by the same persons, so that there would not be a distinction of duties and states in the Church.

Objection 3: Further, the good of the Church seemingly consists chiefly in peace, according to Ps. 147:3, "Who hath placed peace in thy borders," and 2 Cor. 13:11, "Have peace, and the God of peace . . . shall be with you." Now distinction is a hindrance to peace, for peace would seem to result from likeness, according to Ecclus. 13:19, "Every beast loveth its like," while the Philosopher says (Polit. vii, 5) that "a little difference causes dissension in a state." Therefore it would seem that there ought not to be a distinction of states and duties in the Church.

On the contrary, It is written in praise of the Church (Ps. 44:10) that she is "surrounded with variety": and a gloss on these words says that "the Queen," namely the Church, "is bedecked with the teaching of the apostles, the confession of martyrs, the purity of virgins, the sorrowings of penitents."

I answer that, The difference of states and duties in the Church regards three things. In the first place it regards the perfection of the Church. For even as in the order of natural things, perfection, which in God is simple and uniform, is not to be found in the created universe except in a multiform and manifold manner, so too, the fulness of grace, which is centered in Christ as head, flows forth to His members in various ways, for the perfecting of the body of the Church. This is the meaning of the Apostle's words (Eph. 4:11,12): "He gave some apostles, and some prophets, and other some evangelists, and other some pastors and doctors for the perfecting of the saints." Secondly, it regards the need of those actions which are necessary in the Church. For a diversity of actions requires a diversity of men appointed to them, in order that all things may be accomplished without delay or confusion; and this is indicated by the Apostle (Rom. 12:4,5), "As in one body we have many members, but all the members have not the same office, so we being many are one body in Christ." Thirdly, this belongs to the dignity and beauty of the Church, which consist in a certain order; wherefore it is written (3 Kings 10:4,5) that "when the queen of Saba saw all the wisdom of Solomon . . . and the apartments of his servants, and the order of his ministers . . . she had no longer any spirit in her." Hence the Apostle says (2 Tim. 2:20) that "in a great house there are not only vessels of gold and silver, but also of wood and of earth."

Reply to Objection 1: The distinction of states and duties is not an obstacle to the unity of the Church, for this results from the unity of faith, charity, and mutual service, according to the saying of the Apostle (Eph. 4:16): "From whom the whole body being compacted," namely by faith, "and fitly joined together," namely by charity, "by what every joint supplieth," namely by one man serving another.

Reply to Objection 2: Just as nature does not employ many means where one suffices, so neither does it confine itself to one where many are required, according to the saying of the Apostle (1 Cor. 12:17), "If the whole body were the eye, where would be the hearing?" Hence there was need in the Church, which is Christ's body, for the members to be differentiated by various duties, states, and grades.

Reply to Objection 3: Just as in the natural body the various members are held together in unity by the power of the quickening spirit, and are dissociated from one another as soon as that spirit departs, so too in the Church's body the peace of the various members is preserved by the power of the Holy Spirit, Who quickens the body of the Church, as stated in Jn. 6:64. Hence the Apostle says (Eph. 4:3): "Careful to keep the unity of the Spirit in the bond of peace." Now a man departs from this unity of spirit when he seeks his own; just as in an earthly kingdom peace ceases when the citizens seek each man his own. Besides, the peace both of mind and of an earthly commonwealth is the better preserved by a distinction of duties and states, since thereby the greater number have a share in public actions. Wherefore the Apostle says (1 Cor. 12:24,25) that "God hath tempered [the body] together that there might be no schism in the body, but the members might be mutually careful one for another."

Whether duties differ according to their actions?

Objection 1: It would seem that duties do not differ according to their actions. For there are infinite varieties of human acts both in spirituals and in temporals. Now there can be no certain distinction among things that are infinite in number. Therefore human duties cannot be differentiated according to a difference of acts.

Objection 2: Further, the active and the contemplative life differ according to their acts, as stated above ([3747]Q[179], A[1]). But the distinction of duties seems to be other than the distinction of lives. Therefore duties do not differ according to their acts.

Objection 3: Further, even ecclesiastical orders, states, and grades seemingly differ according to their acts. If, then, duties differ according to their acts it would seem that duties, grades, and states differ in the same way. Yet this is not true, since they are divided into their respective parts in different ways. Therefore duties do not differ according to their acts.

On the contrary, Isidore says (Etym. vi, 19) that "officium [duty] takes its name from 'efficere' [to effect], as though it were instead of 'efficium,' by the change of one letter for the sake of the sound." But effecting pertains to action. Therefore duties differ according to their acts.

I answer that, As stated above [3748](A[2]), difference among the members of the Church is directed to three things: perfection, action, and beauty; and according to these three we may distinguish a threefold distinction among the faithful. One, with regard to perfection, and thus we have the difference of states, in reference to which some persons are more perfect than others. Another distinction regards action and this is the distinction of duties: for persons are said to have various duties when they are appointed to various actions. A third distinction regards the order of ecclesiastical beauty: and thus we distinguish various grades according as in the same state or duty one person is above another. Hence according to a variant text [*The Septuagint] it is written (Ps. 47:4): "In her grades shall God be known."

Reply to Objection 1: The material diversity of human acts is infinite. It is not thus that duties differ, but by their formal diversity which results from diverse species of acts, and in this way human acts are not infinite.

Reply to Objection 2: Life is predicated of a thing absolutely: wherefore diversity of acts which are becoming to man considered in himself. But efficiency, whence we have the word "office" (as stated above), denotes action tending to something else according to Metaph. ix, text. 16 [*Ed. Did. viii, 8]. Hence offices differ properly in respect of acts that are referred to other persons; thus a teacher is said to have an office, and so is a judge, and so forth. Wherefore Isidore says (Etym. vi, 19) that "to have an office is to be officious," i.e. harmful "to no one, but to be useful to all."

Reply to Objection 3: Differences of state, offices and grades are taken from different things, as stated above (A[1], ad 3). Yet these three things may concur in the same subject: thus when a person is appointed to a higher action, he attains thereby both office and grade, and sometimes, besides this, a state of perfection, on account of the sublimity of the act, as in the case of a bishop. The ecclesiastical orders are particularly distinct according to divine offices. For Isidore says (Etym. vi): "There are various kinds of offices; but the foremost is that which relates to sacred and Divine things."

Whether the difference of states applies to those who are beginning, progressing, or perfect?

Objection 1: It would seem that the difference of states does not apply to those who are beginning, progressing, or perfect. For "diverse genera have diverse species and differences" [*Aristotle, Categ. ii]. Now this difference of beginning, progress, and perfection is applied to the degrees of charity, as stated above ([3749]Q[24], A[9]), where we were treating of charity. Therefore it would seem that the differences of states should not be assigned in this manner.

Objection 2: Further, as stated above [3750](A[1]), state regards a condition of servitude or freedom, which apparently has no connection with the aforesaid difference of beginning, progress, and perfection. Therefore it is unfitting to divide state in this way.

Objection 3: Further, the distinction of beginning, progress, and perfection seems to refer to "more" and "less," and this seemingly implies the notion of grades. But the distinction of grades differs from that of states, as we have said above ([3751]AA[2],3). Therefore state is unfittingly divided according to beginning, progress, and perfection.

On the contrary, Gregory says (Moral. xxiv, 11): "There are three states of the converted, the beginning, the middle, and the perfection"; and (Hom. xv in Ezech.): "Other is the beginning of virtue, other its progress, and other still its perfection."

I answer that, As stated above [3752](A[1]) state regards freedom or servitude. Now in spiritual things there is a twofold servitude and a twofold freedom: for there is the servitude of sin and the servitude of justice; and there is likewise a twofold freedom, from sin, and from justice, as appears from the words of the Apostle (Rom. 6:20, 22), "When you were the servants of sin, you were free men to justice . . . but now being made free from sin," you are . . . "become servants to God."

Now the servitude of sin or justice consists in being inclined to evil by a habit of sin, or inclined to good by a habit of justice: and in like manner freedom from sin is not to be overcome by the inclination to sin, and freedom from justice is not to be held back from evil for the love of justice. Nevertheless, since man, by his natural reason, is inclined to justice, while sin is contrary to natural reason, it follows that freedom from sin is true freedom which is united to the servitude of justice, since they both incline man to that which is becoming to him. In like manner true servitude is the servitude of sin, which is connected with freedom from justice, because man is thereby hindered from attaining that which is proper to him. That a man become the servant of justice or sin results from his efforts, as the Apostle declares (Rom. 6:16): "To whom you yield yourselves servants to obey, his servants you are whom you obey, whether it be of sin unto death, or of obedience unto justice." Now in every human effort we can distinguish a beginning, a middle, and a term; and consequently the state of spiritual servitude and freedom is differentiated according to these things, namely, the beginning---to which pertains the state of beginners---the middle, to which pertains the state of the proficient---and the term, to which belongs the state of the perfect.

Reply to Objection 1: Freedom from sin results from charity which "is poured forth in our hearts by the Holy Ghost, Who is given to us" (Rom. 5:5). Hence it is written (2 Cor. 3:17): "Where the Spirit of the Lord is, there is liberty." Wherefore the same division applies to charity as to the state of those who enjoy spiritual freedom.

Reply to Objection 2: Men are said to be beginners, proficient, and perfect (so far as these terms indicate different states), not in relation to any occupation whatever, but in relation to such occupations as pertain to spiritual freedom or servitude, as stated above [3753](A[1]).

Reply to Objection 3: As already observed (A[3], ad 3), nothing hinders grade and state from concurring in the same subject. For even in earthly affairs those who are free, not only belong to a different state from those who are in service, but are also of a different grade.

OF THE STATE OF PERFECTION IN GENERAL (EIGHT ARTICLES)

We must now consider those things that pertain to the state of perfection whereto the other states are directed. For the consideration of offices in relation to other acts belongs to the legislator; and in relation to the sacred ministry it comes under the consideration of orders of which we shall treat in the Third Part [*XP, Q[34]].

Concerning the state of the perfect, a three-fold consideration presents itself: (1) The state of perfection in general; (2) Things relating to the perfection of bishops; (3) Things relating to the perfection of religious.

Under the first head there are eight points of inquiry:

(1) Whether perfection bears any relation to charity?

(2) Whether one can be perfect in this life?

(3) Whether the perfection of this life consists chiefly in observing the counsels or the commandments?

(4) Whether whoever is perfect is in the state of perfection?

(5) Whether especially prelates and religious are in the state of perfection?

(6) Whether all prelates are in the state of perfection?

(7) Which is the more perfect, the episcopal or the religious state?

(8) The comparison between religious and parish priests and archdeacons.

Whether the perfection of the Christian life consists chiefly in charity?

Objection 1: It would seem that the perfection of the Christian life does not consist chiefly in charity. For the Apostle says (1 Cor. 14:20): "In malice be children, but in sense be perfect." But charity regards not the senses but the affections. Therefore it would seem that the perfection of the Christian life does not chiefly consist in charity.

Objection 2: Further,'it is written (Eph. 6:13): "Take unto you the armor of God, that you may be able to resist in the evil day, and to stand in all things perfect"; and the text continues (Eph. 6:14, 16), speaking of the armor of God: "Stand therefore having your loins girt about with truth, and having on the breast-plate of justice . . . in all things taking the shield of faith." Therefore the perfection of the Christian life consists not only in charity, but also in other virtues.

Objection 3: Further, virtues like other habits, are specified by their acts. Now it is written (James 1:4) that "patience hath a perfect work." Therefore seemingly the state of perfection consists more specially in patience.

On the contrary, It is written (Col. 3:14): "Above all things have charity, which is the bond of perfection," because it binds, as it were, all the other virtues together in perfect unity.

I answer that, A thing is said to be perfect in so far as it attains its proper end, which is the ultimate perfection thereof. Now it is charity that unites us to God, Who is the last end of the human mind, since "he that abideth in charity abideth in God, and God in him" (1 Jn. 4:16). Therefore the perfection of the Christian life consists radically in charity.

Reply to Objection 1: The perfection of the human senses would seem to consist chiefly in their concurring together in the unity of truth, according to 1 Cor. 1:10, "That you be perfect in the same mind [sensu], and in the same judgment." Now this is effected by charity which operates consent in us men. Wherefore even the perfection of the senses consists radically in the perfection of charity.

Reply to Objection 2: A man may be said to be perfect in two ways. First, simply: and this perfection regards that which belongs to a thing's nature, for instance an animal may be said to be perfect when it lacks nothing in the disposition of its members and in such things as are necessary for an animal's life. Secondly, a thing is said to be perfect relatively: and this perfection regards something connected with the thing externally, such as whiteness or blackness or something of the kind. Now the Christian life consists chiefly in charity whereby the soul is united to God; wherefore it is written (1 Jn. 3:14): "He that loveth not abideth in death." Hence the perfection of the Christian life consists simply in charity, but in the other virtues relatively. And since that which is simply, is paramount and greatest in comparison with other things, it follows that the perfection of charity is paramount in relation to the perfection that regards the other virtues.

Reply to Objection 3: Patience is stated to have a perfect work in relation to charity, in so far as it is an effect of the abundance of charity that a man bears hardships patiently, according to Rom. 8:35, "Who . . . shall separate us from the love of Christ? Shall tribulation? Or distress?" etc.

Whether any one can be perfect in this life?

Objection 1: It would seem that none can be perfect in this life. For the Apostle says (1 Cor. 13:10): "When that which is perfect is come, that which is in part shall be done away." Now in this life that which is in part is not done away; for in this life faith and hope, which are in part, remain. Therefore none can be perfect in this life.

Objection 2: Further, "The perfect is that which lacks nothing" (Phys. iii, 6). Now there is no one in this life who lacks nothing; for it is written (James 3:2): "In many things we all offend"; and (Ps. 138:16): "Thy eyes did see my imperfect being." Therefore none is perfect in this life.

Objection 3: Further, the perfection of the Christian life, as stated [3754](A[1]), relates to charity, which comprises the love of God and of our neighbor. Now, neither as to the love of God can one have perfect charity in this life, since according to Gregory (Hom. xiv in Ezech.) "the furnace of love which begins to burn here, will burn more fiercely when we see Him Whom we love"; nor as to the love of our neighbor, since in this life we cannot love all our neighbors actually, even though we love them habitually; and habitual love is imperfect. Therefore it seems that no one can be perfect in this life.

On the contrary, The Divine law does not prescribe the impossible. Yet it prescribes perfection according to Mat. 5:48, "Be you . . . perfect, as also your heavenly Father is perfect." Therefore seemingly one can be perfect in this life.

I answer that, As stated above [3755](A[1]), the perfection of the Christian life consists in charity. Now perfection implies a certain universality because according to Phys. iii, 6, "the perfect is that which lacks nothing." Hence we may consider a threefold perfection. One is absolute, and answers to a totality not only on the part of the lover, but also on the part of the object loved, so that God be loved as much as He is lovable. Such perfection as this is not possible to any creature, but is competent to God alone, in Whom good is wholly and essentially.

Another perfection answers to an absolute totality on the part of the lover, so that the affective faculty always actually tends to God as much as it possibly can; and such perfection as this is not possible so long as we are on the way, but we shall have it in heaven.

The third perfection answers to a totality neither on the part of the object served, nor on the part of the lover as regards his always actually tending to God, but on the part of the lover as regards the removal of obstacles to the movement of love towards God, in which sense Augustine says (QQ. LXXXIII, qu. 36) that "carnal desire is the bane of charity; to have no carnal desires is the perfection of charity." Such perfection as this can be had in this life, and in two ways. First, by the removal from man's affections of all that is contrary to charity, such as mortal sin; and there can be no charity apart from this perfection, wherefore it is necessary for salvation. Secondly, by the removal from man's affections not only of whatever is contrary to charity, but also of whatever hinders the mind's affections from tending wholly to God. Charity is possible apart from this perfection, for instance in those who are beginners and in those who are proficient.

Reply to Objection 1: The Apostle is speaking there of heavenly perfection which is not possible to those who are on the way.

Reply to Objection 2: Those who are perfect in this life are said to "offend in many things" with regard to venial sins, which result from the weakness of the present life: and in this respect they have an "imperfect being" in comparison with the perfection of heaven.

Reply to Objection 3: As the conditions of the present life do not allow of a man always tending actually to God, so neither does it allow of his tending actually to each individual neighbor; but it suffices for him to tend to all in common and collectively, and to each individual habitually and according to the preparedness of his mind. Now in the love of our neighbor, as in the love of God we may observe a twofold perfection: one without which charity is impossible, and consisting in one's having in one's affections nothing that is contrary to the love of one's neighbor; and another without which it is possible to have charity. The latter perfection may be considered in three ways. First, as to the extent of love, through a man loving not only his friends and acquaintances but also strangers and even his enemies, for as Augustine says (Enchiridion lxxiii) this is a mark of the perfect children of God. Secondly, as to the intensity of love, which is shown by the things which man despises for his neighbor's sake, through his despising not only external goods for the sake of his neighbor, but also bodily hardships and even death, according to Jn. 15:13, "Greater love than this no man hath, that a man lay down his life for his friends." Thirdly, as to the effect of love, so that a man will surrender not only temporal but also spiritual goods and even himself, for his neighbor's sake, according to the words of the Apostle (2 Cor. 12:15), "But I most gladly will spend and be spent myself for your souls."

Whether, in this life, perfection consists in the observance of the commandments or of the counsels?

Objection 1: It would seem that, in this life, perfection consists in the observance not of the commandments but of the counsels. For our Lord said (Mat. 19:21): "If thou wilt be perfect, go sell all [Vulg.: 'what'] thou hast, and give to the poor . . . and come, follow Me." Now this is a counsel. Therefore perfection regards the counsels and not the precepts.

Objection 2: Further, all are bound to the observance of the commandments, since this is necessary for salvation. Therefore, if the perfection of the Christian life consists in observing the commandments, it follows that perfection is necessary for salvation, and that all are bound thereto; and this is evidently false.

Objection 3: Further, the perfection of the Christian life is gauged according to charity, as stated above [3756](A[1]). Now the perfection of charity, seemingly, does not consist in the observance of the commandments, since the perfection of charity is preceded both by its increase and by its beginning, as Augustine says (Super Canonic. Joan. Tract. ix). But the beginning of charity cannot precede the observance of the commandments, since according to Jn. 14:23, "If any one love Me, he will keep My word." Therefore the perfection of life regards not the commandments but the counsels.

On the contrary, It is written (Dt. 6:5): "Thou shalt love the Lord thy God with thy whole heart," and (Lev. 19:18): "Thou shalt love thy neighbor [Vulg.: 'friend'] as thyself"; and these are the commandments of which our Lord said (Mat. 22:40): "On these two commandments dependeth the whole law and the prophets." Now the perfection of charity, in respect of which the Christian life is said to be perfect, consists in our loving God with our whole heart, and our neighbor as ourselves. Therefore it would seem that perfection consists in the observance of the precepts.

I answer that, Perfection is said to consist in a thing in two ways: in one way, primarily and essentially; in another, secondarily and accidentally. Primarily and essentially the perfection of the Christian life consists in charity, principally as to the love of God, secondarily as to the love of our neighbor, both of which are the matter of the chief commandments of the Divine law, as stated above. Now the love of God and of our neighbor is not commanded according to a measure, so that what is in excess of the measure be a matter of counsel. This is evident from the very form of the commandment, pointing, as it does, to perfection---for instance in the words, "Thou shalt love the Lord thy God with thy whole heart": since "the whole" is the same as "the perfect," according to the Philosopher (Phys. iii, 6), and in the words, "Thou shalt love thy neighbor as thyself," since every one loves himself most. The reason of this is that "the end of the commandment is charity," according to the Apostle (1 Tim. 1:5); and the end is not subject to a measure, but only such things as are directed to the end, as the Philosopher observes (Polit. i, 3); thus a physician does not measure the amount of his healing, but how much medicine or diet he shall employ for the purpose of healing. Consequently it is evident that perfection consists essentially in the observance of the commandments; wherefore Augustine says (De Perf. Justit. viii): "Why then should not this perfection be prescribed to man, although no man has it in this life?"

Secondarily and instrumentally, however, perfection consists in the observance of the counsels, all of which, like the commandments, are directed to charity; yet not in the same way. For the commandments, other than the precepts of charity, are directed to the removal of things contrary to charity, with which, namely, charity is incompatible, whereas the counsels are directed to the removal of things that hinder the act of charity, and yet are not contrary to charity, such as marriage, the occupation of worldly business, and so forth. Hence Augustine says (Enchiridion cxxi): "Whatever things God commands, for instance, 'Thou shalt not commit adultery,' and whatever are not commanded, yet suggested by a special counsel, for instance, 'It is good for a man not to touch a woman,' are then done aright when they are referred to the love of God, and of our neighbor for God's sake, both in this world and in the world to come." Hence it is that in the Conferences of the Fathers (Coll. i, cap. vii) the abbot Moses says: "Fastings, watchings, meditating on the Scriptures, penury and loss of all one's wealth, these are not perfection but means to perfection, since not in them does the school of perfection find its end, but through them it achieves its end," and he had already said that "we endeavor to ascend by these steps to the perfection of charity."

Reply to Objection 1: In this saying of our Lord something is indicated as being the way to perfection by the words, "Go, sell all thou hast, and give to the poor"; and something else is added wherein perfection consists, when He said, "And follow Me." Hence Jerome in his commentary on Mat. 19:27, says that "since it is not enough merely to leave, Peter added that which is perfect: 'And have followed Thee'"; and Ambrose, commenting on Lk. 5:27, "Follow Me," says: "He commands him to follow, not with steps of the body, but with devotion of the soul, which is the effect of charity." Wherefore it is evident from the very way of speaking that the counsels are means of attaining to perfection, since it is thus expressed: "If thou wilt be perfect, go, sell," etc., as though He said: "By so doing thou shalt accomplish this end."

Reply to Objection 2: As Augustine says (De Perf. Justit. viii) "the perfection of charity is prescribed to man in this life, because one runs not right unless one knows whither to run. And how shall we know this if no commandment declares it to us?" And since that which is a matter of precept can be fulfilled variously, one does not break a commandment through not fulfilling it in the best way, but it is enough to fulfil it in any way whatever. Now the perfection of Divine love is a matter of precept for all without exception, so that even the perfection of heaven is not excepted from this precept, as Augustine says (De Perf. Justit. viii [*Cf. De Spir. et Lit. XXXVI]), and one escapes transgressing the precept, in whatever measure one attains to the perfection of Divine love. The lowest degree of Divine love is to love nothing more than God, or contrary to God, or equally with God, and whoever fails from this degree of perfection nowise fulfils the precept. There is another degree of the Divine love, which cannot be fulfilled so long as we are on the way, as stated above [3757](A[2]), and it is evident that to fail from this is not to be a transgressor of the precept; and in like manner one does not transgress the precept, if one does not attain to the intermediate degrees of perfection, provided one attain to the lowest.

Reply to Objection 3: Just as man has a certain perfection of his nature as soon as he is born, which perfection belongs to the very essence of his species, while there is another perfection which he acquires by growth, so again there is a perfection of charity which belongs to the very essence of charity, namely that man love God above all things, and love nothing contrary to God, while there is another perfection of charity even in this life, whereto a man attains by a kind of spiritual growth, for instance when a man refrains even from lawful things, in order more freely to give himself to the service of God.

Whether whoever is perfect is in the state of perfection?

Objection 1: It would seem that whoever is perfect is in the state of perfection. For, as stated above (A[3], ad 3), just as bodily perfection is reached by bodily growth, so spiritual perfection is acquired by spiritual growth. Now after bodily growth one is said to have reached the state of perfect age. Therefore seemingly also after spiritual growth, when one has already reached spiritual perfection, one is in the state of perfection.

Objection 2: Further, according to Phys. v, 2, movement "from one contrary to another" has the same aspect as "movement from less to more." Now when a man is changed from sin to grace, he is said to change his state, in so far as the state of sin differs from the state of grace. Therefore it would seem that in the same manner, when one progresses from a lesser to a greater grace, so as to reach the perfect degree, one is in the state of perfection.

Objection 3: Further, a man acquires a state by being freed from servitude. But one is freed from the servitude of sin by charity, because "charity covereth all sins" (Prov. 10:12). Now one is said to be perfect on account of charity, as stated above [3758](A[1]). Therefore, seemingly, whoever has perfection, for this very reason has the state of perfection.

On the contrary, Some are in the state of perfection, who are wholly lacking in charity and grace, for instance wicked bishops or religious. Therefore it would seem that on the other hand some have the perfection of life, who nevertheless have not the state of perfection.

I answer that, As stated above ([3759]Q[183], A[1]), state properly regards a condition of freedom or servitude. Now spiritual freedom or servitude may be considered in man in two ways: first, with respect to his internal actions; secondly, with respect to his external actions. And since according to 1 Kings 16:7, "man seeth those things that appear, but the Lord beholdeth the heart," it follows that with regard to man's internal disposition we consider his spiritual state in relation to the Divine judgment, while with regard to his external actions we consider man's spiritual state in relation to the Church. It is in this latter sense that we are now speaking of states, namely in so far as the Church derives a certain beauty from the variety of states [*Cf.[3760] Q[183], A[2]].

Now it must be observed, that so far as men are concerned, in order that any one attain to a state of freedom or servitude there is required first of all an obligation or a release. For the mere fact of serving someone does not make a man a slave, since even the free serve, according to Gal. 5:13, "By charity of the spirit serve one another": nor again does the mere fact of ceasing to serve make a man free, as in the case of a runaway slave; but properly speaking a man is a slave if he be bound to serve, and a man is free if he be released from service. Secondly, it is required that the aforesaid obligation be imposed with a certain solemnity; even as a certain solemnity is observed in other matters which among men obtain a settlement in perpetuity.

Accordingly, properly speaking, one is said to be in the state of perfection, not through having the act of perfect love, but through binding himself in perpetuity and with a certain solemnity to those things that pertain to perfection. Moreover it happens that some persons bind themselves to that which they do not keep, and some fulfil that to which they have not bound themselves, as in the case of the two sons (Mat. 21:28, 30), one of whom when his father said: "Work in my vineyard," answered: "I will not," and "afterwards . . . he went," while the other "answering said: I go . . . and he went not." Wherefore nothing hinders some from being perfect without being in the state of perfection, and some in the state of perfection without being perfect.

Reply to Objection 1: By bodily growth a man progresses in things pertaining to nature, wherefore he attains to the state of nature; especially since "what is according to nature is," in a way, "unchangeable" [*Ethic. v, 7], inasmuch as nature is determinate to one thing. In like manner by inward spiritual growth a man reaches the state of perfection in relation to the Divine judgment. But as regards the distinctions of ecclesiastical states, a man does not reach the state of perfection except by growth in respect of external actions.

Reply to Objection 2: This argument also regards the interior state. Yet when a man passes from sin to grace, he passes from servitude to freedom; and this does not result from a mere progress in grace, except when a man binds himself to things pertaining to grace.

Reply to Objection 3: Again this argument considers the interior state. Nevertheless, although charity causes the change of condition from spiritual servitude to spiritual freedom, an increase of charity has not the same effect.

Whether religious and prelates are in the state of perfection?

Objection 1: It would seem that prelates and religious are not in the state of perfection. For the state of perfection differs from the state of the beginners and the proficient. Now no class of men is specially assigned to the state of the proficient or of the beginners. Therefore it would seem that neither should any class of men be assigned to the state of perfection.

Objection 2: Further, the outward state should answer to the inward, else one is guilty of lying, "which consists not only in false words, but also in deceitful deeds," according to Ambrose in one of his sermons (xxx de Tempore). Now there are many prelates and religious who have not the inward perfection of charity. Therefore, if all religious and prelates are in the state of perfection, it would follow that all of them that are not perfect are in mortal sin, as deceivers and liars.

Objection 3: Further, as stated above [3761](A[1]), perfection is measured according to charity. Now the most perfect charity would seem to be in the martyrs, according to Jn. 15:13, "Greater love than this no man hath, that a man lay down his life for his friends": and a gloss on Heb. 12:4, "For you have not yet resisted unto blood," says: "In this life no love is more perfect than that to which the holy martyrs attained, who strove against sin even unto blood." Therefore it would seem that the state of perfection should be ascribed to the martyrs rather than to religious and bishops.

On the contrary, Dionysius (Eccl. Hier. v) ascribes perfection to bishops as being perfecters, and (Eccl. Hier. vi) to religious (whom he calls monks or {therapeutai}, i.e. servants of God) as being perfected.

I answer that, As stated above [3762](A[4]), there is required for the state of perfection a perpetual obligation to things pertaining to perfection, together with a certain solemnity. Now both these conditions are competent to religious and bishops. For religious bind themselves by vow to refrain from worldly affairs, which they might lawfully use, in order more freely to give themselves to God, wherein consists the perfection of the present life. Hence Dionysius says (Eccl. Hier. vi), speaking of religious: "Some call them {therapeutai}," i.e. servants, "on account of their rendering pure service and homage to God; others call them {monachoi}" [*i.e. solitaries; whence the English word 'monk'], "on account of the indivisible and single-minded life which by their being wrapped in," i.e. contemplating, "indivisible things, unites them in a Godlike union and a perfection beloved of God" [*Cf. Q[180], A[6]]. Moreover, the obligation in both cases is undertaken with a certain solemnity of profession and consecration; wherefore Dionysius adds (Eccl. Hier. vi): "Hence the holy legislation in bestowing perfect grace on them accords them a hallowing invocation."

In like manner bishops bind themselves to things pertaining to perfection when they take up the pastoral duty, to which it belongs that a shepherd "lay down his life for his sheep," according to Jn. 10:15. Wherefore the Apostle says (1 Tim. 6:12): "Thou . . . hast confessed a good confession before many witnesses," that is to say, "when he was ordained," as a gloss says on this passage. Again, a certain solemnity of consecration is employed together with the aforesaid profession, according to 2 Tim. 1:6: "Stir up the grace of God which is in thee by the imposition of my hands," which the gloss ascribes to the grace of the episcopate. And Dionysius says (Eccl. Hier. v) that "when the high priest," i.e. the bishop, "is ordained, he receives on his head the most holy imposition of the sacred oracles, whereby it is signified that he is a participator in the whole and entire hierarchical power, and that not only is he the enlightener in all things pertaining to his holy discourses and actions, but that he also confers this on others."

Reply to Objection 1: Beginning and increase are sought not for their own sake, but for the sake of perfection; hence it is only to the state of perfection that some are admitted under certain obligations and with solemnity.

Reply to Objection 2: Those who enter the state of perfection do not profess to be perfect, but to tend to perfection. Hence the Apostle says (Phil. 3:12): "Not as though I had already attained, or were already perfect; but I follow after, if I may by any means apprehend": and afterwards (Phil. 3:15): "Let us therefore as many as are perfect, be thus minded." Hence a man who takes up the state of perfection is not guilty of lying or deceit through not being perfect, but through withdrawing his mind from the intention of reaching perfection.

Reply to Objection 3: Martyrdom is the most perfect act of charity. But an act of perfection does not suffice to make the state of perfection, as stated above [3763](A[4]).

Whether all ecclesiastical prelates are in the state of perfection?

Objection 1: It would seem that all ecclesiastical prelates are in a state of perfection. For Jerome commenting on Titus 1:5, "Ordain . . . in every city," etc. says: "Formerly priest was the same as bishop," and afterwards he adds: "Just as priests know that by the custom of the Church they are subject to the one who is placed over them, so too, bishops should recognize that, by custom rather than by the very ordinance of our Lord, they are above the priests, and are together the rightful governors of the Church." Now bishops are in the state of perfection. Therefore those priests also are who have the cure of souls.

Objection 2: Further, just as bishops together with their consecration receive the cure of souls, so also do parish priests and archdeacons, of whom a gloss on Acts 6:3, "Brethren, look ye out . . . seven men of good reputation," says: "The apostles decided here to appoint throughout the Church seven deacons, who were to be of a higher degree, and as it were the supports of that which is nearest to the altar." Therefore it would seem that these also are in the state of perfection.

Objection 3: Further, just as bishops are bound to "lay down their life for their sheep," so too are parish priests and archdeacons. But this belongs to the perfection of charity, as stated above (A[2], ad 3). Therefore it would seem that parish priests and archdeacons also are in the state of perfection.

On the contrary, Dionysius says (Eccl. Hier. v): "The order of pontiffs is consummative and perfecting, that of the priests is illuminative and light-giving, that of the ministers is cleansing and discretive." Hence it is evident that perfection is ascribed to bishops only.

I answer that, In priests and deacons having cure of souls two things may be considered, namely their order and their cure. Their order is directed to some act in the Divine offices. Wherefore it has been stated above ([3764]Q[183], A[3], ad 3) that the distinction of orders is comprised under the distinction of offices. Hence by receiving a certain order a man receives the power of exercising certain sacred acts, but he is not bound on this account to things pertaining to perfection, except in so far as in the Western Church the receiving of a sacred order includes the taking of a vow of continence, which is one of the things pertaining to perfection, as we shall state further on ([3765]Q[186], A[4]). Therefore it is clear that from the fact that a man receives a sacred order a man is not placed simply in the state of perfection, although inward perfection is required in order that one exercise such acts worthily.

In like manner, neither are they placed in the state of perfection on the part of the cure which they take upon themselves. For they are not bound by this very fact under the obligation of a perpetual vow to retain the cure of souls; but they can surrender it---either by entering religion, even without their bishop's permission (cf. Decret. xix, qu. 2, can. Duae sunt)---or again an archdeacon may with his bishop's permission resign his arch-deaconry or parish, and accept a simple prebend without cure, which would be nowise lawful, if he were in the state of perfection; for "no man putting his hand to the plough and looking back is fit for the kingdom of God" (Lk. 9:62). On the other hand bishops, since they are in the state of perfection, cannot abandon the episcopal cure, save by the authority of the Sovereign Pontiff (to whom alone it belongs also to dispense from perpetual vows), and this for certain causes, as we shall state further on ([3766]Q[185], A[4]). Wherefore it is manifest that not all prelates are in the state of perfection, but only bishops.

Reply to Objection 1: We may speak of priest and bishop in two ways. First, with regard to the name: and thus formerly bishops and priests were not distinct. For bishops are so called "because they watch over others," as Augustine observes (De Civ. Dei xix, 19); while the priests according to the Greek are "elders." [*Referring to the Greek {episkopos} and {presbyteros} from which the English 'bishop' and 'priest' are derived.] Hence the Apostle employs the term "priests" in reference to both, when he says (1 Tim. 5:17): "Let the priests that rule well be esteemed worthy of double honor"; and again he uses the term "bishops" in the same way, wherefore addressing the priests of the Church of Ephesus he says (Acts 20:28): "Take heed to yourselves" and "to the whole flock, wherein the Holy Ghost hath placed you bishops, to rule the church of God."

But as regards the thing signified by these terms, there was always a difference between them, even at the time of the apostles. This is clear on the authority of Dionysius (Eccl. Hier. v), and of a gloss on Lk. 10:1, "After these things the Lord appointed," etc. which says: "Just as the apostles were made bishops, so the seventy-two disciples were made priests of the second order." Subsequently, however, in order to avoid schism, it became necessary to distinguish even the terms, by calling the higher ones bishops and the lower ones priests. But to assert that priests nowise differ from bishops is reckoned by Augustine among heretical doctrines (De Heres. liii), where he says that the Arians maintained that "no distinction existed between a priest and a bishop."

Reply to Objection 2: Bishops have the chief cure of the sheep of their diocese, while parish priests and archdeacons exercise an inferior ministry under the bishops. Hence a gloss on 1 Cor. 12:28, "to one, helps, to another, governments [*Vulg.: 'God hath set some in the church . . . helps, governments,' etc.]," says: "Helps, namely assistants to those who are in authority," as Titus was to the Apostle, or as archdeacons to the bishop; "governments, namely persons of lesser authority, such as priests who have to instruct the people": and Dionysius says (Eccl. Hier. v) that "just as we see the whole hierarchy culminating in Jesus, so each office culminates in its respective godlike hierarch or bishop." Also it is said (XVI, qu. i, can. Cunctis): "Priests and deacons must all take care not to do anything without their bishop's permission." Wherefore it is evident that they stand in relation to their bishop as wardens or mayors to the king; and for this reason, just as in earthly governments the king alone receives a solemn blessing, while others are appointed by simple commission, so too in the Church the episcopal cure is conferred with the solemnity of consecration, while the archdeacon or parish priest receives his cure by simple appointment; although they are consecrated by receiving orders before having a cure.

Reply to Objection 3: As parish priests and archdeacons have not the chief cure, but a certain ministry as committed to them by the bishop, so the pastoral office does not belong to them in chief, nor are they bound to lay down their life for the sheep, except in so far as they have a share in their cure. Hence we should say that they have an office pertaining to perfection rather than that they attain the state of perfection.

Whether the religious state is more perfect than that of prelates?

Objection 1: It would seem that the religious state is more perfect than that of prelates. For our Lord said (Mat. 19:21): "If thou wilt be perfect, go" and "sell" all [Vulg.: 'what'] "thou hast, and give to the poor"; and religious do this. But bishops are not bound to do so; for it is said (XII, qu. i, can. Episcopi de rebus): "Bishops, if they wish, may bequeath to their heirs their personal or acquired property, and whatever belongs to them personally." Therefore religious are in a more perfect state than bishops.

Objection 2: Further, perfection consists more especially in the love of God than in the love of our neighbor. Now the religious state is directly ordered to the love of God, wherefore it takes its name from "service and homage to God," as Dionysius says (Eccl. Hier. vi); [*Quoted above A[5]] whereas the bishop's state would seem to be ordered to the love of our neighbor, of whose cure he is the "warden," and from this he takes his name, as Augustine observes (De Civ. Dei. xix, 19). Therefore it would seem that the religious state is more perfect than that of bishops.

Objection 3: Further, the religious state is directed to the contemplative life, which is more excellent than the active life to which the episcopal state is directed. For Gregory says (Pastor. i, 7) that "Isaias wishing to be of profit to his neighbor by means of the active life desired the office of preaching, whereas Jeremias, who was fain to hold fast to the love of his Creator, exclaimed against being sent to preach." Therefore it would seem that the religious state is more perfect than the episcopal state.

On the contrary, It is not lawful for anyone to pass from a more excellent to a less excellent state; for this would be to look back [*Cf. Lk. 9:62]. Yet a man may pass from the religious to the episcopal state, for it is said (XVIII, qu. i, can. Statutum) that "the holy ordination makes a monk to be a bishop." Therefore the episcopal state is more perfect than the religious.

I answer that, As Augustine says (Gen. ad lit. xii, 16), "the agent is ever more excellent than the patient." Now in the genus of perfection according to Dionysius (Eccl. Hier. v, vi), bishops are in the position of "perfecters," whereas religious are in the position of being "perfected"; the former of which pertains to action, and the latter to passion. Whence it is evident that the state of perfection is more excellent in bishops than in religious.

Reply to Objection 1: Renunciation of one's possessions may be considered in two ways. First, as being actual: and thus it is not essential, but a means, to perfection, as stated above [3767](A[3]). Hence nothing hinders the state of perfection from being without renunciation of one's possessions, and the same applies to other outward practices. Secondly, it may be considered in relation to one's preparedness, in the sense of being prepared to renounce or give away all: and this belongs directly to perfection. Hence Augustine says (De QQ. Evang. ii, qu. 11): "Our Lord shows that the children of wisdom understand righteousness to consist neither in eating nor in abstaining, but in bearing want patiently." Wherefore the Apostle says (Phil. 4:12): "I know . . . both to abound and to suffer need." Now bishops especially are bound to despise all things for the honor of God and the spiritual welfare of their flock, when it is necessary for them to do so, either by giving to the poor of their flock, or by suffering "with joy the being stripped of" their "own goods" [*Heb. 10:34].

Reply to Objection 2: That bishops are busy about things pertaining to the love of their neighbor, arises out of the abundance of their love of God. Hence our Lord asked Peter first of all whether he loved Him, and afterwards committed the care of His flock to him. And Gregory says (Pastor. i, 5): "If the pastoral care is a proof of love, he who refuses to feed God's flock, though having the means to do so, is convicted of not loving the supreme Pastor." And it is a sign of greater love if a man devotes himself to others for his friend's sake, than if he be willing only to serve his friend.

Reply to Objection 3: As Gregory says (Pastor. ii, 1), "a prelate should be foremost in action, and more uplifted than others in contemplation," because it is incumbent on him to contemplate, not only for his own sake, but also for the purpose of instructing others. Hence Gregory applies (Hom. v in Ezech.) the words of Ps. 144:7, "They shall publish the memory . . . of Thy sweetness," to perfect men returning after their contemplation.

Whether parish priests and archdeacons are more perfect than religious?

Objection 1: It would seem that also parish priests and archdeacons are more perfect than religious. For Chrysostom says in his Dialogue (De Sacerdot. vi): "Take for example a monk, such as Elias, if I may exaggerate somewhat, he is not to be compared with one who, cast among the people and compelled to carry the sins of many, remains firm and strong." A little further on he says: "If I were given the choice, where would I prefer to please, in the priestly office, or in the monastic solitude, without hesitation I should choose the former." Again in the same book (ch. 5) he says: "If you compare the toils of this project, namely of the monastic life, with a well-employed priesthood, you will find them as far distant from one another as a common citizen is from a king." Therefore it would seem that priests who have the cure of souls are more perfect than religious.

Objection 2: Further, Augustine says (ad Valerium, Ep. xxi): "Let thy religious prudence observe that in this life, and especially at these times, there is nothing so difficult, so onerous, so perilous as the office of bishop, priest, or deacon; while in God's sight there is no greater blessing, if one engage in the fight as ordered by our Commander-in-chief." Therefore religious are not more perfect than priests or deacons.

Objection 3: Further, Augustine says (Ep. lx, ad Aurel.): "It would be most regrettable, were we to exalt monks to such a disastrous degree of pride, and deem the clergy deserving of such a grievous insult," as to assert that 'a bad monk is a good clerk,' "since sometimes even a good monk makes a bad clerk." And a little before this he says that "God's servants," i.e. monks, "must not be allowed to think that they may easily be chosen for something better," namely the clerical state, "if they should become worse thereby," namely by leaving the monastic state. Therefore it would seem that those who are in the clerical state are more perfect than religious.

Objection 4: Further, it is not lawful to pass from a more perfect to a less perfect state. Yet it is lawful to pass from the monastic state to a priestly office with a cure attached, as appears (XVI, qu. i, can. Si quis monachus) from a decree of Pope Gelasius, who says: "If there be a monk, who by the merit of his exemplary life is worthy of the priesthood, and the abbot under whose authority he fights for Christ his King, ask that he be made a priest, the bishop shall take him and ordain him in such place as he shall choose fitting."

And Jerome says (Ad Rustic. Monach., Ep. cxxv): "In the monastery so live as to deserve to be a clerk." Therefore parish priests and archdeacons are more perfect than religious.

Objection 5: Further, bishops are in a more perfect state than religious, as shown above [3768](A[7]). But parish priests and archdeacons. through having cure of souls, are more like bishops than religious are. Therefore they are more perfect.

Objection 6: Further, virtue "is concerned with the difficult and the good" (Ethic. ii, 3). Now it is more difficult to lead a good life in the office of parish priest or archdeacon than in the religious state. Therefore parish priests and archdeacons have more perfect virtue than religious.

On the contrary, It is stated (XIX, qu. ii, cap. Duce): "If a man while governing the people in his church under the bishop and leading a secular life is inspired by the Holy Ghost to desire to work out his salvation in a monastery or under some canonical rule, since he is led by a private law, there is no reason why he should be constrained by a public law." Now a man is not led by the law of the Holy Ghost, which is here called a "private law," except to something more perfect. Therefore it would seem that religious are more perfect than archdeacons or parish priests.

I answer that, When we compare things in the point of super-eminence, we look not at that in which they agree, but at that wherein they differ. Now in parish priests and archdeacons three things may be considered, their state, their order, and their office. It belongs to their state that they are seculars, to their order that they are priests or deacons, to their office that they have the cure of souls committed to them.

Accordingly, if we compare these with one who is a religious by state, a deacon or priest by order, having the cure of souls by office, as many monks and canons regular have, this one will excel in the first point, and in the other points he will be equal. But if the latter differ from the former in state and office, but agree in order, such as religious priests and deacons not having the cure of souls, it is evident that the latter will be more excellent than the former in state, less excellent in office, and equal in order.

We must therefore consider which is the greater, preeminence of state or of office; and here, seemingly, we should take note of two things, goodness and difficulty. Accordingly, if we make the comparison with a view to goodness, the religious state surpasses the office of parish priest or archdeacon, because a religious pledges his whole life to the quest of perfection, whereas the parish priest or archdeacon does not pledge his whole life to the cure of souls, as a bishop does, nor is it competent to him, as it is to a bishop, to exercise the cure of souls in chief, but only in certain particulars regarding the cure of souls committed to his charge, as stated above (A[6], ad 2). Wherefore the comparison of their religious state with their office is like the comparisons of the universal with the particular, and of a holocaust with a sacrifice which is less than a holocaust according to Gregory (Hom. xx in Ezech.). Hence it is said (XIX, qu. i, can. Clerici qui monachorum.): "Clerics who wish to take the monastic vows through being desirous of a better life must be allowed by their bishops the free entrance into the monastery."

This comparison, however, must be considered as regarding the genus of the deed; for as regards the charity of the doer it happens sometimes that a deed which is of less account in its genus is of greater merit if it be done out of greater charity.

On the other hand, if we consider the difficulty of leading a good life in religion, and in the office of one having the cure of souls, in this way it is more difficult to lead a good life together with the exercise of the cure of souls, on account of outward dangers: although the religious life is more difficult as regards the genus of the deed, by reason of the strictness of religious observance. If, however, the religious is also without orders, as in the case of religious lay brethren, then it is evident that the pre-eminence of order excels in the point of dignity, since by holy orders a man is appointed to the most august ministry of serving Christ Himself in the sacrament of the altar. For this requires a greater inward holiness than that which is requisite for the religious state, since as Dionysius says (Eccl. Hier. vi) the monastic order must follow the priestly orders, and ascend to Divine things in imitation of them. Hence, other things being equal, a cleric who is in holy orders, sins more grievously if he do something contrary to holiness than a religious who is not in holy orders: although a religious who is not in orders is bound to regular observance to which persons in holy orders are not bound.

Reply to Objection 1: We might answer briefly these quotations from Chrysostom by saying that he speaks not of a priest of lesser order who has the cure of souls, but of a bishop, who is called a high-priest; and this agrees with the purpose of that book wherein he consoles himself and Basil in that they were chosen to be bishops. We may, however, pass this over and reply that he speaks in view of the difficulty. For he had already said: "When the pilot is surrounded by the stormy sea and is able to bring the ship safely out of the tempest, then he deserves to be acknowledged by all as a perfect pilot"; and afterwards he concludes, as quoted, with regard to the monk, "who is not to be compared with one who, cast among the people . . . remains firm"; and he gives the reason why, because "both in the calm end in the storm he piloted himself to safety." This proves nothing more than that the state of one who has the cure of souls is fraught with more danger than the monastic state; and to keep oneself innocent in face of a greater peril is proof of greater virtue. on the other hand, it also indicates greatness of virtue if a man avoid dangers by entering religion; hence he does not say that "he would prefer the priestly office to the monastic solitude," but that "he would rather please" in the former than in the latter, since this is a proof of greater virtue.

Reply to Objection 2: This passage quoted from Augustine also clearly refers to the question of difficulty which proves the greatness of virtue in those who lead a good life, as stated above (ad 1).

Reply to Objection 3: Augustine there compares monks with clerics as regards the pre-eminence of order, not as regards the distinction between religious and secular life.

Reply to Objection 4: Those who are taken from the religious state to receive the cure of souls, being already in sacred orders, attain to something they had not hitherto, namely the office of the cure, yet they do not put aside what they had already. For it is said in the Decretals (XVI, qu. i, can. De Monachis): "With regard to those monks who after long residence in a monastery attain to the order of clerics, we bid them not to lay aside their former purpose."

On the other hand, parish priests and archdeacons, when they enter religion, resign their cure, in order to enter the state of perfection. This very fact shows the excellence of the religious life. When religious who are not in orders are admitted to the clerical state and to the sacred orders, they are clearly promoted to something better, as stated: this is indicated by the very way in which Jerome expresses himself: "So live in the monastery as to deserve to be a clerk."

Reply to Objection 5: Parish priests and archdeacons are more like bishops than religious are, in a certain respect, namely as regards the cure of souls which they have subordinately; but as regards the obligation in perpetuity, religious are more like a bishop, as appears from what we have said above ([3769]AA[5],6).

Reply to Objection 6: The difficulty that arises from the arduousness of the deed adds to the perfection of virtue; but the difficulty that results from outward obstacles sometimes lessens the perfection of virtue---for instance, when a man loves not virtue so much as to wish to avoid the obstacles to virtue, according to the saying of the Apostle (1 Cor. 9:25), "Everyone that striveth for the mastery refraineth himself from all things": and sometimes it is a sign of perfect virtue---for instance, when a man forsakes not virtue, although he is hindered in the practice of virtue unawares or by some unavoidable cause. In the religious state there is greater difficulty arising from the arduousness of deeds; whereas for those who in any way at all live in the world, there is greater difficulty resulting from obstacles to virtue, which obstacles the religious has had the foresight to avoid.

OF THINGS PERTAINING TO THE EPISCOPAL STATE (EIGHT ARTICLES)
We must now consider things pertaining to the episcopal state. Under this head there are eight points of inquiry:
(1) Whether it is lawful to desire the office of a bishop?
(2) Whether it is lawful to refuse the office of bishop definitively?
(3) Whether the better man should be chosen for the episcopal office?
(4) Whether a bishop may pass over to the religious state?
(5) Whether he may lawfully abandon his subjects in a bodily manner?
(6) Whether he can have anything of his own?
(7) Whether he sins mortally by not distributing ecclesiastical goods to the poor?
(8) Whether religious who are appointed to the episcopal office are bound to religious observances?

Whether it is lawful to desire the office of a bishop?
Objection 1: It would seem that it is lawful to desire the office of a bishop. For the Apostle says (1 Tim. 3:1): "He that desires [Vulg.: 'If a man desire'] the office of a bishop, he desireth a good work." Now it is lawful and praiseworthy to desire a good work. Therefore it is even praiseworthy to desire the office of a bishop.

Objection 2: Further, the episcopal state is more perfect than the religious, as we have said above ([3770]Q[184], A[7]). But it is praiseworthy to desire to enter the religious state. Therefore it is also praiseworthy to desire promotion to the episcopal state.

Objection 3: Further, it is written (Prov. 11:26): "He that hideth up corn shall be cursed among the people; but a blessing upon the head of them that sell." Now a man who is apt, both in manner of life and by knowledge, for the episcopal office, would seem to hide up the spiritual corn, if he shun the episcopal state, whereas by accepting the episcopal office he enters the state of a dispenser of spiritual corn. Therefore it would seem praiseworthy to desire the office of a bishop, and blameworthy to refuse it.

Objection 4: Further, the deeds of the saints related in Holy Writ are set before us as an example, according to Rom. 15:4, "What things soever were written, were written for our learning." Now we read (Is. 6:8) that Isaias offered himself for the office of preacher, which belongs chiefly to bishops. Therefore it would seem praiseworthy to desire the office of a bishop.

On the contrary, Augustine says (De Civ. Dei xix, 19): "The higher place, without which the people cannot be ruled, though it be filled becomingly, is unbecomingly desired."

I answer that, Three things may be considered in the episcopal office. One is principal and final, namely the bishop's work, whereby the good of our neighbor is intended, according to Jn. 21:17, "Feed My sheep." Another thing is the height of degree, for a bishop is placed above others, according to Mat. 24:45, "A faithful and a wise servant, whom his lord hath appointed over his family." The third is something resulting from these, namely reverence, honor, and a sufficiency of temporalities, according to 1 Tim. 5:17, "Let the priests that rule well be esteemed worthy of double honor." Accordingly, to desire the episcopal office on account of these incidental goods is manifestly unlawful, and pertains to covetousness or ambition. Wherefore our Lord said against the Pharisees (Mat. 23:6,7): "They love the first places at feasts, and the first chairs in the synagogues, and salutations in the market-place, and to be called by men, Rabbi." As regards the second, namely the height of degree, it is presumptuous to desire the episcopal office. Hence our Lord reproved His disciples for seeking precedence, by saying to them (Mat. 20:25): "You know that the princes of the gentiles lord it over them." Here Chrysostom says (Hom. lxv in Matth.) that in these words "He points out that it is heathenish to seek precedence; and thus by comparing them to the gentiles He converted their impetuous soul."

On the other hand, to desire to do good to one's neighbor is in itself praiseworthy, and virtuous. Nevertheless, since considered as an episcopal act it has the height of degree attached to it, it would seem that, unless there be manifest and urgent reason for it, it would be presumptuous for any man to desire to be set over others in order to do them good. Thus Gregory says (Pastor. i, 8) that "it was praiseworthy to seek the office of a bishop when it was certain to bring one into graver dangers." Wherefore it was not easy to find a person to accept this burden, especially seeing that it is through the zeal of charity that one divinely instigated to do so, according to Gregory, who says (Pastor. i, 7) that "Isaias being desirous of profiting his neighbor, commendably desired the office of preacher."

Nevertheless, anyone may, without presumption, desire to do such like works if he should happen to be in that office, or to be worthy of doing them; so that the object of his desire is the good work and not the precedence in dignity. Hence Chrysostom* says: "It is indeed good to desire a good work, but to desire the primacy of honor is vanity. For primacy seeks one that shuns it, and abhors one that desires it." [*The quotation is from the Opus Imperfectum in Matth. (Hom. xxxv), falsely ascribed to St. John Chrysostom.]

184

Reply to Objection 1: As Gregory says (Pastor. i, 8), "when the Apostle said this he who was set over the people was the first to be dragged to the torments of martyrdom," so that there was nothing to be desired in the episcopal office, save the good work. Wherefore Augustine says (De Civ. Dei xix, 19) that when the Apostle said, "'Whoever desireth the office of bishop, desireth a good work,' he wished to explain what the episcopacy is: for it denotes work and not honor: since {skopos} signifies 'watching.' Wherefore if we like we may render {episkopein} by the Latin 'superintendere' [to watch over]: thus a man may know himself to be no bishop if he loves to precede rather than to profit others." For, as he observed shortly before, "in our actions we should seek, not honor nor power in this life, since all things beneath the sun are vanity, but the work itself which that honor or power enables us to do." Nevertheless, as Gregory says (Pastor. i, 8), "while praising the desire" (namely of the good work) "he forthwith turns this object of praise into one of fear, when he adds: It behooveth . . . a bishop to be blameless," as though to say: "I praise what you seek, but learn first what it is you seek."

Reply to Objection 2: There is no parity between the religious and the episcopal state, for two reasons. First, because perfection of life is a prerequisite of the episcopal state, as appears from our Lord asking Peter if he loved Him more than the others, before committing the pastoral office to him, whereas perfection is not a prerequisite of the religious state, since the latter is the way to perfection. Hence our Lord did not say (Mat. 19:21): "If thou art perfect, go, sell all [Vulg.: 'what'] thou hast," but "If thou wilt be perfect." The reason for this difference is because, according to Dionysius (Eccl. Hier. vi), perfection pertains actively to the bishop, as the "perfecter," but to the monk passively as one who is "perfected": and one needs to be perfect in order to bring others to perfection, but not in order to be brought to perfection. Now it is presumptuous to think oneself perfect, but it is not presumptuous to tend to perfection. Secondly, because he who enters the religious state subjects himself to others for the sake of a spiritual profit, and anyone may lawfully do this. Wherefore Augustine says (De Civ. Dei xix, 19): "No man is debarred from striving for the knowledge of truth, since this pertains to a praiseworthy ease." On the other hand, he who enters the episcopal state is raised up in order to watch over others, and no man should seek to be raised thus, according to Heb. 5:4, "Neither doth any man take the honor to himself, but he that is called by God": and Chrysostom says: "To desire supremacy in the Church is neither just nor useful. For what wise man seeks of his own accord to submit to such servitude and peril, as to have to render an account of the whole Church? None save him who fears not God's judgment, and makes a secular abuse of his ecclesiastical authority, by turning it to secular uses."

Reply to Objection 3: The dispensing of spiritual corn is not to be carried on in an arbitrary fashion, but chiefly according to the appointment and disposition of God, and in the second place according to the appointment of the higher prelates, in whose person it is said (1 Cor. 4:1): "Let a man so account of us as of the ministers of Christ, and the dispensers of the mysteries of God." Wherefore a man is not deemed to hide spiritual corn if he avoids governing or correcting others, and is not competent to do so, neither in virtue of his office nor of his superior's command; thus alone is he deemed to hide it, when he neglects to dispense it while under obligation to do so in virtue of his office, or obstinately refuses to accept the office when it is imposed on him. Hence Augustine says (De Civ. Dei xix, 19): "The love of truth seeks a holy leisure, the demands of charity undertake an honest labor. If no one imposes this burden upon us, we must devote ourselves to the research and contemplation of truth, but if it be imposed on us, we must bear it because charity demands it of us."

Reply to Objection 4: As Gregory says (Pastor. i, 7), "Isaias, who wishing to be sent, knew himself to be already cleansed by the live coal taken from the altar, shows us that no one should dare uncleansed to approach the sacred ministry. Since, then, it is very difficult for anyone to be able to know that he is cleansed, it is safer to decline the office of preacher."

Whether it is lawful for a man to refuse absolutely an appointment to the episcopate?

Objection 1: It would seem that it is lawful to refuse absolutely an appointment to the episcopate. For as Gregory says (Pastor. i, 7), "Isaias wishing to be of profit to his neighbor by means of the active life, desired the office of preaching, whereas Jeremias who was fain to hold fast to the love of his Creator by contemplation exclaimed against being sent to preach." Now no man sins by being unwilling to forgo better things in order to adhere to things that are not so good. Since then the love of God surpasses the love of our neighbor, and the contemplative life is preferable to the active, as shown above ([3771]Q[25], A[1];[3772] Q[26], A[2];[3773] Q[182], A[1]) it would seem that a man sins not if he refuse absolutely the episcopal office.

Objection 2: Further, as Gregory says (Pastor. i, 7), "it is very difficult for anyone to be able to know that he is cleansed: nor should anyone uncleansed approach the sacred ministry." Therefore if a man perceives that he is not cleansed, however urgently the episcopal office be enjoined him, he ought not to accept it.

Objection 3: Further, Jerome (Prologue, super Marc.) says that "it is related of the Blessed Mark* that after receiving the faith he cut off his thumb that he might be excluded from the priesthood." [*This prologue was falsely ascribed to St. Jerome, and the passage quoted refers, not to St. Mark the Evangelist, but to a hermit of that name. (Cf. Baronius, Anno Christi, 45, num. XLIV)] Likewise some take a vow never to accept a bishopric. Now to place an obstacle to a thing amounts to the same as refusing it altogether. Therefore it would seem that one may, without sin, refuse the episcopal office absolutely.

On the contrary, Augustine says (Ep. xlviii ad Eudox.): "If Mother Church requires your service, neither accept with greedy conceit, nor refuse with fawning indolence"; and afterwards he adds: "Nor prefer your ease to the needs of the Church: for if no good men were willing to assist her in her labor, you would seek in vain how we could be born of her."

I answer that, Two things have to be considered in the acceptance of the episcopal office: first, what a man may fittingly desire according to his own will; secondly, what it behooves a man to do according to the will of another. As regards his own will it becomes a man to look chiefly to his own spiritual welfare, whereas that he look to the spiritual welfare of others becomes a man according to the appointment of another having authority, as stated above (A[1], ad 3). Hence just as it is a mark of an inordinate will that a man of his own choice incline to be appointed to the government of others, so too it indicates an inordinate will if a man definitively refuse the aforesaid office of government in direct opposition to the appointment of his superior: and this for two reasons.

First, because this is contrary to the love of our neighbor, for whose good a man should offer himself according as place and time demand: hence Augustine says (De Civ. Dei xix, 19) that "the demands of charity undertake an honest labor." Secondly, because this is contrary to humility, whereby a man submits to his superior's commands: hence Gregory says (Pastor. i, 6): "In God's sight humility is genuine when it does not obstinately refuse to submit to what is usefully prescribed."

Reply to Objection 1: Although simply and absolutely speaking the contemplative life is more excellent than the active, and the love of God better than the love of our neighbor, yet, on the other hand, the good of the many should be preferred to the good of the individual. Wherefore Augustine says in the passage quoted above: "Nor prefer your own ease to the needs of the Church," and all the more since it belongs to the love of God that a man undertake the pastoral care of Christ's sheep. Hence Augustine, commenting on Jn. 21:17, "Feed My sheep," says (Tract. cxxiii in Joan.): "Be it the task of love to feed the Lord's flock, even as it was the mark of fear to deny the Shepherd."

Moreover prelates are not transferred to the active life, so as to forsake the contemplative; wherefore Augustine says (De Civ. Dei xix, 19) that "if the burden of the pastoral office be imposed, we must not abandon the delights of truth," which are derived from contemplation.

Reply to Objection 2: No one is bound to obey his superior by doing what is unlawful, as appears from what was said above concerning obedience ([3774]Q[104], A[5]). Accordingly it may happen that he who is appointed to the office of prelate perceive something in himself on account of which it is unlawful for him to accept a prelacy. But this obstacle may sometimes be removed by the very person who is appointed to the pastoral cure---for instance, if he have a purpose to sin, he may abandon it---and for this reason he is not excused from being bound to obey definitely the superior who has appointed him. Sometimes, however, he is unable himself to remove the impediment that makes the pastoral office unlawful to him, yet the prelate who appoints him can do so---for instance, if he be irregular or excommunicate. In such a case he ought to make known his defect to the prelate who has appointed him; and if the latter be willing to remove the impediment, he is bound humbly to obey. Hence when Moses had said (Ex. 4:10): "I beseech thee, Lord, I am not eloquent from yesterday, and the day before," the Lord answered (Ex. 4:12): "I will be in thy mouth, and I will teach thee what thou shalt speak." At other times the impediment cannot be removed, neither by the person appointing nor by the one appointed---for instance, if an archbishop be unable to dispense from an irregularity; wherefore a subject, if irregular, would not be bound to obey him by accepting the episcopate or even sacred orders.

Reply to Objection 3: It is not in itself necessary for salvation to accept the episcopal office, but it becomes necessary by reason of the superior's command. Now one may lawfully place an obstacle to things thus necessary for salvation, before the command is given; else it would not be lawful to marry a second time, lest one should thus incur an impediment to the episcopate or holy orders. But this would not be lawful in things necessary for salvation. Hence the Blessed Mark did not act against a precept by cutting off his finger, although it is credible that he did this by the instigation of the Holy Ghost, without which it would be unlawful for anyone to lay hands on himself. If a man take a vow not to accept the bishop's office, and by this intend to bind himself not even to accept it in obedience to his superior prelate, his vow is unlawful; but if he intend to bind himself, so far as it lies with him, not to seek the episcopal office, nor to accept it except under urgent necessity, his vow is lawful, because he vows to do what it becomes a man to do.

Whether he that is appointed to the episcopate ought to be better than others?

Objection 1: It would seem that one who is appointed to the episcopate ought to be better than others. For our Lord, when about to commit the pastoral office to Peter, asked him if he loved Him more than the others. Now a man is the better through loving God the more. Therefore it would seem that one ought not to be appointed to the episcopal office except he be better than others.

Objection 2: Further, Pope Symmachus says (can. Vilissimus I, qu. 1): "A man is of very little worth who though excelling in dignity, excels not in knowledge and holiness." Now he who excels in knowledge and holiness is better. Therefore a man ought not to be appointed to the episcopate unless he be better than others.

Objection 3: Further, in every genus the lesser are governed by the greater, as corporeal things are governed by things spiritual, and the lower bodies by the higher, as Augustine says (De Trin. iii, 3). Now a bishop is appointed to govern others. Therefore he should be better than others.

On the contrary, The Decretal [*Can. Cum dilectus, de Electione] says that "it suffices to choose a good man, nor is it necessary to choose the better man."

I answer that, In designating a man for the episcopal office, something has to be considered on the part of the person designate, and something on the part of the designator. For on the part of the designator, whether by election or by appointment, it is required that he choose such a one as will dispense the divine mysteries faithfully. These should be dispensed for the good of the Church, according to 1 Cor. 14:12, "Seek to abound unto the edifying of the Church"; and the divine mysteries are not committed to men for their own meed, which they should await in the life to come. Consequently he who has to choose or appoint one for a bishop is not bound to take one who is best simply, i.e. according to charity, but one who is best for governing the Church, one namely who is able to instruct, defend, and govern the Church peacefully. Hence Jerome, commenting on Titus 1:5, says against certain persons that "some seek to erect as pillars of the Church, not those whom they know to be more useful to the Church, but those whom they love more, or those by whose obsequiousness they have been cajoled or undone, or for whom some person in authority has spoken, and, not to say worse than this, have succeeded by means of gifts in being made clerics."

Now this pertains to the respect of persons, which in such matters is a grave sin. Wherefore a gloss of Augustine [*Ep. clxvii ad Hieron.] on James 2:1, "Brethren, have not . . . with respect of persons," says: "If this distinction of sitting and standing be referred to ecclesiastical honors, we must not deem it a slight sin to 'have the faith of the Lord of glory with respect of persons.' For who would suffer a rich man to be chosen for the Church's seat of honor, in despite of a poor man who is better instructed and holier?"

On the part of the person appointed, it is not required that he esteem himself better than others, for this would be proud and presumptuous; but it suffices that he perceive nothing in himself which would make it unlawful for him to take up the office of prelate.

Hence although Peter was asked by our Lord if he loved Him more than the others, he did not, in his reply, set himself before the others, but answered simply that he loved Christ.

Reply to Objection 1: Our Lord knew that, by His own bestowal, Peter was in other respects fitted to govern the Church: wherefore He questioned him about his greater love, to show that when we find a man otherwise fitted for the government of the Church, we must look chiefly to his pre-eminence in the love of God.

Reply to Objection 2: This statement refers to the pursuits of the man who is placed in authority. For he should aim at showing himself to be more excellent than others in both knowledge and holiness. Wherefore Gregory says (Pastor. ii, 1) "the occupations of a prelate ought to excel those of the people, as much as the shepherd's life excels that of his flock." But he is not to be blamed and looked upon as worthless if he excelled not before being raised to the prelacy.

Reply to Objection 3: According to 1 Cor. 12:4 seqq., "there are diversities of graces . . . and . . . of ministries . . . and . . . of operations." Hence nothing hinders one from being more fitted for the office of governing, who does not excel in the grace of holiness. It is otherwise in the government of the natural order, where that which is higher in the natural order is for that very reason more fitted to dispose of those that are lower.

Whether a bishop may lawfully forsake the episcopal cure, in order to enter religion?

Objection 1: It seems that a bishop cannot lawfully forsake his episcopal cure in order to enter religion. For no one can lawfully pass from a more perfect to a less perfect state; since this is "to look back," which is condemned by the words of our Lord (Lk. 9:62), "No man putting his hand to the plough, and looking back, is fit for the kingdom of God." Now the episcopal state is more perfect than the religious, as shown above ([3775]Q[184], A[7]). Therefore just as it is unlawful to return to the world from the religious state, so is it unlawful to pass from the episcopal to the religious state.

Objection 2: Further, the order of grace is more congruous than the order of nature. Now according to nature a thing is not moved in contrary directions; thus if a stone be naturally moved downwards, it cannot naturally return upwards from below. But according to the order of grace it is lawful to pass from the religious to the episcopal state. Therefore it is not lawful to pass contrariwise from the episcopal to the religious state.

Objection 3: Further, in the works of grace nothing should be inoperative. Now when once a man is consecrated bishop he retains in perpetuity the spiritual power of giving orders and doing like things that pertain to the episcopal office: and this power would seemingly remain inoperative in one who gives up the episcopal cure. Therefore it would seem that a bishop may not forsake the episcopal cure and enter religion.

On the contrary, No man is compelled to do what is in itself unlawful. Now those who seek to resign their episcopal cure are compelled to resign (Extra, de Renunt. cap. Quidam). Therefore apparently it is not unlawful to give up the episcopal cure.

I answer that, The perfection of the episcopal state consists in this that for love of God a man binds himself to work for the salvation of his neighbor, wherefore he is bound to retain the pastoral cure so long as he is able to procure the spiritual welfare of the subjects entrusted to his care: a matter which he must not neglect---neither for the sake of the quiet of divine contemplation, since the Apostle, on account of the needs of his subjects, suffered patiently to be delayed even from the contemplation of the life to come, according to Phil. 1:22-25, "What I shall choose I know not, but I am straitened between two, having a desire to be dissolved, and to be with Christ, a thing by far better. But to abide still in the flesh is needful for you. And having this confidence, I know that I shall abide"; nor for the sake of avoiding any hardships or of acquiring any gain whatsoever, because as it is written (Jn. 10:11), "the good shepherd giveth his life for his sheep."

At times, however, it happens in several ways that a bishop is hindered from procuring the spiritual welfare of his subjects. Sometimes on account of his own defect, either of conscience (for instance if he be guilty of murder or simony), or of body (for example if he be old or infirm), or of irregularity arising, for instance, from bigamy. Sometimes he is hindered through some defect in his subjects, whom he is unable to profit. Hence Gregory says (Dial. ii, 3): "The wicked must be borne patiently, when there are some good who can be succored, but when there is no profit at all for the good, it is sometimes useless to labor for the wicked. Wherefore the perfect when they find that they labor in vain are often minded to go elsewhere in order to labor with fruit." Sometimes again this hindrance arises on the part of others, as when scandal results from a certain person being in authority: for the Apostle says (1 Cor. 8:13): "If meat scandalize my brother, I will never eat flesh": provided, however, the scandal is not caused by the wickedness of persons desirous of subverting the faith or the righteousness of the Church; because the pastoral cure is not to be laid aside on account of scandal of this kind, according to Mat. 15:14, "Let them alone," those namely who were scandalized at the truth of Christ's teaching, "they are blind, and leaders of the blind."

Nevertheless just as a man takes upon himself the charge of authority at the appointment of a higher superior, so too it behooves him to be subject to the latter's authority in laying aside the accepted charge for the reasons given above. Hence Innocent III says (Extra, de Renunt., cap. Nisi cum pridem): "Though thou hast wings wherewith thou art anxious to fly away into solitude, they are so tied by the bonds of authority, that thou art not free to fly without our permission." For the Pope alone can dispense from the perpetual vow, by which a man binds himself to the care of his subjects, when he took upon himself the episcopal office.

Reply to Objection 1: The perfection of religious and that of bishops are regarded from different standpoints. For it belongs to the perfection of a religious to occupy oneself in working out one's own salvation, whereas it belongs to the perfection of a bishop to occupy oneself in working for the salvation of others. Hence so long as a man can be useful to the salvation of his neighbor, he would be going back, if he wished to pass to the religious state, to busy himself only with his own salvation, since he has bound himself to work not only for his own but also for others' salvation. Wherefore Innocent III says in the Decretal quoted above that "it is more easily allowable for a monk to ascend to the episcopacy, than for a bishop to descend to the monastic life. If, however, he be unable to procure the salvation of others it is meet he should seek his own."

Reply to Objection 2: On account of no obstacle should a man forego the work of his own salvation, which pertains to the religious state. But there may be an obstacle to the procuring of another's salvation; wherefore a monk may be raised to the episcopal state wherein he is able also to work out his own salvation. And a bishop, if he be hindered from procuring the salvation of others, may enter the religious life, and may return to his bishopric should the obstacle cease, for instance by the correction of his subjects, cessation of the scandal, healing of his infirmity, removal of his ignorance by sufficient instruction. Again, if he owed his promotion to simony of which he was in ignorance, and resigning his episcopate entered the religious life, he can be reappointed to another bishopric [*Cap. Post translat., de Renunt.]. On the other hand, if a man be deposed from the episcopal office for some sin, and confined in a monastery that he may do penance, he cannot be reappointed to a bishopric. Hence it is stated (VII, qu. i, can. Hoc nequaquam): "The holy synod orders that any man who has been degraded from the episcopal dignity to the monastic life and a place of repentance, should by no means rise again to the episcopate."

Reply to Objection 3: Even in natural things power remains inactive on account of a supervening obstacle, for instance the act of sight ceases through an affliction of the eye. So neither is it unreasonable if, through the occurrence of some obstacle from without, the episcopal power remain without the exercise of its act.

Whether it is lawful for a bishop on account of bodily persecution to abandon the flock committed to his care?

Objection 1: It would seem that it is unlawful for a bishop, on account of some temporal persecution, to withdraw his bodily presence from the flock committed to his care. For our Lord said (Jn. 10:12) that he is a hireling and no true shepherd, who "seeth the wolf coming, and leaveth the sheep and flieth": and Gregory says (Hom. xiv in Ev.) that "the wolf comes upon the sheep when any man by his injustice and robbery oppresses the faithful and the humble." Therefore if, on account of the persecution of a tyrant, a bishop withdraws his bodily presence from the flock entrusted to his care, it would seem that he is a hireling and not a shepherd.

Objection 2: Further, it is written (Prov. 6:1): "My son, if thou be surety for thy friend, thou hast engaged fast thy hand to a stranger," and afterwards (Prov. 6:3): "Run about, make haste, stir up thy friend." Gregory expounds these words and says (Pastor. iii, 4): "To be surety for a friend, is to vouch for his good conduct by engaging oneself to a stranger. And whoever is put forward as an example to the lives of others, is warned not only to watch but even to rouse his friend." Now he cannot do this if he withdraw his bodily presence from his flock. Therefore it would seem that a bishop should not on account of persecution withdraw his bodily presence from his flock.

Objection 3: Further, it belongs to the perfection of the bishop's state that he devote himself to the care of his neighbor. Now it is unlawful for one who has professed the state of perfection to forsake altogether the things that pertain to perfection. Therefore it would seem unlawful for a bishop to withdraw his bodily presence from the execution of his office, except perhaps for the purpose of devoting himself to works of perfection in a monastery.

On the contrary, our Lord commanded the apostles, whose successors bishops are (Mat. 10:23): "When they shall persecute you in this city, flee into another."

I answer that, In any obligation the chief thing to be considered is the end of the obligation. Now bishops bind themselves to fulfil the pastoral office for the sake of the salvation of their subjects. Consequently when the salvation of his subjects demands the personal presence of the pastor, the pastor should not withdraw his personal presence from his flock, neither for the sake of some temporal advantage, nor even on account of some impending danger to his person, since the good shepherd is bound to lay down his life for his sheep.

On the other hand, if the salvation of his subjects can be sufficiently provided for by another person in the absence of the pastor, it is lawful for the pastor to withdraw his bodily presence from his flock, either for the sake of some advantage to the Church, or on account of some danger to his person. Hence Augustine says (Ep. ccxxviii ad Honorat.): "Christ's servants may flee from one city to another, when one of them is specially sought out by persecutors: in order that the Church be not abandoned by others who are not so sought for. When, however, the same danger threatens all, those who stand in need of others must not be abandoned by those whom they need." For "if it is dangerous for the helmsman to leave the ship when the sea is calm, how much more so when it is stormy," as Pope Nicholas I says (cf. VII, qu. i, can. Sciscitaris).

Reply to Objection 1: To flee as a hireling is to prefer temporal advantage or one's bodily welfare to the spiritual welfare of one's neighbor. Hence Gregory says (Hom. xiv in Ev.): "A man cannot endanger himself for the sake of his sheep, if he uses his authority over them not through love of them but for the sake of earthly gain: wherefore he fears to stand in the way of danger lest he lose what he loves." But he who, in order to avoid danger, leaves the flock without endangering the flock, does not flee as a hireling.

Reply to Objection 2: If he who is surety for another be unable to fulfil his engagement, it suffices that he fulfil it through another. Hence if a superior is hindered from attending personally to the care of his subjects, he fulfils his obligation if he do so through another.

Reply to Objection 3: When a man is appointed to a bishopric, he embraces the state of perfection as regards one kind of perfection; and if he be hindered from the practice thereof, he is not bound to another kind of perfection, so as to be obliged to enter the religious state. Yet he is under the obligation of retaining the intention of devoting himself to his neighbor's salvation, should an opportunity offer, and necessity require it of him.

Whether it is lawful for a bishop to have property of his own?

Objection 1: It would seem that it is not lawful for a bishop to have property of his own. For our Lord said (Mat. 19:21): "If thou wilt be perfect, go sell all [Vulg.: 'what'] thou hast, and give to the poor . . . and come, follow Me"; whence it would seem to follow that voluntary poverty is requisite for perfection. Now bishops are in the state of perfection. Therefore it would seem unlawful for them to possess anything as their own.

Objection 2: Further, bishops take the place of the apostles in the Church, according to a gloss on Lk. 10:1. Now our Lord commanded the apostles to possess nothing of their own, according to Mat. 10:9, "Do not possess gold, nor silver, nor money in your purses"; wherefore Peter said for himself and the other apostles (Mat. 19:27): "Behold we have left all things and have followed Thee." Therefore it would seem that bishops are bound to keep this command, and to possess nothing of their own.

Objection 3: Further, Jerome says (Ep. lii ad Nepotian.): "The Greek {kleros} denotes the Latin 'sors.' Hence clerics are so called either because they are of the Lord's estate, or because the Lord Himself is the estate, i.e. portion of clerics. Now he that possesses the Lord, can have nothing besides God; and if he have gold and silver, possessions, and chattels of all kinds, with such a portion the Lord does not vouchsafe to be his portion also." Therefore it would seem that not only bishops but even clerics should have nothing of their own.

On the contrary, It is stated (XII, qu. i, can. Episcopi de rebus): "Bishops, if they wish, may bequeath to their heirs their personal or acquired property, and whatever belongs to them personally."

I answer that, No one is bound to works of supererogation, unless he binds himself specially thereto by vow. Hence Augustine says (Ep. cxxvii ad Paulin. et Arment.): "Since you have taken the vow, you have already bound yourself, you can no longer do otherwise. Before you were bound by the vow, you were free to submit." Now it is evident that to live without possessing anything is a work of supererogation, for it is a matter not of precept but of counsel. Wherefore our Lord after saying to the young man: "If thou wilt enter into life, keep the commandments," said afterwards by way of addition: "If thou wilt be perfect go sell" all "that thou hast, and give to the poor" (Mat. 19:17, 21). Bishops, however, do not bind themselves at their ordination to live without possessions of their own; nor indeed does the pastoral office, to which they bind themselves, make it necessary for them to live without anything of their own. Therefore bishops are not bound to live without possessions of their own.

Reply to Objection 1: As stated above ([3776]Q[184], A[3], ad 1) the perfection of the Christian life does not essentially consist in voluntary poverty, but voluntary poverty conduces instrumentally to the perfection of life. Hence it does not follow that where there is greater poverty there is greater perfection; indeed the highest perfection is compatible with great wealth, since Abraham, to whom it was said (Gn. 17:1): "Walk before Me and be perfect," is stated to have been rich (Gn. 13:2).

Reply to Objection 2: This saying of our Lord can be understood in three ways. First, mystically, that we should possess neither gold nor silver means that the preacher should not rely chiefly on temporal wisdom and eloquence; thus Jerome expounds the passage.

Secondly, according to Augustine's explanation (De Consens. Ev. ii, 30), we are to understand that our Lord said this not in command but in permission. For he permitted them to go preaching without gold or silver or other means, since they were to receive the means of livelihood from those to whom they preached; wherefore He added: "For the workman is worthy of his meat." And yet if anyone were to use his own means in preaching the Gospel, this would be a work of supererogation, as Paul says in reference to himself (1 Cor. 9:12, 15).

Thirdly, according to the exposition of Chrysostom [*Hom. ii in Rom. xvi, 3], we are to understand that our Lord laid these commands on His disciples in reference to the mission on which they were sent to preach to the Jews, so that they might be encouraged to trust in His power, seeing that He provided for their wants without their having means of their own. But it does not follow from this that they, or their successors, were obliged to preach the Gospel without having means of their own: since we read of Paul (2 Cor. 11:8) that he "received wages" of other churches for preaching to the Corinthians, wherefore it is clear that he possessed something sent to him by others. And it seems foolish to say that so many holy bishops as Athanasius, Ambrose, and Augustine would have disobeyed these commandments if they believed themselves bound to observe them.

Reply to Objection 3: Every part is less than the whole. Accordingly a man has other portions together with God, if he becomes less intent on things pertaining to God by occupying himself with things of the world. Now neither bishops nor clerics ought thus to possess means of their own, that while busy with their own they neglect those that concern the worship of God.

Day 245

Whether bishops sin mortally if they distribute not to the poor the ecclesiastical goods which accrue to them?

Objection 1: It would seem that bishops sin mortally if they distribute not to the poor the ecclesiastical goods which they acquire. For Ambrose [*Basil, Serm. lxiv, de Temp., among the supposititious works of St. Jerome] expounding Lk. 12:16, "The land of a certain . . . man brought forth plenty of fruits," says: "Let no man claim as his own that which he has taken and obtained by violence from the common property in excess of his requirements"; and afterwards he adds: "It is not less criminal to take from him who has, than, when you are able and have plenty to refuse him who has not." Now it is a mortal sin to take another's property by violence. Therefore bishops sin mortally if they give not to the poor that which they have in excess.

Objection 2: Further, a gloss of Jerome on Is. 3:14, "The spoil of the poor is in your house," says that "ecclesiastical goods belong to the poor." Now whoever keeps for himself or gives to others that which belongs to another, sins mortally and is bound to restitution. Therefore if bishops keep for themselves, or give to their relations or friends, their surplus of ecclesiastical goods, it would seem that they are bound to restitution.

Objection 3: Further, much more may one take what is necessary for oneself from the goods of the Church, than accumulate a surplus therefrom. Yet Jerome says in a letter to Pope Damasus [*Cf. Can. Clericos, cause. i, qu. 2; Can. Quoniam; cause. xvi, qu. 1; Regul. Monach. iv, among the supposititious works of St. Jerome]: "It is right that those clerics who receive no goods from their parents and relations should be supported from the funds of the Church. But those who have sufficient income from their parents and their own possessions, if they take what belongs to the poor, they commit and incur the guilt of sacrilege." Wherefore the Apostle says (1 Tim. 5:16): "If any of the faithful have widows, let him minister to them, and let not the Church be charged, that there may be sufficient for them that are widows indeed." Much more therefore do bishops sin mortally if they give not to the poor the surplus of their ecclesiastical goods.

On the contrary, Many bishops do not give their surplus to the poor, but would seem commendably to lay it out so as to increase the revenue of the Church.

I answer that, The same is not to be said of their own goods which bishops may possess, and of ecclesiastical goods. For they have real dominion over their own goods; wherefore from the very nature of the case they are not bound to give these things to others, and may either keep them for themselves or bestow them on others at will. Nevertheless they may sin in this disposal by inordinate affection, which leads them either to accumulate more than they should, or not to assist others, in accordance with the demands of charity; yet they are not bound to restitution, because such things are entrusted to their ownership.

On the other hand, they hold ecclesiastical goods as dispensers or trustees. For Augustine says (Ep. clxxxv ad Bonif.): "If we possess privately what is enough for us, other things belong not to us but to the poor, and we have the dispensing of them; but we can claim ownership of them only by wicked theft." Now dispensing requires good faith, according to 1 Cor. 4:2, "Here now it is required among the dispensers that a man be found faithful." Moreover ecclesiastical goods are to be applied not only to the good of the poor, but also to the divine worship and the needs of its ministers. Hence it is said (XII, qu. ii, can. de reditibus): "Of the Church's revenues or the offerings of the faithful only one part is to be assigned to the bishop, two parts are to be used by the priest, under pain of suspension, for the ecclesiastical fabric, and for the benefit of the poor; the remaining part is to be divided among the clergy according to their respective merits." Accordingly if the goods which are assigned to the use of the bishop are distinct from those which are appointed for the use of the poor, or the ministers, or for the ecclesiastical worship, and if the bishop keeps back for himself part of that which should be given to the poor, or to the ministers for their use, or expended on the divine worship, without doubt he is an unfaithful dispenser, sins mortally, and is bound to restitution.

But as regards those goods which are deputed to his private use, the same apparently applies as to his own property, namely that he sins through immoderate attachment thereto or use thereof, if he exceeds moderation in what he keeps for himself, and fails to assist others according to the demands of charity.

On the other hand, if no distinction is made in the aforesaid goods, their distribution is entrusted to his good faith; and if he fail or exceed in a slight degree, this may happen without prejudice to his good faith, because in such matters a man cannot possibly decide precisely what ought to be done. On the other hand, if the excess be very great he cannot be ignorant of the fact; consequently he would seem to be lacking in good faith, and is guilty of mortal sin. For it is written (Mat. 24:48-51) that "if that evil servant shall say in his heart: My lord is long a-coming," which shows contempt of God's judgment, "and shall begin to strike his fellow-servants," which is a sign of pride, "and shall eat and drink with drunkards," which proceeds from lust, "the lord of that servant shall come in a day that he hopeth not . . . and shall separate him," namely from the fellowship of good men, "and appoint his portion with hypocrites," namely in hell.

Reply to Objection 1: This saying of Ambrose refers to the administration not only of ecclesiastical things but also of any goods whatever from which a man is bound, as a duty of charity, to provide for those who are in need. But it is not possible to state definitely when this need is such as to impose an obligation under pain of mortal sin, as is the case in other points of detail that have to be considered in human acts: for the decision in such matters is left to human prudence.

Reply to Objection 2: As stated above the goods of the Church have to be employed not only for the use of the poor, but also for other purposes. Hence if a bishop or cleric wish to deprive himself of that which is assigned to his own use, and give it to his relations or others, he sins not so long as he observes moderation, so, to wit, that they cease to be in want without becoming the richer thereby. Hence Ambrose says (De Offic. i, 30): "It is a commendable liberality if you overlook not your kindred when you know them to be in want; yet not so as to wish to make them rich with what you can give to the poor."

Reply to Objection 3: The goods of churches should not all be given to the poor, except in a case of necessity: for then, as Ambrose says (De Offic. ii, 28), even the vessels consecrated to the divine worship are to be sold for the ransom of prisoners, and other needs of the poor. In such a case of necessity a cleric would sin if he chose to maintain himself on the goods of the Church, always supposing him to have a patrimony of his own on which to support himself.

Reply to Objection 4: The goods of the churches should be employed for the good of the poor. Consequently a man is to be commended if, there being no present necessity for helping the poor, he spends the surplus from the Church revenue, in buying property, or lays it by for some future use connected with the Church or the needs of the poor. But if there be a pressing need for helping the poor, to lay by for the future is a superfluous and inordinate saving, and is forbidden by our Lord Who said (Mat. 6:34): "Be . . . not solicitous for the morrow."

Whether religious who are raised to the episcopate are bound to religious observances?

Objection 1: It would seem that religious who are raised to the episcopate are not bound to religious observances. For it is said (XVIII, qu. i, can. Statutum) that a "canonical election loosens a monk from the yoke imposed by the rule of the monastic profession, and the holy ordination makes of a monk a bishop." Now the regular observances pertain to the yoke of the rule. Therefore religious who are appointed bishops are not bound to religious observances.

Objection 2: Further, he who ascends from a lower to a higher degree is seemingly not bound to those things which pertain to the lower degree: thus it was stated above ([3777]Q[88], A[12], ad 1) that a religious is not bound to keep the vows he made in the world. But a religious who is appointed to the episcopate ascends to something greater, as stated above (Q[84], A[7]). Therefore it would seem that a bishop is not bound to those things whereto he was bound in the state of religion.

Objection 3: Further, religious would seem to be bound above all to obedience, and to live without property of their own. But religious who are appointed bishops, are not bound to obey the superiors of their order, since they are above them; nor apparently are they bound to poverty, since according to the decree quoted above (OBJ[1]) "when the holy ordination has made of a monk a bishop he enjoys the right, as the lawful heir, of claiming his paternal inheritance." Moreover they are sometimes allowed to make a will. Much less therefore are they bound to other regular observances.

On the contrary, It is said in the Decretals (XVI, qu. i, can. De Monachis): "With regard to those who after long residence in a monastery attain to the order of clerics, we bid them not to lay aside their former purpose."

I answer that, As stated above (A[1], ad 2) the religious state pertains to perfection, as a way of tending to perfection, while the episcopal state pertains to perfection, as a professorship of perfection. Hence the religious state is compared to the episcopal state, as the school to the professorial chair, and as disposition to perfection. Now the disposition is not voided at the advent of perfection, except as regards what perchance is incompatible with perfection, whereas as to that wherein it is in accord with perfection, it is confirmed the more. Thus when the scholar has become a professor it no longer becomes him to be a listener, but it becomes him to read and meditate even more than before. Accordingly we must assert that if there be among religious observances any that instead of being an obstacle to the episcopal office, are a safeguard of perfection, such as continence, poverty, and so forth, a religious, even after he has been made a bishop, remains bound to observe these, and consequently to wear the habit of his order, which is a sign of this obligation.

On the other hand, a man is not bound to keep such religious observances as may be incompatible with the episcopal office, for instance solitude, silence, and certain severe abstinences or watchings and such as would render him bodily unable to exercise the episcopal office. For the rest he may dispense himself from them, according to the needs of his person or office, and the manner of life of those among whom he dwells, in the same way as religious superiors dispense themselves in such matters.

Reply to Objection 1: He who from being a monk becomes a bishop is loosened from the yoke of the monastic profession, not in everything, but in those that are incompatible with the episcopal office, as stated above.

Reply to Objection 2: The vows of those who are living in the world are compared to the vows of religion as the particular to the universal, as stated above ([3778]Q[88], A[12], ad 1). But the vows of religion are compared to the episcopal dignity as disposition to perfection. Now the particular is superfluous when one has the universal, whereas the disposition is still necessary when perfection has been attained.

Reply to Objection 3: It is accidental that religious who are bishops are not bound to obey the superiors of their order, because, to wit, they have ceased to be their subjects; even as those same religious superiors. Nevertheless the obligation of the vow remains virtually, so that if any person be lawfully set above them, they would be bound to obey them, inasmuch as they are bound to obey both the statutes of their rule in the way mentioned above, and their superiors if they have any.

As to property they can nowise have it. For they claim their paternal inheritance not as their own, but as due to the Church. Hence it is added (XVIII, qu. i, can. Statutum) that after he has been ordained bishop at the altar to which he is consecrated and appointed according to the holy canons, he must restore whatever he may acquire.

Nor can he make any testament at all, because he is entrusted with the sole administration of things ecclesiastical, and this ends with his death, after which a testament comes into force according to the Apostle (Heb. 9:17). If, however, by the Pope's permission he make a will, he is not to be understood to bequeath property of his own, but we are to understand that by apostolic authority the power of his administration has been prolonged so as to remain in force after his death.

OF THOSE THINGS IN WHICH THE RELIGIOUS STATE PROPERLY CONSISTS (TEN ARTICLES)

We must now consider things pertaining to the religious state: which consideration will be fourfold. In the first place we shall consider those things in which the religious state consists chiefly; secondly, those things which are lawfully befitting to religious; thirdly, the different kinds of religious orders; fourthly, the entrance into the religious state.

Under the first head there are ten points of inquiry:

(1) Whether the religious state is perfect?

(2) Whether religious are bound to all the counsels?

(3) Whether voluntary poverty is required for the religious state?

(4) Whether continency is necessary?

(5) Whether obedience is necessary?

(6) Whether it is necessary that these should be the matter of a vow?

(7) Of the sufficiency of these vows;

(8) Of their comparison one with another;

(9) Whether a religious sins mortally whenever he transgresses a statute of his rule?

(10) Whether, other things being equal, a religious sins more grievously by the same kind of sin than a secular person?

Whether religion implies a state of perfection?

Objection 1: It would seem that religion does not imply a state of perfection. For that which is necessary for salvation does not seemingly pertain to perfection. But religion is necessary for salvation, whether because "thereby we are bound [religamur] to the one almighty God," as Augustine says (De Vera Relig. 55), or because it takes its name from "our returning [religimus] to God Whom we had lost by neglecting Him" [*Cf.[3779] Q[81], A[1]], according to Augustine (De Civ. Dei x, 3). Therefore it would seem that religion does not denote the state of perfection.

Objection 2: Further, religion according to Tully (De Invent. Rhet. ii, 53) is that "which offers worship and ceremony to the Divine nature." Now the offering of worship and ceremony to God would seem to pertain to the ministry of holy orders rather than to the diversity of states, as stated above ([3780]Q[40], A[2];[3781] Q[183], A[3]). Therefore it would seem that religion does not denote the state of perfection.

Objection 3: Further, the state of perfection is distinct from the state of beginners and that of the proficient. But in religion also some are beginners, and some are proficient. Therefore religion does not denote the state of perfection.

Objection 4: Further, religion would seem a place of repentance; for it is said in the Decrees (VII, qu. i, can. Hoc nequaquam): "The holy synod orders that any man who has been degraded from the episcopal dignity to the monastic life and a place of repentance, should by no means rise again to the episcopate." Now a place of repentance is opposed to the state of perfection; hence Dionysius (Eccl. Hier. vi) places penitents in the lowest place, namely among those who are to be cleansed. Therefore it would seem that religion is not the state of perfection.

On the contrary, In the Conferences of the Fathers (Collat. i, 7) abbot Moses speaking of religious says: "We must recognize that we have to undertake the hunger of fasting, watchings, bodily toil, privation, reading, and other acts of virtue, in order by these degrees to mount to the perfection of charity." Now things pertaining to human acts are specified and denominated from the intention of the end. Therefore religious belong to the state of perfection.

Moreover Dionysius says (Eccl. Hier. vi) that those who are called servants of God, by reason of their rendering pure service and subjection to God, are united to the perfection beloved of Him.

I answer that, As stated above ([3782]Q[141], A[2]) that which is applicable to many things in common is ascribed antonomastically to that to which it is applicable by way of excellence. Thus the name of "fortitude" is claimed by the virtue which preserves the firmness of the mind in regard to most difficult things, and the name of "temperance," by that virtue which tempers the greatest pleasures. Now religion as stated above ([3783]Q[81], A[2]; A[3], ad 2) is a virtue whereby a man offers something to the service and worship of God. Wherefore those are called religious antonomastically, who give themselves up entirely to the divine service, as offering a holocaust to God. Hence Gregory says (Hom. xx in Ezech.): "Some there are who keep nothing for themselves, but sacrifice to almighty God their tongue, their senses, their life, and the property they possess." Now the perfection of man consists in adhering wholly to God, as stated above ([3784]Q[184], A[2]), and in this sense religion denotes the state of perfection.

Reply to Objection 1: To offer something to the worship of God is necessary for salvation, but to offer oneself wholly, and one's possessions to the worship of God belongs to perfection.

Reply to Objection 2: As stated above ([3785]Q[81], A[1], ad 1; A[4], ad 1,2;[3786] Q[85], A[3]) when we were treating of the virtue of religion, religion has reference not only to the offering of sacrifices and other like things that are proper to religion, but also to the acts of all the virtues which in so far as these are referred to God's service and honor become acts of religion. Accordingly if a man devotes his whole life to the divine service, his whole life belongs to religion, and thus by reason of the religious life that they lead, those who are in the state of perfection are called religious.

Reply to Objection 3: As stated above ([3787]Q[184], AA[4],6) religion denotes the state of perfection by reason of the end intended. Hence it does not follow that whoever is in the state of perfection is already perfect, but that he tends to perfection. Hence Origen commenting on Mat. 19:21, "If thou wilt be perfect," etc., says (Tract. viii in Matth.) that "he who has exchanged riches for poverty in order to become perfect does not become perfect at the very moment of giving his goods to the poor; but from that day the contemplation of God will begin to lead him to all the virtues." Thus all are not perfect in religion, but some are beginners, some proficient.

Reply to Objection 4: The religious state was instituted chiefly that we might obtain perfection by means of certain exercises, whereby the obstacles to perfect charity are removed. By the removal of the obstacles of perfect charity, much more are the occasions of sin cut off, for sin destroys charity altogether. Wherefore since it belongs to penance to cut out the causes of sin, it follows that the religious state is a most fitting place for penance. Hence (XXXIII, qu. ii, cap. Admonere) a man who had killed his wife is counseled to enter a monastery which is described as "better and lighter," rather than to do public penance while remaining in the world.

Whether every religious is bound to keep all the counsels?

Objection 1: It would seem that every religious is bound to keep all the counsels. For whoever professes a certain state of life is bound to observe whatever belongs to that state. Now each religious professes the state of perfection. Therefore every religious is bound to keep all the counsels that pertain to the state of perfection.

Objection 2: Further, Gregory says (Hom. xx in Ezech.) that "he who renounces this world, and does all the good he can, is like one who has gone out of Egypt and offers sacrifice in the wilderness." Now it belongs specially to religious to renounce the world. Therefore it belongs to them also to do all the good they can. and so it would seem that each of them is bound to fulfil all the counsels.

Objection 3: Further, if it is not requisite for the state of perfection to fulfil all the counsels, it would seem enough to fulfil some of them. But this is false, since some who lead a secular life fulfil some of the counsels, for instance those who observe continence. Therefore it would seem that every religious who is in the state of perfection is bound to fulfil whatever pertains to perfection: and such are the counsels.

On the contrary, one is not bound, unless one bind oneself, to do works of supererogation. But every religious does not bind himself to keep all the counsels, but to certain definite ones, some to some, others to others. Therefore all are not bound to keep all of them.

I answer that, A thing pertains to perfection in three ways. First, essentially, and thus, as stated above ([3788]Q[184], A[3]) the perfect observance of the precepts of charity belongs to perfection. Secondly, a thing belongs to perfection consequently: such are those things that result from the perfection of charity, for instance to bless them that curse you (Lk. 6:27), and to keep counsels of a like kind, which though they be binding as regards the preparedness of the mind, so that one has to fulfil them when necessity requires; yet are sometimes fulfilled, without there being any necessity, through superabundance of charity. Thirdly, a thing belongs to perfection instrumentally and dispositively, as poverty, continence, abstinence, and the like.

Now it has been stated [3789](A[1]) that the perfection of charity is the end of the religious state. And the religious state is a school or exercise for the attainment of perfection, which men strive to reach by various practices, just as a physician may use various remedies in order to heal. But it is evident that for him who works for an end it is not necessary that he should already have attained the end, but it is requisite that he should by some means tend thereto. Hence he who enters the religious state is not bound to have perfect charity, but he is bound to tend to this, and use his endeavors to have perfect charity.

For the same reason he is not bound to fulfil those things that result from the perfection of charity, although he is bound to intend to fulfil them: against which intention he acts if he contemns them, wherefore he sins not by omitting them but by contempt of them.

In like manner he is not bound to observe all the practices whereby perfection may be attained, but only those which are definitely prescribed to him by the rule which he has professed.

Reply to Objection 1: He who enters religion does not make profession to be perfect, but he professes to endeavor to attain perfection; even as he who enters the schools does not profess to have knowledge, but to study in order to acquire knowledge. Wherefore as Augustine says (De Civ. Dei viii, 2), Pythagoras was unwilling to profess to be a wise man, but acknowledged himself, "a lover of wisdom." Hence a religious does not violate his profession if he be not perfect, but only if he despises to tend to perfection.

Reply to Objection 2: Just as, though all are bound to love God with their whole heart, yet there is a certain wholeness of perfection which cannot be omitted without sin, and another wholeness which can be omitted without sin ([3790]Q[184], A[2], ad 3), provided there be no contempt, as stated above (ad 1), so too, all, both religious and seculars, are bound, in a certain measure, to do whatever good they can, for to all without exception it is said (Eccles. 9:10): "Whatsoever thy hand is able to do, do it earnestly." Yet there is a way of fulfilling this precept, so as to avoid sin, namely if one do what one can as required by the conditions of one's state of life: provided there be no contempt of doing better things, which contempt sets the mind against spiritual progress.

Reply to Objection 3: There are some counsels such that if they be omitted, man's whole life would be taken up with secular business; for instance if he have property of his own, or enter the married state, or do something of the kind that regards the essential vows of religion themselves; wherefore religious are bound to keep all such like counsels. Other counsels there are, however, about certain particular better actions, which can be omitted without one's life being taken up with secular actions; wherefore there is no need for religious to be bound to fulfil all of them.

Whether poverty is required for religious perfection?

Objection 1: It would seem that poverty is not required for religious perfection. For that which it is unlawful to do does not apparently belong to the state of perfection. But it would seem to be unlawful for a man to give up all he possesses; since the Apostle (2 Cor. 8:12) lays down the way in which the faithful are to give alms saying: "If the will be forward, it is accepted according to that which a man hath," i.e. "you should keep back what you need," and afterwards he adds (2 Cor. 8:13): "For I mean not that others should be eased, and you burthened," i.e. "with poverty," according to a gloss. Moreover a gloss on 1 Tim. 6:8, "Having food, and wherewith to be covered," says: "Though we brought nothing, and will carry nothing away, we must not give up these temporal things altogether." Therefore it seems that voluntary poverty is not requisite for religious perfection.

Objection 2: Further, whosoever exposes himself to danger sins. But he who renounces all he has and embraces voluntary poverty exposes himself to danger---not only spiritual, according to Prov. 30:9, "Lest perhaps . . . being compelled by poverty, I should steal and forswear the name of my God," and Ecclus. 27:1, "Through poverty many have sinned"---but also corporal, for it is written (Eccles. 7:13): "As wisdom is a defense, so money is a defense," and the Philosopher says (Ethic. iv, 1) that "the waste of property appears to be a sort of ruining of one's self, since thereby man lives." Therefore it would seem that voluntary poverty is not requisite for the perfection of religious life.

Objection 3: Further, "Virtue observes the mean," as stated in Ethic. ii, 6. But he who renounces all by voluntary poverty seems to go to the extreme rather than to observe the mean. Therefore he does not act virtuously: and so this does not pertain to the perfection of life.

Objection 4: Further, the ultimate perfection of man consists in happiness. Now riches conduce to happiness; for it is written (Ecclus. 31:8): "Blessed is the rich man that is found without blemish," and the Philosopher says (Ethic. i, 8) that "riches contribute instrumentally to happiness." Therefore voluntary poverty is not requisite for religious perfection.

Objection 5: Further, the episcopal state is more perfect than the religious state. But bishops may have property, as stated above ([3791]Q[185], A[6]). Therefore religious may also.

Objection 6: Further, almsgiving is a work most acceptable to God, and as Chrysostom says (Hom. ix in Ep. ad Hebr.) "is a most effective remedy in repentance." Now poverty excludes almsgiving. Therefore it would seem that poverty does not pertain to religious perfection.

On the contrary, Gregory says (Moral. viii, 26): "There are some of the righteous who bracing themselves up to lay hold of the very height of perfection, while they aim at higher objects within, abandon all things without." Now, as stated above, ([3792]AA[1],2), it belongs properly to religious to brace themselves up in order to lay hold of the very height of perfection. Therefore it belongs to them to abandon all outward things by voluntary poverty.

I answer that, As stated above [3793](A[2]), the religious state is an exercise and a school for attaining to the perfection of charity. For this it is necessary that a man wholly withdraw his affections from worldly things; since Augustine says (Confess. x, 29), speaking to God: "Too little doth he love Thee, who loves anything with Thee, which he loveth not for Thee." Wherefore he says (QQ. lxxxiii, qu. 36) that "greater charity means less cupidity, perfect charity means no cupidity." Now the possession of worldly things draws a man's mind to the love of them: hence Augustine says (Ep. xxxi ad Paulin. et Theras.) that "we are more firmly attached to earthly things when we have them than when we desire them: since why did that young man go away sad, save because he had great wealth? For it is one thing not to wish to lay hold of what one has not, and another to renounce what one already has; the former are rejected as foreign to us, the latter are cut off as a limb." And Chrysostom says (Hom. lxiii in Matth.) that "the possession of wealth kindles a greater flame and the desire for it becomes stronger."

Hence it is that in the attainment of the perfection of charity the first foundation is voluntary poverty, whereby a man lives without property of his own, according to the saying of our Lord (Mat. 19:21), "If thou wilt be perfect, go, sell all [Vulg.: 'what'] thou hast, and give to the poor . . . and come, follow Me."

Reply to Objection 1: As the gloss adds, "when the Apostle said this (namely "not that you should be burthened," i.e. with poverty)," he did not mean that "it were better not to give: but he feared for the weak, whom he admonished so to give as not to suffer privation." Hence in like manner the other gloss means not that it is unlawful to renounce all one's temporal goods, but that this is not required of necessity. Wherefore Ambrose says (De Offic. i, 30): "Our Lord does not wish," namely does not command us "to pour out our wealth all at once, but to dispense it; or perhaps to do as did Eliseus who slew his oxen, and fed the poor with that which was his own so that no household care might hold him back."

Reply to Objection 2: He who renounces all his possessions for Christ's sake exposes himself to no danger, neither spiritual nor corporal. For spiritual danger ensues from poverty when the latter is not voluntary; because those who are unwillingly poor, through the desire of money-getting, fall into many sins, according to 1 Tim. 6:9, "They that will become rich, fall into temptation and into the snare of the devil." This attachment is put away by those who embrace voluntary poverty, but it gathers strength in those who have wealth, as stated above. Again bodily danger does not threaten those who, intent on following Christ, renounce all their possessions and entrust themselves to divine providence. Hence Augustine says (De Serm. Dom. in Monte ii, 17): "Those who seek first the kingdom of God and His justice are not weighed down by anxiety lest they lack what is necessary."

Reply to Objection 3: According to the Philosopher (Ethic. ii, 6), the mean of virtue is taken according to right reason, not according to the quantity of a thing. Consequently whatever may be done in accordance with right reason is not rendered sinful by the greatness of the quantity, but all the more virtuous. It would, however, be against right reason to throw away all one's possessions through intemperance, or without any useful purpose; whereas it is in accordance with right reason to renounce wealth in order to devote oneself to the contemplation of wisdom. Even certain philosophers are said to have done this; for Jerome says (Ep. xlviii ad Paulin.): "The famous Theban, Crates, once a very wealthy man, when he was going to Athens to study philosophy, cast away a large amount of gold; for he considered that he could not possess both gold and virtue at the same time." Much more therefore is it according to right reason for a man to renounce all he has, in order perfectly to follow Christ. Wherefore Jerome says (Ep. cxxv ad Rust. Monach.): "Poor thyself, follow Christ poor."

Reply to Objection 4: Happiness or felicity is twofold. One is perfect, to which we look forward in the life to come; the other is imperfect, in respect of which some are said to be happy in this life. The happiness of this life is twofold, one is according to the active life, the other according to the contemplative life, as the Philosopher asserts (Ethic. x, 7,8). Now wealth conduces instrumentally to the happiness of the active life which consists in external actions, because as the Philosopher says (Ethic. i, 8) "we do many things by friends, by riches, by political influence, as it were by instruments." On the other hand, it does not conduce to the happiness of the contemplative life, rather is it an obstacle thereto, inasmuch as the anxiety it involves disturbs the quiet of the soul, which is most necessary to one who contemplates. Hence it is that the Philosopher asserts (Ethic. x, 8) that "for actions many things are needed, but the contemplative man needs no such things," namely external goods, "for his operation; in fact they are obstacles to his contemplation."

Man is directed to future happiness by charity; and since voluntary poverty is an efficient exercise for the attaining of perfect charity, it follows that it is of great avail in acquiring the happiness of heaven. Wherefore our Lord said (Mat. 19:21): "Go, sell all [Vulg.: 'what'] thou hast, and give to the poor, and thou shalt have treasure in heaven." Now riches once they are possessed are in themselves of a nature to hinder the perfection of charity, especially by enticing and distracting the mind. Hence it is written (Mat. 13:22) that "the care of this world and the deceitfulness of riches choketh up the word" of God, for as Gregory says (Hom. xv in Ev.) by "preventing the good desire from entering into the heart, they destroy life at its very outset." Consequently it is difficult to safeguard charity amidst riches: wherefore our Lord said (Mat. 19:23) that "a rich man shall hardly enter into the kingdom of heaven," which we must understand as referring to one who actually has wealth, since He says that this is impossible for him who places his affection in riches, according to the explanation of Chrysostom (Hom. lxiii in Matth.), for He adds (Mat. 19:24): "It is easier for a camel to pass through the eye of a needle, than for a rich man to enter into the kingdom of heaven." Hence it is not said simply that the "rich man" is blessed, but "the rich man that is found without blemish, and that hath not gone after gold," and this because he has done a difficult thing, wherefore the text continues (Mat. 19:9): "Who is he? and we will praise him; for he hath done wonderful things in his life," namely by not loving riches though placed in the midst of them.

Reply to Objection 5: The episcopal state is not directed to the attainment of perfection, but rather to the effect that, in virtue of the perfection which he already has, a man may govern others, by administering not only spiritual but also temporal things. This belongs to the active life, wherein many things occur that may be done by means of wealth as an instrument, as stated (ad 4). Wherefore it is not required of bishops, who make profession of governing Christ's flock, that they have nothing of their own, whereas it is required of religious who make profession of learning to obtain perfection.

Reply to Objection 6: The renouncement of one's own wealth is compared to almsgiving as the universal to the particular, and as the holocaust to the sacrifice. Hence Gregory says (Hom. xx in Ezech.) that those who assist "the needy with the things they possess, by their good deeds offer sacrifice, since they offer up something to God and keep back something for themselves; whereas those who keep nothing for themselves offer a holocaust which is greater than a sacrifice." Wherefore Jerome also says (Contra Vigilant.): "When you declare that those do better who retain the use of their possessions, and dole out the fruits of their possessions to the poor, it is not I but the Lord Who answers you; If thou wilt be perfect," etc., and afterwards he goes on to say: "This man whom you praise belongs to the second and third degree, and we too commend him: provided we acknowledge the first as to be preferred to the second and third." For this reason in order to exclude the error of Vigilantius it is said (De Eccl. Dogm. xxxviii): "It is a good thing to give away one's goods by dispensing them to the poor: it is better to give them away once for all with the intention of following the Lord, and, free of solicitude, to be poor with Christ."

Whether perpetual continence is required for religious perfection?

Objection 1: It would seem that perpetual continence is not required for religious perfection. For all perfection of the Christian life began with Christ's apostles. Now the apostles do not appear to have observed continence, as evidenced by Peter, of whose mother-in-law we read Mat. 8:14. Therefore it would seem that perpetual continence is not requisite for religious perfection.

Objection 2: Further, the first example of perfection is shown to us in the person of Abraham, to whom the Lord said (Gn. 17:1): "Walk before Me, and be perfect." Now the copy should not surpass the example. Therefore perpetual continence is not requisite for religious perfection.

Objection 3: Further, that which is required for religious perfection is to be found in every religious order. Now there are some religious who lead a married life. Therefore religious perfection does not require perpetual continence.

On the contrary, The Apostle says (2 Cor. 7:1): "Let us cleanse ourselves from all defilement of the flesh and of the spirit, perfecting sanctification in the fear of God." Now cleanness of flesh and spirit is safeguarded by continence, for it is said (1 Cor. 7:34): "The unmarried woman and the virgin thinketh on the things of the Lord that she may be holy both in spirit and in body [Vulg.: 'both in body and in spirit']." Therefore religious perfection requires continence.

I answer that, The religious state requires the removal of whatever hinders man from devoting himself entirely to God's service. Now the use of sexual union hinders the mind from giving itself wholly to the service of God, and this for two reasons. First, on account of its vehement delectation, which by frequent repetition increases concupiscence, as also the Philosopher observes (Ethic. iii, 12): and hence it is that the use of venery withdraws the mind from that perfect intentness on tending to God. Augustine expresses this when he says (Solil. i, 10): "I consider that nothing so casts down the manly mind from its height as the fondling of women, and those bodily contacts which belong to the married state." Secondly, because it involves man in solicitude for the control of his wife, his children, and his temporalities which serve for their upkeep. Hence the Apostle says (1 Cor. 7:32,33): "He that is without a wife is solicitous for the things that belong to the Lord, how he may please God: but he that is with a wife is solicitous for the things of the world, how he may please his wife."

Therefore perpetual continence, as well as voluntary poverty, is requisite for religious perfection. Wherefore just as Vigilantius was condemned for equaling riches to poverty, so was Jovinian condemned for equaling marriage to virginity.

Reply to Objection 1: The perfection not only of poverty but also of continence was introduced by Christ Who said (Mat. 19:12): "There are eunuchs who have made themselves eunuchs, for the kingdom of heaven," and then added: "He that can take, let him take it." And lest anyone should be deprived of the hope of attaining perfection, he admitted to the state of perfection those even who were married. Now the husbands could not without committing an injustice forsake their wives, whereas men could without injustice renounce riches. Wherefore Peter whom He found married, He severed not from his wife, while "He withheld from marriage John who wished to marry" [*Prolog. in Joan. among the supposititious works of St. Jerome].

Reply to Objection 2: As Augustine says (De Bono Conjug. xxii), "the chastity of celibacy is better than the chastity of marriage, one of which Abraham had in use, both of them in habit. For he lived chastely, and he might have been chaste without marrying, but it was not requisite then." Nevertheless if the patriarchs of old had perfection of mind together with wealth and marriage, which is a mark of the greatness of their virtue, this is no reason why any weaker person should presume to have such great virtue that he can attain to perfection though rich and married; as neither does a man unarmed presume to attack his enemy, because Samson slew many foes with the jaw-bone of an ass. For those fathers, had it been seasonable to observe continence and poverty, would have been most careful to observe them.

Reply to Objection 3: Such ways of living as admit of the use of marriage are not the religious life simply and absolutely speaking, but in a restricted sense, in so far as they have a certain share in those things that belong to the religious state.

Whether obedience belongs to religious perfection?

Objection 1: It would seem that obedience does not belong to religious perfection. For those things seemingly belong to religious perfection, which are works of supererogation and are not binding upon all. But all are bound to obey their superiors, according to the saying of the Apostle (Heb. 13:17), "Obey your prelates, and be subject to them." Therefore it would seem that obedience does not belong to religious perfection.

Objection 2: Further, obedience would seem to belong properly to those who have to be guided by the sense of others, and such persons are lacking in discernment. Now the Apostle says (Heb. 5:14) that "strong meat is for the perfect, for them who by custom have their senses exercised to the discerning of good and evil." Therefore it would seem that obedience does not belong to the state of the perfect.

Objection 3: Further, if obedience were requisite for religious perfection, it would follow that it is befitting to all religious. But it is not becoming to all; since some religious lead a solitary life, and have no superior whom they obey. Again religious superiors apparently are not bound to obedience. Therefore obedience would seem not to pertain to religious perfection.

Objection 4: Further, if the vow of obedience were requisite for religion, it would follow that religious are bound to obey their superiors in all things, just as they are bound to abstain from all venery by their vow of continence. But they are not bound to obey them in all things, as stated above ([3794]Q[104], A[5]), when we were treating of the virtue of obedience. Therefore the vow of obedience is not requisite for religion.

Objection 5: Further, those services are most acceptable to God which are done freely and not of necessity, according to 2 Cor. 9:7, "Not with sadness or of necessity." Now that which is done out of obedience is done of necessity of precept. Therefore those good works are more deserving of praise which are done of one's own accord. Therefore the vow of obedience is unbecoming to religion whereby men seek to attain to that which is better.

On the contrary, Religious perfection consists chiefly in the imitation of Christ, according to Mat. 19:21, "If thou wilt be perfect, go sell all [Vulg.: 'what'] thou hast, and give to the poor, and follow Me." Now in Christ obedience is commended above all according to Phil. 2:8, "He became [Vulg.: 'becoming'] obedient unto death." Therefore seemingly obedience belongs to religious perfection.

I answer that, As stated above ([3795]AA[2],3) the religious state is a school and exercise for tending to perfection. Now those who are being instructed or exercised in order to attain a certain end must needs follow the direction of someone under whose control they are instructed or exercised so as to attain that end as disciples under a master. Hence religious need to be placed under the instruction and command of someone as regards things pertaining to the religious life; wherefore it is said (VII, qu. i, can. Hoc nequaquam): "The monastic life denotes subjection and discipleship." Now one man is subjected to another's command and instruction by obedience: and consequently obedience is requisite for religious perfection.

Reply to Objection 1: To obey one's superiors in matters that are essential to virtue is not a work of supererogation, but is common to all: whereas to obey in matters pertaining to the practice of perfection belongs properly to religious. This latter obedience is compared to the former as the universal to the particular. For those who live in the world, keep something for themselves, and offer something to God; and in the latter respect they are under obedience to their superiors: whereas those who live in religion give themselves wholly and their possessions to God, as stated above ([3796]AA[1],3). Hence their obedience is universal.

Reply to Objection 2: As the Philosopher says (Ethic. ii, 1,2), by performing actions we contract certain habits, and when we have acquired the habit we are best able to perform the actions. Accordingly those who have not attained to perfection, acquire perfection by obeying, while those who have already acquired perfection are most ready to obey, not as though they need to be directed to the acquisition of perfection, but as maintaining themselves by this means in that which belongs to perfection.

Reply to Objection 3: The subjection of religious is chiefly in reference to bishops, who are compared to them as perfecters to perfected, as Dionysius states (Eccl. Hier. vi), where he also says that the "monastic order is subjected to the perfecting virtues of the bishops, and is taught by their godlike enlightenment." Hence neither hermits nor religious superiors are exempt from obedience to bishops; and if they be wholly or partly exempt from obedience to the bishop of the diocese, they are nevertheless bound to obey the Sovereign Pontiff, not only in matters affecting all in common, but also in those which pertain specially to religious discipline.

Reply to Objection 4: The vow of obedience taken by religious, extends to the disposition of a man's whole life, and in this way it has a certain universality, although it does not extend to all individual acts. For some of these do not belong to religion, through not being of those things that concern the love of God and of our neighbor, such as rubbing one's beard, lifting a stick from the ground and so forth, which do not come under a vow nor under obedience; and some are contrary to religion. Nor is there any comparison with continence whereby acts are excluded which are altogether contrary to religion.

Reply to Objection 5: The necessity of coercion makes an act involuntary and consequently deprives it of the character of praise or merit; whereas the necessity which is consequent upon obedience is a necessity not of coercion but of a free will, inasmuch as a man is willing to obey, although perhaps he would not be willing to do the thing commanded considered in itself. Wherefore since by the vow of obedience a man lays himself under the necessity of doing for God's sake certain things that are not pleasing in themselves, for this very reason that which he does is the more acceptable to God, though it be of less account, because man can give nothing greater to God, than by subjecting his will to another man's for God's sake. Hence in the Conferences of the Fathers (Coll. xviii, 7) it is stated that "the Sarabaitae are the worst class of monks, because through providing for their own needs without being subject to superiors, they are free to do as they will; and yet day and night they are more busily occupied in work than those who live in monasteries."

Whether it is requisite for religious perfection that poverty, continence, and obedience should come under a vow?

Objection 1: It would seem that it is not requisite for religious perfection that the three aforesaid, namely poverty, continence, and obedience, should come under a vow. For the school of perfection is founded on the principles laid down by our Lord. Now our Lord in formulating perfection (Mat. 19:21) said: "If thou wilt be perfect, go, sell all [Vulg.: 'what'] thou hast, and give to the poor," without any mention of a vow. Therefore it would seem that a vow is not necessary for the school of religion.

Objection 2: Further, a vow is a promise made to God, wherefore (Eccles. 5:3) the wise man after saying: "If thou hast vowed anything to God, defer not to pay it," adds at once, "for an unfaithful and foolish promise displeaseth Him." But when a thing is being actually given there is no need for a promise. Therefore it suffices for religious perfection that one keep poverty, continence, and obedience without. vowing them.

Objection 3: Further, Augustine says (Ad Pollent., de Adult. Conjug. i, 14): "The services we render are more pleasing when we might lawfully not render them, yet do so out of love." Now it is lawful not to render a service which we have not vowed, whereas it is unlawful if we have vowed to render it. Therefore seemingly it is more pleasing to God to keep poverty, continence, and obedience without a vow. Therefore a vow is not requisite for religious perfection.

On the contrary, In the Old Law the Nazareans were consecrated by vow according to Num. 6:2, "When a man or woman shall make a vow to be sanctified and will consecrate themselves to the Lord," etc. Now these were a figure of those "who attain the summit of perfection," as a gloss [*Cf. Moral. ii] of Gregory states. Therefore a vow is requisite for religious perfection.

I answer that, It belongs to religious to be in the state of perfection, as shown above (Q[174], A[5]). Now the state of perfection requires an obligation to whatever belongs to perfection: and this obligation consists in binding oneself to God by means of a vow. But it is evident from what has been said ([3797]AA[3],4,5) that poverty, continence, and obedience belong to the perfection of the Christian life. Consequently the religious state requires that one be bound to these three by vow. Hence Gregory says (Hom. xx in Ezech.): "When a man vows to God all his possessions, all his life, all his knowledge, it is a holocaust"; and afterwards he says that this refers to those who renounce the present world.

Reply to Objection 1: Our Lord declared that it belongs to the perfection of life that a man follow Him, not anyhow, but in such a way as not to turn back. Wherefore He says again (Lk. 9:62): "No man putting his hand to the plough, and looking back, is fit for the kingdom of God." And though some of His disciples went back, yet when our Lord asked (Jn. 6:68,69), "Will you also go away?"

Peter answered for the others: "Lord, to whom shall we go?" Hence Augustine says (De Consensu Ev. ii, 17) that "as Matthew and Mark relate, Peter and Andrew followed Him after drawing their boats on to the beach, not as though they purposed to return, but as following Him at His command." Now this unwavering following of Christ is made fast by a vow: wherefore a vow is requisite for religious perfection.

Reply to Objection 2: As Gregory says (Moral. ii) religious perfection requires that a man give "his whole life" to God. But a man cannot actually give God his whole life, because that life taken as a whole is not simultaneous but successive. Hence a man cannot give his whole life to God otherwise than by the obligation of a vow.

Reply to Objection 3: Among other services that we can lawfully give, is our liberty, which is dearer to man than aught else. Consequently when a man of his own accord deprives himself by vow of the liberty of abstaining from things pertaining to God's service, this is most acceptable to God. Hence Augustine says (Ep. cxxvii ad Paulin. et Arment.): "Repent not of thy vow; rejoice rather that thou canst no longer do lawfully, what thou mightest have done lawfully but to thy own cost. Happy the obligation that compels to better things."

Whether it is right to say that religious perfection consists in these three vows?

Objection 1: It would seem that it is not right to say that religious perfection consists in these three vows. For the perfection of life consists of inward rather than of outward acts, according to Rom. 14:17, "The Kingdom of God is not meat and drink, but justice and peace and joy in the Holy Ghost." Now the religious vow binds a man to things belonging to perfection. Therefore vows of inward actions, such as contemplation, love of God and our neighbor, and so forth, should pertain to the religious state, rather than the vows of poverty, continence, and obedience which refer to outward actions.

Objection 2: Further, the three aforesaid come under the religious vow, in so far as they belong to the practice of tending to perfection. But there are many other things that religious practice, such as abstinence, watchings, and the like. Therefore it would seem that these three vows are incorrectly described as pertaining to the state of perfection.

Objection 3: Further, by the vow of obedience a man is bound to do according to his superior's command whatever pertains to the practice of perfection. Therefore the vow of obedience suffices without the two other vows.

Objection 4: Further, external goods comprise not only riches but also honors. Therefore, if religious, by the vow of poverty, renounce earthly riches, there should be another vow whereby they may despise worldly honors.

On the contrary, It is stated (Extra, de Statu Monach., cap. Cum ad monasterium) that "the keeping of chastity and the renouncing of property are affixed to the monastic rule."

I answer that, The religious state may be considered in three ways. First, as being a practice of tending to the perfection of charity: secondly, as quieting the human mind from outward solicitude, according to 1 Cor. 7:32: "I would have you to be without solicitude": thirdly, as a holocaust whereby a man offers himself and his possessions wholly to God; and in corresponding manner the religious state is constituted by these three vows.

First, as regards the practice of perfection a man is required to remove from himself whatever may hinder his affections from tending wholly to God, for it is in this that the perfection of charity consists. Such hindrances are of three kinds. First, the attachment to external goods, which is removed by the vow of poverty; secondly, the concupiscence of sensible pleasures, chief among which are venereal pleasures, and these are removed by the vow of continence; thirdly, the inordinateness of the human will, and this is removed by the vow of obedience. In like manner the disquiet of worldly solicitude is aroused in man in reference especially to three things. First, as regards the dispensing of external things, and this solicitude is removed from man by the vow of poverty; secondly, as regards the control of wife and children, which is cut away by the vow of continence; thirdly, as regards the disposal of one's own actions, which is eliminated by the vow of obedience, whereby a man commits himself to the disposal of another.

Again, "a holocaust is the offering to God of all that one has," according to Gregory (Hom. xx in Ezech.). Now man has a threefold good, according to the Philosopher (Ethic. i, 8). First, the good of external things, which he wholly offers to God by the vow of voluntary poverty: secondly, the good of his own body, and this good he offers to God especially by the vow of continence, whereby he renounces the greatest bodily pleasures. the third is the good of the soul, which man wholly offers to God by the vow of obedience, whereby he offers God his own will by which he makes use of all the powers and habits of the soul. Therefore the religious state is fittingly constituted by the three vows.

Reply to Objection 1: As stated above [3798](A[1]), the end whereunto the religious vow is directed is the perfection of charity, since all the interior acts of virtue belong to charity as to their mother, according to 1 Cor. 13:4, "Charity is patient, is kind," etc. Hence the interior acts of virtue, for instance humility, patience, and so forth, do not come under the religious vow, but this is directed to them as its end.

Reply to Objection 2: All other religious observances are directed to the three aforesaid principal vows; for if any of them are ordained for the purpose of procuring a livelihood, such as labor, questing, and so on, they are to be referred to poverty; for the safeguarding of which religious seek a livelihood by these means. Other observances whereby the body is chastised, such as watching, fasting, and the like, are directly ordained for the observance of the vow of continence. And such religious observances as regard human actions whereby a man is directed to the end of religion, namely the love of God and his neighbor (such as reading, prayer, visiting the sick, and the like), are comprised under the vow of obedience that applies to the will, which directs its actions to the end according to the ordering of another person. The distinction of habit belongs to all three vows, as a sign of being bound by them: wherefore the religious habit is given or blessed at the time of profession.

Reply to Objection 3: By obedience a man offers to God his will, to which though all human affairs are subject, yet some are subject to it alone in a special manner, namely human actions, since passions belong also to the sensitive appetite. Wherefore in order to restrain the passions of carnal pleasures and of external objects of appetite, which hinder the perfection of life, there was need for the vows of continence and poverty; but for the ordering of one's own actions accordingly as the state of perfection requires, there was need for the vow of obedience.

Reply to Objection 4: As the Philosopher says (Ethic. iv, 3), strictly and truly speaking honor is not due save to virtue. Since, however, external goods serve instrumentally for certain acts of virtue, the consequence is that a certain honor is given to their excellence especially by the common people who acknowledge none but outward excellence. Therefore since religious tend to the perfection of virtue it becomes them not to renounce the honor which God and all holy men accord to virtue, according to Ps. 138:17, "But to me Thy friends, O God, are made exceedingly honorable." On the other hand, they renounce the honor that is given to outward excellence, by the very fact that they withdraw from a worldly life: hence no special vow is needed for this.

Day 246

Whether the vow of obedience is the chief of the three religious vows?

Objection 1: It would seem that the vow of obedience is not the chief of the three religious vows. For the perfection of the religious life was inaugurated by Christ. Now Christ gave a special counsel of poverty; whereas He is not stated to have given a special counsel of obedience. Therefore the vow of poverty is greater than the vow of obedience.

Objection 2: Further, it is written (Ecclus. 26:20) that "no price is worthy of a continent soul." Now the vow of that which is more worthy is itself more excellent. Therefore the vow of continence is more excellent than the vow of obedience.

Objection 3: Further, the greater a vow the more indispensable it would seem to be. Now the vows of poverty and continence "are so inseparable from the monastic rule, that not even the Sovereign Pontiff can allow them to be broken," according to a Decretal (De Statu Monach., cap. Cum ad monasterium): yet he can dispense a religious from obeying his superior. Therefore it would seem that the vow of obedience is less than the vow of poverty and continence.

On the contrary, Gregory says (Moral. xxxv, 14): "Obedience is rightly placed before victims, since by victims another's flesh, but by obedience one's own will, is sacrificed." Now the religious vows are holocausts, as stated above ([3799]AA[1],3, ad 6). Therefore the vow of obedience is the chief of all religious vows.

I answer that, The vow of obedience is the chief of the three religious vows, and this for three reasons.

First, because by the vow of obedience man offers God something greater, namely his own will; for this is of more account than his own body, which he offers God by continence, and than external things, which he offers God by the vow of poverty. Wherefore that which is done out of obedience is more acceptable to God than that which is done of one's own will, according to the saying of Jerome (Ep. cxxv ad Rustic Monach.): "My words are intended to teach you not to rely on your own judgment": and a little further on he says: "You may not do what you will; you must eat what you are bidden to eat, you may possess as much as you receive, clothe yourself with what is given to you." Hence fasting is not acceptable to God if it is done of one's own will, according to Is. 58:3, "Behold in the day of your fast your own will is found."

Secondly, because the vow of obedience includes the other vows, but not vice versa: for a religious, though bound by vow to observe continence and poverty, yet these also come under obedience, as well as many other things besides the keeping of continence and poverty.

Thirdly, because the vow of obedience extends properly to those acts that are closely connected with the end of religion; and the more closely a thing is connected with the end, the better it is.

It follows from this that the vow of obedience is more essential to the religious life. For if a man without taking a vow of obedience were to observe, even by vow, voluntary poverty and continence, he would not therefore belong to the religious state, which is to be preferred to virginity observed even by vow; for Augustine says (De Virgin. xlvi): "No one, methinks, would prefer virginity to the monastic life." [*St. Augustine wrote not 'monasterio' but 'martyrio'---to 'martyrdom'; and St. Thomas quotes the passage correctly above[3800], Q[124], A[3] and[3801] Q[152], A[5]].

Reply to Objection 1: The counsel of obedience was included in the very following of Christ, since to obey is to follow another's will. Consequently it is more pertinent to perfection than the vow of poverty, because as Jerome, commenting on Mat. 19:27, "Behold we have left all things," observes, "Peter added that which is perfect when he said: And have followed Thee."

Reply to Objection 2: The words quoted mean that continence is to be preferred, not to all other acts of virtue, but to conjugal chastity, or to external riches of gold and silver which are measured by weight [*'Pondere,' referring to the Latin 'ponderatio' in the Vulgate, which the Douay version renders 'price.']. Or again continence is taken in a general sense for abstinence from all evil, as stated above ([3802]Q[155], A[4], ad 1).

Reply to Objection 3: The Pope cannot dispense a religious from his vow of obedience so as to release him from obedience to every superior in matters relating to the perfection of life, for he cannot exempt him from obedience to himself. He can, however, exempt him from subjection to a lower superior, but this is not to dispense him from his vow of obedience.

Whether a religious sins mortally whenever he transgresses the things contained in his rule?

Objection 1: It would seem that a religious sins mortally whenever he transgresses the things contained in his rule. For to break a vow is a sin worthy of condemnation, as appears from 1 Tim. 5:11,12, where the Apostle says that widows who "will marry have [Vulg.: 'having'] damnation, because they have made void their first faith." But religious are bound to a rule by the vows of their profession. Therefore they sin mortally by transgressing the things contained in their rule.

Objection 2: Further, the rule is enjoined upon a religious in the same way as a law. Now he who transgresses a precept of law sins mortally. Therefore it would seem that a monk sins mortally if he transgresses the things contained in his rule.

Objection 3: Further, contempt involves a mortal sin. Now whoever repeatedly does what he ought not to do seems to sin from contempt. Therefore it would seem that a religious sins mortally by frequently transgressing the things contained in his rule.

On the contrary, The religious state is safer than the secular state; wherefore Gregory at the beginning of his Morals [*Epist. Missoria, ad Leand. Episc. i] compares the secular life to the stormy sea, and the religious life to the calm port. But if every transgression of the things contained in his rule were to involve a religious in mortal sin, the religious life would be fraught with danger of account of its multitude of observances. Therefore not every transgression of the things contained in the rule is a mortal sin.

I answer that, As stated above (A[1], ad 1,2), a thing is contained in the rule in two ways. First, as the end of the rule, for instance things that pertain to the acts of the virtues; and the transgression of these, as regards those which come under a common precept, involves a mortal sin; but as regards those which are not included in the common obligation of a precept, the transgression thereof does not involve a mortal sin, except by reason of contempt, because, as stated above [3803](A[2]), a religious is not bound to be perfect, but to tend to perfection, to which the contempt of perfection is opposed.

Secondly, a thing is contained in the rule through pertaining to the outward practice, such as all external observances, to some of which a religious is bound by the vow of his profession. Now the vow of profession regards chiefly the three things aforesaid, namely poverty, continence, and obedience, while all others are directed to these. Consequently the transgression of these three involves a mortal sin, while the transgression of the others does not involve a mortal sin, except either by reason of contempt of the rule (since this is directly contrary to the profession whereby a man vows to live according to the rule), or by reason of a precept, whether given orally by a superior, or expressed in the rule, since this would be to act contrary to the vow of obedience.

Reply to Objection 1: He who professes a rule does not vow to observe all the things contained in the rule, but he vows the regular life which consists essentially in the three aforesaid things. Hence in certain religious orders precaution is taken to profess, not the rule, but to live according to the rule, i.e. to tend to form one's conduct in accordance with the rule as a kind of model; and this is set aside by contempt. Yet greater precaution is observed in some religious orders by professing obedience according to the rule, so that only that which is contrary to a precept of the rule is contrary to the profession, while the transgression or omission of other things binds only under pain of venial sin, because, as stated above (A[7], ad 2), such things are dispositions to the chief vows. And venial sin is a disposition to mortal, as stated above ([3804]FS, Q[88], A[3]), inasmuch as it hinders those things whereby a man is disposed to keep the chief precepts of Christ's law, namely the precepts of charity.

There is also a religious order, that of the Friars Preachers, where such like transgressions or omissions do not, by their very nature, involve sin, either mortal or venial; but they bind one to suffer the punishment affixed thereto, because it is in this way that they are bound to observe such things. Nevertheless they may sin venially or mortally through neglect, concupiscence, or contempt.

Reply to Objection 2: Not all the contents of the law are set forth by way of precept; for some are expressed under the form of ordinance or statute binding under pain of a fixed punishment. Accordingly, just as in the civil law the transgression of a legal statute does not always render a man deserving of bodily death, so neither in the law of the Church does every ordinance or statute bind under mortal sin; and the same applies to the statutes of the rule.

Reply to Objection 3: An action or transgression proceeds from contempt when a man's will refuses to submit to the ordinance of the law or rule, and from this he proceeds to act against the law or rule. on the other hand, he does not sin from contempt, but from some other cause, when he is led to do something against the ordinance of the law or rule through some particular cause such as concupiscence or anger, even though he often repeat the same kind of sin through the same or some other cause. Thus Augustine says (De Nat. et Grat. xxix) that "not all sins are committed through proud contempt." Nevertheless the frequent repetition of a sin leads dispositively to contempt, according to the words of Prov. 18:3, "The wicked man, when he is come into the depth of sins, contemneth."

Whether a religious sins more grievously than a secular by the same kind of sin?

Objection 1: It would seem that a religious does not sin more grievously than a secular by the same kind of sin. For it is written (2 Paralip 30:18,19): "The Lord Who is good will show mercy to all them who with their whole heart seek the Lord the God of their fathers, and will not impute it to them that they are not sanctified." Now religious apparently follow the Lord the God of their fathers with their whole heart rather than seculars, who partly give themselves and their possessions to God and reserve part for themselves, as Gregory says (Hom. xx in Ezech.). Therefore it would seem that it is less imputed to them if they fall short somewhat of their sanctification.

Objection 2: Further, God is less angered at a man's sins if he does some good deeds, according to 2 Paralip 19:2,3, "Thou helpest the ungodly, and thou art joined in friendship with them that hate the Lord, and therefore thou didst deserve indeed the wrath of the Lord: but good works are found in thee." Now religious do more good works than seculars. Therefore if they commit any sins, God is less angry with them.

Objection 3: Further, this present life is not carried through without sin, according to James 3:2, "In many things we all offend." Therefore if the sins of religious were more grievous than those of seculars it would follow that religious are worse off than seculars: and consequently it would not be a wholesome counsel to enter religion.

On the contrary, The greater the evil the more it would seem to be deplored. But seemingly the sins of those who are in the state of holiness and perfection are the most deplorable, for it is written (Jer. 23:9): "My heart is broken within me," and afterwards (Jer. 23:11): "For the prophet and the priest are defiled; and in My house I have found their wickedness." Therefore religious and others who are in the state of perfection, other things being equal, sin more grievously.

I answer that, A sin committed by a religious may be in three ways more grievous than a like sin committed by a secular. First, if it be against his religious vow; for instance if he be guilty of fornication or theft, because by fornication he acts against the vow of continence, and by theft against the vow of poverty; and not merely against a precept of the divine law. Secondly, if he sin out of contempt, because thereby he would seem to be the more ungrateful for the divine favors which have raised him to the state of perfection. Thus the Apostle says (Heb. 10:29) that the believer "deserveth worse punishments" who through contempt tramples under foot the Son of God. Hence the Lord complains (Jer. 11:15): "What is the meaning that My beloved hath wrought much wickedness in

My house?" Thirdly, the sin of a religious may be greater on account of scandal, because many take note of his manner of life: wherefore it is written (Jer. 23:14): "I have seen the likeness of adulterers, and the way of lying in the Prophets of Jerusalem; and they strengthened the hands of the wicked, that no man should return from his evil doings."

On the other hand, if a religious, not out of contempt, but out of weakness or ignorance, commit a sin that is not against the vow of his profession, without giving scandal (for instance if he commit it in secret) he sins less grievously in the same kind of sin than a secular, because his sin if slight is absorbed as it were by his many good works, and if it be mortal, he more easily recovers from it. First, because he has a right intention towards God, and though it be intercepted for the moment, it is easily restored to its former object. Hence Origen commenting on Ps. 36:24, "When he shall fall he shall not be bruised," says (Hom. iv in Ps. 36): "The wicked man, if he sin, repents not, and fails to make amends for his sin. But the just man knows how to make amends and recover himself; even as he who had said: 'I know not the man,' shortly afterwards when the Lord had looked on him, knew to shed most bitter tears, and he who from the roof had seen a woman and desired her knew to say: 'I have sinned and done evil before Thee.'" Secondly, he is assisted by his fellow-religious to rise again, according to Eccles. 4:10, "If one fall he shall be supported by the other: woe to him that is alone, for when he falleth he hath none to lift him up."

Reply to Objection 1: The words quoted refer to things done through weakness or ignorance, but not to those that are done out of contempt.

Reply to Objection 2: Josaphat also, to whom these words were addressed, sinned not out of contempt, but out of a certain weakness of human affection.

Reply to Objection 3: The just sin not easily out of contempt; but sometimes they fall into a sin through ignorance or weakness from which they easily arise. If, however, they go so far as to sin out of contempt, they become most wicked and incorrigible, according to the word of Jer. 2:20: "Thou hast broken My yoke, thou hast burst My bands, and thou hast said: 'I will not serve.' For on every high hill and under every green tree thou didst prostitute thyself." Hence Augustine says (Ep. lxxviii ad Pleb. Hippon.): "From the time I began to serve God, even as I scarcely found better men than those who made progress in monasteries, so have I not found worse than those who in the monastery have fallen."

OF THOSE THINGS THAT ARE COMPETENT TO RELIGIOUS (SIX ARTICLES)

We must now consider the things that are competent to religious; and under this head there are six points of inquiry:
(1) Whether it is lawful for them to teach, preach, and do like things?
(2) Whether it is lawful for them to meddle in secular business?
(3) Whether they are bound to manual labor?
(4) Whether it is lawful for them to live on alms?
(5) Whether it is lawful for them to quest?
(6) Whether it is lawful for them to wear coarser clothes than other persons?

Whether it is lawful for religious to teach, preach, and the like?

Objection 1: It would seem unlawful for religious to teach, preach, and the like. For it is said (VII, qu. i, can. Hoc nequaquam) in an ordinance of a synod of Constantinople [*Pseudosynod held by Photius in the year 879]: "The monastic life is one of subjection and discipleship, not of teaching, authority, or pastoral care." And Jerome says (ad Ripar. et Desider. [*Contra Vigilant. xvi]): "A monk's duty is not to teach but to lament." Again Pope Leo [*Leo I, Ep. cxx ad Theodoret., 6, cf. XVI, qu. i, can. Adjicimus]: says "Let none dare to preach save the priests of the Lord, be he monk or layman, and no matter what knowledge he may boast of having." Now it is not lawful to exceed the bounds of one's office or transgress the ordinance of the Church. Therefore seemingly it is unlawful for religious to teach, preach, and the like.

Objection 2: Further, in an ordinance of the Council of Nicea (cf. XVI, qu. i, can. Placuit) it is laid down as follows: "It is our absolute and peremptory command addressed to all that monks shall not hear confessions except of one another, as is right, that they shall not bury the dead except those dwelling with them in the monastery, or if by chance a brother happen to die while on a visit." But just as the above belong to the duty of clerics, so also do preaching and teaching. Therefore since "the business of a monk differs from that of a cleric," as Jerome says (Ep. xiv ad Heliod.), it would seem unlawful for religious to preach, teach, and the like.

Objection 3: Further, Gregory says (Regist. v, Ep. 1): "No man can fulfil ecclesiastical duties, and keep consistently to the monastic rule": and this is quoted XVI, qu. i, can. Nemo potest. Now monks are bound to keep consistently to the monastic rule. Therefore it would seem that they cannot fulfil ecclesiastical duties, whereof teaching and preaching are a part. Therefore seemingly it is unlawful for them to preach, teach, and do similar things.

On the contrary, Gregory is quoted (XVI, qu. i, can. Ex auctoritate) as saying: "By authority of this decree framed in virtue of our apostolic power and the duty of our office, be it lawful to monk priests who are configured to the apostles, to preach, baptize, give communion, pray for sinners, impose penance, and absolve from sin."

I answer that, A thing is declared to be unlawful to a person in two ways. First, because there is something in him contrary to that which is declared unlawful to him: thus to no man is it lawful to sin, because each man has in himself reason and an obligation to God's law, to which things sin is contrary. And in this way it is said to be unlawful for a person to preach, teach, or do like things, because there is in him something incompatible with these things, either by reason of a precept---thus those who are irregular by ordinance of the Church may not be raised to the sacred orders---or by reason of sin, according to Ps. 49:16, "But to the sinner God hath said: Why dost thou declare My justice?"

In this way it is not unlawful for religious to preach, teach, and do like things, both because they are bound neither by vow nor by precept of their rule to abstain from these things, and because they are not rendered less apt for these things by any sin committed, but on the contrary they are the more apt through having taken upon themselves the practice of holiness. For it is foolish to say that a man is rendered less fit for spiritual duties through advancing himself in holiness; and consequently it is foolish to declare that the religious state is an obstacle to the fulfilment of such like duties. This error is rejected by Pope Boniface [*Boniface IV] for the reasons given above. His words which are quoted (XVI, qu. i, can. Sunt. nonnulli) are these: "There are some who without any dogmatic proof, and with extreme daring, inspired with a zeal rather of bitterness than of love, assert that monks though they be dead to the world and live to God, are unworthy of the power of the priestly office, and that they cannot confer penance, nor christen, nor absolve in virtue of the power divinely bestowed on them in the priestly office. But they are altogether wrong." He proves this first because it is not contrary to the rule; thus he continues: "For neither did the Blessed Benedict the saintly teacher of monks forbid this in any way," nor is it forbidden in other rules. Secondly, he refutes the above error from the usefulness of the monks, when he adds at the end of the same chapter: "The more perfect a man is, the more effective is he in these, namely in spiritual works."

Secondly, a thing is said to be unlawful for a man, not on account of there being in him something contrary thereto, but because he lacks that which enables him to do it: thus it is unlawful for a deacon to say mass, because he is not in priestly orders; and it is unlawful for a priest to deliver judgment because he lacks the episcopal authority. Here, however, a distinction must be made. Because those things which are a matter of an order, cannot be deputed to one who has not the order, whereas matters of jurisdiction can be deputed to those who have not ordinary jurisdiction: thus the delivery of a judgment is deputed by the bishop to a simple priest. In this sense it is said to be unlawful for monks and other religious to preach, teach, and so forth, because the religious state does not give them the power to do these things. They can, however, do them if they receive orders, or ordinary jurisdiction, or if matters of jurisdiction be delegated to them.

Reply to Objection 1: It results from the words quoted that the fact of their being monks does not give monks the power to do these things, yet it does not involve in them anything contrary to the performance of these acts.

Reply to Objection 2: Again, this ordinance of the Council of Nicea forbids monks to claim the power of exercising those acts on the ground of their being monks, but it does not forbid those acts being delegated to them.

Reply to Objection 3: These two things are incompatible, namely, the ordinary cure of ecclesiastical duties, and the observance of the monastic rule in a monastery. But this does not prevent monks and other religious from being sometimes occupied with ecclesiastical duties through being deputed thereto by superiors having ordinary cure; especially members of religious orders that are especially instituted for that purpose, as we shall say further on ([3805]Q[188], A[4]).

Whether it is lawful for religious to occupy themselves with secular business?

Objection 1: It would seem unlawful for religious to occupy themselves with secular business. For in the decree quoted above [3806](A[1]) of Pope Boniface it is said that the "Blessed Benedict bade them to be altogether free from secular business; and this is most explicitly prescribed by the apostolic doctrine and the teaching of all the Fathers, not only to religious, but also to all the canonical clergy," according to 2 Tim. 2:4, "No man being a soldier to God, entangleth himself with secular business." Now it is the duty of all religious to be soldiers of God. Therefore it is unlawful for them to occupy themselves with secular business.

Objection 2: Further, the Apostle says (1 Thess. 4:11): "That you use your endeavor to be quiet, and that you do your own business," which a gloss explains thus---"by refraining from other people's affairs, so as to be the better able to attend to the amendment of your own life." Now religious devote themselves in a special way to the amendment of their life. Therefore they should not occupy themselves with secular business.

Objection 3: Further, Jerome, commenting on Mat. 11:8, "Behold they that are clothed in soft garments are in the houses of kings," says: "Hence we gather that an austere life and severe preaching should avoid the palaces of kings and the mansions of the voluptuous." But the needs of secular business induce men to frequent the palaces of kings. Therefore it is unlawful for religious to occupy themselves with secular business.

On the contrary, The Apostle says (Rom. 16:1): "I commend to you Phoebe our Sister," and further on (Rom. 16:2), "that you assist her in whatsoever business she shall have need of you."

I answer that, As stated above ([3807]Q[186], AA[1],7, ad 1), the religious state is directed to the attainment of the perfection of charity, consisting principally in the love of God and secondarily in the love of our neighbor. Consequently that which religious intend chiefly and for its own sake is to give themselves to God. Yet if their neighbor be in need, they should attend to his affairs out of charity, according to Gal. 6:2, "Bear ye one another's burthens: and so you shall fulfil the law of Christ," since through serving their neighbor for God's sake, they are obedient to the divine love. Hence it is written (James 1:27): "Religion clean and undefiled before God and the Father, is this: to visit the fatherless and widows in their tribulation," which means, according to a gloss, to assist the helpless in their time of need.

We must conclude therefore that it is unlawful for either monks or clerics to carry on secular business from motives of avarice; but from motives of charity, and with their superior's permission, they may occupy themselves with due moderation in the administration and direction of secular business. Wherefore it is said in the Decretals (Dist. xxxviii, can. Decrevit): "The holy synod decrees that henceforth no cleric shall buy property or occupy himself with secular business, save with a view to the care of the fatherless, orphans, or widows, or when the bishop of the city commands him to take charge of the business connected with the Church." And the same applies to religious as to clerics, because they are both debarred from secular business on the same grounds, as stated above.

Reply to Objection 1: Monks are forbidden to occupy themselves with secular business from motives of avarice, but not from motives of charity.

Reply to Objection 2: To occupy oneself with secular business on account of another's need is not officiousness but charity.

Reply to Objection 3: To haunt the palaces of kings from motives of pleasure, glory, or avarice is not becoming to religious, but there is nothing unseemly in their visiting them from motives of piety. Hence it is written (4 Kings 4:13): "Hast thou any business, and wilt thou that I speak to the king or to the general of the army?" Likewise it becomes religious to go to the palaces of kings to rebuke and guide them, even as John the Baptist rebuked Herod, as related in Mat. 14:4.

Whether religious are bound to manual labor?

Objection 1: It would seem that religious are bound to manual labor. For religious are not exempt from the observance of precepts. Now manual labor is a matter of precept according to 1 Thess. 4:11, "Work with your own hands as we commanded you"; wherefore Augustine says (De oper. Monach. xxx): "But who can allow these insolent men," namely religious that do no work, of whom he is speaking there, "who disregard the most salutary admonishment of the Apostle, not merely to be borne with as being weaker than others, but even to preach as though they were holier than others." Therefore it would seem that religious are bound to manual labor.

Objection 2: Further, a gloss [*St. Augustine, (De oper. Monach. xxi)] on 2 Thess. 3:10, "If any man will not work, neither let him eat," says: "Some say that this command of the Apostle refers to spiritual works, and not to the bodily labor of the farmer or craftsman"; and further on: "But it is useless for them to try to hide from themselves and from others the fact that they are unwilling not only to fulfil, but even to understand the useful admonishments of charity"; and again: "He wishes God's servants to make a living by working with their bodies." Now religious especially are called servants of God, because they give themselves entirely to the service of God, as Dionysius asserts (Eccl. Hier. vi). Therefore it would seem that they are bound to manual labor.

Objection 3: Further, Augustine says (De oper. Monach. xvii): "I would fain know how they would occupy themselves, who are unwilling to work with their body. We occupy our time, say they, with prayers, psalms, reading, and the word of God." Yet these things are no excuse, and he proves this, as regards each in particular. For in the first place, as to prayer, he says: "One prayer of the obedient man is sooner granted than ten thousand prayers of the contemptuous": meaning that those are contemptuous and unworthy to be heard who work not with their hands. Secondly, as to the divine praises he adds: "Even while working with their hands they can easily sing hymns to God." Thirdly, with regard to reading, he goes on to say: "Those who say they are occupied in reading, do they not find there what the Apostle commanded? What sort of perverseness is this, to wish to read but not to obey what one reads?" Fourthly, he adds in reference to preaching [*Cap. xviii]: "If one has to speak, and is so busy that he cannot spare time for manual work, can all in the monastery do this? And since all cannot do this, why should all make this a pretext for being exempt? And even if all were able, they should do so by turns, not only so that the others may be occupied in other works, but also because it suffices that one speak while many listen." Therefore it would seem that religious should not desist from manual labor on account of such like spiritual works to which they devote themselves.

Objection 4: Further, a gloss on Lk. 12:33, "Sell what you possess," says: "Not only give your clothes to the poor, but sell what you possess, that having once for all renounced all your possessions for the Lord's sake, you may henceforth work with the labor of your hands, so as to have wherewith to live or to give alms." Now it belongs properly to religious to renounce all they have. Therefore it would seem likewise to belong to them to live and give alms through the labor of their hands.

Objection 5: Further, religious especially would seem to be bound to imitate the life of the apostles, since they profess the state of perfection. Now the apostles worked with their own hands, according to 1 Cor. 4:12: "We labor, working with our own hands." Therefore it would seem that religious are bound to manual labor.

On the contrary, Those precepts that are commonly enjoined upon all are equally binding on religious and seculars. But the precept of manual labor is enjoined upon all in common, as appears from 2 Thess. 3:6, "Withdraw yourselves from every brother walking disorderly," etc. (for by brother he signifies every Christian, according to 1 Cor. 7:12, "If any brother have a wife that believeth not"). Now it is written in the same passage (2 Thess. 3:10): "If any man will not work, neither let him eat." Therefore religious are not bound to manual labor any more than seculars are.

I answer that, Manual labor is directed to four things. First and principally to obtain food; wherefore it was said to the first man (Gn. 3:19): "In the sweat of thy face shalt thou eat bread," and it is written (Ps. 127:2): "For thou shalt eat the labors of thy hands." Secondly, it is directed to the removal of idleness whence arise many evils; hence it is written (Ecclus. 33:28,29): "Send" thy slave "to work, that he be not idle, for idleness hath taught much evil." Thirdly, it is directed to the curbing of concupiscence, inasmuch as it is a means of afflicting the body; hence it is written (2 Cor. 6:5,6): "In labors, in watchings, in fastings, in chastity." Fourthly, it is directed to almsgiving, wherefore it is written (Eph. 4:28): "He that stole, let him now steal no more; but rather let him labor, working with his hands the thing which is good, that he may have something to give to him that suffereth need." Accordingly, in so far as manual labor is directed to obtaining food, it comes under a necessity of precept in so far as it is necessary for that end: since that which is directed to an end derives its necessity from that end, being, in effect, so far necessary as the end cannot be obtained without it. Consequently he who has no other means of livelihood is bound to work with his hands, whatever his condition may be. This is signified by the words of the Apostle: "If any man will not work, neither let him eat," as though to say: "The necessity of manual labor is the necessity of meat." So that if one could live without eating, one would not be bound to work with one's hands. The same applies to those who have no other lawful means of livelihood: since a man is understood to be unable to do what he cannot do lawfully. Wherefore we find that the Apostle prescribed manual labor merely as a remedy for the sin of those who gained their livelihood by unlawful means. For the Apostle ordered manual labor first of all in order to avoid theft, as appears from Eph. 4:28, "He that stole, let him now steal no more; but rather let him labor, working with his hands." Secondly, to avoid the coveting of others' property, wherefore it is written (1 Thess. 4:11): "Work with your own hands, as we commanded you, and that you walk honestly towards them that are without." Thirdly, to avoid the discreditable pursuits whereby some seek a livelihood. Hence he says (2 Thess. 3:10-12): "When we were with you, this we declared to you: that if any man will not work, neither let him eat. For we have heard that there are some among you who walk disorderly, working not at all, but curiously meddling" (namely, as a gloss explains it, "who make a living by meddling in unlawful things). Now we charge them that are such, and beseech them . . . that working with silence, they would eat their own bread." Hence Jerome states (Super epist. ad Galat. [*Preface to Bk. ii of Commentary]) that the Apostle said this "not so much in his capacity of teacher as on account of the faults of the people."

It must, however, be observed that under manual labor are comprised all those human occupations whereby man can lawfully gain a livelihood, whether by using his hands, his feet, or his tongue. For watchmen, couriers, and such like who live by their labor, are understood to live by their handiwork: because, since the hand is "the organ of organs" [*De Anima iii, 8], handiwork denotes all kinds of work, whereby a man may lawfully gain a livelihood.

In so far as manual labor is directed to the removal of idleness, or the affliction of the body, it does not come under a necessity of precept if we consider it in itself, since there are many other means besides manual labor of afflicting the body or of removing idleness: for the flesh is afflicted by fastings and watchings, and idleness is removed by meditation on the Holy Scriptures and by the divine praises. Hence a gloss on Ps. 118:82, "My eyes have failed for Thy word," says: "He is not idle who meditates only on God's word; nor is he who works abroad any better than he who devotes himself to the study of knowing the truth." Consequently for these reasons religious are not bound to manual labor, as neither are seculars, except when they are so bound by the statutes of their order. Thus Jerome says (Ep. cxxv ad Rustic Monach.): "The Egyptian monasteries are wont to admit none unless they work or labor, not so much for the necessities of life, as for the welfare of the soul, lest it be led astray by wicked thoughts." But in so far as manual labor is directed to almsgiving, it does not come under the necessity of precept, save perchance in some particular case, when a man is under an obligation to give alms, and has no other means of having the wherewithal to assist the poor: for in such a case religious would be bound as well as seculars to do manual labor.

Reply to Objection 1: This command of the Apostle is of natural law: wherefore a gloss on 2 Thess. 3:6, "That you withdraw yourselves from every brother walking disorderly," says, "otherwise than the natural order requires," and he is speaking of those who abstained from manual labor. Hence nature has provided man with hands instead of arms and clothes, with which she has provided other animals, in order that with his hands he may obtain these and all other necessaries. Hence it is clear that this precept, even as all the precepts of the natural law, is binding on both religious and seculars alike. Yet not everyone sins that works not with his hands, because those precepts of the natural law which regard the good of the many are not binding on each individual, but it suffices that one person apply himself to this business and another to that; for instance, that some be craftsmen, others husbandmen, others judges, and others teachers, and so forth, according to the words of the Apostle (1 Cor. 12:17), "If the whole body were the eye, where would be the hearing? If the whole were the hearing, where would be the smelling?"

Reply to Objection 2: This gloss is taken from Augustine's De operibus Monachorum, cap. 21, where he speaks against certain monks who declared it to be unlawful for the servants of God to work with their hands, on account of our Lord's saying (Mat. 6:25): "Be not solicitous for your life, what you shall eat." Nevertheless his words do not imply that religious are bound to work with their hands, if they have other means of livelihood. This is clear from his adding: "He wishes the servants of God to make a living by working with their bodies." Now this does not apply to religious any more than to seculars, which is evident for two reasons. First, on account of the way in which the Apostle expresses himself, by saying: "That you withdraw yourselves from every brother walking disorderly." For he calls all Christians brothers, since at that time religious orders were not as yet founded. Secondly, because religious have no other obligations than what seculars have, except as required by the rule they profess: wherefore if their rule contain nothing about manual labor, religious are not otherwise bound to manual labor than seculars are.

Reply to Objection 3: A man may devote himself in two ways to all the spiritual works mentioned by Augustine in the passage quoted: in one way with a view to the common good, in another with a view to his private advantage. Accordingly those who devote themselves publicly to the aforesaid spiritual works are thereby exempt from manual labor for two reasons: first, because it behooves them to be occupied exclusively with such like works; secondly, because those who devote themselves to such works have a claim to be supported by those for whose advantage they work.

On the other hand, those who devote themselves to such works not publicly but privately as it were, ought not on that account to be exempt from manual labor, nor have they a claim to be supported by the offerings of the faithful, and it is of these that Augustine is speaking. For when he says: "They can sing hymns to God even while working with their hands; like the craftsmen who give tongue to fable telling without withdrawing their hands from their work," it is clear that he cannot refer to those who sing the canonical hours in the church, but to those who tell psalms or hymns as private prayers. Likewise what he says of reading and prayer is to be referred to the private prayer and reading which even lay people do at times, and not to those who perform public prayers in the church, or give public lectures in the schools. Hence he does not say: "Those who say they are occupied in teaching and instructing," but: "Those who say they are occupied in reading." Again he speaks of that preaching which is addressed, not publicly to the people, but to one or a few in particular by way of private admonishment. Hence he says expressly: "If one has to speak." For according to a gloss on 1 Cor. 2:4, "Speech is addressed privately, preaching to many."

Reply to Objection 4: Those who despise all for God's sake are bound to work with their hands, when they have no other means of livelihood, or of almsgiving (should the case occur where almsgiving were a matter of precept), but not otherwise, as stated in the Article. It is in this sense that the gloss quoted is to be understood.

Reply to Objection 5: That the apostles worked with their hands was sometimes a matter of necessity, sometimes a work of supererogation. It was of necessity when they failed to receive a livelihood from others. Hence a gloss on 1 Cor. 4:12, "We labor, working with our own hands," adds, "because no man giveth to us." It was supererogation, as appears from 1 Cor. 9:12, where the Apostle says that he did not use the power he had of living by the Gospel. The Apostle had recourse to this supererogation for three motives. First, in order to deprive the false apostles of the pretext for preaching, for they preached merely for a temporal advantage; hence he says (2 Cor. 11:12): "But what I do, that I will do that I may cut off the occasion from them," etc. Secondly, in order to avoid burdening those to whom he preached; hence he says (2 Cor. 12:13): "What is there that you have had less than the other churches, but that I myself was not burthensome to you?" Thirdly, in order to give an example of work to the idle; hence he says (2 Thess. 3:8,9): "We worked night and day . . . that we might give ourselves a pattern unto you, to imitate us." However, the Apostle did not do this in places like Athens where he had facilities for preaching daily, as Augustine observes (De oper. Monach. xviii). Yet religious are not for this reason bound to imitate the Apostle in this matter, since they are not bound to all works of supererogation: wherefore neither did the other apostles work with their hands.

Whether it is lawful for religious to live on alms?

Objection 1: It would seem unlawful for religious to live on alms. For the Apostle (1 Tim. 5:16) forbids those widows who have other means of livelihood to live on the alms of the Church, so that the Church may have "sufficient for them that are widows indeed." And Jerome says to Pope Damasus [*Cf. Cf. Can. Clericos, cause. i, qu. 2; Can. Quoniam, cause xvi, qu. 1; Regul. Monach. iv among the supposititious works of St. Jerome] that "those who have sufficient income from their parents and their own possessions, if they take what belongs to the poor they commit and incur the guilt of sacrilege, and by the abuse of such things they eat and drink judgment to themselves." Now religious if they be able-bodied can support themselves by the work of their hands. Therefore it would seem that they sin if they consume the alms belonging to the poor.

Objection 2: Further, to live at the expense of the faithful is the stipend appointed to those who preach the Gospel in payment of their labor or work, according to Mat. 10:10: "The workman is worthy of his meat." Now it belongs not to religious to preach the Gospel, but chiefly to prelates who are pastors and teachers. Therefore religious cannot lawfully live on the alms of the faithful.

Objection 3: Further, religious are in the state of perfection. But it is more perfect to give than to receive alms; for it is written (Acts 20:35): "It is a more blessed thing to give, rather than to receive." Therefore they should not live on alms, but rather should they give alms of their handiwork.

Objection 4: Further, it belongs to religious to avoid obstacles to virtue and occasions of sin. Now the receiving of alms offers an occasion of sin, and hinders an act of virtue; hence a gloss on 2 Thess. 3:9, "That we might give ourselves a pattern unto you," says: "He who through idleness eats often at another's table, must needs flatter the one who feeds him." It is also written (Ex. 23:8): "Neither shalt thou take bribes which . . . blind the wise, and pervert the words of the just," and (Prov. 22:7): "The borrower is servant to him that lendeth." This is contrary to religion, wherefore a gloss on 2 Thess. 3:9, "That we might give ourselves a pattern," etc., says, "our religion calls men to liberty." Therefore it would seem that religious should not live on alms.

Objection 5: Further, religious especially are bound to imitate the perfection of the apostles; wherefore the Apostle says (Phil. 3:15): "Let us . . . as many as are perfect, be thus minded." But the Apostle was unwilling to live at the expense of the faithful, either in order to cut off the occasion from the false apostles as he himself says (2 Cor. 11:12), or to avoid giving scandal to the weak, as appears from 1 Cor. 9:12. It would seem therefore that religious ought for the same reasons to refrain from living on alms. Hence Augustine says (De oper. Monach. 28): "Cut off the occasion of disgraceful marketing whereby you lower yourselves in the esteem of others, and give scandal to the weak: and show men that you seek not an easy livelihood in idleness, but the kingdom of God by the narrow and strait way."

On the contrary, Gregory says (Dial. ii, 1): The Blessed Benedict after leaving his home and parents dwelt for three years in a cave, and while there lived on the food brought to him by a monk from Rome. Nevertheless, although he was able-bodied, we do not read that he sought to live by the labor of his hands. Therefore religious may lawfully live on alms.

I answer that, A man may lawfully live on what is his or due to him. Now that which is given out of liberality becomes the property of the person to whom it is given. Wherefore religious and clerics whose monasteries or churches have received from the munificence of princes or of any of the faithful any endowment whatsoever for their support, can lawfully live on such endowment without working with their hands, and yet without doubt they live on alms. Wherefore in like manner if religious receive movable goods from the faithful they can lawfully live on them. For it is absurd to say that a person may accept an alms of some great property but not bread or some small sum of money. Nevertheless since these gifts would seem to be bestowed on religious in order that they may have more leisure for religious works, in which the donors of temporal goods wish to have a share, the use of such gifts would become unlawful for them if they abstained from religious works, because in that case, so far as they are concerned, they would be thwarting the intention of those who bestowed those gifts.

A thing is due to a person in two ways. First, on account of necessity, which makes all things common, as Ambrose [*Basil, Serm. de Temp. lxiv, among the supposititious works of St. Ambrose] asserts. Consequently if religious be in need they can lawfully live on alms. Such necessity may occur in three ways. First, through weakness of body, the result being that they are unable to make a living by working with their hands. Secondly, because that which they gain by their handiwork is insufficient for their livelihood: wherefore Augustine says (De oper. Monach. xvii) that "the good works of the faithful should not leave God's servants who work with their hands without a supply of necessaries, that when the hour comes for them to nourish their souls, so as to make it impossible for them to do these corporal works, they be not oppressed by want." Thirdly, because of the former mode of life of those who were unwont to work with their hands: wherefore Augustine says (De oper. Monach. xxi) that "if they had in the world the wherewithal easily to support this life without working, and gave it to the needy when they were converted to God, we must credit their weakness and bear with it." For those who have thus been delicately brought up are wont to be unable to bear the toil of bodily labor.

In another way a thing becomes due to a person through his affording others something whether temporal or spiritual, according to 1 Cor. 9:11, "If we have sown unto you spiritual things, is it a great matter if we reap your carnal things?" And in this sense religious may live on alms as being due to them in four ways. First, if they preach by the authority of the prelates. Secondly, if they be ministers of the altar, according to 1 Cor. 9:13,14, "They that serve the altar partake with the altar. So also the lord ordained that they who preach the Gospel should live by the Gospel." Hence Augustine says (De oper. Monach. xxi): "If they be gospelers, I allow, they have" (a claim to live at the charge of the faithful): "if they be ministers of the altar and dispensers of the sacraments, they need not insist on it, but it is theirs by perfect right." The reason for this is because the sacrament of the altar wherever it be offered is common to all the faithful. Thirdly, if they devote themselves to the study of Holy Writ to the common profit of the whole Church. Wherefore Jerome says (Contra Vigil. xiii): "It is still the custom in Judea, not only among us but also among the Hebrews, for those who meditate on the law of the Lord day and night, end have no other share on earth but God alone, to be supported by the subscriptions of the synagogues and of the whole world." Fourthly, if they have endowed the monastery with the goods they possessed, they may live on the alms given to the monastery. Hence Augustine says (De oper. Monach. xxv) that "those who renouncing or distributing their means, whether ample or of any amount whatever, have desired with pious and salutary humility to be numbered among the poor of Christ, have a claim on the community and on brotherly love to receive a livelihood in return. They are to be commended indeed if they work with their hands, but if they be unwilling, who will dare to force them? Nor does it matter, as he goes on to say, to which monasteries, or in what place any one of them has bestowed his goods on his needy brethren; for all Christians belong to one commonwealth."

On the other hand, in the default of any necessity, or of their affording any profit to others, it is unlawful for religious to wish to live in idleness on the alms given to the poor. Hence Augustine says (De oper. Monach. xxii): "Sometimes those who enter the profession of God's service come from a servile condition of life, from tilling the soil or working at some trade or lowly occupation. In their case it is not so clear whether they came with the purpose of serving God, or of evading a life of want and toil with a view to being fed and clothed in idleness, and furthermore to being honored by those by whom they were wont to be despised and downtrodden. Such persons surely cannot excuse themselves from work on the score of bodily weakness, for their former mode of life is evidence against them." And he adds further on (De oper. Monach. xxv): "If they be unwilling to work, neither let them eat. For if the rich humble themselves to piety, it is not that the poor may be exalted to pride; since it is altogether unseemly that in a life wherein senators become laborers, laborers should become idle, and that where the lords of the manor have come after renouncing their ease, the serfs should live in comfort."

Reply to Objection 1: These authorities must be understood as referring to cases of necessity, that is to say, when there is no other means of succoring the poor: for then they would be bound not only to refrain from accepting alms, but also to give what they have for the support of the needy.

Reply to Objection 2: Prelates are competent to preach in virtue of their office, but religious may be competent to do so in virtue of delegation; and thus when they work in the field of the Lord, they may make their living thereby, according to 2 Tim. 2:6, "The husbandman that laboreth must first partake of the fruits," which a gloss explains thus, "that is to say, the preacher, who in the field of the Church tills the hearts of his hearers with the plough of God's word." Those also who minister to the preachers may live on alms. Hence a gloss on Rom. 15:27, "If the Gentiles have been made partakers of their spiritual things, they ought also in carnal things to minister to them," says, "namely, to the Jews who sent preachers from Jerusalem." There are moreover other reasons for which a person has a claim to live at the charge of the faithful, as stated above.

Reply to Objection 3: Other things being equal, it is more perfect to give than to receive. Nevertheless to give or to give up all one's possessions for Christ's sake, and to receive a little for one's livelihood is better than to give to the poor part by part, as stated above ([3808]Q[186], A[3], ad 6).

Reply to Objection 4: To receive gifts so as to increase one's wealth, or to accept a livelihood from another without having a claim to it, and without profit to others or being in need oneself, affords an occasion of sin. But this does not apply to religious, as stated above.

Reply to Objection 5: Whenever there is evident necessity for religious living on alms without doing any manual work, as well as an evident profit to be derived by others, it is not the weak who are scandalized, but those who are full of malice like the Pharisees, whose scandal our Lord teaches us to despise (Mat. 15:12-14). If, however, these motives of necessity and profit be lacking, the weak might possibly be scandalized thereby; and this should be avoided. Yet the same scandal might be occasioned through those who live in idleness on the common revenues.

Whether it is lawful for religious to beg?

Objection 1: It would seem unlawful for religious to beg. For Augustine says (De oper. Monach. xxviii): "The most cunning foe has scattered on all sides a great number of hypocrites wearing the monastic habit, who go wandering about the country," and afterwards he adds: "They all ask, they all demand to be supported in their profitable penury, or to be paid for a pretended holiness." Therefore it would seem that the life of mendicant religious is to be condemned.

Objection 2: Further, it is written (1 Thess. 4:11): "That you . . . work with your own hands as we commanded you, and that you walk honestly towards them that are without: and that you want nothing of any man's": and a gloss on this passage says: "You must work and not be idle, because work is both honorable and a light to the unbeliever: and you must not covet that which belongs to another and much less beg or take anything." Again a gloss [*St. Augustine, (De oper. Monach. iii)] on 2 Thess. 3:10, "If any man will not work," etc. says: "He wishes the servants of God to work with the body, so as to gain a livelihood, and not be compelled by want to ask for necessaries." Now this is to beg. Therefore it would seem unlawful to beg while omitting to work with one's hands.

Objection 3: Further, that which is forbidden by law and contrary to justice, is unbecoming to religious. Now begging is forbidden in the divine law; for it is written (Dt. 15:4): "There shall be no poor nor beggar among you," and (Ps. 36:25): "I have not seen the just forsaken, nor his seed seeking bread." Moreover an able-bodied mendicant is punished by civil law, according to the law (XI, xxvi, de Valid. Mendicant.). Therefore it is unfitting for religious to beg.

Objection 4: Further, "Shame is about that which is disgraceful," as Damascene says (De Fide Orth. ii, 15). Now Ambrose says (De Offic. i, 30) that "to be ashamed to beg is a sign of good birth." Therefore it is disgraceful to beg: and consequently this is unbecoming to religious.

Objection 5: Further, according to our Lord's command it is especially becoming to preachers of the Gospel to live on alms, as stated above [3809](A[4]). Yet it is not becoming that they should beg, since a gloss on 2 Tim. 2:6, "The husbandman, that laboreth," etc. says: "The Apostle wishes the gospeler to understand that to accept necessaries from those among whom he labors is not mendicancy but a right." Therefore it would seem unbecoming for religious to beg.

On the contrary, It becomes religious to live in imitation of Christ. Now Christ was a mendicant, according to Ps. 39:18, "But I am a beggar and poor"; where a gloss says: "Christ said this of Himself as bearing the 'form of a servant,'" and further on: "A beggar is one who entreats another, and a poor man is one who has not enough for himself." Again it is written (Ps. 69:6): "I am needy and poor"; where a gloss says: "'Needy,' that is a suppliant; 'and poor,' that is, not having enough for myself, because I have no worldly wealth." And Jerome says in a letter [*Reference unknown]: "Beware lest whereas thy Lord," i.e. Christ, "begged, thou amass other people's wealth." Therefore it becomes religious to beg.

I answer that, Two things may be considered in reference to mendicancy. The first is on the part of the act itself of begging, which has a certain abasement attaching to it; since of all men those would seem most abased who are not only poor, but are so needy that they have to receive their meat from others. In this way some deserve praise for begging out of humility, just as they abase themselves in other ways, as being the most efficacious remedy against pride which they desire to quench either in themselves or in others by their example. For just as a disease that arises from excessive heat is most efficaciously healed by things that excel in cold, so proneness to pride is most efficaciously healed by those things which savor most of abasement. Hence it is said in the Decretals (II, cap. Si quis semel, de Paenitentia): "To condescend to the humblest duties, and to devote oneself to the lowliest service is an exercise of humility; for thus one is able to heal the disease of pride and human glory." Hence Jerome praises Fabiola (Ep. lxxvii ad ocean.) for that she desired "to receive alms, having poured forth all her wealth for Christ's sake." The Blessed Alexis acted in like manner, for, having renounced all his possessions for Christ's sake he rejoiced in receiving alms even from his own servants. It is also related of the Blessed Arsenius in the Lives of the Fathers (v, 6) that he gave thanks because he was forced by necessity to ask for alms. Hence it is enjoined to some people as a penance for grievous sins to go on a pilgrimage begging. Since, however, humility like the other virtues should not be without discretion, it behooves one to be discreet in becoming a mendicant for the purpose of humiliation, lest a man thereby incur the mark of covetousness or of anything else unbecoming. Secondly, mendicancy may be considered on the part of that which one gets by begging: and thus a man may be led to beg by a twofold motive. First, by the desire to have wealth or meat without working for it, and such like mendicancy is unlawful; secondly, by a motive of necessity or usefulness. The motive is one of necessity if a man has no other means of livelihood save begging; and it is a motive of usefulness if he wishes to accomplish something useful, and is unable to do so without the alms of the faithful. Thus alms are besought for the building of a bridge, or church, or for any other work whatever that is conducive to the common good: thus scholars may seek alms that they may devote themselves to the study of wisdom. In this way mendicancy is lawful to religious no less than to seculars.

Reply to Objection 1: Augustine is speaking there explicitly of those who beg from motives of covetousness.

Reply to Objection 2: The first gloss speaks of begging from motives of covetousness, as appears from the words of the Apostle; while the second gloss speaks of those who without effecting any useful purpose, beg their livelihood in order to live in idleness. on the other hand, he lives not idly who in any way lives usefully.

Reply to Objection 3: This precept of the divine law does not forbid anyone to beg, but it forbids the rich to be so stingy that some are compelled by necessity to beg. The civil law imposes a penalty on able-bodied mendicants who beg from motives neither of utility nor of necessity.

Reply to Objection 4: Disgrace is twofold; one arises from lack of honesty [*Cf.[3810] Q[145], A[1]], the other from an external defect, thus it is disgraceful for a man to be sick or poor. Such like uncomeliness of mendicancy does not pertain to sin, but it may pertain to humility, as stated above.

Reply to Objection 5: Preachers have the right to be fed by those to whom they preach: yet if they wish to seek this by begging so as to receive it as a free gift and not as a right this will be a mark of greater humility.

Whether it is lawful for religious to wear coarser clothes than others?

Objection 1: It would seem unlawful for religious to wear coarser clothes than others. For according to the Apostle (1 Thess. 5:22) we ought to "refrain from all appearance of evil." Now coarseness of clothes has an appearance of evil; for our Lord said (Mat. 7:15): "Beware of false prophets who come to you in the clothing of sheep": and a gloss on Apoc. 6:8, "Behold a pale horse," says: "The devil finding that he cannot succeed, neither by outward afflictions nor by manifest heresies, sends in advance false brethren, who under the guise of religion assume the characteristics of the black and red horses by corrupting the faith." Therefore it would seem that religious should not wear coarse clothes.

Objection 2: Further, Jerome says (Ep. lii ad Nepotian.): "Avoid somber," i.e. black, "equally with glittering apparel. Fine and coarse clothes are equally to be shunned, for the one exhales pleasure, the other vainglory." Therefore, since vainglory is a graver sin than the use of pleasure, it would seem that religious who should aim at what is more perfect ought to avoid coarse rather than fine clothes.

Objection 3: Further, religious should aim especially at doing works of penance. Now in works of penance we should use, not outward signs of sorrow, but rather signs of joy; for our Lord said (Mat. 6:16): "When you fast, be not, as the hypocrites, sad," and afterwards He added: "But thou, when thou fastest, anoint thy head and wash thy face." Augustine commenting on these words (De Serm. Dom. in Monte ii, 12): "In this chapter we must observe that not only the glare and pomp of outward things, but even the weeds of mourning may be a subject of ostentation, all the more dangerous as being a decoy under the guise of God's service." Therefore seemingly religious ought not to wear coarse clothes.

On the contrary, The Apostle says (Heb. 11:37): "They wandered about in sheep-skins in goat-skins," and a gloss adds---"as Elias and others." Moreover it is said in the Decretal XXI, qu. iv, can. Omnis jactantia: "If any persons be found to deride those who wear coarse and religious apparel they must be reproved. For in the early times all those who were consecrated to God went about in common and coarse apparel."

I answer that, As Augustine says (De Doctr. Christ. iii, 12), "in all external things, it is not the use but the intention of the user that is at fault." In order to judge of this it is necessary to observe that coarse and homely apparel may be considered in two ways. First, as being a sign of a man's disposition or condition, because according to Ecclus. 19:27, "the attire . . . of the man" shows "what he is." In this way coarseness of attire is sometimes a sign of sorrow: wherefore those who are beset with sorrow are wont to wear coarser clothes, just as on the other hand in times of festivity and joy they wear finer clothes. Hence penitents make use of coarse apparel, for example, the king (Jonah 3:6) who "was clothed with sack-cloth," and Achab (3 Kings 21:27) who "put hair-cloth upon his flesh." Sometimes, however, it is a sign of the contempt of riches and worldly ostentation. Wherefore Jerome says (Ep. cxxv ad Rustico Monach.): "Let your somber attire indicate your purity of mind, your coarse robe prove your contempt of the world, yet so that your mind be not inflated withal, lest your speech belie your habit." In both these ways it is becoming for religious to wear coarse attire, since religion is a state of penance and of contempt of worldly glory.

But that a person wish to signify this to others arises from three motives. First, in order to humble himself: for just as a man's mind is uplifted by fine clothes, so is it humbled by lowly apparel. Hence speaking of Achab who "put hair-cloth on his flesh," the Lord said to Elias: "Hast thou not seen Achab humbled before Me?" (3 Kings 21:29). Secondly, in order to set an example to others; wherefore a gloss on Mat. 3:4, "(John) had his garments of camel's hair," says: "He who preaches penance is clothed in the habit of penance." Thirdly, on account of vainglory; thus Augustine says (cf. OBJ[3]) that "even the weeds of mourning may be a subject of ostentation."

Accordingly in the first two ways it is praiseworthy to wear humble apparel, but in the third way it is sinful.

Secondly, coarse and homely attire may be considered as the result of covetousness or negligence, and thus also it is sinful.

Reply to Objection 1: Coarseness of attire has not of itself the appearance of evil, indeed it has more the appearance of good, namely of the contempt of worldly glory. Hence it is that wicked persons hide their wickedness under coarse clothing. Hence Augustine says (De Serm. Dom. in Monte ii, 24) that "the sheep should not dislike their clothing for the reason that the wolves sometimes hide themselves under it."

Reply to Objection 2: Jerome is speaking there of the coarse attire that is worn on account of human glory.

Reply to Objection 3: According to our Lord's teaching men should do no deeds of holiness for the sake of show: and this is especially the case when one does something strange. Hence Chrysostom [*Hom. xiii in Matth. in the Opus Imperfectum, falsely ascribed to St. John Chrysostom] says: "While praying a man should do nothing strange, so as to draw the gaze of others, either by shouting or striking his breast, or casting up his hands," because the very strangeness draws people's attention to him. Yet blame does not attach to all strange behavior that draws people's attention, for it may be done well or ill. Hence Augustine says (De Serm. Dom. in Monte ii, 12) that "in the practice of the Christian religion when a man draws attention to himself by unwonted squalor and shabbiness, since he acts thus voluntarily and not of necessity, we can gather from his other deeds whether his behavior is motivated by contempt of excessive dress or by affectation." Religious, however, would especially seem not to act thus from affectation, since they wear a coarse habit as a sign of their profession whereby they profess contempt of the world.

Day 247

OF THE DIFFERENT KINDS OF RELIGIOUS LIFE (EIGHT ARTICLES)
We must now consider the different kinds of religious life, and under this head there are eight points of inquiry:
(1) Whether there are different kinds of religious life or only one?
(2) Whether a religious order can be established for the works of the active life?
(3) Whether a religious order can be directed to soldiering?
(4) Whether a religious order can be established for preaching and the exercise of like works?
(5) Whether a religious order can be established for the study of science?
(6) Whether a religious order that is directed to the contemplative life is more excellent than one that is directed to the active life?
(7) Whether religious perfection is diminished by possessing something in common?
(8) Whether the religious life of solitaries is to be preferred to the religious life of those who live in community?

Whether there is only one religious order?
Objection 1: It would seem that there is but one religious order. For there can be no diversity in that which is possessed wholly and perfectly; wherefore there can be only one sovereign good, as stated in the [3811]FP, Q[6] , AA[2],3,4. Now as Gregory says (Hom. xx in Ezech.), "when a man vows to Almighty God all that he has, all his life, all his knowledge, it is a holocaust," without which there is no religious life. Therefore it would seem that there are not many religious orders but only one.

Objection 2: Further, things which agree in essentials differ only accidentally. Now there is no religious order without the three essential vows of religion, as stated above ([3812]Q[186], AA[6],7). Therefore it would seem that religious orders differ not specifically, but only accidentally.

Objection 3: Further, the state of perfection is competent both to religious and to bishops, as stated above ([3813]Q[185], AA[5],7). Now the episcopate is not diversified specifically, but is one wherever it may be; wherefore Jerome says (Ep. cxlvi ad Evan.): "Wherever a bishop is, whether at Rome, or Gubbio, or Constantinople, or Reggio, he has the same excellence, the same priesthood." Therefore in like manner there is but one religious order.

Objection 4: Further, anything that may lead to confusion should be removed from the Church. Now it would seem that a diversity of religious orders might confuse the Christian people, as stated in the Decretal de Statu Monach. et Canon. Reg. [*Cap. Ne Nimia, de Relig. Dom.]. Therefore seemingly there ought not to be different religious orders.

On the contrary, It is written (Ps. 44:10) that it pertains to the adornment of the queen that she is "surrounded with variety."

I answer that, As stated above (Q[186], A, 7;[3814] Q[187], A[2]), the religious state is a training school wherein one aims by practice at the perfection of charity. Now there are various works of charity to which a man may devote himself; and there are also various kinds of exercise. Wherefore religious orders may be differentiated in two ways. First, according to the different things to which they may be directed: thus one may be directed to the lodging of pilgrims, another to visiting or ransoming captives. Secondly, there may be various religious orders according to the diversity of practices; thus in one religious order the body is chastised by abstinence in food, in another by the practice of manual labor, scantiness of clothes, or the like.

Since, however, the end imports most in every matter, [*Arist., Topic. vi 8] religious orders differ more especially according to their various ends than according to their various practices.

Reply to Objection 1: The obligation to devote oneself wholly to God's service is common to every religious order; hence religious do not differ in this respect, as though in one religious order a person retained some one thing of his own, and in another order some other thing. But the difference is in respect of the different things wherein one may serve God, and whereby a man may dispose himself to the service of God.

Reply to Objection 2: The three essential vows of religion pertain to the practice of religion as principles to which all other matters are reduced, as stated above ([3815]Q[186], A[7]). But there are various ways of disposing oneself to the observance of each of them. For instance one disposes oneself to observe the vow of continence, by solitude of place, by abstinence, by mutual fellowship, and by many like means. Accordingly it is evident that the community of the essential vows is compatible with diversity of religious life, both on account of the different dispositions and on account of the different ends, as explained above.

Reply to Objection 3: In matters relating to perfection, the bishop stands in the position of agent, and the religious as passive, as stated above ([3816]Q[184], A[7]). Now the agent, even in natural things, the higher it is, is so much the more one, whereas the things that are passive are various. Hence with reason the episcopal state is one, while religious orders are many.

Reply to Objection 4: Confusion is opposed to distinction and order. Accordingly the multitude of religious orders would lead to confusion, if different religious orders were directed to the same end and in the same way, without necessity or utility. Wherefore to prevent this happening it has been wholesomely forbidden to establish a new religious order without the authority of the Sovereign Pontiff.

Whether a religious order should be established for the works of the active life?

Objection 1: It would seem that no religious order should be established for the works of the active life. For every religious order belongs to the state of perfection, as stated above ([3817]Q[184], A[5];[3818] Q[186], A[1]). Now the perfection of the religious state consists in the contemplation of divine things. For Dionysius says (Eccl. Hier. vi) that they are "called servants of God by reason of their rendering pure service and subjection to God, and on account of the indivisible and singular life which unites them by holy reflections," i.e. contemplations, "on invisible things, to the Godlike unity and the perfection beloved of God." Therefore seemingly no religious order should be established for the works of the active life.

Objection 2: Further, seemingly the same judgment applies to canons regular as to monks, according to Extra, De Postul., cap. Ex parte; and De Statu Monach., cap. Quod Dei timorem: for it is stated that "they are not considered to be separated from the fellowship of monks": and the same would seem to apply to all other religious. Now the monastic rule was established for the purpose of the contemplative life; wherefore Jerome says (Ep. lviii ad Paulin.): "If you wish to be what you are called, a monk," i.e. a solitary, "what business have you in a city?" The same is found stated in Extra, De Renuntiatione, cap. Nisi cum pridem; and De Regular., cap. Licet quibusdam. Therefore it would seem that every religious order is directed to the contemplative life, and none to the active life.

Objection 3: Further, the active life is concerned with the present world. Now all religious are said to renounce the world; wherefore Gregory says (Hom. xx in Ezech.): "He who renounces this world, and does all the good he can, is like one who has gone out of Egypt and offers sacrifice in the wilderness." Therefore it would seem that no religious order can be directed to the active life.

On the contrary, It is written (James 1:27): "Religion clean and undefiled before God and the Father, is this: to visit the fatherless and widows in their tribulation." Now this belongs to the active life. Therefore religious life can be fittingly directed to the active life.

I answer that, As stated above [3819](A[1]), the religious state is directed to the perfection of charity, which extends to the love of God and of our neighbor. Now the contemplative life which seeks to devote itself to God alone belongs directly to the love of God, while the active life, which ministers to our neighbor's needs, belongs directly to the love of one's neighbor. And just as out of charity we love our neighbor for God's sake, so the services we render our neighbor redound to God, according to Mat. 25:40, "What you have done [Vulg.: 'As long as you did it'] to one of these My least brethren, you did it to Me." Consequently those services which we render our neighbor, in so far as we refer them to God, are described as sacrifices, according to Heb. 13:16, "Do not forget to do good and to impart, for by such sacrifices God's favor is obtained." And since it belongs properly to religion to offer sacrifice to God, as stated above (Q[81], A[1], ad 1; A[4], ad 1), it follows that certain religious orders are fittingly directed to the works of the active life. Wherefore in the Conferences of the Fathers (Coll. xiv, 4) the Abbot Nesteros in distinguishing the various aims of religious orders says: "Some direct their intention exclusively to the hidden life of the desert and purity of heart; some are occupied with the instruction of the brethren and the care of the monasteries; while others delight in the service of the guesthouse," i.e. in hospitality.

Reply to Objection 1: Service and subjection rendered to God are not precluded by the works of the active life, whereby a man serves his neighbor for God's sake, as stated in the Article. Nor do these works preclude singularity of life; not that they involve man's living apart from his fellow-men, but in the sense that each man individually devotes himself to things pertaining to the service of God; and since religious occupy themselves with the works of the active life for God's sake, it follows that their action results from their contemplation of divine things. Hence they are not entirely deprived of the fruit of the contemplative life.

Reply to Objection 2: The same judgment applies to monks and to all other religious, as regards things common to all religious orders: for instance as regards their devoting themselves wholly to the divine service, their observance of the essential vows of religion, and their refraining from worldly business. But it does not follow that this likeness extends to other things that are proper to the monastic profession, and are directed especially to the contemplative life. Hence in the aforesaid Decretal, De Postulando, it is not simply stated that "the same judgment applies to canons regular" as "to monks," but that it applies "in matters already mentioned," namely that "they are not to act as advocates in lawsuits." Again the Decretal quoted, De Statu Monach., after the statement that "canons regular are not considered to be separated from the fellowship of monks," goes on to say: "Nevertheless they obey an easier rule." Hence it is evident that they are not bound to all that monks are bound.

Reply to Objection 3: A man may be in the world in two ways: in one way by his bodily presence, in another way by the bent of his mind. Hence our Lord said to His disciples (Jn. 15:19): "I have chosen you out of the world," and yet speaking of them to His Father He said (Jn. 17:11): "These are in the world, and I come to Thee." Although, then, religious who are occupied with the works of the active life are in the world as to the presence of the body, they are not in the world as regards their bent of mind, because they are occupied with external things, not as seeking anything of the world, but merely for the sake of serving God: for "they . . . use this world, as if they used it not," to quote 1 Cor. 7:31. Hence (James 1:27) after it is stated that "religion clean and undefiled . . . is . . . to visit the fatherless and widows in their tribulation," it is added, "and to keep one's self unspotted from this world," namely to avoid being attached to worldly things.

Whether a religious order can be directed to soldiering?

Objection 1: It would seem that no religious order can be directed to soldiering. For all religious orders belong to the state of perfection. Now our Lord said with reference to the perfection of Christian life (Mat. 5:39): "I say to you not to resist evil; but if one strike thee on the right cheek, turn to him also the other," which is inconsistent with the duties of a soldier. Therefore no religious order can be established for soldiering.

Objection 2: Further, the bodily encounter of the battlefield is more grievous than the encounter in words that takes place between counsel at law. Yet religious are forbidden to plead at law, as appears from the Decretal De Postulando quoted above (A[2], OBJ[2]). Therefore it is much less seemly for a religious order to be established for soldiering.

Objection 3: Further, the religious state is a state of penance, as we have said above ([3820]Q[187], A[6]). Now according to the code of laws soldiering is forbidden to penitents. for it is said in the Decretal De Poenit., Dist. v, cap. 3: "It is altogether opposed to the rules of the Church, to return to worldly soldiering after doing penance." Therefore it is unfitting for any religious order to be established for soldiering.

Objection 4: Further, no religious order may be established for an unjust object. But as Isidore says (Etym. xviii, 1), "A just war is one that is waged by order of the emperor." Since then religious are private individuals, it would seem unlawful for them to wage war; and consequently no religious order may be established for this purpose.

On the contrary, Augustine says (Ep. clxxxix; ad Bonifac.), "Beware of thinking that none of those can please God who handle war-like weapons. Of such was holy David to whom the Lord gave great testimony." Now religious orders are established in order that men may please God. Therefore nothing hinders the establishing of a religious order for the purpose of soldiering.

I answer that, As stated above [3821](A[2]), a religious order may be established not only for the works of the contemplative life, but also for the works of the active life, in so far as they are concerned in helping our neighbor and in the service of God, but not in so far as they are directed to a worldly object. Now the occupation of soldiering may be directed to the assistance of our neighbor, not only as regards private individuals, but also as regards the defense of the whole commonwealth. Hence it is said of Judas Machabeus (1 Macc. 3:2,3) that "he [Vulg.: 'they'] fought with cheerfulness the battle of Israel, and he got his people great honor." It can also be directed to the upkeep of divine worship, wherefore (1 Macc. 3:21) Judas is stated to have said: "We will fight for our lives and our laws," and further on (1 Macc. 13:3) Simon said: "You know what great battles I and my brethren, and the house of my father, have fought for the laws and the sanctuary."

Hence a religious order may be fittingly established for soldiering, not indeed for any worldly purpose, but for the defense of divine worship and public safety, or also of the poor and oppressed, according to Ps. 81:4: "Rescue the poor, and deliver the needy out of the hand of the sinner."

Reply to Objection 1: Not to resist evil may be understood in two ways. First, in the sense of forgiving the wrong done to oneself, and thus it may pertain to perfection, when it is expedient to act thus for the spiritual welfare of others. Secondly, in the sense of tolerating patiently the wrongs done to others: and this pertains to imperfection, or even to vice, if one be able to resist the wrongdoer in a becoming manner. Hence Ambrose says (De Offic. i, 27): "The courage whereby a man in battle defends his country against barbarians, or protects the weak at home, or his friends against robbers is full of justice": even so our Lord says in the passage quoted [*Lk. 6:30 "Of him that taketh away thy goods, ask them not again"; Cf. Mat. 5:40], " . . . thy goods, ask them not again." If, however, a man were not to demand the return of that which belongs to another, he would sin if it were his business to do so: for it is praiseworthy to give away one's own, but not another's property. And much less should the things of God be neglected, for as Chrysostom [*Hom. v in Matth. in the Opus Imperfectum, falsely ascribed to St. John Chrysostom] says, "it is most wicked to overlook the wrongs done to God."

Reply to Objection 2: It is inconsistent with any religious order to act as counsel at law for a worldly object, but it is not inconsistent to do so at the orders of one's superior and in favor of one's monastery, as stated in the same Decretal, or for the defense of the poor and widows. Wherefore it is said in the Decretals (Dist. lxxxviii, cap. 1): "The holy synod has decreed that henceforth no cleric is to buy property or occupy himself with secular business, save with a view to the care of the fatherless . . . and widows." Likewise to be a soldier for the sake of some worldly object is contrary to all religious life, but this does not apply to those who are soldiers for the sake of God's service.

Reply to Objection 3: Worldly soldiering is forbidden to penitents, but the soldiering which is directed to the service of God is imposed as a penance on some people, as in the case of those upon whom it is enjoined to take arms in defense of the Holy Land.

Reply to Objection 4: The establishment of a religious order for the purpose of soldiering does not imply that the religious can wage war on their own authority; but they can do so only on the authority of the sovereign or of the Church.

Whether a religious order can be established for preaching or hearing confessions?

Objection 1: It would seem that no religious order may be established for preaching, or hearing confessions. For it is said (VII, qu. i [*Cap. Hoc nequaquam; Cf.[3822] Q[187], A[1], OBJ[1]]): "The monastic life is one of subjection and discipleship, not of teaching, authority, or pastoral care," and the same apparently applies to religious. Now preaching and hearing confessions are the actions of a pastor and teacher. Therefore a religious order should not be established for this purpose.

Objection 2: Further, the purpose for which a religious order is established would seem to be something most proper to the religious life, as stated above [3823](A[1]). Now the aforesaid actions are not proper to religious but to bishops. Therefore a religious order should not be established for the purpose of such actions.

Objection 3: Further, it seems unfitting that the authority to preach and hear confessions should be committed to an unlimited number of men; and there is no fixed number of those who are received into a religious order. Therefore it is unfitting for a religious order to be established for the purpose of the aforesaid actions.

Objection 4: Further, preachers have a right to receive their livelihood from the faithful of Christ, according to 1 Cor. 9. If then the office of preaching be committed to a religious order established for that purpose, it follows that the faithful of Christ are bound to support an unlimited number of persons, which would be a heavy burden on them. Therefore a religious order should not be established for the exercise of these actions.

Objection 5: Further, the organization of the Church should be in accordance with Christ's institution. Now Christ sent first the twelve apostles to preach, as related in Luke 9, and afterwards He sent the seventy-two disciples, as stated in Luke 10. Moreover, according to the gloss of Bede on "And after these things" (Lk. 10:1), "the apostles are represented by the bishops, the seventy-two disciples by the lesser priests," i.e. the parish priests. Therefore in addition to bishops and parish priests, no religious order should be established for the purpose of preaching and hearing confessions.

On the contrary, In the Conferences of the Fathers (Coll. xiv, 4), Abbot Nesteros, speaking of the various kinds of religious orders, says: "Some choosing the care of the sick, others devoting themselves to the relief of the afflicted and oppressed, or applying themselves to teaching, or giving alms to the poor, have been most highly esteemed on account of their devotion and piety." Therefore just as a religious order may be established for the care of the sick, so also may one be established for teaching the people by preaching and like works.

I answer that, As stated above [3824](A[2]), it is fitting for a religious order to be established for the works of the active life, in so far as they are directed to the good of our neighbor, the service of God, and the upkeep of divine worship. Now the good of our neighbor is advanced by things pertaining to the spiritual welfare of the soul rather than by things pertaining to the supplying of bodily needs, in proportion to the excellence of spiritual over corporal things. Hence it was stated above (Q[32], A[3]) that spiritual works of mercy surpass corporal works of mercy. Moreover this is more pertinent to the service of God, to Whom no sacrifice is more acceptable than zeal for souls, as Gregory says (Hom. xii in Ezech.). Furthermore, it is a greater thing to employ spiritual arms in defending the faithful against the errors of heretics and the temptations of the devil, than to protect the faithful by means of bodily weapons. Therefore it is most fitting for a religious order to be established for preaching and similar works pertaining to the salvation of souls.

Reply to Objection 1: He who works by virtue of another, acts as an instrument. And a minister is like an "animated instrument," as the Philosopher says (Polit. i, 2 [*Cf. Ethic. viii, 11]). Hence if a man preach or do something similar by the authority of his superiors, he does not rise above the degree of "discipleship" or "subjection," which is competent to religious.

Reply to Objection 2: Some religious orders are established for soldiering, to wage war, not indeed on their own authority, but on that of the sovereign or of the Church who are competent to wage war by virtue of their office, as stated above (A[3], ad 4). In the same way certain religious orders are established for preaching and hearing confessions, not indeed by their own authority, but by the authority of the higher and lower superiors, to whom these things belong by virtue of their office. Consequently to assist one's superiors in such a ministry is proper to a religious order of this kind.

Reply to Objection 3: Bishops do not allow these religious severally and indiscriminately to preach or hear confessions, but according to the discretion of the religious superiors, or according to their own appointment.

Reply to Objection 4: The faithful are not bound by law to contribute to the support of other than their ordinary prelates, who receive the tithes and offerings of the faithful for that purpose, as well as other ecclesiastical revenues. But if some men are willing to minister to the faithful by exercising the aforesaid acts gratuitously, and without demanding payment as of right, the faithful are not burdened thereby because their temporal contributions can be liberally repaid by those men, nor are they bound by law to contribute, but by charity, and yet not so that they be burdened thereby and others eased, as stated in 2 Cor. 8:13. If, however, none be found to devote themselves gratuitously to services of this kind, the ordinary prelate is bound, if he cannot suffice by himself, to seek other suitable persons and support them himself.

Reply to Objection 5: The seventy-two disciples are represented not only by the parish priests, but by all those of lower order who in any way assist the bishops in their office. For we do not read that our Lord appointed the seventy-two disciples to certain fixed parishes, but that "He sent them two and two before His face into every city and place whither He Himself was to come." It was fitting, however, that in addition to the ordinary prelates others should be chosen for these duties on account of the multitude of the faithful, and the difficulty of finding a sufficient number of persons to be appointed to each locality, just as it was necessary to establish religious orders for military service, on account of the secular princes being unable to cope with unbelievers in certain countries.

Whether a religious order should be established for the purpose of study?

Objection 1: It would seem that a religious order should not be established for the purpose of study. For it is written (Ps. 70:15,16): "Because I have not known letters [Douay: 'learning'], I will enter into the powers of the Lord," i.e. "Christian virtue," according to a gloss. Now the perfection of Christian virtue, seemingly, pertains especially to religious. Therefore it is not for them to apply themselves to the study of letters.

Objection 2: Further, that which is a source of dissent is unbecoming to religious, who are gathered together in the unity of peace. Now study leads to dissent: wherefore different schools of thought arose among the philosophers. Hence Jerome (Super Epist. ad Tit. 1:5) says: "Before a diabolical instinct brought study into religion, and people said: I am of Paul, I of Apollo, I of Cephas," etc. Therefore it would seem that no religious order should be established for the purpose of study.

Objection 3: Further, those who profess the Christian religion should profess nothing in common with the Gentiles. Now among the Gentiles were some who professed philosophy, and even now some secular persons are known as professors of certain sciences. Therefore the study of letters does not become religious.

On the contrary, Jerome (Ep. liii ad Paulin.) urges him to acquire learning in the monastic state, saying: "Let us learn on earth those things the knowledge of which will remain in heaven," and further on: "Whatever you seek to know, I will endeavor to know with you."

I answer that As stated above [3825](A[2]), religion may be ordained to the active and to the contemplative life. Now chief among the works of the active life are those which are directly ordained to the salvation of souls, such as preaching and the like. Accordingly the study of letters is becoming to the religious life in three ways. First, as regards that which is proper to the contemplative life, to which the study of letters helps in a twofold manner. In one way by helping directly to contemplate, namely by enlightening the intellect. For the contemplative life of which we are now speaking is directed chiefly to the consideration of divine things, as stated above (Q[180], A[4]), to which consideration man is directed by study; for which reason it is said in praise of the righteous (Ps. 1:2) that "he shall meditate day and night" on the law of the Lord, and (Ecclus. 39:1): "The wise man will seek out the wisdom of all the ancients, and will be occupied in the prophets." In another way the study of letters is a help to the contemplative life indirectly, by removing the obstacles to contemplation, namely the errors which in the contemplation of divine things frequently beset those who are ignorant of the scriptures. Thus we read in the Conferences of the Fathers (Coll. x, 3) that the Abbot Serapion through simplicity fell into the error of the Anthropomorphites, who thought that God had a human shape. Hence Gregory says (Moral. vi) that "some through seeking in contemplation more than they are able to grasp, fall away into perverse doctrines, and by failing to be the humble disciples of truth become the masters of error." Hence it is written (Eccles. 2:3): "I thought in my heart to withdraw my flesh from wine, that I might turn my mind to wisdom and might avoid folly."

Secondly, the study of letters is necessary in those religious orders that are founded for preaching and other like works; wherefore the Apostle (Titus 1:9), speaking of bishops to whose office these acts belong, says: "Embracing that faithful word which is according to doctrine, that he may be able to exhort in sound doctrine and to convince the gainsayers." Nor does it matter that the apostles were sent to preach without having studied letters, because, as Jerome says (Ep. liii ad Paulin.), "whatever others acquire by exercise and daily meditation in God's law, was taught them by the Holy Ghost."

Thirdly, the study of letters is becoming to religious as regards that which is common to all religious orders. For it helps us to avoid the lusts of the flesh; wherefore Jerome says (Ep. cxxv ad Rust. Monach.): "Love the science of the Scriptures and thou shalt have no love for carnal vice." For it turns the mind away from lustful thoughts, and tames the flesh on account of the toil that study entails according to Ecclus. 31:1, "Watching for riches* consumeth the flesh." [*Vigilia honestatis St. Thomas would seem to have taken 'honestas' in the sense of virtue]. It also helps to remove the desire of riches, wherefore it is written (Wis. 7:8): "I . . . esteemed riches nothing in comparison with her," and (1 Macc. 12:9): "We needed none of these things," namely assistance from without, "having for our comfort the holy books that are in our hands." It also helps to teach obedience, wherefore Augustine says (De oper. Monach. xvii): "What sort of perverseness is this, to wish to read, but not to obey what one reads?" Hence it is clearly fitting that a religious order be established for the study of letters.

Reply to Objection 1: This commentary of the gloss is an exposition of the Old Law of which the Apostle says (2 Cor. 3:6): "The letter killeth." Hence not to know letters is to disapprove of the circumcision of the "letter" and other carnal observances.

Reply to Objection 2: Study is directed to knowledge which, without charity, "puffeth up," and consequently leads to dissent, according to Prov. 13:10, "Among the proud there are always dissensions": whereas, with charity, it "edifieth and begets concord." Hence the Apostle after saying (1 Cor. 1:5): "You are made rich . . . in all utterance and in all knowledge," adds (1 Cor. 1:10): "That you all speak the same thing, and that there be no schisms among you." But Jerome is not speaking here of the study of letters, but of the study of dissensions which heretics and schismatics have brought into the Christian religion.

Reply to Objection 3: The philosophers professed the study of letters in the matter of secular learning: whereas it becomes religious to devote themselves chiefly to the study of letters in reference to the doctrine that is "according to godliness" (Titus 1:1). It becomes not religious, whose whole life is devoted to the service of God, to seek for other learning, save in so far as it is referred to the sacred doctrine. Hence Augustine says at the end of De Musica vi, 17: "Whilst we think that we should not overlook those whom heretics delude by the deceitful assurance of reason and knowledge, we are slow to advance in the consideration of their methods. Yet we should not be praised for doing this, were it not that many holy sons of their most loving mother the Catholic Church had done the same under the necessity of confounding heretics."

Whether a religious order that is devoted to the contemplative life is more excellent than on that is given to the active life?

Objection 1: It would seem that a religious order which is devoted to the contemplative life is not more excellent than one which is given to the active life. For it is said (Extra, de Regular. et Transeunt. ad Relig., cap. Licet), quoting the words of Innocent III: "Even as a greater good is preferred to a lesser, so the common profit takes precedence of private profit: and in this case teaching is rightly preferred to silence, responsibility to contemplation, work to rest." Now the religious order which is directed to the greater good is better. Therefore it would seem that those religious orders that are directed to the active life are more excellent than those which are directed to the contemplative life.

Objection 2: Further, every religious order is directed to the perfection of charity, as stated above ([3826]AA[1],2). Now a gloss on Heb. 12:4, "For you have not yet resisted unto blood," says: "In this life there is no more perfect love than that to which the holy martyrs attained, who fought against sin unto blood." Now to fight unto blood is becoming those religious who are directed to military service, and yet this pertains to the active life. Therefore it would seem that religious orders of this kind are the most excellent.

Objection 3: Further, seemingly the stricter a religious order is, the more excellent it is. But there is no reason why certain religious orders directed to the active life should not be of stricter observance than those directed to the contemplative life. Therefore they are more excellent.

On the contrary, our Lord said (Lk. 10:42) that the "best part" was Mary's, by whom the contemplative life is signified.

I answer that, As stated above [3827](A[1]), the difference between one religious order and another depends chiefly on the end, and secondarily on the exercise. And since one thing cannot be said to be more excellent than another save in respect of that in which it differs therefrom, it follows that the excellence of one religious order over another depends chiefly on their ends, and secondarily on their respective exercises. Nevertheless each of these comparisons is considered in a different way. For the comparison with respect to the end is absolute, since the end is sought for its own sake; whereas the comparison with respect to exercise is relative, since exercise is sought not for its own sake, but for the sake of the end. Hence a religious order is preferable to another, if it be directed to an end that is absolutely more excellent either because it is a greater good or because it is directed to more goods. If, however, the end be the same, the excellence of one religious order over another depends secondarily, not on the amount of exercise, but on the proportion of the exercise to the end in view. Wherefore in the Conferences of the Fathers (Coll. ii, 2) Blessed Antony is quoted, as preferring discretion whereby a man moderates all his actions, to fastings, watchings, and all such observances.

Accordingly we must say that the work of the active life is twofold. one proceeds from the fulness of contemplation, such as teaching and preaching. Wherefore Gregory says (Hom. v in Ezech.) that the words of Ps. 144:7, "They shall publish the memory of . . . Thy sweetness," refer "to perfect men returning from their contemplation." And this work is more excellent than simple contemplation. For even as it is better to enlighten than merely to shine, so is it better to give to others the fruits of one's contemplation than merely to contemplate. The other work of the active life consists entirely in outward occupation, for instance almsgiving, receiving guests, and the like, which are less excellent than the works of contemplation, except in cases of necessity, as stated above ([3828]Q[182], A[1]). Accordingly the highest place in religious orders is held by those which are directed to teaching and preaching, which, moreover, are nearest to the episcopal perfection, even as in other things "the end of that which is first is in conjunction with the beginning of that which is second," as Dionysius states (Div. Nom. vii). The second place belongs to those which are directed to contemplation, and the third to those which are occupied with external actions.

Moreover, in each of these degrees it may be noted that one religious order excels another through being directed to higher action in the same genus; thus among the works of the active life it is better to ransom captives than to receive guests, and among the works of the contemplative life prayer is better than study. Again one will excel another if it be directed to more of these actions than another, or if it have statutes more adapted to the attainment of the end in view.

Reply to Objection 1: This Decretal refers to the active life as directed to the salvation of souls.

Reply to Objection 2: Those religious orders that are established for the purpose of military service aim more directly at shedding the enemy's blood than at the shedding of their own, which latter is more properly competent to martyrs. Yet there is no reason why religious of this description should not acquire the merit of martyrdom in certain cases, and in this respect stand higher than other religious; even as in some cases the works of the active life take precedence of contemplation.

Reply to Objection 3: Strictness of observances, as the Blessed Antony remarks (Conferences of the Fathers; Coll. ii, 2), is not the chief object of commendation in a religious order; and it is written (Is. 58:5): "Is this such a fast as I have chosen, for a man to afflict his soul for a day?" Nevertheless it is adopted in religious life as being necessary for taming the flesh, "which if done without discretion, is liable to make us fail altogether," as the Blessed Antony observes. Wherefore a religious order is not more excellent through having stricter observances, but because its observances are directed by greater discretion to the end of religion. Thus the taming of the flesh is more efficaciously directed to continence by means of abstinence in meat and drink, which pertain to hunger and thirst, than by the privation of clothing, which pertains to cold and nakedness, or by bodily labor.

Whether religious perfection is diminished by possessing something in common?

Objection 1: It would seem that religious perfection is diminished by possessing something in common. For our Lord said (Mat. 19:21): "If thou wilt be perfect, go sell all [Vulg.: 'what'] thou hast and give to the poor." Hence it is clear that to lack worldly wealth belongs to the perfection of Christian life. Now those who possess something in common do not lack worldly wealth. Therefore it would seem that they do not quite reach to the perfection of Christian life.

Objection 2: Further, the perfection of the counsels requires that one should be without worldly solicitude; wherefore the Apostle in giving the counsel of virginity said (1 Cor. 7:32): "I would have you to be without solicitude." Now it belongs to the solicitude of the present life that certain people keep something to themselves for the morrow; and this solicitude was forbidden His disciples by our Lord (Mat. 6:34) saying: "Be not . . . solicitous for tomorrow." Therefore it would seem that the perfection of Christian life is diminished by having something in common.

Objection 3: Further, possessions held in common belong in some way to each member of the community; wherefore Jerome (Ep. lx ad Heliod. Episc.) says in reference to certain people: "They are richer in the monastery than they had been in the world; though serving the poor Christ they have wealth which they had not while serving the rich devil; the Church rejects them now that they are rich, who in the world were beggars." But it is derogatory to religious perfection that one should possess wealth of one's own. Therefore it is also derogatory to religious perfection to possess anything in common.

Objection 4: Further, Gregory (Dial. iii, 14) relates of a very holy man named Isaac, that "when his disciples humbly signified that he should accept the possessions offered to him for the use of the monastery, he being solicitous for the safeguarding of his poverty, held firmly to his opinion, saying: A monk who seeks earthly possessions is no monk at all": and this refers to possessions held in common, and which were offered him for the common use of the monastery. Therefore it would seem destructive of religious perfection to possess anything in common.

Objection 5: Further, our Lord in prescribing religious perfection to His disciples, said (Mat. 10:9,10): "Do not possess gold, nor silver, nor money in your purses, nor script for your journey." By these words, as Jerome says in his commentary, "He reproves those philosophers who are commonly called Bactroperatae [*i.e. staff and scrip bearers], who as despising the world and valuing all things at naught carried their pantry about with them." Therefore it would seem derogatory to religious perfection that one should keep something whether for oneself or for the common use.

On the contrary, Prosper [*Julianus Pomerius, among the works of Prosper] says (De Vita Contempl. ix) and his words are quoted (XII, qu. 1, can. Expedit): "It is sufficiently clear both that for the sake of perfection one should renounce having anything of one's own, and that the possession of revenues, which are of course common property, is no hindrance to the perfection of the Church."

I answer that, As stated above ([3829]Q[184], A[3], ad 1;[3830] Q[185], A[6], ad 1), perfection consists, essentially, not in poverty, but in following Christ, according to the saying of Jerome (Super Matth. xix, 27): "Since it is not enough to leave all, Peter adds that which is perfect, namely, 'We have followed Thee,'" while poverty is like an instrument or exercise for the attainment of perfection. Hence in the Conferences of the Fathers (Coll. i, 7) the abbot Moses says: "Fastings, watchings, meditating on the Scriptures, poverty, and privation of all one's possessions are not perfection, but means of perfection."

Now the privation of one's possessions, or poverty, is a means of perfection, inasmuch as by doing away with riches we remove certain obstacles to charity; and these are chiefly three. The first is the cares which riches bring with them; wherefore our Lord said (Mat. 13:22): "That which was sown [Vulg.: 'He that received the seed'] among thorns, is he that heareth the word, and the care of this world, and the deceitfulness of riches, choketh up the word." The second is the love of riches, which increases with the possession of wealth; wherefore Jerome says (Super Matth. xix, 23) that "since it is difficult to despise riches when we have them, our Lord did not say: 'It is impossible for a rich man to enter the kingdom of heaven,' but: 'It is difficult.'" The third is vainglory or elation which results from riches, according to Ps. 48:7, "They that trust in their own strength, and glory in the multitude of their riches."

Accordingly the first of these three cannot be altogether separated from riches whether great or small. For man must needs take a certain amount of care in acquiring or keeping external things. But so long as external things are sought or possessed only in a small quantity, and as much as is required for a mere livelihood, such like care does not hinder one much; and consequently is not inconsistent with the perfection of Christian life. For our Lord did not forbid all care, but only such as is excessive and hurtful; wherefore Augustine, commenting on Mat. 6:25, "Be not solicitous for your life, what you shall eat," says (De Serm. in Monte [*The words quoted are from De Operibus Monach. xxvi]): "In saying this He does not forbid them to procure these things in so far as they needed them, but to be intent on them, and for their sake to do whatever they are bidden to do in preaching the Gospel." Yet the possession of much wealth increases the weight of care, which is a great distraction to man's mind and hinders him from giving himself wholly to God's service. The other two, however, namely the love of riches and taking pride or glorying in riches, result only from an abundance of wealth.

Nevertheless it makes a difference in this matter if riches, whether abundant or moderate, be possessed in private or in common. For the care that one takes of one's own wealth, pertains to love of self, whereby a man loves himself in temporal matters; whereas the care that is given to things held in common pertains to the love of charity which "seeketh not her own," but looks to the common good. And since religion is directed to the perfection of charity, and charity is perfected in "the love of God extending to contempt of self" [*Augustine, De Civ. Dei xiv, 28], it is contrary to religious perfection to possess anything in private. But the care that is given to common goods may pertain to charity, although it may prove an obstacle to some higher act of charity, such as divine contemplation or the instructing of one's neighbor. Hence it is evident that to have excessive riches in common, whether in movable or in immovable property, is an obstacle to perfection, though not absolutely incompatible with it; while it is not an obstacle to religious perfection to have enough external things, whether movables or immovables, as suffice for a livelihood, if we consider poverty in relation to the common end of religious orders, which is to devote oneself to the service of God. But if we consider poverty in relation to the special end of any religious order, then this end being presupposed, a greater or lesser degree of poverty is adapted to that religious order; and each religious order will be the more perfect in respect of poverty, according as it professes a poverty more adapted to its end. For it is evident that for the purpose of the outward and bodily works of the active life a man needs the assistance of outward things, whereas few are required for contemplation. Hence the Philosopher says (Ethic. x, 8) that "many things are needed for action, and the more so, the greater and nobler the actions are. But the contemplative man requires no such things for the exercise of his act: he needs only the necessaries; other things are an obstacle to his contemplation." Accordingly it is clear that a religious order directed to the bodily actions of the active life, such as soldiering or the lodging of guests, would be imperfect if it lacked common riches; whereas those religious orders which are directed to the contemplative life are the more perfect, according as the poverty they profess burdens them with less care for temporal things. And the care of temporal things is so much a greater obstacle to religious life as the religious life requires a greater care of spiritual things.

Now it is manifest that a religious order established for the purpose of contemplating and of giving to others the fruits of one's contemplation by teaching and preaching, requires greater care of spiritual things than one that is established for contemplation only. Wherefore it becomes a religious order of this kind to embrace a poverty that burdens one with the least amount of care. Again it is clear that to keep what one has acquired at a fitting time for one's necessary use involves the least burden of care. Wherefore a threefold degree of poverty corresponds to the three aforesaid degrees of religious life. For it is fitting that a religious order which is directed to the bodily actions of the active life should have an abundance of riches in common; that the common possession of a religious order directed to contemplation should be more moderate, unless the said religious be bound, either themselves or through others, to give hospitality or to assist the poor; and that those who aim at giving the fruits of their contemplation to others should have their life most exempt from external cares; this being accomplished by their laying up the necessaries of life procured at a fitting time.

213

This, our Lord, the Founder of poverty, taught by His example. For He had a purse which He entrusted to Judas, and in which were kept the things that were offered to Him, as related in Jn. 12:6.

Nor should it be argued that Jerome (Super Matth. xvii, 26) says: "If anyone object that Judas carried money in the purse, we answer that He deemed it unlawful to spend the property of the poor on His own uses," namely by paying the tax---because among those poor His disciples held a foremost place, and the money in Christ's purse was spent chiefly on their needs. For it is stated (Jn. 4:8) that "His disciples were gone into the city to buy meats," and (Jn. 13:29) that the disciples "thought, because Judas had the purse, that Jesus had said to him: But those things which we have need of for the festival day, or that he should give something to the poor." From this it is evident that to keep money by, or any other common property for the support of religious of the same order, or of any other poor, is in accordance with the perfection which Christ taught by His example. Moreover, after the resurrection, the disciples from whom all religious orders took their origin kept the price of the lands, and distributed it according as each one had need (Acts 4:34,35).

Reply to Objection 1: As stated above ([3831]Q[184], A[3], ad 1), this saying of our Lord does not mean that poverty itself is perfection, but that it is the means of perfection. Indeed, as shown above ([3832]Q[186], A[8]), it is the least of the three chief means of perfection; since the vow of continence excels the vow of poverty, and the vow of obedience excels them both. Since, however, the means are sought not for their own sake, but for the sake of the end, a thing is better, not for being a greater instrument, but for being more adapted to the end. Thus a physician does not heal the more the more medicine he gives, but the more the medicine is adapted to the disease. Accordingly it does not follow that a religious order is the more perfect, according as the poverty it professes is more perfect, but according as its poverty is more adapted to the end both common and special. Granted even that the religious order which exceeds others in poverty be more perfect in so far as it is poorer, this would not make it more perfect simply. For possibly some other religious order might surpass it in matters relating to continence, or obedience, and thus be more perfect simply, since to excel in better things is to be better simply.

Reply to Objection 2: Our Lord's words (Mat. 6:34), "Be not solicitous for tomorrow," do not mean that we are to keep nothing for the morrow; for the Blessed Antony shows the danger of so doing, in the Conferences of the Fathers (Coll. ii, 2), where he says: "It has been our experience that those who have attempted to practice the privation of all means of livelihood, so as not to have the wherewithal to procure themselves food for one day, have been deceived so unawares that they were unable to finish properly the work they had undertaken." And, as Augustine says (De oper. Monach. xxiii), "if this saying of our Lord, 'Be not solicitous for tomorrow,' means that we are to lay nothing by for the morrow, those who shut themselves up for many days from the sight of men, and apply their whole mind to a life of prayer, will be unable to provide themselves with these things." Again he adds afterwards: "Are we to suppose that the more holy they are, the less do they resemble the birds?" And further on (De oper. Monach. xxiv): "For if it be argued from the Gospel that they should lay nothing by, they answer rightly: Why then did our Lord have a purse, wherein He kept the money that was collected? Why, in days long gone by, when famine was imminent, was grain sent to the holy fathers? Why did the apostles thus provide for the needs of the saints?"

Accordingly the saying: "Be not solicitous for tomorrow," according to Jerome (Super Matth.) is to be rendered thus: "It is enough that we think of the present; the future being uncertain, let us leave it to God": according to Chrysostom [*Hom. xvi in the Opus Imperfectum, falsely ascribed to St. John Chrysostom], "It is enough to endure the toil for necessary things, labor not in excess for unnecessary things": according to Augustine (De Serm. Dom. in Monte ii, 17): "When we do any good action, we should bear in mind not temporal things which are denoted by the morrow, but eternal things."

Reply to Objection 3: The saying of Jerome applies where there are excessive riches, possessed in private as it were, or by the abuse of which even the individual members of a community wax proud and wanton. But they do not apply to moderate wealth, set by for the common use, merely as a means of livelihood of which each one stands in need. For it amounts to the same that each one makes use of things pertaining to the necessaries of life, and that these things be set by for the common use.

Reply to Objection 4: Isaac refused to accept the offer of possessions, because he feared lest this should lead him to have excessive wealth, the abuse of which would be an obstacle to religious perfection. Hence Gregory adds (Dial. iii, 14): "He was as afraid of forfeiting the security of his poverty, as the rich miser is careful of his perishable wealth." It is not, however, related that he refused to accept such things as are commonly necessary for the upkeep of life.

Reply to Objection 5: The Philosopher says (Polit. i, 5,6) that bread, wine, and the like are natural riches, while money is artificial riches. Hence it is that certain philosophers declined to make use of money, and employed other things, living according to nature. Wherefore Jerome shows by the words of our Lord, Who equally forbade both, that it comes to the same to have money and to possess other things necessary for life. And though our Lord commanded those who were sent to preach not to carry these things on the way, He did not forbid them to be possessed in common. How these words of our Lord should be understood has been shown above (Q[185], A[6] , ad 2; [3833]FS, Q[108], A[2], ad 3).

Whether the religious life of those who live in community is more perfect than that of those who lead a solitary life?

Objection 1: It would seem that the religious life of those who live in community is more perfect than that of those who lead a solitary life. For it is written (Eccles. 4:9): "It is better . . . that two should be together, than one; for they have the advantage of their society." Therefore the religious life of those who live in community would seem to be more perfect.

Objection 2: Further, it is written (Mat. 18:20): "Where there are two or three gathered together in My name, there am I in the midst of them." But nothing can be better than the fellowship of Christ. Therefore it would seem better to live in community than in solitude.

Objection 3: Further, the vow of obedience is more excellent than the other religious vows; and humility is most acceptable to God. Now obedience and humility are better observed in company than in solitude; for Jerome says (Ep. cxxv ad Rustic. Monach.): "In solitude pride quickly takes man unawares, he sleeps as much as he will, he does what he likes"; whereas when instructing one who lives in community, he says: "You may not do what you will, you must eat what you are bidden to eat, you may possess so much as you receive, you must obey one you prefer not to obey, you must be a servant to your brethren, you must fear the superior of the monastery as God, love him as a father." Therefore it would seem that the religious life of those who live in community is more perfect than that of those who lead a solitary life.

Objection 4: Further, our Lord said (Lk. 11:33): "No man lighteth a candle and putteth it in a hidden place, nor under a bushel." Now those who lead a solitary life are seemingly in a hidden place, and to be doing no good to any man. Therefore it would seem that their religious life is not more perfect.

Objection 5: Further, that which is in accord with man's nature is apparently more pertinent to the perfection of virtue. But man is naturally a social animal, as the Philosopher says (Polit. i, 1). Therefore it would seem that to lead a solitary life is not more perfect than to lead a community life.

On the contrary, Augustine says (De oper. Monach. xxiii) that "those are holier who keep themselves aloof from the approach of all, and give their whole mind to a life of prayer."

I answer that, Solitude, like poverty, is not the essence of perfection, but a means thereto. Hence in the Conferences of the Fathers (Coll. i, 7) the Abbot Moses says that "solitude," even as fasting and other like things, is "a sure means of acquiring purity of heart." Now it is evident that solitude is a means adapted not to action but to contemplation, according to Osee 2:14, "I . . . will lead her into solitude [Douay: 'the wilderness']; and I will speak to her heart." Wherefore it is not suitable to those religious orders that are directed to the works whether corporal or spiritual of the active life; except perhaps for a time, after the example of Christ, Who as Luke relates (6:12), "went out into a mountain to pray; and He passed the whole night in the prayer of God." On the other hand, it is suitable to those religious orders that are directed to contemplation.

It must, however, be observed that what is solitary should be self-sufficing by itself. Now such a thing is one "that lacks nothing," and this belongs to the idea of a perfect thing [*Aristotle, Phys. iii, 6]. Wherefore solitude befits the contemplative who has already attained to perfection. This happens in two ways: in one way by the gift only of God, as in the case of John the Baptist, who was "filled with the Holy Ghost even from his mother's womb" (Lk. 1:11), so that he was in the desert even as a boy; in another way by the practice of virtuous action, according to Heb. 5:14: "Strong meat is for the perfect; for them who by custom have their senses exercised to the discerning of good and evil."

Now man is assisted in this practice by the fellowship of others in two ways. First, as regards his intellect, to the effect of his being instructed in that which he has to contemplate; wherefore Jerome says (ad Rustic. Monach., Ep. cxxv): "It pleases me that you have the fellowship of holy men, and teach not yourself. Secondly, as regards the affections, seeing that man's noisome affections are restrained by the example and reproof which he receives from others; for as Gregory says (Moral. xxx, 23), commenting on the words, "To whom I have given a house in the wilderness" (Job 39:6), "What profits solitude of the body, if solitude of the heart be lacking?" Hence a social life is necessary for the practice of perfection. Now solitude befits those who are already perfect; wherefore Jerome says (ad Rustic. Monach., Ep. cxxv): "Far from condemning the solitary life, we have often commended it. But we wish the soldiers who pass from the monastic school to be such as not to be deterred by the hard noviciate of the desert, and such as have given proof of their conduct for a considerable time.

Accordingly, just as that which is already perfect surpasses that which is being schooled in perfection, so the life of the solitaries, if duly practiced, surpasses the community life. But if it be undertaken without the aforesaid practice, it is fraught with very great danger, unless the grace of God supply that which others acquire by practice, as in the case of the Blessed Antony and the Blessed Benedict.

Reply to Objection 1: Solomon shows that two are better than one, on account of the help which one affords the other either by "lifting him" up, or by "warming him," i.e. giving him spiritual heat (Eccles. 4:10,11). But those who have already attained to perfection do not require this help.

Reply to Objection 2: According to 1 Jn. 4:16, "He that abideth in charity abideth in God and God in him." Wherefore just as Christ is in the midst of those who are united together in the fellowship of brotherly love, so does He dwell in the heart of the man who devotes himself to divine contemplation through love of God.

Reply to Objection 3: Actual obedience is required of those who need to be schooled according to the direction of others in the attainment of perfection; but those who are already perfect are sufficiently "led by the spirit of God" so that they need not to obey others actually. Nevertheless they have obedience in the preparedness of the mind.

Reply to Objection 4: As Augustine says (De Civ. Dei xix, 19), "no one is forbidden to seek the knowledge of truth, for this pertains to a praiseworthy leisure." That a man be placed "on a candlestick," does not concern him but his superiors, and "if this burden is not placed on us," as Augustine goes on to say (De Civ. Dei xix, 19), "we must devote ourselves to the contemplation of truth," for which purpose solitude is most helpful. Nevertheless, those who lead a solitary life are most useful to mankind. Hence, referring to them, Augustine says (De Morib. Eccl. xxxi): "They dwell in the most lonely places, content to live on water and the bread that is brought to them from time to time, enjoying colloquy with God to whom they have adhered with a pure mind. To some they seem to have renounced human intercourse more than is right: but these understand not how much such men profit us by the spirit of their prayers, what an example to us is the life of those whom we are forbidden to see in the body."

Reply to Objection 5: A man may lead a solitary life for two motives. one is because he is unable, as it were, to bear with human fellowship on account of his uncouthness of mind; and this is beast-like. The other is with a view to adhering wholly to divine things; and this is superhuman. Hence the Philosopher says (Polit. i, 1) that "he who associates not with others is either a beast or a god," i.e. a godly man.

Day 248

OF THE ENTRANCE INTO RELIGIOUS LIFE (TEN ARTICLES)

We must now consider the entrance into religious life. Under this head there are ten points of inquiry:

(1) Whether those who are not practiced in the observance of the commandments should enter religion?

(2) Whether it is lawful for a person to be bound by vow to enter religion?

(3) Whether those who are bound by vow to enter religion are bound to fulfil their vow?

(4) Whether those who vow to enter religion are bound to remain there in perpetuity?

(5) Whether children should be received into religion?

(6) Whether one should be withheld from entering religion through deference to one's parents?

(7) Whether parish priests or archdeacons may enter religion?

(8) Whether one may pass from one religious order to another?

(9) Whether one ought to induce others to enter religion?

(10) Whether serious deliberation with one's relations and friends is requisite for entrance into religion?

Whether those who are not practiced in keeping the commandments should enter religion?

Objection 1: It would seem that none should enter religion but those who are practiced in the observance of the commandments. For our Lord gave the counsel of perfection to the young man who said that he had kept the commandments "from his youth." Now all religious orders originate from Christ. Therefore it would seem that none should be allowed to enter religion but those who are practiced in the observance of the commandments.

Objection 2: Further, Gregory says (Hom. xv in Ezech., and Moral. xxii): "No one comes suddenly to the summit; but he must make a beginning of a good life in the smallest matters, so as to accomplish great things." Now the great things are the counsels which pertain to the perfection of life, while the lesser things are the commandments which belong to common righteousness. Therefore it would seem that one ought not to enter religion for the purpose of keeping the counsels, unless one be already practiced in the observance of the precepts.

Objection 3: Further, the religious state, like the holy orders, has a place of eminence in the Church. Now, as Gregory writes to the bishop Siagrius [*Regist. ix, Ep. 106], "order should be observed in ascending to orders. For he seeks a fall who aspires to mount to the summit by overpassing the steps." [*The rest of the quotation is from Regist. v, Ep. 53, ad Virgil. Episc.]. "For we are well aware that walls when built receive not the weight of the beams until the new fabric is rid of its moisture, lest if they should be burdened with weight before they are seasoned they bring down the whole building" (Dist. xlviii, can. Sicut neophytus). Therefore it would seem that one should not enter religion unless one be practiced in the observance of the precepts.

Objection 4: Further, a gloss on Ps. 130:2, "As a child that is weaned is towards his mother," says: "First we are conceived in the womb of Mother Church, by being taught the rudiments of faith. Then we are nourished as it were in her womb, by progressing in those same elements. Afterwards we are brought forth to the light by being regenerated in baptism. Then the Church bears us as it were in her hands and feeds us with milk, when after baptism we are instructed in good works and are nourished with the milk of simple doctrine while we progress; until having grown out of infancy we leave our mother's milk for a father's control, that is to say, we pass from simple doctrine, by which we are taught the Word made flesh, to the Word that was in the beginning with God." Afterwards it goes on to say: "For those who are just baptized on Holy Saturday are borne in the hands of the Church as it were and fed with milk until Pentecost, during which time nothing arduous is prescribed, no fasts, no rising at midnight. Afterwards they are confirmed by the Paraclete Spirit, and being weaned so to speak, begin to fast and keep other difficult observances. Many, like the heretics and schismatics, have perverted this order by being weaned before the time. Hence they have come to naught." Now this order is apparently perverted by those who enter religion, or induce others to enter religion, before they are practiced in the easier observance of the commandments. Therefore they would seem to be heretics or schismatics.

Objection 5: Further, one should proceed from that which precedes to that which follows after. Now the commandments precede the counsels, because they are more universal, for "the implication of the one by the other is not convertible" [*Categor. ix], since whoever keeps the counsels keeps the commandments, but the converse does not hold. Seeing then that the right order requires one to pass from that which comes first to that which comes after, it follows that one ought not to pass to the observance of the counsels in religion, without being first of all practiced in the observance of the commandments.

On the contrary, Matthew the publican who was not practiced in the observance of the commandments was called by our Lord to the observance of the counsels. For it is stated (Lk. 5:28) that "leaving all things he . . . followed Him." Therefore it is not necessary for a person to be practiced in the observance of the commandments before passing to the perfection of the counsels.

I answer that, As shown above ([3834]Q[188], A[1]), the religious state is a spiritual schooling for the attainment of the perfection of charity. This is accomplished through the removal of the obstacles to perfect charity by religious observances; and these obstacles are those things which attach man's affections to earthly things. Now the attachment of man's affections to earthly things is not only an obstacle to the perfection of charity, but sometimes leads to the loss of charity, when through turning inordinately to temporal goods man turns away from the immutable good by sinning mortally. Hence it is evident that the observances of the religious state, while removing the obstacles to perfect charity, remove also the occasions of sin: for instance, it is clear that fasting, watching, obedience, and the like withdraw man from sins of gluttony and lust and all other manner of sins.

Consequently it is right that not only those who are practiced in the observance of the commandments should enter religion in order to attain to yet greater perfection, but also those who are not practiced, in order the more easily to avoid sin and attain to perfection.

Reply to Objection 1: Jerome (Super Matth. xix, 20) says: "The young man lies when he says: 'All these have I kept from my youth.' For if he had fulfilled this commandment, 'Thou shalt love thy neighbor as thyself,' why did he go away sad when he heard: Go, sell all thou hast and give to the poor?" But this means that he lied as to the perfect observance of this commandment. Hence Origen says (Tract. viii super Matth.) that "it is written in the Gospel according to the Hebrews that when our Lord had said to him: 'Go, sell all thou hast,' the rich man began to scratch his head; and that our Lord said to him: How sayest thou: I have fulfilled the law and the prophets, seeing that it is written in the law: Thou shalt love thy neighbor as thyself? Behold many of thy brethren, children of Abraham, are clothed in filth, and die of hunger, whilst thy house is full of all manner of good things, and nothing whatever hath passed thence to them. And thus our Lord reproves him saying: If thou wilt be perfect, go, etc. For it is impossible to fulfil the commandment which says, Thou shalt love thy neighbor as thyself, and to be rich, especially to have such great wealth." This also refers to the perfect fulfilment of this precept. on the other hand, it is true that he kept the commandments imperfectly and in a general way. For perfection consists chiefly in the observance of the precepts of charity, as stated above ([3835]Q[184], A[3]). Wherefore in order to show that the perfection of the counsels is useful both to the innocent and to sinners, our Lord called not only the innocent youth but also the sinner Matthew. Yet Matthew obeyed His call, and the youth obeyed not, because sinners are converted to the religious life more easily than those who presume on their innocency. It is to the former that our Lord says (Mat. 21:31): "The publicans and the harlots shall go into the kingdom of God before you."

Reply to Objection 2: The highest and the lowest place can be taken in three ways. First, in reference to the same state and the same man; and thus it is evident that no one comes to the summit suddenly, since every man that lives aright, progresses during the whole course of his life, so as to arrive at the summit. Secondly, in comparison with various states; and thus he who desires to reach to a higher state need not begin from a lower state: for instance, if a man wish to be a cleric he need not first of all be practiced in the life of a layman. Thirdly, in comparison with different persons; and in this way it is clear that one man begins straightway not only from a higher state, but even from a higher degree of holiness, than the highest degree to which another man attains throughout his whole life. Hence Gregory says (Dial. ii, 1): "All are agreed that the boy Benedict began at a high degree of grace and perfection in his daily life."

Reply to Objection 3: As stated above ([3836]Q[184], A[6]) the holy orders prerequire holiness, whereas the religious state is a school for the attainment of holiness. Hence the burden of orders should be laid on the walls when these are already seasoned with holiness, whereas the burden of religion seasons the walls, i.e. men, by drawing out the damp of vice.

Reply to Objection 4: It is manifest from the words of this gloss that it is chiefly a question of the order of doctrine, in so far as one has to pass from easy matter to that which is more difficult. Hence it is clear from what follows that the statement that certain "heretics" and "schismatics have perverted this order" refers to the order of doctrine. For it continues thus: "But he says that he has kept these things, namely the aforesaid order, binding himself by an oath [*Referring to the last words of the verse, and taking 'retributio,' which Douay renders 'reward,' as meaning 'punishment']. Thus I was humble not only in other things but also in knowledge, for 'I was humbly minded'; because I was first of all fed with milk, which is the Word made flesh, so that I grew up to partake of the bread of angels, namely the Word that is in the beginning with God." The example which is given in proof, of the newly baptized not being commanded to fast until Pentecost, shows that no difficult things are to be laid on them as an obligation before the Holy Ghost inspires them inwardly to take upon themselves difficult things of their own choice. Hence after Pentecost and the receiving of the Holy Ghost the Church observes a fast. Now the Holy Ghost, according to Ambrose (Super Luc. 1:15), "is not confined to any particular age; He ceases not when men die, He is not excluded from the maternal womb." Gregory also in a homily for Pentecost (xxx in Ev.) says: "He fills the boy harpist and makes him a psalmist: He fills the boy abstainer and makes him a wise judge [*Dan. 1:8-17]," and afterwards he adds: "No time is needed to learn whatsoever He will, for He teaches the mind by the merest touch." Again it is written (Eccles. 8:8), "It is not in man's power to stop the Spirit," and the Apostle admonishes us (1 Thess. 5:19): "Extinguish not the Spirit," and (Acts 7:51) it is said against certain persons: "You always resist the Holy Ghost."

Reply to Objection 5: There are certain chief precepts which are the ends, so to say, of the commandments and counsels. These are the precepts of charity, and the counsels are directed to them, not that these precepts cannot be observed without keeping the counsels, but that the keeping of the counsels conduces to the better observance of the precepts. The other precepts are secondary and are directed to the precepts of charity; in such a way that unless one observe them it is altogether impossible to keep the precepts of charity. Accordingly in the intention the perfect observance of the precepts of charity precedes the counsels, and yet sometimes it follows them in point of time. For such is the order of the end in relation to things directed to the end. But the observance in a general way of the precepts of charity together with the other precepts, is compared to the counsels as the common to the proper, because one can observe the precepts without observing the counsels, but not vice versa. Hence the common observance of the precepts precedes the counsels in the order of nature; but it does not follow that it precedes them in point of time, for a thing is not in the genus before being in one of the species. But the observance of the precepts apart from the counsels is directed to the observance of the precepts together with the counsels; as an imperfect to a perfect species, even as the irrational to the rational animal. Now the perfect is naturally prior to the imperfect, since "nature," as Boethius says (De Consol. iii, 10), "begins with perfect things." And yet it is not necessary for the precepts first of all to be observed without the counsels, and afterwards with the counsels, just as it is not necessary for one to be an ass before being a man, or married before being a virgin. In like manner it is not necessary for a person first of all to keep the commandments in the world before entering religion; especially as the worldly life does not dispose one to religious perfection, but is more an obstacle thereto.

Whether one ought to be bound by vow to enter religion?

Objection 1: It would seem that one ought not to be bound by vow to enter religion. For in making his profession a man is bound by the religious vow. Now before profession a year of probation is allowed, according to the rule of the Blessed Benedict (lviii) and according to the decree of Innocent IV [*Sext. Decret., cap. Non solum., de Regular. et Transeunt, ad Relig.] who moreover forbade anyone to be bound to the religious life by profession before completing the year of probation. Therefore it would seem that much less ought anyone while yet in the world to be bound by vow to enter religion.

Objection 2: Further, Gregory says (Regist. xi, Ep. 15): Jews "should be persuaded to be converted, not by compulsion but of their own free will" (Dist. xlv, can. De Judaeis). Now one is compelled to fulfil what one has vowed. Therefore no one should be bound by vow to enter religion.

Objection 3: Further, no one should give another an occasion of falling; wherefore it is written (Ex. 21:33,34): "If a man open a pit . . . and an ox or an ass fall into it, the owner of the pit shall pay the price of the beasts." Now through being bound by vow to enter religion it often happens that people fall into despair and various sins. Therefore it would seem that one ought not to be bound by vow to enter religion.

On the contrary, It is written, (Ps. 75:12): "Vow ye, and pay to the Lord your God"; and a gloss of Augustine says that "some vows concern the individual, such as vows of chastity, virginity, and the like." Consequently Holy Scripture invites us to vow these things. But Holy Scripture invites us only to that which is better. Therefore it is better to bind oneself by vow to enter religion.

I answer that, As stated above ([3837]Q[88], A[6]), when we were treating of vows, one and the same work done in fulfilment of a vow is more praiseworthy than if it be done apart from a vow, both because to vow is an act of religion, which has a certain pre-eminence among the virtues, and because a vow strengthens a man's will to do good; and just as a sin is more grievous through proceeding from a will obstinate in evil, so a good work is the more praiseworthy through proceeding from a will confirmed in good by means of a vow. Therefore it is in itself praiseworthy to bind oneself by vow to enter religion.

Reply to Objection 1: The religious vow is twofold. One is the solemn vow which makes a man a monk or a brother in some other religious order. This is called the profession, and such a vow should be preceded by a year's probation, as the objection proves. The other is the simple vow which does not make a man a monk or a religious, but only binds him to enter religion, and such a vow need not be preceded by a year's probation.

Reply to Objection 2: The words quoted from Gregory must be understood as referring to absolute violence. But the compulsion arising from the obligation of a vow is not absolute necessity, but a necessity of end, because after such a vow one cannot attain to the end of salvation unless one fulfil that vow. Such a necessity is not to be avoided; indeed, as Augustine says (Ep. cxxvii ad Armentar. et Paulin.), "happy is the necessity that compels us to better things."

Reply to Objection 3: The vow to enter religion is a strengthening of the will for better things, and consequently, considered in itself, instead of giving a man an occasion of falling, withdraws him from it. But if one who breaks a vow falls more grievously, this does not derogate from the goodness of the vow, as neither does it derogate from the goodness of Baptism that some sin more grievously after being baptized.

Whether one who is bound by a vow to enter religion is under an obligation of entering religion?

Objection 1: It would seem that one who is bound by the vow to enter religion is not under an obligation of entering religion. For it is said in the Decretals (XVII, qu. ii, can. Consaldus): "Consaldus, a priest under pressure of sickness and emotional fervour, promised to become a monk. He did not, however, bind himself to a monastery or abbot; nor did he commit his promise to writing, but he renounced his benefice in the hands of a notary; and when he was restored to health he refused to become a monk." And afterwards it is added: "We adjudge and by apostolic authority we command that the aforesaid priest be admitted to his benefice and sacred duties, and that he be allowed to retain them in peace." Now this would not be if he were bound to enter religion. Therefore it would seem that one is not bound to keep one's vow of entering religion.

Objection 2: Further, no one is bound to do what is not in his power. Now it is not in a person's power to enter religion, since this depends on the consent of those whom he wishes to join. Therefore it would seem that a man is not obliged to fulfil the vow by which he bound himself to enter religion.

Objection 3: Further, a less useful vow cannot remit a more useful one. Now the fulfilment of a vow to enter religion might hinder the fulfilment of a vow to take up the cross in defense of the Holy Land; and the latter apparently is the more useful vow, since thereby a man obtains the forgiveness of his sins. Therefore it would seem that the vow by which a man has bound himself to enter religion is not necessarily to be fulfilled.

On the contrary, It is written (Eccles. 5:3): "If thou hast vowed anything to God, defer not to pay it, for an unfaithful and foolish promise displeaseth him"; and a gloss on Ps. 75:12, "Vow ye, and pay to the Lord your God," says: "To vow depends on the will: but after the vow has been taken the fulfilment is of obligation."

I answer that, As stated above ([3838]Q[88], A[1]), when we were treating of vows, a vow is a promise made to God in matters concerning God. Now, as Gregory says in a letter to Boniface [*Innoc. I, Epist. ii, Victricio Epo. Rotomag., cap. 14; Cf. can. Viduas: cause. xxvii, qu. 1]: "If among men of good faith contracts are wont to be absolutely irrevocable, how much more shall the breaking of this promise given to God be deserving of punishment!" Therefore a man is under an obligation to fulfil what he has vowed, provided this be something pertaining to God.

Now it is evident that entrance into religion pertains very much to God, since thereby man devotes himself entirely to the divine service, as stated above ([3839]Q[186], A[1]). Hence it follows that he who binds himself to enter religion is under an obligation to enter religion according as he intends to bind himself by his vow: so that if he intend to bind himself absolutely, he is obliged to enter as soon as he can, through the cessation of a lawful impediment; whereas if he intend to bind himself to a certain fixed time, or under a certain fixed condition, he is bound to enter religion when the time comes or the condition is fulfilled.

Reply to Objection 1: This priest had made, not a solemn, but a simple vow. Hence he was not a monk in effect, so as to be bound by law to dwell in a monastery and renounce his cure. However, in the court of conscience one ought to advise him to renounce all and enter religion. Hence (Extra, De Voto et Voti Redemptione, cap. Per tuas) the Bishop of Grenoble, who had accepted the episcopate after vowing to enter religion, without having fulfilled his vow, is counseled that if "he wish to heal his conscience he should renounce the government of his see and pay his vows to the Most High."

Reply to Objection 2: As stated above ([3840]Q[88], A[3], ad 2), when we were treating of vows, he who has bound himself by vow to enter a certain religious order is bound to do what is in his power in order to be received in that order; and if he intend to bind himself simply to enter the religious life, if he be not admitted to one, he is bound to go to another; whereas if he intend to bind himself only to one particular order, he is bound only according to the measure of the obligation to which he has engaged himself.

Reply to Objection 3: The vow to enter religion being perpetual is greater than the vow of pilgrimage to the Holy Land, which is a temporal vow; and as Alexander III says (Extra, De Voto et Voti Redemptione, cap. Scripturae), "he who exchanges a temporary service for the perpetual service of religion is in no way guilty of breaking his vow."

Moreover it may be reasonably stated that also by entrance into religion a man obtains remission of all his sins. For if by giving alms a man may forthwith satisfy for his sins, according to Dan. 4:24, "Redeem thou thy sins with alms," much more does it suffice to satisfy for all his sins that a man devote himself wholly to the divine service by entering religion, for this surpasses all manner of satisfaction, even that of public penance, according to the Decretals (XXXIII, qu. i, cap. Admonere) just as a holocaust exceeds a sacrifice, as Gregory declares (Hom. xx in Ezech.). Hence we read in the Lives of the Fathers (vi, 1) that by entering religion one receives the same grace as by being baptized. And yet even if one were not thereby absolved from all debt of punishment, nevertheless the entrance into religion is more profitable than a pilgrimage to the Holy Land, as regards the advancement in good, which is preferable to absolution from punishment.

Whether he who has vowed to enter religion is bound to remain in religion in perpetuity?

Objection 1: It would seem that he who has vowed to enter religion, is bound in perpetuity to remain in religion. For it is better not to enter religion than to leave after entering, according to 2 Pet. 2:21, "It had been better for them not to have known the way of justice, than after they have known it to turn back," and Lk. 9:62, "No man putting his hand to the plough, and looking back, is fit for the kingdom of God." But he who bound himself by the vow to enter religion, is under the obligation to enter, as stated above [3841] (A[3]). Therefore he is also bound to remain for always.

Objection 2: Further, everyone is bound to avoid that which gives rise to scandal, and is a bad example to others. Now by leaving after entering religion a man gives a bad example and is an occasion of scandal to others, who are thereby withdrawn from entering or incited to leave. Therefore it seems that he who enters religion in order to fulfil a vow which he had previously taken, is bound to remain evermore.

Objection 3: Further, the vow to enter religion is accounted a perpetual vow: wherefore it is preferred to temporal vows, as stated above (A[3], ad 3;[3842] Q[88], A[12], ad 1). But this would not be so if a person after vowing to enter religion were to enter with the intention of leaving. It seems, therefore, that he who vows to enter religion is bound also to remain in perpetuity.

On the contrary, The vow of religious profession, for the reason that it binds a man to remain in religion for evermore, has to be preceded by a year of probation; whereas this is not required before the simple vow whereby a man binds himself to enter religion. Therefore it seems that he who vows to enter religion is not for that reason bound to remain there in perpetuity.

I answer that, The obligation of a vow proceeds from the will: because "to vow is an act of the will" according to Augustine [*Gloss of Peter Lombard on Ps. 75:12]. Consequently the obligation of a vow extends as far as the will and intention of the person who takes the vow. Accordingly if in vowing he intend to bind himself not only to enter religion, but also to remain there evermore, he is bound to remain in perpetuity. If, on the other hand, he intend to bind himself to enter religion for the purpose of trial, while retaining the freedom to remain or not remain, it is clear that he is not bound to remain. If, however, in vowing he thought merely of entering religion, without thinking of being free to leave, or of remaining in perpetuity, it would seem that he is bound to enter religion according to the form prescribed by common law, which is that those who enter should be given a year's probation. Wherefore he is not bound to remain for ever.

Reply to Objection 1: It is better to enter religion with the purpose of making a trial than not to enter at all, because by so doing one disposes oneself to remain always. Nor is a person accounted to turn or to look back, save when he omits to do that which he engaged to do: else whoever does a good work for a time, would be unfit for the kingdom of God, unless he did it always, which is evidently false.

Reply to Objection 2: A man who has entered religion gives neither scandal nor bad example by leaving, especially if he do so for a reasonable motive; and if others are scandalized, it will be passive scandal on their part, and not active scandal on the part of the person leaving, since in doing so, he has done what was lawful, and expedient on account of some reasonable motive, such as sickness, weakness, and the like.

Reply to Objection 3: He who enters with the purpose of leaving forthwith, does not seem to fulfil his vow, since this was not his intention in vowing. Hence he must change that purpose, at least so as to wish to try whether it is good for him to remain in religion, but he is not bound to remain for evermore.

Whether children should be received in religion?

Objection 1: It would seem that children ought not to be received in religion. Because it is said (Extra, De Regular. et Transeunt. ad Relig., cap. Nullus): "No one should be tonsured unless he be of legal age and willing." But children, seemingly, are not of legal age; nor have they a will of their own, not having perfect use of reason. Therefore it seems that they ought not to be received in religion.

Objection 2: Further, the state of religion would seem to be a state of repentance; wherefore religion is derived [*Cf.[3843] Q[81], A[1]] from "religare" [to bind] or from "re-eligere" [to choose again], as Augustine says (De Civ. Dei x, 3 [*Cf. De Vera Relig. lv]). But repentance does not become children. Therefore it seems that they should not enter religion.

Objection 3: Further, the obligation of a vow is like that of an oath. But children under the age of fourteen ought not to be bound by oath (Decret. XXII, qu. v, cap. Pueri and cap. Honestum.). Therefore it would seem that neither should they be bound by vow.

Objection 4: Further, it is seemingly unlawful to bind a person to an obligation that can be justly canceled. Now if any persons of unripe age bind themselves to religion, they can be withdrawn by their parents or guardians. For it is written in the Decretals (XX, qu. ii, can. Puella) that "if a maid under twelve years of age shall take the sacred veil of her own accord, her parents or guardians, if they choose, can at once declare the deed null and void." It is therefore unlawful for children, especially of unripe age, to be admitted or bound to religion.

On the contrary, our Lord said (Mat. 19:14): "Suffer the little children, and forbid them not to come to Me." Expounding these words Origen says (Tract. vii in Matth.) that "the disciples of Jesus before they have been taught the conditions of righteousness [*Cf. Mat. 19:16-30], rebuke those who offer children and babes to Christ: but our Lord urges His disciples to stoop to the service of children. We must therefore take note of this, lest deeming ourselves to excel in wisdom we despise the Church's little ones, as though we were great, and forbid the children to come to Jesus."

I answer that, As stated above (A[2], ad 1), the religious vow is twofold. One is the simple vow consisting in a mere promise made to God, and proceeding from the interior deliberation of the mind. Such a vow derives its efficacy from the divine law. Nevertheless it may encounter a twofold obstacle. First, through lack of deliberation, as in the case of the insane, whose vows are not binding [*Extra, De Regular. et Transeunt. ad Relig., cap. Sicut tenor]. The same applies to children who have not reached the required use of reason, so as to be capable of guile, which use boys attain, as a rule, at about the age of fourteen, and girls at the age of twelve, this being what is called "the age of puberty," although in some it comes earlier and in others it is delayed, according to the various dispositions of nature. Secondly, the efficacy of a simple vow encounters an obstacle, if the person who makes a vow to God is not his own master; for instance, if a slave, though having the use of reason, vows to enter religion, or even is ordained, without the knowledge of his master: for his master can annul this, as stated in the Decretals (Dist. LIV, cap. Si servus). And since boys and girls under the age of puberty are naturally in their father's power as regards the disposal of their manner of life, their father may either cancel or approve their vow, if it please him to do so, as it is expressly said with regard to a woman (Num. 30:4).

Accordingly if before reaching the age of puberty a child makes a simple vow, not yet having full use of reason, he is not bound in virtue of the vow; but if he has the use of reason before reaching the age of puberty, he is bound, so far as he is concerned, by his vow; yet this obligation may be removed by his father's authority, under whose control he still remains, because the ordinance of the law whereby one man is subject to another considers what happens in the majority of cases. If, however, the

child has passed the age of puberty, his vow cannot be annulled by the authority of his parents; though if he has not the full use of reason, he would not be bound in the sight of God.

The other is the solemn vow which makes a man a monk or a religious. Such a vow is subject to the ordinance of the Church, on account of the solemnity attached to it. And since the Church considers what happens in the majority of cases, a profession made before the age of puberty, however much the person who makes profession may have the use of reason, or be capable of guile, does not take effect so as to make him a religious (Extra, De Regular., etc. cap. Significatum est.).

Nevertheless, although they cannot be professed before the age of puberty, they can, with the consent of their parents, be received into religion to be educated there: thus it is related of John the Baptist (Lk. 1:80) that "the child grew and was strengthened in spirit, and was in the deserts." Hence, as Gregory states (Dial. ii, 3), "the Roman nobles began to give their sons to the blessed Benedict to be nurtured for Almighty God"; and this is most fitting, according to Lam. 3:27, "It is good for a man when he has borne the yoke from his youth." It is for this reason that by common custom children are made to apply themselves to those duties or arts with which they are to pass their lives.

Reply to Objection 1: The legal age for receiving the tonsure and taking the solemn vow of religion is the age of puberty, when a man is able to make use of his own will; but before the age of puberty it is possible to have reached the lawful age to receive the tonsure and be educated in a religious house.

Reply to Objection 2: The religious state is chiefly directed to the attachment of perfection, as stated above ([3844]Q[186], A[1], ad 4); and accordingly it is becoming to children, who are easily drawn to it. But as a consequence it is called a state of repentance, inasmuch as occasions of sin are removed by religious observances, as stated above ([3845]Q[186], A[1], ad 4).

Reply to Objection 3: Even as children are not bound to take oaths (as the canon states), so are they not bound to take vows. If, however, they bind themselves by vow or oath to do something, they are bound in God's sight, if they have the use of reason, but they are not bound in the sight of the Church before reaching the age of fourteen.

Reply to Objection 4: A woman who has not reached the age of puberty is not rebuked (Num. 30:4) for taking a vow without her parents' consent: but the vow can be made void by her parents. Hence it is evident that she does not sin in vowing. But we are given to understand that she binds herself by vow, so far as she may, without prejudice to her parents' authority.

Whether one ought to be withdrawn from entering religion through deference to one's parents?

Objection 1: It would seem that one ought to be withdrawn from entering religion through deference to one's parents. For it is not lawful to omit that which is of obligation in order to do that which is optional. Now deference to one's parents comes under an obligation of the precept concerning the honoring of our parents (Ex. 20:12); wherefore the Apostle says (1 Tim. 5:4): "If any widow have children or grandchildren, let her learn first to govern her own house, and to make a return of duty to her parents." But the entrance to religion is optional. Therefore it would seem that one ought not to omit deference to one's parents for the sake of entering religion.

Objection 2: Further, seemingly the subjection of a son to his father is greater than that of a slave to his master, since sonship is natural, while slavery results from the curse of sin, as appears from Gn. 9:25. Now a slave cannot set aside the service of his master in order to enter religion or take holy orders, as stated in the Decretals (Dist. LIV, cap. Si servus). Much less therefore can a son set aside the deference due to his father in order to enter religion.

Objection 3: Further, a man is more indebted to his parents than to those to whom he owes money. Now persons who owe money to anyone cannot enter religion. For Gregory says (Regist. viii, Ep. 5) that "those who are engaged in trade must by no means be admitted into a monastery, when they seek admittance, unless first of all they withdraw from public business" (Dist. liii, can. Legem.). Therefore seemingly much less may children enter religion in despite of their duty to their parents.

On the contrary, It is related (Mat. 4:22) that James and John "left their nets and father, and followed our Lord." By this, says Hilary (Can. iii in Matth.), "we learn that we who intend to follow Christ are not bound by the cares of the secular life, and by the ties of home."

I answer that, As stated above ([3846]Q[101], A[2], ad 2) when we were treating of piety, parents as such have the character of a principle, wherefore it is competent to them as such to have the care of their children. Hence it is unlawful for a person having children to enter religion so as altogether to set aside the care for their children, namely without providing for their education. For it is written (1 Tim. 5:8) that "if any man have not care of his own . . . he hath denied the faith, and is worse than an infidel."

Nevertheless it is accidentally competent to parents to be assisted by their children, in so far, to wit, as they are placed in a condition of necessity. Consequently we must say that when their parents are in such need that they cannot fittingly be supported otherwise than by the help of their children, these latter may not lawfully enter religion in despite of their duty to their parents. If, however, the parents' necessity be not such as to stand in great need of their children's assistance, the latter may, in despite of the duty they owe their parents, enter religion even against their parents' command, because after the age of puberty every freeman enjoys freedom in things concerning the ordering of his state of life, especially in such as belong to the service of God, and "we should more obey the Father of spirits that we may live [*'Shall we not much more obey the Father of Spirits, and live?'],." as says the Apostle (Heb. 12:9), than obey our parents. Hence as we read (Mat. 8:22; Lk. 9:62) our Lord rebuked the disciple who was unwilling to follow him forthwith on account of his father's burial: for there were others who could see to this, as Chrysostom remarks [*Hom. xxvii in Matth.].

Reply to Objection 1: The commandment of honoring our parents extends not only to bodily but also to spiritual service, and to the paying of deference. Hence even those who are in religion can fulfil the commandment of honoring their parents, by praying for them and by revering and assisting them, as becomes religious, since even those who live in the world honor their parents in different ways as befits their condition.

Reply to Objection 2: Since slavery was imposed in punishment of sin, it follows that by slavery man forfeits something which otherwise he would be competent to have, namely the free disposal of his person, for "a slave belongs wholly to his master" [*Aristotle, Polit. i, 2]. On the other hand, the son, through being subject to his father, is not hindered from freely disposing of his person by transferring himself to the service of God; which is most conducive to man's good.

Reply to Objection 3: He who is under a certain fixed obligation cannot lawfully set it aside so long as he is able to fulfil it. Wherefore if a person is under an obligation to give an account to someone or to pay a certain fixed debt, he cannot lawfully evade this obligation in order to enter religion. If, however, he owes a sum of money, and has not wherewithal to pay the debt, he must do what he can, namely by surrendering his goods to his creditor. According to civil law [*Cod. IV, x, de Oblig. et Action, 12] money lays an obligation not on the person of a freeman, but on his property, because the person of a freeman "is above all pecuniary consideration" [*Dig. L, xvii, de div. reg. Jur. ant. 106,176]. Hence, after surrendering his property, he may lawfully enter religion, nor is he bound to remain in the world in order to earn the means of paying the debt.

On the other hand, he does not owe his father a special debt, except as may arise in a case of necessity, as stated above.

Whether parish priests may lawfully enter religion?

Objection 1: It would seem that parish priests cannot lawfully enter religion. For Gregory says (Past. iii, 4) that "he who undertakes the cure of souls, receives an awful warning in the words: 'My son, if thou be surety for thy friend, thou hast engaged fast thy hand to a stranger'" (Prov. 6:1); and he goes on to say, "because to be surety for a friend is to take charge of the soul of another on the surety of one's own behavior." Now he who is under an obligation to a man for a debt, cannot enter religion, unless he pay what he owes, if he can. Since then a priest is able to fulfil the cure of souls, to which obligation he has pledged his soul, it would seem unlawful for him to lay aside the cure of souls in order to enter religion.

Objection 2: Further, what is lawful to one is likewise lawful to all. But if all priests having cure of souls were to enter religion, the people would be left without a pastor's care, which would be unfitting. Therefore it seems that parish priests cannot lawfully enter religion.

Objection 3: Further, chief among the acts to which religious orders are directed are those whereby a man gives to others the fruit of his contemplation. Now such acts are competent to parish priests and archdeacons, whom it becomes by virtue of their office to preach and hear confessions. Therefore it would seem unlawful for a parish priest or archdeacon to pass over to religion.

On the contrary, It is said in the Decretals (XIX, qu. ii, cap. Duce sunt leges.): "If a man, while governing the people in his church under the bishop and leading a secular life, is inspired by the Holy Ghost to desire to work out his salvation in a monastery or under some canonical rule, even though his bishop withstand him, we authorize him to go freely."

I answer that, As stated above (A[3], ad 3;[3847] Q[88], A[12], ad 1), the obligation of a perpetual vow stands before every other obligation. Now it belongs properly to bishops and religious to be bound by perpetual vow to devote themselves to the divine service [*Cf.[3848] Q[184], A[5]], while parish priests and archdeacons are not, as bishops are, bound by a perpetual and solemn vow to retain the cure of souls. Wherefore bishops "cannot lay aside their bishopric for any pretext whatever, without the authority of the Roman Pontiff" (Extra, De Regular. et Transeunt. ad Relig., cap. Licet.): whereas archdeacons and parish priests are free to renounce in the hands of the bishop the cure entrusted to them, without the Pope's special permission, who alone can dispense from perpetual vows. Therefore it is evident that archdeacons and parish priests may lawfully enter religion.

Reply to Objection 1: Parish priests and archdeacons have bound themselves to the care of their subjects, as long as they retain their archdeaconry or parish, but they did not bind themselves to retain their archdeaconry or parish for ever.

Reply to Objection 2: As Jerome says (Contra Vigil.): "Although they," namely religious, "are sorely smitten by thy poisonous tongue, about whom you argue, saying; 'If all shut themselves up and live in solitude, who will go to church? who will convert worldlings? who will be able to urge sinners to virtue?' If this holds true, if all are fools with thee, who can be wise? Nor will virginity be commendable, for if all be virgins, and none marry, the human race will perish. Virtue is rare, and is not desired by many." It is therefore evident that this is a foolish alarm; thus might a man fear to draw water lest the river run dry. [*St. Thomas gives no reply to the third objection, which is sufficiently solved in the body of the article.]

Whether it is lawful to pass from one religious order to another?

Objection 1: It seems unlawful to pass from one religious order to another, even a stricter one. For the Apostle says (Heb. 10:25): "Not forsaking our assembly, as some are accustomed"; and a gloss observes: "Those namely who yield through fear of persecution, or who presuming on themselves withdraw from the company of sinners or of the imperfect, that they may appear to be righteous." Now those who pass from one religious order to another more perfect one would seem to do this. Therefore this is seemingly unlawful.

Objection 2: Further, the profession of monks is stricter than that of canons regular (Extra, De Statu Monach. et Canonic. Reg., cap. Quod Dei timorem). But it is unlawful for anyone to pass from the state of canon regular to the monastic state. For it is said in the Decretals (XIX, qu. iii, can. Mandamus): "We ordain and without any exception forbid any professed canon regular to become a monk, unless (which God forbid) he have fallen into public sin." Therefore it would seem unlawful for anyone to pass from one religious order to another of higher rank.

Objection 3: Further, a person is bound to fulfil what he has vowed, as long as he is able lawfully to do so; thus if a man has vowed to observe continence, he is bound, even after contracting marriage by words in the present tense, to fulfil his vow so long as the marriage is not consummated, because he can fulfil the vow by entering religion. Therefore if a person may lawfully pass from one religious order to another, he will be bound to do so if he vowed it previously while in the world. But this would seem objectionable, since in many cases it might give rise to scandal. Therefore a religious may not pass from one religious order to another stricter one.

On the contrary, It is said in the Decretals (XX, qu. iv, can. Virgines): "If sacred virgins design for the good of their soul to pass to another monastery on account of a stricter life, and decide to remain there, the holy synod allows them to do so": and the same would seem to apply to any religious. Therefore one may lawfully pass from one religious order to another.

I answer that, It is not commendable to pass from one religious order to another: both because this frequently gives scandal to those who remain; and because, other things being equal, it is easier to make progress in a religious order to which one is accustomed than in one to which one is not habituated. Hence in the Conferences of the Fathers (Coll. xiv, 5) Abbot Nesteros says: "It is best for each one that he should, according to the resolve he has made, hasten with the greatest zeal and care to reach the perfection of the work he has undertaken, and nowise forsake the profession he has chosen." And further on he adds (cap. 6) by way of reason: "For it is impossible that one and the same man should excel in all the virtues at once, since if he endeavor to practice them equally, he will of necessity, while trying to attain them all, end in acquiring none of them perfectly": because the various religious orders excel in respect of various works of virtue.

Nevertheless one may commendably pass from one religious order to another for three reasons. First, through zeal for a more perfect religious life, which excellence depends, as stated above ([3849]Q[188], A[6]), not merely on severity, but chiefly on the end to which a religious order is directed, and secondarily on the discretion whereby the observances are proportionate to the due end. Secondly, on account of a religious order falling away from the perfection it ought to have: for instance, if in a more severe religious order, the religious begin to live less strictly, it is commendable for one to pass even to a less severe religious order if the observance is better. Hence in the Conferences of the Fathers (Coll. xix, 3,5,6) Abbot John says of himself that he had passed from the solitary life, in which he was professed, to a less severe life, namely of those who lived in community, because the hermetical life had fallen into decline and laxity. Thirdly, on account of sickness or weakness, the result of which sometimes is that one is unable to keep the ordinances of a more severe religious order, though able to observe those of a less strict religion.

There is, however, a difference in these three cases. For in the first case one ought, on account of humility, to seek permission: yet this cannot be denied, provided it be certain that this other religion is more severe. "And if there be a probable doubt about this, one should ask one's superior to decide" (Extra, De Regular. et Transeunt. ad Relig., cap. Licet.). In like manner the superior's decision should be sought in the second case. In the third case it is also necessary to have a dispensation.

Reply to Objection 1: Those who pass to a stricter religious order, do so not out of presumption that they may appear righteous, but out of devotion, that they may become more righteous.

Reply to Objection 2: Religious orders whether of monks or of canons regular are destined to the works of the contemplative life. Chief among these are those which are performed in the divine mysteries, and these are the direct object of the orders of canons regular, the members of which are essentially religious clerics. On the other hand, monastic religious are not essentially clerics, according to the Decretals (XVI, qu. i, cap. Alia causa). Hence although monastic orders are more severe, it would be lawful, supposing the members to be lay monks, to pass from the monastic order to an order of canons regular, according to the statement of Jerome (Ep. cxxv, ad Rustic. Monach.): "So live in the monastery as to deserve to become a cleric"; but not conversely, as expressed in the Decretal quoted (XIX, qu. iii). If, however, the monks be clerics devoting themselves to the sacred ministry, they have this in common with canons regular coupled with greater severity, and consequently it will be lawful to pass from an order of canons regular to a monastic order, provided withal that one seek the superior's permission (XIX, qu. iii; cap. Statuimus).

Reply to Objection 3: The solemn vow whereby a person is bound to a less strict order, is more binding than the simple vow whereby a person is bound to a stricter order. For if after taking a simple vow a person were to be married, his marriage would not be invalid, as it would be after his taking a solemn vow. Consequently a person who is professed in a less severe order is not bound to fulfil a simple vow he has taken on entering a more severe order.

Day 249

Whether one ought to induce others to enter religion?

Objection 1: It would seem that no one ought to induce others to enter religion. For the blessed Benedict prescribes in his Rule (lviii) that "those who seek to enter religion must not easily be admitted, but spirits must be tested whether they be of God"; and Cassian has the same instruction (De Inst. Caenob. iv, 3). Much less therefore is it lawful to induce anyone to enter religion.

Objection 2: Further, our Lord said (Mat. 23:15): "Woe to you . . . because you go round about the sea and the land to make one proselyte, and when he is made you make him the child of hell twofold more than yourselves." Now thus would seem to do those who induce persons to enter religion. Therefore this would seem blameworthy.

Objection 3: Further, no one should induce another to do what is to his prejudice. But those who are induced to enter religion, sometimes take harm therefrom, for sometimes they are under obligation to enter a stricter religion. Therefore it would not seem praiseworthy to induce others to enter religion.

On the contrary, It is written (Ex. 26:3, seqq. [*St. Thomas quotes the sense, not the words]): "Let one curtain draw the other." Therefore one man should draw another to God's service.

I answer that, Those who induce others to enter religion not only do not sin, but merit a great reward. For it is written (James 5:20): "He who causeth a sinner to be converted from the error of his way, shall save his soul from death, and shall cover a multitude of sins"; and (Dan. 12:3): "They that instruct many to justice shall be as stars for all eternity."

Nevertheless such inducement may be affected by a threefold inordinateness. First, if one person force another by violence to enter religion: and this is forbidden in the Decretals (XX, qu. iii, cap. Praesens). Secondly, if one person persuade another simoniacally to enter religion, by giving him presents: and this is forbidden in the Decretal (I, qu. ii, cap. Quam pio). But this does not apply to the case where one provides a poor person with necessaries by educating him in the world for the religious life; or when without any compact one gives a person little presents for the sake of good fellowship. Thirdly, if one person entices another by lies: for it is to be feared that the person thus enticed may turn back on finding himself deceived, and thus "the last state of that man" may become "worse than the first" (Lk. 11:26).

Reply to Objection 1: Those who are induced to enter religion have still a time of probation wherein they make a trial of the hardships of religion, so that they are not easily admitted to the religious life.

Reply to Objection 2: According to Hilary (Can. xxiv in Matth.) this saying of our Lord was a forecast of the wicked endeavors of the Jews, after the preaching of Christ, to draw Gentiles or even Christians to observe the Jewish ritual, thereby making them doubly children of hell, because, to wit, they were not forgiven the former sins which they committed while adherents of Judaism, and furthermore they incurred the guilt of Jewish perfidy; and thus interpreted these words have nothing to do with the case in point.

According to Jerome, however, in his commentary on this passage of Matthew, the reference is to the Jews even at the time when it was yet lawful to keep the legal observances, in so far as he whom they converted to Judaism "from paganism, was merely misled; but when he saw the wickedness of his teachers, he returned to his vomit, and becoming a pagan deserved greater punishment for his treachery." Hence it is manifest that it is not blameworthy to draw others to the service of God or to the religious life, but only when one gives a bad example to the person converted, whence he becomes worse.

Reply to Objection 3: The lesser is included in the greater. Wherefore a person who is bound by vow or oath to enter a lesser order, may be lawfully induced to enter a greater one. unless there be some special obstacle, such as ill-health, or the hope of making greater progress in the lesser order. On the other hand, one who is bound by vow or oath to enter a greater order, cannot be lawfully induced to enter a lesser order, except for some special and evident motive, and then with the superior's dispensation.

Whether it is praiseworthy to enter religion without taking counsel of many, and previously deliberating for a long time?

Objection 1: It would not seem praiseworthy to enter religion without taking counsel of many, and previously deliberating for a long time. For it is written (1 Jn. 4:1): "Believe not every spirit, but try the spirits if they be of God." Now sometimes a man's purpose of entering religion is not of God, since it often comes to naught through his leaving the religious life; for it is written (Acts 5:38,39): "If this counsel or this work be of God, you cannot overthrow it." Therefore it would seem that one ought to make a searching inquiry before entering religion.

Objection 2: Further, it is written (Prov. 25:9): "Treat thy cause with thy friend." Now a man's cause would seem to be especially one that concerns a change in his state of life. Therefore seemingly one ought not to enter religion without discussing the matter with one's friends.

Objection 3: Further, our Lord (Lk. 14:28) in making a comparison with a man who has a mind to build a tower, says that he doth "first sit down and reckon the charges that are necessary, whether he have wherewithal to finish it," lest he become an object of mockery, for that "this man began to build and was not able to finish." Now the wherewithal to build the tower, as Augustine says (Ep. ad Laetum ccxliii), is nothing less than that "each one should renounce all his possessions." Yet it happens sometimes that many cannot do this, nor keep other religious observances; and in signification of this it is stated (1 Kings 17:39) that David could not walk in Saul's armor, for he was not used to it. Therefore it would seem that one ought not to enter religion without long deliberation beforehand and taking counsel of many.

On the contrary, It is stated (Mat. 4:20) that upon our Lord's calling them, Peter and Andrew "immediately leaving their nets, followed Him." Here Chrysostom says (Hom. xiv in Matth.): "Such obedience as this does Christ require of us, that we delay not even for a moment."

I answer that, Long deliberation and the advice of many are required in great matters of doubt, as the Philosopher says (Ethic. iii, 3); while advice is unnecessary in matters that are certain and fixed. Now with regard to entering religion three points may be considered. First, the entrance itself into religion, considered by itself; and thus it is certain that entrance into religion is a greater good, and to doubt about this is to disparage Christ Who gave this counsel. Hence Augustine says (De Verb. Dom., Serm. c, 2): "The East," that is Christ, "calleth thee, and thou turnest to the West," namely mortal and fallible man. Secondly, the entrance into religion may be considered in relation to the strength of the person who intends to enter. And here again there is no room for doubt about the

223

entrance to religion, since those who enter religion trust not to be able to stay by their own power, but by the assistance of the divine power, according to Is. 40:31, "They that hope in the Lord shall renew their strength, they shall take wings as eagles, they shall run and not be weary, they shall walk and not faint." Yet if there be some special obstacle (such as bodily weakness, a burden of debts, or the like) in such cases a man must deliberate and take counsel with such as are likely to help and not hinder him. Hence it is written (Ecclus. 37:12): "Treat with a man without religion concerning holiness [*The Douay version supplies the negative: 'Treat not . . . nor with . . . '], with an unjust man concerning justice," meaning that one should not do so, wherefore the text goes on (Ecclus. 37:14,15), "Give no heed to these in any matter of counsel, but be continually with a holy man." In these matters, however, one should not take long deliberation. Wherefore Jerome says (Ep. and Paulin. liii): "Hasten, I pray thee, cut off rather than loosen the rope that holds the boat to the shore." Thirdly, we may consider the way of entering religion, and which order one ought to enter, and about such matters also one may take counsel of those who will not stand in one's way.

Reply to Objection 1: The saying: "Try the spirits, if they be of God," applies to matters admitting of doubt whether the spirits be of God; thus those who are already in religion may doubt whether he who offers himself to religion be led by the spirit of God, or be moved by hypocrisy. Wherefore they must try the postulant whether he be moved by the divine spirit. But for him who seeks to enter religion there can be no doubt but that the purpose of entering religion to which his heart has given birth is from the spirit of God, for it is His spirit "that leads" man "into the land of uprightness" (Ps. 142:10).

Nor does this prove that it is not of God that some turn back; since not all that is of God is incorruptible: else corruptible creatures would not be of God, as the Manicheans hold, nor could some who have grace from God lose it, which is also heretical. But God's "counsel" whereby He makes even things corruptible and changeable, is imperishable according to Is. 46:10, "My counsel shall stand and all My will shall be done." Hence the purpose of entering religion needs not to be tried whether it be of God, because "it requires no further demonstration," as a gloss says on 1 Thess. 5:21, "Prove all things."

Reply to Objection 2: Even as "the flesh lusteth against the spirit" (Gal. 5:17), so too carnal friends often thwart our spiritual progress, according to Mic. 7:6, "A man's enemies are they of his own household." Wherefore Cyril expounding Lk. 9:61, "Let me first take my leave of them that are at my house," says [*Cf. St. Thomas's Catena Aurea]: "By asking first to take his leave of them that were at his house, he shows he was somewhat of two minds. For to communicate with his neighbors, and consult those who are unwilling to relish righteousness, is an indication of weakness and turning back. Hence he hears our Lord say: 'No man putting his hand to the plough, and looking back, is fit for the kingdom of God,' because he looks back who seeks delay in order to go home and confer with his kinsfolk."

Reply to Objection 3: The building of the tower signifies the perfection of Christian life; and the renunciation of one's possessions is the wherewithal to build this tower. Now no one doubts or deliberates about wishing to have the wherewithal, or whether he is able to build the tower if he have the wherewithal, but what does come under deliberation is whether one has the wherewithal. Again it need not be a matter of deliberation whether one ought to renounce all that one has, or whether by so doing one may be able to attain to perfection; whereas it is a matter of deliberation whether that which one is doing amounts to the renunciation of all that he has, since unless he does renounce (which is to have the wherewithal) he cannot, as the text goes on to state, be Christ's disciple, and this is to build the tower.

The misgiving of those who hesitate as to whether they may be able to attain to perfection by entering religion is shown by many examples to be unreasonable. Hence Augustine says (Confess. viii, 11): "On that side whither I had set my face, and whither I trembled to go, there appeared to me the chaste dignity of continency . . . honestly alluring me to come and doubt not, and stretching forth to receive and embrace me, her holy hands full of multitudes of good examples. There were so many young men and maidens here, a multitude of youth and every age, grave widows and aged virgins . . . And she smiled at me with a persuasive mockery as though to say: Canst not thou what these youths and these maidens can? Or can they either in themselves, and not rather in the Lord their God? . . . Why standest thou in thyself, and so standest not? Cast thyself upon Him; fear not, He will not withdraw Himself that thou shouldst fall. Cast thyself fearlessly upon Him: He will receive and will heal thee."

The example quoted of David is not to the point, because "the arms of Saul," as a gloss on the passage observes, "are the sacraments of the Law, as being burdensome": whereas religion is the sweet yoke of Christ, for as Gregory says (Moral. iv, 33), "what burden does He lay on the shoulders of the mind, Who commands us to shun all troublesome desires, Who warns us to turn aside from the rough paths of this world?"

To those indeed who take this sweet yoke upon themselves He promises the refreshment of the divine fruition and the eternal rest of their souls.

To which may He Who made this promise bring us, Jesus Christ our Lord, "Who is over all things God blessed for ever. Amen."

THIRD PART (TP) OF THE SUMMA THEOLOGICA (QQ[1]-90)

PROLOGUE

Forasmuch as our Saviour the Lord Jesus Christ, in order to "save His people from their sins" (Mat. 1:21), as the angel announced, showed unto us in His own Person the way of truth, whereby we may attain to the bliss of eternal life by rising again, it is necessary, in order to complete the work of theology, that after considering the last end of human life, and the virtues and vices, there should follow the consideration of the Saviour of all, and of the benefits bestowed by Him on the human race.

Concerning this we must consider (1) the Saviour Himself; (2) the sacraments by which we attain to our salvation; (3) the end of immortal life to which we attain by the resurrection.

Concerning the first, a double consideration occurs: the first, about the mystery of the Incarnation itself, whereby God was made man for our salvation; the second, about such things as were done and suffered by our Saviour---i.e. God incarnate.

OF THE FITNESS OF THE INCARNATION (SIX ARTICLES)

Concerning the first, three things occur to be considered: first, the fitness of the Incarnation; secondly, the mode of union of the Word Incarnate; thirdly, what follows this union.

Under the first head there are six points of inquiry:

(1) Whether it is fitting for God to become incarnate?

(2) Whether it was necessary for the restoration of the human race?

(3) Whether if there had been no sin God would have become incarnate?

(4) Whether He became incarnate to take away original sin rather than actual?

(5) Whether it was fitting for God to become incarnate from the beginning of the world?

(6) Whether His Incarnation ought to have been deferred to the end of the world?

Whether it was fitting that God should become incarnate?

Objection 1: It would seem that it was not fitting for God to become incarnate. Since God from all eternity is the very essence of goodness, it was best for Him to be as He had been from all eternity. But from all eternity He had been without flesh. Therefore it was most fitting for Him not to be united to flesh. Therefore it was not fitting for God to become incarnate.

Objection 2: Further, it is not fitting to unite things that are infinitely apart, even as it would not be a fitting union if one were "to paint a figure in which the neck of a horse was joined to the head of a man" [*Horace, Ars. Poet., line 1]. But God and flesh are infinitely apart; since God is most simple, and flesh is most composite---especially human flesh. Therefore it was not fitting that God should be united to human flesh.

Objection 3: Further, a body is as distant from the highest spirit as evil is from the highest good. But it was wholly unfitting that God, Who is the highest good, should assume evil. Therefore it was not fitting that the highest uncreated spirit should assume a body.

Objection 4: Further, it is not becoming that He Who surpassed the greatest things should be contained in the least, and He upon Whom rests the care of great things should leave them for lesser things. But God---Who takes care of the whole world---the whole universe of things cannot contain. Therefore it would seem unfitting that "He should be hid under the frail body of a babe in swathing bands, in comparison with Whom the whole universe is accounted as little; and that this Prince should quit His throne for so long, and transfer the government of the whole world to so frail a body," as Volusianus writes to Augustine (Ep. cxxxv).

On the contrary, It would seem most fitting that by visible things the invisible things of God should be made known; for to this end was the whole world made, as is clear from the word of the Apostle (Rom. 1:20): "For the invisible things of God . . . are clearly seen, being understood by the things that are made." But, as Damascene says (De Fide Orth. iii, 1), by the mystery of the Incarnation are made known at once the goodness, the wisdom, the justice, and the power or might of God---"His goodness, for He did not despise the weakness of His own handiwork; His justice, since, on man's defeat, He caused the tyrant to be overcome by none other than man, and yet He did not snatch men forcibly from death; His wisdom, for He found a suitable discharge for a most heavy debt; His power, or infinite might, for there is nothing greater than for God to become incarnate . . ."

I answer that, To each things, that is befitting which belongs to it by reason of its very nature; thus, to reason befits man, since this belongs to him because he is of a rational nature. But the very nature of God is goodness, as is clear from Dionysius (Div. Nom. i). Hence, what belongs to the essence of goodness befits God. But it belongs to the essence of goodness to communicate itself to others, as is plain from Dionysius (Div. Nom. iv). Hence it belongs to the essence of the highest good to communicate itself in the highest manner to the creature, and this is brought about chiefly by "His so joining created nature to Himself that one Person is made up of these three---the Word, a soul and flesh," as Augustine says (De Trin. xiii). Hence it is manifest that it was fitting that God should become incarnate.

Reply to Objection 1: The mystery of the Incarnation was not completed through God being changed in any way from the state in which He had been from eternity, but through His having united Himself to the creature in a new way, or rather through having united it to Himself. But it is fitting that a creature which by nature is mutable, should not always be in one way. And therefore, as the creature began to be, although it had not been before, so likewise, not having been previously united to God in Person, it was afterwards united to Him.

Reply to Objection 2: To be united to God in unity of person was not fitting to human flesh, according to its natural endowments, since it was above its dignity; nevertheless, it was fitting that God, by reason of His infinite goodness, should unite it to Himself for man's salvation.

Reply to Objection 3: Every mode of being wherein any creature whatsoever differs from the Creator has been established by God's wisdom, and is ordained to God's goodness. For God, Who is uncreated, immutable, and incorporeal, produced mutable and corporeal creatures for His own goodness. And so also the evil of punishment was established by God's justice for God's glory. But evil of fault is committed by withdrawing from the art of the Divine wisdom and from the order of the Divine goodness. And therefore it could be fitting to God to assume a nature created, mutable, corporeal, and subject to penalty, but it did not become Him to assume the evil of fault.

Reply to Objection 4: As Augustine replies (Ep. ad Volusian. cxxxvii): "The Christian doctrine nowhere holds that God was so joined to human flesh as either to desert or lose, or to transfer and as it were, contract within this frail body, the care of governing the universe. This is the thought of men unable to see anything but corporeal things . . . God is great not in mass, but in might. Hence the greatness of His might feels no straits in narrow surroundings. Nor, if the passing word of a man is heard at once by many, and wholly by each, is it incredible that the abiding Word of God should be everywhere at once?" Hence nothing unfitting arises from God becoming incarnate.

Whether it was necessary for the restoration of the human race that the Word of God should become incarnate?

Objection 1: It would seem that it was not necessary for the reparation of the human race that the Word of God should become incarnate. For since the Word of God is perfect God, as has been said ([3850]FP, Q[4], AA[1],2), no power was added to Him by the assumption of flesh. Therefore, if the incarnate Word of God restored human nature. He could also have restored it without assuming flesh.

Objection 2: Further, for the restoration of human nature, which had fallen through sin, nothing more is required than that man should satisfy for sin. Now man can satisfy, as it would seem, for sin; for God cannot require from man more than man can do, and since He is more inclined to be merciful than to punish, as He lays the act of sin to man's charge, so He ought to credit him with the contrary act. Therefore it was not necessary for the restoration of human nature that the Word of God should become incarnate.

Objection 3: Further, to revere God pertains especially to man's salvation; hence it is written (Mal. 1:6): "If, then, I be a father, where is my honor? and if I be a master, where is my fear?" But men revere God the more by considering Him as elevated above all, and far beyond man's senses, hence (Ps. 112:4) it is written: "The Lord is high above all nations, and His glory above the heavens"; and farther on: "Who is as the Lord our God?" which pertains to reverence. Therefore it would seem unfitting to man's salvation that God should be made like unto us by assuming flesh.

On the contrary, What frees the human race from perdition is necessary for the salvation of man. But the mystery of the Incarnation is such; according to Jn. 3:16: "God so loved the world as to give His only-begotten Son, that whosoever believeth in Him may not perish, but may have life everlasting." Therefore it was necessary for man's salvation that God should become incarnate.

I answer that, A thing is said to be necessary for a certain end in two ways. First, when the end cannot be without it; as food is necessary for the preservation of human life. Secondly, when the end is attained better and more conveniently, as a horse is necessary for a journey. In the first way it was not necessary that God should become incarnate for the restoration of human nature. For God with His omnipotent power could have restored human nature in many other ways. But in the second way it was necessary that God should become incarnate for the restoration of human nature. Hence Augustine says (De Trin. xii, 10): "We shall also show that other ways were not wanting to God, to Whose power all things are equally subject; but that there was not a more fitting way of healing our misery."

Now this may be viewed with respect to our "furtherance in good." First, with regard to faith, which is made more certain by believing God Himself Who speaks; hence Augustine says (De Civ. Dei xi, 2): "In order that man might journey more trustfully toward the truth, the Truth itself, the Son of God, having assumed human nature, established and founded faith." Secondly, with regard to hope, which is thereby greatly strengthened; hence Augustine says (De Trin. xiii): "Nothing was so necessary for raising our hope as to show us how deeply God loved us. And what could afford us a stronger proof of this than that the Son of God should become a partner with us of human nature?" Thirdly, with regard to charity, which is greatly enkindled by this; hence Augustine says (De Catech. Rudib. iv): "What greater cause is there of the Lord's coming than to show God's love for us?" And he afterwards adds: "If we have been slow to love, at least let us hasten to love in return." Fourthly, with regard to well-doing, in which He set us an example; hence Augustine says in a sermon (xxii de Temp.): "Man who might be seen was not to be followed; but God was to be followed, Who could not be seen. And therefore God was made man, that He Who might be seen by man, and Whom man might follow, might be shown to man." Fifthly, with regard to the full participation of the Divinity, which is the true bliss of man and end of human life; and this is bestowed upon us by Christ's humanity; for Augustine says in a sermon (xiii de Temp.): "God was made man, that man might be made God."

So also was this useful for our "withdrawal from evil." First, because man is taught by it not to prefer the devil to himself, nor to honor him who is the author of sin; hence Augustine says (De Trin. xiii, 17): "Since human nature is so united to God as to become one person, let not these proud spirits dare to prefer themselves to man, because they have no bodies." Secondly, because we are thereby taught how great is man's dignity, lest we should sully it with sin; hence Augustine says (De Vera Relig. xvi): "God has proved to us how high a place human nature holds amongst creatures, inasmuch as He appeared to men as a true man." And Pope Leo says in a sermon on the Nativity (xxi): "Learn, O Christian, thy worth; and being made a partner of the Divine nature, refuse to return by evil deeds to your former worthlessness." Thirdly, because, "in order to do away with man's presumption, the grace of God is commended in Jesus Christ, though no merits of ours went before," as Augustine says (De Trin. xiii, 17). Fourthly, because "man's pride, which is the greatest stumbling-block to our clinging to God, can be convinced and cured by humility so great," as Augustine says in the same place. Fifthly, in order to free man from the thraldom of sin, which, as Augustine says (De Trin. xiii, 13), "ought to be done in such a way that the devil should be overcome by the justice of the man Jesus Christ," and this was done by Christ satisfying for us. Now a mere man could not have satisfied for the whole human race, and God was not bound to satisfy; hence it behooved Jesus Christ to be both God and man. Hence Pope Leo says in the same sermon: "Weakness is assumed by strength, lowliness by majesty, mortality by eternity, in order that one and the same Mediator of God and men might die in one and rise in the other---for this was our fitting remedy. Unless He was God, He would not have brought a remedy; and unless He was man, He would not have set an example."

And there are very many other advantages which accrued, above man's apprehension.

Reply to Objection 1: This reason has to do with the first kind of necessity, without which we cannot attain to the end.

Reply to Objection 2: Satisfaction may be said to be sufficient in two ways---first, perfectly, inasmuch as it is condign, being adequate to make good the fault committed, and in this way the satisfaction of a mere man cannot be sufficient for sin, both because the whole of human nature has been corrupted by sin, whereas the goodness of any person or persons could not be made up adequately for the harm done to the whole of the nature; and also because a sin committed against God has a kind of infinity from the infinity of the Divine majesty, because the greater the person we offend, the more grievous the offense. Hence for condign satisfaction it was necessary that the act of the one satisfying should have an infinite efficiency, as being of God and man. Secondly, man's satisfaction may be termed sufficient, imperfectly---i.e. in the acceptation of him who is content with it, even though it is not condign, and in this way the satisfaction of a mere man is sufficient. And forasmuch as every imperfect presupposes some perfect thing, by which it is sustained, hence it is that satisfaction of every mere man has its efficiency from the satisfaction of Christ.

Reply to Objection 3: By taking flesh, God did not lessen His majesty; and in consequence did not lessen the reason for reverencing Him, which is increased by the increase of knowledge of Him. But, on the contrary, inasmuch as He wished to draw nigh to us by taking flesh, He greatly drew us to know Him.

Whether, if man had not sinned, God would have become incarnate?

Objection 1: It would seem that if man had not sinned, God would still have become incarnate. For the cause remaining, the effect also remains. But as Augustine says (De Trin. xiii, 17): "Many other things are to be considered in the Incarnation of Christ besides absolution from sin"; and these were discussed above [3851](A[2]). Therefore if man had not sinned, God would have become incarnate.

Objection 2: Further, it belongs to the omnipotence of the Divine power to perfect His works, and to manifest Himself by some infinite effect. But no mere creature can be called an infinite effect, since it is finite of its very essence. Now, seemingly, in the work of the Incarnation alone is an infinite effect of the Divine power manifested in a special manner by which power things infinitely distant are united, inasmuch as it has been brought about that man is God. And in this work especially the universe would seem to be perfected, inasmuch as the last creature---viz. man---is united to the first principle---viz. God. Therefore, even if man had not sinned, God would have become incarnate.

Objection 3: Further, human nature has not been made more capable of grace by sin. But after sin it is capable of the grace of union, which is the greatest grace. Therefore, if man had not sinned, human nature would have been capable of this grace; nor would God have withheld from human nature any good it was capable of. Therefore, if man had not sinned, God would have become incarnate.

Objection 4: Further, God's predestination is eternal. But it is said of Christ (Rom. 1:4): "Who was predestined the Son of God in power." Therefore, even before sin, it was necessary that the Son of God should become incarnate, in order to fulfil God's predestination.

Objection 5: Further, the mystery of the Incarnation was revealed to the first man, as is plain from Gn. 2:23. "This now is bone of my bones," etc. which the Apostle says is "a great sacrament . . . in Christ and in the Church," as is plain from Eph. 5:32. But man could not be fore-conscious of his fall, for the same reason that the angels could not, as Augustine proves (Gen. ad lit. xi, 18). Therefore, even if man had not sinned, God would have become incarnate.

On the contrary, Augustine says (De Verb. Apost. viii, 2), expounding what is set down in Lk. 19:10, "For the Son of Man is come to seek and to save that which was lost"; "Therefore, if man had not sinned, the Son of Man would not have come." And on 1 Tim. 1:15, "Christ Jesus came into this world to save sinners," a gloss says, "There was no cause of Christ's coming into the world, except to save sinners. Take away diseases, take away wounds, and there is no need of medicine."

I answer that, There are different opinions about this question. For some say that even if man had not sinned, the Son of Man would have become incarnate. Others assert the contrary, and seemingly our assent ought rather to be given to this opinion.

For such things as spring from God's will, and beyond the creature's due, can be made known to us only through being revealed in the Sacred Scripture, in which the Divine Will is made known to us. Hence, since everywhere in the Sacred Scripture the sin of the first man is assigned as the reason of the Incarnation, it is more in accordance with this to say that the work of the Incarnation was ordained by God as a remedy for sin; so that, had sin not existed, the Incarnation would not have been. And yet the power of God is not limited to this; even had sin not existed, God could have become incarnate.

Reply to Objection 1: All the other causes which are assigned in the preceding article have to do with a remedy for sin. For if man had not sinned, he would have been endowed with the light of Divine wisdom, and would have been perfected by God with the righteousness of justice in order to know and carry out everything needful. But because man, on deserting God, had stooped to corporeal things, it was necessary that God should take flesh, and by corporeal things should afford him the remedy of salvation. Hence, on Jn. 1:14, "And the Word was made flesh," St. Augustine says (Tract. ii): "Flesh had blinded thee, flesh heals thee; for Christ came and overthrew the vices of the flesh."

Reply to Objection 2: The infinity of Divine power is shown in the mode of production of things from nothing. Again, it suffices for the perfection of the universe that the creature be ordained in a natural manner to God as to an end. But that a creature should be united to God in person exceeds the limits of the perfection of nature.

Reply to Objection 3: A double capability may be remarked in human nature: one, in respect of the order of natural power, and this is always fulfilled by God, Who apportions to each according to its natural capability; the other in respect to the order of the Divine power, which all creatures implicitly obey; and the capability we speak of pertains to this. But God does not fulfil all such capabilities, otherwise God could do only what He has done in creatures, and this is false, as stated above ([3852]FP, Q[105], A[6]). But there is no reason why human nature should not have been raised to something greater after sin. For God allows evils to happen in order to bring a greater good therefrom; hence it is written (Rom. 5:20): "Where sin abounded, grace did more abound." Hence, too, in the blessing of the Paschal candle, we say: "O happy fault, that merited such and so great a Redeemer!"

Reply to Objection 4: Predestination presupposes the foreknowledge of future things; and hence, as God predestines the salvation of anyone to be brought about by the prayers of others, so also He predestined the work of the Incarnation to be the remedy of human sin.

Reply to Objection 5: Nothing prevents an effect from being revealed to one to whom the cause is not revealed. Hence, the mystery of the Incarnation could be revealed to the first man without his being fore-conscious of his fall. For not everyone who knows the effect knows the cause.

Whether God became incarnate in order to take away actual sin, rather than to take away original sin?

Objection 1: It would seem that God became incarnate as a remedy for actual sins rather than for original sin. For the more grievous the sin, the more it runs counter to man's salvation, for which God became incarnate. But actual sin is more grievous than original sin; for the lightest punishment is due to original sin, as Augustine says (Contra Julian. v, 11). Therefore the Incarnation of Christ is chiefly directed to taking away actual sins.

Objection 2: Further, pain of sense is not due to original sin, but merely pain of loss, as has been shown ([3853]FS, Q[87], A[5]). But Christ came to suffer the pain of sense on the Cross in satisfaction for sins---and not the pain of loss, for He had no defect of either the beatific vision or fruition. Therefore He came in order to take away actual sin rather than original sin.

Objection 3: Further, as Chrysostom says (De Compunctione Cordis ii, 3): "This must be the mind of the faithful servant, to account the benefits of his Lord, which have been bestowed on all alike, as though they were bestowed on himself alone. For as if speaking of himself alone, Paul writes to the Galatians 2:20: 'Christ . . . loved me and delivered Himself for me.'" But our individual sins are actual sins; for original sin is the common sin. Therefore we ought to have this conviction, so as to believe that He has come chiefly for actual sins.

On the contrary, It is written (Jn. 1:29): "Behold the Lamb of God, behold Him Who taketh away the sins [Vulg.: 'sin'] of the world."

I answer that, It is certain that Christ came into this world not only to take away that sin which is handed on originally to posterity, but also in order to take away all sins subsequently added to it; not that all are taken away (and this is from men's fault, inasmuch as they do not adhere to Christ, according to Jn. 3:19: "The light is come into the world, and men loved darkness rather than the light"), but because He offered what was sufficient for blotting out all sins. Hence it is written (Rom. 5:15-16): "But not as the offense, so also the gift . . . For judgment indeed was by one unto condemnation, but grace is of many offenses unto justification."

Moreover, the more grievous the sin, the more particularly did Christ come to blot it out. But "greater" is said in two ways: in one way "intensively," as a more intense whiteness is said to be greater, and in this way actual sin is greater than original sin; for it has more of the nature of voluntary, as has been shown ([3854]FS, Q[81], A[1]). In another way a thing is said to be greater "extensively," as whiteness on a greater superficies is said to be greater; and in this way original sin, whereby the whole human race is infected, is greater than any actual sin, which is proper to one person. And in this respect Christ came principally to take away original sin, inasmuch as "the good of the race is a more Divine thing than the good of an individual," as is said Ethic. i, 2.

Reply to Objection 1: This reason looks to the intensive greatness of sin.

Reply to Objection 2: In the future award the pain of sense will not be meted out to original sin. Yet the penalties, such as hunger, thirst, death, and the like, which we suffer sensibly in this life flow from original sin. And hence Christ, in order to satisfy fully for original sin, wished to suffer sensible pain, that He might consume death and the like in Himself.

Reply to Objection 3: Chrysostom says (De Compunctione Cordis ii, 6): "The Apostle used these words, not as if wishing to diminish Christ's gifts, ample as they are, and spreading throughout the whole world, but that he might account himself alone the occasion of them. For what does it matter that they are given to others, if what are given to you are as complete and perfect as if none of them were given to another than yourself?" And hence, although a man ought to account Christ's gifts as given to himself, yet he ought not to consider them not to be given to others. And thus we do not exclude that He came to wipe away the sin of the whole nature rather than the sin of one person. But the sin of the nature is as perfectly healed in each one as if it were healed in him alone. Hence, on account of the union of charity, what is vouchsafed to all ought to be accounted his own by each one.

Whether it was fitting that God should become incarnate in the beginning of the human race?

Objection 1: It would seem that it was fitting that God should become incarnate in the beginning of the human race. For the work of the Incarnation sprang from the immensity of Divine charity, according to Eph. 2:4,5: "But God (Who is rich in mercy), for His exceeding charity wherewith He loved us . . . even when we were dead in sins, hath quickened us together in Christ." But charity does not tarry in bringing assistance to a friend who is suffering need, according to Prov. 3:28: "Say not to thy friend: Go, and come again, and tomorrow I will give to thee, when thou canst give at present." Therefore God ought not to have put off the work of the Incarnation, but ought thereby to have brought relief to the human race from the beginning.

Objection 2: Further, it is written (1 Tim. 1:15): "Christ Jesus came into this world to save sinners." But more would have been saved had God become incarnate at the beginning of the human race; for in the various centuries very many, through not knowing God, perished in their sin. Therefore it was fitting that God should become incarnate at the beginning of the human race.

Objection 3: Further, the work of grace is not less orderly than the work of nature. But nature takes its rise with the more perfect, as Boethius says (De Consol. iii). Therefore the work of Christ ought to have been perfect from the beginning. But in the work of the Incarnation we see the perfection of grace, according to Jn. 1:14: "The Word was made flesh"; and afterwards it is added: "Full of grace and truth." Therefore Christ ought to have become incarnate at the beginning of the human race.

On the contrary, It is written (Gal. 4:4): "But when the fulness of the time was come, God sent His Son, made of a woman, made under the law": upon which a gloss says that "the fulness of the time is when it was decreed by God the Father to send His Son." But God decreed everything by His wisdom. Therefore God became incarnate at the most fitting time; and it was not fitting that God should become incarnate at the beginning of the human race.

I answer that, Since the work of the Incarnation is principally ordained to the restoration of the human race by blotting out sin, it is manifest that it was not fitting for God to become incarnate at the beginning of the human race before sin. For medicine is given only to the sick. Hence our Lord Himself says (Mat. 9:12,13): "They that are in health need not a physician, but they that are ill . . . For I am not come to call the just, but sinners."

Nor was it fitting that God should become incarnate immediately after sin. First, on account of the manner of man's sin, which had come of pride; hence man was to be liberated in such a manner that he might be humbled, and see how he stood in need of a deliverer. Hence on the words in Gal. 3:19, "Being ordained by angels in the hand of a mediator," a gloss says: "With great wisdom was it so ordered that the Son of Man should not be sent immediately after man's fall. For first of all God left man under the natural law, with the freedom of his will, in order that he might know his natural strength; and when he failed in it, he received the law; whereupon, by the fault, not of the law, but of his nature, the disease gained strength; so that having recognized his infirmity he might cry out for a physician, and beseech the aid of grace."

Secondly, on account of the order of furtherance in good, whereby we proceed from imperfection to perfection. Hence the Apostle says (1 Cor. 15:46,47): "Yet that was not first which is spiritual, but that which is natural; afterwards that which is spiritual . . . The first man was of the earth, earthy; the second man from heaven, heavenly."

Thirdly, on account of the dignity of the incarnate Word, for on the words (Gal. 4:4), "But when the fulness of the time was come," a gloss says: "The greater the judge who was coming, the more numerous was the band of heralds who ought to have preceded him."

Fourthly, lest the fervor of faith should cool by the length of time, for the charity of many will grow cold at the end of the world. Hence (Lk. 18:8) it is written: "But yet the Son of Man, when He cometh, shall He find think you, faith on earth?"

Reply to Objection 1: Charity does not put off bringing assistance to a friend: always bearing in mind the circumstances as well as the state of the persons. For if the physician were to give the medicine at the very outset of the ailment, it would do less good, and would hurt rather than benefit. And hence the Lord did not bestow upon the human race the remedy of the Incarnation in the beginning, lest they should despise it through pride, if they did not already recognize their disease.

Reply to Objection 2: Augustine replies to this (De Sex Quest. Pagan., Ep. cii), saying ([3855]Q[2]) that "Christ wished to appear to man and to have His doctrine preached to them when and where He knew those were who would believe in Him. But in such times and places as His Gospel was not preached He foresaw that not all, indeed, but many would so bear themselves towards His preaching as not to believe in His corporeal presence, even were He to raise the dead." But the same Augustine, taking exception to this reply in his book (De Perseverantia ix), says: "How can we say the inhabitants of Tyre and Sidon would not believe when such great wonders were wrought in their midst, or would not have believed had they been wrought, when God Himself bears witness that they would have done penance with great humility if these signs of Divine power had been wrought in their midst?" And he adds in answer (De Perseverantia xi): "Hence, as the Apostle says (Rom. 9:16), 'it is not of him that willeth nor of him that runneth, but of God that showeth mercy'; Who (succors whom He will of) those who, as He foresaw, would believe in His miracles if wrought amongst them, (while others) He succors not, having judged them in His predestination secretly yet justly. Therefore let us unshrinkingly believe His mercy to be with those who are set free, and His truth with those who are condemned." [*The words in brackets are not in the text of St. Augustine].

Reply to Objection 3: Perfection is prior to imperfection, both in time and nature, in things that are different (for what brings others to perfection must itself be perfect); but in one and the same, imperfection is prior in time though posterior in nature. And thus the eternal perfection of God precedes in duration the imperfection of human nature; but the latter's ultimate perfection in union with God follows.

Whether the Incarnation ought to have been put off till the end of the world?

Objection 1: It would seem that the work of the Incarnation ought to have been put off till the end of the world. For it is written (Ps. 91:11): "My old age in plentiful mercy"---i.e. "in the last days," as a gloss says. But the time of the Incarnation is especially the time of mercy, according to Ps. 101:14: "For it is time to have mercy on it." Therefore the Incarnation ought to have been put off till the end of the world.

Objection 2: Further, as has been said (A[5], ad 3), in the same subject, perfection is subsequent in time to imperfection. Therefore, what is most perfect ought to be the very last in time. But the highest perfection of human nature is in the union with the Word, because "in Christ it hath pleased the Father that all the fulness of the Godhead should dwell," as the Apostle says (Col. 1:19, and 2:9). Therefore the Incarnation ought to have been put off till the end of the world.

Objection 3: Further, what can be done by one ought not to be done by two. But the one coming of Christ at the end of the world was sufficient for the salvation of human nature. Therefore it was not necessary for Him to come beforehand in His Incarnation; and hence the Incarnation ought to have been put off till the end of the world.

On the contrary, It is written (Hab. 3:2): "In the midst of the years Thou shalt make it known." Therefore the mystery of the Incarnation which was made known to the world ought not to have been put off till the end of the world.

I answer that, As it was not fitting that God should become incarnate at the beginning of the world, so also it was not fitting that the Incarnation should be put off till the end of the world. And this is shown first from the union of the Divine and human nature. For, as it has been said (A[5], ad 3), perfection precedes imperfection in time in one way, and contrariwise in another way imperfection precedes perfection. For in that which is made perfect from being imperfect, imperfection precedes perfection in time, whereas in that which is the efficient cause of perfection, perfection precedes imperfection in time. Now in the work of the Incarnation both concur; for by the Incarnation human nature is raised to its highest perfection; and in this way it was not becoming that the Incarnation should take place at the beginning of the human race. And the Word incarnate is the efficient cause of the perfection of human nature, according to Jn. 1:16: "Of His fulness we have all received"; and hence the work of the Incarnation ought not to have been put off till the end of the world. But the perfection of glory to which human nature is to be finally raised by the Word Incarnate will be at the end of the world.

Secondly, from the effect of man's salvation; for, as is said Qq. Vet et Nov. Test., qu. 83, "it is in the power of the Giver to have pity when, or as much as, He wills. Hence He came when He knew it was fitting to succor, and when His boons would be welcome. For when by the feebleness of the human race men's knowledge of God began to grow dim and their morals lax, He was pleased to choose Abraham as a standard of the restored knowledge of God and of holy living; and later on when reverence grew weaker, He gave the law to Moses in writing; and because the gentiles despised it and would not take it upon themselves, and they who received it would not keep it, being touched with pity, God sent His Son, to grant to all remission of their sin and to offer them, justified, to God the Father." But if this remedy had been put off till the end of the world, all knowledge and reverence of God and all uprightness of morals would have been swept away from the earth.

Thirdly, this appears fitting to the manifestation of the Divine power, which has saved men in several ways---not only by faith in some future thing, but also by faith in something present and past.

Reply to Objection 1: This gloss has in view the mercy of God, which leads us to glory. Nevertheless, if it is referred to the mercy shown the human race by the Incarnation of Christ, we must reflect that, as Augustine says (Retract. i), the time of the Incarnation may be compared to the youth of the human race, "on account of the strength and fervor of faith, which works by charity"; and to old age--- i.e. the sixth age---on account of the number of centuries, for Christ came in the sixth age. And although youth and old age cannot be together in a body, yet they can be together in a soul, the former on account of quickness, the latter on account of gravity. And hence Augustine says elsewhere (Qq. lxxxiii, qu. 44) that "it was not becoming that the Master by Whose imitation the human race was to be formed to the highest virtue should come from heaven, save in the time of youth." But in another work (De Gen. cont. Manich. i, 23) he says: that Christ came in the sixth age---i.e. in the old age---of the human race.

Reply to Objection 2: The work of the Incarnation is to be viewed not as merely the terminus of a movement from imperfection to perfection, but also as a principle of perfection to human nature, as has been said.

Reply to Objection 3: As Chrysostom says on Jn. 3:11, "For God sent not His Son into the world to judge the world" (Hom. xxviii): "There are two comings of Christ: the first, for the remission of sins; the second, to judge the world. For if He had not done so, all would have perished together, since all have sinned and need the glory of God." Hence it is plain that He ought not to have put off the coming in mercy till the end of the world.

OF THE MODE OF UNION OF THE WORD INCARNATE (TWELVE ARTICLES)

Now we must consider the mode of union of the Incarnate Word; and, first, the union itself; secondly, the Person assuming; thirdly, the nature assumed.

Under the first head there are twelve points of inquiry:

(1) Whether the union of the Word Incarnate took place in the nature?
(2) Whether it took place in the Person?
(3) Whether it took place in the suppositum or hypostasis?
(4) Whether the Person or hypostasis of Christ is composite after the Incarnation?
(5) Whether any union of body and soul took place in Christ?
(6) Whether the human nature was united to the Word accidentally?
(7) Whether the union itself is something created?
(8) Whether it is the same as assumption?
(9) Whether the union of the two natures is the greatest union?
(10) Whether the union of the two natures in Christ was brought about by grace?
(11) Whether any merits preceded it?
(12) Whether the grace of union was natural to the man Christ?

Whether the Union of the Incarnate Word took place in the nature?

Objection 1: It would seem that the Union of the Word Incarnate took place in the nature. For Cyril says (he is quoted in the acts of the Council of Chalcedon, part ii, act. 1): "We must understand not two natures, but one incarnate nature of the Word of God"; and this could not be unless the union took place in the nature. Therefore the union of the Word Incarnate took place in the nature.

Objection 2: Further, Athanasius says that, as the rational soul and the flesh together form the human nature, so God and man together form a certain one nature; therefore the union took place in the nature.

Objection 3: Further, of two natures one is not denominated by the other unless they are to some extent mutually transmuted. But the Divine and human natures in Christ are denominated one by the other; for Cyril says (quoted in the acts of the Council of Chalcedon, part ii, act. 1) that the Divine nature "is incarnate"; and Gregory Nazianzen says (Ep. i ad Cledon.) that the human nature is "deified," as appears from Damascene (De Fide Orth. iii, 6,11). Therefore from two natures one seems to have resulted.

On the contrary, It is said in the declaration of the Council of Chalcedon: "We confess that in these latter times the only-begotten Son of God appeared in two natures, without confusion, without change, without division, without separation---the distinction of natures not having been taken away by the union." Therefore the union did not take place in the nature.

I answer that, To make this question clear we must consider what is "nature." Now it is to be observed that the word "nature" comes from nativity. Hence this word was used first of all to signify the begetting of living beings, which is called "birth" or "sprouting forth," the word "natura" meaning, as it were, "nascitura." Afterwards this word "nature" was taken to signify the principle of this begetting; and because in living things the principle of generation is an intrinsic principle, this word "nature" was further employed to signify any intrinsic principle of motion: thus the Philosopher says (Phys. ii) that "nature is the principle of motion in that in which it is essentially and not accidentally." Now this principle is either form or matter. Hence sometimes form is called nature, and sometimes matter. And because the end of natural generation, in that which is generated, is the essence of the species, which the definition signifies, this essence of the species is called the "nature." And thus Boethius defines nature (De Duab. Nat.): "Nature is what informs a thing with its specific difference,"---i.e. which perfects the specific definition. But we are now speaking of nature as it signifies the essence, or the "what-it-is," or the quiddity of the species.

Now, if we take nature in this way, it is impossible that the union of the Incarnate Word took place in the nature. For one thing is made of two or more in three ways. First, from two complete things which remain in their perfection. This can only happen to those whose form is composition, order, or figure, as a heap is made up of many stones brought together without any order, but solely with juxtaposition; and a house is made of stones and beams arranged in order, and fashioned to a figure. And in this way some said the union was by manner of confusion (which is without order) or by manner of commensuration (which is with order). But this cannot be. First, because neither composition nor order nor figure is a substantial form, but accidental; and hence it would follow that the union of the Incarnation was not essential, but accidental, which will be disproved later on [3856](A[6]). Secondly, because thereby we should not have an absolute unity, but relative only, for there remain several things actually. Thirdly, because the form of such is not a nature, but an art, as the form of a house; and thus one nature would not be constituted in Christ, as they wish.

Secondly, one thing is made up of several things, perfect but changed, as a mixture is made up of its elements; and in this way some have said that the union of the Incarnation was brought about by manner of combination. But this cannot be. First, because the Divine Nature is altogether immutable, as has been said ([3857]FP, Q[9], AA[1],2), hence neither can it be changed into something else, since it is incorruptible; nor can anything else be changed into it, for it cannot be generated. Secondly, because what is mixed is of the same species with none of the elements; for flesh differs in species from any of its elements. And thus Christ would be of the same nature neither with His Father nor with His Mother. Thirdly, because there can be no mingling of things widely apart; for the species of one of them is absorbed, e.g. if we were to put a drop of water in a flagon of wine. And hence, since the Divine Nature infinitely exceeds the human nature, there could be no mixture, but the Divine Nature alone would remain.

Thirdly, a thing is made up of things not mixed nor changed, but imperfect; as man is made up of soul and body, and likewise of divers members. But this cannot be said of the mystery of the Incarnation. First, because each nature, i.e. the Divine and the human, has its specific perfection. Secondly, because the Divine and human natures cannot constitute anything after the manner of quantitative parts, as the members make up the body; for the Divine Nature is incorporeal; nor after the manner of form and matter, for the Divine Nature cannot be the form of anything, especially of anything corporeal, since it would follow that the species resulting therefrom would be communicable to several, and thus there would be several Christs. Thirdly, because Christ would exist neither in human nature nor in the Divine Nature: since any difference varies the species, as unity varies number, as is said (Metaph. viii, text. 10).

Reply to Objection 1: This authority of Cyril is expounded in the Fifth Synod (i.e. Constantinople II, coll. viii, can. 8) thus: "If anyone proclaiming one nature of the Word of God to be incarnate does not receive it as the Fathers taught, viz. that from the Divine and human natures (a union in subsistence having taken place) one Christ results, but endeavors from these words to introduce one nature or substance of the Divinity and flesh of Christ, let such a one be anathema." Hence the sense is not that from two natures one results; but that the Nature of the Word of God united flesh to Itself in Person.

Reply to Objection 2: From the soul and body a double unity, viz. of nature and person---results in each individual---of nature inasmuch as the soul is united to the body, and formally perfects it, so that one nature springs from the two as from act and potentiality or from matter and form. But the comparison is not in this sense, for the Divine Nature cannot be the form of a body, as was proved ([3858]FP, Q[3], A[8]). Unity of person results from them, however, inasmuch as there is an individual subsisting in flesh and soul; and herein lies the likeness, for the one Christ subsists in the Divine and human natures.

Reply to Objection 3: As Damascene says (De Fide Orth. iii, 6,11), the Divine Nature is said to be incarnate because It is united to flesh personally, and not that It is changed into flesh. So likewise the flesh is said to be deified, as he also says (De Fide Orth. 15,17), not by change, but by union with the Word, its natural properties still remaining, and hence it may be considered as deified, inasmuch as it becomes the flesh of the Word of God, but not that it becomes God.

Whether the union of the Incarnate Word took place in the Person?

Objection 1: It would seem that the union of the Incarnate Word did not take place in the person. For the Person of God is not distinct from His Nature, as we said ([3859]FP, Q[39], A[1]). If, therefore, the union did not take place in the nature, it follows that it did not take place in the person.

Objection 2: Further, Christ's human nature has no less dignity than ours. But personality belongs to dignity, as was stated above ([3860]FP, Q[29], A[3], ad 2). Hence, since our human nature has its proper personality, much more reason was there that Christ's should have its proper personality.

Objection 3: Further, as Boethius says (De Duab. Nat.), a person is an individual substance of rational nature. But the Word of God assumed an individual human nature, for "universal human nature does not exist of itself, but is the object of pure thought," as Damascene says (De Fide Orth. iii, 11). Therefore the human nature of Christ has its personality. Hence it does not seem that the union took place in the person.

On the contrary, We read in the Synod of Chalcedon (Part ii, act. 5): "We confess that our Lord Jesus Christ is not parted or divided into two persons, but is one and the same only-Begotten Son and Word of God." Therefore the union took place in the person.

I answer that, Person has a different meaning from "nature." For nature, as has been said [3861](A[1]), designates the specific essence which is signified by the definition. And if nothing was found to be added to what belongs to the notion of the species, there would be no need to distinguish the nature from the suppositum of the nature (which is the individual subsisting in this nature), because every individual subsisting in a nature would be altogether one with its nature. Now in certain subsisting things we happen to find what does not belong to the notion of the species, viz. accidents and individuating principles, which appears chiefly in such as are composed of matter and form. Hence in such as these the nature and the suppositum really differ; not indeed as if they were wholly separate, but because the suppositum includes the nature, and in addition certain other things outside the notion of the species. Hence the suppositum is taken to be a whole which has the nature as its formal part to perfect it; and consequently in such as are composed of matter and form the nature is not predicated of the suppositum, for we do not say that this man is his manhood. But if there is a thing in which there is nothing outside the species or its nature (as in God), the suppositum and the nature are not really distinct in it, but only in our way of thinking, inasmuch it is called "nature" as it is an essence, and a "suppositum" as it is subsisting. And what is said of a suppositum is to be applied to a person in rational or intellectual creatures; for a person is nothing else than "an individual substance of rational nature," according to Boethius. Therefore, whatever adheres to a person is united to it in person, whether it belongs to its nature or not. Hence, if the human nature is not united to God the Word in person, it is nowise united to Him; and thus belief in the Incarnation is altogether done away with, and Christian faith wholly overturned. Therefore, inasmuch as the Word has a human nature united to Him, which does not belong to His Divine Nature, it follows that the union took place in the Person of the Word, and not in the nature.

Reply to Objection 1: Although in God Nature and Person are not really distinct, yet they have distinct meanings, as was said above, inasmuch as person signifies after the manner of something subsisting. And because human nature is united to the Word, so that the Word subsists in it, and not so that His Nature receives therefrom any addition or change, it follows that the union of human nature to the Word of God took place in the person, and not in the nature.

Reply to Objection 2: Personality pertains of necessity to the dignity of a thing, and to its perfection so far as it pertains to the dignity and perfection of that thing to exist by itself (which is understood by the word "person"). Now it is a greater dignity to exist in something nobler than oneself than to exist by oneself. Hence the human nature of Christ has a greater dignity than ours, from this very fact that in us, being existent by itself, it has its own personality, but in Christ it exists in the Person of the Word. Thus to perfect the species belongs to the dignity of a form, yet the sensitive part in man, on account of its union with the nobler form which perfects the species, is more noble than in brutes, where it is itself the form which perfects.

Reply to Objection 3: The Word of God "did not assume human nature in general, but 'in atomo'"---that is, in an individual---as Damascene says (De Fide Orth. iii, 11) otherwise every man would be the Word of God, even as Christ was. Yet we must bear in mind that not every individual in the genus of substance, even in rational nature, is a person, but that alone which exists by itself, and not that which exists in some more perfect thing. Hence the hand of Socrates, although it is a kind of individual, is not a person, because it does not exist by itself, but in something more perfect, viz. in the whole. And hence, too, this is signified by a "person" being defined as "an individual substance," for the hand is not a complete substance, but part of a substance. Therefore, although this human nature is a kind of individual in the genus of substance, it has not its own personality, because it does not exist separately, but in something more perfect, viz. in the Person of the Word. Therefore the union took place in the person.

Day 250

Whether the union of the Word Incarnate took place in the suppositum or hypostasis?

Objection 1: It would seem that the union of the Word Incarnate did not take place in the suppositum or hypostasis. For Augustine says (Enchiridion xxxv, xxxviii): "Both the Divine and human substance are one Son of God, but they are one thing [aliud] by reason of the Word and another thing [aliud] by reason of the man." And Pope Leo says in his letter to Flavian (Ep. xxviii): "One of these is glorious with miracles, the other succumbs under injuries." But "one" [aliud] and "the other" [aliud] differ in suppositum. Therefore the union of the Word Incarnate did not take place in the suppositum.

Objection 2: Further, hypostasis is nothing more than a "particular substance," as Boethius says (De Duab. Nat.). But it is plain that in Christ there is another particular substance beyond the hypostasis of the Word, viz. the body and the soul and the resultant of these. Therefore there is another hypostasis in Him besides the hypostasis of the Word.

Objection 3: Further, the hypostasis of the Word is not included in any genus or species, as is plain from [3862]FP, Q[3], A[5]. But Christ, inasmuch as He is made man, is contained under the species of man; for Dionysius says (Div. Nom. 1): "Within the limits of our nature He came, Who far surpasses the whole order of nature supersubstantially." Now nothing is contained under the human species unless it be a hypostasis of the human species. Therefore in Christ there is another hypostasis besides the hypostasis of the Word of God; and hence the same conclusion follows as above.

On the contrary, Damascene says (De Fide Orth. iii, 3,4,5): "In our Lord Jesus Christ we acknowledge two natures and one hypostasis."

I answer that, Some who did not know the relation of hypostasis to person, although granting that there is but one person in Christ, held, nevertheless, that there is one hypostasis of God and another of man, and hence that the union took place in the person and not in the hypostasis. Now this, for three reasons, is clearly erroneous. First, because person only adds to hypostasis a determinate nature, viz. rational, according to what Boethius says (De Duab. Nat.), "a person is an individual substance of rational nature"; and hence it is the same to attribute to the human nature in Christ a proper hypostasis and a proper person. And the holy Fathers, seeing this, condemned both in the Fifth Council held at Constantinople, saying: "If anyone seeks to introduce into the mystery of the Incarnation two subsistences or two persons, let him be anathema. For by the incarnation of one of the Holy Trinity, God the Word, the Holy Trinity received no augment of person or subsistence." Now "subsistence" is the same as the subsisting thing, which is proper to hypostasis, as is plain from Boethius (De Duab. Nat.). Secondly, because if it is granted that person adds to hypostasis something in which the union can take place, this something is nothing else than a property pertaining to dignity; according as it is said by some that a person is a "hypostasis distinguished by a property pertaining to dignity." If, therefore, the union took place in the person and not in the hypostasis, it follows that the union only took place in regard to some dignity. And this is what Cyril, with the approval of the Council of Ephesus (part iii, can. 3), condemned in these terms: "If anyone after the uniting divides the subsistences in the one Christ, only joining them in a union of dignity or authority or power, and not rather in a concourse of natural union, let him be anathema."

Thirdly, because to the hypostasis alone are attributed the operations and the natural properties, and whatever belongs to the nature in the concrete; for we say that this man reasons, and is risible, and is a rational animal. So likewise this man is said to be a suppositum, because he underlies [supponitur] whatever belongs to man and receives its predication. Therefore, if there is any hypostasis in Christ besides the hypostasis of the Word, it follows that whatever pertains to man is verified of some other than the Word, e.g. that He was born of a Virgin, suffered, was crucified, was buried. And this, too, was condemned with the approval of the Council of Ephesus (part iii, can. 4) in these words: "If anyone ascribes to two persons or subsistences such words as are in the evangelical and apostolic Scriptures, or have been said of Christ by the saints, or by Himself of Himself, and, moreover, applies some of them to the man, taken as distinct from the Word of God, and some of them (as if they could be used of God alone) only to the Word of God the Father, let him be anathema." Therefore it is plainly a heresy condemned long since by the Church to say that in Christ there are two hypostases, or two supposita, or that the union did not take place in the hypostasis or suppositum. Hence in the same Synod (can. 2) it is said: "If anyone does not confess that the Word was united to flesh in subsistence, and that Christ with His flesh is both---to wit, God and man---let him be anathema."

Reply to Objection 1: As accidental difference makes a thing "other" [alterum], so essential difference makes "another thing" [aliud]. Now it is plain that the "otherness" which springs from accidental difference may pertain to the same hypostasis or suppositum in created things, since the same thing numerically can underlie different accidents. But it does not happen in created things that the same numerically can subsist in divers essences or natures. Hence just as when we speak of "otherness" in regard to creatures we do not signify diversity of suppositum, but only diversity of accidental forms, so likewise when Christ is said to be one thing or another thing, we do not imply diversity of suppositum or hypostasis, but diversity of nature. Hence Gregory Nazianzen says in a letter to Chelidonius (Ep. ci): "In the Saviour we may find one thing and another, yet He is not one person and another. And I say 'one thing and another'; whereas, on the contrary, in the Trinity we say one Person and another (so as not to confuse the subsistences), but not one thing and another."

Reply to Objection 2: Hypostasis signifies a particular substance, not in every way, but as it is in its complement. Yet as it is in union with something more complete, it is not said to be a hypostasis, as a hand or a foot. So likewise the human nature in Christ, although it is a particular substance, nevertheless cannot be called a hypostasis or suppositum, seeing that it is in union with a completed thing, viz. the whole Christ, as He is God and man. But the complete being with which it concurs is said to be a hypostasis or suppositum.

Reply to Objection 3: In created things a singular thing is placed in a genus or species, not on account of what belongs to its individuation, but on account of its nature, which springs from its form, and in composite things individuation is taken more from matter. Hence we say that Christ is in the human species by reason of the nature assumed, and not by reason of the hypostasis.

Whether after the Incarnation the Person or Hypostasis of Christ is composite?

Objection 1: It would seem that the Person of Christ is not composite. For the Person of Christ is naught else than the Person or hypostasis of the Word, as appears from what has been said [3863](A[2]). But in the Word, Person and Nature do not differ, as appears from [3864]FP, Q[39], A[1]. Therefore since the Nature of the Word is simple, as was shown above ([3865]FP, Q[3], A[7]), it is impossible that the Person of Christ be composite.

Objection 2: Further, all composition requires parts. But the Divine Nature is incompatible with the notion of a part, for every part implicates the notion of imperfection. Therefore it is impossible that the Person of Christ be composed of two natures.

Objection 3: Further, what is composed of others would seem to be homogeneous with them, as from bodies only a body can be composed. Therefore if there is anything in Christ composed of the two natures, it follows that this will not be a person but a nature; and hence the union in Christ will take place in the nature, which is contrary to A[2].

On the contrary, Damascene says (De Fide Orth. iii, 3,4,5), "In the Lord Jesus Christ we acknowledge two natures, but one hypostasis composed from both."

I answer that, The Person or hypostasis of Christ may be viewed in two ways. First as it is in itself, and thus it is altogether simple, even as the Nature of the Word. Secondly, in the aspect of person or hypostasis to which it belongs to subsist in a nature; and thus the Person of Christ subsists in two natures. Hence though there is one subsisting being in Him, yet there are different aspects of subsistence, and hence He is said to be a composite person, insomuch as one being subsists in two.

And thereby the solution to the first is clear.

Reply to Objection 2: This composition of a person from natures is not so called on account of parts, but by reason of number, even as that in which two things concur may be said to be composed of them.

Reply to Objection 3: It is not verified in every composition, that the thing composed is homogeneous with its component parts, but only in the parts of a continuous thing; for the continuous is composed solely of continuous [parts]. But an animal is composed of soul and body, and neither of these is an animal.

Whether in Christ there is any union of soul and body?

Objection 1: It would seem that in Christ there was no union of soul and body. For from the union of soul and body in us a person or a human hypostasis is caused. Hence if the soul and body were united in Christ, it follows that a hypostasis resulted from their union. But this was not the hypostasis of God the Word, for It is eternal. Therefore in Christ there would be a person or hypostasis besides the hypostasis of the Word, which is contrary to [3866]AA[2],3.

Objection 2: Further, from the union of soul and body results the nature of the human species. But Damascene says (De Fide Orth. iii, 3), that "we must not conceive a common species in the Lord Jesus Christ." Therefore there was no union of soul and body in Him.

Objection 3: Further, the soul is united to the body for the sole purpose of quickening it. But the body of Christ could be quickened by the Word of God Himself, seeing He is the fount and principle of life. Therefore in Christ there was no union of soul and body.

On the contrary, The body is not said to be animated save from its union with the soul. Now the body of Christ is said to be animated, as the Church chants: "Taking an animate body, He deigned to be born of a Virgin" [*Feast of the Circumcision, Ant. ii, Lauds]. Therefore in Christ there was a union of soul and body.

I answer that, Christ is called a man univocally with other men, as being of the same species, according to the Apostle (Phil. 2:7), "being made in the likeness of a man." Now it belongs essentially to the human species that the soul be united to the body, for the form does not constitute the species, except inasmuch as it becomes the act of matter, and this is the terminus of generation through which nature intends the species. Hence it must be said that in Christ the soul was united to the body; and the contrary is heretical, since it destroys the truth of Christ's humanity.

Reply to Objection 1: This would seem to be the reason which was of weight with such as denied the union of the soul and body in Christ, viz. lest they should thereby be forced to admit a second person or hypostasis in Christ, since they saw that the union of soul and body in mere men resulted in a person. But this happens in mere men because the soul and body are so united in them as to exist by themselves. But in Christ they are united together, so as to be united to something higher, which subsists in the nature composed of them. And hence from the union of the soul and body in Christ a new hypostasis or person does not result, but what is composed of them is united to the already existing hypostasis or Person. Nor does it therefore follow that the union of the soul and body in Christ is of less effect than in us, for its union with something nobler does not lessen but increases its virtue and worth; just as the sensitive soul in animals constitutes the species, as being considered the ultimate form, yet it does not do so in man, although it is of greater effect and dignity, and this because of its union with a further and nobler perfection, viz. the rational soul, as has been said above (A[2], ad 2).

Reply to Objection 2: This saying of Damascene may be taken in two ways: First, as referring to human nature, which, as it is in one individual alone, has not the nature of a common species, but only inasmuch as either it is abstracted from every individual, and considered in itself by the mind, or according as it is in all individuals. Now the Son of God did not assume human nature as it exists in the pure thought of the intellect, since in this way He would not have assumed human nature in reality, unless it be said that human nature is a separate idea, just as the Platonists conceived of man without matter. But in this way the Son of God would not have assumed flesh, contrary to what is written (Lk. 24:39), "A spirit hath not flesh and bones as you see Me to have." Neither can it be said that the Son of God assumed human nature as it is in all the individuals of the same species, otherwise He would have assumed all men. Therefore it remains, as Damascene says further on (De Fide Orth. iii, 11) that He assumed human nature "in atomo," i.e. in an individual; not, indeed, in another individual which is a suppositum or a person of that nature, but in the Person of the Son of God.

Secondly, this saying of Damascene may be taken not as referring to human nature, as if from the union of soul and body one common nature (viz. human) did not result, but as referring to the union of the two natures Divine and human: which do not combine so as to form a third something that becomes a common nature, for in this way it would become predicable of many, and this is what he is aiming at, since he adds: "For there was not generated, neither will there ever be generated, another Christ, Who from the Godhead and manhood, and in the Godhead and manhood, is perfect God and perfect man."

Reply to Objection 3: There are two principles of corporeal life: one the effective principle, and in this way the Word of God is the principle of all life; the other, the formal principle of life, for since "in living things to be is to live," as the Philosopher says (De Anima ii, 37), just as everything is formally by its form, so likewise the body lives by the soul: in this way a body could not live by the Word, Which cannot be the form of a body.

Whether the human nature was united to the Word of God accidentally?

Objection 1: It would seem that the human nature was united to the Word of God accidentally. For the Apostle says (Phil. 2:7) of the Son of God, that He was "in habit found as a man." But habit is accidentally associated with that to which it pertains, whether habit be taken for one of the ten predicaments or as a species of quality. Therefore human nature is accidentally united to the Son of God.

Objection 2: Further, whatever comes to a thing that is complete in being comes to it accidentally, for an accident is said to be what can come or go without the subject being corrupted. But human nature came to Christ in time, Who had perfect being from eternity. Therefore it came to Him accidentally.

Objection 3: Further, whatever does not pertain to the nature or the essence of a thing is its accident, for whatever is, is either a substance or an accident. But human nature does not pertain to the Divine Essence or Nature of the Son of God, for the union did not take place in the nature, as was said above [3867](A[1]). Hence the human nature must have accrued accidentally to the Son of God.

Objection 4: Further, an instrument accrues accidentally. But the human nature was the instrument of the Godhead in Christ, for Damascene says (De Fide Orth. iii, 15), that "the flesh of Christ is the instrument of the Godhead." Therefore it seems that the human nature was united to the Son of God accidentally.

On the contrary, Whatever is predicated accidentally, predicates, not substance, but quantity, or quality, or some other mode of being. If therefore the human nature accrues accidentally, when we say Christ is man, we do not predicate substance, but quality or quantity, or some other mode of being, which is contrary to the Decretal of Pope Alexander III, who says (Conc. Later. iii): "Since Christ is perfect God and perfect man, what foolhardiness have some to dare to affirm that Christ as man is not a substance?"

I answer that, In evidence of this question we must know that two heresies have arisen with regard to the mystery of the union of the two natures in Christ. The first confused the natures, as Eutyches and Dioscorus, who held that from the two natures one nature resulted, so that they confessed Christ to be "from" two natures (which were distinct before the union), but not "in" two natures (the distinction of nature coming to an end after the union). The second was the heresy of Nestorius and Theodore of Mopsuestia, who separated the persons. For they held the Person of the Son of God to be distinct from the Person of the Son of man, and said these were mutually united: first, "by indwelling," inasmuch as the Word of God dwelt in the man, as in a temple; secondly, "by unity of intention," inasmuch as the will of the man was always in agreement with the will of the Word of God; thirdly, "by operation," inasmuch as they said the man was the instrument of the Word of God; fourthly, "by greatness of honor," inasmuch as all honor shown to the Son of God was equally shown to the Son of man, on account of His union with the Son of God; fifthly, "by equivocation," i.e. communication of names, inasmuch as we say that this man is God and the Son of God. Now it is plain that these modes imply an accidental union.

But some more recent masters, thinking to avoid these heresies, through ignorance fell into them. For some conceded one person in Christ, but maintained two hypostases, or two supposita, saying that a man, composed of body and soul, was from the beginning of his conception assumed by the Word of God. And this is the first opinion set down by the Master (Sent. iii, D, 6). But others desirous of keeping the unity of person, held that the soul of Christ was not united to the body, but that these two were mutually separate, and were united to the Word accidentally, so that the number of persons might not be increased. And this is the third opinion which the Master sets down (Sent. iii, D, 6).

But both of these opinions fall into the heresy of Nestorius; the first, indeed, because to maintain two hypostases or supposita in Christ is the same as to maintain two persons, as was shown above [3868](A[3]). And if stress is laid on the word "person," we must have in mind that even Nestorius spoke of unity of person on account of the unity of dignity and honor. Hence the fifth Council (Constantinople II, coll. viii, can. 5) directs an anathema against such a one as holds "one person in dignity, honor and adoration, as Theodore and Nestorius foolishly wrote." But the other opinion falls into the error of Nestorius by maintaining an accidental union. For there is no difference in saying that the Word of God is united to the Man Christ by indwelling, as in His temple (as Nestorius said), or by putting on man, as a garment, which is the third opinion; rather it says something worse than Nestorius---to wit, that the soul and body are not united.

Now the Catholic faith, holding the mean between the aforesaid positions, does not affirm that the union of God and man took place in the essence or nature, nor yet in something accidental, but midway, in a subsistence or hypostasis. Hence in the fifth Council (Constantinople II, coll. viii, can. 5) we read: "Since the unity may be understood in many ways, those who follow the impiety of Apollinaris and Eutyches, professing the destruction of what came together" (i.e. destroying both natures), "confess a union by mingling; but the followers of Theodore and Nestorius, maintaining division, introduce a union of purpose. But the Holy Church of God, rejecting the impiety of both these treasons, confesses a union of the Word of God with flesh, by composition, which is in subsistence." Therefore it is plain that the second of the three opinions, mentioned by the Master (Sent. iii, D, 6), which holds one hypostasis of God and man, is not to be called an opinion, but an article of Catholic faith. So likewise the first opinion which holds two hypostases, and the third which holds an accidental union, are not to be styled opinions, but heresies condemned by the Church in Councils.

Reply to Objection 1: As Damascene says (De Fide Orth. iii, 26): "Examples need not be wholly and at all points similar, for what is wholly similar is the same, and not an example, and especially in Divine things, for it is impossible to find a wholly similar example in the Theology," i.e. in the Godhead of Persons, "and in the Dispensation," i.e. the mystery of the Incarnation. Hence the human nature in Christ is likened to a habit, i.e. a garment, not indeed in regard to accidental union, but inasmuch as the Word is seen by the human nature, as a man by his garment, and also inasmuch as the garment is changed, for it is shaped according to the figure of him who puts it on, and yet he is not changed from his form on account of the garment. So likewise the human nature assumed by the Word of God is ennobled, but the Word of God is not changed, as Augustine says (Qq. 83, qu. 73).

Reply to Objection 2: Whatever accrues after the completion of the being comes accidentally, unless it be taken into communion with the complete being, just as in the resurrection the body comes to the soul which pre-exists, yet not accidentally, because it is assumed unto the same being, so that the body has vital being through the soul; but it is not so with whiteness, for the being of whiteness is other than the being of man to which whiteness comes. But the Word of God from all eternity had complete being in hypostasis or person; while in time the human nature accrued to it, not as if it were assumed unto one being inasmuch as this is of the nature (even as the body is assumed to the being of the soul), but to one being inasmuch as this is of the hypostasis or person. Hence the human nature is not accidentally united to the Son of God.

Reply to Objection 3: Accident is divided against substance. Now substance, as is plain from Metaph. v, 25, is taken in two ways: first, for essence or nature; secondly, for suppositum or hypostasis---hence the union having taken place in the hypostasis, is enough to show that it is not an accidental union, although the union did not take place in the nature.

Reply to Objection 4: Not everything that is assumed as an instrument pertains to the hypostasis of the one who assumes, as is plain in the case of a saw or a sword; yet nothing prevents what is assumed into the unity of the hypostasis from being as an instrument, even as the body of man or his members. Hence Nestorius held that the human nature was assumed by the Word merely as an instrument, and not into the unity of the hypostasis. And therefore he did not concede that the man was really the Son of God, but His instrument. Hence Cyril says (Epist. ad Monach. Aegyptii): "The Scripture does not affirm that this Emmanuel," i.e. Christ, "was assumed for the office of an instrument, but as God truly humanized," i.e. made man. But Damascene held that the human nature in Christ is an instrument belonging to the unity of the hypostasis.

Whether the union of the Divine nature and the human is anything created?

Objection 1: It would seem that the union of the Divine and human natures is not anything created. For there can be nothing created in God, because whatever is in God is God. But the union is in God, for God Himself is united to human nature. Therefore it seems that the union is not anything created.

Objection 2: Further, the end holds first place in everything. But the end of the union is the Divine hypostasis or Person in which the union is terminated. Therefore it seems that this union ought chiefly to be judged with reference to the dignity of the Divine hypostasis, which is not anything created. Therefore the union is nothing created.

Objection 3: Further, "That which is the cause of a thing being such is still more so" (Poster. i). But man is said to be the Creator on account of the union. Therefore much more is the union itself nothing created, but the Creator.

On the contrary, Whatever has a beginning in time is created. Now this union was not from eternity, but began in time. Therefore the union is something created.

I answer that, The union of which we are speaking is a relation which we consider between the Divine and the human nature, inasmuch as they come together in one Person of the Son of God. Now, as was said above ([3869]FP, Q[13], A[7]), every relation which we consider between God and the creature is really in the creature, by whose change the relation is brought into being; whereas it is not really in God, but only in our way of thinking, since it does not arise from any change in God. And hence we must say that the union of which we are speaking is not really in God, except only in our way of thinking; but in the human nature, which is a creature, it is really. Therefore we must say it is something created.

Reply to Objection 1: This union is not really in God, but only in our way of thinking, for God is said to be united to a creature inasmuch as the creature is really united to God without any change in Him.

Reply to Objection 2: The specific nature of a relation, as of motion, depends on the subject. And since this union has its being nowhere save in a created nature, as was said above, it follows that it has a created being.

Reply to Objection 3: A man is called Creator and is God because of the union, inasmuch as it is terminated in the Divine hypostasis; yet it does not follow that the union itself is the Creator or God, because that a thing is said to be created regards its being rather than its relation.

Whether union is the same as assumption?

Objection 1: It would seem that union is the same as assumption. For relations, as motions, are specified by their termini. Now the term of assumption and union is one and the same, viz. the Divine hypostasis. Therefore it seems that union and assumption are not different.

Objection 2: Further, in the mystery of the Incarnation the same thing seems to be what unites and what assumes, and what is united and what is assumed. But union and assumption seem to follow the action and passion of the thing uniting and the united, of the thing assuming and the assumed. Therefore union seems to be the same as assumption.

Objection 3: Further, Damascene says (De Fide Orth. iii, 11): "Union is one thing, incarnation is another; for union demands mere copulation, and leaves unsaid the end of the copulation; but incarnation and humanation determine the end of copulation." But likewise assumption does not determine the end of copulation. Therefore it seems that union is the same as assumption.

On the contrary, The Divine Nature is said to be united, not assumed.

I answer that, As was stated above [3870](A[7]), union implies a certain relation of the Divine Nature and the human, according as they come together in one Person. Now all relations which begin in time are brought about by some change; and change consists in action and passion. Hence the "first" and principal difference between assumption and union must be said to be that union implies the relation: whereas assumption implies the action, whereby someone is said to assume, or the passion, whereby something is said to be assumed. Now from this difference another "second" difference arises, for assumption implies "becoming," whereas union implies "having become," and therefore the thing uniting is said to be united, but the thing assuming is not said to be assumed. For the human nature is taken to be in the terminus of assumption unto the Divine hypostasis when man is spoken of; and hence we can truly say that the Son of God, Who assumes human nature unto Himself, is man. But human nature, considered in itself, i.e. in the abstract, is viewed as assumed; and we do not say the Son of God is human nature. From this same follows a "third" difference, which is that a relation, especially one of equiparance, is no more to one extreme than to the other, whereas action and passion bear themselves differently to the agent and the patient, and to different termini. And hence assumption determines the term whence and the term whither; for assumption means a taking to oneself from another. But union determines none of these things. hence it may be said indifferently that the human nature is united with the Divine, or conversely. But the Divine Nature is not said to be assumed by the human, but conversely, because the human nature is joined to the Divine personality, so that the Divine Person subsists in human nature.

Reply to Objection 1: Union and assumption have not the same relation to the term, but a different relation, as was said above.

Reply to Objection 2: What unites and what assumes are not the same. For whatsoever Person assumes unites, and not conversely. For the Person of the Father united the human nature to the Son, but not to Himself; and hence He is said to unite and not to assume. So likewise the united and the assumed are not identical, for the Divine Nature is said to be united, but not assumed.

Reply to Objection 3: Assumption determines with whom the union is made on the part of the one assuming, inasmuch as assumption means taking unto oneself [ad se sumere], whereas incarnation and humanation (determine with whom the union is made) on the part of the thing assumed, which is flesh or human nature. And thus assumption differs logically both from union and from incarnation or humanation.

Whether the union of the two natures in Christ is the greatest of all unions?

Objection 1: It would seem that the union of the two natures in Christ is not the greatest of all unions. For what is united falls short of the unity of what is one, since what is united is by participation, but one is by essence. Now in created things there are some that are simply one, as is shown especially in unity itself, which is the principle of number. Therefore the union of which we are speaking does not imply the greatest of all unions.

Objection 2: Further, the greater the distance between things united, the less the union. Now, the things united by this union are most distant---namely, the Divine and human natures; for they are infinitely apart. Therefore their union is the least of all.

Objection 3: Further, from union there results one. But from the union of soul and body in us there arises what is one in person and nature; whereas from the union of the Divine and human nature there results what is one in person only. Therefore the union of soul and body is greater than that of the Divine and human natures; and hence the union of which we speak does not imply the greatest unity.

On the contrary, Augustine says (De Trin. i, 10) that "man is in the Son of God, more than the Son in the Father." But the Son is in the Father by unity of essence, and man is in the Son by the union of the Incarnation. Therefore the union of the Incarnation is greater than the unity of the Divine Essence, which nevertheless is the greatest union; and thus the union of the Incarnation implies the greatest unity.

I answer that, Union implies the joining of several in some one thing. Therefore the union of the Incarnation may be taken in two ways: first, in regard to the things united; secondly, in regard to that in which they are united. And in this regard this union has a pre-eminence over other unions; for the unity of the Divine Person, in which the two natures are united, is the greatest. But it has no pre-eminence in regard to the things united.

Reply to Objection 1: The unity of the Divine Person is greater than numerical unity, which is the principle of number. For the unity of a Divine Person is an uncreated and self-subsisting unity, not received into another by participation. Also, it is complete in itself, having in itself whatever pertains to the nature of unity; and therefore it is not compatible with the nature of a part, as in numerical unity, which is a part of number, and which is shared in by the things numbered. And hence in this respect the union of the Incarnation is higher than numerical unity by reason of the unity of the Divine Person, and not by reason of the human nature, which is not the unity of the Divine Person, but is united to it.

Reply to Objection 2: This reason regards the things united, and not the Person in Whom the union takes place.

Reply to Objection 3: The unity of the Divine Person is greater than the unity of person and nature in us; and hence the union of the Incarnation is greater than the union of soul and body in us.

And because what is urged in the argument "on the contrary" rests upon what is untrue---namely, that the union of the Incarnation is greater than the unity of the Divine Persons in Essence---we must say to the authority of Augustine that the human nature is not more in the Son of God than the Son of God in the Father, but much less. But the man in some respects is more in the Son than the Son in the Father---namely, inasmuch as the same suppositum is signified when I say "man," meaning Christ, and when I say "Son of God"; whereas it is not the same suppositum of Father and Son.

Whether the union of the Incarnation took place by grace?

Objection 1: It would seem that the union of the Incarnation did not take place by grace. For grace is an accident, as was shown above ([3871]FS, Q[110], A[2]). But the union of the human nature to the Divine did not take place accidentally, as was shown above [3872](A[6]). Therefore it seems that the union of the Incarnation did not take place by grace.

Objection 2: Further, the subject of grace is the soul. But it is written (Col. 2:9): "In Christ [Vulg.: 'Him'] dwelleth all the fulness of the Godhead corporeally." Therefore it seems that this union did not take place by grace.

Objection 3: Further, every saint is united to God by grace. If, therefore, the union of the Incarnation was by grace, it would seem that Christ is said to be God no more than other holy men.

On the contrary, Augustine says (De Praed. Sanct. xv): "By the same grace every man is made a Christian, from the beginning of his faith, as this man from His beginning was made Christ." But this man became Christ by union with the Divine Nature. Therefore this union was by grace.

I answer that, As was said above ([3873]FS, Q[110], A[1]), grace is taken in two ways:--first, as the will of God gratuitously bestowing something; secondly, as the free gift of God. Now human nature stands in need of the gratuitous will of God in order to be lifted up to God, since this is above its natural capability. Moreover, human nature is lifted up to God in two ways: first, by operation, as the saints know and love God; secondly, by personal being, and this mode belongs exclusively to Christ, in Whom human nature is assumed so as to be in the Person of the Son of God. But it is plain that for the perfection of operation the power needs to be perfected by a habit, whereas that a nature has being in its own suppositum does not take place by means of a habit.

And hence we must say that if grace be understood as the will of God gratuitously doing something or reputing anything as well-pleasing or acceptable to Him, the union of the Incarnation took place by grace, even as the union of the saints with God by knowledge and love. But if grace be taken as the free gift of God, then the fact that the human nature is united to the Divine Person may be called a grace, inasmuch as it took place without being preceded by any merits---but not as though there were an habitual grace, by means of which the union took place.

Reply to Objection 1: The grace which is an accident is a certain likeness of the Divinity participated by man. But by the Incarnation human nature is not said to have participated a likeness of the Divine nature, but is said to be united to the Divine Nature itself in the Person of the Son. Now the thing itself is greater than a participated likeness of it.

Reply to Objection 2: Habitual grace is only in the soul; but the grace, i.e. the free gift of God, of being united to the Divine Person belongs to the whole human nature, which is composed of soul and body. And hence it is said that the fulness of the Godhead dwelt corporeally in Christ because the Divine Nature is united not merely to the soul, but to the body also. Although it may also be said that it dwelt in Christ corporeally, i.e. not as in a shadow, as it dwelt in the sacraments of the old law, of which it is said in the same place (Col. 2:17) that they are the "shadow of things to come but the body is Christ" [Vulg.: 'Christ's'], inasmuch as the body is opposed to the shadow. And some say that the Godhead is said to have dwelt in Christ corporeally, i.e. in three ways, just as a body has three dimensions: first, by essence, presence, and power, as in other creatures; secondly, by sanctifying grace, as in the saints; thirdly, by personal union, which is proper to Christ.

Hence the reply to the third is manifest, viz. because the union of the Incarnation did not take place by habitual grace alone, but in subsistence or person.

Day 251

Whether any merits preceded the union of the Incarnation?

237

Objection 1: It would seem that the union of the Incarnation followed upon certain merits, because upon Ps. 32:22, "Let Thy mercy, o Lord, be upon us, as," etc. a gloss says: "Here the prophet's desire for the Incarnation and its merited fulfilment are hinted at." Therefore the Incarnation falls under merit.

Objection 2: Further, whoever merits anything merits that without which it cannot be. But the ancient Fathers merited eternal life, to which they were able to attain only by the Incarnation; for Gregory says (Moral. xiii): "Those who came into this world before Christ's coming, whatsoever eminency of righteousness they may have had, could not, on being divested of the body, at once be admitted into the bosom of the heavenly country, seeing that He had not as yet come Who, by His own descending, should place the souls of the righteous in their everlasting seat." Therefore it would seem that they merited the Incarnation.

Objection 3: Further, of the Blessed Virgin it is sung that "she merited to bear the Lord of all" [*Little Office of B. V. M., Dominican Rite, Ant. at Benedictus], and this took place through the Incarnation. Therefore the Incarnation falls under merit.

On the contrary, Augustine says (De Praed. Sanct. xv): "Whoever can find merits preceding the singular generation of our Head, may also find merits preceding the repeated regeneration of us His members." But no merits preceded our regeneration, according to Titus 3:5: "Not by the works of justice which we have done, but according to His mercy He saved us, by the laver of regeneration." Therefore no merits preceded the generation of Christ.

I answer that, With regard to Christ Himself, it is clear from the above [3874](A[10]) that no merits of His could have preceded the union. For we do not hold that He was first of all a mere man, and that afterwards by the merits of a good life it was granted Him to become the Son of God, as Photinus held; but we hold that from the beginning of His conception this man was truly the Son of God, seeing that He had no other hypostasis but that of the Son of God, according to Luke 1:35: "The Holy which shall be born of thee shall be called the Son of God." And hence every operation of this man followed the union. Therefore no operation of His could have been meritorious of the union.

Neither could the needs of any other man whatsoever have merited this union condignly: first, because the meritorious works of man are properly ordained to beatitude, which is the reward of virtue, and consists in the full enjoyment of God. Whereas the union of the Incarnation, inasmuch as it is in the personal being, transcends the union of the beatified mind with God, which is by the act of the soul in fruition; and therefore it cannot fall under merit. Secondly, because grace cannot fall under merit, for the principle of merit does not fall under merit; and therefore neither does grace, for it is the principle of merit. Hence, still less does the Incarnation fall under merit, since it is the principle of grace, according to Jn. 1:17: "Grace and truth came by Jesus Christ." Thirdly, because the Incarnation is for the reformation of the entire human nature, and therefore it does not fall under the merit of any individual man, since the goodness of a mere man cannot be the cause of the good of the entire nature. Yet the holy Fathers merited the Incarnation congruously by desiring and beseeching; for it was becoming that God should harken to those who obeyed Him.

And thereby the reply to the First Objection is manifest.

Reply to Objection 2: It is false that under merit falls everything without which there can be no reward. For there is something pre-required not merely for reward, but also for merit, as the Divine goodness and grace and the very nature of man. And again, the mystery of the Incarnation is the principle of merit, because "of His fulness we all have received" (Jn. 1:16).

Reply to Objection 3: The Blessed Virgin is said to have merited to bear the Lord of all; not that she merited His Incarnation, but because by the grace bestowed upon her she merited that grade of purity and holiness, which fitted her to be the Mother of God.

Whether the grace of union was natural to the man Christ?

Objection 1: It would seem that the grace of union was not natural to the man Christ. For the union of the Incarnation did not take place in the nature, but in the Person, as was said above [3875](A[2]). Now a thing is denominated from its terminus. Therefore this grace ought rather to be called personal than natural.

Objection 2: Further, grace is divided against nature, even as gratuitous things, which are from God, are distinguished from natural things, which are from an intrinsic principle. But if things are divided in opposition to one another, one is not denominated by the other. Therefore the grace of Christ was not natural to Him.

Objection 3: Further, natural is that which is according to nature. But the grace of union is not natural to Christ in regard to the Divine Nature, otherwise it would belong to the other Persons; nor is it natural to Him according to the human nature, otherwise it would belong to all men, since they are of the same nature as He. Therefore it would seem that the grace of union is nowise natural to Christ.

On the contrary, Augustine says (Enchiridion xl): "In the assumption of human nature, grace itself became somewhat natural to that man, so as to leave no room for sin in Him."

I answer that, According to the Philosopher (Metaph. v, 5), nature designates, in one way, nativity; in another, the essence of a thing. Hence natural may be taken in two ways: first, for what is only from the essential principles of a thing, as it is natural to fire to mount; secondly, we call natural to man what he has had from his birth, according to Eph. 2:3: "We were by nature children of wrath"; and Wis. 12:10: "They were a wicked generation, and their malice natural." Therefore the grace of Christ, whether of union or habitual, cannot be called natural as if caused by the principles of the human nature of Christ, although it may be called natural, as if coming to the human nature of Christ by the causality of His Divine Nature. But these two kinds of grace are said to be natural to Christ, inasmuch as He had them from His nativity, since from the beginning of His conception the human nature was united to the Divine Person, and His soul was filled with the gift of grace.

Reply to Objection 1: Although the union did not take place in the nature, yet it was caused by the power of the Divine Nature, which is truly the nature of Christ, and it, moreover, belonged to Christ from the beginning of His nativity.

Reply to Objection 2: The union is not said to be grace and natural in the same respect; for it is called grace inasmuch as it is not from merit; and it is said to be natural inasmuch as by the power of the Divine Nature it was in the humanity of Christ from His nativity.

Reply to Objection 3: The grace of union is not natural to Christ according to His human nature, as if it were caused by the principles of the human nature, and hence it need not belong to all men. Nevertheless, it is natural to Him in regard to the human nature on account of the "property" of His birth, seeing that He was conceived by the Holy Ghost, so that He might be the natural Son of God and of man. But it is natural to Him in regard to the Divine Nature, inasmuch as the Divine Nature is the active principle of this grace; and this belongs to the whole Trinity---to wit, to be the active principle of this grace.

Day 252

OF THE MODE OF UNION ON THE PART OF THE PERSON ASSUMING (EIGHT ARTICLES)
We must now consider the union on the part of the Person assuming, and under this head there are eight points of inquiry:
(1) Whether to assume is befitting to a Divine Person?
(2) Whether it is befitting to the Divine Nature?
(3) Whether the Nature abstracted from the Personality can assume?
(4) Whether one Person can assume without another?
(5) Whether each Person can assume?
(6) Whether several Persons can assume one individual nature?
(7) Whether one Person can assume two individual natures?
(8) Whether it was more fitting for the Person of the Son of God to assume human nature than for another Divine Person?

Whether it is befitting for a Divine Person to assume?
Objection 1: It would seem that it is not befitting to a Divine Person to assume a created nature. For a Divine Person signifies something most perfect. Now no addition can be made to what is perfect. Therefore, since to assume is to take to oneself, and consequently what is assumed is added to the one who assumes, it does not seem to be befitting to a Divine Person to assume a created nature.

Objection 2: Further, that to which anything is assumed is communicated in some degree to what is assumed to it, just as dignity is communicated to whosoever is assumed to a dignity. But it is of the nature of a person to be incommunicable, as was said above ([3876]FP, Q[29], A[1]). Therefore it is not befitting to a Divine Person to assume, i.e. to take to Himself.

Objection 3: Further, person is constituted by nature. But it is repugnant that the thing constituted should assume the constituent, since the effect does not act on its cause. Hence it is not befitting to a Person to assume a nature.

On the contrary, Augustine [*Fulgentius] says (De Fide ad Petrum ii): "This God, i.e. the only-Begotten one, took the form," i.e. the nature, "of a servant to His own Person." But the only-Begotten God is a Person. Therefore it is befitting to a Person to take, i.e. to assume a nature.

I answer that, In the word "assumption" are implied two things, viz. the principle and the term of the act, for to assume is to take something to oneself. Now of this assumption a Person is both the principle and the term. The principle---because it properly belongs to a person to act, and this assuming of flesh took place by the Divine action. Likewise a Person is the term of this assumption, because, as was said above ([3877]Q[2], AA[1] ,2), the union took place in the Person, and not in the nature. Hence it is plain that to assume a nature is most properly befitting to a Person.

Reply to Objection 1: Since the Divine Person is infinite, no addition can be made to it: Hence Cyril says [*Council of Ephesus, Part I, ch. 26]: "We do not conceive the mode of conjunction to be according to addition"; just as in the union of man with God, nothing is added to God by the grace of adoption, but what is Divine is united to man; hence, not God but man is perfected.

Reply to Objection 2: A Divine Person is said to be incommunicable inasmuch as It cannot be predicated of several supposita, but nothing prevents several things being predicated of the Person. Hence it is not contrary to the nature of person to be communicated so as to subsist in several natures, for even in a created person several natures may concur accidentally, as in the person of one man we find quantity and quality. But this is proper to a Divine Person, on account of its infinity, that there should be a concourse of natures in it, not accidentally, but in subsistence.

Reply to Objection 3: As was said above ([3878]Q[2], A[1]), the human nature constitutes a Divine Person, not simply, but forasmuch as the Person is denominated from such a nature. For human nature does not make the Son of Man to be simply, since He was from eternity, but only to be man. It is by the Divine Nature that a Divine Person is constituted simply. Hence the Divine Person is not said to assume the Divine Nature, but to assume the human nature.

Whether it is befitting to the Divine Nature to assume?
Objection 1: It would seem that it is not befitting to the Divine Nature to assume. Because, as was said above [3879](A[1]), to assume is to take to oneself. But the Divine Nature did not take to Itself human nature, for the union did not take place in the nature, as was said above (Q[2], AA[1],3). Hence it is not befitting to the Divine Nature to assume human nature.

Objection 2: Further, the Divine Nature is common to the three Persons. If, therefore, it is befitting to the Divine Nature to assume, it consequently is befitting to the three Persons; and thus the Father assumed human nature even as the Son, which is erroneous.

Objection 3: Further, to assume is to act. But to act befits a person, not a nature, which is rather taken to be the principle by which the agent acts. Therefore to assume is not befitting to the nature.

On the contrary, Augustine (Fulgentius) says (De Fide ad Petrum ii): "That nature which remains eternally begotten of the Father" (i.e. which is received from the Father by eternal generation) "took our nature free of sin from His Mother."

I answer that, As was said above [3880](A[1]), in the word assumption two things are signified---to wit, the principle and the term of the action. Now to be the principle of the assumption belongs to the Divine Nature in itself, because the assumption took place by

Its power; but to be the term of the assumption does not belong to the Divine Nature in itself, but by reason of the Person in Whom It is considered to be. Hence a Person is primarily and more properly said to assume, but it may be said secondarily that the Nature assumed a nature to Its Person. And after the same manner the Nature is also said to be incarnate, not that it is changed to flesh, but that it assumed the nature of flesh. Hence Damascene says (De Fide Orth. iii, 6): "Following the blessed Athanasius and Cyril we say that the Nature of God is incarnate."

Reply to Objection 1: "Oneself" is reciprocal, and points to the same suppositum. But the Divine Nature is not a distinct suppositum from the Person of the Word. Hence, inasmuch as the Divine Nature took human nature to the Person of the Word, It is said to take it to Itself. But although the Father takes human nature to the Person of the Word, He did not thereby take it to Himself, for the suppositum of the Father and the Son is not one. and hence it cannot properly be said that the Father assumes human nature.

Reply to Objection 2: What is befitting to the Divine Nature in Itself is befitting to the three Persons, as goodness, wisdom, and the like. But to assume belongs to It by reason of the Person of the Word, as was said above, and hence it is befitting to that Person alone.

Reply to Objection 3: As in God "what is" and "whereby it is" are the same, so likewise in Him "what acts" and "whereby it acts" are the same, since everything acts, inasmuch as it is a being. Hence the Divine Nature is both that whereby God acts, and the very God Who acts.

Whether the Nature abstracted from the Personality can assume?

Objection 1: It would seem that if we abstract the Personality by our mind, the Nature cannot assume. For it was said above [3881] (A[1]) that it belongs to the Nature to assume by reason of the Person. But what belongs to one by reason of another cannot belong to it if the other is removed; as a body, which is visible by reason of color, without color cannot be seen. Hence if the Personality be mentally abstracted, the Nature cannot assume.

Objection 2: Further, assumption implies the term of union, as was said above [3882](A[1]). But the union cannot take place in the nature, but only in the Person. Therefore, if the Personality be abstracted, the Divine Nature cannot assume.

Objection 3: Further, it has been said above ([3883]FP, Q[40], A[3]) that in the Godhead if the Personality is abstracted, nothing remains. But the one who assumes is something. Therefore, if the Personality is abstracted, the Divine Nature cannot assume.

On the contrary, In the Godhead Personality signifies a personal property; and this is threefold, viz. Paternity, Filiation and Procession, as was said above ([3884]FP, Q[30], A[2]). Now if we mentally abstract these, there still remains the omnipotence of God, by which the Incarnation was wrought, as the angel says (Lk. 1:37): "No word shall be impossible with God." Therefore it seems that if the Personality be removed, the Divine Nature can still assume.

I answer that, The intellect stands in two ways towards God. First, to know God as He is, and in this manner it is impossible for the intellect to circumscribe something in God and leave the rest, for all that is in God is one, except the distinction of Persons; and as regards these, if one is removed the other is taken away, since they are distinguished by relations only which must be together at the same time. Secondly, the intellect stands towards God, not indeed as knowing God as He is, but in its own way, i.e. understanding manifoldly and separately what in God is one: and in this way our intellect can understand the Divine goodness and wisdom, and the like, which are called essential attributes, without understanding Paternity or Filiation, which are called Personalities. And hence if we abstract Personality by our intellect, we may still understand the Nature assuming.

Reply to Objection 1: Because in God "what is," and "whereby it is," are one, if any one of the things which are attributed to God in the abstract is considered in itself, abstracted from all else, it will still be something subsisting, and consequently a Person, since it is an intellectual nature. Hence just as we now say three Persons, on account of holding three personal properties, so likewise if we mentally exclude the personal properties there will still remain in our thought the Divine Nature as subsisting and as a Person. And in this way It may be understood to assume human nature by reason of Its subsistence or Personality.

Reply to Objection 2: Even if the personal properties of the three Persons are abstracted by our mind, nevertheless there will remain in our thoughts the one Personality of God, as the Jews consider. And the assumption can be terminated in It, as we now say it is terminated in the Person of the Word.

Reply to Objection 3: If we mentally abstract the Personality, it is said that nothing remains by way of resolution, i.e. as if the subject of the relation and the relation itself were distinct because all we can think of in God is considered as a subsisting suppositum. However, some of the things predicated of God can be understood without others, not by way of resolution, but by the way mentioned above.

Whether one Person without another can assume a created nature?

Objection 1: It would seem that one Person cannot assume a created nature without another assuming it. For "the works of the Trinity are inseparable," as Augustine says (Enchiridion xxxviii). But as the three Persons have one essence, so likewise They have one operation. Now to assume is an operation. Therefore it cannot belong to one without belonging to another.

Objection 2: Further, as we say the Person of the Son became incarnate, so also did the Nature; for "the whole Divine Nature became incarnate in one of Its hypostases," as Damascene says (De Fide Orth. iii, 6). But the Nature is common to the three Persons. Therefore the assumption is.

Objection 3: Further, as the human nature in Christ is assumed by God, so likewise are men assumed by Him through grace, according to Rom. 14:3: "God hath taken him to Him." But this assumption pertains to all the Persons; therefore the first also.

On the contrary, Dionysius says (Div. Nom. ii) that the mystery of the Incarnation pertains to "discrete theology," i.e. according to which something "distinct" is said of the Divine Persons.

I answer that, As was said above [3885](A[1]), assumption implies two things, viz. the act of assuming and the term of assumption. Now the act of assumption proceeds from the Divine power, which is common to the three Persons, but the term of the assumption is a Person, as stated above [3886](A[2]). Hence what has to do with action in the assumption is common to the three Persons; but what pertains to the nature of term belongs to one Person in such a manner as not to belong to another; for the three Persons caused the human nature to be united to the one Person of the Son.

Reply to Objection 1: This reason regards the operation, and the conclusion would follow if it implied this operation only, without the term, which is a Person.

Reply to Objection 2: The Nature is said to be incarnate, and to assume by reason of the Person in Whom the union is terminated, as stated above ([3887]AA[1],2), and not as it is common to the three Persons. Now "the whole Divine Nature is" said to be "incarnate"; not that It is incarnate in all the Persons, but inasmuch as nothing is wanting to the perfection of the Divine Nature of the Person incarnate, as Damascene explains there.

Reply to Objection 3: The assumption which takes place by the grace of adoption is terminated in a certain participation of the Divine Nature, by an assimilation to Its goodness, according to 2 Pet. 1:4: "That you may be made partakers of the Divine Nature"; and hence this assumption is common to the three Persons, in regard to the principle and the term. But the assumption which is by the grace of union is common on the part of the principle, but not on the part of the term, as was said above.

Whether each of the Divine Persons could have assumed human nature?

Objection 1: It would seem that no other Divine Person could have assumed human nature except the Person of the Son. For by this assumption it has been brought about that God is the Son of Man. But it was not becoming that either the Father or the Holy Ghost should be said to be a Son; for this would tend to the confusion of the Divine Persons. Therefore the Father and Holy Ghost could not have assumed flesh.

Objection 2: Further, by the Divine Incarnation men have come into possession of the adoption of sons, according to Rom. 8:15: "For you have not received the spirit of bondage again in fear, but the spirit of adoption of sons." But sonship by adoption is a participated likeness of natural sonship which does not belong to the Father nor the Holy Ghost; hence it is said (Rom. 8:29): "For whom He foreknew He also predestinated to be made conformable to the image of His Son." Therefore it seems that no other Person except the Person of the Son could have become incarnate.

Objection 3: Further, the Son is said to be sent and to be begotten by the temporal nativity, inasmuch as He became incarnate. But it does not belong to the Father to be sent, for He is innascible, as was said above ([3888]FP, Q[32], A[3]; [3889]FP, Q[43], A[4]). Therefore at least the Person of the Father cannot become incarnate.

On the contrary, Whatever the Son can do, so can the Father and the Holy Ghost, otherwise the power of the three Persons would not be one. But the Son was able to become incarnate. Therefore the Father and the Holy Ghost were able to become incarnate.

I answer that, As was said above ([3890]AA[1],2,4), assumption implies two things, viz. the act of the one assuming and the term of the assumption. Now the principle of the act is the Divine power, and the term is a Person. But the Divine power is indifferently and commonly in all the Persons. Moreover, the nature of Personality is common to all the Persons, although the personal properties are different. Now whenever a power regards several things indifferently, it can terminate its action in any of them indifferently, as is plain in rational powers, which regard opposites, and can do either of them. Therefore the Divine power could have united human nature to the Person of the Father or of the Holy Ghost, as It united it to the Person of the Son. And hence we must say that the Father or the Holy Ghost could have assumed flesh even as the Son.

Reply to Objection 1: The temporal sonship, whereby Christ is said to be the Son of Man, does not constitute His Person, as does the eternal Sonship; but is something following upon the temporal nativity. Hence, if the name of son were transferred to the Father or the Holy Ghost in this manner, there would be no confusion of the Divine Persons.

Reply to Objection 2: Adoptive sonship is a certain participation of natural sonship; but it takes place in us, by appropriation, by the Father, Who is the principle of natural sonship, and by the gift of the Holy Ghost, Who is the love of the Father and Son, according to Gal. 4:6: "God hath sent the Spirit of His Son into your hearts crying, Abba, Father." And therefore, even as by the Incarnation of the Son we receive adoptive sonship in the likeness of His natural sonship, so likewise, had the Father become incarnate, we should have received adoptive sonship from Him, as from the principle of the natural sonship, and from the Holy Ghost as from the common bond of Father and Son.

Reply to Objection 3: It belongs to the Father to be innascible as to eternal birth, and the temporal birth would not destroy this. But the Son of God is said to be sent in regard to the Incarnation, inasmuch as He is from another, without which the Incarnation would not suffice for the nature of mission.

Whether several Divine Persons can assume one and the same individual nature?

Objection 1: It would seem that two Divine Persons cannot assume one and the same individual nature. For, this being granted, there would either be several men or one. But not several, for just as one Divine Nature in several Persons does not make several gods, so one human nature in several persons does not make several men. Nor would there be only one man, for one man is "this man," which signifies one person; and hence the distinction of three Divine Persons would be destroyed, which cannot be allowed. Therefore neither two nor three Persons can take one human nature.

Objection 2: Further, the assumption is terminated in the unity of Person, as has been said above [3891](A[2]). But the Father, Son, and Holy Ghost are not one Person. Therefore the three Persons cannot assume one human nature.

Objection 3: Further, Damascene says (De Fide Orth. iii, 3,4), and Augustine (De Trin. i, 11,12,13), that from the Incarnation of God the Son it follows that whatever is said of the Son of God is said of the Son of Man, and conversely. Hence, if three Persons were to assume one human nature, it would follow that whatever is said of each of the three Persons would be said of the man; and conversely, what was said of the man could be said of each of the three Persons. Therefore what is proper to the Father, viz. to beget the Son, would be said of the man, and consequently would be said of the Son of God; and this could not be. Therefore it is impossible that the three Persons should assume one human nature.

On the contrary, The Incarnate Person subsists in two natures. But the three Persons can subsist in one Divine Nature. Therefore they can also subsist in one human nature in such a way that the human nature be assumed by the three Persons.

I answer that, As was said above ([3892]Q[2], A[5], ad 1), by the union of the soul and body in Christ neither a new person is made nor a new hypostasis, but one human nature is assumed to the Divine Person or hypostasis, which, indeed, does not take place by the power of the human nature, but by the power of the Divine Person. Now such is the characteristic of the Divine Persons that one does not exclude another from communicating in the same nature, but only in the same Person. Hence, since in the mystery of the Incarnation "the whole reason of the deed is the power of the doer," as Augustine says (Ep. ad Volusianum cxxxvii), we must judge of it in regard to the quality of the Divine Person assuming, and not according to the quality of the human nature assumed. Therefore it is not impossible that two or three Divine Persons should assume one human nature, but it would be impossible for them to assume one human hypostasis or person; thus Anselm says in the book De Concep. Virg. (Cur Deus Homo ii, 9), that "several Persons cannot assume one and the same man to unity of Person."

Reply to Objection 1: In the hypothesis that three Persons assume one human nature, it would be true to say that the three Persons were one man, because of the one human nature. For just as it is now true to say the three Persons are one God on account of the one Divine Nature, so it would be true to say they are one man on account of the one human nature. Nor would "one" imply unity of person, but unity in human nature; for it could not be argued that because the three Persons were one man they were one simply. For nothing hinders our saying that men, who are many simply, are in some respect one, e.g. one people, and as Augustine says (De Trin. vi, 3): "The Spirit of God and the spirit of man are by nature different, but by inherence one spirit results," according to 1 Cor. 6:17: "He who is joined to the Lord is one spirit."

Reply to Objection 2: In this supposition the human nature would be assumed to the unity, not indeed of one Person, but to the unity of each Person, so that even as the Divine Nature has a natural unity with each Person, so also the human nature would have a unity with each Person by assumption.

Reply to Objection 3: In the mystery of the Incarnation, there results a communication of the properties belonging to the nature, because whatever belongs to the nature can be predicated of the Person subsisting in that nature, no matter to which of the natures it may apply. Hence in this hypothesis, of the Person of the Father may be predicated what belongs to the human nature and what belongs to the Divine; and likewise of the Person of the Son and of the Holy Ghost. But what belongs to the Person of the Father by reason of His own Person could not be attributed to the Person of the Son or Holy Ghost on account of the distinction of Persons which would still remain. Therefore it might be said that as the Father was unbegotten, so the man was unbegotten, inasmuch as "man" stood for the Person of the Father. But if one were to go on to say, "The man is unbegotten; the Son is man; therefore the Son is unbegotten," it would be the fallacy of figure of speech or of accident; even as we now say God is unbegotten, because the Father is unbegotten, yet we cannot conclude that the Son is unbegotten, although He is God.

Whether one Divine Person can assume two human natures?

Objection 1: It would seem that one Divine Person cannot assume two human natures. For the nature assumed in the mystery of the Incarnation has no other suppositum than the suppositum of the Divine Person, as is plain from what has been stated above ([3893]Q[2], AA[3],6). Therefore, if we suppose one Person to assume two human natures, there would be one suppositum of two natures of the same species; which would seem to imply a contradiction, for the nature of one species is only multiplied by distinct supposita.

Objection 2: Further, in this hypothesis it could not be said that the Divine Person incarnate was one man, seeing that He would not have one human nature; neither could it be said that there were several, for several men have distinct supposita, whereas in this case there would be only one suppositum. Therefore the aforesaid hypothesis is impossible.

Objection 3: Further, in the mystery of the Incarnation the whole Divine Nature is united to the whole nature assumed, i.e. to every part of it, for Christ is "perfect God and perfect man, complete God and complete man," as Damascene says (De Fide Orth. iii, 7). But two human natures cannot be wholly united together, inasmuch as the soul of one would be united to the body of the other; and, again, two bodies would be together, which would give rise to confusion of natures. Therefore it is not possibly for one Divine Person to assume two human natures.

On the contrary, Whatever the Father can do, that also can the Son do. But after the Incarnation the Father can still assume a human nature distinct from that which the Son has assumed; for in nothing is the power of the Father or the Son lessened by the Incarnation of the Son. Therefore it seems that after the Incarnation the Son can assume another human nature distinct from the one He has assumed.

I answer that, What has power for one thing, and no more, has a power limited to one. Now the power of a Divine Person is infinite, nor can it be limited by any created thing. Hence it may not be said that a Divine Person so assumed one human nature as to be unable to assume another. For it would seem to follow from this that the Personality of the Divine Nature was so comprehended by one human nature as to be unable to assume another to its Personality; and this is impossible, for the Uncreated cannot be comprehended by any creature. Hence it is plain that, whether we consider the Divine Person in regard to His power, which is the principle of the union, or in regard to His Personality, which is the term of the union, it has to be said that the Divine Person, over and beyond the human nature which He has assumed, can assume another distinct human nature.

Reply to Objection 1: A created nature is completed in its essentials by its form, which is multiplied according to the division of matter. And hence, if the composition of matter and form constitutes a new suppositum, the consequence is that the nature is multiplied by the multiplication of supposita. But in the mystery of the Incarnation the union of form and matter, i.e. of soul and body, does not constitute a new suppositum, as was said above [3894](A[6]). Hence there can be a numerical multitude on the part of the nature, on account of the division of matter, without distinction of supposita.

Reply to Objection 2: It might seem possible to reply that in such a hypothesis it would follow that there were two men by reason of the two natures, just as, on the contrary, the three Persons would be called one man, on account of the one nature assumed, as was said above (A[6], ad 1). But this does not seem to be true; because we must use words according to the purpose of their signification, which is in relation to our surroundings. Consequently, in order to judge of a word's signification or co-signification, we must consider the things which are around us, in which a word derived from some form is never used in the plural unless there are several supposita. For a man who has on two garments is not said to be "two persons clothed," but "one clothed with two garments"; and whoever has two qualities is designated in the singular as "such by reason of the two qualities." Now the assumed nature is, as it were, a garment, although this similitude does not fit at all points, as has been said above ([3895]Q[2], A[6], ad 1). And hence, if the Divine Person were to assume two human natures, He would be called, on account of the unity of suppositum, one man having two human natures. Now many men are said to be one people, inasmuch as they have some one thing in common, and not on account of the unity of suppositum. So likewise, if two Divine Persons were to assume one singular human nature, they would be said to be one man, as stated (A[6], ad 1), not from the unity of suppositum, but because they have some one thing in common.

Reply to Objection 3: The Divine and human natures do not bear the same relation to the one Divine Person, but the Divine Nature is related first of all thereto, inasmuch as It is one with It from eternity; and afterwards the human nature is related to the Divine Person, inasmuch as it is assumed by the Divine Person in time, not indeed that the nature is the Person, but that the Person of God subsists in human nature. For the Son of God is His Godhead, but is not His manhood. And hence, in order that the human nature may be assumed by the Divine Person, the Divine Nature must be united by a personal union with the whole nature assumed, i.e. in all its parts. Now in the two natures assumed there would be a uniform relation to the Divine Person, nor would one assume the other. Hence it would not be necessary for one of them to be altogether united to the other, i.e. all the parts of one with all the parts of the other.

Whether it was more fitting that the Person of the Son rather than any other Divine Person should assume human nature?

Objection 1: It would seem that it was not more fitting that the Son of God should become incarnate than the Father or the Holy Ghost. For by the mystery of the Incarnation men are led to the true knowledge of God, according to Jn. 18:37: "For this was I born, and for this came I into the world, to give testimony to the truth." But by the Person of the Son of God becoming incarnate many have been kept back from the true knowledge of God, since they referred to the very Person of the Son what was said of the Son in His human nature, as Arius, who held an inequality of Persons, according to what is said (Jn. 14:28): "The Father is greater than I." Now this error would not have arisen if the Person of the Father had become incarnate, for no one would have taken the Father to be less than the Son. Hence it seems fitting that the Person of the Father, rather than the Person of the Son, should have become incarnate.

Objection 2: Further, the effect of the Incarnation would seem to be, as it were, a second creation of human nature, according to Gal. 6:15: "For in Christ Jesus neither circumcision availeth anything, nor uncircumcision, but a new creature." But the power of creation is appropriated to the Father. Therefore it would have been more becoming to the Father than to the Son to become incarnate.

Objection 3: Further, the Incarnation is ordained to the remission of sins, according to Mat. 1:21: "Thou shalt call His name Jesus. For He shall save His people from their sins." Now the remission of sins is attributed to the Holy Ghost according to Jn. 20:22,23: "Receive ye the Holy Ghost. Whose sins you shall forgive, they are forgiven them." Therefore it became the Person of the Holy Ghost rather than the Person of the Son to become incarnate.

On the contrary, Damascene says (De Fide Orth. iii, 1): "In the mystery of the Incarnation the wisdom and power of God are made known: the wisdom, for He found a most suitable discharge for a most heavy debt; the power, for He made the conquered conquer." But power and wisdom are appropriated to the Son, according to 1 Cor. 1:24: "Christ, the power of God and the wisdom of God." Therefore it was fitting that the Person of the Son should become incarnate.

I answer that, It was most fitting that the Person of the Son should become incarnate. First, on the part of the union; for such as are similar are fittingly united. Now the Person of the Son, Who is the Word of God, has a certain common agreement with all creatures, because the word of the craftsman, i.e. his concept, is an exemplar likeness of whatever is made by him. Hence the Word of God, Who is His eternal concept, is the exemplar likeness of all creatures. And therefore as creatures are established in their proper species, though movably, by the participation of this likeness, so by the non-participated and personal union of the Word with a creature, it was fitting that the creature should be restored in order to its eternal and unchangeable perfection; for the craftsman by the intelligible form of his art, whereby he fashioned his handiwork, restores it when it has fallen into ruin. Moreover, He has a particular agreement with human nature, since the Word is a concept of the eternal Wisdom, from Whom all man's wisdom is derived. And hence man is perfected in wisdom (which is his proper perfection, as he is rational) by participating the Word of God, as the disciple is instructed by receiving the word of his master. Hence it is said (Ecclus. 1:5): "The Word of God on high is the fountain of wisdom." And hence for the consummate perfection of man it was fitting that the very Word of God should be personally united to human nature.

Secondly, the reason of this fitness may be taken from the end of the union, which is the fulfilling of predestination, i.e. of such as are preordained to the heavenly inheritance, which is bestowed only on sons, according to Rom. 8:17: "If sons, heirs also." Hence it was fitting that by Him Who is the natural Son, men should share this likeness of sonship by adoption, as the Apostle says in the same chapter (Rom. 8:29): "For whom He foreknew, He also predestinated to be made conformable to the image of His Son."

Thirdly, the reason for this fitness may be taken from the sin of our first parent, for which the Incarnation supplied the remedy. For the first man sinned by seeking knowledge, as is plain from the words of the serpent, promising to man the knowledge of good and evil. Hence it was fitting that by the Word of true knowledge man might be led back to God, having wandered from God through an inordinate thirst for knowledge.

Reply to Objection 1: There is nothing which human malice cannot abuse, since it even abuses God's goodness, according to Rom. 2:4: "Or despisest thou the riches of His goodness?" Hence, even if the Person of the Father had become incarnate, men would have been capable of finding an occasion of error, as though the Son were not able to restore human nature.

Reply to Objection 2: The first creation of things was made by the power of God the Father through the Word; hence the second creation ought to have been brought about through the Word, by the power of God the Father, in order that restoration should correspond to creation according to 2 Cor. 5:19: "For God indeed was in Christ reconciling the world to Himself."

Reply to Objection 3: To be the gift of the Father and the Son is proper to the Holy Ghost. But the remission of sins is caused by the Holy Ghost, as by the gift of God. And hence it was more fitting to man's justification that the Son should become incarnate, Whose gift the Holy Ghost is.

OF THE MODE OF UNION ON THE PART OF THE HUMAN NATURE (SIX ARTICLES)

We must now consider the union on the part of what was assumed. About which we must consider first what things were assumed by the Word of God; secondly, what were co-assumed, whether perfections or defects.

Now the Son of God assumed human nature and its parts. Hence a threefold consideration arises. First, with regard to the nature; secondly, with regard to its parts; thirdly, with regard to the order of the assumption.

Under the first head there are six points of inquiry:

(1) Whether human nature was more capable of being assumed than any other nature?

(2) Whether He assumed a person?

(3) Whether He assumed a man?

(4) Whether it was becoming that He should assume human nature abstracted from all individuals?

(5) Whether it was becoming that He should assume human nature in all its individuals?

(6) Whether it was becoming that He should assume human nature in any man begotten of the stock of Adam?

Whether human nature was more assumable by the Son of God than any other nature?

Objection 1: It would seem that human nature is not more capable of being assumed by the Son of God than any other nature. For Augustine says (Ep. ad Volusianum cxxxvii): "In deeds wrought miraculously the whole reason of the deed is the power of the doer." Now the power of God Who wrought the Incarnation, which is a most miraculous work, is not limited to one nature, since the power of God is infinite. Therefore human nature is not more capable of being assumed than any other creature.

Objection 2: Further, likeness is the foundation of the fittingness of the Incarnation of the Divine Person, as above stated ([3896]Q[3], A[8]). But as in rational creatures we find the likeness of image, so in irrational creatures we find the image of trace. Therefore the irrational creature was as capable of assumption as human nature.

Objection 3: Further, in the angelic nature we find a more perfect likeness than in human nature, as Gregory says: (Hom. de Cent. Ovib.; xxxiv in Ev.), where he introduces Ezech. 28:12: "Thou wast the seal of resemblance." And sin is found in angels, even as in man, according to Job 4:18: "And in His angels He found wickedness." Therefore the angelic nature was as capable of assumption as the nature of man.

Objection 4: Further, since the highest perfection belongs to God, the more like to God a thing is, the more perfect it is. But the whole universe is more perfect than its parts, amongst which is human nature. Therefore the whole universe is more capable of being assumed than human nature.

On the contrary, It is said (Prov. 8:31) by the mouth of Begotten Wisdom: "My delights were to be with the children of men"; and hence there would seem some fitness in the union of the Son of God with human nature.

I answer that, A thing is said to be assumable as being capable of being assumed by a Divine Person, and this capability cannot be taken with reference to the natural passive power, which does not extend to what transcends the natural order, as the personal union of a creature with God transcends it. Hence it follows that a thing is said to be assumable according to some fitness for such a union. Now this fitness in human nature may be taken from two things, viz. according to its dignity, and according to its need. According to its dignity, because human nature, as being rational and intellectual, was made for attaining to the Word to some extent by its operation, viz. by knowing and loving Him. According to its need---because it stood in need of restoration, having fallen under original sin. Now these two things belong to human nature alone. For in the irrational creature the fitness of dignity is wanting, and in the angelic nature the aforesaid fitness of need is wanting. Hence it follows that only human nature was assumable.

Reply to Objection 1: Creatures are said to be "such" with reference to their proper causes, not with reference to what belongs to them from their first and universal causes; thus we call a disease incurable, not that it cannot be cured by God, but that it cannot be cured by the proper principles of the subject. Therefore a creature is said to be not assumable, not as if we withdrew anything from the power of God, but in order to show the condition of the creature, which has no capability for this.

Reply to Objection 2: The likeness of image is found in human nature, forasmuch as it is capable of God, viz. by attaining to Him through its own operation of knowledge and love. But the likeness of trace regards only a representation by Divine impression, existing in the creature, and does not imply that the irrational creature, in which such a likeness is, can attain to God by its own operation alone. For what does not come up to the less, has no fitness for the greater; as a body which is not fitted to be perfected by a sensitive soul is much less fitted for an intellectual soul. Now much greater and more perfect is the union with God in personal being than the union by operation. And hence the irrational creature which falls short of the union with God by operation has no fitness to be united with Him in personal being.

Reply to Objection 3: Some say that angels are not assumable, since they are perfect in their personality from the beginning of their creation, inasmuch as they are not subject to generation and corruption; hence they cannot be assumed to the unity of a Divine Person, unless their personality be destroyed, and this does not befit the incorruptibility of their nature nor the goodness of the one assuming, to Whom it does not belong to corrupt any perfection in the creature assumed. But this would not seem totally to disprove the fitness of the angelic nature for being assumed. For God by producing a new angelic nature could join it to Himself in unity of Person, and in this way nothing pre-existing would be corrupted in it. But as was said above, there is wanting the fitness of need, because, although the angelic nature in some is the subject of sin, their sin is irremediable, as stated above ([3897]FP, Q[64], A[2]).

Reply to Objection 4: The perfection of the universe is not the perfection of one person or suppositum, but of something which is one by position or order, whereof very many parts are not capable of assumption, as was said above. Hence it follows that only human nature is capable of being assumed.

Whether the Son of God assumed a person?

Objection 1: It would seem that the Son of God assumed a person. For Damascene says (De Fide Orth. iii, 11) that the Son of God "assumed human nature 'in atomo,'" i.e. in an individual. But an individual in rational nature is a person, as is plain from Boethius (De Duab. Nat.). Therefore the Son of God assumed a person.

Objection 2: Further, Damascene says (De Fide Orth. iii, 6) that the Son of God "assumed what He had sown in our nature." But He sowed our personality there. Therefore the Son of God assumed a person.

Objection 3: Further, nothing is absorbed unless it exist. But Innocent III [*Paschas. Diac., De Spiritu Sanct. ii] says in a Decretal that "the Person of God absorbed the person of man." Therefore it would seem that the person of man existed previous to its being assumed.

On the contrary, Augustine [*Fulgentius] says (De Fide ad Petrum ii) that "God assumed the nature, not the person, of man."

I answer that, A thing is said to be assumed inasmuch as it is taken into another. Hence, what is assumed must be presupposed to the assumption, as what is moved locally is presupposed to the motion. Now a person in human nature is not presupposed to assumption; rather, it is the term of the assumption, as was said ([3898]Q[3], AA[1],2). For if it were presupposed, it must either have been corrupted---in which case it was useless; or it remains after the union---and thus there would be two persons, one assuming and the other assumed, which is false, as was shown above ([3899]Q[2], A[6]). Hence it follows that the Son of God nowise assumed a human person.

Reply to Objection 1: The Son of God assumed human nature "in atomo," i.e. in an individual, which is no other than the uncreated suppositum, the Person of the Son of God. Hence it does not follow that a person was assumed.

Reply to Objection 2: Its proper personality is not wanting to the nature assumed through the loss of anything pertaining to the perfection of the human nature but through the addition of something which is above human nature, viz. the union with a Divine Person.

Reply to Objection 3: Absorption does not here imply the destruction of anything pre-existing, but the hindering what might otherwise have been. For if the human nature had not been assumed by a Divine Person, the human nature would have had its own personality; and in this way is it said, although improperly, that the Person "absorbed the person," inasmuch as the Divine Person by His union hindered the human nature from having its personality.

Whether the Divine Person assumed a man?

Objection 1: It would seem that the Divine Person assumed a man. For it is written (Ps. 64:5): "Blessed is he whom Thou hast chosen and taken to Thee," which a gloss expounds of Christ; and Augustine says (De Agone Christ. xi): "The Son of God assumed a man, and in him bore things human."

Objection 2: Further, the word "man" signifies a human nature. But the Son of God assumed a human nature. Therefore He assumed a man.

Objection 3: Further, the Son of God is a man. But He is not one of the men He did not assume, for with equal reason He would be Peter or any other man. Therefore He is the man whom He assumed.

On the contrary, Is the authority of Felix, Pope and Martyr, which is quoted by the Council of Ephesus: "We believe in our Lord Jesus Christ, born of the Virgin Mary, because He is the Eternal Son and Word of God, and not a man assumed by God, in such sort that there is another besides Him. For the Son of God did not assume a man, so that there be another besides Him."

I answer that, As has been said above [3900](A[2]), what is assumed is not the term of the assumption, but is presupposed to the assumption. Now it was said (Q[3], AA[1],2) that the individual to Whom the human nature is assumed is none other than the Divine Person, Who is the term of the assumption. Now this word "man" signifies human nature, as it is in a suppositum, because, as Damascene says (De Fide Orth. iii, 4,11), this word God signifies Him Who has human nature. And hence it cannot properly be said that the Son assumed a man, granted (as it must be, in fact) that in Christ there is but one suppositum and one hypostasis. But according to such as hold that there are two hypostases or two supposita in Christ, it may fittingly and properly be said that the Son of God assumed a man. Hence the first opinion quoted in Sent. iii, D. 6, grants that a man was assumed. But this opinion is erroneous, as was said above (Q[2], A[6]).

Reply to Objection 1: These phrases are not to be taken too literally, but are to be loyally explained, wherever they are used by holy doctors; so as to say that a man was assumed, inasmuch as his nature was assumed; and because the assumption terminated in this--- that the Son of God is man.

Reply to Objection 2: The word "man" signifies human nature in the concrete, inasmuch as it is in a suppositum; and hence, since we cannot say a suppositum was assumed, so we cannot say a man was assumed.

Reply to Objection 3: The Son of God is not the man whom He assumed, but the man whose nature He assumed.

Whether the Son of God ought to have assumed human nature abstracted from all individuals?

Objection 1: It would seem that the Son of God ought to have assumed human nature abstracted from all individuals. For the assumption of human nature took place for the common salvation of all men; hence it is said of Christ (1 Tim. 4:10) that He is "the

Saviour of all men, especially of the faithful." But nature as it is in individuals withdraws from its universality. Therefore the Son of God ought to have assumed human nature as it is abstracted from all individuals.

Objection 2: Further, what is noblest in all things ought to be attributed to God. But in every genus what is of itself is best. Therefore the Son of God ought to have assumed self-existing [per se] man, which, according to Platonists, is human nature abstracted from its individuals. Therefore the Son of God ought to have assumed this.

Objection 3: Further, human nature was not assumed by the Son of God in the concrete as is signified by the word "man," as was said above [3901](A[3]). Now in this way it signifies human nature as it is in individuals, as is plain from what has been said [3902] (A[3]). Therefore the Son of God assumed human nature as it is separated from individuals.

On the contrary, Damascene says (De Fide Orth. iii, 11): "God the Word Incarnate did not assume a nature which exists in pure thought; for this would have been no Incarnation, but a false and fictitious Incarnation." But human nature as it is separated or abstracted from individuals is "taken to be a pure conception, since it does not exist in itself," as Damascene says (De Fide Orth. iii, 11). Therefore the Son of God did not assume human nature, as it is separated from individuals.

I answer that, The nature of man or of any other sensible thing, beyond the being which it has in individuals, may be taken in two ways: first, as if it had being of itself, away from matter, as the Platonists held; secondly, as existing in an intellect either human or Divine. Now it cannot subsist of itself, as the Philosopher proves (Metaph. vii, 26,27,29,51), because sensible matter belongs to the specific nature of sensible things, and is placed in its definition, as flesh and bones in the definition of man. Hence human nature cannot be without sensible matter. Nevertheless, if human nature were subsistent in this way, it would not be fitting that it should be assumed by the Word of God. First, because this assumption is terminated in a Person, and it is contrary to the nature of a common form to be thus individualized in a person. Secondly, because to a common nature can only be attributed common and universal operations, according to which man neither merits nor demerits, whereas, on the contrary, the assumption took place in order that the Son of God, having assumed our nature, might merit for us. Thirdly, because a nature so existing would not be sensible, but intelligible. But the Son of God assumed human nature in order to show Himself in men's sight, according to Baruch 3:38: "Afterwards He was seen upon earth, and conversed with men."

Likewise, neither could human nature have been assumed by the Son of God, as it is in the Divine intellect, since it would be none other than the Divine Nature; and, according to this, human nature would be in the Son of God from eternity. Neither can we say that the Son of God assumed human nature as it is in a human intellect, for this would mean nothing else but that He is understood to assume a human nature; and thus if He did not assume it in reality, this would be a false understanding; nor would this assumption of the human nature be anything but a fictitious Incarnation, as Damascene says (De Fide Orth. iii, 11).

Reply to Objection 1: The incarnate Son of God is the common Saviour of all, not by a generic or specific community, such as is attributed to the nature separated from the individuals, but by a community of cause, whereby the incarnate Son of God is the universal cause of human salvation.

Reply to Objection 2: Self-existing [per se] man is not to be found in nature in such a way as to be outside the singular, as the Platonists held, although some say Plato believed that the separate man was only in the Divine intellect. And hence it was not necessary for it to be assumed by the Word, since it had been with Him from eternity.

Reply to Objection 3: Although human nature was not assumed in the concrete, as if the suppositum were presupposed to the assumption, nevertheless it is assumed in an individual, since it is assumed so as to be in an individual.

Whether the Son of God ought to have assumed human nature in all individuals?

Objection 1: It would seem that the Son of God ought to have assumed human nature in all individuals. For what is assumed first and by itself is human nature. But what belongs essentially to a nature belongs to all who exist in the nature. Therefore it was fitting that human nature should be assumed by the Word of God in all its supposita.

Objection 2: Further, the Divine Incarnation proceeded from Divine Love; hence it is written (Jn. 3:16): "God so loved the world as to give His only-begotten Son." But love makes us give ourselves to our friends as much as we can, and it was possible for the Son of God to assume several human natures, as was said above ([3903]Q[3], A[7]), and with equal reason all. Hence it was fitting for the Son of God to assume human nature in all its supposita.

Objection 3: Further, a skilful workman completes his work in the shortest manner possible. But it would have been a shorter way if all men had been assumed to the natural sonship than for one natural Son to lead many to the adoption of sons, as is written Gal. 4:5 (cf. Heb. 2:10). Therefore human nature ought to have been assumed by God in all its supposita.

On the contrary, Damascene says (De Fide Orth. iii, 11) that the Son of God "did not assume human nature as a species, nor did He assume all its hypostases."

I answer that, It was unfitting for human nature to be assumed by the Word in all its supposita. First, because the multitude of supposita of human nature, which are natural to it, would have been taken away. For since we must not see any other suppositum in the assumed nature, except the Person assuming, as was said above [3904](A[3]), if there was no human nature except what was assumed, it would follow that there was but one suppositum of human nature, which is the Person assuming. Secondly, because this would have been derogatory to the dignity of the incarnate Son of God, as He is the First-born of many brethren, according to the human nature, even as He is the First-born of all creatures according to the Divine, for then all men would be of equal dignity. Thirdly, because it is fitting that as one Divine suppositum is incarnate, so He should assume one human nature, so that on both sides unity might be found.

Reply to Objection 1: To be assumed belongs to the human nature of itself, because it does not belong to it by reason of a person, as it belongs to the Divine Nature to assume by reason of the Person; not, however, that it belongs to it of itself as if belonging to its essential principles, or as its natural property in which manner it would belong to all its supposita.

Reply to Objection 2: The love of God to men is shown not merely in the assumption of human nature, but especially in what He suffered in human nature for other men, according to Rom. 5:8: "But God commendeth His charity towards us; because when as yet we were sinners . . . Christ died for us," which would not have taken place had He assumed human nature in all its supposita.

Reply to Objection 3: In order to shorten the way, which every skilful workman does, what can be done by one must not be done by many. Hence it was most fitting that by one man all the rest should be saved.

Whether it was fitting for the Son of God to assume human nature of the stock of Adam?

Objection 1: It would seem that it was not fitting for the Son of God to assume human nature of the stock of Adam, for the Apostle says (Heb. 7:26): "For it was fitting that we should have such a high priest . . . separated from sinners." But He would have been still further separated from sinners had He not assumed human nature of the stock of Adam, a sinner. Hence it seems that He ought not to have assumed human nature of the stock of Adam.

Objection 2: Further, in every genus the principle is nobler than what is from the principle. Hence, if He wished to assume human nature, He ought to have assumed it in Adam himself.

Objection 3: Further, the Gentiles were greater sinners than the Jews, as a gloss says on Gal. 2:15: "For we by nature are Jews, and not of the Gentiles, sinners." Hence, if He wished to assume human nature from sinners, He ought rather to have assumed it from the Gentiles than from the stock of Abraham, who was just.

On the contrary, (Lk. 3), the genealogy of our Lord is traced back to Adam.

I answer that, As Augustine says (De Trin. xiii, 18): "God was able to assume human nature elsewhere than from the stock of Adam, who by his sin had fettered the whole human race; yet God judged it better to assume human nature from the vanquished race, and thus to vanquish the enemy of the human race." And this for three reasons: First, because it would seem to belong to justice that he who sinned should make amends; and hence that from the nature which he had corrupted should be assumed that whereby satisfaction was to be made for the whole nature. Secondly, it pertains to man's greater dignity that the conqueror of the devil should spring from the stock conquered by the devil. Thirdly, because God's power is thereby made more manifest, since, from a corrupt and weakened nature, He assumed that which was raised to such might and glory.

Reply to Objection 1: Christ ought to be separated from sinners as regards sin, which He came to overthrow, and not as regards nature which He came to save, and in which "it behooved Him in all things to be made like to His brethren," as the Apostle says (Heb. 2:17). And in this is His innocence the more wonderful, seeing that though assumed from a mass tainted by sin, His nature was endowed with such purity.

Reply to Objection 2: As was said above (ad 1) it behooved Him Who came to take away sins to be separated from sinners as regards sin, to which Adam was subject, whom Christ "brought out of his sin," as is written (Wis. 10:2). For it behooved Him Who came to cleanse all, not to need cleansing Himself; just as in every genus of motion the first mover is immovable as regards that motion, and the first to alter is itself unalterable. Hence it was not fitting that He should assume human nature in Adam himself.

Reply to Objection 3: Since Christ ought especially to be separated from sinners as regards sin, and to possess the highest innocence, it was fitting that between the first sinner and Christ some just men should stand midway, in whom certain forecasts of (His) future holiness should shine forth. And hence, even in the people from whom Christ was to be born, God appointed signs of holiness, which began in Abraham, who was the first to receive the promise of Christ, and circumcision, as a sign that the covenant should be kept, as is written (Gn. 17:11).

OF THE PARTS OF HUMAN NATURE WHICH WERE ASSUMED (FOUR ARTICLES)

We must now consider the assumption of the parts of human nature; and under this head there are four points of inquiry:
(1) Whether the Son of God ought to have assumed a true body?
(2) Whether He ought to have assumed an earthly body, i.e. one of flesh and blood?
(3) Whether He ought to have assumed a soul?
(4) Whether He ought to have assumed an intellect?

Whether the Son of God ought to have assumed a true body?

Objection 1: It would seem that the Son of God did not assume a true body. For it is written (Phil. 2:7), that He was "made in the likeness of men." But what is something in truth is not said to be in the likeness thereof. Therefore the Son of God did not assume a true body.

Objection 2: Further, the assumption of a body in no way diminishes the dignity of the Godhead; for Pope Leo says (Serm. de Nativ.) that "the glorification did not absorb the lesser nature, nor did the assumption lessen the higher." But it pertains to the dignity of God to be altogether separated from bodies. Therefore it seems that by the assumption God was not united to a body.

Objection 3: Further, signs ought to correspond to the realities. But the apparitions of the Old Testament which were signs of the manifestation of Christ were not in a real body, but by visions in the imagination, as is plain from Is. 60:1: "I saw the Lord sitting," etc. Hence it would seem that the apparition of the Son of God in the world was not in a real body, but only in imagination.

On the contrary, Augustine says (Qq. lxxxiii, qu. 13): "If the body of Christ was a phantom, Christ deceived us, and if He deceived us, He is not the Truth. But Christ is the Truth. Therefore His body was not a phantom." Hence it is plain that He assumed a true body.

I answer that, As is said (De Eccles. Dogm. ii). The Son of God was not born in appearance only, as if He had an imaginary body; but His body was real. The proof of this is threefold. First, from the essence of human nature to which it pertains to have a true body. Therefore granted, as already proved ([3905]Q[4], A[1]), that it was fitting for the Son of God to assume human nature, He must consequently have assumed a real body. The second reason is taken from what was done in the mystery of the Incarnation. For if His body was not real but imaginary, He neither underwent a real death, nor of those things which the Evangelists recount of Him, did He do any in very truth, but only in appearance; and hence it would also follow that the real salvation of man has not taken place; since the effect must be proportionate to the cause. The third reason is taken from the dignity of the Person assuming, Whom it did not become to have anything fictitious in His work, since He is the Truth. Hence our Lord Himself deigned to refute this error (Lk. 24:37, 39), when the disciples, "troubled and frighted, supposed that they saw a spirit," and not a true body; wherefore He offered Himself to their touch, saying: "Handle, and see; for a spirit hath not flesh and bones, as you see Me to have."

Reply to Objection 1: This likeness indicates the truth of the human nature in Christ---just as all that truly exist in human nature are said to be like in species---and not a mere imaginary likeness. In proof of this the Apostle subjoins (Phil. 2:8) that He became "obedient unto death, even to the death of the cross"; which would have been impossible, had it been only an imaginary likeness.

Reply to Objection 2: By assuming a true body the dignity of the Son of God is nowise lessened. Hence Augustine [*Fulgentius] says (De Fide ad Petrum ii): "He emptied Himself, taking the form of a servant, that He might become a servant; yet did He not lose the fulness of the form of God." For the Son of God assumed a true body, not so as to become the form of a body, which is repugnant to the Divine simplicity and purity---for this would be to assume a body to the unity of the nature, which is impossible, as is plain from what has been stated above ([3906]Q[2], A[1]): but, the natures remaining distinct, He assumed a body to the unity of Person.

Reply to Objection 3: The figure ought to correspond to the reality as regards the likeness and not as regards the truth of the thing. For if they were alike in all points, it would no longer be a likeness but the reality itself, as Damascene says (De Fide Orth. iii, 26). Hence it was more fitting that the apparitions of the old Testament should be in appearance only, being figures; and that the apparition of the Son of God in the world should be in a real body, being the thing prefigured by these figures. Hence the Apostle says (Col. 2:17): "Which are a shadow of things to come, but the body is Christ's."

Whether the Son of God ought to have assumed a carnal or earthly body?

Objection 1: It would seem that Christ had not a carnal or earthly, but a heavenly body. For the Apostle says (1 Cor. 15:41): "The first man was of the earth, earthy; the second man from heaven, heavenly." But the first man, i.e. Adam, was of the earth as regards his body, as is plain from Gn. 1. Therefore the second man, i.e. Christ, was of heaven as regards the body.

Objection 2: Further, it is said (1 Cor. 15:50): "Flesh and blood shall not [Vulg.: 'cannot'] possess the kingdom of God." But the kingdom of God is in Christ chiefly. Therefore there is no flesh or blood in Him, but rather a heavenly body.

Objection 3: Further, whatever is best is to be attributed to God. But of all bodies a heavenly body is the best. Therefore it behooved Christ to assume such a body.

On the contrary, our Lord says (Lk. 24:39): "A spirit hath not flesh and bones, as you see Me to have." Now flesh and bones are not of the matter of heavenly bodies, but are composed of the inferior elements. Therefore the body of Christ was not a heavenly, but a carnal and earthly body.

I answer that, By the reasons which proved that the body of Christ was not an imaginary one, it may also be shown that it was not a heavenly body. First, because even as the truth of the human nature of Christ would not have been maintained had His body been an imaginary one, such as Manes supposed, so likewise it would not have been maintained if we supposed, as did Valentine, that it was a heavenly body. For since the form of man is a natural thing, it requires determinate matter, to wit, flesh and bones, which must be placed in the definition of man, as is plain from the Philosopher (Metaph. vii, 39). Secondly, because this would lessen the truth of such things as Christ did in the body. For since a heavenly body is impassible and incorruptible, as is proved De Coel. i, 20, if the Son of God had assumed a heavenly body, He would not have truly hungered or thirsted, nor would he have undergone His passion and death. Thirdly, this would have detracted from God's truthfulness. For since the Son of God showed Himself to men, as if He had a carnal and earthly body, the manifestation would have been false, had He had a heavenly body. Hence (De Eccles. Dogm. ii) it is said: "The Son of God was born, taking flesh of the Virgin's body, and not bringing it with Him from heaven."

Reply to Objection 1: Christ is said in two ways to have come down from heaven. First, as regards His Divine Nature; not indeed that the Divine Nature ceased to be in heaven, but inasmuch as He began to be here below in a new way, viz. by His assumed. nature, according to Jn. 3:13: "No man hath ascended into heaven, but He that descended from heaven, the Son of Man, Who is in heaven."

Secondly, as regards His body, not indeed that the very substance of the body of Christ descended from heaven, but that His body was formed by a heavenly power, i.e. by the Holy Ghost. Hence Augustine, explaining the passage quoted, says (Ad Orosium [*Dial. Qq. lxv, qu. 4, work of an unknown author]): "I call Christ a heavenly man because He was not conceived of human seed." And Hilary expounds it in the same way (De Trin. x).

Reply to Objection 2: Flesh and blood are not taken here for the substance of flesh and blood, but for the corruption of flesh, which was not in Christ as far as it was sinful; but as far as it was a punishment; thus, for a time, it was in Christ, that He might carry through the work of our redemption.

Reply to Objection 3: It pertains to the greatest glory of God to have raised a weak and earthly body to such sublimity. Hence in the General Council of Ephesus (P. II, Act. I) we read the saying of St. Theophilus: "Just as the best workmen are esteemed not merely for displaying their skill in precious materials, but very often because by making use of the poorest . . . lay and commonest earth, they show the power of their craft; so the best of all workmen, the Word of God, did not come down to us by taking a heavenly body of some most precious matter, but shewed the greatness of His skill in clay."

Day 253

Whether the Son of God assumed a soul?

Objection 1: It would seem that the Son of God did not assume a soul. For John has said, teaching the mystery of the Incarnation (Jn. 1:14): "The Word was made flesh"---no mention being made of a soul. Now it is not said that "the Word was made flesh" as if changed to flesh, but because He assumed flesh. Therefore He seems not to have assumed a soul.

Objection 2: Further, a soul is necessary to the body, in order to quicken it. But this was not necessary for the body of Christ, as it would seem, for of the Word of God it is written (Ps. 35:10): Lord, "with Thee is the fountain of life." Therefore it would seem altogether superfluous for the soul to be there, when the Word was present. But "God and nature do nothing uselessly," as the Philosopher says (De Coel. i, 32; ii, 56). Therefore the Word would seem not to have assumed a soul.

Objection 3: Further, by the union of soul and body is constituted the common nature, which is the human species. But "in the Lord Jesus Christ we are not to look for a common species," as Damascene says (De Fide Orth. iii, 3). Therefore He did not assume a soul.

On the contrary, Augustine says (De Agone Christ. xxi): "Let us not hearken to such as say that only a human body was assumed by the Word of God; and take 'the Word was made flesh' to mean that the man had no soul nor any other part of a man, save flesh."

I answer that, As Augustine says (De Haeres. 69,55), it was first of all the opinion of Arius and then of Apollinaris that the Son of God assumed only flesh, without a soul, holding that the Word took the place of a soul to the body. And consequently it followed that there were not two natures in Christ, but only one; for from a soul and body one human nature is constituted. But this opinion cannot hold, for three reasons. First, because it is counter to the authority of Scripture, in which our Lord makes mention of His soul, Mat. 26:38: "My soul is sorrowful even unto death"; and Jn. 10:18: "I have power to lay down My soul [animam meam: Douay: 'My life']." But to this Apollinaris replied that in these words soul is taken metaphorically, in which way mention is made in the Old Testament of the soul of God (Is. 1:14): "My soul hateth your new moons and your solemnities." But, as Augustine says (Qq. lxxxiii, qu. 80), the Evangelists relate how Jesus wondered, was angered, sad, and hungry. Now these show that He had a true soul, just as that He ate, slept and was weary shows that He had a true human body: otherwise, if these things are a metaphor, because the like are said of God in the Old Testament, the trustworthiness of the Gospel story is undermined. For it is one thing that things were foretold in a figure, and another that historical events were related in very truth by the Evangelists. Secondly, this error lessens the utility of the Incarnation, which is man's liberation. For Augustine [*Vigilius Tapsensis] argues thus (Contra Felician. xiii): "If the Son of God in taking flesh passed over the soul, either He knew its sinlessness, and trusted it did not need a remedy; or He considered it unsuitable to Him, and did not bestow on it the boon of redemption; or He reckoned it altogether incurable, and was unable to heal it; or He cast it off as worthless and seemingly unfit for any use. Now two of these reasons imply a blasphemy against God. For how shall we call Him omnipotent, if He is unable to heal what is beyond hope? Or God of all, if He has not made our soul. And as regards the other two reasons, in one the cause of the soul is ignored, and in the other no place is given to merit. Is He to be considered to understand the cause of the soul, Who seeks to separate it from the sin of wilful transgression, enabled as it is to receive the law by the endowment of the habit of reason? Or how can His generosity be known to any one who says it was despised on account of its ignoble sinfulness? If you look at its origin, the substance of the soul is more precious than the body: but if at the sin of transgression, on account of its intelligence it is worse than the body. Now I know and declare that Christ is perfect wisdom, nor have I any doubt that He is most loving; and because of the first of these He did not despise what was better and more capable of prudence; and because of the second He protected what was most wounded." Thirdly, this position is against the truth of the Incarnation. For flesh and the other parts of man receive their species through the soul. Hence, if the soul is absent, there are no bones nor flesh, except equivocally, as is plain from the Philosopher (De Anima ii, 9; Metaph. vii, 34).

Reply to Objection 1: When we say, "The Word was made flesh," "flesh" is taken for the whole man, as if we were to say, "The Word was made man," as Is. 40:5: "All flesh together shall see that the mouth of the Lord hath spoken." And the whole man is signified by flesh, because, as is said in the authority quoted, the Son of God became visible by flesh; hence it is subjoined: "And we saw His glory." Or because, as Augustine says (Qq. lxxxiii, qu. 80), "in all that union the Word is the highest, and flesh the last and lowest. Hence, wishing to commend the love of God's humility to us, the Evangelist mentioned the Word and flesh, leaving the soul on one side, since it is less than the Word and nobler than flesh." Again, it was reasonable to mention flesh, which, as being farther away from the Word, was less assumable, as it would seem.

Reply to Objection 2: The Word is the fountain of life, as the first effective cause of life; but the soul is the principle of the life of the body, as its form. Now the form is the effect of the agent. Hence from the presence of the Word it might rather have been concluded that the body was animated, just as from the presence of fire it may be concluded that the body, in which fire adheres, is warm.

Reply to Objection 3: It is not unfitting, indeed it is necessary to say that in Christ there was a nature which was constituted by the soul coming to the body. But Damascene denied that in Jesus Christ there was a common species, i.e. a third something resulting from the Godhead and the humanity.

Whether the Son of God assumed a human mind or intellect?

Objection 1: It would seem that the Son of God did not assume a human mind or intellect. For where a thing is present, its image is not required. But man is made to God's image, as regards his mind, as Augustine says (De Trin. xiv, 3,6). Hence, since in Christ there was the presence of the Divine Word itself, there was no need of a human mind.

Objection 2: Further, the greater light dims the lesser. But the Word of God, Who is "the light, which enlighteneth every man that cometh into this world," as is written Jn. 1:9, is compared to the mind as the greater light to the lesser; since our mind is a light, being as it were a lamp enkindled by the First Light (Prov. 20:27): "The spirit of a man is the lamp of the Lord." Therefore in Christ Who is the Word of God, there is no need of a human mind.

Objection 3: Further, the assumption of human nature by the Word of God is called His Incarnation. But the intellect or human mind is nothing carnal, either in its substance or in its act. for it is not the act of a body, as is proved De Anima iii, 6. Hence it would seem that the Son of God did not assume a human mind.

On the contrary, Augustine [*Fulgentius] says (De Fide ad Petrum xiv): "Firmly hold and nowise doubt that Christ the Son of God has true flesh and a rational soul of the same kind as ours, since of His flesh He says (Lk. 24:39): 'Handle, and see; for a spirit hath not flesh and bones, as you see Me to have.' And He proves that He has a soul, saying (Jn. 10:17): 'I lay down My soul [Douay: 'life'] that I may take it again.' And He proves that He has an intellect, saying (Mat. 11:29): 'Learn of Me, because I am meek and humble of heart.' And God says of Him by the prophet (Is. 52:13): 'Behold my servant shall understand.'"

I answer that, As Augustine says (De Haeres. 49,50), "the Apollinarists thought differently from the Catholic Church concerning the soul of Christ, saying with the Arians, that Christ took flesh alone, without a soul; and on being overcome on this point by the Gospel witness, they went on to say that the mind was wanting to Christ's soul, but that the Word supplied its place." But this position is refuted by the same arguments as the preceding. First, because it runs counter to the Gospel story, which relates how He marveled (as is plain from Mat. 8:10). Now marveling cannot be without reason, since it implies the collation of effect and cause, i.e. inasmuch as when we see an effect and are ignorant of its cause, we seek to know it, as is said Metaph. i, 2. Secondly, it is inconsistent with the purpose of the Incarnation, which is the justification of man from sin. For the human soul is not capable of sin nor of justifying grace except through the mind. Hence it was especially necessary for the mind to be assumed. Hence Damascene says (De Fide Orth. iii, 6) that "the Word of God assumed a body and an intellectual and rational soul," and adds afterwards: "The whole was united to the whole, that He might bestow salvation on me wholly; for what was not assumed is not curable." Thirdly, it is against the truth of the Incarnation. For since the body is proportioned to the soul as matter to its proper form, it is not truly human flesh if it is not perfected by human, i.e. a rational soul. And hence if Christ had had a soul without a mind, He would not have had true human flesh, but irrational flesh, since our soul differs from an animal soul by the mind alone. Hence Augustine says (Qq. lxxxiii, qu. 80) that from this error it would have followed that the Son of God "took an animal with the form of a human body," which, again, is against the Divine truth, which cannot suffer any fictitious untruth.

Reply to Objection 1: Where a thing is by its presence, its image is not required to supply the place of the thing, as where the emperor is the soldiers do not pay homage to his image. Yet the image of a thing is required together with its presence, that it may be perfected by the presence of the thing, just as the image in the wax is perfected by the impression of the seal, and as the image of man is reflected in the mirror by his presence. Hence in order to perfect the human mind it was necessary that the Word should unite it to Himself.

Reply to Objection 2: The greater light dims the lesser light of another luminous body; but it does not dim, rather it perfects the light of the body illuminated---at the presence of the sun the light of the stars is put out, but the light of the air is perfected. Now the intellect or mind of man is, as it were, a light lit up by the light of the Divine Word; and hence by the presence of the Word the mind of man is perfected rather than overshadowed.

Reply to Objection 3: Although the intellective power is not the act of a body, nevertheless the essence of the human soul, which is the form of the body, requires that it should be more noble, in order that it may have the power of understanding; and hence it is necessary that a better disposed body should correspond to it.

OF THE ORDER OF ASSUMPTION (SIX ARTICLES)
We must now consider the order of the foregoing assumption, and under this head there are six points of inquiry:
(1) Whether the Son of God assumed flesh through the medium of the soul?
(2) Whether He assumed the soul through the medium of the spirit or mind?
(3) Whether the soul was assumed previous to the flesh?
(4) Whether the flesh of Christ was assumed by the Word previous to being united to the soul?
(5) Whether the whole human nature was assumed through the medium of the parts?
(6) Whether it was assumed through the medium of grace?

Whether the Son of God assumed flesh through the medium of the soul?
Objection 1: It would seem that the Son of God did not assume flesh through the medium of the soul. For the mode in which the Son of God is united to human nature and its parts, is more perfect than the mode whereby He is in all creatures. But He is in all creatures immediately by essence, power and presence. Much more, therefore, is the Son of God united to flesh without the medium of the soul.

Objection 2: Further, the soul and flesh are united to the Word of God in unity of hypostasis or person. But the body pertains immediately to the human hypostasis or person, even as the soul. Indeed, the human body, since it is matter, would rather seem to be nearer the hypostasis than the soul, which is a form, since the principle of individuation, which is implied in the word "hypostasis," would seem to be matter. Hence the Son of God did not assume flesh through the medium of the soul.

Objection 3: Further, take away the medium and you separate what were joined by the medium; for example, if the superficies be removed color would leave the body, since it adheres to the body through the medium of the superficies. But though the soul was separated from the body by death, yet there still remained the union of the Word to the flesh, as will be shown ([3907]Q[50], AA[2],3). Hence the Word was not joined to flesh through the medium of the soul.

On the contrary, Augustine says (Ep. ad Volusianum cxxxvi): "The greatness of the Divine power fitted to itself a rational soul, and through it a human body, so as to raise the whole man to something higher."

I answer that, A medium is in reference to a beginning and an end. Hence as beginning and end imply order, so also does a medium. Now there is a twofold order: one, of time; the other, of nature. But in the mystery of the Incarnation nothing is said to be a medium in the order of time, for the Word of God united the whole human nature to Himself at the same time, as will appear ([3908]Q[30], A[3]). An order of nature between things may be taken in two ways: first, as regards rank of dignity, as we say the angels are midway between man and God; secondly, as regards the idea of causality, as we say a cause is midway between the first cause and the last effect. And this second order follows the first to some extent; for as Dionysius says (Coel. Hier. xiii), God acts upon the more remote substances through the less remote. Hence if we consider the rank of dignity, the soul is found to be midway between God and flesh; and in this way it may be said that the Son of God united flesh to Himself, through the medium of the soul. But even as regards the second order of causality the soul is to some extent the cause of flesh being united to the Son of God. For the flesh would not have been assumable, except by its relation to the rational soul, through which it becomes human flesh. For it was said above ([3909]Q[4], A[1]) that human nature was assumable before all others.

Reply to Objection 1: We may consider a twofold order between creatures and God: the first is by reason of creatures being caused by God and depending on Him as on the principle of their being; and thus on account of the infinitude of His power God touches each thing immediately, by causing and preserving it, and so it is that God is in all things by essence, presence and power. But the second order is by reason of things being directed to God as to their end; and it is here that there is a medium between the creature and God, since lower creatures are directed to God by higher, as Dionysius says (Eccl. Hier. v); and to this order pertains the assumption of human nature by the Word of God, Who is the term of the assumption; and hence it is united to flesh through the soul.

Reply to Objection 2: If the hypostasis of the Word of God were constituted simply by human nature, it would follow that the body was nearest to it, since it is matter which is the principle of individuation; even as the soul, being the specific form, would be nearer the human nature. But because the hypostasis of the Word is prior to and more exalted than the human nature, the more exalted any part of the human nature is, the nearer it is to the hypostasis of the Word. And hence the soul is nearer the Word of God than the body is.

Reply to Objection 3: Nothing prevents one thing being the cause of the aptitude and congruity of another, and yet if it be taken away the other remains; because although a thing's becoming may depend on another, yet when it is in being it no longer depends on it, just as a friendship brought about by some other may endure when the latter has gone; or as a woman is taken in marriage on account of her beauty, which makes a woman's fittingness for the marriage tie, yet when her beauty passes away, the marriage tie still remains. So likewise, when the soul was separated, the union of the Word with flesh still endured.

Whether the Son of God assumed a soul through the medium of the spirit or mind?

Objection 1: It would seem that the Son of God did not assume a soul through the medium of the spirit or mind. For nothing is a medium between itself and another. But the spirit is nothing else in essence but the soul itself, as was said above ([3910]FP, Q[77], A[1], ad 1). Therefore the Son of God did not assume a soul through the medium of the spirit or mind.

Objection 2: Further, what is the medium of the assumption is itself more assumable. But the spirit or mind is not more assumable than the soul; which is plain from the fact that angelic spirits are not assumable, as was said above ([3911]Q[4], A[1]). Hence it seems that the Son of God did not assume a soul through the medium of the spirit.

Objection 3: Further, that which comes later is assumed by the first through the medium of what comes before. But the soul implies the very essence, which naturally comes before its power---the mind. Therefore it would seem that the Son of God did not assume a soul through the medium of the spirit or mind.

On the contrary, Augustine says (De Agone Christ. xviii): "The invisible and unchangeable Truth took a soul by means of the spirit, and a body by means of the soul."

I answer that, As stated above [3912](A[1]), the Son of God is said to have assumed flesh through the medium of the soul, on account of the order of dignity, and the congruity of the assumption. Now both these may be applied to the intellect, which is called the spirit, if we compare it with the other parts of the soul. For the soul is assumed congruously only inasmuch as it has a capacity for God, being in His likeness: which is in respect of the mind that is called the spirit, according to Eph. 4:23: "Be renewed in the spirit of your mind." So, too, the intellect is the highest and noblest of the parts of the soul, and the most like to God, and hence Damascene says (De Fide Orth. iii, 6) that "the Word of God is united to flesh through the medium of the intellect; for the intellect is the purest part of the soul, God Himself being an intellect."

Reply to Objection 1: Although the intellect is not distinct from the soul in essence, it is distinct from the other parts of the soul as a power; and it is in this way that it has the nature of a medium.

Reply to Objection 2: Fitness for assumption is wanting to the angelic spirits, not from any lack of dignity, but because of the irremediableness of their fall, which cannot be said of the human spirit, as is clear from what has been said above ([3913]FP, Q[62], A[8]; [3914]FP, Q[64], A[2]).

Reply to Objection 3: The soul, between which and the Word of God the intellect is said to be a medium, does not stand for the essence of the soul, which is common to all the powers, but for the lower powers, which are common to every soul.

Whether the soul was assumed before the flesh by the Son of God?

Objection 1: It would seem that the soul of Christ was assumed before the flesh by the Word. For the Son of God assumed flesh through the medium of the soul, as was said above [3915](A[1]). Now the medium is reached before the end. Therefore the Son of God assumed the soul before the body.

Objection 2: Further, the soul of Christ is nobler than the angels, according to Ps. 96:8: "Adore Him, all you His angels." But the angels were created in the beginning, as was said above ([3916]FP, Q[46], A[3]). Therefore the soul of Christ also (was created in the beginning). But it was not created before it was assumed, for Damascene says (De Fide Orth. iii, 2,3,9), that "neither the soul nor the body of Christ ever had any hypostasis save the hypostasis of the Word." Therefore it would seem that the soul was assumed before the flesh, which was conceived in the womb of the Virgin.

Objection 3: Further, it is written (Jn. 1:14): "We saw Him [Vulg.: 'His glory'] full of grace and truth," and it is added afterwards that "of His fulness we have all received" (Jn. 1:16), i.e. all the faithful of all time, as Chrysostom expounds it (Hom. xiii in Joan.).

Now this could not have been unless the soul of Christ had all fulness of grace and truth before all the saints, who were from the beginning of the world, for the cause is not subsequent to the effect. Hence since the fulness of grace and truth was in the soul of Christ from union with the Word, according to what is written in the same place: "We saw His glory, the glory as it were of the Only-begotten of the Father, full of grace and truth," it would seem in consequence that from the beginning of the world the soul of Christ was assumed by the Word of God.

On the contrary, Damascene says (De Fide Orth. iv, 6): "The intellect was not, as some untruthfully say, united to the true God, and henceforth called Christ, before the Incarnation which was of the Virgin."

I answer that, Origen (Peri Archon i, 7,8; ii, 8) maintained that all souls, amongst which he placed Christ's soul, were created in the beginning. But this is not fitting, if we suppose that it was first of all created, but not at once joined to the Word, since it would follow that this soul once had its proper subsistence without the Word; and thus, since it was assumed by the Word, either the union did not take place in the subsistence, or the pre-existing subsistence of the soul was corrupted. So likewise it is not fitting to suppose that this soul was united to the Word from the beginning, and that it afterwards became incarnate in the womb of the Virgin; for thus His soul would not seem to be of the same nature as ours, which are created at the same time that they are infused into bodies. Hence Pope Leo says (Ep. ad Julian. xxxv) that "Christ's flesh was not of a different nature to ours, nor was a different soul infused into it in the beginning than into other men."

Reply to Objection 1: As was said above [3917](A[1]), the soul of Christ is said to be the medium in the union of the flesh with the Word, in the order of nature; but it does not follow from this that it was the medium in the order of time.

Reply to Objection 2: As Pope Leo says in the same Epistle, Christ's soul excels our soul "not by diversity of genus, but by sublimity of power"; for it is of the same genus as our souls, yet excels even the angels in "fulness of grace and truth." But the mode of creation is in harmony with the generic property of the soul; and since it is the form of the body, it is consequently created at the same time that it is infused into and united with the body; which does not happen to angels, since they are substances entirely free from matter.

Reply to Objection 3: Of the fulness of Christ all men receive according to the faith they have in Him; for it is written (Rom. 3:22) that "the justice of God is by faith of Jesus Christ unto all and upon all them that believe in Him." Now just as we believe in Him as already born; so the ancients believed in Him as about to be born, since "having the same spirit of faith . . . we also believe," as it is written (2 Cor. 4:13). But the faith which is in Christ has the power of justifying by reason of the purpose of the grace of God, according to Rom. 4:5: "But to him that worketh not, yet believeth in Him that justifieth the ungodly, his faith is reputed to justice according to the purpose of the grace of God." Hence because this purpose is eternal, there is nothing to hinder some from being justified by the faith of Jesus Christ, even before His soul was full of grace and truth.

Whether the flesh of Christ was assumed by the Word before being united to the soul?

Objection 1: It would seem that the flesh of Christ was assumed by the Word before being united to the soul. For Augustine [*Fulgentius] says (De Fide ad Petrum xviii): "Most firmly hold, and nowise doubt that the flesh of Christ was not conceived in the womb of the Virgin without the Godhead before it was assumed by the Word." But the flesh of Christ would seem to have been conceived before being united to the rational soul, because matter or disposition is prior to the completive form in order of generation. Therefore the flesh of Christ was assumed before being united to the soul.

Objection 2: Further, as the soul is a part of human nature, so is the body. But the human soul in Christ had no other principle of being than in other men, as is clear from the authority of Pope Leo, quoted above (A[3]). Therefore it would seem that the body of Christ had no other principle of being than we have. But in us the body is begotten before the rational soul comes to it. Therefore it was the same in Christ; and thus the flesh was assumed by the Word before being united to the soul.

Objection 3: Further, as is said (De Causis), the first cause excels the second in bringing about the effect, and precedes it in its union with the effect. But the soul of Christ is compared to the Word as a second cause to a first. Hence the Word was united to the flesh before it was to the soul.

On the contrary, Damascene says (De Fide Orth. iii, 2): "At the same time the Word of God was made flesh, and flesh was united to a rational and intellectual soul." Therefore the union of the Word with the flesh did not precede the union with the soul.

I answer that, The human flesh is assumable by the Word on account of the order which it has to the rational soul as to its proper form. Now it has not this order before the rational soul comes to it, because when any matter becomes proper to any form, at the same time it receives that form; hence the alteration is terminated at the same instant in which the substantial form is introduced. And hence it is that the flesh ought not to have been assumed before it was human flesh; and this happened when the rational soul came to it. Therefore since the soul was not assumed before the flesh, inasmuch as it is against the nature of the soul to be before it is united to the body, so likewise the flesh ought not to have been assumed before the soul, since it is not human flesh before it has a rational soul.

Reply to Objection 1: Human flesh depends upon the soul for its being; and hence, before the coming of the soul, there is no human flesh, but there may be a disposition towards human flesh. Yet in the conception of Christ, the Holy Ghost, Who is an agent of infinite might, disposed the matter and brought it to its perfection at the same time.

Reply to Objection 2: The form actually gives the species; but the matter in itself is in potentiality to the species. And hence it would be against the nature of a form to exist before the specific nature. And therefore the dissimilarity between our origin and Christ's origin, inasmuch as we are conceived before being animated, and Christ's flesh is not, is by reason of what precedes the perfection of the nature, viz. that we are conceived from the seed of man, and Christ is not. But a difference which would be with reference to the origin of the soul, would bespeak a diversity of nature.

Reply to Objection 3: The Word of God is understood to be united to the flesh before the soul by the common mode whereby He is in the rest of creatures by essence, power, and presence. Yet I say "before," not in time, but in nature; for the flesh is understood as a being, which it has from the Word, before it is understood as animated, which it has from the soul. But by the personal union we understand the flesh as united to the soul before it is united to the Word, for it is from its union with the soul that it is capable of being united to the Word in Person; especially since a person is found only in the rational nature

Whether the whole human nature was assumed through the medium of the parts?

Objection 1: It would seem that the Son of God assumed the whole human nature through the medium of its parts. For Augustine says (De Agone Christ. xviii) that "the invisible and unchangeable Truth assumed the soul through the medium of the spirit, and the body through the medium of the soul, and in this way the whole man." But the spirit, soul, and body are parts of the whole man. Therefore He assumed all, through the medium of the parts.

Objection 2: Further, the Son of God assumed flesh through the medium of the soul because the soul is more like to God than the body. But the parts of human nature, since they are simpler than the body, would seem to be more like to God, Who is most simple, than the whole. Therefore He assumed the whole through the medium of the parts.

Objection 3: Further, the whole results from the union of parts. But the union is taken to be the term of the assumption, and the parts are presupposed to the assumption. Therefore He assumed the whole by the parts.

On the contrary, Damascene says (De Fide Orth. iii, 16): "In our Lord Jesus Christ we do not behold parts of parts, but such as are immediately joined, i.e. the Godhead and the manhood." Now the humanity is a whole, which is composed of soul and body, as parts. Therefore the Son of God assumed the parts through the medium of the whole.

I answer that, When anything is said to be a medium in the assumption of the Incarnation, we do not signify order of time, because the assumption of the whole and the parts was simultaneous. For it has been shown ([3918]AA[3] ,4) that the soul and body were mutually united at the same time in order to constitute the human nature of the Word. But it is order of nature that is signified. Hence by what is prior in nature, that is assumed which is posterior in nature. Now a thing is prior in nature in two ways: First on the part of the agent, secondly on the part of the matter; for these two causes precede the thing. On the part of the agent---that is simply first, which is first included in his intention; but that is relatively first, with which his operation begins---and this because the intention is prior to the operation. On the part of the matter---that is first which exists first in the transmutation of the matter. Now in the Incarnation the order depending on the agent must be particularly considered, because, as Augustine says (Ep. ad Volusianum cxxxvii), "in such things the whole reason of the deed is the power of the doer." But it is manifest that, according to the intention of the doer, what is complete is prior to what is incomplete, and, consequently, the whole to the parts. Hence it must be said that the Word of God assumed the parts of human nature, through the medium of the whole; for even as He assumed the body on account of its relation to the rational soul, so likewise He assumed a body and soul on account of their relation to human nature.

Reply to Objection 1: From these words nothing may be gathered, except that the Word, by assuming the parts of human nature, assumed the whole human nature. And thus the assumption of parts is prior in the order of the intellect, if we consider the operation, but not in order of time; whereas the assumption of the nature is prior if we consider the intention: and this is to be simply first, as was said above.

Reply to Objection 2: God is so simple that He is also most perfect; and hence the whole is more like to God than the parts, inasmuch as it is more perfect.

Reply to Objection 3: It is a personal union wherein the assumption is terminated, not a union of nature, which springs from a conjunction of parts.

Whether the human nature was assumed through the medium of grace?

Objection 1: It would seem that the Son of God assumed human nature through the medium of grace. For by grace we are united to God. But the human nature in Christ was most closely united to God. Therefore the union took place by grace.

Objection 2: Further, as the body lives by the soul, which is its perfection, so does the soul by grace. But the human nature was fitted for the assumption by the soul. Therefore the Son of God assumed the soul through the medium of grace.

Objection 3: Further, Augustine says (De Trin. xv, 11) that the incarnate Word is like our spoken word. But our word is united to our speech by means of "breathing" [spiritus]. Therefore the Word of God is united to flesh by means of the Holy Spirit, and hence by means of grace, which is attributed to the Holy Spirit, according to 1 Cor. 12:4: "Now there are diversities of graces, but the same Spirit."

On the contrary, Grace is an accident in the soul, as was shown above ([3919]FS, Q[110], A[2]). Now the union of the Word with human nature took place in the subsistence, and not accidentally, as was shown above (Q[2], A[6]). Therefore the human nature was not assumed by means of grace.

I answer that, In Christ there was the grace of union and habitual grace. Therefore grace cannot be taken to be the medium of the assumption of the human nature, whether we speak of the grace of union or of habitual grace. For the grace of union is the personal being that is given gratis from above to the human nature in the Person of the Word, and is the term of the assumption. Whereas the habitual grace pertaining to the spiritual holiness of the man is an effect following the union, according to Jn. 1:14: "We saw His glory . . . as it were of the Only-begotten of the Father, full of grace and truth"---by which we are given to understand that because this Man (as a result of the union) is the Only-begotten of the Father, He is full of grace and truth. But if by grace we understand the will of God doing or bestowing something gratis, the union took place by grace, not as a means, but as the efficient cause.

Reply to Objection 1: Our union with God is by operation, inasmuch as we know and love Him; and hence this union is by habitual grace, inasmuch as a perfect operation proceeds from a habit. Now the union of the human nature with the Word of God is in personal being, which depends not on any habit, but on the nature itself.

Reply to Objection 2: The soul is the substantial perfection of the body; grace is but an accidental perfection of the soul. Hence grace cannot ordain the soul to personal union, which is not accidental, as the soul ordains the body.

Reply to Objection 3: Our word is united to our speech, by means of breathing [spiritus], not as a formal medium, but as a moving medium. For from the word conceived within, the breathing proceeds, from which the speech is formed. And similarly from the eternal Word proceeds the Holy Spirit, Who formed the body of Christ, as will be shown ([3920]Q[32], A[1]). But it does not follow from this that the grace of the Holy Spirit is the formal medium in the aforesaid union.

Day 254

OF THE GRACE OF CHRIST AS AN INDIVIDUAL MAN (THIRTEEN ARTICLES)
We must now consider such things as were co-assumed by the Son of God in human nature; and first what belongs to perfection; secondly, what belongs to defect.
Concerning the first, there are three points of consideration: (1) The grace of Christ; (2) His knowledge; (3) His power.
With regard to His grace we must consider two things: (1) His grace as He is an individual man; (2) His grace as He is the Head of the Church. Of the grace of union we have already spoken ([3921]Q[2]).
Under the first head there are thirteen points of inquiry:
(1) Whether in the soul of Christ there was any habitual grace?
(2) Whether in Christ there were virtues?
(3) Whether He had faith?
(4) Whether He had hope?
(5) Whether in Christ there were the gifts?
(6) Whether in Christ there was the gift of fear?
(7) Whether in Christ there were any gratuitous graces?
(8) Whether in Christ there was prophecy?
(9) Whether there was the fulness of grace in Him?
(10) Whether such fulness was proper to Christ?
(11) Whether the grace of Christ was infinite?
(12) Whether it could have been increased?
(13) How this grace stood towards the union?

Whether in the Soul of Christ there was any habitual grace?
Objection 1: It would seem there was no habitual grace in the soul assumed by the Word. For grace is a certain partaking of the Godhead by the rational creature, according to 2 Pet. 1:4: "By Whom He hath given us most great and precious promises, that by these you may be made partakers of the Divine Nature." Now Christ is God not by participation, but in truth. Therefore there was no habitual grace in Him.
Objection 2: Further, grace is necessary to man, that he may operate well, according to 1 Cor. 15:10: "I have labored more abundantly than all they; yet not I, but the grace of God with me"; and in order that he may reach eternal life, according to Rom. 6:23: "The grace of God (is) life everlasting." Now the inheritance of everlasting life was due to Christ by the mere fact of His being the natural Son of God; and by the fact of His being the Word, by Whom all things were made, He had the power of doing all things well. Therefore His human nature needed no further grace beyond union with the Word.
Objection 3: Further, what operates as an instrument does not need a habit for its own operations, since habits are rooted in the principal agent. Now the human nature in Christ was "as the instrument of the Godhead," as Damascene says (De Fide Orth. iii, 15). Therefore there was no need of habitual grace in Christ.
On the contrary, It is written (Is. 11:2): "The Spirit of the Lord shall rest upon Him"---which (Spirit), indeed, is said to be in man by habitual grace, as was said above ([3922]FP, Q[8], A[3]; [3923]FP, Q[43], AA[3],6). Therefore there was habitual grace in Christ.
I answer that, It is necessary to suppose habitual grace in Christ for three reasons. First, on account of the union of His soul with the Word of God. For the nearer any recipient is to an inflowing cause, the more does it partake of its influence. Now the influx of grace is from God, according to Ps. 83:12: "The Lord will give grace and glory." And hence it was most fitting that His soul should receive the influx of Divine grace. Secondly, on account of the dignity of this soul, whose operations were to attain so closely to God by knowledge and love, to which it is necessary for human nature to be raised by grace. Thirdly, on account of the relation of Christ to the human race. For Christ, as man, is the "Mediator of God and men," as is written, 1 Tim. 2:5; and hence it behooved Him to have grace which would overflow upon others, according to Jn. 1:16: "And of His fulness we have all received, and grace for grace."
Reply to Objection 1: Christ is the true God in Divine Person and Nature. Yet because together with unity of person there remains distinction of natures, as stated above ([3924]Q[2], AA[1],2), the soul of Christ. is not essentially Divine. Hence it behooves it to be Divine by participation, which is by grace.
Reply to Objection 2: To Christ, inasmuch as He is the natural Son of God, is due an eternal inheritance, which is the uncreated beatitude through the uncreated act of knowledge and love of God, i.e. the same whereby the Father knows and loves Himself. Now the soul was not capable of this act, on account of the difference of natures. Hence it behooved it to attain to God by a created act of fruition which could not be without grace. Likewise, inasmuch as He was the Word of God, He had the power of doing all things well by the Divine operation. And because it is necessary to admit a human operation, distinct from the Divine operation, as will be shown ([3925]Q[19], A[1]), it was necessary for Him to have habitual grace, whereby this operation might be perfect in Him.
Reply to Objection 3: The humanity of Christ is the instrument of the Godhead---not, indeed, an inanimate instrument, which nowise acts, but is merely acted upon; but an instrument animated by a rational soul, which is so acted upon as to act. And hence the nature of the action demanded that he should have habitual grace.

Whether in Christ there were virtues?

Objection 1: It would seem that in Christ there were no virtues. For Christ had the plenitude of grace. Now grace is sufficient for every good act, according to 2 Cor. 12:9: "My grace is sufficient for thee." Therefore there were no virtues in Christ.

Objection 2: Further, according to the Philosopher (Ethic. vii, 1), virtue is contrasted with a "certain heroic or godlike habit" which is attributed to godlike men. But this belongs chiefly to Christ. Therefore Christ had not virtues, but something higher than virtue.

Objection 3: Further, as was said above ([3926]FS, Q[65], AA[1],2), all the virtues are bound together. But it was not becoming for Christ to have all the virtues, as is clear in the case of liberality and magnificence, for these have to do with riches, which Christ spurned, according to Mat. 8:20: "The Son of man hath not where to lay His head." Temperance and continence also regard wicked desires, from which Christ was free. Therefore Christ had not the virtues.

On the contrary, on Ps. 1:2, "But His will is in the law of the Lord," a gloss says: "This refers to Christ, Who is full of all good." But a good quality of the mind is a virtue. Therefore Christ was full of all virtue.

I answer that, As was said above ([3927]FS, Q[110], AA[3],4), as grace regards the essence of the soul, so does virtue regard its power. Hence it is necessary that as the powers of the soul flow from its essence, so do the virtues flow from grace. Now the more perfect a principle is, the more it impresses its effects. Hence, since the grace of Christ was most perfect, there flowed from it, in consequence, the virtues which perfect the several powers of the soul for all the soul's acts; and thus Christ had all the virtues.

Reply to Objection 1: Grace suffices a man for all whereby he is ordained to beatitude; nevertheless, it effects some of these by itself---as to make him pleasing to God, and the like; and some others through the medium of the virtues which proceed from grace.

Reply to Objection 2: A heroic or godlike habit only differs from virtue commonly so called by a more perfect mode, inasmuch as one is disposed to good in a higher way than is common to all. Hence it is not hereby proved that Christ had not the virtues, but that He had them most perfectly beyond the common mode. In this sense Plotinus gave to a certain sublime degree of virtue the name of "virtue of the purified soul" (cf. [3928]FS, Q[61] , A[5]).

Reply to Objection 3: Liberality and magnificence are praiseworthy in regard to riches, inasmuch as anyone does not esteem wealth to the extent of wishing to retain it, so as to forego what ought to be done. But he esteems them least who wholly despises them, and casts them aside for love of perfection. And hence by altogether contemning all riches, Christ showed the highest kind of liberality and magnificence; although He also performed the act of liberality, as far as it became Him, by causing to be distributed to the poor what was given to Himself. Hence, when our Lord said to Judas (Jn. 13:21), "That which thou dost do quickly," the disciples understood our Lord to have ordered him to give something to the poor. But Christ had no evil desires whatever, as will be shown ([3929]Q[15], AA[1],2); yet He was not thereby prevented from having temperance, which is the more perfect in man, as he is without evil desires. Hence, according to the Philosopher (Ethic. vii, 9), the temperate man differs from the continent in this---that the temperate has not the evil desires which the continent suffers. Hence, taking continence in this sense, as the Philosopher takes it, Christ, from the very fact that He had all virtue, had not continence, since it is not a virtue, but something less than virtue.

Whether in Christ there was faith?

Objection 1: It would seem that there was faith in Christ. For faith is a nobler virtue than the moral virtues, e.g. temperance and liberality. Now these were in Christ, as stated above [3930](A[2]). Much more, therefore, was there faith in Him.

Objection 2: Further, Christ did not teach virtues which He had not Himself, according to Acts 1:1: "Jesus began to do and to teach." But of Christ it is said (Heb. 12:2) that He is "the author and finisher of our faith." Therefore there was faith in Him before all others.

Objection 3: Further, everything imperfect is excluded from the blessed. But in the blessed there is faith; for on Rom. 1:17, "the justice of God is revealed therein from faith to faith," a gloss says: "From the faith of words and hope to the faith of things and sight." Therefore it would seem that in Christ also there was faith, since it implies nothing imperfect.

On the contrary, It is written (Heb. 11:1): "Faith is the evidence of things that appear not." But there was nothing that did not appear to Christ, according to what Peter said to Him (Jn. 21:17): "Thou knowest all things." Therefore there was no faith in Christ.

I answer that, As was said above ([3931]SS, Q[1], A[4]), the object of faith is a Divine thing not seen. Now the habit of virtue, as every other habit, takes its species from the object. Hence, if we deny that the Divine thing was not seen, we exclude the very essence of faith. Now from the first moment of His conception Christ saw God's Essence fully, as will be made clear (Q[34], A[1]). Hence there could be no faith in Him.

Reply to Objection 1: Faith is a nobler virtue than the moral virtues, seeing that it has to do with nobler matter; nevertheless, it implies a certain defect with regard to that matter; and this defect was not in Christ. And hence there could be no faith in Him, although the moral virtues were in Him, since in their nature they imply no defect with regard to their matter.

Reply to Objection 2: The merit of faith consists in this---that man through obedience assents to what things he does not see, according to Rom. 1:5: "For obedience to the faith in all nations for His name." Now Christ had most perfect obedience to God, according to Phil. 2:8: "Becoming obedient unto death." And hence He taught nothing pertaining to merit which He did not fulfil more perfectly Himself.

Reply to Objection 3: As a gloss says in the same place, faith is that "whereby such things as are not seen are believed." But faith in things seen is improperly so called, and only after a certain similitude with regard to the certainty and firmness of the assent.

Whether in Christ there was hope?

Objection 1: It would seem that there was hope in Christ. For it is said in the Person of Christ (Ps. 30:1): "In Thee, O Lord, have I hoped." But the virtue of hope is that whereby a man hopes in God. Therefore the virtue of hope was in Christ.

Objection 2: Further, hope is the expectation of the bliss to come, as was shown above ([3932]SS, Q[17], A[5], ad 3). But Christ awaited something pertaining to bliss, viz. the glorifying of His body. Therefore it seems there was hope in Him.

Objection 3: Further, everyone may hope for what pertains to his perfection, if it has yet to come. But there was something still to come pertaining to Christ's perfection, according to Eph. 4:12: "For the perfecting of the saints, for the work of the ministry, for the building up [Douay: 'edifying'] of the body of Christ." Hence it seems that it befitted Christ to have hope.

On the contrary, It is written (Rom. 8:24): "What a man seeth, why doth he hope for?" Thus it is clear that as faith is of the unseen, so also is hope. But there was no faith in Christ, as was said above [3933](A[1]): neither, consequently, was there hope.

I answer that, As it is of the nature of faith that one assents to what one sees not, so is it of the nature of hope that one expects what as yet one has not; and as faith, forasmuch as it is a theological virtue, does not regard everything unseen, but only God; so likewise hope, as a theological virtue, has God Himself for its object, the fruition of Whom man chiefly expects by the virtue of hope; yet, in consequence, whoever has the virtue of hope may expect the Divine aid in other things, even as he who has the virtue of faith believes God not only in Divine things, but even in whatsoever is divinely revealed. Now from the beginning of His conception Christ had the Divine fruition fully, as will be shown ([3934]Q[34], A[4]), and hence he had not the virtue of hope. Nevertheless He had hope as regards such things as He did not yet possess, although He had not faith with regard to anything; because, although He knew all things fully, wherefore faith was altogether wanting to Him, nevertheless He did not as yet fully possess all that pertained to His perfection, viz. immortality and glory of the body, which He could hope for.

Reply to Objection 1: This is said of Christ with reference to hope, not as a theological virtue, but inasmuch as He hoped for some other things not yet possessed, as was said above.

Reply to Objection 2: The glory of the body does not pertain to beatitude as being that in which beatitude principally consists, but by a certain outpouring from the soul's glory, as was said above ([3935]FS, Q[4], A[6]). Hence hope, as a theological virtue, does not regard the bliss of the body but the soul's bliss, which consists in the Divine fruition.

Reply to Objection 3: The building up of the church by the conversion of the faithful does not pertain to the perfection of Christ, whereby He is perfect in Himself, but inasmuch as it leads others to a share of His perfection. And because hope properly regards what is expected by him who hopes, the virtue of hope cannot properly be said to be in Christ, because of the aforesaid reason.

Whether in Christ there were the gifts?

Objection 1: It would seem that the gifts were not in Christ. For, as is commonly said, the gifts are given to help the virtues. But what is perfect in itself does not need an exterior help. Therefore, since the virtues of Christ were perfect, it seems there were no gifts in Him.

Objection 2: Further, to give and to receive gifts would not seem to belong to the same; since to give pertains to one who has, and to receive pertains to one who has not. But it belongs to Christ to give gifts according to Ps. 67:19. "Thou hast given gifts to men [Vulg.: 'Thou hast received gifts in men']." Therefore it was not becoming that Christ should receive gifts of the Holy Ghost.

Objection 3: Further, four gifts would seem to pertain to the contemplation of earth, viz. wisdom, knowledge, understanding, and counsel which pertains to prudence; hence the Philosopher (Ethic. vi, 3) enumerates these with the intellectual virtues. But Christ had the contemplation of heaven. Therefore He had not these gifts.

On the contrary, It is written (Is. 4:1): "Seven women shall take hold of one man": on which a gloss says: "That is, the seven gifts of the Holy Ghost shall take hold of Christ."

I answer that, As was said above ([3936]FS, Q[68], A[1]), the gifts, properly, are certain perfections of the soul's powers, inasmuch a[9] these have a natural aptitude to be moved by the Holy Ghost, according to Luke 4:1: "And Jesus, being full of the Holy Ghost, returned from the Jordan, and was led by the Spirit into the desert." Hence it is manifest that in Christ the gifts were in a pre-eminent degree.

Reply to Objection 1: What is perfect in the order of its nature needs to be helped by something of a higher nature; as man, however perfect, needs to be helped by God. And in this way the virtues, which perfect the powers of the soul, as they are controlled by reason, no matter how perfect they are, need to be helped by the gifts, which perfect the soul's powers, inasmuch as these are moved by the Holy Ghost.

Reply to Objection 2: Christ is not a recipient and a giver of the gifts of the Holy Ghost, in the same respect; for He gives them as God and receives them as man. Hence Gregory says (Moral. ii) that "the Holy Ghost never quitted the human nature of Christ, from Whose Divine nature He proceedeth."

Reply to Objection 3: In Christ there was not only heavenly knowledge, but also earthly knowledge, as will be said (Q[15], A[10]). And yet even in heaven the gifts of the Holy Ghost will still exist, in a certain manner, as was said above ([3937]FS, Q[68], A[6]).

Whether in Christ there was the gift of fear?

Objection 1: It would seem that in Christ there was not the gift of fear. For hope would seem to be stronger than fear; since the object of hope is goodness, and of fear, evil. as was said above ([3938]FS, Q[40], A[1]; [3939]FS, Q[42], A[1]). But in Christ there was not the virtue of hope, as was said above [3940](A[4]). Hence, likewise, there was not the gift of fear in Him.

Objection 2: Further, by the gift of fear we fear either to be separated from God, which pertains to "chaste" fear---or to be punished by Him, which pertains to "servile" fear, as Augustine says (In Joan. Tract. ix). But Christ did not fear being separated from God by sin, nor being punished by Him on account of a fault, since it was impossible for Him to sin, as will be said ([3941]Q[15], AA[1],2). Now fear is not of the impossible. Therefore in Christ there was not the gift of fear.

Objection 3: Further, it is written (1 Jn. 4:18) that "perfect charity casteth out fear." But in Christ there was most perfect charity, according to Eph. 3:19: "The charity of Christ which surpasseth all knowledge." Therefore in Christ there was not the gift of fear.

On the contrary, It is written (Is. 11:3): "And He shall be filled with the spirit of the fear of the Lord."

I answer that, As was said above ([3942]FS, Q[42], A[1]), fear regards two objects, one of which is an evil causing terror; the other is that by whose power an evil can be inflicted, as we fear the king inasmuch as he has the power of putting to death. Now whoever can hurt would not be feared unless he had a certain greatness of might, to which resistance could not easily be offered; for what we easily repel we do not fear. And hence it is plain that no one is feared except for some pre-eminence. And in this way it is said that in Christ there was the fear of God, not indeed as it regards the evil of separation from God by fault, nor as it regards the evil of punishment for fault; but inasmuch as it regards the Divine pre-eminence, on account of which the soul of Christ, led by the Holy Spirit, was borne towards God in an act of reverence. Hence it is said (Heb. 5:7) that in all things "he was heard for his reverence." For Christ as man had this act of reverence towards God in a fuller sense and beyond all others. And hence Scripture attributes to Him the fulness of the fear of the Lord.

Reply to Objection 1: The habits of virtues and gifts regard goodness properly and of themselves; but evil, consequently; since it pertains to the nature of virtue to render acts good, as is said Ethic. ii, 6. And hence the nature of the gift of fear regards not that evil which fear is concerned with, but the pre-eminence of that goodness, viz. of God, by Whose power evil may be inflicted. on the other hand, hope, as a virtue, regards not only the author of good, but even the good itself, as far as it is not yet possessed. And hence to Christ, Who already possessed the perfect good of beatitude, we do not attribute the virtue of hope, but we do attribute the gift of fear.

Reply to Objection 2: This reason is based on fear in so far as it regards the evil object.

Reply to Objection 3: Perfect charity casts out servile fear, which principally regards punishment. But this kind of fear was not in Christ.

Whether the gratuitous graces were in Christ?

Objection 1: It would seem that the gratuitous graces were not in Christ. For whoever has anything in its fulness, to him it does not pertain to have it by participation. Now Christ has grace in its fulness, according to Jn. 1:14: "Full of grace and truth." But the gratuitous graces would seem to be certain participations, bestowed distributively and particularly upon divers subjects, according to 1 Cor. 12:4: "Now there are diversities of graces." Therefore it would seem that there were no gratuitous graces in Christ.

Objection 2: Further, what is due to anyone would not seem to be gratuitously bestowed on him. But it was due to the man Christ that He should abound in the word of wisdom and knowledge, and to be mighty in doing wonderful works and the like, all of which pertain to gratuitous graces: since He is "the power of God and the wisdom of God," as is written 1 Cor. 1:24. Therefore it was not fitting for Christ to have the gratuitous graces.

Objection 3: Further, gratuitous graces are ordained to the benefit of the faithful. But it does not seem that a habit which a man does not use is for the benefit of others, according to Ecclus. 20:32: "Wisdom that is hid and treasure that is not seen: what profit is there in them both?" Now we do not read that Christ made use of these gratuitously given graces, especially as regards the gift of tongues. Therefore not all the gratuitous graces were in Christ.

On the contrary, Augustine says (Ep. ad Dardan. cclxxxvii) that "as in the head are all the senses, so in Christ were all the graces."

I answer that, As was said above ([3943]FS, Q[3], AA[1],4), the gratuitous graces are ordained for the manifestation of faith and spiritual doctrine. For it behooves him who teaches to have the means of making his doctrine clear; otherwise his doctrine would be useless. Now Christ is the first and chief teacher of spiritual doctrine and faith, according to Heb. 2:3,4: "Which having begun to be declared by the Lord was confirmed unto us by them that heard Him, God also bearing them witness by signs and wonders." Hence it is clear that all the gratuitous graces were most excellently in Christ, as in the first and chief teacher of the faith.

Reply to Objection 1: As sanctifying grace is ordained to meritorious acts both interior and exterior, so likewise gratuitous grace is ordained to certain exterior acts manifestive of the faith, as the working of miracles, and the like. Now of both these graces Christ had the fulness. since inasmuch as His soul was united to the Godhead, He had the perfect power of effecting all these acts. But other saints who are moved by God as separated and not united instruments, receive power in a particular manner in order to bring about this or that act. And hence in other saints these graces are divided, but not in Christ.

Reply to Objection 2: Christ is said to be the power of God and the wisdom of God, inasmuch as He is the Eternal Son of God. But in this respect it does not pertain to Him to have grace, but rather to be the bestower of grace. but it pertains to Him in His human nature to have grace.

Reply to Objection 3: The gift of tongues was bestowed on the apostles, because they were sent to teach all nations; but Christ wished to preach personally only in the one nation of the Jews, as He Himself says (Mat. 15:24): "I was not sent but to the sheep that are lost of the house of Israel"; and the Apostle says (Rom. 15:8): "I say that Christ Jesus was minister of the circumcision." And hence it was not necessary for Him to speak several languages. Yet was a knowledge of all languages not wanting to Him, since even the secrets of hearts, of which all words are signs, were not hidden from Him, as will be shown ([3944]Q[10], A[2]). Nor was this knowledge uselessly possessed. just as it is not useless to have a habit, which we do not use when there is no occasion.

Whether in Christ there was the gift of prophecy?

Objection 1: It would seem that in Christ there was not the gift of prophecy. For prophecy implies a certain obscure and imperfect knowledge, according to Num. 12:6: "If there be among you a prophet of the Lord, I will appear to him in a vision, or I will speak to him in a dream." But Christ had full and unveiled knowledge, much more than Moses, of whom it is subjoined that "plainly and not by riddles and figures doth he see God" (Num. 6:8). Therefore we ought not to admit prophecy in Christ.

Objection 2: Further, as faith has to do with what is not seen, and hope with what is not possessed, so prophecy has to do with what is not present, but distant; for a prophet means, as it were, a teller of far-off things. But in Christ there could be neither faith nor hope, as was said above ([3945]AA[3],4). Hence prophecy also ought not to be admitted in Christ.

Objection 3: Further, a prophet is in an inferior order to an angel; hence Moses, who was the greatest of the prophets, as was said above ([3946]SS, Q[174], A[4]) is said (Acts 7:38) to have spoken with an angel in the desert. But Christ was "made lower than the angels," not as to the knowledge of His soul, but only as regards the sufferings of His body, as is shown Heb. 2:9. Therefore it seems that Christ was not a prophet.

On the contrary, It is written of Him (Dt. 18:15): "Thy God will raise up to thee a prophet of thy nation and of thy brethren," and He says of Himself (Mat. 13:57; Jn. 4:44): "A prophet is not without honor, save in his own country."

I answer that, A prophet means, as it were, a teller or seer of far-off things, inasmuch as he knows and announces what things are far from men's senses, as Augustine says (Contra Faust. xvi, 18). Now we must bear in mind that no one can be called a prophet for knowing and announcing what is distant from others, with whom he is not. And this is clear in regard to place and time. For if anyone living in France were to know and announce to others living in France what things were transpiring in Syria, it would be prophetical, as Eliseus told Giezi (4 Kings 5:26) how the man had leaped down from his chariot to meet him. But if anyone living in Syria were to announce what things were there, it would not be prophetical. And the same appears in regard to time. For it was prophetical of Isaias to announce that Cyrus, King of the Persians, would rebuild the temple of God, as is clear from Is. 44:28. But it was not prophetical of Esdras to write it, in whose time it took place. Hence if God or angels, or even the blessed, know and announce what is beyond our knowing, this does not pertain to prophecy, since they nowise touch our state. Now Christ before His passion touched our state, inasmuch as He was not merely a "comprehensor," but a "wayfarer." Hence it was prophetical in Him to know and announce what was beyond the knowledge of other "wayfarers": and for this reason He is called a prophet.

Reply to Objection 1: These words do not prove that enigmatical knowledge, viz. by dream and vision, belongs to the nature of prophecy; but the comparison is drawn between other prophets, who saw Divine things in dreams and visions, and Moses, who saw God plainly and not by riddles, and who yet is called a prophet, according to Dt. 24:10: "And there arose no more a prophet in Israel like unto Moses." Nevertheless it may be said that although Christ had full and unveiled knowledge as regards the intellective part, yet in the imaginative part He had certain similitudes, in which Divine things could be viewed, inasmuch as He was not only a "comprehensor," but a "wayfarer."

Reply to Objection 2: Faith regards such things as are unseen by him who believes; and hope, too, is of such things as are not possessed by the one who hopes; but prophecy is of such things as are beyond the sense of men, with whom the prophet dwells and converses in this state of life. And hence faith and hope are repugnant to the perfection of Christ's beatitude; but prophecy is not.

Reply to Objection 3: Angels, being "comprehensors," are above prophets, who are merely "wayfarers"; but not above Christ, Who was both a "comprehensor" and a "wayfarer."

Whether in Christ there was the fulness of grace?

Objection 1: It would seem that in Christ there was not the fulness of grace. For the virtues flow from grace, as was said above ([3947]FS, Q[110], A[4]). But in Christ there were not all the virtues; for there was neither faith nor hope in Him, as was shown above ([3948]AA[3],4). Therefore in Christ there was not the fulness of grace.

Objection 2: Further, as is plain from what was said above ([3949]FS, Q[111], A[2]), grace is divided into operating and cooperating. Now operating grace signifies that whereby the ungodly is justified, which has no place in Christ, Who never lay under any sin. Therefore in Christ there was not the fulness of grace.

Objection 3: Further, it is written (James 1:17): "Every best gift and every perfect gift is from above, coming down from the Father of lights." But what comes thus is possessed partially, and not fully. Therefore no creature, not even the soul of Christ, can have the fulness of the gifts of grace.

On the contrary, It is written (Jn. 1:14): "We saw Him [Vulg.: 'His glory'] full of grace and truth."

I answer that, To have fully is to have wholly and perfectly. Now totality and perfection can be taken in two ways: First as regards their "intensive" quantity; for instance, I may say that some man has whiteness fully, because he has as much of it as can naturally be in him; secondly, "as regards power"; for instance, if anyone be said to have life fully, inasmuch as he has it in all the effects or works of life; and thus man has life fully, but senseless animals or plants have not. Now in both these ways Christ has the fulness of grace. First, since He has grace in its highest degree, in the most perfect way it can be had. And this appears, first, from the nearness of Christ's soul to the cause of grace. For it was said above [3950](A[1]) that the nearer a recipient is to the inflowing cause, the more it receives. And hence the soul of Christ, which is more closely united to God than all other rational creatures, receives the greatest outpouring of His grace. Secondly, in His relation to the effect. For the soul of Christ so received grace, that, in a manner, it is poured out from it upon others. And hence it behooved Him to have the greatest grace; as fire which is the cause of heat in other hot things, is of all things the hottest.

Likewise, as regards the "virtue" of grace, He had grace fully, since He had it for all the operations and effects of grace; and this, because grace was bestowed on Him, as upon a universal principle in the genus of such as have grace. Now the virtue of the first principle of a genus universally extends itself to all the effects of that genus; thus the force of the sun, which is the universal cause of generation, as Dionysius says (Div. Nom. i), extends to all things that come under generation. Hence the second fulness of grace is seen in Christ inasmuch as His grace extends to all the effects of grace, which are the virtues, gifts, and the like.

Reply to Objection 1: Faith and hope signify effects of grace with certain defects on the part of the recipient of grace, inasmuch as faith is of the unseen, and hope of what is not yet possessed. Hence it was not necessary that in Christ, Who is the author of grace, there should be any defects such as faith and hope imply; but whatever perfection is in faith and hope was in Christ most perfectly; as in fire there are not all the modes of heat which are defective by the subject's defect, but whatever belongs to the perfection of heat.

Reply to Objection 2: It pertains essentially to operating grace to justify; but that it makes the ungodly to be just is accidental to it on the part of the subject, in which sin is found. Therefore the soul of Christ was justified by operating grace, inasmuch as it was rendered just and holy by it from the beginning of His conception; not that it was until then sinful, or even not just.

Reply to Objection 3: The fulness of grace is attributed to the soul of Christ according to the capacity of the creature and not by comparison with the infinite fulness of the Divine goodness.

Whether the fulness of grace is proper to Christ?

Objection 1: It would seem that the fulness of grace is not proper to Christ. For what is proper to anyone belongs to him alone. But to be full of grace is attributed to some others; for it was said to the Blessed Virgin (Lk. 1:28): "Hail, full of grace"; and again it is written (Acts 6:8): "Stephen, full of grace and fortitude." Therefore the fulness of grace is not proper to Christ.

Objection 2: Further, what can be communicated to others through Christ does not seem to be proper to Christ. But the fulness of grace can be communicated to others through Christ, since the Apostle says (Eph. 3:19): "That you may be filled unto all the fulness of God." Therefore the fulness of grace is not proper to Christ.

Objection 3: Further, the state of the wayfarer seems to be proportioned to the state of the comprehensor. But in the state of the comprehensor there will be a certain fulness, since "in our heavenly country with its fulness of all good, although some things are bestowed in a pre-eminent way, yet nothing is possessed singularly," as is clear from Gregory (Hom. De Cent. Ovib.; xxxiv in Ev.). Therefore in the state of the comprehensor the fulness of grace is possessed by everyone, and hence the fulness of grace is not proper to Christ. on the contrary, The fulness of grace is attributed to Christ inasmuch as He is the only-begotten of the Father, according to Jn. 1:14: "We saw Him [Vulg.: 'His glory'] as it were . . . the Only-begotten of the Father, full of grace and truth." But to be the Only-begotten of the Father is proper to Christ. Therefore it is proper to Him to be full of grace and truth.

I answer that, The fulness of grace may be taken in two ways: First, on the part of grace itself, or secondly on the part of the one who has grace. Now on the part of grace itself there is said to be the fulness of grace when the limit of grace is attained, as to essence and power, inasmuch as grace is possessed in its highest possible excellence and in its greatest possible extension to all its effects. And this fulness of grace is proper to Christ. But on the part of the subject there is said to be the fulness of grace when anyone fully possesses grace according to his condition---whether as regards intensity, by reason of grace being intense in him, to the limit assigned by God, according to Eph. 4:1: "But to every one of us is given grace according to the measure of the giving of Christ"---or "as regards power," by reason of a man having the help of grace for all that belongs to his office or state, as the Apostle says (Eph. 3:8): "To me, the least of all the saints, is given this grace . . . to enlighten all men." And this fulness of grace is not proper to Christ, but is communicated to others by Christ.

Reply to Objection 1: The Blessed Virgin is said to be full of grace, not on the part of grace itself---since she had not grace in its greatest possible excellence---nor for all the effects of grace; but she is said to be full of grace in reference to herself, i.e. inasmuch as she had sufficient grace for the state to which God had chosen her, i.e. to be the mother of His Only-begotten. So, too, Stephen is said to be full of grace, since he had sufficient grace to be a fit minister and witness of God, to which office he had been called. And the same must be said of others. Of these fulnesses one is greater than another, according as one is divinely pre-ordained to a higher or lower state.

Reply to Objection 2: The Apostle is there speaking of that fulness which has reference to the subject, in comparison with what man is divinely pre-ordained to; and this is either something in common, to which all the saints are pre-ordained, or something special, which pertains to the pre-eminence of some. And in this manner a certain fulness of grace is common to all the saints, viz. to have grace enough to merit eternal life, which consists in the enjoyment of God. And this is the fulness of grace which the Apostle desires for the faithful to whom he writes.

Reply to Objection 3: These gifts which are in common in heaven, viz.: vision, possession and fruition, and the like, have certain gifts corresponding to them in this life which are also common to all the saints. Yet there are certain prerogatives of saints, both in heaven and on earth, which are not possessed by all.

Whether the grace of Christ is infinite?

Objection 1: It would seem that Christ's grace is infinite. For everything immeasurable is infinite. But the grace of Christ is immeasurable; since it is written (Jn. 3:34): "For God doth not give the Spirit by measure to His Son [*'To His Son' is lacking in the Vulgate], namely Christ." Therefore the grace of Christ is infinite.

Objection 2: Further, an infinite effect betokens an infinite power which can only spring from an infinite essence. But the effect of Christ's grace is infinite, since it extends to the salvation of the whole human race; for He is the propitiation for our sins . . . and for those of the whole world, as is said (1 Jn. 2:2). Therefore the grace of Christ is infinite.

Objection 3: Further, every finite thing by addition can attain to the quantity of any other finite thing. Therefore if the grace of Christ is finite the grace of any other man could increase to such an extent as to reach to an equality with Christ's grace, against what is written (Job 28:17): "Gold nor crystal cannot equal it," as Gregory expounds it (Moral. xviii). Therefore the grace of Christ is infinite.

On the contrary, Grace is something created in the soul. But every created thing is finite, according to Wis. 11:21: "Thou hast ordered all things in measure and number and weight." Therefore the grace of Christ is not infinite.

I answer that, As was made clear above ([3951]Q[2], A[10]), a twofold grace may be considered in Christ; the first being the grace of union, which, as was said ([3952]Q[6], A[6]), is for Him to be personally united to the Son of God, which union has been bestowed gratis on the human nature; and it is clear that this grace is infinite, as the Person of God is infinite. The second is habitual grace; which may be taken in two ways: first as a being, and in this way it must be a finite being, since it is in the soul of Christ, as in a subject, and Christ's soul is a creature having a finite capacity; hence the being of grace cannot be infinite, since it cannot exceed its subject. Secondly it may be viewed in its specific nature of grace; and thus the grace of Christ can be termed infinite, since it is not limited, i.e. it has whatsoever can pertain to the nature of grace, and what pertains to the nature of grace is not bestowed on Him in a fixed measure; seeing that "according to the purpose" of God to Whom it pertains to measure grace, it is bestowed on Christ's soul as on a universal principle for bestowing grace on human nature, according to Eph. 1:5,6, "He hath graced us in His beloved Son"; thus we might say that the light of the sun is infinite, not indeed in being, but in the nature of light, as having whatever can pertain to the nature of light.

Reply to Objection 1: When it is said that the Father "doth not give the Spirit by measure," it may be expounded of the gift which God the Father from all eternity gave the Son, viz. the Divine Nature, which is an infinite gift. Hence the comment of a certain gloss: "So that the Son may be as great as the Father is." Or again, it may be referred to the gift which is given the human nature, to be united to the Divine Person, and this also is an infinite gift. Hence a gloss says on this text: "As the Father begot a full and perfect Word, it is united thus full and perfect to human nature." Thirdly, it may be referred to habitual grace, inasmuch as the grace of Christ extends to whatever belongs to grace. Hence Augustine expounding this (Tract. xiv in Joan.) says: "The division of the gifts is a measurement. For to one indeed by the Spirit is given the word of wisdom, to another the word of knowledge." But Christ the giver does not receive by measure.

Reply to Objection 2: The grace of Christ has an infinite effect, both because of the aforesaid infinity of grace, and because of the unity [*Perhaps we should read 'infinity'---Ed.] of the Divine Person, to Whom Christ's soul is united.

Reply to Objection 3: The lesser can attain by augment to the quantity of the greater, when both have the same kind of quantity. But the grace of any man is compared to the grace of Christ as a particular to a universal power; hence as the force of fire, no matter how much it increases, can never equal the sun's strength, so the grace of a man, no matter how much it increases, can never equal the grace of Christ.

Whether the grace of Christ could increase?

Objection 1: It would seem that the grace of Christ could increase. For to every finite thing addition can be made. But the grace of Christ was finite. Therefore it could increase.

Objection 2: Further, it is by Divine power that grace is increased, according to 2 Cor. 9:8: "And God is able to make all grace abound in you." But the Divine power, being infinite, is confined by no limits. Therefore it seems that the grace of Christ could have been greater.

Objection 3: Further, it is written (Lk. 2:52) that the child "Jesus advanced in wisdom and age and grace with God and men." Therefore the grace of Christ could increase.

On the contrary, It is written (Jn. 1:14): "We saw Him [Vulg.: 'His glory'] as it were . . . the Only-begotten of the Father, full of grace and truth." But nothing can be or can be thought greater than that anyone should be the Only-begotten of the Father. Therefore no greater grace can be or can be thought than that of which Christ was full.

I answer that, For a form to be incapable of increase happens in two ways: First on the part of the subject; secondly, on the part of the form itself. On the part of the subject, indeed, when the subject reaches the utmost limit wherein it partakes of this form, after its own manner, e.g. if we say that air cannot increase in heat, when it has reached the utmost limit of heat which can exist in the nature of air, although there may be greater heat in actual existence, viz. the heat of fire. But on the part of the form, the possibility of increase is excluded when a subject reaches the utmost perfection which this form can have by nature, e.g. if we say the heat of fire cannot be increased because there cannot be a more perfect grade of heat than that to which fire attains. Now the proper measure of grace, like that of other forms, is determined by the Divine wisdom, according to Wis. 11:21: "Thou hast ordered all things in number, weight and measure." And it is with reference to its end that a measure is set to every form. as there is no greater gravity than that of the earth, because there is no lower place than that of the earth. Now the end of grace is the union of the rational creature with God. But there can neither be nor be thought a greater union of the rational creature with God than that which is in the Person. And hence the grace of Christ reached the highest measure of grace. Hence it is clear that the grace of Christ cannot be increased on the part of grace. But neither can it be increased on the part of the subject, since Christ as man was a true and full comprehensor from the first instant of His conception. Hence there could have been no increase of grace in Him, as there could be none in the rest of the blessed, whose grace could not increase, seeing that they have reached their last end. But as regards men who are wholly wayfarers, their grace can be increased not merely on the part of the form, since they have not attained the highest degree of grace, but also on the part of the subject, since they have not yet attained their end.

Reply to Objection 1: If we speak of mathematical quantity, addition can be made to any finite quantity, since there is nothing on the part of finite quantity which is repugnant to addition. But if we speak of natural quantity, there may be repugnance on the part of the form to which a determined quantity is due, even as other accidents are determined. Hence the Philosopher says (De Anima ii, 41) that "there is naturally a term of all things, and a fixed limit of magnitude and increase." And hence to the quantity of the whole there can be no addition. And still more must we suppose a term in the forms themselves, beyond which they may not go. Hence it is not necessary that addition should be capable of being made to Christ's grace, although it is finite in its essence.

Reply to Objection 2: Although the Divine power can make something greater and better than the habitual grace of Christ, yet it could not make it to be ordained to anything greater than the personal union with the Only-begotten Son of the Father; and to this union, by the purpose of the Divine wisdom, the measure of grace is sufficient.

Reply to Objection 3: Anyone may increase in wisdom and grace in two ways. First inasmuch as the very habits of wisdom and grace are increased; and in this way Christ did not increase. Secondly, as regards the effects, i.e. inasmuch as they do wiser and greater works; and in this way Christ increased in wisdom and grace even as in age, since in the course of time He did more perfect works, to prove Himself true man, both in the things of God, and in the things of man.

Whether the habitual grace of Christ followed after the union?

Objection 1: It would seem that the habitual grace did not follow after the union. For nothing follows itself. But this habitual grace seems to be the same as the grace of union; for Augustine says (De Praedest. Sanct. xv): "Every man becomes a Christian from the beginning of his belief, by the same grace whereby this Man from His beginning became Christ"; and of these two the first pertains to habitual grace and the second to the grace of union. Therefore it would seem that habitual grace did not follow upon the union.

Objection 2: Further, disposition precedes perfection, if not in time, at least in thought. But the habitual grace seems to be a disposition in human nature for the personal union. Therefore it seems that the habitual grace did not follow but rather preceded the union.

Objection 3: Further, the common precedes the proper. But habitual grace is common to Christ and other men; and the grace of union is proper to Christ. Therefore habitual grace is prior in thought to the union. Therefore it does not follow it.

On the contrary, It is written (Is. 42:1): "Behold my servant, I will uphold Him . . . "and farther on: "I have given My Spirit upon Him"; and this pertains to the gift of habitual grace. Hence it remains that the assumption of human nature to the unity of the Person preceded the habitual grace of Christ.

I answer that, The union of the human nature with the Divine Person, which, as we have said above ([3953]Q[2], A[10];[3954] Q[6], A[6]), is the grace of union, precedes the habitual grace of Christ, not in order of time, but by nature and in thought; and this for a triple reason: First, with reference to the order of the principles of both. For the principle of the union is the Person of the Son assuming human nature, Who is said to be sent into the world, inasmuch as He assumed human nature; but the principle of habitual grace, which is given with charity, is the Holy Ghost, Who is said to be sent inasmuch as He dwells in the mind by charity. Now the mission of the Son is prior, in the order of nature, to the mission of the Holy Ghost, even as in the order of nature the Holy Ghost proceeds from the Son, and love from wisdom. Hence the personal union, according to which the mission of the Son took place, is prior in the order of nature to habitual grace, according to which the mission of the Holy Ghost takes place. Secondly, the reason of this order may be taken from the relation of grace to its cause. For grace is caused in man by the presence of the Godhead, as light in the air by the presence of the sun. Hence it is written (Ezech. 43:2): "The glory of the God of Israel came in by the way of the east . . . and the earth shone with His majesty." But the presence of God in Christ is by the union of human nature with the Divine Person. Hence the habitual grace of Christ is understood to follow this union, as light follows the sun. Thirdly, the reason of this union can be taken from the end of grace, since it is ordained to acting rightly, and action belongs to the suppositum and the individual. Hence action and, in consequence, grace ordaining thereto, presuppose the hypostasis which operates. Now the hypostasis did not exist in the human nature before the union, as is clear from[3955] Q[4], A[2]. Therefore the grace of union precedes, in thought, habitual grace.

Reply to Objection 1: Augustine here means by grace the gratuitous will of God, bestowing benefits gratis; and hence every man is said to be made a Christian by the same grace whereby a Man became Christ, since both take place by the gratuitous will of God without merits.

Reply to Objection 2: As disposition in the order of generation precedes the perfection to which it disposes, in such things as are gradually perfected; so it naturally follows the perfection which one has already obtained; as heat, which was a disposition to the form of fire, is an effect flowing from the form of already existing fire. Now the human nature in Christ is united to the Person of the Word from the beginning without succession. Hence habitual grace is not understood to have preceded the union, but to have followed it; as a natural property. Hence, as Augustine says (Enchiridion xl): "Grace is in a manner natural to the Man Christ."

Reply to Objection 3: The common precedes the proper, when both are of the same genus; but when they are of divers genera, there is nothing to prevent the proper being prior to the common. Now the grace of union is not in the same genus as habitual grace; but is above all genera even as the Divine Person Himself. Hence there is nothing to prevent this proper from being before the common since it does not result from something being added to the common, but is rather the principle and source of that which is common.

OF THE GRACE OF CHRIST, AS HE IS THE HEAD OF THE CHURCH (EIGHT ARTICLES)

We must now consider the grace of Christ as the Head of the Church; and under this head there are eight points of inquiry:
(1) Whether Christ is the Head of the Church?
(2) Whether He is the Head of men as regards their bodies or only as regards their souls?
(3) Whether He is the Head of all men?
(4) Whether He is the Head of the angels?
(5) Whether the grace of Christ as Head of the Church is the same as His habitual grace as an individual man?
(6) Whether to be Head of the Church is proper to Christ?
(7) Whether the devil is the head of all the wicked?
(8) Whether Anti-christ can be called the head of all the wicked?

Whether Christ is the Head of the Church?

Objection 1: It would seem that it does not belong to Christ as man to be Head of the Church. For the head imparts sense and motion to the members. Now spiritual sense and motion which are by grace, are not imparted to us by the Man Christ, because, as Augustine says (De Trin. i, 12; xv, 24), "not even Christ, as man, but only as God, bestows the Holy Ghost." Therefore it does not belong to Him as man to be Head of the Church.

Objection 2: Further, it is not fitting for the head to have a head. But God is the Head of Christ, as man, according to 1 Cor. 11:3, "The Head of Christ is God." Therefore Christ Himself is not a head.

Objection 3: Furthermore, the head of a man is a particular member, receiving an influx from the heart. But Christ is the universal principle of the whole Church. Therefore He is not the Head of the Church.

On the contrary, It is written (Eph. 1:22): "And He . . . hath made Him head over all the Church."

I answer that, As the whole Church is termed one mystic body from its likeness to the natural body of a man, which in divers members has divers acts, as the Apostle teaches (Rom. 12; 1 Cor. 12), so likewise Christ is called the Head of the Church from a likeness with the human head, in which we may consider three things, viz. order, perfection, and power: "Order," indeed; for the head is the first part of man, beginning from the higher part; and hence it is that every principle is usually called a head according to Ezech. 16:25: "At every head of the way, thou hast set up a sign of thy prostitution"---"Perfection," inasmuch as in the head dwell all the senses, both interior and exterior, whereas in the other members there is only touch, and hence it is said (Is. 9:15): "The aged and honorable, he is the head"---"Power," because the power and movement of the other members, together with the direction of them in their acts, is from the head, by reason of the sensitive and motive power there ruling; hence the ruler is called the head of a people, according to 1 Kings 15:17: "When thou wast a little one in thy own eyes, wast thou not made the head of the tribes of Israel?" Now these three things belong spiritually to Christ. First, on account of His nearness to God His grace is the highest and first, though not in time, since all have received grace on account of His grace, according to Rom. 8:29: "For whom He foreknew, He also predestinated to be made conformable to the image of His Son; that He might be the first-born amongst many brethren." Secondly, He had perfection as regards the fulness of all graces, according to Jn. 1:14, "We saw Him [Vulg.: 'His glory'] . . . full of grace and truth," as was shown[3956], Q[7], A[9]. Thirdly, He has the power of bestowing grace on all the members of the Church, according to Jn. 1:16: "Of His fulness we have all received." And thus it is plain that Christ is fittingly called the Head of the Church.

Reply to Objection 1: To give grace or the Holy Ghost belongs to Christ as He is God, authoritatively; but instrumentally it belongs also to Him as man, inasmuch as His manhood is the instrument of His Godhead. And hence by the power of the Godhead His actions were beneficial, i.e. by causing grace in us, both meritoriously and efficiently. But Augustine denies that Christ as man gives the Holy Ghost authoritatively. Even other saints are said to give the Holy Ghost instrumentally, or ministerially, according to Gal. 3:5: "He . . . who giveth to you the Spirit."

Reply to Objection 2: In metaphorical speech we must not expect a likeness in all respects; for thus there would be not likeness but identity. Accordingly a natural head has not another head because one human body is not part of another; but a metaphorical body, i.e. an ordered multitude, is part of another multitude as the domestic multitude is part of the civil multitude; and hence the father who is head of the domestic multitude has a head above him, i.e. the civil governor. And hence there is no reason why God should not be the Head of Christ, although Christ Himself is Head of the Church.

Reply to Objection 3: The head has a manifest pre-eminence over the other exterior members; but the heart has a certain hidden influence. And hence the Holy Ghost is likened to the heart, since He invisibly quickens and unifies the Church; but Christ is likened to the Head in His visible nature in which man is set over man.

Whether Christ is the Head of men as to their bodies or only as to their souls?

Objection 1: It would seem that Christ is not the Head of men as to their bodies. For Christ is said to be the Head of the Church inasmuch as He bestows spiritual sense and the movement of grace on the Church. But a body is not capable of this spiritual sense and movement. Therefore Christ is not the Head of men as regards their bodies.

Objection 2: Further, we share bodies with the brutes. If therefore Christ was the Head of men as to their bodies, it would follow that He was the Head of brute animals; and this is not fitting.

Objection 3: Further, Christ took His body from other men, as is clear from Mat. 1 and Luke 3. But the head is the first of the members, as was said above (A[1], ad 3). Therefore Christ is not the Head of the Church as regards bodies.

On the contrary, It is written (Phil. 3:21): "Who will reform the body of our lowness, made like to the body of His glory."

I answer that, The human body has a natural relation to the rational soul, which is its proper form and motor. Inasmuch as the soul is its form, it receives from the soul life and the other properties which belong specifically to man; but inasmuch as the soul is its motor, the body serves the soul instrumentally. Therefore we must hold that the manhood of Christ had the power of "influence," inasmuch as it is united to the Word of God, to Whom His body is united through the soul, as stated above ([3957]Q[6], A[1]). Hence the whole manhood of Christ, i.e. according to soul and body, influences all, both in soul and body; but principally the soul, and secondarily the body: First, inasmuch as the "members of the body are presented as instruments of justice" in the soul that lives through Christ, as the Apostle says (Rom. 6:13): secondly, inasmuch as the life of glory flows from the soul on to the body, according to Rom. 8:11: "He that raised up Jesus from the dead shall quicken also your mortal bodies, because of His Spirit that dwelleth in you."

Reply to Objection 1: The spiritual sense of grace does not reach to the body first and principally, but secondarily and instrumentally, as was said above.

Reply to Objection 2: The body of an animal has no relation to a rational soul, as the human body has. Hence there is no parity.

Reply to Objection 3: Although Christ drew the matter of His body from other men, yet all draw from Him the immortal life of their body, according to 1 Cor. 15:22: "And as in Adam all die, so also in Christ all shall be made alive."

Whether Christ is the Head of all men?

Objection 1: It would seem that Christ is not the Head of all men. For the head has no relation except to the members of its body. Now the unbaptized are nowise members of the Church which is the body of Christ, as it is written (Eph. 1:23). Therefore Christ is not the Head of all men.

Objection 2: Further, the Apostle writes to the Ephesians (5:25,27): "Christ delivered Himself up for" the Church "that He might present it to Himself a glorious Church, not having spot or wrinkle or any such thing." But there are many of the faithful in whom is found the spot or the wrinkle of sin. Therefore Christ is not the Head of all the faithful.

Objection 3: Further, the sacraments of the Old Law are compared to Christ as the shadow to the body, as is written (Col. 2:17). But the fathers of the Old Testament in their day served unto these sacraments, according to Heb. 8:5: "Who serve unto the example and shadow of heavenly things." Hence they did not pertain to Christ's body, and therefore Christ is not the Head of all men.

On the contrary, It is written (1 Tim. 4:10): "Who is the Saviour of all men, especially of the faithful," and (1 Jn. 2:2): "He is the propitiation for our sins, and not for ours only, but also for those of the whole world." Now to save men and to be a propitiation for their sins belongs to Christ as Head. Therefore Christ is the Head of all men.

I answer that, This is the difference between the natural body of man and the Church's mystical body, that the members of the natural body are all together, and the members of the mystical are not all together---neither as regards their natural being, since the body of the Church is made up of the men who have been from the beginning of the world until its end---nor as regards their supernatural being, since, of those who are at any one time, some there are who are without grace, yet will afterwards obtain it, and some have it already. We must therefore consider the members of the mystical body not only as they are in act, but as they are in potentiality. Nevertheless, some are in potentiality who will never be reduced to act, and some are reduced at some time to act; and this according to the triple class, of which the first is by faith, the second by the charity of this life, the third by the fruition of the life to come. Hence we must say that if we take the whole time of the world in general, Christ is the Head of all men, but diversely. For, first and principally, He is the Head of such as are united to Him by glory; secondly, of those who are actually united to Him by charity; thirdly, of those who are actually united to Him by faith; fourthly, of those who are united to Him merely in potentiality, which is not yet reduced to act, yet will be reduced to act according to Divine predestination; fifthly, of those who are united to Him in potentiality, which will never be reduced to act; such are those men existing in the world, who are not predestined, who, however, on their departure from this world, wholly cease to be members of Christ, as being no longer in potentiality to be united to Christ.

Reply to Objection 1: Those who are unbaptized, though not actually in the Church, are in the Church potentially. And this potentiality is rooted in two things---first and principally, in the power of Christ, which is sufficient for the salvation of the whole human race; secondly, in free-will.

Reply to Objection 2: To be "a glorious Church not having spot or wrinkle" is the ultimate end to which we are brought by the Passion of Christ. Hence this will be in heaven, and not on earth, in which "if we say we have no sin, we deceive ourselves," as is written (1 Jn. 1:8). Nevertheless, there are some, viz. mortal, sins from which they are free who are members of Christ by the actual union of charity; but such as are tainted with these sins are not members of Christ actually, but potentially; except, perhaps, imperfectly, by formless faith, which unites to God, relatively but not simply, viz. so that man partake of the life of grace. For, as is written (James 2:20): "Faith without works is dead." Yet such as these receive from Christ a certain vital act, i.e. to believe, as if a lifeless limb were moved by a man to some extent.

Reply to Objection 3: The holy Fathers made use of the legal sacraments, not as realities, but as images and shadows of what was to come. Now it is the same motion to an image as image, and to the reality, as is clear from the Philosopher (De Memor. et Remin. ii). Hence the ancient Fathers, by observing the legal sacraments, were borne to Christ by the same faith and love whereby we also are borne to Him, and hence the ancient Fathers belong to the same Church as we.

Whether Christ is the Head of the angels?

Objection 1: It would seem that Christ as man is not the head of the angels. For the head and members are of one nature. But Christ as man is not of the same nature with the angels, but only with men, since, as is written (Heb. 2:16): "For nowhere doth He take hold of the angels, but of the seed of Abraham He taketh hold." Therefore Christ as man is not the head of the angels.

Objection 2: Further, Christ is the head of such as belong to the Church, which is His Body, as is written (Eph. 1:23). But the angels do not belong to the Church. For the Church is the congregation of the faithful: and in the angels there is no faith, for they do not "walk by faith" but "by sight," otherwise they would be "absent from the Lord," as the Apostle argues (2 Cor. 5:6,7). Therefore Christ as man is not head of the angels.

Objection 3: Further, Augustine says (Tract. xix; xxiii in Joan.), that as "the Word" which "was in the beginning with the Father" quickens souls, so the "Word made flesh" quickens bodies, which angels lack. But the Word made flesh is Christ as man. Therefore Christ as man does not give life to angels, and hence as man He is not the head of the angels.

On the contrary, The Apostle says (Col. 2:10), "Who is the head of all Principality and Power," and the same reason holds good with the other orders of angels. Therefore Christ is the Head of the angels.

I answer that, As was said above (A[1], ad 2), where there is one body we must allow that there is one head. Now a multitude ordained to one end, with distinct acts and duties, may be metaphorically called one body. But it is manifest that both men and angels are ordained to one end, which is the glory of the Divine fruition. Hence the mystical body of the Church consists not only of men but of angels. Now of all this multitude Christ is the Head, since He is nearer God, and shares His gifts more fully, not only than man, but even than angels; and of His influence not only men but even angels partake, since it is written (Eph. 1:20-22): that God the Father set "Him," namely Christ, "on His right hand in the heavenly places, above all Principality and Power and Virtue and Dominion and every name that is named not only in this world, but also in that which is to come. And He hath subjected all things under His feet." Therefore Christ is not only the Head of men, but of angels. Hence we read (Mat. 4:11) that "angels came and ministered to Him."

Reply to Objection 1: Christ's influence over men is chiefly with regard to their souls; wherein men agree with angels in generic nature, though not in specific nature. By reason of this agreement Christ can be said to be the Head of the angels, although the agreement falls short as regards the body.

Reply to Objection 2: The Church, on earth, is the congregation of the faithful; but, in heaven, it is the congregation of comprehensors. Now Christ was not merely a wayfarer, but a comprehensor. And therefore He is the Head not merely of the faithful, but of comprehensors, as having grace and glory most fully.

Reply to Objection 3: Augustine here uses the similitude of cause and effect, i.e. inasmuch as corporeal things act on bodies, and spiritual things on spiritual things. Nevertheless, the humanity of Christ, by virtue of the spiritual nature, i.e. the Divine, can cause something not only in the spirits of men, but also in the spirits of angels, on account of its most close conjunction with God, i.e. by personal union.

Whether the grace of Christ, as Head of the Church, is the same as His habitual grace, inasmuch as He is Man?

Objection 1: It would seem that the grace whereby Christ is Head of the Church and the individual grace of the Man are not the same. For the Apostle says (Rom. 5:15): "If by the offense of one many died, much more the grace of God and the gift, by the grace of one man, Jesus Christ, hath abounded unto many." But the actual sin of Adam is distinct from original sin which he transmitted to his posterity. Hence the personal grace which is proper to Christ is distinct from His grace, inasmuch as He is the Head of the Church, which flows to others from Him.

Objection 2: Further, habits are distinguished by acts. But the personal grace of Christ is ordained to one act, viz. the sanctification of His soul; and the capital grace is ordained to another, viz. to sanctifying others. Therefore the personal grace of Christ is distinct from His grace as He is the Head of the Church.

Objection 3: Further, as was said above ([3958]Q[6], A[6]), in Christ we distinguish a threefold grace, viz. the grace of union, capital grace, and the individual grace of the Man. Now the individual grace of Christ is distinct from the grace of union. Therefore it is also distinct from the capital grace.

On the contrary, It is written (Jn. 1:16): "Of His fulness we all have received." Now He is our Head, inasmuch as we receive from Him. Therefore He is our Head, inasmuch as He has the fulness of grace. Now He had the fulness of grace, inasmuch as personal grace was in Him in its perfection, as was said above ([3959]Q[7], A[9]). Hence His capital and personal grace are not distinct.

I answer that, Since everything acts inasmuch as it is a being in act, it must be the same act whereby it is in act and whereby it acts, as it is the same heat whereby fire is hot and whereby it heats. Yet not every act whereby anything is in act suffices for its being the principle of acting upon others. For since the agent is nobler than the patient, as Augustine says (Gen. ad lit. xii, 16) and the Philosopher (De Anima iii, 19), the agent must act on others by reason of a certain pre-eminence. Now it was said above [3960](A[1]; Q[7], A[9]) grace was received by the soul of Christ in the highest way; and therefore from this pre-eminence of grace which He received, it is from Him that this grace is bestowed on others---and this belongs to the nature of head. Hence the personal grace, whereby the soul of Christ is justified, is essentially the same as His grace, as He is the Head of the Church, and justifies others; but there is a distinction of reason between them.

Reply to Objection 1: Original sin in Adam, which is a sin of the nature, is derived from his actual sin, which is a personal sin, because in him the person corrupted the nature; and by means of this corruption the sin of the first man is transmitted to posterity, inasmuch as the corrupt nature corrupts the person. Now grace is not vouchsafed us by means of human nature, but solely by the personal action of Christ Himself. Hence we must not distinguish a twofold grace in Christ, one corresponding to the nature, the other to the person as in Adam we distinguish the sin of the nature and of the person.

Reply to Objection 2: Different acts, one of which is the reason and the cause of the other, do not diversify a habit. Now the act of the personal grace which is formally to sanctify its subject, is the reason of the justification of others, which pertains to capital grace. Hence it is that the essence of the habit is not diversified by this difference.

Reply to Objection 3: Personal and capital grace are ordained to an act; but the grace of union is not ordained to an act, but to the personal being. Hence the personal and the capital grace agree in the essence of the habit; but the grace of union does not, although the personal grace can be called in a manner the grace of union, inasmuch as it brings about a fitness for the union; and thus the grace of union, the capital, and the personal grace are one in essence, though there is a distinction of reason between them.

Day 256

Whether it is proper to Christ to be Head of the Church?

Objection 1: It seems that it is not proper to Christ to be Head of the Church. For it is written (1 Kings 15:17): "When thou wast a little one in thy own eyes, wast thou not made the head of the tribes of Israel?" Now there is but one Church in the New and the Old Testament. Therefore it seems that with equal reason any other man than Christ might be head of the Church.

Objection 2: Further, Christ is called Head of the Church from His bestowing grace on the Church's members. But it belongs to others also to grant grace to others, according to Eph. 4:29: "Let no evil speech proceed from your mouth; but that which is good to the edification of faith, that it may administer grace to the hearers." Therefore it seems to belong also to others than Christ to be head of the Church.

Objection 3: Further, Christ by His ruling over the Church is not only called "Head," but also "Shepherd" and "Foundation." Now Christ did not retain for Himself alone the name of Shepherd, according to 1 Pet. 5:4, "And when the prince of pastors shall appear, you shall receive a never-fading crown of glory"; nor the name of Foundation, according to Apoc. 21:14: "And the wall of the city had twelve foundations." Therefore it seems that He did not retain the name of Head for Himself alone.

On the contrary, It is written (Col. 2:19): "The head" of the Church is that "from which the whole body, by joints and bands being supplied with nourishment and compacted groweth unto the increase of God." But this belongs only to Christ. Therefore Christ alone is Head of the Church.

I answer that, The head influences the other members in two ways. First, by a certain intrinsic influence, inasmuch as motive and sensitive force flow from the head to the other members; secondly, by a certain exterior guidance, inasmuch as by sight and the senses, which are rooted in the head, man is guided in his exterior acts. Now the interior influx of grace is from no one save Christ, Whose manhood, through its union with the Godhead, has the power of justifying; but the influence over the members of the Church, as regards their exterior guidance, can belong to others; and in this way others may be called heads of the Church, according to Amos 6:1, "Ye great men, heads of the people"; differently, however, from Christ. First, inasmuch as Christ is the Head of all who pertain to the Church in every place and time and state; but all other men are called heads with reference to certain special places, as bishops of their Churches. Or with reference to a determined time as the Pope is the head of the whole Church, viz. during the time of his

264

Pontificate, and with reference to a determined state, inasmuch as they are in the state of wayfarers. Secondly, because Christ is the Head of the Church by His own power and authority; while others are called heads, as taking Christ's place, according to 2 Cor. 2:10, "For what I have pardoned, if I have pardoned anything, for your sakes I have done it in the person of Christ," and 2 Cor. 5:20, "For Christ therefore we are ambassadors, God, as it were, exhorting by us."

Reply to Objection 1: The word "head" is employed in that passage in regard to exterior government; as a king is said to be the head of his kingdom.

Reply to Objection 2: Man does not distribute grace by interior influx, but by exteriorly persuading to the effects of grace.

Reply to Objection 3: As Augustine says (Tract. xlvi in Joan.): "If the rulers of the Church are Shepherds, how is there one Shepherd, except that all these are members of one Shepherd?" So likewise others may be called foundations and heads, inasmuch as they are members of the one Head and Foundation. Nevertheless, as Augustine says (Tract. xlvii), "He gave to His members to be shepherds; yet none of us calleth himself the Door. He kept this for Himself alone." And this because by door is implied the principal authority, inasmuch as it is by the door that all enter the house; and it is Christ alone by "Whom also we have access . . . into this grace, wherein we stand" (Rom. 5:2); but by the other names above-mentioned there may be implied not merely the principal but also the secondary authority.

Whether the devil is the head of all the wicked?

Objection 1: It would seem that the devil is not the head of the wicked. For it belongs to the head to diffuse sense and movement into the members, as a gloss says, on Eph. 1:22, "And made Him head," etc. But the devil has no power of spreading the evil of sin, which proceeds from the will of the sinner. Therefore the devil cannot be called the head of the wicked.

Objection 2: Further, by every sin a man is made evil. But not every sin is from the devil; and this is plain as regards the demons, who did not sin through the persuasion of another; so likewise not every sin of man proceeds from the devil, for it is said (De Eccles. Dogm. lxxxii): "Not all our wicked thoughts are always raised up by the suggestion of the devil; but sometimes they spring from the movement of our will." Therefore the devil is not the head of all the wicked.

Objection 3: Further, one head is placed on one body. But the whole multitude of the wicked do not seem to have anything in which they are united, for evil is contrary to evil and springs from divers defects, as Dionysius says (Div. Nom. iv). Therefore the devil cannot be called the head of all the wicked.

On the contrary, A gloss [*St. Gregory, Moral. xiv] on Job 18:17, "Let the memory of him perish from the earth," says: "This is said of every evil one, yet so as to be referred to the head," i.e. the devil.

I answer that, As was said above [3961](A[6]), the head not only influences the members interiorly, but also governs them exteriorly, directing their actions to an end. Hence it may be said that anyone is the head of a multitude, either as regards both, i.e. by interior influence and exterior governance, and thus Christ is the Head of the Church, as was stated [3962](A[6]); or as regards exterior governance, and thus every prince or prelate is head of the multitude subject to him. And in this way the devil is head of all the wicked. For, as is written (Job 41:25): "He is king over all the children of pride." Now it belongs to a governor to lead those whom he governs to their end. But the end of the devil is the aversion of the rational creature from God; hence from the beginning he has endeavored to lead man from obeying the Divine precept. But aversion from God has the nature of an end, inasmuch as it is sought for under the appearance of liberty, according to Jer. 2:20: "Of old time thou hast broken my yoke, thou hast burst my bands, and thou saidst, 'I will not serve.'" Hence, inasmuch as some are brought to this end by sinning, they fall under the rule and government of the devil, and therefore he is called their head.

Reply to Objection 1: Although the devil does not influence the rational mind interiorly, yet he beguiles it to evil by persuasion.

Reply to Objection 2: A governor does not always suggest to his subjects to obey his will; but proposes to all the sign of his will, in consequence of which some are incited by inducement, and some of their own free-will, as is plain in the leader of an army, whose standard all the soldiers follow, though no one persuades them. Therefore in the same way, the first sin of the devil, who "sinneth from the beginning" (1 Jn. 3:8), is held out to all to be followed, and some imitate at his suggestion, and some of their own will without any suggestion. And hence the devil is the head of all the wicked, inasmuch as they imitate Him, according to Wis. 2:24,25: "By the envy of the devil, death came into the world. And they follow him that are of his side."

Reply to Objection 3: All sins agree in aversion from God, although they differ by conversion to different changeable goods.

Whether Anti-christ may be called the head of all the wicked?

Objection 1: It would seem that Antichrist is not the head of the wicked. For there are not several heads of one body. But the devil is the head of the multitude of the wicked. Therefore Anti-christ is not their head.

Objection 2: Further, Anti-christ is a member of the devil. Now the head is distinguished from the members. Therefore Anti-christ is not the head of the wicked.

Objection 3: Further, the head has an influence over the members. But Anti-christ has no influence over the wicked who have preceded him. Therefore Anti-christ is not the head of the wicked.

On the contrary, A gloss [*St. Gregory, Moral. xv] on Job 21:29, "Ask any of them that go by the way," says: "Whilst he was speaking of the body of all the wicked, suddenly he turned his speech to Anti-christ the head of all evil-doers."

I answer that, As was said above [3963](A[1]), in the head are found three things: order, perfection, and the power of influencing. But as regards the order of the body, Anti-christ is not said to be the head of the wicked as if his sin had preceded, as the sin of the devil preceded. So likewise he is not called the head of the wicked from the power of influencing, although he will pervert some in his day by exterior persuasion; nevertheless those who were before him were not beguiled into wickedness by him nor have imitated his wickedness. Hence he cannot be called the head of all the wicked in this way, but of some. Therefore it remains to be said that he is the head of all the wicked by reason of the perfection of his wickedness. Hence, on 2 Thess. 2:4, "Showing himself as if he were God," a gloss says: "As in Christ dwelt the fulness of the Godhead, so in Anti-christ the fulness of all wickedness." Not indeed as if his humanity were assumed by the devil into unity of person, as the humanity of Christ by the Son of God; but that the devil by suggestion infuses his wickedness more copiously into him than into all others. And in this way all the wicked who have gone before are signs of Anti-christ, according to 2 Thess. 2:7, "For the mystery of iniquity already worketh."

Reply to Objection 1: The devil and Anti-christ are not two heads, but one; since Anti-christ is called the head, inasmuch as the wickedness of the devil is most fully impressed on him. Hence, on 2 Thess. 2:4, "Showing himself as if he were God," a gloss says: "The head of all the wicked, namely the devil, who is king over all the children of pride will be in him." Now he is said to be in him not by personal union, nor by indwelling, since "the Trinity alone dwells in the mind" (as is said De Eccles. Dogm. lxxxiii), but by the effect of wickedness.

Reply to Objection 2: As the head of Christ is God, and yet He is the Head of the Church, as was said above (A[1], ad 2), so likewise Anti-christ is a member of the devil and yet is head of the wicked.

Reply to Objection 3: Anti-christ is said to be the head of all the wicked not by a likeness of influence, but by a likeness of perfection. For in him the devil, as it were, brings his wickedness to a head, in the same way that anyone is said to bring his purpose to a head when he executes it.

OF CHRIST'S KNOWLEDGE IN GENERAL (FOUR ARTICLES)

We must now consider Christ's knowledge; concerning which the consideration will be twofold. First, of Christ's knowledge in general; secondly, of each particular kind of knowledge He had.

Under the first head there are four points of inquiry:

(1) Whether Christ had any knowledge besides the Divine?

(2) Whether He had the knowledge which the blessed or comprehensors have?

(3) Whether He had an imprinted or infused knowledge?

(4) Whether He had any acquired knowledge?

Whether Christ had any knowledge besides the Divine?

Objection 1: It would seem that in Christ there was no knowledge except the Divine. For knowledge is necessary that things may be known thereby. But by His Divine knowledge Christ knew all things. Therefore any other knowledge would have been superfluous in Him.

Objection 2: Further, the lesser light is dimmed by the greater. But all created knowledge in comparison with the uncreated knowledge of God is as the lesser to the greater light. Therefore there shone in Christ no other knowledge except the Divine.

Objection 3: Further, the union of the human nature with the Divine took place in the Person, as is clear from[3964] Q[2], A[2]. Now, according to some there is in Christ a certain "knowledge of the union," whereby Christ knew what belongs to the mystery of the Incarnation more fully than anyone else. Hence, since the personal union contains two natures, it would seem that there are not two knowledges in Christ, but one only, pertaining to both natures.

On the contrary, Ambrose says (De Incarnat. vii): "God assumed the perfection of human nature in the flesh; He took upon Himself the sense of man, but not the swollen sense of the flesh." But created knowledge pertains to the sense of man. Therefore in Christ there was created knowledge.

I answer that, As said above ([3965]Q[5]), the Son of God assumed an entire human nature, i.e. not only a body, but also a soul, and not only a sensitive, but also a rational soul. And therefore it behooved Him to have created knowledge, for three reasons. First, on account of the soul's perfection. For the soul, considered in itself, is in potentiality to knowing intelligible things. since it is like "a tablet on which nothing is written," and yet it may be written upon through the possible intellect, whereby it may become all things, as is said De Anima iii, 18. Now what is in potentiality is imperfect unless reduced to act. But it was fitting that the Son of God should assume, not an imperfect, but a perfect human nature, since the whole human race was to be brought back to perfection by its means. Hence it behooved the soul of Christ to be perfected by a knowledge, which would be its proper perfection. And therefore it was necessary that there should be another knowledge in Christ besides the Divine knowledge, otherwise the soul of Christ would have been more imperfect than the souls of the rest of men. Secondly, because, since everything is on account of its operation, as stated De Coel. ii, 17, Christ would have had an intellective soul to no purpose if He had not understood by it; and this pertains to created knowledge. Thirdly, because some created knowledge pertains to the nature of the human soul, viz. that whereby we naturally know first principles; since we are here taking knowledge for any cognition of the human intellect. Now nothing natural was wanting to Christ, since He took the whole human nature, as stated above ([3966]Q[5]). And hence the Sixth Council [*Third Council of Constantinople, Act. 4] condemned the opinion of those who denied that in Christ there are two knowledges or wisdoms.

Reply to Objection 1: Christ knew all things with the Divine knowledge by an uncreated operation which is the very Essence of God; since God's understanding is His substance, as the Philosopher proves (Metaph. xii, text. 39). Hence this act could not belong to the human soul of Christ, seeing that it belongs to another nature. Therefore, if there had been no other knowledge in the soul of Christ, it would have known nothing; and thus it would have been assumed to no purpose, since everything is on account of its operation.

Reply to Objection 2: If the two lights are supposed to be in the same order, the lesser is dimmed by the greater, as the light of the sun dims the light of a candle, both being in the class of illuminants. But if we suppose two lights, one of which is in the class of illuminants and the other in the class of illuminated, the lesser light is not dimmed by the greater, but rather is strengthened, as the light of the air by the light of the sun. And in this manner the light of knowledge is not dimmed, but rather is heightened in the soul of

Christ by the light of the Divine knowledge, which is "the true light which enlighteneth every man that cometh into this world," as is written Jn. 1:9.

Reply to Objection 3: On the part of what are united we hold there is a knowledge in Christ, both as to His Divine and as to His human nature; so that, by reason of the union whereby there is one hypostasis of God and man, the things of God are attributed to man, and the things of man are attributed to God, as was said above ([3967]Q[3], AA[1],6). But on the part of the union itself we cannot admit any knowledge in Christ. For this union is in personal being, and knowledge belongs to person only by reason of a nature.

Whether Christ had the knowledge which the blessed or comprehensors have?

Objection 1: It would seem that in Christ there was not the knowledge of the blessed or comprehensors. For the knowledge of the blessed is a participation of Divine light, according to Ps. 35:10: "In Thy light we shall see light." Now Christ had not a participated light, but He had the Godhead Itself substantially abiding in Him, according to Col. 2:9: "For in Him dwelleth all the fulness of the Godhead corporeally." Therefore in Christ there was not the knowledge of the blessed.

Objection 2: Further, the knowledge of the blessed makes them blessed, according to Jn. 17:3: "This is eternal life: that they may know Thee, the only true God, and Jesus Christ Whom Thou hast sent." But this Man was blessed through being united to God in person, according to Ps. 64:5: "Blessed is He Whom Thou hast chosen and taken to Thee." Therefore it is not necessary to suppose the knowledge of the blessed in Him.

Objection 3: Further, to man belongs a double knowledge---one by nature, one above nature. Now the knowledge of the blessed, which consists in the vision of God, is not natural to man, but above his nature. But in Christ there was another and much higher supernatural knowledge, i.e. the Divine knowledge. Therefore there was no need of the knowledge of the blessed in Christ.

On the contrary, The knowledge of the blessed consists in the knowledge of God. But He knew God fully, even as He was man, according to Jn. 8:55: "I do know Him, and do keep His word." Therefore in Christ there was the knowledge of the blessed.

I answer that, What is in potentiality is reduced to act by what is in act; for that whereby things are heated must itself be hot. Now man is in potentiality to the knowledge of the blessed, which consists in the vision of God; and is ordained to it as to an end; since the rational creature is capable of that blessed knowledge, inasmuch as he is made in the image of God. Now men are brought to this end of beatitude by the humanity of Christ, according to Heb. 2:10: "For it became Him, for Whom are all things, and by Whom are all things, Who had brought many children unto glory, to perfect the author of their salvation by His passion." And hence it was necessary that the beatific knowledge, which consists in the vision of God, should belong to Christ pre-eminently, since the cause ought always to be more efficacious than the effect.

Reply to Objection 1: The Godhead is united to the manhood of Christ in Person, not in essence or nature; yet with the unity of Person remains the distinction of natures. And therefore the soul of Christ, which is a part of human nature, through a light participated from the Divine Nature, is perfected with the beatific knowledge whereby it sees God in essence.

Reply to Objection 2: By the union this Man is blessed with the uncreated beatitude, even as by the union He is God; yet besides the uncreated beatitude it was necessary that there should be in the human nature of Christ a created beatitude, whereby His soul was established in the last end of human nature.

Reply to Objection 3: The beatific vision and knowledge are to some extent above the nature of the rational soul, inasmuch as it cannot reach it of its own strength; but in another way it is in accordance with its nature, inasmuch as it is capable of it by nature, having been made to the likeness of God, as stated above. But the uncreated knowledge is in every way above the nature of the human soul.

Whether Christ had an imprinted or infused knowledge?

Objection 1: It would seem that there was not in Christ another infused knowledge besides the beatific knowledge. For all other knowledge compared to the beatific knowledge is like imperfect to perfect. But imperfect knowledge is removed by the presence of perfect knowledge, as the clear "face-to-face" vision removes the enigmatical vision of faith, as is plain from 1 Cor. 13:10,12. Since, therefore, in Christ there was the beatific knowledge, as stated above [3968](A[2]), it would seem that there could not be any other imprinted knowledge.

Objection 2: Further, an imperfect mode of cognition disposes towards a more perfect, as opinion, the result of dialectical syllogisms, disposes towards science, which results from demonstrative syllogisms. Now, when perfection is reached, there is no further need of the disposition, even as on reaching the end motion is no longer necessary. Hence, since every created cognition is compared to beatific cognition, as imperfect to perfect and as disposition to its term, it seems that since Christ had beatific knowledge, it was not necessary for Him to have any other knowledge.

Objection 3: Further, as corporeal matter is in potentiality to sensible forms, so the possible intellect is in potentiality to intelligible forms. Now corporeal matter cannot receive two forms at once! one more perfect and the other less perfect. Therefore neither can the soul receive a double knowledge at once, one more perfect and the other less perfect; and hence the same conclusion as above.

On the contrary, It is written (Col. 2:3) that in Christ "are hid all the treasures of wisdom and knowledge."

I answer that, As stated above [3969](A[1]), it was fitting that the human nature assumed by the Word of God should not be imperfect. Now everything in potentiality is imperfect unless it be reduced to act. But the passive intellect of man is in potentiality to all intelligible things. and it is reduced to act by intelligible species, which are its completive forms, as is plain from what is said De Anima iii, 32,38. And hence we must admit in the soul of Christ an infused knowledge, inasmuch as the Word of God imprinted upon the soul of Christ, which is personally united to Him, intelligible species of all things to which the possible intellect is in potentiality; even as in the beginning of the creation of things, the Word of God imprinted intelligible species upon the angelic mind, as is clear from Augustine (Gen. ad lit. ii, 8). And therefore, even as in the angels, according to Augustine (Gen. ad lit. iv, 22,24,30), there is a double knowledge---one the morning knowledge, whereby they know things in the Word; the other the evening knowledge, whereby they know things in their proper natures by infused species; so likewise, besides the Divine and uncreated knowledge in Christ, there is in His soul a beatific knowledge, whereby He knows the Word, and things in the Word; and an infused or imprinted knowledge, whereby He knows things in their proper nature by intelligible species proportioned to the human mind.

Reply to Objection 1: The imperfect vision of faith is essentially opposed to manifest vision, seeing that it is of the essence of faith to have reference to the unseen, as was said above ([3970]SS, Q[1], A[4]). But cognition by infused species includes no opposition to beatific cognition. Therefore there is no parity.

Reply to Objection 2: Disposition is referred to perfection in two ways: first, as a way leading to perfection; secondly, as an effect proceeding from perfection; thus matter is disposed by heat to receive the form of fire, and, when this comes, the heat does not cease, but remains as an effect of this form. So, too, opinion caused by a dialectical syllogism is a way to knowledge, which is acquired by demonstration, yet, when this has been acquired, there may still remain the knowledge gained by the dialectical syllogism, following, so to say, the demonstrative knowledge, which is based on the cause, since he who knows the cause is thereby enabled the better to understand the probable signs from which dialectical syllogisms proceed. So likewise in Christ, together with the beatific knowledge, there still remains infused knowledge, not as a way to beatitude, but as strengthened by beatitude.

Reply to Objection 3: The beatific knowledge is not by a species, that is a similitude of the Divine Essence, or of whatever is known in the Divine Essence, as is plain from what has been said in the [3971]FP, Q[12], A[2]; but it is a knowledge of the Divine Essence immediately, inasmuch as the Divine Essence itself is united to the beatified mind as an intelligible to an intelligent being; and the Divine Essence is a form exceeding the capacity of any creature whatsoever. Hence, together with this super-exceeding form, there is nothing to hinder from being in the rational mind, intelligible species, proportioned to its nature.

Whether Christ had any acquired knowledge?

Objection 1: It would seem that in Christ there was no empiric and acquired knowledge. For whatever befitted Christ, He had most perfectly. Now Christ did not possess acquired knowledge most perfectly, since He did not devote Himself to the study of letters, by which knowledge is acquired in its perfection; for it is said (Jn. 7:15): "The Jews wondered, saying: How doth this Man know letters, having never learned?" Therefore it seems that in Christ there was no acquired knowledge.

Objection 2: Further, nothing can be added to what is full. But the power of Christ's soul was filled with intelligible species divinely infused, as was said above (A. 3). Therefore no acquired species could accrue to His soul.

Objection 3: Further, he who already has the habit of knowledge, acquires no new habit, through what he receives from the senses (otherwise two forms of the same species would be in the same thing together); but the habit which previously existed is strengthened and increased. Therefore, since Christ had the habit of infused knowledge, it does not seem that He acquired a new knowledge through what He perceived by the senses.

On the contrary, It is written (Heb. 5:8): "Whereas . . . He was the Son of God, He learned obedience by the things which He suffered," i.e. "experienced," says a gloss. Therefore there was in the soul of Christ an empiric knowledge, which is acquired knowledge.

I answer that, As is plain from A[1], nothing that God planted in our nature was wanting to the human nature assumed by the Word of God. Now it is manifest that God planted in human nature not only a passive, but an active intellect. Hence it is necessary to say that in the soul of Christ there was not merely a passive, but also an active intellect. But if in other things God and nature make nothing in vain, as the Philosopher says (De Coel. i, 31; ii, 59), still less in the soul of Christ is there anything in vain. Now what has not its proper operation is useless, as is said in De Coel. ii, 17. Now the proper operation of the active intellect is to make intelligible species in act, by abstracting them from phantasms; hence, it is said (De Anima iii, 18) that the active intellect is that "whereby everything is made actual." And thus it is necessary to say that in Christ there were intelligible species received in the passive intellect by the action of the active intellect---which means that there was acquired knowledge in Him, which some call empiric. And hence, although I wrote differently (Sent. iii, D, xiv, A[3]; D, xviii, A[3]), it must be said that in Christ there was acquired knowledge, which is properly knowledge in a human fashion, both as regards the subject receiving and as regards the active cause. For such knowledge springs from Christ's active intellect, which is natural to the human soul. But infused knowledge is attributed to the soul, on account of a light infused from on high, and this manner of knowing is proportioned to the angelic nature. But the beatific knowledge, whereby the very Essence of God is seen, is proper and natural to God alone, as was said in the [3972]FP, Q[12], A[4].

Reply to Objection 1: Since there is a twofold way of acquiring knowledge---by discovery and by being taught---the way of discovery is the higher, and the way of being taught is secondary. Hence it is said (Ethic. i, 4): "He indeed is the best who knows everything by himself: yet he is good who obeys him that speaks aright." And hence it was more fitting for Christ to possess a knowledge acquired by discovery than by being taught, especially since He was given to be the Teacher of all, according to Joel 2:23: "Be joyful in the Lord your God, because He hath given you a Teacher of justice."

Reply to Objection 2: The human mind has two relations---one to higher things, and in this respect the soul of Christ was full of the infused knowledge. The other relation is to lower things, i.e. to phantasms, which naturally move the human mind by virtue of the active intellect. Now it was necessary that even in this respect the soul of Christ should be filled with knowledge, not that the first fulness was insufficient for the human mind in itself, but that it behooved it to be also perfected with regard to phantasms.

Reply to Objection 3: Acquired and infused habits are not to be classed together; for the habit of knowledge is acquired by the relation of the human mind to phantasms; hence, another habit of the same kind cannot be again acquired. But the habit of infused knowledge is of a different nature, as coming down to the soul from on high, and not from phantasms. And hence there is no parity between these habits.

OF THE BEATIFIC KNOWLEDGE OF CHRIST'S SOUL (FOUR ARTICLES)

Now we must consider each of the aforesaid knowledges. Since, however, we have treated of the Divine knowledge in the FP, Q[14], it now remains to speak of the three others: (1) of the beatific knowledge; (2) of the infused knowledge; (3) of the acquired knowledge.

But again, because much has been said in the FP, Q[12], of the beatific knowledge, which consists in the vision of God, we shall speak here only of such things as belong properly to the soul of Christ. Under this head there are four points of inquiry:

(1) Whether the soul of Christ comprehended the Word or the Divine Essence?
(2) Whether it knew all things in the Word?
(3) Whether the soul of Christ knew the infinite in the Word?
(4) Whether it saw the Word or the Divine Essence clearer than did any other creature?

Whether the soul of Christ comprehended the Word or the Divine Essence?

Objection 1: It would seem that the soul of Christ comprehended and comprehends the Word or Divine Essence. For Isidore says (De Summo Bono i, 3) that "the Trinity is known only to Itself and to the Man assumed." Therefore the Man assumed communicates with the Holy Trinity in that knowledge of Itself which is proper to the Trinity. Now this is the knowledge of comprehension. Therefore the soul of Christ comprehends the Divine Essence.

Objection 2: Further, to be united to God in personal being is greater than to be united by vision. But as Damascene says (De Fide Orth. iii, 6), "the whole Godhead in one Person is united to the human nature in Christ." Therefore much more is the whole Divine Nature seen by the soul of Christ; and hence it would seem that the soul of Christ comprehended the Divine Essence.

Objection 3: Further, what belongs by nature to the Son of God belongs by grace to the Son of Man, as Augustine says (De Trin. i, 13). But to comprehend the Divine Essence belongs by nature to the Son of God. Therefore it belongs by grace to the Son of Man; and thus it seems that the soul of Christ comprehended the Divine Essence by grace.

On the contrary, Augustine says (Qq. lxxxiii, qu. 14): "Whatsoever comprehends itself is finite to itself." But the Divine Essence is not finite with respect to the soul of Christ, since It infinitely exceeds it. Therefore the soul of Christ does not comprehend the Word.

I answer that, As is plain from Q[2], AA[1],6, the union of the two natures in the Person of Christ took place in such a way that the properties of both natures remained unconfused, i.e. "the uncreated remained uncreated, and the created remained within the limits of the creature," as Damascene says (De Fide Orth. iii, 3,4). Now it is impossible for any creature to comprehend the Divine Essence, as was shown in the [3973]FP, Q[12], AA[1],4,7, seeing that the infinite is not comprehended by the finite. And hence it must be said that the soul of Christ nowise comprehends the Divine Essence.

Reply to Objection 1: The Man assumed is reckoned with the Divine Trinity in the knowledge of Itself, not indeed as regards comprehension, but by reason of a certain most excellent knowledge above the rest of creatures.

Reply to Objection 2: Not even in the union by personal being does the human nature comprehend the Word of God or the Divine Nature, for although it was wholly united to the human nature in the one Person of the Son, yet the whole power of the Godhead was not circumscribed by the human nature. Hence Augustine says (Ep. ad Volusian. cxxxvii): "I would have you know that it is not the Christian doctrine that God was united to flesh in such a manner as to quit or lose the care of the world's government, neither did Ne narrow or reduce it when He transferred it to that little body." So likewise the soul of Christ sees the whole Essence of God, yet does not comprehend It; since it does not see It totally, i.e. not as perfectly as It is knowable, as was said in the [3974]FP, Q[12], A[7].

Reply to Objection 3: This saying of Augustine is to be understood of the grace of union, by reason of which all that is said of the Son of God in His Divine Nature is also said of the Son of Man on account of the identity of suppositum. And in this way it may be said that the Son of Man is a comprehensor of the Divine Essence, not indeed by His soul, but in His Divine Nature; even as we may also say that the Son of Man is the Creator.

Whether the Son of God knew all things in the Word?

Objection 2: It would seem that the soul of Christ does not know all things in the Word. For it is written (Mk. 13:32): "But of that day or hour no man knoweth, neither the angels in heaven nor the Son, but the Father." Therefore He does not know all things in the Word.

Objection 2: Further, the more perfectly anyone knows a principle the more he knows in the principle. But God sees His Essence more perfectly than the soul of Christ does. Therefore He knows more than the soul of Christ knows in the Word. Therefore the soul of Christ does not know all things in the Word.

Objection 3: Further, the extent depends on the number of things known. If, therefore, the soul of Christ knew in the Word all that the Word knows, it would follow that the knowledge of the soul of Christ would equal the Divine knowledge, i.e. the created would equal the uncreated, which is impossible.

On the contrary, on Apoc. 5:12, "The Lamb that was slain is worthy to receive . . . divinity and wisdom," a gloss says, i.e. "the knowledge of all things."

I answer that, When it is inquired whether Christ knows all things in the Word, "all things" may be taken in two ways: First, properly, to stand for all that in any way whatsoever is, will be, or was done, said, or thought, by whomsoever and at any time. And in this way it must be said that the soul of Christ knows all things in the Word. For every created intellect knows in the Word, not all simply, but so many more things the more perfectly it sees the Word. Yet no beatified intellect fails to know in the Word whatever pertains to itself. Now to Christ and to His dignity all things to some extent belong, inasmuch as all things are subject to Him. Moreover, He has been appointed Judge of all by God, "because He is the Son of Man," as is said Jn. 5:27; and therefore the soul of Christ knows in the Word all things existing in whatever time, and the thoughts of men, of which He is the Judge, so that what is said of Him (Jn. 2:25), "For He knew what was in man," can be understood not merely of the Divine knowledge, but also of His soul's knowledge, which it had in the Word. Secondly, "all things" may be taken widely, as extending not merely to such things as are in act at some time, but even to such things as are in potentiality, and never have been nor ever will be reduced to act. Now some of these are in the Divine power alone, and not all of these does the soul of Christ know in the Word. For this would be to comprehend all that God could do, which would be to comprehend the Divine power, and, consequently, the Divine Essence. For every power is known from the knowledge of all it can do. Some, however, are not only in the power of God, but also in the power of the creature; and all of these the soul of Christ knows in the Word; for it comprehends in the Word the essence of every creature, and, consequently, its power and virtue, and all things that are in the power of the creature.

Reply to Objection 1: Arius and Eunomius understood this saying, not of the knowledge of the soul, which they did not hold to be in Christ, as was said above ([3975]Q[9], A[1]), but of the Divine knowledge of the Son, Whom they held to be less than the Father as regards knowledge. But this will not stand, since all things were made by the Word of God, as is said Jn. 1:3, and, amongst other things, all times were made by Him. Now He is not ignorant of anything that was made by Him.

He is said, therefore, not to know the day and the hour of the Judgment, for that He does not make it known, since, on being asked by the apostles (Acts 1:7), He was unwilling to reveal it; and, on the contrary, we read (Gn. 22:12): "Now I know that thou fearest God," i.e. "Now I have made thee know." But the Father is said to know, because He imparted this knowledge to the Son. Hence, by saying but the Father, we are given to understand that the Son knows, not merely in the Divine Nature, but also in the human, because, as Chrysostom argues (Hom. lxxviii in Matth.), if it is given to Christ as man to know how to judge---which is greater---much more is it given to Him to know the less, viz. the time of Judgment. Origen, however (in Matth. Tract. xxx), expounds it of His body, which is the Church, which is ignorant of this time. Lastly, some say this is to be understood of the adoptive, and not of the natural Son of God.

Reply to Objection 2: God knows His Essence so much the more perfectly than the soul of Christ, as He comprehends it. And hence He knows all things, not merely whatever are in act at any time, which things He is said to know by knowledge of vision, but also what ever He Himself can do, which He is said to know by simple intelligence, as was shown in the [3976]FP, Q[14], A[9]. Therefore the soul of Christ knows all things that God knows in Himself by the knowledge of vision, but not all that God knows in Himself by knowledge of simple intelligence; and thus in Himself God knows many more things than the soul of Christ.

Reply to Objection 3: The extent of knowledge depends not merely on the number of knowable things, but also on the clearness of the knowledge. Therefore, although the knowledge of the soul of Christ which He has in the Word is equal to the knowledge of vision as regards the number of things known, nevertheless the knowledge of God infinitely exceeds the knowledge of the soul of Christ in clearness of cognition, since the uncreated light of the Divine intellect infinitely exceeds any created light received by the soul of Christ; although, absolutely speaking, the Divine knowledge exceeds the knowledge of the soul of Christ, not only as regards the mode of knowing, but also as regards the number of things known, as was stated above.

Day 257

Whether the soul of Christ can know the infinite in the Word?

Objection 1: It would seem that the soul of Christ cannot know the infinite in the Word. For that the infinite should be known is repugnant to the definition of the infinite which (Phys. iii, 63) is said to be that "from which, however much we may take, there always remains something to be taken." But it is impossible for the definition to be separated from the thing defined, since this would mean that contradictories exist together. Therefore it is impossible that the soul of Christ knows the infinite.

Objection 2: Further, the knowledge of the infinite is infinite. But the knowledge of the soul of Christ cannot be infinite, because its capacity is finite, since it is created. Therefore the soul of Christ cannot know the infinite.

Objection 3: Further, there can be nothing greater than the infinite. But more is contained in the Divine knowledge, absolutely speaking, than in the knowledge of Christ's soul, as stated above [3977](A[2]). Therefore the soul of Christ does not know the infinite.

On the contrary, The soul of Christ knows all its power and all it can do. Now it can cleanse infinite sins, according to 1 Jn. 2:2: "He is the propitiation for our sins, and not for ours only, but also for those of the whole world." Therefore the soul of Christ knows the infinite.

I answer that, Knowledge regards only being, since being and truth are convertible. Now a thing is said to be a being in two ways: First, simply, i.e. whatever is a being in act; secondly, relatively, i.e. whatever is a being in potentiality. And because, as is said Metaph. ix, 20, everything is known as it is in act, and not as it is in potentiality, knowledge primarily and essentially regards being in act, and secondarily regards being in potentiality, which is not knowable of itself, but inasmuch as that in whose power it exists is known. Hence, with regard to the first mode of knowledge, the soul of Christ does not know the infinite. Because there is not an infinite number in act, even though we were to reckon all that are in act at any time whatsoever, since the state of generation and corruption will not last for ever: consequently there is a certain number not only of things lacking generation and corruption, but also of things capable of generation and corruption. But with regard to the other mode of knowing, the soul of Christ knows infinite things in the Word, for it knows, as stated above [3978](A[2]), all that is in the power of the creature. Hence, since in the power of the creature there is an infinite number of things, it knows the infinite, as it were, by a certain knowledge of simple intelligence, and not by a knowledge of vision.

Reply to Objection 1: As we said in the [3979]FP, Q[8], A[1], the infinite is taken in two ways. First, on the part of a form, and thus we have the negatively infinite, i.e. a form or act not limited by being received into matter or a subject; and this infinite of itself is most knowable on account of the perfection of the act, although it is not comprehensible by the finite power of the creature; for thus God is said to be infinite. And this infinite the soul of Christ knows, yet does not comprehend. Secondly, there is the infinite as regards matter, which is taken privatively, i.e. inasmuch as it has not the form it ought naturally to have, and in this way we have infinite in quantity. Now such an infinite of itself, is unknown: inasmuch as it is, as it were, matter with privation of form as is said Phys. iii, 65. But all knowledge is by form or act. Therefore if this infinite is to be known according to its mode of being, it cannot be known. For its mode is that part be taken after part, as is said Phys. iii, 62,63. And in this way it is true that, if we take something from it, i.e. taking part after part, there always remains something to be taken. But as material things can be received by the intellect immaterially, and many things unitedly, so can infinite things be received by the intellect, not after the manner of infinite, but finitely; and thus what are in themselves infinite are, in the intellect of the knower, finite. And in this way the soul of Christ knows an infinite number of things, inasmuch as it knows them not by discoursing from one to another, but in a certain unity, i.e. in any creature in whose potentiality infinite things exist, and principally in the Word Himself.

Reply to Objection 2: There is nothing to hinder a thing from being infinite in one way and finite in another, as when in quantities we imagine a surface infinite in length and finite in breadth. Hence, if there were an infinite number of men, they would have a relative infinity, i.e. in multitude; but, as regards the essence, they would be finite, since the essence of all would be limited to one specific nature. But what is simply infinite in its essence is God, as was said in the [3980]FP, Q[7], A[2]. Now the proper object of the intellect is "what a thing is," as is said De Anima iii, 26, to which pertains the notion of the species. And thus the soul of Christ, since it has a finite capacity, attains to, but does not comprehend, what is simply infinite in essence, as stated above (A[1]). But the infinite in potentiality which is in creatures can be comprehended by the soul of Christ, since it is compared to that soul according to its essence, in which respect it is not infinite. For even our intellect understands a universal---for example, the nature of a genus or species, which in a manner has infinity, inasmuch as it can be predicated of an infinite number.

Reply to Objection 3: That which is infinite in every way can be but one. Hence the Philosopher says (De Coel. i, 2,3,) that, since bodies have dimensions in every part, there cannot be several infinite bodies. Yet if anything were infinite in one way only, nothing would hinder the existence of several such infinite things; as if we were to suppose several lines of infinite length drawn on a surface of finite breadth. Hence, because infinitude is not a substance, but is accidental to things that are said to be infinite, as the Philosopher says (Phys. iii, 37,38); as the infinite is multiplied by different subjects, so, too, a property of the infinite must be multiplied, in such a way that it belongs to each of them according to that particular subject. Now it is a property of the infinite that nothing is greater than it. Hence, if we take one infinite line, there is nothing greater in it than the infinite; so, too, if we take any one of other infinite lines, it is plain that each has infinite parts. Therefore of necessity in this particular line there is nothing greater than all these infinite parts; yet in another or a third line there will be more infinite parts besides these. We observe this in numbers also, for the species of even numbers are infinite, and likewise the species of odd numbers are infinite; yet there are more even and odd numbers than even. And thus it must be said that nothing is greater than the simply and in every way infinite; but than the infinite which is limited in some respect, nothing is greater in that order; yet we may suppose something greater outside that order. In this way, therefore, there are infinite things in the potentiality of the creature, and yet there are more in the power of God than in the potentiality of the creature. So, too, the soul of Christ knows infinite things by the knowledge of simple intelligence; yet God knows more by this manner of knowledge or understanding.

Whether the soul of Christ sees the Word or the Divine Essence more clearly than does any other creature?

Objection 1: It would seem that the soul of Christ does not see the Word more perfectly than does any other creature. For the perfection of knowledge depends upon the medium of knowing; as the knowledge we have by means of a demonstrative syllogism is more perfect than that which we have by means of a probable syllogism. But all the blessed see the Word immediately in the Divine Essence Itself, as was said in the [3981]FP, Q[12], A[2]. Therefore the soul of Christ does not see the Word more perfectly than any other creature.

Objection 2: Further, the perfection of vision does not exceed the power of seeing. But the rational power of a soul such as is the soul of Christ is below the intellective power of an angel, as is plain from Dionysius (Coel. Hier. iv). Therefore the soul of Christ did not see the Word more perfectly than the angels.

Objection 3: Further, God sees His Word infinitely more perfectly than does the soul of Christ. Hence there are infinite possible mediate degrees between the manner in which God sees His Word, and the manner in which the soul of Christ sees the Word. Therefore we cannot assert that the soul of Christ sees the Word or the Divine Essence more perfectly than does every other creature.

On the contrary, The Apostle says (Eph. 1:20,21) that God set Christ "on His right hand in the heavenly places, above all principality and power and virtue and dominion and every name that is named not only in this world, but also in that which is to come." But in that heavenly glory the higher anyone is the more perfectly does he know God. Therefore the soul of Christ sees God more perfectly than does any other creature.

I answer that, The vision of the Divine Essence is granted to all the blessed by a partaking of the Divine light which is shed upon them from the fountain of the Word of God, according to Ecclus. 1:5: "The Word of God on high is the fountain of Wisdom." Now the soul of Christ, since it is united to the Word in person, is more closely joined to the Word of God than any other creature. Hence it more fully receives the light in which God is seen by the Word Himself than any other creature. And therefore more perfectly than the rest of creatures it sees the First Truth itself, which is the Essence of God; hence it is written (Jn. 1:14): "And we saw His glory, the glory as it were of the Only-begotten of the Father," "full" not only of "grace" but also of "truth."

Reply to Objection 1: Perfection of knowledge, on the part of the thing known, depends on the medium; but as regards the knower, it depends on the power or habit. And hence it is that even amongst men one sees a conclusion in a medium more perfectly than another does. And in this way the soul of Christ, which is filled with a more abundant light, knows the Divine Essence more perfectly than do the other blessed, although all see the Divine Essence in itself.

Reply to Objection 2: The vision of the Divine Essence exceeds the natural power of any creature, as was said in the [3982]FP, Q[12], A[4]. And hence the degrees thereof depend rather on the order of grace in which Christ is supreme, than on the order of nature, in which the angelic nature is placed before the human.

Reply to Objection 3: As stated above ([3983]Q[7], A[12]), there cannot be a greater grace than the grace of Christ with respect to the union with the Word; and the same is to be said of the perfection of the Divine vision; although, absolutely speaking, there could be a higher and more sublime degree by the infinity of the Divine power.

OF THE KNOWLEDGE IMPRINTED OR INFUSED IN THE SOUL OF CHRIST (SIX ARTICLES)

We must now consider the knowledge imprinted or infused in the soul of Christ, and under this head there are six points of inquiry:
(1) Whether Christ knows all things by this knowledge?
(2) Whether He could use this knowledge by turning to phantasms?
(3) Whether this knowledge was collative?
(4) Of the comparison of this knowledge with the angelic knowledge;
(5) Whether it was a habitual knowledge?
(6) Whether it was distinguished by various habits?

Whether by this imprinted or infused knowledge Christ knew all things?

Objection 1: It would seem that by this knowledge Christ did not know all things. For this knowledge is imprinted upon Christ for the perfection of the passive intellect. Now the passive intellect of the human soul does not seem to be in potentiality to all things simply, but only to those things with regard to which it can be reduced to act by the active intellect, which is its proper motor; and these are knowable by natural reason. Therefore by this knowledge Christ did not know what exceeded the natural reason.

Objection 2: Further, phantasms are to the human intellect as colors to sight, as is said De Anima iii, 18,31,39. But it does not pertain to the perfection of the power of seeing to know what is without color. Therefore it does not pertain to the perfection of human intellect to know things of which there are no phantasms, such as separate substances. Hence, since this knowledge was in Christ for the perfection of His intellective soul, it seems that by this knowledge He did not know separate substances.

Objection 3: Further, it does not belong to the perfection of the intellect to know singulars. Hence it would seem that by this knowledge the soul of Christ did not know singulars.

On the contrary, It is written (Is. 11:2) that "the Spirit of wisdom and understanding, of knowledge and counsel shall fill Him [*Vulg.: 'The Spirit of the Lord shall rest upon Him, the Spirit of wisdom and understanding, the Spirit of counsel . . . the Spirit of knowledge . . . '; cf. Ecclus. 15:5]," under which are included all that may be known; for the knowledge of all Divine things belongs to wisdom, the knowledge of all immaterial things to understanding, the knowledge of all conclusions to knowledge [scientia], the knowledge of all practical things to counsel. Hence it would seem that by this knowledge Christ had the knowledge of all things.

I answer that, As was said above ([3984]Q[9], A[1]), it was fitting that the soul of Christ should be wholly perfected by having each of its powers reduced to act. Now it must be borne in mind that in the human soul, as in every creature, there is a double passive power: one in comparison with a natural agent; the other in comparison with the first agent, which can reduce any creature to a higher act than a natural agent can reduce it, and this is usually called the obediential power of a creature. Now both powers of Christ's soul were reduced to act by this divinely imprinted knowledge. And hence, by it the soul of Christ knew: First, whatever can be known by force of a man's active intellect, e.g. whatever pertains to human sciences; secondly, by this knowledge Christ knew all things made known to man by Divine revelation, whether they belong to the gift of wisdom or the gift of prophecy, or any other gift of the Holy Ghost; since the soul of Christ knew these things more fully and completely than others. Yet He did not know the Essence of God by this knowledge, but by the first alone, of which we spoke above ([3985]Q[10]).

Reply to Objection 1: This reason refers to the natural power of an intellective soul in comparison with its natural agent, which is the active intellect.

Reply to Objection 2: The human soul in the state of this life, since it is somewhat fettered by the body, so as to be unable to understand without phantasms, cannot understand separate substances. But after the state of this life the separated soul will be able, in a measure, to know separate substances by itself, as was said in the [3986]FP, Q[89], AA[1],2, and this is especially clear as regards the souls of the blessed. Now before His Passion, Christ was not merely a wayfarer but also a comprehensor; hence His soul could know separate substances in the same way that a separated soul could.

Reply to Objection 3: The knowledge of singulars pertains to the perfection of the intellective soul, not in speculative knowledge, but in practical knowledge, which is imperfect without the knowledge of singulars, in which operations exist, as is said Ethic. vi, 7. Hence for prudence are required the remembrance of past things, knowledge of present things, and foresight of future things, as Tully says (De Invent. ii). Therefore, since Christ had the fulness of prudence by the gift of counsel, He consequently knew all singular things---present, past, and future.

Whether Christ could use this knowledge by turning to phantasms?

Objection 1: It would seem that the soul of Christ could not understand by this knowledge except by turning to phantasms, because, as is stated De Anima iii, 18,31,39, phantasms are compared to man's intellective soul as colors to sight. But Christ's power of seeing could not become actual save by turning to colors. Therefore His intellective soul could understand nothing except by turning to phantasms.

Objection 2: Further, Christ's soul is of the same nature as ours. otherwise He would not be of the same species as we, contrary to what the Apostle says (Phil. 2:7) " . . . being made in the likeness of men." But our soul cannot understand except by turning to phantasms. Hence, neither can Christ's soul otherwise understand.

Objection 3: Further, senses are given to man to help his intellect. Hence, if the soul of Christ could understand without turning to phantasms, which arise in the senses, it would follow that in the soul of Christ the senses were useless, which is not fitting. Therefore it seems that the soul of Christ can only understand by turning to phantasms.

On the contrary, The soul of Christ knew certain things which could not be known by the senses, viz. separate substances. Therefore it could understand without turning to phantasms.

I answer that, In the state before His Passion Christ was at the same time a wayfarer and a comprehensor, as will be more clearly shown ([3987]Q[15], A[10]). Especially had He the conditions of a wayfarer on the part of the body, which was passible; but the conditions of a comprehensor He had chiefly on the part of the soul. Now this is the condition of the soul of a comprehensor, viz. that it is nowise subject to its body, or dependent upon it, but wholly dominates it. Hence after the resurrection glory will flow from the soul to the body. But the soul of man on earth needs to turn to phantasms, because it is fettered by the body and in a measure subject to and dependent upon it. And hence the blessed both before and after the resurrection can understand without turning to phantasms. And this must be said of the soul of Christ, which had fully the capabilities of a comprehensor.

Reply to Objection 1: This likeness which the Philosopher asserts is not with regard to everything. For it is manifest that the end of the power of seeing is to know colors; but the end of the intellective power is not to know phantasms, but to know intelligible species, which it apprehends from and in phantasms, according to the state of the present life. Therefore there is a likeness in respect of what both powers regard, but not in respect of that in which the condition of both powers is terminated. Now nothing prevents a thing in different states from reaching its end by different ways: albeit there is never but one proper end of a thing. Hence, although the sight knows nothing without color; nevertheless in a certain state the intellect can know without phantasms, but not without intelligible species.

Reply to Objection 2: Although the soul of Christ was of the same nature as our souls, yet it had a state which our souls have not yet in fact, but only in hope, i.e. the state of comprehension.

Reply to Objection 3: Although the soul of Christ could understand without turning to phantasms, yet it could also understand by turning to phantasms. Hence the senses were not useless in it; especially as the senses are not afforded to man solely for intellectual knowledge, but for the need of animal life.

Whether this knowledge is collative?

Objection 1: It would seem that the soul of Christ had not this knowledge by way of comparison. For Damascene says (De Fide Orth. iii, 14): "We do not uphold counsel or choice in Christ." Now these things are withheld from Christ only inasmuch as they imply comparison and discursion. Therefore it seems that there was no collative or discursive knowledge in Christ.

Objection 2: Further, man needs comparison and discursion of reason in order to find out the unknown. But the soul of Christ knew everything, as was said above ([3988]Q[10], A[2]). Hence there was no discursive or collative knowledge in Him.

Objection 3: Further, the knowledge in Christ's soul was like that of comprehensors, who are likened to the angels, according to Mat. 22:30. Now there is no collative or discursive knowledge in the angels, as Dionysius shows (Div. Nom. vii). Therefore there was no discursive or collative knowledge in the soul of Christ.

On the contrary, Christ had a rational soul, as was shown ([3989]Q[5], A[4]). Now the proper operation of a rational soul consists in comparison and discursion from one thing to another. Therefore there was collative and discursive knowledge in Christ.

I answer that, Knowledge may be discursive or collative in two ways. First, in the acquisition of the knowledge, as happens to us, who proceed from one thing to the knowledge of another, as from causes to effects, and conversely. And in this way the knowledge in Christ's soul was not discursive or collative, since this knowledge which we are now considering was divinely infused, and not acquired by a process of reasoning. Secondly, knowledge may be called discursive or collative in use; as at times those who know, reason from cause to effect, not in order to learn anew, but wishing to use the knowledge they have. And in this way the knowledge in Christ's soul could be collative or discursive; since it could conclude one thing from another, as it pleased, as in Mat. 17:24,25, when our Lord asked Peter: "Of whom do the kings of the earth receive tribute, of their own children, or of strangers?" On Peter replying: "Of strangers," He concluded: "Then the children are free."

Reply to Objection 1: From Christ is excluded that counsel which is with doubt; and consequently choice, which essentially includes such counsel; but the practice of using counsel is not excluded from Christ.

Reply to Objection 2: This reason rests upon discursion and comparison, as used to acquire knowledge.

Reply to Objection 3: The blessed are likened to the angels in the gifts of graces; yet there still remains the difference of natures. And hence to use comparison and discursion is connatural to the souls of the blessed, but not to angels.

Whether in Christ this knowledge was greater than the knowledge of the angels?

Objection 1: It would seem that this knowledge was not greater in Christ than in the angels. For perfection is proportioned to the thing perfected. But the human soul in the order of nature is below the angelic nature. Therefore since the knowledge we are now speaking of is imprinted upon Christ's soul for its perfection, it seems that this knowledge is less than the knowledge by which the angelic nature is perfected.

Objection 2: Further, the knowledge of Christ's soul was in a measure comparative and discursive, which cannot be said of the angelic knowledge. Therefore the knowledge of Christ's soul was less than the knowledge of the angels.

Objection 3: Further, the more immaterial knowledge is, the greater it is. But the knowledge of the angels is more immaterial than the knowledge of Christ's soul, since the soul of Christ is the act of a body, and turns to phantasms, which cannot be said of the angels. Therefore the knowledge of angels is greater than the knowledge of Christ's soul.

On the contrary, The Apostle says (Heb. 2:9): "For we see Jesus, Who was made a little lower than the angels, for the suffering of death, crowned with glory and honor"; from which it is plain that Christ is said to be lower than the angels only in regard to the suffering of death. And hence, not in knowledge.

I answer that, The knowledge imprinted on Christ's soul may be looked at in two ways: First, as regards what it has from the inflowing cause; secondly, as regards what it has from the subject receiving it. Now with regard to the first, the knowledge imprinted upon the soul of Christ was more excellent than the knowledge of the angels, both in the number of things known and in the certainty of the knowledge; since the spiritual light, which is imprinted on the soul of Christ, is much more excellent than the light which pertains to the angelic nature. But as regards the second, the knowledge imprinted on the soul of Christ is less than the angelic knowledge, in the manner of knowing that is natural to the human soul, i.e. by turning to phantasms, and by comparison and discursion.

And hereby the reply to the objections is made clear.

Whether this knowledge was habitual?

Objection 1: It would seem that in Christ there was no habitual knowledge. For it has been said ([3990]Q[9], A[1]) that the highest perfection of knowledge befitted Christ's soul. But the perfection of an actually existing knowledge is greater than that of a potentially or habitually existing knowledge. Therefore it was fitting for Him to know all things actually. Therefore He had not habitual knowledge.

Objection 2: Further, since habits are ordained to acts, a habitual knowledge which is never reduced to act would seem useless. Now, since Christ knew all things, as was said[3991] Q[10], A[2], He could not have considered all things actually, thinking over one after another, since the infinite cannot be passed over by enumeration. Therefore the habitual knowledge of certain things would have been useless to Him---which is unfitting. Therefore He had an actual and not a habitual knowledge of what He knew.

Objection 3: Further, habitual knowledge is a perfection of the knower. But perfection is more noble than the thing perfected. If, therefore, in the soul of Christ there was any created habit of knowledge, it would follow that this created thing was nobler than the soul of Christ. Therefore there was no habitual knowledge in Christ's soul.

On the contrary, The knowledge of Christ we are now speaking about was univocal with our knowledge, even as His soul was of the same species as ours. But our knowledge is in the genus of habit. Therefore the knowledge of Christ was habitual.

I answer that, As stated above [3992](A[4]), the mode of the knowledge impressed on the soul of Christ befitted the subject receiving it. For the received is in the recipient after the mode of the recipient. Now the connatural mode of the human soul is that it should understand sometimes actually, and sometimes potentially. But the medium between a pure power and a completed act is a habit: and extremes and medium are of the same genus. Thus it is plain that it is the connatural mode of the human soul to receive knowledge as a habit. Hence it must be said that the knowledge imprinted on the soul of Christ was habitual, for He could use it when He pleased.

Reply to Objection 1: In Christ's soul there was a twofold knowledge---each most perfect of its kind: the first exceeding the mode of human nature, as by it He saw the Essence of God, and other things in It, and this was the most perfect, simply. Nor was this knowledge habitual, but actual with respect to everything He knew in this way. But the second knowledge was in Christ in a manner proportioned to human nature, i.e. inasmuch as He knew things by species divinely imprinted upon Him, and of this knowledge we are now speaking. Now this knowledge was not most perfect, simply, but merely in the genus of human knowledge; hence it did not behoove it to be always in act.

Reply to Objection 2: Habits are reduced to act by the command of the will, since a habit is that "with which we act when we wish." Now the will is indeterminate in regard to infinite things. Yet it is not useless, even when it does not actually tend to all; provided it actually tends to everything in fitting place and time. And hence neither is a habit useless, even if all that it extends to is not reduced to act; provided that that which befits the due end of the will be reduced to act according as the matter in hand and the time require.

Reply to Objection 3: Goodness and being are taken in two ways: First, simply; and thus a substance, which subsists in its being and goodness, is a good and a being; secondly, being and goodness are taken relatively, and in this way an accident is a being and a good, not that it has being and goodness, but that its subject is a being and a good. And hence habitual knowledge is not simply better or more excellent than the soul of Christ; but relatively, since the whole goodness of habitual knowledge is added to the goodness of the subject.

Whether this knowledge was distinguished by divers habits?

Objection 1: It would seem that in the soul of Christ there was only one habit of knowledge. For the more perfect knowledge is, the more united it is; hence the higher angels understand by the more universal forms, as was said in the [3993]FP, Q[55], A[3]. Now Christ's knowledge was most perfect. Therefore it was most one. Therefore it was not distinguished by several habits.

Objection 2: Further, our faith is derived from Christ's knowledge; hence it is written (Heb. 12:2): "Looking on Jesus the author and finisher of faith." But there is only one habit of faith about all things believed, as was said in the [3994]SS, Q[4], A[6]. Much more, therefore, was there only one habit of knowledge in Christ.

Objection 3: Further, knowledge is distinguished by the divers formalities of knowable things. But the soul of Christ knew everything under one formality, i.e. by a divinely infused light. Therefore in Christ there was only one habit of knowledge.

On the contrary, It is written (Zech. 3:9) that on "one" stone, i.e. Christ, "there are seven eyes." Now by the eye is understood knowledge. Therefore it would seem that in Christ there were several habits of knowledge.

I answer that, As stated above ([3995]AA[4],5), the knowledge imprinted on Christ's soul has a mode connatural to a human soul. Now it is connatural to a human soul to receive species of a lesser universality than the angels receive; so that it knows different specific natures by different intelligible species. But it so happens that we have different habits of knowledge, because there are different classes of knowable things, inasmuch as what are in one genus are known by one habit; thus it is said (Poster. i, 42) that "one science is of one class of object." And hence the knowledge imprinted on Christ's soul was distinguished by different habits.

Reply to Objection 1: As was said [3996](A[4]), the knowledge of Christ's soul is most perfect, and exceeds the knowledge of angels with regard to what is in it on the part of God's gift; but it is below the angelic knowledge as regards the mode of the recipient. And it pertains to this mode that this knowledge is distinguished by various habits, inasmuch as it regards more particular species.

Reply to Objection 2: Our faith rests upon the First Truth; and hence Christ is the author of our faith by the Divine knowledge, which is simply one.

Reply to Objection 3: The divinely infused light is the common formality for understanding what is divinely revealed, as the light of the active intellect is with regard to what is naturally known. Hence, in the soul of Christ there must be the proper species of singular things, in order to know each with proper knowledge; and in this way there must be divers habits of knowledge in Christ's soul, as stated above.

Day 258

OF THE ACQUIRED OR EMPIRIC KNOWLEDGE OF CHRIST'S SOUL (FOUR ARTICLES)
We must now consider the acquired or empiric knowledge of Christ's soul; and under this head there are four points of inquiry:
(1) Whether Christ knew all things by this knowledge?
(2) Whether He advanced in this knowledge?
(3) Whether He learned anything from man?
(4) Whether He received anything from angels?

Whether Christ knew all things by this acquired or empiric knowledge?
Objection 1: It would seem that Christ did not know everything by this knowledge. For this knowledge is acquired by experience. But Christ did not experience everything. Therefore He did not know everything by this knowledge.
Objection 2: Further, man acquires knowledge through the senses. But not all sensible things were subjected to Christ's bodily senses. Therefore Christ did not know everything by this knowledge.
Objection 3: Further, the extent of knowledge depends on the things knowable. Therefore if Christ knew all things by this knowledge, His acquired knowledge would have been equal to His infused and beatific knowledge; which is not fitting. Therefore Christ did not know all things by this knowledge.
On the contrary, Nothing imperfect was in Christ's soul. Now this knowledge of His would have been imperfect if He had not known all things by it, since the imperfect is that to which addition may be made. Hence Christ knew all things by this knowledge.
I answer that, Acquired knowledge is held to be in Christ's soul, as we have said[3997] Q[9], A[4], by reason of the active intellect, lest its action, which is to make things actually intelligible, should be wanting; even as imprinted or infused knowledge is held to be in Christ's soul for the perfection of the passive intellect. Now as the passive intellect is that by which "all things are in potentiality," so the active intellect is that by which "all are in act," as is said De Anima iii, 18. And hence, as the soul of Christ knew by infused knowledge all things to which the passive intellect is in any way in potentiality, so by acquired knowledge it knew whatever can be known by the action of the active intellect.
Reply to Objection 1: The knowledge of things may be acquired not merely by experiencing the things themselves, but by experiencing other things; since by virtue of the light of the active intellect man can go on to understand effects from causes, and causes from effects, like from like, contrary from contrary. Therefore Christ, though He did not experience all things, came to the knowledge of all things from what He did experience.
Reply to Objection 2: Although all sensible things were not subjected to Christ's bodily senses, yet other sensible things were subjected to His senses; and from this He could come to know other things by the most excellent force of His reason, in the manner described in the previous reply; just as in seeing heavenly bodies He could comprehend their powers and the effects they have upon things here below, which were not subjected to His senses; and for the same reason, from any other things whatsoever, He could come to the knowledge of yet other things.
Reply to Objection 3: By this knowledge the soul of Christ did not know all things simply, but all such as are knowable by the light of man's active intellect. Hence by this knowledge He did not know the essences of separate substances, nor past, present, or future singulars, which, nevertheless, He knew by infused knowledge, as was said above ([3998]Q[11]).

Whether Christ advanced in acquired or empiric knowledge?
Objection 1: It would seem that Christ did not advance in this knowledge. For even as Christ knew all things by His beatific and His infused knowledge, so also did He by this acquired knowledge, as is plain from what has been said [3999](A[1]). But He did not advance in these knowledges. Therefore neither in this.
Objection 2: Further, to advance belongs to the imperfect, since the perfect cannot be added to. Now we cannot suppose an imperfect knowledge in Christ. Therefore Christ did not advance in this knowledge.
Objection 3: Further, Damascene says (De Fide Orth. iii, 22): "Whoever say that Christ advanced in wisdom and grace, as if receiving additional sensations, do not venerate the union which is in hypostasis." But it is impious not to venerate this union. Therefore it is impious to say that His knowledge received increase.

On the contrary, It is written (Lk. 2:52): "Jesus advanced in wisdom and age and grace with God and men"; and Ambrose says (De Incar. Dom. vii) that "He advanced in human wisdom." Now human wisdom is that which is acquired in a human manner, i.e. by the light of the active intellect. Therefore Christ advanced in this knowledge.

I answer that, There is a twofold advancement in knowledge: one in essence, inasmuch as the habit of knowledge is increased; the other in effect---e.g. if someone were with one and the same habit of knowledge to prove to someone else some minor truths at first, and afterwards greater and more subtle conclusions. Now in this second way it is plain that Christ advanced in knowledge and grace, even as in age, since as His age increased He wrought greater deeds, and showed greater knowledge and grace.

But as regards the habit of knowledge, it is plain that His habit of infused knowledge did not increase, since from the beginning He had perfect infused knowledge of all things; and still less could His beatific knowledge increase; while in the [4000]FP, Q[14], A[15], we have already said that His Divine knowledge could not increase. Therefore, if in the soul of Christ there was no habit of acquired knowledge, beyond the habit of infused knowledge, as appears to some [*Blessed Albert the Great, Alexander of Hales, St. Bonaventure], and sometime appeared to me (Sent. iii, D, xiv), no knowledge in Christ increased in essence, but merely by experience, i.e. by comparing the infused intelligible species with phantasms. And in this way they maintain that Christ's knowledge grew in experience, e.g. by comparing the infused intelligible species with what He received through the senses for the first time. But because it seems unfitting that any natural intelligible action should be wanting to Christ, and because to extract intelligible species from phantasms is a natural action of man's active intellect, it seems becoming to place even this action in Christ. And it follows from this that in the soul of Christ there was a habit of knowledge which could increase by this abstraction of species; inasmuch as the active intellect, after abstracting the first intelligible species from phantasms, could abstract others, and others again.

Reply to Objection 1: Both the infused knowledge and the beatific knowledge of Christ's soul were the effects of an agent of infinite power, which could produce the whole at once; and thus in neither knowledge did Christ advance; since from the beginning He had them perfectly. But the acquired knowledge of Christ is caused by the active intellect which does not produce the whole at once, but successively; and hence by this knowledge Christ did not know everything from the beginning, but step by step, and after a time, i.e. in His perfect age; and this is plain from what the Evangelist says, viz. that He increased in "knowledge and age" together.

Reply to Objection 2: Even this knowledge was always perfect for the time being, although it was not always perfect, simply and in comparison to the nature; hence it could increase.

Reply to Objection 3: This saying of Damascene regards those who say absolutely that addition was made to Christ's knowledge, i.e. as regards any knowledge of His, and especially as regards the infused knowledge which is caused in Christ's soul by union with the Word; but it does not regard the increase of knowledge caused by the natural agent.

Whether Christ learned anything from man?

Objection 1: It would seem that Christ learned something from man. For it is written (Lk. 2:46,47) that, "They found Him in the temple in the midst of the doctors, hearing them, and asking them questions." But to ask questions and to reply pertains to a learner. Therefore Christ learned something from man.

Objection 2: Further, to acquire knowledge from a man's teaching seems more noble than to acquire it from sensible things, since in the soul of the man who teaches the intelligible species are in act; but in sensible things the intelligible species are only in potentiality. Now Christ received empiric knowledge from sensible things, as stated above [4001](A[2]). Much more, therefore, could He receive knowledge by learning from men.

Objection 3: Further, by empiric knowledge Christ did not know everything from the beginning, but advanced in it, as was said above [4002](A[2]). But anyone hearing words which mean something, may learn something he does not know. Therefore Christ could learn from men something He did not know by this knowledge.

On the contrary, It is written (Ps. 45:4): "Behold, I have given Him for a witness to the people, for a leader and a master to the Gentiles." Now a master is not taught, but teaches. Therefore Christ did not receive any knowledge by the teaching of any man.

I answer that, In every genus that which is the first mover is not moved according to the same species of movement; just as the first alterative is not itself altered. Now Christ is established by God the Head of the Church---yea, of all men, as was said above ([4003]Q[8], A[3]), so that not only all might receive grace through Him, but that all might receive the doctrine of Truth from Him. Hence He Himself says (Jn. 18:37): "For this was I born, and for this came I into the world; that I should give testimony to the truth." And thus it did not befit His dignity that He should be taught by any man.

Reply to Objection 1: As Origen says (Hom. xix in Luc.): "Our Lord asked questions not in order to learn anything, but in order to teach by questioning. For from the same well of knowledge came the question and the wise reply." Hence the Gospel goes on to say that "all that heard Him were astonished at His wisdom and His answers."

Reply to Objection 2: Whoever learns from man does not receive knowledge immediately from the intelligible species which are in his mind, but through sensible words, which are signs of intelligible concepts. Now as words formed by a man are signs of his intellectual knowledge; so are creatures, formed by God, signs of His wisdom. Hence it is written (Ecclus. 1:10) that God "poured" wisdom "out upon all His works." Hence, just as it is better to be taught by God than by man, so it is better to receive our knowledge from sensible creatures and not by man's teaching.

Reply to Objection 3: Jesus advanced in empiric knowledge, as in age, as stated above [4004](A[2]). Now as a fitting age is required for a man to acquire knowledge by discovery, so also that he may acquire it by being taught. But our Lord did nothing unbecoming to His age; and hence He did not give ear to hearing the lessons of doctrine until such time as He was able to have reached that grade of knowledge by way of experience. Hence Gregory says (Sup. Ezech. Lib. i, Hom. ii): "In the twelfth year of His age He deigned to question men on earth, since in the course of reason, the word of doctrine is not vouchsafed before the age of perfection."

Whether Christ received knowledge from the angels?

Objection 1: It would seem that Christ received knowledge from the angels. For it is written (Lk. 22:43) that "there appeared to Him an angel from heaven, strengthening Him." But we are strengthened by the comforting words of a teacher, according to Job 4:3,4: "Behold thou hast taught many and hast strengthened the weary hand. Thy words have confirmed them that were staggering." Therefore Christ was taught by angels.

Objection 2: Further, Dionysius says (Coel. Hier. iv): "For I see that even Jesus---the super-substantial substance of supercelestial substances---when without change He took our substance upon Himself, was subject in obedience to the instructions of the Father and God by the angels." Hence it seems that even Christ wished to be subject to the ordinations of the Divine law, whereby men are taught by means of angels.

Objection 3: Further, as in the natural order the human body is subject to the celestial bodies, so likewise is the human mind to angelic minds. Now Christ's body was subject to the impressions of the heavenly bodies, for He felt the heat in summer and the cold in winter, and other human passions. Therefore His human mind was subject to the illuminations of supercelestial spirits.

On the contrary, Dionysius says (Coel. Hier. vii) that "the highest angels question Jesus, and learn the knowledge of His Divine work, and of the flesh assumed for us; and Jesus teaches them directly." Now to teach and to be taught do not belong to the same. Therefore Christ did not receive knowledge from the angels.

I answer that, Since the human soul is midway between spiritual substances and corporeal things, it is perfected naturally in two ways. First by knowledge received from sensible things; secondly, by knowledge imprinted or infused by the illumination of spiritual substances. Now in both these ways the soul of Christ was perfected; first by empirical knowledge of sensible things, for which there is no need of angelic light, since the light of the active intellect suffices; secondly, by the higher impression of infused knowledge, which He received directly from God. For as His soul was united to the Word above the common mode, in unity of person, so above the common manner of men was it filled with knowledge and grace by the Word of God Himself; and not by the medium of angels, who in their beginning received the knowledge of things by the influence of the Word, as Augustine says (Gen. ad lit. ii, 8).

Reply to Objection 1: This strengthening by the angel was for the purpose not of instructing Him, but of proving the truth of His human nature. Hence Bede says (on Lk. 22:43): "In testimony of both natures are the angels said to have ministered to Him and to have strengthened Him. For the Creator did not need help from His creature; but having become man, even as it was for our sake that He was sad, so was it for our sake that He was strengthened," i.e. in order that our faith in the Incarnation might be strengthened.

Reply to Objection 2: Dionysius says that Christ was subject to the angelic instructions, not by reason of Himself, but by reason of what happened at His Incarnation, and as regards the care of Him whilst He was a child. Hence in the same place he adds that "Jesus' withdrawal to Egypt decreed by the Father is announced to Joseph by angels, and again His return to Judaea from Egypt."

Reply to Objection 3: The Son of God assumed a passible body (as will be said hereafter ([4005]Q[14], A[1])) and a soul perfect in knowledge and grace ([4006]Q[14] , A[1], ad 1; A[4]). Hence His body was rightly subject to the impression of heavenly bodies; but His soul was not subject to the impression of heavenly spirits.

OF THE POWER OF CHRIST'S SOUL (FOUR ARTICLES)

We must now consider the power of Christ's soul; and under this head there are four points of inquiry:

(1) Whether He had omnipotence simply?
(2) Whether He had omnipotence with regard to corporeal creatures?
(3) Whether He had omnipotence with regard to His own body?
(4) Whether He had omnipotence as regards the execution of His own will?

Whether the soul of Christ had omnipotence?

Objection 1: It would seem that the soul of Christ had omnipotence. For Ambrose [*Gloss, Ord.] says on Lk. 1:32: "The power which the Son of God had naturally, the Man was about to receive in time." Now this would seem to regard the soul principally, since it is the chief part of man. Hence since the Son of God had omnipotence from all eternity, it would seem that the soul of Christ received omnipotence in time.

Objection 2: Further, as the power of God is infinite, so is His knowledge. But the soul of Christ in a manner had the knowledge of all that God knows, as was said above ([4007]Q[10], A[2]). Therefore He had all power; and thus He was omnipotent.

Objection 3: Further, the soul of Christ has all knowledge. Now knowledge is either practical or speculative. Therefore He has a practical knowledge of what He knows, i.e. He knew how to do what He knows; and thus it seems that He can do all things.

On the contrary, What is proper to God cannot belong to any creature. But it is proper to God to be omnipotent, according to Ex. 15:2,3: "He is my God and I will glorify Him," and further on, "Almighty is His name." Therefore the soul of Christ, as being a creature, has not omnipotence.

I answer that, As was said above ([4008]Q[2], A[1];[4009] Q[10], A[1]) in the mystery of the Incarnation the union in person so took place that there still remained the distinction of natures, each nature still retaining what belonged to it. Now the active principle of a thing follows its form, which is the principle of action. But the form is either the very nature of the thing, as in simple things; or is the constituent of the nature of the thing; as in such as are composed of matter and form.

And it is in this way that omnipotence flows, so to say, from the Divine Nature. For since the Divine Nature is the very uncircumscribed Being of God, as is plain from Dionysius (Div. Nom. v), it has an active power over everything that can have the nature of being; and this is to have omnipotence; just as every other thing has an active power over such things as the perfection of its nature extends to; as what is hot gives heat. Therefore since the soul of Christ is a part of human nature, it cannot possibly have omnipotence.

Reply to Objection 1: By union with the Person, the Man receives omnipotence in time, which the Son of God had from eternity; the result of which union is that as the Man is said to be God, so is He said to be omnipotent; not that the omnipotence of the Man is distinct (as neither is His Godhead) from that of the Son of God, but because there is one Person of God and man.

Reply to Objection 2: According to some, knowledge and active power are not in the same ratio; for an active power flows from the very nature of the thing, inasmuch as action is considered to come forth from the agent; but knowledge is not always possessed by the very essence or form of the knower, since it may be had by assimilation of the knower to the thing known by the aid of received species. But this reason seems not to suffice, because even as we may understand by a likeness obtained from another, so also may we act by a form obtained from another, as water or iron heats, by heat borrowed from fire. Hence there would be no reason why the soul of Christ, as it can know all things by the similitudes of all things impressed upon it by God, cannot do these things by the same similitudes.

It has, therefore, to be further considered that what is received in the lower nature from the higher is possessed in an inferior manner; for heat is not received by water in the perfection and strength it had in fire. Therefore, since the soul of Christ is of an inferior nature to the Divine Nature, the similitudes of things are not received in the soul of Christ in the perfection and strength they had in the Divine Nature. And hence it is that the knowledge of Christ's soul is inferior to Divine knowledge as regards the manner of knowing, for God knows (things) more perfectly than the soul of Christ; and also as regards the number of things known, since the soul of Christ does not know all that God can do, and these God knows by the knowledge of simple intelligence; although it knows all things present, past, and future, which God knows by the knowledge of vision. So, too, the similitudes of things infused into Christ's soul do not equal the Divine power in acting, i.e. so as to do all that God can do, or to do in the same manner as God does, Who acts with an infinite might whereof the creature is not capable. Now there is no thing, to know which in some way an infinite power is needed, although a certain kind of knowledge belongs to an infinite power; yet there are things which can be done only by an infinite power, as creation and the like, as is plain from what has been said in the [4010]FP, Q[45]. Hence Christ's soul which, being a creature, is finite in might, can know, indeed, all things, but not in every way; yet it cannot do all things, which pertains to the nature of omnipotence; and, amongst other things, it is clear it cannot create itself.

Reply to Objection 3: Christ's soul has practical and speculative knowledge; yet it is not necessary that it should have practical knowledge of those things of which it has speculative knowledge. Because for speculative knowledge a mere conformity or assimilation of the knower to the thing known suffices; whereas for practical knowledge it is required that the forms of the things in the intellect should be operative. Now to have a form and to impress this form upon something else is more than merely to have the form; as to be lightsome and to enlighten is more than merely to be lightsome. Hence the soul of Christ has a speculative knowledge of creation (for it knows the mode of God's creation), but it has no practical knowledge of this mode, since it has no knowledge operative of creation.

Whether the soul of Christ had omnipotence with regard to the transmutation of creatures?

Objection 1: It would seem that the soul of Christ had omnipotence with regard to the transmutation of creatures. For He Himself says (Mat. 28:18): "All power is given to Me in heaven and on earth." Now by the words "heaven and earth" are meant all creatures, as is plain from Gn. 1:1: "In the beginning God created heaven and earth." Therefore it seems that the soul of Christ had omnipotence with regard to the transmutation of creatures.

Objection 2: Further, the soul of Christ is the most perfect of all creatures. But every creature can be moved by another creature; for Augustine says (De Trin. iii, 4) that "even as the denser and lower bodies are ruled in a fixed way by the subtler and stronger bodies; so are all bodies by the spirit of life, and the irrational spirit of life by the rational spirit of life, and the truant and sinful rational spirit of life by the rational, loyal, and righteous spirit of life." But the soul of Christ moves even the highest spirits, enlightening them, as Dionysius says (Coel. Hier. vii). Therefore it seems that the soul of Christ has omnipotence with regard to the transmutation of creatures.

Objection 3: Further, Christ's soul had in its highest degree the "grace of miracles" or works of might. But every transmutation of the creature can belong to the grace of miracles; since even the heavenly bodies were miraculously changed from their course, as Dionysius proves (Ep. ad Polycarp). Therefore Christ's soul had omnipotence with regard to the transmutation of creatures.

On the contrary, To transmute creatures belongs to Him Who preserves them. Now this belongs to God alone, according to Heb. 1:3: "Upholding all things by the word of His power." Therefore God alone has omnipotence with regard to the transmutation of creatures. Therefore this does not belong to Christ's soul.

I answer that, Two distinctions are here needed. of these the first is with respect to the transmutation of creatures, which is three-fold. The first is natural, being brought about by the proper agent naturally; the second is miraculous, being brought about by a supernatural agent above the wonted order and course of nature, as to raise the dead; the third is inasmuch as every creature may be brought to nothing.

The second distinction has to do with Christ's soul, which may be looked at in two ways: first in its proper nature and with its power of nature or of grace; secondly, as it is the instrument of the Word of God, personally united to Him. Therefore if we speak of the soul of Christ in its proper nature and with its power of nature or of grace, it had power to cause those effects proper to a soul (e.g. to rule the body and direct human acts, and also, by the fulness of grace and knowledge to enlighten all rational creatures falling short of its perfection), in a manner befitting a rational creature. But if we speak of the soul of Christ as it is the instrument of the Word united to Him, it had an instrumental power to effect all the miraculous transmutations ordainable to the end of the Incarnation, which is "to re-establish all things that are in heaven and on earth" [*Eph. 1:10]. But the transmutation of creatures, inasmuch as they may be brought to nothing, corresponds to their creation, whereby they were brought from nothing. And hence even as God alone can create, so, too, He alone can bring creatures to nothing, and He alone upholds them in being, lest they fall back to nothing. And thus it must be said that the soul of Christ had not omnipotence with regard to the transmutation of creatures.

Reply to Objection 1: As Jerome says (on the text quoted): "Power is given Him," i.e. to Christ as man, "Who a little while before was crucified, buried in the tomb, and afterwards rose again." But power is said to have been given Him, by reason of the union whereby it was brought about that a Man was omnipotent, as was said above (A[1], ad 1). And although this was made known to the angels before the Resurrection, yet after the Resurrection it was made known to all men, as Remigius says (cf. Catena Aurea). Now, "things are said to happen when they are made known" [*Hugh of St. Victor: Qq. in Ep. ad Philip.]. Hence after the Resurrection our Lord says "that all power is given" to Him "in heaven and on earth."

Reply to Objection 2: Although every creature is transmutable by some other creature, except, indeed, the highest angel, and even it can be enlightened by Christ's soul; yet not every transmutation that can be made in a creature can be made by a creature; since some transmutations can be made by God alone. Yet all transmutations that can be made in creatures can be made by the soul of Christ, as the instrument of the Word, but not in its proper nature and power, since some of these transmutations pertain to the soul neither in the order of nature nor in the order of grace.

Reply to Objection 3: As was said in the [4011]SS, Q[178], A[1], ad 1, the grace of mighty works or miracles is given to the soul of a saint, so that these miracles are wrought not by his own, but by Divine power. Now this grace was bestowed on Christ's soul most excellently, i.e. not only that He might work miracles, but also that He might communicate this grace to others. Hence it is written (Mat. 10:1) that, "having called His twelve disciples together, He gave them power over unclean spirits, to cast them out, and to heal all manner of diseases, and all manner of infirmities."

Whether the soul of Christ had omnipotence with regard to His own body?

Objection 1: It would seem that Christ's soul had omnipotence with regard to His own body. For Damascene says (De Fide Orth. iii, 20,23) that "all natural things were voluntary to Christ; He willed to hunger, He willed to thirst, He willed to fear, He willed to die." Now God is called omnipotent because "He hath done all things whatsoever He would" (Ps. 113:11). Therefore it seems that Christ's soul had omnipotence with regard to the natural operations of the body.

Objection 2: Further, human nature was more perfect in Christ than in Adam, who had a body entirely subject to the soul, so that nothing could happen to the body against the will of the soul---and this on account of the original justice which it had in the state of innocence. Much more, therefore, had Christ's soul omnipotence with regard to His body.

Objection 3: Further, the body is naturally changed by the imaginations of the soul; and so much more changed, the stronger the soul's imagination, as was said in the [4012]FP, Q[117], A[3], ad 3. Now the soul of Christ had most perfect strength as regards both the imagination and the other powers. Therefore the soul of Christ was omnipotent with regard to His own body.

On the contrary, It is written (Heb. 2:17) that "it behooved Him in all things to be made like unto His brethren," and especially as regards what belongs to the condition of human nature. But it belongs to the condition of human nature that the health of the body and its nourishment and growth are not subject to the bidding of reason or will, since natural things are subject to God alone Who is the author of nature. Therefore they were not subject in Christ. Therefore Christ's soul was not omnipotent with regard to His own body.

I answer that, As stated above [4013](A[2]), Christ's soul may be viewed in two ways. First, in its proper nature and power; and in this way, as it was incapable of making exterior bodies swerve from the course and order of nature, so, too, was it incapable of changing its own body from its natural disposition, since the soul, of its own nature, has a determinate relation to its body. Secondly, Christ's soul may be viewed as an instrument united in person to God's Word; and thus every disposition of His own body was wholly subject to His power. Nevertheless, since the power of an action is not properly attributed to the instrument, but to the principal agent, this omnipotence is attributed to the Word of God rather than to Christ's soul.

Reply to Objection 1: This saving of Damascene refers to the Divine will of Christ, since, as he says in the preceding chapter (De Fide Orth. xix, 14,15), it was by the consent of the Divine will that the flesh was allowed to suffer and do what was proper to it.

Reply to Objection 2: It was no part of the original justice which Adam had in the state of innocence that a man's soul should have the power of changing his own body to any form, but that it should keep it from any hurt. Yet Christ could have assumed even this power if He had wished. But since man has three states---viz. innocence, sin, and glory, even as from the state of glory He assumed comprehension and from the state of innocence, freedom from sin---so also from the state of sin did He assume the necessity of being under the penalties of this life, as will be said ([4014]Q[14], A[2]).

Reply to Objection 3: If the imagination be strong, the body obeys naturally in some things, e.g. as regards falling from a beam set on high, since the imagination was formed to be a principle of local motion, as is said De Anima iii, 9,10. So, too, as regards alteration in heat and cold, and their consequences; for the passions of the soul, wherewith the heart is moved, naturally follow the imagination, and thus by commotion of the spirits the whole body is altered. But the other corporeal dispositions which have no natural relation to the imagination are not transmuted by the imagination, however strong it is, e.g. the shape of the hand, or foot, or such like.

Whether the soul of Christ had omnipotence as regards the execution of His will?

Objection 1: It would seem that the soul of Christ had not omnipotence as regards the execution of His own will. For it is written (Mk. 7:24) that "entering into a house, He would that no man should know it, and He could not be hid." Therefore He could not carry out the purpose of His will in all things.

Objection 2: Further, a command is a sign of will, as was said in the [4015]FP, Q[19], A[12]. But our Lord commanded certain things to be done, and the contrary came to pass, for it is written (Mat. 9:30, 31) that Jesus strictly charged them whose eyes had been opened, saying: "See that no man know this. But they going out spread His fame abroad in all that country." Therefore He could not carry out the purpose of His will in everything.

Objection 3: Further, a man does not ask from another for what he can do himself. But our Lord besought the Father, praying for what He wished to be done, for it is written (Lk. 6:12): "He went out into a mountain to pray, and He passed the whole night in the prayer of God." Therefore He could not carry out the purpose of His will in all things.

On the contrary, Augustine says (Qq. Nov. et Vet. Test., qu. 77): "It is impossible for the will of the Saviour not to be fulfilled: nor is it possible for Him to will what He knows ought not to come to pass."

I answer that, Christ's soul willed things in two ways. First, what was to be brought about by Himself; and it must be said that He was capable of whatever He willed thus, since it would not befit His wisdom if He willed to do anything of Himself that was not subject to His will. Secondly, He wished things to be brought about by the Divine power, as the resurrection of His own body and such like miraculous deeds, which He could not effect by His own power, except as the instrument of the Godhead, as was said above [4016](A[2]).

Reply to Objection 1: As Augustine says (Qq. Nov. et Vet. Test., qu. 77): "What came to pass, this Christ must be said to have willed. For it must be remarked that this happened in the country of the Gentiles, to whom it was not yet time to preach. Yet it would have been invidious not to welcome such as came spontaneously for the faith. Hence He did not wish to be heralded by His own, and yet He wished to be sought; and so it came to pass." Or it may be said that this will of Christ was not with regard to what was to be carried out by it, but with regard to what was to be done by others, which did not come under His human will. Hence in the letter of Pope Agatho, which was approved in the Sixth Council [*Third Council of Constantinople, Act. iv], we read: "When He, the Creator and Redeemer of all, wished to be hid and could not, must not this be referred only to His human will which He deigned to assume in time?"

Reply to Objection 2: As Gregory says (Moral. xix), by the fact that "Our Lord charged His mighty works to be kept secret, He gave an example to His servants coming after Him that they should wish their miracles to be hidden; and yet, that others may profit by their example, they are made public against their will." And thus this command signified His will to fly from human glory, according to Jn. 8:50, "I seek not My own glory." Yet He wished absolutely, and especially by His Divine will, that the miracle wrought should be published for the good of others.

Reply to Objection 3: Christ prayed both for things that were to be brought about by the Divine power, and for what He Himself was to do by His human will, since the power and operation of Christ's soul depended on God, "Who works in all [Vulg.: 'you'], both to will and to accomplish" (Phil. 2:13).

Day 259

OF THE DEFECTS OF BODY ASSUMED BY THE SON OF GOD (FOUR ARTICLES)

We must now consider the defects Christ assumed in the human nature; and first, of the defects of body; secondly, of the defects of soul.

Under the first head there are four points of inquiry:

(1) Whether the Son of God should have assumed in human nature defects of body?

(2) Whether He assumed the obligation of being subject to these defects?

(3) Whether He contracted these defects?

(4) Whether He assumed all these defects?

Whether the Son of God in human nature ought to have assumed defects of body?

Objection 1: It would seem that the Son of God ought not to have assumed human nature with defects of body. For as His soul is personally united to the Word of God, so also is His body. But the soul of Christ had every perfection, both of grace and truth, as was said above ([4017]Q[7], A[9]; Q[9], seqq.). Hence, His body also ought to have been in every way perfect, not having any imperfection in it.

Objection 2: Further, the soul of Christ saw the Word of God by the vision wherein the blessed see, as was said above ([4018]Q[9], A[2]), and thus the soul of Christ was blessed. Now by the beatification of the soul the body is glorified; since, as Augustine says (Ep. ad Dios. cxviii), "God made the soul of a nature so strong that from the fulness of its blessedness there pours over even into the lower nature" (i.e. the body), "not indeed the bliss proper to the beatific fruition and vision, but the fulness of health" (i.e. the vigor of incorruptibility). Therefore the body of Christ was incorruptible and without any defect.

Objection 3: Further, penalty is the consequence of fault. But there was no fault in Christ, according to 1 Pet. 2:22: "Who did no guile." Therefore defects of body, which are penalties, ought not to have been in Him.

Objection 4: Further, no reasonable man assumes what keeps him from his proper end. But by such like bodily defects, the end of the Incarnation seems to be hindered in many ways. First, because by these infirmities men were kept back from knowing Him, according to Is. 53:2,3: "[There was no sightliness] that we should be desirous of Him. Despised and the most abject of men, a man of sorrows and acquainted with infirmity, and His look was, as it were, hidden and despised, whereupon we esteemed Him not." Secondly, because the de. sire of the Fathers would not seem to be fulfilled, in whose person it is written (Is. 51:9): "Arise, arise, put on Thy strength, O Thou Arm of the Lord." Thirdly, because it would seem more fitting for the devil's power to be overcome and man's weakness healed, by strength than by weakness. Therefore it does not seem to have been fitting that the Son of God assumed human nature with infirmities or defects of body.

On the contrary, It is written (Heb. 2:18): "For in that, wherein He Himself hath suffered and been tempted, He is able to succor them also that are tempted." Now He came to succor us. hence David said of Him (Ps. 120:1): "I have lifted up my eyes to the mountains, from whence help shall come to me." Therefore it was fitting for the Son of God to assume flesh subject to human infirmities, in order to suffer and be tempted in it and so bring succor to us.

I answer that, It was fitting for the body assumed by the Son of God to be subject to human infirmities and defects; and especially for three reasons. First, because it was in order to satisfy for the sin of the human race that the Son of God, having taken flesh, came into the world. Now one satisfies for another's sin by taking on himself the punishment due to the sin of the other. But these bodily defects, to wit, death, hunger, thirst, and the like, are the punishment of sin, which was brought into the world by Adam, according to Rom. 5:12: "By one man sin entered into this world, and by sin death." Hence it was useful for the end of the Incarnation that He should assume these penalties in our flesh and in our stead, according to Is. 53:4, "Surely He hath borne our infirmities." Secondly, in order to cause belief in the Incarnation. For since human nature is known to men only as it is subject to these defects, if the Son of God had assumed human nature without these defects, He would not have seemed to be true man, nor to have true, but imaginary, flesh, as the Manicheans held. And so, as is said, Phil. 2:7: "He . . . emptied Himself, taking the form of a servant, being made in the likeness of men, and in habit found as a man." Hence, Thomas, by the sight of His wounds, was recalled to the faith, as related Jn. 20:26. Thirdly, in order to show us an example of patience by valiantly bearing up against human passibility and defects. Hence it is said (Heb. 12:3) that He "endured such opposition from sinners against Himself, that you be not wearied. fainting in your minds."

Reply to Objection 1: The penalties one suffers for another's sin are the matter, as it were, of the satisfaction for that sin; but the principle is the habit of soul, whereby one is inclined to wish to satisfy for another, and from which the satisfaction has its efficacy, for satisfaction would not be efficacious unless it proceeded from charity, as will be explained ([4019]XP, Q[14], A[2]). Hence, it behooved the soul of Christ to be perfect as regards the habit of knowledge and virtue, in order to have the power of satisfying; but His body was subject to infirmities, that the matter of satisfaction should not be wanting.

Reply to Objection 2: From the natural relationship which is between the soul and the body, glory flows into the body from the soul's glory. Yet this natural relationship in Christ was subject to the will of His Godhead, and thereby it came to pass that the beatitude remained in the soul, and did not flow into the body; but the flesh suffered what belongs to a passible nature; thus Damascene says (De Fide Orth. iii, 15) that, "it was by the consent of the Divine will that the flesh was allowed to suffer and do what belonged to it."

Reply to Objection 3: Punishment always follows sin actual or original, sometimes of the one punished, sometimes of the one for whom he who suffers the punishment satisfies. And so it was with Christ, according to Is. 53:5: "He was wounded for our iniquities, He was bruised for our sins."

Reply to Objection 4: The infirmity assumed by Christ did not impede, but greatly furthered the end of the Incarnation, as above stated. And although these infirmities concealed His Godhead, they made known His Manhood, which is the way of coming to the Godhead, according to Rom. 5:1,2: "By Jesus Christ we have access to God." Moreover, the ancient Fathers did not desire bodily strength in Christ, but spiritual strength, wherewith He vanquished the devil and healed human weakness.

Whether Christ was of necessity subject to these defects?

Objection 1: It would seem that Christ was not of necessity subject to these defects. For it is written (Is. 53:7): "He was offered because it was His own will"; and the prophet is speaking of the offering of the Passion. But will is opposed to necessity. Therefore Christ was not of necessity subject to bodily defects.

Objection 2: Further, Damascene says (De Fide Orth. iii, 20): "Nothing obligatory is seen in Christ: all is voluntary." Now what is voluntary is not necessary. Therefore these defects were not of necessity in Christ.

Objection 3: Further, necessity is induced by something more powerful. But no creature is more powerful than the soul of Christ, to which it pertained to preserve its own body. Therefore these defects were not of necessity in Christ.

On the contrary, The Apostle says (Rom. 8:3) that "God" sent "His own Son in the likeness of sinful flesh." Now it is a condition of sinful flesh to be under the necessity of dying, and suffering other like passions. Therefore the necessity of suffering these defects was in Christ's flesh.

I answer that, Necessity is twofold. one is a necessity of "constraint," brought about by an external agent; and this necessity is contrary to both nature and will, since these flow from an internal principle. The other is "natural" necessity, resulting from the natural principles---either the form (as it is necessary for fire to heat), or the matter (as it is necessary for a body composed of contraries to be dissolved). Hence, with this necessity, which results from the matter, Christ's body was subject to the necessity of death and other like defects, since, as was said (A[1], ad 2), "it was by the consent of the Divine will that the flesh was allowed to do and suffer what belonged to it." And this necessity results from the principles of human nature, as was said above in this article. But if we speak of necessity of constraint, as repugnant to the bodily nature, thus again was Christ's body in its own natural condition subject to necessity in regard to the nail that pierced and the scourge that struck. Yet inasmuch as such necessity is repugnant to the will, it is clear that in Christ these defects were not of necessity as regards either the Divine will, or the human will of Christ considered absolutely, as following the deliberation of reason; but only as regards the natural movement of the will, inasmuch as it naturally shrinks from death and bodily hurt.

Reply to Objection 1: Christ is said to be "offered because it was His own will," i.e. Divine will and deliberate human will; although death was contrary to the natural movement of His human will, as Damascene says (De Fide Orth. iii, 23,24).

Reply to Objection 2: This is plain from what has been said.

Reply to Objection 3: Nothing was more powerful than Christ's soul, absolutely; yet there was nothing to hinder a thing being more powerful in regard to this or that effect, as a nail for piercing. And this I say, in so far as Christ's soul is considered in its own proper nature and power.

Whether Christ contracted these defects?

Objection 1: It would seem that Christ contracted bodily defects. For we are said to contract what we derive with our nature from birth. But Christ, together with human nature, derived His bodily defects and infirmities through His birth from His mother, whose flesh was subject to these defects. Therefore it seems that He contracted these defects.

Objection 2: Further, what is caused by the principles of nature is derived together with nature, and hence is contracted. Now these penalties are caused by the principles of human nature. Therefore Christ contracted them.

Objection 3: Further, Christ is likened to other men in these defects, as is written Heb. 2:17. But other men contract these defects. Therefore it seems that Christ contracted these defects.

On the contrary, These defects are contracted through sin, according to Rom. 5:12: "By one man sin entered into this world and by sin, death." Now sin had no place in Christ. Therefore Christ did not contract these defects.

I answer that, In the verb "to contract" is understood the relation of effect to cause, i.e. that is said to be contracted which is derived of necessity together with its cause. Now the cause of death and such like defects in human nature is sin, since "by sin death entered into this world," according to Rom. 5:12. And hence they who incur these defects, as due to sin, are properly said to contract them. Now Christ had not these defects, as due to sin, since, as Augustine [*Alcuin in the Gloss, Ord.], expounding Jn. 3:31, "He that cometh from above, is above all," says: "Christ came from above, i.e. from the height of human nature, which it had before the fall of the first man." For He received human nature without sin, in the purity which it had in the state of innocence. In the same way He might have assumed human nature without defects. Thus it is clear that Christ did not contract these defects as if taking them upon Himself as due to sin, but by His own will.

Reply to Objection 1: The flesh of the Virgin was conceived in original sin, [*See introductory note to Q[27]] and therefore contracted these defects. But from the Virgin, Christ's flesh assumed the nature without sin, and He might likewise have assumed the nature without its penalties. But He wished to bear its penalties in order to carry out the work of our redemption, as stated above [4020](A[1]). Therefore He had these defects---not that He contracted them, but that He assumed them.

Reply to Objection 2: The cause of death and other corporeal defects of human nature is twofold: the first is remote, and results from the material principles of the human body, inasmuch as it is made up of contraries. But this cause was held in check by original justice. Hence the proximate cause of death and other defects is sin, whereby original justice is withdrawn. And thus, because Christ was without sin, He is said not to have contracted these defects, but to have assumed them.

Reply to Objection 3: Christ was made like to other men in the quality and not in the cause of these defects; and hence, unlike others, He did not contract them.

Whether Christ ought to have assumed all the bodily defects of men?

Objection 1: It would seem that Christ ought to have assumed all the bodily defects of men. For Damascene says (De Fide Orth. iii, 6,18): "What is unassumable is incurable." But Christ came to cure all our defects. Therefore He ought to have assumed all our defects.

Objection 2: Further it was said [4021](A[1]), that in order to satisfy for us, Christ ought to have had perfective habits of soul and defects of body. Now as regards the soul, He assumed the fulness of all grace. Therefore as regards the body, He ought to have assumed all defects.

Objection 3: Further, amongst all bodily defects death holds the chief place. Now Christ assumed death. Much more, therefore, ought He to have assumed other defects.

On the contrary, Contraries cannot take place simultaneously in the same. Now some infirmities are contrary to each other, being caused by contrary principles. Hence it could not be that Christ assumed all human infirmities.

I answer that, As stated above ([4022]AA[1],2), Christ assumed human defects in order to satisfy for the sin of human nature, and for this it was necessary for Him to have the fulness of knowledge and grace in His soul. Hence Christ ought to have assumed those defects which flow from the common sin of the whole nature, yet are not incompatible with the perfection of knowledge and grace. And thus it was not fitting for Him to assume all human defects or infirmities. For there are some defects that are incompatible with the perfection of knowledge and grace, as ignorance, a proneness towards evil, and a difficulty in well-doing. Some other defects do not flow from the whole of human nature in common on account of the sin of our first parent, but are caused in some men by certain particular causes, as leprosy, epilepsy, and the like; and these defects are sometimes brought about by the fault of the man, e.g. from inordinate eating; sometimes by a defect in the formative power. Now neither of these pertains to Christ, since His flesh was conceived of the Holy Ghost, Who has infinite wisdom and power, and cannot err or fail; and He Himself did nothing wrong in the order of His life. But there are some third defects, to be found amongst all men in common, by reason of the sin of our first parent, as death, hunger, thirst, and the like; and all these defects Christ assumed, which Damascene (De Fide Orth. i, 11; iii, 20) calls "natural and indetractible passions" ---natural, as following all human nature in common; indetractible, as implying no defect of knowledge or grace.

Reply to Objection 1: All particular defects of men are caused by the corruptibility and passibility of the body, some particular causes being added; and hence, since Christ healed the passibility and corruptibility of our body by assuming it, He consequently healed all other defects.

Reply to Objection 2: The fulness of all grace and knowledge was due to Christ's soul of itself, from the fact of its being assumed by the Word of God; and hence Christ assumed all the fulness of knowledge and wisdom absolutely. But He assumed our defects economically, in order to satisfy for our sin, and not that they belonged to Him of Himself. Hence it was not necessary for Him to assume them all, but only such as sufficed to satisfy for the sin of the whole nature.

Reply to Objection 3: Death comes to all men from the sin of our first parent; but not other defects, although they are less than death. Hence there is no parity.

OF THE DEFECTS OF SOUL ASSUMED BY CHRIST (TEN ARTICLES)

We must now consider the defects pertaining to the soul; and under this head there are ten points of inquiry:

(1) Whether there was sin in Christ?

(2) Whether there was the "fomes" of sin in Him?

(3) Whether there was ignorance?

(4) Whether His soul was passible?

(5) Whether in Him there was sensible pain?

(6) Whether there was sorrow?

(7) Whether there was fear?

(8) Whether there was wonder?

(9) Whether there was anger?

(10) Whether He was at once wayfarer and comprehensor?

Whether there was sin in Christ?

Objection 1: It would seem that there was sin in Christ. For it is written (Ps. 21:2): "O God, My God . . . why hast Thou forsaken Me? Far from My salvation are the words of My sins." Now these words are said in the person of Christ Himself, as appears from His having uttered them on the cross. Therefore it would seem that in Christ there were sins.

Objection 2: Further, the Apostle says (Rom. 5:12) that "in Adam all have sinned"---namely, because all were in Adam by origin. Now Christ also was in Adam by origin. Therefore He sinned in him.

Objection 3: Further, the Apostle says (Heb. 2:18) that "in that, wherein He Himself hath suffered and been tempted, He is able to succor them also that are tempted." Now above all do we require His help against sin. Therefore it seems that there was sin in Him.

Objection 4: Further, it is written (2 Cor. 5:21) that "Him that knew no sin" (i.e. Christ), "for us" God "hath made sin." But that really is, which has been made by God. Therefore there was really sin in Christ.

Objection 5: Further, as Augustine says (De Agone Christ. xi), "in the man Christ the Son of God gave Himself to us as a pattern of living." Now man needs a pattern not merely of right living, but also of repentance for sin. Therefore it seems that in Christ there ought to have been sin, that He might repent of His sin, and thus afford us a pattern of repentance.

On the contrary, He Himself says (Jn. 8:46): "Which of you shall convince Me of sin?"

I answer that, As was said above ([4023]Q[14], A[1]), Christ assumed our defects that He might satisfy for us, that He might prove the truth of His human nature, and that He might become an example of virtue to us. Now it is plain that by reason of these three things He ought not to have assumed the defect of sin. First, because sin nowise works our satisfaction; rather, it impedes the power of satisfying, since, as it is written (Ecclus. 34:23), "The Most High approveth not the gifts of the wicked." Secondly, the truth of His human nature is not proved by sin, since sin does not belong to human nature, whereof God is the cause; but rather has been sown in it against its nature by the devil, as Damascene says (De Fide Orth. iii, 20). Thirdly, because by sinning He could afford no example of virtue, since sin is opposed to virtue. Hence Christ nowise assumed the defect of sin---either original or actual---according to what is written (1 Pet. 2:22): "Who did no sin, neither was guile found in His mouth."

Reply to Objection 1: As Damascene says (De Fide Orth. iii, 25), things are said of Christ, first, with reference to His natural and hypostatic property, as when it is said that God became man, and that He suffered for us; secondly, with reference to His personal and relative property, when things are said of Him in our person which nowise belong to Him of Himself. Hence, in the seven rules of Tichonius which Augustine quotes in De Doctr. Christ. iii, 31, the first regards "Our Lord and His Body," since "Christ and His Church are taken as one person." And thus Christ, speaking in the person of His members, says (Ps. 21:2): "The words of My sins"---not that there were any sins in the Head.

Reply to Objection 2: As Augustine says (Gen. ad lit. x, 20), Christ was in Adam and the other fathers not altogether as we were. For we were in Adam as regards both seminal virtue and bodily substance, since, as he goes on to say: "As in the seed there is a visible bulk and an invisible virtue, both have come from Adam. Now Christ took the visible substance of His flesh from the Virgin's flesh; but the virtue of His conception did not spring from the seed of man, but far otherwise---from on high." Hence He was not in Adam according to seminal virtue, but only according to bodily substance. And therefore Christ did not receive human nature from Adam actively, but only materially---and from the Holy Ghost actively; even as Adam received his body materially from the slime of the earth---actively from God. And thus Christ did not sin in Adam, in whom He was only as regards His matter.

Reply to Objection 3: In His temptation and passion Christ has succored us by satisfying for us. Now sin does not further satisfaction, but hinders it, as has been said. Hence, it behooved Him not to have sin, but to be wholly free from sin; otherwise the punishment He bore would have been due to Him for His own sin.

Reply to Objection 4: God "made Christ sin"---not, indeed, in such sort that He had sin, but that He made Him a sacrifice for sin: even as it is written (Osee 4:8): "They shall eat the sins of My people"---they, i.e. the priests, who by the law ate the sacrifices offered for sin. And in that way it is written (Is. 53:6) that "the Lord hath laid on Him the iniquity of us all" (i.e. He gave Him up to be a victim for the sins of all men); or "He made Him sin" (i.e. made Him to have "the likeness of sinful flesh"), as is written (Rom. 8:3), and this on account of the passible and mortal body He assumed.

Reply to Objection 5: A penitent can give a praiseworthy example, not by having sinned, but by freely bearing the punishment of sin. And hence Christ set the highest example to penitents, since He willingly bore the punishment, not of His own sin, but of the sins of others.

Whether there was the "fomes" of sin in Christ?

Objection 1: It would seem that in Christ there was the "fomes" of sin. For the "fomes" of sin, and the passibility and mortality of the body spring from the same principle, to wit, from the withdrawal of original justice, whereby the inferior powers of the soul were subject to the reason, and the body to the soul. Now passibility and mortality of body were in Christ. Therefore there was also the "fomes" of sin.

Objection 2: Further, as Damascene says (De Fide Orth. iii, 19), "it was by consent of the Divine will that the flesh of Christ was allowed to suffer and do what belonged to it." But it is proper to the flesh to lust after its pleasures. Now since the "fomes" of sin is nothing more than concupiscence, as the gloss says on Rom. 7:8, it seems that in Christ there was the "fomes" of sin.

Objection 3: Further, it is by reason of the "fomes" of sin that "the flesh lusteth against the spirit," as is written (Gal. 5:17). But the spirit is shown to be so much the stronger and worthier to be crowned according as the more completely it overcomes its enemy---to wit, the concupiscence of the flesh, according to 2 Tim. 2:5, he "is not crowned except he strive lawfully." Now Christ had a most valiant and conquering spirit, and one most worthy of a crown, according to Apoc. 6:2: "There was a crown given Him, and He went forth conquering that He might conquer." Therefore it would especially seem that the "fomes" of sin ought to have been in Christ.

On the contrary, It is written (Mat. 1:20): "That which is conceived in her is of the Holy Ghost." Now the Holy Ghost drives out sin and the inclination to sin, which is implied in the word "fomes." Therefore in Christ there ought not to have been the "fomes" of sin.

I answer that, As was said above (Q[7], AA[2],9), Christ had grace and all the virtues most perfectly. Now moral virtues, which are in the irrational part of the soul, make it subject to reason, and so much the more as the virtue is more perfect; thus, temperance controls the concupiscible appetite, fortitude and meekness the irascible appetite, as was said in the [4024]FS, Q[56], A[4]. But there belongs to the very nature of the "fomes" of sin an inclination of the sensual appetite to what is contrary to reason. And hence it is plain that the more perfect the virtues are in any man, the weaker the "fomes" of sin becomes in him. Hence, since in Christ the virtues were in their highest degree, the "fomes" of sin was nowise in Him; inasmuch, also, as this defect cannot be ordained to satisfaction, but rather inclined to what is contrary to satisfaction.

Reply to Objection 1: The inferior powers pertaining to the sensitive appetite have a natural capacity to be obedient to reason; but not the bodily powers, nor those of the bodily humors, nor those of the vegetative soul, as is made plain Ethic. i, 13. And hence perfection of virtue, which is in accordance with right reason, does not exclude possibility of body; yet it excludes the "fomes" of sin, the nature of which consists in the resistance of the sensitive appetite to reason.

Reply to Objection 2: The flesh naturally seeks what is pleasing to it by the concupiscence of the sensitive appetite; but the flesh of man, who is a rational animal, seeks this after the manner and order of reason. And thus with the concupiscence of the sensitive appetite Christ's flesh naturally sought food, drink, and sleep, and all else that is sought in right reason, as is plain from Damascene (De Fide Orth. iii, 14). Yet it does not therefore follow that in Christ there was the "fomes" of sin, for this implies the lust after pleasurable things against the order of reason.

Reply to Objection 3: The spirit gives evidence of fortitude to some extent by resisting that concupiscence of the flesh which is opposed to it; yet a greater fortitude of spirit is shown, if by its strength the flesh is thoroughly overcome, so as to be incapable of lusting against the spirit. And hence this belonged to Christ, whose spirit reached the highest degree of fortitude. And although He suffered no internal assault on the part of the "fomes" of sin, He sustained an external assault on the part of the world and the devil, and won the crown of victory by overcoming them.

Whether in Christ there was ignorance?

Objection 1: It would seem that there was ignorance in Christ. For that is truly in Christ which belongs to Him in His human nature, although it does not belong to Him in His Divine Nature, as suffering and death. But ignorance belongs to Christ in His human nature; for Damascene says (De Fide Orth. iii, 21) that "He assumed an ignorant and enslaved nature." Therefore ignorance was truly in Christ.

Objection 2: Further, one is said to be ignorant through defect of knowledge. Now some kind of knowledge was wanting to Christ, for the Apostle says (2 Cor. 5:21) "Him that knew no sin, for us He hath made sin." Therefore there was ignorance in Christ.

Objection 3: Further, it is written (Is. 8:4): "For before the child know to call his Father and his mother, the strength of Damascus . . . shall be taken away." Therefore in Christ there was ignorance of certain things.

On the contrary, Ignorance is not taken away by ignorance. But Christ came to take away our ignorance; for "He came to enlighten them that sit in darkness and in the shadow of death" (Lk. 1:79). Therefore there was no ignorance in Christ.

I answer that, As there was the fulness of grace and virtue in Christ, so too there was the fulness of all knowledge, as is plain from what has been said above ([4025]Q[7], A[9];[4026] Q[9]). Now as the fulness of grace and virtue in Christ excluded the "fomes" of sin, so the fulness of knowledge excluded ignorance, which is opposed to knowledge. Hence, even as the "fomes" of sin was not in Christ, neither was there ignorance in Him.

Reply to Objection 1: The nature assumed by Christ may be viewed in two ways. First, in its specific nature, and thus Damascene calls it "ignorant and enslaved"; hence he adds: "For man's nature is a slave of Him" (i.e. God) "Who made it; and it has no knowledge of future things." Secondly, it may be considered with regard to what it has from its union with the Divine hypostasis, from which it has the fulness of knowledge and grace, according to Jn. 1:14: "We saw Him [Vulg.: 'His glory'] as it were the Only-begotten of the Father, full of grace and truth"; and in this way the human nature in Christ was not affected with ignorance.

Reply to Objection 2: Christ is said not to have known sin, because He did not know it by experience; but He knew it by simple cognition.

Reply to Objection 3: The prophet is speaking in this passage of the human knowledge of Christ; thus he says: "Before the Child" (i.e. in His human nature) "know to call His father" (i.e. Joseph, who was His reputed father), "and His mother" (i.e. Mary), "the strength of Damascus . . . shall be taken away." Nor are we to understand this as if He had been some time a man without knowing it; but "before He know" (i.e. before He is a man having human knowledge)---literally, "the strength of Damascus and the spoils of Samaria shall be taken away by the King of the Assyrians"---or spiritually, "before His birth He will save His people solely by invocation," as a gloss expounds it. Augustine however (Serm. xxxii de Temp.) says that this was fulfilled in the adoration of the Magi. For he says: "Before He uttered human words in human flesh, He received the strength of Damascus, i.e. the riches which Damascus vaunted (for in riches the first place is given to gold). They themselves were the spoils of Samaria. Because Samaria is taken to signify idolatry; since this people, having turned away from the Lord, turned to the worship of idols. Hence these were the first spoils which the child took from the domination of idolatry." And in this way "before the child know" may be taken to mean "before he show himself to know."

Whether Christ's soul was passible?

Objection 1: It would seem that the soul of Christ was not passible. For nothing suffers except by reason of something stronger; since "the agent is greater than the patient," as is clear from Augustine (Gen. ad lit. xii, 16), and from the Philosopher (De Anima iii, 5). Now no creature was stronger than Christ's soul. Therefore Christ's soul could not suffer at the hands of any creature; and hence it was not passible; for its capability of suffering would have been to no purpose if it could not have suffered at the hands of anything.

Objection 2: Further, Tully (De Tusc. Quaes. iii) says that the soul's passions are ailments [*Cf. [4027]FS, Q[24], A[2]]. But Christ's soul had no ailment; for the soul's ailment results from sin, as is plain from Ps. 40:5: "Heal my soul, for I have sinned against Thee." Therefore in Christ's soul there were no passions.

Objection 3: Further, the soul's passions would seem to be the same as the "fomes" of sin, hence the Apostle (Rom. 7:5) calls them the "passions of sins." Now the "fomes" of sin was not in Christ, as was said A[2]. Therefore it seems that there were no passions in His soul; and hence His soul was not passible.

On the contrary, It is written (Ps. 87:4) in the person of Christ: "My soul is filled with evils"---not sins, indeed, but human evils, i.e. "pains," as a gloss expounds it. Hence the soul of Christ was passible.

I answer that, A soul placed in a body may suffer in two ways: first with a bodily passion; secondly, with an animal passion. It suffers with a bodily passion through bodily hurt; for since the soul is the form of the body, soul and body have but one being; and hence, when the body is disturbed by any bodily passion, the soul, too, must be disturbed, i.e. in the being which it has in the body. Therefore, since Christ's body was passible and mortal, as was said above (Q[14], A[2]), His soul also was of necessity passible in like manner. But the soul suffers with an animal passion, in its operations---either in such as are proper to the soul, or in such as are of the soul more than of the body. And although the soul is said to suffer in this way through sensation and intelligence, as was said in the [4028]FS, Q[22], A[3]; [4029]FS, Q[41], A[1]; nevertheless the affections of the sensitive appetite are most properly called passions of the soul. Now these were in Christ, even as all else pertaining to man's nature. Hence Augustine says (De Civ. Dei xiv, 9): "Our Lord having deigned to live in the form of a servant, took these upon Himself whenever He judged they ought to be assumed; for there was no false human affection in Him Who had a true body and a true human soul."

Nevertheless we must know that the passions were in Christ otherwise than in us, in three ways. First, as regards the object, since in us these passions very often tend towards what is unlawful, but not so in Christ. Secondly, as regards the principle, since these passions in us frequently forestall the judgment of reason; but in Christ all movements of the sensitive appetite sprang from the disposition of the reason. Hence Augustine says (De Civ. Dei xiv, 9), that "Christ assumed these movements, in His human soul, by an unfailing dispensation, when He willed; even as He became man when He willed." Thirdly, as regards the effect, because in us these movements, at times, do not remain in the sensitive appetite, but deflect the reason; but not so in Christ, since by His disposition the movements that are naturally becoming to human flesh so remained in the sensitive appetite that the reason was nowise hindered in doing what was right. Hence Jerome says (on Mat. 26:37) that "Our Lord, in order to prove the reality of the assumed manhood, 'was sorrowful' in very deed; yet lest a passion should hold sway over His soul, it is by a propassion that He is said to have 'begun to grow sorrowful and to be sad'"; so that it is a perfect "passion" when it dominates the soul, i.e. the reason; and a "propassion" when it has its beginning in the sensitive appetite, but goes no further.

Reply to Objection 1: The soul of Christ could have prevented these passions from coming upon it, and especially by the Divine power; yet of His own will He subjected Himself to these corporeal and animal passions.

Reply to Objection 2: Tully is speaking there according to the opinions of the Stoics, who did not give the name of passions to all, but only to the disorderly movements of the sensitive appetite. Now, it is manifest that passions like these were not in Christ.

Reply to Objection 3: The "passions of sins" are movements of the sensitive appetite that tend to unlawful things; and these were not in Christ, as neither was the "fomes" of sin.

Day 260

Whether there was sensible pain in Christ?

Objection 1: It would seem that there was no true sensible pain in Christ. For Hilary says (De Trin. x): "Since with Christ to die was life, what pain may He be supposed to have suffered in the mystery of His death, Who bestows life on such as die for Him?" And further on he says: "The Only-begotten assumed human nature, not ceasing to be God; and although blows struck Him and wounds were inflicted on Him, and scourges fell upon Him, and the cross lifted Him up, yet these wrought in deed the vehemence of the passion, but brought no pain; as a dart piercing the water." Hence there was no true pain in Christ.

Objection 2: Further, it would seem to be proper to flesh conceived in original sin, to be subject to the necessity of pain. But the flesh of Christ was not conceived in sin, but of the Holy Ghost in the Virgin's womb. Therefore it lay under no necessity of suffering pain.

Objection 3: Further, the delight of the contemplation of Divine things dulls the sense of pain; hence the martyrs in their passions bore up more bravely by thinking of the Divine love. But Christ's soul was in the perfect enjoyment of contemplating God, Whom He saw in essence, as was said above ([4030]Q[9], A[2]). Therefore He could feel no pain.

On the contrary, It is written (Is. 53:4): "Surely He hath borne our infirmities and carried our sorrows."

I answer that, As is plain from what has been said in the [4031]FS, Q[35], A[7], for true bodily pain are required bodily hurt and the sense of hurt. Now Christ's body was able to be hurt, since it was passible and mortal, as above stated (Q[14], AA[1],2); neither was the sense of hurt wanting to it, since Christ's soul possessed perfectly all natural powers. Therefore no one should doubt but that in Christ there was true pain.

Reply to Objection 1: In all these and similar words, Hilary does not intend to exclude the reality of the pain, but the necessity of it. Hence after the foregoing he adds: "Nor, when He thirsted, or hungered, or wept, was the Lord seen to drink, or eat, or grieve. But in order to prove the reality of the body, the body's customs were assumed, so that the custom of our body was atoned for by the custom of our nature. Or when He took drink or food, He acceded, not to the body's necessity, but to its custom." And he uses the word "necessity" in reference to the first cause of these defects, which is sin, as above stated ([4032]Q[14], AA[1],3), so that Christ's flesh is said not to have lain under the necessity of these defects, in the sense that there was no sin in it. Hence he adds: "For He" (i.e. Christ) "had a body---one proper to His origin, which did not exist through the unholiness of our conception, but subsisted in the form of our body by the strength of His power." But as regards the proximate cause of these defects, which is composition of contraries, the flesh of Christ lay under the necessity of these defects, as was said above ([4033]Q[14] , A[2]).

Reply to Objection 2: Flesh conceived in sin is subject to pain, not merely on account of the necessity of its natural principles, but from the necessity of the guilt of sin. Now this necessity was not in Christ; but only the necessity of natural principles.

Reply to Objection 3: As was said above ([4034]Q[14], A[1], ad 2), by the power of the Godhead of Christ the beatitude was economically kept in the soul, so as not to overflow into the body, lest His passibility and mortality should be taken away; and for the same reason the delight of contemplation was so kept in the mind as not to overflow into the sensitive powers, lest sensible pain should thereby be prevented.

Whether there was sorrow in Christ?

Objection 1: It would seem that in Christ there was no sorrow. For it is written of Christ (Is. 42:4): "He shall not be sad nor troublesome."

Objection 2: Further, it is written (Prov. 12:21): "Whatever shall befall the just man, it shall not make him sad." And the reason of this the Stoics asserted to be that no one is saddened save by the loss of his goods. Now the just man esteems only justice and virtue as his goods, and these he cannot lose; otherwise the just man would be subject to fortune if he was saddened by the loss of the goods fortune has given him. But Christ was most just, according to Jer. 23:6: "This is the name that they shall call Him: The Lord, our just one." Therefore there was no sorrow in Him.

Objection 3: Further, the Philosopher says (Ethic. vii, 13,14) that all sorrow is "evil, and to be shunned." But in Christ there was no evil to be shunned. Therefore there was no sorrow in Christ.

Objection 4: Furthermore, as Augustine says (De Civ. Dei xiv, 6): "Sorrow regards the things we suffer unwillingly." But Christ suffered nothing against His will, for it is written (Is. 53:7): "He was offered because it was His own will." Hence there was no sorrow in Christ.

On the contrary, Our Lord said (Mat. 26:38): "My soul is sorrowful even unto death." And Ambrose says (De Trin. ii.) that "as a man He had sorrow; for He bore my sorrow. I call it sorrow, fearlessly, since I preach the cross."

I answer that, As was said above (A[5], ad 3), by Divine dispensation the joy of contemplation remained in Christ's mind so as not to overflow into the sensitive powers, and thereby shut out sensible pain. Now even as sensible pain is in the sensitive appetite, so also is sorrow. But there is a difference of motive or object; for the object and motive of pain is hurt perceived by the sense of touch, as when anyone is wounded; but the object and motive of sorrow is anything hurtful or evil interiorly, apprehended by the reason or the imagination, as was said in the [4035]FS, Q[35], AA[2],7, as when anyone grieves over the loss of grace or money. Now Christ's soul could apprehend things as hurtful either to Himself, as His passion and death---or to others, as the sin of His disciples, or of the Jews that killed Him. And hence, as there could be true pain in Christ, so too could there be true sorrow; otherwise, indeed, than in us, in the three ways above stated [4036](A[4]), when we were speaking of the passions of Christ's soul in general.

Reply to Objection 1: Sorrow was not in Christ, as a perfect passion; yet it was inchoatively in Him as a "propassion." Hence it is written (Mat. 26:37): "He began to grow sorrowful and to be sad." For "it is one thing to be sorrowful and another to grow sorrowful," as Jerome says, on this text.

Reply to Objection 2: As Augustine says (De Civ. Dei xiv, 8), "for the three passions"---desire, joy, and fear---the Stoics held three {eupatheias} i.e. good passions, in the soul of the wise man, viz. for desire, will---for joy, delight---for fear, caution. But as regards sorrow, they denied it could be in the soul of the wise man, for sorrow regards evil already present, and they thought that no evil could befall a wise man; and for this reason, because they believed that only the virtuous is good, since it makes men good, and that nothing is evil, except what is sinful, whereby men become wicked. Now although what is virtuous is man's chief good, and what is sinful is man's chief evil, since these pertain to reason which is supreme in man, yet there are certain secondary goods of man, which pertain to the body, or to the exterior things that minister to the body. And hence in the soul of the wise man there may be sorrow in the sensitive appetite by his apprehending these evils; without this sorrow disturbing the reason. And in this way are we to understand that "whatsoever shall befall the just man, it shall not make him sad," because his reason is troubled by no misfortune. And thus Christ's sorrow was a propassion, and not a passion.

Reply to Objection 3: All sorrow is an evil of punishment; but it is not always an evil of fault, except only when it proceeds from an inordinate affection. Hence Augustine says (De Civ. Dei xiv, 9): "Whenever these affections follow reason, and are caused when and where needed, who will dare to call them diseases or vicious passions?"

Reply to Objection 4: There is no reason why a thing may not of itself be contrary to the will, and yet be willed by reason of the end, to which it is ordained, as bitter medicine is not of itself desired, but only as it is ordained to health. And thus Christ's death and passion were of themselves involuntary, and caused sorrow, although they were voluntary as ordained to the end, which is the redemption of the human race.

Whether there was fear in Christ?

Objection 1: It would seem that there was no fear in Christ. For it is written (Prov. 28:1): "The just, bold as a lion, shall be without dread." But Christ was most just. Therefore there was no fear in Christ.

Objection 2: Further, Hilary says (De Trin. x): "I ask those who think thus, does it stand to reason that He should dread to die, Who by expelling all dread of death from the Apostles, encouraged them to the glory of martyrdom?" Therefore it is unreasonable that there should be fear in Christ.

Objection 3: Further, fear seems only to regard what a man cannot avoid. Now Christ could have avoided both the evil of punishment which He endured, and the evil of fault which befell others. Therefore there was no fear in Christ.

On the contrary, It is written (Mk. 4:33): Jesus "began to fear and to be heavy."

I answer that, As sorrow is caused by the apprehension of a present evil, so also is fear caused by the apprehension of a future evil. Now the apprehension of a future evil, if the evil be quite certain, does not arouse fear. Hence the Philosopher says (Rhet. ii, 5) that we do not fear a thing unless there is some hope of avoiding it. For when there is no hope of avoiding it the evil is considered present, and thus it causes sorrow rather than fear. Hence fear may be considered in two ways. First, inasmuch as the sensitive appetite naturally shrinks from bodily hurt, by sorrow if it is present, and by fear if it is future; and thus fear was in Christ, even as sorrow. Secondly, fear may be considered in the uncertainty of the future event, as when at night we are frightened at a sound, not knowing what it is; and in this way there was no fear in Christ, as Damascene says (De Fide Orth. iii, 23).

Reply to Objection 1: The just man is said to be "without dread," in so far as dread implies a perfect passion drawing man from what reason dictates. And thus fear was not in Christ, but only as a propassion. Hence it is said (Mk. 14:33) that Jesus "began to fear and to be heavy," with a propassion, as Jerome expounds (Mat. 26:37).

Reply to Objection 2: Hilary excludes fear from Christ in the same way that he excludes sorrow, i.e. as regards the necessity of fearing. And yet to show the reality of His human nature, He voluntarily assumed fear, even as sorrow.

Reply to Objection 3: Although Christ could have avoided future evils by the power of His Godhead, yet they were unavoidable, or not easily avoidable by the weakness of the flesh.

Whether there was wonder in Christ?

Objection 1: It would seem that in Christ there was no wonder. For the Philosopher says (Metaph. i, 2) that wonder results when we see an effect without knowing its cause; and thus wonder belongs only to the ignorant. Now there was no ignorance in Christ, as was said A[3]. Therefore there was no wonder in Christ.

Objection 2: Further, Damascene says (De Fide Orth. ii, 15) that "wonder is fear springing from the imagination of something great"; and hence the Philosopher says (Ethic. iv, 3) that the "magnanimous man does not wonder." But Christ was most magnanimous. Therefore there was no wonder in Christ.

Objection 3: Further, no man wonders at what he himself can do. Now Christ could do whatsoever was great. Therefore it seems that He wondered at nothing.

On the contrary, It is written (Mat. 8:10): "Jesus hearing this," i.e. the words of the centurion, "marveled."

I answer that, Wonder properly regards what is new and unwonted. Now there could be nothing new and unwonted as regards Christ's Divine knowledge, whereby He saw things in the Word; nor as regards the human knowledge, whereby He saw things by infused species. Yet things could be new and unwonted with regard to His empiric knowledge, in regard to which new things could occur to Him day by day. Hence, if we speak of Christ with respect to His Divine knowledge, and His beatific and even His infused knowledge, there was no wonder in Christ. But if we speak of Him with respect to empiric knowledge, wonder could be in Him; and He assumed this affection for our instruction, i.e. in order to teach us to wonder at what He Himself wondered at. Hence Augustine says (Super Gen. Cont. Manich. i, 8): "Our Lord wondered in order to show us that we, who still need to be so affected, must wonder. Hence all these emotions are not signs of a disturbed mind, but of a master teaching."

Reply to Objection 1: Although Christ was ignorant of nothing, yet new things might occur to His empiric knowledge, and thus wonder would be caused.

Reply to Objection 2: Christ did not marvel at the Centurion's faith as if it was great with respect to Himself, but because it was great with respect to others.

Reply to Objection 3: He could do all things by the Divine power, for with respect to this there was no wonder in Him, but only with respect to His human empiric knowledge, as was said above.

Whether there was anger in Christ?

Objection 1: It would seem that there was no anger in Christ. For it is written (James 1:20): "The anger of man worketh not the justice of God." Now whatever was in Christ pertained to the justice of God, since of Him it is written (1 Cor. 1:30): "For He [Vulg.: 'Who'] of God is made unto us . . . justice." Therefore it seems that there was no anger in Christ.

Objection 2: Further, anger is opposed to meekness, as is plain from Ethic. iv, 5. But Christ was most meek. Therefore there was no anger in Him.

Objection 3: Further, Gregory says (Moral. v, 45) that "anger that comes of evil blinds the eye of the mind, but anger that comes of zeal disturbs it." Now the mind's eye in Christ was neither blinded nor disturbed. Therefore in Christ there was neither sinful anger nor zealous anger.

On the contrary, It is written (Jn. 2:17) that the words of Ps. 58:10, "the zeal of Thy house hath eaten me up," were fulfilled in Him.

I answer that, As was said in the [4037]FS, Q[46], A[3], ad 3, and [4038]SS, Q[158], A[2], ad 3, anger is an effect of sorrow. or when sorrow is inflicted upon someone, there arises within him a desire of the sensitive appetite to repel this injury brought upon himself or others. Hence anger is a passion composed of sorrow and the desire of revenge. Now it was said [4039](A[6]) that sorrow could be in Christ. As to the desire of revenge it is sometimes with sin, i.e. when anyone seeks revenge beyond the order of reason: and in this way anger could not be in Christ, for this kind of anger is sinful. Sometimes, however, this desire is without sin---nay, is praiseworthy, e.g. when anyone seeks revenge according to justice, and this is zealous anger. For Augustine says (on Jn. 2:17) that "he is eaten up by zeal for the house of God, who seeks to better whatever He sees to be evil in it, and if he cannot right it, bears with it and sighs." Such was the anger that was in Christ.

Reply to Objection 1: As Gregory says (Moral. v), anger is in man in two ways---sometimes it forestalls reason, and causes it to operate, and in this way it is properly said to work, for operations are attributed to the principal agent. It is in this way that we must understand that "the anger of man worketh not the justice of God." Sometimes anger follows reason, and is, as it were, its instrument, and then the operation, which pertains to justice, is not attributed to anger but to reason.

Reply to Objection 2: It is the anger which outsteps the bounds of reason that is opposed to meekness, and not the anger which is controlled and brought within its proper bounds by reason, for meekness holds the mean in anger.

Reply to Objection 3: In us the natural order is that the soul's powers mutually impede each other, i.e. if the operation of one power is intense, the operation of the other is weakened. This is the reason why any movement whatsoever of anger, even if it be tempered by reason, dims the mind's eye of him who contemplates. But in Christ, by control of the Divine power, "every faculty was allowed to do what was proper to it," and one power was not impeded by another. Hence, as the joy of His mind in contemplation did not impede the sorrow or pain of the inferior part, so, conversely, the passions of the inferior part no-wise impeded the act of reason.

Whether Christ was at once a wayfarer and a comprehensor?

Objection 1: It would seem that Christ was not at once a wayfarer and a comprehensor. For it belongs to a wayfarer to be moving toward the end of beatitude, and to a comprehensor it belongs to be resting in the end. Now to be moving towards the end and to be resting in the end cannot belong to the same. Therefore Christ could not be at once wayfarer and comprehensor.

Objection 2: Further, to tend to beatitude, or to obtain it, does not pertain to man's body, but to his soul; hence Augustine says (Ep. ad Dios. cxviii) that "upon the inferior nature, which is the body, there overflows, not indeed the beatitude which belongs to such as enjoy and understand, the fulness of health, i.e. the vigor of incorruption." Now although Christ had a passible body, He fully enjoyed God in His mind. Therefore Christ was not a wayfarer but a comprehensor.

Objection 3: Further, the Saints, whose souls are in heaven and whose bodies are in the tomb, enjoy beatitude in their souls, although their bodies are subject to death, yet they are called not wayfarers, but only comprehensors. Hence, with equal reason, would it seem that Christ was a pure comprehensor and nowise a wayfarer, since His mind enjoyed God although His body was mortal.

On the contrary, It is written (Jer. 14:8): "Why wilt Thou be as a stranger in the land, and as a wayfaring man turning in to lodge?"

I answer that, A man is called a wayfarer from tending to beatitude, and a comprehensor from having already obtained beatitude, according to 1 Cor. 9:24: "So run that you may comprehend [Douay: 'obtain']"; and Phil. 3:12: "I follow after, if by any means I may comprehend [Douay: 'obtain']". Now man's perfect beatitude consists in both soul and body, as stated in the [4040]FS, Q[4], A[6]. In the soul, as regards what is proper to it, inasmuch as the mind sees and enjoys God; in the body, inasmuch as the body "will rise spiritual in power and glory and incorruption," as is written 1 Cor. 15:42. Now before His passion Christ's mind saw God fully, and thus He had beatitude as far as it regards what is proper to the soul; but beatitude was wanting with regard to all else, since His soul was passible, and His body both passible and mortal, as is clear from the above [4041](A[4]; Q[14], AA[1],2). Hence He was at once comprehensor, inasmuch as He had the beatitude proper to the soul, and at the same time wayfarer, inasmuch as He was tending to beatitude, as regards what was wanting to His beatitude.

Reply to Objection 1: It is impossible to be moving towards the end and resting in the end, in the same respect; but there is nothing against this under a different respect---as when a man is at once acquainted with what he already knows, and yet is a learner with regard to what he does not know.

Reply to Objection 2: Beatitude principally and properly belongs to the soul with regard to the mind, yet secondarily and, so to say, instrumentally, bodily goods are required for beatitude; thus the Philosopher says (Ethic. i, 8), that exterior goods minister "organically" to beatitude.

Reply to Objection 3: There is no parity between the soul of a saint and of Christ, for two reasons: first, because the souls of saints are not passible, as Christ's soul was; secondly, because their bodies do nothing by which they tend to beatitude, as Christ by His bodily sufferings tended to beatitude as regards the glory of His body.

OF THOSE THINGS WHICH ARE APPLICABLE TO CHRIST IN HIS BEING AND BECOMING
(TWELVE ARTICLES)

We must now consider the consequences of the union; and first as to what belongs to Christ in Himself; secondly, as to what belongs to Christ in relation with His Father; thirdly, as to what belongs to Christ in relation to us.

Concerning the first, there occurs a double consideration. The first is about such things as belong to Christ in being and becoming; the second regards such things as belong to Christ by reason of unity.

Under the first head there are twelve points of inquiry:

(1) Whether this is true: "God is man"?

(2) Whether this is true: "Man is God"?

(3) Whether Christ may be called a lordly man?

(4) Whether what belongs to the Son of Man may be predicated of the Son of God, and conversely?

(5) Whether what belongs to the Son of Man may be predicated of the Divine Nature, and what belongs to the Son of God of the human nature?

(6) Whether this is true: "The Son of God was made man"?

(7) Whether this is true: "Man became God"?

(8) Whether this is true: "Christ is a creature"?

(9) Whether this is true: "This man," pointing out Christ, "began to be"? or "always was"?

(10) Whether this is true: "Christ as man is a creature"?

(11) Whether this is true: "Christ as man is God"?

(12) Whether this is true: "Christ as man is a hypostasis or person"?

Whether this is true: "God is man"?

Objection 1: It would seem that this is false: "God is man." For every affirmative proposition of remote matter is false. Now this proposition, "God is man," is on remote matter, since the forms signified by the subject and predicate are most widely apart. Therefore, since the aforesaid proposition is affirmative, it would seem to be false.

Objection 2: Further, the three Divine Persons are in greater mutual agreement than the human nature and the Divine. But in the mystery of the Incarnation one Person is not predicated of another; for we do not say that the Father is the Son, or conversely. Therefore it seems that the human nature ought not to be predicated of God by saying that God is man.

Objection 3: Further, Athanasius says (Symb. Fid.) that, "as the soul and the flesh are one man, so are God and man one Christ." But this is false: "The soul is the body." Therefore this also is false: "God is man."

Objection 4: Further, it was said in the [4042]FP, Q[39], A[4] that what is predicated of God not relatively but absolutely, belongs to the whole Trinity and to each of the Persons. But this word "man" is not relative, but absolute. Hence, if it is predicated of God, it would follow that the whole Trinity and each of the Persons is man; and this is clearly false.

On the contrary, It is written (Phil. 2:6,7): "Who being in the form of God . . . emptied Himself, taking the form of a servant, being made in the likeness of men, and in habit found as a man"; and thus He Who is in the form of God is man. Now He Who is in the form of God is God. Therefore God is man.

I answer that, This proposition "God is man," is admitted by all Christians, yet not in the same way by all. For some admit the proposition, but not in the proper acceptation of the terms. Thus the Manicheans say the Word of God is man, not indeed true, but fictitious man, inasmuch as they say that the Son of God assumed an imaginary body, and thus God is called man as a bronze figure is called man if it has the figure of a man. So, too, those who held that Christ's body and soul were not united, could not say that God is true man, but that He is figuratively called man by reason of the parts. Now both these opinions were disproved above ([4043]Q[2], A[5];[4044] Q[5], A[1]).

Some, on the contrary, hold the reality on the part of man, but deny the reality on the part of God. For they say that Christ, Who is God and man, is God not naturally, but by participation, i.e. by grace; even as all other holy men are called gods---Christ being more excellently so than the rest, on account of His more abundant grace. And thus, when it is said that "God is man," God does not stand for the true and natural God. And this is the heresy of Photinus, which was disproved above ([4045]Q[2], AA[10],11). But some admit this proposition, together with the reality of both terms, holding that Christ is true God and true man; yet they do not preserve the truth of the predication. For they say that man is predicated of God by reason of a certain conjunction either of dignity, or of authority, or of affection or indwelling. It was thus that Nestorius held God to be man---nothing further being meant than that God is joined to man by such a conjunction that man is dwelt in by God, and united to Him in affection, and in a share of the Divine authority and honor. And into the same error fall those who suppose two supposita or hypostases in Christ, since it is impossible to understand how, of two things distinct in suppositum or hypostasis, one can be properly predicated of the other: unless merely by a figurative expression, inasmuch as they are united in something, as if we were to say that Peter is John because they are somehow mutually joined together. And these opinions also were disproved above ([4046]Q[2], AA[3],6).

Hence, supposing the truth of the Catholic belief, that the true Divine Nature is united with true human nature not only in person, but also in suppositum or hypostasis; we say that this proposition is true and proper, "God is man"---not only by the truth of its terms, i.e. because Christ is true God and true man, but by the truth of the predication. For a word signifying the common nature in the concrete may stand for all contained in the common nature, as this word "man" may stand for any individual man. And thus this word "God," from its very mode of signification, may stand for the Person of the Son of God, as was said in the [4047]FP, Q[39], A[4]. Now of every suppositum of any nature we may truly and properly predicate a word signifying that nature in the concrete, as "man" may properly and truly be predicated of Socrates and Plato. Hence, since the Person of the Son of God for Whom this word "God" stands, is a suppositum of human nature this word man may be truly and properly predicated of this word "God," as it stands for the Person of the Son of God.

Reply to Objection 1: When different forms cannot come together in one suppositum, the proposition is necessarily in remote matter, the subject signifying one form and the predicate another. But when two forms can come together in one suppositum, the matter is not remote, but natural or contingent, as when I say: "Something white is musical." Now the Divine and human natures, although most widely apart, nevertheless come together by the mystery of the Incarnation in one suppositum, in which neither exists accidentally, but [both] essentially. Hence this proposition is neither in remote nor in contingent, but in natural matter; and man is not predicated of God accidentally, but essentially, as being predicated of its hypostasis---not, indeed, by reason of the form signified by this word "God," but by reason of the suppositum, which is a hypostasis of human nature.

Reply to Objection 2: The three Divine Persons agree in one Nature, and are distinguished in suppositum; and hence they are not predicated one of another. But in the mystery of the Incarnation the natures, being distinct, are not predicated one of the other, in the abstract. For the Divine Nature is not the human nature. But because they agree in suppositum, they are predicated of each other in the concrete.

Reply to Objection 3: "Soul" and "flesh" are taken in the abstract, even as Godhead and manhood; but in the concrete we say "animate" and "carnal" or "corporeal," as, on the other hand, "God" and "man." Hence in both cases the abstract is not predicated of the abstract, but only the concrete of the concrete.

Reply to Objection 4: This word "man" is predicated of God, because of the union in person, and this union implies a relation. Hence it does not follow the rule of those words which are absolutely predicated of God from eternity.

Whether this is true: "Man is God"?

Objection 1: It would seem that this is false: "Man is God." For God is an incommunicable name; hence (Wis. 13:10; 14:21) idolaters are rebuked for giving the name of God, which is incommunicable, to wood and stones. Hence with equal reason does it seem unbecoming that this word "God" should be predicated of man.

Objection 2: Further, whatever is predicated of the predicate may be predicated of the subject. But this is true: "God is the Father," or "God is the Trinity." Therefore, if it is true that "Man is God," it seems that this also is true: "Man is the Father," or "Man is the Trinity." But these are false. Therefore the first is false.

Objection 3: Further, it is written (Ps. 80:10): "There shall be no new God in thee." But man is something new; for Christ was not always man. Therefore this is false: "Man is God."

On the contrary, It is written (Rom. 9:5): "Of whom is Christ according to the flesh, Who is over all things, God blessed for ever." Now Christ, according to the flesh, is man. Therefore this is true: "Man is God."

I answer that, Granted the reality of both natures, i.e. Divine and human, and of the union in person and hypostasis, this is true and proper: "Man is God," even as this: "God is man." For this word "man" may stand for any hypostasis of human nature; and thus it may stand for the Person of the Son of God, Whom we say is a hypostasis of human nature. Now it is manifest that the word "God" is truly and properly predicated of the Person of the Son of God, as was said in the [4048]FP, Q[39], A[4]. Hence it remains that this is true and proper: "Man is God."

Reply to Objection 1: Idolaters attributed the name of the Deity to stones and wood, considered in their own nature, because they thought there was something divine in them. But we do not attribute the name of the Deity to the man in His human nature, but in the eternal suppositum, which by union is a suppositum of human nature, as stated above.

Reply to Objection 2: This word "Father" is predicated of this word "God," inasmuch as this word "God" stands for the Person of the Father. And in this way it is not predicated of the Person of the Son, because the Person of the Son is not the Person of the Father. And, consequently, it is not necessary that this word "Father" be predicated of this word "Man," of which the Word "God" is predicated, inasmuch as "Man" stands for the Person of the Son.

Reply to Objection 3: Although the human nature in Christ is something new, yet the suppositum of the human nature is not new, but eternal. And because this word "God" is predicated of man not on account of the human nature, but by reason of the suppositum, it does not follow that we assert a new God. But this would follow, if we held that "Man" stands for a created suppositum: even as must be said by those who assert that there are two supposita in Christ [*Cf.[4049] Q[2], AA[3],6].

Day 261

Whether Christ can be called a lordly man?

[*The question is hardly apposite in English. St. Thomas explains why we can say in Latin, e.g. 'oratio dominica' (the Lord's Prayer) or 'passio dominica' (Our Lord's Passion), but not speak of our Lord as 'homo dominicus' (a lordly man)].

Objection 1: It would seem that Christ can be called a lordly man. For Augustine says (Qq. lxxxiii, qu. 36) that "we are to be counseled to hope for the goods that were in the Lordly Man"; and he is speaking of Christ. Therefore it seems that Christ was a lordly man.

Objection 2: Further, as lordship belongs to Christ by reason of His Divine Nature, so does manhood belong to the human nature. Now God is said to be "humanized," as is plain from Damascene (De Fide Orth. iii, 11), where he says that "being humanized manifests the conjunction with man." Hence with like reason may it be said denominatively that this man is lordly.

Objection 3: Further, as "lordly" is derived from "lord," so is Divine derived from "Deus" [God]. But Dionysius (Eccl. Hier. iv) calls Christ the "most Divine Jesus." Therefore with like reason may Christ be called a lordly man.

On the contrary, Augustine says (Retract. i, 19): "I do not see that we may rightly call Jesus Christ a lordly man, since He is the Lord Himself."

I answer that, As was said above (A[2], ad 3), when we say "the Man Christ Jesus," we signify the eternal suppositum, which is the Person of the Son of God, because there is only one suppositum of both natures. Now "God" and "Lord" are predicated essentially of the Son of God; and hence they ought not to be predicated denominatively, since this is derogatory to the truth of the union. Hence, since we say "lordly" denominatively from lord, it cannot truly and properly be said that this Man is lordly, but rather that He is Lord. But if, when we say "the Man Christ Jesus," we mean a created suppositum, as those who assert two supposita in Christ, this man might be called lordly, inasmuch as he is assumed to a participation of Divine honor, as the Nestorians said. And, even in this way, the human nature is not called "divine" by essence, but "deified"---not, indeed, by its being converted into the Divine Nature, but by its conjunction with the Divine Nature in one hypostasis, as is plain from Damascene (De Fide Orth. iii, 11,17).

Reply to Objection 1: Augustine retracts these and the like words (Retract. i, 19); hence, after the foregoing words (Retract. i, 19), he adds: "Wherever I have said this," viz. that Christ Jesus is a lordly man, "I wish it unsaid, having afterwards seen that it ought not to be said although it may be defended with some reason," i.e. because one might say that He was called a lordly man by reason of the human nature, which this word "man" signifies, and not by reason of the suppositum.

Reply to Objection 2: This one suppositum, which is of the human and Divine natures, was first of the Divine Nature, i.e. from eternity. Afterwards in time it was made a suppositum of human nature by the Incarnation. And for this reason it is said to be "humanized"---not that it assumed a man, but that it assumed human nature. But the converse of this is not true, viz. that a suppositum of human nature assumed the Divine Nature; hence we may not say a "deified" or "lordly" man.

Reply to Objection 3: This word Divine is wont to be predicated even of things of which the word God is predicated essentially; thus we say that "the Divine Essence is God," by reason of identity; and that "the Essence belongs to God," or is "Divine," on account of the different way of signifying; and we speak of the "Divine Word," though the Word is God. So, too, we say "a Divine Person," just as we say "the person of Plato," on account of its different mode of signification. But "lordly" is not predicated of those of which "lord" is predicated; for we are not wont to call a man who is a lord, lordly; but whatsoever belongs to a lord is called lordly, as the "lordly will," or the "lordly hand," or the "lordly possession." And hence the man Christ, Who is our Lord, cannot be called lordly; yet His flesh can be called "lordly flesh" and His passion the "lordly passion."

Whether what belongs to the human nature can be predicated of God?

Objection 1: It would seem that what belongs to the human nature cannot be said of God. For contrary things cannot be said of the same. Now, what belongs to human nature is contrary to what is proper to God, since God is uncreated, immutable, and eternal, and it belongs to the human nature to be created temporal and mutable. Therefore what belongs to the human nature cannot be said of God.

Objection 2: Further, to attribute to God what is defective seems to be derogatory to the Divine honor, and to be a blasphemy. Now what pertains to the human nature contains a kind of defect, as to suffer, to die, and the like. Hence it seems that what pertains to the human nature can nowise be said of God.

Objection 3: Further, to be assumed pertains to the human nature; yet it does not pertain to God. Therefore what belongs to the human nature cannot be said of God.

On the contrary, Damascene says (De Fide Orth. iii, 4) that "God assumed the idioms," i.e. the properties, "of flesh, since God is said to be passible, and the God of glory was crucified."

I answer that, On this question there was a difference of opinion between Nestorians and Catholics. The Nestorians wished to divide words predicated of Christ, in this way, viz. that such as pertained to human nature should not be predicated of God, and that such as pertained to the Divine Nature should not be predicated of the Man. Hence Nestorius said: "If anyone attempt to attribute sufferings to the Word, let him be anathema" [*Council of Ephesus, Part I, ch. 29]. But if there are any words applicable to both natures, of them they predicated what pertained to both natures, as "Christ" or "Lord." Hence they granted that Christ was born of a Virgin, and that He was from eternity; but they did not say that God was born of a virgin, or that the Man was from eternity. Catholics on the other hand maintained that words which are said of Christ either in His Divine or in His human nature may be said either of God or of man. Hence Cyril says [*Council of Ephesus, Part I, ch. 26]: "If anyone ascribes to two persons or substances," i.e. hypostases, "such words as are in the evangelical and apostolic Scriptures, or have been said of Christ by the Saints, or by Himself of Himself, and believes that some are to be applied to the Man, and apportions some to the Word alone---let him be anathema." And the reason of this is that, since there is one hypostasis of both natures, the same hypostasis is signified by the name of either nature. Thus whether we say "man" or "God," the hypostasis of Divine and human nature is signified. And hence, of the Man may be said what belongs to the Divine Nature, as of a hypostasis of the Divine Nature; and of God may be said what belongs to the human nature, as of a hypostasis of human nature.

Nevertheless, it must be borne in mind that in a proposition in which something is predicated of another, we must not merely consider what the predicate is predicated of, but also the reason of its being predicated. Thus, although we do not distinguish things predicated of Christ, yet we distinguish that by reason of which they are predicated, since those things that belong to the Divine Nature are predicated of Christ in His Divine Nature, and those that belong to the human nature are predicated of Christ in His human nature. Hence Augustine says (De Trin. i, 11): "We must distinguish what is said by Scripture in reference to the form of God, wherein He is equal to the Father, and what in reference to the form of a servant, wherein He is less than the Father": and further on he says (De Trin. i, 13): "The prudent, careful, and devout reader will discern the reason and point of view of what is said."

Reply to Objection 1: It is impossible for contraries to be predicated of the same in the same respects, but nothing prevents their being predicated of the same in different aspects. And thus contraries are predicated of Christ, not in the same, but in different natures.

Reply to Objection 2: If the things pertaining to defect were attributed to God in His Divine Nature, it would be a blasphemy, since it would be derogatory to His honor. But there is no kind of wrong done to God if they are attributed to Him in His assumed nature. Hence in a discourse of the Council of Ephesus [*Part III, ch. 10] it is said: "God accounts nothing a wrong which is the occasion of man's salvation. For no lowliness that He assumed for us injures that Nature which can be subject to no injury, yet makes lower things Its own, to save our nature. Therefore, since these lowly and worthless things do no harm to the Divine Nature, but bring about our salvation, how dost thou maintain that what was the cause of our salvation was the occasion of harm to God?"

Reply to Objection 3: To be assumed pertains to human nature, not in its suppositum, but in itself; and thus it does not belong to God.

Whether what belongs to the human nature can be predicated of the Divine Nature?

Objection 1: It would seem that what belongs to the human nature can be said of the Divine Nature. For what belongs to the human nature is predicated of the Son of God, and of God. But God is His own Nature. Therefore, what belongs to the human nature may be predicated of the Divine Nature.

Objection 2: Further, the flesh pertains to human nature. But as Damascene says (De Fide Orth. iii, 6), "we say, after the blessed Athanasius and Cyril, that the Nature of the Word was incarnate." Therefore it would seem with equal reason that what belongs to the human nature may be said of the Divine Nature.

Objection 3: Further, what belongs to the Divine Nature belongs to Christ's human nature; such as to know future things and to possess saving power. Therefore it would seem with equal reason that what belongs to the human may be said of the Divine Nature.

On the contrary, Damascene says (De Fide Orth. iii, 4): "When we mention the Godhead we do not predicate of it the idioms," i.e. the properties, "of the humanity; for we do not say that the Godhead is passible or creatable." Now the Godhead is the Divine Nature. Therefore what is proper to the human nature cannot be said of the Divine Nature.

I answer that, What belongs to one cannot be said of another, unless they are both the same; thus "risible" can be predicated only of man. Now in the mystery of the Incarnation the Divine and human natures are not the same; but the hypostasis of the two natures is the same. And hence what belongs to one nature cannot be predicated of the other if they are taken in the abstract. Now concrete words stand for the hypostasis of the nature; and hence of concrete words we may predicate indifferently what belongs to either nature---whether the word of which they are predicated refers to one nature, as the word "Christ," by which is signified "both the Godhead anointing and the manhood anointed"; or to the Divine Nature alone, as this word "God" or "the Son of God"; or to the manhood alone, as this word "Man" or "Jesus." Hence Pope Leo says (Ep. ad Palaest. cxxiv): "It is of no consequence from what substance we name Christ; because since the unity of person remains inseparably, one and the same is altogether Son of Man by His flesh, and altogether Son of God by the Godhead which He has with the Father."

Reply to Objection 1: In God, Person and Nature are really the same; and by reason of this identity the Divine Nature is predicated of the Son of God. Nevertheless, its mode of predication is different; and hence certain things are said of the Son of God which are not said of the Divine Nature; thus we say that the Son of God is born, yet we do not say that the Divine Nature is born; as was said in the [4050]FP, Q[39], A[5]. So, too, in the mystery of the Incarnation we say that the Son of God suffered, yet we do not say that the Divine Nature suffered.

Reply to Objection 2: Incarnation implies union with flesh, rather than any property of flesh. Now in Christ each nature is united to the other in person; and by reason of this union the Divine Nature is said to be incarnate and the human nature deified, as stated above ([4051]Q[2], A[1], ad 3).

Reply to Objection 3: What belongs to the Divine Nature is predicated of the human nature---not, indeed, as it belongs essentially to the Divine Nature, but as it is participated by the human nature. Hence, whatever cannot be participated by the human nature (as to be uncreated and omnipotent), is nowise predicated of the human nature. But the Divine Nature received nothing by participation from the human nature; and hence what belongs to the human nature can nowise be predicated of the Divine Nature.

Whether this is true: "God was made man"?
Objection 1: It would seem that this is false: "God was made man." For since man signifies a substance, to be made man is to be made simply. But this is false: "God was made simply." Therefore this is false: "God was made man."

Objection 2: Further, to be made man is to be changed. But God cannot be the subject of change, according to Malachi 3:6: "I am the Lord, and I change not." Hence this is false: "God was made man."

Objection 3: Further, man as predicated of Christ stands for the Person of the Son of God. But this is false: "God was made the Person of the Son of God." Therefore this is false: "God was made man."

On the contrary, It is written (Jn. 1:14): "The Word was made flesh": and as Athanasius says (Ep. ad Epictetum), "when he said, 'The Word was made flesh,' it is as if it were said that God was made man."

I answer that, A thing is said to be made that which begins to be predicated of it for the first time. Now to be man is truly predicated of God, as stated above [4052](A[1]), yet in such sort that it pertains to God to be man, not from eternity, but from the time of His assuming human nature. Hence, this is true, "God was made man"; though it is understood differently by some: even as this, "God is man," as we said above [4053](A[1]).

Reply to Objection 1: To be made man is to be made simply, in all those in whom human nature begins to be in a newly created suppositum. But God is said to have been made man, inasmuch as the human nature began to be in an eternally pre-existing suppositum of the Divine Nature. And hence for God to be made man does not mean that God was made simply.

Reply to Objection 2: As stated above, to be made implies that something. is newly predicated of another. Hence, whenever anything is predicated of another, and there is a change in that of which it is predicated, then to be made is to be changed; and this takes place in whatever is predicated absolutely, for whiteness or greatness cannot newly affect anything, unless it be newly changed to whiteness or greatness. But whatever is predicated relatively can be newly predicated of anything without its change, as a man may be made to be on the right side without being changed and merely by the change of him on whose left side he was. Hence in such cases, not all that is said to be made is changed, since it may happen by the change of something else. And it is thus we say of God: "Lord, Thou art made [Douay: 'hast been'] our refuge" (Ps. 89:1). Now to be man belongs to God by reason of the union, which is a relation. And hence to be man is newly predicated of God without any change in Him, by a change in the human nature, which is assumed to a Divine Person. And hence, when it is said, "God was made man," we understand no change on the part of God, but only on the part of the human nature.

Reply to Objection 3: Man stands not for the bare Person of the Son of God, but inasmuch as it subsists in human nature. Hence, although this is false, "God was made the Person of the Son of God," yet this is true: "God was made man" by being united to human nature.

Whether this is true: "Man was made God"?
Objection 1: It would seem that this is true: "Man was made God." For it is written (Rom. 1:2,3): "Which He had promised before by His prophets in the holy Scriptures, concerning His Son Who was made to Him of the seed of David according to the flesh." Now Christ, as man, is of the seed of David according to the flesh. Therefore man was made the Son of God.

Objection 2: Further, Augustine says (De Trin. i, 13) that "such was this assumption, which made God man, and man God." But by reason of this assumption this is true: "God was made man." Therefore, in like manner, this is true: "Man was made God."

Objection 3: Further, Gregory Nazianzen says (Ep. ad Chelid. ci): "God was humanized and man was deified, or whatever else one may like to call it." Now God is said to be humanized by being made man. Therefore with equal reason man is said to be deified by being made God; and thus it is true that "Man was made God."

Objection 4: Further, when it is said that "God was made man," the subject of the making or uniting is not God, but human nature, which the word "man" signifies. Now that seems to be the subject of the making, to which the making is attributed. Hence "Man was made God" is truer than "God was made man."

On the contrary, Damascene says (De Fide Orth. iii, 2): "We do not say that man was deified, but that God was humanized." Now to be made God is the same as to be deified. Hence this is false: "Man was made God."

I answer that, This proposition, Man was made God, may be understood in three ways. First, so that the participle "made" absolutely determines either the subject or the predicate; and in this sense it is false, since neither the Man of Whom it is predicated was made, nor is God made, as will be said ([4054]AA[8],9). And in the same sense this is false: "God was made man." But it is not of this sense that we are now speaking. Secondly, it may be so understood that the word "made" determines the composition, with this meaning: "Man was made God, i.e. it was brought about that Man is God." And in this sense both are true, viz. that "Man was made God" and that "God was made Man." But this is not the proper sense of these phrases; unless, indeed, we are to understand that "man" has not a personal but a simple supposition. For although "this man" was not made God, because this suppositum, viz. the Person of the Son of God, was eternally God, yet man, speaking commonly, was not always God. Thirdly, properly understood, this participle "made" attaches making to man with relation to God, as the term of the making. And in this sense, granted that the Person or hypostasis in Christ are the same as the suppositum of God and Man, as was shown ([4055]Q[2], AA[2],3), this proposition is false, because, when it is said, "Man was made God," "man" has a personal suppositum: because, to be God is not verified of the Man in His human nature, but in His suppositum. Now the suppositum of human nature, of Whom "to be God" is verified, is the same as the hypostasis or Person of the Son of God, Who was always God. Hence it cannot be said that this Man began to be God, or is made God, or that He was made God.

But if there were a different hypostasis of God and man, so that "to be God" was predicated of the man, and, conversely, by reason of a certain conjunction of supposita, or of personal dignity, or of affection or indwelling, as the Nestorians said, then with equal reason might it be said that Man was made God, i.e. joined to God, and that God was made Man, i.e. joined to man.

Reply to Objection 1: In these words of the Apostle the relative "Who" which refers to the Person of the Son of God ought not to be considered as affecting the predicate, as if someone already existing of the "seed of David according to the flesh" was made the Son of God---and it is in this sense that the objection takes it. But it ought to be taken as affecting the subject, with this meaning---that the "Son of God was made to Him ('namely to the honor of the Father,' as a gloss expounds it), being of the seed of David according to the flesh," as if to say "the Son of God having flesh of the seed of David to the honor of God."

Reply to Objection 2: This saying of Augustine is to be taken in the sense that by the assumption that took place in the Incarnation it was brought about that Man is God and God is Man; and in this sense both sayings are true as stated above.

The same is to be said in reply to the third, since to be deified is the same as to be made God.

Reply to Objection 4: A term placed in the subject is taken materially, i.e. for the suppositum; placed in the predicate it is taken formally, i.e. for the nature signified. Hence when it is said that "Man was made God," the being made is not attributed to the human nature but to the suppositum of the human nature, Which is God from eternity, and hence it does not befit Him to be made God. But when it is said that "God was made Man," the making is taken to be terminated in the human nature. Hence, properly speaking, this is true: "God was made Man," and this is false: "Man was made God"; even as if Socrates, who was already a man, were made white, and were pointed out, this would be true: "This man was made white today," and this would be false; "This white thing was made man today." Nevertheless, if on the part of the subject there is added some word signifying human nature in the abstract, it might be taken in this way for the subject of the making, e.g. if it were said that "human nature was made the Son of God's."

Whether this is true: "Christ is a creature"?

Objection 1: It would seem that this is true: "Christ is a creature." For Pope Leo says [*Cf. Append. Opp. August., Serm. xii de Nativ.]: "A new and unheard of covenant: God Who is and was, is made a creature." Now we may predicate of Christ whatever the Son of God became by the Incarnation. Therefore this is true; Christ is a creature.

Objection 2: Further, the properties of both natures may be predicated of the common hypostasis of both natures, no matter by what word they are signified, as stated above [4056](A[5]). But it is the property of human nature to be created, as it is the property of the Divine Nature to be Creator. Hence both may be said of Christ, viz. that He is a creature and that he is uncreated and Creator.

Objection 3: Further, the principal part of a man is the soul rather than the body. But Christ, by reason of the body which He took from the Virgin, is said simply to be born of the Virgin. Therefore by reason of the soul which is created by God, it ought simply to be said that He is a creature.

On the contrary, Ambrose says (De Trin. i): "Was Christ made by a word? Was Christ created by a command?" as if to say: "No!" Hence he adds: "How can there be a creature in God? For God has a simple not a composite Nature." Therefore it must not be granted that "Christ is a creature."

I answer that, As Jerome [*Gloss, Ord. in Osee 2:16] says, "words spoken amiss lead to heresy"; hence with us and heretics the very words ought not to be in common, lest we seem to countenance their error. Now the Arian heretics said that Christ was a creature and less than the Father, not only in His human nature, but even in His Divine Person. And hence we must not say absolutely that Christ is a "creature" or "less than the Father"; but with a qualification, viz. "in His human nature." But such things as could not be considered to belong to the Divine Person in Itself may be predicated simply of Christ by reason of His human nature; thus we say simply that Christ suffered, died and was buried: even as in corporeal and human beings, things of which we may doubt whether they belong to the whole or the part, if they are observed to exist in a part, are not predicated of the whole simply, i.e. without qualification, for we do not say that the Ethiopian is white but that he is white as regards his teeth; but we say without qualification that he is curly, since this can only belong to him as regards his hair.

Reply to Objection 1: Sometimes, for the sake of brevity, the holy doctors use the word "creature" of Christ, without any qualifying term; we should however take as understood the qualification, "as man."

Reply to Objection 2: All the properties of the human, just as of the Divine Nature, may be predicated equally of Christ. Hence Damascene says (De Fide Orth. iii, 4) that "Christ Who God and Man, is called created and uncreated, passible and impassible." Nevertheless things of which we may doubt to what nature they belong, are not to be predicated without a qualification. Hence he afterwards adds (De Fide Orth. iv, 5) that "the one hypostasis," i.e. of Christ, "is uncreated in its Godhead and created in its manhood": even so conversely, we may not say without qualification, "Christ is incorporeal" or "impassible"; in order to avoid the error of Manes, who held that Christ had not a true body, nor truly suffered, but we must say, with a qualification, that Christ was incorporeal and impassible "in His Godhead."

Reply to Objection 3: There can be no doubt how the birth from the Virgin applies to the Person of the Son of God, as there can be in the case of creation; and hence there is no parity.

Whether this Man, i.e. Christ, began to be?

Objection 1: It would seem that this Man, i.e. Christ, began to be. For Augustine says (Tract. cv in Joan.) that "before the world was, neither were we, nor the Mediator of God and men---the Man Jesus Christ." But what was not always, has begun to be. Therefore this Man, i.e. Christ, began to be.

Objection 2: Further, Christ began to be Man. But to be man is to be simply. Therefore this man began to be, simply.

Objection 3: Further, "man" implies a suppositum of human nature. But Christ was not always a suppositum of human nature. Therefore this Man began to be.

On the contrary, It is written (Heb. 13:8): "Jesus Christ yesterday and today: and the same for ever."

I answer that, We must not say that "this Man"---pointing to Christ---"began to be," unless we add something. And this for a twofold reason. First, for this proposition is simply false, in the judgment of the Catholic Faith, which affirms that in Christ there is one suppositum and one hypostasis, as also one Person. For according to this, when we say "this Man," pointing to Christ, the eternal suppositum is necessarily meant, with Whose eternity a beginning in time is incompatible. Hence this is false: "This Man began to be." Nor does it matter that to begin to be refers to the human nature, which is signified by this word "man"; because the term placed in the subject is not taken formally so as to signify the nature, but is taken materially so as to signify the suppositum, as was said (A[1], ad 4). Secondly, because even if this proposition were true, it ought not to be made use of without qualification; in order to avoid the heresy of Arius, who, since he pretended that the Person of the Son of God is a creature, and less than the Father, so he maintained that He began to be, saying "there was a time when He was not."

Reply to Objection 1: The words quoted must be qualified, i.e. we must say that the Man Jesus Christ was not, before the world was, "in His humanity."

Reply to Objection 2: With this word "begin" we cannot argue from the lower species to the higher. For it does not follow if "this began to be white," that therefore "it began to be colored." And this because "to begin" implies being now and not heretofore: for it does not follow if "this was not white hitherto" that "therefore it was not colored hitherto." Now, to be simply is higher than to be man. Hence this does not follow: "Christ began to be Man---therefore He began to be."

Reply to Objection 3: This word "Man," as it is taken for Christ, although it signifies the human nature, which began to be, nevertheless signifies the eternal suppositum which did not begin to be. Hence, since it signifies the suppositum when placed in the subject, and refers to the nature when placed in the predicate, therefore this is false: "The Man Christ began to be": but this is true: "Christ began to be Man."

Whether this is true: "Christ as Man is a creature"?

Objection 1: It would seem that this is false: "Christ as Man is a creature," or "began to be." For nothing in Christ is created except the human nature. But this is false: "Christ as Man is the human nature." Therefore this is also false; Christ as Man is a creature.

Objection 2: Further, the predicate is predicated of the term placed in reduplication, rather than of the subject of the proposition; as when I say: "A body as colored is visible," it follows that the colored is visible. But as stated ([4057]AA[8],9) we must not absolutely grant that "the Man Christ is a creature"; nor consequently that "Christ as Man is a creature."

Objection 3: Further, whatever is predicated of a man as man is predicated of him "per se" and simply, for "per se" is the same as "inasmuch as itself," as is said Metaph. v, text. 23. But this is false: "Christ as Man is per se and simply a creature." Hence this, too, is false; "Christ as Man is a creature."

On the contrary, Whatever is, is either Creator or creature. But this is false: "Christ as Man is Creator." Therefore this is true: "Christ as Man is a creature."

I answer that, When we say "Christ as Man" this word "man" may be added in the reduplication, either by reason of the suppositum or by reason of the nature. If it be added by reason of the suppositum, since the suppositum of the human nature in Christ is eternal and uncreated, this will be false: "Christ as Man is a creature." But if it be added by reason of the human nature, it is true, since by reason of the human nature or in the human nature, it belongs to Him to be a creature, as was said [4058](A[8]).

It must however be borne in mind that the term covered by the reduplication signifies the nature rather than the suppositum, since it is added as a predicate, which is taken formally, for it is the same to say "Christ as Man" and to say "Christ as He is a Man." Hence this is to be granted rather than denied: "Christ as Man is a creature." But if something further be added whereby [the term covered by

294

the reduplication] is attracted to the suppositum, this proposition is to be denied rather than granted, for instance were one to say: "Christ as 'this' Man is a creature."

Reply to Objection 1: Although Christ is not the human nature, He has human nature. Now the word "creature" is naturally predicated not only of abstract, but also of concrete things; since we say that "manhood is a creature" and that "man is a creature."

Reply to Objection 2: Man as placed in the subject refers to the suppositum---and as placed in the reduplication refers to the nature, as was stated above. And because the nature is created and the suppositum uncreated, therefore, although it is not granted that "this man is a creature," yet it is granted that "Christ as Man is a creature."

Reply to Objection 3: It belongs to every man who is a suppositum of human nature alone to have his being only in human nature. Hence of every such suppositum it follows that if it is a creature as man, it is a creature simply. But Christ is a suppositum not merely of human nature, but also of the Divine Nature, in which He has an uncreated being. Hence it does not follow that, if He is a creature as Man, He is a creature simply.

Day 262

Whether this is true: "Christ as Man is God"?

Objection 1: It would seem that Christ, as Man, is God. For Christ is God by the grace of union. But Christ, as Man, has the grace of union. Therefore Christ as Man is God.

Objection 2: Further, to forgive sins is proper to God, according to Is. 43:25: "I am He that blot out thy iniquities for My own sake." But Christ as Man forgives sin, according to Mat. 9:6: "But that you may know that the Son of Man hath power on earth to forgive sins," etc. Therefore Christ as Man is God.

Objection 3: Further, Christ is not Man in common, but is this particular Man. Now Christ, as this Man, is God, since by "this Man" we signify the eternal suppositum which is God naturally. Therefore Christ as Man is God.

On the contrary, Whatever belongs to Christ as Man belongs to every man. Now, if Christ as Man is God, it follows that every man is God---which is clearly false.

I answer that, This term "man" when placed in the reduplication may be taken in two ways. First as referring to the nature; and in this way it is not true that Christ as Man is God, because the human nature is distinct from the Divine by a difference of nature. Secondly it may be taken as referring to the suppositum; and in this way, since the suppositum of the human nature in Christ is the Person of the Son of God, to Whom it essentially belongs to be God, it is true that Christ, as Man, is God. Nevertheless because the term placed in the reduplication signifies the nature rather than the suppositum, as stated above [4059](A[10]), hence this is to be denied rather than granted: "Christ as Man is God."

Reply to Objection 1: It is not with regard to the same, that a thing moves towards, and that it is, something; for to move belongs to a thing because of its matter or subject---and to be in act belongs to it because of its form. So too it is not with regard to the same, that it belongs to Christ to be ordained to be God by the grace of union, and to be God. For the first belongs to Him in His human nature, and the second, in His Divine Nature. Hence this is true: "Christ as Man has the grace of union"; yet not this: "Christ as Man is God."

Reply to Objection 2: The Son of Man has on earth the power of forgiving sins, not by virtue of the human nature, but by virtue of the Divine Nature, in which Divine Nature resides the power of forgiving sins authoritatively; whereas in the human nature it resides instrumentally and ministerially. Hence Chrysostom expounding this passage says [*Implicitly. Hom. xxx in Matth; cf. St. Thomas, Catena Aurea on Mk. 2:10]: "He said pointedly 'on earth to forgive sins,' in order to show that by an indivisible union He united human nature to the power of the Godhead, since although He was made Man, yet He remained the Word of God."

Reply to Objection 3: When we say "this man," the demonstrative pronoun "this" attracts "man" to the suppositum; and hence "Christ as this Man, is God, is a truer proposition than Christ as Man is God."

Whether this is true: "Christ as Man is a hypostasis or person"?

Objection 1: It would seem that Christ as Man is a hypostasis or person. For what belongs to every man belongs to Christ as Man, since He is like other men according to Phil. 2:7: "Being made in the likeness of men." But every man is a person. Therefore Christ as Man is a person.

Objection 2: Further, Christ as Man is a substance of rational nature. But He is not a universal substance: therefore He is an individual substance. Now a person is nothing else than an individual substance of rational nature; as Boethius says (De Duab. Nat.). Therefore Christ as Man is a person.

Objection 3: Further, Christ as Man is a being of human nature, and a suppositum and a hypostasis of the same nature. But every hypostasis and suppositum and being of human nature is a person. Therefore Christ as Man is a person.

On the contrary, Christ as Man is not an eternal person. Therefore if Christ as Man is a person it would follow that in Christ there are two persons---one temporal and the other eternal, which is erroneous, as was said above ([4060]Q[2], A[6];[4061] Q[4], A[2]).

I answer that, As was said ([4062]AA[10],11), the term "Man" placed in the reduplication may refer either to the suppositum or to the nature. Hence when it is said: "Christ as Man is a person," if it is taken as referring to the suppositum, it is clear that Christ as Man is a person, since the suppositum of human nature is nothing else than the Person of the Son of God. But if it be taken as referring to the nature, it may be understood in two ways. First, we may so understand it as if it belonged to human nature to be in a person, and in this way it is true, for whatever subsists in human nature is a person. Secondly it may be taken that in Christ a proper personality, caused by the principles of the human nature, is due to the human nature; and in this way Christ as Man is not a person, since the human nature does not exist of itself apart from the Divine Nature, and yet the notion of person requires this.

Reply to Objection 1: It belongs to every man to be a person, inasmuch as everything subsisting in human nature is a person. Now this is proper to the Man Christ that the Person subsisting in His human nature is not caused by the principles of the human nature, but is eternal. Hence in one way He is a person, as Man; and in another way He is not, as stated above.

Reply to Objection 2: The "individual substance," which is included in the definition of a person, implies a complete substance subsisting of itself and separate from all else; otherwise, a man's hand might be called a person, since it is an individual substance; nevertheless, because it is an individual substance existing in something else, it cannot be called a person; nor, for the same reason, can the human nature in Christ, although it may be called something individual and singular.

Reply to Objection 3: As a person signifies something complete and self-subsisting in rational nature, so a hypostasis, suppositum, and being of nature in the genus of substance, signify something that subsists of itself. Hence, as human nature is not of itself a person apart from the Person of the Son of God, so likewise it is not of itself a hypostasis or suppositum or a being of nature. Hence in the sense in which we deny that "Christ as Man is a person" we must deny all the other propositions.

OF CHRIST'S UNITY OF BEING (TWO ARTICLES)

We must now consider what pertains to Christ's unity in common. For, in their proper place, we must consider what pertains to unity and plurality in detail: thus we concluded ([4063]Q[9]) that there is not only one knowledge in Christ, and it will be concluded hereafter ([4064]Q[35], A[2]) that there is not only one nativity in Christ.

Hence we must consider Christ's unity (1) of being; (2) of will; (3) of operation.

Under the first head there are two points of inquiry:

(1) Whether Christ is one or two?

(2) Whether there is only one being in Christ?

Whether Christ is one or two?

Objection 1: It would seem that Christ is not one, but two. For Augustine says (De Trin. i, 7): "Because the form of God took the form of a servant, both are God by reason of God Who assumed, yet both are Man by reason of the man assumed." Now "both" may only be said when there are two. Therefore Christ is two.

Objection 2: Further, where there is one thing and another there are two. Now Christ is one thing and another; for Augustine says (Enchiridion xxxv): "Being in the form of God . . . He took the form of a servant . . . being both in one; but He was one of these as Word, and the other as man." Therefore Christ is two.

Objection 3: Further, Christ is not only man; for, if He were a mere man, He would not be God. Therefore He is something else than man, and thus in Christ there is one thing and another. Therefore Christ is two.

Objection 4: Further, Christ is something that the Father is, and something that the Father is not. Therefore Christ is one thing and another. Therefore Christ is two.

Objection 5: Further, as in the mystery of the Trinity there are three Persons in one Nature, so in the mystery of the Incarnation there are two natures in one Person. But on account of the unity of the Nature, notwithstanding the distinction of Person, the Father and Son are one, according to Jn. 10:30: "I and the Father are one." Therefore, notwithstanding the unity of Person, Christ is two on account of the duality of nature.

Objection 6: Further, the Philosopher says (Phys. iii, text. 18) that "one" and "two" are predicated denominatively. Now Christ has a duality of nature. Therefore Christ is two.

Objection 7: Further, as accidental form makes a thing otherwise [alterum] so does substantial form make another thing [aliud] as Porphyry says (Praedic.). Now in Christ there are two substantial natures, the human and the Divine. Therefore Christ is one thing and another. Therefore Christ is two.

On the contrary, Boethius says (De Duab. Nat.): "Whatever is, inasmuch as it is, is one." But we confess that Christ is. Therefore Christ is one.

I answer that, Nature, considered in itself, as it is used in the abstract, cannot truly be predicated of the suppositum or person, except in God, in Whom "what it is" and "whereby it is" do not differ, as stated in the [4065]FP, Q[29], A[4], ad 1. But in Christ, since there are two natures, viz. the Divine and the human, one of them, viz. the Divine, may be predicated of Him both in the abstract and in the concrete, for we say that the Son of God, Who is signified by the word Christ, is the Divine Nature and is God. But the human nature cannot be predicated of Christ in the abstract, but only in the concrete, i.e. as it is signified by the suppositum. For we cannot truly say that "Christ is human nature," because human nature is not naturally predicated of its suppositum. But we say that Christ is a man, even as Christ is God. Now God signifies one having the Godhead, and man signifies one having manhood. Yet one having manhood is differently signified by the word "man" and by the word "Jesus" or "Peter." For this word "man" implies one having manhood indistinctly, even as the word "God" implies indistinctly one having the Godhead; but the word "Peter" or "Jesus" implies one having manhood distinctly, i.e. with its determinate individual properties, as "Son of God" implies one having the Godhead under a determinate personal property. Now the dual number is placed in Christ with regard to the natures. Hence, if both the natures were predicated in the abstract of Christ, it would follow that Christ is two. But because the two natures are not predicated of Christ, except as they are signified in the suppositum, it must be by reason of the suppositum that "one" or "two" be predicated of Christ.

Now some placed two supposita in Christ, and one Person, which, in their opinion, would seem to be the suppositum completed with its final completion. Hence, since they placed two supposita in Christ, they said that God is two, in the neuter. But because they asserted one Person, they said that Christ is one, in the masculine, for the neuter gender signifies something unformed and imperfect, whereas the masculine signifies something formed and perfect. on the other hand, the Nestorians, who asserted two Persons in Christ, said that Christ is two not only in the neuter, but also in the masculine. But since we maintain one person and one suppositum in

Christ, as is clear from[4066] Q[2], AA[2],3, it follows that we say that Christ is one not merely in the masculine, but also in the neuter.

Reply to Objection 1: This saying of Augustine is not to be taken as if "both" referred to the predicate, so as to mean that Christ is both; but it refers to the subject. And thus "both" does not stand for two supposita, but for two words signifying two natures in the concrete. For I can say that "both, viz. God and Man, are God" on account of God Who assumes; and "both, viz. God and Man," are Man on account of the man assumed.

Reply to Objection 2: When it is said that "Christ is one thing and another," this saying is to be explained in this sense---"having this nature and another." And it is in this way that Augustine explains it (Contra Felic. xi), where, after saying, "In the mediator of God and man, the Son of God is one thing, and the Son of Man another," he adds: "I say another thing by reason of the difference of substance, and not another thing by reason of the unity of person." Hence Gregory Nazianzen says (Ep. ad Chelid. ci): "If we must speak briefly, that of which the Saviour is, is one thing and another; thus the invisible is not the same as the visible; and what is without time is not the same as what is in time. Yet they are not one and another: far from it; for both these are one."

Reply to Objection 3: This is false, "Christ is only man"; because it does not exclude another suppositum, but another nature, since terms placed in the predicate are taken formally. But if anything is added whereby it is drawn to the suppositum, it would be a true proposition---for instance, "Christ is only that which is man." Nevertheless, it would not follow that He is "any other thing than man," because "another thing," inasmuch as it refers to a diversity of substance, properly refers to the suppositum. even as all relative things bearing a personal relation. But it does follow: "Therefore He has another nature."

Reply to Objection 4: When it is said, "Christ is something that the Father is"; "something" signifies the Divine Nature, which is predicated even in the abstract of the Father and Son. But when it is said: "Christ is something that is not the Father"; "something" signifies, not the human nature as it is in the abstract, but as it is in the concrete; not, indeed, in a distinct, but in an indistinct suppositum, i.e. inasmuch as it underlies the nature and not the individuating properties. Hence it does not follow that Christ is one thing and another, or that He is two, since the suppositum of the human nature in Christ, which is the Person of the Son of God, does not reckon numerically with the Divine Nature, which is predicated of the Father and Son.

Reply to Objection 5: In the mystery of the Divine Trinity the Divine Nature is predicated, even in the abstract of the three Persons; hence it may be said simply that the three Persons are one. But in the mystery of the Incarnation both natures are not predicated in the abstract of Christ; hence it cannot be said simply that Christ is two.

Reply to Objection 6: Two signifies what has duality, not in another, but in the same thing of which "two" is predicated. Now what is predicated is said of the suppositum, which is implied by the word "Christ." Hence, although Christ has duality of nature, yet, because He has not duality of suppositum, it cannot be said that Christ is two.

Reply to Objection 7: Otherwise implies diversity of accident. Hence diversity of accident suffices for anything to be called "otherwise" simply. But "another thing" implies diversity of substance. Now not merely the nature, but also the suppositum is said to be a substance, as is said Metaph. v, text. 15. Hence diversity of nature does not suffice for anything to be called "another thing" simply, unless there is diversity of suppositum. But diversity of nature makes "another thing" relatively, i.e. in nature, if there is no diversity of suppositum.

Whether there is only one being in Christ?

Objection 1: It would seem that in Christ there is not merely one being, but two. For Damascene says (De Fide Orth. iii, 13) that whatever follows the nature is doubled in Christ. But being follows the nature, for being is from the form. Hence in Christ there are two beings.

Objection 2: Further, the being of the Son of God is the Divine Nature itself, and is eternal: whereas the being of the Man Christ is not the Divine Nature, but is a temporal being. Therefore there is not only one being in Christ.

Objection 3: Further, in the Trinity, although there are three Persons, yet on account of the unity of nature there is only one being. But in Christ there are two natures, though there is one Person. Therefore in Christ there is not only one being.

Objection 4: Further, in Christ the soul gives some being to the body, since it is its form. But it does not give the Divine being, since this is uncreated. Therefore in Christ there is another being besides the Divine being; and thus in Christ there is not only one being.

On the contrary, Everything is said to be a being, inasmuch as it is one, for one and being are convertible. Therefore, if there were two beings in Christ, and not one only, Christ would be two, and not one.

I answer that, Because in Christ there are two natures and one hypostasis, it follows that things belonging to the nature in Christ must be two; and that those belonging to the hypostasis in Christ must be only one. Now being pertains both to the nature and to the hypostasis; to the hypostasis as to that which has being---and to the nature as to that whereby it has being. For nature is taken after the manner of a form, which is said to be a being because something is by it; as by whiteness a thing is white, and by manhood a thing is man. Now it must be borne in mind that if there is a form or nature which does not pertain to the personal being of the subsisting hypostasis, this being is not said to belong to the person simply, but relatively; as to be white is the being of Socrates, not as he is Socrates, but inasmuch as he is white. And there is no reason why this being should not be multiplied in one hypostasis or person; for the being whereby Socrates is white is distinct from the being whereby he is a musician. But the being which belongs to the very hypostasis or person in itself cannot possibly be multiplied in one hypostasis or person, since it is impossible that there should not be one being for one thing.

If, therefore, the human nature accrued to the Son of God, not hypostatically or personally, but accidentally, as some maintained, it would be necessary to assert two beings in Christ---one, inasmuch as He is God---the other, inasmuch as He is Man; even as in Socrates we place one being inasmuch as he is white, and another inasmuch as he is a man, since "being white" does not pertain to the personal being of Socrates. But being possessed of a head, being corporeal, being animated---all these pertain to the one person of

Socrates, and hence there arises from these only the one being of Socrates. And if it so happened that after the person of Socrates was constituted there accrued to him hands or feet or eyes, as happened to him who was born blind, no new being would be thereby added to Socrates, but only a relation to these, i.e. inasmuch as he would be said to be, not only with reference to what he had previously, but also with reference to what accrued to him afterwards. And thus, since the human nature is united to the Son of God, hypostatically or personally as was said above ([4067]Q[2], AA[5],6), and not accidentally, it follows that by the human nature there accrued to Him no new personal being, but only a new relation of the pre-existing personal being to the human nature, in such a way that the Person is said to subsist not merely in the Divine, but also in the human nature.

Reply to Objection 1: Being is consequent upon nature, not as upon that which has being, but as upon that whereby a thing is: whereas it is consequent upon person or hypostasis, as upon that which has being. Hence it has unity from the unity of hypostasis, rather than duality from the duality of the nature.

Reply to Objection 2: The eternal being of the Son of God, which is the Divine Nature, becomes the being of man, inasmuch as the human nature is assumed by the Son of God to unity of Person.

Reply to Objection 3: As was said in the [4068]FP, Q[50], A[2], ad 3; [4069]FP, Q[75], A[5], ad 4, since the Divine Person is the same as the Nature, there is no distinction in the Divine Persons between the being of the Person and the being of the Nature, and, consequently, the three Persons have only one being. But they would have a triple being if the being of the Person were distinct in them from the being of the Nature.

Reply to Objection 4: In Christ the soul gives being to the body, inasmuch as it makes it actually animated, which is to give it the complement of its nature and species. But if we consider the body perfected by the soul, without the hypostasis having both---this whole, composed of soul and body, as signified by the word "humanity," does not signify "what is," but "whereby it is." Hence being belongs to the subsisting person, inasmuch as it has a relation to such a nature, and of this relation the soul is the cause, inasmuch as it perfects human nature by informing the body.

OF CHRIST'S UNITY OF WILL (SIX ARTICLES)
We must now consider unity as regards the will; and under this head there are six points of inquiry:
(1) Whether the Divine will and the human are distinct in Christ?
(2) Whether in Christ's human nature the will of sensuality is distinct from the will of reason?
(3) Whether as regards the reason there were several wills in Christ?
(4) Whether there was free-will in Christ?
(5) Whether Christ's human will was always conformed to the Divine will in the thing willed?
(6) Whether there was any contrariety of wills in Christ?

Whether there are two wills in Christ?
Objection 1: It would seem that in Christ there are not two wills, one Divine, the other human. For the will is the first mover and first commander in whoever wills. But in Christ the first mover and commander was the Divine will, since in Christ everything human was moved by the Divine will. Hence it seems that in Christ there was only one will, viz. the Divine.

Objection 2: Further, an instrument is not moved by its own will but by the will of its mover. Now the human nature of Christ was the instrument of His Godhead. Hence the human nature of Christ was not moved by its own will, but by the Divine will.

Objection 3: Further, that alone is multiplied in Christ which belongs to the nature. But the will does not seem to pertain to nature: for natural things are of necessity; whereas what is voluntary is not of necessity. Therefore there is but one will in Christ.

Objection 4: Further, Damascene says (De Fide Orth. iii, 14) that "to will in this or that way belongs not to our nature but to our intellect," i.e. our personal intellect. But every will is this or that will, since there is nothing in a genus which is not at the same time in some one of its species. Therefore all will belongs to the person. But in Christ there was and is but one person. Therefore in Christ there is only one will.

On the contrary, our Lord says (Lk. 22:42): "Father, if Thou wilt, remove this chalice from Me. But yet not My will but Thine be done." And Ambrose, quoting this to the Emperor Gratian (De Fide ii, 7) says: "As He assumed my will, He assumed my sorrow;" and on Lk. 22:42 he says: "His will, He refers to the Man---the Father's, to the Godhead. For the will of man is temporal, and the will of the Godhead eternal."

I answer that, Some placed only one will in Christ; but they seem to have had different motives for holding this. For Apollinaris did not hold an intellectual soul in Christ, but maintained that the Word was in place of the soul, or even in place of the intellect. Hence since "the will is in the reason," as the Philosopher says (De Anima iii, 9), it followed that in Christ there was no human will; and thus there was only one will in Him. So, too, Eutyches and all who held one composite nature in Christ were forced to place one will in Him. Nestorius, too, who maintained that the union of God and man was one of affection and will, held only one will in Christ. But later on, Macarius, Patriarch of Antioch, Cyrus of Alexandria, and Sergius of Constantinople and some of their followers, held that there is one will in Christ, although they held that in Christ there are two natures united in a hypostasis; because they believed that Christ's human nature never moved with its own motion, but only inasmuch as it was moved by the Godhead, as is plain from the synodical letter of Pope Agatho [*Third Council of Constantinople, Act. 4].

And hence in the sixth Council held at Constantinople [*Act. 18] it was decreed that it must be said that there are two wills in Christ, in the following passage: "In accordance with what the Prophets of old taught us concerning Christ, and as He taught us Himself, and the Symbol of the Holy Fathers has handed down to us, we confess two natural wills in Him and two natural operations." And this much it was necessary to say. For it is manifest that the Son of God assumed a perfect human nature, as was shown above (Q[5]; Q[9], A[1]). Now the will pertains to the perfection of human nature, being one of its natural powers, even as the intellect, as was stated in the FP, QQ[79],80. Hence we must say that the Son of God assumed a human will, together with human nature. Now by the assumption of human nature the Son of God suffered no diminution of what pertains to His Divine Nature, to which it belongs to have a will, as was said in the [4070]FP, Q[19], A[1]. Hence it must be said that there are two wills in Christ, i.e. one human, the other Divine.

Reply to Objection 1: Whatever was in the human nature of Christ was moved at the bidding of the Divine will; yet it does not follow that in Christ there was no movement of the will proper to human nature, for the good wills of other saints are moved by God's will, "Who worketh" in them "both to will and to accomplish," as is written Phil. 2:13. For although the will cannot be inwardly moved by any creature, yet it can be moved inwardly by God, as was said in the [4071]FP, Q[105], A[4]. And thus, too, Christ by His human will followed the Divine will according to Ps. 39:9; "That I should do Thy will, O my God, I have desired it." Hence Augustine says (Contra Maxim. ii, 20): "Where the Son says to the Father, 'Not what I will, but what Thou willest,' what do you gain by adding your own words and saying 'He shows that His will was truly subject to His Father,' as if we denied that man's will ought to be subject to God's will?"

Reply to Objection 2: It is proper to an instrument to be moved by the principal agent, yet diversely, according to the property of its nature. For an inanimate instrument, as an axe or a saw, is moved by the craftsman with only a corporeal movement; but an instrument animated by a sensitive soul is moved by the sensitive appetite, as a horse by its rider; and an instrument animated with a rational soul is moved by its will, as by the command of his lord the servant is moved to act, the servant being like an animate instrument, as the Philosopher says (Polit. i, 2,4; Ethic. viii, 11). And hence it was in this manner that the human nature of Christ was the instrument of the Godhead, and was moved by its own will.

Reply to Objection 3: The power of the will is natural, and necessarily follows upon the nature; but the movement or act of this power---which is also called will---is sometimes natural and necessary, e.g. with respect to beatitude; and sometimes springs from free-will and is neither necessary nor natural, as is plain from what has been stated in the [4072]FS, Q[10], AA[1],[2] [*Cf. [4073]FP, Q[82], A[2]]. And yet even reason itself, which is the principle of this movement, is natural. Hence besides the Divine will it is necessary to place in Christ a human will, not merely as a natural power, or a natural movement, but even as a rational movement.

Reply to Objection 4: When we say "to will in a certain way," we signify a determinate mode of willing. Now a determinate mode regards the thing of which it is the mode. Hence since the will pertains to the nature, "to will in a certain way" belongs to the nature, not indeed considered absolutely, but as it is in the hypostasis. Hence the human will of Christ had a determinate mode from the fact of being in a Divine hypostasis, i.e. it was always moved in accordance with the bidding of the Divine will.

Whether in Christ there was a will of sensuality besides the will of reason?

Objection 1: It would seem that in Christ there was no will of sensuality besides the will of reason. For the Philosopher says (De Anima iii, text. 42) that "the will is in the reason, and in the sensitive appetite are the irascible and concupiscible parts." Now sensuality signifies the sensitive appetite. Hence in Christ there was no will of sensuality.

Objection 2: Further, according to Augustine (De Trin. xii, 12,13) the sensuality is signified by the serpent. But there was nothing serpent-like in Christ; for He had the likeness of a venomous animal without the venom, as Augustine says (De Pecc. Merit. et Remiss. i, 32). Hence in Christ there was no will of sensuality.

Objection 3: Further, will is consequent upon nature, as was said [4074](A[1]). But in Christ there was only one nature besides the Divine. Hence in Christ there was only one human will.

On the contrary, Ambrose says (De Fide ii, 7): "Mine is the will which He calls His own; because as Man He assumed my sorrow." From this we are given to understand that sorrow pertains to the human will of Christ. Now sorrow pertains to the sensuality, as was said in the [4075]FS, Q[23], A[1]; [4076]FS, Q[25], A[1]. Therefore, seemingly, in Christ there is a will of sensuality besides the will of reason.

I answer that, As was said ([4077]Q[9], A[1]), the Son of God assumed human nature together with everything pertaining to the perfection of human nature. Now in human nature is included animal nature, as the genus in its species. Hence the Son of God must have assumed together with the human nature whatever belongs to animal nature; one of which things is the sensitive appetite, which is called the sensuality. Consequently it must be allowed that in Christ there was a sensual appetite, or sensuality. But it must be borne in mind that sensuality or the sensual appetite, inasmuch as it naturally obeys reason, is said to be "rational by participation," as is clear from the Philosopher (Ethic. i, 13). And because "the will is in the reason," as stated above, it may equally be said that the sensuality is "a will by participation."

Reply to Objection 1: This argument is based on the will, essentially so called, which is only in the intellectual part; but the will by participation can be in the sensitive part, inasmuch as it obeys reason.

Reply to Objection 2: The sensuality is signified by the serpent---not as regards the nature of the sensuality, which Christ assumed, but as regards the corruption of the "fomes," which was not in Christ.

Reply to Objection 3: "Where there is one thing on account of another, there seems to be only one" (Aristotle, Topic. iii); thus a surface which is visible by color is one visible thing with the color. So, too, because the sensuality is called the will, only because it partakes of the rational will, there is said to be but one human will in Christ, even as there is but one human nature.

Whether in Christ there were two wills as regards the reason?

Objection 1: It would seem that in Christ there were two wills as regards the reason. For Damascene says (De Fide Orth. ii, 22) that there is a double will in man, viz. the natural will which is called {thelesis}, and the rational will which is called {boulesis}. Now Christ in His human nature had whatever belongs to the perfection of human nature. Hence both the foregoing wills were in Christ.

Objection 2: Further, the appetitive power is diversified in man by the difference of the apprehensive power, and hence according to the difference of sense and intellect is the difference of sensitive and intellective appetite in man. But in the same way as regards man's apprehension, we hold the difference of reason and intellect; both of which were in Christ. Therefore there was a double will in Him, one intellectual and the other rational.

Objection 3: Further, some [*Hugh of St. Victor, De Quat. Volunt. Christ.] ascribe to Christ "a will of piety," which can only be on the part of reason. Therefore in Christ on the part of reason there are several wills.

On the contrary, In every order there is one first mover. But the will is the first mover in the genus of human acts. Therefore in one man there is only one will, properly speaking, which is the will of reason. But Christ is one man. Therefore in Christ there is only one human will.

I answer that, As stated above (A[1], ad 3), the will is sometimes taken for the power, and sometimes for the act. Hence if the will is taken for the act, it is necessary to place two wills, i.e. two species of acts of the will in Christ on the part of the reason. For the will, as was said in the [4078]FS, Q[8], AA[2],3, regards both the end and the means; and is affected differently towards both. For towards the end it is borne simply and absolutely, as towards what is good in itself; but towards the means it is borne under a certain relation, as the goodness of the means depends on something else. Hence the act of the will, inasmuch as it is drawn to anything desired of itself, as health, which act is called by Damascene {thelesis}---i.e. simple will, and by the masters "will as nature," is different from the act of the will as it is drawn to anything that is desired only in order to something else, as to take medicine; and this act of the will Damascene calls {boulesis}---i.e. counseling will, and the masters, "will as reason." But this diversity of acts does not diversify the power, since both acts regard the one common ratio of the object, which is goodness. Hence we must say that if we are speaking of the power of the will, in Christ there is but one human will, essentially so called and not by participation; but if we are speaking of the will as an act, we thus distinguish in Christ a will as nature, which is called {thelesis}, and a will as reason, which is called {boulesis}.

Reply to Objection 1: These two wills do not diversify the power but only the act, as we have said.

Reply to Objection 2: The intellect and the reason are not distinct powers, as was said in the [4079]FP, Q[79], A[8].

Reply to Objection 3: The "will of piety" would not seem to be distinct from the will considered as nature, inasmuch as it shrinks from another's evil, absolutely considered.

Whether there was free-will in Christ?

Objection 1: It would seem that in Christ there was no free-will. For Damascene says (De Fide Orth. iii, 14) that {gnome}, i.e. opinion, thinking or cogitation, and {proairesis}, i.e. choice, "cannot possibly be attributed to our Lord, if we wish to speak with propriety." But in the things of faith especially we must speak with propriety. Therefore there was no choice in Christ and consequently no free-will, of which choice is the act.

Objection 2: Further, the Philosopher says (Ethic. iii, 2) that choice is "a desire of something after taking counsel." Now counsel does not appear to be in Christ, because we do not take counsel concerning such things as we are certain of. But Christ was certain of everything. Hence there was no counsel and consequently no free-will in Christ.

Objection 3: Further, free-will is indifferent. But Christ's will was determined to good, since He could not sin; as stated above ([4080]Q[15], AA[1],2). Hence there was no free-will in Christ.

On the contrary, It is written (Is. 7:15): "He shall eat butter and honey, that He may know to refuse the evil and to choose the good," which is an act of the free-will. Therefore there was free-will in Christ.

I answer that, As was said above [4081](A[3]), there was a twofold act of the will in Christ; one whereby He was drawn to anything willed in itself, which implies the nature of an end; the other whereby His will was drawn to anything willed on account of its being ordained to another---which pertains to the nature of means. Now, as the Philosopher says (Ethic. iii, 2) choice differs from will in this, that will of itself regards the end, while choice regards the means. And thus simple will is the same as the "will as nature"; but choice is the same as the "will as reason," and is the proper act of free-will, as was said in the [4082]FP, Q[83], A[3]. Hence, since "will as reason" is placed in Christ, we must also place choice, and consequently free-will, whose act is choice, as was said in the [4083]FP, Q[83], A[3]; [4084]FS, Q[13], A[1].

Reply to Objection 1: Damascene excludes choice from Christ, in so far as he considers that doubt is implied in the word choice. Nevertheless doubt is not necessary to choice, since it belongs even to God Himself to choose, according to Eph. 1:4: "He chose us in Him before the foundation of the world," although in God there is no doubt. Yet doubt is accidental to choice when it is in an ignorant nature. We may also say the same of whatever else is mentioned in the passage quoted.

Reply to Objection 2: Choice presupposes counsel; yet it follows counsel only as determined by judgment. For what we judge to be done, we choose, after the inquiry of counsel, as is stated (Ethic. iii, 2,3). Hence if anything is judged necessary to be done, without any preceding doubt or inquiry, this suffices for choice. Therefore it is plain that doubt or inquiry belong to choice not essentially, but only when it is in an ignorant nature.

Reply to Objection 3: The will of Christ, though determined to good, is not determined to this or that good. Hence it pertains to Christ, even as to the blessed, to choose with a free-will confirmed in good.

Day 263

Whether the human will of Christ was altogether conformed to the Divine will in the thing willed?

Objection 1: It would seem that the human will in Christ did not will anything except what God willed. For it is written (Ps. 39:9) in the person of Christ: "That I should do Thy will: O my God, I have desired it." Now he who desires to do another's will, wills what the other wills. Hence it seems that Christ's human will willed nothing but what was willed by His Divine will.

Objection 2: Further, Christ's soul had most perfect charity, which, indeed, surpasses the comprehension of all our knowledge, according to Eph. 3:19, "the charity of Christ, which surpasseth all knowledge." Now charity makes men will what God wills; hence the Philosopher says (Ethic. ix, 4) that one mark of friendship is "to will and choose the same." Therefore the human will in Christ willed nothing else than was willed by His Divine will.

Objection 3: Further, Christ was a true comprehensor. But the Saints who are comprehensors in heaven will only what God wills, otherwise they would not be happy, because they would not obtain whatever they will, for "blessed is he who has what he wills, and wills nothing amiss," as Augustine says (De Trin. xiii, 5). Hence in His human will Christ wills nothing else than does the Divine will.

On the contrary, Augustine says (Contra Maxim. ii, 20): "When Christ says 'Not what I will, but what Thou wilt' He shows Himself to have willed something else than did His Father; and this could only have been by His human heart, since He did not transfigure our weakness into His Divine but into His human will."

I answer that, As was said ([4085]AA[2],3), in Christ according to His human nature there is a twofold will, viz. the will of sensuality, which is called will by participation, and the rational will, whether considered after the manner of nature, or after the manner of reason. Now it was said above (Q[13], A[3], ad 1; Q[14], A[1], ad 2) that by a certain dispensation the Son of God before His Passion "allowed His flesh to do and suffer what belonged to it." And in like manner He allowed all the powers of His soul to do what belonged to them. Now it is clear that the will of sensuality naturally shrinks from sensible pains and bodily hurt. In like manner, the will as nature turns from what is against nature and what is evil in itself, as death and the like; yet the will as reason may at time choose these things in relation to an end, as in a mere man the sensuality and the will absolutely considered shrink from burning, which, nevertheless, the will as reason may choose for the sake of health. Now it was the will of God that Christ should undergo pain, suffering, and death, not that these of themselves were willed by God, but for the sake of man's salvation. Hence it is plain that in His will of sensuality and in His rational will considered as nature, Christ could will what God did not; but in His will as reason He always willed the same as God, which appears from what He says (Mat. 26:39): "Not as I will, but as Thou wilt." For He willed in His reason that the Divine will should be fulfilled although He said that He willed something else by another will.

Reply to Objection 1: By His rational will Christ willed the Divine will to be fulfilled; but not by His will of sensuality, the movement of which does not extend to the will of God---nor by His will considered as nature which regards things absolutely considered and not in relation to the Divine will.

Reply to Objection 2: The conformity of the human will to the Divine regards the will of reason: according to which the wills even of friends agree, inasmuch as reason considers something willed in its relation to the will of a friend.

Reply to Objection 3: Christ was at once comprehensor and wayfarer, inasmuch as He was enjoying God in His mind and had a passible body. Hence things repugnant to His natural will and to His sensitive appetite could happen to Him in His passible flesh.

Whether there was contrariety of wills in Christ?

Objection 1: It would seem that there was contrariety of wills in Christ. For contrariety of wills regards contrariety of objects, as contrariety of movements springs from contrariety of termini, as is plain from the Philosopher (Phys. v, text. 49, seq.). Now Christ in His different wills wished contrary things. For in His Divine will He wished for death, from which He shrank in His human will, hence Athanasius says [*De Incarnat. et Cont. Arianos, written against Apollinarius]: "When Christ says 'Father, if it be possible, let this chalice pass from Me; yet not My will, but Thine be done,' and again, 'The spirit indeed is willing, but the flesh weak,' He denotes two wills---the human, which through the weakness of the flesh shrank from the passion---and His Divine will eager for the passion." Hence there was contrariety of wills in Christ.

Objection 2: Further, it is written (Gal. 5:17) that "the flesh lusteth against the spirit, and the spirit against the flesh." Now when the spirit desires one thing, and the flesh another, there is contrariety of wills. But this was in Christ; for by the will of charity which the Holy Spirit was causing in His mind, He willed the passion, according to Is. 53:7: "He was offered because it was His own will," yet in His flesh He shrank from the passion. Therefore there was contrariety of wills in Him.

Objection 3: Further, it is written (Lk. 22:43) that "being in an agony, He prayed the longer." Now agony seems to imply a certain struggle [*Greek, {agonia}] in a soul drawn to contrary things. Hence it seems that there was contrariety of will in Christ.

On the contrary, In the decisions of the Sixth Council [*Third Council of Constantinople, Act. 18] it is said: "We confess two natural wills, not in opposition, as evil-minded heretics assert, but following His human will, and neither withstanding nor striving against, but rather being subject to, His Divine and omnipotent will."

I answer that, Contrariety can exist only where there is opposition in the same and as regards the same. For if the diversity exists as regards diverse things, and in diverse subjects, this would not suffice for the nature of contrariety, nor even for the nature of contradiction, e.g. if a man were well formed or healthy as regards his hand, but not as regards his foot. Hence for there to be contrariety of wills in anyone it is necessary, first, that the diversity of wills should regard the same. For if the will of one regards the doing of something with reference to some universal reason, and the will of another regards the not doing the same with reference to some particular reason, there is not complete contrariety of will, e.g. when a judge wishes a brigand to be hanged for the good of the commonwealth, and one of the latter's kindred wishes him not to be hanged on account of a private love, there is no contrariety of wills; unless, indeed, the desire of the private good went so far as to wish to hinder the public good for the private good---in that case the opposition of wills would regard the same.

Secondly, for contrariety of wills it is necessary that it should be in the same will. For if a man wishes one thing with his rational appetite, and wishes another thing with his sensitive appetite, there is no contrariety, unless the sensitive appetite so far prevailed as to change or at least keep back the rational appetite; for in this case something of the contrary movement of the sensitive appetite would reach the rational will.

And hence it must be said that although the natural and the sensitive will in Christ wished what the Divine will did not wish, yet there was no contrariety of wills in Him. First, because neither the natural will nor the will of sensuality rejected the reason for which the Divine will and the will of the human reason in Christ wished the passion. For the absolute will of Christ wished the salvation of the human race, although it did not pertain to it to will this for the sake of something further; but the movement of sensuality could nowise extend so far. Secondly, because neither the Divine will nor the will of reason in Christ was impeded or retarded by the natural will or the appetite of sensuality. So, too, on the other hand, neither the Divine will nor the will of reason in Christ shrank from or retarded the movement of the natural human will and the movement of the sensuality in Christ. For it pleased Christ, in His Divine will, and in His will of reason, that His natural will and will of sensuality should be moved according to the order of their nature. Hence it is clear that in Christ there was no opposition or contrariety of wills.

Reply to Objection 1: The fact of any will in Christ willing something else than did the Divine will, proceeded from the Divine will, by whose permission the human nature in Christ was moved by its proper movements, as Damascene says (De Fide Orth. ii, 15,18,19).

Reply to Objection 2: In us the desires of the spirit are impeded or retarded by the desires of the flesh: this did not occur in Christ. Hence in Christ there was no contrariety of flesh and spirit, as in us.

Reply to Objection 3: The agony in Christ was not in the rational soul, in as far as it implies a struggle in the will arising from a diversity of motives, as when anyone, on his reason considering one, wishes one thing, and on its considering another, wishes the contrary. For this springs from the weakness of the reason, which is unable to judge which is the best simply. Now this did not occur in Christ, since by His reason He judged it best that the Divine will regarding the salvation of the human race should be fulfilled by His passion. Nevertheless, there was an agony in Christ as regards the sensitive part, inasmuch as it implied a dread of coming trial, as Damascene says (De Fide Orth. ii, 15; iii, 18,23).

OF THE UNITY OF CHRIST'S OPERATION (FOUR ARTICLES)

We must now consider the unity of Christ's operation; and under this head there are four points of inquiry:
(1) Whether in Christ there was one or several operations of the Godhead and Manhood?
(2) Whether in Christ there were several operations of the human nature?
(3) Whether Christ by His human operation merited anything for Himself?
(4) Whether He merited anything for us by it?

Whether in Christ there is only one operation of the Godhead and Manhood?

Objection 1: It would seem that in Christ there is but one operation of the Godhead and the Manhood. For Dionysius says (Div. Nom. ii): "The most loving operation of God is made manifest to us by the supersubstantial Word having taken flesh integrally and truly, and having operated and suffered whatsoever befits His human and Divine operation." But he here mentions only one human and Divine operation, which is written in Greek {theandrike}, i.e. God-manlike. Hence it seems that there is but one composite operation in Christ.

Objection 2: Further, there is but one operation of the principal and instrumental agent. Now the human nature in Christ was the instrument of the Divine, as was said above ([4086]Q[7], A[1], ad 3;[4087] Q[8], A[1], ad 1;[4088] Q[18], A[1], ad 2). Hence the operations of the Divine and human natures in Christ are the same.

Objection 3: Further, since in Christ there are two natures in one hypostasis or person, whatever pertains to the hypostasis or person is one and the same. But operation pertains to the hypostasis or person, for it is only a subsisting suppositum that operates; hence, according to the Philosopher (Metaph. i, 1), acts belong to singulars. Hence in Christ there is only one operation of the Godhead and the Manhood.

Objection 4: Further, as being belongs to a subsisting hypostasis, so also does operation. But on account of the unity of hypostasis there is only one operation of the Godhead and the ([4089]Q[17], A[2]). Hence, on account of the same unity, there is one operation in Christ.

Objection 5: Further, as being belongs to a sub-operated there is one operation. But the same thing was operated by the Godhead and the Manhood, as the healing of the lepers or the raising of the dead. Hence it seems that in Christ there is but one operation of the Godhead and the Manhood.

On the contrary, Ambrose says (De Fide ii, 8): "How can the same operation spring from different powers? Cannot the lesser operate as the greater? And can there be one operation where there are different substances?"

I answer that, As was said above ([4090]Q[18], A[1]), the aforesaid heretics who placed one will in Christ placed one operation in Christ. Now in order better to understand their erroneous opinion, we must bear in mind that wherever there are several mutually ordained agents, the inferior is moved by the superior, as in man the body is moved by the soul and the lower powers by the reason. And thus the actions and movements of the inferior principle are things operated rather than operations. Now what pertains to the highest principle is properly the operation; thus we say of man that to walk, which belongs to the feet, and to touch, which belongs to the hand, are things operated by the man---one of which is operated by the soul through the feet, the other through the hands. And because it is the same soul that operates in both cases, there is only one indifferent operation, on the part of the thing operating, which is the first moving principle; but difference is found on the part of what is operated. Now, as in a mere man the body is moved by the soul, and the sensitive by the rational appetite, so in the Lord Jesus Christ the human nature is moved and ruled by the Divine. Hence they said that there is one indifferent operation on the part of the Godhead operating, but divers things operated, inasmuch as the Godhead of Christ did one thing by Itself, as to uphold all things by the word of His power---and another thing by His human nature, as to walk in body. Hence the Sixth Council [*Third Council of Constantinople, Act. 10] quotes the words of Severus the heretic, who said: "What things were done and wrought by the one Christ, differ greatly; for some are becoming to God, and some are human, as to walk bodily on the earth is indeed human, but to give hale steps to sickly limbs, wholly unable to walk on the ground, is becoming to God. Yet one, i.e. the Incarnate Word, wrought one and the other---neither was this from one nature, and that from another; nor can we justly affirm that because there are distinct things operated there are therefore two operating natures and forms."

But herein they were deceived, for what is moved by another has a twofold action---one which it has from its own form---the other, which it has inasmuch as it is moved by another; thus the operation of an axe of itself is to cleave; but inasmuch as it is moved by the craftsman, its operation is to make benches. Hence the operation which belongs to a thing by its form is proper to it, nor does it belong to the mover, except in so far as he makes use of this kind of thing for his work: thus to heat is the proper operation of fire, but not of a smith, except in so far as he makes use of fire for heating iron. But the operation which belongs to the thing, as moved by another, is not distinct from the operation of the mover; thus to make a bench is not the work of the axe independently of the workman. Hence, wheresoever the mover and the moved have different forms or operative faculties, there must the operation of the mover and the proper operation of the moved be distinct; although the moved shares in the operation of the mover, and the mover makes use of the operation of the moved, and, consequently, each acts in communion with the other.

Therefore in Christ the human nature has its proper form and power whereby it acts; and so has the Divine. Hence the human nature has its proper operation distinct from the Divine, and conversely. Nevertheless, the Divine Nature makes use of the operation of the human nature, as of the operation of its instrument; and in the same way the human nature shares in the operation of the Divine Nature, as an instrument shares in the operation of the principal agent. And this is what Pope Leo says (Ep. ad Flavian. xxviii): "Both forms" (i.e. both the Divine and the human nature in Christ) "do what is proper to each in union with the other, i.e. the Word operates what belongs to the Word, and the flesh carries out what belongs to flesh."

But if there were only one operation of the Godhead and manhood in Christ, it would be necessary to say either that the human nature had not its proper form and power (for this could not possibly be said of the Divine), whence it would follow that in Christ there was only the Divine operation; or it would be necessary to say that from the Divine and human power there was made up one power. Now both of these are impossible. For by the first the human nature in Christ is supposed to be imperfect; and by the second a confusion of the natures is supposed. Hence it is with reason that the Sixth Council (Act. 18) condemned this opinion, and decreed as follows: "We confess two natural, indivisible, unconvertible, unconfused, and inseparable operations in the same Lord Jesus Christ our true God"; i.e. the Divine operation and the human operation.

Reply to Objection 1: Dionysius places in Christ a theandric, i.e. a God-manlike or Divino-human, operation not by any confusion of the operations or powers of both natures, but inasmuch as His Divine operation employs the human, and His human operation shares in the power of the Divine. Hence, as he says in a certain epistle (Ad Caium iv), "what is of man He works beyond man; and this is shown by the Virgin conceiving supernaturally and by the unstable waters bearing up the weight of bodily feet." Now it is clear that to be begotten belongs to human nature, and likewise to walk; yet both were in Christ supernaturally. So, too, He wrought Divine things humanly, as when He healed the leper with a touch. Hence in the same epistle he adds: "He performed Divine works not as God does, and human works not as man does, but, God having been made man, by a new operation of God and man."

Now, that he understood two operations in Christ, one of the Divine and the other of the human nature, is clear from what he says, Div. Nom. ii: "Whatever pertains to His human operation the Father and the Holy Ghost no-wise share in, except, as one might say, by their most gracious and merciful will," i.e. inasmuch as the Father and the Holy Ghost in their mercy wished Christ to do and to suffer human things. And he adds: "He is truly the unchangeable God, and God's Word by the sublime and unspeakable operation of God, which, being made man for us, He wrought." Hence it is clear that the human operation, in which the Father and the Holy Ghost do not share, except by Their merciful consent, is distinct from His operation, as the Word of God, wherein the Father and the Holy Ghost share.

Reply to Objection 2: The instrument is said to act through being moved by the principal agent; and yet, besides this, it can have its proper operation through its own form, as stated above of fire. And hence the action of the instrument as instrument is not distinct from the action of the principal agent; yet it may have another operation, inasmuch as it is a thing. Hence the operation of Christ's human nature, as the instrument of the Godhead, is not distinct from the operation of the Godhead; for the salvation wherewith the manhood of Christ saves us and that wherewith His Godhead saves us are not distinct; nevertheless, the human nature in Christ, inasmuch as it is a certain nature, has a proper operation distinct from the Divine, as stated above.

Reply to Objection 3: To operate belongs to a subsisting hypostasis; in accordance, however, with the form and nature from which the operation receives its species. Hence from the diversity of forms or natures spring the divers species of operations, but from the unity of hypostasis springs the numerical unity as regards the operation of the species: thus fire has two operations specifically different, namely, to illuminate and to heat, from the difference of light and heat, and yet the illumination of the fire that illuminates at one and the same time is numerically one. So, likewise, in Christ there are necessarily two specifically different operations by reason of His two natures; nevertheless, each of the operations at one and the same time is numerically one, as one walking and one healing.

Reply to Objection 4: Being and operation belong to the person by reason of the nature; yet in a different manner. For being belongs to the very constitution of the person, and in this respect it has the nature of a term; consequently, unity of person requires unity of the complete and personal being. But operation is an effect of the person by reason of a form or nature. Hence plurality of operations is not incompatible with personal unity.

Reply to Objection 5: The proper work of the Divine operation is different from the proper work of the human operation. Thus to heal a leper is a proper work of the Divine operation, but to touch him is the proper work of the human operation. Now both these operations concur in one work, inasmuch as one nature acts in union with the other.

Whether in Christ there are several human operations?

Objection 1: It would seem that in Christ there are several human operations. For Christ as man communicates with plants by His nutritive soul, with the brutes by His sensitive soul, and with the angels by His intellective soul, even as other men do. Now the operations of a plant as plant and of an animal as animal are different. Therefore Christ as man has several operations.

Objection 2: Further, powers and habits are distinguished by their acts. Now in Christ's soul there were divers powers and habits; therefore also divers operations.

Objection 3: Further, instruments ought to be proportioned to their operations. Now the human body has divers members of different form, and consequently fitted to divers operations. Therefore in Christ there are divers operations in the human nature.

On the contrary, As Damascene says (De Fide Orth. iii, 15), "operation is consequent upon the nature." But in Christ there is only one human nature. Therefore in Christ there is only one human operation.

I answer that, Since it is by his reason that man is what he is; that operation is called human simply, which proceeds from the reason through the will, which is the rational appetite. Now if there is any operation in man which does not proceed from the reason and the will, it is not simply a human operation, but belongs to man by reason of some part of human nature---sometimes by reason of the nature of elementary bodies, as to be borne downwards---sometimes by reason of the force of the vegetative soul, as to be nourished, and to grow---sometimes by reason of the sensitive part, as to see and hear, to imagine and remember, to desire and to be angry. Now between these operations there is a difference. For the operations of the sensitive soul are to some extent obedient to reason, and consequently they are somewhat rational and human inasmuch as they obey reason, as is clear from the Philosopher (Ethic. i, 13). But the operations that spring from the vegetative soul, or from the nature of elemental bodies, are not subject to reason; consequently they are nowise rational; nor simply human, but only as regards a part of human nature. Now it was said [4091](A[1]) that when a subordinate agent acts by its own form, the operations of the inferior and of the superior agent are distinct; but when the inferior agent acts only as moved by the superior agent, then the operation of the superior and the inferior agent is one.

And hence in every mere man the operations of the elemental body and of the vegetative soul are distinct from the will's operation, which is properly human; so likewise the operations of the sensitive soul inasmuch as it is not moved by reason; but inasmuch as it is moved by reason, the operations of the sensitive and the rational part are the same. Now there is but one operation of the rational part if we consider the principle of the operation, which is the reason and the will; but the operations are many if we consider their relationship to various objects. And there were some who called this a diversity of things operated rather than of operations, judging the unity of the operation solely from the operative principle. And it is in this respect that we are now considering the unity and plurality of operations in Christ.

Hence in every mere man there is but one operation, which is properly called human; but besides this there are in a mere man certain other operations, which are not strictly human, as was said above. But in the Man Jesus Christ there was no motion of the sensitive part which was not ordered by reason. Even the natural and bodily operations pertained in some respects to His will, inasmuch as it was His will "that His flesh should do and suffer what belonged to it," as stated above ([4092]Q[18], A[5]). Much more, therefore, is there one operation in Christ, than in any other man whatsoever.

Reply to Objection 1: The operations of the sensitive and nutritive parts are not strictly human, as stated above; yet in Christ these operations were more human than in others.

Reply to Objection 2: Powers and habits are diversified by comparison with their objects. Hence in this way the diversity of operations corresponds to the divers powers and habits, as likewise to the divers objects. Now we do not wish to exclude this diversity of operations from Christ's humanity, nor that which springs from a diversity of time, but only that which regards the first active principle, as was said above.

(St. Thomas gives no reply to OBJ[3]; some codices add: Hence may be gathered the reply to the third objection.)

Whether the human action of Christ could be meritorious to Him?

Objection 1: It would seem that the human action of Christ could not be meritorious to Him. For before His death Christ was a comprehensor even as He is now. But comprehensors do not merit: because the charity of the comprehensor belongs to the reward of beatitude, since fruition depends upon it. Hence it does not seem to be the principle of merit, since merit and reward are not the same. Therefore Christ before His passion did not merit, even as He does not merit now.

Objection 2: Further, no one merits what is due to him. But because Christ is the Son of God by nature, the eternal inheritance is due to Him, which other men merit by their works. And hence Christ Who, from the beginning, was the Word of God, could not merit anything for Himself.

Objection 3: Further, whoever has the principle does not properly merit what flows from its possession. But Christ has the glory of the soul, whence, in the natural course, flowed the glory of the body, as Augustine says (Ep. ad Dios cxviii); though by a dispensation it was brought about that in Christ the glory of the soul should not overflow to the body. Hence Christ did not merit the glory of the body.

Objection 4: Further, the manifestation of Christ's excellence is a good, not of Christ Himself, but of those who know Him. Hence it is promised as a reward to such as love Christ that He will be manifested to them, according to Jn. 14:21: "He that loveth Me, shall be loved of My Father, and I will love him and will manifest Myself to him." Therefore Christ did not merit the manifestation of His greatness.

On the contrary, The Apostle says (Phil. 2:8,9): "Becoming obedient unto death . . . For which cause God also hath exalted Him." Therefore by obeying He merited His exaltation and thus He merited something for Himself.

I answer that, To have any good thing of oneself is more excellent than to have it from another, for "what is of itself a cause is always more excellent than what is a cause through another," as is said Phys. viii, 5. Now a thing is said to have, of itself, that of which it is to some extent the cause. But of whatever good we possess the first cause by authority is God; and in this way no creature has any good of itself, according to 1 Cor. 4:7: "What hast thou that thou hast not received?" Nevertheless, in a secondary manner anyone may be a cause, to himself, of having certain good things, inasmuch as he cooperates with God in the matter, and thus whoever has anything by his own merit has it, in a manner, of himself. Hence it is better to have a thing by merit than without merit.

Now since all perfection and greatness must be attributed to Christ, consequently He must have by merit what others have by merit; unless it be of such a nature that its want would detract from Christ's dignity and perfection more than would accrue to Him by merit. Hence He merited neither grace nor knowledge nor the beatitude of His soul, nor the Godhead, because, since merit regards only what is not yet possessed, it would be necessary that Christ should have been without these at some time; and to be without them would have diminished Christ's dignity more than His merit would have increased it. But the glory of the body, and the like, are less than the dignity of meriting, which pertains to the virtue of charity. Hence we must say that Christ had, by merit, the glory of His body and whatever pertained to His outward excellence, as His Ascension, veneration, and the rest. And thus it is clear that He could merit for Himself.

Reply to Objection 1: Fruition, which is an act of charity, pertains to the glory of the soul, which Christ did not merit. Hence if He merited by charity, it does not follow that the merit and the reward are the same. Nor did He merit by charity inasmuch as it was the charity of a comprehensor, but inasmuch as it was that of a wayfarer. For He was at once a wayfarer and a comprehensor, as was said above ([4093]Q[15], A[10]). And therefore, since He is no longer a wayfarer, He is not in the state of meriting.

Reply to Objection 2: Because by nature Christ is God and the Son of God, the Divine glory and the lordship of all things are due to Him, as to the first and supreme Lord. Nevertheless a glory is due to Him as a beatified man; and this He has partly without merit, and partly with merit, as is clear from what has been said.

Reply to Objection 3: It is by Divine appointment that there is an overflow of glory from the soul to the body, in keeping with human merit; so that as man merits by the act of the soul which he performs in the body, so he may be rewarded by the glory of the soul overflowing to the body. And hence not only the glory of the soul, but also the glory of the body falls under merit, according to Rom. 8:11: "He . . . shall quicken also our [Vulg.: 'your'] mortal bodies, because of His Spirit that dwelleth in us [Vulg.: 'you']." And thus it could fall under Christ's merit.

Reply to Objection 4: The manifestation of Christ's excellence is His good as regards the being which it has in the knowledge of others; although in regard to the being which they have in themselves it chiefly belongs to the good of those who know Him. Yet even this is referred to Christ inasmuch as they are His members.

Whether Christ could merit for others?

Objection 1: It would seem that Christ could not merit for others. For it is written (Ezech. 18:4): "The soul that sinneth, the same shall die." Hence, for a like reason, the soul that meriteth, the same shall be recompensed. Therefore it is not possible that Christ merited for others.

Objection 2: Further, of the fulness of Christ's grace we all receive, as is written Jn. 1:16. Now other men having Christ's grace cannot merit for others. For it is written (Ezech. 14:20) that if "Noe and Daniel and Job be in the city [Vulg.: 'the midst thereof'] . . . they shall deliver neither son nor daughter; but they shall only deliver their own souls by their justice." Hence Christ could not merit anything for us.

Objection 3: Further, the "reward" that we merit is due "according to justice [Vulg.: 'debt'] and not according to grace," as is clear from Rom. 4:4. Therefore if Christ merited our salvation it follows that our salvation is not by God's grace but by justice, and that He acts unjustly with those whom He does not save, since Christ's merit extends to all.

On the contrary, It is written (Rom. 5:18): "As by the offense of one, unto all men to condemnation; so also by the justice of one, unto all men to justification of life." But Adam's demerits reached to the condemnation of others. Much more, therefore, does the merit of Christ reach others.

I answer that, As stated above ([4094]Q[8], AA[1],5), grace was in Christ not merely as in an individual, but also as in the Head of the whole Church, to Whom all are united, as members to a head, who constitute one mystical person. And hence it is that Christ's merit extends to others inasmuch as they are His members; even as in a man the action of the head reaches in a manner to all his members, since it perceives not merely for itself alone, but for all the members.

Reply to Objection 1: The sin of an individual harms himself alone; but the sin of Adam, who was appointed by God to be the principle of the whole nature, is transmitted to others by carnal propagation. So, too, the merit of Christ, Who has been appointed by God to be the head of all men in regard to grace, extends to all His members.

Reply to Objection 2: Others receive of Christ's fulness not indeed the fount of grace, but some particular grace. And hence it need not be that men merit for others, as Christ did.

Reply to Objection 3: As the sin of Adam reaches others only by carnal generation, so, too, the merit of Christ reaches others only by spiritual regeneration, which takes place in baptism; wherein we are incorporated with Christ, according to Gal. 3:27, "As many of you as have been baptized in Christ, have put on Christ"; and it is by grace that it is granted to man to be incorporated with Christ. And thus man's salvation is from grace.

OF CHRIST'S SUBJECTION TO THE FATHER (TWO ARTICLES)

We must now consider such things as belong to Christ in relation to the Father. Some of these things are predicated of Him because of His relation to the Father, e.g. that He was subject to Him, that He prayed to Him, that He ministered, to Him by priesthood. And some are predicated, or may be predicated, of Him because of the Father's relation to Him, e.g. that the Father adopted Him and that He predestined Him.

Hence we must consider (1) Christ's subjection to the Father; (2) His prayer; (3) His priesthood; (4) Adoption---whether it is becoming to Him; (5) His predestination.

Under the first head there are two points of inquiry:

(1) Whether Christ is subject to the Father?

(2) Whether He is subject to Himself?

Whether we may say that Christ is subject to the Father?

Objection 1: It would seem that we may not say that Christ was subject to the Father. For everything subject to the Father is a creature, since, as is said in De Eccles. Dogm. iv, "in the Trinity there is no dependence or subjection." But we cannot say simply that Christ is a creature, as was stated above ([4095]Q[16], A[8]). Therefore we cannot say simply that Christ is subject to God the Father.

Objection 2: Further, a thing is said to be subject to God when it is subservient to His dominion. But we cannot attribute subservience to the human nature of Christ; for Damascene says (De Fide Orth. iii, 21): "We must bear in mind that we may not call it" (i.e. Christ's human nature) "a servant; for the words 'subservience' and 'domination' are not names of the nature, but of relations, as the words 'paternity' and 'filiation.'" Hence Christ in His human nature is not subject to God the Father.

Objection 3: Further, it is written (1 Cor. 15:28): "And when all things shall be subdued unto Him, then the Son also Himself shall be subject unto Him that put all things under Him." But, as is written (Heb. 2:8): "We see not as yet all things subject to Him." Hence He is not yet subject to the Father, Who has subjected all things to Him.

On the contrary, Our Lord says (Jn. 14:28), "The Father is greater than I"; and Augustine says (De Trin. i, 7): "It is not without reason that the Scripture mentions both, that the Son is equal to the Father and the Father greater than the Son, for the first is said on account of the form of God, and the second on account of the form of a servant, without any confusion." Now the less is subject to the greater. Therefore in the form of a servant Christ is subject to the Father.

I answer that, Whoever has a nature is competent to have what is proper to that nature. Now human nature from its beginning has a threefold subjection to God. The first regards the degree of goodness, inasmuch as the Divine Nature is the very essence of goodness as is clear from Dionysius (Div. Nom. i) while a created nature has a participation of the Divine goodness, being subject, so to say, to the rays of this goodness. Secondly, human nature is subject to God, as regards God's power, inasmuch as human nature, even as every creature, is subject to the operation of the Divine ordinance. Thirdly, human nature is especially subject to God through its proper act, inasmuch as by its own will it obeys His command. This triple subjection to God Christ professes of Himself. The first (Mat. 19:17): "Why askest thou Me concerning good? One is good, God." And on this Jerome remarks: "He who had called Him a good master, and had not confessed Him to be God or the Son of God, learns that no man, however holy, is good in comparison with God." And hereby He gave us to understand that He Himself, in His human nature, did not attain to the height of Divine goodness. And because "in such things as are great, but not in bulk, to be great is the same as to be good," as Augustine says (De Trin. vi, 8), for this reason the Father is said to be greater than Christ in His human nature. The second subjection is attributed to Christ, inasmuch as all that befell Christ is believed to have happened by Divine appointment; hence Dionysius says (Coel. Hier. iv) that Christ "is subject to the ordinance of God the Father." And this is the subjection of subservience, whereby "every creature serves God" (Judith 16:17), being subject to His ordinance, according to Wis. 16:24: "The creature serving Thee the Creator." And in this way the Son of God (Phil. 2:7) is said to have taken "the form of a servant." The third subjection He attributes to Himself, saying (Jn. 8:29): "I do always the things that please Him." And this is the subjection to the Father, of obedience unto death. Hence it is written (Phil. 2:8) that he became "obedient" to the Father "unto death."

Reply to Objection 1: As we are not to understand that Christ is a creature simply, but only in His human nature, whether this qualification be added or not, as stated above ([4096]Q[16], A[8]), so also we are to understand that Christ is subject to the Father not simply but in His human nature, even if this qualification be not added; and yet it is better to add this qualification in order to avoid the error of Arius, who held the Son to be less than the Father.

Reply to Objection 2: The relation of subservience and dominion is based upon action and passion, inasmuch as it belongs to a servant to be moved by the will of his master. Now to act is not attributed to the nature as agent, but to the person, since "acts belong to supposita and to singulars," according to the Philosopher (Metaph. i, 1). Nevertheless action is attributed to the nature as to that whereby the person or hypostasis acts. Hence, although the nature is not properly said to rule or serve, yet every hypostasis or person may be properly said to be ruling or serving in this or that nature. And in this way nothing prevents Christ being subject or servant to the Father in human nature.

Reply to Objection 3: As Augustine says (De Trin. i, 8): "Christ will give the kingdom to God and the Father, when He has brought the faithful, over whom He now reigns by faith, to the vision," i.e. to see the essence common to the Father and the Son: and then He will be totally subject to the Father not only in Himself, but also in His members by the full participation of the Godhead. And then all things will be fully subject to Him by the final accomplishment of His will concerning them; although even now all things are subject to Him as regards His power, according to Mat. 28:18: "All power is given to Me in heaven and in earth."

Whether Christ is subject to Himself?

Objection 1: It would seem that Christ is not subject to Himself. For Cyril says in a synodal letter which the Council of Ephesus (Part I, ch. xxvi) received: "Christ is neither servant nor master of Himself. It is foolish, or rather impious, to think or say this." And Damascene says the same (De Fide Orth. iii, 21): "The one Being, Christ, cannot be the servant or master of Himself." Now Christ is said to be the servant of the Father inasmuch as He is subject to Him. Hence Christ is not subject to Himself.

Objection 2: Further, servant has reference to master. Now nothing has a relation to itself, hence Hilary says (De Trin. vii) that nothing is like or equal to itself. Hence Christ cannot be said to be the servant of Himself, and consequently to be subject to Himself.

Objection 3: Further, "as the rational soul and flesh are one man; so God and man are one Christ," as Athanasius says (Symb. Fid.). Now man is not said to be subject to himself or servant to himself or greater than himself because his body is subject to his soul. Therefore, Christ is not said to be subject to Himself because His Manhood is subject to His Godhead.

On the contrary, Augustine says (De Trin. i, 7): "Truth shows in this way" (i.e. whereby the Father is greater than Christ in human nature) "that the Son is less than Himself."

Further, as he argues (De Trin. i, 7), the form of a servant was so taken by the Son of God that the form of God was not lost. But because of the form of God, which is common to the Father and the Son, the Father is greater than the Son in human nature. Therefore the Son is greater than Himself in human nature.

Further, Christ in His human nature is the servant of God the Father, according to Jn. 20:17: "I ascend to My Father and to your Father to My God and your God." Now whoever is the servant of the Father is the servant of the Son; otherwise not everything that belongs to the Father would belong to the Son. Therefore Christ is His own servant and is subject to Himself.

I answer that, As was said above (A[1], ad 2), to be master or servant is attributed to a person or hypostasis according to a nature. Hence when it is said that Christ is the master or servant of Himself, or that the Word of God is the Master of the Man Christ, this may be understood in two ways. First, so that this is understood to be said by reason of another hypostasis or person, as if there was the person of the Word of God ruling and the person of the man serving; and this is the heresy of Nestorius. Hence in the condemnation of Nestorius it is said in the Council of Ephesus (Part III, ch. i, anath. 6): "If anyone say that the Word begotten of God the Father is the God or Lord of Christ, and does not rather confess the same to be at once God and man as the Word made flesh, according to the Scriptures, let him be anathema." And in this sense it is denied by Cyril and Damascene (OBJ[1]); and in the same sense must it be denied that Christ is less than Himself or subject to Himself. Secondly, it may be understood of the diversity of natures in the one person or hypostasis. And thus we may say that in one of them, in which He agrees with the Father, He presides and rules together with the Father; and in the other nature, in which He agrees with us, He is subject and serves, and in this sense Augustine says that "the Son is less than Himself."

Yet it must be borne in mind that since this name "Christ" is the name of a Person, even as the name "Son," those things can be predicated essentially and absolutely of Christ which belong to Him by reason of the Person, Which is eternal; and especially those relations which seem more properly to pertain to the Person or the hypostasis. But whatever pertains to Him in His human nature is rather to be attributed to Him with a qualification; so that we say that Christ is simply greatest, Lord, Ruler, whereas to be subject or servant or less is to be attributed to Him with the qualification, in His human nature.

Reply to Objection 1: Cyril and Damascene deny that Christ is the head of Himself inasmuch as this implies a plurality of supposita, which is required in order that anyone may be the master of another.

Reply to Objection 2: Simply speaking it is necessary that the master and the servant should be distinct; yet a certain notion of mastership and subservience may be preserved inasmuch as the same one is master of Himself in different respects.

Reply to Objection 3: On account of the divers parts of man, one of which is superior and the other inferior, the Philosopher says (Ethic. v, 11) that there is justice between a man and himself inasmuch as the irascible and concupiscible powers obey reason. Hence this way a man may be said to be subject and subservient to Himself as regards His different parts.

To the other arguments, the reply is clear from what has been said. For Augustine asserts that the Son is less than, or subject to, Himself in His human nature, and not by a diversity of supposita.

Day 264

OF CHRIST'S PRAYER (FOUR ARTICLES)
We must now consider Christ's prayer; and under this head there are four points of inquiry:
(1) Whether it is becoming that Christ should pray?
(2) Whether it pertains to Him in respect of His sensuality?
(3) Whether it is becoming to Him to pray for Himself or only for others?
(4) Whether every prayer of His was heard?

Whether it is becoming of Christ to pray?
Objection 1: It would seem unbecoming that Christ should pray. For, as Damascene says (De Fide Orth. iii, 24), "prayer is the asking for becoming things from God." But since Christ could do all things, it does not seem becoming to Him to ask anything from anyone. Therefore it does not seem fitting that Christ should pray.

Objection 2: Further, we need not ask in prayer for what we know for certain will happen; thus, we do not pray that the sun may rise tomorrow. Nor is it fitting that anyone should ask in prayer for what he knows will not happen. But Christ in all things knew what would happen. Therefore it was not fitting that He should ask anything in prayer.

Objection 3: Further, Damascene says (De Fide Orth. iii, 24) that "prayer is the raising up of the mind to God." Now Christ's mind needed no uplifting to God, since His mind was always united to God, not only by the union of the hypostasis, but by the fruition of beatitude. Therefore it was not fitting that Christ should pray.

On the contrary, It is written (Lk. 6:12): "And it came to pass in those days, that He went out into a mountain, and He passed the whole night in the prayer of God."

I answer that, As was said in the [4097]SS, Q[83], AA[1],2, prayer is the unfolding of our will to God, that He may fulfill it. If, therefore, there had been but one will in Christ, viz. the Divine, it would nowise belong to Him to pray, since the Divine will of itself is effective of whatever He wishes by it, according to Ps. 134:6: "Whatsoever the Lord pleased, He hath done." But because the Divine and the human wills are distinct in Christ, and the human will of itself is not efficacious enough to do what it wishes, except by Divine power, hence to pray belongs to Christ as man and as having a human will.

Reply to Objection 1: Christ as God and not as man was able to carry out all He wished, since as man He was not omnipotent, as stated above ([4098]Q[13], A[1]). Nevertheless being both God and man, He wished to offer prayers to the Father, not as though He were incompetent, but for our instruction. First, that He might show Himself to be from the Father; hence He says (Jn. 11:42): "Because of the people who stand about I have said it" (i.e. the words of the prayer) "that they may believe that Thou hast sent Me." Hence Hilary says (De Trin. x): "He did not need prayer. It was for us He prayed, lest the Son should be unknown." Secondly, to give us an example of prayer; hence Ambrose says (on Lk. 6:12): "Be not deceived, nor think that the Son of God prays as a weakling, in order to beseech what He cannot effect. For the Author of power, the Master of obedience persuades us to the precepts of virtue by His example." Hence Augustine says (Tract. civ in Joan.): "Our Lord in the form of a servant could have prayed in silence, if need be, but He wished to show Himself a suppliant of the Father, in such sort as to bear in mind that He was our Teacher."

Reply to Objection 2: Amongst the other things which He knew would happen, He knew that some would be brought about by His prayer; and for these He not unbecomingly besought God.

Reply to Objection 3: To rise is nothing more than to move towards what is above. Now movement is taken in two ways, as is said De Anima iii, 7; first, strictly, according it implies the passing from potentiality to act, inasmuch as it is the act of something imperfect, and thus to rise pertains to what is potentially and not actually above. Now in this sense, as Damascene says (De Fide Orth. iii, 24), "the human mind of Christ did not need to rise to God, since it was ever united to God both by personal being and by the blessed vision." Secondly, movement signifies the act of something perfect, i.e. something existing in act, as to understand and to feel are called movements; and in this sense the mind of Christ was always raised up to God, since He was always contemplating Him as existing above Himself.

Whether it pertains to Christ to pray according to His sensuality?

Objection 1: It would seem that it pertains to Christ to pray according to His sensuality. For it is written (Ps. 83:3) in the person of Christ: "My heart and My flesh have rejoiced in the Living God." Now sensuality is called the appetite of the flesh. Hence Christ's sensuality could ascend to the Living God by rejoicing; and with equal reason by praying.

Objection 2: Further, prayer would seem to pertain to that which desires what is besought. Now Christ besought something that His sensuality desired when He said (Mat. 26:39): "Let this chalice pass from Me." Therefore Christ's sensuality prayed.

Objection 3: Further, it is a greater thing to be united to God in person than to mount to Him in prayer. But the sensuality was assumed by God to the unity of Person, even as every other part of human nature. Much more, therefore, could it mount to God by prayer.

On the contrary, It is written (Phil. 2:7) that the Son of God in the nature that He assumed was "made in the likeness of men." But the rest of men do not pray with their sensuality. Therefore, neither did Christ pray according to His sensuality.

I answer that, To pray according to sensuality may be understood in two ways. First as if prayer itself were an act of the sensuality; and in this sense Christ did not pray with His sensuality, since His sensuality was of the same nature and species in Christ as in us. Now in us the sensuality cannot pray for two reasons; first because the movement of the sensuality cannot transcend sensible things, and, consequently, it cannot mount to God, which is required for prayer; secondly, because prayer implies a certain ordering inasmuch as we desire something to be fulfilled by God; and this is the work of reason alone. Hence prayer is an act of the reason, as was said in the [4099]SS, Q[83], A[1].

Secondly, we may be said to pray according to the sensuality when our prayer lays before God what is in our appetite of sensuality; and in this sense Christ prayed with His sensuality inasmuch as His prayer expressed the desire of His sensuality, as if it were the advocate of the sensuality---and this, that He might teach us three things. First, to show that He had taken a true human nature, with all its natural affections: secondly, to show that a man may wish with his natural desire what God does not wish: thirdly, to show that man should subject his own will to the Divine will. Hence Augustine says in the Enchiridion (Serm. 1 in Ps. 32): "Christ acting as a man, shows the proper will of a man when He says 'Let this chalice pass from Me'; for this was the human will desiring something proper to itself and, so to say, private. But because He wishes man to be righteous and to be directed to God, He adds: 'Nevertheless not as I will but as Thou wilt,' as if to say, 'See thyself in Me, for thou canst desire something proper to thee, even though God wishes something else.'"

Reply to Objection 1: The flesh rejoices in the Living God, not by the act of the flesh mounting to God, but by the outpouring of the heart into the flesh, inasmuch as the sensitive appetite follows the movement of the rational appetite.

Reply to Objection 2: Although the sensuality wished what the reason besought, it did not belong to the sensuality to seek this by praying, but to the reason, as stated above.

Reply to Objection 3: The union in person is according to the personal being, which pertains to every part of the human nature; but the uplifting of prayer is by an act which pertains only to the reason, as stated above. Hence there is no parity.

Whether it was fitting that Christ should pray for Himself?

Objection 1: It would seem that it was not fitting that Christ should pray for Himself. For Hilary says (De Trin. x): "Although His word of beseeching did not benefit Himself, yet He spoke for the profit of our faith." Hence it seems that Christ prayed not for Himself but for us.

Objection 2: Further, no one prays save for what He wishes, because, as was said [4100](A[1]), prayer is an unfolding of our will to God that He may fulfil it. Now Christ wished to suffer what He suffered. For Augustine says (Contra Faust. xxvi): "A man, though unwilling, is often angry; though unwilling, is sad; though unwilling, sleeps; though unwilling, hungers and thirsts. But He" (i.e. Christ) "did all these things, because He wished." Therefore it was not fitting that He should pray for Himself.

Objection 3: Further, Cyprian says (De Orat. Dom.): "The Doctor of Peace and Master of Unity did not wish prayers to be offered individually and privately, lest when we prayed we should pray for ourselves alone." Now Christ did what He taught, according to Acts 1:1: "Jesus began to do and to teach." Therefore Christ never prayed for Himself alone.

On the contrary, our Lord Himself said while praying (Jn. 17:1): "Glorify Thy Son."

I answer that, Christ prayed for Himself in two ways. First, by expressing the desire of His sensuality, as stated above [4101](A[2]); or also of His simple will, considered as a nature; as when He prayed that the chalice of His Passion might pass from Him (Mat. 26:39). Secondly, by expressing the desire of His deliberate will, which is considered as reason; as when He prayed for the glory of His Resurrection (Jn. 17:1). And this is reasonable. For as we have said above (A[1], ad 1) Christ wished to pray to His Father in order to give us an example of praying; and also to show that His Father is the author both of His eternal procession in the Divine Nature, and of all the good that He possesses in the human nature. Now just as in His human nature He had already received certain gifts from His Father. so there were other gifts which He had not yet received, but which He expected to receive. And therefore, as He gave thanks to the Father for gifts already received in His human nature, by acknowledging Him as the author thereof, as we read (Mat. 26:27; Jn. 11:41): so also, in recognition of His Father, He besought Him in prayer for those gifts still due to Him in His human nature, such as the glory of His body, and the like. And in this He gave us an example, that we should give thanks for benefits received, and ask in prayer for those we have not as yet.

Reply to Objection 1: Hilary is speaking of vocal prayer, which was not necessary to Him for His own sake, but only for ours. Whence he says pointedly that "His word of beseeching did not benefit Himself." For if "the Lord hears the desire of the poor," as is said in the Ps. 9:38, much more the mere will of Christ has the force of a prayer with the Father: wherefore He said (Jn. 11:42): "I know that Thou hearest Me always, but because of the people who stand about have I said it, that they may believe that Thou hast sent Me."

Reply to Objection 2: Christ wished indeed to suffer what He suffered, at that particular time: nevertheless He wished to obtain, after His passion, the glory of His body, which as yet He had not. This glory He expected to receive from His Father as the author thereof, and therefore it was fitting that He should pray to Him for it.

Reply to Objection 3: This very glory which Christ, while praying, besought for Himself, pertained to the salvation of others according to Rom. 4:25: "He rose again for our justification." Consequently the prayer which He offered for Himself was also in a manner offered for others. So also anyone that asks a boon of God that he may use it for the good of others, prays not only for himself, but also for others.

Whether Christ's prayer was always heard?

Objection 1: It would seem that Christ's prayer was not always heard. For He besought that the chalice of His passion might be taken from Him, as we read (Mat. 26:39): and yet it was not taken from Him. Therefore it seems that not every prayer of His was heard.

Objection 2: Further, He prayed that the sin of those who crucified Him might be forgiven, as is related (Lk. 23:34). Yet not all were pardoned this sin, since the Jews were punished on account thereof. Therefore it seems that not every prayer of His was heard.

Objection 3: Further, our Lord prayed for them "who would believe in Him through the word" of the apostles, that they "might all be one in Him," and that they might attain to being with Him (Jn. 17:20, 21, 24). But not all attain to this. Therefore not every prayer of His was heard.

Objection 4: Further, it is said (Ps. 21:3) in the person of Christ: "I shall cry by day, and Thou wilt not hear." Not every prayer of His, therefore, was heard.

On the contrary, The Apostle says (Heb. 5:7): "With a strong cry and tears offering up prayers . . . He was heard for His reverence."

I answer that, As stated above [4102](A[1]), prayer is a certain manifestation of the human will. Wherefore, then is the request of one who prays granted, when his will is fulfilled. Now absolutely speaking the will of man is the will of reason; for we will absolutely that which we will in accordance with reason's deliberation. Whereas what we will in accordance with the movement of sensuality, or even of the simple will, which is considered as nature is willed not absolutely but conditionally [secundum quid]---that is, provided no obstacle be discovered by reason's deliberation. Wherefore such a will should rather be called a "velleity" than an absolute will; because one would will [vellet] if there were no obstacle.

But according to the will of reason, Christ willed nothing but what He knew God to will. Wherefore every absolute will of Christ, even human, was fulfilled, because it was in conformity with God; and consequently His every prayer was fulfilled. For in this respect also is it that other men's prayers are fulfilled, in that their will is in conformity with God, according to Rom. 8:27: "And He that searcheth the hearts knoweth," that is, approves of, "what the Spirit desireth," that is, what the Spirit makes the saints to desire: "because He asketh for the saints according to God," that is, in conformity with the Divine will.

Reply to Objection 1: This prayer for the passing of the chalice is variously explained by the Saints. For Hilary (Super Matth. 31) says: "When He asks that this may pass from Him, He does not pray that it may pass by Him, but that others may share in that which passes on from Him to them; So that the sense is: As I am partaking of the chalice of the passion, so may others drink of it, with unfailing hope, with unflinching anguish, without fear of death."

Or according to Jerome (on Mat. 26:39): "He says pointedly, 'This chalice,' that is of the Jewish people, who cannot allege ignorance as an excuse for putting Me to death, since they have the Law and the Prophets, who foretold concerning Me."

Or, according to Dionysius of Alexandria (De Martyr. ad Origen 7): "When He says 'Remove this chalice from Me,' He does not mean, 'Let it not come to Me'; for if it come not, it cannot be removed. But, as that which passes is neither untouched nor yet permanent, so the Saviour beseeches, that a slightly pressing trial may be repulsed."

Lastly, Ambrose, Origen and Chrysostom say that He prayed thus "as man," being reluctant to die according to His natural will.

Thus, therefore, whether we understand, according to Hilary, that He thus prayed that other martyrs might be imitators of His Passion, or that He prayed that the fear of drinking His chalice might not trouble Him, or that death might not withhold Him, His prayer was entirely fulfilled. But if we understand that He prayed that He might not drink the chalice of His passion and death; or that He might not drink it at the hands of the Jews; what He besought was not indeed fulfilled, because His reason which formed the petition did not desire its fulfilment, but for our instruction, it was His will to make known to us His natural will, and the movement of His sensuality, which was His as man.

Reply to Objection 2: Our Lord did not pray for all those who crucified Him, as neither did He for all those who would believe in Him; but for those only who were predestinated to obtain eternal life through Him.

Wherefore the reply to the third objection is also manifest.

Reply to Objection 4: When He says: "I shall cry and Thou wilt not hear," we must take this as referring to the desire of sensuality, which shunned death. But He is heard as to the desire of His reason, as stated above.

OF THE PRIESTHOOD OF CHRIST (SIX ARTICLES)
We have now to consider the Priesthood of Christ; and under this head there are six points of inquiry:
(1) Whether it is fitting that Christ should be a priest?
(2) Of the victim offered by this priest;
(3) Of the effect of this priesthood;
(4) Whether the effect of His priesthood pertains to Himself, or only to others?
(5) Of the eternal duration of His priesthood;
(6) Whether He should be called "a priest according to the order of Melchisedech"?

Whether it is fitting that Christ should be a priest?
Objection 1: It would seem unfitting that Christ should be a priest. For a priest is less than an angel; whence it is written (Zech. 3:1): "The Lord showed me the high-priest standing before the angel of the Lord." But Christ is greater than the angels, according to Heb. 1:4: "Being made so much better than the angels, as He hath inherited a more excellent name than they." Therefore it is unfitting that Christ should be a priest.
Objection 2: Further, things which were in the Old Testament were figures of Christ, according to Col. 2:17: "Which are a shadow of things to come, but the body is Christ's." But Christ was not descended from the priests of the Old Law, for the Apostle says (Heb. 7:14): "It is evident that our Lord sprang out of Judah, in which tribe Moses spoke nothing concerning priests." Therefore it is not fitting that Christ should be a priest.
Objection 3: Further, in the Old Law, which is a figure of Christ, the lawgivers and the priests were distinct: wherefore the Lord said to Moses the lawgiver (Ex. 28:1): "Take unto thee Aaron, thy brother . . . that he [Vulg.: 'they'] may minister to Me in the priest's office." But Christ is the giver of the New Law, according to Jer. 31:33: "I will give My law in their bowels." Therefore it is unfitting that Christ should be a priest.
On the contrary, It is written (Heb. 4:14): "We have [Vulg.: 'Having'] therefore a great high-priest that hath passed into the heavens, Jesus, the Son of God."
I answer that, The office proper to a priest is to be a mediator between God and the people: to wit, inasmuch as He bestows Divine things on the people, wherefore "sacerdos" [priest] means a giver of sacred things [sacra dans], according to Malachi 2:7: "They shall seek the law at his," i.e. the priest's, "mouth"; and again, forasmuch as he offers up the people's prayers to God, and, in a manner, makes satisfaction to God for their sins; wherefore the Apostle says (Heb. 5:1): "Every high-priest taken from among men is ordained for men in the things that appertain to God, that he may offer up gifts and sacrifices for sins." Now this is most befitting to Christ. For through Him are gifts bestowed on men, according to 2 Pet. 1:4: "By Whom" (i.e. Christ) "He hath given us most great and precious promises, that by these you may be made partakers of the Divine Nature." Moreover, He reconciled the human race to God, according to Col. 1:19,20: "In Him" (i.e. Christ) "it hath well pleased (the Father) that all fulness should dwell, and through Him to reconcile all things unto Himself." Therefore it is most fitting that Christ should be a priest.
Reply to Objection 1: Hierarchical power appertains to the angels, inasmuch as they also are between God and man, as Dionysius explains (Coel. Hier. ix), so that the priest himself, as being between God and man, is called an angel, according to Malachi 2:7: "He is the angel of the Lord of hosts." Now Christ was greater than the angels, not only in His Godhead, but also in His humanity, as having the fulness of grace and glory. Wherefore also He had the hierarchical or priestly power in a higher degree than the angels, so that even the angels were ministers of His priesthood, according to Mat. 4:11: "Angels came and ministered unto Him." But, in regard to His passibility, He "was made a little lower than the angels," as the Apostle says (Heb. 2:9): and thus He was conformed to those wayfarers who are ordained to the priesthood.
Reply to Objection 2: As Damascene says (De Fide Orth. iii, 26): "What is like in every particular must be, of course, identical, and not a copy." Since, therefore, the priesthood of the Old Law was a figure of the priesthood of Christ, He did not wish to be born of the stock of the figurative priests, that it might be made clear that His priesthood is not quite the same as theirs, but differs therefrom as truth from figure.
Reply to Objection 3: As stated above ([4103]Q[7], A[7], ad 1), other men have certain graces distributed among them: but Christ, as being the Head of all, has the perfection of all graces. Wherefore, as to others, one is a lawgiver, another is a priest, another is a king; but all these concur in Christ, as the fount of all grace. Hence it is written (Is. 33:22): "The Lord is our Judge, the Lord is our law-giver, the Lord is our King: He will" come and "save us."

Whether Christ was Himself both priest and victim?
Objection 1: It would seem that Christ Himself was not both priest and victim. For it is the duty of the priest to slay the victim. But Christ did not kill Himself. Therefore He was not both priest and victim.
Objection 2: Further, the priesthood of Christ has a greater similarity to the Jewish priesthood, instituted by God, than to the priesthood of the Gentiles, by which the demons were worshiped. Now in the old Law man was never offered up in sacrifice: whereas this was very much to be reprehended in the sacrifices of the Gentiles, according to Ps. 105:38: "They shed innocent blood; the blood of their sons and of their daughters, which they sacrificed to the idols of Chanaan." Therefore in Christ's priesthood the Man Christ should not have been the victim.

Objection 3: Further, every victim, through being offered to God, is consecrated to God. But the humanity of Christ was from the beginning consecrated and united to God. Therefore it cannot be said fittingly that Christ as man was a victim.

On the contrary, The Apostle says (Eph. 5:2): "Christ hath loved us, and hath delivered Himself for us, an oblation and a victim [Douay: 'sacrifice'] to God for an odor of sweetness."

I answer that, As Augustine says (De Civ. Dei x, 5): "Every visible sacrifice is a sacrament, that is a sacred sign, of the invisible sacrifice." Now the invisible sacrifice is that by which a man offers his spirit to God, according to Ps. 50:19: "A sacrifice to God is an afflicted spirit." Wherefore, whatever is offered to God in order to raise man's spirit to Him, may be called a sacrifice.

Now man is required to offer sacrifice for three reasons. First, for the remission of sin, by which he is turned away from God. Hence the Apostle says (Heb. 5:1) that it appertains to the priest "to offer gifts and sacrifices for sins." Secondly, that man may be preserved in a state of grace, by ever adhering to God, wherein his peace and salvation consist. Wherefore under the old Law the sacrifice of peace-offerings was offered up for the salvation of the offerers, as is prescribed in the third chapter of Leviticus. Thirdly, in order that the spirit of man be perfectly united to God: which will be most perfectly realized in glory. Hence, under the Old Law, the holocaust was offered, so called because the victim was wholly burnt, as we read in the first chapter of Leviticus.

Now these effects were conferred on us by the humanity of Christ. For, in the first place, our sins were blotted out, according to Rom. 4:25: "Who was delivered up for our sins." Secondly, through Him we received the grace of salvation, according to Heb. 5:9: "He became to all that obey Him the cause of eternal salvation." Thirdly, through Him we have acquired the perfection of glory, according to Heb. 10:19: "We have [Vulg.: 'Having'] a confidence in the entering into the Holies" (i.e. the heavenly glory) "through His Blood." Therefore Christ Himself, as man, was not only priest, but also a perfect victim, being at the same time victim for sin, victim for a peace-offering, and a holocaust.

Reply to Objection 1: Christ did not slay Himself, but of His own free-will He exposed Himself to death, according to Is. 53:7: "He was offered because it was His own will." Thus He is said to have offered Himself.

Reply to Objection 2: The slaying of the Man Christ may be referred to a twofold will. First, to the will of those who slew Him: and in this respect He was not a victim: for the slayers of Christ are not accounted as offering a sacrifice to God, but as guilty of a great crime: a similitude of which was borne by the wicked sacrifices of the Gentiles, in which they offered up men to idols. Secondly, the slaying of Christ may be considered in reference to the will of the Sufferer, Who freely offered Himself to suffering. In this respect He is a victim, and in this He differs from the sacrifices of the Gentiles.

(The reply to the third objection is wanting in the original manuscripts, but it may be gathered from the above.--Ed.)

[*Some editions, however, give the following reply:

Reply to Objection 3: The fact that Christ's manhood was holy from its beginning does not prevent that same manhood, when it was offered to God in the Passion, being sanctified in a new way---namely, as a victim actually offered then. For it acquired then the actual holiness of a victim, from the charity which it had from the beginning, and from the grace of union sanctifying it absolutely.]

Whether the effect of Christ's priesthood is the expiation of sins?

Objection 1: It would seem that the effect of Christ's priesthood is not the expiation of sins. For it belongs to God alone to blot out sins, according to Is. 43:25: "I am He that blot out thy iniquities for My own sake." But Christ is priest, not as God, but as man. Therefore the priesthood of Christ does not expiate sins.

Objection 2: Further, the Apostle says (Heb. 10:1-3) that the victims of the Old Testament could not "make" (the comers thereunto) "perfect: for then they would have ceased to be offered; because the worshipers once cleansed should have no conscience of sin any longer; but in them there is made a commemoration of sins every year." But in like manner under the priesthood of Christ a commemoration of sins is made in the words: "Forgive us our trespasses" (Mat. 6:12). Moreover, the Sacrifice is offered continuously in the Church; wherefore again we say: "Give us this day our daily bread." Therefore sins are not expiated by the priesthood of Christ.

Objection 3: Further, in the sin-offerings of the Old Law, a he-goat was mostly offered for the sin of a prince, a she-goat for the sin of some private individual, a calf for the sin of a priest, as we gather from Lev. 4:3,23,28. But Christ is compared to none of these, but to the lamb, according to Jer. 11:19: "I was as a meek lamb, that is carried to be a victim." Therefore it seems that His priesthood does not expiate sins.

On the contrary, The Apostle says (Heb. 9:14): "The blood of Christ, Who by the Holy Ghost offered Himself unspotted unto God, shall cleanse our conscience from dead works, to serve the living God." But dead works denote sins. Therefore the priesthood of Christ has the power to cleanse from sins.

I answer that, Two things are required for the perfect cleansing from sins, corresponding to the two things comprised in sin--- namely, the stain of sin and the debt of punishment. The stain of sin is, indeed, blotted out by grace, by which the sinner's heart is turned to God: whereas the debt of punishment is entirely removed by the satisfaction that man offers to God. Now the priesthood of Christ produces both these effects. For by its virtue grace is given to us, by which our hearts are turned to God, according to Rom. 3:24,25: "Being justified freely by His grace, through the redemption that is in Christ Jesus, Whom God hath proposed to be a propitiation, through faith in His blood." Moreover, He satisfied for us fully, inasmuch as "He hath borne our infirmities and carried our sorrows" (Is. 53:4). Wherefore it is clear that the priesthood of Christ has full power to expiate sins.

Reply to Objection 1: Although Christ was a priest, not as God, but as man, yet one and the same was both priest and God. Wherefore in the Council of Ephesus [*Part III, ch. i, anath. 10] we read: "If anyone say that the very Word of God did not become our High-Priest and Apostle, when He became flesh and a man like us, but altogether another one, the man born of a woman, let him be anathema." Hence in so far as His human nature operated by virtue of the Divine, that sacrifice was most efficacious for the blotting out of sins. For this reason Augustine says (De Trin. iv, 14): "So that, since four things are to be observed in every sacrifice---to whom it is offered, by whom it is offered, what is offered, for whom it is offered; the same one true Mediator reconciling us to God by the sacrifice of peace, was one with Him to Whom it was offered, united in Himself those for whom He offered it, at the same time offered it Himself, and was Himself that which He offered."

Reply to Objection 2: Sins are commemorated in the New Law, not on account of the inefficacy of the priesthood of Christ, as though sins were not sufficiently expiated by Him: but in regard to those who either are not willing to be participators in His sacrifice, such as unbelievers, for whose sins we pray that they be converted; or who, after taking part in this sacrifice, fall away from it by whatsoever kind of sin. The Sacrifice which is offered every day in the Church is not distinct from that which Christ Himself offered, but is a commemoration thereof. Wherefore Augustine says (De Civ. De. x, 20): "Christ Himself both is the priest who offers it and the victim: the sacred token of which He wished to be the daily Sacrifice of the Church."

Reply to Objection 3: As Origen says (Sup. Joan. i, 29), though various animals were offered up under the Old Law, yet the daily sacrifice, which was offered up morning and evening, was a lamb, as appears from Num. 38:3,4. By which it was signified that the offering up of the true lamb, i.e. Christ, was the culminating sacrifice of all. Hence (Jn. 1:29) it is said: "Behold the Lamb of God, behold Him Who taketh away the sins [Vulg.: 'sin'] of the world."

Whether the effect of the priesthood of Christ pertained not only to others, but also to Himself?

Objection 1: It would seem that the effect of the priesthood of Christ pertained not only to others, but also to Himself. For it belongs to the priest's office to pray for the people, according to 2 Macc. 1:23: "The priests made prayer while the sacrifice was consuming." Now Christ prayed not only for others, but also for Himself, as we have said above ([4104]Q[21], A[3]), and as expressly stated (Heb. 5:7): "In the days of His flesh, with a strong cry and tears He offered [Vulg.: 'offering'] up prayers and supplications to Him that was able to save Him from death." Therefore the priesthood of Christ had an effect not only in others, but also in Himself.

Objection 2: Further, in His passion Christ offered Himself as a sacrifice. But by His passion He merited, not only for others, but also for Himself, as stated above ([4105]Q[19], AA[3],4). Therefore the priesthood of Christ had an effect not only in others, but also in Himself.

Objection 3: Further, the priesthood of the Old Law was a figure of the priesthood of Christ. But the priest of the Old Law offered sacrifice not only for others, but also for himself: for it is written (Lev. 16:17) that "the high-priest goeth into the sanctuary to pray for himself and his house, and for the whole congregation of Israel." Therefore the priesthood of Christ also had an effect not merely in others, but also in Himself.

On the contrary, We read in the acts of the Council of Ephesus [*Part III, ch. i, anath. 10]: "If anyone say that Christ offered sacrifice for Himself, and not rather for us alone (for He Who knew not sin needed no sacrifice), let him be anathema." But the priest's office consists principally in offering sacrifice. Therefore the priesthood of Christ had no effect in Himself.

I answer that, As stated above [4106](A[1]), a priest is set between God and man. Now he needs someone between himself and God, who of himself cannot approach to God; and such a one is subject to the priesthood by sharing in the effect thereof. But this cannot be said of Christ; for the Apostle says (Heb. 7:25): "Coming of Himself to God, always living to make intercession for us [Vulg.: 'He is able to save for ever them that come to God by Him; always living,' etc.]." And therefore it is not fitting for Christ to be the recipient of the effect of His priesthood, but rather to communicate it to others. For the influence of the first agent in every genus is such that it receives nothing in that genus: thus the sun gives but does not receive light; fire gives but does not receive heat. Now Christ is the fountain-head of the entire priesthood: for the priest of the Old Law was a figure of Him; while the priest of the New Law works in His person, according to 2 Cor. 2:10: "For what I have pardoned, if I have pardoned anything, for your sakes have I done it in the person of Christ." Therefore it is not fitting that Christ should receive the effect of His priesthood.

Reply to Objection 1: Although prayer is befitting to priests, it is not their proper office, for it is befitting to everyone to pray both for himself and for others, according to James 5:16: "Pray for one another that you may be saved." And so we may say that the prayer by which Christ prayed for Himself was not an action of His priesthood. But this answer seems to be precluded by the Apostle, who, after saying (Heb. 5:6), "Thou art a priest for ever according to the order of Melchisedech," adds, "Who in the days of His flesh offering up payers," etc., as quoted above (OBJ[1]): so that it seems that the prayer which Christ offered pertained to His priesthood. We must therefore say that other priests partake in the effect of their priesthood, not as priests, but as sinners, as we shall state farther on (ad 3). But Christ had, simply speaking, no sin; though He had the "likeness of sin in the flesh [Vulg.,: 'sinful flesh']," as is written Rom. 8:3. And, consequently, we must not say simply that He partook of the effect of His priesthood but with this qualification---in regard to the passibility of the flesh. Wherefore he adds pointedly, "that was able to save Him from death."

Reply to Objection 2: Two things may be considered in the offering of a sacrifice by any priest---namely, the sacrifice itself which is offered, and the devotion of the offerer. Now the proper effect of priesthood is that which results from the sacrifice itself. But Christ obtained a result from His passion, not as by virtue of the sacrifice, which is offered by way of satisfaction, but by the very devotion with which out of charity He humbly endured the passion.

Reply to Objection 3: A figure cannot equal the reality, wherefore the figural priest of the Old Law could not attain to such perfection as not to need a sacrifice of satisfaction. But Christ did not stand in need of this. Consequently, there is no comparison between the two; and this is what the Apostle says (Heb. 7:28): "The Law maketh men priests, who have infirmity; but the word of the oath, which was since the Law, the Son Who is perfected for evermore."

Day 265

Whether the priesthood of Christ endures for ever?

Objection 1: It would seem that the priesthood of Christ does not endure for ever. For as stated above (A[4], ad 1,3) those alone need the effect of the priesthood who have the weakness of sin, which can be expiated by the priest's sacrifice. But this will not be for ever. For in the Saints there will be no weakness, according to Is. 60:21: "Thy people shall be all just": while no expiation will be possible for the weakness of sin, since "there is no redemption in hell" (Office of the Dead, Resp. vii). Therefore the priesthood of Christ endures not for ever.

Objection 2: Further, the priesthood of Christ was made manifest most of all in His passion and death, when "by His own blood He entered into the Holies" (Heb. 9:12). But the passion and death of Christ will not endure for ever, as stated Rom. 6:9: "Christ rising again from the dead, dieth now no more." Therefore the priesthood of Christ will not endure for ever.

Objection 3: Further, Christ is a priest, not as God, but as man. But at one time Christ was not man, namely during the three days He lay dead. Therefore the priesthood of Christ endures not for ever.

On the contrary, It is written (Ps. 109:4): "Thou art a priest for ever."

I answer that, In the priestly office, we may consider two things: first, the offering of the sacrifice; secondly, the consummation of the sacrifice, consisting in this, that those for whom the sacrifice is offered, obtain the end of the sacrifice. Now the end of the sacrifice which Christ offered consisted not in temporal but in eternal good, which we obtain through His death, according to Heb. 9:11: "Christ is [Vulg.: 'being come'] a high-priest of the good things to come"; for which reason the priesthood of Christ is said to be eternal. Now this consummation of Christ's sacrifice was foreshadowed in this, that the high-priest of the Old Law, once a year, entered into the Holy of Holies with the blood of a he-goat and a calf, as laid down, Lev. 16:11, and yet he offered up the he-goat and calf not within the Holy of Holies, but without. In like manner Christ entered into the Holy of Holies---that is, into heaven---and prepared the way for us, that we might enter by the virtue of His blood, which He shed for us on earth.

Reply to Objection 1: The Saints who will be in heaven will not need any further expiation by the priesthood of Christ, but having expiated, they will need consummation through Christ Himself, on Whom their glory depends, as is written (Apoc. 21:23): "The glory of God hath enlightened it"---that is, the city of the Saints---"and the Lamb is the lamp thereof."

Reply to Objection 2: Although Christ's passion and death are not to be repeated, yet the virtue of that Victim endures for ever, for, as it is written (Heb. 10:14), "by one oblation He hath perfected for ever them that are sanctified."

Wherefore the reply to the third objection is clear.

As to the unity of this sacrifice, it was foreshadowed in the Law in that, once a year, the high-priest of the Law entered into the Holies, with a solemn oblation of blood, as set down, Lev. 16:11. But the figure fell short of the reality in this, that the victim had not an everlasting virtue, for which reason those sacrifices were renewed every year.

Whether the priesthood of Christ was according to the order of Melchisedech?

Objection 1: It would seem that Christ's priesthood was not according to the order of Melchisedech. For Christ is the fountain-head of the entire priesthood, as being the principal priest. Now that which is principal is not . secondary in regard to others, but others are secondary in its regard. Therefore Christ should not be called a priest according to the order of Melchisedech.

Objection 2: Further, the priesthood of the Old Law was more akin to Christ's priesthood than was the priesthood that existed before the Law. But the nearer the sacraments were to Christ, the more clearly they signified Him; as is clear from what we have said in the [4107]SS, Q[2], A[7]. Therefore the priesthood of Christ should be denominated after the priesthood of the Law, rather than after the order of Melchisedech, which was before the Law.

Objection 3: Further, it is written (Heb. 7:2,3): "That is 'king of peace,' without father, without mother, without genealogy; having neither beginning of days nor ending of life": which can be referred only to the Son of God. Therefore Christ should not be called a priest according to the order of Melchisedech, as of some one else, but according to His own order.

On the contrary, It is written (Ps. 109:4): "Thou art a priest for ever according to the order of Melchisedech."

I answer that, As stated above (A[4], ad 3) the priesthood of the Law was a figure of the priesthood of Christ, not as adequately representing the reality, but as falling far short thereof: both because the priesthood of the Law did not wash away sins, and because it was not eternal, as the priesthood of Christ. Now the excellence of Christ's over the Levitical priesthood was foreshadowed in the priesthood of Melchisedech, who received tithes from Abraham, in whose loins the priesthood of the Law was tithed. Consequently the priesthood of Christ is said to be "according to the order of Melchisedech," on account of the excellence of the true priesthood over the figural priesthood of the Law.

Reply to Objection 1: Christ is said to be according to the order of Melchisedech not as though the latter were a more excellent priest, but because he foreshadowed the excellence of Christ's over the Levitical priesthood.

Reply to Objection 2: Two things may be considered in Christ's priesthood: namely, the offering made by Christ, and (our) partaking thereof. As to the actual offering, the priesthood of Christ was more distinctly foreshadowed by the priesthood of the Law, by reason of the shedding of blood, than by the priesthood of Melchisedech in which there was no blood-shedding. But if we consider the participation of this sacrifice and the effect thereof, wherein the excellence of Christ's priesthood over the priesthood of the Law principally consists, then the former was more distinctly foreshadowed by the priesthood of Melchisedech, who offered bread and wine, signifying, as Augustine says (Tract. xxvi in Joan.) ecclesiastical unity, which is established by our taking part in the sacrifice of Christ [*Cf.[4108] Q[79], A[1]]. Wherefore also in the New Law the true sacrifice of Christ is presented to the faithful under the form of bread and wine.

Reply to Objection 3: Melchisedech is described as "without father, without mother, without genealogy," and as "having neither beginning of days nor ending of life," not as though he had not these things, but because these details in his regard are not supplied by Holy Scripture. And this it is that, as the Apostle says in the same passage, he is "likened unto the Son of God," Who had no earthly father, no heavenly mother, and no genealogy, according to Is. 53:8: "Who shall declare His generation?" and Who in His Godhead has neither beginning nor end of days.

OF ADOPTION AS BEFITTING TO CHRIST (FOUR ARTICLES)

We must now come to consider whether adoption befits Christ: and under this head there are four points of inquiry:

(1) Whether it is fitting that God should adopt sons?
(2) Whether this is fitting to God the Father alone?
(3) Whether it is proper to man to be adopted to the sonship of God?
(4) Whether Christ can be called the adopted Son?

Whether it is fitting that God should adopt sons?

Objection 1: It would seem that it is not fitting that God should adopt sons. For, as jurists say, no one adopts anyone but a stranger as his son. But no one is a stranger in relation to God, Who is the Creator of all. Therefore it seems unfitting that God should adopt.

Objection 2: Further, adoption seems to have been introduced in default of natural sonship. But in God there is natural sonship, as set down in the [4109]FP, Q[27], A[2]. Therefore it is unfitting that God should adopt.

Objection 3: Further, the purpose of adopting anyone is that he may succeed, as heir, the person who adopts him. But it does not seem possible for anyone to succeed God as heir, for He can never die. Therefore it is unfitting that God should adopt.

On the contrary, It is written (Eph. 1:5) that "He hath predestinated us unto the adoption of children of God." But the predestination of God is not ineffectual. Therefore God does adopt some as His sons.

I answer that, A man adopts someone as his son forasmuch as out of goodness he admits him as heir to his estate. Now God is infinitely good: for which reason He admits His creatures to a participation of good things; especially rational creatures, who forasmuch as they are made to the image of God, are capable of Divine beatitude. And this consists in the enjoyment of God, by which also God Himself is happy and rich in Himself---that is, in the enjoyment of Himself. Now a man's inheritance is that which makes him rich. Wherefore, inasmuch as God, of His goodness, admits men to the inheritance of beatitude, He is said to adopt them. Moreover Divine exceeds human adoption, forasmuch as God, by bestowing His grace, makes man whom He adopts worthy to receive the heavenly inheritance; whereas man does not make him worthy whom he adopts; but rather in adopting him he chooses one who is already worthy.

Reply to Objection 1: Considered in his nature man is not a stranger in respect to God, as to the natural gifts bestowed on him: but he is as to the gifts of grace and glory; in regard to which he is adopted.

Reply to Objection 2: Man works in order to supply his wants: not so God, Who works in order to communicate to others the abundance of His perfection. Wherefore, as by the work of creation the Divine goodness is communicated to all creatures in a certain likeness, so by the work of adoption the likeness of natural sonship is communicated to men, according to Rom. 8:29: "Whom He foreknew . . . to be made conformable to the image of His Son."

Reply to Objection 3: Spiritual goods can be possessed by many at the same time; not so material goods. Wherefore none can receive a material inheritance except the successor of a deceased person: whereas all receive the spiritual inheritance at the same time in its entirety without detriment to the ever-living Father.

Yet it might be said that God ceases to be, according as He is in us by faith, so as to begin to be in us by vision, as a gloss says on Rom. 8:17: "If sons, heirs also."

Whether it is fitting that the whole Trinity should adopt?

Objection 1: It would seem unfitting that the whole Trinity should adopt. For adoption is said of God in likeness to human custom. But among men those only adopt who can beget: and in God this can be applied only to the Father. Therefore in God the Father alone can adopt.

Objection 2: Further, by adoption men become the brethren of Christ, according to Rom. 8:29: "That He might be the first-born among many brethren." Now brethren are the sons of the same father; wherefore our Lord says (Jn. 20:17): "I ascend to My Father and to your Father." Therefore Christ's Father alone has adopted sons.

Objection 3: Further, it is written (Gal. 4:4, 5, 6): "God sent His Son . . . that we might receive the adoption of sons. And because you are sons of God, God hath sent the Spirit of His Son into your hearts, crying: 'Abba' [Father]." Therefore it belongs to Him to adopt, Who has the Son and the Holy Ghost. But this belongs to the Father alone. Therefore it befits the Father alone to adopt.

On the contrary, It belongs to Him to adopt us as sons, Whom we can call Father; whence it is written (Rom. 8:15): "You have received the spirit of adoption of sons, whereby we cry: 'Abba' [Father]." But when we say to God, "Our Father," we address the whole Trinity: as is the case with the other names which are said of God in respect of creatures, as stated in the [4110]FP, Q[33], A[3], OBJ[1]; cf. [4111]FP, Q[45], A[6]. Therefore to adopt is befitting to the whole Trinity.

I answer that, There is this difference between an adopted son of God and the natural Son of God, that the latter is "begotten not made"; whereas the former is made, according to Jn. 1:12: "He gave them power to be made the sons of God." Yet sometimes the adopted son is said to be begotten, by reason of the spiritual regeneration which is by grace, not by nature; wherefore it is written (James 1:18): "Of His own will hath He begotten us by the word of truth." Now although, in God, to beget belongs to the Person of the Father, yet to produce any effect in creatures is common to the whole Trinity, by reason of the oneness of their Nature: since, where there is one nature, there must needs be one power and one operation: whence our Lord says (Jn. 5:19): "What things soever the Father doth, these the Son also doth in like manner." Therefore it belongs to the whole Trinity to adopt men as sons of God.

Reply to Objection 1: All human individuals are not of one individual nature, so that there need be one operation and one effect of them all, as is the case in God. Consequently in this respect no comparison is possible.

Reply to Objection 2: By adoption we are made the brethren of Christ, as having with Him the same Father: Who, nevertheless, is His Father in one way, and ours in another. Whence pointedly our Lord says, separately, "My Father," and "Your Father" (Jn. 20:17). For He is Christ's Father by natural generation; and this is proper to Him: whereas He is our Father by a voluntary operation, which is common to Him and to the Son and Holy Ghost: so that Christ is not the Son of the whole Trinity, as we are.

Reply to Objection 3: As stated above (A[1], ad 2), adoptive sonship is a certain likeness of the eternal Sonship: just as all that takes place in time is a certain likeness of what has been from eternity. Now man is likened to the splendor of the Eternal Son by reason of the light of grace which is attributed to the Holy Ghost. Therefore adoption, though common to the whole Trinity, is appropriated to the Father as its author; to the Son, as its exemplar; to the Holy Ghost, as imprinting on us the likeness of this exemplar.

Whether it is proper to the rational nature to be adopted?

Objection 1: It would seem that it is not proper to the rational nature to be adopted. For God is not said to be the Father of the rational creature, save by adoption. But God is called the Father even of the irrational creature, according to Job 38:28: "Who is father of the rain? Or who begot the drops of dew?" Therefore it is not proper to the rational creature to be adopted.

Objection 2: Further, by reason of adoption some are called sons of God. But to be sons of God seems to be properly attributed by the Scriptures to the angels; according to Job 1:6: "On a certain day when the sons of God came to stand before the Lord." Therefore it is not proper to the rational creature to be adopted.

Objection 3: Further, whatever is proper to a nature, belongs to all that have that nature: just as risibility belongs to all men. But to be adopted does not belong to every rational nature. Therefore it is not proper to human nature.

On the contrary, Adopted sons are the "heirs of God," as is stated Rom. 8:17. But such an inheritance belongs to none but the rational nature. Therefore it is proper to the rational nature to be adopted.

I answer that, As stated above (A[2], ad 3), the sonship of adoption is a certain likeness of natural sonship. Now the Son of God proceeds naturally from the Father as the Intellectual Word, in oneness of nature with the Father. To this Word, therefore, something may be likened in three ways. First, on the part of the form but not on the part of its intelligibility: thus the form of a house already built is like the mental word of the builder in its specific form, but not in intelligibility, because the material form of a house is not intelligible, as it was in the mind of the builder. In this way every creature is like the Eternal Word; since it was made through the Word. Secondly, the creature is likened to the Word, not only as to its form, but also as to its intelligibility: thus the knowledge which is begotten in the disciple's mind is likened to the word in the mind of the master. In this way the rational creature, even in its nature, is likened to the Word of God. Thirdly, a creature is likened to the Eternal Word, as to the oneness of the Word with the Father, which is by reason of grace and charity: wherefore our Lord prays (Jn. 17:21,22): "That they may be one in Us . . . as We also are one." And this likeness perfects the adoption: for to those who are thus like Him the eternal inheritance is due. It is therefore clear that to be adopted belongs to the rational creature alone: not indeed to all, but only to those who have charity; which is "poured forth in our hearts by the Holy Ghost" (Rom. 5:5); for which reason (Rom. 8:15) the Holy Ghost is called "the Spirit of adoption of sons."

Reply to Objection 1: God is called the Father of the irrational creature, not properly speaking, by reason of adoption, but by reason of creation; according to the first-mentioned participation of likeness.

Reply to Objection 2: Angels are called sons of God by adoptive sonship, not that it belongs to them first; but because they were the first to receive the adoption of sons.

Reply to Objection 3: Adoption is a property resulting not from nature, but from grace, of which the rational nature is capable. Therefore it need not belong to every rational nature: but every rational creature must needs be capable of adoption.

Whether Christ as man is the adopted Son of God?

Objection 1: It would seem that Christ as man is the adopted Son of God. For Hilary says (De Trin. ii) speaking of Christ: "The dignity of power is not forfeited when carnal humanity [*Some editions read 'humilitas'---'the humility or lowliness of the flesh'] is adopted." Therefore Christ as man is the adopted Son of God.

Objection 2: Further, Augustine says (De Praedest. Sanct. xv) that "by the same grace that Man is Christ, as from the birth of faith every man is a Christian." But other men are Christians by the grace of adoption. Therefore this Man is Christ by adoption: and consequently He would seem to be an adopted son.

Objection 3: Further, Christ, as man, is a servant. But it is of greater dignity to be an adopted son than to be a servant. Therefore much more is Christ, as man, an adopted Son.

On the contrary, Ambrose says (De Incarn. viii): "We do not call an adopted son a natural son: the natural son is a true son." But Christ is the true and natural Son of God, according to 1 Jn. 5:20: "That we may . . . be in His true Son, Jesus Christ." Therefore Christ, as Man, is not an adopted Son.

I answer that, Sonship belongs properly to the hypostasis or person, not to the nature; whence in the [4112]FP, Q[32], A[3] we have stated that Filiation is a personal property. Now in Christ there is no other than the uncreated person or hypostasis, to Whom it belongs by nature to be the Son. But it has been said above (A[1], ad 2), that the sonship of adoption is a participated likeness of natural sonship: nor can a thing be said to participate in what it has essentially. Therefore Christ, Who is the natural Son of God, can nowise be called an adopted Son.

But according to those who suppose two persons or two hypostases or two supposita in Christ, no reason prevents Christ being called the adopted Son of God.

Reply to Objection 1: As sonship does not properly belong to the nature, so neither does adoption. Consequently, when it is said that "carnal humanity is adopted," the expression is metaphorical: and adoption is used to signify the union of human nature to the Person of the Son.

Reply to Objection 2: This comparison of Augustine is to be referred to the principle because, to wit, just as it is granted to any man without meriting it to be a Christian, so did it happen that this man without meriting it was Christ. But there is a difference on the part of the term: because by the grace of union Christ is the natural Son; whereas another man by habitual grace is an adopted son. Yet habitual grace in Christ does not make one who was not a son to be an adopted son, but is a certain effect of Filiation in the soul of Christ, according to Jn. 1:14: "We saw His glory . . . as it were of the Only-begotten of the Father; full of grace and truth."

Reply to Objection 3: To be a creature, as also to be subservient or subject to God, regards not only the person, but also the nature: but this cannot be said of sonship. Wherefore the comparison does not hold.

OF THE PREDESTINATION OF CHRIST (FOUR ARTICLES)

We shall now consider the predestination of Christ. Under this head there are four points of inquiry:

(1) Whether Christ was predestinated?

(2) Whether He was predestinated as man?

(3) Whether His predestination is the exemplar of ours?

(4) Whether it is the cause of our predestination?

Whether it is befitting that Christ should be predestinated?

Objection 1: It would seem unfitting that Christ should be predestinated. For the term of anyone's predestination seems to be the adoption of sons, according to Eph. 1:5: "Who hath predestinated us unto the adoption of children." But it is not befitting to Christ to be an adopted Son, as stated above ([4113]Q[23], A[4]). Therefore it is not fitting that Christ be predestinated.

Objection 2: Further, we may consider two things in Christ: His human nature and His person. But it cannot be said that Christ is predestinated by reason of His human nature; for this proposition is false---"The human nature is Son of God." In like manner neither by reason of the person; for this person is the Son of God, not by grace, but by nature: whereas predestination regards what is of grace, as stated in the [4114]FP, Q[23], AA[2],5. Therefore Christ was not predestinated to be the Son of God.

Objection 3: Further, just as that which has been made was not always, so also that which was predestinated; since predestination implies a certain antecedence. But, because Christ was always God and the Son of God, it cannot be said that that Man was "made the Son of God." Therefore, for a like reason, we ought not to say that Christ was "predestinated the Son of God."

On the contrary, The Apostle says, speaking of Christ (Rom. 1:4): "Who was predestinated the Son of God in power."

I answer that, As is clear from what has been said in the [4115]FP, Q[23], AA[1],2, predestination, in its proper sense, is a certain Divine preordination from eternity of those things which are to be done in time by the grace of God. Now, that man is God, and that God is man, is something done in time by God through the grace of union. Nor can it be said that God has not from eternity pre-ordained to do this in time: since it would follow that something would come anew into the Divine Mind. And we must needs admit that the union itself of natures in the Person of Christ falls under the eternal predestination of God. For this reason do we say that Christ was predestinated.

Reply to Objection 1: The Apostle there speaks of that predestination by which we are predestinated to be adopted sons. And just as Christ in a singular manner above all others is the natural Son of God, so in a singular manner is He predestinated.

Reply to Objection 2: As a gloss [*From St. Augustine, De Praed. Sanct. xv] says on Rom. 1:4, some understood that predestination to refer to the nature and not to the Person---that is to say, that on human nature was bestowed the grace of being united to the Son of God in unity of Person.

But in that case the phrase of the Apostle would be improper, for two reasons. First, for a general reason: for we do not speak of a person's nature, but of his person, as being predestinated: because to be predestinated is to be directed towards salvation, which belongs to a suppositum acting for the end of beatitude. Secondly, for a special reason. Because to be Son of God is not befitting to human nature; for this proposition is false: "The human nature is the Son of God": unless one were to force from it such an exposition as: "Who was predestinated the Son of God in power"---that is, "It was predestinated that the Human nature should be united to the Son of God in the Person."

Hence we must attribute predestination to the Person of Christ: not, indeed, in Himself or as subsisting in the Divine Nature, but as subsisting in the human nature. Wherefore the Apostle, after saying, "Who was made to Him of the seed of David according to the flesh," added, "Who was predestinated the Son of God in power": so as to give us to understand that in respect of His being of the seed of David according to the flesh, He was predestinated the Son of God in power. For although it is natural to that Person, considered in Himself, to be the Son of God in power, yet this is not natural to Him, considered in the human nature, in respect of which this befits Him according to the grace of union.

Reply to Objection 3: Origen commenting on Rom. 1:4 says that the true reading of this passage of the Apostle is: "Who was destined to be the Son of God in power"; so that no antecedence is implied. And so there would be no difficulty. Others refer the antecedence implied in the participle "predestinated," not to the fact of being the Son of God, but to the manifestation thereof, according to the customary way of speaking in Holy Scripture, by which things are said to take place when they are made known; so that the sense would be---"Christ was predestinated to be made known as the Son of God." But this is an improper signification of predestination. For a person is properly said to be predestinated by reason of his being directed to the end of beatitude: but the beatitude of Christ does not depend on our knowledge thereof.

It is therefore better to say that the antecedence implied in the participle "predestinated" is to be referred to the Person not in Himself, but by reason of the human nature: since, although that Person was the Son of God from eternity, it was not always true that one subsisting in human nature was the Son of God. Hence Augustine says (De Praedest. Sanct. xv): "Jesus was predestinated, so that He Who according to the flesh was to be the son of David, should be nevertheless Son of God in power."

Moreover, it must be observed that, although the participle "predestinated," just as this participle "made," implies antecedence, yet there is a difference. For "to be made" belongs to the thing in itself: whereas "to be predestinated" belongs to someone as being in the apprehension of one who pre-ordains. Now that which is the subject of a form or nature in reality, can be apprehended either as under that form or absolutely. And since it cannot be said absolutely of the Person of Christ that He began to be the Son of God, yet this is becoming to Him as understood or apprehended to exist in human nature, because at one time it began to be true that one existing in human nature was the Son of God; therefore this proposition---"Christ was predestinated the Son of God"---is truer than this---"Christ was made the Son of God."

Whether this proposition is false: "Christ as man was predestinated to be the Son of God"?

Objection 1: It would seem that this proposition is false: "Christ as man was predestinated to be the Son of God." For at some time a man is that which he was predestinated to be: since God's predestination does not fail. If, therefore, Christ as man was predestinated the Son of God, it seems to follow that as man He is the Son of God. But the latter is false. Therefore the former is false.

Objection 2: Further, what is befitting to Christ as man is befitting to any man; since He belongs to the same species as other men. If, therefore, Christ, as man, was predestinated the Son of God, it will follow that this is befitting to any other man. But the latter is false. Therefore the former is false.

Objection 3: Further, that is predestinated from eternity which is to take place at some time. But this proposition, "The Son of God was made man," is truer than this, "Man was made the Son of God." Therefore this proposition, "Christ, as the Son of God, was predestinated to be man," is truer than this, "Christ as Man was predestinated to be the Son of God."

On the contrary, Augustine (De Praedest. Sanct. xv) says: "Forasmuch as God the Son was made Man, we say that the Lord of Glory was predestinated."

I answer that, Two things may be considered in predestination. One on the part of eternal predestination itself: and in this respect it implies a certain antecedence in regard to that which comes under predestination. Secondly, predestination may be considered as regards its temporal effect, which is some gratuitous gift of God. Therefore from both points of view we must say that predestination is ascribed to Christ by reason of His human nature alone: for human nature was not always united to the Word; and by grace bestowed an it was it united in Person to the Son of God. Consequently, by reason of human nature alone can predestination be attributed to Christ. Wherefore Augustine says (De Praedest. Sanct. xv): "This human nature of ours was predestinated to be raised to so great, so lofty, so exalted a position, that it would be impossible to raise it higher." Now that is said to belong to anyone as man which belongs to him by reason of human nature. Consequently, we must say that "Christ, as Man, was predestinated the Son of God."

Reply to Objection 1: When we say, "Christ, as Man, was predestinated the Son of God," this qualification, "as Man," can be referred in two ways to the action signified by the participle. First, as regards what comes under predestination materially, and thus it is false. For the sense would be that it was predestinated that Christ, as Man, should be the Son of God. And in this sense the objection takes it.

Secondly, it may be referred to the very nature of the action itself: that is, forasmuch as predestination implies antecedence and gratuitous effect. And thus predestination belongs to Christ by reason of His human nature, as stated above. And in this sense He is said to be predestinated as Man.

Reply to Objection 2: Something may be befitting to a man by reason of human nature, in two ways. First, so that human nature be the cause thereof: thus risibility is befitting to Socrates by reason of human nature, being caused by its principles. In this manner predestination is not befitting either to Christ or to any other man, by reason of human nature. This is the sense of the objection. Secondly, a thing may be befitting to someone by reason of human nature, because human nature is susceptible of it. And in this sense we say that Christ was predestinated by reason of human nature; because predestination refers to the exaltation of human nature in Him, as stated above.

Reply to Objection 3: As Augustine says (Praedest. Sanct. xv): "The Word of God assumed Man to Himself in such a singular and ineffable manner that at the same time He may be truly and correctly called the Son of Man, because He assumed Men to Himself; and the Son of God, because it was the Only-begotten of God Who assumed human nature." Consequently, since this assumption comes under predestination by reason of its being gratuitous, we can say both that the Son of God was predestinated to be man, and that the Son of Man was predestinated to be the Son of God. But because grace was not bestowed on the Son of God that He might be man, but rather on human nature, that it might be united to the Son of God; it is more proper to say that "Christ, as Man, was predestinated to be the Son of God," than that, "Christ, as Son of God, was predestinated to be Man."

Whether Christ's predestination is the exemplar of ours?

Objection 1: It would seem that Christ's predestination is not the exemplar of ours. For the exemplar exists before the exemplate. But nothing exists before the eternal. Since, therefore, our predestination is eternal, it seems that Christ's predestination is not the exemplar of ours.

Objection 2: Further, the exemplar leads us to knowledge of the exemplate. But there was no need for God to be led from something else to knowledge of our predestination; since it is written (Rom. 8:29): "Whom He foreknew, He also predestinated." Therefore Christ's predestination is not the exemplar of ours.

Objection 3: Further, the exemplar is conformed to the exemplate. But Christ's predestination seems to be of a different nature from ours: because we are predestinated to the sonship of adoption, whereas Christ was predestinated "Son of God in power," as is written (Rom. 1:4). Therefore His predestination is not the exemplar of ours.

On the contrary, Augustine says (De Praedest. Sanct. xv): "The Saviour Himself, the Mediator of God and men, the Man Christ Jesus is the most splendid light of predestination and grace." Now He is called the light of predestination and grace, inasmuch as our predestination is made manifest by His predestination and grace; and this seems to pertain to the nature of an exemplar. Therefore Christ's predestination is the exemplar of ours.

I answer that, Predestination may be considered in two ways. First, on the part of the act of predestination: and thus Christ's predestination cannot be said to be the exemplar of ours: for in the same way and by the same eternal act God predestinated us and Christ.

Secondly, predestination may be considered on the part of that to which anyone is predestinated, and this is the term and effect of predestination. In this sense Christ's predestination is the exemplar of ours, and this in two ways. First, in respect of the good to which we are predestinated: for He was predestinated to be the natural Son of God, whereas we are predestinated to the adoption of sons, which is a participated likeness of natural sonship. Whence it is written (Rom. 8:29): "Whom He foreknew, He also predestinated to be made conformable to the image of His Son." Secondly, in respect of the manner of obtaining this good---that is, by grace. This is most manifest in Christ; because human nature in Him, without any antecedent merits, was united to the Son of God: and of the fulness of His grace we all have received, as it is written (Jn. 1:16).

Reply to Objection 1: This argument considers the aforesaid act of the predestinator.

The same is to be said of the second objection.

Reply to Objection 3: The exemplate need not be conformed to the exemplar in all respects: it is sufficient that it imitate it in some.

Whether Christ's predestination is the cause of ours?

Objection 1: It would seem that Christ's predestination is not the cause of ours. For that which is eternal has no cause. But our predestination is eternal. Therefore Christ's predestination is not the cause of ours.

Objection 2: Further, that which depends on the simple will of God has no other cause but God's will. Now, our predestination depends on the simple will of God, for it is written (Eph. 1:11): "Being predestinated according to the purpose of Him, Who worketh all things according to the counsel of His will." Therefore Christ's predestination is not the cause of ours.

Objection 3: Further, if the cause be taken away, the effect is also taken away. But if we take away Christ's predestination, ours is not taken away; since even if the Son of God were not incarnate, our salvation might yet have been achieved in a different manner, as Augustine says (De Trin. xiii, 10). Therefore Christ's predestination is. not the cause of ours.

On the contrary, It is written (Eph. 1:5): "(Who) hath predestinated us unto the adoption of children through Jesus Christ."

I answer that, if we consider predestination on the part of the very act of predestinating, then Christ's predestination is not the cause of ours; because by one and the same act God predestinated both Christ and us. But if we consider predestination on the part of its term, thus Christ's predestination is the cause of ours: for God, by predestinating from eternity, so decreed our salvation, that it should be achieved through Jesus Christ. For eternal predestination covers not only that which is to be accomplished in time, but also the mode and order in which it is to be accomplished in time.

Replies OBJ 1 and 2: These arguments consider predestination on the part of the act of predestinating.

Reply to Objection 3: If Christ were not to have been incarnate, God would have decreed men's salvation by other means. But since He decreed the Incarnation of Christ, He decreed at the same time that He should be the cause of our salvation.

Day 266

OF THE ADORATION OF CHRIST (SIX ARTICLES)

We have now to consider things pertaining to Christ in reference to us; and first, the adoration of Christ, by which we adore Him; secondly, we must consider how He is our Mediator with God.

Under the first head there are six points of inquiry:

(1) Whether Christ's Godhead and humanity are to be adored with one and the same adoration?

(2) Whether His flesh is to be adored with the adoration of "latria"?

(3) Whether the adoration of "latria" is to be given to the image of Christ?

(4) Whether "latria" is to be given to the Cross of Christ?

(5) Whether to His Mother?

(6) Concerning the adoration of the relics of Saints.

Whether Christ's humanity and Godhead are to be adored with the same adoration?

Objection 1: It would seem that Christ's humanity and Godhead are not to be adored with the same adoration. For Christ's Godhead is to be adored, as being common to Father and Son; wherefore it is written (Jn. 5:23): "That all may honor the Son, as they honor the Father." But Christ's humanity is not common to Him and the Father. Therefore Christ's humanity and Godhead are not to be adored with the same adoration.

Objection 2: Further, honor is properly "the reward of virtue," as the Philosopher says (Ethic. iv, 3). But virtue merits its reward by action. Since, therefore, in Christ the action of the Divine Nature is distinct from that of the human nature, as stated above ([4116]Q[19], A[1]), it seems that Christ's humanity is to be adored with a different adoration from that which is given to His Godhead.

Objection 3: Further, if the soul of Christ were not united to the Word, it would have been worthy of veneration on account of the excellence of its wisdom and grace. But by being united to the Word it lost nothing of its worthiness. Therefore His human nature should receive a certain veneration proper thereto, besides the veneration which is given to His Godhead.

On the contrary, We read in the chapters of the Fifth Council [*Second Council of Constantinople, coll. viii, can. 9]: "If anyone say that Christ is adored in two natures, so as to introduce two distinct adorations, and does not adore God the Word made flesh with the one and the same adoration as His flesh, as the Church has handed down from the beginning; let such a one be anathema."

I answer that, We may consider two things in a person to whom honor is given: the person himself, and the cause of his being honored. Now properly speaking honor is given to a subsistent thing in its entirety: for we do not speak of honoring a man's hand, but the man himself. And if at any time it happen that we speak of honoring a man's hand or foot, it is not by reason of these members being honored of themselves: but by reason of the whole being honored in them. In this way a man may be honored even in something external; for instance in his vesture, his image, or his messenger.

The cause of honor is that by reason of which the person honored has a certain excellence. for honor is reverence given to something on account of its excellence, as stated in the [4117]SS, Q[103], A[1]. If therefore in one man there are several causes of honor, for instance, rank, knowledge, and virtue, the honor given to him will be one in respect of the person honored, but several in respect of the causes of honor: for it is the man that is honored, both on account of knowledge and by reason of his virtue.

Since, therefore, in Christ there is but one Person of the Divine and human natures, and one hypostasis, and one suppositum, He is given one adoration and one honor on the part of the Person adored: but on the part of the cause for which He is honored, we can say that there are several adorations, for instance that He receives one honor on account of His uncreated knowledge, and another on account of His created knowledge.

But if it be said that there are several persons or hypostases in Christ, it would follow that there would be, absolutely speaking, several adorations. And this is what is condemned in the Councils. For it is written in the chapters of Cyril [*Council of Ephesus, Part I, ch. 26]: "If anyone dare to say that the man assumed should be adored besides the Divine Word, as though these were distinct persons; and does not rather honor the Emmanuel with one single adoration, inasmuch as the Word was made flesh; let him be anathema."

Reply to Objection 1: In the Trinity there are three Who are honored, but only one cause of honor. In the mystery of the Incarnation it is the reverse: and therefore only one honor is given to the Trinity and only one to Christ, but in a different way.

Reply to Objection 2: Operation is not the object but the motive of honor. And therefore there being two operations in Christ proves, not two adorations, but two causes of adoration.

Reply to Objection 3: If the soul of Christ were not united to the Word of God, it would be the principal thing in that Man. Wherefore honor would be due to it principally, since man is that which is principal in him [*Cf. Ethic. ix, 8]. But since Christ's soul is united to a Person of greater dignity, to that Person is honor principally due to Whom Christ's soul is united. Nor is the dignity of Christ's soul hereby diminished, but rather increased, as stated above ([4118]Q[2], A[2], ad 2).

Whether Christ's humanity should be adored with the adoration of "latria"?

Objection 1: It would seem that Christ's soul should not be adored with the adoration of "latria." For on the words of Ps. 98:5, "Adore His foot-stool for it is holy," a gloss says: "The flesh assumed by the Word of God is rightly adored by us: for no one partakes spiritually of His flesh unless he first adore it; but not indeed with the adoration called 'latria,' which is due to the Creator alone." Now the flesh is part of the humanity. Therefore Christ's humanity is not to be adored with the adoration of "latria."

Objection 2: Further, the worship of "latria" is not to be given to any creature: since for this reason were the Gentiles reproved, that they "worshiped and served the creature," as it is written (Rom. 1:25). But Christ's humanity is a creature. Therefore it should not be adored with the adoration of "latria."

Objection 3: Further, the adoration of "latria" is due to God in recognition of His supreme dominion, according to Dt. 6:13: "Thou shalt adore [Vulg.: 'fear'; cf. Mat. 4:10] the Lord thy God, and shalt serve Him only." But Christ as man is less than the Father. Therefore His humanity is not to be adored with the adoration of "latria."

On the contrary, Damascene says (De Fide Orth. iv, 3): "On account of the incarnation of the Divine Word, we adore the flesh of Christ not for its own sake, but because the Word of God is united thereto in person." And on Ps. 98:5, "Adore His foot-stool," a gloss says: "He who adores the body of Christ, regards not the earth, but rather Him whose foot-stool it is, in Whose honor he adores the foot-stool." But the incarnate Word is adored with the adoration of "latria." Therefore also His body or His humanity.

I answer that, As stated above [4119](A[1]) adoration is due to the subsisting hypostasis: yet the reason for honoring may be something non-subsistent, on account of which the person, in whom it is, is honored. And so the adoration of Christ's humanity may be understood in two ways. First, so that the humanity is the thing adored: and thus to adore the flesh of Christ is nothing else than to adore the incarnate Word of God: just as to adore a King's robe is nothing else than to adore a robed King. And in this sense the adoration of Christ's humanity is the adoration of "latria." Secondly, the adoration of Christ's humanity may be taken as given by reason of its being perfected with every gift of grace. And so in this sense the adoration of Christ's humanity is the adoration not of "latria" but of "dulia." So that one and the same Person of Christ is adored with "latria" on account of His Divinity, and with "dulia" on account of His perfect humanity.

Nor is this unfitting. For the honor of "latria" is due to God the Father Himself on account of His Godhead; and the honor of "dulia" on account of the dominion by which He rules over creatures. Wherefore on Ps. 7:1, "O Lord my God, in Thee have I hoped," a gloss says: "Lord of all by power, to Whom 'dulia' is due: God of all by creation, to Whom 'latria' is due."

Reply to Objection 1: That gloss is not to be understood as though the flesh of Christ were adored separately from its Godhead: for this could happen only, if there were one hypostasis of God, and another of man. But since, as Damascene says (De Fide Orth. iv, 3): "If by a subtle distinction you divide what is seen from what is understood, it cannot be adored because it is a creature"---that is, with adoration of "latria." And then thus understood as distinct from the Word of God, it should be adored with the adoration of "dulia"; not any kind of "dulia," such as is given to other creatures, but with a certain higher adoration, which is called "hyperdulia."

Hence appear the answers to the second and third objections. Because the adoration of "latria" is not given to Christ's humanity in respect of itself; but in respect of the Godhead to which it is united, by reason of which Christ is not less than the Father.

Whether the image of Christ should be adored with the adoration of "latria"?

Objection 1: It would seem that Christ's image should not be adored with the adoration of "latria." For it is written (Ex. 20:4): "Thou shalt not make to thyself a graven thing, nor the likeness of anything." But no adoration should be given against the commandment of God. Therefore Christ's image should not be adored with the adoration of "latria."

Objection 2: Further, we should have nothing in common with the works of the Gentiles, as the Apostle says (Eph. 5:11). But the Gentiles are reproached principally for that "they changed the glory of the incorruptible God into the likeness of the image of a corruptible man," as is written (Rom. 1:23). Therefore Christ's image is not to be adored with the adoration of "latria."

Objection 3: Further, to Christ the adoration of "latria" is due by reason of His Godhead, not of His humanity. But the adoration of "latria" is not due to the image of His Godhead, which is imprinted on the rational soul. Much less, therefore, is it due to the material image which represents the humanity of Christ Himself.

Objection 4: Further, it seems that nothing should be done in the Divine worship that is not instituted by God; wherefore the Apostle (1 Cor. 11:23) when about to lay down the doctrine of the sacrifice of the Church, says: "I have received of the Lord that which also I delivered unto you." But Scripture does not lay down anything concerning the adoration of images. Therefore Christ's image is not to be adored with the adoration of "latria."

On the contrary, Damascene (De Fide Orth. iv, 16) quotes Basil as saying: "The honor given to an image reaches to the prototype," i.e. the exemplar. But the exemplar itself---namely, Christ---is to be adored with the adoration of "latria"; therefore also His image.

I answer that, As the Philosopher says (De Memor. et Remin. i), there is a twofold movement of the mind towards an image: one indeed towards the image itself as a certain thing; another, towards the image in so far as it is the image of something else. And between these movements there is this difference; that the former, by which one is moved towards an image as a certain thing, is different from the movement towards the thing: whereas the latter movement, which is towards the image as an image, is one and the same as that which is towards the thing. Thus therefore we must say that no reverence is shown to Christ's image, as a thing---for instance, carved or painted wood: because reverence is not due save to a rational creature. It follow therefore that reverence should be shown to it, in so far only as it is an image. Consequently the same reverence should be shown to Christ's image as to Christ Himself. Since, therefore, Christ is adored with the adoration of "latria," it follows that His image should be adored with the adoration of "latria."

Reply to Objection 1: This commandment does not forbid the making of any graven thing or likeness, but the making thereof for the purpose of adoration, wherefore it is added: "Thou shalt not adore them nor serve them." And because, as stated above, the movement towards the image is the same as the movement towards the thing, adoration thereof is forbidden in the same way as adoration of the thing whose image it is. Wherefore in the passage quoted we are to understand the prohibition to adore those images which the Gentiles made for the purpose of venerating their own gods, i.e. the demons, and so it is premised: "Thou shalt not have strange gods before Me." But no corporeal image could be raised to the true God Himself, since He is incorporeal; because, as Damascene observes (De Fide Orth. iv, 16): "It is the highest absurdity and impiety to fashion a figure of what is Divine." But because in the New Testament God was made man, He can be adored in His corporeal image.

Reply to Objection 2: The Apostle forbids us to have anything in common with the "unfruitful works" of the Gentiles, but not with their useful works. Now the adoration of images must be numbered among the unfruitful works in two respects. First, because some of the Gentiles used to adore the images themselves, as things, believing that there was something Divine therein, on account of the answers which the demons used to give in them, and on account of other such like wonderful effects. Secondly on account of the things of which they were images; for they set up images to certain creatures, to whom in these images they gave the veneration of "latria." Whereas we give the adoration of "latria" to the image of Christ, Who is true God, not for the sake of the image, but for the sake of the thing whose image it is, as stated above.

Reply to Objection 3: Reverence is due to the rational creature for its own sake. Consequently, if the adoration of "latria" were shown to the rational creature in which this image is, there might be an occasion of error---namely, lest the movement of adoration might stop short at the man, as a thing, and not be carried on to God, Whose image he is. This cannot happen in the case of a graven or painted image in insensible material.

Reply to Objection 4: The Apostles, led by the inward instinct of the Holy Ghost, handed down to the churches certain instructions which they did not put in writing, but which have been ordained, in accordance with the observance of the Church as practiced by the faithful as time went on. Wherefore the Apostle says (2 Thess. 2:14): "Stand fast; and hold the traditions which you have learned, whether by word"---that is by word of mouth---"or by our epistle"---that is by word put into writing. Among these traditions is the worship of Christ's image. Wherefore it is said that Blessed Luke painted the image of Christ, which is in Rome.

Whether Christ's cross should be worshipped with the adoration of "latria"?

Objection 1: It would seem that Christ's cross should not be worshiped with the adoration of "latria." For no dutiful son honors that which dishonors his father, as the scourge with which he was scourged, or the gibbet on which he was hanged; rather does he abhor it. Now Christ underwent the most shameful death on the cross; according to Wis. 2:20: "Let us condemn Him to a most shameful death." Therefore we should not venerate the cross but rather we should abhor it.

Objection 2: Further, Christ's humanity is worshiped with the adoration of "latria," inasmuch as it is united to the Son of God in Person. But this cannot be said of the cross. Therefore Christ's cross should not be worshiped with the adoration of "latria."

Objection 3: Further, as Christ's cross was the instrument of His passion and death, so were also many other things, for instance, the nails, the crown, the lance; yet to these we do not show the worship of "latria." It seems, therefore, that Christ's cross should not be worshiped with the adoration of "latria."

On the contrary, We show the worship of "latria" to that in which we place our hope of salvation. But we place our hope in Christ's cross, for the Church sings:

"Dear Cross, best hope o'er all beside,

That cheers the solemn passion-tide:
Give to the just increase of grace,
Give to each contrite sinner peace."
[*Hymn Vexilla Regis: translation of Father Aylward, O.P.]
Therefore Christ's cross should be worshiped with the adoration of "latria."

I answer that, As stated above [4120](A[3]), honor or reverence is due to a rational creature only; while to an insensible creature, no honor or reverence is due save by reason of a rational nature. And this in two ways. First, inasmuch as it represents a rational nature: secondly, inasmuch as it is united to it in any way whatsoever. In the first way men are wont to venerate the king's image; in the second way, his robe. And both are venerated by men with the same veneration as they show to the king.

If, therefore, we speak of the cross itself on which Christ was crucified, it is to be venerated by us in both ways---namely, in one way in so far as it represents to us the figure of Christ extended thereon; in the other way, from its contact with the limbs of Christ, and from its being saturated with His blood. Wherefore in each way it is worshiped with the same adoration as Christ, viz. the adoration of "latria." And for this reason also we speak to the cross and pray to it, as to the Crucified Himself. But if we speak of the effigy of Christ's cross in any other material whatever---for instance, in stone or wood, silver or gold---thus we venerate the cross merely as Christ's image, which we worship with the adoration of "latria," as stated above [4121](A[3]).

Reply to Objection 1: If in Christ's cross we consider the point of view and intention of those who did not believe in Him, it will appear as His shame: but if we consider its effect, which is our salvation, it will appear as endowed with Divine power, by which it triumphed over the enemy, according to Col. 2:14,15: "He hath taken the same out of the way, fastening it to the cross, and despoiling the principalities and powers, He hath exposed them confidently, in open show, triumphing over them in Himself." Wherefore the Apostle says (1 Cor. 1:18): "The Word of the cross to them indeed that perish is foolishness; but to them that are saved---that is, to us---it is the power of God."

Reply to Objection 2: Although Christ's cross was not united to the Word of God in Person, yet it was united to Him in some other way, viz. by representation and contact. And for this sole reason reverence is shown to it.

Reply to Objection 3: By reason of the contact of Christ's limbs we worship not only the cross, but all that belongs to Christ. Wherefore Damascene says (De Fide Orth. iv, 11): "The precious wood, as having been sanctified by the contact of His holy body and blood, should be meetly worshiped; as also His nails, His lance, and His sacred dwelling-places, such as the manger, the cave and so forth." Yet these very things do not represent Christ's image as the cross does, which is called "the Sign of the Son of Man" that "will appear in heaven," as it is written (Mat. 24:30). Wherefore the angel said to the women (Mk. 16:6): "You seek Jesus of Nazareth, Who was crucified": he said not "pierced," but "crucified." For this reason we worship the image of Christ's cross in any material, but not the image of the nails or of any such thing.

Whether the Mother of God should be worshipped with the adoration of "latria"?

Objection 1: It would seem that the Mother of God is to be worshiped with the adoration of "latria." For it seems that the same honor is due to the king's mother as to the king: whence it is written (3 Kings 2:19) that "a throne was set for the king's mother, and she sat on His right hand." Moreover, Augustine [*Sermon on the Assumption, work of an anonymous author] says: "It is right that the throne of God, the resting-place of the Lord of Heaven, the abode of Christ, should be there where He is Himself." But Christ is worshiped with the adoration of "latria." Therefore His Mother also should be.

Objection 2: Further, Damascene says (De Fide Orth. iv, 16): "The honor of the Mother reflects on the Son." But the Son is worshiped with the adoration of "latria." Therefore the Mother also.

Objection 3: Further, Christ's Mother is more akin to Him than the cross. But the cross is worshiped with the adoration of "latria." Therefore also His Mother is to be worshiped with the same adoration.

On the contrary, The Mother of God is a mere creature. Therefore the worship of "latria" is not due to her.

I answer that, Since "latria" is due to God alone, it is not due to a creature so far as we venerate a creature for its own sake. For though insensible creatures are not capable of being venerated for their own sake, yet the rational creature is capable of being venerated for its own sake. Consequently the worship of "latria" is not due to any mere rational creature for its own sake. Since, therefore, the Blessed Virgin is a mere rational creature, the worship of "latria" is not due to her, but only that of "dulia": but in a higher degree than to other creatures, inasmuch as she is the Mother of God. For this reason we say that not any kind of "dulia" is due to her, but "hyperdulia."

Reply to Objection 1: The honor due to the king's mother is not equal to the honor which is due to the king: but is somewhat like it, by reason of a certain excellence on her part. This is what is meant by the authorities quoted.

Reply to Objection 2: The honor given to the Mother reflects on her Son, because the Mother is to be honored for her Son's sake. But not in the same way as honor given to an image reflects on its exemplar: because the image itself, considered as a thing, is not to be venerated in any way at all.

Reply to Objection 3: The cross, considered in itself, is not an object of veneration, as stated above ([4122]AA[4],5). But the Blessed Virgin is in herself an object of veneration. Hence there is no comparison.

Whether any kind of worship is due to the relics of the saints?

Objection 1: It would seem that the relics of the saints are not to be worshiped at all. For we should avoid doing what may be the occasion of error. But to worship the relics of the dead seems to savor of the error of the Gentiles, who gave honor to dead men. Therefore the relics of the saints are not to be honored.

Objection 2: Further, it seems absurd to venerate what is insensible. But the relics of the saints are insensible. Therefore it is absurd to venerate them.

Objection 3: Further, a dead body is not of the same species as a living body: consequently it does not seem to be identical with it. Therefore, after a saint's death, it seems that his body should not be worshiped.

On the contrary, It is written (De Eccles. Dogm. xl): "We believe that the bodies of the saints, above all the relics of the blessed martyrs, as being the members of Christ, should be worshiped in all sincerity": and further on: "If anyone holds a contrary opinion, he is not accounted a Christian, but a follower of Eunomius and Vigilantius."

I answer that, As Augustine says (De Civ. Dei i, 13): "If a father's coat or ring, or anything else of that kind, is so much more cherished by his children, as love for one's parents is greater, in no way are the bodies themselves to be despised, which are much more intimately and closely united to us than any garment; for they belong to man's very nature." It is clear from this that he who has a certain affection for anyone, venerates whatever of his is left after his death, not only his body and the parts thereof, but even external things, such as his clothes, and such like. Now it is manifest that we should show honor to the saints of God, as being members of Christ, the children and friends of God, and our intercessors. Wherefore in memory of them we ought to honor any relics of theirs in a fitting manner: principally their bodies, which were temples, and organs of the Holy Ghost dwelling and operating in them, and are destined to be likened to the body of Christ by the glory of the Resurrection. Hence God Himself fittingly honors such relics by working miracles at their presence.

Reply to Objection 1: This was the argument of Vigilantius, whose words are quoted by Jerome in the book he wrote against him (ch. ii) as follows: "We see something like a pagan rite introduced under pretext of religion; they worship with kisses I know not what tiny heap of dust in a mean vase surrounded with precious linen." To him Jerome replies (Ep. ad Ripar. cix): "We do not adore, I will not say the relics of the martyrs, but either the sun or the moon or even the angels"---that is to say, with the worship of "latria." "But we honor the martyrs' relics, so that thereby we give honor to Him Whose martyrs [*The original meaning of the word 'martyr,' i.e. the Greek {martys} is 'a witness'] they are: we honor the servants, that the honor shown to them may reflect on their Master." Consequently, by honoring the martyrs' relics we do not fall into the error of the Gentiles, who gave the worship of "latria" to dead men.

Reply to Objection 2: We worship that insensible body, not for its own sake, but for the sake of the soul, which was once united thereto, and now enjoys God; and for God's sake, whose ministers the saints were.

Reply to Objection 3: The dead body of a saint is not identical with that which the saint had during life, on account of the difference of form, viz. the soul: but it is the same by identity of matter, which is destined to be reunited to its form.

OF CHRIST AS CALLED THE MEDIATOR OF GOD AND MAN (TWO ARTICLES)

We have now to consider how Christ is called the Mediator of God and man, and under this head there are two points of inquiry:

(1) Whether it is proper to Christ to be the Mediator of God and man?

(2) Whether this belongs to Him by reason of His human nature?

Whether it is proper to Christ to be the Mediator of God and man?

Objection 1: It would seem that it is not proper to Christ to be the Mediator of God and man. For a priest and a prophet seem to be mediators between God and man, according to Dt. 5:5: "I was the mediator and stood between God [Vulg.: 'the Lord'] and you at that time." But it is not proper to Christ to be a priest and a prophet. Neither, therefore, is it proper to Him to be Mediator.

Objection 2: Further, that which is fitting to angels, both good and bad, cannot be said to be proper to Christ. But to be between God and man is fitting to the good angels, as Dionysius says (Div. Nom. iv). It is also fitting to the bad angels---that is, the demons: for they have something in common with God---namely, "immortality"; and something they have in common with men---namely, "passibility of soul" and consequently unhappiness; as appears from what Augustine says (De Civ. Dei ix, 13,15). Therefore it is not proper to Christ to be a Mediator of God and man.

Objection 3: Further, it belongs to the office of Mediator to beseech one of those, between whom he mediates, for the other. But the Holy Ghost, as it is written (Rom. 8:26), "asketh" God "for us with unspeakable groanings." Therefore the Holy Ghost is a Mediator between God and man. Therefore this is not proper to Christ.

On the contrary, It is written (1 Tim. 2:5): "There is . . . one Mediator of God and man, the man Christ Jesus."

I answer that, Properly speaking, the office of a mediator is to join together and unite those between whom he mediates: for extremes are united in the mean [medio]. Now to unite men to God perfectively belongs to Christ, through Whom men are reconciled to God, according to 2 Cor. 5:19: "God was in Christ reconciling the world to Himself." And, consequently, Christ alone is the perfect Mediator of God and men, inasmuch as, by His death, He reconciled the human race to God. Hence the Apostle, after saying, "Mediator of God and man, the man Christ Jesus," added: "Who gave Himself a redemption for all."

However, nothing hinders certain others from being called mediators, in some respect, between God and man, forasmuch as they cooperate in uniting men to God, dispositively or ministerially.

Reply to Objection 1: The prophets and priests of the Old Law were called mediators between God and man, dispositively and ministerially: inasmuch as they foretold and foreshadowed the true and perfect Mediator of God and men. As to the priests of the New Law, they may be called mediators of God and men, inasmuch as they are the ministers of the true Mediator by administering, in His stead, the saving sacraments to men.

Reply to Objection 2: The good angels, as Augustine says (De Civ. Dei ix, 13), cannot rightly be called mediators between God and men. "For since, in common with God, they have both beatitude and immortality, and none of these things in common with unhappy and mortal man, how much rather are they not aloof from men and akin to God, than established between them?" Dionysius, however, says that they do occupy a middle place, because, in the order of nature, they are established below God and above man. Moreover, they fulfill the office of mediator, not indeed principally and perfectively, but ministerially and dispositively: whence (Mat. 4:11) it is said that "angels came and ministered unto Him"---namely, Christ. As to the demons, it is true that they have immortality in common with God, and unhappiness in common with men. "Hence for this purpose does the immortal and unhappy demon intervene, in order that he may hinder men from passing to a happy immortality," and may allure them to an unhappy immortality. Whence he is like "an evil mediator, who separates friends" [*Augustine, De Civ. Dei xv].

But Christ had beatitude in common with God, mortality in common with men. Hence "for this purpose did He intervene, that having fulfilled the span of His mortality, He might from dead men make immortal---which He showed in Himself by rising again; and that He might confer beatitude on those who were deprived of it---for which reason He never forsook us." Wherefore He is "the good Mediator, Who reconciles enemies" (De Civ. Dei xv).

Reply to Objection 3: Since the Holy Ghost is in everything equal to God, He cannot be said to be between, or a Mediator of, God and men: but Christ alone, Who, though equal to the Father in His Godhead, yet is less than the Father in His human nature, as stated above ([4123]Q[20], A[1]). Hence on Gal. 3:20, "Christ is a Mediator [Vulg.: 'Now a mediator is not of one, but God is one']," the gloss says: "Not the Father nor the Holy Ghost." The Holy Ghost, however, is said "to ask for us," because He makes us ask.

Whether Christ, is the Mediator of God and men?

Objection 1: It would seem that Christ is not, as man, the Mediator of God and men. For Augustine says (Contra Felic. x): "One is the Person of Christ: lest there be not one Christ, not one substance; lest, the office of Mediator being denied, He be called the Son either of God alone, or merely the Son of a man." But He is the Son of God and man, not as man, but as at the same time God and man. Therefore neither should we say that, as man alone, He is Mediator of God and man.

Objection 2: Further, just as Christ, as God, has a common nature with the Father and the Holy Ghost; so, as man, He has a common nature with men. But for the reason that, as God, He has the same nature as the Father and the Holy Ghost, He cannot be called Mediator, as God: for on 1 Tim. 2:5, "Mediator of God and man," a gloss says: "As the Word, He is not a Mediator, because He is equal to God, and God 'with God,' and at the same time one God." Therefore neither, as man, can He be called Mediator, on account of His having the same nature as men.

Objection 3: Further, Christ is called Mediator, inasmuch as He reconciled us to God: and this He did by taking away sin, which separated us from God. But to take away sin belongs to Christ, not as man, but as God. Therefore Christ is our Mediator, not as man, but as God.

On the contrary, Augustine says (De Civ. Dei ix, 15): "Not because He is the Word, is Christ Mediator, since He Who is supremely immortal and supremely happy is far from us unhappy mortals; but He is Mediator, as man."

I answer that, We may consider two things in a mediator: first, that he is a mean; secondly, that he unites others. Now it is of the nature of a mean to be distant from each extreme: while it unites by communicating to one that which belongs to the other. Now neither of these can be applied to Christ as God, but only as man. For, as God, He does not differ from the Father and the Holy Ghost in nature and power of dominion: nor have the Father and the Holy Ghost anything that the Son has not, so that He be able to communicate to others something belonging to the Father or the Holy Ghost, as though it were belonging to others than Himself. But both can be applied to Him as man. Because, as man, He is distant both from God, by nature, and from man by dignity of both grace and glory. Again, it belongs to Him, as man, to unite men to God, by communicating to men both precepts and gifts, and by offering satisfaction and prayers to God for men. And therefore He is most truly called Mediator, as man.

Reply to Objection 1: If we take the Divine Nature from Christ, we consequently take from Him the singular fulness of grace, which belongs to Him as the Only-begotten of the Father, as it is written (Jn. 1:14). From which fulness it resulted that He was established over all men, and approached nearer to God.

Reply to Objection 2: Christ, as God, is in all things equal to the Father. But even in the human nature He is above all men. Therefore, as man, He can be Mediator, but not as God.

Reply to Objection 3: Although it belongs to Christ as God to take away sin authoritatively, yet it belongs to Him, as man, to satisfy for the sin of the human race. And in this sense He is called the Mediator of God and men.

ST. THOMAS AND THE IMMACULATE CONCEPTION (EDITORIAL NOTE)

The privilege of the Virgin-Mother of God and the supreme prerogative of her Son may be seen from the following diagram:

THE LAW AND THE COURSE OF ORIGINAL SIN UNDER THE LAW . . . . . all descendants from Adam . . . . . spring from Adam materially and seminally . . . . . the body lies (not under the guilty, but) under the effects of original sin . . . . . the stricken body dispositively causes the soul to contract the guilt of original sin . . . . . all contract both debt and stain . . . . . all need a Redeemer to destroy the stain contracted PARTIALLY EXEMPT FROM THE LAW; PRIVILEGE OF IMMACULATE CONCEPTION . . . . . the Blessed Virgin . . . . . springs from Adam materially and seminally . . . . . the body lies (not under the guilt, but) under the effects of original sin . . . . . the stricken body would have dispositively caused the soul to contract the guilt of original sin . . . . . the soul at the moment of union with the body was prevented by the infusion of grace from contracting sin . . . . . Mary contracted the debt, but not the stain . . . . . Mary needed a Redeemer to prevent her from contracting the stain WHOLLY EXEMPT FROM THE LAW; MIRACULOUS CONCEPTION . . . . . Our Blessed Lord . . . . . springs from Adam materially, not seminally ([4124]Q[31], A[1]) . . . . . His body lay under neither guilt nor effects of original sin . . . . . the body being entirely free, could not transmit the stain to His soul . . . . . no preventive grace needed . . . . . Jesus Christ contracted neither debt nor stain . . . . . Jesus Christ is not redeemed, but the Redeemer

It will thus be seen how accurately St. Thomas speaks of the "flesh" or body of our Blessed Lady. For it should be remembered that, according to St. Thomas, the human body is animated in succession by (1) a vegetative, (2) a sensitive, and (3) a rational soul. Hence his assertion that "the flesh of the Blessed Virgin was conceived in original sin" ([4125]Q[14], A[3], ad 1) means that the body of the Blessed Virgin, being descended from Adam both materially and seminally, contracted the bodily defects which are conveyed by seminal generation, and are the results of the privation of original justice ([4126]Q[69], A[4], ad 3). Before animation, therefore the body of the Blessed Virgin would not be infected with the guilt of original sin, because privation of grace can only be in that which is the subject of grace, viz. the rational soul. Nevertheless, before animation the body of the Blessed Virgin, being seminally descended from Adam, was such that it would have been the means of transmitting the taint of original sin to the rational soul at the very first instant of animation, unless the grace of the Redeemer intervened and sanctified her soul "in that self-same instant," thus redeeming her and preventing her from contracting the guilt of original sin.

Why, then, does St. Thomas say that because the Blessed Virgin was not sanctified before animation, therefore she could be sanctified only after animation?

Such a conclusion would hold if it were a question of the order of Nature: "a thing must be before it is such [prius est esse quam esse tale]"; and therefore the soul must be, before it is sanctified. But if St. Thomas held for a posteriority of time, no matter how short, we ask how it was that he did not perceive the fallacy of the argument, since it might be neither before nor after, but in the very instant of, animation.

The question is answered thus: St. Thomas as a Doctor of the Church and in matters which were not then "de fide," is a witness to the expression of the faith of his time. Hence his line of argument coincides with, because it follows, that of St. Bernard, Peter Lombard, Alexander of Hales, Albert the Great, St. Bonaventure. It was not likely that St. Thomas would differ from the great masters of his time, who failed to understand that the grace of redemption might at the same time be one of preservation and prevention. Nor is it likely that St. Thomas had any reliable information about the movement* in progress at that time towards a belief in the Immaculate Conception. [*Principally in England, where, owing to the influence of St. Anselm (1109), the doctrine was maintained by Eadmer (1137). Nicolas of St. Albans (1175), Osbert of Clare (1170), Robert Grosseteste, Bishop of Lincoln (1253), William of Ware (1300), who was the master of Duns Scotus (1308)]. No doubt he knew something of it, but the names of its promoters would have weighed little with him as against those of Bernard, Albert, Peter, Alexander, and Bonaventure. And it must not be forgotten that among those who upheld the doctrine of the Immaculate Conception, not a few ascribed the privilege as being absolute and not one of preservation and Redemption. Hence it is that St. Thomas insists on two things: (1) that the Mother of God was redeemed, and (2) that the grace of her sanctification was a grace of preservation. And, be it remarked in conclusion, these two points, so much insisted on by St. Thomas, are at the very basis of the Catholic doctrine of the Immaculate Conception.

Day 267

OF THE SANCTIFICATION OF THE BLESSED VIRGIN (SIX ARTICLES)

After the foregoing treatise of the union of God and man and the consequences thereof, it remains for us to consider what things the Incarnate Son of God did or suffered in the human nature united to Him. This consideration will be fourfold. For we shall consider: (1) Those things that relate to His coming into the world; (2) Those things that relate to the course of His life in this world; (3) His departure from this world; (4) Those things that concern His exaltation after this life.

The first of these offers four points of consideration: (1) The Conception of Christ; (2) His Birth; (3) His Circumcision; (4) His Baptism. Concerning His Conception there are some points to be considered: (1) As to the Mother who conceived Him; (2) as to the mode of His Conception; (3) as to the perfection of the offspring conceived.

On the part of the Mother four points offer themselves to our consideration: (1) Her sanctification. (2) her virginity; (3) her espousals; (4) her annunciation, or preparation for conception.

Concerning the first there are six points of inquiry:

(1) Whether the Blessed Virgin, Mother of God, was sanctified before her birth from the womb?
(2) Whether she was sanctified before animation?
(3) Whether in virtue of this sanctification the fomes of sin was entirely taken away from her?
(4) Whether the result of this sanctification was that she never sinned?
(5) Whether in virtue of this sanctification she received the fulness of grace?
(6) Whether it was proper to her to be thus sanctified?

Whether the Blessed Virgin was sanctified before her birth from the womb?

Objection 1: It would seem that the Blessed Virgin was not sanctified before her birth from the womb. For the Apostle says (1 Cor. 15:46): "That was not first which is spiritual but that which is natural; afterwards that which is spiritual." But by sanctifying grace man is born spiritually into a son of God according to Jn. 1:13: "(who) are born of God." But birth from the womb is a natural birth. Therefore the Blessed Virgin was not sanctified before her birth from the womb.

Objection 2: Further, Augustine says (Ep. ad Dardan.): "The sanctification, by which we become temples of God, is only of those who are born again." But no one is born again, who was not born previously. Therefore the Blessed Virgin was not sanctified before her birth from the womb.

Objection 3: Further, whoever is sanctified by grace is cleansed from sin, both original and actual. If, therefore, the Blessed Virgin was sanctified before her birth from the womb, it follows that she was then cleansed from original sin. Now nothing but original sin could hinder her from entering the heavenly kingdom. If therefore she had died then, it seems that she would have entered the gates of heaven. But this was not possible before the Passion of Christ, according to the Apostle (Heb. 10:19): "We have [Vulg.: 'having'] therefore a confidence in the entering into the Holies by His blood." It seems therefore that the Blessed Virgin was not sanctified before her birth from the womb.

Objection 4: Further, original sin is contracted through the origin, just as actual sin is contracted through an act. But as long as one is in the act of sinning, one cannot be cleansed from actual sin. Therefore neither could the Blessed Virgin be cleansed from original sin as long as she was in the act of origin, by existence in her mother's womb.

On the contrary, The Church celebrates the feast of our Lady's Nativity. Now the Church does not celebrate feasts except of those who are holy. Therefore even in her birth the Blessed Virgin was holy. Therefore she was sanctified in the womb.

I answer that, Nothing is handed down in the canonical Scriptures concerning the sanctification of the Blessed Mary as to her being sanctified in the womb; indeed, they do not even mention her birth. But as Augustine, in his tractate on the Assumption of the Virgin, argues with reason, since her body was assumed into heaven, and yet Scripture does not relate this; so it may be reasonably argued that she was sanctified in the womb. For it is reasonable to believe that she, who brought forth "the Only-Begotten of the Father full of grace and truth," received greater privileges of grace than all others: hence we read (Lk. 1:28) that the angel addressed her in the words: "Hail full of grace!"

Moreover, it is to be observed that it was granted, by way of privilege, to others, to be sanctified in the womb; for instance, to Jeremias, to whom it was said (Jer. 1:5): "Before thou camest forth out of the womb, I sanctified thee"; and again, to John the Baptist, of whom it is written (Lk. 1:15): "He shall be filled with the Holy Ghost even from his mother's womb." It is therefore with reason that we believe the Blessed Virgin to have been sanctified before her birth from the womb.

Reply to Objection 1: Even in the Blessed Virgin, first was that which is natural, and afterwards that which is spiritual: for she was first conceived in the flesh, and afterwards sanctified in the spirit.

Reply to Objection 2: Augustine speaks according to the common law, by reason of which no one is regenerated by the sacraments, save those who are previously born. But God did not so limit His power to the law of the sacraments, but that He can bestow His grace, by special privilege, on some before they are born from the womb.

Reply to Objection 3: The Blessed Virgin was sanctified in the womb from original sin, as to the personal stain; but she was not freed from the guilt to which the whole nature is subject, so as to enter into Paradise otherwise than through the Sacrifice of Christ; the same also is to be said of the Holy Fathers who lived before Christ.

Reply to Objection 4: Original sin is transmitted through the origin, inasmuch as through the origin the human nature is transmitted, and original sin, properly speaking, affects the nature. And this takes place when the off-spring conceived is animated. Wherefore nothing hinders the offspring conceived from being sanctified after animation: for after this it remains in the mother's womb not for the purpose of receiving human nature, but for a certain perfecting of that which it has already received.

Whether the Blessed Virgin was sanctified before animation?

Objection 1: It would seem that the Blessed Virgin was sanctified before animation. Because, as we have stated [4127](A[1]), more grace was bestowed on the Virgin Mother of God than on any saint. Now it seems to have been granted to some, to be sanctified before animation. For it is written (Jer. 1:5): "Before I formed thee in the bowels of thy mother, I knew thee": and the soul is not infused before the formation of the body. Likewise Ambrose says of John the Baptist (Comment. in Luc. i, 15): "As yet the spirit of life was not in him and already he possessed the Spirit of grace." Much more therefore could the Blessed Virgin be sanctified before animation.

Objection 2: Further, as Anselm says (De Concep. Virg. xviii), "it was fitting that this Virgin should shine with such a purity that under God none greater can be imagined": wherefore it is written (Canticles 4:7): "Thou art all fair, O my love, and there is not a spot in thee." But the purity of the Blessed Virgin would have been greater, if she had never been stained by the contagion of original sin. Therefore it was granted to her to be sanctified before her flesh was animated.

Objection 3: Further, as it has been stated above, no feast is celebrated except of some saint. But some keep the feast of the Conception of the Blessed Virgin. Therefore it seems that in her very Conception she was holy; and hence that she was sanctified before animation.

Objection 4: Further, the Apostle says (Rom. 11:16): "If the root be holy, so are the branches." Now the root of the children is their parents. Therefore the Blessed Virgin could be sanctified even in her parents, before animation.

On the contrary, The things of the Old Testament were figures of the New, according to 1 Cor. 10:11: "All things happened to them in figure." Now the sanctification of the tabernacle, of which it is written (Ps. 45:5): "The most High hath sanctified His own tabernacle," seems to signify the sanctification of the Mother of God, who is called "God's Tabernacle," according to Ps. 18:6: "He hath set His tabernacle in the sun." But of the tabernacle it is written (Ex. 40:31,32): "After all things were perfected, the cloud covered the tabernacle of the testimony, and the glory of the Lord filled it." Therefore also the Blessed Virgin was not sanctified until after all in her was perfected, viz. her body and soul.

I answer that, The sanctification of the Blessed Virgin cannot be understood as having taken place before animation, for two reasons. First, because the sanctification of which we are speaking, is nothing but the cleansing from original sin: for sanctification is a "perfect cleansing," as Dionysius says (Div. Nom. xii). Now sin cannot be taken away except by grace, the subject of which is the rational creature alone. Therefore before the infusion of the rational soul, the Blessed Virgin was not sanctified.

Secondly, because, since the rational creature alone can be the subject of sin; before the infusion of the rational soul, the offspring conceived is not liable to sin. And thus, in whatever manner the Blessed Virgin would have been sanctified before animation, she could never have incurred the stain of original sin: and thus she would not have needed redemption and salvation which is by Christ, of whom it is written (Mat. 1:21): "He shall save His people from their sins." But this is unfitting, through implying that Christ is not the "Saviour of all men," as He is called (1 Tim. 4:10). It remains, therefore, that the Blessed Virgin was sanctified after animation.

Reply to Objection 1: The Lord says that He "knew" Jeremias before he was formed in the womb, by knowledge, that is to say, of predestination: but He says that He "sanctified" him, not before formation, but before he "came forth out of the womb," etc.

As to what Ambrose says, viz. that in John the Baptist there was not the spirit of life when there was already the Spirit of grace, by spirit of life we are not to understand the life-giving soul, but the air which we breathe out [respiratus]. Or it may be said that in him as yet there was not the spirit of life, that is the soul, as to its manifest and complete operations.

Reply to Objection 2: If the soul of the Blessed Virgin had never incurred the stain of original sin, this would be derogatory to the dignity of Christ, by reason of His being the universal Saviour of all. Consequently after Christ, who, as the universal Saviour of all, needed not to be saved, the purity of the Blessed Virgin holds the highest place. For Christ did not contract original sin in any way whatever, but was holy in His very Conception, according to Lk. 1:35: "The Holy which shall be born of thee, shall be called the Son of God." But the Blessed Virgin did indeed contract original sin, but was cleansed therefrom before her birth from the womb. This is what is signified (Job 3:9) where it is written of the night of original sin: "Let it expect light," i.e. Christ, "and not see it"---(because "no defiled thing cometh into her," as is written Wis. 7:25), "nor the rising of the dawning of the day," that is of the Blessed Virgin, who in her birth was immune from original sin.

Reply to Objection 3: Although the Church of Rome does not celebrate the Conception of the Blessed Virgin, yet it tolerates the custom of certain churches that do keep that feast, wherefore this is not to be entirely reprobated. Nevertheless the celebration of this feast does not give us to understand that she was holy in her conception. But since it is not known when she was sanctified, the feast of her Sanctification, rather than the feast of her Conception, is kept on the day of her conception.

Reply to Objection 4: Sanctification is twofold. one is that of the whole nature: inasmuch as the whole human nature is freed from all corruption of sin and punishment. This will take place at the resurrection. The other is personal sanctification. This is not transmitted to the children begotten of the flesh: because it does not regard the flesh but the mind. Consequently, though the parents of the Blessed Virgin were cleansed from original sin, nevertheless she contracted original sin, since she was conceived by way of fleshly concupiscence and the intercourse of man and woman: for Augustine says (De Nup. et Concup. i): "All flesh born of carnal intercourse is sinful."

Whether the Blessed Virgin was cleansed from the infection of the fomes?

Objection 1: It would seem that the Blessed Virgin was not cleansed from the infection of the fomes. For just as the fomes, consisting in the rebellion of the lower powers against the reason, is a punishment of original sin; so also are death and other corporeal penalties. Therefore the fomes was not entirely removed from her.

Objection 2: Further, it is written (2 Cor. 12:9): "Power is made perfect in infirmity," which refers to the weakness of the fomes, by reason of which he (the Apostle) felt the "sting of the flesh." But it was not fitting that anything should be taken away from the Blessed Virgin, pertaining to the perfection of virtue. Therefore it was unfitting that the fomes should be entirely taken away from her.

Objection 3: Further, Damascene says (De Fide Orth. iii) that "the Holy Ghost came upon" the Blessed Virgin, "purifying her," before she conceived the Son of God. But this can only be understood of purification from the fomes: for she committed no sin, as Augustine says (De Nat. et Grat. xxvi). Therefore by the sanctification in the womb she was not absolutely cleansed from the fomes.

On the contrary, It is written (Canticles 4:7): "Thou art all fair, O my love, and there is not a spot in thee!" But the fomes implies a blemish, at any rate in the flesh. Therefore the fomes was not in the Blessed Virgin.

I answer that, on this point there are various opinions. For some have held that the fomes was entirely taken away in that sanctification whereby the Blessed Virgin was sanctified in the womb. Others say that it remained as far as it causes a difficulty in doing good, but was taken away as far as it causes a proneness to evil. Others again, that it was taken away as to the personal corruption, by which it makes us quick to do evil and slow to do good: but that it remained as to the corruption of nature, inasmuch as it is the cause of transmitting original sin to the offspring. Lastly, others say that, in her first sanctification, the fomes remained essentially, but was fettered; and that, when she conceived the Son of God, it was entirely taken away. In order to understand the question at issue, it must be observed that the fomes is nothing but a certain inordinate, but habitual, concupiscence of the sensitive appetite. for actual concupiscence is a sinful motion. Now sensual concupiscence is said to be inordinate, in so far as it rebels against reason; and this it does by inclining to evil, or hindering from good. Consequently it is essential to the fomes to incline to evil, or hinder from good. Wherefore to say that the fomes was in the Blessed Virgin without an inclination to evil, is to combine two contradictory statements.

In like manner it seems to imply a contradiction to say that the fomes remained as to the corruption of nature, but not as to the personal corruption. For, according to Augustine (De Nup. et Concup. i.), it is lust that transmits original sin to the offspring. Now lust implies inordinate concupiscence, not entirely subject to reason: and therefore, if the fomes were entirely taken away as to personal corruption, it could not remain as to the corruption of nature.

It remains, therefore, for us to say, either that the fomes was entirely taken away from her by her first sanctification or that it was fettered. Now that the fomes was entirely taken away, might be understood in this way, that, by the abundance of grace bestowed on the Blessed Virgin, such a disposition of the soul's powers was granted to her, that the lower powers were never moved without the command of her reason: just as we have stated to have been the case with Christ ([4128]Q[15], A[2]), who certainly did not have the fomes of sin; as also was the case with Adam, before he sinned, by reason of original justice: so that, in this respect, the grace of sanctification in the Virgin had the force of original justice. And although this appears to be part of the dignity of the Virgin Mother, yet it is somewhat derogatory to the dignity of Christ, without whose power no one had been freed from the first sentence of condemnation. And though, through faith in Christ, some were freed from that condemnation, according to the spirit, before Christ's Incarnation, yet it does not seem fitting that any one should be freed from that condemnation, according to the flesh, except after His Incarnation, for it was then that immunity from condemnation was first to appear. Consequently, just as before the immortality of the flesh of Christ rising again, none obtained immortality of the flesh, so it seems unfitting to say that before Christ appeared in sinless flesh, His Virgin Mother's or anyone else's flesh should be without the fomes, which is called "the law of the flesh" or "of the members" (Rom. 7:23, 25).

Therefore it seems better to say that by the sanctification in the womb, the Virgin was not freed from the fomes in its essence, but that it remained fettered: not indeed by an act of her reason, as in holy men, since she had not the use of reason from the very first moment of her existence in her mother's womb, for this was the singular privilege of Christ: but by reason of the abundant grace bestowed on her in her sanctification, and still more perfectly by Divine Providence preserving her sensitive soul, in a singular manner, from any inordinate movement. Afterwards, however, at the conception of Christ's flesh, in which for the first time immunity from sin was to be conspicuous, it is to be believed that entire freedom from the fomes redounded from the Child to the Mother. This indeed is signified (Ezech. 43:2): "Behold the glory of the God of Israel came in by the way of the east," i.e. by the Blessed Virgin, "and the earth," i.e. her flesh, "shone with His," i.e. Christ's, "majesty."

Reply to Objection 1: Death and such like penalties do not of themselves incline us to sin. Wherefore though Christ assumed them, He did not assume the fomes. Consequently in order that the Blessed Virgin might be conformed to her Son, from "whose fulness" her grace was derived, the fomes was at first fettered and afterwards taken away: while she was not freed from death and other such penalties.

Reply to Objection 2: The "infirmity" of the flesh, that pertains to the fomes, is indeed to holy men an occasional cause of perfect virtue: but not the "sine qua non" of perfection: and it is quite enough to ascribe to the Blessed Virgin perfect virtue and abundant grace: nor is there any need to attribute to her every occasional cause of perfection.

Reply to Objection 3: The Holy Ghost effected a twofold purification in the Blessed Virgin. The first was, as it were, preparatory to Christ's conception: which did not cleanse her from the stain of sin or fomes, but rather gave her mind a unity of purpose and disengaged it from a multiplicity of things (Cf. Dionysius, Div. Nom. iv), since even the angels are said to be purified, in whom there is no stain, as Dionysius says (Eccl. Hier. vi). The second purification effected in her by the Holy Ghost was by means of the conception of Christ which was the operation of the Holy Ghost. And in respect of this, it may be said that He purified her entirely from the fomes.

Whether by being sanctified in the womb the Blessed Virgin was preserved from all actual sin?

Objection 1: It would seem that by being sanctified in the womb the Blessed Virgin was not preserved from all actual sin. For, as we have already stated [4129](A[3]), after her first sanctification the fomes remained in the Virgin. Now the motion of the fomes, even if it precede the act of the reason, is a venial sin, albeit extremely slight, as Augustine says in his work De Trinitate [*Cf. Sent. ii, D, 24]. Therefore there was some venial sin in the Blessed Virgin.

Objection 2: Further, Augustine (Qq. Nov. et Vet. Test. lxxiii on Lk. 2:35: "Thy own soul a sword shall pierce") says that the Blessed Virgin "was troubled with wondering doubt at the death of our Lord." But doubt in matters of faith is a sin. Therefore the Blessed Virgin was not preserved from all actual sin.

Objection 3: Further, Chrysostom (Hom. xlv in Matth.) expounding the text: "Behold thy mother and thy brethren stand without, seeking thee," says: "It is clear that they did this from mere vain glory." Again, on Jn. 2:3: "They have no wine," the same Chrysostom says that "she wished to do them a favor, and raise herself in their esteem, by means of her Son: and perchance she succumbed to human frailty, just as did His brethren when they said: 'Manifest Thyself to the world.'" And a little further on he says: "For as yet she did not believe in Him as she ought." Now it is quite clear that all this was sinful. Therefore the Blessed Virgin was not preserved from all sin.

On the contrary, Augustine says (De Nat. et Grat. xxxvi): "In the matter of sin, it is my wish to exclude absolutely all questions concerning the holy Virgin Mary, on account of the honor due to Christ. For since she conceived and brought forth Him who most certainly was guilty of no sin, we know that an abundance of grace was given her that she might be in every way the conqueror of sin."

I answer that, God so prepares and endows those, whom He chooses for some particular office, that they are rendered capable of fulfilling it, according to 2 Cor. 3:6: "(Who) hath made us fit ministers of the New Testament." Now the Blessed Virgin was chosen by God to be His Mother. Therefore there can be no doubt that God, by His grace, made her worthy of that office, according to the words spoken to her by the angel (Lk. 1:30,31): "Thou hast found grace with God: behold thou shalt conceive," etc. But she would not have been worthy to be the Mother of God, if she had ever sinned. First, because the honor of the parents reflects on the child, according to Prov. 17:6: "The glory of children are their fathers": and consequently, on the other hand, the Mother's shame would have reflected on her Son. Secondly, because of the singular affinity between her and Christ, who took flesh from her: and it is written (2 Cor. 6:15): "What concord hath Christ with Belial?" Thirdly, because of the singular manner in which the Son of God, who is the "Divine Wisdom" (1 Cor. 1:24) dwelt in her, not only in her soul but in her womb. And it is written (Wis. 1:4): "Wisdom will not enter into a malicious soul, nor dwell in a body subject to sins."

We must therefore confess simply that the Blessed Virgin committed no actual sin, neither mortal nor venial; so that what is written (Cant 4:7) is fulfilled: "Thou art all fair, O my love, and there is not a spot in thee," etc.

Reply to Objection 1: After her sanctification the fomes remained in the Blessed Virgin, but fettered; lest she should be surprised by some sudden inordinate act, antecedent to the act of reason. And although the grace of her sanctification contributed to this effect, yet it did not suffice; for otherwise the result of her sanctification would have been to render impossible in her any sensual movement not preceded by an act of reason, and thus she would. not have had the fomes, which is contrary to what we have said above [4130](A[3]). We must therefore say that the above mentioned fettering (of the fomes) was perfected by divine providence not permitting any inordinate motion to result from the fomes.

Reply to Objection 2: Origen (Hom. xvii in Luc.) and certain other doctors expound these words of Simeon as referring to the sorrow which she suffered at the time of our Lord's Passion. Ambrose (in Luc. 2:35) says that the sword signifies "Mary's prudence which took note of the heavenly mystery. For the word of God is living and effectual, and more piercing than any two-edged sword" (Heb. 4:12).

Others again take the sword to signify doubt. But this is to be understood of the doubt, not of unbelief, but of wonder and discussion. Thus Basil says (Ep. ad Optim.) that "the Blessed Virgin while standing by the cross, and observing every detail, after the message of Gabriel, and the ineffable knowledge of the Divine Conception, after that wondrous manifestation of miracles, was troubled in mind": that is to say, on the one side seeing Him suffer such humiliation, and on the other considering His marvelous works.

Reply to Objection 3: In those words Chrysostom goes too far. They may, however, be explained as meaning that our Lord corrected in her, not the inordinate motion of vain glory in regard to herself, but that which might be in the thoughts of others.

Whether, by her sanctification in the womb, the Blessed Virgin received the fulness of grace?

Objection 1: It would seem that, by her sanctification in the womb, the Blessed Virgin did not receive the fulness or perfection of grace. For this seems to be Christ's privilege, according to Jn. 1:14: "We saw Him [Vulg.: 'His glory'] as the Only-Begotten [Vulg.: 'as it were of the Only-Begotten'] full of grace and truth." But what is proper to Christ ought not to be ascribed to some one else. Therefore the Blessed Virgin did not receive the fulness of grace at the time of her sanctification.

Objection 2: Further, nothing remains to be added to that which is full and perfect: for "the perfect is that which lacks nothing," as is said Phys. iii. But the Blessed Virgin received additional grace afterwards when she conceived Christ; for to her was it said (Lk. 1:35): "The Holy Ghost shall come upon thee: and again, when she was assumed into glory." Therefore it seems that she did not receive the fulness of grace at the time of her first sanctification.

Objection 3: Further, "God does nothing useless," as is said De Coelo et Mundo i. But it would have been useless for her to have certain graces, for she would never have put them to use: since we do not read that she taught which is the act of wisdom; or that she worked miracles, which is the act of one of the gratuitous graces. Therefore she had not the fulness of grace.

On the contrary, The angel said to her: "Hail, full of grace" (Lk. 1:28); which words Jerome expounds as follows, in a sermon on the Assumption (cf. Ep. ad Paul. et Eustoch.): "Full indeed of grace: for to others it is given in portions; whereas on Mary the fulness of grace was showered all at once."

I answer that, In every genus, the nearer a thing is to the principle, the greater the part which it has in the effect of that principle, whence Dionysius says (Coel. Hier. iv) that angels, being nearer to God, have a greater share than men, in the effects of the Divine goodness. Now Christ is the principle of grace, authoritatively as to His Godhead, instrumentally as to His humanity: whence (Jn. 1:17) it is written: "Grace and truth came by Jesus Christ." But the Blessed Virgin Mary was nearest to Christ in His humanity: because He received His human nature from her. Therefore it was due to her to receive a greater fulness of grace than others.

Reply to Objection 1: God gives to each one according to the purpose for which He has chosen him. And since Christ as man was predestinated and chosen to be "predestinated the Son of God in power . . . of sanctification" (Rom. 1:4), it was proper to Him to have such a fulness of grace that it overflowed from Him into all, according to Jn. 1:16: "Of His fulness we have all received." Whereas the Blessed Virgin Mary received such a fulness of grace that she was nearest of all to the Author of grace; so that she received within her Him Who is full of all grace; and by bringing Him forth, she, in a manner, dispensed grace to all.

Reply to Objection 2: In natural things at first there is perfection of disposition, for instance when matter is perfectly disposed for the form. Secondly, there is the perfection of the form; and this is the more excellent, for the heat that proceeds from the form of fire is more perfect than that which disposed to the form of fire. Thirdly, there is the perfection of the end: for instance when fire has its qualities in the most perfect degree, having mounted to its own place.

In like manner there was a threefold perfection of grace in the Blessed Virgin. The first was a kind of disposition, by which she was made worthy to be the mother of Christ: and this was the perfection of her sanctification. The second perfection of grace in the Blessed Virgin was through the presence of the Son of God Incarnate in her womb. The third perfection of the end is that which she has in glory.

That the second perfection excels the first, and the third the second, appears (1) from the point of view of deliverance from evil. For at first in her sanctification she was delivered from original sin: afterwards, in the conception of the Son of God, she was entirely cleansed from the fomes: lastly, in her glorification she was also delivered from all affliction whatever. It appears (2) from the point of view of ordering to good. For at first in her sanctification she received grace inclining her to good: in the conception of the Son of God she received consummate grace confirming her in good; and in her glorification her grace was further consummated so as to perfect her in the enjoyment of all good.

Reply to Objection 3: There is no doubt that the Blessed Virgin received in a high degree both the gift of wisdom and the grace of miracles and even of prophecy, just as Christ had them. But she did not so receive them, as to put them and such like graces to every use, as did Christ: but accordingly as it befitted her condition of life. For she had the use of wisdom in contemplation, according to Lk. 2:19: "But Mary kept all these words, pondering them in her heart." But she had not the use of wisdom as to teaching: since this befitted not the female sex, according to 1 Tim. 2:12: "But I suffer not a woman to teach." The use of miracles did not become her while she lived: because at that time the Teaching of Christ was to be confirmed by miracles, and therefore it was befitting that Christ alone, and His disciples who were the bearers of His doctrine, should work miracles. Hence of John the Baptist it is written (Jn. 10:41) that he "did no sign"; that is, in order that all might fix their attention on Christ. As to the use of prophecy, it is clear that she had it, from the canticle spoken by her: "My soul doth magnify the Lord" (Lk. 1:46, etc.).

Whether after Christ, it was proper to the Blessed Virgin to be sanctified in the womb?

Objection 1: It would seem that it was proper for the Blessed Virgin, after Christ, to be sanctified in the womb. For it has been said [4131](A[4]) that the Blessed Virgin was sanctified in the womb, in order that she might be worthy to be the mother of God. But this is proper to her. Therefore she alone was sanctified in the womb.

Objection 2: Further, some men seem to have been more closely connected with Christ than Jeremias and John the Baptist, who are said to have been sanctified in the womb. For Christ is specially called the Son of David and of Abraham, by reason of the promise specially made to them concerning Christ. Isaias also prophesied of Christ in the most express terms. And the apostles were in converse with Christ Himself. And yet these are not mentioned as having been sanctified in the womb. Therefore it was not befitting that either Jeremias or John the Baptist should be sanctified in the womb.

Objection 3: Further, Job says of himself (Job 31:18): "From my infancy mercy grew up with me; and it came out with me from [my mother's] womb." Nevertheless we do not for this reason say that he was sanctified in the womb. Neither therefore are we bound to say that Jeremias and John the Baptist were sanctified in the womb.

On the contrary, It is written of Jeremias (Jer. 1:5): "Before thou camest forth out of the womb I sanctified thee." And of John the Baptist it is written (Lk. 1:15): "He shall be filled with the Holy Ghost, even from his mother's womb."

I answer that, Augustine (Ep. ad Dardan.) seems to speak dubiously of their (Jeremias' and John the Baptist's) sanctification in the womb. For the leaping of John in the womb "might," as he says, "signify the great truth," viz. that the woman was the mother of God, "which was to be made known to his elders, though as yet unknown to the infant. Hence in the Gospel it is written, not that the infant in her womb believed, but that it 'leaped': and our eyes are witness that not only infants leap but also cattle. But this was unwonted because it was in the womb. And therefore, just as other miracles are wont to be done, this was done divinely, in the infant; not humanly by the infant. Perhaps also in this child the use of reason and will was so far accelerated that while yet in his mother's womb he was able to acknowledge, believe, and consent, whereas in other children we have to wait for these things till they grow older: this again I count as a miraculous result of the divine power."

But since it is expressly said (of John) in the Gospel that "he shall be filled with the Holy Ghost, even from his mother's womb"; and of Jeremias, "Before thou camest forth out of the womb, I sanctified thee"; it seems that we must needs assert that they were sanctified in the womb, although, while in the womb, they had not the use of reason (which is the point discussed by Augustine); just as neither do children enjoy the use of free will as soon as they are sanctified by baptism.

Nor are we to believe that any others, not mentioned by Scripture, were sanctified in the womb. For such privileges of grace, which are bestowed on some, outside the common law, are ordered for the salvation of others, according to 1 Cor. 12:7: "The manifestation of the Spirit is given to every man unto profit," which would not result from the sanctification of anyone unless it were made known to the Church.

And although it is not possible to assign a reason for God's judgments, for instance, why He bestows such a grace on one and not on another, yet there seems to be a certain fittingness in both of these being sanctified in the womb, by their foreshadowing the sanctification which was to be effected through Christ. First, as to His Passion, according to Heb. 13:12: "Jesus, that He might sanctify the people by His own blood, suffered without the gate": which Passion Jeremias foretold openly by words and by symbols, and most clearly foreshadowed by his own sufferings. Secondly, as to His Baptism (1 Cor. 6:11): "But you are washed, but you are sanctified"; to which Baptism John prepared men by his baptism.

Reply to Objection 1: The blessed Virgin, who was chosen by God to be His Mother, received a fuller grace of sanctification than John the Baptist and Jeremias, who were chosen to foreshadow in a special way the sanctification effected by Christ. A sign of this is that it was granted to the Blessed Virgin thence-forward never to sin either mortally or venially: whereas to the others who were thus sanctified it was granted thenceforward not to sin mortally, through the protection of God's grace.

Reply to Objection 2: In other respects these saints might be more closely united to Christ than Jeremias and John the Baptist. But the latter were most closely united to Him by clearly foreshadowing His sanctification, as explained above.

Reply to Objection 3: The mercy of which Job speaks is not the infused virtue; but a certain natural inclination to the act of that virtue.

OF THE VIRGINITY OF THE MOTHER OF GOD (FOUR ARTICLES)

We now have to consider the virginity of the Mother of God; concerning which there are four points of inquiry:
(1) Whether she was a virgin in conceiving?
(2) Whether she was a virgin in His Birth?
(3) Whether she remained a virgin after His Birth?
(4) Whether she took a vow of virginity?

Whether the Mother of God was a virgin in conceiving Christ?

Objection 1: It would seem that the Mother of God was not a virgin in conceiving Christ. For no child having father and mother is conceived by a virgin mother. But Christ is said to have had not only a mother, but also a father, according to Lk. 2:33: "His father and mother were wondering at those things which were spoken concerning Him": and further on (Lk. 2:48) in the same chapter she says: "Behold I and Thy father [Vulg.: 'Thy father and I'] have sought Thee sorrowing." Therefore Christ was not conceived of a virgin mother.

Objection 2: Further (Mat. 1) it is proved that Christ was the Son of Abraham and David, through Joseph being descended from David. But this proof would have availed nothing if Joseph were not the father of Christ. Therefore it seems that Christ's Mother conceived Him of the seed of Joseph; and consequently that she was not a virgin in conceiving Him.

Objection 3: Further, it is written (Gal. 4:4): "God sent His Son, made of a woman." But according to the customary mode of speaking, the term "woman" applies to one who is known of a man. Therefore Christ was not conceived by a virgin mother.

Objection 4: Further, things of the same species have the same mode of generation: since generation is specified by its terminus just as are other motions. But Christ belonged to the same species as other men, according to Phil. 2:7: "Being made in the likeness of men, and in habit found as a man." Since therefore other men are begotten of the mingling of male and female, it seems that Christ was begotten in the same manner; and that consequently He was not conceived of a virgin mother.

Objection 5: Further, every natural form has its determinate matter, outside which it cannot be. But the matter of human form appears to be the semen of male and female. If therefore Christ's body was not conceived of the semen of male and female, it would not have been truly a human body; which cannot be asserted. It seems therefore that He was not conceived of a virgin mother.

On the contrary, It is written (Is. 7:14): "Behold a virgin shall conceive."

I answer that, We must confess simply that the Mother of Christ was a virgin in conceiving for to deny this belongs to the heresy of the Ebionites and Cerinthus, who held Christ to be a mere man, and maintained that He was born of both sexes.

It is fitting for four reasons that Christ should be born of a virgin. First, in order to maintain the dignity or the Father Who sent Him. For since Christ is the true and natural Son of God, it was not fitting that He should have another father than God: lest the dignity belonging to God be transferred to another.

Secondly, this was befitting to a property of the Son Himself, Who is sent. For He is the Word of God: and the word is conceived without any interior corruption: indeed, interior corruption is incompatible with perfect conception of the word. Since therefore flesh was so assumed by the Word of God, as to be the flesh of the Word of God, it was fitting that it also should be conceived without corruption of the mother.

Thirdly, this was befitting to the dignity of Christ's humanity in which there could be no sin, since by it the sin of the world was taken away, according to Jn. 1:29: "Behold the Lamb of God" (i.e. the Lamb without stain) "who taketh away the sin of the world." Now it was not possible in a nature already corrupt, for flesh to be born from sexual intercourse without incurring the infection of original sin. Whence Augustine says (De Nup. et Concup. i): "In that union," viz. the marriage of Mary and Joseph, "the nuptial intercourse alone was lacking: because in sinful flesh this could not be without fleshly concupiscence which arises from sin, and without which He wished to be conceived, Who was to be without sin."

Fourthly, on account of the very end of the Incarnation of Christ, which was that men might be born again as sons of God, "not of the will of the flesh, nor of the will of man, but of God" (Jn. 1:13), i.e. of the power of God, of which fact the very conception of Christ was to appear as an exemplar. Whence Augustine says (De Sanct. Virg.): "It behooved that our Head, by a notable miracle, should be born, after the flesh, of a virgin, that He might thereby signify that His members would be born, after the Spirit, of a virgin Church."

Reply to Objection 1: As Bede says on Lk. 1:33: Joseph is called the father of the Saviour, not that he really was His father, as the Photinians pretended: but that he was considered by men to be so, for the safeguarding of Mary's good name. Wherefore Luke adds (Lk. 3:23): "Being, as it was supposed, the son of Joseph."

Or, according to Augustine (De Cons. Evang. ii), Joseph is called the father of Christ just as "he is called the husband of Mary, without fleshly mingling, by the mere bond of marriage: being thereby united to Him much more closely than if he were adopted from another family. Consequently that Christ was not begotten of Joseph by fleshly union is no reason why Joseph should not be called His father; since he would be the father even of an adopted son not born of his wife."

Reply to Objection 2: As Jerome says on Mat. 1:18: "Though Joseph was not the father of our Lord and Saviour, the order of His genealogy is traced down to Joseph"---first, because "the Scriptures are not wont to trace the female line in genealogies": secondly, "Mary and Joseph were of the same tribe"; wherefore by law he was bound to take her as being of his kin. Likewise, as Augustine says (De Nup. et Concup. i), "it was befitting to trace the genealogy down to Joseph, lest in that marriage any slight should be offered to the male sex, which is indeed the stronger: for truth suffered nothing thereby, since both Joseph and Mary were of the family of David."

Reply to Objection 3: As the gloss says on this passage, the word "'mulier,' is here used instead of 'femina,' according to the custom of the Hebrew tongue: which applies the term signifying woman to those of the female sex who are virgins."

Reply to Objection 4: This argument is true of those things which come into existence by the way of nature: since nature, just as it is fixed to one particular effect, so it is determinate to one mode of producing that effect. But as the supernatural power of God extends to the infinite: just as it is not determinate to one effect, so neither is it determinate to one mode of producing any effect whatever. Consequently, just as it was possible for the first man to be produced, by the Divine power, "from the slime of the earth," so too was it possible for Christ's body to be made, by Divine power, from a virgin without the seed of the male.

Reply to Objection 5: According to the Philosopher (De Gener. Animal. i, ii, iv), in conception the seed of the male is not by way of matter, but by way of agent: and the female alone supplies the matter. Wherefore though the seed of the male was lacking in Christ's conception, it does not follow that due matter was lacking.

But if the seed of the male were the matter of the fetus in animal conception, it is nevertheless manifest that it is not a matter remaining under one form, but subject to transformation. And though the natural power cannot transmute other than determinate matter to a determinate form; nevertheless the Divine power, which is infinite, can transmute all matter to any form whatsoever. Consequently, just as it transmuted the slime of the earth into Adam's body, so could it transmute the matter supplied by His Mother into Christ's body, even though it were not the sufficient matter for a natural conception.

Whether Christ's Mother was a virgin in His birth?

Objection 1: It would seem that Christ's Mother was not a virgin in His Birth. For Ambrose says on Lk. 2:23: "He who sanctified a strange womb, for the birth of a prophet, He it is who opened His Mother's womb, that He might go forth unspotted." But opening of the womb excludes virginity. Therefore Christ's Mother was not a virgin in His Birth.

Objection 2: Further, nothing should have taken place in the mystery of Christ, which would make His body to seem unreal. Now it seems to pertain not to a true but to an unreal body, to be able to go through a closed passage; since two bodies cannot be in one place at the same time. It was therefore unfitting that Christ's body should come forth from His Mother's closed womb: and consequently that she should remain a virgin in giving birth to Him.

Objection 3: Further, as Gregory says in the Homily for the octave of Easter [*xxvi in Evang.], that by entering after His Resurrection where the disciples were gathered, the doors being shut, our Lord "showed that His body was the same in nature but differed in glory": so that it seems that to go through a closed passage pertains to a glorified body. But Christ's body was not glorified in its conception, but was passible, having "the likeness of sinful flesh," as the Apostle says (Rom. 8:3). Therefore He did not come forth through the closed womb of the Virgin.

On the contrary, In a sermon of the Council of Ephesus (P. III, Cap. ix) it is said: "After giving birth, nature knows not a virgin: but grace enhances her fruitfulness, and effects her motherhood, while in no way does it injure her virginity." Therefore Christ's Mother was a virgin also in giving birth to Him.

I answer that, Without any doubt whatever we must assert that the Mother of Christ was a virgin even in His Birth: for the prophet says not only: "Behold a virgin shall conceive," but adds: "and shall bear a son." This indeed was befitting for three reasons. First, because this was in keeping with a property of Him whose Birth is in question, for He is the Word of God. For the word is not only conceived in the mind without corruption, but also proceeds from the mind without corruption. Wherefore in order to show that body to be the body of the very Word of God, it was fitting that it should be born of a virgin incorrupt. Whence in the sermon of the Council of Ephesus (quoted above) we read: "Whosoever brings forth mere flesh, ceases to be a virgin. But since she gave birth to the Word made flesh, God safeguarded her virginity so as to manifest His Word, by which Word He thus manifested Himself: for neither does our word, when brought forth, corrupt the mind; nor does God, the substantial Word, deigning to be born, destroy virginity."

Secondly, this is fitting as regards the effect of Christ's Incarnation: since He came for this purpose, that He might take away our corruption. Wherefore it is unfitting that in His Birth He should corrupt His Mother's virginity. Thus Augustine says in a sermon on the Nativity of Our Lord: "It was not right that He who came to heal corruption, should by His advent violate integrity."

Thirdly, it was fitting that He Who commanded us to honor our father and mother should not in His Birth lessen the honor due to His Mother.

Reply to Objection 1: Ambrose says this in expounding the evangelist's quotation from the Law: "Every male opening the womb shall be called holy to the Lord." This, says Bede, "is said in regard to the wonted manner of birth; not that we are to believe that our Lord in coming forth violated the abode of her sacred womb, which His entrance therein had hallowed." Wherefore the opening here spoken of does not imply the unlocking of the enclosure of virginal purity; but the mere coming forth of the infant from the maternal womb.

Reply to Objection 2: Christ wished so to show the reality of His body, as to manifest His Godhead at the same time. For this reason He mingled wondrous with lowly things. Wherefore, to show that His body was real, He was born of a woman. But in order to manifest His Godhead, He was born of a virgin, for "such a Birth befits a God," as Ambrose says in the Christmas hymn.

Reply to Objection 3: Some have held that Christ, in His Birth, assumed the gift of "subtlety," when He came forth from the closed womb of a virgin; and that He assumed the gift of "agility" when with dry feet He walked on the sea. But this is not consistent with what has been decided above (Q[14]). For these gifts of a glorified body result from an overflow of the soul's glory on to the body, as we shall explain further on, in treating of glorified bodies ([4132]XP, Q[82]): and it has been said above (Q[13], A[3], ad 1; Q[16], A[1], ad 2) that before His Passion Christ "allowed His flesh to do and to suffer what was proper to it" (Damascene, De Fide Orth. iii): nor was there such an overflow of glory from His soul on to His body.

We must therefore say that all these things took place miraculously by Divine power. Whence Augustine says (Sup. Joan. Tract. 121): "To the substance of a body in which was the Godhead closed doors were no obstacle. For truly He had power to enter in by doors not open, in Whose Birth His Mother's virginity remained inviolate." And Dionysius says in an epistle (Ad Caium iv) that "Christ excelled man in doing that which is proper to man: this is shown in His supernatural conception, of a virgin, and in the unstable waters bearing the weight of earthly feet."

Day 268

Whether Christ's Mother remained a virgin after His birth?

Objection 1: It would seem that Christ's Mother did not remain a virgin after His Birth. For it is written (Mat. 1:18): "Before Joseph and Mary came together, she was found with child of the Holy Ghost." Now the Evangelist would not have said this---"before they came together"---unless he were certain of their subsequent coming together; for no one says of one who does not eventually dine "before he dines" (cf. Jerome, Contra Helvid.). It seems, therefore, that the Blessed Virgin subsequently had intercourse with Joseph; and consequently that she did not remain a virgin after (Christ's) Birth.

Objection 2: Further, in the same passage (Mat. 1:20) are related the words of the angel to Joseph: "Fear not to take unto thee Mary thy wife." But marriage is consummated by carnal intercourse. Therefore it seems that this must have at some time taken place between Mary and Joseph: and that, consequently she did not remain a virgin after (Christ's) Birth.

Objection 3: Further, again in the same passage a little further on (Mat. 1:24,25) we read: "And" (Joseph) "took unto him his wife; and he knew her not till she brought forth her first-born Son." Now this conjunction "till" is wont to designate a fixed time, on the completion of which that takes place which previously had not taken place. And the verb "knew" refers here to knowledge by intercourse (cf. Jerome, Contra Helvid.); just as (Gn. 4:1) it is said that "Adam knew his wife." Therefore it seems that after (Christ's) Birth, the Blessed Virgin was known by Joseph; and, consequently, that she did not remain a virgin after the Birth (of Christ).

Objection 4: Further, "first-born" can only be said of one who has brothers afterwards: wherefore (Rom. 8:29): "Whom He foreknew, He also predestinated to be made conformable to the image of His Son; that He might be the first-born among many brethren." But the evangelist calls Christ the first-born by His Mother. Therefore she had other children after Christ. And therefore it seems that Christ's Mother did not remain a virgin after His Birth.

Objection 5: Further, it is written (Jn. 2:12): "After this He went down to Capharnaum, He"---that is, Christ---"and His Mother and His brethren." But brethren are those who are begotten of the same parent. Therefore it seems that the Blessed Virgin had other sons after Christ.

Objection 6: Further, it is written (Mat. 27:55,56): "There were there"---that is, by the cross of Christ---"many women afar off, who had followed Jesus from Galilee, ministering unto Him; among whom was Mary Magdalen, and Mary the mother of James and Joseph, and the mother of the sons of Zebedee." Now this Mary who is called "the mother of James and Joseph" seems to have been also the Mother of Christ; for it is written (Jn. 19:25) that "there stood by the cross of Jesus, Mary His Mother." Therefore it seems that Christ's Mother did not remain a virgin after His Birth.

On the contrary, It is written (Ezech. 44:2): "This gate shall be shut, it shall not be opened, and no man shall pass through it; because the Lord the God of Israel hath entered in by it." Expounding these words, Augustine says in a sermon (De Annunt. Dom. iii): "What means this closed gate in the House of the Lord, except that Mary is to be ever inviolate? What does it mean that 'no man shall pass through it,' save that Joseph shall not know her? And what is this---'The Lord alone enters in and goeth out by it'---except that the Holy Ghost shall impregnate her, and that the Lord of angels shall be born of her? And what means this---'it shall be shut for evermore'---but that Mary is a virgin before His Birth, a virgin in His Birth, and a virgin after His Birth?"

I answer that, Without any hesitation we must abhor the error of Helvidius, who dared to assert that Christ's Mother, after His Birth, was carnally known by Joseph, and bore other children. For, in the first place, this is derogatory to Christ's perfection: for as He is in His Godhead the Only-Begotten of the Father, being thus His Son in every respect perfect, so it was becoming that He should be the Only-begotten son of His Mother, as being her perfect offspring.

Secondly, this error is an insult to the Holy Ghost, whose "shrine" was the virginal womb [*"Sacrarium Spiritus Sancti" (Office of B. M. V., Ant. ad Benedictus, T. P.)], wherein He had formed the flesh of Christ: wherefore it was unbecoming that it should be desecrated by intercourse with man.

Thirdly, this is derogatory to the dignity and holiness of God's Mother: for thus she would seem to be most ungrateful, were she not content with such a Son; and were she, of her own accord, by carnal intercourse to forfeit that virginity which had been miraculously preserved in her.

Fourthly, it would be tantamount to an imputation of extreme presumption in Joseph, to assume that he attempted to violate her whom by the angel's revelation he knew to have conceived by the Holy Ghost.

We must therefore simply assert that the Mother of God, as she was a virgin in conceiving Him and a virgin in giving Him birth, did she remain a virgin ever afterwards.

Reply to Objection 1: As Jerome says (Contra Helvid. i): "Although this particle 'before' often indicates a subsequent event, yet we must observe that it not infrequently points merely to some thing previously in the mind: nor is there need that what was in the mind take place eventually, since something may occur to prevent its happening. Thus if a man say: 'Before I dined in the port, I set sail,' we do not understand him to have dined in port after he set sail: but that his mind was set on dining in port." In like manner the evangelist says: "Before they came together" Mary "was found with child, of the Holy Ghost," not that they came together afterwards: but that, when it seemed that they would come together, this was forestalled through her conceiving by the Holy Ghost, the result being that afterwards they did not come together.

Reply to Objection 2: As Augustine says (De Nup. et Concup. i): "The Mother of God is called (Joseph's) wife from the first promise of her espousals, whom he had not known nor ever was to know by carnal intercourse." For, as Ambrose says on Lk. 1:27: "The fact of her marriage is declared, not to insinuate the loss of virginity, but to witness to the reality of the union."

Reply to Objection 3: Some have said that this is not to be understood of carnal knowledge, but of acquaintance. Thus Chrysostom says [*Opus Imperf. in Matth., Hom. 1: among the spurious works ascribed to Chrysostom] that "Joseph did not know her, until she gave birth, being unaware of her dignity: but after she had given birth, then did he know her. Because by reason of her child she surpassed the whole world in beauty and dignity: since she alone in the narrow abode of her womb received Him Whom the world cannot contain."

Others again refer this to knowledge by sight. For as, while Moses was speaking with God, his face was so bright "that the children of Israel could not steadfastly behold it"; so Mary, while being "overshadowed" by the brightness of the "power of the Most High," could not be gazed on by Joseph, until she gave birth. But afterwards she is acknowledged by Joseph, by looking on her face, not by lustful contact.

Jerome, however, grants that this is to be understood of knowledge by intercourse; but he observes that "before" or "until" has a twofold sense in Scripture. For sometimes it indicates a fixed time, as Gal. 3:19: The law "was set because of transgressions, until the seed should come, to whom He made the promise." On the other hand, it sometimes indicates an indefinite time, as in Ps. 122:2: "Our eyes are unto the Lord our God, until He have mercy on us"; from which it is not to be gathered that our eyes are turned from God as soon as His mercy has been obtained. In this sense those things are indicated "of which we might doubt if they had not been written down: while others are left out to be supplied by our understanding. Thus the evangelist says that the Mother of God was not known by her husband until she gave birth, that we may be given to understand that still less did he know her afterwards" (Adversus Helvid. v).

Reply to Objection 4: The Scriptures are wont to designate as the first-born, not only a child who is followed by others, but also the one that is born first. "Otherwise, if a child were not first-born unless followed by others, the first-fruits would not be due as long as there was no further produce" [*Jerome, Adversus Helvid. x]: which is clearly false, since according to the law the first-fruits had to be redeemed within a month (Num. 18:16).

Reply to Objection 5: Some, as Jerome says on Mat. 12:49,50, "suppose that the brethren of the Lord were Joseph's sons by another wife. But we understand the brethren of the Lord to be not sons of Joseph, but cousins of the Saviour, the sons of Mary, His Mother's sister." For "Scripture speaks of brethren in four senses; namely, those who are united by being of the same parents, of the same nation, of the same family, by common affection." Wherefore the brethren of the Lord are so called, not by birth, as being born of the same mother; but by relationship, as being blood-relations of His. But Joseph, as Jerome says (Contra Helvid. ix), is rather to be believed to have remained a virgin, "since he is not said to have had another wife," and "a holy man does not live otherwise than chastely."

Reply to Objection 6: Mary who is called "the mother of James and Joseph" is not to be taken for the Mother of our Lord, who is not wont to be named in the Gospels save under this designation of her dignity---"the Mother of Jesus." This Mary is to be taken for the wife of Alphaeus, whose son was James the less, known as the "brother of the Lord" (Gal. 1:19).

Whether the Mother of God took a vow of virginity?

Objection 1: It would seem that the Mother of God did not take a vow of virginity. For it is written (Dt. 7:14): "No one shall be barren among you of either sex." But sterility is a consequence of virginity. Therefore the keeping of virginity was contrary to the commandment of the Old Law. But before Christ was born the old law was still in force. Therefore at that time the Blessed Virgin could not lawfully take a vow of virginity.

Objection 2: Further, the Apostle says (1 Cor. 7:25): "Concerning virgins I have no commandment of the Lord; but I give counsel." But the perfection of the counsels was to take its beginning from Christ, who is the "end of the Law," as the Apostle says (Rom. 10:4). It was not therefore becoming that the Virgin should take a vow of virginity.

Objection 3: Further, the gloss of Jerome says on 1 Tim. 5:12, that "for those who are vowed to virginity, it is reprehensible not only to marry, but also to desire to be married." But the Mother of Christ committed no sin for which she could be reprehended, as stated above ([4133]Q[27], A[4]). Since therefore she was "espoused," as related by Lk. 1:27 it seems that she did not take a vow of virginity.

On the contrary, Augustine says (De Sanct. Virg. iv): "Mary answered the announcing angel: 'How shall this be done, because I know not man?' She would not have said this unless she had already vowed her virginity to God."

I answer that, As we have stated in the [4134]SS, Q[88], A[6], works of perfection are more praiseworthy when performed in fulfilment of a vow. Now it is clear that for reasons already given ([4135]AA[1],2,3) virginity had a special place in the Mother of God. It was therefore fitting that her virginity should be consecrated to God by vow. Nevertheless because, while the Law was in force both men and women were bound to attend to the duty of begetting, since the worship of God was spread according to carnal origin, until Christ was born of that people; the Mother of God is not believed to have taken an absolute vow of virginity, before being espoused to Joseph, although she desired to do so, yet yielding her own will to God's judgment. Afterwards, however, having taken a husband, according as the custom of the time required, together with him she took a vow of virginity.

Reply to Objection 1: Because it seemed to be forbidden by the law not to take the necessary steps for leaving a posterity on earth, therefore the Mother of God did not vow virginity absolutely, but under the condition that it were pleasing to God. When, however, she knew that it was acceptable to God, she made the vow absolute, before the angel's Annunciation.

Reply to Objection 2: Just as the fulness of grace was in Christ perfectly, yet some beginning of the fulness preceded in His Mother; so also the observance of the counsels, which is an effect of God's grace, began its perfection in Christ, but was begun after a fashion in His Virgin Mother.

Reply to Objection 3: These words of the Apostle are to be understood of those who vow chastity absolutely. Christ's Mother did not do this until she was espoused to Joseph. After her espousals, however, by their common consent she took a vow of virginity together with her spouse.

OF THE ESPOUSALS OF THE MOTHER OF GOD (TWO ARTICLES)

We now consider the espousals of God's Mother: concerning which two points arise for inquiry:
(1) Whether Christ should have been born of an espoused virgin?
(2) Whether there was true marriage between our Lord's Mother and Joseph?

Whether Christ should have been born of an espoused virgin?

Objection 1: It would seem that Christ should not have been born of an espoused virgin. For espousals are ordered to carnal intercourse. But our Lord's Mother never wished to have carnal intercourse with her husband; because this would be derogatory to the virginity of her mind. Therefore she should not have been espoused.

Objection 2: Further, that Christ was born of a virgin was miraculous, whence Augustine says (Ep. ad Volus. cxxxvii): "This same power of God brought forth the infant's limbs out of the virginal womb of His inviolate Mother, by which in the vigor of manhood He passed through the closed doors. If we are told why this happened, it will cease to be wonderful; if another instance be alleged, it will no longer be unique." But miracles that are wrought in confirmation of the Faith should be manifest. Since, therefore, by her Espousals this miracle would be less evident, it seems that it was unfitting that Christ should be born of an espoused virgin.

Objection 3: Further, the martyr Ignatius, as Jerome says on Mat. 1:18, gives as a reason of the espousals of the Mother of God, "that the manner of His Birth might be hidden from the devil, who would think Him to be begotten not of a virgin but of a wife." But this seems to be no reason at all. First, because by his natural cunning he knows whatever takes place in bodies. Secondly, because later on the demons, through many evident signs, knew Christ after a fashion: whence it is written (Mk. 1:23,24): "A man with an unclean spirit . . . cried out, saying: What have we to do with Thee, Jesus of Nazareth? Art Thou come to destroy us? I know . . . Thou art the Holy one of God." Therefore it does not seem fitting that the Mother of God should have been espoused.

Objection 4: Further, Jerome gives as another reason, "lest the Mother of God should be stoned by the Jews as an adulteress." But this reason seems to have no weight, for if she were not espoused, she could not be condemned for adultery. Therefore it does not seem reasonable that Christ should be born of an espoused virgin.

On the contrary, It is written (Mat. 1:18): "When as His Mother Mary was espoused to Joseph": and (Lk. 1:26,27): "The angel Gabriel was sent . . . to a virgin espoused to a man whose name was Joseph."

I answer that, It was fitting that Christ should be born of an espoused virgin; first, for His own sake; secondly, for His Mother's sake; thirdly, for our sake. For the sake of Christ Himself, for four reasons. First, lest He should be rejected by unbelievers as illegitimate: wherefore Ambrose says on Lk. 1:26,27: "How could we blame Herod or the Jews if they seem to persecute one who was born of adultery?"

Secondly, in order that in the customary way His genealogy might be traced through the male line. Thus Ambrose says on Lk. 3:23: "He Who came into the world, according to the custom of the world had to be enrolled Now for this purpose, it is the men that are required, because they represent the family in the senate and other courts. The custom of the Scriptures, too, shows that the ancestry of the men is always traced out."

Thirdly, for the safety of the new-born Child: lest the devil should plot serious hurt against Him. Hence Ignatius says that she was espoused "that the manner of His Birth might be hidden from the devil."

Fourthly, that He might be fostered by Joseph: who is therefore called His "father," as bread-winner.

It was also fitting for the sake of the Virgin. First, because thus she was rendered exempt from punishment; that is, "lest she should be stoned by the Jews as an adulteress," as Jerome says.

Secondly, that thus she might be safeguarded from ill fame. Whence Ambrose says on Lk. 1:26,27: "She was espoused lest she be wounded by the ill-fame of violated virginity, in whom the pregnant womb would betoken corruption."

Thirdly, that, as Jerome says, Joseph might administer to her wants.

This was fitting, again, for our sake. First, because Joseph is thus a witness to Christ's being born of a virgin. Wherefore Ambrose says: "Her husband is the more trustworthy witness of her purity, in that he would deplore the dishonor, and avenge the disgrace, were it not that he acknowledged the mystery."

Secondly, because thereby the very words of the Virgin are rendered more credible by which she asserted her virginity. Thus Ambrose says: "Belief in Mary's words is strengthened, the motive for a lie is removed. If she had not been espoused when pregnant, she would seem to have wished to hide her sin by a lie: being espoused, she had no motive for lying, since a woman's pregnancy is the reward of marriage and gives grace to the nuptial bond." These two reasons add strength to our faith.

Thirdly, that all excuse be removed from those virgins who, through want of caution, fall into dishonor. Hence Ambrose says: "It was not becoming that virgins should expose themselves to evil report, and cover themselves with the excuse that the Mother of the Lord had also been oppressed by ill-fame."

Fourthly, because by this the universal Church is typified, which is a virgin and yet is espoused to one Man, Christ, as Augustine says (De Sanct. Virg. xii).

A fifth reason may be added: since the Mother of the Lord being both espoused and a virgin, both virginity and wedlock are honored in her person, in contradiction to those heretics who disparaged one or the other.

Reply to Objection 1: We must believe that the Blessed Virgin, Mother of God, desired, from an intimate inspiration of the Holy Ghost, to be espoused, being confident that by the help of God she would never come to have carnal intercourse: yet she left this to God's discretion. Wherefore she suffered nothing in detriment to her virginity.

Reply to Objection 2: As Ambrose says on Lk. 1:26: "Our Lord preferred that men should doubt of His origin rather than of His Mother's purity. For he knew the delicacy of virgin modesty, and how easily the fair name of chastity is disparaged: nor did He choose that our faith in His Birth should be strengthened in detriment to His Mother." We must observe, however, that some miracles wrought by God are the direct object of faith; such are the miracles of the virginal Birth, the Resurrection of our Lord, and the Sacrament of the Altar. Wherefore our Lord wished these to be more hidden, that belief in them might have greater merit. Whereas other miracles are for the strengthening of faith: and these it behooves to be manifest.

Reply to Objection 3: As Augustine says (De Trin. iii), the devil can do many things by his natural power which he is hindered by the Divine power from doing. Thus it may be that by his natural power the devil could know that the Mother of God knew not man, but was a virgin; yet was prevented by God from knowing the manner of the Divine Birth. That afterwards the devil after a fashion knew that He was the Son of God, makes no difficulty: because then the time had already come for Christ to make known His power against the devil, and to suffer persecution aroused by him. But during His infancy it behooved the malice of the devil to be withheld, lest he should persecute Him too severely: for Christ did not wish to suffer such things then, nor to make His power known, but to show Himself to be in all things like other infants. Hence Pope Leo (Serm. in Epiph. iv) says that "the Magi found the Child Jesus small in body, dependent on others, unable to speak, and in no way differing from the generality of human infants." Ambrose, however, expounding Lk. 1:26, seems to understand this of the devil's members. For, after giving the above reason---namely, that the prince of the world might be deceived---he continues thus: "Yet still more did He deceive the princes of the world, since the evil disposition of the demons easily discovers even hidden things: but those who spend their lives in worldly vanities can have no acquaintance of Divine things."

Reply to Objection 4: The sentence of adulteresses according to the Law was that they should be stoned, not only if they were already espoused or married, but also if their maidenhood were still under the protection of the paternal roof, until the day when they enter the married state. Thus it is written (Dt. 22:20,21): "If . . . virginity be not found in the damsel . . . the men of the city shall stone her to death, and she shall die; because she hath done a wicked thing in Israel, to play the whore in her father's house."

It may also be said, according to some writers, that the Blessed Virgin was of the family or kindred of Aaron, so that she was related to Elizabeth, as we are told (Lk. 1:36). Now a virgin of the priestly tribe was condemned to death for whoredom; for we read (Lev. 21:9): "If the daughter of a priest be taken in whoredom, and dishonor the name of her father, she shall be burnt with fire."

Lastly, some understand the passage of Jerome to refer to the throwing of stones by ill-fame.

Whether there was a true marriage between Mary and Joseph?

Objection 1: It would seem that there was no true marriage between Mary and Joseph. For Jerome says against Helvidius that Joseph "was Mary's guardian rather than her husband." But if this was a true marriage, Joseph was truly her husband. Therefore there was no true marriage between Mary and Joseph.

Objection 2: Further, on Mat. 1:16: "Jacob begot Joseph the husband of Mary," Jerome says: "When thou readest 'husband' suspect not a marriage; but remember that Scripture is wont to speak of those who are betrothed as husband and wife." But a true marriage is not effected by the betrothal, but by the wedding. Therefore, there was no true marriage between the Blessed Virgin and Joseph.

Objection 3: Further, it is written (Mat. 1:19): "Joseph, her husband, being a just man, and not willing to take her away [*Douay: 'publicly to expose her'], i.e. to take her to his home in order to cohabit with her, was minded to put her away privately, i.e. to postpone the wedding," as Remigius [*Cf. Catena Aurea in Matth.] expounds. Therefore, it seems that, as the wedding was not yet solemnized, there was no true marriage: especially since, after the marriage contract, no one can lawfully put his wife away.

On the contrary, Augustine says (De Consensu Evang. ii): "It cannot be allowed that the evangelist thought that Joseph ought to sever his union with Mary" (since he said that Joseph was Mary's husband) "on the ground that in giving birth to Christ, she had not conceived of him, but remained a virgin. For by this example the faithful are taught that if after marriage they remain continent by mutual consent, their union is still and is rightly called marriage, even without intercourse of the sexes."

I answer that, Marriage or wedlock is said to be true by reason of its attaining its perfection. Now perfection of anything is twofold; first, and second. The first perfection of a thing consists in its very form, from which it receives its species; while the second perfection of a thing consists in its operation, by which in some way a thing attains its end. Now the form of matrimony consists in a certain inseparable union of souls, by which husband and wife are pledged by a bond of mutual affection that cannot be sundered. And the end of matrimony is the begetting and upbringing of children: the first of which is attained by conjugal intercourse; the second by the other duties of husband and wife, by which they help one another in rearing their offspring.

Thus we may say, as to the first perfection, that the marriage of the Virgin Mother of God and Joseph was absolutely true: because both consented to the nuptial bond, but not expressly to the bond of the flesh, save on the condition that it was pleasing to God. For this reason the angel calls Mary the wife of Joseph, saying to him (Mat. 1:20): "Fear not to take unto thee Mary thy wife": on which words Augustine says (De Nup. et Concup. i): "She is called his wife from the first promise of her espousals, whom he had not known nor ever was to know by carnal intercourse."

But as to the second perfection which is attained by the marriage act, if this be referred to carnal intercourse, by which children are begotten; thus this marriage was not consummated. Wherefore Ambrose says on Lk. 1:26,27: "Be not surprised that Scripture calls Mary a wife. The fact of her marriage is declared, not to insinuate the loss of virginity, but to witness to the reality of the union." Nevertheless, this marriage had the second perfection, as to upbringing of the child. Thus Augustine says (De Nup. et Concup. i): "All the nuptial blessings are fulfilled in the marriage of Christ's parents, offspring, faith and sacrament. The offspring we know to have been the Lord Jesus; faith, for there was no adultery: sacrament, since there was no divorce. Carnal intercourse alone there was none."

Reply to Objection 1: Jerome uses the term "husband" in reference to marriage consummated.

Reply to Objection 2: By marriage Jerome means the nuptial intercourse.

Reply to Objection 3: As Chrysostom says (Hom. i super Matth. [*Opus Imperfectum among the supposititious works ascribed to St. Chrysostom]) the Blessed Virgin was so espoused to Joseph that she dwelt in his home: "for just as she who conceives in her husband's house is understood to have conceived of him, so she who conceives elsewhere is suspect." Consequently sufficient precaution would not have been taken to safeguard the fair fame of the Blessed Virgin, if she had not the entry of her husband's house. Wherefore the words, "not willing to take her away" are better rendered as meaning, "not willing publicly to expose her," than understood of taking her to his house. Hence the evangelist adds that "he was minded to put her away privately." But although she had the entry of Joseph's house by reason of her first promise of espousals, yet the time had not yet come for the solemnizing of the wedding; for which reason they had not yet consummated the marriage. Therefore, as Chrysostom says (Hom. iv in Matth.): "The evangelist does not say, 'before she was taken to the house of her husband,' because she was already in the house. For it was the custom among the ancients for espoused maidens to enter frequently the houses of them to whom they were betrothed." Therefore the angel also said to Joseph: "Fear not to take unto thee Mary thy wife"; that is: "Fear not to solemnize your marriage with her." Others, however, say that she was not yet admitted to his house, but only betrothed to him. But the first is more in keeping with the Gospel narrative.

OF THE ANNUNCIATION OF THE BLESSED VIRGIN (FOUR ARTICLES)

We now have to consider the Blessed Virgin's Annunciation, concerning which there are four points of inquiry:

(1) Whether it was befitting that announcement should be made to her of that which was to be begotten of her?
(2) By whom should this announcement be made?
(3) In what manner should this announcement be made?
(4) Of the order observed in the Annunciation.

Whether it was necessary to announce to the Blessed Virgin that which was to be done in her?

Objection 1: It would seem that it was unnecessary to announce to the Blessed Virgin that which was to be done in her. For there seems to have been no need of the Annunciation except for the purpose of receiving the Virgin's consent. But her consent seems to have been unnecessary: because the Virginal Conception was foretold by a prophecy of "predestination," which is "fulfilled without our consent," as a gloss says on Mat. 1:22. There was no need, therefore, for this Annunciation.

Objection 2: Further, the Blessed Virgin believed in the Incarnation, for to disbelieve therein excludes man from the way of salvation; because, as the Apostle says (Rom. 3:22): "The justice of God (is) by faith of Jesus Christ." But one needs no further instruction concerning what one believes without doubt. Therefore the Blessed Virgin had no need for the Incarnation of her Son to be announced to her.

Objection 3: Further, just as the Blessed Virgin conceived Christ in her body, so every pious soul conceives Him spiritually. Thus the Apostle says (Gal. 4:19): "My little children, of whom I am in labor again, until Christ be formed in you." But to those who conceive Him spiritually no announcement is made of this conception. Therefore neither should it have been announced to the Blessed Virgin that she was to conceive the Son of God in her womb.

On the contrary, It is related (Lk. 1:31) that the angel said to her: "Behold, thou shalt conceive in thy womb, and shalt bring forth a son."

I answer that, It was reasonable that it should be announced to the Blessed Virgin that she was to conceive Christ. First, in order to maintain a becoming order in the union of the Son of God with the Virgin---namely, that she should be informed in mind concerning Him, before conceiving Him in the flesh. Thus Augustine says (De Sancta Virgin. iii): "Mary is more blessed in receiving the faith of Christ, than in conceiving the flesh of Christ"; and further on he adds: "Her nearness as a Mother would have been of no profit to Mary, had she not borne Christ in her heart after a more blessed manner than in her flesh."

Secondly, that she might be a more certain witness of this mystery, being instructed therein by God.

Thirdly, that she might offer to God the free gift of her obedience: which she proved herself right ready to do, saying: "Behold the handmaid of the Lord."

Fourthly, in order to show that there is a certain spiritual wedlock between the Son of God and human nature. Wherefore in the Annunciation the Virgin's consent was besought in lieu of that of the entire human nature.

Reply to Objection 1: The prophecy of predestination is fulfilled without the causality of our will; not without its consent.

Reply to Objection 2: The Blessed Virgin did indeed believe explicitly in the future Incarnation; but, being humble, she did not think such high things of herself. Consequently she required instruction in this matter.

Reply to Objection 3: The spiritual conception of Christ through faith is preceded by the preaching of the faith, for as much as "faith is by hearing" (Rom. 10:17). Yet man does not know for certain thereby that he has grace; but he does know that the faith, which he has received, is true.

Whether the annunciation should have been made by an angel to the Blessed Virgin?

Objection 1: It would seem that the Annunciation should not have been made by an angel to our Blessed Lady. For revelations to the highest angels are made immediately by God, as Dionysius says (Coel. Hier. vii). But the Mother of God is exalted above all the angels. Therefore it seems that the mystery of the Incarnation should have been announced to her by God immediately, and not by an angel.

Objection 2: Further, if in this matter it behooved the common order to be observed, by which Divine things are announced to men by angels; in like manner Divine things are announced to a woman by a man: wherefore the Apostle says (1 Cor. 14:34,35): "Let women keep silence in the churches . . . but if they would learn anything, let them ask their husbands at home." Therefore it seems that the mystery of the Incarnation should have been announced to the Blessed Virgin by some man: especially seeing that Joseph, her husband, was instructed thereupon by an angel, as is related (Mat. 1:20,21)

Objection 3: Further, none can becomingly announce what he knows not. But the highest angels did not fully know the mystery of the Incarnation: wherefore Dionysius says (Coel. Hier. vii) that the question, "Who is this that cometh from Edom?" (Is. 63:1) is to be understood as made by them. Therefore it seems that the announcement of the Incarnation could not be made becomingly by any angel.

Objection 4: Further, greater things should be announced by messengers of greater dignity. But the mystery of the Incarnation is the greatest of all things announced by angels to men. It seems, therefore, if it behooved to be announced by an angel at all, that this should have been done by an angel of the highest order. But Gabriel is not of the highest order, but of the order of archangels, which is the last but one: wherefore the Church sings: "We know that the archangel Gabriel brought thee a message from God" [*Feast of Purification B.V.M. ix Resp. Brev. O.P.]. Therefore this announcement was not becomingly made by the archangel Gabriel.

On the contrary, It is written (Lk. 1:26): "The angel Gabriel was sent by God," etc.

I answer that, It was fitting for the mystery of the Incarnation to be announced to the Mother of God by an angel, for three reasons. First, that in this also might be maintained the order established by God, by which Divine things are brought to men by means of the angels. Wherefore Dionysius says (Coel. Hier. iv) that "the angels were the first to be taught the Divine mystery of the loving kindness of Jesus: afterwards the grace of knowledge was imparted to us through them. Thus, then, the most god-like Gabriel made known to Zachary that a prophet son would be born to him; and, to Mary, how the Divine mystery of the ineffable conception of God would be realized in her."

Secondly, this was becoming to the restoration of human nature which was to be effected by Christ. Wherefore Bede says in a homily (in Annunt.): "It was an apt beginning of man's restoration that an angel should be sent by God to the Virgin who was to be hallowed by the Divine Birth: since the first cause of man's ruin was through the serpent being sent by the devil to cajole the woman by the spirit of pride."

Thirdly, because this was becoming to the virginity of the Mother of God. Wherefore Jerome says in a sermon on the Assumption [*Ascribed to St. Jerome but not his work]: "It is well that an angel be sent to the Virgin; because virginity is ever akin to the angelic nature. Surely to live in the flesh and not according to the flesh is not an earthly but a heavenly life."

Reply to Objection 1: The Mother of God was above the angels as regards the dignity to which she was chosen by God. But as regards the present state of life, she was beneath the angels. For even Christ Himself, by reason of His passible life, "was made a little lower than the angels," according to Heb. 2:9. But because Christ was both wayfarer and comprehensor, He did not need to be instructed by angels, as regards knowledge of Divine things. The Mother of God, however, was not yet in the state of comprehension: and therefore she had to be instructed by angels concerning the Divine Conception.

Reply to Objection 2: As Augustine says in a sermon on the Assumption (De Assump. B.V.M. [*Work of another author: among the works of St. Augustine]) a true estimation of the Blessed Virgin excludes her from certain general rules. For "neither did she 'multiply her conceptions' nor was she 'under man's, i.e. her husband's,' power (Gn. 3:16), who in her spotless womb conceived Christ of the Holy Ghost." Therefore it was fitting that she should be informed of the mystery of the Incarnation by means not of a man, but of an angel. For this reason it was made known to her before Joseph: since the message was brought to her before she conceived, but to Joseph after she had conceived.

Reply to Objection 3: As may be gathered from the passage quoted from Dionysius, the angels were acquainted with the mystery of the Incarnation: and yet they put this question, being desirous that Christ should give them more perfect knowledge of the details of this mystery, which are incomprehensible to any created intellect. Thus Maximus [*Maximus of Constantinople] says that "there can be no question that the angels knew that the Incarnation was to take place. But it was not given to them to trace the manner of our Lord's conception, nor how it was that He remained whole in the Father, whole throughout the universe, and was whole in the narrow abode of the Virgin."

Reply to Objection 4: Some say that Gabriel was of the highest order; because Gregory says (Hom. de Centum Ovibus [*34 in Evang.]): "It was right that one of the highest angels should come, since his message was most sublime." But this does nat imply that he was of the highest order of all, but in regard to the angels: since he was an archangel. Thus the Church calls him an archangel, and Gregory himself in a homily (De Centum Ovibus 34) says that "those are called archangels who announce sublime things." It is therefore sufficiently credible that he was the highest of the archangels. And, as Gregory says (De Centum Ovibus 34), this name agrees with his office: for "Gabriel means 'Power of God.' This message therefore was fittingly brought by the 'Power of God,' because the Lord of hosts and mighty in battle was coming to overcome the powers of the air."

Whether the angel of annunciation should have appeared to the Virgin in a bodily vision?

Objection 1: It would seem that the angel of the Annunciation should not have appeared to the Virgin in a bodily vision. For "intellectual vision is more excellent than bodily vision," as Augustine says (Gen. ad lit. xii), and especially more becoming to an angel: since by intellectual vision an angel is seen in his substance; whereas in a bodily vision he is seen in the bodily shape which he assumes. Now since it behooved a sublime messenger to come to announce the Divine Conception, so, seemingly, he should have appeared in the most excellent kind of vision. Therefore it seems that the angel of the Annunciation appeared to the Virgin in an intellectual vision.

Objection 2: Further, imaginary vision also seems to excel bodily vision: just as the imagination is a higher power than the senses. But "the angel . . . appeared to Joseph in his sleep" (Mat. 1:20), which was clearly an imaginary vision. Therefore it seems that he should have appeared to the Blessed Virgin also in an imaginary vision.

Objection 3: Further, the bodily vision of a spiritual substance stupefies the beholder; thus we sing of the Virgin herself: "And the Virgin seeing the light was filled with fear" [*Feast of Annunciation, B.V.M. ii Resp. Brev. O.P.]. But it was better that her mind should be preserved from being thus troubled. Therefore it was not fitting that this announcement should be made in a bodily vision.

On the contrary, Augustine in a sermon (De Annunt. iii) pictures the Blessed Virgin as speaking thus: "To me came the archangel Gabriel with glowing countenance, gleaming robe, and wondrous step." But these cannot pertain to other than bodily vision. Therefore the angel of the Annunciation appeared in a bodily vision to the Blessed Virgin.

I answer that, The angel of the Annunciation appeared in a bodily vision to the Blessed Virgin. And this indeed was fitting, first in regard to that which was announced. For the angel came to announce the Incarnation of the invisible God. Wherefore it was becoming that, in order to make this known, an invisible creature should assume a form in which to appear visibly: forasmuch as all the apparitions of the Old Testament are ordered to that apparition in which the Son of God appeared in the flesh.

Secondly, it was fitting as regards the dignity of the Mother of God, who was to receive the Son of God not only in her mind, but in her bodily womb. Therefore it behooved not only her mind, but also her bodily senses to be refreshed by the angelic vision.

Thirdly, it is in keeping with the certainty of that which was announced. For we apprehend with greater certainty that which is before our eyes, than what is in our imagination. Thus Chrysostom says (Hom. iv in Matth.) that the angel "came to the Virgin not in her sleep, but visibly. For since she was receiving from the angel a message exceeding great, before such an event she needed a vision of great solemnity."

Reply to Objection 1: Intellectual vision excels merely imaginary and merely bodily vision. But Augustine himself says (De Annunt. iii) that prophecy is more excellent if accompanied by intellectual and imaginary vision, than if accompanied by only one of them. Now the Blessed Virgin perceived not only the bodily vision, but also the intellectual illumination. Wherefore this was a more excellent vision. Yet it would have been more excellent if she had perceived the angel himself in his substance by her intellectual vision. But it was incompatible with her state of wayfarer that she should see an angel in his essence.

Reply to Objection 2: The imagination is indeed a higher power than the exterior sense: but because the senses are the principle of human knowledge, the greatest certainty is in them, for the principles of knowledge must needs always be most certain. Consequently Joseph, to whom the angel appeared in his sleep, did not have so excellent a vision as the Blessed Virgin.

Reply to Objection 3: As Ambrose says on Lk. 1:11: "We are disturbed, and lose our presence of mind, when we are confronted by the presence of a superior power." And this happens not only in bodily, but also in imaginary vision. Wherefore it is written (Gn. 15:12) that "when the sun was setting, a deep sleep fell upon Abram, and a great and darksome horror seized upon him." But by being thus disturbed man is not harmed to such an extent that therefore he ought to forego the vision of an angel. First because from the very fact that man is raised above himself, in which matter his dignity is concerned, his inferior powers are weakened; and from this results the aforesaid disturbance: thus, also, when the natural heat is drawn within a body, the exterior parts tremble. Secondly, because, as Origen says (Hom. iv in Luc.): "The angel who appeared, knowing hers was a human nature, first sought to remedy the disturbance of mind to which a man is subject." Wherefore both to Zachary and to Mary, as soon as they were disturbed, he said: "Fear not." For this reason, as we read in the life of Anthony, "it is difficult to discern good from evil spirits. For if joy succeed fear, we should know that the help is from the Lord: because security of soul is a sign of present majesty. But if the fear with which we are stricken persevere, it is an enemy that we see."

Moreover it was becoming to virginal modesty that the Virgin should be troubled. Because, as Ambrose says on Lk. 1:20: "It is the part of a virgin to be timid, to fear the advances of men, and to shrink from men's addresses."

But others says that as the Blessed Virgin was accustomed to angelic visions, she was not troubled at seeing this angel, but with wonder at hearing what the angel said to her, for she did not think so highly of herself. Wherefore the evangelist does not say that she was troubled at seeing the angel, but "at his saying."

Whether the Annunciation took place in becoming order?

Objection 1: It would seem that the Annunciation did not take place in becoming order. For the dignity of the Mother of God results from the child she conceived. But the cause should be made known before the effect. Therefore the angel should have announced to the Virgin the conception of her child before acknowledging her dignity in greeting her.

Objection 2: Further, proof should be omitted in things which admit of no doubt; and premised where doubt is possible. But the angel seems first to have announced what the virgin might doubt, and which, because of her doubt, would make her ask: "How shall this be done?" and afterwards to have given the proof, alleging both the instance of Elizabeth and the omnipotence of God. Therefore the Annunciation was made by the angel in unbecoming order.

Objection 3: Further, the greater cannot be adequately proved by the less. But it was a greater wonder for a virgin than for an old woman to be with child. Therefore the angel's proof was insufficient to demonstrate the conception of a virgin from that of an old woman.

On the contrary, it is written (Rom. 13:1): "Those that are of God, are well ordered [Vulg.: 'Those that are, are ordained of God']." Now the angel was "sent by God" to announce unto the Virgin, as is related Lk. 1:26. Therefore the Annunciation was made by the angel in the most perfect order.

I answer that, The Annunciation was made by the angel in a becoming manner. For the angel had a threefold purpose in regard to the Virgin. First, to draw her attention to the consideration of a matter of such moment. This he did by greeting her by a new and unwonted salutation. Wherefore Origen says, commenting on Luke (Hom. vi), that if "she had known that similar words had been addressed to anyone else, she, who had knowledge of the Law, would never have been astonished at the seeming strangeness of the salutation." In which salutation he began by asserting her worthiness of the conception, by saying, "Full of grace"; then he announced the conception in the words, "The Lord is with thee"; and then foretold the honor which would result to her therefrom, by saying, "Blessed art thou among women."

Secondly, he purposed to instruct her about the mystery of the Incarnation, which was to be fulfilled in her. This he did by foretelling the conception and birth, saying: "Behold, thou shalt conceive in thy womb," etc.; and by declaring the dignity of the child conceived, saying: "He shall be great"; and further, by making known the mode of conception, when he said: "The Holy Ghost shall come upon thee."

Thirdly, he purposed to lead her mind to consent. This he did by the instance of Elizabeth, and by the argument from Divine omnipotence.

Reply to Objection 1: To a humble mind nothing is more astonishing than to hear its own excellence. Now, wonder is most effective in drawing the mind's attention. Therefore the angel, desirous of drawing the Virgin's attention to the hearing of so great a mystery, began by praising her.

Reply to Objection 2: Ambrose says explicitly on Lk. 1:34, that the Blessed Virgin did not doubt the angel's words. For he says: "Mary's answer is more temperate than the words of the priest. She says: How shall this be? He replies: Whereby shall I know this? He denies that he believes, since he denies that he knows this. She does not doubt fulfilment when she asks how it shall be done."

Augustine, however, seems to assert that she doubted. For he says (De Qq. Vet. et Nov. Test. qu. li): "To Mary, in doubt about the conception, the angel declares the possibility thereof." But such a doubt is one of wonder rather than of unbelief. And so the angel adduces a proof, not as a cure for unbelief, but in order to remove her astonishment.

Reply to Objection 3: As Ambrose says (Hexaemeron v): "For this reason had many barren women borne children, that the virginal birth might be credible."

The conception of the sterile Elizabeth is therefore adduced, not as a sufficient argument, but as a kind of figurative example.: consequently in support of this instance, the convincing argument is added taken from the Divine omnipotence.

Day 269

OF THE MATTER FROM WHICH THE SAVIOUR'S BODY WAS CONCEIVED (EIGHT ARTICLES)

We have now to consider the Saviour's conception. First, as to the matter from which His body was conceived; secondly, as to the author of His conception; thirdly, as to the manner and order of His conception.

Concerning the first there are eight points of inquiry:

(1) Whether the flesh of Christ was derived from Adam?

(2) Whether it was derived from David?

(3) Of the genealogy of Christ which is given in the Gospels;

(4) Whether it was fitting for Christ to be born of a woman?

(5) Whether His body was formed from the purest blood of the Virgin?

(6) Whether the flesh of Christ was in the patriarchs as to something signate?

(7) Whether the flesh of Christ in the patriarchs was subject to sin?

(8) Whether Christ paid tithes in the loins of Abraham?

Whether the flesh of Christ was derived from Adam?

Objection 1: It would seem that Christ's flesh was not derived from Adam. For the Apostle says (1 Cor. 15:47): "The first man was of the earth, earthly: the second man, from heaven, heavenly." Now, the first man is Adam: and the second man is Christ. Therefore Christ is not derived from Adam, but has an origin distinct from him.

Objection 2: Further, the conception of Christ should have been most miraculous. But it is a greater miracle to form man's body from the slime of the earth, than from human matter derived from Adam. It seems therefore unfitting that Christ should take flesh from Adam. Therefore the body of Christ should not have been formed from the mass of the human race derived from Adam, but of some other matter.

Objection 3: Further, by "one man sin entered into this world," i.e. by Adam, because in him all nations sinned originally, as is clear from Rom. 5:12. But if Christ's body was derived from Adam, He would have been in Adam originally when he sinned: therefore he would have contracted original sin; which is unbecoming in His purity. Therefore the body of Christ was not formed of matter derived from Adam.

On the contrary, The Apostle says (Heb. 2:16): "Nowhere doth He"---that is, the Son of God---"take hold of the angels: but of the seed of Abraham He taketh hold." But the seed of Abraham was derived from Adam. Therefore Christ's body was formed of matter derived from Adam.

I answer that, Christ assumed human nature in order to cleanse it of corruption. But human nature did not need to be cleansed save in as far as it was soiled in its tainted origin whereby it was descended from Adam. Therefore it was becoming that He should assume flesh of matter derived from Adam, that the nature itself might be healed by the assumption.

Reply to Objection 1: The second man, i.e. Christ, is said to be of heaven, not indeed as to the matter from which His body was formed, but either as to the virtue whereby it was formed; or even as to His very Godhead. But as to matter, Christ's body was earthly, as Adam's body was.

Reply to Objection 2: As stated above ([4136]Q[29], A[1], ad 2) the mystery of Christ's Incarnation is miraculous, not as ordained to strengthen faith, but as an article of faith. And therefore in the mystery of the Incarnation we do not seek that which is most miraculous, as in those miracles that are wrought for the confirmation of faith' but what is most becoming to Divine wisdom, and most expedient to the salvation of man, since this is what we seek in all matters of faith.

It may also be said that in the mystery of the Incarnation the miracle is not only in reference to the matter of the conception, but rather in respect of the manner of the conception and birth; inasmuch as a virgin conceived and gave birth to God.

Reply to Objection 3: As stated above ([4137]Q[15], A[1], ad 2), Christ's body was in Adam in respect of a bodily substance---that is to say, that the corporeal matter of Christ's body was derived from Adam: but it was not there by reason of seminal virtue, because it was not conceived from the seed of man. Thus it did not contract original sin, as others who are descended from Adam by man's seed.

Whether Christ took flesh of the seed of David?

Objection 1: It would seem that Christ did not take flesh of the seed of David. For Matthew, in tracing the genealogy of Christ, brings it down to Joseph. But Joseph was not Christ's father, as shown above ([4138]Q[28], A[1], ad 1,2). Therefore it seems that Christ was not descended from David.

Objection 2: Further, Aaron was of the tribe of Levi, as related Ex. 6. Now Mary the Mother of Christ is called the cousin of Elizabeth, who was a daughter of Aaron, as is clear from Lk. 1:5,36. Therefore, since David was of the tribe of Juda, as is shown Mat. 1, it seems that Christ was not descended from David.

Objection 3: Further, it is written of Jechonias (Jer. 22:30): "Write this man barren . . . for there shall not be a man of his seed that shall sit upon the throne of David." Whereas of Christ it is written (Is. 9:7): "He shall sit upon the throne of David." Therefore Christ was not of the seed of Jechonias: nor, consequently, of the family of David, since Matthew traces the genealogy from David through Jechonias.

On the contrary, It is written (Rom. 1:3): "Who was made to him of the seed of David according to the flesh."

I answer that, Christ is said to have been the son especially of two of the patriarchs, Abraham and David, as is clear from Mat. 1:1. There are many reasons for this. First to these especially was the promise made concerning Christ. For it was said to Abraham (Gn. 22:18): "In thy seed shall all the nations of the earth be blessed": which words the Apostle expounds of Christ (Gal. 3:16): "To Abraham were the promises made and to his seed. He saith not, 'And to his seeds' as of many; but as of one, 'And to thy seed,' which is Christ." And to David it was said (Ps. 131:11): "Of the fruit of thy womb I will set upon thy throne." Wherefore the Jewish people, receiving Him with kingly honor, said (Mat. 21:9): "Hosanna to the Son of David."

A second reason is because Christ was to be king, prophet, and priest. Now Abraham was a priest; which is clear from the Lord saying unto him (Gn. 15:9): "Take thee [Vulg.: 'Me'] a cow of three years old," etc. He was also a prophet, according to Gn. 20:7: "He is a prophet; and he shall pray for thee." Lastly David was both king and prophet.

A third reason is because circumcision had its beginning in Abraham: while in David God's election was most clearly made manifest, according to 1 Kings 13:14: "The Lord hath sought Him a man according to His own heart." And consequently Christ is called in a most special way the Son of both, in order to show that He came for the salvation both of the circumcised and of the elect among the Gentiles.

Reply to Objection 1: Faustus the Manichean argued thus, in the desire to prove that Christ is not the Son of David, because He was not conceived of Joseph, in whom Matthew's genealogy terminates. Augustine answered this argument thus (Contra Faust. xxii): "Since the same evangelist affirms that Joseph was Mary's husband and that Christ's mother was a virgin, and that Christ was of the seed of Abraham, what must we believe, but that Mary was not a stranger to the family of David: and that it is not without reason that she was called the wife of Joseph, by reason of the close alliance of their hearts, although not mingled in the flesh; and that the genealogy is traced down to Joseph rather than to her by reason of the dignity of the husband? So therefore we believe that Mary was also of the family of David: because we believe the Scriptures, which assert both that Christ was of the seed of David according to the flesh, and that Mary was His Mother, not by sexual intercourse but retaining her virginity." For as Jerome says on Mat. 1:18: "Joseph and Mary were of the same tribe: wherefore he was bound by law to marry her as she was his kinswoman. Hence it was that they were enrolled together at Bethlehem, as being descended from the same stock."

Reply to Objection 2: Gregory of Nazianzum answers this objection by saying that it happened by God's will, that the royal family was united to the priestly race, so that Christ, who is both king and priest, should be born of both according to the flesh. Wherefore Aaron, who was the first priest according to the Law, married a wife of the tribe of Juda, Elizabeth, daughter of Aminadab. It is therefore possible that Elizabeth's father married a wife of the family of David, through whom the Blessed Virgin Mary, who was of the family of David, would be a cousin of Elizabeth. or conversely, and with greater likelihood, that the Blessed Mary's father, who was of the family of David, married a wife of the family of Aaron.

Again, it may be said with Augustine (Contra Faust. xxii) that if Joachim, Mary's father, was of the family of Aaron (as the heretic Faustus pretended to prove from certain apocryphal writings), then we must believe that Joachim's mother, or else his wife, was of the family of David, so long as we say that Mary was in some way descended from David.

Reply to Objection 3: As Ambrose says on Lk. 3:25, this prophetical passage does not deny that a posterity will be born of the seed of Jechonias. And so Christ is of his seed. Neither is the fact that Christ reigned contrary to prophecy, for He did not reign with worldly honor; since He declared: "My kingdom is not of this world."

Whether Christ's genealogy is suitably traced by the evangelists?

Objection 1: It would seem that Christ's genealogy is not suitably traced by the Evangelists. For it is written (Is. 53:8): "Who shall declare His generation?" Therefore Christ's genealogy should not have been set down.

Objection 2: Further, one man cannot possibly have two fathers. But Matthew says that "Jacob begot Joseph, the husband of Mary": whereas Luke says that Joseph was the son of Heli. Therefore they contradict one another.

Objection 3: Further, there seem to be divergencies between them on several points. For Matthew, at the commencement of his book, beginning from Abraham and coming down to Joseph, enumerates forty-two generations. Whereas Luke sets down Christ's genealogy after His Baptism, and beginning from Christ traces the series of generations back to God, counting in all seventy-seven generations, the first and last included. It seems therefore that their accounts of Christ's genealogy do not agree.

Objection 4: Further, we read (4 Kings 8:24) that Joram begot Ochozias, who was succeeded by his son Joas: who was succeeded by his son Amasius: after whom reigned his son Azarias, called Ozias; who was succeeded by his son Joathan. But Matthew says that Joram begot Ozias. Therefore it seems that his account of Christ's genealogy is unsuitable, since he omits three kings in the middle thereof.

Objection 5: Further, all those who are mentioned in Christ's genealogy had both a father and a mother, and many of them had brothers also. Now in Christ's genealogy Matthew mentions only three mothers---namely, Thamar, Ruth, and the wife of Urias. He also mentions the brothers of Judas and Jechonias, and also Phares and Zara. But Luke mentions none of these. Therefore the evangelists seem to have described the genealogy of Christ in an unsuitable manner.

On the contrary, The authority of Scripture suffices.

I answer that, As is written (2 Tim. 3:16), "All Holy Scripture is inspired of God [Vulg.: 'All scripture inspired of God is profitable'], etc. Now what is done by God is done in perfect order, according to Rom. 13:1: "Those that are of God are ordained [Vulg.: 'Those that are, are ordained of God']. Therefore Christ's genealogy is set down by the evangelists in a suitable order.

Reply to Objection 1: As Jerome says on Mat. 1, Isaias speaks of the generation of Christ's Godhead. Whereas Matthew relates the generation of Christ in His humanity; not indeed by explaining the manner of the Incarnation, which is also unspeakable; but by enumerating Christ's forefathers from whom He was descended according to the flesh.

Reply to Objection 2: Various answers have been made by certain writers to this objection which was raised by Julian the Apostate; for some, as Gregory of Nazianzum, say that the people mentioned by the two evangelists are the same, but under different names, as though they each had two. But this will not stand: because Matthew mentions one of David's sons---namely, Solomon; whereas Luke mentions another---namely, Nathan, who according to the history of the kings (2 Kings 5:14) were clearly brothers.

Wherefore others said that Matthew gave the true genealogy of Christ: while Luke gave the supposititious genealogy; hence he began: "Being (as it was supposed) the son of Joseph." For among the Jews there were some who believed that, on account of the crimes of the kings of Juda, Christ would be born of the family of David, not through the kings, but through some other line of private individuals.

Others again have supposed that Matthew gave the forefathers according to the flesh: whereas Luke gave these according to the spirit, that is, righteous men, who are called (Christ's) forefathers by likeness of virtue.

But an answer is given in the Qq. Vet. et Nov. Test. [*Part i, qu. lvi; part 2, qu. vi] to the effect that we are not to understand that Joseph is said by Luke to be the son of Heli: but that at the time of Christ, Heli and Joseph were differently descended from David. Hence Christ is said to have been supposed to be the son of Joseph, and also to have been the son of Heli as though (the Evangelist) were to say that Christ, from the fact that He was the son of Joseph, could be called the son of Heli and of all those who were descended from David; as the Apostle says (Rom. 9:5): "Of whom" (viz. the Jews) "is Christ according to the flesh."

Augustine again gives three solutions (De Qq. Evang. ii), saying: "There are three motives by one or other of which the evangelist was guided. For either one evangelist mentions Joseph's father of whom he was begotten; whilst the other gives either his maternal grandfather or some other of his later forefathers; or one was Joseph's natural father: the other is father by adoption. Or, according to the Jewish custom, one of those having died without children, a near relation of his married his wife, the son born of the latter union being reckoned as the son of the former": which is a kind of legal adoption, as Augustine himself says (De Consensu Evang. ii, Cf. Retract. ii).

This last motive is the truest: Jerome also gives it commenting on Mat. 1:16; and Eusebius of Caesarea in his Church history (I, vii), says that it is given by Africanus the historian. For these writers says that Mathan and Melchi, at different times, each begot a son of one and the same wife, named Estha. For Mathan, who traced his descent through Solomon, had married her first, and died, leaving one son, whose name was Jacob: and after his death, as the law did not forbid his widow to remarry, Melchi, who traced his descent through Mathan, being of the same tribe though not of the same family as Mathan, married his widow, who bore him a son, called Heli; so that Jacob and Heli were uterine brothers born to different fathers. Now one of these, Jacob, on his brother Heli dying without issue, married the latter's widow, according to the prescription of the law, of whom he had a son, Joseph, who by nature was his own son, but by law was accounted the son of Heli. Wherefore Matthew says "Jacob begot Joseph": whereas Luke, who was giving the legal genealogy, speaks of no one as begetting.

And although Damascene (De Fide Orth. iv) says that the Blessed Virgin Mary was connected with Joseph in as far as Heli was accounted as his father, for he says that she was descended from Melchi: yet must we also believe that she was in some way descended from Solomon through those patriarchs enumerated by Matthew, who is said to have set down Christ's genealogy according to the flesh; and all the more since Ambrose states that Christ was of the seed of Jechonias.

Reply to Objection 3: According to Augustine (De Consensu Evang. ii) "Matthew purposed to delineate the royal personality of Christ; Luke the priestly personality: so that in Matthew's genealogy is signified the assumption of our sins by our Lord Jesus Christ": inasmuch as by his carnal origin "He assumed 'the likeness of sinful flesh.' But in Luke's genealogy the washing away of our sins is signified," which is effected by Christ's sacrifice. "For which reason Matthew traces the generations downwards, Luke upwards." For the same reason too "Matthew descends from David through Solomon, in whose mother David sinned; whereas Luke ascends to David through Nathan, through whose namesake, the prophet, God expiated his sin." And hence it is also that, because "Matthew wished to signify that Christ had condescended to our mortal nature, he set down the genealogy of Christ at the very outset of his Gospel, beginning with Abraham and descending to Joseph and the birth of Christ Himself. Luke, on the contrary, sets forth Christ's genealogy not at the outset, but after Christ's Baptism, and not in the descending but in the ascending order: as though giving prominence to the office of the priest in expiating our sins, to which John bore witness, saying: 'Behold Him who taketh away the sin of the world.' And in the ascending order, he passes Abraham and continues up to God, to whom we are reconciled by cleansing and expiating. With reason too he follows the origin of adoption; because by adoption we become children of God: whereas by carnal generation the Son of God became the Son of Man. Moreover he shows sufficiently that he does not say that Joseph was the son of Heli as though begotten by him, but because he was adopted by him, since he says that Adam was the son of God, inasmuch as he was created by God."

Again, the number forty pertains to the time of our present life: because of the four parts of the world in which we pass this mortal life under the rule of Christ. And forty is the product of four multiplied by ten: while ten is the sum of the numbers from one to four. The number ten may also refer to the decalogue; and the number four to the present life; or again to the four Gospels, according to which Christ reigns in us. And thus "Matthew, putting forward the royal personality of Christ, enumerates forty persons not counting Him" (cf. Augustine, De Consensu Evang. ii). But this is to be taken on the supposition that it be the same Jechonias at the end of the second, and at the commencement of the third series of fourteen, as Augustine understands it. According to him this was done in order to signify "that under Jechonias there was a certain defection to strange nations during the Babylonian captivity; which also foreshadowed the fact that Christ would pass from the Jews to the Gentiles."

On the other hand, Jerome (on Mat. 1:12-15) says that there were two Joachims---that is, Jechonias, father and son: both of whom are mentioned in Christ's genealogy, so as to make clear the distinction of the generations, which the evangelist divides into three series of fourteen; which amounts in all to forty-two persons. Which number may also be applied to the Holy Church: for it is the product of six, which signifies the labor of the present life, and seven, which signifies the rest of the life to come: for six times seven are forty-two. The number fourteen, which is the sum of ten and four, can also be given the same signification as that given to the number forty, which is the product of the same numbers by multiplication.

But the number used by Luke in Christ's genealogy signifies the generality of sins. "For the number ten is shown in the ten precepts of the Law to be the number of righteousness. Now, to sin is to go beyond the restriction of the Law. And eleven is the number beyond ten." And seven signifies universality: because "universal time is involved in seven days." Now seven times eleven are seventy-seven: so that this number signifies the generality of sins which are taken away by Christ.

Reply to Objection 4: As Jerome says on Mat. 1:8, 11: "Because Joram allied himself with the family of the most wicked Jezabel, therefore his memory is omitted down to the third generation, lest it should be inserted among the holy predecessors of the Nativity." Hence as Chrysostom [*Cf. Opus Imperf. in Matth. Hom. i, falsely ascribed to Chrysostom] says: "Just as great was the blessing conferred on Jehu, who wrought vengeance on the house of Achab and Jezabel, so also great was the curse on the house of Joram, through the wicked daughter of Achab and Jezabel, so that until the fourth generation his posterity is cut off from the number of kings, according to Ex. 20:5: I shall visit [Vulg.: 'Visiting'] the iniquity of the fathers upon the children unto the third and fourth generations."

It must also be observed that there were other kings who sinned and are mentioned in Christ's genealogy: but their impiety was not continuous. For, as it is stated in the book De Qq. Vet. et Nov. Test. qu. lxxxv: "Solomon through his father's merits is included in the series of kings; and Roboam . . . through the merits of Asa," who was son of his (Roboam's) son, Abiam. "But the impiety of those three [*i.e. Ochozias, Joas, and Amasias, of whom St. Augustine asks in this question lxxxv, why they were omitted by St. Matthew] was continuous."

Reply to Objection 5: As Jerome says on Mat. 1:3: "None of the holy women are mentioned in the Saviour's genealogy, but only those whom Scripture censures, so that He who came for the sake of sinners, by being born of sinners, might blot out all sin." Thus Thamar is mentioned, who is censured for her sin with her father-in-law; Rahab who was a whore; Ruth who was a foreigner; and Bethsabee, the wife of Urias, who was an adulteress. The last, however, is not mentioned by name, but is designated through her husband; both on account of his sin, for he was cognizant of the adultery and murder; and further in order that, by mentioning the husband by name, David's sin might be recalled. And because Luke purposes to delineate Christ as the expiator of our sins, he makes no mention of these women. But he does mention Juda's brethren, in order to show that they belong to God's people: whereas Ismael, the brother of Isaac, and Esau, Jacob's brother, were cut off from God's people, and for this reason are not mentioned in Christ's genealogy. Another motive was to show the emptiness of pride of birth: for many of Juda's brethren were born of hand-maidens, and yet all were patriarchs and heads of tribes. Phares and Zara are mentioned together, because, as Ambrose says on Lk. 3:23, "they are the type of the twofold life of man: one, according to the Law," signified by Zara; "the other by Faith," of which Phares is the type. The brethren of Jechonias are included, because they all reigned at various times: which was not the case with other kings: or, again, because they were alike in wickedness and misfortune.

Whether the matter of Christ's body should have been taken from a woman?

Objection 1: It would seem that the matter of Christ's body should not have been taken from a woman. For the male sex is more noble than the female. But it was most suitable that Christ should assume that which is perfect in human nature. Therefore it seems that He should not have taken flesh from a woman but rather from man: just as Eve was formed from the rib of a man.

Objection 2: Further, whoever is conceived of a woman is shut up in her womb. But it ill becomes God, Who fills heaven and earth, as is written Jer. 23:24, to be shut up within the narrow limits of the womb. Therefore it seems that He should not have been conceived of a woman.

Objection 3: Further, those who are conceived of a woman contract a certain uncleanness: as it is written (Job 25:4): "Can man be justified compared with God? Or he that is born of a woman appear clean?" But it was unbecoming that any uncleanness should be in Christ: for He is the Wisdom of God, of whom it is written (Wis. 7:25) that "no defiled thing cometh into her." Therefore it does not seem right that He should have taken flesh from a woman.

On the contrary, It is written (Gal. 4:4): "God sent His Son, made of a woman."

I answer that, Although the Son of God could have taken flesh from whatever matter He willed, it was nevertheless most becoming that He should take flesh from a woman. First because in this way the entire human nature was ennobled. Hence Augustine says (QQ. lxxxiii, qu. 11): "It was suitable that man's liberation should be made manifest in both sexes. Consequently, since it behooved a man, being of the nobler sex, to assume, it was becoming that the liberation of the female sex should be manifested in that man being born of a woman."

Secondly, because thus the truth of the Incarnation is made evident. Wherefore Ambrose says (De Incarn. vi): "Thou shalt find in Christ many things both natural, and supernatural. In accordance with nature He was within the womb," viz. of a woman's body: "but it was above nature that a virgin should conceive and give birth: that thou mightest believe that He was God, who was renewing nature; and that He was man who, according to nature, was being born of a man." And Augustine says (Ep. ad Volus. cxxxvii): "If Almighty God had created a man formed otherwise than in a mother's womb, and had suddenly produced him to sight . . . would He not have strengthened an erroneous opinion, and made it impossible for us to believe that He had become a true man? And whilst He is doing all things wondrously, would He have taken away that which He accomplished in mercy? But now, He, the mediator between God and man, has so shown Himself, that, uniting both natures in the unity of one Person, He has given a dignity to ordinary by extraordinary things, and tempered the extraordinary by the ordinary."

Thirdly, because in this fashion the begetting of man is accomplished in every variety of manner. For the first man was made from the "slime of the earth," without the concurrence of man or woman: Eve was made of man but not of woman: and other men are made from both man and woman. So that this fourth manner remained as it were proper to Christ, that He should be made of a woman without the concurrence of a man.

Reply to Objection 1: The male sex is more noble than the female, and for this reason He took human nature in the male sex. But lest the female sex should be despised, it was fitting that He should take flesh of a woman. Hence Augustine says (De Agone Christ. xi): "Men, despise not yourselves: the Son of God became a man: despise not yourselves, women; the Son of God was born of a woman."

Reply to Objection 2: Augustine thus (Contra Faust. xxiii) replies to Faustus, who urged this objection; "By no means," says he, "does the Catholic Faith, which believes that Christ the Son of God was born of a virgin, according to the flesh, suppose that the same Son of God was so shut up in His Mother's womb, as to cease to be elsewhere, as though He no longer continued to govern heaven and earth, and as though He had withdrawn Himself from the Father. But you, Manicheans, being of a mind that admits of nought but material images, are utterly unable to grasp these things." For, as he again says (Ep. ad Volus. cxxxvii), "it belongs to the sense of man to form conceptions only through tangible bodies, none of which can be entire everywhere, because they must of necessity be diffused through their innumerable parts in various places . . . Far otherwise is the nature of the soul from that of the body: how much more the nature of God, the Creator of soul and body! . . . He is able to be entire everywhere, and to be contained in no place. He is able to come without moving from the place where He was; and to go without leaving the spot whence He came."

Reply to Objection 3: There is no uncleanness in the conception of man from a woman, as far as this is the work of God: wherefore it is written (Acts 10:15): "That which God hath cleansed do not thou call common," i.e. unclean. There is, however, a certain uncleanness therein, resulting from sin, as far as lustful desire accompanies conception by sexual union. But this was not the case with Christ, as shown above ([4139]Q[28], A[1]). But if there were any uncleanness therein, the Word of God would not have been sullied thereby, for He is utterly unchangeable. Wherefore Augustine says (Contra Quinque Haereses v): "God saith, the Creator of man: What is it that troubles thee in My Birth? I was not conceived by lustful desire. I made Myself a mother of whom to be born. If the sun's rays can dry up the filth in the drain, and yet not be defiled: much more can the Splendor of eternal light cleanse whatever It shines upon, but Itself cannot be sullied."

Whether the flesh of Christ was conceived of the Virgin's purest blood?

Objection 1: It would seem that the flesh of Christ was not conceived of the Virgin's purest blood: For it is said in the collect (Feast of the Annunciation) that God "willed that His Word should take flesh from a Virgin." But flesh differs from blood. Therefore Christ's body was not taken from the Virgin's blood.

Objection 2: Further, as the woman was miraculously formed from the man, so Christ's body was formed miraculously from the Virgin. But the woman is not said to have been formed from the man's blood, but rather from his flesh and bones, according to Gn. 2:23: "This now is bone of my bones, and flesh of my flesh." It seems therefore that neither should Christ's body have been formed from the Virgin's blood, but from her flesh and bones.

Objection 3: Further, Christ's body was of the same species as other men's bodies. But other men's bodies are not formed from the purest blood but from the semen and the menstrual blood. Therefore it seems that neither was Christ's body conceived of the purest blood of the Virgin.

On the contrary, Damascene says (De Fide Orth. iii) that "the Son of God, from the Virgin's purest blood, formed Himself flesh, animated with a rational soul."

I answer that, As stated above [4140](A[4]), in Christ's conception His being born of a woman was in accordance with the laws of nature, but that He was born of a virgin was above the laws of nature. Now, such is the law of nature that in the generation of an animal the female supplies the matter, while the male is the active principle of generation; as the Philosopher proves (De Gener. Animal. i). But a woman who conceives of a man is not a virgin. And consequently it belongs to the supernatural mode of Christ's generation, that the active principle of generation was the supernatural power of God: but it belongs to the natural mode of His generation, that the matter from which His body was conceived is similar to the matter which other women supply for the conception of their offspring. Now, this matter, according to the Philosopher (De Gener. Animal.), is the woman's blood, not any of her blood, but brought to a more perfect stage of secretion by the mother's generative power, so as to be apt for conception. And therefore of such matter was Christ's body conceived.

Reply to Objection 1: Since the Blessed Virgin was of the same nature as other women, it follows that she had flesh and bones of the same nature as theirs. Now, flesh and bones in other women are actual parts of the body, the integrity of which results therefrom: and consequently they cannot be taken from the body without its being corrupted or diminished. But as Christ came to heal what was corrupt, it was not fitting that He should bring corruption or diminution to the integrity of His Mother. Therefore it was becoming that Christ's body should be formed not from the flesh or bones of the Virgin, but from her blood, which as yet is not actually a part, but is potentially the whole, as stated in De Gener. Animal. i. Hence He is said to have taken flesh from the Virgin, not that the matter from which His body was formed was actual flesh, but blood, which is flesh potentially.

Reply to Objection 2: As stated in the [4141]FP, Q[92], A[3], ad 2, Adam, through being established as a kind of principle of human nature, had in his body a certain proportion of flesh and bone, which belonged to him, not as an integral part of his personality, but in regard to his state as a principle of human nature. And from this was the woman formed, without detriment to the man. But in the Virgin's body there was nothing of this sort, from which Christ's body could be formed without detriment to His Mother's body.

Reply to Objection 3: Woman's semen is not apt for generation, but is something imperfect in the seminal order, which, on account of the imperfection of the female power, it has not been possible to bring to complete seminal perfection. Consequently this semen is not the necessary matter of conception; as the Philosopher says (De Gener. Animal. i): wherefore there was none such in Christ's conception: all the more since, though it is imperfect in the seminal order, a certain concupiscence accompanies its emission, as also that of the male semen: whereas in that virginal conception there could be no concupiscence. Wherefore Damascene says (De Fide Orth. iii) that Christ's body was not conceived "seminally." But the menstrual blood, the flow of which is subject to monthly periods, has a certain natural impurity of corruption: like other superfluities, which nature does not heed, and therefore expels. Of such menstrual blood infected with corruption and repudiated by nature, the conception is not formed; but from a certain secretion of the pure blood which by a process of elimination is prepared for conception, being, as it were, more pure and more perfect than the rest of the blood. Nevertheless, it is tainted with the impurity of lust in the conception of other men: inasmuch as by sexual intercourse this blood is drawn to a place apt for conception. This, however, did not take place in Christ's conception: because this blood was brought together in the Virgin's womb and fashioned into a child by the operation of the Holy Ghost. Therefore is Christ's body said to be "formed of the most chaste and purest blood of the Virgin."

Whether Christ's body was in Adam and the other patriarchs, as to something signate?

Objection 1: It would seem that Christ's body was in Adam and the patriarchs as to something signate. For Augustine says (Gen. ad lit. x) that the flesh of Christ was in Adam and Abraham "by way of a bodily substance." But bodily substance is something signate. Therefore Christ's flesh was in Adam, Abraham, and the other patriarchs, according to something signate.

Objection 2: Further, it is said (Rom. 1:3) that Christ "was made . . . of the seed of David according to the flesh." But the seed of David was something signate in him. Therefore Christ was in David, according to something signate, and for the same reason in the other patriarchs.

Objection 3: Further, the human race is Christ's kindred, inasmuch as He took flesh therefrom. But if that flesh were not something signate in Adam, the human race, which is descended from Adam, would seem to have no kindred with Christ: but rather with those other things from which the matter of His flesh was taken. Therefore it seems that Christ's flesh was in Adam and the other patriarchs according to something signate.

On the contrary, Augustine says (Gen. ad lit. x) that in whatever way Christ was in Adam and Abraham, other men were there also; but not conversely. But other men were not in Adam and Abraham by way of some signate matter, but only according to origin, as stated in the [4142]FP, Q[119] , A[1], A[2], ad 4. Therefore neither was Christ in Adam and Abraham according to something signate; and, for the same reason, neither was He in the other patriarchs.

I answer that, As stated above (A[5], ad 1), the matter of Christ's body was not the flesh and bones of the Blessed Virgin, nor anything that was actually a part of her body, but her blood which was her flesh potentially. Now, whatever was in the Blessed Virgin, as received from her parents, was actually a part of her body. Consequently that which the Blessed Virgin received from her parents was not the matter of Christ's body. Therefore we must say that Christ's body was not in Adam and the other patriarchs according to something signate, in the sense that some part of Adam's or of anyone else's body could be singled out and designated as the very matter from which Christ's body was to be formed: but it was there according to origin, just as was the flesh of other men. For Christ's body is related to Adam and the other patriarchs through the medium of His Mother's body. Consequently Christ's body was in the patriarchs, in no other way than was His Mother's body, which was not in the patriarchs according to signate matter: as neither were the bodies of other men, as stated in the [4143]FP, Q[119], A[1], A[2], ad 4.

Reply to Objection 1: The expression "Christ was in Adam according to bodily substance," does not mean that Christ's body was a bodily substance in Adam: but that the bodily substance of Christ's body, i.e. the matter which He took from the Virgin, was in Adam as in its active principle, but not as in its material principle: in other words, by the generative power of Adam and his descendants down to the Blessed Virgin, this matter was prepared for Christ's conception. But this matter was not fashioned into Christ's body by the seminal power derived from Adam. Therefore Christ is said to have been in Adam by way of origin, according to bodily substance: but not according to seminal virtue.

Reply to Objection 2: Although Christ's body was not in Adam and the other patriarchs, according to seminal virtue, yet the Blessed Virgin's body was thus in them, through her being conceived from the seed of a man. For this reason, through the medium of the Blessed Virgin, Christ is said to be of the seed of David, according to the flesh, by way of origin.

Reply to Objection 3: Christ and the human race are kindred, through the likeness of species. Now, specific likeness results not from remote but from proximate matter, and from the active principle which begets its like in species. Thus, then, the kinship of Christ and the human race is sufficiently preserved by His body being formed from the Virgin's blood, derived in its origin from Adam and the other patriarchs. Nor is this kinship affected by the matter whence this blood is taken, as neither is it in the generation of other men, as stated in the [4144]FP, Q[119], A[2], ad 3.

Whether Christ's flesh in the patriarchs was infected by sin?

Objection 1: It would seem that Christ's flesh was not infected by sin in the patriarchs. For it is written (Wis. 7:25) that "no defiled thing cometh into" Divine Wisdom. But Christ is the Wisdom of God according to 1 Cor. 1:24. Therefore Christ's flesh was never defiled by sin.

Objection 2: Further, Damascene says (De Fide Orth. iii) that Christ "assumed the first-fruits of our nature." But in the primitive state human flesh was not infected by sin. Therefore Christ's flesh was not infected either in Adam or in the other patriarchs.

Objection 3: Further, Augustine says (Gen. ad lit. x) that "human nature ever had, together with the wound, the balm with which to heal it." But that which is infected cannot heal a wound; rather does it need to be healed itself. Therefore in human nature there was ever something preserved from infection, from which afterwards Christ's body was formed.

On the contrary, Christ's body is not related to Adam and the other patriarchs, save through the medium of the Blessed Virgin's body, of whom He took flesh. But the body of the Blessed Virgin was wholly conceived in original sin, as stated above ([4145]Q[14], A[3], ad 1), and thus, as far as it was in the patriarchs, it was subject to sin. Therefore the flesh of Christ, as far as it was in the patriarchs, was subject to sin.

I answer that, When we say that Christ or His flesh was in Adam and the other patriarchs, we compare Him, or His flesh, to Adam and the other patriarchs. Now, it is manifest that the condition of the patriarchs differed from that of Christ: for the patriarchs were subject to sin, whereas Christ was absolutely free from sin. Consequently a twofold error may occur on this point. First, by attributing to Christ, or to His flesh, that condition which was in the patriarchs; by saying, for instance, that Christ sinned in Adam, since after some fashion He was in him. But this is false; because Christ was not in Adam in such a way that Adam's sin belonged to Christ: forasmuch as He is not descended from him according to the law of concupiscence, or according to seminal virtue; as stated above (A[1], ad 3, A[6], ad 1;[4146] Q[15], A[1], ad 2).

Secondly, error may occur by attributing the condition of Christ or of His flesh to that which was actually in the patriarchs: by saying, for instance, that, because Christ's flesh, as existing in Christ, was not subject to sin, therefore in Adam also and in the patriarchs there was some part of his body that was not subject to sin, and from which afterwards Christ's body was formed; as some indeed held. For this is quite impossible. First, because Christ's flesh was not in Adam and in the other patriarchs, according to something signate, distinguishable from the rest of his flesh, as pure from impure; as already stated (A[6]). Secondly, because since human flesh is infected by sin, through being conceived in lust, just as the entire flesh of a man is conceived through lust, so also is it entirely defiled by sin. Consequently we must say that the entire flesh of the patriarchs was subjected to sin, nor was there anything in them that was free from sin, and from which afterwards Christ's body could be formed.

Reply to Objection 1: Christ did not assume the flesh of the human race subject to sin, but cleansed from all infection of sin. Thus it is that "no defiled thing cometh into the Wisdom of God."

Reply to Objection 2: Christ is said to have assumed the first-fruits of our nature, as to the likeness of condition; forasmuch as He assumed flesh not infected by sin, like unto the flesh of man before sin. But this is not to be understood to imply a continuation of that primitive purity, as though the flesh of innocent man was preserved in its freedom from sin until the formation of Christ's body.

Reply to Objection 3: Before Christ, there was actually in human nature a wound, i.e. the infection of original sin. But the balm to heal the wound was not there actually, but only by a certain virtue of origin, forasmuch as from those patriarchs the flesh of Christ was to be propagated.

Whether Christ paid tithes in Abraham's loins?

Objection 1: It would seem that Christ "paid tithes" in Abraham's loins. For the Apostle says (Heb. 7:6-9) that Levi, the great-grandson of Abraham, "paid tithes in Abraham," because, when the latter paid tithes to Melchisedech, "he was yet in his loins." In like manner Christ was in Abraham's loins when the latter paid tithes. Therefore Christ Himself also paid tithes in Abraham.

Objection 2: Further, Christ is of the seed of Abraham according to the flesh which He received from His Mother. But His Mother paid tithes in Abraham. Therefore for a like reason did Christ.

Objection 3: Further, "in Abraham tithe was levied on that which needed healing," as Augustine says (Gen. ad lit. x). But all flesh subject to sin needed healing. Since therefore Christ's flesh was the subject of sin, as stated above [4147](A[7]), it seems that Christ's flesh paid tithes in Abraham.

Objection 4: Further, this does not seem to be at all derogatory to Christ's dignity. For the fact that the father of a bishop pays tithes to a priest does not hinder his son, the bishop, from being of higher rank than an ordinary priest. Consequently, although we may say that Christ paid tithes when Abraham paid them to Melchisedech, it does not follow that Christ was not greater than Melchisedech.

On the contrary, Augustine says (Gen. ad lit. x) that "Christ did not pay tithes there," i.e. in Abraham, "for His flesh derived from him, not the heat of the wound, but the matter of the antidote."

I answer that, It behooves us to say that the sense of the passage quoted from the Apostle is that Christ did not pay tithes in Abraham. For the Apostle proves that the priesthood according to the order of Melchisedech is greater than the Levitical priesthood, from the fact that Abraham paid tithes to Melchisedech, while Levi, from whom the legal priesthood was derived, was yet in his loins. Now, if Christ had also paid tithes in Abraham, His priesthood would not have been according to the order of Melchisedech, but of a lower order. Consequently we must say that Christ did not pay tithes in Abraham's loins, as Levi did.

For since he who pays a tithe keeps nine parts to himself, and surrenders the tenth to another, inasmuch as the number ten is the sign of perfection, as being, in a sort, the terminus of all numbers which mount from one to ten, it follows that he who pays a tithe bears witness to his own imperfection and to the perfection of another. Now, to sin is due the imperfection of the human race, which needs to be perfected by Him who cleanses from sin. But to heal from sin belongs to Christ alone, for He is the "Lamb that taketh away the sin of the world" (Jn. 1:29), whose figure was Melchisedech, as the Apostle proves (Heb. 7). Therefore by giving tithes to Melchisedech, Abraham foreshadowed that he, as being conceived in sin, and all who were to be his descendants in contracting original sin, needed that healing which is through Christ. And Isaac, Jacob, and Levi, and all the others were in Abraham in such a way so as to be descended from him, not only as to bodily substance, but also as to seminal virtue, by which original sin is transmitted. Consequently, they all paid tithes in Abraham, i.e. foreshadowed as needing to be healed by Christ. And Christ alone was in Abraham in such a manner as to descend from him, not by seminal virtue, but according to bodily substance. Therefore He was not in Abraham so as to need to be healed, but rather "as the balm with which the wound was to be healed." Therefore He did not pay tithes in Abraham's loins.

Thus the answer to the first objection is made manifest.

Reply to Objection 2: Because the Blessed Virgin was conceived in original sin, she was in Abraham as needing to be healed. Therefore she paid tithes in him, as descending from him according to seminal virtue. But this is not true of Christ's body, as stated above.

Reply to Objection 3: Christ's flesh is said to have been subject to sin, according as it was in the patriarchs, by reason of the condition in which it was in His forefathers, who paid the tithes: but not by reason of its condition as actually in Christ, who did not pay the tithes.

Reply to Objection 4: The levitical priesthood was handed down through carnal origin: wherefore it was not less in Abraham than in Levi. Consequently, since Abraham paid tithes to Melchisedech as to one greater than he, it follows that the priesthood of Melchisedech, inasmuch as he was a figure of Christ, was greater than that of Levi. But the priesthood of Christ does not result from carnal origin, but from spiritual grace. Therefore it is possible that a father pay tithes to a priest, as the less to the greater, and yet his son, if he be a bishop, is greater than that priest, not through carnal origin, but through the spiritual grace which he has received from Christ.

Day 270

OF THE ACTIVE PRINCIPLE IN CHRIST'S CONCEPTION (FOUR ARTICLES)

We shall now consider the active principle in Christ's conception: concerning which there are four points of inquiry:

(1) Whether the Holy Ghost was the active principle of Christ's conception?
(2) Whether it can be said that Christ was conceived of the Holy Ghost?
(3) Whether it can be said that the Holy Ghost is Christ's father according to the flesh?
(4) Whether the Blessed Virgin cooperated actively in Christ's conception?

Whether the accomplishment of Christ's conception should be attributed to the Holy Ghost?

Objection 1: It would seem that the accomplishment of Christ's conception should not be attributed to the Holy Ghost, because. as Augustine says (De Trin. i), "The works of the Trinity are indivisible, just as the Essence of the Trinity is indivisible." But the accomplishment of Christ's conception was the work of God. Therefore it seems that it should not be attributed to the Holy Ghost any more than to the Father or the Son.

Objection 2: Further, the Apostle says (Gal. 4:4): "When the fulness of time was come, God sent His Son, made of a woman"; which words Augustine expounds by saying (De Trin. iv): "Sent, in so far as made of a woman." But the sending of the Son is especially attributed to the Father, as stated in the [4148]FP, Q[43], A[8]. Therefore His conception also, by reason of which He was "made of a woman," should be attributed principally to the Father.

Objection 3: Further, it is written (Prov. 9:1): "Wisdom hath built herself a house." Now, Christ is Himself the Wisdom of God; according to 1 Cor. 1:24: "Christ the Power of God and the Wisdom of God." And the house of this Wisdom is Christ's body, which is also called His temple, according to Jn. 2:21: "But He spoke of the temple of His body." Therefore it seems that the accomplishment of Christ's conception should be attributed principally to the Son, and not, therefore, to the Holy Ghost.

On the contrary, It is written (Lk. 1:35): "The Holy Ghost shall come upon Thee."

I answer that, The whole Trinity effected the conception of Christ's body: nevertheless, this is attributed to the Holy Ghost, for three reasons. First, because this is befitting to the cause of the Incarnation, considered on the part of God. For the Holy Ghost is the love of Father and Son, as stated in the [4149]FP, Q[37], A[1]. Now, that the Son of God took to Himself flesh from the Virgin's womb was due to the exceeding love of God: wherefore it is said (Jn. 3:16): "God so loved the world as to give His only-begotten Son."

Secondly, this is befitting to the cause of the Incarnation, on the part of the nature assumed. Because we are thus given to understand that human nature was assumed by the Son of God into the unity of Person, not by reason of its merits, but through grace alone; which is attributed to the Holy Ghost, according to 1 Cor. 12:4: "There are diversities of graces, but the same Spirit." Wherefore Augustine says (Enchiridion xl): "The manner in which Christ was born of the Holy Ghost . . . suggests to us the grace of God, whereby man, without any merits going before, in the very beginning of his nature when he began to exist was joined to God the Word, into so great unity of Person, that He Himself should be the Son of God."

Thirdly, because this is befitting the term of the Incarnation. For the term of the Incarnation was that that man, who was being conceived, should be the Holy one and the Son of God. Now, both of these are attributed to the Holy Ghost. For by Him men are made to be sons of God, according to Gal. 4:6: "Because you are sons, God hath sent the Spirit of His Son into your [Vulg.: 'our'] hearts, crying: Abba, Father." Again, He is the "Spirit of sanctification," according to Rom. 1:4. Therefore, just as other men are sanctified spiritually by the Holy Ghost; so as to be the adopted sons of God, so was Christ conceived in sanctity by the Holy Ghost, so as to be the natural Son of God. Hence, according to a gloss on Rom. 1:4, the words, "Who was predestinated the Son of God, in power," are explained by what immediately follows: "According to the Spirit of sanctification, i.e. through being conceived of the Holy Ghost." And the Angel of the Annunciation himself, after saying, "The Holy Ghost shall come upon thee," draws the conclusion: "Therefore also the Holy which shall be born of thee shall be called the Son of God."

Reply to Objection 1: The work of the conception is indeed common to the whole Trinity; yet in some way it is attributed to each of the Persons. For to the Father is attributed authority in regard to the Person of the Son, who by this conception took to Himself (human nature). The taking itself (of human nature) is attributed to the Son: but the formation of the body taken by the Son is attributed to the Holy Ghost. For the Holy Ghost is the Spirit of the Son, according to Gal. 4:6: "God sent the Spirit of His Son." For just as the power of the soul which is in the semen, through the spirit enclosed therein, fashions the body in the generation of other men, so the Power of God, which is the Son Himself, according to 1 Cor. 1:24: "Christ, the Power of God," through the Holy Ghost formed the body which He assumed. This is also shown by the words of the angel: "The Holy Ghost shall come upon thee," as it were, in order to prepare and fashion the matter of Christ's body; "and the Power of the Most High," i.e. Christ, "shall overshadow thee---that is to say, the incorporeal Light of the Godhead shall in thee take the corporeal substance of human nature: for a shadow is formed by light and body," as Gregory says (Moral. xviii). The "Most High" is the Father, whose Power is the Son.

Reply to Objection 2: The mission refers to the Person assuming, who is sent by the Father; but the conception refers to the body assumed, which is formed by the operation of the Holy Ghost. And therefore, though mission and conception are in the same subject; since they differ in our consideration of them, mission is attributed to the Father, but the accomplishment of the conception to the Holy Ghost; whereas the assumption of flesh is attributed to the Son.

Reply to Objection 3: As Augustine says (QQ. Vet. et Nov. Test., qu. 52): "This may be understood in two ways. For, first, Christ's house is the Church, which He built with His blood. Secondly, His body may be called His house, just as it is called His temple . . . and what is done by the Holy Ghost is done by the Son of God, because Theirs is one Nature and one Will."

Whether it should be said that Christ was conceived of [de] the Holy Ghost?

Objection 1: It would seem that we should not say that Christ was conceived of [de] the Holy Ghost. Because on Rom. 11:36: "For of Him [ex ipso] and by Him, and in Him, are all things," the gloss of Augustine says: "Notice that he does not say, 'of Him' [de ipso], but 'of Him' [ex ipso]. For of Him [ex ipso], are heaven and earth, since He made them: but not of Him [de ipso], since they are not made of His substance." But the Holy Ghost did not form Christ's body of [de] His own substance. Therefore we should not say that Christ was conceived of [de] the Holy Ghost.

Objection 2: Further, the active principle of [de] which something is conceived is as the seed in generation. But the Holy Ghost did not take the place of seed in Christ's conception. For Jerome says (Expos. Cathol. Fidei) [*Written by Pelagius]: "We do not say, as some wicked wretches hold, that the Holy Ghost took the place of seed: but we say that Christ's body was wrought," i.e. formed, "by the power and might of the Creator." Therefore we should not say that Christ's body was conceived of [de] the Holy Ghost.

Objection 3: Further, no one thing is made of two, except they be in some way mingled. But Christ's body was formed of [de] the Virgin Mary. If therefore we say that Christ was conceived of [de] the Holy Ghost, it seems that a mingling took place of the Holy Ghost with the matter supplied by the Virgin: and this is clearly false. Therefore we should not say that Christ was conceived of [de] the Holy Ghost.

On the contrary, It is written (Mat. 1:18): "Before they came together, she was found with child, of [de] the Holy Ghost."

I answer that, Conception is not attributed to Christ's body alone, but also to Christ Himself by reason of His body. Now, in the Holy Ghost we may observe a twofold habitude to Christ. For to the Son of God Himself, who is said to have been conceived, He has a habitude of consubstantiality: while to His body He has the habitude of efficient cause. And this preposition of [de] signifies both habitudes: thus we say that a certain man is "of [de] his father." And therefore we can fittingly say that Christ was conceived of the Holy Ghost in such a way that the efficiency of the Holy Ghost be referred to the body assumed, and the consubstantiality to the Person assuming.

Reply to Objection 1: Christ's body, through not being consubstantial with the Holy Ghost, cannot properly be said to be conceived "of" [de] the Holy Ghost, but rather "from [ex] the Holy Ghost," as Ambrose says (De Spir. Sanct. ii.): "What is from someone is either from his substance or from his power: from his substance, as the Son who is from the Father; from his power, as all things are from God, just as Mary conceived from the Holy Ghost."

Reply to Objection 2: It seems that on this point there is a difference of opinion between Jerome and certain other Doctors, who assert that the Holy Ghost took the place of seed in this conception. For Chrysostom says (Hom. i in Matth. [*Opus Imperf., among the supposititious writings]): "When God's Only-Begotten was about to enter into the Virgin, the Holy Ghost preceded Him; that by the previous entrance of the Holy Ghost, Christ might be born unto sanctification according to His body, the Godhead entering instead of the seed." And Damascene says (De Fide Orth. iii): "God's wisdom and power overshadowed her, like unto a Divine seed."

But these expressions are easily explained. Because Chrysostom and Damascene compare the Holy Ghost, or also the Son, who is the Power of the Most High, to seed, by reason of the active power therein; while Jerome denies that the Holy Ghost took the place of seed, considered as a corporeal substance which is transformed in conception.

Reply to Objection 3: As Augustine says (Enchiridion xl), Christ is said to be conceived or born of the Holy Ghost in one sense; of the Virgin Mary in another---of the Virgin Mary materially; of the Holy Ghost efficiently. Therefore there was no mingling here.

Whether the Holy Ghost should be called Christ's father in respect of His humanity?

Objection 1: It would seem that the Holy Ghost should be called Christ's father in respect of His humanity. Because, according to the Philosopher (De Gener. Animal. i): "The Father is the active principle in generation, the Mother supplies the matter." But the Blessed Virgin is called Christ's Mother, by reason of the matter which she supplied in His conception. Therefore it seems that the Holy Ghost can be called His father, through being the active principle in His conception.

Objection 2: Further, as the minds of other holy men are fashioned by the Holy Ghost, so also was Christ's body fashioned by the Holy Ghost. But other holy men, on account of the aforesaid fashioning, are called the children of the whole Trinity, and consequently of the Holy Ghost. Therefore it seems that Christ should be called the Son of the Holy Ghost, forasmuch as His body was fashioned by the Holy Ghost.

Objection 3: Further, God is called our Father by reason of His having made us, according to Dt. 32:6: "Is not He thy Father, that hath possessed thee, and made thee and created thee?" But the Holy Ghost made Christ's body, as stated above ([4150]AA[1],2). Therefore the Holy Ghost should be called Christ's Father in respect of the body fashioned by Him.

On the contrary, Augustine says (Enchiridion xl): "Christ was born of the Holy Ghost not as a Son, and of the Virgin Mary as a Son."

I answer that, The words "fatherhood," "motherhood," and "sonship," result from generation; yet not from any generation, but from that of living things, especially animals. For we do not say that fire generated is the son of the fire generating it, except, perhaps, metaphorically; we speak thus only of animals in whom generation is more perfect. Nevertheless, the word "son" is not applied to everything generated in animals, but only to that which is generated into likeness of the generator. Wherefore, as Augustine says (Enchiridion xxxix), we do not say that a hair which is generated in a man is his son; nor do we say that a man who is born is the son of the seed; for neither is the hair like the man nor is the man born like the seed, but like the man who begot him. And if the likeness be perfect, the sonship is perfect, whether in God or in man. But if the likeness be imperfect, the sonship is imperfect. Thus in man there is a certain imperfect likeness to God, both as regards his being created to God's image and as regards His being created unto the likeness of grace. Therefore in both ways man can be called His son, both because he is created to His image and because he is likened to Him by grace. Now, it must be observed that what is said in its perfect sense of a thing should not be said thereof in its imperfect sense: thus, because Socrates is said to be naturally a man, in the proper sense of "man," never is he called man in the sense in which the portrait of a man is called a man, although, perhaps, he may resemble another man. Now, Christ is the Son of God in the perfect sense of sonship. Wherefore, although in His human nature He was created and justified, He ought not to be called the Son of God, either in respect of His being created or of His being justified, but only in respect of His eternal generation, by reason of which He is the Son of the Father alone. Therefore nowise should Christ be called the Son of the Holy Ghost, nor even of the whole Trinity.

Reply to Objection 1: Christ was conceived of the Virgin Mary, who supplied the matter of His conception unto likeness of species. For this reason He is called her Son. But as man He was conceived of the Holy Ghost as the active principle of His conception, but not unto likeness of species, as a man is born of his father. Therefore Christ is not called the Son of the Holy Ghost.

Reply to Objection 2: Men who are fashioned spiritually by the Holy Ghost cannot be called sons of God in the perfect sense of sonship. And therefore they are called sons of God in respect of imperfect sonship, which is by reason of the likeness of grace, which flows from the whole Trinity.

But with Christ it is different, as stated above.

The same reply avails for the Third Objection.

Whether the Blessed Virgin cooperated actively in the conception of Christ's body?

Objection 1: It would seem that the Blessed Virgin cooperated actively in the conception of Christ's body. For Damascene says (De Fide Orth. iii) that "the Holy Ghost came upon the Virgin, purifying her, and bestowing on her the power to receive and to bring forth the Word of God." But she had from nature the passive power of generation, like any other woman. Therefore He bestowed on her an active power of generation. And thus she cooperated actively in Christ's conception.

Objection 2: Further, all the powers of the vegetative soul are active, as the Commentator says (De Anima ii). But the generative power, in both man and woman, belongs to the vegetative soul. Therefore, both in man and woman, it cooperates actively in the conception of the child.

Objection 3: Further, in the conception of a child the woman supplies the matter from which the child's body is naturally formed. But nature is an intrinsic principle of movement. Therefore it seems that in the very matter supplied by the Blessed Virgin there was an active principle.

On the contrary, The active principle in generation is called the "seminal virtue." But, as Augustine says (Gen. ad lit. x), Christ's body "was taken from the Virgin, only as to corporeal matter, by the Divine power of conception and formation, but not by any human seminal virtue." Therefore the Blessed Virgin did not cooperate actively in, the conception of Christ's body.

I answer that, Some say that the Blessed Virgin cooperated actively in Christ's conception, both by natural and by a supernatural power. By natural power, because they hold that in all natural matter there is an active principle. otherwise they believe that there would be no such thing as natural transformation. But in this they are deceived. Because a transformation is said to be natural by reason not only of an active but also of a passive intrinsic principle: for the Philosopher says expressly (Phys. viii) that in heavy and light things there is a passive, and not an active, principle of natural movement. Nor is it possible for matter to be active in its own formation, since it is not in act. Nor, again, is it possible for anything to put itself in motion except it be divided into two parts, one being the mover, the other being moved: which happens in animate things only, as is proved Phys. viii.

By a supernatural power, because they say that the mother requires not only to supply the matter, which is the menstrual blood, but also the semen, which, being mingled with that of the male, has an active power in generation. And since in the Blessed Virgin there was no resolution of semen, by reason of her inviolate virginity, they say that the Holy Ghost supernaturally bestowed on her an active power in the conception of Christ's body, which power other mothers have by reason of the semen resolved. But this cannot stand, because, since "each thing is on account of its operation" (De Coel. ii), nature would not, for the purpose of the act of generation, distinguish the male and female sexes, unless the action of the male were distinct from that of the female. Now, in generation there are two distinct operations---that of the agent and that of the patient. Wherefore it follows that the entire active operation is on the part of the male, and the passive on the part of the female. For this reason in plants, where both forces are mingled, there is no distinction of male and female.

Since, therefore, the Blessed Virgin was not Christ's Father, but His Mother, it follows that it was not given to her to exercise an active power in His conception: whether to cooperate actively so as to be His Father, or not to cooperate at all, as some say. whence it would follow that this active power was bestowed on her to no purpose. We must therefore say that in Christ's conception itself she did not cooperate actively, but merely supplied the matter thereof. Nevertheless, before the conception she cooperated actively in the preparation of the matter so that it should be apt for the conception.

Reply to Objection 1: This conception had three privileges---namely, that it was without original sin; that it was not that of a man only, but of God and man; and that it was a virginal conception. And all three were effected by the Holy Ghost. Therefore Damascene says, as to the first, that the Holy Ghost "came upon the Virgin, purifying her"---that is, preserving her from conceiving with original sin. As to the second, he says: "And bestowing on her the power to receive," i.e. to conceive, "the Word of God." As to the third, he says: "And to give birth" to Him, i.e. that she might, while remaining a virgin, bring Him forth, not actively, but passively, just as other mothers achieve this through the action of the male seed.

Reply to Objection 2: The generative power of the female is imperfect compared to that of the male. And, therefore, just as in the arts the inferior art gives a disposition to the matter to which the higher art gives the form, as is stated Phys. ii, so also the generative power of the female prepares the matter, which is then fashioned by the active power of the male.

Reply to Objection 3: In order for a transformation to be natural, there is no need for an active principle in matter, but only for a passive principle, as stated above.

OF THE MODE AND ORDER OF CHRIST'S CONCEPTION (FOUR ARTICLES)

We have now to consider the mode and order of Christ's conception, concerning which there are four points of inquiry:

(1) Whether Christ's body was formed in the first instant of its conception?

(2) Whether it was animated in the first instant of its conception?

(3) Whether it was assumed by the Word in the first instant of its conception?

(4) Whether this conception was natural or miraculous?

Whether Christ's body was formed in the first instant of its conception?

Objection 1: It would seem that Christ's body was not formed in the first instant of its conception. For it is written (Jn. 2:20): "Six-and-forty years was this Temple in building"; on which words Augustine comments as follows (De Trin. iv): "This number applies manifestly to the perfection of our Lord's body." He says, further (QQ. lxxxiii, qu. 56): "It is not without reason that the Temple, which was a type of His body, is said to have been forty-six years in building: so that as many years as it took to build the Temple, in so many days was our Lord's body perfected." Therefore Christ's body was not perfectly formed in the first instant of its conception.

Objection 2: Further, there was need of local movement for the formation of Christ's body in order that the purest blood of the Virgin's body might be brought where generation might aptly take place. Now, no body can be moved locally in an instant: since the time taken in movement is divided according to the division of the thing moved, as is proved Phys. vi. Therefore Christ's body was not formed in an instant.

Objection 3: Further, Christ's body was formed of the purest blood of the Virgin, as stated above ([4151]Q[31], A[5]). But that matter could not be in the same instant both blood and flesh, because thus matter would have been at the same time the subject of two forms. Therefore the last instant in which it was blood was distinct from the first instant in which it was flesh. But between any two instants there is an interval of time. Therefore Christ's body was not formed in an instant, but during a space of time.

Objection 4: Further, as the augmentative power requires a fixed time for its act, so also does the generative power: for both are natural powers belonging to the vegetative soul. But Christ's body took a fixed time to grow, like the bodies of other men: for it is written (Lk. 2:52) that He "advanced in wisdom and age." Therefore it seems for the same reason that the formation of His body, since that, too, belongs to the generative power, was not instantaneous, but took a fixed time, like the bodies of other men.

On the contrary, Gregory says (Moral. xviii): "As soon as the angel announced it, as soon as the Spirit came down, the Word was in the womb, within the womb the Word was made flesh."

I answer that, In the conception of Christ's body three points may be considered: first, the local movement of the blood to the place of generation; secondly, the formation of the body from that matter; thirdly, the development whereby it was brought to perfection of quantity. of these, the second is the conception itself; the first is a preamble; the third, a result of the conception.

Now, the first could not be instantaneous: since this would be contrary to the very nature of the local movement of any body whatever, the parts of which come into a place successively. The third also requires a succession of time: both because there is no increase without local movement, and because increase is effected by the power of the soul already informing the body, the operation of which power is subject to time.

But the body's very formation, in which conception principally consists, was instantaneous, for two reasons. First, because of the infinite power of the agent, viz. the Holy Ghost, by whom Christ's body was formed, as stated above ([4152]Q[32], A[1]). For the greater the power of an agent, the more quickly can it dispose matter; and, consequently, an agent of infinite power can dispose matter instantaneously to its due form. Secondly, on the part of the Person of the Son, whose body was being formed. For it was unbecoming that He should take to Himself a body as yet unformed. While, if the conception had been going on for any time before the perfect formation of the body, the whole conception could not be attributed to the Son of God, since it is not attributed to Him except by reason of the assumption of that body. Therefore in the first instant in which the various parts of the matter were united together in the place of generation, Christ's body was both perfectly formed and assumed. And thus is the Son of God said to have been conceived; nor could it be said otherwise.

Reply to Objection 1: Neither quotation from Augustine refers to formation alone of Christ's body, but to its formation, together with a fixed development up to the time of His birth. Wherefore in the aforesaid number are foreshadowed the number of months during which Christ was in the Virgin's womb.

Reply to Objection 2: This local movement is not comprised within the conception itself, but is a preamble thereto.

Reply to Objection 3: It is not possible to fix the last instant in which that matter was blood: but it is possible to fix the last period of time which continued without any interval up to the first instant in which Christ's body was formed. And this instant was the terminus of the time occupied by the local movement of the matter towards the place of generation.

Reply to Objection 4: Increase is caused by the augmentative power of that which is the subject of increase: but the formation of the body is caused by the generative power, not of that which is generated, but of the father generating from seed, in which the formative power derived from the father's soul has its operation. But Christ's body was not formed by the seed of man, as stated above ([4153]Q[31], A[5], ad 3), but by the operation of the Holy Ghost. Therefore the formation thereof should be such as to be worthy of the Holy Ghost. But the development of Christ's body was the effect of the augmentative power in Christ's soul: and since this was of the same species as ours, it behooved His body to develop in the same way as the bodies of other men, so as to prove the reality of His human nature.

Whether Christ's body was animated in the first instant of its conception?

Objection 1: It would seem that Christ's body was not animated in the first instant of its conception. For Pope Leo says (Ep. ad Julian.): "Christ's flesh was not of another nature than ours: nor was the beginning of His animation different from that of other men." But the soul is not infused into other men at the first instant of their conception. Therefore neither should Christ's soul have been infused into His body in the first instant of its conception.

Objection 2: Further, the soul, like any natural form, requires determinate quantity in its matter. But in the first instant of its conception Christ's body was not of the same quantity as the bodies of other men when they are animated: otherwise, if afterwards its development had been continuous, either its birth would have occurred sooner, or at the time of birth He would have been a bigger child than others. The former alternative is contrary to what Augustine says (De Trin. iv), where he proves that Christ was in the Virgin's womb for the space of nine months: while the latter is contrary to what Pope Leo says (Serm. iv in Epiph.): "They found the child Jesus nowise differing from the generality of infants." Therefore Christ's body was not animated in the first instant of its conception.

Objection 3: Further, whenever there is "before" and "after" there must be several instants. But according to the Philosopher (De Gener. Animal. ii) in the generation of a man there must needs be "before" and "after": for he is first of all a living thing, and afterwards, an animal, and after that, a man. Therefore the animation of Christ could not be effected in the first instant of His conception.

On the contrary, Damascene says (De Fide Orth. iii): "At the very instant that there was flesh, it was the flesh of the Word of God, it was flesh animated with a rational and intellectual soul."

I answer that, For the conception to be attributed to the very Son of God, as we confess in the Creed, when we say, "who was conceived by the Holy Ghost," we must needs say that the body itself, in being conceived, was assumed by the Word of God. Now it has been shown above ([4154]Q[6], AA[1],2) that the Word of God assumed the body by means of the soul, and the soul by means of the spirit, i.e. the intellect. Wherefore in the first instant of its conception Christ's body must needs have been animated by the rational soul.

Reply to Objection 1: The beginning of the infusion of the soul may be considered in two ways. First, in regard to the disposition of the body. And thus, the beginning of the infusion of the soul into Christ's body was the same as in other men's bodies: for just as the soul is infused into another man's body as soon as it is formed, so was it with Christ. Secondly, this beginning may be considered merely in regard to time. And thus, because Christ's body was perfectly formed in a shorter space of time, so after a shorter space of time was it animated.

Reply to Objection 2: The soul requires due quantity in the matter into which it is infused: but this quantity allows of a certain latitude because it is not fixed to a certain amount. Now the quantity that a body has when the soul is first infused into it is in proportion to the perfect quantity to which it will attain by development: that is to say, men of greater stature have greater bodies at the time of first animation. But Christ at the perfect age was of becoming and middle stature: in proportion to which was the quantity of His body at the time when other men's bodies are animated; though it was less than theirs at the first instant of His conception. Nevertheless that quantity was not too small to safeguard the nature of an animated body; since it would have sufficed for the animation of a small man's body.

Reply to Objection 3: What the Philosopher says is true in the generation of other men, because the body is successively formed and disposed for the soul: whence, first, as being imperfectly disposed, it receives an imperfect soul; and afterwards, when it is perfectly disposed, it receives a perfect soul. But Christ's body, on account of the infinite power of the agent, was perfectly disposed instantaneously. Wherefore, at once and in the first instant it received a perfect form, that is, the rational soul.

Whether Christ's flesh was first of all conceived and afterwards assumed?

Objection 1: It would seem that Christ's flesh was first of all conceived, and afterwards assumed. Because what is not cannot be assumed. But Christ's flesh began to exist when it was conceived. Therefore it seems that it was assumed by the Word of God after it was conceived.

Objection 2: Further, Christ's flesh was assumed by the Word of God, by means of the rational soul. But it received the rational soul at the term of the conception. Therefore it was assumed at the term of the conception. But at the term of the conception it was already conceived. Therefore it was first of all conceived and afterwards assumed.

Objection 3: Further, in everything generated, that which is imperfect precedes in time that which is perfect: which is made clear by the Philosopher (Metaph. ix). But Christ's body is something generated. Therefore it did not attain to its ultimate perfection, which consisted in the union with the Word of God, at the first instant of its conception; but, first of all, the flesh was conceived and afterwards assumed.

On the contrary, Augustine says (De Fide ad Petrum xviii [*Written by Fulgentius]): "Hold steadfastly, and doubt not for a moment that Christ's flesh was not conceived in the Virgin's womb, before being assumed by the Word."

I answer that, As stated above, we may say properly that "God was made man," but not that "man was made God": because God took to Himself that which belongs to man---and that which belongs to man did not pre-exist, as subsisting in itself, before being assumed by the Word. But if Christ's flesh had been conceived before being assumed by the Word, it would have had at some time an hypostasis other than that of the Word of God. And this is against the very nature of the Incarnation, which we hold to consist in this, that the Word of God was united to human nature and to all its parts in the unity of hypostasis: nor was it becoming that the Word of God should, by assuming human nature, destroy a pre-existing hypostasis of human nature or of any part thereof. It is consequently contrary to faith to assert that Christ's flesh was first of all conceived and afterwards assumed by the Word of God.

Reply to Objection 1: If Christ's flesh had been formed or conceived, not instantaneously, but successively, one of two things would follow: either that what was assumed was not yet flesh, or that the flesh was conceived before it was assumed. But since we hold that the conception was effected instantaneously, it follows that in that flesh the beginning and the completion of its conception were in the same instant. So that, as Augustine [*Fulgentius, De Fide ad Petrum xviii] says: "We say that the very Word of God was conceived in taking flesh, and that His very flesh was conceived by the Word taking flesh."

From the above the reply to the Second Objection is clear. For in the same moment that this flesh began to be conceived, its conception and animation were completed.

Reply to Objection 3: The mystery of the Incarnation is not to be looked upon as an ascent, as it were, of a man already existing and mounting up to the dignity of the Union: as the heretic Photinus maintained. Rather is it to be considered as a descent, by reason of the perfect Word of God taking unto Himself the imperfection of our nature; according to Jn. 6:38: "I came down from heaven."

Whether Christ's conception was natural?

Objection 1: It would seem that Christ's conception was natural. For Christ is called the Son of Man by reason of His conception in the flesh. But He is a true and natural Son of Man: as also is He the true and natural Son of God. Therefore His conception was natural.

Objection 2: Further, no creature can be the cause of a miraculous effect. But Christ's conception is attributed to the Blessed Virgin, who is a mere creature: for we say that the Virgin conceived Christ. Therefore it seems that His conception was not miraculous, but natural.

Objection 3: Further, for a transformation to be natural, it is enough that the passive principle be natural, as stated above ([4155]Q[32], A[4]). But in Christ's conception the passive principle on the part of His Mother was natural, as we have shown ([4156]Q[32], A[4]). Therefore Christ's conception was natural.

On the contrary, Dionysius says (Ep. ad Caium Monach.): "Christ does in a superhuman way those things that pertain to man: this is shown in the miraculous virginal conception."

I answer that, As Ambrose says (De Incarn. vi): "In this mystery thou shalt find many things that are natural, and many that are supernatural." For if we consider in this conception anything connected with the matter thereof, which was supplied by the mother, it was in all such things natural. But if we consider it on the part of the active power, thus it was entirely miraculous. And since judgment of a thing should be pronounced in respect of its form rather than of its matter: and likewise in respect of its activity rather than of its passiveness: therefore is it that Christ's conception should be described simply as miraculous and supernatural, although in a certain respect it was natural.

Reply to Objection 1: Christ is said to be a natural Son of Man, by reason of His having a true human nature, through which He is a Son of Man, although He had it miraculously; thus, too, the blind man to whom sight has been restored sees naturally by sight miraculously received.

Reply to Objection 2: The conception is attributed to the Blessed Virgin, not as the active principle thereof, but because she supplied the matter, and because the conception took place in her womb.

Reply to Objection 3: A natural passive principle suffices for a transformation to be natural, when it is moved by its proper active principle in a natural and wonted way. But this is not so in the case in point. Therefore this conception cannot be called simply natural.

Day 271

OF THE PERFECTION OF THE CHILD CONCEIVED (FOUR ARTICLES)
We must now consider the perfection of the child conceived: and concerning this there are four points of inquiry:
(1) Whether Christ was sanctified by grace in the first instant of His conception?
(2) Whether in that same instant He had the use of free-will?
(3) Whether in that same instant He could merit?
(4) Whether in that same instant He was a perfect comprehensor?

Whether Christ was sanctified in the first instant of His conception?
Objection 1: It would seem that Christ was not sanctified in the first instant of His conception. For it is written (1 Cor. 15:46): "That was not first which is spiritual, but that which is natural: afterwards that which is spiritual." But sanctification by grace is something spiritual. Therefore Christ received the grace of sanctification, not at the very beginning of His conception, but after a space of time.

Objection 2: Further, sanctification seems to be a cleansing from sin: according to 1 Cor. 6:1: "And such some of you were," namely, sinners, "but you are washed, but you are sanctified." But sin was never in Christ. Therefore it was not becoming that He should be sanctified by grace.

Objection 3: Further, as by the Word of God "all things were made," so from the Word incarnate all men who are made holy receive holiness, according to Heb. 2:11: "Both he that sanctifieth and they who are sanctified are all of one." But "the Word of God, by whom all things were made, was not Himself made"; as Augustine says (De Trin. i). Therefore Christ, by whom all are made holy, was not Himself made holy.

On the contrary, It is written (Lk. 1:35): "The Holy which shall be born of thee shall be called the Son of God"; and (Jn. 10:36): "Whom the Father hath sanctified and sent into the world."

I answer that, As stated above ([4157]Q[7], AA[9],10,12), the abundance of grace sanctifying Christ's soul flows from the very union of the Word, according to Jn. 1:14: "We saw His glory . . . as it were of the Only-Begotten of the Father, full of grace and truth." For it has been shown above ([4158]Q[33], AA[2],3) that in the first instant of conception, Christ's body was both animated and assumed by the Word of God. Consequently, in the first instant of His conception, Christ had the fulness of grace sanctifying His body and His soul.

Reply to Objection 1: The order set down by the Apostle in this passage refers to those who by advancing attain to the spiritual state. But the mystery of the Incarnation is considered as a condescension of the fulness of the Godhead into human nature rather than as the promotion of human nature, already existing, as it were, to the Godhead. Therefore in the man Christ there was perfection of spiritual life from the very beginning.

Reply to Objection 2: To be sanctified is to be made holy. Now something is made not only from its contrary, but also from that which is opposite to it, either by negation or by privation: thus white is made either from black or from not-white. We indeed from being sinners are made holy: so that our sanctification is a cleansing from sin. Whereas Christ, as man, was made holy, because He was not always thus sanctified by grace: yet He was not made holy from being a sinner, because He never sinned; but He was made holy from not-holy as man, not indeed by privation, as though He were at some time a man and not holy; but by negation---that is,

351

when He was not man He had not human sanctity. Therefore at the same time He was made man and a holy man. For this reason the angel said (Lk. 1:35): "The Holy which shall be born of thee." Which words Gregory expounds as follows (Moral. xviii): "In order to show the distinction between His holiness and ours, it is declared that He shall be born holy. For we, though we are made holy, yet are not born holy, because by the mere condition of a corruptible nature we are tied . . . But He alone is truly born holy who . . . was not conceived by the combining of carnal union."

Reply to Objection 3: The Father creates things through the Son, and the whole Trinity sanctifies men through the Man Christ, but not in the same way. For the Word of God has the same power and operation as God the Father: hence the Father does not work through the Son as an instrument, which is both mover and moved. Whereas the humanity of Christ is as the instrument of the Godhead, as stated above ([4159]Q[7], A[1], ad 3;[4160] Q[8], A[1], ad 1). Therefore Christ's humanity is both sanctified and sanctifier.

Whether Christ as man had the use of free-will in the first instant of His conception?

Objection 1: It would seem that Christ as man had not the use of free-will in the first instant of His conception. For a thing is, before it acts or operates. Now the use of free-will is an operation. Since, therefore, Christ's soul began to exist in the first instant of His conception, as was made clear above ([4161]Q[33], A[2]), it seems impossible that He should have the use of free-will in the first instant of His conception.

Objection 2: Further, the use of free-will consists in choice. But choice presupposes the deliberation of counsel: for the Philosopher says (Ethic. iii) that choice is "the desire of what has been previously the object of deliberation." Therefore it seems impossible that Christ should have had the use of free-will in the first instant of His conception.

Objection 3: Further, the free-will is "a faculty of the will and reason," as stated in the [4162]FP, Q[83], A[2], OBJ[2]: consequently the use of free-will is an act of the will and the reason or intellect. But the act of the intellect presupposes an act of the senses; and this cannot exist without proper disposition of the organs---a condition which would seem impossible in the first instant of Christ's conception. Therefore it seems that Christ could not have the use of free-will at the first instant of His conception.

On the contrary, Augustine says in his book on the Trinity (Gregory: Regist. ix, Ep. 61): "As soon as the Word entered the womb, while retaining the reality of His Nature, He was made flesh, and a perfect man." But a perfect man has the use of free-will. Therefore Christ had the use of free-will in the first instant of His conception.

I answer that, As stated above [4163](A[1]), spiritual perfection was becoming to the human nature which Christ took, which perfection He attained not by making progress, but by receiving it from the very first. Now ultimate perfection does not consist in power or habit, but in operation; wherefore it is said (De Anima ii, text. 5) that operation is a "second act." We must, therefore, say that in the first instant of His conception Christ had that operation of the soul which can be had in an instant. And such is the operation of the will and intellect, in which the use of free-will consists. For the operation of the intellect and will is sudden and instantaneous, much more, indeed, than corporeal vision; inasmuch as to understand, to will, and to feel, are not movements that may be described as "acts of an imperfect being," which attains perfection successively, but are "the acts of an already perfect being," as is said, De Anima iii, text. 28. We must therefore say that Christ had the use of free-will in the first instant of His conception.

Reply to Objection 1: Existence precedes action by nature, but not in time; but at the same time the agent has perfect existence, and begins to act unless it is hindered. Thus fire, as soon as it is generated, begins to give heat and light. The action of heating, however, is not terminated in an instant, but continues for a time; whereas the action of giving light is perfected in an instant. And such an operation is the use of free-will, as stated above.

Reply to Objection 2: As soon as counsel or deliberation is ended, there may be choice. But those who need the deliberation of counsel, as soon as this comes to an end are certain of what ought to be chosen: and consequently they choose at once. From this it is clear that the deliberation of counsel does not of necessity precede choice save for the purpose of inquiring into what is uncertain. But Christ, in the first instant of His conception, had the fulness of sanctifying grace, and in like manner the fulness of known truth; according to Jn. 1:14: "Full of grace and truth." Wherefore, as being possessed of certainty about all things, He could choose at once in an instant.

Reply to Objection 3: Christ's intellect, in regard to His infused knowledge, could understand without turning to phantasms, as stated above ([4164]Q[11], A[2]). Consequently His intellect and will could act without any action of the senses.

Nevertheless it was possible for Him, in the first instant of His conception, to have an operation of the senses: especially as to the sense of touch, which the infant can exercise in the womb even before it has received the rational soul, as is said, De Gener. Animal. ii, 3,4. Wherefore, since Christ had the rational soul in the first instant of His conception, through His body being already fashioned and endowed with sensible organs, much more was it possible for Him to exercise the sense of touch in that same instant.

Whether Christ could merit in the first instant of His conception?

Objection 1: It would seem that Christ could not merit in the first instant of His conception. For the free-will bears the same relation to merit as to demerit. But the devil could not sin in the first instant of his creation, as was shown in the [4165]FP, Q[63], A[5]. Therefore neither could Christ's soul merit in the first instant of its creation---that is, in the first instant of Christ's conception.

Objection 2: Further, that which man has in the first instant of his conception seems to be natural to him: for it is in this that his natural generation is terminated. But we do not merit by what is natural to us, as is clear from what has been said in the [4166]FS, Q[109], A[5]; [4167]FS, Q[114], A[2]. Therefore it seems that the use of free-will, which Christ as man had in the first instant of His conception, was not meritorious.

Objection 3: Further, that which a man has once merited he makes, in a way, his own: consequently it seems that he cannot merit the same thing again: for no one merits what is already his. If, therefore, Christ merited in the first instant of His conception, it follows that afterwards He merited nothing. But this is evidently untrue. Therefore Christ did not merit in the first instant of His conception.

On the contrary, Augustine [*Paterius, Expos. Vet. et Nov. Test. super Ex. 40] says: "Increase of merit was absolutely impossible to the soul of Christ." But increase of merit would have been possible had He not merited in the first instant of His conception. Therefore Christ merited in the first instant of His conception.

I answer that, As stated above [4168](A[1]), Christ was sanctified by grace in the first instant of His conception. Now, sanctification is twofold: that of adults who are sanctified in consideration of their own act; and that of infants who are sanctified in consideration of, not their own act of faith, but that of their parents or of the Church. The former sanctification is more perfect than the latter: just as act is more perfect than habit; and "that which is by itself, than that which is by another" [*Aristotle, Phys. viii]. Since, therefore, the sanctification of Christ was most perfect, because He was so sanctified that He might sanctify others; consequently He was sanctified by reason of His own movement of the free-will towards God. Which movement, indeed, of the free-will is meritorious. Consequently, Christ did merit in the first instant of His conception.

Reply to Objection 1: Free-will does not bear the same relation to good as to evil: for to good it is related of itself, and naturally; whereas to evil it is related as to a defect, and beside nature. Now, as the Philosopher says (De Coelo ii, text. 18): "That which is beside nature is subsequent to that which is according to nature; because that which is beside nature is an exception to nature." Therefore the free-will of a creature can be moved to good meritoriously in the first instant of its creation, but not to evil sinfully; provided, however, its nature be unimpaired.

Reply to Objection 2: That which man has at the first moment of his creation, in the ordinary course of nature, is natural to him. but nothing hinders a creature from receiving from God a gift of grace at the very beginning of its creation. In this way did Christ's soul in the first instant of its creation receive grace by which it could merit. And for this reason is that grace, by way of a certain likeness, said to be natural to this Man, as explained by Augustine (Enchiridion xl).

Reply to Objection 3: Nothing prevents the same thing belonging to someone from several causes. And thus it is that Christ was able by subsequent actions and sufferings to merit the glory of immortality, which He also merited in the first instant of His conception: not, indeed, so that it became thereby more due to Him than before, but so that it was due to Him from more causes than before.

Whether Christ was a perfect comprehensor in the first instant of His conception?

Objection 1: It would seem that Christ was not a perfect comprehensor in the first instant of His conception. For merit precedes reward, as fault precedes punishment. But Christ merited in the first instant of His conception, as stated above [4169](A[3]). Since, therefore, the state of comprehension is the principal reward, it seems that Christ was not a comprehensor in the first instant of His conception.

Objection 2: Further, our Lord said (Lk. 24:26): "Ought not Christ to have suffered these things, and so to enter into His glory?" But glory belongs to the state of comprehension. Therefore Christ was not in the state of comprehension in the first instant of His conception, when as yet He had not suffered.

Objection 3: Further, what befits neither man nor angel seems proper to God; and therefore is not becoming to Christ as man. But to be always in the state of beatitude befits neither man nor angel: for if they had been created in beatitude, they would not have sinned afterwards. Therefore Christ, as man, was not in the state of beatitude in the first instant of His conception.

On the contrary, It is written (Ps. 64:5): "Blessed is he whom Thou hast chosen, end taken to Thee"; which words, according to the gloss, refer to Christ's human nature, which "was taken by the Word of God unto the unity of Person." But human nature was taken by the Word of God in the first instant of His conception. Therefore, in the first instant of His conception, Christ, as man, was in the state of beatitude; which is to be a comprehensor.

I answer that, As appears from what was said above [4170](A[3]), it was unbecoming that in His conception Christ should receive merely habitual grace without the act. Now, He received grace "not by measure" (Jn. 3:34), as stated above (Q[7], A[11]). But the grace of the "wayfarer," being short of that of the "comprehensor," is in less measure than that of the comprehensor. Wherefore it is manifest that in the first instant of His conception Christ received not only as much grace as comprehensors have, but also greater than that which they all have. And because that grace was not without its act, it follows that He was a comprehensor in act, seeing God in His Essence more clearly than other creatures.

Reply to Objection 1: As stated above ([4171]Q[19], A[3]), Christ did not merit the glory of the soul, in respect of which He is said to have been a comprehensor, but the glory of the body, to which He came through His Passion.

Wherefore the reply to the Second Objection is clear.

Reply to Objection 3: Since Christ was both God and man, He had, even in His humanity, something more than other creatures--- namely, that He was in the state of beatitude from the very beginning.

OF CHRIST'S NATIVITY (EIGHT ARTICLES)

After considering Christ's conception, we must treat of His nativity. First, as to the nativity itself; secondly, as to His manifestation after birth.

Concerning the first there are eight points of inquiry:

(1) Whether nativity regards the nature or the person?
(2) Whether another, besides His eternal, birth should be attributed to Christ?
(3) Whether the Blessed Virgin is His Mother in respect of His temporal birth?
(4) Whether she ought to be called the Mother of God?
(5) Whether Christ is the Son of God the Father and of the Virgin Mother in respect of two filiations?
(6) Of the mode of the Nativity;

(7) Of its place;

(8) Of the time of the Nativity.

Whether nativity regards the nature rather than the person?

Objection 1: It would seem that nativity regards the nature rather than the person. For Augustine [*Fulgentius] says (De Fide ad Petrum): "The eternal Divine Nature could not be conceived and born of human nature, except in a true human nature." Consequently it becomes the Divine Nature to be conceived and born by reason of the human nature. Much more, therefore, does it regard human nature itself.

Objection 2: Further, according to the Philosopher (Metaph. v), "nature" is so denominated from "nativity." But things are denominated from one another by reason of some likeness. Therefore it seems that nativity regards the nature rather than the person.

Objection 3: Further, properly speaking, that is born which begins to exist by nativity. But Christ's Person did not begin to exist by His nativity, whereas His human nature did. Therefore it seems that the nativity properly regards the nature, and not the person.

On the contrary, Damascene says (De Fide Orth. iii): "Nativity regards the hypostasis, not the nature."

I answer that, Nativity can be attributed to someone in two ways: first, as to its subject; secondly, as to its terminus. To him that is born it is attributed as to its subject: and this, properly speaking, is the hypostasis, not the nature. For since to be born is to be generated; as a thing is generated in order for it to be, so is a thing born in order for it to be. Now, to be, properly speaking, belongs to that which subsists; since a form that does not subsist is said to be only inasmuch as by it something is: and whereas person or hypostasis designates something as subsisting, nature designates form, whereby something subsists. Consequently, nativity is attributed to the person or hypostasis as to the proper subject of being born, but not to the nature.

But to the nature nativity is attributed as to its terminus. For the terminus of generation and of every nativity is the form. Now, nature designates something as a form: wherefore nativity is said to be "the road to nature," as the Philosopher states (Phys. ii): for the purpose of nature is terminated in the form or nature of the species.

Reply to Objection 1: On account of the identity of nature and hypostasis in God, nature fs sometimes put instead of person or hypostasis. And in this sense Augustine says that the Divine Nature was conceived and born, inasmuch as the Person of the Son was conceived and born in the human nature.

Reply to Objection 2: No movement or change is denominated from the subject moved, but from the terminus of the movement, whence the subject has its species. For this reason nativity is not denominated from the person born, but from nature, which is the terminus of nativity.

Reply to Objection 3: Nature, properly speaking, does not begin to exist: rather is it the person that begins to exist in some nature. Because, as stated above, nature designates that by which something is; whereas person designates something as having subsistent being.

Whether a temporal nativity should be attributed to Christ?

Objection 1: It would seem that temporal nativity is not to be attributed to Christ. For "to be born is a certain movement of a thing that did not exist before it was born, which movement procures for it the benefit of existence" [*Cf. Augustine, De Unit. Trin. xii]. But Christ was from all eternity. Therefore He could not be born in time.

Objection 2: Further, what is perfect in itself needs not to be born. But the Person of the Son of God was perfect from eternity. Therefore He needs not to be born in time. Therefore it seems that He had no temporal birth.

Objection 3: Further, properly speaking, nativity regards the person. But in Christ there is only one person. Therefore in Christ there is but one nativity.

Objection 4: Further, what is born by two nativities is born twice. But this proposition is false; "Christ was born twice": because the nativity whereby He was born of the Father suffers no interruption; since it is eternal. Whereas interruption is required to warrant the use of the adverb "twice": for a man is said to run twice whose running is interrupted. Therefore it seems that we should not admit a double nativity in Christ.

On the contrary, Damascene says (De Fide Orth. iii): "We confess two nativities in Christ: one of the Father---eternal; and one which occurred in these latter times for our sake."

I answer that, As stated above [4172](A[1]), nature is compared to nativity, as the terminus to movement or change. Now, movement is diversified according to the diversity of its termini, as the Philosopher shows (Phys. v). But, in Christ there is a twofold nature: one which He received of the Father from eternity, the other which He received from His Mother in time. Therefore we must needs attribute to Christ a twofold nativity: one by which He was born of the Father from all eternity; one by which He was born of His Mother in time.

Reply to Objection 1: This was the argument of a certain heretic, Felician, and is solved thus by Augustine (Contra Felic. xii). "Let us suppose," says he, "as many maintain, that in the world there is a universal soul, which, by its ineffable movement, so gives life to all seed, that it is not compounded with things begotten, but bestows life that they may be begotten. Without doubt, when this soul reaches the womb, being intent on fashioning the passible matter to its own purpose, it unites itself to the personality thereof, though manifestly it is not of the same substance; and thus of the active soul and passive matter, one man is made out of two substances. And so we confess that the soul is born from out the womb; but not as though, before birth, it was nothing at all in itself. Thus, then, but in a way much more sublime, the Son of God was born as man, just as the soul is held to be born together with the body: not as though they both made one substance, but that from both, one person results. Yet we do not say that the Son of God began thus to exist: lest it be thought that His Divinity is temporal. Nor do we acknowledge the flesh of the Son of God to have been from eternity: lest it be thought that He took, not a true human body, but some resemblance thereof."

Reply to Objection 2: This was an argument of Nestorius, and it is thus solved by Cyril in an epistle [*Cf. Acta Concil. Ephes., p. 1, cap. viii]: "We do not say that the Son of God had need, for His own sake, of a second nativity, after that which is from the Father: for it is foolish and a mark of ignorance to say that He who is from all eternity, and co-eternal with the Father, needs to begin again to exist. But because for us and for our salvation, uniting the human nature to His Person, He became the child of a woman, for this reason do we say that He was born in the flesh."

Reply to Objection 3: Nativity regards the person as its subject, the nature as its terminus. Now, it is possible for several transformations to be in the same subject: yet must they be diversified in respect of their termini. But we do not say this as though the eternal nativity were a transformation or a movement, but because it is designated by way of a transformation or movement.

Reply to Objection 4: Christ can be said to have been born twice in respect of His two nativities. For just as he is said to run twice who runs at two different times, so can He be said to be born twice who is born once from eternity and once in time: because eternity and time differ much more than two different times, although each signifies a measure of duration.

Whether the Blessed Virgin can be called Christ's Mother in respect of His temporal nativity?

Objection 1: It would seem that the Blessed Virgin cannot be called Christ's Mother in respect of His temporal nativity. For, as stated above ([4173]Q[32], A[4]), the Blessed Virgin Mary did not cooperate actively in begetting Christ, but merely supplied the matter. But this does not seem sufficient to make her His Mother: otherwise wood might be called the mother of the bed or bench. Therefore it seems that the Blessed Virgin cannot be called the Mother of Christ.

Objection 2: Further, Christ was born miraculously of the Blessed Virgin. But a miraculous begetting does not suffice for motherhood or sonship: for we do not speak of Eve as being the daughter of Adam. Therefore neither should Christ be called the Son of the Blessed Virgin.

Objection 3: Further, motherhood seems to imply partial separation of the semen. But, as Damascene says (De Fide Orth. iii), "Christ's body was formed, not by a seminal process, but by the operation of the Holy Ghost." Therefore it seems that the Blessed Virgin should not be called the Mother of Christ.

On the contrary, It is written (Mat. 1:18): "The generation of Christ was in this wise. When His Mother Mary was espoused to Joseph," etc.

I answer that, The Blessed Virgin Mary is in truth and by nature the Mother of Christ. For, as we have said above ([4174]Q[5], A[2];[4175] Q[31], A[5]), Christ's body was not brought down from heaven, as the heretic Valentine maintained, but was taken from the Virgin Mother, and formed from her purest blood. And this is all that is required for motherhood, as has been made clear above ([4176]Q[31], A[5];[4177] Q[32], A[4]). Therefore the Blessed Virgin is truly Christ's Mother.

Reply to Objection 1: As stated above ([4178]Q[32], A[3]), not every generation implies fatherhood or motherhood and sonship, but only the generation of living things. Consequently when inanimate things are made from some matter, the relationship of motherhood and sonship does not follow from this, but only in the generation of living things, which is properly called nativity.

Reply to Objection 2: As Damascene says (De Fide Orth. iii): "The temporal nativity by which Christ was born for our salvation is, in a way, natural, since a Man was born of a woman, and after the due lapse of time from His conception: but it is also supernatural, because He was begotten, not of seed, but of the Holy Ghost and the Blessed Virgin, above the law of conception." Thus, then, on the part of the mother, this nativity was natural, but on the part of the operation of the Holy Ghost it was supernatural. Therefore the Blessed Virgin is the true and natural Mother of Christ.

Reply to Objection 3: As stated above ([4179]Q[31], A[5], ad 3;[4180] Q[32], A[4]), the resolution of the woman's semen is not necessary for conception; neither, therefore, is it required for motherhood.

Whether the Blessed Virgin should be called the Mother of God?

Objection 1: It would seem that the Blessed Virgin should not be called the Mother of God. For in the Divine mysteries we should not make any assertion that is not taken from Holy Scripture. But we read nowhere in Holy Scripture that she is the mother or parent of God, but that she is the "mother of Christ" or of "the Child," as may be seen from Mat. 1:18. Therefore we should not say that the Blessed Virgin is the Mother of God.

Objection 2: Further, Christ is called God in respect of His Divine Nature. But the Divine Nature did not first originate from the Virgin. Therefore the Blessed Virgin should not be called the Mother of God.

Objection 3: Further, the word "God" is predicated in common of Father, Son, and Holy Ghost. If, therefore, the Blessed Virgin is Mother of God it seems to follow that she was the Mother of Father, Son, and Holy Ghost, which cannot be allowed. Therefore the Blessed Virgin should not be called Mother of God.

On the contrary, In the chapters of Cyril, approved in the Council of Ephesus (P. 1, Cap. xxvi), we read: "If anyone confess not that the Emmanuel is truly God, and that for this reason the Holy Virgin is the Mother of God, since she begot of her flesh the Word of God made flesh, let him be anathema."

I answer that, As stated above ([4181]Q[16], A[1]), every word that signifies a nature in the concrete can stand for any hypostasis of that nature. Now, since the union of the Incarnation took place in the hypostasis, as above stated ([4182]Q[2], A[3]), it is manifest that this word "God" can stand for the hypostasis, having a human and a Divine nature. Therefore whatever belongs to the Divine and to the human nature can be attributed to that Person: both when a word is employed to stand for it, signifying the Divine Nature, and when a word is used signifying the human nature. Now, conception and birth are attributed to the person and hypostasis in respect of that nature in which it is conceived and born. Since, therefore, the human nature was taken by the Divine Person in the very beginning of the conception, as stated above ([4183]Q[33], A[3]), it follows that it can be truly said that God was conceived and born of the Virgin. Now from this is a woman called a man's mother, that she conceived him and gave birth to him. Therefore the Blessed Virgin is truly called the Mother of God. For the only way in which it could be denied that the Blessed Virgin is the Mother of God would be either if the humanity were first subject to conception and birth, before this man were the Son of God, as Photinus said; or if the humanity were not assumed unto unity of the Person or hypostasis of the Word of God, as Nestorius maintained. But both of these are erroneous. Therefore it is heretical to deny that the Blessed Virgin is the Mother of God.

Reply to Objection 1: This was an argument of Nestorius, and it is solved by saying that, although we do not find it said expressly in Scripture that the Blessed Virgin is the Mother of God, yet we do find it expressly said in Scripture that "Jesus Christ is true God," as may be seen 1 Jn. 5:20, and that the Blessed Virgin is the "Mother of Jesus Christ," which is clearly expressed Mat. 1:18. Therefore, from the words of Scripture it follows of necessity that she is the Mother of God.

Again, it is written (Rom. 9:5) that Christ is of the Jews "according to the flesh, who is over all things, God blessed for ever." But He is not of the Jews except through the Blessed Virgin. Therefore He who is "above all things, God blessed for ever," is truly born of the Blessed Virgin as of His Mother.

Reply to Objection 2: This was an argument of Nestorius. But Cyril, in a letter against Nestorius [*Cf. Acta Conc. Ephes., p. 1, cap. ii], answers it thus: "Just as when a man's soul is born with its body, they are considered as one being: and if anyone wish to say that the mother of the flesh is not the mother of the soul, he says too much. Something like this may be perceived in the generation of Christ. For the Word of God was born of the substance of God the Father: but because He took flesh, we must of necessity confess that in the flesh He was born of a woman." Consequently we must say that the Blessed Virgin is called the Mother of God, not as though she were the Mother of the Godhead, but because she is the mother, according to His human nature, of the Person who has both the divine and the human nature.

Reply to Objection 3: Although the name "God" is common to the three Persons, yet sometimes it stands for the Person of the Father alone, sometimes only for the Person of the Son or of the Holy Ghost, as stated above (Q[16], A[1]; [4184]FP, Q[39], A[4]). So that when we say, "The Blessed Virgin is the Mother of God," this word "God" stands only for the incarnate Person of the Son.

Day 272

Whether there are two filiations in Christ?

Objection 1: It would seem that there are two filiations in Christ. For nativity is the cause of filiation. But in Christ there are two nativities. Therefore in Christ there are also two filiations.

Objection 2: Further, filiation, which is said of a man as being the son of someone, his father or his mother, depends, in a way, on him: because the very being of a relation consists "in being referred to another"; wherefore if one of two relatives be destroyed, the other is destroyed also. But the eternal filiation by which Christ is the Son of God the Father depends not on His Mother, because nothing eternal depends on what is temporal. Therefore Christ is not His Mother's Son by temporal filiation. Either, therefore, He is not her Son at all, which is in contradiction to what has been said above ([4185]AA[3],4), or He must needs be her Son by some other temporal filiation. Therefore in Christ there are two filiations.

Objection 3: Further, one of two relatives enters the definition of the other; hence it is clear that of two relatives, one is specified from the other. But one and the same cannot be in diverse species. Therefore it seems impossible that one and the same relation be referred to extremes which are altogether diverse. But Christ is said to be the Son of the Eternal Father and a temporal mother, who are terms altogether diverse. Therefore it seems that Christ cannot, by the same relation, be called the Son of the Father and of His Mother Therefore in Christ there are two filiations.

On the contrary, As Damascene says (De Fide Orth. iii), things pertaining to the nature are multiple in Christ; but not those things that pertain to the Person. But filiation belongs especially to the Person, since it is a personal property, as appears from what was said in the [4186]FP, Q[32], A[3]; [4187]FP, Q[40], A[2]. Therefore there is but one filiation in Christ.

I answer that, opinions differ on this question. For some, considering only the cause of filiation, which is nativity, put two filiations in Christ, just as there are two nativities. On the contrary, others, considering only the subject of filiation, which is the person or hypostasis, put only one filiation in Christ, just as there is but one hypostasis or person. Because the unity or plurality of a relation is considered in respect, not of its terms, but of its cause or of its subject. For if it were considered in respect of its terms, every man would of necessity have in himself two filiations---one in reference to his father, and another in reference to his mother. But if we consider the question aright, we shall see that every man bears but one relation to both his father and his mother, on account of the unity of the cause thereof. For man is born by one birth of both father and mother: whence he bears but one relation to both. The same is said of one master who teaches many disciples the same doctrine, and of one lord who governs many subjects by the same power. But if there be various causes specifically diverse, it seems that in consequence the relations differ in species: wherefore nothing hinders several such relations being in the same subject. Thus if a man teach grammar to some and logic to others, his teaching is of a different kind in one case and in the other; and therefore one and the same man may have different relations as the master of different disciples, or of the same disciples in regard to diverse doctrines. Sometimes, however, it happens that a man bears a relation to several in respect of various causes, but of the same species: thus a father may have several sons by several acts of generation. Wherefore the paternity cannot differ specifically, since the acts of generation are specifically the same. And because several forms of the same species cannot at the same time be in the same subject, it is impossible for several paternities to be in a man who is the father of several sons by natural generation. But it would not be so were he the father of one son by natural generation and of another by adoption.

Now, it is manifest that Christ was not born by one and the same nativity, of the Father from eternity, and of His Mother in time: indeed, these two nativities differ specifically. Wherefore, as to this, we must say that there are various filiations, one temporal and the other eternal. Since, however, the subject of filiation is neither the nature nor part of the nature, but the person or hypostasis alone; and since in Christ there is no other hypostasis or person than the eternal, there can be no other filiation in Christ but that which is in the eternal hypostasis. Now, every relation which is predicated of God from time does not put something real in the eternal God, but only

356

something according to our way of thinking, as we have said in the [4188]FP, Q[13], A[7]. Therefore the filiation by which Christ is referred to His Mother cannot be a real relation, but only a relation of reason.

Consequently each opinion is true to a certain extent. For if we consider the adequate causes of filiation, we must needs say that there are two filiations in respect of the twofold nativity. But if we consider the subject of filiation, which can only be the eternal suppositum, then no other than the eternal filiation in Christ is a real relation. Nevertheless, He has the relation of Son in regard to His Mother, because it is implied in the relation of motherhood to Christ. Thus God is called Lord by a relation which is implied in the real relation by which the creature is subject to God. And although lordship is not a real relation in God, yet is He really Lord through the real subjection of the creature to Him. In the same way Christ is really the Son of the Virgin Mother through the real relation of her motherhood to Christ.

Reply to Objection 1: Temporal nativity would cause a real temporal filiation in Christ if there were in Him a subject capable of such filiation. But this cannot be; since the eternal suppositum cannot be receptive of a temporal relation, as stated above. Nor can it be said that it is receptive of temporal filiation by reason of the human nature, just as it is receptive of the temporal nativity; because human nature would need in some way to be the subject of filiation, just as in a way it is the subject of nativity; for since an Ethiopian is said to be white by reason of his teeth, it must be that his teeth are the subject of whiteness. But human nature can nowise be the subject of filiation, because this relation regards directly the person.

Reply to Objection 2: Eternal filiation does not depend on a temporal mother, but together with this eternal filiation we understand a certain temporal relation dependent on the mother, in respect of which relation Christ is called the Son of His Mother.

Reply to Objection 3: One and being are mutually consequent, as is said Metaph. iv. Therefore, just as it happens that in one of the extremes of a relation there is something real, whereas in the other there is not something real, but merely a certain aspect, as the Philosopher observes of knowledge and the thing known; so also it happens that on the part of one extreme there is one relation, whereas on the part of the other there are many. Thus in man on the part of his parents there is a twofold relation, the one of paternity, the other of motherhood, which are specifically diverse, inasmuch as the father is the principle of generation in one way, and the mother in another (whereas if many be the principle of one action and in the same way---for instance, if many. together draw a ship along---there would be one and the same relation in all of them); but on the part of the child there is but one filiation in reality, though there be two in aspect, corresponding to the two relations in the parents, as considered by the intellect. And thus in one way there is only one real filiation in Christ, which is in respect of the Eternal Father: yet there is another temporal relation in regard to His temporal mother.

Whether Christ was born without His Mother suffering?

Objection 1: It would seem that Christ was not born without His Mother suffering. For just as man's death was a result of the sin of our first parents, according to Gn. 2:17: "In what day soever ye shall eat, ye shall [Vulg.: 'thou shalt eat of it, thou shalt] die"; so were the pains of childbirth, according to Gn. 3:16: "In sorrow shalt thou bring forth children." But Christ was willing to undergo death. Therefore for the same reason it seems that His birth should have been with pain.

Objection 2: Further, the end is proportionate to the beginning. But Christ ended His life in pain, according to Is. 53:4: "Surely . . . He hath carried our sorrows." Therefore it seems that His nativity was not without the pains of childbirth.

Objection 3: Further, in the book on the birth of our Saviour [*Protevangelium Jacobi xix, xx] it is related that midwives were present at Christ's birth; and they would be wanted by reason of the mother's suffering pain. Therefore it seems that the Blessed Virgin suffered pain in giving birth to her Child.

On the contrary, Augustine says (Serm. de Nativ. [*Supposititious]), addressing himself to the Virgin-Mother: "In conceiving thou wast all pure, in giving birth thou wast without pain."

I answer that, The pains of childbirth are caused by the infant opening the passage from the womb. Now it has been said above ([4189]Q[28], A[2], Replies to objections), that Christ came forth from the closed womb of His Mother, and, consequently, without opening the passage. Consequently there was no pain in that birth, as neither was there any corruption; on the contrary, there was much joy therein for that God-Man "was born into the world," according to Is. 35:1,2: "Like the lily, it shall bud forth and blossom, and shall rejoice with joy and praise."

Reply to Objection 1: The pains of childbirth in the woman follow from the mingling of the sexes. Wherefore (Gn. 3:16) after the words, "in sorrow shalt thou bring forth children," the following are added: "and thou shalt be under thy husband's power." But, as Augustine says (Serm. de Assumpt. B. Virg., [*Supposititious]), from this sentence we must exclude the Virgin-Mother of God; who, "because she conceived Christ without the defilement of sin, and without the stain of sexual mingling, therefore did she bring Him forth without pain, without violation of her virginal integrity, without detriment to the purity of her maidenhood." Christ, indeed, suffered death, but through His own spontaneous desire, in order to atone for us, not as a necessary result of that sentence, for He was not a debtor unto death.

Reply to Objection 2: As "by His death" Christ "destroyed our death" [*Preface of the Mass in Paschal-time], so by His pains He freed us from our pains; and so He wished to die a painful death. But the mother's pains in childbirth did not concern Christ, who came to atone for our sins. And therefore there was no need for His Mother to suffer in giving birth.

Reply to Objection 3: We are told (Lk. 2:7) that the Blessed Virgin herself "wrapped up in swaddling clothes" the Child whom she had brought forth, "and laid Him in a manger." Consequently the narrative of this book, which is apocryphal, is untrue. Wherefore Jerome says (Adv. Helvid. iv): "No midwife was there, no officious women interfered. She was both mother and midwife. 'With swaddling clothes,' says he, 'she wrapped up the child, and laid Him in a manger.'" These words prove the falseness of the apocryphal ravings.

Whether Christ should have been born in Bethlehem?

Objection 1: It would seem that Christ should not have been born in Bethlehem. For it is written (Is. 2:3): "The law shall come forth from Sion, and the Word of the Lord from Jerusalem." But Christ is truly the Word of God. Therefore He should have come into the world at Jerusalem.

Objection 2: Further, it is said (Mat. 2:23) that it is written of Christ that "He shall be called a Nazarene"; which is taken from Is. 11:1: "A flower shall rise up out of his root"; for "Nazareth" is interpreted "a flower." But a man is named especially from the place of his birth. Therefore it seems that He should have been born in Nazareth, where also He was conceived and brought up.

Objection 3: Further, for this was our Lord born into the world, that He might make known the true faith. according to Jn. 18:37: "For this was I born, and for this came I into the world; that I should give testimony to the truth." But this would have been easier if He had been born in the city of Rome, which at that time ruled the world; whence Paul, writing to the Romans (1:8) says: "Your faith is spoken of in the whole world." Therefore it seems that He should not have been born in Bethlehem.

On the contrary, It is written (Mic. 5:2): "And thou, Bethlehem, Ephrata . . . out of thee shall He come forth unto Me, that is to be the ruler in Israel."

I answer that, Christ willed to be born in Bethlehem for two reasons. First, because "He was made . . . of the seed of David according to the flesh," as it is written (Rom. 1:3); to whom also was a special promise made concerning Christ; according to 2 Kings 23:1: "The man to whom it was appointed concerning the Christ of the God of Jacob . . . said." Therefore He willed to be born at Bethlehem, where David was born, in order that by the very birthplace the promise made to David might be shown to be fulfilled. The Evangelist points this out by saying: "Because He was of the house and of the family of David." Secondly, because, as Gregory says (Hom. viii in Evang.): "Bethlehem is interpreted 'the house of bread.' It is Christ Himself who said, 'I am the living Bread which came down from heaven.'"

Reply to Objection 1: As David was born in Bethlehem, so also did he choose Jerusalem to set up his throne there, and to build there the Temple of God, so that Jerusalem was at the same time a royal and a priestly city. Now, Christ's priesthood and kingdom were "consummated" principally in His Passion. Therefore it was becoming that He should choose Bethlehem for His Birthplace and Jerusalem for the scene of His Passion.

At the same time, too, He put to silence the vain boasting of men who take pride in being born in great cities, where also they desire especially to receive honor. Christ, on the contrary, willed to be born in a mean city, and to suffer reproach in a great city.

Reply to Objection 2: Christ wished "to flower" by His holy life, not in His carnal birth. Therefore He wished to be fostered and brought up at Nazareth. But He wished to be born at Bethlehem away from home; because, as Gregory says (Hom. viii in Evang.), through the human nature which He had taken, He was born, as it were, in a foreign place---foreign not to His power, but to His Nature. And, again, as Bede says on Lk. 2:7: "In order that He who found no room at the inn might prepare many mansions for us in His Father's house."

Reply to Objection 3: According to a sermon in the Council of Ephesus [*P. iii, cap. ix]: "If He had chosen the great city of Rome, the change in the world would be ascribed to the influence of her citizens. If He had been the son of the Emperor, His benefits would have been attributed to the latter's power. But that we might acknowledge the work of God in the transformation of the whole earth, He chose a poor mother and a birthplace poorer still."

"But the weak things of the world hath God chosen, that He may confound the strong" (1 Cor. 1:27). And therefore, in order the more to show His power, He set up the head of His Church in Rome itself, which was the head of the world, in sign of His complete victory, in order that from that city the faith might spread throughout the world; according to Is. 26:5,6: "The high city He shall lay low . . . the feet of the poor," i.e. of Christ, "shall tread it down; the steps of the needy," i.e. of the apostles Peter and Paul.

Whether Christ was born at a fitting time?

Objection 1: It would seem that Christ was not born at a fitting time. Because Christ came in order to restore liberty to His own. But He was born at a time of subjection---namely, when the whole world, as it were, tributary to Augustus, was being enrolled, at his command as Luke relates (2:1). Therefore it seems that Christ was not born at a fitting time.

Objection 2: Further, the promises concerning the coming of Christ were not made to the Gentiles; according to Rom. 9:4: "To whom belong . . . the promises." But Christ was born during the reign of a foreigner, as appears from Mat. 2:1: "When Jesus was born in the days of King Herod." Therefore it seems that He was not born at a fitting time.

Objection 3: Further, the time of Christ's presence on earth is compared to the day, because He is the "Light of the world"; wherefore He says Himself (Jn. 9:4): "I must work the works of Him that sent Me, whilst it is day." But in summer the days are longer than in winter. Therefore, since He was born in the depth of winter, eight days before the Kalends of January, it seems that He was not born at a fitting time.

On the contrary, It is written (Gal. 4:4): "When the fulness of the time was come, God sent His Son, made of a woman, made under the law."

I answer that, There is this difference between Christ and other men, that, whereas they are born subject to the restrictions of time, Christ, as Lord and Maker of all time, chose a time in which to be born, just as He chose a mother and a birthplace. And since "what is of God is well ordered" and becomingly arranged, it follows that Christ was born at a most fitting time.

Reply to Objection 1: Christ came in order to bring us back from a state of bondage to a state of liberty. And therefore, as He took our mortal nature in order to restore us to life, so, as Bede says (Super Luc. ii, 4,5), "He deigned to take flesh at such a time that, shortly after His birth, He would be enrolled in Caesar's census, and thus submit Himself to bondage for the sake of our liberty."

Moreover, at that time, when the whole world lived under one ruler, peace abounded on the earth. Therefore it was a fitting time for the birth of Christ, for "He is our peace, who hath made both one," as it is written (Eph. 2:14). Wherefore Jerome says on Is. 2:4: "If we search the page of ancient history, we shall find that throughout the whole world there was discord until the twenty-eighth year of Augustus Caesar: but when our Lord was born, all war ceased"; according to Is. 2:4: "Nation shall not lift up sword against nation."

Again, it was fitting that Christ should be born while the world was governed by one ruler, because "He came to gather His own [Vulg.: 'the children of God'] together in one" (Jn. 11:52), that there might be "one fold and one shepherd" (Jn. 10:16).

Reply to Objection 2: Christ wished to be born during the reign of a foreigner, that the prophecy of Jacob might be fulfilled (Gn. 49:10): "The sceptre shall not be taken away from Juda, nor a ruler from his thigh, till He come that is to be sent." Because, as Chrysostom says (Hom. ii in Matth. [*Opus Imperf., falsely ascribed to Chrysostom]), as long as the Jewish "people was governed by Jewish kings, however wicked, prophets were sent for their healing. But now that the Law of God is under the power of a wicked king, Christ is born; because a grave and hopeless disease demanded a more skilful physician."

Reply to Objection 3: As says the author of the book De Qq. Nov. et Vet. Test., "Christ wished to be born, when the light of day begins to increase in length," so as to show that He came in order that man might come nearer to the Divine Light, according to Lk. 1:79: "To enlighten them that sit in darkness and in the shadow of death."

In like manner He chose to be born in the rough winter season, that He might begin from then to suffer in body for us.

OF THE MANIFESTATION OF THE NEWLY BORN CHRIST (EIGHT ARTICLES)

We must now consider the manifestation of the newly born Christ: concerning which there are eight points of inquiry:

(1) Whether Christ's birth should have been made known to all?
(2) Whether it should have been made known to some?
(3) To whom should it have been made known?
(4) Whether He should have made Himself known, or should He rather have been manifested by others?
(5) By what other means should it have been made known?
(6) Of the order of these manifestations;
(7) Of the star by means of which His birth was made known;
(8) of the adoration of the Magi, who were informed of Christ's nativity by means of the star.

Whether Christ's birth should have been made known to all?

Objection 1: It would seem that Christ's birth should have been made known to all. Because fulfilment should correspond to promise. Now, the promise of Christ's coming is thus expressed (Ps. 49:3): "God shall come manifestly. But He came by His birth in the flesh." Therefore it seems that His birth should have been made known to the whole world.

Objection 2: Further, it is written (1 Tim. 1:15): "Christ came into this world to save sinners." But this is not effected save in as far as the grace of Christ is made known to them; according to Titus 2:11,12: "The grace of God our Saviour hath appeared to all men, instructing us, that denying ungodliness and worldly desires, we should live soberly, and justly, and godly in this world." Therefore it seems that Christ's birth should have been made known to all.

Objection 3: Further, God is most especially inclined to mercy; according to Ps. 144:9: "His tender mercies are over all His works." But in His second coming, when He will "judge justices" (Ps. 70:3), He will come before the eyes of all; according to Mat. 24:27: "As lightning cometh out of the east, and appeareth even into the west, so shall also the coming of the Son of Man be." Much more, therefore, should His first coming, when He was born into the world according to the flesh, have been made known to all.

On the contrary, It is written (Is. 45:15): "Thou art a hidden God, the Holy [Vulg.: 'the God] of Israel, the Saviour." And, again (Is. 43:3): "His look was, as it were, hidden and despised."

I answer that, It was unfitting that Christ's birth should be made known to all men without distinction. First, because this would have been a hindrance to the redemption of man, which was accomplished by means of the Cross; for, as it is written (1 Cor. 2:8): "If they had known it, they would never have crucified the Lord of glory."

Secondly, because this would have lessened the merit of faith, which He came to offer men as the way to righteousness. according to Rom. 3:22: "The justice of God by faith of Jesus Christ." For if, when Christ was born, His birth had been made known to all by evident signs, the very nature of faith would have been destroyed, since it is "the evidence of things that appear not," as stated, Heb. 11:1.

Thirdly, because thus the reality of His human nature would have come into doubt. Whence Augustine says (Ep. ad Volusianum cxxxvii): "If He had not passed through the different stages of age from babyhood to youth, had neither eaten nor slept, would He not have strengthened an erroneous opinion, and made it impossible for us to believe that He had become true man? And while He is doing all things wondrously, would He have taken away that which He accomplished in mercy?"

Reply to Objection 1: According to the gloss, the words quoted must be understood of Christ's coming as judge.

Reply to Objection 2: All men were to be instructed unto salvation, concerning the grace of God our Saviour, not at the very time of His birth, but afterwards, in due time, after He had "wrought salvation in the midst of the earth" (Ps. 73:12). Wherefore after His Passion and Resurrection, He said to His disciples (Mat. 28:19): "Going . . . teach ye all nations."

Reply to Objection 3: For judgment to be passed, the authority of the judge needs to be known: and for this reason it behooves that the coming of Christ unto judgment should be manifest. But His first coming was unto the salvation of all, which is by faith that is of things not seen. And therefore it was fitting that His first coming should be hidden.

Whether Christ's birth should have been made known to some?

Objection 1: It would seem that Christ's birth should not have been made known to anyone. For, as stated above (A[1], ad 3), it befitted the salvation of mankind that Christ's first coming should be hidden. But Christ came to save all; according to 1 Tim. 4:10: "Who is the Saviour of all men, especially of the faithful." Therefore Christ's birth should not have been made known to anyone.

Objection 2: Further, before Christ was born, His future birth was made known to the Blessed Virgin and Joseph. Therefore it was not necessary that it should be made known to others after His birth.

Objection 3: Further, no wise man makes known that from which arise disturbance and harm to others. But, when Christ's birth was made known, disturbance arose: for it is written (Mat. 2:3) that "King Herod, hearing" of Christ's birth, "was troubled, and all Jerusalem with him." Moreover, this brought harm to others; because it was the occasion of Herod's killing "all the male children that were in Bethlehem . . . from two years old and under." Therefore it seems unfitting for Christ's birth to have been made known to anyone.

On the contrary, Christ's birth would have been profitable to none if it had been hidden from all. But it behooved Christ's birth to be profitable: else He were born in vain. Therefore it seems that Christ's birth should have been made known to some.

I answer that, As the Apostle says (Rom. 13:1) "what is of God is well ordered." Now it belongs to the order of Divine wisdom that God's gifts and the secrets of His wisdom are not bestowed on all equally, but to some immediately, through whom they are made known to others. Wherefore, with regard to the mystery of the Resurrection it is written (Acts 10:40,41): "God . . . gave" Christ rising again "to be made manifest, not to all the people, but to witnesses pre-ordained by God." Consequently, that His birth might be consistent with this, it should have been made known, not to all, but to some, through whom it could be made known to others.

Reply to Objection 1: As it would have been prejudicial to the salvation of mankind if God's birth had been made known to all men, so also would it have been if none had been informed of it. Because in either case faith is destroyed, whether a thing be perfectly manifest, or whether it be entirely unknown, so that no one can hear it from another; for "faith cometh by hearing" (Rom. 10:17).

Reply to Objection 2: Mary and Joseph needed to be instructed concerning Christ's birth before He was born, because it devolved on them to show reverence to the child conceived in the womb, and to serve Him even before He was born. But their testimony, being of a domestic character, would have aroused suspicion in regard to Christ's greatness: and so it behooved it to be made known to others, whose testimony could not be suspect.

Reply to Objection 3: The very disturbance that arose when it was known that Christ was born was becoming to His birth. First, because thus the heavenly dignity of Christ is made manifest. Wherefore Gregory says (Hom. x in Evang.): "After the birth of the King of heaven, the earthly king is troubled: doubtless because earthly grandeur is covered with confusion when the heavenly majesty is revealed."

Secondly, thereby the judicial power of Christ was foreshadowed. Thus Augustine says in a sermon (30 de Temp.) on the Epiphany: "What will He be like in the judgment-seat; since from His cradle He struck terror into the heart of a proud king?"

Thirdly, because thus the overthrow of the devil's kingdom was foreshadowed. For, as Pope Leo says in a sermon on the Epiphany (Serm. v [*Opus Imperfectum in Matth., Hom. ii, falsely ascribed to St. John Chrysostom]): "Herod was not so much troubled in himself as the devil in Herod. For Herod thought Him to be a man, but the devil thought Him to be God. Each feared a successor to his kingdom: the devil, a heavenly successor; Herod, an earthly successor." But their fear was needless: since Christ had not come to set up an earthly kingdom, as Pope Leo says, addressing himself to Herod: "Thy palace cannot hold Christ: nor is the Lord of the world content with the paltry power of thy scepter." That the Jews were troubled, who, on the contrary, should have rejoiced, was either because, as Chrysostom says, "wicked men could not rejoice at the coming of the Holy one," or because they wished to court favor with Herod, whom they feared; for "the populace is inclined to favor too much those whose cruelty it endures."

And that the children were slain by Herod was not harmful to them, but profitable. For Augustine says in a sermon on the Epiphany (66 de Diversis): "It cannot be questioned that Christ, who came to set man free, rewarded those who were slain for Him; since, while hanging on the cross, He prayed for those who were putting Him to death."

Whether those to whom Christ's birth was made known were suitably chosen?

Objection 1: It would seem that those to whom Christ's birth was made known were not suitably chosen. For our Lord (Mat. 10:5) commanded His disciples, "Go ye not into the way of the Gentiles," so that He might be made known to the Jews before the Gentiles. Therefore it seems that much less should Christ's birth have been at once revealed to the Gentiles who "came from the east," as stated Mat. 2:1.

Objection 2: Further, the revelation of Divine truth should be made especially to the friends of God, according to Job 37 [Vulg.: Job 36:33]: "He sheweth His friend concerning it." But the Magi seem to be God's foes; for it is written (Lev. 19:31): "Go not aside after wizards [magi], neither ask anything of soothsayers." Therefore Christ's birth should not have been made known to the Magi.

Objection 3: Further, Christ came in order to set free the whole world from the power of the devil; whence it is written (Malachi 1:11): "From the rising of the sun even to the going down, My name is great among the Gentiles." Therefore He should have been made known, not only to those who dwelt in the east, but also to some from all parts of the world.

Objection 4: Further, all the sacraments of the Old Law were figures of Christ. But the sacraments of the Old Law were dispensed through the ministry of the legal priesthood. Therefore it seems that Christ's birth should have been made known rather to the priests in the Temple than to the shepherds in the fields.

Objection 5: Further, Christ was born of a Virgin-Mother, and was as yet a little child. It was therefore more suitable that He should be made known to youths and virgins than to old and married people or to widows, such as Simeon and Anna.

On the contrary, It is written (Jn. 13:18): "I know whom I have chosen." But what is done by God's wisdom is done becomingly. Therefore those to whom Christ's birth was made known were suitably chosen.

I answer that, Salvation, which was to be accomplished by Christ, concerns all sorts and conditions of men: because, as it is written (Col. 3:11), in Christ "there is neither male nor female, [*These words are in reality from Gal. 3:28] neither Gentile nor Jew . . . bond nor free," and so forth. And in order that this might be foreshadowed in Christ's birth, He was made known to men of all conditions. Because, as Augustine says in a sermon on the Epiphany (32 de Temp.), "the shepherds were Israelites, the Magi were Gentiles. The former were nigh to Him, the latter far from Him. Both hastened to Him together as to the cornerstone." There was also another point of contrast: for the Magi were wise and powerful; the shepherds simple and lowly. He was also made known to the righteous as Simeon and Anna; and to sinners, as the Magi. He was made known both to men, and to women---namely, to Anna---so as to show no condition of men to be excluded from Christ's redemption.

Reply to Objection 1: That manifestation of Christ's birth was a kind of foretaste of the full manifestation which was to come. And as in the later manifestation the first announcement of the grace of Christ was made by Him and His Apostles to the Jews and afterwards to the Gentiles, so the first to come to Christ were the shepherds, who were the first-fruits of the Jews, as being near to Him; and afterwards came the Magi from afar, who were "the first-fruits of the Gentiles," as Augustine says (Serm. 30 de Temp. cc.).

Reply to Objection 2: As Augustine says in a sermon on the Epiphany (Serm. 30 de Temp.): "As unskilfulness predominates in the rustic manners of the shepherd, so ungodliness abounds in the profane rites of the Magi. Yet did this Corner-Stone draw both to Itself; inasmuch as He came 'to choose the foolish things that He might confound the wise,' and 'not to call the just, but sinners,'" so that "the proud might not boast, nor the weak despair." Nevertheless, there are those who say that these Magi were not wizards, but wise astronomers, who are called Magi among the Persians or Chaldees.

Reply to Objection 3: As Chrysostom says [*Hom. ii in Matth. in the Opus Imperf., among the supposititious works of Chrysostom]: "The Magi came from the east, because the first beginning of faith came from the land where the day is born; since faith is the light of the soul." Or, "because all who come to Christ come from Him and through Him": whence it is written (Zech. 6:12): "Behold a Man, the Orient is His name." Now, they are said to come from the east literally, either because, as some say, they came from the farthest parts of the east, or because they came from the neighboring parts of Judea that lie to the east of the region inhabited by the Jews. Yet it is to be believed that certain signs of Christ's birth appeared also in other parts of the world: thus, at Rome the river flowed with oil [*Eusebius, Chronic. II, Olymp. 185]; and in Spain three suns were seen, which gradually merged into one [*Cf. Eusebius, Chronic. II, Olymp. 184].

Reply to Objection 4: As Chrysostom observes (Theophylact., Enarr. in Luc. ii, 8), the angel who announced Christ's birth did not go to Jerusalem, nor did he seek the Scribes and Pharisees, for they were corrupted, and full of ill-will. But the shepherds were single-minded, and were like the patriarchs and Moses in their mode of life.

Moreover, these shepherds were types of the Doctors of the Church, to whom are revealed the mysteries of Christ that were hidden from the Jews.

Reply to Objection 5: As Ambrose says (on Lk. 2:25): "It was right that our Lord's birth should be attested not only by the shepherds, but also by people advanced in age and virtue": whose testimony is rendered the more credible by reason of their righteousness.

Whether Christ Himself should have made His birth know?

Objection 1: It would seem that Christ should have Himself made His birth known. For "a direct cause is always of greater power than an indirect cause," as is stated Phys. viii. But Christ made His birth known through others---for instance, to the shepherds through the angels, and to the Magi through the star. Much more, therefore, should He Himself have made His birth known.

Objection 2: Further, it is written (Ecclus. 20:32): "Wisdom that is hid and treasure that is not seen; what profit is there in them both?" But Christ had, to perfection, the treasure of wisdom and grace from the beginning of His conception. Therefore, unless He had made the fulness of these gifts known by words and deeds, wisdom and grace would have been given Him to no purpose. But this is unreasonable: because "God and nature do nothing without a purpose" (De Coelo i).

Objection 3: Further, we read in the book De Infantia Salvatoris that in His infancy Christ worked many miracles. It seems therefore that He did Himself make His birth known.

On the contrary, Pope Leo says (Serm. xxxiv) that the Magi found the "infant Jesus in no way different from the generality of human infants." But other infants do not make themselves known. Therefore it was not fitting that Christ should Himself make His birth known.

I answer that, Christ's birth was ordered unto man's salvation, which is by faith. But saving faith confesses Christ's Godhead and humanity. It behooved, therefore, Christ's birth to be made known in such a way that the proof of His Godhead should not be prejudicial to faith in His human nature. But this took place while Christ presented a likeness of human weakness, and yet, by means of God's creatures, He showed the power of the Godhead in Himself. Therefore Christ made His birth known, not by Himself, but by means of certain other creatures.

Reply to Objection 1: By the way of generation and movement we must of necessity come to the imperfect before the perfect. And therefore Christ was made known first through other creatures, and afterwards He Himself manifested Himself perfectly.

Reply to Objection 2: Although hidden wisdom is useless, yet there is no need for a wise man to make himself known at all times, but at a suitable time; for it is written (Ecclus. 20:6): "There is one that holdeth his peace because he knoweth not what to say: and there is another that holdeth his peace, knowing the proper time." Hence the wisdom given to Christ was not useless, because at a suitable time He manifested Himself. And the very fact that He was hidden at a suitable time is a sign of wisdom.

Reply to Objection 3: The book De Infantia Salvatoris is apocryphal. Moreover, Chrysostom (Hom. xxi super Joan.) says that Christ worked no miracles before changing the water into wine, according to Jn. 2:11: "'This beginning of miracles did Jesus.' For if He had worked miracles at an early age, there would have been no need for anyone else to manifest Him to the Israelites; whereas John the Baptist says (Jn. 1:31): 'That He may be made manifest in Israel; therefore am I come baptizing with water.' Moreover, it was fitting that He should not begin to work miracles at an early age. For people would have thought the Incarnation to be unreal, and, out of sheer spite, would have crucified Him before the proper time."

Day 273

361

Whether Christ's birth should have been manifested by means of the angels and the star?

Objection 1: It would seem that Christ's birth should not have been manifested by means of the angels. For angels are spiritual substances, according to Ps. 103:4: "Who maketh His [Vulg.: 'makest Thy'] angels, spirits." But Christ's birth was in the flesh, and not in His spiritual substance. Therefore it should not have been manifested by means of angels.

Objection 2: Further, the righteous are more akin to the angels than to any other, according to Ps. 33:8: "The angel of the Lord shall encamp round about them that fear Him, and shall deliver them." But Christ's birth was not announced to the righteous, viz. Simeon and Anna, through the angels. Therefore neither should it have been announced to the shepherds by means of the angels.

Objection 3: Further, it seems that neither ought it to have been announced to the Magi by means of the star. For this seems to favor the error of those who think that man's birth is influenced by the stars. But occasions of sin should be taken away from man. Therefore it was not fitting that Christ's birth should be announced by a star.

Objection 4: Further, a sign should be certain, in order that something be made known thereby. But a star does not seem to be a certain sign of Christ's birth. Therefore Christ's birth was not suitably announced by a star.

On the contrary, It is written (Dt. 32:4): "The works of God are perfect." But this manifestation is the work of God. Therefore it was accomplished by means of suitable signs.

I answer that, As knowledge is imparted through a syllogism from something which we know better, so knowledge given by signs must be conveyed through things which are familiar to those to whom the knowledge is imparted. Now, it is clear that the righteous have, through the spirit of prophecy, a certain familiarity with the interior instinct of the Holy Ghost, and are wont to be taught thereby, without the guidance of sensible signs. Whereas others, occupied with material things, are led through the domain of the senses to that of the intellect. The Jews, however, were accustomed to receive Divine answers through the angels; through whom they also received the Law, according to Acts 7:53: "You [Vulg.: 'who'] . . . have received the Law by the disposition of angels." And the Gentiles, especially astrologers, were wont to observe the course of the stars. And therefore Christ's birth was made known to the righteous, viz. Simeon and Anna, by the interior instinct of the Holy Ghost, according to Lk. 2:26: "He had received an answer from the Holy Ghost that he should not see death before he had seen the Christ of the Lord." But to the shepherds and Magi, as being occupied with material things, Christ's birth was made known by means of visible apparitions. And since this birth was not only earthly, but also, in a way, heavenly, to both (shepherds and Magi) it is revealed through heavenly signs: for, as Augustine says in a sermon on the Epiphany (cciv): "The angels inhabit, and the stars adorn, the heavens: by both, therefore, do the 'heavens show forth the glory of God.'" Moreover, it was not without reason that Christ's birth was made known, by means of angels, to the shepherds, who, being Jews, were accustomed to frequent apparitions of the angels: whereas it was revealed by means of a star to the Magi, who were wont to consider the heavenly bodies. Because, as Chrysostom says (Hom. vi in Matth.): "Our Lord deigned to call them through things to which they were accustomed." There is also another reason. For, as Gregory says (Hom. x in Evang.): "To the Jews, as rational beings, it was fitting that a rational animal [*Cf. [4190]FP, Q[51], A[1], ad 2]," viz. an angel, "should preach. Whereas the Gentiles, who were unable to come to the knowledge of God through the reason, were led to God, not by words, but by signs. And as our Lord, when He was able to speak, was announced by heralds who spoke, so before He could speak He was manifested by speechless elements." Again, there is yet another reason. For, as Augustine [*Pope Leo] says in a sermon on the Epiphany: "To Abraham was promised an innumerable progeny, begotten, not of carnal propagation, but of the fruitfulness of faith. For this reason it is compared to the multitude of stars; that a heavenly progeny might be hoped for." Wherefore the Gentiles, "who are thus designated by the stars, are by the rising of a new star stimulated" to seek Christ, through whom they are made the seed of Abraham.

Reply to Objection 1: That which of itself is hidden needs to be manifested, but not that which in itself is manifest. Now, the flesh of Him who was born was manifest, whereas the Godhead was hidden. And therefore it was fitting that this birth should be made known by angels, who are the ministers of God. Wherefore also a certain "brightness" (Lk. 2:9) accompanied the angelic apparition, to indicate that He who was just born was the "Brightness of" the Father's "glory."

Reply to Objection 2: The righteous did not need the visible apparition of the angel; on account of their perfection the interior instinct of the Holy Ghost was enough for them.

Reply to Objection 3: The star which manifested Christ's birth removed all occasion of error. For, as Augustine says (Contra Faust. ii): "No astrologer has ever so far connected the stars with man's fate at the time of his birth as to assert that one of the stars, at the birth of any man, left its orbit and made its way to him who was just born": as happened in the case of the star which made known the birth of Christ. Consequently this does not corroborate the error of those who "think there is a connection between man's birth and the course of the stars, for they do not hold that the course of the stars can be changed at a man's birth."

In the same sense Chrysostom says (Hom. vi in Matth.): "It is not an astronomer's business to know from the stars those who are born, but to tell the future from the hour of a man's birth: whereas the Magi did not know the time of the birth, so as to conclude therefrom some knowledge of the future; rather was it the other way about."

Reply to Objection 4: Chrysostom relates (Hom. ii in Matth.) that, according to some apocryphal books, a certain tribe in the far east near the ocean was in the possession of a document written by Seth, referring to this star and to the presents to be offered: which tribe watched attentively for the rising of this star, twelve men being appointed to take observations, who at stated times repaired to the summit of a mountain with faithful assiduity: whence they subsequently perceived the star containing the figure of a small child, and above it the form of a cross.

Or we may say, as may be read in the book De Qq. Vet. et Nov. Test., qu. lxiii, that "these Magi followed the tradition of Balaam," who said, "'A star shall rise out of Jacob.' Wherefore observing this star to be a stranger to the system of this world, they gathered that it was the one foretold by Balaam to indicate the King of the Jews."

Or again, it may be said with Augustine, in a sermon on the Epiphany (ccclxxiv), that "the Magi had received a revelation through the angels" that the star was a sign of the birth of Christ: and he thinks it probable that these were "good angels; since in adoring Christ they were seeking for salvation."

Or with Pope Leo, in a sermon on the Epiphany (xxxiv), that "besides the outward form which aroused the attention of their corporeal eyes, a more brilliant ray enlightened their minds with the light of faith."

Whether Christ's birth was made known in a becoming order?

Objection 1: It would seem that Christ's birth was made known in an unbecoming order. For Christ's birth should have been made known to them first who were nearest to Christ, and who longed for Him most; according to Wis. 6:14: "She preventeth them that covet her, so that she first showeth herself unto them." But the righteous were nearest to Christ by faith, and longed most for His coming; whence it is written (Lk. 2:25) of Simeon that "he was just and devout, waiting for the consolation of Israel." Therefore Christ's birth should have been made known to Simeon before the shepherds and Magi.

Objection 2: Further, the Magi were the "first-fruits of the Gentiles," who were to believe in Christ. But first the "fulness of the Gentiles . . . come in" unto faith, and afterwards "all Israel" shall "be saved," as is written (Rom. 11:25). Therefore Christ's birth should have been made known to the Magi before the shepherds.

Objection 3: Further, it is written (Mat. 2:16) that "Herod killed all the male children that were in Bethlehem, and in all the borders thereof, from two years old and under, according to the time which he had diligently inquired from the wise men": so that it seems that the Magi were two years in coming to Christ after His birth. It was therefore unbecoming that Christ should be made known to the Gentiles so long after His birth.

On the contrary, It is written (Dan. 2:21): "He changes time and ages." Consequently the time of the manifestation of Christ's birth seems to have been arranged in a suitable order.

I answer that, Christ's birth was first made known to the shepherds on the very day that He was born. For, as it is written (Lk. 2:8, 15, 16): "There were in the same country shepherds watching, and keeping the night-watches over their flock . . . And it came to pass, after the angels departed from them into heaven they [Vulg.: 'the shepherds'] said one to another: Let us go over to Bethlehem . . . and they came with haste." Second in order were the Magi, who came to Christ on the thirteenth day after His birth, on which day is kept the feast of the Epiphany. For if they had come after a year, or even two years, they would not have found Him in Bethlehem, since it is written (Lk. 2:39) that "after they had performed all things according to the law of the Lord"---that is to say, after they had offered up the Child Jesus in the Temple---"they returned into Galilee, to their city"---namely, "Nazareth." In the third place, it was made known in the Temple to the righteous on the fortieth day after His birth, as related by Luke (2:22).

The reason of this order is that the shepherds represent the apostles and other believers of the Jews, to whom the faith of Christ was made known first; among whom there were "not many mighty, not many noble," as we read 1 Cor. 1:26. Secondly, the faith of Christ came to the "fulness of the Gentiles"; and this is foreshadowed in the Magi. Thirdly it came to the fulness of the Jews, which is foreshadowed in the righteous. Wherefore also Christ was manifested to them in the Jewish Temple.

Reply to Objection 1: As the Apostle says (Rom. 9:30,31): "Israel, by following after the law of justice, is not come unto the law of justice": but the Gentiles, "who followed not after justice," forestalled the generality of the Jews in the justice which is of faith. As a figure of this, Simeon, "who was waiting for the consolation of Israel," was the last to know Christ born: and he was preceded by the Magi and the shepherds, who did not await the coming of Christ with such longing.

Reply to Objection 2: Although the "fulness of the Gentiles came in" unto faith before the fulness of the Jews, yet the first-fruits of the Jews preceded the first-fruits of the Gentiles in faith. For this reason the birth of Christ was made known to the shepherds before the Magi.

Reply to Objection 3: There are two opinions about the apparition of the star seen by the Magi. For Chrysostom (Hom. ii in Matth. [*Opus Imperf. in Matth., falsely ascribed to Chrysostom]), and Augustine in a sermon on the Epiphany (cxxxi, cxxxii), say that the star was seen by the Magi during the two years that preceded the birth of Christ: and then, having first considered the matter and prepared themselves for the journey, they came from the farthest east to Christ, arriving on the thirteenth day after His birth. Wherefore Herod, immediately after the departure of the Magi, "perceiving that He was deluded by them," commanded the male children to be killed "from two years old and under," being doubtful lest Christ were already born when the star appeared, according as he had heard from the Magi.

But others say that the star first appeared when Christ was born, and that the Magi set off as soon as they saw the star, and accomplished a journey of very great length in thirteen days, owing partly to the Divine assistance, and partly to the fleetness of the dromedaries. And I say this on the supposition that they came from the far east. But others, again, say that they came from a neighboring country, whence also was Balaam, to whose teaching they were heirs; and they are said to have come from the east, because their country was to the east of the country of the Jews. In this case Herod killed the babes, not as soon as the Magi departed, but two years after: and that either because he is said to have gone to Rome in the meanwhile on account of an accusation brought against him, or because he was troubled at some imminent peril, and for the time being desisted from his anxiety to slay the child, or because he may have thought that the Magi, "being deceived by the illusory appearance of the star, and not finding the child, as they had expected to, were ashamed to return to him": as Augustine says (De Consensu Evang. ii). And the reason why he killed not only those who were two years old, but also the younger children, would be, as Augustine says in a sermon on the Innocents, because he feared lest a child whom the stars obey, might make himself appear older or younger.

Whether the star which appeared to the Magi belonged to the heavenly system?

Objection 1: It would seem that the star which appeared to the Magi belonged to the heavenly system. For Augustine says in a sermon on the Epiphany (cxxii): "While God yet clings to the breast, and suffers Himself to be wrapped in humble swaddling clothes, suddenly a new star shines forth in the heavens." Therefore the star which appeared to the Magi belonged to the heavenly system.

Objection 2: Further, Augustine says in a sermon on the Epiphany (cci): "Christ was made known to the shepherds by angels, to the Magi by a star. A heavenly tongue speaks to both, because the tongue of the prophets spoke no longer." But the angels who appeared to the shepherds were really angels from heaven. Therefore also the star which appeared to the Magi was really a star from the heavens.

Objection 3: Further, stars which are not in the heavens but in the air are called comets, which do not appear at the birth of kings, but rather are signs of their approaching death. But this star was a sign of the King's birth: wherefore the Magi said (Mat. 2:2): "Where is He that is born King of the Jews? For we have seen His star in the east." Therefore it seems that it was a star from the heavens.

On the contrary, Augustine says (Contra Faust. ii): "It was not one of those stars which since the beginning of the creation observe the course appointed to them by the Creator; but this star was a stranger to the heavens, and made its appearance at the strange sight of a virgin in childbirth."

I answer that, As Chrysostom says (Hom. vi in Matth.), it is clear, for many reasons, that the star which appeared to the Magi did not belong to the heavenly system. First, because no other star approaches from the same quarter as this star, whose course was from north to south, these being the relative positions of Persia, whence the Magi came, and Judea. Secondly, from the time [at which it was seen]. For it appeared not only at night, but also at midday: and no star can do this, not even the moon. Thirdly, because it was visible at one time and hidden at another. For when they entered Jerusalem it hid itself: then, when they had left Herod, it showed itself again. Fourthly, because its movement was not continuous, but when the Magi had to continue their journey the star moved on; when they had to stop the star stood still; as happened to the pillar of a cloud in the desert. Fifthly, because it indicated the virginal Birth, not by remaining aloft, but by coming down below. For it is written (Mat. 2:9) that "the star which they had seen in the east went before them, until it came and stood over where the child was." Whence it is evident that the words of the Magi, "We have seen His star in the east," are to be taken as meaning, not that when they were in the east the star appeared over the country of Judea, but that when they saw the star it was in the east, and that it preceded them into Judea (although this is considered doubtful by some). But it could not have indicated the house distinctly, unless it were near the earth. And, as he [Chrysostom] observes, this does not seem fitting to a star, but "of some power endowed with reason." Consequently "it seems that this was some invisible force made visible under the form of a star."

Wherefore some say that, as the Holy Ghost, after our Lord's Baptism, came down on Him under the form of a dove, so did He appear to the Magi under the form of a star. While others say that the angel who, under a human form, appeared to the shepherds, under the form of a star, appeared to the Magi. But it seems more probable that it was a newly created star, not in the heavens, but in the air near the earth, and that its movement varied according to God's will. Wherefore Pope Leo says in a sermon on the Epiphany (xxxi): "A star of unusual brightness appeared to the three Magi in the east, which, through being more brilliant and more beautiful than the other stars, drew men's gaze and attention: so that they understood at once that such an unwonted event could not be devoid of purpose."

Reply to Objection 1: In Holy Scripture the air is sometimes called the heavens---for instance, "The birds of the heavens [Douay: 'air'] and the fishes of the sea."

Reply to Objection 2: The angels of heaven, by reason of their very office, come down to us, being "sent to minister." But the stars of heaven do not change their position. Wherefore there is no comparison.

Reply to Objection 3: As the star did not follow the course of the heavenly stars, so neither did it follow the course of the comets, which neither appear during the daytime nor vary their customary course. Nevertheless in its signification it has something in common with the comets. Because the heavenly kingdom of Christ "shall break in pieces, and shall consume all the kingdoms" of the earth, "and itself shall stand for ever" (Dan. 2:44).

Whether it was becoming that the Magi should come to adore Christ and pay homage to Him?

Objection 1: It would seem that it was unbecoming that the Magi should come to adore Christ and pay homage to Him. For reverence is due to a king from his subjects. But the Magi did not belong to the kingdom of the Jews. Therefore, since they knew by seeing the star that He that was born was the "King of the Jews," it seems unbecoming that they should come to adore Him.

Objection 2: Further, it seems absurd during the reign of one king to proclaim a stranger. But in Judea Herod was reigning. Therefore it was foolish of the Magi to proclaim the birth of a king.

Objection 3: Further, a heavenly sign is more certain than a human sign. But the Magi had come to Judea from the east, under the guidance of a heavenly sign. Therefore it was foolish of them to seek human guidance besides that of the star, saying: "Where is He that is born King of the Jews?"

Objection 4: Further, the offering of gifts and the homage of adoration are not due save to kings already reigning. But the Magi did not find Christ resplendent with kingly grandeur. Therefore it was unbecoming for them to offer Him gifts and homage.

On the contrary, It is written (Is. 60:3): "[The Gentiles] shall walk in the light, and kings in the brightness of thy rising." But those who walk in the Divine light do not err. Therefore the Magi were right in offering homage to Christ.

I answer that, As stated above (A[3], ad 1), the Magi are the "first-fruits of the Gentiles" that believed in Christ; because their faith was a presage of the faith and devotion of the nations who were to come to Christ from afar. And therefore, as the devotion and faith of the nations is without any error through the inspiration of the Holy Ghost, so also we must believe that the Magi, inspired by the Holy Ghost, did wisely in paying homage to Christ.

Reply to Objection 1: As Augustine says in a sermon on the Epiphany (cc.): "Though many kings of the Jews had been born and died, none of them did the Magi seek to adore. And so they who came from a distant foreign land to a kingdom that was entirely strange to them, had no idea of showing such great homage to such a king as the Jews were wont to have. But they had learnt that such a King was born that by adoring Him they might be sure of obtaining from Him the salvation which is of God."

Reply to Objection 2: By proclaiming [Christ King] the Magi foreshadowed the constancy of the Gentiles in confessing Christ even until death. Whence Chrysostom says (Hom. ii in Matth.) that, while they thought of the King who was to come, the Magi feared not the king who was actually present. They had not yet seen Christ, and they were already prepared to die for Him.

Reply to Objection 3: As Augustine says in a sermon on the Epiphany (cc.): "The star which led the Magi to the place where the Divine Infant was with His Virgin-Mother could bring them to the town of Bethlehem, in which Christ was born. Yet it hid itself until the Jews also bore testimony of the city in which Christ was to be born: so that, being encouraged by a twofold witness," as Pope Leo says (Serm. xxxiv), "they might seek with more ardent faith Him, whom both the brightness of the star and the authority of prophecy revealed." Thus they "proclaim" that Christ is born, and "inquire where; they believe and ask, as it were, betokening those who walk by faith and desire to see," as Augustine says in a sermon on the Epiphany (cxcix). But the Jews, by indicating to them the place of Christ's birth, "are like the carpenters who built the Ark of Noe, who provided others with the means of escape, and themselves perished in the flood. Those who asked, heard and went their way: the teachers spoke and stayed where they were; like the milestones that point out the way but walk not" (Augustine, Serm. cclxxiii). It was also by God's will that, when they no longer saw the star, the Magi, by human instinct, went to Jerusalem, to seek in the royal city the new-born King, in order that Christ's birth might be publicly proclaimed first in Jerusalem, according to Is. 2:3: "The Law shall come forth from Sion, and the Word of the Lord from Jerusalem"; and also "in order that by the zeal of the Magi who came from afar, the indolence of the Jews who lived near at hand, might be proved worthy of condemnation" (Remig., Hom. in Matth. ii, 1).

Reply to Objection 4: As Chrysostom says (Hom. ii in Matth. [*From the supposititious Opus Imperfectum]): "If the Magi had come in search of an earthly King, they would have been disconcerted at finding that they had taken the trouble to come such a long way for nothing. Consequently they would have neither adored nor offered gifts. But since they sought a heavenly King, though they found in Him no signs of royal pre-eminence, yet, content with the testimony of the star alone, they adored: for they saw a man, and they acknowledged a God." Moreover, they offer gifts in keeping with Christ's greatness: "gold, as to the great King; they offer up incense as to God, because it is used in the Divine Sacrifice; and myrrh, which is used in embalming the bodies of the dead, is offered as to Him who is to die for the salvation of all" (Gregory, Hom. x in Evang.). And hereby, as Gregory says (Hom. x in Evang.), we are taught to offer gold, "which signifies wisdom, to the new-born King, by the luster of our wisdom in His sight." We offer God incense, "which signifies fervor in prayer, if our constant prayers mount up to God with an odor of sweetness"; and we offer myrrh, "which signifies mortification of the flesh, if we mortify the ill-deeds of the flesh by refraining from them."

OF CHRIST'S CIRCUMCISION, AND OF THE OTHER LEGAL OBSERVANCES ACCOMPLISHED IN
REGARD TO THE CHILD CHRIST (FOUR ARTICLES)

We must now consider Christ's circumcision. And since the circumcision is a kind of profession of observing the Law, according to Gal. 5:3: "I testify . . . to every man circumcising himself that he is a debtor to do the whole Law," we shall have at the same time to inquire about the other legal observances accomplished in regard to the Child Christ. Therefore there are four points of inquiry:

(1) His circumcision;
(2) The imposition of His name;
(3) His presentation;
(4) His Mother's purification.

Whether Christ should have been circumcised?

Objection 1: It would seem that Christ should not have been circumcised. For on the advent of the reality, the figure ceases. But circumcision was prescribed to Abraham as a sign of the covenant concerning his posterity, as may be seen from Gn. 17. Now this covenant was fulfilled in Christ's birth. Therefore circumcision should have ceased at once.

Objection 2: Further, "every action of Christ is a lesson to us" [*Innoc. III, Serm. xxii de Temp.]; wherefore it is written (Jn. 3:15): "I have given you an example, that as I have done to you, so you do also." But we ought not to be circumcised; according to Gal. 5:2: "If you be circumcised, Christ shall profit you nothing." Therefore it seems that neither should Christ have been circumcised.

Objection 3: Further, circumcision was prescribed as a remedy of original sin. But Christ did not contract original sin, as stated above ([4191]Q[14], A[3];[4192] Q[15], A[1]). Therefore Christ should not have been circumcised.

On the contrary, It is written (Lk. 2:21): "After eight days were accomplished, that the child should be circumcised."

I answer that, For several reasons Christ ought to have been circumcised. First, in order to prove the reality of His human nature, in contradiction to the Manicheans, who said that He had an imaginary body: and in contradiction to Apollinarius, who said that Christ's body was consubstantial with His Godhead; and in contradiction to Valentine, who said that Christ brought His body from heaven. Secondly, in order to show His approval of circumcision, which God had instituted of old. Thirdly, in order to prove that He was descended from Abraham, who had received the commandment of circumcision as a sign of his faith in Him. Fourthly, in order to take away from the Jews an excuse for not receiving Him, if He were uncircumcised. Fifthly, "in order by His example to exhort us to be obedient" [*Bede, Hom. x in Evang.]. Wherefore He was circumcised on the eighth day according to the prescription of the Law (Lev. 12:3). Sixthly, "that He who had come in the likeness of sinful flesh might not reject the remedy whereby sinful flesh was wont to be healed." Seventhly, that by taking on Himself the burden of the Law, He might set others free therefrom, according to Gal. 4:4,5: "God sent His Son . . . made under the Law, that He might redeem them who were under the Law."

Reply to Objection 1: Circumcision by the removal of the piece of skin in the member of generation, signified "the passing away of the old generation" [*Athanasius, De Sabb. et Circumcis.]: from the decrepitude of which we are freed by Christ's Passion. Consequently this figure was not completely fulfilled in Christ's birth, but in His Passion, until which time the circumcision retained its virtue and status. Therefore it behooved Christ to be circumcised as a son of Abraham before His Passion.

Reply to Objection 2: Christ submitted to circumcision while it was yet of obligation. And thus His action in this should be imitated by us, in fulfilling those things which are of obligation in our own time. Because "there is a time and opportunity for every business" (Eccl 8:6).

Moreover, according to Origen (Hom. xiv in Luc.), "as we died when He died, and rose again when Christ rose from the dead, so were we circumcised spiritually through Christ: wherefore we need no carnal circumcision." And this is what the Apostle says (Col. 2:11): "In whom," [i.e. Christ] "you are circumcised with circumcision not made by hand in despoiling of the body of the flesh, but in the circumcision of" our Lord Jesus "Christ."

Reply to Objection 3: As Christ voluntarily took upon Himself our death, which is the effect of sin, whereas He had no sin Himself, in order to deliver us from death, and to make us to die spiritually unto sin, so also He took upon Himself circumcision, which was a remedy against original sin, whereas He contracted no original sin, in order to deliver us from the yoke of the Law, and to accomplish a spiritual circumcision in us---in order, that is to say, that, by taking upon Himself the shadow, He might accomplish the reality.

Whether His name was suitably given to Christ?

Objection 1: It would seem that an unsuitable name was given to Christ. For the Gospel reality should correspond to the prophetic foretelling. But the prophets foretold another name for Christ: for it is written (Is. 7:14): "Behold a virgin shall conceive and bear a son, and His name shall be called Emmanuel"; and (Is. 8:3): "Call His name, Hasten to take away the spoils; Make haste to take away the prey"; and (Is. 9:6): "His name shall be called Wonderful, Counselor God the Mighty, the Father of the world to come, the Prince of Peace"; and (Zech. 6:12): "Behold a Man, the Orient is His name." Thus it was unsuitable that His name should be called Jesus.

Objection 2: Further, it is written (Is. 62:2): "Thou shalt be called by a new name, which the mouth of the Lord hath named [Vulg.: 'shall name']." But the name Jesus is not a new name, but was given to several in the Old Testament: as may be seen in the genealogy of Christ (Lk. 3:29), "Therefore it seems that it was unfitting for His name to be called Jesus."

Objection 3: Further, the name Jesus signifies "salvation"; as is clear from Mat. 1:21: "She shall bring forth a son, and thou shalt call His name Jesus. For He shall save His people from their sins." But salvation through Christ was accomplished not only in the circumcision, but also in uncircumcision, as is declared by the Apostle (Rom. 4:11,12). Therefore this name was not suitably given to Christ at His circumcision.

On the contrary is the authority of Scripture, in which it is written (Lk. 2:21): "After eight days were accomplished, that the child should be circumcised, His name was called Jesus."

I answer that, A name should answer to the nature of a thing. This is clear in the names of genera and species, as stated Metaph. iv: "Since a name is but an expression of the definition" which designates a thing's proper nature.

Now, the names of individual men are always taken from some property of the men to whom they are given. Either in regard to time; thus men are named after the Saints on whose feasts they are born: or in respect of some blood relation; thus a son is named after his father or some other relation; and thus the kinsfolk of John the Baptist wished to call him "by his father's name Zachary," not by the name John, because "there" was "none of" his "kindred that" was "called by this name," as related Lk. 1:59-61. Or, again, from some occurrence; thus Joseph "called the name of" the "first-born Manasses, saying: God hath made me to forget all my labors" (Gn. 41:51). Or, again, from some quality of the person who receives the name; thus it is written (Gn. 25:25) that "he that came forth first was red and hairy like a skin; and his name was called Esau," which is interpreted "red."

But names given to men by God always signify some gratuitous gift bestowed on them by Him; thus it was said to Abraham (Gn. 17:5): "Thou shalt be called Abraham; because I have made thee a father of many nations": and it was said to Peter (Mat. 16:18): "Thou art Peter, and upon this rock I will build My Church." Since, therefore, this prerogative of grace was bestowed on the Man Christ that through Him all men might be saved, therefore He was becomingly named Jesus, i.e. Saviour: the angel having foretold this name not only to His Mother, but also to Joseph, who was to be his foster-father.

Reply to Objection 1: All these names in some way mean the same as Jesus, which means "salvation." For the name "Emmanuel, which being interpreted is 'God with us,'" designates the cause of salvation, which is the union of the Divine and human natures in the Person of the Son of God, the result of which union was that "God is with us."

When it was said, "Call his name, Hasten to take away," etc., these words indicate from what He saved us, viz. from the devil, whose spoils He took away, according to Col. 2:15: "Despoiling the principalities and powers, He hath exposed them confidently."

When it was said, "His name shall be called Wonderful," etc., the way and term of our salvation are pointed out: inasmuch as "by the wonderful counsel and might of the Godhead we are brought to the inheritance of the life to come," in which the children of God will enjoy "perfect peace" under "God their Prince."

When it was said, "Behold a Man, the Orient is His name," reference is made to the same, as in the first, viz. to the mystery of the Incarnation, by reason of which "to the righteous a light is risen up in darkness" (Ps. 111:4).

Reply to Objection 2: The name Jesus could be suitable for some other reason to those who lived before Christ---for instance, because they were saviours in a particular and temporal sense. But in the sense of spiritual and universal salvation, this name is proper to Christ, and thus it is called a "new" name.

Reply to Objection 3: As is related Gn. 17, Abraham received from God and at the same time both his name and the commandment of circumcision. For this reason it was customary among the Jews to name children on the very day of circumcision, as though before being circumcised they had not as yet perfect existence: just as now also children receive their names in Baptism. Wherefore on Prov. 4:3, "I was my father's son, tender, and as an only son in the sight of my mother," the gloss says: "Why does Solomon call himself an only son in the sight of his mother, when Scripture testifies that he had an elder brother of the same mother, unless it be that the latter died unnamed soon after birth?" Therefore it was that Christ received His name at the time of His circumcision.

Whether Christ was becomingly presented in the temple?

Objection 1: It would seem that Christ was unbecomingly presented in the Temple. For it is written (Ex. 13:2): "Sanctify unto Me every first-born that openeth the womb among the children of Israel." But Christ came forth from the closed womb of the Virgin; and thus He did not open His Mother's womb. Therefore Christ was not bound by this law to be presented in the Temple.

Objection 2: Further, that which is always in one's presence cannot be presented to one. But Christ's humanity was always in God's presence in the highest degree, as being always united to Him in unity of person. Therefore there was no need for Him to be presented to the Lord.

Objection 3: Further, Christ is the principal victim, to whom all the victims of the old Law are referred, as the figure to the reality. But a victim should not be offered up for a victim. Therefore it was not fitting that another victim should be offered up for Christ.

Objection 4: Further, among the legal victims the principal was the lamb, which was a "continual sacrifice" [Vulg.: 'holocaust'], as is stated Num. 28:6: for which reason Christ is also called "the Lamb---Behold the Lamb of God" (Jn. 1: 29). It was therefore more fitting that a lamb should be offered for Christ than "a pair of turtle doves or two young pigeons."

On the contrary is the authority of Scripture which relates this as having taken place (Lk. 2:22).

I answer that, As stated above [4193](A[1]), Christ wished to be "made under the Law, that He might redeem them who were under the Law" (Gal. 4:4,5), and that the "justification of the Law might be" spiritually "fulfilled" in His members. Now, the Law contained a twofold precept touching the children born. one was a general precept which affected all---namely, that "when the days of the mother's purification were expired," a sacrifice was to be offered either "for a son or for a daughter," as laid down Lev. 12:6. And this sacrifice was for the expiation of the sin in which the child was conceived and born; and also for a certain consecration of the child, because it was then presented in the Temple for the first time. Wherefore one offering was made as a holocaust and another for sin.

The other was a special precept in the law concerning the first-born of "both man and beast": for the Lord claimed for Himself all the first-born in Israel, because, in order to deliver the Israelites, He "slew every first-born in the land of Egypt, both men and cattle" (Ex. 12:12, 13, 29), the first-born of Israel being saved; which law is set down Ex. 13. Here also was Christ foreshadowed, who is "the First-born amongst many brethren" (Rom. 8:29).

Therefore, since Christ was born of a woman and was her first-born, and since He wished to be "made under the Law," the Evangelist Luke shows that both these precepts were fulfilled in His regard. First, as to that which concerns the first-born, when he says (Lk. 2:22,23): "They carried Him to Jerusalem to present Him to the Lord: as it is written in the law of the Lord, 'Every male opening the womb shall be called holy to the Lord.'" Secondly, as to the general precept which concerned all, when he says (Lk. 2:24): "And to offer a sacrifice according as it is written in the law of the Lord, a pair of turtle doves or two young pigeons."

Reply to Objection 1: As Gregory of Nyssa says (De Occursu Dom.): "It seems that this precept of the Law was fulfilled in God incarnate alone in a special manner exclusively proper to Him. For He alone, whose conception was ineffable, and whose birth was incomprehensible, opened the virginal womb which had been closed to sexual union, in such a way that after birth the seal of chastity remained inviolate." Consequently the words "opening the womb" imply that nothing hitherto had entered or gone forth therefrom. Again, for a special reason is it written "'a male,' because He contracted nothing of the woman's sin": and in a singular way "is He called 'holy,' because He felt no contagion of earthly corruption, whose birth was wondrously immaculate" (Ambrose, on Lk. 2:23).

Reply to Objection 2: As the Son of God "became man, and was circumcised in the flesh, not for His own sake, but that He might make us to be God's through grace, and that we might be circumcised in the spirit; so, again, for our sake He was presented to the Lord, that we may learn to offer ourselves to God" [*Athanasius, on Lk. 2:23]. And this was done after His circumcision, in order to show that "no one who is not circumcised from vice is worthy of Divine regard" [*Bede, on Lk. 2:23].

Reply to Objection 3: For this very reason He wished the legal victims to be offered for Him who was the true Victim, in order that the figure might be united to and confirmed by the reality, against those who denied that in the Gospel Christ preached the God of the Law. "For we must not think," says Origen (Hom. xiv in Luc.) "that the good God subjected His Son to the enemy's law, which He Himself had not given."

Reply to Objection 4: The law ofLev. 12:6, 8 "commanded those who could, to offer, for a son or a daughter, a lamb and also a turtle dove or a pigeon: but those who were unable to offer a lamb were commanded to offer two turtle doves or two young pigeons" [*Bede, Hom. xv in Purif.]. "And so the Lord, who, 'being rich, became poor for our [Vulg.: 'your'] sakes, that through His poverty we [you] might be rich," as is written 2 Cor. 8:9, "wished the poor man's victim to be offered for Him" just as in His birth He was "wrapped in swaddling clothes and laid in a manger" [*Bede on Lk. 1]. Nevertheless, these birds have a figurative sense. For the turtle dove, being a loquacious bird, represents the preaching and confession of faith; and because it is a chaste animal, it signifies chastity; and being a solitary animal, it signifies contemplation. The pigeon is a gentle and simple animal, and therefore signifies gentleness and simplicity. It is also a gregarious animal; wherefore it signifies the active life. Consequently this sacrifice signified the perfection of Christ and His members. Again, "both these animals, by the plaintiveness of their song, represented the mourning of the saints in this life: but the turtle dove, being solitary, signifies the tears of prayer; whereas the pigeon, being gregarious, signifies the public prayers of the Church" [*Bede, Hom. xv in Purif.]. Lastly, two of each of these animals are offered, to show that holiness should be not only in the soul, but also in the body.

Whether it was fitting that the Mother of God should go to the temple to be purified?

Objection 1: It would seem that it was unfitting for the Mother of God to go to the Temple to be purified. For purification presupposes uncleanness. But there was no uncleanness in the Blessed Virgin, as stated above (QQ[27],28). Therefore she should not have gone to the Temple to be purified.

Objection 2: Further, it is written (Lev. 12:2-4): "If a woman, having received seed, shall bear a man-child, she shall be unclean seven days"; and consequently she is forbidden "to enter into the sanctuary until the days of her purification be fulfilled." But the Blessed Virgin brought forth a male child without receiving the seed of man. Therefore she had no need to come to the Temple to be purified.

Objection 3: Further, purification from uncleanness is accomplished by grace alone. But the sacraments of the Old Law did not confer grace; rather, indeed, did she have the very Author of grace with her. Therefore it was not fitting that the Blessed Virgin should come to the Temple to be purified.

On the contrary is the authority of Scripture, where it is stated (Lk. 2:22) that "the days of" Mary's "purification were accomplished according to the law of Moses."

I answer that, As the fulness of grace flowed from Christ on to His Mother, so it was becoming that the mother should be like her Son in humility: for "God giveth grace to the humble," as is written James 4:6. And therefore, just as Christ, though not subject to the Law, wished, nevertheless, to submit to circumcision and the other burdens of the Law, in order to give an example of humility and obedience; and in order to show His approval of the Law; and, again, in order to take away from the Jews an excuse for calumniating Him: for the same reasons He wished His Mother also to fulfil the prescriptions of the Law, to which, nevertheless, she was not subject.

Reply to Objection 1: Although the Blessed Virgin had no uncleanness, yet she wished to fulfil the observance of purification, not because she needed it, but on account of the precept of the Law. Thus the Evangelist says pointedly that the days of her purification "according to the Law" were accomplished; for she needed no purification in herself.

Reply to Objection 2: Moses seems to have chosen his words in order to exclude uncleanness from the Mother of God, who was with child "without receiving seed." It is therefore clear that she was not bound to fulfil that precept, but fulfilled the observance of purification of her own accord, as stated above.

Reply to Objection 3: The sacraments of the Law did not cleanse from the uncleanness of sin which is accomplished by grace, but they foreshadowed this purification: for they cleansed by a kind of carnal purification, from the uncleanness of a certain irregularity, as stated in the [4194]FS, Q[102], A[5]; [4195]FS, Q[103], A[2]. But the Blessed Virgin contracted neither uncleanness, and consequently did not need to be purified.

Day 274

OF THE BAPTISM OF JOHN (SIX ARTICLES)

We now proceed to consider the baptism wherewith Christ was baptized. And since Christ was baptized with the baptism of John, we shall consider (1) the baptism of John in general; (2) the baptizing of Christ. In regard to the former there are six points of inquiry:

(1) Whether it was fitting that John should baptize?
(2) Whether that baptism was from God?
(3) Whether it conferred grace?
(4) Whether others besides Christ should have received that baptism?
(5) Whether that baptism should have ceased when Christ was baptized?
(6) Whether those who received John's baptism had afterwards to receive Christ's baptism?

Whether it was fitting that John should baptize?

Objection 1: It would seem that it was not fitting that John should baptize. For every sacramental rite belongs to some law. But John did not introduce a new law. Therefore it was not fitting that he should introduce the new rite of baptism.

Objection 2: Further, John "was sent by God . . . for a witness" (Jn. 1:6,7) as a prophet; according to Lk. 1:76: "Thou, child, shalt be called the prophet of the Highest." But the prophets who lived before Christ did not introduce any new rite, but persuaded men to observe the rites of the Law. as is clearly stated Malachi 4:4: "Remember the law of Moses My servant." Therefore neither should John have introduced a new rite of baptism.

Objection 3: Further, when there is too much of anything, nothing should be added to it. But the Jews observed a superfluity of baptisms; for it is written (Mk. 7:3,4) that "the Pharisees and all the Jews eat not without often washing their hands . . . and when they come from the market, unless they be washed, they eat not; and many other things there are that have been delivered to them to observe, the washings of cups and of pots, and of brazen vessels, and of beds." Therefore it was unfitting that John should baptize.

On the contrary is the authority of Scripture (Mat. 3:5,6), which, after stating the holiness of John, adds many went out to him, "and were baptized in the Jordan."

I answer that, It was fitting for John to baptize, for four reasons: first, it was necessary for Christ to be baptized by John, in order that He might sanctify baptism; as Augustine observes, super Joan. (Tract. xiii in Joan.).

Secondly, that Christ might be manifested. Whence John himself says (Jn. 1:31): "That He," i.e. Christ, "may be made manifest in Israel, therefore am I come baptizing with water." For he announced Christ to the crowds that gathered around him; which was thus done much more easily than if he had gone in search of each individual, as Chrysostom observes, commenting on St. John (Hom. x in Matth.).

Thirdly, that by his baptism he might accustom men to the baptism of Christ; wherefore Gregory says in a homily (Hom. vii in Evang.) that therefore did John baptize, "that, being consistent with his office of precursor, as he had preceded our Lord in birth, so he might also by baptizing precede Him who was about to baptize."

Fourthly, that by persuading men to do penance, he might prepare men to receive worthily the baptism of Christ. Wherefore Bede [*Cf. Scot. Erig. in Joan. iii, 24] says that "the baptism of John was as profitable before the baptism of Christ, as instruction in the faith profits the catechumens not yet baptized. For just as he preached penance, and foretold the baptism of Christ, and drew men to the knowledge of the Truth that hath appeared to the world, so do the ministers of the Church, after instructing men, chide them for their sins, and lastly promise them forgiveness in the baptism of Christ."

Reply to Objection 1: The baptism of John was not a sacrament properly so called [per se], but a kind of sacramental, preparatory to the baptism of Christ. Consequently, in a way, it belonged to the law of Christ, but not to the law of Moses.

Reply to Objection 2: John was not only a prophet, but "more than a prophet," as stated Mat. 11:9: for he was the term of the Law and the beginning of the Gospel. Therefore it was in his province to lead men, both by word and deed, to the law of Christ rather than to the observance of the Old Law.

Reply to Objection 3: Those baptisms of the Pharisees were vain, being ordered merely unto carnal cleanliness. But the baptism of John was ordered unto spiritual cleanliness, since it led men to do penance, as stated above.

Whether the baptism of John was from God?

Objection 1: It would seem that the baptism of John was not from God. For nothing sacramental that is from God is named after a mere man: thus the baptism of the New Law is not named after Peter or Paul, but after Christ. But that baptism is named after John, according to Mat. 21:25: "The baptism of John . . . was it from heaven or from men?" Therefore the baptism of John was not from God.

Objection 2: Further, every doctrine that proceeds from God anew is confirmed by some signs: thus the Lord (Ex. 4) gave Moses the power of working signs; and it is written (Heb. 2:3,4) that our faith "having begun to be declared by the Lord, was confirmed unto us by them that heard Him, God also bearing them witness by signs and wonders." But it is written of John the Baptist (Jn. 10:41) that "John did no sign." Therefore it seems that the baptism wherewith he baptized was not from God.

Objection 3: Further, those sacraments which are instituted by God are contained in certain precepts of Holy Scripture. But there is no precept of Holy Writ commanding the baptism of John. Therefore it seems that it was not from God.

On the contrary, It is written (Jn. 1:33): "He who sent me to baptize with water said to me: 'He upon whom thou shalt see the Spirit,'" etc.

I answer that, Two things may be considered in the baptism of John---namely, the rite of baptism and the effect of baptism. The rite of baptism was not from men, but from God, who by an interior revelation of the Holy Ghost sent John to baptize. But the effect of that baptism was from man, because it effected nothing that man could not accomplish. Wherefore it was not from God alone, except in as far as God works in man.

Reply to Objection 1: By the baptism of the New Law men are baptized inwardly by the Holy Ghost, and this is accomplished by God alone. But by the baptism of John the body alone was cleansed by the water. Wherefore it is written (Mat. 3:11): "I baptize you in water; but . . . He shall baptize you in the Holy Ghost." For this reason the baptism of John was named after him, because it effected nothing that he did not accomplish. But the baptism of the New Law is not named after the minister thereof, because he does not accomplish its principal effect, which is the inward cleansing.

Reply to Objection 2: The whole teaching and work of John was ordered unto Christ, who, by many miracles confirmed both His own teaching and that of John. But if John had worked signs, men would have paid equal attention to John and to Christ. Wherefore, in order that men might pay greater attention to Christ, it was not given to John to work a sign. Yet when the Jews asked him why he baptized, he confirmed his office by the authority of Scripture, saying: "I am the voice of one crying in the wilderness," etc. as related, Jn. 1:23 (cf. Is. 40:3). Moreover, the very austerity of his life was a commendation of his office, because, as Chrysostom says, commenting on Matthew (Hom. x in Matth.), "it was wonderful to witness such endurance in a human body."

Reply to Objection 3: The baptism of John was intended by God to last only for a short time, for the reasons given above [4196] (A[1]). Therefore it was not the subject of a general commandment set down in Sacred Writ, but of a certain interior revelation of the Holy Ghost, as stated above.

Whether grace was given in the baptism of John?

Objection 1: It would seem that grace was given in the baptism of John. For it is written (Mk. 1:4): "John was in the desert baptizing and preaching the baptism of penance unto remission of sins." But penance and remission of sins are the effect of grace. Therefore the baptism of John conferred grace.

Objection 2: Further, those who were about to be baptized by John "confessed their sins," as related Mat. 3:6 and Mk. 1:5. But the confession of sins is ordered to their remission, which is effected by grace. Therefore grace was conferred in the baptism of John.

Objection 3: Further, the baptism of John was more akin than circumcision to the baptism of Christ. But original sin was remitted through circumcision: because, as Bede says (Hom. x in Circumcis.), "under the Law, circumcision brought the same saving aid to heal the wound of original sin as baptism is wont to bring now that grace is revealed." Much more, therefore, did the baptism of John effect the remission of sins, which cannot be accomplished without grace.

On the contrary, It is written (Mat. 3:11): "I indeed baptize you in water unto penance." Which words Gregory thus expounds in a certain homily (Hom. vii in Evang.): "John baptized, not in the Spirit, but in water: because he could not forgive sins." But grace is given by the Holy Ghost, and by means thereof sins are taken away. Therefore the baptism of John did not confer grace.

I answer that, As stated above (A[2], ad 2), the whole teaching and work of John was in preparation for Christ: just as it is the duty of the servant and of the under-craftsman to prepare the matter for the form which is accomplished by the head-craftsman. Now grace was to be conferred on men through Christ, according to Jn. 1:17: "Grace and truth came through Jesus Christ." Therefore the baptism of John did not confer grace, but only prepared the way for grace; and this in three ways: first, by John's teaching, which led men to faith in Christ; secondly, by accustoming men to the rite of Christ's baptism; thirdly, by penance, preparing men to receive the effect of Christ's baptism.

Reply to Objection 1: In these words, as Bede says (on Mk. 1:4), a twofold baptism of penance may be understood. one is that which John conferred by baptizing, which is called "a baptism of penance," etc., by reason of its inducing men to do penance, and of its being a kind of protestation by which men avowed their purpose of doing penance. The other is the baptism of Christ, by which sins are remitted, and which John could not give, but only preach, saying: "He will baptize you in the Holy Ghost."

Or it may be said that he preached the "baptism of penance," i.e. which induced men to do penance, which penance leads men on to "the remission of sins."

Or again, it may be said with Jerome [*Another author on Mk. 1 (inter op. Hier.)] that "by the baptism of Christ grace is given, by which sins are remitted gratis; and that what is accomplished by the bridegroom is begun by the bridesman," i.e. by John. Consequently it is said that "he baptized and preached the baptism of penance unto remission of sins," not as though he accomplished this himself, but because he began it by preparing the way for it.

Reply to Objection 2: That confession of sins was made unto the remission of sins, to be realized immediately through the baptism of John, but to be obtained through subsequent penance and through the baptism of Christ, for which that penance was a preparation.

Reply to Objection 3: Circumcision was instituted as a remedy for original sin. Whereas the baptism of John was not instituted for this purpose, but was merely in preparation for the baptism of Christ, as stated above; whereas the sacraments attain their effect through the force of their institution.

Whether Christ alone should have been baptized with the baptism of John?

Objection 1: It would seem that Christ alone should have been baptized with the baptism of John. For, as stated above [4197] (A[1]), "the reason why John baptized was that Christ might receive baptism," as Augustine says (Super Joan., Tract. xiii). But what is proper to Christ should not be applicable to others. Therefore no others should have received that baptism.

Objection 2: Further, whoever is baptized either receives something from the baptism or confers something on the baptism. But no one could receive anything from the baptism of John, because thereby grace was not conferred, as stated above [4198](A[3]). On the other hand, no one could confer anything on baptism save Christ, who "sanctified the waters by the touch of His most pure flesh" [*Mag. Sent. iv, 3]. Therefore it seems that Christ alone should have been baptized with the baptism of John.

Objection 3: Further, if others were baptized with that baptism, this was only in order that they might be prepared for the baptism of Christ: and thus it would seem fitting that the baptism of John should be conferred on all, old and young, Gentile and Jew, just as the baptism of Christ. But we do not read that either children or Gentiles were baptized by the latter; for it is written (Mk. 1:5) that "there went out to him . . . all they of Jerusalem, and were baptized by him." Therefore it seems that Christ alone should have been baptized by John.

On the contrary, It is written (Lk. 3:21): "It came to pass, when all the people were baptized, that Jesus also being baptized and praying, heaven was opened."

I answer that, For two reasons it behooved others besides Christ to be baptized with the baptism of John. First, as Augustine says (Super Joan., Tract. iv, v), "if Christ alone had been baptized with the baptism of John, some would have said that John's baptism, with which Christ was baptized, was more excellent than that of Christ, with which others are baptized."

Secondly, because, as above stated, it behooved others to be prepared by John's baptism for the baptism of Christ.

Reply to Objection 1: The baptism of John was instituted not only that Christ might be baptized, but also for other reasons, as stated above [4199](A[1]). And yet, even if it were instituted merely in order that Christ might be baptized therewith, it was still necessary for others to receive this baptism, in order to avoid the objection mentioned above.

Reply to Objection 2: Others who approached to be baptized by John could not, indeed, confer anything on his baptism: yet neither did they receive anything therefrom, save only the sign of penance.

Reply to Objection 3: This was the baptism of "penance," for which children were not suited; wherefore they were not baptized therewith. But to bring the nations into the way of salvation was reserved to Christ alone, who is the "expectation of the nations," as we read Gn. 49:10. Indeed, Christ forbade the apostles to preach the Gospel to the Gentiles before His Passion and Resurrection. Much less fitting, therefore, was it for the Gentiles to be baptized by John.

Whether John's baptism should have ceased after Christ was baptized?

Objection 1: It would seem that John's baptism should have ceased after Christ was baptized. For it is written (Jn. 1:31): "That He may be made manifest in Israel, therefore am I come baptizing in water." But when Christ had been baptized, He was made sufficiently manifest, both by the testimony of John and by the dove coming down upon Him, and again by the voice of the Father bearing witness to Him. Therefore it seems that John's baptism should not have endured thereafter.

Objection 2: Further, Augustine says (Super Joan., Tract. iv): "Christ was baptized, and John's baptism ceased to avail." Therefore it seems that, after Christ's baptism, John should not have continued to baptize.

Objection 3: Further, John's baptism prepared the way for Christ's. But Christ's baptism began as soon as He had been baptized; because "by the touch of His most pure flesh He endowed the waters with a regenerating virtue," as Bede asserts (Mag. Sent. iv, 3). Therefore it seems that John's baptism ceased when Christ had been baptized.

On the contrary, It is written (Jn. 3:22,23): "Jesus . . . came into the land of Judea . . . and baptized: and John also was baptizing." But Christ did not baptize before being baptized. Therefore it seems that John continued to baptize after Christ had been baptized.

I answer that, It was not fitting for the baptism of John to cease when Christ had been baptized. First, because, as Chrysostom says (Hom. xxix in Joan.), "if John had ceased to baptize" when Christ had been baptized, "men would think that he was moved by jealousy or anger." Secondly, if he had ceased to baptize when Christ baptized, "he would have given His disciples a motive for yet greater envy." Thirdly, because, by continuing to baptize, "he sent his hearers to Christ" (Hom. xxix in Joan.). Fourthly, because, as Bede [*Scot. Erig. Comment. in Joan.] says, "there still remained a shadow of the Old Law: nor should the forerunner withdraw until the truth be made manifest."

Reply to Objection 1: When Christ was baptized, He was not as yet fully manifested: consequently there was still need for John to continue baptizing.

Reply to Objection 2: The baptism of John ceased after Christ had been baptized, not immediately, but when the former was cast into prison. Thus Chrysostom says (Hom. xxix in Joan.): "I consider that John's death was allowed to take place, and that Christ's preaching began in a great measure after John had died, so that the undivided allegiance of the multitude was transferred to Christ, and there was no further motive for the divergence of opinions concerning both of them."

Reply to Objection 3: John's baptism prepared the way not only for Christ to be baptized, but also for others to approach to Christ's baptism: and this did not take place as soon as Christ was baptized.

Whether those who had been baptized with John's baptism had to be baptized with the baptism of Christ?

Objection 1: It would seem that those who had been baptized with John's baptism had not to be baptized with the baptism of Christ. For John was not less than the apostles, since of him is it written (Mat. 11:11): "There hath not risen among them that are born of women a greater than John the Baptist." But those who were baptized by the apostles were not baptized again, but only received the imposition of hands; for it is written (Acts 8:16,17) that some were "only baptized" by Philip "in the name of the Lord Jesus": then the apostles---namely, Peter and John---"laid their hands upon them, and they received the Holy Ghost." Therefore it seems that those who had been baptized by John had not to be baptized with the baptism of Christ.

Objection 2: Further, the apostles were baptized with John's baptism, since some of them were his disciples, as is clear from Jn. 1:37. But the apostles do not seem to have been baptized with the baptism of Christ: for it is written (Jn. 4:2) that "Jesus did not baptize, but His disciples." Therefore it seems that those who had been baptized with John's baptism had not to be baptized with the baptism of Christ.

Objection 3: Further, he who is baptized is less than he who baptizes. But we are not told that John himself was baptized with the baptism of Christ. Therefore much less did those who had been baptized by John need to receive the baptism of Christ.

Objection 4: Further, it is written (Acts 19:1-5) that "Paul . . . found certain disciples; and he said to them: Have you received the Holy Ghost since ye believed? But they said to him: We have not so much as heard whether there be a Holy Ghost. And he said: In what then were you baptized? Who said: In John's baptism." Wherefore "they were" again "baptized in the name of our [Vulg.: 'the'] Lord Jesus Christ." Hence it seems that they needed to be baptized again, because they did not know of the Holy Ghost: as Jerome says on Joel 2:28 and in an epistle (lxix De Viro unius uxoris), and likewise Ambrose (De Spiritu Sancto). But some were baptized with John's baptism who had full knowledge of the Trinity. Therefore these had no need to be baptized again with Christ's baptism.

Objection 5: Further, on Rom. 10:8, "This is the word of faith, which we preach," the gloss of Augustine says: "Whence this virtue in the water, that it touches the body and cleanses the heart, save by the efficacy of the word, not because it is uttered, but because it is believed?" Whence it is clear that the virtue of baptism depends on faith. But the form of John's baptism signified the faith in which we are baptized; for Paul says (Acts 19:4): "John baptized the people with the baptism of penance, saying: That they should believe in Him who was to come after him---that is to say, in Jesus." Therefore it seems that those who had been baptized with John's baptism had no need to be baptized again with the baptism of Christ.

On the contrary, Augustine says (Super Joan., Tract. v): "Those who were baptized with John's baptism needed to be baptized with the baptism of our Lord."

I answer that, According to the opinion of the Master (Sent. iv, D, 2), "those who had been baptized by John without knowing of the existence of the Holy Ghost, and who based their hopes on his baptism, were afterwards baptized with the baptism of Christ: but those who did not base their hope on John's baptism, and who believed in the Father, Son, and Holy Ghost, were not baptized afterwards, but received the Holy Ghost by the imposition of hands made over them by the apostles."

And this, indeed, is true as to the first part, and is confirmed by many authorities. But as to the second part, the assertion is altogether unreasonable. First, because John's baptism neither conferred grace nor imprinted a character, but was merely "in water," as he says himself (Mat. 3:11). Wherefore the faith or hope which the person baptized had in Christ could not supply this defect. Secondly, because, when in a sacrament, that is omitted which belongs of necessity to the sacrament, not only must the omission be supplied, but the whole must be entirely renewed. Now, it belongs of necessity to Christ's baptism that it be given not only in water, but also in the Holy Ghost, according to Jn. 3:5: "Unless a man be born of water and the Holy Ghost, he cannot enter into the kingdom of God." Wherefore in the case of those who had been baptized with John's baptism in water only, not merely had the omission to be supplied by giving them the Holy Ghost by the imposition of hands, but they had to be baptized wholly anew "in water and the Holy Ghost."

Reply to Objection 1: As Augustine says (Super Joan., Tract. v): "After John, baptism was administered, and the reason why was because he gave not Christ's baptism, but his own . . . That which Peter gave . . . and if any were given by Judas, that was Christ's. And therefore if Judas baptized anyone, yet were they not rebaptized . . . For the baptism corresponds with him by whose authority it is given, not with him by whose ministry it is given." For the same reason those who were baptized by the deacon Philip, who gave the baptism of Christ, were not baptized again, but received the imposition of hands by the apostles, just as those who are baptized by priests are confirmed by bishops.

Reply to Objection 2: As Augustine says to Seleucianus (Ep. cclxv), "we deem that Christ's disciples were baptized either with John's baptism, as some maintain, or with Christ's baptism, which is more probable. For He would not fail to administer baptism so as to have baptized servants through whom He baptized others, since He did not fail in His humble service to wash their feet."

Reply to Objection 3: As Chrysostom says (Hom. iv in Matth. [*From the supposititious Opus Imperfectum]): "Since, when John said, 'I ought to be baptized by Thee,' Christ answered, 'Suffer it to be so now': it follows that afterwards Christ did baptize John." Moreover, he asserts that "this is distinctly set down in some of the apocryphal books." At any rate, it is certain, as Jerome says on Mat. 3:13, that, "as Christ was baptized in water by John, so had John to be baptized in the Spirit by Christ."

Reply to Objection 4: The reason why these persons were baptized after being baptized by John was not only because they knew not of the Holy Ghost, but also because they had not received the baptism of Christ.

Reply to Objection 5: As Augustine says (Contra Faust. xix), our sacraments are signs of present grace, whereas the sacraments of the Old Law were signs of future grace. Wherefore the very fact that John baptized in the name of one who was to come, shows that he did not give the baptism of Christ, which is a sacrament of the New Law.

OF THE BAPTIZING OF CHRIST (EIGHT ARTICLES)

We have now to consider the baptizing of Christ, concerning which there are eight points of inquiry:

(1) Whether Christ should have been baptized?
(2) Whether He should have been baptized with the baptism of John?
(3) Of the time when He was baptized;
(4) Of the place;
(5) Of the heavens being opened unto Him;
(6) Of the apparition of the Holy Ghost under the form of a dove;
(7) Whether that dove was a real animal?
(8) Of the voice of the Father witnessing unto Him.

Whether it was fitting that Christ should be baptized?

Objection 1: It would seem that it was not fitting for Christ to be baptized. For to be baptized is to be washed. But it was not fitting for Christ to be washed, since there was no uncleanness in Him. Therefore it seems unfitting for Christ to be baptized.

Objection 2: Further, Christ was circumcised in order to fulfil the law. But baptism was not prescribed by the law. Therefore He should not have been baptized.

Objection 3: Further, the first mover in every genus is unmoved in regard to that movement; thus the heaven, which is the first cause of alteration, is unalterable. But Christ is the first principle of baptism, according to Jn. 1:33: "He upon whom thou shalt see the Spirit descending and remaining upon Him, He it is that baptizeth." Therefore it was unfitting for Christ to be baptized.

On the contrary, It is written (Mat. 3:13) that "Jesus cometh from Galilee to the Jordan, unto John, to be baptized by him."

I answer that, It was fitting for Christ to be baptized. First, because, as Ambrose says on Lk. 3:21: "Our Lord was baptized because He wished, not to be cleansed, but to cleanse the waters, that, being purified by the flesh of Christ that knew no sin, they might have the virtue of baptism"; and, as Chrysostom says (Hom. iv in Matth.), "that He might bequeath the sanctified waters to those who were to be baptized afterwards." Secondly, as Chrysostom says (Hom. iv in Matth.), "although Christ was not a sinner, yet did He take a sinful nature and 'the likeness of sinful flesh.' Wherefore, though He needed not baptism for His own sake, yet carnal nature in others had need thereof." And, as Gregory Nazianzen says (Orat. xxxix) "Christ was baptized that He might plunge the old Adam entirely in the water." Thirdly, He wished to be baptized, as Augustine says in a sermon on the Epiphany (cxxxvi), "because He wished to do what He had commanded all to do." And this is what He means by saying: "So it becometh us to fulfil all justice" (Mat. 3:15). For, as Ambrose says (on Lk. 3:21), "this is justice, to do first thyself that which thou wishest another to do, and so encourage others by thy example."

Reply to Objection 1: Christ was baptized, not that He might be cleansed, but that He might cleanse, as stated above.

Reply to Objection 2: It was fitting that Christ should not only fulfil what was prescribed by the Old Law, but also begin what appertained to the New Law. Therefore He wished not only to be circumcised, but also to be baptized.

Reply to Objection 3: Christ is the first principle of baptism's spiritual effect. Unto this He was not baptized, but only in water.

Whether it was fitting for Christ to be baptized with John's baptism?

Objection 1: It would seem that it was unfitting for Christ to be baptized with John's baptism. For John's baptism was the "baptism of penance." But penance is unbecoming to Christ, since He had no sin. Therefore it seems that He should not have been baptized with John's baptism.

Objection 2: Further, John's baptism, as Chrysostom says (Hom. de Bapt. Christi), "was a mean between the baptism of the Jews and that of Christ." But "the mean savors of the nature of the extremes" (Aristotle, De Partib. Animal.). Since, therefore, Christ was not baptized with the Jewish baptism, nor yet with His own, on the same grounds He should not have been baptized with the baptism of John.

Objection 3: Further, whatever is best in human things should be ascribed to Christ. But John's baptism does not hold the first place among baptisms. Therefore it was not fitting for Christ to be baptized with John's baptism.

On the contrary, It is written (Mat. 3:13) that "Jesus cometh to the Jordan, unto John, to be baptized by him."

I answer that, As Augustine says (Super Joan., Tract. xiii): "After being baptized, the Lord baptized, not with that baptism wherewith He was baptized." Wherefore, since He Himself baptized with His own baptism, it follows that He was not baptized with His own, but with John's baptism. And this was befitting: first, because John's baptism was peculiar in this, that he baptized, not in the Spirit, but only "in water"; while Christ did not need spiritual baptism, since He was filled with the grace of the Holy Ghost from the beginning of His conception, as we have made clear above ([4200]Q[34], A[1]). And this is the reason given by Chrysostom (Hom. de Bapt. Christi). Secondly, as Bede says on Mk. 1:9, He was baptized with the baptism of John, that, "by being thus baptized, He might show His approval of John's baptism." Thirdly, as Gregory Nazianzen says (Orat. xxxix), "by going to John to be baptized by him, He sanctified baptism."

Reply to Objection 1: As stated above [4201](A[1]), Christ wished to be baptized in order by His example to lead us to baptism. And so, in order that He might lead us thereto more efficaciously, He wished to be baptized with a baptism which He clearly needed not, that men who needed it might approach unto it. Wherefore Ambrose says on Lk. 3:21: "Let none decline the laver of grace, since Christ did not refuse the laver of penance."

Reply to Objection 2: The Jewish baptism prescribed by the law was merely figurative, whereas John's baptism, in a measure, was real, inasmuch as it induced men to refrain from sin; but Christ's baptism is efficacious unto the remission of sin and the conferring of grace. Now Christ needed neither the remission of sin, which was not in Him, nor the bestowal of grace, with which He was filled. Moreover, since He is "the Truth," it was not fitting that He should receive that which was no more than a figure. Consequently it was more fitting that He should receive the intermediate baptism than one of the extremes.

Reply to Objection 3: Baptism is a spiritual remedy. Now, the more perfect a thing is, the less remedy does it need. Consequently, from the very fact that Christ is most perfect, it follows that it was fitting that He should not receive the most perfect baptism: just as one who is healthy does not need a strong medicine.

Day 275

Whether Christ was baptized at a fitting time?

Objection 1: It would seem that Christ was baptized at an unfitting time. For Christ was baptized in order that He might lead others to baptism by His example. But it is commendable that the faithful of Christ should be baptized, not merely before their thirtieth year, but even in infancy. Therefore it seems that Christ should not have been baptized at the age of thirty.

Objection 2: Further, we do not read that Christ taught or worked miracles before being baptized. But it would have been more profitable to the world if He had taught for a longer time, beginning at the age of twenty, or even before. Therefore it seems that Christ, who came for man's profit, should have been baptized before His thirtieth year.

Objection 3: Further, the sign of wisdom infused by God should have been especially manifest in Christ. But in the case of Daniel this was manifested at the time of his boyhood; according to Dan. 13:45: "The Lord raised up the holy spirit of a young boy, whose name was Daniel." Much more, therefore, should Christ have been baptized or have taught in His boyhood.

Objection 4: Further, John's baptism was ordered to that of Christ as to its end. But "the end is first in intention and last in execution." Therefore He should have been baptized by John either before all the others, or after them.

On the contrary, It is written (Lk. 3:21): "It came to pass, when all the people were baptized, that Jesus also being baptized, and praying;" and further on (Lk. 3:23): "And Jesus Himself was beginning about the age of thirty years."

I answer that, Christ was fittingly baptized in His thirtieth year. First, because Christ was baptized as though for the reason that He was about forthwith to begin to teach and preach: for which purpose perfect age is required, such as is the age of thirty. Thus we read (Gn. 41:46) that "Joseph was thirty" years old when he undertook the government of Egypt. In like manner we read (2 Kings 5:4) that "David was thirty years old when he began to reign." Again, Ezechiel began to prophesy in "his thirtieth year," as we read Ezech. 1:1.

Secondly, because, as Chrysostom says (Hom. x in Matth.), "the law was about to pass away after Christ's baptism: wherefore Christ came to be baptized at this age which admits of all sins; in order that by His observing the law, no one might say that because He Himself could not fulfil it, He did away with it."

Thirdly, because by Christ's being baptized at the perfect age, we are given to understand that baptism brings forth perfect men, according to Eph. 4:13: "Until we all meet into the unity of faith, and of the knowledge of the Son of God, unto a perfect man, unto the measure of the age of the fulness of Christ." Hence the very property of the number seems to point to this. For thirty is product of three and ten: and by the number three is implied faith in the Trinity, while ten signifies the fulfilment of the commandments of the Law: in which two things the perfection of Christian life consists.

Reply to Objection 1: As Gregory Nazianzen says (Orat. xl), Christ was baptized, not "as though He needed to be cleansed, or as though some peril threatened Him if He delayed to be baptized. But no small danger besets any other man who departs from this life without being clothed with the garment of incorruptibility"---namely, grace. And though it be a good thing to remain clean after baptism, "yet is it still better," as he says, "to be slightly sullied now and then than to be altogether deprived of grace."

Reply to Objection 2: The profit which accrues to men from Christ is chiefly through faith and humility: to both of which He conduced by beginning to teach not in His boyhood or youth, but at the perfect age. To faith, because in this manner His human nature is shown to be real, by its making bodily progress with the advance of time; and lest this progress should be deemed imaginary, He did not wish to show His wisdom and power before His body had reached the perfect age: to humility, lest anyone should presume to govern or teach others before attaining to perfect age.

Reply to Objection 3: Christ was set before men as an example to all. Wherefore it behooved that to be shown forth in Him, which is becoming to all according to the common law---namely, that He should teach after reaching the perfect age. But, as Gregory Nazianzen says (Orat. xxxix), that which seldom occurs is not the law of the Church; as "neither does one swallow make the spring." For by special dispensation, in accordance with the ruling of Divine wisdom, it has been granted to some, contrary to the common law, to exercise the functions of governing or teaching. such as Solomon, Daniel, and Jeremias.

Reply to Objection 4: It was not fitting that Christ should be baptized by John either before or after all others. Because, as Chrysostom says (Hom. iv in Matth. [*From the supposititious Opus Imperfectum]), for this was Christ baptized, "that He might confirm the preaching and the baptism of John, and that John might bear witness to Him." Now, men would not have had faith in John's testimony except after many had been baptized by him. Consequently it was not fitting that John should baptize Him before baptizing anyone else. In like manner, neither was it fitting that he should baptize Him last. For as he (Chrysostom) says in the same passage: "As the light of the sun does not wait for the setting of the morning star, but comes forth while the latter is still above the horizon, and by its brilliance dims its shining: so Christ did not wait till John had run his course, but appeared while he was yet teaching and baptizing."

Whether Christ should have been baptized in the Jordan?

Objection 1: It would seem that Christ should not have been baptized in the Jordan. For the reality should correspond to the figure. But baptism was prefigured in the crossing of the Red Sea, where the Egyptians were drowned, just as our sins are blotted out in baptism. Therefore it seems that Christ should rather have been baptized in the sea than in the river Jordan.

Objection 2: Further, "Jordan" is interpreted a "going down." But by baptism a man goes up rather than down: wherefore it is written (Mat. 3:16) that "Jesus being baptized, forthwith came up [Douay: 'out'] from the water." Therefore it seems unfitting that Christ should be baptized in the Jordan.

Objection 3: Further, while the children of Israel were crossing, the waters of the Jordan "were turned back," as it is related Jos. 4, and as it is written Ps. 113:3,5. But those who are baptized go forward, not back. Therefore it was not fitting that Christ should be baptized in the Jordan.

On the contrary, It is written (Mk. 1:9) that "Jesus was baptized by John in the Jordan."

I answer that, It was through the river Jordan that the children of Israel entered into the land of promise. Now, this is the prerogative of Christ's baptism over all other baptisms: that it is the entrance to the kingdom of God, which is signified by the land of promise; wherefore it is said (Jn. 3:5): "Unless a man be born again of water and the Holy Ghost, he cannot enter into the kingdom of God." To this also is to be referred the dividing of the water of the Jordan by Elias, who was to be snatched up into heaven in a fiery chariot, as it is related 4 Kings 2: because, to wit, the approach to heaven is laid open by the fire of the Holy Ghost, to those who pass through the waters of baptism. Therefore it was fitting that Christ should be baptized in the Jordan.

Reply to Objection 1: The crossing of the Red Sea foreshadowed baptism in this---that baptism washes away sin: whereas the crossing of the Jordan foreshadows it in this---that it opens the gate to the heavenly kingdom: and this is the principal effect of baptism, and accomplished through Christ alone. And therefore it was fitting that Christ should be baptized in the Jordan rather than in the sea.

Reply to Objection 2: In baptism we "go up" by advancing in grace: for which we need to "go down" by humility, according to James 4:6: "He giveth grace to the humble." And to this "going down" must the name of the Jordan be referred.

Reply to Objection 3: As Augustine says in a sermon for the Epiphany (x): "As of yore the waters of the Jordan were held back, so now, when Christ was baptized, the torrent of sin was held back." Or else this may signify that against the downward flow of the waters the river of blessings flowed upwards.

Whether the heavens should have been opened unto Christ at His baptism?

Objection 1: It would seem that the heavens should not have been opened unto Christ at His baptism. For the heavens should be opened unto one who needs to enter heaven, by reason of his being out of heaven. But Christ was always in heaven, according to Jn. 3:13: "The Son of Man who is in heaven." Therefore it seems that the heavens should not have been opened unto Him.

Objection 2: Further, the opening of the heavens is understood either in a corporal or in a spiritual sense. But it cannot be understood in a corporal sense: because the heavenly bodies are impassible and indissoluble, according to Job 37:18: "Thou perhaps hast made the heavens with Him, which are most strong, as if they were of molten brass." In like manner neither can it be understood in a spiritual sense, because the heavens were not previously closed to the eyes of the Son of God. Therefore it seems unbecoming to say that when Christ was baptized "the heavens were opened."

Objection 3: Further, heaven was opened to the faithful through Christ's Passion, according to Heb. 10:19: "We have [Vulg.: 'Having'] a confidence in the entering into the holies by the blood of Christ." Wherefore not even those who were baptized with Christ's baptism, and died before His Passion, could enter heaven. Therefore the heavens should have been opened when Christ was suffering rather than when He was baptized.

On the contrary, It is written (Lk. 3:21): "Jesus being baptized and praying, heaven was opened."

I answer that, As stated above [4202](A[1]; Q[38], A[1]), Christ wished to be baptized in order to consecrate the baptism wherewith we were to be baptized. And therefore it behooved those things to be shown forth which belong to the efficacy of our baptism: concerning which efficacy three points are to be considered. First, the principal power from which it is derived; and this, indeed, is a heavenly power. For which reason, when Christ was baptized, heaven was opened, to show that in future the heavenly power would sanctify baptism.

Secondly, the faith of the Church and of the person baptized conduces to the efficacy of baptism: wherefore those who are baptized make a profession of faith, and baptism is called the "sacrament of faith." Now by faith we gaze on heavenly things, which surpass the senses and human reason. And in order to signify this, the heavens were opened when Christ was baptized.

Thirdly, because the entrance to the heavenly kingdom was opened to us by the baptism of Christ in a special manner, which entrance had been closed to the first man through sin. Hence, when Christ was baptized, the heavens were opened, to show that the way to heaven is open to the baptized.

Now after baptism man needs to pray continually, in order to enter heaven: for though sins are remitted through baptism, there still remain the fomes of sin assailing us from within, and the world and the devils assailing us from without. And therefore it is said pointedly (Lk. 3:21) that "Jesus being baptized and praying, heaven was opened": because, to wit, the faithful after baptism stand in need of prayer. Or else, that we may be led to understand that the very fact that through baptism heaven is opened to believers is in virtue of the prayer of Christ. Hence it is said pointedly (Mat. 3:16) that "heaven was opened to Him"---that is, "to all for His sake." Thus, for example, the Emperor might say to one asking a favor for another: "Behold, I grant this favor, not to him, but to thee"---that is, "to him for thy sake," as Chrysostom says (Hom. iv in Matth. [*From the supposititious Opus Imperfectum]).

Reply to Objection 1: According to Chrysostom (Hom. iv in Matth.; from the supposititious Opus Imperfectum), as Christ was baptized for man's sake, though He needed no baptism for His own sake, so the heavens were opened unto Him as man, whereas in respect of His Divine Nature He was ever in heaven.

Reply to Objection 2: As Jerome says on Mat. 3:16,17, the heavens were opened to Christ when He was baptized, not by an unfolding of the elements, but by a spiritual vision: thus does Ezechiel relate the opening of the heavens at the beginning of his book. And Chrysostom proves this (Hom. iv in Matth.; from the supposititious Opus Imperfectum) by saying that "if the creature"---namely, heaven---"had been sundered he would not have said, 'were opened to Him,' since what is opened in a corporeal sense is open to all." Hence it is said expressly (Mk. 1:10) that Jesus "forthwith coming up out of the water, saw the heavens opened"; as though the opening of the heavens were to be considered as seen by Christ. Some, indeed, refer this to the corporeal vision, and say that such a brilliant light shone round about Christ when He was baptized, that the heavens seemed to be opened. It can also be referred to the imaginary vision, in which manner Ezechiel saw the heavens opened: since such a vision was formed in Christ's imagination by the Divine power and by His rational will, so as to signify that the entrance to heaven is opened to men through baptism. Lastly, it can be referred to intellectual vision: forasmuch as Christ, when He had sanctified baptism, saw that heaven was opened to men: nevertheless He had seen before that this would be accomplished.

Reply to Objection 3: Christ's Passion is the common cause of the opening of heaven to men. But it behooves this cause to be applied to each one, in order that he enter heaven. And this is effected by baptism, according to Rom. 6:3: "All we who are baptized in Christ Jesus are baptized in His death." Wherefore mention is made of the opening of the heavens at His baptism rather than at His Passion.

Or, as Chrysostom says (Hom. iv in Matth.; from the supposititious Opus Imperfectum): "When Christ was baptized, the heavens were merely opened: but after He had vanquished the tyrant by the cross; since gates were no longer needed for a heaven which thenceforth would be never closed, the angels said, not 'open the gates,' but 'Take them away.'" Thus Chrysostom gives us to understand that the obstacles which had hitherto hindered the souls of the departed from entering into heaven were entirely removed by the Passion: but at Christ's baptism they were opened, as though the way had been shown by which men were to enter into heaven.

Whether it is fitting to say that when Christ was baptized the Holy Ghost came down on Him in the form of a dove?

Objection 1: It would seem that it is not fitting to say that when Christ was baptized the Holy Ghost came down on Him in the form of a dove. For the Holy Ghost dwells in man by grace. But the fulness of grace was in the Man-Christ from the beginning of His conception, because He was the "Only-begotten of the Father," as is clear from what has been said above ([4203]Q[7], A[12];[4204] Q[34], A[1]). Therefore the Holy Ghost should not have been sent to Him at His baptism.

Objection 2: Further, Christ is said to have "descended" into the world in the mystery of the Incarnation, when "He emptied Himself, taking the form of a servant" (Phil. 2:7). But the Holy Ghost did not become incarnate. Therefore it is unbecoming to say that the Holy Ghost "descended upon Him."

Objection 3: Further, that which is accomplished in our baptism should have been shown in Christ's baptism, as in an exemplar. But in our baptism no visible mission of the Holy Ghost takes place. Therefore neither should a visible mission of the Holy Ghost have taken place in Christ's baptism.

Objection 4: Further, the Holy Ghost is poured forth on others through Christ, according to Jn. 1:16: "Of His fulness we all have received." But the Holy Ghost came down on the apostles in the form, not of a dove, but of fire. Therefore neither should He have come down on Christ in the form of a dove, but in the form of fire.

On the contrary, It is written (Lk. 3:22): "The Holy Ghost descended in a bodily shape as a dove upon Him."

I answer that, What took place with respect to Christ in His baptism, as Chrysostom says (Hom. iv in Matth. [*From the supposititious Opus Imperfectum]), "is connected with the mystery accomplished in all who were to be baptized afterwards." Now, all those who are baptized with the baptism of Christ receive the Holy Ghost, unless they approach unworthily; according to Mat. 3:11: "He shall baptize you in the Holy Ghost." Therefore it was fitting that when our Lord was baptized the Holy Ghost should descend upon Him.

Reply to Objection 1: As Augustine says (De Trin. xv): "It is most absurd to say that Christ received the Holy Ghost, when He was already thirty years old: for when He came to be baptized, since He was without sin, therefore was He not without the Holy Ghost. For if it is written of John that 'he shall be filled with the Holy Ghost from his mother's womb,' what must we say of the Man-Christ, whose conception in the flesh was not carnal, but spiritual? Therefore now," i.e. at His baptism, "He deigned to foreshadow His body," i.e. the Church, "in which those who are baptized receive the Holy Ghost in a special manner."

Reply to Objection 2: As Augustine says (De Trin. ii), the Holy Ghost is said to have descended on Christ in a bodily shape, as a dove, not because the very substance of the Holy Ghost was seen, for He is invisible: nor as though that visible creature were assumed into the unity of the Divine Person; since it is not said that the Holy Ghost was the dove, as it is said that the Son of God is man by reason of the union. Nor, again, was the Holy Ghost seen under the form of a dove, after the manner in which John saw the slain Lamb in the Apocalypse (5:6): "For the latter vision took place in the spirit through spiritual images of bodies; whereas no one ever doubted that this dove was seen by the eyes of the body." Nor, again, did the Holy Ghost appear under the form of a dove in the sense in which it is said (1 Cor. 10:4): "'Now, the rock was Christ': for the latter had already a created existence, and through the manner of its action was called by the name of Christ, whom it signified: whereas this dove came suddenly into existence, to fulfil the purpose of its signification, and afterwards ceased to exist, like the flame which appeared in the bush to Moses."

Hence the Holy Ghost is said to have descended upon Christ, not by reason of His being united to the dove: but either because the dove itself signified the Holy Ghost, inasmuch as it "descended" when it came upon Him; or, again, by reason of the spiritual grace, which is poured out by God, so as to descend, as it were, on the creature, according to James 1:17: "Every best gift and every perfect gift is from above, coming down from the Father of lights."

Reply to Objection 3: As Chrysostom says (Hom. xii in Matth.): "At the beginning of all spiritual transactions sensible visions appear, for the sake of them who cannot conceive at all an incorporeal nature . . . so that, though afterwards no such thing occur, they may shape their faith according to that which has occurred once for all." And therefore the Holy Ghost descended visibly, under a bodily shape, on Christ at His baptism, in order that we may believe Him to descend invisibly on all those who are baptized.

Reply to Objection 4: The Holy Ghost appeared over Christ at His baptism, under the form of a dove, for four reasons. First, on account of the disposition required in the one baptized---namely, that he approach in good faith: since! as it is written (Wis. 1:5): "The holy spirit of discipline will flee from the deceitful." For the dove is an animal of a simple character, void of cunning and deceit: whence it is said (Mat. 10:16): "Be ye simple as doves."

Secondly, in order to designate the seven gifts of the Holy Ghost, which are signified by the properties of the dove. For the dove dwells beside the running stream, in order that, on perceiving the hawk, it may plunge in and escape. This refers to the gift of wisdom, whereby the saints dwell beside the running waters of Holy Scripture, in order to escape the assaults of the devil. Again, the dove prefers the more choice seeds. This refers to the gift of knowledge, whereby the saints make choice of sound doctrines, with which they nourish themselves. Further, the dove feeds the brood of other birds. This refers to the gift of counsel, with which the saints, by teaching and example, feed men who have been the brood, i.e. imitators, of the devil. Again, the dove tears not with its beak. This refers to the gift of understanding, wherewith the saints do not rend sound doctrines, as heretics do. Again, the dove has no gall. This refers to the gift of piety, by reason of which the saints are free from unreasonable anger. Again, the dove builds its nest in the cleft of a rock. This refers to the gift of fortitude, wherewith the saints build their nest, i.e. take refuge and hope, in the death wounds of Christ, who is the Rock of strength. Lastly, the dove has a plaintive song. This refers to the gift of fear, wherewith the saints delight in bewailing sins.

Thirdly, the Holy Ghost appeared under the form of a dove on account of the proper effect of baptism, which is the remission of sins and reconciliation with God: for the dove is a gentle creature. Wherefore, as Chrysostom says, (Hom. xii in Matth.), "at the Deluge this creature appeared bearing an olive branch, and publishing the tidings of the universal peace of the whole world: and now again the dove appears at the baptism, pointing to our Deliverer."

Fourthly, the Holy Ghost appeared over our Lord at His baptism in the form of a dove, in order to designate the common effect of baptism---namely, the building up of the unity of the Church. Hence it is written (Eph. 5:25-27): "Christ delivered Himself up . . . that He might present . . . to Himself a glorious Church, not having spot or wrinkle, or any such thing . . . cleansing it by the laver of water in the word of life." Therefore it was fitting that the Holy Ghost should appear at the baptism under the form of a dove, which is a creature both loving and gregarious. Wherefore also it is said of the Church (Cant 6:8): "One is my dove."

But on the apostles the Holy Ghost descended under the form of fire, for two reasons. First, to show with what fervor their hearts were to be moved, so as to preach Christ everywhere, though surrounded by opposition. And therefore He appeared as a fiery tongue. Hence Augustine says (Super Joan., Tract. vi): Our Lord "manifests" the Holy Ghost "visibly in two ways"---namely, "by the dove corning upon the Lord when He was baptized; by fire, coming upon the disciples when they were met together . . . In the former case simplicity is shown, in the latter fervor . . . We learn, then, from the dove, that those who are sanctified by the Spirit should be without guile: and from the fire, that their simplicity should not be left to wax cold. Nor let it disturb anyone that the tongues were cloven . . . in the dove recognize unity."

Secondly, because, as Chrysostom says (Gregory, Hom. xxx in Ev.): "Since sins had to be forgiven," which is effected in baptism, "meekness was required"; this is shown by the dove: "but when we have obtained grace we must look forward to be judged"; and this is signified by the fire.

Whether the dove in which the Holy Ghost appeared was real?

Objection 1: It would seem that the dove in which the Holy Ghost appeared was not real. For that seems to be a mere apparition which appears in its semblance. But it is stated (Lk. 3:22) that the "Holy Ghost descended in a bodily shape as a dove upon Him." Therefore it was not a real dove, but a semblance of a dove.

Objection 2: Further, just as "Nature does nothing useless, so neither does God" (De Coelo i). Now since this dove came merely "in order to signify something and pass away," as Augustine says (De Trin. ii), a real dove would have been useless: because the semblance of a dove was sufficient for that purpose. Therefore it was not a real dove.

Objection 3: Further, the properties of a thing lead us to a knowledge of that thing. If, therefore, this were a real dove, its properties would have signified the nature of the real animal, and not the effect of the Holy Ghost. Therefore it seems that it was not a real dove.

On the contrary, Augustine says (De Agone Christ. xxii): "Nor do we say this as though we asserted that our Lord Jesus Christ alone had a real body, and that the Holy Ghost appeared to men's eyes in a fallacious manner: but we say that both those bodies were real."

I answer that, As stated above ([4205]Q[5], A[1]), it was unbecoming that the Son of God, who is the Truth of the Father, should make use of anything unreal; wherefore He took, not an imaginary, but a real body. And since the Holy Ghost is called the Spirit of Truth, as appears from Jn. 16:13, therefore He too made a real dove in which to appear, though He did not assume it into unity of person. Wherefore, after the words quoted above, Augustine adds: "Just as it behooved the Son of God not to deceive men, so it behooved the Holy Ghost not to deceive. But it was easy for Almighty God, who created all creatures out of nothing, to frame the body of a real dove without the help of other doves, just as it was easy for Him to form a true body in Mary's womb without the seed of a man: since the corporeal creature obeys its Lord's command and will, both in the mother's womb in forming a man, and in the world itself in forming a dove."

Reply to Objection 1: The Holy Ghost is said to have descended in the shape or semblance of a dove, not in the sense that the dove was not real, but in order to show that He did not appear in the form of His substance.

Reply to Objection 2: It was not superfluous to form a real dove, in which the Holy Ghost might appear, because by the very reality of the dove the reality of the Holy Ghost and of His effects is signified.

Reply to Objection 3: The properties of the dove lead us to understand the dove's nature and the effects of the Holy Ghost in the same way. Because from the very fact that the dove has such properties, it results that it signifies the Holy Ghost.

Whether it was becoming, when Christ was baptized that the Father's voice should be heard, bearing witness to the Son?

Objection 1: It would seem that it was unbecoming when Christ was baptized for the Father's voice to be heard bearing witness to the Son. For the Son and the Holy Ghost, according as they have appeared visibly, are said to have been visibly sent. But it does not become the Father to be sent, as Augustine makes it clear (De Trin. ii). Neither, therefore, (does it become Him) to appear.

Objection 2: Further, the voice gives expression to the word conceived in the heart. But the Father is not the Word. Therefore He is unfittingly manifested by a voice.

Objection 3: Further, the Man-Christ did not begin to be Son of God at His baptism, as some heretics have stated: but He was the Son of God from the beginning of His conception. Therefore the Father's voice should have proclaimed Christ's Godhead at His nativity rather than at His baptism.

On the contrary, It is written (Mat. 3:17): "Behold a voice from heaven, saying: This is My beloved Son in whom I am well pleased."

I answer that, As stated above [4206](A[5]), that which is accomplished in our baptism should be manifested in Christ's baptism, which was the exemplar of ours. Now the baptism which the faithful receive is hallowed by the invocation and the power of the Trinity; according to Mat. 28:19: "Go ye and teach all nations, baptizing them in the name of the Father, and of the Son, and of the Holy Ghost." Wherefore, as Jerome says on Mat. 3:16,17: "The mystery of the Trinity is shown forth in Christ's baptism. our Lord Himself is baptized in His human nature; the Holy Ghost descended in the shape of a dove: the Father's voice is heard bearing witness to the Son." Therefore it was becoming that in that baptism the Father should be manifested by a voice.

Reply to Objection 1: The visible mission adds something to the apparition, to wit, the authority of the sender. Therefore the Son and the Holy Ghost who are from another, are said not only to appear, but also to be sent visibly. But the Father, who is not from another, can appear indeed, but cannot be sent visibly.

Reply to Objection 2: The Father is manifested by the voice, only as producing the voice or speaking by it. And since it is proper to the Father to produce the Word---that is, to utter or to speak---therefore was it most becoming that the Father should be manifested by a voice, because the voice designates the word. Wherefore the very voice to which the Father gave utterance bore witness to the Sonship of the Word. And just as the form of the dove, in which the Holy Ghost was made manifest, is not the Nature of the Holy Ghost, nor is the form of man in which the Son Himself was manifested, the very Nature of the Son of God, so neither does the voice belong to the Nature of the Word or of the Father who spoke. Hence (Jn. 5:37) our Lord says: "Neither have you heard His," i.e. the Father's, "voice at any time, nor seen His shape." By which words, as Chrysostom says (Hom. xl in Joan.), "He gradually leads them to the knowledge of the philosophical truth, and shows them that God has neither voice nor shape, but is above all such forms and utterances." And just as the whole Trinity made both the dove and the human nature assumed by Christ, so also they formed the voice: yet the Father alone as speaking is manifested by the voice, just as the Son alone assumed human nature, and the Holy Ghost alone is manifested in the dove, as Augustine [*Fulgentius, De Fide ad Petrum] makes evident.

Reply to Objection 3: It was becoming that Christ's Godhead should not be proclaimed to all in His nativity, but rather that It should be hidden while He was subject to the defects of infancy. But when He attained to the perfect age, when the time came for Him to teach, to work miracles, and to draw men to Himself then did it behoove His Godhead to be attested from on high by the Father's testimony, so that His teaching might become the more credible. Hence He says (Jn. 5:37): "The Father Himself who sent Me, hath given testimony of Me." And specially at the time of baptism, by which men are born again into adopted sons of God; since God's sons by adoption are made to be like unto His natural Son, according to Rom. 8:29: "Whom He foreknew, He also predestinated to be made conformable to the image of His Son." Hence Hilary says (Super Matth. ii) that when Jesus was baptized, the Holy Ghost descended on Him, and the Father's voice was heard saying: "'This is My beloved Son,' that we might know, from what was accomplished in Christ, that after being washed in the waters of baptism the Holy Ghost comes down upon us from on high, and that the Father's voice declares us to have become the adopted sons of God."

OF CHRIST'S MANNER OF LIFE (FOUR ARTICLES)

Having considered those things which relate to Christ's entrance into the world, or to His beginning, it remains for us to consider those that relate to the process of His life. And we must consider (1) His manner of life; (2) His temptation; (3) His doctrine; (4) His miracles.

Concerning the first there are four points of inquiry:

(1) Whether Christ should have led a solitary life, or have associated with men?

(2) Whether He should have led an austere life as regards food, drink, and clothing? Or should He have conformed Himself to others in these respects?

(3) Whether He should have adopted a lowly state of life, or one of wealth and honor?

(4) Whether He should have lived in conformity with the Law?

Whether Christ should have associated with men, or led a solitary life?

Objection 1: It would seem that Christ should not have associated with men, but should have led a solitary life. For it behooved Christ to show by His manner of life not only that He was man, but also that He was God. But it is not becoming that God should associate with men, for it is written (Dan. 2:11): "Except the gods, whose conversation is not with men"; and the Philosopher says

(Polit. i) that he who lives alone is "either a beast"---that is, if he do this from being wild---"or a god," if his motive be the contemplation of truth. Therefore it seems that it was not becoming for Christ to associate with men.

Objection 2: Further, while He lived in mortal flesh, it behooved Christ to lead a most perfect life. But the most perfect is the contemplative life, as we have stated in the [4207]SS, Q[182], AA[1],2. Now, solitude is most suitable to the contemplative life; according to Osee 2:14: "I will lead her into the wilderness, and I will speak to her heart." Therefore it seems that Christ should have led a solitary life.

Objection 3: Further, Christ's manner of life should have been uniform: because it should always have given evidence of that which is best. But at times Christ avoided the crowd and sought lonely places: hence Remigius [*Cf. Catena Aurea, Matth. 5:1], commenting on Matthew, says: "We read that our Lord had three places of refuge: the ship, the mountain, the desert; to one or other of which He betook Himself whenever he was harassed by the crowd." Therefore He ought always to have led a solitary life.

On the contrary, It is written (Baruch 3:38): "Afterwards He was seen upon earth and conversed with men."

I answer that, Christ's manner of life had to be in keeping with the end of His Incarnation, by reason of which He came into the world. Now He came into the world, first, that He might publish the truth. thus He says Himself (Jn. 18:37): "For this was I born, and for this came I into the world, that I should give testimony to the truth." Hence it was fitting not that He should hide Himself by leading a solitary life, but that He should appear openly and preach in public. Wherefore (Lk. 4:42,43) He says to those who wished to stay Him: "To other cities also I must preach the kingdom of God: for therefore am I sent."

Secondly, He came in order to free men from sin; according to 1 Tim. 1:15: "Christ Jesus came into this world to save sinners." And hence, as Chrysostom says, "although Christ might, while staying in the same place, have drawn all men to Himself, to hear His preaching, yet He did not do so; thus giving us the example to go about and seek those who perish, like the shepherd in his search of the lost sheep, and the physician in his attendance on the sick."

Thirdly, He came that by Him "we might have access to God," as it is written (Rom. 5:2). And thus it was fitting that He should give men confidence in approaching Him by associating familiarly with them. Wherefore it is written (Mat. 9:10): "It came to pass as He was sitting . . . in the house, behold, many publicans and sinners came, and sat down with Jesus and His disciples." On which Jerome comments as follows: "They had seen the publican who had been converted from a sinful to a better life: and consequently they did not despair of their own salvation."

Reply to Objection 1: Christ wished to make His Godhead known through His human nature. And therefore, since it is proper to man to do so, He associated with men, at the same time manifesting His Godhead to all, by preaching and working miracles, and by leading among men a blameless and righteous life.

Reply to Objection 2: As stated in the [4208]SS, Q[182], A[1]; [4209]SS, Q[188], A[6], the contemplative life is, absolutely speaking, more perfect than the active life, because the latter is taken up with bodily actions: yet that form of active life in which a man, by preaching and teaching, delivers to others the fruits of his contemplation, is more perfect than the life that stops at contemplation, because such a life is built on an abundance of contemplation, and consequently such was the life chosen by Christ.

Reply to Objection 3: Christ's action is our instruction. And therefore, in order to teach preachers that they ought not to be for ever before the public, our Lord withdrew Himself sometimes from the crowd. We are told of three reasons for His doing this. First, for the rest of the body: hence (Mk. 6:31) it is stated that our Lord said to His disciples: "Come apart into a desert place, and rest a little. For there were many coming and going: and they had not so much as time to eat." But sometimes it was for the sake of prayer; thus it is written (Lk. 6:12): "It came to pass in those days, that He went out into a mountain to pray; and He passed the whole night in the prayer of God." On this Ambrose remarks that "by His example He instructs us in the precepts of virtue." And sometimes He did so in order to teach us to avoid the favor of men. Wherefore Chrysostom, commenting on Mat. 5:1, Jesus, "seeing the multitude, went up into a mountain," says: "By sitting not in the city and in the market-place, but on a mountain and in a place of solitude, He taught us to do nothing for show, and to withdraw from the crowd, especially when we have to discourse of needful things."

Whether it was becoming that Christ should lead an austere life in this world?

Objection 1: It would seem that it was becoming that Christ should lead an austere life in this world. For Christ preached the perfection of life much more than John did. But John led an austere life in order that he might persuade men by his example to embrace a perfect life; for it is written (Mat. 3:4) that "the same John had his garment of camel's hair and a leathern girdle about his loins: and his meat was locusts and wild honey"; on which Chrysostom comments as follows (Hom. x): "It was a marvelous and strange thing to behold such austerity in a human frame: which thing also particularly attracted the Jews." Therefore it seems that an austere life was much more becoming to Christ.

Objection 2: Further, abstinence is ordained to continency; for it is written (Osee 4:10): "They shall eat and shall not be filled; they have committed fornication, and have not ceased." But Christ both observed continency in Himself and proposed it to be observed by others when He said (Mat. 19:12): "There are eunuchs who have made themselves eunuchs for the kingdom of heaven: he that can take it let him take it." Therefore it seems that Christ should have observed an austere life both in Himself and in His disciples.

Objection 3: Further, it seems absurd for a man to begin a stricter form of life and to return to an easier life: for one might quote to his discredit that which is written, Lk. 14:30: "This man began to build, and was not able to finish." Now Christ began a very strict life after His baptism, remaining in the desert and fasting for "forty days and forty nights." Therefore it seems unbecoming that, after leading such a strict life, He should return to the common manner of living.

On the contrary, It is written (Mat. 11:19): "The Son of Man came eating and drinking."

I answer that, As stated above [4210](A[1]), it was in keeping with the end of the Incarnation that Christ should not lead a solitary life, but should associate with men. Now it is most fitting that he who associates with others should conform to their manner of living; according to the words of the Apostle (1 Cor. 9:22): "I became all things to all men." And therefore it was most fitting that Christ should conform to others in the matter of eating and drinking. Hence Augustine says (Contra Faust. xvi) that "John is described as 'neither eating nor drinking,' because he did not take the same food as the Jews. Therefore, unless our Lord had taken it, it would not be said of Him, in contrast, 'eating and drinking.'"

Reply to Objection 1: In His manner of living our Lord gave an example of perfection as to all those things which of themselves relate to salvation. Now abstinence in eating and drinking does not of itself relate to salvation, according to Rom. 14:17: "The kingdom of God is not meat and drink." And Augustine (De Qq. Evang. ii, qu. 11) explains Mat. 11:19, "Wisdom is justified by her children," saying that this is because the holy apostles "understood that the kingdom of God does not consist in eating and drinking, but in suffering indigence with equanimity," for they are neither uplifted by affluence, nor distressed by want. Again (De Doctr. Christ. iii), he says that in all such things "it is not making use of them, but the wantonness of the user, that is sinful." Now both these lives are lawful and praiseworthy---namely, that a man withdraw from the society of other men and observe abstinence; and that he associate with other men and live like them. And therefore our Lord wished to give men an example of either kind of life.

As to John, according to Chrysostom (Hom. xxxvii super Matth.), "he exhibited no more than his life and righteous conduct . . . but Christ had the testimony also of miracles. Leaving, therefore, John to be illustrious by his fasting, He Himself came the opposite way, both coming unto publicans' tables and eating and drinking."

Reply to Objection 2: Just as by abstinence other men acquire the power of self-restraint, so also Christ, in Himself and in those that are His, subdued the flesh by the power of His Godhead. Wherefore, as we read Mat. 9:14, the Pharisees and the disciples of John fasted, but not the disciples of Christ. On which Bede comments, saying that "John drank neither wine nor strong drink: because abstinence is meritorious where the nature is weak. But why should our Lord, whose right by nature it is to forgive sins, avoid those whom He could make holier than such as abstain?"

Reply to Objection 3: As Chrysostom says (Hom. xiii super Matth.), "that thou mightest learn how great a good is fasting, and how it is a shield against the devil, and that after baptism thou shouldst give thyself up, not to luxury, but to fasting---for this cause did He fast, not as needing it Himself, but as teaching us . . . And for this did He proceed no further than Moses and Elias, lest His assumption of our flesh might seem incredible." The mystical meaning, as Gregory says (Hom. xvi in Evang.), is that by Christ's example the number "forty" is observed in His fast, because the power of the "decalogue is fulfilled throughout the four books of the Holy Gospel: since ten multiplied by four amounts to forty." Or, because "we live in this mortal body composed of the four elements, and by its lusts we transgress the commandments of the Lord, which are expressed in the decalogue." Or, according to Augustine (QQ. lxxxiii, qu. 81): "To know the Creator and the creature is the entire teaching of wisdom. The Creator is the Trinity, the Father, the Son, and the Holy Ghost. Now the creature is partly invisible, as the soul, to which the number three may be ascribed, for we are commanded to love God in three ways, 'with our whole heart, our whole soul, and our whole mind'; and partly visible, as the body, to which the number four is applicable on account of its being subject to heat, moisture, cold, and dryness. Hence if we multiply ten, which may be referred to the entire moral code, by four, which number may be applied to the body, because it is the body that executes the law, the product is the number forty: in which," consequently, "the time during which we sigh and grieve is shown forth." And yet there was no inconsistency in Christ's returning to the common manner of living, after fasting and (retiring into the) desert. For it is becoming to that kind of life, which we hold Christ to have embraced, wherein a man delivers to others the fruits of his contemplation, that he devote himself first of all to contemplation, and that he afterwards come down to the publicity of active life by associating with other men. Hence Bede says on Mk. 2:18: "Christ fasted, that thou mightest not disobey the commandment; He ate with sinners, that thou mightest discern His sanctity and acknowledge His power."

Day 276

Whether Christ should have led a life of poverty in this world?

Objection 1: It would seem that Christ should not have led a life of poverty in this world. Because Christ should have embraced the most eligible form of life. But the most eligible form of life is that which is a mean between riches and poverty; for it is written (Prov. 30:8): "Give me neither beggary nor riches; give me only the necessaries of life." Therefore Christ should have led a life, not of poverty, but of moderation.

Objection 2: Further, external wealth is ordained to bodily use as to food and raiment. But Christ conformed His manner of life to those among whom He lived, in the matter of food and raiment. Therefore it seems that He should have observed the ordinary manner of life as to riches and poverty, and have avoided extreme poverty.

Objection 3: Further, Christ specially invited men to imitate His example of humility, according to Mat. 11:29: "Learn of Me, because I am meek and humble of heart." But humility is most commendable in the rich; thus it is written (1 Tim. 6:11): "Charge the rich of this world not to be high-minded." Therefore it seems that Christ should not have chosen a life of poverty.

On the contrary, It is written (Mat. 8:20): "The Son of Man hath not where to lay His head": as though He were to say as Jerome observes: "Why desirest thou to follow Me for the sake of riches and worldly gain, since I am so poor that I have not even the smallest dwelling-place, and I am sheltered by a roof that is not Mine?" And on Mat. 17:26: "That we may not scandalize them, go to the sea," Jerome says: "This incident, taken literally, affords edification to those who hear it when they are told that our Lord was so poor that He had not the wherewithal to pay the tax for Himself and His apostles."

I answer that, It was fitting for Christ to lead a life of poverty in this world. First, because this was in keeping with the duty of preaching, for which purpose He says that He came (Mk. 1:38): "Let us go into the neighboring towns and cities, that I may preach there also: for to this purpose am I come." Now in order that the preachers of God's word may be able to give all their time to preaching, they must be wholly free from care of worldly matters: which is impossible for those who are possessed of wealth. Wherefore the Lord Himself, when sending the apostles to preach, said to them (Mat. 10:9): "Do not possess gold nor silver." And the apostles (Acts 6:2) say: "It is not reasonable that we should leave the word of God and serve tables."

Secondly, because just as He took upon Himself the death of the body in order to bestow spiritual life on us, so did He bear bodily poverty, in order to enrich us spiritually, according to 2 Cor. 8:9: "You know the grace of our Lord Jesus Christ: that . . . He became poor for our [Vulg.: 'your'] sakes that through His poverty we [Vulg.: 'you'] might be rich."

Thirdly, lest if He were rich His preaching might be ascribed to cupidity. Wherefore Jerome says on Mat. 10:9, that if the disciples had been possessed of wealth, "they had seemed to preach for gain, not for the salvation of mankind." And the same reason applies to Christ.

Fourthly, that the more lowly He seemed by reason of His poverty, the greater might the power of His Godhead be shown to be. Hence in a sermon of the Council of Ephesus (P. iii, c. ix) we read: "He chose all that was poor and despicable, all that was of small account and hidden from the majority, that we might recognize His Godhead to have transformed the terrestrial sphere. For this reason did He choose a poor maid for His Mother, a poorer birthplace; for this reason did He live in want. Learn this from the manger."

Reply to Objection 1: Those who wish to live virtuously need to avoid abundance of riches and beggary, in as far as these are occasions of sin: since abundance of riches is an occasion for being proud; and beggary is an occasion of thieving and lying, or even of perjury. But forasmuch as Christ was incapable of sin, He had not the same motive as Solomon for avoiding these things. Yet neither is every kind of beggary an occasion of theft and perjury, as Solomon seems to add (Prov. 30:8); but only that which is involuntary, in order to avoid which, a man is guilty of theft and perjury. But voluntary poverty is not open to this danger: and such was the poverty chosen by Christ.

Reply to Objection 2: A man may feed and clothe himself in conformity with others, not only by possessing riches, but also by receiving the necessaries of life from those who are rich. This is what happened in regard to Christ: for it is written (Lk. 8:2,3) that certain women followed Christ and "ministered unto Him of their substance." For, as Jerome says on Mat. 27:55, "It was a Jewish custom, nor was it thought wrong for women, following the ancient tradition of their nation, out of their private means to provide their instructors with food and clothing. But as this might give scandal to the heathens, Paul says that he gave it up": thus it was possible for them to be fed out of a common fund, but not to possess wealth, without their duty of preaching being hindered by anxiety.

Reply to Objection 3: Humility is not much to be praised in one who is poor of necessity. But in one who, like Christ, is poor willingly, poverty itself is a sign of very great humility.

Whether Christ conformed His conduct to the Law?

Objection 1: It would seem that Christ did not conform His conduct to the Law. For the Law forbade any work whatsoever to be done on the Sabbath, since God "rested on the seventh day from all His work which He had done." But He healed a man on the Sabbath, and commanded him to take up his bed. Therefore it seems that He did not conform His conduct to the Law.

Objection 2: Further, what Christ taught, that He also did, according to Acts 1:1: "Jesus began to do and to teach." But He taught (Mat. 15:11) that "not" all "that which goeth into the mouth defileth a man": and this is contrary to the precept of the Law, which declared that a man was made unclean by eating and touching certain animals, as stated Lev. 11. Therefore it seems that He did not conform His conduct to the Law.

Objection 3: Further, he who consents to anything is of the same mind as he who does it, according to Rom. 1:32: "Not only they that do them, but they also that consent to them that do them." But Christ, by excusing His disciples, consented to their breaking the Law by plucking the ears of corn on the Sabbath; as is related Mat. 12:1-8. Therefore it seems that Christ did not conform His conduct to the Law.

On the contrary, It is written (Mat. 5:17): "Do not think that I am come to destroy the Law or the Prophets." Commenting on these words, Chrysostom says: "He fulfilled the Law . . . in one way, by transgressing none of the precepts of the Law; secondly, by justifying us through faith, which the Law, in the letter, was unable to do."

I answer that, Christ conformed His conduct in all things to the precepts of the Law. In token of this He wished even to be circumcised; for the circumcision is a kind of protestation of a man's purpose of keeping the Law, according to Gal. 5:3: "I testify to every man circumcising himself, that he is a debtor to do the whole Law."

And Christ, indeed, wished to conform His conduct to the Law, first, to show His approval of the Old Law. Secondly, that by obeying the Law He might perfect it and bring it to an end in His own self, so as to show that it was ordained to Him. Thirdly, to deprive the Jews of an excuse for slandering Him. Fourthly, in order to deliver men from subjection to the Law, according to Gal. 4:4,5: "God sent His Son . . . made under the Law that He might redeem them who were under the Law."

Reply to Objection 1: Our Lord excuses Himself from any transgression of the Law in this matter, for three reasons. First, the precept of the hallowing of the Sabbath forbids not Divine work, but human work: for though God ceased on the seventh day from the creation of new creatures, yet He ever works by keeping and governing His creatures. Now that Christ wrought miracles was a Divine work: hence He says (Jn. 5:17): "My Father worketh until now; and I work."

Secondly, He excuses Himself on the ground that this precept does not forbid works which are needful for bodily health. Wherefore He says (Lk. 13:15): "Doth not every one of you on the Sabbath-day loose his ox or his ass from the manger, and lead them to water?" And farther on (Lk. 14:5): "Which of you shall have an ass or an ox fall into a pit, and will not immediately draw him out on the Sabbath-day?" Now it is manifest that the miraculous works done by Christ related to health of body and soul.

Thirdly, because this precept does not forbid works pertaining to the worship of God. Wherefore He says (Mat. 12:5): "Have ye not read in the Law that on the Sabbath-days the priests in the Temple break the Sabbath, and are without blame?" And (Jn. 7:23) it is written that a man receives circumcision on the Sabbath-day. Now when Christ commanded the paralytic to carry his bed on the Sabbath-day, this pertained to the worship of God, i.e. to the praise of God's power. And thus it is clear that He did not break the Sabbath: although the Jews threw this false accusation in His face, saying (Jn. 9:16): "This man is not of God, who keepeth not the Sabbath."

Reply to Objection 2: By those words Christ wished to show that man is made unclean as to his soul, by the use of any sort of foods considered not in their nature, but only in some signification. And that certain foods are in the Law called "unclean" is due to some signification; whence Augustine says (Contra Faust. vi): "If a question be raised about swine and lambs, both are clean by nature, since 'all God's creatures are good'; but by a certain signification lambs are clean and swine unclean."

Reply to Objection 3: The disciples also, when, being hungry, they plucked the ears of corn on the Sabbath, are to be excused from transgressing the Law, since they were pressed by hunger: just as David did not transgress the Law when, through being compelled by hunger, he ate the loaves which it was not lawful for him to eat.

OF CHRIST'S TEMPTATION (FOUR ARTICLES)

We have now to consider Christ's temptation, concerning which there are four points of inquiry:

(1) Whether it was becoming that Christ should be tempted?

(2) Of the place;

(3) Of the time;

(4) Of the mode and order of the temptation.

Whether it was becoming that Christ should be tempted?

Objection 1: It would seem that it was not becoming for Christ to be tempted. For to tempt is to make an experiment, which is not done save in regard to something unknown. But the power of Christ was known even to the demons; for it is written (Lk. 4:41) that "He suffered them not to speak, for they knew that He was Christ." Therefore it seems that it was unbecoming for Christ to be tempted.

Objection 2: Further, Christ was come in order to destroy the works of the devil, according to 1 Jn. 3:8: "For this purpose the Son of God appeared, that He might destroy the works of the devil." But it is not for the same to destroy the works of a certain one and to suffer them. Therefore it seems unbecoming that Christ should suffer Himself to be tempted by the devil.

Objection 3: Further, temptation is from a threefold source---the flesh, the world, and the devil. But Christ was not tempted either by the flesh or by the world. Therefore neither should He have been tempted by the devil.

On the contrary, It is written (Mat. 4:1): "Jesus was led by the Spirit into the desert to be tempted by the devil."

I answer that, Christ wished to be tempted; first that He might strengthen us against temptations. Hence Gregory says in a homily (xvi in Evang.): "It was not unworthy of our Redeemer to wish to be tempted, who came also to be slain; in order that by His temptations He might conquer our temptations, just as by His death He overcame our death."

Secondly, that we might be warned, so that none, however holy, may think himself safe or free from temptation. Wherefore also He wished to be tempted after His baptism, because, as Hilary says (Super Matth., cap. iii.): "The temptations of the devil assail those principally who are sanctified, for he desires, above all, to overcome the holy. Hence also it is written (Ecclus. 2): Son, when thou comest to the service of God, stand in justice and in fear, and prepare thy soul for temptation."

Thirdly, in order to give us an example: to teach us, to wit, how to overcome the temptations of the devil. Hence Augustine says (De Trin. iv) that Christ "allowed Himself to be tempted" by the devil, "that He might be our Mediator in overcoming temptations, not only by helping us, but also by giving us an example."

Fourthly, in order to fill us with confidence in His mercy. Hence it is written (Heb. 4:15): "We have not a high-priest, who cannot have compassion on our infirmities, but one tempted in all things like as we are, without sin."

Reply to Objection 1: As Augustine says (De Civ. Dei ix): "Christ was known to the demons only so far as He willed; not as the Author of eternal life, but as the cause of certain temporal effects," from which they formed a certain conjecture that Christ was the Son of God. But since they also observed in Him certain signs of human frailty, they did not know for certain that He was the Son of God: wherefore (the devil) wished to tempt Him. This is implied by the words of Mat. 4:2,3, saying that, after "He was hungry, the tempter" came "to Him," because, as Hilary says (Super Matth., cap. iii), "Had not Christ's weakness in hungering betrayed His human nature, the devil would not have dared to tempt Him." Moreover, this appears from the very manner of the temptation, when he said: "If Thou be the Son of God." Which words Ambrose explains as follows (In Luc. iv): "What means this way of addressing Him, save that, though he knew that the Son of God was to come, yet he did not think that He had come in the weakness of the flesh?"

Reply to Objection 2: Christ came to destroy the works of the devil, not by powerful deeds, but rather by suffering from him and his members, so as to conquer the devil by righteousness, not by power; thus Augustine says (De Trin. xiii) that "the devil was to be overcome, not by the power of God, but by righteousness." And therefore in regard to Christ's temptation we must consider what He did of His own will and what He suffered from the devil. For that He allowed Himself to be tempted was due to His own will. Wherefore it is written (Mat. 4:1): "Jesus was led by the Spirit into the desert, to be tempted by the devil"; and Gregory (Hom. xvi in Evang.) says this is to be understood of the Holy Ghost, to wit, that "thither did His Spirit lead Him, where the wicked spirit would find Him and tempt Him." But He suffered from the devil in being "taken up" on to "the pinnacle of the Temple" and again "into a very high mountain." Nor is it strange, as Gregory observes, "that He allowed Himself to be taken by him on to a mountain, who allowed Himself to be crucified by His members." And we understand Him to have been taken up by the devil, not, as it were, by force, but because, as Origen says (Hom. xxi super Luc.), "He followed Him in the course of His temptation like a wrestler advancing of his own accord."

Reply to Objection 3: As the Apostle says (Heb. 4:15), Christ wished to be "tempted in all things, without sin." Now temptation which comes from an enemy can be without sin: because it comes about by merely outward suggestion. But temptation which comes from the flesh cannot be without sin, because such a temptation is caused by pleasure and concupiscence; and, as Augustine says (De

Civ. Dei xix), "it is not without sin that 'the flesh desireth against the spirit.'" And hence Christ wished to be tempted by an enemy, but not by the flesh.

Whether Christ should have been tempted in the desert?

Objection 1: It would seem that Christ should not have been tempted in the desert. Because Christ wished to be tempted in order to give us an example, as stated above [4211](A[1]). But an example should be set openly before those who are to follow it. Therefore He should not have been tempted in the desert.

Objection 2: Further, Chrysostom says (Hom. xii in Matth.): "Then most especially does the devil assail by tempting us, when he sees us alone. Thus did he tempt the woman in the beginning when he found her apart from her husband." Hence it seems that, by going into the desert to be tempted, He exposed Himself to temptation. Since, therefore, His temptation is an example to us, it seems that others too should take such steps as will lead them into temptation. And yet this seems a dangerous thing to do, since rather should we avoid the occasion of being tempted.

Objection 3: Further, Mat. 4:5, Christ's second temptation is set down, in which "the devil took" Christ up "into the Holy City, and set Him upon the pinnacle of the Temple": which is certainly not in the desert. Therefore He was not tempted in the desert only.

On the contrary, It is written (Mk. 1:13) that Jesus "was in the desert forty days and forty nights, and was tempted by Satan."

I answer that, As stated above (A[1], ad 2), Christ of His own free-will exposed Himself to be tempted by the devil, just as by His own free-will He submitted to be killed by His members; else the devil would not have dared to approach Him. Now the devil prefers to assail a man who is alone, for, as it is written (Eccles. 4:12), "if a man prevail against one, two shall withstand him." And so it was that Christ went out into the desert, as to a field of battle, to be tempted there by the devil. Hence Ambrose says on Lk. 4:1, that "Christ was led into the desert for the purpose of provoking the devil. For had he," i.e. the devil, "not fought, He," i.e. Christ, "would not have conquered." He adds other reasons, saying that "Christ in doing this set forth the mystery of Adam's delivery from exile," who had been expelled from paradise into the desert, and "set an example to us, by showing that the devil envies those who strive for better things."

Reply to Objection 1: Christ is set as an example to all through faith, according to Heb. 12:2: "Looking on Jesus, the author and finisher of faith." Now faith, as it is written (Rom. 10:17), "cometh by hearing," but not by seeing: nay, it is even said (Jn. 20:29): "Blessed are they that have not seen and have believed." And therefore, in order that Christ's temptation might be an example to us, it behooved that men should not see it, and it was enough that they should hear it related.

Reply to Objection 2: The occasions of temptation are twofold. one is on the part of man---for instance, when a man causes himself to be near to sin by not avoiding the occasion of sinning. And such occasions of temptation should be avoided, as it is written of Lot (Gn. 19:17): "Neither stay thou in all the country about" Sodom.

Another occasion of temptation is on the part of the devil, who always "envies those who strive for better things," as Ambrose says (In Luc. iv, 1). And such occasions of temptation are not to be avoided. Hence Chrysostom says (Hom. v in Matth. [*From the supposititious Opus Imperfectum]): "Not only Christ was led into the desert by the Spirit, but all God's children that have the Holy Ghost. For it is not enough for them to sit idle; the Holy Ghost urges them to endeavor to do something great: which is for them to be in the desert from the devil's standpoint, for no unrighteousness, in which the devil delights, is there. Again, every good work, compared to the flesh and the world, is the desert; because it is not according to the will of the flesh and of the world." Now, there is no danger in giving the devil such an occasion of temptation; since the help of the Holy Ghost, who is the Author of the perfect deed, is more powerful* than the assault of the envious devil. [*All the codices read 'majus.' One of the earliest printed editions has 'magis,' which has much to commend it, since St. Thomas is commenting the text quoted from St. Chrysostom. The translation would run thus: 'since rather is it (the temptation) a help from the Holy Ghost, who,' etc.].

Reply to Objection 3: Some say that all the temptations took place in the desert. Of these some say that Christ was led into the Holy City, not really, but in an imaginary vision; while others say that the Holy City itself, i.e. Jerusalem, is called "a desert," because it was deserted by God. But there is no need for this explanation. For Mark says that He was tempted in the desert by the devil, but not that He was tempted in the desert only.

Whether Christ's temptation should have taken place after His fast?

Objection 1: It would seem that Christ's temptation should not have taken place after His fast. For it has been said above ([4212]Q[40], A[2]) that an austere mode of life was not becoming to Christ. But it savors of extreme austerity that He should have eaten nothing for forty days and forty nights, for Gregory (Hom. xvi inn Evang.) explains the fact that "He fasted forty days and forty nights," saying that "during that time He partook of no food whatever." It seems, therefore, that He should not thus have fasted before His temptation.

Objection 2: Further, it is written (Mk. 1:13) that "He was in the desert forty days and forty nights; and was tempted by Satan." Now, He fasted forty days and forty nights. Therefore it seems that He was tempted by the devil, not after, but during, His fast.

Objection 3: Further, we read that Christ fasted but once. But He was tempted by the devil, not only once, for it is written (Lk. 4:13) "that all the temptation being ended, the devil departed from Him for a time." As, therefore, He did not fast before the second temptation, so neither should He have fasted before the first.

On the contrary, It is written (Mat. 4:2,3): "When He had fasted forty days and forty nights, afterwards He was hungry": and then "the tempter came to Him."

I answer that, It was becoming that Christ should wish to fast before His temptation. First, in order to give us an example. For since we are all in urgent need of strengthening ourselves against temptation, as stated above [4213](A[1]), by fasting before being tempted, He teaches us the need of fasting in order to equip ourselves against temptation. Hence the Apostle (2 Cor. 6:5, 7) reckons "fastings" together with the "armor of justice."

Secondly, in order to show that the devil assails with temptations even those who fast, as likewise those who are given to other good works. And so Christ's temptation took place after His fast, as also after His baptism. Hence since rather Chrysostom says (Hom. xiii super Matth.): "To instruct thee how great a good is fasting, and how it is a most powerful shield against the devil; and that after baptism thou shouldst give thyself up, not to luxury, but to fasting; for this cause Christ fasted, not as needing it Himself, but as teaching us."

Thirdly, because after the fast, hunger followed, which made the devil dare to approach Him, as already stated (A[1], ad 1). Now, when "our Lord was hungry," says Hilary (Super Matth. iii), "it was not because He was overcome by want of food, but because He abandoned His manhood to its nature. For the devil was to be conquered, not by God, but by the flesh." Wherefore Chrysostom too says: "He proceeded no farther than Moses and Elias, lest His assumption of our flesh might seem incredible."

Reply to Objection 1: It was becoming for Christ not to adopt an extreme form of austere life in order to show Himself outwardly in conformity with those to whom He preached. Now, no one should take up the office of preacher unless he be already cleansed and perfect in virtue, according to what is said of Christ, that "Jesus began to do and to teach" (Acts 1:1). Consequently, immediately after His baptism Christ adopted an austere form of life, in order to teach us the need of taming the flesh before passing on to the office of preaching, according to the Apostle (1 Cor. 9:27): "I chastise my body, and bring it into subjection, lest perhaps when I have preached to others, I myself should become a castaway."

Reply to Objection 2: These words of Mark may be understood as meaning that "He was in the desert forty days and forty nights," and that He fasted during that time: and the words, "and He was tempted by Satan," may be taken as referring, not to the time during which He fasted, but to the time that followed: since Matthew says that "after He had fasted forty days and forty nights, afterwards He was hungry," thus affording the devil a pretext for approaching Him. And so the words that follow, and the angels ministered to Him, are to be taken in sequence, which is clear from the words of Matthew (4:11): "Then the devil left Him," i.e. after the temptation, "and behold angels came and ministered to Him." And as to the words inserted by Mark, "and He was with the beasts," according to Chrysostom (Hom. xiii in Matth.), they are set down in order to describe the desert as being impassable to man and full of beasts.

On the other hand, according to Bede's exposition of Mk. 1:12,13, our Lord was tempted forty days and forty nights. But this is not to be understood of the visible temptations which are related by Matthew and Luke, and occurred after the fast, but of certain other assaults which perhaps Christ suffered from the devil during that time of His fast.

Reply to Objection 3: As Ambrose says on Lk. 4:13, the devil departed from Christ "for a time, because, later on, he returned, not to tempt Him, but to assail Him openly"---namely, at the time of His Passion. Nevertheless, He seemed in this later assault to tempt Christ to dejection and hatred of His neighbor; just as in the desert he had tempted Him to gluttonous pleasure and idolatrous contempt of God.

Whether the mode and order of the temptation were becoming?

Objection 1: It would seem that the mode and order of the temptation were unbecoming. For the devil tempts in order to induce us to sin. But if Christ had assuaged His bodily hunger by changing the stones into bread, He would not have sinned; just as neither did He sin when He multiplied the loaves, which was no less a miracle, in order to succor the hungry crowd. Therefore it seems that this was nowise a temptation.

Objection 2: Further, a counselor is inconsistent if he persuades the contrary to what he intends. But when the devil set Christ on a pinnacle of the Temple, he purposed to tempt Him to pride or vainglory. Therefore it was inconsistent to urge Him to cast Himself thence: for this would be contrary to pride or vainglory, which always seeks to rise.

Objection 3: Further, one temptation should lead to one sin. But in the temptation on the mountain he counseled two sins---namely, covetousness and idolatry. Therefore the mode of the temptation was unfitting.

Objection 4: Further, temptations are ordained to sin. But there are seven deadly sins, as we have stated in the [4214]FS, Q[84], A[4]. But the tempter only deals with three, viz. gluttony, vainglory, and covetousness. Therefore the temptation seems to have been incomplete.

Objection 5: Further, after overcoming all the vices, man is still tempted to pride or vainglory: since pride "worms itself in stealthily, and destroys even good works," as Augustine says (Ep. ccxi). Therefore Matthew unfittingly gives the last place to the temptation to covetousness on the mountain, and the second place to the temptation to vainglory in the Temple, especially since Luke puts them in the reverse order.

Objection 6: Further, Jerome says on Mat. 4:4 that "Christ purposed to overcome the devil by humility, not by might." Therefore He should not have repulsed him with a haughty rebuke, saying: "Begone, Satan."

Objection 7: Further, the gospel narrative seems to be false. For it seems impossible that Christ could have been set on a pinnacle of the Temple without being seen by others. Nor is there to be found a mountain so high that all the world can be seen from it, so that all the kingdoms of the earth could be shown to Christ from its summit. It seems, therefore, that Christ's temptation is unfittingly described.

On the contrary is the authority of Scripture.

I answer that, The temptation which comes from the enemy takes the form of a suggestion, as Gregory says (Hom. xvi in Evang.). Now a suggestion cannot be made to everybody in the same way; it must arise from those things towards which each one has an inclination. Consequently the devil does not straight away tempt the spiritual man to grave sins, but he begins with lighter sins, so as gradually to lead him to those of greater magnitude. Wherefore Gregory (Moral. xxxi), expounding Job 39:25, "He smelleth the battle afar off, the encouraging of the captains and the shouting of the army," says: "The captains are fittingly described as encouraging, and the army as shouting. Because vices begin by insinuating themselves into the mind under some specious pretext: then they come on the mind in such numbers as to drag it into all sorts of folly, deafening it with their bestial clamor."

Thus, too, did the devil set about the temptation of the first man. For at first he enticed his mind to consent to the eating of the forbidden fruit, saying (Gn. 3:1): "Why hath God commanded you that you should not eat of every tree of paradise?" Secondly [he tempted him] to vainglory by saying: "Your eyes shall be opened." Thirdly, he led the temptation to the extreme height of pride, saying: "You shall be as gods, knowing good and evil." This same order did he observe in tempting Christ. For at first he tempted Him to that which men desire, however spiritual they may be---namely, the support of the corporeal nature by food. Secondly, he advanced to that matter in which spiritual men are sometimes found wanting, inasmuch as they do certain things for show, which pertains to vainglory. Thirdly, he led the temptation on to that in which no spiritual men, but only carnal men, have a part---namely, to desire worldly riches and fame, to the extent of holding God in contempt. And so in the first two temptations he said: "If Thou be the Son of God"; but not in the third, which is inapplicable to spiritual men, who are sons of God by adoption, whereas it does apply to the two preceding temptations.

And Christ resisted these temptations by quoting the authority of the Law, not by enforcing His power, "so as to give more honor to His human nature and a greater punishment to His adversary, since the foe of the human race was vanquished, not as by God, but as by man"; as Pope Leo says (Serm. 1, De Quadrag. 3).

Reply to Objection 1: To make use of what is needful for self-support is not the sin of gluttony; but if a man do anything inordinate out of the desire for such support, it can pertain to the sin of gluttony. Now it is inordinate for a man who has human assistance at his command to seek to obtain food miraculously for mere bodily support. Hence the Lord miraculously provided the children of Israel with manna in the desert, where there was no means of obtaining food otherwise. And in like fashion Christ miraculously provided the crowds with food in the desert, when there was no other means of getting food. But in order to assuage His hunger, He could have done otherwise than work a miracle, as did John the Baptist, according to Matthew (3:4); or He could have hastened to the neighboring country. Consequently the devil esteemed that if Christ was a mere man, He would fall into sin by attempting to assuage His hunger by a miracle.

Reply to Objection 2: It often happens that a man seeks to derive glory from external humiliation, whereby he is exalted by reason of spiritual good. Hence Augustine says (De Serm. Dom. in Monte ii, 12): "It must be noted that it is possible to boast not only of the beauty and splendor of material things, but even of filthy squalor." And this is signified by the devil urging Christ to seek spiritual glory by casting His body down.

Reply to Objection 3: It is a sin to desire worldly riches and honors in an inordinate fashion. And the principal sign of this is when a man does something wrong in order to acquire such things. And so the devil was not satisfied with instigating to a desire for riches and honors, but he went so far as to tempt Christ, for the sake of gaining possession of these things, to fall down and adore him, which is a very great crime, and against God. Nor does he say merely, "if Thou wilt adore me," but he adds, "if, falling down"; because, as Ambrose says on Lk. 4:5: "Ambition harbors yet another danger within itself: for, while seeking to rule, it will serve; it will bow in submission that it may be crowned with honor; and the higher it aims, the lower it abases itself."

In like manner [the devil] in the preceding temptations tried to lead [Christ] from the desire of one sin to the commission of another; thus from the desire of food he tried to lead Him to the vanity of the needless working of a miracle; and from the desire of glory to tempt God by casting Himself headlong.

Reply to Objection 4: As Ambrose says on Lk. 4:13, Scripture would not have said that "'all the temptation being ended, the devil departed from Him,' unless the matter of all sins were included in the three temptations already related. For the causes of temptations are the causes of desires"---namely, "lust of the flesh, hope of glory, eagerness for power."

Reply to Objection 5: As Augustine says (De Consensu Evang. ii): "It is not certain which happened first; whether the kingdoms of the earth were first shown to Him, and afterwards He was set on the pinnacle of the Temple; or the latter first, and the former afterwards. However, it matters not, provided it be made clear that all these things did take place." It may be that the Evangelists set these things in different orders, because sometimes cupidity arises from vainglory, sometimes the reverse happens.

Reply to Objection 6: When Christ had suffered the wrong of being tempted by the devil saying, "If Thou be the Son of God cast Thyself down," He was not troubled, nor did He upbraid the devil. But when the devil usurped to himself the honor due to God, saying, "All these things will I give Thee, if, falling down, Thou wilt adore me," He was exasperated, and repulsed him, saying, "Begone, Satan": that we might learn from His example to bear bravely insults leveled at ourselves, but not to allow ourselves so much as to listen to those which are aimed at God.

Reply to Objection 7: As Chrysostom says (Hom. v in Matth.): "The devil set Him" (on a pinnacle of the Temple) "that He might be seen by all, whereas, unawares to the devil, He acted in such sort that He was seen by none."

In regard to the words, "'He showed Him all the kingdoms of the world, and the glory of them,' we are not to understand that He saw the very kingdoms, with the cities and inhabitants, their gold and silver: but that the devil pointed out the quarters in which each kingdom or city lay, and set forth to Him in words their glory and estate." Or, again, as Origen says (Hom. xxx in Luc.), "he showed Him how, by means of the various vices, he was the lord of the world."

OF CHRIST'S DOCTRINE (FOUR ARTICLES)

We have now to consider Christ's doctrine, about which there are four points of inquiry:

(1) Whether Christ should have preached to the Jews only, or to the Gentiles also?

(2) Whether in preaching He should have avoided the opposition of the Jews?

(3) Whether He should have preached in an open or in a hidden manner?

(4) Whether He should have preached by word only, or also by writing?

Concerning the time when He began to teach, we have spoken above when treating of His baptism (Q[29], A[3]).

Whether Christ should have preached not only to the Jews, but also to the Gentiles?

Objection 1: It would seem that Christ should have preached not only to the Jews, but also to the Gentiles. For it is written (Is. 49:6): "It is a small thing that thou shouldst be My servant to raise up the tribes of Israel [Vulg.: 'Jacob'] and to convert the dregs of Jacob [Vulg.: 'Israel']: behold, I have given thee to be the light of the Gentiles, that thou mayest be my salvation even to the farthest part of the earth." But Christ gave light and salvation through His doctrine. Therefore it seems that it was "a small thing" that He preached to Jews alone, and not to the Gentiles.

Objection 2: Further, as it is written (Mat. 7:29): "He was teaching them as one having power." Now the power of doctrine is made more manifest in the instruction of those who, like the Gentiles, have received no tidings whatever; hence the Apostle says (Rom. 15:20): "I have so preached the [Vulg.: 'this'] gospel, not where Christ was named, lest I should build upon another man's foundation." Therefore much rather should Christ have preached to the Gentiles than to the Jews.

Objection 3: Further, it is more useful to instruct many than one. But Christ instructed some individual Gentiles, such as the Samaritan woman (Jn. 4) and the Chananaean woman (Mat. 15). Much more reason, therefore, was there for Christ to preach to the Gentiles in general.

On the contrary, our Lord said (Mat. 15:24): "I was not sent but to the sheep that are lost of the house of Israel." And (Rom. 10:15) it is written: "How shall they preach unless they be sent?" Therefore Christ should not have preached to the Gentiles.

I answer that, It was fitting that Christ's preaching, whether through Himself or through His apostles, should be directed at first to the Jews alone. First, in order to show that by His coming the promises were fulfilled which had been made to the Jews of old, and not to the Gentiles. Thus the Apostle says (Rom. 15:8): "I say that Christ . . . was minister of the circumcision," i.e. the apostle and preacher of the Jews, "for the truth of God, to confirm the promises made unto the fathers."

Secondly, in order to show that His coming was of God; because, as is written Rom. 13:1: "Those things which are of God are well ordered [Vulg.: 'those that are, are ordained of God']" [*See Scriptural Index on this passage]. Now the right order demanded that the doctrine of Christ should be made known first to the Jews, who, by believing in and worshiping one God, were nearer to God, and that it should be transmitted through them to the Gentiles: just as in the heavenly hierarchy the Divine enlightenment comes to the lower angels through the higher. Hence on Mat. 15:24, "I was not sent but to the sheep that are lost in the house of Israel," Jerome says: "He does not mean by this that He was not sent to the Gentiles, but that He was sent to the Jews first." And so we read (Is. 66:19): "I will send of them that shall be saved," i.e. of the Jews, "to the Gentiles . . . and they shall declare My glory unto the Gentiles."

Thirdly, in order to deprive the Jews of ground for quibbling. Hence on Mat. 10:5, "Go ye not into the way of the Gentiles." Jerome says: "It behooved Christ's coming to be announced to the Jews first, lest they should have a valid excuse, and say that they had rejected our Lord because He had sent His apostles to the Gentiles and Samaritans."

Fourthly, because it was through the triumph of the cross that Christ merited power and lordship over the Gentiles. Hence it is written (Apoc. 2:26, 28): "He that shall overcome . . . I will give him power over the nations . . . as I also have received of My Father"; and that because He became "obedient unto the death of the cross, God hath exalted Him . . . that in the name of Jesus every knee should bow . . ." and that "every tongue should confess Him" (Phil. 2:8-11). Consequently He did not wish His doctrine to be preached to the Gentiles before His Passion: it was after His Passion that He said to His disciples (Mat. 28:19): "Going, teach ye all nations." For this reason it was that, when, shortly before His Passion, certain Gentiles wished to see Jesus, He said: "Unless the grain of wheat falling into the ground dieth, itself remaineth alone: but if it die it bringeth forth much fruit" (Jn. 12:20-25); and as Augustine says, commenting on this passage: "He called Himself the grain of wheat that must be mortified by the unbelief of the Jews, multiplied by the faith of the nations."

Reply to Objection 1: Christ was given to be the light and salvation of the Gentiles through His disciples, whom He sent to preach to them.

Reply to Objection 2: It is a sign, not of lesser, but of greater power to do something by means of others rather than by oneself. And thus the Divine power of Christ was specially shown in this, that He bestowed on the teaching of His disciples such a power that they converted the Gentiles to Christ, although these had heard nothing of Him.

Now the power of Christ's teaching is to be considered in the miracles by which He confirmed His doctrine, in the efficacy of His persuasion, and in the authority of His words, for He spoke as being Himself above the Law when He said: "But I say to you" (Mat. 5:22,28,32,34,39,44); and, again, in the force of His righteousness shown in His sinless manner of life.

Reply to Objection 3: Just as it was unfitting that Christ should at the outset make His doctrine known to the Gentiles equally with the Jews, in order that He might appear as being sent to the Jews, as to the first-born people; so neither was it fitting for Him to neglect the Gentiles altogether, lest they should be deprived of the hope of salvation. For this reason certain individual Gentiles were admitted, on account of the excellence of their faith and devotedness.

Whether Christ should have preached to the Jews without offending them?

Objection 1: It would seem that Christ should have preached to the Jews without offending them. For, as Augustine says (De Agone Christ. xi): "In the Man Jesus Christ, a model of life is given us by the Son of God." But we should avoid offending not only the faithful, but even unbelievers, according to 1 Cor. 10:32: "Be without offense to the Jews, and to the Gentiles, and to the Church of God." Therefore it seems that, in His teaching, Christ should also have avoided giving offense to the Jews.

Objection 2: Further, no wise man should do anything that will hinder the result of his labor. Now through the disturbance which His teaching occasioned among the Jews, it was deprived of its results; for it is written (Lk. 11:53,54) that when our Lord reproved the Pharisees and Scribes, they "began vehemently to urge Him, end to oppress His mouth about many things; lying in wait for Him, and seeking to catch something from His mouth, that they might accuse Him." It seems therefore unfitting that He should have given them offense by His teaching.

Objection 3: Further, the Apostle says (1 Tim. 5:1): "An ancient man rebuke not; but entreat him as a father." But the priests and princes of the Jews were the elders of that people. Therefore it seems that they should not have been rebuked with severity.

On the contrary, It was foretold (Is. 8:14) that Christ would be "for a stone of stumbling and for a rock of offense to the two houses of Israel."

I answer that, The salvation of the multitude is to be preferred to the peace of any individuals whatsoever. Consequently, when certain ones, by their perverseness, hinder the salvation of the multitude, the preacher and the teacher should not fear to offend those men, in order that he may insure the salvation of the multitude. Now the Scribes and Pharisees and the princes of the Jews were by their malice a considerable hindrance to the salvation of the people, both because they opposed themselves to Christ's doctrine, which was the only way to salvation, and because their evil ways corrupted the morals of the people. For which reason our Lord, undeterred by their taking offense, publicly taught the truth which they hated, and condemned their vices. Hence we read (Mat. 15:12, 14) that when the disciples of our Lord said: "Dost Thou know that the Pharisees, when they heard this word, were scandalized?" He answered: "Let them alone: they are blind and leaders of the blind; and if the blind lead the blind, both fall into the pit."

Reply to Objection 1: A man ought so to avoid giving offense, as neither by wrong deed or word to be the occasion of anyone's downfall. "But if scandal arise from truth, the scandal should be borne rather than the truth be set aside," as Gregory says (Hom. vii in Ezech.).

Reply to Objection 2: By publicly reproving the Scribes and Pharisees, Christ promoted rather than hindered the effect of His teaching. Because when the people came to know the vices of those men, they were less inclined to be prejudiced against Christ by hearing what was said of Him by the Scribes and Pharisees, who were ever withstanding His doctrine.

Reply to Objection 3: This saying of the Apostle is to be understood of those elders whose years are reckoned not only in age and authority, but also in probity; according to Num. 11:16: "Gather unto Me seventy men of the ancients of Israel, whom thou knowest to be ancients . . . of the people." But if by sinning openly they turn the authority of their years into an instrument of wickedness, they should be rebuked openly and severely, as also Daniel says (Dan. 13:52): "O thou that art grown old in evil days," etc.

Day 277

Whether Christ should have taught all things openly?

Objection 1: It would seem that Christ should not have taught all things openly. For we read that He taught many things to His disciples apart: as is seen clearly in the sermon at the Supper. Wherefore He said: "That which you heard in the ear in the chambers shall be preached on the housetops" [*St. Thomas, probably quoting from memory, combines Mat. 10:27 with Lk. 12:3]. Therefore He did not teach all things openly.

Objection 2: Further, the depths of wisdom should not be expounded save to the perfect, according to 1 Cor. 2:6: "We speak wisdom among the perfect." Now Christ's doctrine contained the most profound wisdom. Therefore it should not have been made known to the imperfect crowd.

Objection 3: Further, it comes to the same, to hide the truth, whether by saying nothing or by making use of a language that is difficult to understand. Now Christ, by speaking to the multitudes a language they would not understand, hid from them the truth that He preached; since "without parables He did not speak to them" (Mat. 13:34). In the same way, therefore, He could have hidden it from them by saying nothing at all.

On the contrary, He says Himself (Jn. 18:20): "In secret I have spoken nothing."

I answer that, Anyone's doctrine may be hidden in three ways. First, on the part of the intention of the teacher, who does not wish to make his doctrine known to many, but rather to hide it. And this may happen in two ways---sometimes through envy on the part of the teacher, who desires to excel in his knowledge, wherefore he is unwilling to communicate it to others. But this was not the case with Christ, in whose person the following words are spoken (Wis. 7:13): "Which I have learned without guile, and communicate without envy, and her riches I hide not." But sometimes this happens through the vileness of the things taught; thus Augustine says on Jn. 16:12: "There are some things so bad that no sort of human modesty can bear them." Wherefore of heretical doctrine it is written (Prov. 9:17): "Stolen waters are sweeter." Now, Christ's doctrine is "not of error nor of uncleanness" (1 Thess. 2:3). Wherefore our Lord says (Mk. 4:21): "Doth a candle," i.e. true and pure doctrine, "come in to be put under a bushel?"

Secondly, doctrine is hidden because it is put before few. And thus, again, did Christ teach nothing in secret: for He propounded His entire doctrine either to the whole crowd or to His disciples gathered together. Hence Augustine says on Jn. 18:20: "How can it be said that He speaks in secret when He speaks before so many men? . . . especially if what He says to few He wishes through them to be made known to many?"

Thirdly, doctrine is hidden, as to the manner in which it is propounded. And thus Christ spoke certain things in secret to the crowds, by employing parables in teaching them spiritual mysteries which they were either unable or unworthy to grasp: and yet it was better for them to be instructed in the knowledge of spiritual things, albeit hidden under the garb of parables, than to be deprived of it altogether. Nevertheless our Lord expounded the open and unveiled truth of these parables to His disciples, so that they might hand it down to others worthy of it; according to 2 Tim. 2:2: "The things which thou hast heard of me by many witnesses, the same command to faithful men, who shall be fit to teach others." This is foreshadowed, Num. 4, where the sons of Aaron are commanded to wrap up the sacred vessels that were to be carried by the Levites.

Reply to Objection 1: As Hilary says, commenting on the passage quoted, "we do not read that our Lord was wont to preach at night, and expound His doctrine in the dark: but He says this because His speech is darkness to the carnal-minded, and His words are night to the unbeliever. His meaning, therefore, is that whatever He said we also should say in the midst of unbelievers, by openly believing and professing it."

Or, according to Jerome, He speaks comparatively---that is to say, because He was instructing them in Judea, which was a small place compared with the whole world, where Christ's doctrine was to be published by the preaching of the apostles.

Reply to Objection 2: By His doctrine our Lord did not make known all the depths of His wisdom, neither to the multitudes, nor, indeed, to His disciples, to whom He said (Jn. 16:12): "I have yet many things to say to you, but you cannot bear them now." Yet whatever things out of His wisdom He judged it right to make known to others, He expounded, not in secret, but openly; although He was not understood by all. Hence Augustine says on Jn. 18:20: "We must understand this, 'I have spoken openly to the world,' as though our Lord had said, 'Many have heard Me' . . . and, again, it was not 'openly,' because they did not understand."

Reply to Objection 3: As stated above, our Lord spoke to the multitudes in parables, because they were neither able nor worthy to receive the naked truth, which He revealed to His disciples.

And when it is said that "without parables He did not speak to them," according to Chrysostom (Hom. xlvii in Matth.), we are to understand this of that particular sermon, since on other occasions He said many things to the multitude without parables. Or, as Augustine says (De Qq. Evang., qu. xvii), this means, "not that He spoke nothing literally, but that He scarcely ever spoke without introducing a parable, although He also spoke some things in the literal sense."

Whether Christ should have committed His doctrine to writing?

Objection 1: It would seem that Christ should have committed His doctrine to writing. For the purpose of writing is to hand down doctrine to posterity. Now Christ's doctrine was destined to endure for ever, according to Lk. 21:33: "Heaven and earth shall pass away, but My words shall not pass away." Therefore it seems that Christ should have committed His doctrine to writing.

Objection 2: Further, the Old Law was a foreshadowing of Christ, according to Heb. 10:1: "The Law has [Vulg.: 'having'] a shadow of the good things to come." Now the Old Law was put into writing by God, according to Ex. 24:12: "I will give thee" two "tables of stone and the law, and the commandments which I have written." Therefore it seems that Christ also should have put His doctrine into writing.

Objection 3: Further, to Christ, who came to enlighten them that sit in darkness (Lk. 1:79), it belonged to remove occasions of error, and to open out the road to faith. Now He would have done this by putting His teaching into writing: for Augustine says (De Consensu Evang. i) that "some there are who wonder why our Lord wrote nothing, so that we have to believe what others have written about Him. Especially do those pagans ask this question who dare not blame or blaspheme Christ, and who ascribe to Him most excellent, but merely human, wisdom. These say that the disciples made out the Master to be more than He really was when they said that He was the Son of God and the Word of God, by whom all things were made." And farther on he adds: "It seems as though they were prepared to believe whatever He might have written of Himself, but not what others at their discretion published about Him." Therefore it seems that Christ should have Himself committed His doctrine to writing.

On the contrary, No books written by Him were to be found in the canon of Scripture.

I answer that, It was fitting that Christ should not commit His doctrine to writing. First, on account of His dignity: for the more excellent the teacher, the more excellent should be his manner of teaching. Consequently it was fitting that Christ, as the most excellent of teachers, should adopt that manner of teaching whereby His doctrine is imprinted on the hearts of His hearers; wherefore it is written (Mat. 7:29) that "He was teaching them as one having power." And so it was that among the Gentiles, Pythagoras and Socrates, who were teachers of great excellence, were unwilling to write anything. For writings are ordained, as to an end, unto the imprinting of doctrine in the hearts of the hearers.

Secondly, on account of the excellence of Christ's doctrine, which cannot be expressed in writing; according to Jn. 21:25: "There are also many other things which Jesus did: which, if they were written everyone, the world itself, I think, would not be able to contain the books that should be written." Which Augustine explains by saying: "We are not to believe that in respect of space the world could not contain them . . . but that by the capacity of the readers they could not be comprehended." And if Christ had committed His doctrine to writing, men would have had no deeper thought of His doctrine than that which appears on the surface of the writing.

Thirdly, that His doctrine might reach all in an orderly manner: Himself teaching His disciples immediately, and they subsequently teaching others, by preaching and writing: whereas if He Himself had written, His doctrine would have reached all immediately.

Hence it is said of Wisdom (Prov. 9:3) that "she hath sent her maids to invite to the tower." It is to be observed, however, that, as Augustine says (De Consensu Evang. i), some of the Gentiles thought that Christ wrote certain books treating of the magic art whereby He worked miracles: which art is condemned by the Christian learning. "And yet they who claim to have read those books of Christ do none of those things which they marvel at His doing according to those same books. Moreover, it is by a Divine judgment that they err so far as to assert that these books were, as it were, entitled as letters to Peter and Paul, for that they found them in several places depicted in company with Christ. No wonder that the inventors were deceived by the painters: for as long as Christ lived in the mortal flesh with His disciples, Paul was no disciple of His."

Reply to Objection 1: As Augustine says in the same book: "Christ is the head of all His disciples who are members of His body. Consequently, when they put into writing what He showed forth and said to them, by no means must we say that He wrote nothing: since His members put forth that which they knew under His dictation. For at His command they, being His hands, as it were, wrote whatever He wished us to read concerning His deeds and words."

Reply to Objection 2: Since the old Law was given under the form of sensible signs, therefore also was it fittingly written with sensible signs. But Christ's doctrine, which is "the law of the spirit of life" (Rom. 8:2), had to be "written not with ink, but with the Spirit of the living God; not in tables of stone, but in the fleshly tables of the heart," as the Apostle says (2 Cor. 3:3).

Reply to Objection 3: Those who were unwilling to believe what the apostles wrote of Christ would have refused to believe the writings of Christ, whom they deemed to work miracles by the magic art.

OF THE MIRACLES WORKED BY CHRIST, IN GENERAL (FOUR ARTICLES)

We must now consider the miracles worked by Christ: (1) In general; (2) Specifically, of each kind of miracle; (3) In particular, of His transfiguration.

Concerning the first, there are four points of inquiry:

(1) Whether Christ should have worked miracles?

(2) Whether He worked them by Divine power?

(3) When did He begin to work miracles?

(4) Whether His miracles are a sufficient proof of His Godhead?

Whether Christ should have worked miracles?

Objection 1: It would seem that Christ should not have worked miracles. For Christ's deeds should have been consistent with His words. But He Himself said (Mat. 16:4): "A wicked and adulterous generation seeketh after a sign; and a sign shall not be given it, but the sign of Jonas the prophet." Therefore He should not have worked miracles.

Objection 2: Further, just as Christ, at His second coming, is to come "with" great power and majesty, as is written Mat. 24:30, so at His first coming He came in infirmity, according to Is. 53:3: "A man of sorrows and acquainted with infirmity." But the working of miracles belongs to power rather than to infirmity. Therefore it was not fitting that He should work miracles in His first coming.

Objection 3: Further, Christ came that He might save men by faith; according to Heb. 12:2: "Looking on Jesus, the author and finisher of faith." But miracles lessen the merit of faith; hence our Lord says (Jn. 4:48): "Unless you see signs and wonders you believe not." Therefore it seems that Christ should not have worked miracles.

On the contrary, It was said in the person of His adversaries (Jn. 11:47): "What do we; for this man doth many miracles?"

I answer that, God enables man to work miracles for two reasons. First and principally, in confirmation of the doctrine that a man teaches. For since those things which are of faith surpass human reason, they cannot be proved by human arguments, but need to be proved by the argument of Divine power: so that when a man does works that God alone can do, we may believe that what he says is from God: just as when a man is the bearer of letters sealed with the king's ring, it is to be believed that what they contain expresses the king's will.

Secondly, in order to make known God's presence in a man by the grace of the Holy Ghost: so that when a man does the works of God we may believe that God dwells in him by His grace. Wherefore it is written (Gal. 3:5): "He who giveth to you the Spirit, and worketh miracles among you."

Now both these things were to be made known to men concerning Christ---namely, that God dwelt in Him by grace, not of adoption, but of union: and that His supernatural doctrine was from God. And therefore it was most fitting that He should work miracles. Wherefore He Himself says (Jn. 10:38): "Though you will not believe Me, believe the works"; and (Jn. 5:36): "The works which the Father hath given Me to perfect . . . themselves . . . give testimony to Me."

Reply to Objection 1: These words, "a sign shall not be given it, but the sign of Jonas," mean, as Chrysostom says (Hom. xliii in Matth.), that "they did not receive a sign such as they sought, viz. from heaven": but not that He gave them no sign at all. Or that "He worked signs not for the sake of those whom He knew to be hardened, but to amend others." Therefore those signs were given, not to them, but to others.

Reply to Objection 2: Although Christ came "in the infirmity" of the flesh, which is manifested in the passions, yet He came "in the power of God" [*Cf. 2 Cor. 13:4], and this had to be made manifest by miracles.

Reply to Objection 3: Miracles lessen the merit of faith in so far as those are shown to be hard of heart who are unwilling to believe what is proved from the Scriptures unless (they are convinced) by miracles. Yet it is better for them to be converted to the faith even by miracles than that they should remain altogether in their unbelief. For it is written (1 Cor. 14:22) that signs are given "to unbelievers," viz. that they may be converted to the faith.

Whether Christ worked miracles by Divine power?

Objection 1: It would seem that Christ did not work miracles by Divine power. For the Divine power is omnipotent. But it seems that Christ was not omnipotent in working miracles; for it is written (Mk. 6:5) that "He could not do any miracles there," i.e. in His own country. Therefore it seems that He did not work miracles by Divine power.

Objection 2: Further, God does not pray. But Christ sometimes prayed when working miracles; as may be seen in the raising of Lazarus (Jn. 11:41,42), and in the multiplication of the loaves, as related Mat. 14:19. Therefore it seems that He did not work miracles by Divine power.

Objection 3: Further, what is done by Divine power cannot be done by the power of any creature. But the things which Christ did could be done also by the power of a creature: wherefore the Pharisees said (Lk. 11:15) that He cast out devils "by Beelzebub the prince of devils." Therefore it seems that Christ did not work miracles by Divine power.

On the contrary, our Lord said (Jn. 14:10): "The Father who abideth in Me, He doth the works."

I answer that, as stated in the [4215]FP, Q[110], A[4], true miracles cannot be wrought save by Divine power: because God alone can change the order of nature; and this is what is meant by a miracle. Wherefore Pope Leo says (Ep. ad Flav. xxviii) that, while there are two natures in Christ, there is "one," viz. the Divine, which shines forth in miracles; and "another," viz. the human, "which submits to insults"; yet "each communicates its actions to the other": in as far as the human nature is the instrument of the Divine action, and the human action receives power from the Divine Nature, as stated above (Q[19], A[1]).

Reply to Objection 1: When it is said that "He could not do any miracles there," it is not to be understood that He could not do them absolutely, but that it was not fitting for Him to do them: for it was unfitting for Him to work miracles among unbelievers. Wherefore it is said farther on: "And He wondered because of their unbelief." In like manner it is said (Gn. 18:17): "Can I hide from Abraham what I am about to do?" and Gn. 19:22: "I cannot do anything till thou go in thither."

Reply to Objection 2: As Chrysostom says on Mat. 14:19, "He took the five loaves and the two fishes, and, looking up to heaven, He blessed and brake: It was to be believed of Him, both that He is of the Father and that He is equal to Him . . . Therefore that He might prove both, He works miracles now with authority, now with prayer . . . in the lesser things, indeed, He looks up to heaven"---for instance, in multiplying the loaves---"but in the greater, which belong to God alone, He acts with authority; for example, when He forgave sins and raised the dead."

When it is said that in raising Lazarus He lifted up His eyes (Jn. 11:41), this was not because He needed to pray, but because He wished to teach us how to pray. Wherefore He said: "Because of the people who stand about have I said it: that they may believe that Thou hast sent Me."

Reply to Objection 3: Christ cast out demons otherwise than they are cast out by the power of demons. For demons are cast out from bodies by the power of higher demons in such a way that they retain their power over the soul: since the devil does not work against his own kingdom. On the other hand, Christ cast out demons, not only from the body, but still more from the soul. For this reason our Lord rebuked the blasphemy of the Jews, who said that He cast out demons by the power of the demons: first, by saying that Satan is not divided against himself; secondly, by quoting the instance of others who cast out demons by the Spirit of God; thirdly, because He could not have cast out a demon unless He had overcome Him by Divine power; fourthly, because there was nothing in common between His works and their effects and those of Satan; since Satan's purpose was to "scatter" those whom Christ "gathered" together [*Cf. Mat. 12:24-30; Mk. 3:22; Lk. 11:15-32].

Whether Christ began to work miracles when He changed water into wine at the marriage feast?

Objection 1: It would seem that Christ did not begin to work miracles when He changed water into wine at the marriage feast. For we read in the book De Infantia Salvatoris that Christ worked many miracles in His childhood. But the miracle of changing water into wine at the marriage feast took place in the thirtieth or thirty-first year of His age. Therefore it seems that it was not then that He began to work miracles.

Objection 2: Further, Christ worked miracles by Divine power. Now He was possessed of Divine power from the first moment of His conception; for from that instant He was both God and man. Therefore it seems that He worked miracles from the very first.

Objection 3: Further, Christ began to gather His disciples after His baptism and temptation, as related Mat. 4:18 and Jn. 1:35. But the disciples gathered around Him, principally on account of His miracles: thus it is written (Lk. 5:4) that He called Peter when "he was astonished at" the miracle which He had worked in "the draught of fishes." Therefore it seems that He worked other miracles before that of the marriage feast.

On the contrary, It is written (Jn. 2:11): "This beginning of miracles did Jesus in Cana of Galilee."

I answer that, Christ worked miracles in order to confirm His doctrine, and in order to show forth His Divine power. Therefore, as to the first, it was unbecoming for Him to work miracles before He began to teach. And it was unfitting that He should begin to teach until He reached the perfect age, as we stated above, in speaking of His baptism ([4216]Q[39], A[3]). But as to the second, it was right that He should so manifest His Godhead by working miracles that men should believe in the reality of His manhood. And, consequently, as Chrysostom says (Hom. xxi in Joan.), "it was fitting that He should not begin to work wonders from His early years: for men would have deemed the Incarnation to be imaginary and would have crucified Him before the proper time."

Reply to Objection 1: As Chrysostom says (Hom. xvii in Joan.), in regard to the saying of John the Baptist, "'That He may be made manifest in Israel, therefore am I come baptizing with water,' it is clear that the wonders which some pretend to have been worked by Christ in His childhood are untrue and fictitious. For had Christ worked miracles from His early years, John would by no means have been unacquainted with Him, nor would the rest of the people have stood in need of a teacher to point Him out to them."

Reply to Objection 2: What the Divine power achieved in Christ was in proportion to the needs of the salvation of mankind, the achievement of which was the purpose of His taking flesh. Consequently He so worked miracles by the Divine power as not to prejudice our belief in the reality of His flesh.

Reply to Objection 3: The disciples were to be commended precisely because they followed Christ "without having seen Him work any miracles," as Gregory says in a homily (Hom. v in Evang.). And, as Chrysostom says (Hom. xxiii in Joan.), "the need for working miracles arose then, especially when the disciples were already gathered around and attached to Him, and attentive to what was going on around them. Hence it is added: 'And His disciples believed in Him,'" not because they then believed in Him for the first time, but because then "they believed with greater discernment and perfection." Or they are called "disciples" because "they were to be disciples later on," as Augustine observes (De Consensu Evang. ii).

Whether the miracles which Christ worked were a sufficient proof of His Godhead?

Objection 1: It would seem that the miracles which Christ worked were not a sufficient proof of His Godhead. For it is proper to Christ to be both God and man. But the miracles which Christ worked have been done by others also. Therefore they were not a sufficient proof of His Godhead.

Objection 2: Further, no power surpasses that of the Godhead. But some have worked greater miracles than Christ, for it is written (Jn. 14:12): "He that believeth in Me, the works that I do, he also shall do, and greater than these shall he do." Therefore it seems that the miracles which Christ worked are not sufficient proof of His Godhead.

Objection 3: Further, the particular is not a sufficient proof of the universal. But any one of Christ's miracles was one particular work. Therefore none of them was a sufficient proof of His Godhead, by reason of which He had universal power over all things.

On the contrary, our Lord said (Jn. 5:36): "The works which the Father hath given Me to perfect . . . themselves . . . give testimony of Me."

I answer that, The miracles which Christ worked were a sufficient proof of His Godhead in three respects. First, as to the very nature of the works, which surpassed the entire capability of created power, and therefore could not be done save by Divine power. For this reason the blind man, after his sight had been restored, said (Jn. 9:32,33): "From the beginning of the world it has not been heard, that any man hath opened the eyes of one born blind. Unless this man were of God, he could not do anything."

Secondly, as to the way in which He worked miracles---namely, because He worked miracles as though of His own power, and not by praying, as others do. Wherefore it is written (Lk. 6:19) that "virtue went out from Him and healed all." Whereby it is proved, as Cyril says (Comment. in Lucam) that "He did not receive power from another, but, being God by nature, He showed His own power over the sick. And this is how He worked countless miracles." Hence on Mat. 8:16: "He cast out spirits with His word, and all that were sick He healed," Chrysostom says: "Mark how great a multitude of persons healed, the Evangelists pass quickly over, not mentioning one by one . . . but in one word traversing an unspeakable sea of miracles." And thus it was shown that His power was co-equal with that of God the Father, according to Jn. 5:19: "What things soever" the Father "doth, these the Son doth also in like manner"; and, again (Jn. 5:21): "As the Father raiseth up the dead and giveth life, so the Son also giveth life to whom He will."

Thirdly, from the very fact that He taught that He was God; for unless this were true it would not be confirmed by miracles worked by Divine power. Hence it was said (Mk. 1:27): "What is this new doctrine? For with power He commandeth the unclean spirits, and they obey Him."

Reply to Objection 1: This was the argument of the Gentiles. Wherefore Augustine says (Ep. ad Volusian. cxxxvii): "No suitable wonders; say they, show forth the presence of so great majesty, for the ghostly cleansing" whereby He cast out demons, "the cure of the sick, the raising of the dead to life, if other miracles be taken into account, are small things before God." To this Augustine answers thus: "We own that the prophets did as much . . . But even Moses himself and the other prophets made Christ the Lord the object of their prophecy, and gave Him great glory . . . He, therefore, chose to do similar things to avoid the inconsistency of failing to do what He had done through others. Yet still He was bound to do something which no other had done: to be born of a virgin, to rise from the dead, and to ascend into heaven. If anyone deem this a slight thing for God to do, I know not what more he can expect. Having become man, ought He to have made another world, that we might believe Him to be Him by whom the world was made? But in this world neither a greater world could be made nor one equal to it: and if He had made a lesser world in comparison with this, that too would have been deemed a small thing."

As to the miracles worked by others, Christ did greater still. Hence on Jn. 15:24: "If I had not done in [Douay: 'among'] them the works that no other men hath done," etc., Augustine says: "None of the works of Christ seem to be greater than the raising of the dead: which thing we know the ancient prophets also did . . . Yet Christ did some works 'which no other man hath done.' But we are told in answer that others did works which He did not, and which none other did . . . But to heal with so great a power so many defects and ailments and grievances of mortal men, this we read concerning none soever of the men of old. To say nothing of those, each of whom by His bidding, as they came in His way, He made whole . . . Mark saith (6:56): 'Whithersoever He entered, into towns or into villages or into cities, they laid the sick in the streets, and besought Him that they might touch but the hem of His garment: and as many as touched Him were made whole.' These things none other did in them; for when He saith 'In them,' it is not to be understood to mean 'Among them,' or 'In their presence,' but wholly 'In them,' because He healed them . . . Therefore whatever works He did in them are works that none ever did; since if ever any other man did any one of them, by His doing he did it; whereas these works He did, not by their doing, but by Himself."

Reply to Objection 2: Augustine explains this passage of John as follows (Tract. lxxi): "What are these 'greater works' which believers in Him would do? That, as they passed by, their very shadow healed the sick? For it is greater that a shadow should heal than the hem of a garment . . . When, however, He said these words, it was the deeds and works of His words that He spoke of: for when He said . . . 'The Father who abideth in Me, He doth the works,' what works did He mean, then, but the words He was speaking? . . . and the fruits of those same words was the faith of those (who believed): but when the disciples preached the Gospel, not some few like those, but the very nations believed . . . (Tract. lxxii). Did not that rich man go away from His presence sorrowful? . . . and yet afterwards, what one individual, having heard from Him, did not, that many did when He spake by the mouth of His disciples . . . Behold, He did greater works when spoken of by men believing than when speaking to men hearing. But there is yet this difficulty: that He did these 'greater works' by the apostles: whereas He saith as meaning not only them: . . . 'He that believeth in Me' . . . Listen! . . . 'He that believeth in Me, the works that I do, he also shall do': first, 'I do,' then 'he also shall do,' because I do that he may do. What works---but that from ungodly he should be made righteous? . . . Which thing Christ worketh in him, truly, but not without him. Yes, I may affirm this to be altogether greater than to create" [*The words 'to create' are not in the text of St. Augustine] "heaven and earth . . . for 'heaven and earth shall pass away'; but the salvation and justification of the predestinate shall remain . . . But also in the heavens . . . the angels are the works of Christ: and does that man do greater works than these, who co-operates with Christ in the work of his justification? . . . let him, who can, judge whether it be greater to create a righteous being than to justify an ungodly one. Certainly if both are works of equal power, the latter is a work of greater mercy."

"But there is no need for us to understand all the works of Christ, where He saith 'Greater than these shall he do.' For by 'these' He meant, perhaps, those which He was doing at that hour: now at that time He was speaking words of faith: . . . and certainly it is less to preach words of righteousness, which thing He did without us, than to justify the ungodly, which thing He so doth in us that we also do it ourselves."

Reply to Objection 3: When some particular work is proper to some agent, then that particular work is a sufficient proof of the whole power of that agent: thus, since the act of reasoning is proper to man, the mere fact that someone reasons about any particular proposition proves him to be a man. In like manner, since it is proper to God to work miracles by His own power, any single miracle worked by Christ by His own power is a sufficient proof that He is God.

OF (CHRIST'S) MIRACLES CONSIDERED SPECIFICALLY (FOUR ARTICLES)

We have now to consider each kind of miracle:
(1) The miracles which He worked in spiritual substances;
(2) The miracles which He worked in heavenly bodies;
(3) The miracles which He worked in man;
(4) The miracles which He worked in irrational creatures.

Whether those miracles were fitting which Christ worked in spiritual substances?

Objection 1: It would seem that those miracles were unfitting which Christ worked in spiritual substances. For among spiritual substances the holy angels are above the demons; for, as Augustine says (De Trin. iii): "The treacherous and sinful rational spirit of life is ruled by the rational, pious, and just spirit of life." But we read of no miracles worked by Christ in the good angels. Therefore neither should He have worked miracles in the demons.

Objection 2: Further, Christ's miracles were ordained to make known His Godhead. But Christ's Godhead was not to be made known to the demons: since this would have hindered the mystery of His Passion, according to 1 Cor. 2:8: "If they had known it, they would never have crucified the Lord of glory." Therefore He should not have worked miracles in the demons.

Objection 3: Further, Christ's miracles were ordained to the glory of God: hence it is written (Mat. 9:8) that "the multitudes seeing" that the man sick of the palsy had been healed by Christ, "feared, and glorified God that gave such power to men." But the demons have no part in glorifying God; since "praise is not seemly in the mouth of a sinner" (Ecclus. 15:9). For which reason also "He suffered them not to speak" (Mk. 1:34; Lk. 4:41) those things which reflected glory on Him. Therefore it seems that it was unfitting for Him to work miracles in the demons.

Objection 4: Further, Christ's miracles are ordained to the salvation of mankind. But sometimes the casting out of demons from men was detrimental to man, in some cases to the body: thus it is related (Mk. 9:24,25) that a demon at Christ's command, "crying out and greatly tearing" the man, "went out of him; and he became as dead, so that many said: He is dead"; sometimes also to things: as when He sent the demons, at their own request, into the swine, which they cast headlong into the sea; wherefore the inhabitants of those parts "besought Him that He would depart from their coasts" (Mat. 8:31-34). Therefore it seems unfitting that He should have worked such like miracles.

On the contrary, this was foretold (Zech. 13:2), where it is written: "I will take away . . . the unclean spirit out of the earth."

I answer that, The miracles worked by Christ were arguments for the faith which He taught. Now, by the power of His Godhead He was to rescue those who would believe in Him, from the power of the demons; according to Jn. 12:31: "Now shall the prince of this world be cast out." Consequently it was fitting that, among other miracles, He should also deliver those who were obsessed by demons.

Reply to Objection 1: Just as men were to be delivered by Christ from the power of the demons, so by Him were they to be brought to the companionship of the angels, according to Col. 1:20: "Making peace through the blood of His cross, both as to the things on earth and the things that are in heaven." Therefore it was not fitting to show forth to men other miracles as regards the angels, except by angels appearing to men: as happened in His Nativity, His Resurrection, and His Ascension.

Reply to Objection 2: As Augustine says (De Civ. Dei ix): "Christ was known to the demons just as much as He willed; and He willed just as far as there was need. But He was known to them, not as to the holy angels, by that which is eternal life, but by certain temporal effects of His power." First, when they saw that Christ was hungry after fasting they deemed Him not to be the Son of God. Hence, on Lk. 4:3, "If Thou be the Son of God," etc., Ambrose says: "What means this way of addressing Him? save that, though He knew that the Son of God was to come, yet he did not think that He had come in the weakness of the flesh?" But afterwards, when he saw Him work miracles, he had a sort of conjectural suspicion that He was the Son of God. Hence on Mk. 1:24, "I know who Thou art, the Holy one of God," Chrysostom [*Victor of Antioch. Cf. Catena Aurea] says that "he had no certain or firm knowledge of God's coming." Yet he knew that He was "the Christ promised in the Law," wherefore it is said (Lk. 4:41) that "they knew that He was Christ." But it was rather from suspicion than from certainty that they confessed Him to be the Son of God. Hence Bede says on Lk. 4:41: "The demons confess the Son of God, and, as stated farther on, 'they knew that He was Christ.' For when the devil saw Him weakened by His fast, He knew Him to be a real man: but when He failed to overcome Him by temptation, He doubted lest He should be the Son of God. And now from the power of His miracles He either knew, or rather suspected that He was the Son of God. His reason therefore for persuading the Jews to crucify Him was not that he deemed Him not to be Christ or the Son of God, but because he did not foresee that he would be the loser by His death. For the Apostle says of this mystery" (1 Cor. 2:7,8), "which is hidden from the beginning, that 'none of the princes of this world knew it,' for if they had known it they would never have crucified the Lord of glory."

Reply to Objection 3: The miracles which Christ worked in expelling demons were for the benefit, not of the demons, but of men, that they might glorify Him. Wherefore He forbade them to speak in His praise. First, to give us an example. For, as Athanasius says, "He restrained his speech, although he was confessing the truth; to teach us not to care about such things, although it may seem that what is said is true. For it is wrong to seek to learn from the devil when we have the Divine Scripture": Besides, it is dangerous, since the demons frequently mix falsehood with truth. Or, as Chrysostom [*Cyril of Alexandria, Comment. in Luc.] says: "It was not meet for them to usurp the prerogative of the apostolic office. Nor was it fitting that the mystery of Christ should be proclaimed by a corrupt tongue" because "praise is not seemly in the mouth of a sinner" [*Cf. Theophylact, Enarr. in Luc.]. Thirdly, because, as Bede says, "He did not wish the envy of the Jews to be aroused thereby" [*Bede, Expos. in Luc. iv, 41]. Hence "even the apostles are commanded to be silent about Him, lest, if His Divine majesty were proclaimed, the gift of His Passion should be deferred."

Reply to Objection 4: Christ came specially to teach and to work miracles for the good of man, and principally as to the salvation of his soul. Consequently, He allowed the demons, that He cast out, to do man some harm, either in his body or in his goods, for the salvation of man's soul---namely, for man's instruction. Hence Chrysostom says on Mat. 8:32 that Christ let the demons depart into the swine, "not as yielding to the demons, but first, to show . . . how harmful are the demons who attack men; secondly, that all might learn that the demons would not dare to hurt even the swine, except He allow them; thirdly, that they would have treated those men more grievously than they treated the swine, unless they had been protected by God's providence."

And for the same motives He allowed the man, who was being delivered from the demons, to suffer grievously for the moment; yet did He release him at once from that distress. By this, moreover, we are taught, as Bede says on Mk. 9:25, that "often, when after falling into sin we strive to return to God, we experience further and more grievous attacks from the old enemy. This he does, either that he may inspire us with a distaste for virtue, or that he may avenge the shame of having been cast out." For the man who was healed "became as dead," says Jerome, "because to those who are healed it is said, 'You are dead; and your life is hid with Christ in God'" (Col. 3:3)

Whether it was fitting that Christ should work miracles in the heavenly bodies?

Objection 1: It would seem that it was unfitting that Christ should work miracles in the heavenly bodies. For, as Dionysius says (Div. Nom. iv), "it beseems Divine providence not to destroy, but to preserve, nature." Now, the heavenly bodies are by nature incorruptible and unchangeable, as is proved De Coelo i. Therefore it was unfitting that Christ should cause any change in the order of the heavenly bodies.

Objection 2: Further, the course of time is marked out by the movement of the heavenly bodies, according to Gn. 1:14: "Let there be lights made in the firmament of heaven . . . and let them be for signs, and for seasons, and for days and years." Consequently if the movement of the heavenly bodies be changed, the distinction and order of the seasons is changed. But there is no report of this having been perceived by astronomers, "who gaze at the stars and observe the months," as it is written (Is. 47:13). Therefore it seems that Christ did not work any change in the movements of the heavenly bodies.

Objection 3: Further, it was more fitting that Christ should work miracles in life and when teaching, than in death: both because, as it is written (2 Cor. 13:4), "He was crucified through weakness, yet He liveth by the power of God," by which He worked miracles; and because His miracles were in confirmation of His doctrine. But there is no record of Christ having worked any miracles in the heavenly bodies during His lifetime: nay, more; when the Pharisees asked Him to give "a sign from heaven," He refused, as Matthew relates (12,16). Therefore it seems that neither in His death should He have worked any miracles in the heavenly bodies.

On the contrary, It is written (Lk. 23:44,45): "There was darkness over all the earth until the ninth hour; and the sun was darkened."

I answer that, As stated above ([4217]Q[43], A[4]) it behooved Christ's miracles to be a sufficient proof of His Godhead. Now this is not so sufficiently proved by changes wrought in the lower bodies, which changes can be brought about by other causes, as it is by changes wrought in the course of the heavenly bodies, which have been established by God alone in an unchangeable order. This is what Dionysius says in his epistle to Polycarp: "We must recognize that no alteration can take place in the order end movement of the heavens that is not caused by Him who made all and changes all by His word." Therefore it was fitting that Christ should work miracles even in the heavenly bodies.

Reply to Objection 1: Just as it is natural to the lower bodies to be moved by the heavenly bodies, which are higher in the order of nature, so is it natural to any creature whatsoever to be changed by God, according to His will. Hence Augustine says (Contra Faust. xxvi; quoted by the gloss on Rom. 11:24: "Contrary to nature thou wert grafted," etc.): "God, the Creator and Author of all natures, does nothing contrary to nature: for whatsoever He does in each thing, that is its nature." Consequently the nature of a heavenly body is not destroyed when God changes its course: but it would be if the change were due to any other cause.

Reply to Objection 2: The order of the seasons was not disturbed by the miracle worked by Christ. For, according to some, this gloom or darkening of the sun, which occurred at the time of Christ's passion, was caused by the sun withdrawing its rays, without any change in the movement of the heavenly bodies, which measures the duration of the seasons. Hence Jerome says on Mat. 27:45: "It seems as though the 'greater light' withdrew its rays, lest it should look on its Lord hanging on the Cross, or bestow its radiancy on the impious blasphemers." And this withdrawal of the rays is not to be understood as though it were in the sun's power to send forth or withdraw its rays: for it sheds its light, not from choice, but by nature, as Dionysius says (Div. Nom. iv). But the sun is said to withdraw its rays in so far as the Divine power caused the sun's rays not to reach the earth. On the other hand, Origen says this was caused by clouds coming between (the earth and the sun). Hence on Mat. 27:45 he says: "We must therefore suppose that many large and very dense clouds were massed together over Jerusalem and the land of Judea; so that it was exceedingly dark from the sixth to the ninth hour. Hence I am of opinion that, just as the other signs which occurred at the time of the Passion"---namely, "the rending of the veil, the quaking of the earth," etc.---"took place in Jerusalem only, so this also: . . . or if anyone prefer, it may be extended to the whole of Judea," since it is said that "'there was darkness over the whole earth,' which expression refers to the land of Judea, as may be gathered from 3 Kings 18:10, where Abdias says to Elias: 'As the Lord thy God liveth, there is no nation or kingdom whither my lord hath not sent to seek thee': which shows that they sought him among the nations in the neighborhood of Judea."

On this point, however, credence is to be given rather to Dionysius, who is an eyewitness as to this having occurred by the moon eclipsing the sun. For he says (Ep. ad Polycarp): "Without any doubt we saw the moon encroach on the sun," he being in Egypt at the time, as he says in the same letter. And in this he points out four miracles. The first is that the natural eclipse of the sun by interposition of the moon never takes place except when the sun and moon are in conjunction. But then the sun and moon were in opposition, it being the fifteenth day, since it was the Jewish Passover. Wherefore he says: "For it was not the time of conjunction."---The second miracle is that whereas at the sixth hour the moon was seen, together with the sun, in the middle of the heavens, in the evening it was seen to be in its place, i.e. in the east, opposite the sun. Wherefore he says: "Again we saw it," i.e. the moon, "return supernaturally into opposition with the sun," so as to be diametrically opposite, having withdrawn from the sun "at the ninth hour," when the darkness ceased, "until evening." From this it is clear that the wonted course of the seasons was not disturbed, because the Divine power caused the moon both to approach the sun supernaturally at an unwonted season, and to withdraw from the sun and return to its proper place according to the season. The third miracle was that the eclipse of the sun naturally always begins in that part of the sun which is to the west and spreads towards the east: and this is because the moon's proper movement from west to east is more rapid than that of the sun, and consequently the moon, coming up from the west, overtakes the sun and passes it on its eastward course. But in this case the moon had already passed the sun, and was distant from it by the length of half the heavenly circle, being opposite to it: consequently it had to return eastwards towards the sun, so as to come into apparent contact with it from the east, and continue in a westerly direction. This is what he refers to when he says: "Moreover, we saw the eclipse begin to the east and spread towards the western edge of the sun," for it was a total eclipse, "and afterwards pass away." The fourth miracle consisted in this, that in a natural eclipse that part of the sun which is first eclipsed is the first to reappear (because the moon, coming in front of the sun, by its natural movement passes on to the east, so as to come away first from the western portion of the sun, which was the first part to be eclipsed), whereas in this case the moon, while returning miraculously from the east to the west, did not pass the sun so as to be to the west of it: but having reached the western edge of the sun returned towards the east: so that the last portion of the sun to be eclipsed was the first to reappear. Consequently the eclipse began towards the east, whereas the sun began to reappear towards the west. And to this he refers by saying: "Again we observed that the occultation and emersion did not begin from the same point," i.e. on the same side of the sun, "but on opposite sides."

Chrysostom adds a fifth miracle (Hom. lxxxviii in Matth.), saying that "the darkness in this case lasted for three hours, whereas an eclipse of the sun lasts but a short time, for it is soon over, as those know who have seen one." Hence we are given to understand that the moon was stationary below the sun, except we prefer to say that the duration of the darkness was measured from the first moment of occultation of the sun to the moment when the sun had completely emerged from the eclipse.

But, as Origen says (on Mat. 27:45), "against this the children of this world object: How is it such a phenomenal occurrence is not related by any writer, whether Greek or barbarian?" And he says that someone of the name of Phlegon "relates in his chronicles that this took place during the reign of Tiberius Caesar, but he does not say that it occurred at the full moon." It may be, therefore, that because it was not the time for an eclipse, the various astronomers living then throughout the world were not on the look-out for one, and that they ascribed this darkness to some disturbance of the atmosphere. But in Egypt, where clouds are few on account of the tranquillity of the air, Dionysius and his companions were considerably astonished so as to make the aforesaid observations about this darkness.

Reply to Objection 3: Then, above all, was there need for miraculous proof of Christ's Godhead, when the weakness of human nature was most apparent in Him. Hence it was that at His birth a new star appeared in the heavens. Wherefore Maximus says (Serm. de Nativ. viii): "If thou disdain the manger, raise thine eyes a little and gaze on the new star in the heavens, proclaiming to the world the birth of our Lord." But in His Passion yet greater weakness appeared in His manhood. Therefore there was need for yet greater miracles in the greater lights of the world. And, as Chrysostom says (Hom. lxxxviii in Matth.): "This is the sign which He promised to them who sought for one saying: 'An evil and adulterous generation seeketh a sign; and a sign shall not be given it, but the sign of Jonas the prophet,' referring to His Cross . . . and Resurrection . . . For it was much more wonderful that this should happen when He was crucified than when He was walking on earth."

Day 278

Whether Christ worked miracles fittingly on men?

Objection 1: It would seem that Christ worked miracles unfittingly on men. For in man the soul is of more import than the body. Now Christ worked many miracles on bodies, but we do not read of His working any miracles on souls: for neither did He convert any unbelievers to the faith mightily, but by persuading and convincing them with outward miracles, nor is it related of Him that He made wise men out of fools. Therefore it seems that He worked miracles on men in an unfitting manner.

Objection 2: Further, as stated above ([4218]Q[43], A[2]), Christ worked miracles by Divine power: to which it is proper to work suddenly, perfectly, and without any assistance. Now Christ did not always heal men suddenly as to their bodies: for it is written (Mk. 8:22-25) that, "taking the blind man by the hand, He led him out of the town; and, spitting upon his eyes, laying His hands on him, He asked him if he saw anything. And, looking up, he said: I see men as it were trees walking. After that again He laid His hands upon his eyes, and he began to see, and was restored, so that he saw all things clearly." It is clear from this that He did not heal him suddenly, but at first imperfectly, and by means of His spittle. Therefore it seems that He worked miracles on men unfittingly.

Objection 3: Further, there is no need to remove at the same time things which do not follow from one another. Now bodily ailments are not always the result of sin, as appears from our Lord's words (Jn. 9:3): "Neither hath this man sinned, nor his parents, that he should be born blind." It was unseemly, therefore, for Him to forgive the sins of those who sought the healing of the body, as He is related to have done in the case of the man sick of the palsy (Mat. 9:2): the more that the healing of the body, being of less account than the forgiveness of sins, does not seem a sufficient argument for the power of forgiving sins.

Objection 4: Further, Christ's miracles were worked in order to confirm His doctrine, and witness to His Godhead, as stated above ([4219]Q[43], A[4]). Now no man should hinder the purpose of his own work. Therefore it seems unfitting that Christ commanded those who had been healed miraculously to tell no one, as appears from Mat. 9:30 and Mk. 8:26: the more so, since He commanded others to proclaim the miracles worked on them; thus it is related (Mk. 5:19) that, after delivering a man from the demons, He said to him: "Go into thy house to thy friends, and tell them, how great things the Lord hath done for thee."

On the contrary, It is written (Mk. 7:37): "He hath done all things well: He hath made both the deaf to hear and the dumb to speak."

I answer that, The means should be proportionate to the end. Now Christ came into the world and taught in order to save man, according to Jn. 3:17: "For God sent not His Son into the world to judge the world, but that the world may be saved by Him." Therefore it was fitting that Christ, by miraculously healing men in particular, should prove Himself to be the universal and spiritual Saviour of all.

Reply to Objection 1: The means are distinct from the end. Now the end for which Christ's miracles were worked was the health of the rational part, which is healed by the light of wisdom, and the gift of righteousness: the former of which presupposes the latter, since, as it is written (Wis. 1:4): "Wisdom will not enter into a malicious soul, nor dwell in a body subject to sins." Now it was unfitting that man should be made righteous unless he willed: for this would be both against the nature of righteousness, which implies rectitude of the will, and contrary to the very nature of man, which requires to be led to good by the free-will, not by force. Christ, therefore, justified man inwardly by the Divine power, but not against man's will. Nor did this pertain to His miracles, but to the end of His miracles. In like manner by the Divine power He infused wisdom into the simple minds of His disciples: hence He said to them (Lk. 21:15): "I will give you a mouth and wisdom" which "all your adversaries will not be able to resist and gainsay." And this, in so far as the enlightenment was inward, is not to be reckoned as a miracle, but only as regards the outward action---namely, in so far as men saw that those who had been unlettered and simple spoke with such wisdom and constancy. Wherefore it is written (Acts 4:13) that the Jews, "seeing the constancy of Peter and of John, understanding that they were illiterate and ignorant men . . . wondered."--- And though such like spiritual effects are different from visible miracles, yet do they testify to Christ's doctrine and power, according to Heb. 2:4: "God also bearing them witness by signs and wonders and divers miracles, and distributions of the Holy Ghost."

Nevertheless Christ did work some miracles on the soul of man, principally by changing its lower powers. Hence Jerome, commenting on Mat. 9:9, "He rose up and followed Him," says: "Such was the splendor and majesty of His hidden Godhead, which shone forth even in His human countenance, that those who gazed on it were drawn to Him at first sight." And on Mat. 21:12, "(Jesus) cast out all them that sold and bought," the same Jerome says: "Of all the signs worked by our Lord, this seems to me the most wondrous---that one man, at that time despised, could, with the blows of one scourge, cast out such a multitude. For a fiery and heavenly light flashed from His eyes, and the majesty of His Godhead shone in His countenance." And Origen says on Jn. 2:15 that "this was a greater miracle than when He changed water into wine, for there He shows His power over inanimate matter, whereas here He tames the minds of thousands of men." Again, on Jn. 18:6, "They went backward and fell to the ground," Augustine says: "Though that crowd was fierce in hate and terrible with arms, yet did that one word . . . without any weapon, smite them through, drive them back, lay them prostrate: for God lay hidden in that flesh." Moreover, to this must be referred what Luke says (4:30) ---namely, that Jesus, "passing through the midst of them, went His way," on which Chrysostom observes (Hom. xlviii in Joan.): "That He stood in the midst of those who were lying in wait for Him, and was not seized by them, shows the power of His Godhead"; and, again, that which is written Jn. 8:59, "Jesus hid Himself and went out of the Temple," on which Theophylact says: "He did not hide Himself in a corner of the Temple, as if afraid, or take shelter behind a wall or pillar; but by His heavenly power making Himself invisible to those who were threatening Him, He passed through the midst of them."

From all these instances it is clear that Christ, when He willed, changed the minds of men by His Divine power, not only by the bestowal of righteousness and the infusion of wisdom, which pertains to the end of miracles, but also by outwardly drawing men to Himself, or by terrifying or stupefying them, which pertains to the miraculous itself.

Reply to Objection 2: Christ came to save the world, not only by Divine power, but also through the mystery of His Incarnation. Consequently in healing the sick He frequently not only made use of His Divine power, healing by way of command, but also by applying something pertaining to His human nature. Hence on Lk. 4:40, "He, laying His hands on every one of them, healed them," Cyril says: "Although, as God, He might, by one word, have driven out all diseases, yet He touched them, showing that His own flesh was endowed with a healing virtue." And on Mk. 8:23, "Spitting upon his eyes, laying His hands on him," etc., Chrysostom [*Victor of Antioch] says: "He spat and laid His hands upon the blind man, wishing to show that His Divine word, accompanied by His operation, works wonders: for the hand signifies operation; the spittle signifies the word which proceeds from the mouth." Again, on Jn. 9:6, "He made clay of the spittle, and spread the clay upon the eyes of the blind man," Augustine says: "Of His spittle He made clay---because 'the Word was made flesh.'" Or, again, as Chrysostom says, to signify that it was He who made man of "the slime of the earth."

It is furthermore to be observed concerning Christ's miracles that generally what He did was most perfect. Hence on Jn. 2:10, "Every man at first setteth forth good wine," Chrysostom says: "Christ's miracles are such as to far surpass the works of nature in splendor and usefulness." Likewise in an instant He conferred perfect health on the sick. Hence on Mat. 8:15, "She arose and ministered to them," Jerome says: "Health restored by our Lord returns wholly and instantly."

There was, however, special reason for the contrary happening in the case of the man born blind, and this was his want of faith, as Chrysostom [*Victor of Antioch] says. Or as Bede observes on Mk. 8:23: "Whom He might have healed wholly and instantly by a single word, He heals little by little, to show the extent of human blindness, which hardly, and that only by degrees, can come back to the light: and to point out that each step forward in the way of perfection is due to the help of His grace."

Reply to Objection 3: As stated above ([4220]Q[43], A[2]), Christ worked miracles by Divine power. Now "the works of God are perfect" (Dt. 32:4). But nothing is perfect except it attain its end. Now the end of the outward healing worked by Christ is the healing of the soul. Consequently it was not fitting that Christ should heal a man's body without healing his soul. Wherefore on Jn. 7:23, "I have healed the whole man on a Sabbath day," Augustine says: "Because he was cured, so as to be whole in body; he believed, so as to be whole in soul." To the man sick of the palsy it is said specially, "Thy sins are forgiven thee," because, as Jerome observes on Mat. 9:5,6: "We are hereby given to understand that ailments of the body are frequently due to sin: for which reason, perhaps, first are his sins forgiven, that the cause of the ailment being removed, health may return." Wherefore, also (Jn. 4:14), it is said: "Sin no more, lest some worse thing happen to thee." Whence, says Chrysostom, "we learn that his sickness was the result of sin."

Nevertheless, as Chrysostom says on Mat. 9:5: "By how much a soul is of more account than a body, by so much is the forgiving of sins a greater work than healing the body; but because the one is unseen He does the lesser and more manifest thing in order to prove the greater and more unseen."

Reply to Objection 4: On Mat. 9:30, "See that no man know this," Chrysostom says: "If in another place we find Him saying, 'Go and declare the glory of God' (cf. Mk. 5:19; Lk. 8:39), that is not contrary to this. For He instructs us to forbid them that would praise us on our own account: but if the glory be referred to God, then we must not forbid, but command, that it be done."

Whether Christ worked miracles fittingly on irrational creatures?

Objection 1: It would seem that Christ worked miracles unfittingly on irrational creatures. For brute animals are more noble than plants. But Christ worked a miracle on plants as when the fig-tree withered away at His command (Mat. 21:19). Therefore Christ should have worked miracles also on brute animals.

Objection 2: Further, punishment is not justly inflicted save for fault. But it was not the fault of the fig-tree that Christ found no fruit on it, when fruit was not in season (Mk. 11:13). Therefore it seems unfitting that He withered it up.

Objection 3: Further, air and water are between heaven and earth. But Christ worked some miracles in the heavens, as stated above [4221](A[2]), and likewise in the earth, when it quaked at the time of His Passion (Mat. 27:51). Therefore it seems that He should also have worked miracles in the air and water, such as to divide the sea, as did Moses (Ex. 14:21); or a river, as did Josue (Josh. 3:16) and Elias (4 Kings 2:8); and to cause thunder to be heard in the air, as occurred on Mount Sinai when the Law was given (Ex. 19:16), and like to what Elias did (3 Kings 18:45).

Objection 4: Further, miraculous works pertain to the work of Divine providence in governing the world. But this work presupposes creation. It seems, therefore, unfitting that in His miracles Christ made use of creation: when, to wit, He multiplied the loaves. Therefore His miracles in regard to irrational creatures seem to have been unfitting.

On the contrary, Christ is "the wisdom of God" (1 Cor. 1:24), of whom it is said (Wis. 8:1) that "she ordereth all things sweetly."

I answer that, As stated above, Christ's miracles were ordained to the end that He should be recognized as having Divine power, unto the salvation of mankind. Now it belongs to the Divine power that every creature be subject thereto. Consequently it behooved Him to work miracles on every kind of creature, not only on man, but also on irrational creatures.

Reply to Objection 1: Brute animals are akin generically to man, wherefore they were created on the same day as man. And since He had worked many miracles on the bodies of men, there was no need for Him to work miracles on the bodies of brute animals. and so much the less that, as to their sensible and corporeal nature, the same reason applies to both men and animals, especially terrestrial. But fish, from living in water, are more alien from human nature; wherefore they were made on another day. On them Christ worked a miracle in the plentiful draught of fishes, related Lk. 5 and Jn. 21; and, again, in the fish caught by Peter, who found a stater in it (Mat. 17:26). As to the swine who were cast headlong into the sea, this was not the effect of a Divine miracle, but of the action of the demons, God permitting.

Reply to Objection 2: As Chrysostom says on Mat. 21:19: "When our Lord does any such like thing" on plants or brute animals, "ask not how it was just to wither up the fig-tree, since it was not the fruit season; to ask such a question is foolish in the extreme," because such things cannot commit a fault or be punished: "but look at the miracle, and wonder at the worker." Nor does the Creator "inflict" any hurt on the owner, if He choose to make use of His own creature for the salvation of others; rather, as Hilary says on Mat. 21:19, "we should see in this a proof of God's goodness, for when He wished to afford an example of salvation as being procured by Him, He exercised His mighty power on the human body: but when He wished to picture to them His severity towards those who wilfully disobey Him, He foreshadows their doom by His sentence on the tree." This is the more noteworthy in a fig-tree which, as Chrysostom observes (on Mat. 21:19), "being full of moisture, makes the miracle all the more remarkable."

Reply to Objection 3: Christ also worked miracles befitting to Himself in the air and water: when, to wit, as related Mat. 8:26, "He commanded the winds, and the sea, and there came a great calm." But it was not befitting that He who came to restore all things to a state of peace and calm should cause either a disturbance in the atmosphere or a division of waters. Hence the Apostle says (Heb. 12:18): "You are not come to a fire that may be touched and approached [Vulg.: 'a mountain that might be touched, and a burning fire'], and a whirlwind, and darkness, and storm."

At the time of His Passion, however, the "veil was rent," to signify the unfolding of the mysteries of the Law; "the graves were opened," to signify that His death gave life to the dead; "the earth quaked and the rocks were rent," to signify that man's stony heart would be softened, and the whole world changed for the better by the virtue of His Passion.

Reply to Objection 4: The multiplication of the loaves was not effected by way of creation, but by an addition of extraneous matter transformed into loaves; hence Augustine says on Jn. 6:1-14: "Whence He multiplieth a few grains into harvests, thence in His hands He multiplied the five loaves": and it is clearly by a process of transformation that grains are multiplied into harvests.

OF CHRIST'S TRANSFIGURATION (FOUR ARTICLES)

We now consider Christ's transfiguration; and here there are four points of inquiry:
(1) Whether it was fitting that Christ should be transfigured?
(2) Whether the clarity of the transfiguration was the clarity of glory?
(3) Of the witnesses of the transfiguration;
(4) Of the testimony of the Father's voice.

Whether it was fitting that Christ should be transfigured?

Objection 1: It would seem that it was not fitting that Christ should be transfigured. For it is not fitting for a true body to be changed into various shapes [figuras], but only for an imaginary body. Now Christ's body was not imaginary, but real, as stated above ([4222]Q[5], A[1]). Therefore it seems that it should not have been transfigured.

Objection 2: Further, figure is in the fourth species of quality, whereas clarity is in the third, since it is a sensible quality. Therefore Christ's assuming clarity should not be called a transfiguration.

Objection 3: Further, a glorified body has four gifts, as we shall state farther on ([4223]XP, Q[82]), viz. impassibility, agility, subtlety, and clarity. Therefore His transfiguration should not have consisted in an assumption of clarity rather than of the other gifts.

On the contrary, It is written (Mat. 17:2) that Jesus "was transfigured" in the presence of three of His disciples.

I answer that, Our Lord, after foretelling His Passion to His disciples, had exhorted them to follow the path of His sufferings (Mat. 16:21, 24). Now in order that anyone go straight along a road, he must have some knowledge of the end: thus an archer will not shoot the arrow straight unless he first see the target. Hence Thomas said (Jn. 14:5): "Lord, we know not whither Thou goest; and how can we know the way?" Above all is this necessary when hard and rough is the road, heavy the going, but delightful the end. Now by His Passion Christ achieved glory, not only of His soul, not only of His soul, which He had from the first moment of His conception, but also of His body; according to Luke (24:26): "Christ ought [Vulg.: 'ought not Christ'] to have suffered these things, and so to enter into His glory (?)." To which glory He brings those who follow the footsteps of His Passion, according to Acts 14:21: "Through many tribulations we must enter into the kingdom of God." Therefore it was fitting that He should show His disciples the glory of His clarity (which is to be transfigured), to which He will configure those who are His; according to Phil. 3:21: "(Who) will reform the body of our lowness configured [Douay: 'made like'] to the body of His glory." Hence Bede says on Mk. 8:39: "By His loving foresight He allowed them to taste for a short time the contemplation of eternal joy, so that they might bear persecution bravely."

Reply to Objection 1: As Jerome says on Mat. 17:2: "Let no one suppose that Christ," through being said to be transfigured, "laid aside His natural shape and countenance, or substituted an imaginary or aerial body for His real body. The Evangelist describes the manner of His transfiguration when he says: 'His face did shine as the sun, and His garments became white as snow.' Brightness of face and whiteness of garments argue not a change of substance, but a putting on of glory."

Reply to Objection 2: Figure is seen in the outline of a body, for it is "that which is enclosed by one or more boundaries" [*Euclid, bk i, def. xiv]. Therefore whatever has to do with the outline of a body seems to pertain to the figure. Now the clarity, just as the color, of a non-transparent body is seen on its surface, and consequently the assumption of clarity is called transfiguration.

Reply to Objection 3: Of those four gifts, clarity alone is a quality of the very person in himself; whereas the other three are not perceptible, save in some action or movement, or in some passion. Christ, then, did show in Himself certain indications of those three gifts---of agility, for instance, when He walked on the waves of the sea; of subtlety, when He came forth from the closed womb of the Virgin; of impassibility, when He escaped unhurt from the hands of the Jews who wished to hurl Him down or to stone Him. And yet He is not said, on account of this, to be transfigured, but only on account of clarity, which pertains to the aspect of His Person.

Whether this clarity was the clarity of glory?

Objection 1: It would seem that this clarity was not the clarity of glory. For a gloss of Bede on Mat. 17:2, "He was transfigured before them," says: "In His mortal body He shows forth, not the state of immortality, but clarity like to that of future immortality." But the clarity of glory is the clarity of immortality. Therefore the clarity which Christ showed to His disciples was not the clarity of glory.

Objection 2: Further, on Lk. 9:27 "(That) shall not taste death unless [Vulg.: 'till'] they see the kingdom of God," Bede's gloss says: "That is, the glorification of the body in an imaginary vision of future beatitude." But the image of a thing is not the thing itself. Therefore this was not the clarity of beatitude.

Objection 3: Further, the clarity of glory is only in a human body. But this clarity of the transfiguration was seen not only in Christ's body, but also in His garments, and in "the bright cloud" which "overshaded" the disciples. Therefore it seems that this was not the clarity of glory.

On the contrary, Jerome says on the words "He was transfigured before them" (Mat. 17:2): "He appeared to the Apostles such as He will appear on the day of judgment." And on Mat. 16:28, "Till they see the Son of Man coming in His kingdom," Chrysostom says: "Wishing to show with what kind of glory He is afterwards to come, so far as it was possible for them to learn it, He showed it to them in their present life, that they might not grieve even over the death of their Lord."

I answer that, The clarity which Christ assumed in His transfiguration was the clarity of glory as to its essence, but not as to its mode of being. For the clarity of the glorified body is derived from that of the soul, as Augustine says (Ep. ad Diosc. cxviii). And in like manner the clarity of Christ's body in His transfiguration was derived from His God. head, as Damascene says (Orat. de Transfig.) and from the glory of His soul. That the glory of His soul did not overflow into His body from the first moment of Christ's conception was due to a certain Divine dispensation, that, as stated above ([4224]Q[14], A[1], ad 2), He might fulfil the mysteries of our redemption in a passible body. This did not, however, deprive Christ of His power of outpouring the glory of His soul into His body. And this He did, as to clarity, in His transfiguration, but otherwise than in a glorified body. For the clarity of the soul overflows into a glorified body, by way of a permanent quality affecting the body. Hence bodily refulgence is not miraculous in a glorified body. But in Christ's transfiguration clarity overflowed from His Godhead and from His soul into His body, not as an immanent quality affecting His very body, but rather after the manner of a transient passion, as when the air is lit up by the sun. Consequently the refulgence, which appeared in Christ's body then, was miraculous: just as was the fact of His walking on the waves of the sea. Hence Dionysius says (Ep. ad Cai. iv): "Christ excelled man in doing that which is proper to man: this is shown in His supernatural conception of a virgin and in the unstable waters bearing the weight of material and earthly feet."

Wherefore we must not say, as Hugh of St. Victor [*Innocent III, De Myst. Miss. iv] said, that Christ assumed the gift of clarity in the transfiguration, of agility in walking on the sea, and of subtlety in coming forth from the Virgin's closed womb: because the gifts are immanent qualities of a glorified body. On the contrary, whatever pertained to the gifts, that He had miraculously. The same is to be said, as to the soul, of the vision in which Paul saw God in a rapture, as we have stated in the [4225]SS, Q[175], A[3], ad 2.

Reply to Objection 1: The words quoted prove, not that the clarity of Christ was not that of glory, but that it was not the clarity of a glorified body, since Christ's body was not as yet immortal. And just as it was by dispensation that in Christ the glory of the soul should not overflow into the body so was it possible that by dispensation it might overflow as to the gift of clarity and not as to that of impassibility.

Reply to Objection 2: This clarity is said to have been imaginary, not as though it were not really the clarity of glory, but because it was a kind of image representing that perfection of glory, in virtue of which the body will be glorious.

Reply to Objection 3: Just as the clarity which was in Christ's body was a representation of His body's future clarity, so the clarity which was in His garments signified the future clarity of the saints, which will be surpassed by that of Christ, just as the brightness of the snow is surpassed by that of the sun. Hence Gregory says (Moral. xxxii) that Christ's garments became resplendent, "because in the height of heavenly clarity all the saints will cling to Him in the refulgence of righteousness. For His garments signify the righteous, because He will unite them to Himself," according to Is. 49:18: "Thou shalt be clothed with all these as with an ornament."

The bright cloud signifies the glory of the Holy Ghost or the "power of the Father," as Origen says (Tract. iii in Matth.), by which in the glory to come the saints will be covered. Or, again, it may be said fittingly that it signifies the clarity of the world redeemed, which clarity will cover the saints as a tent. Hence when Peter proposed to make tents, "a bright cloud overshaded" the disciples.

Whether the witnesses of the transfiguration were fittingly chosen?

Objection 1: It would seem that the witnesses of the transfiguration were unfittingly chosen. For everyone is a better witness of things that he knows. But at the time of Christ's transfiguration no one but the angels had as yet any knowledge from experience of the glory to come. Therefore the witnesses of the transfiguration should have been angels rather than men.

Objection 2: Further, truth, not fiction, is becoming in a witness of the truth. Now, Moses and Elias were there, not really, but only in appearance; for a gloss on Lk. 9:30, "They were Moses and Elias," says: "It must be observed that Moses and Elias were there neither in body nor in soul"; but that those bodies were formed "of some available matter. It is also credible that this was the result of the angelic ministries, through the angels impersonating them." Therefore it seems that they were unsuitable witnesses.

Objection 3: Further, it is said (Acts 10:43) that "all the prophets give testimony" to Christ. Therefore not only Moses and Elias, but also all the prophets, should have been present as witnesses.

Objection 4: Further, Christ's glory is promised as a reward to all the faithful (2 Cor. 3:18; Phil. 3:21), in whom He wished by His transfiguration to enkindle a desire of that glory. Therefore He should have taken not only Peter, James, and John, but all His disciples, to be witnesses of His transfiguration.

On the contrary is the authority of the Gospel.

I answer that, Christ wished to be transfigured in order to show men His glory, and to arouse men to a desire of it, as stated above [4226](A[1]). Now men are brought to the glory of eternal beatitude by Christ---not only those who lived after Him, but also those who preceded Him; therefore, when He was approaching His Passion, both "the multitude that followed" and that "which went before," cried saying: 'Hosanna,'" as related Mat. 21:9, beseeching Him, as it were, to save them. Consequently it was fitting that witnesses should be present from among those who preceded Him---namely, Moses and Elias---and from those who followed after Him---namely, Peter, James, and John---that "in the mouth of two or three witnesses" this word might stand.

Reply to Objection 1: By His transfiguration Christ manifested to His disciples the glory of His body, which belongs to men only. It was therefore fitting that He should choose men and not angels as witnesses.

Reply to Objection 2: This gloss is said to be taken from a book entitled On the Marvels of Holy Scripture. It is not an authentic work, but is wrongly ascribed to St. Augustine; consequently we need not stand by it. For Jerome says on Mat. 17:3: "Observe that when the Scribes and Pharisees asked for a sign from heaven, He refused to give one; whereas here in order to increase the apostles' faith, He gives a sign from heaven, Elias coming down thence, whither he had ascended, and Moses arising from the nether world." This is not to be understood as though the soul of Moses was reunited to his body, but that his soul appeared through some assumed body, just as the angels do. But Elias appeared in his own body, not that he was brought down from the empyrean heaven, but from some place on high whither he was taken up in the fiery chariot.

Reply to Objection 3: As Chrysostom says on Mat. 17:3: "Moses and Elias are brought forward for many reasons." And, first of all, "because the multitude said He was Elias or Jeremias or one of the prophets, He brings the leaders of the prophets with Him; that hereby at least they might see the difference between the servants and their Lord." Another reason was " . . . that Moses gave the Law . . . while Elias . . . was jealous for the glory of God." Therefore by appearing together with Christ, they show how falsely the Jews "accused Him of transgressing the Law, and of blasphemously appropriating to Himself the glory of God." A third reason was "to show that He has power of death and life, and that He is the judge of the dead and the living; by bringing with Him Moses who had died, and Elias who still lived." A fourth reason was because, as Luke says (9:31), "they spoke" with Him "of His decease that He should accomplish in Jerusalem," i.e. of His Passion and death. Therefore, "in order to strengthen the hearts of His disciples with a view to this," He sets before them those who had exposed themselves to death for God's sake: since Moses braved death in opposing Pharaoh, and Elias in opposing Achab. A fifth reason was that "He wished His disciples to imitate the meekness of Moses and the zeal of Elias." Hilary adds a sixth reason---namely, in order to signify that He had been foretold by the Law, which Moses gave them, and by the prophets, of whom Elias was the principal.

Reply to Objection 4: Lofty mysteries should not be immediately explained to everyone, but should be handed down through superiors to others in their proper turn. Consequently, as Chrysostom says (on Mat. 17:3), "He took these three as being superior to the rest." For "Peter excelled in the love" he bore to Christ and in the power bestowed on him; John in the privilege of Christ's love for him on account of his virginity, and, again, on account of his being privileged to be an Evangelist; James on account of the privilege of martyrdom. Nevertheless He did not wish them to tell others what they had seen before His Resurrection; "lest," as Jerome says on Mat. 17:19, "such a wonderful thing should seem incredible to them; and lest, after hearing of so great glory, they should be scandalized at the Cross" that followed; or, again, "lest [the Cross] should be entirely hindered by the people" [*Bede, Hom. xviii; cf.

Catena Aurea]; and "in order that they might then be witnesses of spiritual things when they should be filled with the Holy Ghost" [*Hilary, in Matth. xvii].

Whether the testimony of the Father's voice, saying, "This is My beloved Son," was fittingly added?

Objection 1: It would seem that the testimony of the Father's voice, saying, "This is My beloved Son," was not fittingly added; for, as it is written (Job 33:14), "God speaketh once, and repeateth not the selfsame thing the second time." But the Father's voice had testified to this at the time of (Christ's) baptism. Therefore it was not fitting that He should bear witness to it a second time.

Objection 2: Further, at the baptism the Holy Ghost appeared under the form of a dove at the same time as the Father's voice was heard. But this did not happen at the transfiguration. Therefore it seems that the testimony of the Father was made in an unfitting manner.

Objection 3: Further, Christ began to teach after His baptism. Nevertheless, the Father's voice did not then command men to hear him. Therefore neither should it have so commanded at the transfiguration.

Objection 4: Further, things should not be said to those who cannot bear them, according to Jn. 16:12: "I have yet many things to say to you, but you cannot bear them now." But the disciples could not bear the Father's voice; for it is written (Mat. 17:6) that "the disciples hearing, fell upon their face, and were very much afraid." Therefore the Father's voice should not have been addressed to them.

On the contrary is the authority of the Gospel.

I answer that, The adoption of the sons of God is through a certain conformity of image to the natural Son of God. Now this takes place in two ways: first, by the grace of the wayfarer, which is imperfect conformity; secondly, by glory, which is perfect conformity, according to 1 Jn. 3:2: "We are now the sons of God, and it hath not yet appeared what we shall be: we know that, when He shall appear, we shall be like to Him, because we shall see Him as He is." Since, therefore, it is in baptism that we acquire grace, while the clarity of the glory to come was foreshadowed in the transfiguration, therefore both in His baptism and in His transfiguration the natural sonship of Christ was fittingly made known by the testimony of the Father: because He alone with the Son and Holy Ghost is perfectly conscious of that perfect generation.

Reply to Objection 1: The words quoted are to be understood of God's eternal speaking, by which God the Father uttered the only-begotten and co-eternal Word. Nevertheless, it can be said that God uttered the same thing twice in a bodily voice, yet not for the same purpose, but in order to show the divers modes in which men can be partakers of the likeness of the eternal Sonship.

Reply to Objection 2: Just as in the Baptism, where the mystery of the first regeneration was proclaimed, the operation of the whole Trinity was made manifest, because the Son Incarnate was there, the Holy Ghost appeared under the form of a dove, and the Father made Himself known in the voice; so also in the transfiguration, which is the mystery of the second regeneration, the whole Trinity appears---the Father in the voice, the Son in the man, the Holy Ghost in the bright cloud; for just as in baptism He confers innocence, signified by the simplicity of the dove, so in the resurrection will He give His elect the clarity of glory and refreshment from all sorts of evil, which are signified by the bright cloud.

Reply to Objection 3: Christ came to give grace actually, and to promise glory by His words. Therefore it was fitting at the time of His transfiguration, and not at the time of His baptism, that men should be commanded to hear Him.

Reply to Objection 4: It was fitting that the disciples should be afraid and fall down on hearing the voice of the Father, to show that the glory which was then being revealed surpasses in excellence the sense and faculty of all mortal beings; according to Ex. 33:20: "Man shall not see Me and live." This is what Jerome says on Mat. 17:6: "Such is human frailty that it cannot bear to gaze on such great glory." But men are healed of this frailty by Christ when He brings them into glory. And this is signified by what He says to them: "Arise, and fear not."

THE PASSION OF CHRIST (TWELVE ARTICLES)

In proper sequence we have now to consider all that relates to Christ's leaving the world. In the first place, His Passion; secondly, His death; thirdly, His burial; and, fourthly, His descent into hell.

With regard to the Passion, there arises a threefold consideration: (1) The Passion itself; (2) the efficient cause of the Passion; (3) the fruits of the Passion.

Under the first heading there are twelve points of inquiry:

(1) Whether it was necessary for Christ to suffer for men's deliverance?
(2) Whether there was any other possible means of delivering men?
(3) Whether this was the more suitable means?
(4) Whether it was fitting for Christ to suffer on the cross?
(5) The extent of His sufferings;
(6) Whether the pain which He endured was the greatest?
(7) Whether His entire soul suffered?
(8) Whether His Passion hindered the joy of fruition?
(9) The time of the Passion;
(10) The place;
(11) Whether it was fitting for Him to be crucified with robbers?
(12) Whether Christ's Passion is to be attributed to the Godhead?

Whether it was necessary for Christ to suffer for the deliverance of the human race?

Objection 1: It would seem that it was not necessary for Christ to suffer for the deliverance of the human race. For the human race could not be delivered except by God, according to Is. 45:21: "Am not I the Lord, and there is no God else besides Me? A just God and a Saviour, there is none besides Me." But no necessity can compel God, for this would be repugnant to His omnipotence. Therefore it was not necessary for Christ to suffer.

Objection 2: Further, what is necessary is opposed to what is voluntary. But Christ suffered of His own will; for it is written (Is. 53:7): "He was offered because it was His own will." Therefore it was not necessary for Him to suffer.

Objection 3: Further, as is written (Ps. 24:10): "All the ways of the Lord are mercy and truth." But it does not seem necessary that He should suffer on the part of the Divine mercy, which, as it bestows gifts freely, so it appears to condone debts without satisfaction: nor, again, on the part of Divine justice, according to which man had deserved everlasting condemnation. Therefore it does not seem necessary that Christ should have suffered for man's deliverance.

Objection 4: Further, the angelic nature is more excellent than the human, as appears from Dionysius (Div. Nom. iv). But Christ did not suffer to repair the angelic nature which had sinned. Therefore, apparently, neither was it necessary for Him to suffer for the salvation of the human race.

On the contrary, It is written (Jn. 3:14): "As Moses lifted up the serpent in the desert, so must the Son of man be lifted up, that whosoever believeth in Him may not perish, but may have life everlasting."

I answer that, As the Philosopher teaches (Metaph. v), there are several acceptations of the word "necessary." In one way it means anything which of its nature cannot be otherwise; and in this way it is evident that it was not necessary either on the part of God or on the part of man for Christ to suffer. In another sense a thing may be necessary from some cause quite apart from itself; and should this be either an efficient or a moving cause then it brings about the necessity of compulsion; as, for instance, when a man cannot get away owing to the violence of someone else holding him. But if the external factor which induces necessity be an end, then it will be said to be necessary from presupposing such end---namely, when some particular end cannot exist at all, or not conveniently, except such end be presupposed. It was not necessary, then, for Christ to suffer from necessity of compulsion, either on God's part, who ruled that Christ should suffer, or on Christ's own part, who suffered voluntarily. Yet it was necessary from necessity of the end proposed; and this can be accepted in three ways. First of all, on our part, who have been delivered by His Passion, according to John (3:14): "The Son of man must be lifted up, that whosoever believeth in Him may not perish, but may have life everlasting." Secondly, on Christ's part, who merited the glory of being exalted, through the lowliness of His Passion: and to this must be referred Lk. 24:26: "Ought not Christ to have suffered these things, and so to enter into His glory?" Thirdly, on God's part, whose determination regarding the Passion of Christ, foretold in the Scriptures and prefigured in the observances of the Old Testament, had to be fulfilled. And this is what St. Luke says (22:22): "The Son of man indeed goeth, according to that which is determined"; and (Lk. 24:44, 46): "These are the words which I spoke to you while I was yet with you, that all things must needs be fulfilled which are written in the law of Moses, and in the prophets, and in the psalms concerning Me: for it is thus written, and thus it behooved Christ to suffer, and to rise again from the dead."

Reply to Objection 1: This argument is based on the necessity of compulsion on God's part.

Reply to Objection 2: This argument rests on the necessity of compulsion on the part of the man Christ.

Reply to Objection 3: That man should be delivered by Christ's Passion was in keeping with both His mercy and His justice. With His justice, because by His Passion Christ made satisfaction for the sin of the human race; and so man was set free by Christ's justice: and with His mercy, for since man of himself could not satisfy for the sin of all human nature, as was said above ([4227]Q[1], A[2]), God gave him His Son to satisfy for him, according to Rom. 3:24,25: "Being justified freely by His grace, through the redemption that is in Christ Jesus, whom God hath proposed to be a propitiation, through faith in His blood." And this came of more copious mercy than if He had forgiven sins without satisfaction. Hence it is said (Eph. 2:4): "God, who is rich in mercy, for His exceeding charity wherewith He loved us, even when we were dead in sins, hath quickened us together in Christ."

Reply to Objection 4: The sin of the angels was irreparable; not so the sin of the first man ([4228]FP, Q[64], A[2]).

Whether there was any other possible way of human deliverance besides the Passion of Christ?

Objection 1: It would seem that there was no other possible way of human deliverance besides Christ's Passion. For our Lord says (Jn. 12:24): "Amen, amen I say to you, unless the grain of wheat falling into the ground dieth, itself remaineth alone; but if it die, it bringeth forth much fruit." Upon this St. Augustine (Tract. li) observes that "Christ called Himself the seed." Consequently, unless He suffered death, He would not otherwise have produced the fruit of our redemption.

Objection 2: Further, our Lord addresses the Father (Mat. 26:42): "My Father, if this chalice may not pass away but I must drink it, Thy will be done." But He spoke there of the chalice of the Passion. Therefore Christ's Passion could not pass away; hence Hilary says (Comm. 31 in Matth.): "Therefore the chalice cannot pass except He drink of it, because we cannot be restored except through His Passion."

Objection 3: Further, God's justice required that Christ should satisfy by the Passion in order that man might be delivered from sin. But Christ cannot let His justice pass; for it is written (2 Tim. 2:13): "If we believe not, He continueth faithful, He cannot deny Himself." But He would deny Himself were He to deny His justice, since He is justice itself. It seems impossible, then, for man to be delivered otherwise than by Christ's Passion.

Objection 4: Further, there can be no falsehood underlying faith. But the Fathers of old believed that Christ would suffer. Consequently, it seems that it had to be that Christ should suffer.

On the contrary, Augustine says (De Trin. xiii): "We assert that the way whereby God deigned to deliver us by the man Jesus Christ, who is mediator between God and man, is both good and befitting the Divine dignity; but let us also show that other possible means were not lacking on God's part, to whose power all things are equally subordinate."

I answer that, A thing may be said to be possible or impossible in two ways: first of all, simply and absolutely; or secondly, from supposition. Therefore, speaking simply and absolutely, it was possible for God to deliver mankind otherwise than by the Passion of Christ, because "no word shall be impossible with God" (Lk. 1:37). Yet it was impossible if some supposition be made. For since it is impossible for God's foreknowledge to be deceived and His will or ordinance to be frustrated, then, supposing God's foreknowledge and ordinance regarding Christ's Passion, it was not possible at the same time for Christ not to suffer, and for mankind to be delivered otherwise than by Christ's Passion. And the same holds good of all things foreknown and preordained by God, as was laid down in the [4229]FP, Q[14], A[13].

Reply to Objection 1: Our Lord is speaking there presupposing God's foreknowledge and predetermination, according to which it was resolved that the fruit of man's salvation should not follow unless Christ suffered.

Reply to Objection 2: In the same way we must understand what is here objected to in the second instance: "If this chalice may not pass away but I must drink of it"---that is to say, because Thou hast so ordained it---hence He adds: "Thy will be done."

Reply to Objection 3: Even this justice depends on the Divine will, requiring satisfaction for sin from the human race. But if He had willed to free man from sin without any satisfaction, He would not have acted against justice. For a judge, while preserving justice, cannot pardon fault without penalty, if he must visit fault committed against another---for instance, against another man, or against the State, or any Prince in higher authority. But God has no one higher than Himself, for He is the sovereign and common good of the whole universe. Consequently, if He forgive sin, which has the formality of fault in that it is committed against Himself, He wrongs no one: just as anyone else, overlooking a personal trespass, without satisfaction, acts mercifully and not unjustly. And so David exclaimed when he sought mercy: "To Thee only have I sinned" (Ps. 50:6), as if to say: "Thou canst pardon me without injustice."

Reply to Objection 4: Human faith, and even the Divine Scriptures upon which faith is based, are both based on the Divine foreknowledge and ordinance. And the same reason holds good of that necessity which comes of supposition, and of the necessity which arises of the Divine foreknowledge and will.

Day 279

Whether there was any more suitable way of delivering the human race than by Christ's Passion?

Objection 1: It would seem that there was some other more suitable way of delivering the human race besides Christ's Passion. For nature in its operation imitates the Divine work, since it is moved and regulated by God. But nature never employs two agents where one will suffice. Therefore, since God could have liberated mankind solely by His Divine will, it does not seem fitting that Christ's Passion should have been added for the deliverance of the human race.

Objection 2: Further, natural actions are more suitably performed than deeds of violence, because violence is "a severance or lapse from what is according to nature," as is said in De Coelo ii. But Christ's Passion brought about His death by violence. Therefore it would have been more appropriate had Christ died a natural death rather than suffer for man's deliverance.

Objection 3: Further, it seems most fitting that whatsoever keeps something unjustly and by violence, should be deprived of it by some superior power; hence Isaias says (52:3): "You were sold gratis, and you shall be redeemed without money." But the devil possessed no right over man, whom he had deceived by guile, and whom he held subject in servitude by a sort of violence. Therefore it seems most suitable that Christ should have despoiled the devil solely by His power and without the Passion.

On the contrary, St. Augustine says (De Trin. xiii): "There was no other more suitable way of healing our misery" than by the Passion of Christ.

I answer that, Among means to an end that one is the more suitable whereby the various concurring means employed are themselves helpful to such end. But in this that man was delivered by Christ's Passion, many other things besides deliverance from sin concurred for man's salvation. In the first place, man knows thereby how much God loves him, and is thereby stirred to love Him in return, and herein lies the perfection of human salvation; hence the Apostle says (Rom. 5:8): "God commendeth His charity towards us; for when as yet we were sinners . . . Christ died for us." Secondly, because thereby He set us an example of obedience, humility, constancy, justice, and the other virtues displayed in the Passion, which are requisite for man's salvation. Hence it is written (1 Pet. 2:21): "Christ also suffered for us, leaving you an example that you should follow in His steps." Thirdly, because Christ by His Passion not only delivered man from sin, but also merited justifying grace for him and the glory of bliss, as shall be shown later ([4230]Q[48], A[1];[4231] Q[49], AA[1], 5). Fourthly, because by this man is all the more bound to refrain from sin, according to 1 Cor. 6:20: "You are bought with a great price: glorify and bear God in your body." Fifthly, because it redounded to man's greater dignity, that as man was overcome and deceived by the devil, so also it should be a man that should overthrow the devil; and as man deserved death, so a man by dying should vanquish death. Hence it is written (1 Cor. 15:57): "Thanks be to God who hath given us the victory through our Lord Jesus Christ." It was accordingly more fitting that we should be delivered by Christ's Passion than simply by God's good-will.

Reply to Objection 1: Even nature uses several means to one intent, in order to do something more fittingly: as two eyes for seeing; and the same can be observed in other matters.

Reply to Objection 2: As Chrysostom [*Athanasius, Orat. De Incarn. Verb.] says: "Christ had come in order to destroy death, not His own, (for since He is life itself, death could not be His), but men's death. Hence it was not by reason of His being bound to die that He laid His body aside, but because the death He endured was inflicted on Him by men. But even if His body had sickened and dissolved in the sight of all men, it was not befitting Him who healed the infirmities of others to have his own body afflicted with the same. And even had He laid His body aside without any sickness, and had then appeared, men would not have believed Him when He spoke of His resurrection. For how could Christ's victory over death appear, unless He endured it in the sight of all men, and so proved that death was vanquished by the incorruption of His body?"

Reply to Objection 3: Although the devil assailed man unjustly, nevertheless, on account of sin, man was justly left by God under the devil's bondage. And therefore it was fitting that through justice man should be delivered from the devil's bondage by Christ making satisfaction on his behalf in the Passion. This was also a fitting means of overthrowing the pride of the devil, "who is a deserter from justice, and covetous of sway"; in that Christ "should vanquish him and deliver man, not merely by the power of His Godhead, but likewise by the justice and lowliness of the Passion," as Augustine says (De Trin. xiii).

Whether Christ ought to have suffered on the cross?

Objection 1: It would seem that Christ ought not to have suffered on the cross. For the truth ought to conform to the figure. But in all the sacrifices of the Old Testament which prefigured Christ the beasts were slain with a sword and afterwards consumed by fire. Therefore it seems that Christ ought not to have suffered on a cross, but rather by the sword or by fire.

Objection 2: Further, Damascene says (De Fide Orth. iii) that Christ ought not to assume "dishonoring afflictions." But death on a cross was most dishonoring and ignominious; hence it is written (Wis. 2:20): "Let us condemn Him to a most shameful death." Therefore it seems that Christ ought not to have undergone the death of the cross.

Objection 3: Further, it was said of Christ (Mat. 21:9): "Blessed is He that cometh in the name of the Lord." But death upon the cross was a death of malediction, as we read Dt. 21:23: "He is accursed of God that hangeth on a tree." Therefore it does not seem fitting for Christ to be crucified.

On the contrary, It is written (Phil. 2:8): "He became obedient unto death, even the death of the cross."

I answer that, It was most fitting that Christ should suffer the death of the cross.

First of all, as an example of virtue. For Augustine thus writes (QQ. lxxxiii, qu. 25): "God's Wisdom became man to give us an example in righteousness of living. But it is part of righteous living not to stand in fear of things which ought not to be feared. Now there are some men who, although they do not fear death in itself, are yet troubled over the manner of their death. In order, then, that no kind of death should trouble an upright man, the cross of this Man had to be set before him, because, among all kinds of death, none was more execrable, more fear-inspiring, than this."

Secondly, because this kind of death was especially suitable in order to atone for the sin of our first parent, which was the plucking of the apple from the forbidden tree against God's command. And so, to atone for that sin, it was fitting that Christ should suffer by being fastened to a tree, as if restoring what Adam had purloined; according to Ps. 68:5: "Then did I pay that which I took not away." Hence Augustine says in a sermon on the Passion [*Cf. Serm. ci De Tempore]: "Adam despised the command, plucking the apple from the tree: but all that Adam lost, Christ found upon the cross."

The third reason is because, as Chrysostom says in a sermon on the Passion (De Cruce et Latrone i, ii): "He suffered upon a high rood and not under a roof, in order that the nature of the air might be purified: and the earth felt a like benefit, for it was cleansed by the flowing of the blood from His side." And on Jn. 3:14: "The Son of man must be lifted up," Theophylact says: "When you hear that He was lifted up, understand His hanging on high, that He might sanctify the air who had sanctified the earth by walking upon it."

The fourth reason is, because, by dying on it, He prepares for us an ascent into heaven, as Chrysostom [*Athanasius, vide A, III, ad 2] says. Hence it is that He says (Jn. 12:32): "If I be lifted up from the earth, I will draw all things to Myself."

The fifth reason is because it is befitting the universal salvation of the entire world. Hence Gregory of Nyssa observes (In Christ. Resurr., Orat. i) that "the shape of the cross extending out into four extremes from their central point of contact denotes the power and the providence diffused everywhere of Him who hung upon it." Chrysostom [*Athanasius, vide A. III, ad 2] also says that upon the cross "He dies with outstretched hands in order to draw with one hand the people of old, and with the other those who spring from the Gentiles."

The sixth reason is because of the various virtues denoted by this class of death. Hence Augustine in his book on the grace of the Old and New Testament (Ep. cxl) says: "Not without purpose did He choose this class of death, that He might be a teacher of that breadth, and height, and length, and depth," of which the Apostle speaks (Eph. 3:18): "For breadth is in the beam, which is fixed transversely above; this appertains to good works, since the hands are stretched out upon it. Length is the tree's extent from the beam to the ground; and there it is planted---that is, it stands and abides---which is the note of longanimity. Height is in that portion of the tree which remains over from the transverse beam upwards to the top, and this is at the head of the Crucified, because He is the supreme desire of souls of good hope. But that part of the tree which is hidden from view to hold it fixed, and from which the entire rood springs, denotes the depth of gratuitous grace." And, as Augustine says (Tract. cxix in Joan.): "The tree upon which were fixed the members of Him dying was even the chair of the Master teaching."

The seventh reason is because this kind of death responds to very many figures. For, as Augustine says in a sermon on the Passion (Serm. ci De Tempore), an ark of wood preserved the human race from the waters of the Deluge; at the exodus of God's people from Egypt, Moses with a rod divided the sea, overthrew Pharaoh and saved the people of God. the same Moses dipped his rod into the water, changing it from bitter to sweet; at the touch of a wooden rod a salutary spring gushed forth from a spiritual rock; likewise, in order to overcome Amalec, Moses stretched forth his arms with rod in hand; lastly, God's law is entrusted to the wooden Ark of the Covenant; all of which are like steps by which we mount to the wood of the cross.

Reply to Objection 1: The altar of holocausts, upon which the sacrifices of animals were immolated, was constructed of timbers, as is set forth Ex. 27:, and in this respect the truth answers to the figure; but "it is not necessary for it to be likened in every respect, otherwise it would not be a likeness," but the reality, as Damascene says (De Fide Orth. iii). But. in particular, as Chrysostom [*Athanasius, vide A, III, ad 2] says: "His head is not cut off, as was done to John; nor was He sawn in twain, like Isaias, in order that His entire and indivisible body might obey death, and that there might be no excuse for them who want to divide the Church." While, instead of material fire, there was the spiritual fire of charity in Christ's holocaust.

Reply to Objection 2: Christ refused to undergo dishonorable sufferings which are allied with defects of knowledge, or of grace, or even of virtue, but not those injuries inflicted from without---nay, more, as is written Heb. 12:2: "He endured the cross, despising the shame."

Reply to Objection 3: As Augustine says (Contra Faust. xiv), sin is accursed, and, consequently, so is death, and mortality, which comes of sin. "But Christ's flesh was mortal, 'having the resemblance of the flesh of sin'"; and hence Moses calls it "accursed," just as the Apostle calls it "sin," saying (2 Cor. 5:21): "Him that knew no sin, for us He hath made sin"---namely, because of the penalty of sin. "Nor is there greater ignominy on that account, because he said: 'He is accursed of God.'" For, "unless God had hated sin, He would never have sent His Son to take upon Himself our death, and to destroy it. Acknowledge, then, that it was for us He took the curse upon Himself, whom you confess to have died for us." Hence it is written (Gal. 3:13): "Christ hath redeemed us from the curse of the law, being made a curse for us."

Whether Christ endured all suffering?

Objection 1: It would seem that Christ did endure all sufferings, because Hilary (De Trin. x) says: "God's only-begotten Son testifies that He endured every kind of human sufferings in order to accomplish the sacrament of His death, when with bowed head He gave up the ghost." It seems, therefore, that He did endure all human sufferings.

Objection 2: Further, it is written (Is. 52:13): "Behold My servant shall understand, He shall be exalted and extolled, and shall be exceeding high; as many as have been astonished at Him [Vulg.: 'thee'], so shall His visage be inglorious among men, and His form among the sons of men." But Christ was exalted in that He had all grace and all knowledge, at which many were astonished in admiration thereof. Therefore it seems that He was "inglorious," by enduring every human suffering.

Objection 3: Further, Christ's Passion was ordained for man's deliverance from sin, as stated above [4232](A[3]). But Christ came to deliver men from every kind of sin. Therefore He ought to have endured every kind of suffering.

On the contrary, It is written (Jn. 19:32): "The soldiers therefore came: and they broke the legs of the first, and of the other who was crucified with Him; but after they were come to Jesus, when they saw that He was already dead, they did not break His legs." Consequently, He did not endure every human suffering.

I answer that, Human sufferings may be considered under two aspects. First of all, specifically, and in this way it was not necessary for Christ to endure them all, since many are mutually exclusive, as burning and drowning; for we are dealing now with sufferings inflicted from without, since it was not beseeming for Him to endure those arising from within, such as bodily ailments, as already stated ([4233]Q[14], A[4]). But, speaking generically, He did endure every human suffering. This admits of a threefold acceptance. First of all, on the part of men: for He endured something from Gentiles and from Jews; from men and from women, as is clear from the women servants who accused Peter. He suffered from the rulers, from their servants and from the mob, according to Ps. 2:1,2: "Why have the Gentiles raged, and the people devised vain things? The kings of the earth stood up, and the princes met together, against the Lord and against His Christ." He suffered from friends and acquaintances, as is manifest from Judas betraying and Peter denying Him.

Secondly, the same is evident on the part of the sufferings which a man can endure. For Christ suffered from friends abandoning Him; in His reputation, from the blasphemies hurled at Him; in His honor and glory, from the mockeries and the insults heaped upon Him; in things, for He was despoiled of His garments; in His soul, from sadness, weariness, and fear; in His body, from wounds and scourgings.

Thirdly, it may be considered with regard to His bodily members. In His head He suffered from the crown of piercing thorns; in His hands and feet, from the fastening of the nails; on His face from the blows and spittle; and from the lashes over His entire body. Moreover, He suffered in all His bodily senses: in touch, by being scourged and nailed; in taste, by being given vinegar and gall to drink; in smell, by being fastened to the gibbet in a place reeking with the stench of corpses, "which is called Calvary"; in hearing, by being tormented with the cries of blasphemers and scorners; in sight, by beholding the tears of His Mother and of the disciple whom He loved.

Reply to Objection 1: Hilary's words are to be understood as to all classes of sufferings, but not as to their kinds.

Reply to Objection 2: The likeness is sustained, not as to the number of the sufferings and graces, but as to their greatness; for, as He was uplifted above others in gifts of graces, so was He lowered beneath others by the ignominy of His sufferings.

Reply to Objection 3: The very least one of Christ's sufferings was sufficient of itself to redeem the human race from all sins; but as to fittingness, it sufficed that He should endure all classes of sufferings, as stated above.

Whether the pain of Christ's Passion was greater than all other pains?

Objection 1: It would seem that the pain of Christ's Passion was not greater than all other pains. For the sufferer's pain is increased by the sharpness and the duration of the suffering. But some of the martyrs endured sharper and more prolonged pains than Christ, as is seen in St. Lawrence, who was roasted upon a gridiron; and in St. Vincent, whose flesh was torn with iron pincers. Therefore it seems that the pain of the suffering Christ was not the greatest.

Objection 2: Further, strength of soul mitigates pain, so much so that the Stoics held there was no sadness in the soul of a wise man; and Aristotle (Ethic. ii) holds that moral virtue fixes the mean in the passions. But Christ had most perfect strength of soul. Therefore it seems that the greatest pain did not exist in Christ.

Objection 3: Further, the more sensitive the sufferer is, the more acute will the pain be. But the soul is more sensitive than the body, since the body feels in virtue of the soul; also, Adam in the state of innocence seems to have had a body more sensitive than Christ had, who assumed a human body with its natural defects. Consequently, it seems that the pain of a sufferer in purgatory, or in hell, or even Adam's pain, if he suffered at all, was greater than Christ's in the Passion.

Objection 4: Further, the greater the good lost, the greater the pain. But by sinning the sinner loses a greater good than Christ did when suffering; since the life of grace is greater than the life of nature: also, Christ, who lost His life, but was to rise again after three days, seems to have lost less than those who lose their lives and abide in death. Therefore it seems that Christ's pain was not the greatest of all.

Objection 5: Further, the victim's innocence lessens the sting of his sufferings. But Christ died innocent, according to Jer. 9:19: "I was as a meek lamb, that is carried to be a victim." Therefore it seems that the pain of Christ's Passion was not the greatest.

Objection 6: Further, there was nothing superfluous in Christ's conduct. But the slightest pain would have sufficed to secure man's salvation, because from His Divine Person it would have had infinite virtue. Therefore it would have been superfluous to choose the greatest of all pains.

On the contrary, It is written (Lam. 1:12) on behalf of Christ's Person: "O all ye that pass by the way attend, and see if there be any sorrow like unto My sorrow."

I answer that, As we have stated, when treating of the defects assumed by Christ ([4234]Q[15], AA[5],6), there was true and sensible pain in the suffering Christ, which is caused by something hurtful to the body: also, there was internal pain, which is caused from the apprehension of something hurtful, and this is termed "sadness." And in Christ each of these was the greatest in this present life. This arose from four causes. First of all, from the sources of His pain. For the cause of the sensitive pain was the wounding of His body; and this wounding had its bitterness, both from the extent of the suffering already mentioned (A[5]) and from the kind of suffering, since the death of the crucified is most bitter, because they are pierced in nervous and highly sensitive parts---to wit, the hands and feet; moreover, the weight of the suspended body intensifies the agony. and besides this there is the duration of the suffering because they do not die at once like those slain by the sword. The cause of the interior pain was, first of all, all the sins of the human race, for which He made satisfaction by suffering; hence He ascribes them, so to speak, to Himself, saying (Ps. 21:2): "The words of my sins." Secondly, especially the fall of the Jews and of the others who sinned in His death chiefly of the apostles, who were scandalized at His Passion. Thirdly, the loss of His bodily life, which is naturally horrible to human nature.

The magnitude of His suffering may be considered, secondly, from the susceptibility of the sufferer as to both soul and body. For His body was endowed with a most perfect constitution, since it was fashioned miraculously by the operation of the Holy Ghost; just as some other things made by miracles are better than others, as Chrysostom says (Hom. xxii in Joan.) respecting the wine into which Christ changed the water at the wedding-feast. And, consequently, Christ's sense of touch, the sensitiveness of which is the reason for our feeling pain, was most acute. His soul likewise, from its interior powers, apprehended most vehemently all the causes of sadness.

Thirdly, the magnitude of Christ's suffering can be estimated from the singleness of His pain and sadness. In other sufferers the interior sadness is mitigated, and even the exterior suffering, from some consideration of reason, by some derivation or redundance from the higher powers into the lower; but it was not so with the suffering Christ, because "He permitted each one of His powers to exercise its proper function," as Damascene says (De Fide Orth. iii).

Fourthly, the magnitude of the pain of Christ's suffering can be reckoned by this, that the pain and sorrow were accepted voluntarily, to the end of men's deliverance from sin; and consequently He embraced the amount of pain proportionate to the magnitude of the fruit which resulted therefrom.

From all these causes weighed together, it follows that Christ's pain was the very greatest.

Reply to Objection 1: This argument follows from only one of the considerations adduced---namely, from the bodily injury, which is the cause of sensitive pain; but the torment of the suffering Christ is much more intensified from other causes, as above stated.

Reply to Objection 2: Moral virtue lessens interior sadness in one way, and outward sensitive pain in quite another; for it lessens interior sadness directly by fixing the mean, as being its proper matter, within limits. But, as was laid down in the [4235]FS, Q[64], A[2], moral virtue fixes the mean in the passions, not according to mathematical quantity, but according to quantity of proportion, so that the passion shall not go beyond the rule of reason. And since the Stoics held all sadness to be unprofitable, they accordingly believed it to be altogether discordant with reason, and consequently to be shunned altogether by a wise man. But in very truth some sadness is praiseworthy, as Augustine proves (De Civ. Dei xiv)---namely, when it flows from holy love, as, for instance, when a man is saddened over his own or others' sins. Furthermore, it is employed as a useful means of satisfying for sins, according to the saying of the Apostle (2 Cor. 7:10): "The sorrow that is according to God worketh penance, steadfast unto salvation." And so to atone for the sins of all men, Christ accepted sadness, the greatest in absolute quantity, yet not exceeding the rule of reason. But moral virtue does not lessen outward sensitive pain, because such pain is not subject to reason, but follows the nature of the body; yet it lessens it indirectly by redundance of the higher powers into the lower. But this did not happen in Christ's case, as stated above (cf. Q[14], A[1], ad 2; Q[45], A[2]).

Reply to Objection 3: The pain of a suffering, separated soul belongs to the state of future condemnation, which exceeds every evil of this life, just as the glory of the saints surpasses every good of the present life. Accordingly, when we say that Christ's pain was the greatest, we make no comparison between His and the pain of a separated soul. But Adam's body could not suffer, except he sinned. so that he would become mortal, and passible. And, though actually suffering, it would have felt less pain than Christ's body, for the reasons already stated. From all this it is clear that even if by impassibility Adam had suffered in the state of innocence, his pain would have been less than Christ's.

Reply to Objection 4: Christ grieved not only over the loss of His own bodily life, but also over the sins of all others. And this grief in Christ surpassed all grief of every contrite heart, both because it flowed from a greater wisdom and charity, by which the pang of contrition is intensified, and because He grieved at the one time for all sins, according to Is. 53:4: "Surely He hath carried our sorrows." But such was the dignity of Christ's life in the body, especially on account of the Godhead united with it, that its loss, even for one hour, would be a matter of greater grief than the loss of another man's life for howsoever long a time. Hence the Philosopher says (Ethic. iii) that the man of virtue loves his life all the more in proportion as he knows it to be better; and yet he exposes it for virtue's sake. And in like fashion Christ laid down His most beloved life for the good of charity, according to Jer. 12:7: "I have given My dear soul into the hands of her enemies."

Reply to Objection 5: The sufferer's innocence does lessen numerically the pain of the suffering, since, when a guilty man suffers, he grieves not merely on account of the penalty, but also because of the crime. whereas the innocent man grieves only for the penalty: yet this pain is more intensified by reason of his innocence, in so far as he deems the hurt inflicted to be the more undeserved. Hence it is that even others are more deserving of blame if they do not compassionate him. according to Is. 57:1: "The just perisheth, and no man layeth it to heart."

Reply to Objection 6: Christ willed to deliver the human race from sins not merely by His power, but also according to justice. And therefore He did not simply weigh what great virtue His suffering would have from union with the Godhead, but also how much, according to His human nature, His pain would avail for so great a satisfaction.

Whether Christ suffered in His whole soul?

Objection 1: It would seem that Christ did not suffer in His whole soul. For the soul suffers indirectly when the body suffers, inasmuch as it is the "act of the body." But the soul is not, as to its every part, the "act of the body"; because the intellect is the act of no body, as is said De Anima iii. Therefore it seems that Christ did not suffer in His whole soul.

Objection 2: Further, every power of the soul is passive in regard to its proper object. But the higher part of reason has for its object the eternal types, "to the consideration and consultation of which it directs itself," as Augustine says (De Trin. xii). But Christ could suffer no hurt from the eternal types, since they are nowise opposed to Him. Therefore it seems that He did not suffer in His whole soul.

Objection 3: Further, a sensitive passion is said to be complete when it comes into contact with the reason. But there was none such in Christ, but only "pro-passions"; as Jerome remarks on Mat. 26:37. Hence Dionysius says in a letter to John the Evangelist that "He endured only mentally the sufferings inflicted upon Him." Consequently it does not seem that Christ suffered in His whole soul.

Objection 4: Further, suffering causes pain: but there is no pain in the speculative intellect, because, as the Philosopher says (Topic. i), "there is no sadness in opposition to the pleasure which comes of consideration." Therefore it seems that Christ did not suffer in His whole soul.

On the contrary, It is written (Ps. 87:4) on behalf of Christ: "My soul is filled with evils": upon which the gloss adds: "Not with vices, but with woes, whereby the soul suffers with the flesh; or with evils, viz. of a perishing people, by compassionating them." But His soul would not have been filled with these evils except He had suffered in His whole soul. Therefore Christ suffered in His entire soul.

I answer that, A whole is so termed with respect to its parts. But the parts of a soul are its faculties. So, then, the whole soul is said to suffer in so far as it is afflicted as to its essence, or as to all its faculties. But it must be borne in mind that a faculty of the soul can suffer in two ways: first of all, by its own passion; and this comes of its being afflicted by its proper object; thus, sight may suffer from superabundance of the visible object. In another way a faculty suffers by a passion in the subject on which it is based; as sight suffers when the sense of touch in the eye is affected, upon which the sense of sight rests, as, for instance, when the eye is pricked, or is disaffected by heat.

So, then, we say that if the soul be considered with respect to its essence, it is evident that Christ's whole soul suffered. For the soul's whole essence is allied with the body, so that it is entire in the whole body and in its every part. Consequently, when the body suffered and was disposed to separate from the soul, the entire soul suffered. But if we consider the whole soul according to its faculties, speaking thus of the proper passions of the faculties, He suffered indeed as to all His lower powers; because in all the soul's lower powers, whose operations are but temporal, there was something to be found which was a source of woe to Christ, as is evident from what was said above [4236](A[6]). But Christ's higher reason did not suffer thereby on the part of its object, which is God, who was the cause, not of grief, but rather of delight and joy, to the soul of Christ. Nevertheless, all the powers of Christ's soul did suffer according as any faculty is said to be affected as regards its subject, because all the faculties of Christ's soul were rooted in its essence, to which suffering extended when the body, whose act it is, suffered.

Reply to Objection 1: Although the intellect as a faculty is not the act of the body, still the soul's essence is the act of the body, and in it the intellective faculty is rooted, as was shown in the [4237]FP, Q[77], AA[6],8.

Reply to Objection 2: This argument proceeds from passion on the part of the proper object, according to which Christ's higher reason did not suffer.

Reply to Objection 3: Grief is then said to be a true passion, by which the soul is troubled, when the passion in the sensitive part causes reason to deflect from the rectitude of its act, so that it then follows the passion, and has no longer free-will with regard to it. In this way passion of the sensitive part did not extend to reason in Christ, but merely subjectively, as was stated above.

Reply to Objection 4: The speculative intellect can have no pain or sadness on the part of its object, which is truth considered absolutely, and which is its perfection: nevertheless, both grief and its cause can reach it in the way mentioned above.

Whether Christ's entire soul enjoyed blessed fruition during the Passion?

Objection 1: It would seem that Christ's entire soul did not enjoy blessed fruition during the Passion. For it is not possible to be sad and glad at the one time, since sadness and gladness are contraries. But Christ's whole soul suffered grief during the Passion, as was stated above [4238](A[7]). Therefore His whole soul could not enjoy fruition.

Objection 2: Further, the Philosopher says (Ethic. vii) that, if sadness be vehement, it not only checks the contrary delight, but every delight; and conversely. But the grief of Christ's Passion was the greatest, as shown above [4239](A[6]); and likewise the enjoyment of fruition is also the greatest, as was laid down in the first volume of the [4240]FS, Q[34], A[3]. Consequently, it was not possible for Christ's whole soul to be suffering and rejoicing at the one time.

Objection 3: Further, beatific "fruition" comes of the knowledge and love of Divine things, as Augustine says (Doctr. Christ. i). But all the soul's powers do not extend to the knowledge and love of God. Therefore Christ's whole soul did not enjoy fruition.

On the contrary, Damascene says (De Fide Orth. iii): Christ's Godhead "permitted His flesh to do and to suffer what was proper to it." In like fashion, since it belonged to Christ's soul, inasmuch as it was blessed, to enjoy fruition, His Passion did not impede fruition.

I answer that, As stated above [4241](A[7]), the whole soul can be understood both according to its essence and according to all its faculties. If it be understood according to its essence, then His whole soul did enjoy fruition, inasmuch as it is the subject of the higher part of the soul, to which it belongs, to enjoy the Godhead: so that as passion, by reason of the essence, is attributed to the higher part of the soul, so, on the other hand, by reason of the superior part of the soul, fruition is attributed to the essence. But if we take the whole soul as comprising all its faculties, thus His entire soul did not enjoy fruition: not directly, indeed, because fruition is not the act of any one part of the soul; nor by any overflow of glory, because, since Christ was still upon earth, there was no overflowing of glory from the higher part into the lower, nor from the soul into the body. But since, on the contrary, the soul's higher part was not hindered in its proper acts by the lower, it follows that the higher part of His soul enjoyed fruition perfectly while Christ was suffering.

Reply to Objection 1: The joy of fruition is not opposed directly to the grief of the Passion, because they have not the same object. Now nothing prevents contraries from being in the same subject, but not according to the same. And so the joy of fruition can appertain to the higher part of reason by its proper act; but grief of the Passion according to the subject. Grief of the Passion belongs to the essence of the soul by reason of the body, whose form the soul is; whereas the joy of fruition (belongs to the soul) by reason of the faculty in which it is subjected.

Reply to Objection 2: The Philosopher's contention is true because of the overflow which takes place naturally of one faculty of the soul into another; but it was not so with Christ, as was said above.

Reply to Objection 3: Such argument holds good of the totality of the soul with regard to its faculties.

Whether Christ suffered at a suitable time?

Objection 1: It would seem that Christ did not suffer at a suitable time. For Christ's Passion was prefigured by the sacrifice of the Paschal lamb: hence the Apostle says (1 Cor. 5:7): "Christ our Pasch is sacrificed." But the paschal lamb was slain "on the fourteenth day at eventide," as is stated in Ex. 12:6. Therefore it seems that Christ ought to have suffered then; which is manifestly false: for He was then celebrating the Pasch with His disciples, according to Mark's account (14:12): "On the first day of the unleavened bread, when they sacrificed the Pasch"; whereas it was on the following day that He suffered.

Objection 2: Further, Christ's Passion is called His uplifting, according to Jn. 3:14: "So must the Son of man be lifted up." And Christ is Himself called the Sun of Justice, as we read Mal. 4:2. Therefore it seems that He ought to have suffered at the sixth hour, when the sun is at its highest point, and yet the contrary appears from Mk. 15:25: "It was the third hour, and they crucified Him."

Objection 3: Further, as the sun is at its highest point in each day at the sixth hour, so also it reaches its highest point in every year at the summer solstice. Therefore Christ ought to have suffered about the time of the summer solstice rather than about the vernal equinox.

Objection 4: Further, the world was enlightened by Christ's presence in it, according to Jn. 9:5: "As long as I am in the world I am the light of the world." Consequently it was fitting for man's salvation that Christ should have lived longer in the world, so that He should have suffered, not in young, but in old, age.

On the contrary, It is written (Jn. 13:1): "Jesus, knowing that His hour was come for Him to pass out of this world to the Father"; and (Jn. 2:4): "My hour is not yet come." Upon which texts Augustine observes: "When He had done as much as He deemed sufficient, then came His hour, not of necessity, but of will, not of condition, but of power." Therefore Christ died at an opportune time.

I answer that, As was observed above [4242](A[1]), Christ's Passion was subject to His will. But His will was ruled by the Divine wisdom which "ordereth all things" conveniently and "sweetly" (Wis. 8:1). Consequently it must be said that Christ's Passion was enacted at an opportune time. Hence it is written in De Qq. Vet. et Nov. Test., qu. lv: "The Saviour did everything in its proper place and season."

Reply to Objection 1: Some hold that Christ did die on the fourteenth day of the moon, when the Jews sacrificed the Pasch: hence it is stated (Jn. 18:28) that the Jews "went not into Pilate's hall" on the day of the Passion, "that they might not be defiled, but that they might eat the Pasch." Upon this Chrysostom observes (Hom. lxxxii in Joan.): "The Jews celebrated the Pasch then; but He celebrated the Pasch on the previous day, reserving His own slaying until the Friday, when the old Pasch was kept." And this appears to tally with the statement (Jn. 13:1-5) that "before the festival day of the Pasch . . . when supper was done" . . . Christ washed "the feet of the disciples."

But Matthew's account (26:17) seems opposed to this; that "on the first day of the Azymes the disciples came to Jesus, saying: Where wilt Thou that we prepare for Thee to eat the Pasch?" From which, as Jerome says, "since the fourteenth day of the first month is called the day of the Azymes, when the lamb was slain, and when it was full moon," it is quite clear that Christ kept the supper on the fourteenth and died on the fifteenth. And this comes out more clearly from Mk. 14:12: "On the first day of the unleavened bread, when they sacrificed the Pasch," etc.; and from Lk. 22:7: "The day of the unleavened bread came, on which it was necessary that the Pasch should be killed."

Consequently, then, others say that Christ ate the Pasch with His disciples on the proper day---that is, on the fourteenth day of the moon---"showing thereby that up to the last day He was not opposed to the law," as Chrysostom says (Hom. lxxxi in Matth.): but that the Jews, being busied in compassing Christ's death against the law, put off celebrating the Pasch until the following day. And on this account it is said of them that on the day of Christ's Passion they were unwilling to enter Pilate's hall, "that they might not be defiled, but that they might eat the Pasch."

But even this solution does not tally with Mark, who says: "On the first day of the unleavened bread, when they sacrificed the Pasch." Consequently Christ and the Jews celebrated the ancient Pasch at the one time. And as Bede says on Lk. 22:7,8: "Although Christ who is our Pasch was slain on the following day---that is, on the fifteenth day of the moon---nevertheless, on the night when the Lamb was sacrificed, delivering to the disciples to be celebrated, the mysteries of His body and blood, and being held and bound by the Jews, He hallowed the opening of His own immolation---that is, of His Passion."

But the words (Jn. 13:1) "Before the festival day of the Pasch" are to be understood to refer to the fourteenth day of the moon, which then fell upon the Thursday: for the fifteenth day of the moon was the most solemn day of the Pasch with the Jews: and so the same day which John calls "before the festival day of the Pasch," on account of the natural distinction of days, Matthew calls the first day of the unleavened bread, because, according to the rite of the Jewish festivity, the solemnity began from the evening of the preceding day. When it is said, then, that they were going to eat the Pasch on the fifteenth day of the month, it is to be understood that the Pasch there is not called the Paschal lamb, which was sacrificed on the fourteenth day, but the Paschal food---that is, the unleavened bread---which had to be eaten by the clean. Hence Chrysostom in the same passage gives another explanation, that the Pasch can be taken as meaning the whole feast of the Jews, which lasted seven days.

Reply to Objection 2: As Augustine says (De Consensu Evang. iii): "'It was about the sixth hour' when the Lord was delivered up by Pilate to be crucified," as John relates. For it "was not quite the sixth hour, but about the sixth---that is, it was after the fifth, and when part of the sixth had been entered upon until the sixth hour was ended---that the darkness began, when Christ hung upon the cross. It is understood to have been the third hour when the Jews clamored for the Lord to be crucified: and it is most clearly shown that they crucified Him when they clamored out. Therefore, lest anyone might divert the thought of so great a crime from the Jews to the soldiers, he says: 'It was the third hour, and they crucified Him,' that they before all may be found to have crucified Him, who at the third hour clamored for His crucifixion. Although there are not wanting some persons who wish the Parasceve to be understood as the third hour, which John recalls, saying: 'It was the Parasceve, about the sixth hour.' For 'Parasceve' is interpreted 'preparation.' But the true Pasch, which was celebrated in the Lord's Passion, began to be prepared from the ninth hour of the night---namely, when the chief priests said: 'He is deserving of death.'" According to John, then, "the sixth hour of the Parasceve" lasts from that hour of the night down to Christ's crucifixion; while, according to Mark, it is the third hour of the day.

Still, there are some who contend that this discrepancy is due to the error of a Greek transcriber: since the characters employed by them to represent 3 and 6 are somewhat alike.

Reply to Objection 3: According to the author of De Qq. Vet. et Nov. Test., qu. lv, "our Lord willed to redeem and reform the world by His Passion, at the time of year at which He had created it---that is, at the equinox. It is then that day grows upon night; because by our Saviour's Passion we are brought from darkness to light." And since the perfect enlightening will come about at Christ's second coming, therefore the season of His second coming is compared (Mat. 24:32,33) to the summer in these words: "When the branch thereof is now tender, and the leaves come forth, you know that summer is nigh: so you also, when you shall see all these things, know ye that it is nigh even at the doors." And then also shall be Christ's greatest exaltation.

Reply to Objection 4: Christ willed to suffer while yet young, for three reasons. First of all, to commend the more His love by giving up His life for us when He was in His most perfect state of life. Secondly, because it was not becoming for Him to show any decay of nature nor to be subject to disease, as stated above ([4243]Q[14], A[4]). Thirdly, that by dying and rising at an early age Christ might exhibit beforehand in His own person the future condition of those who rise again. Hence it is written (Eph. 4:13): "Until we all meet into the unity of faith, and of the knowledge of the Son of God, unto a perfect man, unto the measure of the age of the fulness of Christ."

Whether Christ suffered in a suitable place?

Objection 1: It would seem that Christ did not suffer in a suitable place. For Christ suffered according to His human nature, which was conceived in Nazareth and born in Bethlehem. Consequently it seems that He ought not to have suffered in Jerusalem, but in Nazareth or Bethlehem.

Objection 2: Further, the reality ought to correspond with the figure. But Christ's Passion was prefigured by the sacrifices of the Old Law, and these were offered up in the Temple. Therefore it seems that Christ ought to have suffered in the Temple, and not outside the city gate.

Objection 3: Further, the medicine should correspond with the disease. But Christ's Passion was the medicine against Adam's sin: and Adam was not buried in Jerusalem, but in Hebron; for it is written (Josh. 14:15): "The name of Hebron before was called Cariath-Arbe: Adam the greatest in the land of [Vulg.: 'among'] the Enacims was laid there."

On the contrary, It is written (Lk. 13:33): "It cannot be that a prophet perish out of Jerusalem." Therefore it was fitting that He should die in Jerusalem.

I answer that, According to the author of De Qq. Vet. et Nov. Test., qu. lv, "the Saviour did everything in its proper place and season," because, as all things are in His hands, so are all places: and consequently, since Christ suffered at a suitable time, so did He in a suitable place.

Reply to Objection 1: Christ died most appropriately in Jerusalem. First of all, because Jerusalem was God's chosen place for the offering of sacrifices to Himself: and these figurative sacrifices foreshadowed Christ's Passion, which is a true sacrifice, according to Eph. 5:2: "He hath delivered Himself for us, an oblation and a sacrifice to God for an odor of sweetness." Hence Bede says in a Homily (xxiii): "When the Passion drew nigh, our Lord willed to draw nigh to the place of the Passion"---that is to say, to Jerusalem---whither He came five days before the Pasch; just as, according to the legal precept, the Paschal lamb was led to the place of immolation five days before the Pasch, which is the tenth day of the moon.

Secondly, because the virtue of His Passion was to be spread over the whole world, He wished to suffer in the center of the habitable world---that is, in Jerusalem. Accordingly it is written (Ps. 73:12): "But God is our King before ages: He hath wrought salvation in the midst of the earth"---that is, in Jerusalem, which is called "the navel of the earth" [*Cf. Jerome's comment on Ezech. 5:5].

Thirdly, because it was specially in keeping with His humility: that, as He chose the most shameful manner of death, so likewise it was part of His humility that He did not refuse to suffer in so celebrated a place. Hence Pope Leo says (Serm. I in Epiph.): "He who had taken upon Himself the form of a servant chose Bethlehem for His nativity and Jerusalem for His Passion."

Fourthly, He willed to suffer in Jerusalem, where the chief priests dwelt, to show that the wickedness of His slayers arose from the chiefs of the Jewish people. Hence it is written (Acts 4:27): "There assembled together in this city against Thy holy child Jesus whom Thou hast anointed, Herod, and Pontius Pilate, with the Gentiles and the people of Israel."

Reply to Objection 2: For three reasons Christ suffered outside the gate, and not in the Temple nor in the city. First of all, that the truth might correspond with the figure. For the calf and the goat which were offered in most solemn sacrifice for expiation on behalf of the entire multitude were burnt outside the camp, as commanded in Lev. 16:27. Hence it is written (Heb. 13:27): "For the bodies of those beasts, whose blood is brought into the holies by the high-priest for sin, are burned without the camp. Wherefore Jesus also, that He might sanctify the people by His own blood, suffered without the gate."

Secondly, to set us the example of shunning worldly conversation. Accordingly the passage continues: "Let us go forth therefore to Him without the camp, bearing His reproach."

Thirdly, as Chrysostom says in a sermon on the Passion (Hom. i De Cruce et Latrone): "The Lord was not willing to suffer under a roof, nor in the Jewish Temple, lest the Jews might take away the saving sacrifice, and lest you might think He was offered for that people only. Consequently, it was beyond the city and outside the walls, that you may learn it was a universal sacrifice, an oblation for the whole world, a cleansing for all."

Reply to Objection 3: According to Jerome, in his commentary on Mat. 27:33, "someone explained 'the place of Calvary' as being the place where Adam was buried; and that it was so called because the skull of the first man was buried there. A pleasing interpretation indeed, and one suited to catch the ear of the people, but, still, not the true one. For the spots where the condemned are beheaded are outside the city and beyond the gates, deriving thence the name of Calvary---that is, of the beheaded. Jesus, accordingly, was crucified there, that the standards of martyrdom might be uplifted over what was formerly the place of the condemned. But Adam was buried close by Hebron and Arbe, as we read in the book of Jesus Ben Nave." But Jesus was to be crucified in the common spot of the condemned rather than beside Adam's sepulchre, to make it manifest that Christ's cross was the remedy, not only for Adam's personal sin, but also for the sin of the entire world.

Whether it was fitting for Christ to be crucified with thieves?

Objection 1: It would seem unfitting for Christ to have been crucified with thieves, because it is written (2 Cor. 6:14): "What participation hath justice with injustice?" But for our sakes Christ "of God is made unto us justice" (1 Cor. 1:30); whereas iniquity applies to thieves. Therefore it was not fitting for Christ to be crucified with thieves.

Objection 2: Further, on Mat. 26:35, "Though I should die with Thee, I will not deny Thee," Origen (Tract. xxxv in Matth.) observes: "It was not men's lot to die with Jesus, since He died for all." Again, on Lk. 22:33, "I am ready to go with Thee, both into prison and death," Ambrose says: "Our Lord's Passion has followers, but not equals." It seems, then, much less fitting for Christ to suffer with thieves.

Objection 3: Further, it is written (Mat. 27:44) that "the thieves who were crucified with Him reproached Him." But in Lk. 22:42 it is stated that one of them who were crucified with Christ cried out to Him: "Lord, remember me when Thou shalt come into Thy kingdom." It seems, then, that besides the blasphemous thieves there was another man who did not blaspheme Him: and so the Evangelist's account does not seem to be accurate when it says that Christ was crucified with thieves.

On the contrary, It was foretold by Isaias (53:12): "And He was reputed with the wicked."

I answer that, Christ was crucified between thieves from one intention on the part of the Jews, and from quite another on the part of God's ordaining. As to the intention of the Jews, Chrysostom remarks (Hom. lxxxvii in Matth.) that they crucified the two thieves, one on either side, "that He might be made to share their guilt. But it did not happen so; because mention is never made of them; whereas His cross is honored everywhere. Kings lay aside their crowns to take up the cross: on their purple robes, on their diadems, on their weapons, on the consecrated table, everywhere the cross shines forth."

As to God's ordinance, Christ was crucified with thieves, because, as Jerome says on Mat. 27:33: "As Christ became accursed of the cross for us, so for our salvation He was crucified as a guilty one among the guilty." Secondly, as Pope Leo observes (Serm. iv de Passione): "Two thieves were crucified, one on His right hand and one on His left, to set forth by the very appearance of the gibbet that separation of all men which shall be made in His hour of judgment." And Augustine on Jn. 7:36: "The very cross, if thou mark it well, was a judgment-seat: for the judge being set in the midst, the one who believed was delivered, the other who mocked Him was condemned. Already He has signified what He shall do to the quick and the dead; some He will set on His right, others on His left hand." Thirdly, according to Hilary (Comm. xxxiii in Matth.): "Two thieves are set, one upon His right and one upon His left, to show that all mankind is called to the sacrament of His Passion. But because of the cleavage between believers and unbelievers, the multitude is divided into right and left, those on the right being saved by the justification of faith." Fourthly, because, as Bede says on Mk. 15:27: "The thieves crucified with our Lord denote those who, believing in and confessing Christ, either endure the conflict of martyrdom or keep the institutes of stricter observance. But those who do the like for the sake of everlasting glory are denoted by the faith of the thief on the right; while others who do so for the sake of human applause copy the mind and behavior of the one on the left."

Reply to Objection 1: Just as Christ was not obliged to die, but willingly submitted to death so as to vanquish death by His power: so neither deserved He to be classed with thieves; but willed to be reputed with the ungodly that He might destroy ungodliness by His power. Accordingly, Chrysostom says (Hom. lxxxiv in Joan.) that "to convert the thief upon the cross, and lead him into paradise, was no less a wonder than to shake the rocks."

Reply to Objection 2: It was not fitting that anyone else should die with Christ from the same cause as Christ: hence Origen continues thus in the same passage: "All had been under sin, and all required that another should die for them, not they for others."

Reply to Objection 3: As Augustine says (De Consensu Evang. iii): We can understand Matthew "as putting the plural for the singular" when he said "the thieves reproached Him." Or it may be said, with Jerome, that "at first both blasphemed Him, but afterwards one believed in Him on witnessing the wonders."

Day 280

Whether Christ's Passion is to be attributed to His Godhead?

Objection 1: It would seem that Christ's Passion is to be attributed to His Godhead; for it is written (1 Cor. 2:8): "If they had known it, they would never have crucified the Lord of glory." But Christ is the Lord of glory in respect of His Godhead. Therefore Christ's Passion is attributed to Him in respect of His Godhead.

Objection 2: Further, the principle of men's salvation is the Godhead Itself, according to Ps. 36:39: "But the salvation of the just is from the Lord." Consequently, if Christ's Passion did not appertain to His Godhead, it would seem that it could not produce fruit in us.

Objection 3: Further, the Jews were punished for slaying Christ as for murdering God Himself; as is proved by the gravity of the punishment. Now this would not be so if the Passion were not attributed to the Godhead. Therefore Christ's Passion should be so attributed.

On the contrary, Athanasius says (Ep. ad Epict.): "The Word is impassible whose Nature is Divine." But what is impassible cannot suffer. Consequently, Christ's Passion did not concern His Godhead.

I answer that, As stated above ([4244]Q[2], AA[1],2,3,6), the union of the human nature with the Divine was effected in the Person, in the hypostasis, in the suppositum, yet observing the distinction of natures; so that it is the same Person and hypostasis of the Divine and human natures, while each nature retains that which is proper to it. And therefore, as stated above ([4245]Q[16], A[4]), the Passion is to be attributed to the suppositum of the Divine Nature, not because of the Divine Nature, which is impassible, but by reason of the human nature. Hence, in a Synodal Epistle of Cyril [*Act. Conc. Ephes., P. i, cap. 26] we read: "If any man does not confess that the Word of God suffered in the flesh and was crucified in the flesh, let him be anathema." Therefore Christ's Passion belongs to the "suppositum" of the Divine Nature by reason of the passible nature assumed, but not on account of the impassible Divine Nature.

Reply to Objection 1: The Lord of glory is said to be crucified, not as the Lord of glory, but as a man capable of suffering.

Reply to Objection 2: As is said in a sermon of the Council of Ephesus [*P. iii, cap. 10], "Christ's death being, as it were, God's death"---namely, by union in Person---"destroyed death"; since He who suffered "was both God and man. For God's Nature was not wounded, nor did It undergo any change by those sufferings."

Reply to Objection 3: As the passage quoted goes on to say: "The Jews did not crucify one who was simply a man; they inflicted their presumptions upon God. For suppose a prince to speak by word of mouth, and that his words are committed to writing on a parchment and sent out to the cities, and that some rebel tears up the document, he will be led forth to endure the death sentence, not for merely tearing up a document, but as destroying the imperial message. Let not the Jew, then, stand in security, as crucifying a mere man; since what he saw was as the parchment, but what was hidden under it was the imperial Word, the Son by nature, not the mere utterance of a tongue."

OF THE EFFICIENT CAUSE OF CHRIST'S PASSION (SIX ARTICLES)

We have now to consider the efficient cause of Christ's Passion, concerning which there are six points of inquiry:

(1) Whether Christ was slain by others, or by Himself?
(2) From what motive did He deliver Himself up to the Passion?
(3) Whether the Father delivered Him up to suffer?
(4) Whether it was fitting that He should suffer at the hands of the Gentiles, or rather of the Jews?
(5) Whether His slayers knew who He was?
(6) Of the sin of them who slew Christ.

Whether Christ was slain by another or by Himself?

Objection 1: It would seem that Christ was not slain by another, but by Himself. For He says Himself (Jn. 10:18): "No men taketh My life from Me, but I lay it down of Myself." But he is said to kill another who takes away his life. Consequently, Christ was not slain by others, but by Himself.

Objection 2: Further, those slain by others sink gradually from exhausted nature, and this is strikingly apparent in the crucified: for, as Augustine says (De Trin. iv): "Those who were crucified were tormented with a lingering death." But this did not happen in Christ's case, since "crying out, with a loud voice, He yielded up the ghost" (Mat. 27:50). Therefore Christ was not slain by others, but by Himself.

Objection 3: Further, those slain by others suffer a violent death, and hence die unwillingly, because violent is opposed to voluntary. But Augustine says (De Trin. iv): "Christ's spirit did not quit the flesh unwillingly, but because He willed it, when He willed it, and as He willed it." Consequently Christ was not slain by others, but by Himself.

On the contrary, It is written (Lk. 18:33): "After they have scourged Him, they will put him to death."

408

I answer that, A thing may cause an effect in two ways: in the first instance by acting directly so as to produce the effect; and in this manner Christ's persecutors slew Him because they inflicted on Him what was a sufficient cause of death, and with the intention of slaying Him, and the effect followed, since death resulted from that cause. In another way someone causes an effect indirectly---that is, by not preventing it when he can do so; just as one person is said to drench another by not closing the window through which the shower is entering: and in this way Christ was the cause of His own Passion and death. For He could have prevented His Passion and death. Firstly, by holding His enemies in check, so that they would not have been eager to slay Him, or would have been powerless to do so. Secondly, because His spirit had the power of preserving His fleshly nature from the infliction of any injury; and Christ's soul had this power, because it was united in unity of person with the Divine Word, as Augustine says (De Trin. iv). Therefore, since Christ's soul did not repel the injury inflicted on His body, but willed His corporeal nature to succumb to such injury, He is said to have laid down His life, or to have died voluntarily.

Reply to Objection 1: When we hear the words, "No man taketh away My life from Me," we must understand "against My will": for that is properly said to be "taken away" which one takes from someone who is unwilling and unable to resist.

Reply to Objection 2: In order for Christ to show that the Passion inflicted by violence did not take away His life, He preserved the strength of His bodily nature, so that at the last moment He was able to cry out with a loud voice: and hence His death should be computed among His other miracles. Accordingly it is written (Mk. 15:39): "And the centurion who stood over against Him, seeing that crying out in this manner, He had given up the ghost, said: Indeed, this man was the Son of God." It was also a subject of wonder in Christ's death that He died sooner than the others who were tormented with the same suffering. Hence John says (19:32) that "they broke the legs of the first, and of the other that was crucified with Him," that they might die more speedily; "but after they were come to Jesus, when they saw that He was already dead, they did not break His legs." Mark also states (15:44) that "Pilate wondered that He should be already dead." For as of His own will His bodily nature kept its vigor to the end, so likewise, when He willed, He suddenly succumbed to the injury inflicted.

Reply to Objection 3: Christ at the same time suffered violence in order to die, and died, nevertheless, voluntarily; because violence was inflicted on His body, which, however, prevailed over His body only so far as He willed it.

Whether Christ died out of obedience?

Objection 1: It would seem that Christ did not die out of obedience. For obedience is referred to a command. But we do not read that Christ was commanded to suffer. Therefore He did not suffer out of obedience.

Objection 2: Further, a man is said to do from obedience what he does from necessity of precept. But Christ did not suffer necessarily, but voluntarily. Therefore He did not suffer out of obedience.

Objection 3: Further, charity is a more excellent virtue than obedience. But we read that Christ suffered out of charity, according to Eph. 5:2: "Walk in love, as Christ also has loved us, and delivered Himself up for us." Therefore Christ's Passion ought to be ascribed rather to charity than to obedience.

On the contrary, It is written (Phil. 2:8): "He became obedient" to the Father "unto death."

I answer that, It was befitting that Christ should suffer out of obedience. First of all, because it was in keeping with human justification, that "as by the disobedience of one man, many were made sinners: so also by the obedience of one, many shall be made just," as is written Rom. 5:19. Secondly, it was suitable for reconciling man with God: hence it is written (Rom. 5:10): "We are reconciled to God by the death of His Son," in so far as Christ's death was a most acceptable sacrifice to God, according to Eph. 5:2: "He delivered Himself for us an oblation and a sacrifice to God for an odor of sweetness." Now obedience is preferred to all sacrifices. according to 1 Kings 15:22: "Obedience is better than sacrifices." Therefore it was fitting that the sacrifice of Christ's Passion and death should proceed from obedience. Thirdly, it was in keeping with His victory whereby He triumphed over death and its author; because a soldier cannot conquer unless he obey his captain. And so the Man-Christ secured the victory through being obedient to God, according to Prov. 21:28: "An obedient man shall speak of victory."

Reply to Objection 1: Christ received a command from the Father to suffer. For it is written (Jn. 10:18): "I have power to lay down My life, and I have power to take it up again: (and) this commandment have I received of My Father"---namely, of laying down His life and of resuming it again. "From which," as Chrysostom says (Hom. lix in Joan.), it is not to be understood "that at first He awaited the command, and that He had need to be told, but He showed the proceeding to be a voluntary one, and destroyed suspicion of opposition" to the Father. Yet because the Old Law was ended by Christ's death, according to His dying words, "It is consummated" (Jn. 19:30), it may be understood that by His suffering He fulfilled all the precepts of the Old Law. He fulfilled those of the moral order which are founded on the precepts of charity, inasmuch as He suffered both out of love of the Father, according to Jn. 14:31: "That the world may know that I love the Father, and as the Father hath given Me commandment, so do I: arise, let us go hence"---namely, to the place of His Passion: and out of love of His neighbor, according to Gal. 2:20: "He loved me, and delivered Himself up for me." Christ likewise by His Passion fulfilled the ceremonial precepts of the Law, which are chiefly ordained for sacrifices and oblations, in so far as all the ancient sacrifices were figures of that true sacrifice which the dying Christ offered for us. Hence it is written (Col. 2:16,17): "Let no man judge you in meat or drink, or in respect of a festival day, or of the new moon, or of the sabbaths, which are a shadow of things to come, but the body is Christ's," for the reason that Christ is compared to them as a body is to a shadow. Christ also by His Passion fulfilled the judicial precepts of the Law, which are chiefly ordained for making compensation to them who have suffered wrong, since, as is written Ps. 68:5: He "paid that which" He "took not away," suffering Himself to be fastened to a tree on account of the apple which man had plucked from the tree against God's command.

Reply to Objection 2: Although obedience implies necessity with regard to the thing commanded, nevertheless it implies free-will with regard to the fulfilling of the precept. And, indeed, such was Christ's obedience, for, although His Passion and death, considered in themselves, were repugnant to the natural will, yet Christ resolved to fulfill God's will with respect to the same, according to Ps.

39:9: "That I should do Thy will: O my God, I have desired it." Hence He said (Mat. 26:42): "If this chalice may not pass away, but I must drink it, Thy will be done."

Reply to Objection 3: For the same reason Christ suffered out of charity and out of obedience; because He fulfilled even the precepts of charity out of obedience only; and was obedient, out of love, to the Father's command.

Whether God the Father delivered up Christ to the Passion?

Objection 1: It would seem that God the Father did not deliver up Christ to the Passion. For it is a wicked and cruel act to hand over an innocent man to torment and death. But, as it is written (Dt. 32:4): "God is faithful, and without any iniquity." Therefore He did not hand over the innocent Christ to His Passion and death.

Objection 2: Further, it is not likely that a man be given over to death by himself and by another also. But Christ gave Himself up for us, as it is written (Is. 53:12): "He hath delivered His soul unto death." Consequently it does not appear that God the Father delivered Him up.

Objection 3: Further, Judas is held to be guilty because he betrayed Christ to the Jews, according to Jn. 6:71: "One of you is a devil," alluding to Judas, who was to betray Him. The Jews are likewise reviled for delivering Him up to Pilate; as we read in Jn. 18:35: "Thy own nation, and the chief priests have delivered Thee up to me." Moreover, as is related in Jn. 19:16: Pilate "delivered Him to them to be crucified"; and according to 2 Cor. 6:14: there is no "participation of justice with injustice." It seems, therefore, that God the Father did not deliver up Christ to His Passion.

On the contrary, It is written (Rom. 8:32): "God hath not spared His own Son, but delivered Him up for us all."

I answer that, As observed above [4246](A[2]), Christ suffered voluntarily out of obedience to the Father. Hence in three respects God the Father did deliver up Christ to the Passion. In the first way, because by His eternal will He preordained Christ's Passion for the deliverance of the human race, according to the words of Isaias (53:6): "The Lord hath laid on Him the iniquities of us all"; and again (Is. 53:10): "The Lord was pleased to bruise Him in infirmity." Secondly, inasmuch as, by the infusion of charity, He inspired Him with the will to suffer for us; hence we read in the same passage: "He was offered because it was His own will" (Is. 53:7). Thirdly, by not shielding Him from the Passion, but abandoning Him to His persecutors: thus we read (Mat. 27:46) that Christ, while hanging upon the cross, cried out: "My God, My God, why hast Thou forsaken Me?" because, to wit, He left Him to the power of His persecutors, as Augustine says (Ep. cxl).

Reply to Objection 1: It is indeed a wicked and cruel act to hand over an innocent man to torment and to death against his will. Yet God the Father did not so deliver up Christ, but inspired Him with the will to suffer for us. God's "severity" (cf. Rom. 11:22) is thereby shown, for He would not remit sin without penalty: and the Apostle indicates this when (Rom. 8:32) he says: "God spared not even His own Son." Likewise His "goodness" (Rom. 11:22) shines forth, since by no penalty endured could man pay Him enough satisfaction: and the Apostle denotes this when he says: "He delivered Him up for us all": and, again (Rom. 3:25): "Whom"---that is to say, Christ---God "hath proposed to be a propitiation through faith in His blood."

Reply to Objection 2: Christ as God delivered Himself up to death by the same will and action as that by which the Father delivered Him up; but as man He gave Himself up by a will inspired of the Father. Consequently there is no contrariety in the Father delivering Him up and in Christ delivering Himself up.

Reply to Objection 3: The same act, for good or evil, is judged differently, accordingly as it proceeds from a different source. The Father delivered up Christ, and Christ surrendered Himself, from charity, and consequently we give praise to both: but Judas betrayed Christ from greed, the Jews from envy, and Pilate from worldly fear, for he stood in fear of Caesar; and these accordingly are held guilty.

Whether it was fitting for Christ to suffer at the hands of the Gentiles?

Objection 1: It would seem unfitting that Christ should suffer at the hands of the Gentiles. For since men were to be freed from sin by Christ's death, it would seem fitting that very few should sin in His death. But the Jews sinned in His death, on whose behalf it is said (Mat. 21:38): "This is the heir; come, let us kill him." It seems fitting, therefore, that the Gentiles should not be implicated in the sin of Christ's slaying.

Objection 2: Further, the truth should respond to the figure. Now it was not the Gentiles but the Jews who offered the figurative sacrifices of the Old Law. Therefore neither ought Christ's Passion, which was a true sacrifice, to be fulfilled at the hands of the Gentiles.

Objection 3: Further, as related Jn. 5:18, "the Jews sought to kill" Christ because "He did not only break the sabbath, but also said God was His Father, making Himself equal to God." But these things seemed to be only against the Law of the Jews: hence they themselves said (Jn. 19:7): "According to the Law He ought to die because He made Himself the Son of God." It seems fitting, therefore, that Christ should suffer, at the hands not of the Gentiles, but of the Jews, and that what they said was untrue: "It is not lawful for us to put any man to death," since many sins are punishable with death according to the Law, as is evident from Lev. 20.

On the contrary, our Lord Himself says (Mat. 20:19): "They shall deliver Him to the Gentiles to be mocked, and scourged, and crucified."

I answer that, The effect of Christ's Passion was foreshown by the very manner of His death. For Christ's Passion wrought its effect of salvation first of all among the Jews, very many of whom were baptized in His death, as is evident from Acts 2:41 and Acts 4:4. Afterwards, by the preaching of Jews, Christ's Passion passed on to the Gentiles. Consequently it was fitting that Christ should begin His sufferings at the hands of the Jews, and, after they had delivered Him up, finish His Passion at the hands of the Gentiles.

Reply to Objection 1: In order to demonstrate the fulness of His love, on account of which He suffered, Christ upon the cross prayed for His persecutors. Therefore, that the fruits of His petition might accrue to Jews and Gentiles, Christ willed to suffer from both.

Reply to Objection 2: Christ's Passion was the offering of a sacrifice, inasmuch as He endured death of His own free-will out of charity: but in so far as He suffered from His persecutors it was not a sacrifice, but a most grievous sin.

Reply to Objection 3: As Augustine says (Tract. cxiv in Joan.): "The Jews said that 'it is not lawful for us to put any man to death,' because they understood that it was not lawful for them to put any man to death" owing to the sacredness of the feast-day, which they had already begun to celebrate. or, as Chrysostom observes (Hom. lxxxiii in Joan.), because they wanted Him to be slain, not as a transgressor of the Law, but as a public enemy, since He had made Himself out to be a king, of which it was not their place to judge. Or, again, because it was not lawful for them to crucify Him (as they wanted to), but to stone Him, as they did to Stephen. Better still is it to say that the power of putting to death was taken from them by the Romans, whose subjects they were.

Whether Christ's persecutors knew who He was?

Objection 1: It would seem that Christ's persecutors did know who He was. For it is written (Mat. 21:38) that the husbandmen seeing the son said within themselves: "This is the heir; come, let us kill him." On this Jerome remarks: "Our Lord proves most manifestly by these words that the rulers of the Jews crucified the Son of God, not from ignorance, but out of envy: for they understood that it was He to whom the Father says by the Prophet: 'Ask of Me, and I will give Thee the Gentiles for Thy inheritance.'" It seems, therefore, that they knew Him to be Christ or the Son of God.

Objection 2: Further, our Lord says (Jn. 15:24): "But now they have both seen and hated both Me and My Father." Now what is seen is known manifestly. Therefore the Jews, knowing Christ, inflicted the Passion on Him out of hatred.

Objection 3: Further, it is said in a sermon delivered in the Council of Ephesus (P. iii, cap. x): "Just as he who tears up the imperial message is doomed to die, as despising the prince's word; so the Jew, who crucified Him whom he had seen, will pay the penalty for daring to lay his hands on God the Word Himself." Now this would not be so had they not known Him to be the Son of God, because their ignorance would have excused them. Therefore it seems that the Jews in crucifying Christ knew Him to be the Son of God.

On the contrary, It is written (1 Cor. 2:8): "If they had known it, they would never have crucified the Lord of glory." And (Acts 3:17), Peter, addressing the Jews, says: "I know that you did it through ignorance, as did also your rulers." Likewise the Lord hanging upon the cross said: "Father, forgive them, for they know not what they do" (Lk. 23:34).

I answer that, Among the Jews some were elders, and others of lesser degree. Now according to the author of De Qq. Nov. et Vet. Test., qu. lxvi, the elders, who were called "rulers, knew," as did also the devils, "that He was the Christ promised in the Law: for they saw all the signs in Him which the prophets said would come to pass: but they did not know the mystery of His Godhead." Consequently the Apostle says: "If they had known it, they would never have crucified the Lord of glory." It must, however, be understood that their ignorance did not excuse them from crime, because it was, as it were, affected ignorance. For they saw manifest signs of His Godhead; yet they perverted them out of hatred and envy of Christ; neither would they believe His words, whereby He avowed that He was the Son of God. Hence He Himself says of them (Jn. 15:22): "If I had not come, and spoken to them, they would not have sin; but now they have no excuse for their sin." And afterwards He adds (Jn. 15:24): "If I had not done among them the works that no other man hath done, they would not have sin." And so the expression employed by Job (21:14) can be accepted on their behalf: "(Who) said to God: depart from us, we desire not the knowledge of Thy ways."

But those of lesser degree---namely, the common folk---who had not grasped the mysteries of the Scriptures, did not fully comprehend that He was the Christ or the Son of God. For although some of them believed in Him, yet the multitude did not; and if they doubted sometimes whether He was the Christ, on account of the manifold signs and force of His teaching, as is stated Jn. 7:31,41, nevertheless they were deceived afterwards by their rulers, so that they did not believe Him to be the Son of God or the Christ. Hence Peter said to them: "I know that you did it through ignorance, as did also your rulers"---namely, because they were seduced by the rulers.

Reply to Objection 1: Those words are spoken by the husbandmen of the vineyard; and these signify the rulers of the people, who knew Him to be the heir, inasmuch as they knew Him to be the Christ promised in the Law, but the words of Ps. 2:8 seem to militate against this answer: "Ask of Me, and I will give Thee the Gentiles for Thy inheritance"; which are addressed to Him of whom it is said: "Thou art My Son, this day have I begotten Thee." If, then, they knew Him to be the one to whom the words were addressed: "Ask of Me, and I will give Thee the Gentiles for Thy inheritance," it follows that they knew Him to be the Son of God. Chrysostom, too, says upon the same passage that "they knew Him to be the Son of God." Bede likewise, commenting on the words, "For they know not what they do" (Lk. 23:34), says: "It is to be observed that He does not pray for them who, understanding Him to be the Son of God, preferred to crucify Him rather than acknowledge Him." But to this it may be replied that they knew Him to be the Son of God, not from His Nature, but from the excellence of His singular grace.

Yet we may hold that they are said to have known also that He was verily the Son of God, in that they had evident signs thereof: yet out of hatred and envy, they refused credence to these signs, by which they might have known that He was the Son of God.

Reply to Objection 2: The words quoted are preceded by the following: "If I had not done among them the works that no other man hath done, they would not have sin"; and then follow the words: "But now they have both seen and hated both Me and My Father." Now all this shows that while they beheld Christ's marvelous works, it was owing to their hatred that they did not know Him to be the Son of God.

Reply to Objection 3: Affected ignorance does not excuse from guilt, but seems, rather, to aggravate it: for it shows that a man is so strongly attached to sin that he wishes to incur ignorance lest he avoid sinning. The Jews therefore sinned, as crucifiers not only of the Man-Christ, but also as of God.

Whether the sin of those who crucified Christ was most grievous?

Objection 1: It would seem that the sin of Christ's crucifiers was not the most grievous. Because the sin which has some excuse cannot be most grievous. But our Lord Himself excused the sin of His crucifiers when He said: "Father, forgive them: for they know not what they do" (Lk. 23:34). Therefore theirs was not the most grievous sin.

Objection 2: Further, our Lord said to Pilate (Jn. 19:11): "He that hath delivered Me to thee hath the greater sin." But it was Pilate who caused Christ to be crucified by his minions. Therefore the sin of Judas the traitor seems to be greater than that of those who crucified Him.

Objection 3: Further, according to the Philosopher (Ethic. v): "No one suffers injustice willingly"; and in the same place he adds: "Where no one suffers injustice, nobody works injustice." Consequently nobody wreaks injustice upon a willing subject. But Christ suffered willingly, as was shown above ([4247]AA[1],2). Therefore those who crucified Christ did Him no injustice; and hence their sin was not the most grievous.

On the contrary, Chrysostom, commenting on the words, "Fill ye up, then, the measure of your fathers" (Mat. 23:32), says: "In very truth they exceeded the measure of their fathers; for these latter slew men, but they crucified God."

I answer that, As stated above [4248](A[5]), the rulers of the Jews knew that He was the Christ: and if there was any ignorance in them, it was affected ignorance, which could not excuse them. Therefore their sin was the most grievous, both on account of the kind of sin, as well as from the malice of their will. The Jews also of the common order sinned most grievously as to the kind of their sin: yet in one respect their crime was lessened by reason of their ignorance. Hence Bede, commenting on Lk. 23:34, "Father, forgive them, for they know not what they do," says: "He prays for them who know not what they are doing, as having the zeal of God, but not according to knowledge." But the sin of the Gentiles, by whose hands He was crucified, was much more excusable, since they had no knowledge of the Law.

Reply to Objection 1: As stated above, the excuse made by our Lord is not to be referred to the rulers among the Jews, but to the common people.

Reply to Objection 2: Judas did not deliver up Christ to Pilate, but to the chief priests who gave Him up to Pilate, according to Jn. 18:35: "Thy own nation and the chief priests have delivered Thee up to me." But the sin of all these was greater than that of Pilate, who slew Christ from fear of Caesar; and even greater than the sin of the soldiers who crucified Him at the governor's bidding, not out of cupidity like Judas, nor from envy and hate like the chief priests.

Reply to Objection 3: Christ, indeed willed His Passion just as the Father willed it; yet He did not will the unjust action of the Jews. Consequently Christ's slayers are not excused of their injustice. Nevertheless, whoever slays a man not only does a wrong to the one slain, but likewise to God and to the State; just as he who kills himself, as the Philosopher says (Ethic. v). Hence it was that David condemned to death the man who "did not fear to lay hands upon the Lord's anointed," even though he (Saul) had requested it, as related 2 Kings 1:5-14.

OF THE EFFICIENCY OF CHRIST'S PASSION (SIX ARTICLES)

We now have to consider Christ's Passion as to its effect; first of all, as to the manner in which it was brought about; and, secondly, as to the effect in itself. Under the first heading there are six points for inquiry:

(1) Whether Christ's Passion brought about our salvation by way of merit?

(2) Whether it was by way of atonement?

(3) Whether it was by way of sacrifice?

(4) Whether it was by way of redemption?

(5) Whether it is proper to Christ to be the Redeemer?

(6) Whether (the Passion) secured man's salvation efficiently?

Whether Christ's Passion brought about our salvation by way of merit?

Objection 1: It would seem that Christ's Passion did not bring about our salvation by way of merit. For the sources of our sufferings are not within us. But no one merits or is praised except for that whose principle lies within him. Therefore Christ's Passion wrought nothing by way of merit.

Objection 2: Further, from the beginning of His conception Christ merited for Himself and for us, as stated above ([4249]Q[9], A[4];[4250] Q[34], A[3]). But it is superfluous to merit over again what has been merited before. Therefore by His Passion Christ did not merit our salvation.

Objection 3: Further, the source of merit is charity. But Christ's charity was not made greater by the Passion than it was before. Therefore He did not merit our salvation by suffering more than He had already.

On the contrary, on the words of Phil. 2:9, "Therefore God exalted Him," etc., Augustine says (Tract. civ in Joan.): "The lowliness" of the Passion "merited glory; glory was the reward of lowliness." But He was glorified, not merely in Himself, but likewise in His faithful ones, as He says Himself (Jn. 17:10). Therefore it appears that He merited the salvation of the faithful.

I answer that, As stated above ([4251]Q[7], AA[1],9;[4252] Q[8], AA[1],5), grace was bestowed upon Christ, not only as an individual, but inasmuch as He is the Head of the Church, so that it might overflow into His members; and therefore Christ's works are referred to Himself and to His members in the same way as the works of any other man in a state of grace are referred to himself. But it is evident that whosoever suffers for justice's sake, provided that he be in a state of grace, merits his salvation thereby, according to Mat. 5:10: "Blessed are they that suffer persecution for justice's sake." Consequently Christ by His Passion merited salvation, not only for Himself, but likewise for all His members.

Reply to Objection 1: Suffering, as such, is caused by an outward principle: but inasmuch as one bears it willingly, it has an inward principle.

Reply to Objection 2: From the beginning of His conception Christ merited our eternal salvation; but on our side there were some obstacles, whereby we were hindered from securing the effect of His preceding merits: consequently, in order to remove such hindrances, "it was necessary for Christ to suffer," as stated above ([4253]Q[46], A[3]).

Reply to Objection 3: Christ's Passion has a special effect, which His preceding merits did not possess, not on account of greater charity, but because of the nature of the work, which was suitable for such an effect, as is clear from the arguments brought forward above all the fittingness of Christ's Passion (Q[46], AA, 3,4).

Day 281

Whether Christ's Passion brought about our salvation by way of atonement?

Objection 1: It would seem that Christ's Passion did not bring about our salvation by way of atonement. For it seems that to make the atonement devolves on him who commits the sin; as is clear in the other parts of penance, because he who has done the wrong must grieve over it and confess it. But Christ never sinned, according to 1 Pet. 2:22: "Who did no sin." Therefore He made no atonement by His personal suffering.

Objection 2: Further, no atonement is made to another by committing a graver offense. But in Christ's Passion the gravest of all offenses was perpetrated, because those who slew Him sinned most grievously, as stated above ([4254]Q[47], A[6]). Consequently it seems that atonement could not be made to God by Christ's Passion.

Objection 3: Further, atonement implies equality with the trespass, since it is an act of justice. But Christ's Passion does not appear equal to all the sins of the human race, because Christ did not suffer in His Godhead, but in His flesh, according to 1 Pet. 4:1: "Christ therefore having suffered in the flesh." Now the soul, which is the subject of sin, is of greater account than the flesh. Therefore Christ did not atone for our sins by His Passion.

On the contrary, It is written (Ps. 68:5) in Christ's person: "Then did I pay that which I took not away." But he has not paid who has not fully atoned. Therefore it appears that Christ by His suffering has fully atoned for our sins.

I answer that, He properly atones for an offense who offers something which the offended one loves equally, or even more than he detested the offense. But by suffering out of love and obedience, Christ gave more to God than was required to compensate for the offense of the whole human race. First of all, because of the exceeding charity from which He suffered; secondly, on account of the dignity of His life which He laid down in atonement, for it was the life of one who was God and man; thirdly, on account of the extent of the Passion, and the greatness of the grief endured, as stated above ([4255]Q[46], A[6]). And therefore Christ's Passion was not only a sufficient but a superabundant atonement for the sins of the human race; according to 1 Jn. 2:2: "He is the propitiation for our sins: and not for ours only, but also for those of the whole world."

Reply to Objection 1: The head and members are as one mystic person; and therefore Christ's satisfaction belongs to all the faithful as being His members. Also, in so far as any two men are one in charity, the one can atone for the other as shall be shown later ([4256]XP, Q[13], A[2]). But the same reason does not hold good of confession and contrition, because atonement consists in an outward action, for which helps may be used, among which friends are to be computed.

Reply to Objection 2: Christ's love was greater than His slayers' malice: and therefore the value of His Passion in atoning surpassed the murderous guilt of those who crucified Him: so much so that Christ's suffering was sufficient and superabundant atonement for His murderer's crime.

Reply to Objection 3: The dignity of Christ's flesh is not to be estimated solely from the nature of flesh, but also from the Person assuming it---namely, inasmuch as it was God's flesh, the result of which was that it was of infinite worth.

Whether Christ's Passion operated by way of sacrifice?

Objection 1: It would seem that Christ's Passion did not operate by way of sacrifice. For the truth should correspond with the figure. But human flesh was never offered up in the sacrifices of the Old Law, which were figures of Christ: nay, such sacrifices were reputed as impious, according to Ps. 105:38: "And they shed innocent blood: the blood of their sons and of their daughters, which they sacrificed to the idols of Chanaan." It seems therefore that Christ's Passion cannot be called a sacrifice.

Objection 2: Further, Augustine says (De Civ. Dei x) that "a visible sacrifice is a sacrament---that is, a sacred sign---of an invisible sacrifice." Now Christ's Passion is not a sign, but rather the thing signified by other signs. Therefore it seems that Christ's Passion is not a sacrifice.

Objection 3: Further, whoever offers sacrifice performs some sacred rite, as the very word "sacrifice" shows. But those men who slew Christ did not perform any sacred act, but rather wrought a great wrong. Therefore Christ's Passion was rather a malefice than a sacrifice.

On the contrary, The Apostle says (Eph. 5:2): "He delivered Himself up for us, an oblation and a sacrifice to God for an odor of sweetness."

I answer that, A sacrifice properly so called is something done for that honor which is properly due to God, in order to appease Him: and hence it is that Augustine says (De Civ. Dei x): "A true sacrifice is every good work done in order that we may cling to God in holy fellowship, yet referred to that consummation of happiness wherein we can be truly blessed." But, as is added in the same place, "Christ offered Himself up for us in the Passion": and this voluntary enduring of the Passion was most acceptable to God, as coming from charity. Therefore it is manifest that Christ's Passion was a true sacrifice. Moreover, as Augustine says farther on in the same book, "the primitive sacrifices of the holy Fathers were many and various signs of this true sacrifice, one being prefigured by many, in the same way as a single concept of thought is expressed in many words, in order to commend it without tediousness": and, as Augustine observe, (De Trin. iv), "since there are four things to be noted in every sacrifice---to wit, to whom it is offered, by whom it is offered, what is offered, and for whom it is offered---that the same one true Mediator reconciling us with God through the peace-sacrifice might continue to be one with Him to whom He offered it, might be one with them for whom He offered it, and might Himself be the offerer and what He offered."

Reply to Objection 1: Although the truth answers to the figure in some respects, yet it does not in all, since the truth must go beyond the figure. Therefore the figure of this sacrifice, in which Christ's flesh is offered, was flesh right fittingly, not the flesh of men, but of animals, as denoting Christ's. And this is a most perfect sacrifice. First of all, since being flesh of human nature, it is fittingly offered for men, and is partaken of by them under the Sacrament. Secondly, because being passible and mortal, it was fit for immolation. Thirdly, because, being sinless, it had virtue to cleanse from sins. Fourthly, because, being the offerer's own flesh, it was acceptable to God on account of His charity in offering up His own flesh. Hence it is that Augustine says (De Trin. iv): "What else could be so fittingly partaken of by men, or offered up for men, as human flesh? What else could be so appropriate for this immolation as mortal flesh? What else is there so clean for cleansing mortals as the flesh born in the womb without fleshly concupiscence, and coming from a virginal womb? What could be so favorably offered and accepted as the flesh of our sacrifice, which was made the body of our Priest?"

Reply to Objection 2: Augustine is speaking there of visible figurative sacrifices: and even Christ's Passion, although denoted by other figurative sacrifices, is yet a sign of something to be observed by us, according to 1 Pet. 4:1: "Christ therefore, having suffered in the flesh, be you also armed with the same thought: for he that hath suffered in the flesh hath ceased from sins: that now he may live the rest of his time in the flesh, not after the desires of men, but according to the will of God."

Reply to Objection 3: Christ's Passion was indeed a malefice on His slayers' part; but on His own it was the sacrifice of one suffering out of charity. Hence it is Christ who is said to have offered this sacrifice, and not the executioners.

Whether Christ's Passion brought about our salvation by way of redemption?

Objection 1: It would seem that Christ's Passion did not effect our salvation by way of redemption. For no one purchases or redeems what never ceased to belong to him. But men never ceased to belong to God according to Ps. 23:1: "The earth is the Lord's and the fulness thereof: the world and all they that dwell therein." Therefore it seems that Christ did not redeem us by His Passion.

Objection 2: Further, as Augustine says (De Trin. xiii): "The devil had to be overthrown by Christ's justice." But justice requires that the man who has treacherously seized another's property shall be deprived of it, because deceit and cunning should not benefit anyone, as even human laws declare. Consequently, since the devil by treachery deceived and subjugated to himself man, who is God's creature, it seems that man ought not to be rescued from his power by way of redemption.

Objection 3: Further, whoever buys or redeems an object pays the price to the holder. But it was not to the devil, who held us in bondage, that Christ paid His blood as the price of our redemption. Therefore Christ did not redeem us by His Passion.

On the contrary, It is written (1 Pet. 1:18): "You were not redeemed with corruptible things as gold or silver from your vain conversation of the tradition of your fathers: but with the precious blood of Christ, as of a lamb unspotted and undefiled." And (Gal. 3:13): "Christ hath redeemed us from the curse of the law, being made a curse for us." Now He is said to be a curse for us inasmuch as He suffered upon the tree, as stated above ([4257]Q[46], A[4]). Therefore He did redeem us by His Passion.

I answer that, Man was held captive on account of sin in two ways: first of all, by the bondage of sin, because (Jn. 8:34): "Whosoever committeth sin is the servant of sin"; and (2 Pet. 2:19): "By whom a man is overcome, of the same also he is the slave." Since, then, the devil had overcome man by inducing him to sin, man was subject to the devil's bondage. Secondly, as to the debt of punishment, to the payment of which man was held fast by God's justice: and this, too, is a kind of bondage, since it savors of bondage for a man to suffer what he does not wish, just as it is the free man's condition to apply himself to what he wills.

Since, then, Christ's Passion was a sufficient and a superabundant atonement for the sin and the debt of the human race, it was as a price at the cost of which we were freed from both obligations. For the atonement by which one satisfies for self or another is called the price, by which he ransoms himself or someone else from sin and its penalty, according to Dan. 4:24: "Redeem thou thy sins with alms." Now Christ made satisfaction, not by giving money or anything of the sort, but by bestowing what was of greatest price---Himself---for us. And therefore Christ's Passion is called our redemption.

Reply to Objection 1: Man is said to belong to God in two ways. First of all, in so far as he comes under God's power: in which way he never ceased to belong to God; according to Dan. 4:22: "The Most High ruleth over the kingdom of men, and giveth it to whomsoever he will." Secondly, by being united to Him in charity, according to Rom. 8:9: "If any man have not the Spirit of Christ, he is none of His." In the first way, then, man never ceased to belong to God, but in the second way he did cease because of sin. And therefore in so far as he was delivered from sin by the satisfaction of Christ's Passion, he is said to be redeemed by the Passion of Christ.

Reply to Objection 2: Man by sinning became the bondsman both of God and of the devil. Through guilt he had offended God, and put himself under the devil by consenting to him; consequently he did not become God's servant on account of his guilt, but rather, by withdrawing from God's service, he, by God's just permission, fell under the devil's servitude on account of the offense perpetrated. But as to the penalty, man was chiefly bound to God as his sovereign judge, and to the devil as his torturer, according to Mat. 5:25: "Lest perhaps the adversary deliver thee to the judge, and the judge deliver thee to the officer"---that is, "to the relentless avenging angel," as Chrysostom says (Hom. xi). Consequently, although, after deceiving man, the devil, so far as in him lay, held him unjustly in bondage as to both sin and penalty, still it was just that man should suffer it. God so permitting it as to the sin and ordaining it as to the penalty. And therefore justice required man's redemption with regard to God, but not with regard to the devil.

Reply to Objection 3: Because, with regard to God, redemption was necessary for man's deliverance, but not with regard to the devil, the price had to be paid not to the devil, but to God. And therefore Christ is said to have paid the price of our redemption---His own precious blood---not to the devil, but to God.

Whether it is proper to Christ to be the Redeemer?

Objection 1: It would seem that it is not proper to Christ to be the Redeemer, because it is written (Ps. 30:6): "Thou hast redeemed me, O Lord, the God of Truth." But to be the Lord God of Truth belongs to the entire Trinity. Therefore it is not proper to Christ.

Objection 2: Further, he is said to redeem who pays the price of redemption. But God the Father gave His Son in redemption for our sins, as is written (Ps. 110:9): "The Lord hath sent redemption to His people," upon which the gloss adds, "that is, Christ, who gives redemption to captives." Therefore not only Christ, but the Father also, redeemed us.

Objection 3: Further, not only Christ's Passion, but also that of other saints conduced to our salvation, according to Col. 1:24: "I now rejoice in my sufferings for you, and fill up those things that are wanting of the sufferings of Christ, in my flesh for His body, which is the Church." Therefore the title of Redeemer belongs not only to Christ, but also to the other saints.

On the contrary, It is written (Gal. 3:13): "Christ redeemed us from the curse of the Law, being made a curse for us." But only Christ was made a curse for us. Therefore only Christ ought to be called our Redeemer.

I answer that, For someone to redeem, two things are required---namely, the act of paying and the price paid. For if in redeeming something a man pays a price which is not his own, but another's, he is not said to be the chief redeemer, but rather the other is, whose price it is. Now Christ's blood or His bodily life, which "is in the blood," is the price of our redemption (Lev. 17:11, 14), and that life He paid. Hence both of these belong immediately to Christ as man; but to the Trinity as to the first and remote cause, to whom Christ's life belonged as to its first author, and from whom Christ received the inspiration of suffering for us. Consequently it is proper to Christ as man to be the Redeemer immediately; although the redemption may be ascribed to the whole Trinity as its first cause.

Reply to Objection 1: A gloss explains the text thus: "Thou, O Lord God of Truth, hast redeemed me in Christ, crying out, 'Lord, into Thy hands I commend my spirit.'" And so redemption belongs immediately to the Man-Christ, but principally to God.

Reply to Objection 2: The Man-Christ paid the price of our redemption immediately, but at the command of the Father as the original author.

Reply to Objection 3: The sufferings of the saints are beneficial to the Church, as by way, not of redemption, but of example and exhortation, according to 2 Cor. 1:6: "Whether we be in tribulation, it is for your exhortation and salvation."

Whether Christ's Passion brought about our salvation efficiently?

Objection 1: It would seem that Christ's Passion did not bring about our salvation efficiently. For the efficient cause of our salvation is the greatness of the Divine power, according to Is. 59:1: "Behold the hand of the Lord is not shortened that it cannot save." But "Christ was crucified through weakness," as it is written (2 Cor. 13:4). Therefore, Christ's Passion did not bring about our salvation efficiently.

Objection 2: Further, no corporeal agency acts efficiently except by contact: hence even Christ cleansed the leper by touching him "in order to show that His flesh had saving power," as Chrysostom [*Theophylact, Enarr. in Luc.] says. But Christ's Passion could not touch all mankind. Therefore it could not efficiently bring about the salvation of all men.

Objection 3: Further, it does not seem to be consistent for the same agent to operate by way of merit and by way of efficiency, since he who merits awaits the result from someone else. But it was by way of merit that Christ's Passion accomplished our salvation. Therefore it was not by way of efficiency.

On the contrary, It is written (1 Cor. 1:18) that "the word of the cross to them that are saved . . . is the power of God." But God's power brings about our salvation efficiently. Therefore Christ's Passion on the cross accomplished our salvation efficiently.

I answer that, There is a twofold efficient agency---namely, the principal and the instrumental. Now the principal efficient cause of man's salvation is God. But since Christ's humanity is the "instrument of the Godhead," as stated above ([4258]Q[43], A[2]), therefore all Christ's actions and sufferings operate instrumentally in virtue of His Godhead for the salvation of men. Consequently, then, Christ's Passion accomplishes man's salvation efficiently.

Reply to Objection 1: Christ's Passion in relation to His flesh is consistent with the infirmity which He took upon Himself, but in relation to the Godhead it draws infinite might from It, according to 1 Cor. 1:25: "The weakness of God is stronger than men"; because Christ's weakness, inasmuch as He is God, has a might exceeding all human power.

Reply to Objection 2: Christ's Passion, although corporeal, has yet a spiritual effect from the Godhead united: and therefore it secures its efficacy by spiritual contact---namely, by faith and the sacraments of faith, as the Apostle says (Rom. 3:25): "Whom God hath proposed to be a propitiation, through faith in His blood."

Reply to Objection 3: Christ's Passion, according as it is compared with His Godhead, operates in an efficient manner: but in so far as it is compared with the will of Christ's soul it acts in a meritorious manner: considered as being within Christ's very flesh, it acts by way of satisfaction, inasmuch as we are liberated by it from the debt of punishment; while inasmuch as we are freed from the servitude of guilt, it acts by way of redemption: but in so far as we are reconciled with God it acts by way of sacrifice, as shall be shown farther on ([4259]Q[49]).

OF THE EFFECTS OF CHRIST'S PASSION (SIX ARTICLES)

We have now to consider what are the effects of Christ's Passion, concerning which there are six points of inquiry:

(1) Whether we were freed from sin by Christ's Passion?
(2) Whether we were thereby delivered from the power of the devil?
(3) Whether we were freed thereby from our debt of punishment?
(4) Whether we were thereby reconciled with God?
(5) Whether heaven's gate was opened to us thereby?
(6) Whether Christ derived exaltation from it?

Whether we were delivered from sin through Christ's Passion?

Objection 1: It would seem that we were not delivered from sin through Christ's Passion. For to deliver from sin belongs to God alone, according to Is. 43:25: "I am He who blot out your iniquities for My own sake." But Christ did not suffer as God, but as man. Therefore Christ's Passion did not free us from sin.

Objection 2: Further, what is corporeal does not act upon what is spiritual. But Christ's Passion is corporeal, whereas sin exists in the soul, which is a spiritual creature. Therefore Christ's Passion could not cleanse us from sin.

Objection 3: Further, one cannot be purged from a sin not yet committed, but which shall be committed hereafter. Since, then, many sins have been committed since Christ's death, and are being committed daily, it seems that we were not delivered from sin by Christ's death.

Objection 4: Further, given an efficient cause, nothing else is required for producing the effect. But other things besides are required for the forgiveness of sins, such as baptism and penance. Consequently it seems that Christ's Passion is not the sufficient cause of the forgiveness of sins.

Objection 5: Further, it is written (Prov. 10:12): "Charity covereth all sins"; and (Prov. 15:27): "By mercy and faith, sins are purged away." But there are many other things of which we have faith, and which excite charity. Therefore Christ's Passion is not the proper cause of the forgiveness of sins.

On the contrary, It is written (Apoc. 1:5): "He loved us, and washed us from our sins in His own blood."

I answer that, Christ's Passion is the proper cause of the forgiveness of sins in three ways. First of all, by way of exciting our charity, because, as the Apostle says (Rom. 5:8): "God commendeth His charity towards us: because when as yet we were sinners, according to the time, Christ died for us." But it is by charity that we procure pardon of our sins, according to Lk. 7:47: "Many sins are forgiven her because she hath loved much." Secondly, Christ's Passion causes forgiveness of sins by way of redemption. For since He is our head, then, by the Passion which He endured from love and obedience, He delivered us as His members from our sins, as by the price of His Passion: in the same way as if a man by the good industry of his hands were to redeem himself from a sin committed with his feet. For, just as the natural body is one though made up of diverse members, so the whole Church, Christ's mystic body, is reckoned as one person with its head, which is Christ. Thirdly, by way of efficiency, inasmuch as Christ's flesh, wherein He endured the Passion, is the instrument of the Godhead, so that His sufferings and actions operate with Divine power for expelling sin.

Reply to Objection 1: Although Christ did not suffer as God, nevertheless His flesh is the instrument of the Godhead; and hence it is that His Passion has a kind of Divine Power of casting out sin, as was said above.

Reply to Objection 2: Although Christ's Passion is corporeal, still it derives a kind of spiritual energy from the Godhead, to which the flesh is united as an instrument: and according to this power Christ's Passion is the cause of the forgiveness of sins.

Reply to Objection 3: Christ by His Passion delivered us from our sins causally---that is, by setting up the cause of our deliverance, from which cause all sins whatsoever, past, present, or to come, could be forgiven: just as if a doctor were to prepare a medicine by which all sicknesses can be cured even in future.

Reply to Objection 4: As stated above, since Christ's Passion preceded, as a kind of universal cause of the forgiveness of sins, it needs to be applied to each individual for the cleansing of personal sins. Now this is done by baptism and penance and the other sacraments, which derive their power from Christ's Passion, as shall be shown later ([4260]Q[62], A[5]).

Reply to Objection 5: Christ's Passion is applied to us even through faith, that we may share in its fruits, according to Rom. 3:25: "Whom God hath proposed to be a propitiation, through faith in His blood." But the faith through which we are cleansed from sin is not "lifeless faith," which can exist even with sin, but "faith living" through charity; that thus Christ's Passion may be applied to us, not only as to our minds, but also as to our hearts. And even in this way sins are forgiven through the power of the Passion of Christ.

Whether we were delivered from the devil's power through Christ's Passion?

Objection 1: It would seem that we were not delivered from the power of the devil through Christ's Passion. For he has no power over others, who can do nothing to them without the sanction of another. But without the Divine permission the devil could never do hurt to any man, as is evident in the instance of Job (1,2), where, by power received from God, the devil first injured him in his possessions, and afterwards in his body. In like manner it is stated (Mat. 8:31,32) that the devils could not enter into the swine except with Christ's leave. Therefore the devil never had power over men: and hence we are not delivered from his power through Christ's Passion.

Objection 2: Further, the devil exercises his power over men by tempting them and molesting their bodies. But even after the Passion he continues to do the same to men. Therefore we are not delivered from his power through Christ's Passion.

Objection 3: Further, the might of Christ's Passion endures for ever, as, according to Heb. 10:14: "By one oblation He hath perfected for ever them that are sanctified." But deliverance rom the devil's power is not found everywhere, since there are still idolaters in many regions of the world; nor will it endure for ever, because in the time of Antichrist he will be especially active in using his power to the hurt of men; because it is said of him (2 Thess. 2:9): "Whose coming is according to the working of Satan, in all power, and signs, and lying wonders, and in all seduction of iniquity." Consequently it seems that Christ's Passion is not the cause of the human race being delivered from the power of the devil.

On the contrary, our Lord said (Jn. 12:31), when His Passion was drawing nigh: "Now shall the prince of this world be cast out; and I, if I be lifted up from the earth, will draw all things to Myself." Now He was lifted up from the earth by His Passion on the cross. Therefore by His Passion the devil was deprived of his power over man.

I answer that, There are three things to be considered regarding the power which the devil exercised over men previous to Christ's Passion. The first is on man's own part, who by his sin deserved to be delivered over to the devil's power, and was overcome by his tempting. Another point is on God's part, whom man had offended by sinning, and who with justice left man under the devil's power. The third is on the devil's part, who out of his most wicked will hindered man from securing his salvation.

As to the first point, by Christ's Passion man was delivered from the devil's power, in so far as the Passion is the cause of the forgiveness of sins, as stated above [4261](A[1]). As to the second, it must be said that Christ's Passion freed us from the devil's power, inasmuch as it reconciled us with God, as shall be shown later [4262](A[4]). But as to the third, Christ's Passion delivered us from the devil, inasmuch as in Christ's Passion he exceeded the limit of power assigned him by God, by conspiring to bring about Christ's death, Who, being sinless, did not deserve to die. Hence Augustine says (De Trin. xiii, cap. xiv): "The devil was vanquished by Christ's justice: because, while discovering in Him nothing deserving of death, nevertheless he slew Him. And it is certainly just that the debtors whom he held captive should be set at liberty since they believed in Him whom the devil slew, though He was no debtor."

Reply to Objection 1: The devil is said to have had such power over men not as though he were able to injure them without God's sanction, but because he was justly permitted to injure men whom by tempting he had induced to give consent.

Reply to Objection 2: God so permitting it, the devil can still tempt men's souls and harass their bodies: yet there is a remedy provided for man through Christ's Passion, whereby he can safeguard himself against the enemy's assaults, so as not to be dragged down into the destruction of everlasting death. And all who resisted the devil previous to the Passion were enabled to do so through faith in the Passion, although it was not yet accomplished. Yet in one respect no one was able to escape the devil's hands, i.e. so as not to descend into hell. But after Christ's Passion, men can defend themselves from this by its power.

Reply to Objection 3: God permits the devil to deceive men by certain persons, and in times and places, according to the hidden motive of His judgments; still, there is always a remedy provided through Christ's Passion, for defending themselves against the wicked snares of the demons, even in Antichrist's time. But if any man neglect to make use of this remedy, it detracts nothing from the efficacy of Christ's Passion.

Whether men were freed from the punishment of sin through Christ's Passion?

Objection 1: It would seem that men were not freed from the punishment of sin by Christ's Passion. For the chief punishment of sin is eternal damnation. But those damned in hell for their sins were not set free by Christ's Passion, because "in hell there is no redemption" [*Office of the Dead, Resp. vii]. It seems, therefore, that Christ's Passion did not deliver men from the punishment of sin.

Objection 2: Further, no punishment should be imposed upon them who are delivered from the debt of punishment. But a satisfactory punishment is imposed upon penitents. Consequently, men were not freed from the debt of punishment by Christ's Passion.

Objection 3: Further, death is a punishment of sin, according to Rom. 6:23: "The wages of sin is death." But men still die after Christ's Passion. Therefore it seems that we have not been delivered from the debt of punishment.

On the contrary, It is written (Is. 53:4): "Surely He hath borne our iniquities and carried our sorrows."

I answer that, Through Christ's Passion we have been delivered from the debt of punishment in two ways. First of all, directly---namely, inasmuch as Christ's Passion was sufficient and superabundant satisfaction for the sins of the whole human race: but when sufficient satisfaction has been paid, then the debt of punishment is abolished. In another way---indirectly, that is to say---in so far as Christ's Passion is the cause of the forgiveness of sin, upon which the debt of punishment rests.

Reply to Objection 1: Christ's Passion works its effect in them to whom it is applied, through faith and charity and the sacraments of faith. And, consequently, the lost in hell cannot avail themselves of its effects, since they are not united to Christ in the aforesaid manner.

Reply to Objection 2: As stated above (A[1], ad 4,5), in order to secure the effects of Christ's Passion, we must be likened unto Him. Now we are likened unto Him sacramentally in Baptism, according to Rom. 6:4: "For we are buried together with Him by baptism into death." Hence no punishment of satisfaction is imposed upon men at their baptism, since they are fully delivered by Christ's satisfaction. But because, as it is written (1 Pet. 3:18), "Christ died" but "once for our sins," therefore a man cannot a second time be likened unto Christ's death by the sacrament of Baptism. Hence it is necessary that those who sin after Baptism be likened unto Christ suffering by some form of punishment or suffering which they endure in their own person; yet, by the co-operation of Christ's satisfaction, much lighter penalty suffices than one that is proportionate to the sin.

Reply to Objection 3: Christ's satisfaction works its effect in us inasmuch as we are incorporated with Him, as the members with their head, as stated above [4263](A[1]). Now the members must be conformed to their head. Consequently, as Christ first had grace in His soul with bodily passibility, and through the Passion attained to the glory of immortality, so we likewise, who are His members, are freed by His Passion from all debt of punishment, yet so that we first receive in our souls "the spirit of adoption of sons," whereby our names are written down for the inheritance of immortal glory, while we yet have a passible and mortal body: but afterwards, "being made conformable" to the sufferings and death of Christ, we are brought into immortal glory, according to the saying of the Apostle (Rom. 8:17): "And if sons, heirs also: heirs indeed of God, and joint heirs with Christ; yet so if we suffer with Him, that we may be also glorified with Him."

Day 282

Whether we were reconciled to God through Christ's Passion?

Objection 1: It would seem that we were not reconciled to God through Christ's Passion. For there is no need of reconciliation between friends. But God always loved us, according to Wis. 11:25: "Thou lovest all the things that are, and hatest none of the things which Thou hast made." Therefore Christ's Passion did not reconcile us to God.

Objection 2: Further, the same thing cannot be cause and effect: hence grace, which is the cause of meriting, does not come under merit. But God's love is the cause of Christ's Passion, according to Jn. 3:16: "God so loved the world, as to give His only-begotten Son." It does not appear, then, that we were reconciled to God through Christ's Passion, so that He began to love us anew.

Objection 3: Further, Christ's Passion was completed by men slaying Him; and thereby they offended God grievously. Therefore Christ's Passion is rather the cause of wrath than of reconciliation to God.

On the contrary, The Apostle says (Rom. 5:10): "We are reconciled to God by the death of His Son."

I answer that, Christ's Passion is in two ways the cause of our reconciliation to God. In the first way, inasmuch as it takes away sin by which men became God's enemies, according to Wis. 14:9: "To God the wicked and his wickedness are hateful alike"; and Ps. 5:7: "Thou hatest all the workers of iniquity." In another way, inasmuch as it is a most acceptable sacrifice to God. Now it is the proper effect of sacrifice to appease God: just as man likewise overlooks an offense committed against him on account of some pleasing act of homage shown him. Hence it is written (1 Kings 26:19): "If the Lord stir thee up against me, let Him accept of sacrifice." And in like fashion Christ's voluntary suffering was such a good act that, because of its being found in human nature, God was appeased for every offense of the human race with regard to those who are made one with the crucified Christ in the aforesaid manner (A[1], ad 4).

Reply to Objection 1: God loves all men as to their nature, which He Himself made; yet He hates them with respect to the crimes they commit against Him, according to Ecclus. 12:3: "The Highest hateth sinners."

Reply to Objection 2: Christ is not said to have reconciled us with God, as if God had begun anew to love us, since it is written (Jer. 31:3): "I have loved thee with an everlasting love"; but because the source of hatred was taken away by Christ's Passion, both through sin being washed away and through compensation being made in the shape of a more pleasing offering.

Reply to Objection 3: As Christ's slayers were men, so also was the Christ slain. Now the charity of the suffering Christ surpassed the wickedness of His slayers. Accordingly Christ's Passion prevailed more in reconciling God to the whole human race than in provoking Him to wrath.

Whether Christ opened the gate of heaven to us by His Passion?

Objection 1: It would seem that Christ did not open the gate of heaven to us by His Passion. For it is written (Prov. 11:18): "To him that soweth justice, there is a faithful reward." But the reward of justice is the entering into the kingdom of heaven. It seems, therefore, that the holy Fathers who wrought works of justice, obtained by faith the entering into the heavenly kingdom even without Christ's Passion. Consequently Christ's Passion is not the cause of the opening of the gate of the kingdom of heaven.

Objection 2: Further, Elias was caught up to heaven previous to Christ's Passion (4 Kings 2). But the effect never precedes the cause. Therefore it seems that the opening of heaven's gate is not the result of Christ's Passion.

Objection 3: Further, as it is written (Mat. 3:16), when Christ was baptized the heavens were opened to Him. But His baptism preceded the Passion. Consequently the opening of heaven is not the result of Christ's Passion.

Objection 4: Further, it is written (Mic. 2:13): "For He shall go up that shall open the way before them." But to open the way to heaven seems to be nothing else than to throw open its gate. Therefore it seems that the gate of heaven was opened to us, not by Christ's Passion, but by His Ascension.

On the contrary, is the saying of the Apostle (Heb. 10:19): "We have [Vulg.: 'having a'] confidence in the entering into the Holies"---that is, of the heavenly places---"through the blood of Christ."

I answer that, The shutting of the gate is the obstacle which hinders men from entering in. But it is on account of sin that men were prevented from entering into the heavenly kingdom, since, according to Is. 35:8: "It shall be called the holy way, and the unclean shall not pass over it." Now there is a twofold sin which prevents men from entering into the kingdom of heaven. The first is common to the whole race, for it is our first parents' sin, and by that sin heaven's entrance is closed to man. Hence we read in Gn. 3:24 that after our first parents' sin God "placed . . . cherubim and a flaming sword, turning every way, to keep the way of the tree of life." The other is the personal sin of each one of us, committed by our personal act.

Now by Christ's Passion we have been delivered not only from the common sin of the whole human race, both as to its guilt and as to the debt of punishment, for which He paid the penalty on our behalf; but, furthermore, from the personal sins of individuals, who share in His Passion by faith and charity and the sacraments of faith. Consequently, then the gate of heaven's kingdom is thrown open to us through Christ's Passion. This is precisely what the Apostle says (Heb. 9:11,12): "Christ being come a high-priest of the good things to come . . . by His own blood entered once into the Holies, having obtained eternal redemption." And this is foreshadowed (Num. 35:25, 28), where it is said that the slayer* "shall abide there"---that is to say, in the city of refuge---"until the death of the high-priest, that is anointed with the holy oil: but after he is dead, then shall he return home." [*The Septuagint has 'slayer', the Vulgate, 'innocent'---i.e. the man who has slain 'without hatred and enmity'.]

Reply to Objection 1: The holy Fathers, by doing works of justice, merited to enter into the heavenly kingdom, through faith in Christ's Passion, according to Heb. 11:33: The saints "by faith conquered kingdoms, wrought justice," and each of them was thereby cleansed from sin, so far as the cleansing of the individual is concerned. Nevertheless the faith and righteousness of no one of them sufficed for removing the barrier arising from the guilt of the whole human race: but this was removed at the cost of Christ's blood. Consequently, before Christ's Passion no one could enter the kingdom of heaven by obtaining everlasting beatitude, which consists in the full enjoyment of God.

Reply to Objection 2: Elias was taken up into the atmospheric heaven, but not in to the empyrean heaven, which is the abode of the saints: and likewise Enoch was translated into the earthly paradise, where he is believed to live with Elias until the coming of Antichrist.

Reply to Objection 3: As was stated above ([4264]Q[39], A[5]), the heavens were opened at Christ's baptism, not for Christ's sake, to whom heaven was ever open, but in order to signify that heaven is opened to the baptized, through Christ's baptism, which has its efficacy from His Passion.

Reply to Objection 4: Christ by His Passion merited for us the opening of the kingdom of heaven, and removed the obstacle; but by His ascension He, as it were, brought us to the possession of the heavenly kingdom. And consequently it is said that by ascending He "opened the way before them."

Whether by His Passion Christ merited to be exalted?

Objection 1: It seems that Christ did not merit to be exalted on account of His Passion. For eminence of rank belongs to God alone, just as knowledge of truth, according to Ps. 112:4: "The Lord is high above all nations, and His glory above the heavens." But Christ as man had the knowledge of all truth, not on account of any preceding merit, but from the very union of God and man, according to Jn. 1:14: "We saw His glory . . . as it were of the only-Begotten of the Father, full of grace and of truth." Therefore neither had He exaltation from the merit of the Passion but from the union alone.

Objection 2: Further, Christ merited for Himself from the first instant of His conception, as stated above ([4265]Q[34], A[3]). But His love was no greater during the Passion than before. Therefore, since charity is the principle of merit, it seems that He did not merit exaltation from the Passion more than before.

Objection 3: Further, the glory of the body comes from the glory of the soul, as Augustine says (Ep. ad Dioscor.). But by His Passion Christ did not merit exaltation as to the glory of His soul, because His soul was beatified from the first instant of His conception. Therefore neither did He merit exaltation, as to the glory of His body, from the Passion.

On the contrary, It is written (Phil. 2:8): "He became obedient unto death, even the death of the cross; for which cause God also exalted Him."

I answer that, Merit implies a certain equality of justice: hence the Apostle says (Rom. 4:4): "Now to him that worketh, the reward is reckoned according to debt." But when anyone by reason of his unjust will ascribes to himself something beyond his due, it is only just that he be deprived of something else which is his due; thus, "when a man steals a sheep he shall pay back four" (Ex. 22:1). And he is said to deserve it, inasmuch as his unjust will is chastised thereby. So likewise when any man through his just will has stripped himself of what he ought to have, he deserves that something further be granted to him as the reward of his just will. And hence it is written (Lk. 14:11): "He that humbleth himself shall be exalted."

Now in His Passion Christ humbled Himself beneath His dignity in four respects. In the first place as to His Passion and death, to which He was not bound; secondly, as to the place, since His body was laid in a sepulchre and His soul in hell; thirdly, as to the shame and mockeries He endured; fourthly, as to His being delivered up to man's power, as He Himself said to Pilate (Jn. 19:11): "Thou shouldst not have any power against Me, unless it were given thee from above." And, consequently, He merited a four-fold exaltation from His Passion. First of all, as to His glorious Resurrection: hence it is written (Ps. 138:1): "Thou hast known my sitting down"--- that is, the lowliness of My Passion---"and My rising up." Secondly, as to His ascension into heaven: hence it is written (Eph. 4:9): "Now that He ascended, what is it, but because He also descended first into the lower parts of the earth? He that descended is the same also that ascended above all the heavens." Thirdly, as to the sitting on the right hand of the Father and the showing forth of His Godhead, according to Is. 52:13: "He shall be exalted and extolled, and shall be exceeding high: as many have been astonished at him, so shall His visage be inglorious among men." Moreover (Phil. 2:8) it is written: "He humbled Himself, becoming obedient unto death, even to the death of the cross: for which cause also God hath exalted Him, and hath given Him a name which is above all names"---that is to say, so that He shall be hailed as God by all; and all shall pay Him homage as God. And this is expressed in what follows: "That in the name of Jesus every knee should bow, of those that are in heaven, on earth, and under the earth." Fourthly, as to His judiciary power: for it is written (Job 36:17): "Thy cause hath been judged as that of the wicked cause and judgment Thou shalt recover."

Reply to Objection 1: The source of meriting comes of the soul, while the body is the instrument of the meritorious work. And consequently the perfection of Christ's soul, which was the source of meriting, ought not to be acquired in Him by merit, like the perfection of the body, which was the subject of suffering, and was thereby the instrument of His merit.

Reply to Objection 2: Christ by His previous merits did merit exaltation on behalf of His soul, whose will was animated with charity and the other virtues; but in the Passion He merited His exaltation by way of recompense even on behalf of His body: since it is only just that the body, which from charity was subjected to the Passion, should receive recompense in glory.

Reply to Objection 3: It was owing to a special dispensation in Christ that before the Passion the glory of His soul did not shine out in His body, in order that He might procure His bodily glory with greater honor, when He had merited it by His Passion. But it was not beseeming for the glory of His soul to be postponed, since the soul was united immediately with the Word; hence it was beseeming that its glory should be filled by the Word Himself. But the body was united with the Word through the soul.

OF THE DEATH OF CHRIST (SIX ARTICLES)

We have now to consider the death of Christ; concerning which there are six subjects of inquiry:

(1) Whether it was fitting that Christ should die?
(2) Whether His death severed the union of Godhead and flesh?
(3) Whether His Godhead was separated from His soul?
(4) Whether Christ was a man during the three days of His death?
(5) Whether His was the same body, living and dead?
(6) Whether His death conduced in any way to our salvation?

Whether it was fitting that Christ should die?

Objection 1: It would seem that it was not fitting that Christ should die. For a first principle in any order is not affected by anything contrary to such order: thus fire, which is the principle of heat, can never become cold. But the Son of God is the fountain-head and principle of all life, according to Ps. 35:10: "With Thee is the fountain of life." Therefore it does not seem fitting for Christ to die.

Objection 2: Further, death is a greater defect than sickness, because it is through sickness that one comes to die. But it was not beseeming for Christ to languish from sickness, as Chrysostom [*Athanasius, Orat. de Incarn. Verbi] says. Consequently, neither was it becoming for Christ to die.

Objection 3: Further, our Lord said (Jn. 10:10): "I am come that they may have life, and may have it more abundantly." But one opposite does not lead to another. Therefore it seems that neither was it fitting for Christ to die.

On the contrary, It is written, (Jn. 11:50): "It is expedient that one man should die for the people . . . that the whole nation perish not": which words were spoken prophetically by Caiphas, as the Evangelist testifies.

I answer that, It was fitting for Christ to die. First of all to satisfy for the whole human race, which was sentenced to die on account of sin, according to Gn. 2:17: "In what day soever ye shall [Vulg.: 'thou shalt'] eat of it ye shall [Vulg.: 'thou shalt'] die the death." Now it is a fitting way of satisfying for another to submit oneself to the penalty deserved by that other. And so Christ resolved to die, that by dying He might atone for us, according to 1 Pet. 3:18: "Christ also died once for our sins." Secondly, in order to show the reality of the flesh assumed. For, as Eusebius says (Orat. de Laud. Constant. xv), "if, after dwelling among men Christ were suddenly to disappear from men's sight, as though shunning death, then by all men He would be likened to a phantom." Thirdly, that by dying He might deliver us from fearing death: hence it is written (Heb. 2:14,15) that He communicated "to flesh and blood, that through death He might destroy him who had the empire of death and might deliver them who, through the fear of death, were all their lifetime subject to servitude." Fourthly, that by dying in the body to the likeness of sin---that is, to its penalty---He might set us the example of dying to sin spiritually. Hence it is written (Rom. 6:10): "For in that He died to sin, He died once, but in that He liveth, He liveth unto God: so do you also reckon that you are dead to sin, but alive unto God." Fifthly, that by rising from the dead, and manifesting His power whereby He overthrew death, He might instill into us the hope of rising from the dead. Hence the Apostle says (1 Cor. 15:12): "If Christ be preached that He rose again from the dead, how do some among you say, that there is no resurrection from the dead?"

Reply to Objection 1: Christ is the fountain of life, as God, and not as man: but He died as man, and not as God. Hence Augustine [*Vigilius Tapsensis] says against Felician: "Far be it from us to suppose that Christ so felt death that He lost His life inasmuch as He is life in Himself; for, were it so, the fountain of life would have run dry. Accordingly, He experienced death by sharing in our human feeling, which of His own accord He had taken upon Himself, but He did not lose the power of His Nature, through which He gives life to all things."

Reply to Objection 2: Christ did not suffer death which comes of sickness, lest He should seem to die of necessity from exhausted nature: but He endured death inflicted from without, to which He willingly surrendered Himself, that His death might be shown to be a voluntary one.

Reply to Objection 3: One opposite does not of itself lead to the other, yet it does so indirectly at times: thus cold sometimes is the indirect cause of heat: and in this way Christ by His death brought us back to life, when by His death He destroyed our death; just as he who bears another's punishment takes such punishment away.

Whether the Godhead was separated from the flesh when Christ died?

Objection 1: It would seem that the Godhead was separated from the flesh when Christ died. For as Matthew relates (27:46), when our Lord was hanging upon the cross He cried out: "My God, My God, why hast Thou forsaken Me?" which words Ambrose, commenting on Lk. 23:46, explains as follows: "The man cried out when about to expire by being severed from the Godhead; for since the Godhead is immune from death, assuredly death could not be there, except life departed, for the Godhead is life." And so it seems that when Christ died, the Godhead was separated from His flesh.

Objection 2: Further, extremes are severed when the mean is removed. But the soul was the mean through which the Godhead was united with the flesh, as stated above ([4266]Q[6], A[1]). Therefore since the soul was severed from the flesh by death, it seems that, in consequence, His Godhead was also separated from it.

Objection 3: Further, God's life-giving power is greater than that of the soul. But the body could not die unless the soul quitted it. Therefore, much less could it die unless the Godhead departed.

On the contrary, As stated above ([4267]Q[16], AA[4],5), the attributes of human nature are predicated of the Son of God only by reason of the union. But what belongs to the body of Christ after death is predicated of the Son of God---namely, being buried: as is evident from the Creed, in which it is said that the Son of God "was conceived and born of a Virgin, suffered, died, and was buried." Therefore Christ's Godhead was not separated from the flesh when He died.

I answer that, What is bestowed through God's grace is never withdrawn except through fault. Hence it is written (Rom. 11:29): "The gifts and the calling of God are without repentance." But the grace of union whereby the Godhead was united to the flesh in Christ's Person, is greater than the grace of adoption whereby others are sanctified: also it is more enduring of itself, because this grace is ordained for personal union, whereas the grace of adoption is referred to a certain affective union. And yet we see that the grace of adoption is never lost without fault. Since, then there was no sin in Christ, it was impossible for the union of the Godhead with the flesh to be dissolved. Consequently, as before death Christ's flesh was united personally and hypostatically with the Word of God, it remained so after His death, so that the hypostasis of the Word of God was not different from that of Christ's flesh after death, as Damascene says (De Fide Orth. iii).

Reply to Objection 1: Such forsaking is not to be referred to the dissolving of the personal union, but to this, that God the Father gave Him up to the Passion: hence there "to forsake" means simply not to protect from persecutors. or else He says there that He is forsaken, with reference to the prayer He had made: "Father, if it be possible, let this chalice pass away from Me," as Augustine explains it (De Gratia Novi Test.).

Reply to Objection 2: The Word of God is said to be united with the flesh through the medium of the soul, inasmuch as it is through the soul that the flesh belongs to human nature, which the Son of God intended to assume; but not as though the soul were the medium linking them together. But it is due to the soul that the flesh is human even after the soul has been separated from it---namely, inasmuch as by God's ordinance there remains in the dead flesh a certain relation to the resurrection. And therefore the union of the Godhead with the flesh is not taken away.

Reply to Objection 3: The soul formally possesses the life-giving energy, and therefore, while it is present, and united formally, the body must necessarily be a living one, whereas the Godhead has not the life-giving energy formally, but effectively; because It cannot be the form of the body: and therefore it is not necessary for the flesh to be living while the union of the Godhead with the flesh remains, since God does not act of necessity, but of His own will.

Whether in Christ's death there was a severance between His Godhead and His soul?

Objection 1: It would seem that there was a severance in death between Christ's Godhead and His soul, because our Lord said (Jn. 10:18): "No man taketh away My soul from Me: but I lay it down of Myself, and I have power to lay it down, and I have power to take it up again." But it does not appear that the body can set the soul aside, by separating the soul from itself, because the soul is not subject to the power of the body, but rather conversely: and so it appears that it belongs to Christ, as the Word of God, to lay down His soul: but this is to separate it from Himself. Consequently, by death His soul was severed from the Godhead.

Objection 2: Further, Athanasius [*Vigilius Tapsensis, De Trin. vi; Bardenhewer assigns it to St. Athanasius: 45, iii. The full title is De Trinitate et Spiritu Sancto] says that he "is accursed who does not confess that the entire man, whom the Son of God took to Himself, after being assumed once more or delivered by Him, rose again from the dead on the third day." But the entire man could not be assumed again, unless the entire man was at one time separated from the Word of God: and the entire man is made of soul and body. Therefore there was a separation made at one time of the Godhead from both the body and the soul.

Objection 3: Further, the Son of God is truly styled a man because of the union with the entire man. If then, when the union of the soul with the body was dissolved by death, the Word of God continued united with the soul, it would follow that the Son of God could be truly called a soul. But this is false, because since the soul is the form of the body, it would result in the Word of God being the form of the body; which is impossible. Therefore, in death the soul of Christ was separated from the Word of God.

Objection 4: Further, the separated soul and body are not one hypostasis, but two. Therefore, if the Word of God remained united with Christ's soul and body, then, when they were severed by Christ's death, it seems to follow that the Word of God was two hypostases during such time as Christ was dead; which cannot be admitted. Therefore after Christ's death His soul did not continue to be united with the Word.

On the contrary, Damascene says (De Fide Orth. iii): "Although Christ died as man, and His holy soul was separated from His spotless body, nevertheless His Godhead remained unseparated from both---from the soul, I mean, and from the body."

I answer that, The soul is united with the Word of God more immediately and more primarily than the body is, because it is through the soul that the body is united with the Word of God, as stated above ([4268]Q[6], A[1]). Since, then, the Word of God was not separated from the body at Christ's death, much less was He separated from the soul. Accordingly, since what regards the body severed from the soul is affirmed of the Son of God---namely, that "it was buried"---so is it said of Him in the Creed that "He descended into hell," because His soul when separated from the body did go down into hell.

Reply to Objection 1: Augustine (Tract. xlvii in Joan.), in commenting on the text of John, asks, since Christ is Word and soul and body, "whether He putteth down His soul, for that He is the Word? Or, for that He is a soul?" Or, again, "for that He is flesh?" And he says that, "should we say that the Word of God laid down His soul" . . . it would follow that "there was a time when that soul was severed from the Word"---which is untrue. "For death severed the body and soul . . . but that the soul was severed from the Word I do not affirm . . . But should we say that the soul laid itself down," it follows "that it is severed from itself: which is most absurd." It remains, therefore, that "the flesh itself layeth down its soul and taketh it again, not by its own power, but by the power of the Word dwelling in the flesh": because, as stated above [4269](A[2]), the Godhead of the Word was not severed from the flesh in death.

Reply to Objection 2: In those words Athanasius never meant to say that the whole man was reassumed---that is, as to all his parts---as if the Word of God had laid aside the parts of human nature by His death; but that the totality of the assumed nature was restored once more in the resurrection by the resumed union of soul and body.

Reply to Objection 2: Through being united to human nature, the Word of God is not on that account called human nature: but He is called a man---that is, one having human nature. Now the soul and the body are essential parts of human nature. Hence it does not follow that the Word is a soul or a body through being united with both, but that He is one possessing a soul or a body.

Reply to Objection 4: As Damascene says (De Fide Orth. iii): "In Christ's death the soul was separated from the flesh: not one hypostasis divided into two: because both soul and body in the same respect had their existence from the beginning in the hypostasis of the Word; and in death, though severed from one another, each one continued to have the one same hypostasis of the Word. Wherefore the one hypostasis of the Word was the hypostasis of the Word, of the soul, and of the body. For neither soul nor body ever had an hypostasis of its own, besides the hypostasis of the Word: for there was always one hypostasis of the Word, and never two."

Whether Christ was a man during the three days of His death?

Objection 1: It would seem that Christ was a man during the three days of His death, because Augustine says (De Trin. iii): "Such was the assuming [of nature] as to make God to be man, and man to be God." But this assuming [of nature] did not cease at Christ's death. Therefore it seems that He did not cease to be a man in consequence of death.

Objection 2: Further, the Philosopher says (Ethic. ix) that "each man is his intellect"; consequently, when we address the soul of Peter after his death we say: "Saint Peter, pray for us." But the Son of God after death was not separated from His intellectual soul. Therefore, during those three days the Son of God was a man.

Objection 3: Further, every priest is a man. But during those three days of death Christ was a priest: otherwise what is said in Ps. 109:4 would not be true: "Thou art a priest for ever." Therefore Christ was a man during those three days.

On the contrary, When the higher [species] is removed, so is the lower. But the living or animated being is a higher species than animal and man, because an animal is a sensible animated substance. Now during those three days of death Christ's body was not living or animated. Therefore He was not a man.

I answer that, It is an article of faith that Christ was truly dead: hence it is an error against faith to assert anything whereby the truth of Christ's death is destroyed. Accordingly it is said in the Synodal epistle of Cyril [*Act. Conc. Ephes. P. I, cap. xxvi]: "If any man does not acknowledge that the Word of God suffered in the flesh, and was crucified in the flesh and tasted death in the flesh, let him be anathema." Now it belongs to the truth of the death of man or animal that by death the subject ceases to be man or animal; because the death of the man or animal results from the separation of the soul, which is the formal complement of the man or animal. Consequently, to say that Christ was a man during the three days of His death simply and without qualification, is erroneous. Yet it can be said that He was "a dead man" during those three days.

However, some writers have contended that Christ was a man during those three days, uttering words which are indeed erroneous, yet without intent of error in faith: as Hugh of Saint Victor, who (De Sacram. ii) contended that Christ, during the three days that followed His death, was a man, because he held that the soul is a man: but this is false, as was shown in the [4270]FP, Q[75], A[4]. Likewise the Master of the Sentences (iii, D, 22) held Christ to be a man during the three days of His death for quite another reason. For he believed the union of soul and flesh not to be essential to a man, and that for anything to be a man it suffices if it have a soul and body, whether united or separated: and that this is likewise false is clear both from what has been said in the [4271]FP, Q[75], A[4], and from what has been said above regarding the mode of union (Q[2], A[5]).

Reply to Objection 1: The Word of God assumed a united soul and body: and the result of this assumption was that God is man, and man is God. But this assumption did not cease by the separation of the Word from the soul or from the flesh; yet the union of soul and flesh ceased.

Reply to Objection 2: Man is said to be his own intellect, not because the intellect is the entire man, but because the intellect is the chief part of man, in which man's whole disposition lies virtually; just as the ruler of the city may be called the whole city, since its entire disposal is vested in him.

Reply to Objection 3: That a man is competent to be a priest is by reason of the soul, which is the subject of the character of order: hence a man does not lose his priestly order by death, and much less does Christ, who is the fount of the entire priesthood.

Whether Christ's was identically the same body living and dead?

Objection 1: It would seem that Christ's was not identically the same body living and dead. For Christ truly died just as other men do. But the body of everyone else is not simply identically the same, dead and living, because there is an essential difference between them. Therefore neither is the body of Christ identically the same, dead and living.

Objection 2: Further, according to the Philosopher (Metaph. v, text. 12), things specifically diverse are also numerically diverse. But Christ's body, living and dead, was specifically diverse: because the eye or flesh of the dead is only called so equivocally, as is evident from the Philosopher (De Anima ii, text. 9; Metaph. vii). Therefore Christ's body was not simply identically the same, living and dead.

Objection 3: Further, death is a kind of corruption. But what is corrupted by substantial corruption after being corrupted, exists no longer, since corruption is change from being to non-being. Therefore, Christ's body, after it was dead, did not remain identically the same, because death is a substantial corruption.

On the contrary, Athanasius says (Epist. ad Epict.): "In that body which was circumcised and carried, which ate, and toiled, and was nailed on the tree, there was the impassible and incorporeal Word of God: the same was laid in the tomb." But Christ's living body was circumcised and nailed on the tree; and Christ's dead body was laid in the tomb. Therefore it was the same body living and dead.

I answer that, The expression "simply" can be taken in two senses. In the first instance by taking "simply" to be the same as "absolutely"; thus "that is said simply which is said without addition," as the Philosopher put it (Topic. ii): and in this way the dead and living body of Christ was simply identically the same: since a thing is said to be "simply" identically the same from the identity of the subject. But Christ's body living and dead was identical in its suppositum because alive and dead it had none other besides the Word of God, as was stated above [4272](A[2]). And it is in this sense that Athanasius is speaking in the passage quoted.

In another way "simply" is the same as "altogether" or "totally": in which sense the body of Christ, dead and alive, was not "simply" the same identically, because it was not "totally" the same, since life is of the essence of a living body; for it is an essential and not an accidental predicate: hence it follows that a body which ceases to be living does not remain totally the same. Moreover, if it were to be said that Christ's dead body did continue "totally" the same, it would follow that it was not corrupted---I mean, by the corruption of death: which is the heresy of the Gaianites, as Isidore says (Etym. viii), and is to be found in the Decretals (xxiv, qu. iii). And Damascene says (De Fide Orth. iii) that "the term 'corruption' denotes two things: in one way it is the separation of the soul from the body and other things of the sort; in another way, the complete dissolving into elements. Consequently it is impious to say with Julian and Gaian that the Lord's body was incorruptible after the first manner of corruption before the resurrection: because Christ's body would not be consubstantial with us, nor truly dead, nor would we have been saved in very truth. But in the second way Christ's body was incorrupt."

Reply to Objection 1: The dead body of everyone else does not continue united to an abiding hypostasis, as Christ's dead body did; consequently the dead body of everyone else is not the same "simply," but only in some respect: because it is the same as to its matter, but not the same as to its form. But Christ's body remains the same simply, on account of the identity of the suppositum, as stated above.

Reply to Objection 2: Since a thing is said to be the same identically according to suppositum, but the same specifically according to form: wherever the suppositum subsists in only one nature, it follows of necessity that when the unity of species is taken away the unity of identity is also taken away. But the hypostasis of the Word of God subsists in two natures; and consequently, although in others the body does not remain the same according to the species of human nature, still it continues identically the same in Christ according to the suppositum of the Word of God.

Reply to Objection 3: Corruption and death do not belong to Christ by reason of the suppositum, from which suppositum follows the unity of identity; but by reason of the human nature, according to which is found the difference of death and of life in Christ's body.

Whether Christ's death conduced in any way to our salvation?

Objection 1: It would seem that Christ's death did not conduce in any way to our salvation. For death is a sort of privation, since it is the privation of life. But privation has not any power of activity, because it is nothing positive. Therefore it could not work anything for our salvation.

Objection 2: Further, Christ's Passion wrought our salvation by way of merit. But Christ's death could not operate in this way, because in death the body is separated from the soul, which is the principle of meriting. Consequently, Christ's death did not accomplish anything towards our salvation.

Objection 3: Further, what is corporeal is not the cause of what is spiritual. But Christ's death was corporeal. Therefore it could not be the cause of our salvation, which is something spiritual.

On the contrary, Augustine says (De Trin. iv): "The one death of our Saviour," namely, that of the body, "saved us from our two deaths," that is, of the soul and the body.

I answer that, We may speak of Christ's death in two ways, "in becoming" and "in fact." Death is said to be "in becoming" when anyone from natural or enforced suffering is tending towards death: and in this way it is the same thing to speak of Christ's death as of His Passion: so that in this sense Christ's death is the cause of our salvation, according to what has been already said of the Passion ([4273]Q[48]). But death is considered in fact, inasmuch as the separation of soul and body has already taken place: and it is in this sense that we are now speaking of Christ's death. In this way Christ's death cannot be the cause of our salvation by way of merit, but only by way of causality, that is to say, inasmuch as the Godhead was not separated from Christ's flesh by death; and therefore, whatever befell Christ's flesh, even when the soul was departed, was conducive to salvation in virtue of the Godhead united. But the effect of any cause is properly estimated according to its resemblance to the cause. Consequently, since death is a kind of privation of one's own life, the effect of Christ's death is considered in relation to the removal of the obstacles to our salvation: and these are the death of the soul and of the body. Hence Christ's death is said to have destroyed in us both the death of the soul, caused by sin, according to Rom. 4:25: "He was delivered up [namely unto death] for our sins": and the death of the body, consisting in the separation of the soul, according to 1 Cor. 15:54: "Death is swallowed up in victory."

Reply to Objection 1: Christ's death wrought our salvation from the power of the Godhead united, and not consisted merely as His death.

Reply to Objection 2: Though Christ's death, considered "in fact" did not effect our salvation by way of merit, yet it did so by way of causality, as stated above.

Reply to Objection 3: Christ's death was indeed corporeal; but the body was the instrument of the Godhead united to Him, working by Its power, although dead.

Day 283

OF CHRIST'S BURIAL (FOUR ARTICLES)
We have now to consider Christ's burial, concerning which there are four points of inquiry:
(1) Whether it was fitting for Christ to be buried?
(2) Concerning the manner of His burial;
(3) Whether His body was decomposed in the tomb?
(4) Concerning the length of time He lay in the tomb.

Whether it was fitting for Christ to be buried?

Objection 1: It would seem unfitting for Christ to have been buried, because it is said of Him (Ps. 87:6): "He is [Vulg.: 'I am'] become as a man without help, free among the dead." But the bodies of the dead are enclosed in a tomb; which seems contrary to liberty. Therefore it does not seem fitting for Christ to have been buried.

Objection 2: Further, nothing should be done to Christ except it was helpful to our salvation. But Christ's burial seems in no way to be conducive to our salvation. Therefore, it was not fitting for Him to be buried.

Objection 3: Further, it seems out of place for God who is above the high heavens to be laid in the earth. But what befalls the dead body of Christ is attributed to God by reason of the union. Therefore it appears to be unbecoming for Christ to be buried.

On the contrary, our Lord said (Mat. 26:10) of the woman who anointed Him: "She has wrought a good work upon Me," and then He added (Mat. 26:12)---"for she, in pouring this ointment upon My body, hath done it for My burial."

I answer that, It was fitting for Christ to be buried. First of all, to establish the truth of His death; for no one is laid in the grave unless there be certainty of death. Hence we read (Mk. 15:44,45), that Pilate by diligent inquiry assured himself of Christ's death before granting leave for His burial. Secondly, because by Christ's rising from the grave, to them who are in the grave, hope is given of rising again through Him, according to Jn. 5:25,28: "All that are in their graves shall hear the voice of the Son of God . . . and they that hear shall live." Thirdly, as an example to them who dying spiritually to their sins are hidden away "from the disturbance of men" (Ps. 30:21). Hence it is said (Col. 3:3): "You are dead, and your life is hid with Christ in God." Wherefore the baptized likewise who through Christ's death die to sins, are as it were buried with Christ by immersion, according to Rom. 6:4: "We are buried together with Christ by baptism into death."

Reply to Objection 1: Though buried, Christ proved Himself "free among the dead": since, although imprisoned in the tomb, He could not be hindered from going forth by rising again.

Reply to Objection 2: As Christ's death wrought our salvation, so likewise did His burial. Hence Jerome says (Super Marc. xiv): "By Christ's burial we rise again"; and on Is. 53:9: "He shall give the ungodly for His burial," a gloss says: "He shall give to God and the Father the Gentiles who were without godliness, because He purchased them by His death and burial."

Reply to Objection 3: As is said in a discourse made at the Council of Ephesus [*P. iii, cap. 9], "Nothing that saves man is derogatory to God; showing Him to be not passible, but merciful": and in another discourse of the same Council [*P. iii, cap. 10]: "God does not repute anything as an injury which is an occasion of men's salvation. Thus thou shalt not deem God's Nature to be so vile, as though It may sometimes be subjected to injuries."

Whether Christ was buried in a becoming manner?

Objection 1: It would seem that Christ was buried in an unbecoming manner. For His burial should be in keeping with His death. But Christ underwent a most shameful death, according to Wis. 2:20: "Let us condemn Him to a most shameful death." It seems therefore unbecoming for honorable burial to be accorded to Christ, inasmuch as He was buried by men of position---namely, by Joseph of Arimathea, who was "a noble counselor," to use Mark's expression (Mk. 15:43), and by Nicodemus, who was "a ruler of the Jews," as John states (Jn. 3:1).

Objection 2: Further, nothing should be done to Christ which might set an example of wastefulness. But it seems to savor of waste that in order to bury Christ Nicodemus came "bringing a mixture of myrrh and aloes about a hundred pounds weight," as recorded by John (19:39), especially since a woman came beforehand to anoint His body for the burial, as Mark relates (Mk. 14:28). Consequently, this was not done becomingly with regard to Christ.

Objection 3: Further, it is not becoming for anything done to be inconsistent with itself. But Christ's burial on the one hand was simple, because "Joseph wrapped His body in a clean linen cloth," as is related by Matthew (27:59), "but not with gold or gems, or silk," as Jerome observes: yet on the other hand there appears to have been some display, inasmuch as they buried Him with fragrant spices (Jn. 19:40). Consequently, the manner of Christ's burial does not seem to have been seemly.

Objection 4: Further, "What things soever were written," especially of Christ, "were written for our learning," according to Rom. 15:4. But some of the things written in the Gospels touching Christ's burial in no wise seem to pertain to our instruction---as that He was buried "in a garden . . . "in a tomb which was not His own, which was "new," and "hewed out in a rock." Therefore the manner of Christ's burial was not becoming.

On the contrary, It is written (Is. 11:10): "And His sepulchre shall be glorious."

I answer that, The manner of Christ's burial is shown to be seemly in three respects. First, to confirm faith in His death and resurrection. Secondly, to commend the devotion of those who gave Him burial. Hence Augustine says (De Civ. Dei i): "The Gospel mentions as praiseworthy the deed of those who received His body from the cross, and with due care and reverence wrapped it up and buried it." Thirdly, as to the mystery whereby those are molded who "are buried together with Christ into death" (Rom. 6:4).

Reply to Objection 1: With regard to Christ's death, His patience and constancy in enduring death are commended, and all the more that His death was the more despicable: but in His honorable burial we can see the power of the dying Man, who, even in death, frustrated the intent of His murderers, and was buried with honor: and thereby is foreshadowed the devotion of the faithful who in the time to come were to serve the dead Christ.

Reply to Objection 2: On that expression of the Evangelist (Jn. 19:40) that they buried Him "as the manner of the Jews is to bury," Augustine says (Tract. in Joan. cxx): "He admonishes us that in offices of this kind which are rendered to the dead, the custom of each nation should be observed." Now it was the custom of this people to anoint bodies with various spices in order the longer to preserve them from corruption [*Cf. Catena Aurea in Joan. xix]. Accordingly it is said in De Doctr. Christ. iii that "in all such things, it is not the use thereof, but the luxury of the user that is at fault"; and, farther on: "what in other persons is frequently criminal, in a divine or prophetic person is a sign of something great." For myrrh and aloes by their bitterness denote penance, by which man keeps Christ within himself without the corruption of sin; while the odor of the ointments expresses good report.

Reply to Objection 3: Myrrh and aloes were used on Christ's body in order that it might be preserved from corruption, and this seemed to imply a certain need (in the body): hence the example is set us that we may lawfully use precious things medicinally, from the need of preserving our body. But the wrapping up of the body was merely a question of becoming propriety. And we ought to content ourselves with simplicity in such things. Yet, as Jerome observes, by this act was denoted that "he swathes Jesus in clean linen, who receives Him with a pure soul." Hence, as Bede says on Mark 15:46: "The Church's custom has prevailed for the sacrifice of the altar to be offered not upon silk, nor upon dyed cloth, but on linen of the earth; as the Lord's body was buried in a clean winding-sheet."

Reply to Objection 4: Christ was buried "in a garden" to express that by His death and burial we are delivered from the death which we incur through Adam's sin committed in the garden of paradise. But for this "was our Lord buried in the grave of a stranger," as Augustine says in a sermon (ccxlviii), "because He died for the salvation of others; and a sepulchre is the abode of death." Also the extent of the poverty endured for us can be thereby estimated: since He who while living had no home, after death was laid to rest in another's tomb, and being naked was clothed by Joseph. But He is laid in a "new" sepulchre, as Jerome observes on Mat. 27:60, "lest after the resurrection it might be pretended that someone else had risen, while the other corpses remained. The new sepulchre can also denote Mary's virginal womb." And furthermore it may be understood that all of us are renewed by Christ's burial; death and corruption being destroyed. Moreover, He was buried in a monument "hewn out of a rock," as Jerome says on Mat. 27:64, "lest, if it had been constructed of many stones, they might say that He was stolen away by digging away the foundations of the tomb." Hence the "great stone" which was set shows that "the tomb could not be opened except by the help of many hands. Again, if He had been buried in the earth, they might have said: They dug up the soil and stole Him away," as Augustine observes [*Cf. Catena Aurea]. Hilary (Comment. in Matth. cap. xxxiii) gives the mystical interpretation, saying that "by the teaching of the apostles, Christ is borne into the stony heart of the gentile; for it is hewn out by the process of teaching, unpolished and new, untenanted and open to the entrance of the fear of God. And since naught besides Him must enter into our hearts, a great stone is rolled against the door." Furthermore, as Origen says (Tract. xxxv in Matth.): "It was not written by hazard: 'Joseph wrapped Christ's body in a clean winding-sheet, and placed it in a new monument,'" and that "'he rolled a great stone,' because all things around the body of Jesus are clean, and new, and exceeding great."

Whether Christ's body was reduced to dust in the tomb?

Objection 1: It would seem that Christ's body was reduced to dust in the tomb. For just as man dies in punishment of his first parent's sin, so also does he return to dust, since it was said to the first man after his sin: "Dust thou art, and into dust thou shalt return" (Gn. 3:19). But Christ endured death in order to deliver us from death. Therefore His body ought to be made to return to dust, so as to free us from the same penalty.

Objection 2: Further, Christ's body was of the same nature as ours. But directly after death our bodies begin to dissolve into dust, and are disposed towards putrefaction, because when the natural heat departs, there supervenes heat from without which causes corruption. Therefore it seems that the same thing happened to Christ's body.

Objection 3: Further, as stated above [4274](A[1]), Christ willed to be buried in order to furnish men with the hope of rising likewise from the grave. Consequently, He sought likewise to return to dust so as to give to them who have returned to dust the hope of rising from the dust.

On the contrary, It is written (Ps. 15:10): "Nor wilt Thou suffer Thy holy one to see corruption": and Damascene (De Fide Orth. iii) expounds this of the corruption which comes of dissolving into elements.

I answer that, It was not fitting for Christ's body to putrefy, or in any way be reduced to dust, since the putrefaction of any body comes of that body's infirmity of nature, which can no longer hold the body together. But as was said above ([4275]Q[50], A[1], ad 2), Christ's death ought not to come from weakness of nature, lest it might not be believed to be voluntary: and therefore He willed to die, not from sickness, but from suffering inflicted on Him, to which He gave Himself up willingly. And therefore, lest His death might be ascribed to infirmity of nature, Christ did not wish His body to putrefy in any way or dissolve no matter how; but for the manifestation of His Divine power He willed that His body should continue incorrupt. Hence Chrysostom says (Cont. Jud. et Gent. quod 'Christus sit Deus') that "with other men, especially with such as have wrought strenuously, their deeds shine forth in their lifetime; but as soon as they die, their deeds go with them. But it is quite the contrary with Christ: because previous to the cross all is sadness and weakness, but as soon as He is crucified, everything comes to light, in order that you may learn it was not an ordinary man that was crucified."

Reply to Objection 1: Since Christ was not subject to sin, neither was He prone to die or to return to dust. Yet of His own will He endured death for our salvation, for the reasons alleged above ([4276]Q[51], A[1]). But had His body putrefied or dissolved, this fact would have been detrimental to man's salvation, for it would not have seemed credible that the Divine power was in Him. Hence it is on His behalf that it is written (Ps. 19:10): "What profit is there in my blood, whilst I go down to corruption?" as if He were to say: "If My body corrupt, the profit of the blood shed will be lost."

Reply to Objection 2: Christ's body was a subject of corruption according to the condition of its passible nature, but not as to the deserving cause of putrefaction, which is sin: but the Divine power preserved Christ's body from putrefying, just as it raised it up from death.

Reply to Objection 3: Christ rose from the tomb by Divine power, which is not narrowed within bounds. Consequently, His rising from the grave was a sufficient argument to prove that men are to be raised up by Divine power, not only from their graves, but also from any dust whatever.

Whether Christ was in the tomb only one day and two nights?

Objection 1: It would seem that Christ was not in the tomb during only one day and two nights; because He said (Mat. 12:40): "As Jonas was in the whale's belly three days and three nights: so shall the Son of man be in the heart of the earth three days and three nights." But He was in the heart of the earth while He was in the grave. Therefore He was not in the tomb for only one day and two nights.

Objection 2: Gregory says in a Paschal Homily (Hom. xxi): "As Samson carried off the gates of Gaza during the night, even so Christ rose in the night, taking away the gates of hell." But after rising He was not in the tomb. Therefore He was not two whole nights in the grave.

Objection 3: Further, light prevailed over darkness by Christ's death. But night belongs to darkness, and day to light. Therefore it was more fitting for Christ's body to be in the tomb for two days and a night, rather than conversely.

On the contrary, Augustine says (De Trin. iv): "There were thirty-six hours from the evening of His burial to the dawn of the resurrection, that is, a whole night with a whole day, and a whole night."

I answer that, The very time during which Christ remained in the tomb shows forth the effect of His death. For it was said above ([4277]Q[50], A[6]) that by Christ's death we were delivered from a twofold death, namely, from the death of the soul and of the body: and this is signified by the two nights during which He remained in the tomb. But since His death did not come of sin, but was endured from charity, it has not the semblance of night, but of day: consequently it is denoted by the whole day during which Christ was in the sepulchre. And so it was fitting for Christ to be in the sepulchre during one day and two nights.

Reply to Objection 1: Augustine says (De Consens. Evang. iii): "Some men, ignorant of Scriptural language, wished to compute as night those three hours, from the sixth to the ninth hour, during which the sun was darkened, and as day those other three hours during which it was restored to the earth, that is, from the ninth hour until its setting: for the coming night of the Sabbath follows, and if this be reckoned with its day, there will be already two nights and two days. Now after the Sabbath there follows the night of the first day of the Sabbath, that is, of the dawning Sunday, on which the Lord rose. Even so, the reckoning of the three days and three nights will not stand. It remains then to find the solution in the customary usage of speech of the Scriptures, whereby the whole is understood from the part": so that we are able to take a day and a night as one natural day. And so the first day is computed from its ending, during which Christ died and was buried on the Friday; while the second. day is an entire day with twenty-four hours of night and day; while the night following belongs to the third day. "For as the primitive days were computed from light to night on account of man's future fall, so these days are computed from the darkness to the daylight on account of man's restoration" (De Trin. iv).

Reply to Objection 2: As Augustine says (De Trin. iv; cf. De Consens. Evang. iii), Christ rose with the dawn, when light appears in part, and still some part of the darkness of the night remains. Hence it is said of the women that "when it was yet dark" they came "to the sepulchre" (Jn. 20:1). Therefore, in consequence of this darkness, Gregory says (Hom. xxi) that Christ rose in the middle of the night, not that night is divided into two equal parts, but during the night itself: for the expression "early" can be taken as partly night and partly day, from its fittingness with both.

Reply to Objection 3: The light prevailed so far in Christ's death (which is denoted by the one day) that it dispelled the darkness of the two nights, that is, of our twofold death, as stated above.

OF CHRIST'S DESCENT INTO HELL (EIGHT ARTICLES)

We have now to consider Christ's descent into hell; concerning which there are eight points of inquiry:

(1) Whether it was fitting for Christ to descend into hell?
(2) Into which hell did He descend?
(3) Whether He was entirely in hell?
(4) Whether He made any stay there?
(5) Whether He delivered the Holy Fathers from hell?
(6) Whether He delivered the lost from hell?
(7) Whether He delivered the children who died in original sin?
(8) Whether He delivered men from Purgatory?

Whether it was fitting for Christ to descend into hell?

Objection 1: It would seem that it was not fitting for Christ to descend into hell, because Augustine says (Ep. ad Evod. cliv.): "Nor could I find anywhere in the Scriptures hell mentioned as something good." But Christ's soul did not descend into any evil place, for neither do the souls of the just. Therefore it does not seem fitting for Christ's soul to descend into hell.

Objection 2: Further, it cannot belong to Christ to descend into hell according to His Divine Nature, which is altogether immovable; but only according to His assumed nature. But that which Christ did or suffered in His assumed nature is ordained for man's salvation: and to secure this it does not seem necessary for Christ to descend into hell, since He delivered us from both guilt and penalty by His Passion which He endured in this world, as stated above ([4278]Q[49], AA[1],3). Consequently, it was not fitting that Christ should descend into hell.

Objection 3: Further, by Christ's death His soul was separated from His body, and this was laid in the sepulchre, as stated above ([4279]Q[51]). But it seems that He descended into hell, not according to His soul only, because seemingly the soul, being incorporeal, cannot be a subject of local motion; for this belongs to bodies, as is proved in Phys. vi, text. 32; while descent implies corporeal motion. Therefore it was not fitting for Christ to descend into hell.

On the contrary, It is said in the Creed: "He descended into hell": and the Apostle says (Eph. 4:9): "Now that He ascended, what is it, but because He also descended first into the lower parts of the earth?" And a gloss adds: "that is---into hell."

I answer that It was fitting for Christ to descend into hell. First of all, because He came to bear our penalty in order to free us from penalty, according to Is. 53:4: "Surely He hath borne our infirmities and carried our sorrows." But through sin man had incurred not only the death of the body, but also descent into hell. Consequently since it was fitting for Christ to die in order to deliver us from death, so it was fitting for Him to descend into hell in order to deliver us also from going down into hell. Hence it is written (Osee 13:14): "O death, I will be thy death; O hell, I will be thy bite." Secondly, because it was fitting when the devil was overthrown by the Passion that Christ should deliver the captives detained in hell, according to Zech. 9:11: "Thou also by the blood of Thy Testament hast sent forth Thy prisoners out of the pit." And it is written (Col. 2:15): "Despoiling the principalities and powers, He hath exposed them confidently." Thirdly, that as He showed forth His power on earth by living and dying, so also He might manifest it in hell, by visiting it and enlightening it. Accordingly it is written (Ps. 23:7): "Lift up your gates, O ye princes," which the gloss thus interprets: "that is---Ye princes of hell, take away your power, whereby hitherto you held men fast in hell"; and so "at the name of Jesus every knee should bow," not only "of them that are in heaven," but likewise "of them that are in hell," as is said in Phil. 2:10.

Reply to Objection 1: The name of hell stands for an evil of penalty, and not for an evil of guilt. Hence it was becoming that Christ should descend into hell, not as liable to punishment Himself, but to deliver them who were.

Reply to Objection 2: Christ's Passion was a kind of universal cause of men's salvation, both of the living and of the dead. But a general cause is applied to particular effects by means of something special. Hence, as the power of the Passion is applied to the living through the sacraments which make us like unto Christ's Passion, so likewise it is applied to the dead through His descent into hell. On which account it is written (Zech. 9:11) that "He sent forth prisoners out of the pit, in the blood of His testament," that is, by the power of His Passion.

Reply to Objection 3: Christ's soul descended into hell not by the same kind of motion as that whereby bodies are moved, but by that kind whereby the angels are moved, as was said in the [4280]FP, Q[53], A[1].

Whether Christ went down into the hell of the lost?

Objection 1: It would seem that Christ went down into the hell of the lost, because it is said by the mouth of Divine Wisdom (Ecclus. 24:45): "I will penetrate to all the lower parts of the earth." But the hell of the lost is computed among the lower parts of the earth according to Ps. 62:10: "They shall go into the lower parts of the earth." Therefore Christ who is the Wisdom of God, went down even into the hell of the lost.

Objection 2: Further, Peter says (Acts 2:24) that "God hath raised up Christ, having loosed the sorrows of hell, as it was impossible that He should be holden by it." But there are no sorrows in the hell of the Fathers, nor in the hell of the children, since they are not punished with sensible pain on account of any actual sin, but only with the pain of loss on account of original sin. Therefore Christ went down into the hell of the lost, or else into Purgatory, where men are tormented with sensible pain on account of actual sins.

Objection 3: Further, it is written (1 Pet. 3:19) that "Christ coming in spirit preached to those spirits that were in prison, which had some time been incredulous": and this is understood of Christ's descent into hell, as Athanasius says (Ep. ad Epict.). For he says that "Christ's body was laid in the sepulchre when He went to preach to those spirits who were in bondage, as Peter said." But it is clear the unbelievers were in the hell of the lost. Therefore Christ went down into the hell of the lost.

Objection 4: Further, Augustine says (Ep. ad Evod. clxiv): "If the sacred Scriptures had said that Christ came into Abraham's bosom, without naming hell or its woes, I wonder whether any person would dare to assert that He descended into hell. But since evident testimonies mention hell and its sorrows, there is no reason for believing that Christ went there except to deliver men from the same woes." But the place of woes is the hell of the lost. Therefore Christ descended into the hell of the lost.

Objection 5: Further, as Augustine says in a sermon upon the Resurrection: Christ descending into hell "set free all the just who were held in the bonds of original sin." But among them was Job, who says of himself (Job 17:16): "All that I have shall go down into the deepest pit." Therefore Christ descended into the deepest pit.

On the contrary, Regarding the hell of the lost it is written (Job 10:21): "Before I go, and return no more, to a land that is dark and covered with the mist of death." Now there is no "fellowship of light with darkness," according to 2 Cor. 6:14. Therefore Christ, who is "the light," did not descend into the hell of the lost.

I answer that, A thing is said to be in a place in two ways. First of all, through its effect, and in this way Christ descended into each of the hells, but in different manner. For going down into the hell of the lost He wrought this effect, that by descending thither He put them to shame for their unbelief and wickedness: but to them who were detained in Purgatory He gave hope of attaining to glory: while upon the holy Fathers detained in hell solely on account of original sin, He shed the light of glory everlasting.

In another way a thing is said to be in a place through its essence: and in this way Christ's soul descended only into that part of hell wherein the just were detained. so that He visited them "in place," according to His soul, whom He visited "interiorly by grace," according to His Godhead. Accordingly, while remaining in one part of hell, He wrought this effect in a measure in every part of hell, just as while suffering in one part of the earth He delivered the whole world by His Passion.

Reply to Objection 1: Christ, who is the Wisdom of God, penetrated to all the lower parts of the earth, not passing through them locally with His soul, but by spreading the effects of His power in a measure to them all: yet so that He enlightened only the just: because the text quoted continues: "And I will enlighten all that hope in the Lord."

Reply to Objection 2: Sorrow is twofold: one is the suffering of pain which men endure for actual sin, according to Ps. 17:6: "The sorrows of hell encompassed me." Another sorrow comes of hoped-for glory being deferred, according to Prov. 13:12: "Hope that is deferred afflicteth the soul": and such was the sorrow which the holy Fathers suffered in hell, and Augustine refers to it in a sermon on the Passion, saying that "they besought Christ with tearful entreaty." Now by descending into hell Christ took away both sorrows, yet in different ways: for He did away with the sorrows of pains by preserving souls from them, just as a physician is said to free a man from sickness by warding it off by means of physic. Likewise He removed the sorrows caused by glory deferred, by bestowing glory.

Reply to Objection 3: These words of Peter are referred by some to Christ's descent into hell: and they explain it in this sense: "Christ preached to them who formerly were unbelievers, and who were shut up in prison"---that is, in hell---"in spirit"---that is, by His soul. Hence Damascene says (De Fide Orth. iii): "As He evangelized them who are upon the earth, so did He those who were in hell"; not in order to convert unbelievers unto belief, but to put them to shame for their unbelief, since preaching cannot be understood otherwise than as the open manifesting of His Godhead. which was laid bare before them in the lower regions by His descending in power into hell.

Augustine, however, furnishes a better exposition of the text in his Epistle to Evodius quoted above, namely, that the preaching is not to be referred to Christ's descent into hell, but to the operation of His Godhead, to which He gave effect from the beginning of the world. Consequently, the sense is, that "to those (spirits) that were in prison"---that is, living in the mortal body, which is, as it were, the soul's prison-house---"by the spirit" of His Godhead "He came and preached" by internal inspirations, and from without by the admonitions spoken by the righteous: to those, I say, He preached "which had been some time incredulous," i.e. not believing in the preaching of Noe, "when they waited for the patience of God," whereby the chastisement of the Deluge was put off: accordingly (Peter) adds: "In the days of Noe, when the Ark was being built."

Reply to Objection 4: The expression "Abraham's bosom" may be taken in two senses. First of all, as implying that restfulness, existing there, from sensible pain; so that in this sense it cannot be called hell, nor are there any sorrows there. In another way it can be taken as implying the privation of longed-for glory: in this sense it has the character of hell and sorrow. Consequently, that rest of the blessed is now called Abraham's bosom, yet it is not styled hell, nor are sorrows said to be now in Abraham's bosom.

Reply to Objection 5: As Gregory says (Moral. xiii): "Even the higher regions of hell he calls the deepest hell . . . For if relatively to the height of heaven this darksome air is infernal, then relatively to the height of this same air the earth lying beneath can be considered as infernal and deep. And again in comparison with the height of the same earth, those parts of hell which are higher than the other infernal mansions, may in this way be designated as the deepest hell."

Whether the whole Christ was in hell?

Objection 1: It would seem that the whole Christ was not in hell. For Christ's body is one of His parts. But His body was not in hell. Therefore, the whole Christ was not in hell.

Objection 2: Further, nothing can be termed whole when its parts are severed. But the soul and body, which are the parts of human nature, were separated at His death, as stated above ([4281]Q[50], AA[3],4), and it was after death that He descended into hell. Therefore the whole (Christ) could not be in hell.

Objection 3: Further, the whole of a thing is said to be in a place when no part of it is outside such place. But there were parts of Christ outside hell; for instance, His body was in the grave, and His Godhead everywhere. Therefore the whole Christ was not in hell.

On the contrary, Augustine says (De Symbolo iii): "The whole Son is with the Father, the whole Son in heaven, on earth, in the Virgin's womb, on the Cross, in hell, in paradise, into which He brought the robber."

I answer that, It is evident from what was said in the [4282]FP, Q[31], A[2], ad 4, the masculine gender is referred to the hypostasis or person, while the neuter belongs to the nature. Now in the death of Christ, although the soul was separated from the body, yet neither was separated from the Person of the Son of God, as stated above (Q[50], A[2]). Consequently, it must be affirmed that during the three days of Christ's death the whole Christ was in the tomb, because the whole Person was there through the body united with Him, and likewise He was entirely in hell, because the whole Person of Christ was there by reason of the soul united with Him, and the whole Christ was then everywhere by reason of the Divine Nature.

Reply to Objection 1: The body which was then in the grave is not a part of the uncreated Person, but of the assumed nature. Consequently, the fact of Christ's body not being in hell does not prevent the whole Christ from being there: but proves that not everything appertaining to human nature was there.

Reply to Objection 2: The whole human nature is made up of the united soul and body; not so the Divine Person. Consequently when death severed the union of the soul with the body, the whole Christ remained, but His whole human nature did not remain.

Reply to Objection 3: Christ's Person is whole in each single place, but not wholly, because it is not circumscribed by any place: indeed, all places put together could not comprise His immensity; rather is it His immensity that embraces all things. But it happens in those things which are in a place corporeally and circumscriptively, that if a whole be in some place, then no part of it is outside that place. But this is not the case with God. Hence Augustine says (De Symbolo iii): "It is not according to times or places that we say that the whole Christ is everywhere, as if He were at one time whole in one place, at another time whole in another: but as being whole always and everywhere."

Whether Christ made any stay in hell?

Objection 1: It would seem that Christ did not make any stay in hell. For Christ went down into hell to deliver men from thence. But He accomplished this deliverance at once by His descent, for, according to Ecclus. 11:23: "It is easy in the eyes of God on a sudden to make the poor man rich." Consequently He does not seem to have tarried in hell.

Objection 2: Further, Augustine says in a sermon on the Passion (clx) that "of a sudden at our Lord and Saviour's bidding all 'the bars of iron were burst'" (Cf. Is. 45:2). Hence on behalf of the angels accompanying Christ it is written (Ps. 23:7, 9): "Lift up your gates, O ye princes." Now Christ descended thither in order to break the bolts of hell. Therefore He did not make any stay in hell.

Objection 3: Further, it is related (Lk. 23:43) that our Lord while hanging on the cross said to the thief: "This day thou shalt be with Me in paradise": from which it is evident that Christ was in paradise on that very day. But He was not there with His body. for that was in the grave. Therefore He was there with the soul which had gone down into hell: and consequently it appears that He made no stay in hell.

On the contrary, Peter says (Acts 2:24): "Whom God hath raised up, having loosed the sorrows of hell, as it was impossible that He should be held by it." Therefore it seems that He remained in hell until the hour of the Resurrection.

I answer that, As Christ, in order to take our penalties upon Himself, willed His body to be laid in the tomb, so likewise He willed His soul to descend into hell. But the body lay in the tomb for a day and two nights, so as to demonstrate the truth of His death. Consequently, it is to be believed that His soul was in hell, in order that it might be brought back out of hell simultaneously with His body from the tomb.

Reply to Objection 1: When Christ descended into hell He delivered the saints who were there, not by leading them out at once from the confines of hell, but by enlightening them with the light of glory in hell itself. Nevertheless it was fitting that His soul should abide in hell as long as His body remained in the tomb.

Reply to Objection 2: By the expression "bars of hell" are understood the obstacles which kept the holy Fathers from quitting hell, through the guilt of our first parent's sin; and these bars Christ burst asunder by the power of His Passion on descending into hell: nevertheless He chose to remain in hell for some time, for the reason stated above.

Reply to Objection 3: Our Lord's expression is not to be understood of the earthly corporeal paradise, but of a spiritual one, in which all are said to be who enjoy the Divine glory. Accordingly, the thief descended locally into hell with Christ, because it was said to him: "This day thou shalt be with Me in paradise"; still as to reward he was in paradise, because he enjoyed Christ's Godhead just as the other saints did.

Whether Christ descending into hell delivered the holy Fathers from thence?

Objection 1: It would seem that Christ descending into hell did not deliver the holy Fathers from thence. For Augustine (Epist. ad Evod. clxiv) says: "I have not yet discovered what Christ descending into hell bestowed upon those righteous ones who were in

Abraham's bosom, from whom I fail to see that He ever departed according to the beatific presence of His Godhead." But had He delivered them, He would have bestowed much upon them. Therefore it does not appear that Christ delivered the holy Fathers from hell.

Objection 2: Further, no one is detained in hell except on account of sin. But during life the holy Fathers were justified from sin through faith in Christ. Consequently they did not need to be delivered from hell on Christ's descent thither.

Objection 3: Further, if you remove the cause, you remove the effect. But that Christ went down into hell was due to sin which was taken away by the Passion, as stated above ([4283]Q[49], A[1]). Consequently, the holy Fathers were not delivered on Christ's descent into hell.

On the contrary, Augustine says in the sermon on the Passion already quoted that when Christ descended into hell "He broke down the gate and 'iron bars' of hell, setting at liberty all the righteous who were held fast through original sin."

I answer that, As stated above (A[4], ad 2), when Christ descended into hell He worked through the power of His Passion. But through Christ's Passion the human race was delivered not only from sin, but also from the debt of its penalty, as stated above (Q[49], AA[1],3). Now men were held fast by the debt of punishment in two ways: first of all for actual sin which each had committed personally: secondly, for the sin of the whole human race, which each one in his origin contracts from our first parent, as stated in Rom. 5 of which sin the penalty is the death of the body as well as exclusion from glory, as is evident from Gn. 2 and 3: because God cast out man from paradise after sin, having beforehand threatened him with death should he sin. Consequently, when Christ descended into hell, by the power of His Passion He delivered the saints from the penalty whereby they were excluded from the life of glory, so as to be unable to see God in His Essence, wherein man's beatitude lies, as stated in the [4284]FS, Q[3], A[8]. But the holy Fathers were detained in hell for the reason, that, owing to our first parent's sin, the approach to the life of glory was not opened. And so when Christ descended into hell He delivered the holy Fathers from thence. And this is what is written Zech. 9:11: "Thou also by the blood of Thy testament hast sent forth Thy prisoners out of the pit, wherein is no water." And (Col. 2:15) it is written that "despoiling the principalities and powers," i.e. "of hell, by taking out Isaac and Jacob, and the other just souls," "He led them," i.e. "He brought them far from this kingdom of darkness into heaven," as the gloss explains.

Reply to Objection 1: Augustine is speaking there against such as maintained that the righteous of old were subject to penal sufferings before Christ's descent into hell. Hence shortly before the passage quoted he says: "Some add that this benefit was also bestowed upon the saints of old, that on the Lord's coming into hell they were freed from their sufferings. But I fail to see how Abraham, into whose bosom the poor man was received, was ever in such sufferings." Consequently, when he afterwards adds that "he had not yet discovered what Christ's descent into hell had brought to the righteous of old," this must be understood as to their being freed from penal sufferings. Yet Christ bestowed something upon them as to their attaining glory: and in consequence He dispelled the suffering which they endured through their glory being delayed: still they had great joy from the very hope thereof, according to Jn. 8:56: "Abraham your father rejoiced that he might see my day." And therefore he adds: "I fail to see that He ever departed, according to the beatific presence of His Godhead," that is, inasmuch as even before Christ's coming they were happy in hope, although not yet fully happy in fact.

Reply to Objection 2: The holy Fathers while yet living were delivered from original as well as actual sin through faith in Christ; also from the penalty of actual sins, but not from the penalty of original sin, whereby they were excluded from glory, since the price of man's redemption was not yet paid: just as the faithful are now delivered by baptism from the penalty of actual sins, and from the penalty of original sin as to exclusion from glory, yet still remain bound by the penalty of original sin as to the necessity of dying in the body because they are renewed in the spirit, but not yet in the flesh, according to Rom. 8:10: "The body indeed is dead, because of sin; but the spirit liveth, because of justification."

Reply to Objection 3: Directly Christ died His soul went down into hell, and bestowed the fruits of His Passion on the saints detained there; although they did not go out as long as Christ remained in hell, because His presence was part of the fulness of their glory.

Day 284

Whether Christ delivered any of the lost from hell?

Objection 1: It would seem that Christ did deliver some of the lost from hell, because it is written (Is. 24:22): "And they shall be gathered together as in the gathering of one bundle into the pit, end they shall be shut up there in prison: and after many days they shall be visited." But there he is speaking of the lost, who "had adored the host of heaven," according to Jerome's commentary. Consequently it seems that even the lost were visited at Christ's descent into hell; and this seems to imply their deliverance.

Objection 2: Further, on Zech. 9:11: "Thou also by the blood of Thy testament hast sent forth Thy prisoners out of the pit wherein is no water," the gloss observes: "Thou hast delivered them who were held bound in prisons, where no mercy refreshed them, which that rich man prayed for." But only the lost are shut up in merciless prisons. Therefore Christ did deliver some from the hell of the lost.

Objection 3: Further, Christ's power was not less in hell than in this world, because He worked in every place by the power of His Godhead. But in this world He delivered some persons of every state. Therefore, in hell also, He delivered some from the state of the lost.

On the contrary, It is written (Osee 13:14): "O death, I will be thy death; O hell, I will be thy bite": upon which the gloss says: "By leading forth the elect, and leaving there the reprobate." But only the reprobate are in the hell of the lost. Therefore, by Christ's descent into hell none were delivered from the hell of the lost.

I answer that, As stated above [4285](A[5]), when Christ descended into hell He worked by the power of His Passion. Consequently, His descent into hell brought the fruits of deliverance to them only who were united to His Passion through faith quickened by charity, whereby sins are taken away. Now those detained in the hell of the lost either had no faith in Christ's Passion, as

429

infidels; or if they had faith, they had no conformity with the charity of the suffering Christ: hence they could not be cleansed from their sins. And on this account Christ's descent into hell brought them no deliverance from the debt of punishment in hell.

Reply to Objection 1: When Christ descended into hell, all who were in any part of hell were visited in some respect: some to their consolation and deliverance, others, namely, the lost, to their shame and confusion. Accordingly the passage continues: "And the moon shall blush, and the sun be put to shame," etc.

This can also be referred to the visitation which will come upon them in the Day of Judgment, not for their deliverance, but for their yet greater confusion, according to Sophon. i, 12: "I will visit upon the men that are settled on their lees."

Reply to Objection 2: When the gloss says "where no mercy refreshed them," this is to be understood of the refreshing of full deliverance, because the holy Fathers could not be delivered from this prison of hell before Christ's coming.

Reply to Objection 3: It was not due to any lack of power on Christ's part that some were not delivered from every state in hell, as out of every state among men in this world; but it was owing to the very different condition of each state. For, so long as men live here below, they can be converted to faith and charity, because in this life men are not confirmed either in good or in evil, as they are after quitting this life.

Whether the children who died in original sin were delivered by Christ?

Objection 1: It would seem that the children who died in original sin were delivered from hell by Christ's descending thither. For, like the holy Fathers, the children were kept in hell simply because of original sin. But the holy Fathers were delivered from hell, as stated above [4286](A[5]). Therefore the children were similarly delivered from hell by Christ.

Objection 2: Further, the Apostle says (Rom. 5:15): "If by the offense of one, many died; much more the grace of God and the gift, by the grace of one man, Jesus Christ, hath abounded unto many." But the children who die with none but original sin are detained in hell owing to their first parent's sin. Therefore, much more were they delivered from hell through the grace of Christ.

Objection 3: Further, as Baptism works in virtue of Christ's Passion, so also does Christ's descent into hell, as is clear from what has been said (A[4], ad 2, AA[5],6). But through Baptism children are delivered from original sin and hell. Therefore, they were similarly delivered by Christ's descent into hell.

On the contrary, The Apostle says (Rom. 3:25): "God hath proposed Christ to be a propitiation, through faith in His blood." But the children who had died with only original sin were in no wise sharers of faith in Christ. Therefore, they did not receive the fruits of Christ's propitiation, so as to be delivered by Him from hell.

I answer that, As stated above [4287](A[6]), Christ's descent into hell had its effect of deliverance on them only who through faith and charity were united to Christ's Passion, in virtue whereof Christ's descent into hell was one of deliverance. But the children who had died in original sin were in no way united to Christ's Passion by faith and love: for, not having the use of free will, they could have no faith of their own; nor were they cleansed from original sin either by their parents' faith or by any sacrament of faith. Consequently, Christ's descent into hell did not deliver the children from thence. And furthermore, the holy Fathers were delivered from hell by being admitted to the glory of the vision of God, to which no one can come except through grace; according to Rom. 6:23: "The grace of God is life everlasting." Therefore, since children dying in original sin had no grace, they were not delivered from hell.

Reply to Objection 1: The holy Fathers, although still held bound by the debt of original sin, in so far as it touches human nature, were nevertheless delivered from all stain of sin by faith in Christ: consequently, they were capable of that deliverance which Christ brought by descending into hell. But the same cannot be said of the children, as is evident from what was said above.

Reply to Objection 2: When the Apostle says that the grace of God "hath abounded unto many," the word "many" [*The Vulgate reads 'plures,' i.e. 'many more'] is to be taken, not comparatively, as if more were saved by Christ's grace than lost by Adam's sin: but absolutely, as if he said that the grace of the one Christ abounded unto many, just as Adam's sin was contracted by many. But as Adam's sin was contracted by those only who descended seminally from him according to the flesh, so Christ's grace reached those only who became His members by spiritual regeneration: which does not apply to children dying in original sin.

Reply to Objection 3: Baptism is applied to men in this life, in which man's state can be changed from sin into grace: but Christ's descent into hell was vouchsafed to the souls after this life when they are no longer capable of the said change. And consequently by baptism children are delivered from original sin and from hell, but not by Christ's descent into hell.

Whether Christ by His descent into hell delivered souls from purgatory?

Objection 1: It would seem that Christ by His descent into hell delivered souls from Purgatory---for Augustine says (Ep. ad Evod. clxiv): "Because evident testimonies speak of hell and its pains, there is no reason for believing that the Saviour came thither except to rescue men from those same pains: but I still wish to know whether it was all whom He found there, or some whom He deemed worthy of such a benefit. Yet I do not doubt that Christ went into hell, and granted this favor to them who were suffering from its pains." But, as stated above [4288](A[6]), He did not confer the benefit of deliverance upon the lost: and there are no others in a state of penal suffering except those in Purgatory. Consequently Christ delivered souls from Purgatory.

Objection 2: Further, the very presence of Christ's soul had no less effect than His sacraments have. But souls are delivered from Purgatory by the sacraments, especially by the sacrament of the Eucharist, as shall be shown later ([4289]XP, Q[71], A[9]). Therefore much more were souls delivered from Purgatory by the presence of Christ descending into hell.

Objection 3: Further, as Augustine says (De Poenit. ix), those whom Christ healed in this life He healed completely. Also, our Lord says (Jn. 7:23): "I have healed the whole man on the sabbath-day." But Christ delivered them who were in Purgatory from the punishment of the pain of loss, whereby they were excluded from glory. Therefore, He also delivered them from the punishment of Purgatory.

On the contrary, Gregory says (Moral. xiii): "Since our Creator and Redeemer, penetrating the bars of hell, brought out from thence the souls of the elect, He does not permit us to go thither, from whence He has already by descending set others free." But He permits us to go to Purgatory. Therefore, by descending into hell, He did not deliver souls from Purgatory.

I answer that, As we have stated more than once (A[4], ad 2, AA[5],6,7), Christ's descent into hell was one of deliverance in virtue of His Passion. Now Christ's Passion had a virtue which was neither temporal nor transitory, but everlasting, according to Heb. 10:14: "For by one oblation He hath perfected for ever them that are sanctified." And so it is evident that Christ's Passion had no greater efficacy then than it has now. Consequently, they who were such as those who are now in Purgatory, were not set free from Purgatory by Christ's descent into hell. But if any were found such as are now set free from Purgatory by virtue of Christ's Passion, then there was nothing to hinder them from being delivered from Purgatory by Christ's descent into hell.

Reply to Objection 1: From this passage of Augustine it cannot be concluded that all who were in Purgatory were delivered from it, but that such a benefit was bestowed upon some persons, that is to say, upon such as were already cleansed sufficiently, or who in life, by their faith and devotion towards Christ's death, so merited, that when He descended, they were delivered from the temporal punishment of Purgatory.

Reply to Objection 2: Christ's power operates in the sacraments by way of healing and expiation. Consequently, the sacrament of the Eucharist delivers men from Purgatory inasmuch as it is a satisfactory sacrifice for sin. But Christ's descent into hell was not satisfactory; yet it operated in virtue of the Passion, which was satisfactory, as stated above ([4290]Q[48], A[2]), but satisfactory in general, since its virtue had to be applied to each individual by something specially personal ([4291]Q[49], A[1], ad 4,5). Consequently, it does not follow of necessity that all were delivered from Purgatory by Christ's descent into hell.

Reply to Objection 3: Those defects from which Christ altogether delivered men in this world were purely personal, and concerned the individual; whereas exclusion from God's glory was a general defect and common to all human nature. Consequently, there was nothing to prevent those detained in Purgatory being delivered by Christ from their privation of glory, but not from the debt of punishment in Purgatory which pertains to personal defect. Just as on the other hand, the holy Fathers before Christ's coming were delivered from their personal defects, but not from the common defect, as was stated above (A[7], ad 1;[4292] Q[49], A[5], ad 1).

OF CHRIST'S RESURRECTION (FOUR ARTICLES)

We have now to consider those things that concern Christ's Exaltation; and we shall deal with (1) His Resurrection; (2) His Ascension; (3) His sitting at the right hand of God the Father; (4) His Judiciary Power. Under the first heading there is a fourfold consideration: (1) Christ's Resurrection in itself; (2) the quality of the Person rising; (3) the manifestation of the Resurrection; (4) its causality. Concerning the first there are four points of inquiry:

(1) The necessity of His Resurrection;

(2) The time of the Resurrection;

(3) Its order;

(4) Its cause.

Whether it was necessary for Christ to rise again?

Objection 1: It would seem that it was not necessary for Christ to rise again. For Damascene says (De Fide Orth. iv): "Resurrection is the rising again of an animate being, which was disintegrated and fallen." But Christ did not fall by sinning, nor was His body dissolved, as is manifest from what was stated above ([4293]Q[51], A[3]). Therefore, it does not properly belong to Him to rise again.

Objection 2: Further, whoever rises again is promoted to a higher state, since to rise is to be uplifted. But after death Christ's body continued to be united with the Godhead, hence it could not be uplifted to any higher condition. Therefore, it was not due to it to rise again.

Objection 3: Further, all that befell Christ's humanity was ordained for our salvation. But Christ's Passion sufficed for our salvation, since by it we were loosed from guilt and punishment, as is clear from what was said above ([4294]Q[49], A[1],3). Consequently, it was not necessary for Christ to rise again from the dead.

On the contrary, It is written (Lk. 24:46): "It behooved Christ to suffer and to rise again from the dead."

I answer that, It behooved Christ to rise again, for five reasons. First of all; for the commendation of Divine Justice, to which it belongs to exalt them who humble themselves for God's sake, according to Lk. 1:52: "He hath put down the mighty from their seat, and hath exalted the humble." Consequently, because Christ humbled Himself even to the death of the Cross, from love and obedience to God, it behooved Him to be uplifted by God to a glorious resurrection; hence it is said in His Person (Ps. 138:2): "Thou hast known," i.e. approved, "my sitting down," i.e. My humiliation and Passion, "and my rising up," i.e. My glorification in the resurrection; as the gloss expounds.

Secondly, for our instruction in the faith, since our belief in Christ's Godhead is confirmed by His rising again, because, according to 2 Cor. 13:4, "although He was crucified through weakness, yet He liveth by the power of God." And therefore it is written (1 Cor. 15:14): "If Christ be not risen again, then is our preaching vain, and our [Vulg.: 'your'] faith is also vain": and (Ps. 29:10): "What profit is there in my blood?" that is, in the shedding of My blood, "while I go down," as by various degrees of evils, "into corruption?" As though He were to answer: "None. 'For if I do not at once rise again but My body be corrupted, I shall preach to no one, I shall gain no one,'" as the gloss expounds.

Thirdly, for the raising of our hope, since through seeing Christ, who is our head, rise again, we hope that we likewise shall rise again. Hence it is written (1 Cor. 15:12): "Now if Christ be preached that He rose from the dead, how do some among you say, that there is no resurrection of the dead?" And (Job 19:25, 27): "I know," that is with certainty of faith, "that my Redeemer," i.e. Christ, "liveth," having risen from the dead; "and" therefore "in the last day I shall rise out of the earth . . . this my hope is laid up in my bosom."

Fourthly, to set in order the lives of the faithful: according to Rom. 6:4: "As Christ is risen from the dead by the glory of the Father, so we also may walk in newness of life": and further on; "Christ rising from the dead dieth now no more; so do you also reckon that you are dead to sin, but alive to God."

Fifthly, in order to complete the work of our salvation: because, just as for this reason did He endure evil things in dying that He might deliver us from evil, so was He glorified in rising again in order to advance us towards good things; according to Rom. 4:25: "He was delivered up for our sins, and rose again for our justification."

Reply to Objection 1: Although Christ did not fall by sin, yet He fell by death, because as sin is a fall from righteousness, so death is a fall from life: hence the words of Mic. 7:8 can be taken as though spoken by Christ: "Rejoice not thou, my enemy, over me, because I am fallen: I shall rise again." Likewise, although Christ's body was not disintegrated by returning to dust, yet the separation of His soul and body was a kind of disintegration.

Reply to Objection 2: The Godhead was united with Christ's flesh after death by personal union, but not by natural union; thus the soul is united with the body as its form, so as to constitute human nature. Consequently, by the union of the body and soul, the body was uplifted to a higher condition of nature, but not to a higher personal state.

Reply to Objection 3: Christ's Passion wrought our salvation, properly speaking, by removing evils; but the Resurrection did so as the beginning and exemplar of all good things.

Whether it was fitting for Christ to rise again on the third day?

Objection 1: It would seem unfitting that Christ should have risen again on the third day. For the members ought to be in conformity with their head. But we who are His members do not rise from death on the third day, since our rising is put off until the end of the world. Therefore, it seems that Christ, who is our head, should not have risen on the third day, but that His Resurrection ought to have been deferred until the end of the world.

Objection 2: Further, Peter said (Acts 2:24) that "it was impossible for Christ to be held fast by hell" and death. Therefore it seems that Christ's rising ought not to have been deferred until the third day, but that He ought to have risen at once on the same day; especially since the gloss quoted above [4295](A[1]) says that "there is no profit in the shedding of Christ's blood, if He did not rise at once."

Objection 3: The day seems to start with the rising of the sun, the presence of which causes the day. But Christ rose before sunrise: for it is related (Jn. 20:1) that "Mary Magdalen cometh early, when it was yet dark, unto the sepulchre": but Christ was already risen, for it goes on to say: "And she saw the stone taken away from the sepulchre." Therefore Christ did not rise on the third day.

On the contrary, It is written (Mat. 20:19): "They shall deliver Him to the Gentiles to be mocked, and scourged, and crucified, and the third day He shall rise again."

I answer that, As stated above [4296](A[1]) Christ's Resurrection was necessary for the instruction of our faith. But our faith regards Christ's Godhead and humanity, for it is not enough to believe the one without the other, as is evident from what has been said (Q[36], A[4]; cf. [4297]SS, Q[2], AA[7],8). Consequently, in order that our faith in the truth of His Godhead might be confirmed it was necessary that He should rise speedily, and that His Resurrection should not be deferred until the end of the world. But to confirm our faith regarding the truth of His humanity and death, it was needful that there should be some interval between His death and rising. For if He had risen directly after death, it might seem that His death was not genuine and consequently neither would His Resurrection be true. But to establish the truth of Christ's death, it was enough for His rising to be deferred until the third day, for within that time some signs of life always appear in one who appears to be dead whereas he is alive.

Furthermore, by His rising on the third day, the perfection of the number "three" is commended, which is "the number of everything," as having "beginning, middle, and end," as is said in De Coelo i. Again in the mystical sense we are taught that Christ by "His one death" (i.e. of the body) which was light, by reason of His righteousness, "destroyed our two deaths" (i.e. of soul and body), which are as darkness on account of sin; consequently, He remained in death for one day and two nights, as Augustine observes (De Trin. iv).

And thereby is also signified that a third epoch began with the Resurrection: for the first was before the Law; the second under the Law; and the third under grace. Moreover the third state of the saints began with the Resurrection of Christ: for, the first was under figures of the Law; the second under the truth of faith; while the third will be in the eternity of glory, which Christ inaugurated by rising again.

Reply to Objection 1: The head and members are likened in nature, but not in power; because the power of the head is more excellent than that of the members. Accordingly, to show forth the excellence of Christ's power, it was fitting that He should rise on the third day, while the resurrection of the rest is put off until the end of the world.

Reply to Objection 2: Detention implies a certain compulsion. But Christ was not held fast by any necessity of death, but was "free among the dead": and therefore He abode a while in death, not as one held fast, but of His own will, just so long as He deemed necessary for the instruction of our faith. And a task is said to be done "at once" which is performed within a short space of time.

Reply to Objection 3: As stated above ([4298]Q[51], A[4], ad 1,2), Christ rose early when the day was beginning to dawn, to denote that by His Resurrection He brought us to the light of glory; just as He died when the day was drawing to its close, and nearing to darkness, in order to signify that by His death He would destroy the darkness of sin and its punishment. Nevertheless He is said to have risen on the third day, taking day as a natural day which contains twenty-four hours. And as Augustine says (De Trin. iv): "The night until the dawn, when the Lord's Resurrection was proclaimed, belongs to the third day. Because God, who made the light to shine forth from darkness, in order that by the grace of the New Testament and partaking of Christ's rising we might hear this---'once ye were darkness, but now light in the Lord'---insinuates in a measure to us that day draws its origin from night: for, as the first days are computed from light to darkness on account of man's coming fall, so these days are reckoned from darkness to light owing to man's restoration." And so it is evident that even if He had risen at midnight, He could be said to have risen on the third day, taking it as a natural day. But now that He rose early, it can be affirmed that He rose on the third day, even taking the artificial day which is caused by the sun's presence, because the sun had already begun to brighten the sky. Hence it is written (Mk. 16:2) that "the women come to the sepulchre, the sun being now risen"; which is not contrary to John's statement "when it was yet dark," as Augustine says (De Cons. Evang. iii), "because, as the day advances the more the light rises, the more are the remaining shadows dispelled." But when Mark says "'the sun being now risen,' it is not to be taken as if the sun were already apparent over the horizon, but as coming presently into those parts."

Whether Christ was the first to rise from the dead?

Objection 1: It would seem that Christ was not the first to rise from the dead, because we read in the Old Testament of some persons raised to life by Elias and Eliseus, according to Heb. 11:35: "Women received their dead raised to life again": also Christ before His Passion raised three dead persons to life. Therefore Christ was not the first to rise from the dead.

Objection 2: Further, among the other miracles which happened during the Passion, it is narrated (Mat. 27:52) that "the monuments were opened, and many bodies of the saints who had slept rose again." Therefore Christ was not the first to rise from the dead.

Objection 3: Further, as Christ by His own rising is the cause of our resurrection, so by His grace He is the cause of our grace, according to Jn. 1:16: "Of His fulness we all have received." But in point of time some others had grace previous to Christ---for instance all the fathers of the Old Testament. Therefore some others came to the resurrection of the body before Christ.

On the contrary, It is written (1 Cor. 15:20): "Christ is risen from the dead, the first fruits of them that sleep---because," says the gloss, "He rose first in point of time and dignity."

I answer that, Resurrection is a restoring from death to life. Now a man is snatched from death in two ways: first of all, from actual death, so that he begins in any way to live anew after being actually dead: in another way, so that he is not only rescued from death, but from the necessity, nay more, from the possibility of dying again. Such is a true and perfect resurrection, because so long as a man lives, subject to the necessity of dying, death has dominion over him in a measure, according to Rom. 8:10: "The body indeed is dead because of sin." Furthermore, what has the possibility of existence, is said to exist in some respect, that is, in potentiality. Thus it is evident that the resurrection, whereby one is rescued from actual death only, is but an imperfect one.

Consequently, speaking of perfect resurrection, Christ is the first of them who rise, because by rising He was the first to attain life utterly immortal, according to Rom. 6:9: "Christ rising from the dead dieth now no more." But by an imperfect resurrection, some others have risen before Christ, so as to be a kind of figure of His Resurrection.

And thus the answer to the first objection is clear: because both those raised from the dead in the old Testament, and those raised by Christ, so returned to life that they had to die again.

Reply to Objection 2: There are two opinions regarding them who rose with Christ. Some hold that they rose to life so as to die no more, because it would be a greater torment for them to die a second time than not to rise at all. According to this view, as Jerome observes on Mat. 27:52,53, we must understand that "they had not risen before our Lord rose." Hence the Evangelist says that "coming out of the tombs after His Resurrection, they came into the holy city, and appeared to many." But Augustine (Ep. ad Evod. clxiv) while giving this opinion, says: "I know that it appears some, that by the death of Christ the Lord the same resurrection was bestowed upon the righteous as is promised to us in the end; and if they slept not again by laying aside their bodies, it remains to be seen how Christ can be understood to be 'the first-born of the dead,' if so many preceded Him unto that resurrection. Now if reply be made that this is said by anticipation, so that the monuments be understood to have been opened by the earthquake while Christ was still hanging on the cross, but that the bodies of the just did not rise then but after He had risen, the difficulty still arises---how is it that Peter asserts that it was predicted not of David but of Christ, that His body would not see corruption, since David's tomb was in their midst; and thus he did not convince them, if David's body was no longer there; for even if he had risen soon after his death, and his flesh had not seen corruption, his tomb might nevertheless remain. Now it seems hard that David from whose seed Christ is descended, was not in that rising of the just, if an eternal rising was conferred upon them. Also that saying in the Epistle to the Hebrews (11:40) regarding the ancient just would be hard to explain, 'that they should not be perfected without us,' if they were already established in that incorruption of the resurrection which is promised at the end when we shall be made perfect": so that Augustine would seem to think that they rose to die again. In this sense Jerome also in commenting on Matthew (27:52,53) says: "As Lazarus rose, so also many of the bodies of the saints rose, that they might bear witness to the risen Christ." Nevertheless in a sermon for the Assumption [*Ep. ix ad Paul. et Eustoch.; among the supposititious works ascribed to St. Jerome] he seems to leave the matter doubtful. But Augustine's reasons seem to be much more cogent.

Reply to Objection 3: As everything preceding Christ's coming was preparatory for Christ, so is grace a disposition for glory. Consequently, it behooved all things appertaining to glory, whether they regard the soul, as the perfect fruition of God, or whether they regard the body, as the glorious resurrection, to be first in Christ as the author of glory: but that grace should be first in those that were ordained unto Christ.

Whether Christ was the cause of His own Resurrection?

Objection 1: It seems that Christ was not the cause of His own Resurrection. For whoever is raised up by another is not the cause of his own rising. But Christ was raised up by another, according to Acts 2:24: "Whom God hath raised up, having loosed the sorrows of hell": and Rom. 8:11: "He that raised up Jesus Christ from the dead, shall quicken also your mortal bodies." Therefore Christ is not the cause of His own Resurrection.

Objection 2: Further, no one is said to merit, or ask from another, that of which he is himself the cause. But Christ by His Passion merited the Resurrection, as Augustine says (Tract. civ in Joan.): "The lowliness of the Passion is the meritorious cause of the glory of the Resurrection." Moreover He asked the Father that He might be raised up again, according to Ps. 40:11: "But thou, O Lord, have mercy on me, and raise me up again." Therefore He was not the cause of His rising again.

Objection 3: Further, as Damascene proves (De Fide Orth. iv), it is not the soul that rises again, but the body, which is stricken by death. But the body could not unite the soul with itself, since the soul is nobler. Therefore what rose in Christ could not be the cause of His Resurrection.

On the contrary, Our Lord says (Jn. 10:18): "No one taketh My soul from Me, but I lay it down, and I take it up again." But to rise is nothing else than to take the soul up again. Consequently, it appears that Christ rose again of His own power.

I answer that, As stated above ([4299]Q[50], AA[2],3) in consequence of death Christ's Godhead was not separated from His soul, nor from His flesh. Consequently, both the soul and the flesh of the dead Christ can be considered in two respects: first, in respect of His Godhead; secondly, in respect of His created nature. Therefore, according to the virtue of the Godhead united to it, the body took back again the soul which it had laid aside, and the soul took back again the body which it had abandoned: and thus Christ rose by His own power. And this is precisely what is written (2 Cor. 13:4): "For although He was crucified through" our "weakness, yet He liveth by the power of God." But if we consider the body and soul of the dead Christ according to the power of created nature, they could not thus be reunited, but it was necessary for Christ to be raised up by God.

Reply to Objection 1: The Divine power is the same thing as the operation of the Father and the Son; accordingly these two things are mutually consequent, that Christ was raised up by the Divine power of the Father, and by His own power.

Reply to Objection 2: Christ by praying besought and merited His Resurrection, as man and not as God.

Reply to Objection 3: According to its created nature Christ's body is not more powerful than His soul; yet according to its Divine power it is more powerful. Again the soul by reason of the Godhead united to it is more powerful than the body in respect of its created nature. Consequently, it was by the Divine power that the body and soul mutually resumed each other, but not by the power of their created nature.

OF THE QUALITY OF CHRIST RISING AGAIN (FOUR ARTICLES)

We have now to consider the quality of the rising Christ, which presents four points of inquiry:

(1) Whether Christ had a true body after His Resurrection?

(2) Whether He rose with His complete body?

(3) Whether His was a glorified body?

(4) Of the scars which showed in His body.

Whether Christ had a true body after His Resurrection?

Objection 1: It would seem that Christ did not have a true body after His Resurrection. For a true body cannot be in the same place at the same time with another body. But after the Resurrection Christ's body was with another at the same time in the same place: since He entered among the disciples "the doors being shut," as is related in Jn. 20:26. Therefore it seems that Christ did not have a true body after His Resurrection.

Objection 2: Further, a true body does not vanish from the beholder's sight unless perchance it be corrupted. But Christ's body "vanished out of the sight" of the disciples as they gazed upon Him, as is related in Lk. 24:31. Therefore, it seems that Christ did not have a true body after His Resurrection.

Objection 3: Further, every true body has its determinate shape. But Christ's body appeared before the disciples "in another shape," as is evident from Mk. 15:12. Therefore it seems that Christ did not possess a true body after His Resurrection.

On the contrary, It is written (Lk. 24:37) that when Christ appeared to His disciples "they being troubled and frightened, supposed that they saw a spirit," as if He had not a true but an imaginary body: but to remove their fears He presently added: "Handle and see, for a spirit hath not flesh and bones, as you see Me to have." Consequently, He had not an imaginary but a true body.

I answer that, As Damascene says (De Fide Orth. iv): that is said to rise, which fell. But Christ's body fell by death; namely, inasmuch as the soul which was its formal perfection was separated from it. Hence, in order for it to be a true resurrection, it was necessary for the same body of Christ to be once more united with the same soul. And since the truth of the body's nature is from its form it follows that Christ's body after His Resurrection was a true body, and of the same nature as it was before. But had His been an imaginary body, then His Resurrection would not have been true, but apparent.

Reply to Objection 1: Christ's body after His Resurrection, not by miracle but from its glorified condition, as some say, entered in among the disciples while the doors were shut, thus existing with another body in the same place. But whether a glorified body can have this from some hidden property, so as to be with another body at the same time in the same place, will be discussed later ([4300]XP, Q[83], A[4]) when the common resurrection will be dealt with. For the present let it suffice to say that it was not from any property within the body, but by virtue of the Godhead united to it, that this body, although a true one, entered in among the disciples while the doors were shut. Accordingly Augustine says in a sermon for Easter (ccxlvii) that some men argue in this fashion: "If it were a body; if what rose from the sepulchre were what hung upon the tree, how could it enter through closed doors?" And he answers: "If you understand how, it is no miracle: where reason fails, faith abounds." And (Tract. cxxi super Joan.) he says: "Closed doors were no obstacle to the substance of a Body wherein was the Godhead; for truly He could enter in by doors not open, in whose Birth His Mother's virginity remained inviolate." And Gregory says the same in a homily for the octave of Easter (xxvi in Evang.).

Reply to Objection 2: As stated above ([4301]Q[53], A[3]), Christ rose to the immortal life of glory. But such is the disposition of a glorified body that it is spiritual, i.e. subject to the spirit, as the Apostle says (1 Cor. 15:44). Now in order for the body to be entirely subject to the spirit, it is necessary for the body's every action to be subject to the will of the spirit. Again, that an object be seen is due to the action of the visible object upon the sight, as the Philosopher shows (De Anima ii). Consequently, whoever has a glorified body has it in his power to be seen when he so wishes, and not to be seen when he does not wish it. Moreover Christ had this not only from the condition of His glorified body, but also from the power of His Godhead, by which power it may happen that even bodies not glorified are miraculously unseen: as was by a miracle bestowed on the blessed Bartholomew, that "if he wished he could be seen, and not be seen if he did not wish it" [*Apocryphal Historia Apost. viii, 2]. Christ, then, is said to have vanished from the eyes of the disciples, not as though He were corrupted or dissolved into invisible elements; but because He ceased, of His own will, to be seen by them, either while He was present or while He was departing by the gift of agility.

Reply to Objection 3: As Severianus [*Peter Chrysologus: Serm. lxxxii] says in a sermon for Easter: "Let no one suppose that Christ changed His features at the Resurrection." This is to be understood of the outline of His members; since there was nothing out of keeping or deformed in the body of Christ which was conceived of the Holy Ghost, that had to be righted at the Resurrection. Nevertheless He received the glory of clarity in the Resurrection: accordingly the same writer adds: "but the semblance is changed, when, ceasing to be mortal, it becomes immortal; so that it acquired the glory of countenance, without losing the substance of the countenance." Yet He did not come to those disciples in glorified appearance; but, as it lay in His power for His body to be seen or not, so it was within His power to present to the eyes of the beholders His form either glorified or not glorified, or partly glorified and partly not, or in any fashion whatsoever. Still it requires but a slight difference for anyone to seem to appear another shape.

Day 285

Whether Christ's body rose glorified? [*Some editions give this article as the third, following the order of the introduction to the question. But this is evident from the first sentence of the body of A[3] (A[2] in the aforesaid editions), that the order of the Leonine edition is correct.]

Objection 1: It seems that Christ's body did not rise glorified. For glorified bodies shine, according to Mat. 13:43: "Then shall the just shine as the sun in the kingdom of their Father." But shining bodies are seen under the aspect of light, but not of color. Therefore, since Christ's body was beheld under the aspect of color, as it had been hitherto, it seems that it was not a glorified one.

Objection 2: Further, a glorified body is incorruptible. But Christ's body seems not to have been incorruptible; because it was palpable, as He Himself says in Lk. 24:39: "Handle, and see." Now Gregory says (Hom. in Evang. xxvi) that "what is handled must be corruptible, and that which is incorruptible cannot be handled." Consequently, Christ's body was not glorified.

Objection 3: Further, a glorified body is not animal, but spiritual, as is clear from 1 Cor. 15. But after the Resurrection Christ's body seems to have been animal, since He ate and drank with His disciples, as we read in the closing chapters of Luke and John. Therefore, it seems that Christ's body was not glorified.

On the contrary, The Apostle says (Phil. 3:21): "He will reform the body of our lowness, made like to the body of His glory."

I answer that, Christ's was a glorified body in His Resurrection, and this is evident from three reasons. First of all, because His Resurrection was the exemplar and the cause of ours, as is stated in 1 Cor. 15:43. But in the resurrection the saints will have glorified bodies, as is written in the same place: "It is sown in dishonor, it shall rise in glory." Hence, since the cause is mightier than the effect, and the exemplar than the exemplate; much more glorious, then, was the body of Christ in His Resurrection. Secondly, because He merited the glory of His Resurrection by the lowliness of His Passion. Hence He said (Jn. 12:27): "Now is My soul troubled," which refers to the Passion; and later He adds: "Father, glorify Thy name," whereby He asks for the glory of the Resurrection. Thirdly, because as stated above ([4302]Q[34], A[4]), Christ's soul was glorified from the instant of His conception by perfect fruition of the Godhead. But, as stated above ([4303]Q[14], A[1], ad 2), it was owing to the Divine economy that the glory did not pass from His soul to His body, in order that by the Passion He might accomplish the mystery of our redemption. Consequently, when this mystery of Christ's Passion and death was finished, straightway the soul communicated its glory to the risen body in the Resurrection; and so that body was made glorious.

Reply to Objection 1: Whatever is received within a subject is received according to the subject's capacity. Therefore, since glory flows from the soul into the body, it follows that, as Augustine says (Ep. ad Dioscor. cxviii), the brightness or splendor of a glorified body is after the manner of natural color in the human body; just as variously colored glass derives its splendor from the sun's radiance, according to the mode of the color. But as it lies within the power of a glorified man whether his body be seen or not, as stated above (A[1], ad 2), so is it in his power whether its splendor be seen or not. Accordingly it can be seen in its color without its brightness. And it was in this way that Christ's body appeared to the disciples after the Resurrection.

Reply to Objection 2: We say that a body can be handled not only because of its resistance, but also on account of its density. But from rarity and density follow weight and lightness, heat and cold, and similar contraries, which are the principles of corruption in elementary bodies. Consequently, a body that can be handled by human touch is naturally corruptible. But if there be a body that resists touch, and yet is not disposed according to the qualities mentioned, which are the proper objects of human touch, such as a heavenly body, then such body cannot be said to be handled. But Christ's body after the Resurrection was truly made up of elements, and had tangible qualities such as the nature of a human body requires, and therefore it could naturally be handled; and if it had nothing beyond the nature of a human body, it would likewise be corruptible. But it had something else which made it incorruptible, and this was not the nature of a heavenly body, as some maintain, and into which we shall make fuller inquiry later ([4304]XP, Q[82], A[1]), but it was glory flowing from a beatified soul: because, as Augustine says (Ep. ad Dioscor. cxviii): "God made the soul of such powerful nature, that from its fullest beatitude the fulness of health overflows into the body, that is, the vigor of incorruption." And therefore Gregory says (Hom. in Evang. xxvi): "Christ's body is shown to be of the same nature, but of different glory, after the Resurrection."

Reply to Objection 3: As Augustine says (De Civ. Dei xiii): "After the Resurrection, our Saviour in spiritual but true flesh partook of meat with the disciples, not from need of food, but because it lay in His power." For as Bede says on Lk. 24:41: "The thirsty earth sucks in the water, and the sun's burning ray absorbs it; the former from need, the latter by its power." Hence after the Resurrection He ate, "not as needing food, but in order thus to show the nature of His risen body." Nor does it follow that His was an animal body that stands in need of food.

Whether Christ's body rose again entire?

Objection 1: It would seem that Christ's body did not rise entire. For flesh and blood belong to the integrity of the body: whereas Christ seems not to have had both, for it is written (1 Cor. 15:50): "Flesh and blood can not possess the kingdom of God." But Christ rose in the glory of the kingdom of God. Therefore it seems that He did not have flesh and blood.

Objection 2: Further, blood is one of the four humors. Consequently, if Christ had blood, with equal reason He also had the other humors, from which corruption is caused in animal bodies. It would follow, then, that Christ's body was corruptible, which is unseemly. Therefore Christ did not have flesh and blood.

Objection 3: Further, the body of Christ which rose, ascended to heaven. But some of His blood is kept as relics in various churches. Therefore Christ's body did not rise with the integrity of all its parts.

On the contrary, our Lord said (Lk. 24:39) while addressing His disciples after the Resurrection: "A spirit hath not flesh and bones as you see Me to have."

I answer that, As stated above [4305](A[2]), Christ's body in the Resurrection was "of the same nature, but differed in glory." Accordingly, whatever goes with the nature of a human body, was entirely in the body of Christ when He rose again. Now it is clear that flesh, bones, blood, and other such things, are of the very nature of the human body. Consequently, all these things were in Christ's body when He rose again; and this also integrally, without any diminution; otherwise it would not have been a complete resurrection, if whatever was lost by death had not been restored. Hence our Lord assured His faithful ones by saying (Mat. 10:30): "The very hairs of your head are all numbered": and (Lk. 21:18): "A hair of your head shall not perish."

But to say that Christ's body had neither flesh, nor bones, nor the other natural parts of a human body, belongs to the error of Eutyches, Bishop of Constantinople, who maintained that "our body in that glory of the resurrection will be impalpable, and more subtle than wind and air: and that our Lord, after the hearts of the disciples who handled Him were confirmed, brought back to subtlety whatever could be handled in Him" [*St. Gregory, Moral. in Job 14:56]. Now Gregory condemns this in the same book, because Christ's body was not changed after the Resurrection, according to Rom. 6:9: "Christ rising from the dead, dieth now no more." Accordingly, the very man who had said these things, himself retracted them at his death. For, if it be unbecoming for Christ to take a body of another nature in His conception, a heavenly one for instance, as Valentine asserted, it is much more unbecoming for Him at His Resurrection to resume a body of another nature, because in His Resurrection He resumed unto an everlasting life, the body which in His conception He had assumed to a mortal life.

Reply to Objection 1: Flesh and blood are not to be taken there for the nature of flesh and blood, but, either for the guilt of flesh and blood, as Gregory says [*St. Gregory, Moral. in Job 14:56], or else for the corruption of flesh and blood: because, as Augustine says (Ad Consent., De Resur. Carn.), "there will be neither corruption there, nor mortality of flesh and blood." Therefore flesh according to its substance possesses the kingdom of God, according to Lk. 24:39: "A spirit hath not flesh and bones, as you see Me to have." But flesh, if understood as to its corruption, will not possess it; hence it is straightway added in the words of the Apostle: "Neither shall corruption possess incorruption."

Reply to Objection 2: As Augustine says in the same book: "Perchance by reason of the blood some keener critic will press us and say; If the blood was" in the body of Christ when He rose, "why not the rheum?" that is, the phlegm; "why not also the yellow gall?" that is, the gall proper; "and why not the black gall?" that is, the bile, "with which four humors the body is tempered, as medical science bears witness. But whatever anyone may add, let him take heed not to add corruption, lest he corrupt the health and purity of his own faith; because Divine power is equal to taking away such qualities as it wills from the visible and tractable body, while allowing others to remain, so that there be no defilement," i.e. of corruption, "though the features be there; motion without weariness, the power to eat, without need of food."

Reply to Objection 3: All the blood which flowed from Christ's body, belonging as it does to the integrity of human nature, rose again with His body: and the same reason holds good for all the particles which belong to the truth and integrity of human nature. But the blood preserved as relics in some churches did not flow from Christ's side, but is said to have flowed from some maltreated image of Christ.

Whether Christ's body ought to have risen with its scars?

Objection 1: It would seem that Christ's body ought not to have risen with its scars. For it is written (1 Cor. 15:52): "The dead shall rise incorrupt." But scars and wounds imply corruption and defect. Therefore it was not fitting for Christ, the author of the resurrection, to rise again with scars.

Objection 2: Further, Christ's body rose entire, as stated above [4306](A[3]). But open scars are opposed to bodily integrity, since they interfere with the continuity of the tissue. It does not therefore seem fitting for the open wounds to remain in Christ's body; although the traces of the wounds might remain, which would satisfy the beholder; thus it was that Thomas believed, to whom it was said: "Because thou hast seen Me, Thomas, thou hast believed" (Jn. 20:29).

Objection 3: Further, Damascene says (De Fide Orth. iv) that "some things are truly said of Christ after the Resurrection, which He did not have from nature but from special dispensation, such as the scars, in order to make it sure that it was the body which had suffered that rose again." Now when the cause ceases, the effect ceases. Therefore it seems that when the disciples were assured of the Resurrection, He bore the scars no longer. But it ill became the unchangeableness of His glory that He should assume anything which was not to remain in Him for ever. Consequently, it seems that He ought not at His Resurrection to have resumed a body with scars.

On the contrary, Our Lord said to Thomas (Jn. 20:27): "Put in thy finger hither, and see My hands; and bring hither thy hand, and put it into My side, and be not faithless but believing."

I answer that, It was fitting for Christ's soul at His Resurrection to resume the body with its scars. In the first place, for Christ's own glory. For Bede says on Lk. 24:40 that He kept His scars not from inability to heal them, "but to wear them as an everlasting trophy of His victory." Hence Augustine says (De Civ. Dei xxii): "Perhaps in that kingdom we shall see on the bodies of the Martyrs the traces of the wounds which they bore for Christ's name: because it will not be a deformity, but a dignity in them; and a certain kind of beauty will shine in them, in the body, though not of the body." Secondly, to confirm the hearts of the disciples as to "the faith in His Resurrection" (Bede, on Lk. 24:40). Thirdly, "that when He pleads for us with the Father, He may always show the manner of death He endured for us" (Bede, on Lk. 24:40). Fourthly, "that He may convince those redeemed in His blood, how mercifully they have been helped, as He exposes before them the traces of the same death" (Bede, on Lk. 24:40). Lastly, "that in the Judgment-day He may upbraid them with their just condemnation" (Bede, on Lk. 24:40). Hence, as Augustine says (De Symb. ii): "Christ knew why He kept the scars in His body. For, as He showed them to Thomas who would not believe except he handled and saw them, so will He show His wounds to His enemies, so that He who is the Truth may convict them, saying: 'Behold the man whom you crucified; see the wounds you inflicted; recognize the side you pierced, since it was opened by you and for you, yet you would not enter.'"

Reply to Objection 1: The scars that remained in Christ's body belong neither to corruption nor defect, but to the greater increase of glory, inasmuch as they are the trophies of His power; and a special comeliness will appear in the places scarred by the wounds.

Reply to Objection 2: Although those openings of the wounds break the continuity of the tissue, still the greater beauty of glory compensates for all this, so that the body is not less entire, but more perfected. Thomas, however, not only saw, but handled the wounds, because as Pope Leo [*Cf. Append. Opp. August., Serm. clxii] says: "It sufficed for his personal faith for him to have seen what he saw; but it was on our behalf that he touched what he beheld."

Reply to Objection 3: Christ willed the scars of His wounds to remain on His body, not only to confirm the faith of His disciples, but for other reasons also. From these it seems that those scars will always remain on His body; because, as Augustine says (Ad Consent., De Resurr. Carn.): "I believe our Lord's body to be in heaven, such as it was when He ascended into heaven." And Gregory (Moral. xiv) says that "if aught could be changed in Christ's body after His Resurrection, contrary to Paul's truthful teaching, then the Lord after His Resurrection returned to death; and what fool would dare to say this, save he that denies the true resurrection of the flesh?" Accordingly, it is evident that the scars which Christ showed on His body after His Resurrection, have never since been removed from His body.

OF THE MANIFESTATION OF THE RESURRECTION (SIX ARTICLES)

We have now to consider the manifestation of the Resurrection: concerning which there are six points of inquiry:
(1) Whether Christ's Resurrection ought to have been manifested to all men or only to some special individuals?
(2) Whether it was fitting that they should see Him rise?
(3) Whether He ought to have lived with the disciples after the Resurrection?
(4) Whether it was fitting for Him to appeal to the disciples "in another shape"?
(5) Whether He ought to have demonstrated the Resurrection by proofs?
(6) Of the cogency of those proofs.

Whether Christ's Resurrection ought to have been manifested to all?

Objection 1: It would seem that Christ's Resurrection ought to have been manifested to all. For just as a public penalty is due for public sin, according to 1 Tim. 5:20: "Them that sin reprove before all," so is a public reward due for public merit. But, as Augustine says (Tract. civ in Joan.), "the glory of the Resurrection is the reward of the humility of the Passion." Therefore, since Christ's Passion was manifested to all while He suffered in public, it seems that the glory of the Resurrection ought to have been manifested to all.

Objection 2: Further, as Christ's Passion is ordained for our salvation, so also is His Resurrection, according to Rom. 4:25: "He rose again for our justification." But what belongs to the public weal ought to be manifested to all. Therefore Christ's Resurrection ought to have been manifested to all, and not to some specially.

Objection 3: Further, they to whom it was manifested were witnesses of the Resurrection: hence it is said (Acts 3:15): "Whom God hath raised from the dead, of which we are witnesses." Now they bore witness by preaching in public: and this is unbecoming in women, according to 1 Cor. 14:34: "Let women keep silence in the churches": and 1 Tim. 2:12: "I suffer not a woman to teach." Therefore, it does not seem becoming for Christ's Resurrection to be manifested first of all to the women and afterwards to mankind in general.

On the contrary, It is written (Acts 10:40): "Him God raised up the third day, and gave Him to be made manifest, not to all the people, but to witnesses preordained by God."

I answer that, Some things come to our knowledge by nature's common law, others by special favor of grace, as things divinely revealed. Now, as Dionysius says (Coel. Hier. iv), the divinely established law of such things is that they be revealed immediately by God to higher persons, through whom they are imparted to others, as is evident in the ordering of the heavenly spirits. But such things as concern future glory are beyond the common ken of mankind, according to Is. 64:4: "The eye hath not seen, O God, besides Thee, what things Thou hast prepared for them that wait for Thee." Consequently, such things are not known by man except through Divine revelation, as the Apostle says (1 Cor. 2:10): "God hath revealed them to us by His spirit." Since, then, Christ rose by a glorious Resurrection, consequently His Resurrection was not manifested to everyone, but to some, by whose testimony it could be brought to the knowledge of others.

Reply to Objection 1: Christ's Passion was consummated in a body that still had a passible nature, which is known to all by general laws: consequently His Passion could be directly manifested to all. But the Resurrection was accomplished "through the glory of the Father," as the Apostle says (Rom. 6:4). Therefore it was manifested directly to some, but not to all.

But that a public penance is imposed upon public sinners, is to be understood of the punishment of this present life. And in like manner public merits should be rewarded in public, in order that others may be stirred to emulation. But the punishments and rewards of the future life are not publicly manifested to all, but to those specially who are preordained thereto by God.

Reply to Objection 2: Just as Christ's Resurrection is for the common salvation of all, so it came to the knowledge of all; yet not so that it was directly manifested to all, but only to some, through whose testimony it could be brought to the knowledge of all.

Reply to Objection 3: A woman is not to be allowed to teach publicly in church; but she may be permitted to give familiar instruction to some privately. And therefore as Ambrose says on Lk. 24:22, "a woman is sent to them who are of her household," but not to the people to bear witness to the Resurrection. But Christ appeared to the woman first, for this reason, that as a woman was the first to bring the source of death to man, so she might be the first to announce the dawn of Christ's glorious Resurrection. Hence Cyril says on Jn. 20:17: "Woman who formerly was the minister of death, is the first to see and proclaim the adorable mystery of the Resurrection: thus womankind has procured absolution from ignominy, and removal of the curse." Hereby, moreover, it is shown, so far as the state of glory is concerned, that the female sex shall suffer no hurt; but if women burn with greater charity, they shall also attain greater glory from the Divine vision: because the women whose love for our Lord was more persistent---so much so that "when even the disciples withdrew" from the sepulchre "they did not depart" [*Gregory, Hom. xxv in Evang.]---were the first to see Him rising in glory.

Whether it was fitting that the disciples should see Him rise again?

Objection 1: It would seem fitting that the disciples should have seen Him rise again, because it was their office to bear witness to the Resurrection, according to Acts 4:33: "With great power did the apostles give testimony to the Resurrection of Jesus Christ our Lord." But the surest witness of all is an eye-witness. Therefore it would have been fitting for them to see the very Resurrection of Christ.

Objection 2: Further, in order to have the certainty of faith the disciples saw Christ ascend into heaven, according to Acts 1:9: "While they looked on, He was raised up." But it was also necessary for them to have faith in the Resurrection. Therefore it seems that Christ ought to have risen in sight of the disciples.

Objection 3: Further, the raising of Lazarus was a sign of Christ's coming Resurrection. But the Lord raised up Lazarus in sight of the disciples. Consequently, it seems that Christ ought to have risen in sight of the disciples.

On the contrary, It is written (Mk. 16:9): The Lord "rising early the first day of the week, appeared first to Mary Magdalen." Now Mary Magdalen did not see Him rise; but, while searching for Him in the sepulchre, she heard from the angel: "He is risen, He is not here." Therefore no one saw Him rise again.

I answer that, As the Apostle says (Rom. 13:1): "Those things that are of God, are well ordered [Vulg.: 'Those that are, are ordained of God]." Now the divinely established order is this, that things above men's ken are revealed to them by angels, as Dionysius says (Coel. Hier. iv). But Christ on rising did not return to the familiar manner of life, but to a kind of immortal and God-like condition, according to Rom. 6:10: "For in that He liveth, He liveth unto God." And therefore it was fitting for Christ's Resurrection not to be witnessed by men directly, but to be proclaimed to them by angels. Accordingly, Hilary (Comment. Matth. cap. ult.) says: "An angel is therefore the first herald of the Resurrection, that it might be declared out of obedience to the Father's will."

Reply to Objection 1: The apostles were able to testify to the Resurrection even by sight, because from the testimony of their own eyes they saw Christ alive, whom they had known to be dead. But just as man comes from the hearing of faith to the beatific vision, so did men come to the sight of the risen Christ through the message already received from angels.

Reply to Objection 2: Christ's Ascension as to its term wherefrom, was not above men's common knowledge, but only as to its term whereunto. Consequently, the disciples were able to behold Christ's Ascension as to the term wherefrom, that is, according as He was uplifted from the earth; but they did not behold Him as to the term whereunto, because they did not see how He was received into heaven. But Christ's Resurrection transcended common knowledge as to the term wherefrom, according as His soul returned from hell and His body from the closed sepulchre; and likewise as to the term whereunto, according as He attained to the life of glory. Consequently, the Resurrection ought not to be accomplished so as to be seen by man.

Reply to Objection 3: Lazarus was raised so that he returned to the same life as before, which life is not beyond man's common ken. Consequently, there is no parity.

Whether Christ ought to have lived constantly with His disciples after the Resurrection?

Objection 1: It would seem that Christ ought to have lived constantly with His Disciples, because He appeared to them after His Resurrection in order to confirm their faith in the Resurrection, and to bring them comfort in their disturbed state, according to Jn. 20:20: "The disciples were glad when they saw the Lord." But they would have been more assured and consoled had He constantly shown them His presence. Therefore it seems that He ought to have lived constantly with them.

Objection 2: Further, Christ rising from the dead did not at once ascend to heaven, but after forty days, as is narrated in Acts 1:3. But meanwhile He could have been in no more suitable place than where the disciples were met together. Therefore it seems that He ought to have lived with them continually.

Objection 3: Further, as Augustine says (De Consens. Evang. iii), we read how Christ appeared five times on the very day of His Resurrection: first "to the women at the sepulchre; secondly to the same on the way from the sepulchre; thirdly to Peter; fourthly to the two disciples going to the town; fifthly to several of them in Jerusalem when Thomas was not present." Therefore it also seems that He ought to have appeared several times on the other days before the Ascension.

Objection 4: Further, our Lord had said to them before the Passion (Mat. 26:32): "But after I shall be risen again, I will go before you into Galilee"; moreover an angel and our Lord Himself repeated the same to the women after the Resurrection: nevertheless He was seen by them in Jerusalem on the very day of the Resurrection, as stated above (OBJ[3]); also on the eighth day, as we read in Jn. 20:26. It seems, therefore, that He did not live with the disciples in a fitting way after the Resurrection.

On the contrary, It is written (Jn. 20:26) that "after eight days" Christ appeared to the disciples. Therefore He did not live constantly with them.

I answer that, Concerning the Resurrection two things had to be manifested to the disciples, namely, the truth of the Resurrection, and the glory of Him who rose. Now in order to manifest the truth of the Resurrection, it sufficed for Him to appear several times before them, to speak familiarly to them, to eat and drink, and let them touch Him. But in order to manifest the glory of the risen Christ, He was not desirous of living with them constantly as He had done before, lest it might seem that He rose unto the same life as before. Hence (Lk. 24:44) He said to them: "These are the words which I spoke to you, while I was yet with you." For He was there with them by His bodily presence, but hitherto He had been with them not merely by His bodily presence, but also in mortal semblance. Hence Bede in explaining those words of Luke, "while I was with you," says: "that is, while I was still in mortal flesh, in which you are yet: for He had then risen in the same flesh, but was not in the same state of mortality as they."

Reply to Objection 1: Christ's frequent appearing served to assure the disciples of the truth of the Resurrection; but continual intercourse might have led them into the error of believing that He had risen to the same life as was His before. Yet by His constant presence He promised them comfort in another life, according to Jn. 16:22: "I will see you again, and your heart shall rejoice; and your joy no man shall take from you."

Reply to Objection 2: That Christ did not stay continually with the disciples was not because He deemed it more expedient for Him to be elsewhere: but because He judged it to be more suitable for the apostles' instruction that He should not abide continually with them, for the reason given above. But it is quite unknown in what places He was bodily present in the meantime, since Scripture is silent, and His dominion is in every place (Cf. Ps. 102:22).

Reply to Objection 3: He appeared oftener on the first day, because the disciples were to be admonished by many proofs to accept the faith in His Resurrection from the very out set: but after they had once accepted it, they had no further need of being instructed by so many apparitions. Accordingly one reads in the Gospel that after the first day He appeared again only five times. For, as Augustine says (De Consens. Evang. iii), after the first five apparitions "He came again a sixth time when Thomas saw Him; a seventh time was by the sea of Tiberias at the capture of the fishes; the eighth was on the mountain of Galilee, according to Matthew; the ninth occasion is expressed by Mark, 'at length when they were at table,' because no more were they going to eat with Him upon earth; the tenth was on the very day, when no longer upon the earth, but uplifted into the cloud, He was ascending into heaven. But, as John admits, not all things were written down. And He visited them frequently before He went up to heaven," in order to comfort them. Hence it is written (1 Cor. 15:6,7) that "He was seen by more than five hundred brethren at once . . . after that He was seen by James"; of which apparitions no mention is made in the Gospels.

Reply to Objection 4: Chrysostom in explaining Mat. 26:32---"after I shall be risen again, I will go before you into Galilee," says (Hom. lxxxiii in Matth.), "He goes not to some far off region in order to appear to them, but among His own people, and in those very places" in which for the most part they had lived with Him; "in order that they might thereby believe that He who was crucified was the same as He who rose again." And on this account "He said that He would go into Galilee, that they might be delivered from fear of the Jews."

Consequently, as Ambrose says (Expos. in Luc.), "The Lord had sent word to the disciples that they were to see Him in Galilee; yet He showed Himself first to them when they were assembled together in the room out of fear. (Nor is there any breaking of a promise here, but rather a hastened fulfilling out of kindness)" [*Cf. Catena Aurea in Luc. xxiv, 36]: "afterwards, however, when their minds were comforted, they went into Galilee. Nor is there any reason to prevent us from supposing that there were few in the room, and many more on the mountain." For, as Eusebius [*Of Caesarea; Cf. Migne, P. G., xxii, 1003] says, "Two Evangelists, Luke and John, write that He appeared in Jerusalem to the eleven only; but the other two said that an angel and our Saviour commanded not merely the eleven, but all the disciples and brethren, to go into Galilee. Paul makes mention of them when he says (1 Cor. 15:6): 'Then He appeared to more then five hundred brethren at once.'" The truer solution, however, is this, that while they were in hiding in Jerusalem He appeared to them at first in order to comfort them; but in Galilee it was not secretly, nor once or twice, that He made Himself known to them with great power, "showing Himself to them alive after His Passion, by many proofs," as Luke says (Acts 1:3). Or as Augustine writes (De Consens. Evang. iii): "What was said by the angel and by our Lord---that He would 'go before them into Galilee,' must be taken prophetically. For if we take Galilee as meaning 'a passing,' we must understand that they were going to pass from the people of Israel to the Gentiles, who would not believe in the preaching of the apostles unless He prepared the way for them in men's hearts: and this is signified by the words 'He shall go before you into Galilee.' But if by Galilee we understand 'revelation,' we are to understand this as applying to Him not in the form of a servant, but in that form wherein He is equal to the Father, and which He has promised to them that love Him. Although He has gone before us in this sense, He has not abandoned us."

Whether Christ should have appeared to the disciples "in another shape"?

Objection 1: It would seem that Christ ought not to have appeared to the disciples "in another shape." For a thing cannot appear in very truth other than it is. But there was only one shape in Christ. Therefore if He appeared under another, it was not a true but a false apparition. Now this is not at all fitting, because as Augustine says (QQ. lxxxiii, qu. 14): "If He deceives He is not the Truth; yet Christ is the Truth." Consequently, it seems that Christ ought not to have appeared to the disciples "in another shape."

Objection 2: Further, nothing can appear in another shape than the one it has, except the beholder's eyes be captivated by some illusions. But since such illusions are brought about by magical arts, they are unbecoming in Christ, according to what is written (2 Cor. 6:15): "What concord hath Christ with Belial?" Therefore it seems that Christ ought not to have appeared in another shape.

Objection 3: Further, just as our faith receives its surety from Scripture, so were the disciples assured of their faith in the Resurrection by Christ appearing to them. But, as Augustine says in an Epistle to Jerome (xxviii), if but one untruth be admitted into the Sacred Scripture, the whole authority of the Scriptures is weakened. Consequently, if Christ appeared to the disciples, in but one apparition, otherwise than He was, then whatever they saw in Christ after the Resurrection will be of less import, which is not fitting. Therefore He ought not to have appeared in another shape.

On the contrary, It is written (Mk. 16:12): "After that He appeared in another shape to two of them walking, as they were going into the country."

I answer that, As stated above ([4307]AA[1],2), Christ's Resurrection was to be manifested to men in the same way as Divine things are revealed. But Divine things are revealed to men in various ways, according as they are variously disposed. For, those who have minds well disposed, perceive Divine things rightly, whereas those not so disposed perceive them with a certain confusion of doubt or error: "for, the sensual men perceiveth not those things that are of the Spirit of God," as is said in 1 Cor. 2:14. Consequently, after His Resurrection Christ appeared in His own shape to some who were well disposed to belief, while He appeared in another shape to them who seemed to be already growing tepid in their faith: hence these said (Lk. 24:21): "We hoped that it was He that should have redeemed Israel." Hence Gregory says (Hom. xxiii in Evang.), that "He showed Himself to them in body such as He was in their minds: for, because He was as yet a stranger to faith in their hearts, He made pretense of going on farther," that is, as if He were a stranger.

Reply to Objection 1: As Augustine says (De Qq. Evang. ii), "not everything of which we make pretense is a falsehood; but when what we pretend has no meaning then is it a falsehood. But when our pretense has some signification, it is not a lie, but a figure of the truth; otherwise everything said figuratively by wise and holy men, or even by our Lord Himself, would be set down as a falsehood, because it is not customary to take such expressions in the literal sense. And deeds, like words, are feigned without falsehood, in order to denote something else." And so it happened here. as has been said.

Reply to Objection 2: As Augustine says (De Consens. Evang. iii): "Our Lord could change His flesh so that His shape really was other than they were accustomed to behold; for, before His Passion He was transfigured on the mountain, so that His face shone like the sun. But it did not happen thus now." For not without reason do we "understand this hindrance in their eyes to have been of Satan's doing, lest Jesus might be recognized." Hence Luke says (24:16) that "their eyes were held, that they should not know Him."

Reply to Objection 3: Such an argument would prove, if they had not been brought back from the sight of a strange shape to that of Christ's true countenance. For, as Augustine says (De Consens. Evang. iii): "The permission was granted by Christ," namely, that their eyes should be held fast in the aforesaid way, "until the Sacrament of the bread; that when they had shared in the unity of His body, the enemy's hindrance may be understood to have been taken away, so that Christ might be recognized." Hence he goes on to say that "'their eyes were opened, and they knew Him'; not that they were hitherto walking with their eyes shut; but there was something in them whereby they were not permitted to recognize what they saw. This could be caused by the darkness or by some kind of humor."

Whether Christ should have demonstrated the truth of His Resurrection by proofs?

Objection 1: It would seem that Christ should not have demonstrated the truth of His Resurrection by proofs. For Ambrose says (De Fide, ad Gratian. i): "Let there be no proofs where faith is required." But faith is required regarding the Resurrection. Therefore proofs are out of place there.

Objection 2: Further, Gregory says (Hom. xxvi): "Faith has no merit where human reason supplies the test." But it was no part of Christ's office to void the merit of faith. Consequently, it was not for Him to confirm the Resurrection by proofs.

Objection 3: Further, Christ came into the world in order that men might attain beatitude through Him, according to Jn. 10:10: "I am come that they may have life, and may have it more abundantly." But supplying proofs seems to be a hindrance in the way of man's beatitude; because our Lord Himself said (Jn. 20:29): "Blessed are they that have not seen, and have believed." Consequently, it seems that Christ ought not to manifest His Resurrection by any proofs.

On the contrary, It is related in Acts 1:3, that Christ appeared to His disciples "for forty days by many proofs, speaking of the Kingdom of God."

I answer that, The word "proof" is susceptible of a twofold meaning: sometimes it is employed to designate any sort "of reason in confirmation of what is a matter of doubt" [*Tully, Topic. ii]: and sometimes it means a sensible sign employed to manifest the truth; thus also Aristotle occasionally uses the term in his works [*Cf. Prior. Anal. ii; Rhetor. i]. Taking "proof" in the first sense, Christ did not demonstrate His Resurrection to the disciples by proofs, because such argumentative proof would have to be grounded on some principles: and if these were not known to the disciples, nothing would thereby be demonstrated to them, because nothing can be known from the unknown. And if such principles were known to them, they would not go beyond human reason, and consequently would not be efficacious for establishing faith in the Resurrection, which is beyond human reason, since principles must be assumed which are of the same order, according to 1 Poster. But it was from the authority of the Sacred Scriptures that He proved to them the truth of His Resurrection, which authority is the basis of faith, when He said: "All things must needs be fulfilled which are written in the Law, and in the prophets, and in the Psalms, concerning Me": as is set forth Lk. 24:44.

But if the term "proof" be taken in the second sense, then Christ is said to have demonstrated His Resurrection by proofs, inasmuch as by most evident signs He showed that He was truly risen. Hence where our version has "by many proofs," the Greek text, instead of proof has {tekmerion}, i.e. "an evident sign affording positive proof" [*Cf. Prior. Anal. ii]. Now Christ showed these signs of the Resurrection to His disciples, for two reasons. First, because their hearts were not disposed so as to accept readily the faith in the Resurrection. Hence He says Himself (Lk. 24:25): "O foolish and slow of heart to believe": and (Mk. 16:14): "He upbraided them with their incredulity and hardness of heart." Secondly, that their testimony might be rendered more efficacious through the signs shown them, according to 1 Jn. 1:1, 3: "That which we have seen, and have heard, and our hands have handled . . . we declare."

Reply to Objection 1: Ambrose is speaking there of proofs drawn from human reason, which are useless for demonstrating things of faith, as was shown above.

Reply to Objection 2: The merit of faith arises from this, that at God's bidding man believes what he does not see. Accordingly, only that reason debars merit of faith which enables one to see by knowledge what is proposed for belief: and this is demonstrative argument. But Christ did not make use of any such argument for demonstrating His Resurrection.

Reply to Objection 3: As stated already (ad 2), the merit of beatitude, which comes of faith, is not entirely excluded except a man refuse to believe only such things as he can see. But for a man to believe from visible signs the things he does not see, does not entirely deprive him of faith nor of the merit of faith: just as Thomas, to whom it was said (Jn. 20:29): "'Because thou hast seen Me, Thomas, thou hast believed,' saw one thing and believed another" [*Gregory, Hom. xxvi]: the wounds were what he saw, God was the object of His belief. But his is the more perfect faith who does not require such helps for belief. Hence, to put to shame the faith of some men, our Lord said (Jn. 4:48): "Unless you see signs and wonders, you believe not." From this one can learn how they who are so ready to believe God, even without beholding signs, are blessed in comparison with them who do not believe except they see the like.

Whether the proofs which Christ made use of manifested sufficiently the truth of His Resurrection?

Objection 1: It would seem that the proofs which Christ made use of did not sufficiently manifest the truth of His Resurrection. For after the Resurrection Christ showed nothing to His disciples which angels appearing to men did not or could not show; because angels have frequently shown themselves to men under human aspect, have spoken and lived with them, and eaten with them, just as if they were truly men, as is evident from Genesis 18, of the angels whom Abraham entertained. and in the Book of Tobias, of the angel who "conducted" him "and brought" him back. Nevertheless, angels have not true bodies naturally united to them; which is required for a resurrection. Consequently, the signs which Christ showed His disciples were not sufficient for manifesting His Resurrection.

Objection 2: Further, Christ rose again gloriously, that is, having a human nature with glory. But some of the things which Christ showed to His disciples seem contrary to human nature, as for instance, that "He vanished out of their sight," and entered in among them "when the doors were shut": and some other things seem contrary to glory, as for instance, that He ate and drank, and bore the scars of His wounds. Consequently, it seems that those proofs were neither sufficient nor fitting for establishing faith in the Resurrection.

Objection 3: Further, after the Resurrection Christ's body was such that it ought not to be touched by mortal man; hence He said to Magdalen (Jn. 20:17): "Do not touch Me; for I am not yet ascended to My Father." Consequently, it was not fitting for manifesting the truth of His Resurrection, that He should permit Himself to be handled by His disciples.

Objection 4: Further, clarity seems to be the principal of the qualities of a glorified body: yet He gave no sign thereof in His Resurrection. Therefore it seems that those proofs were insufficient for showing the quality of Christ's Resurrection.

Objection 5: [*This objection is wanting in the older codices, and in the text of the Leonine edition, which, however, gives it in a note as taken from one of the more recent codices of the Vatican.]

Further, the angels introduced as witnesses for the Resurrection seem insufficient from the want of agreement on the part of the Evangelists. Because in Matthew's account the angel is described as sitting upon the stone rolled back, while Mark states that he was seen after the women had entered the tomb; and again, whereas these mention one angel, John says that there were two sitting, and Luke says that there were two standing. Consequently, the arguments for the Resurrection do not seem to agree.

On the contrary, Christ, who is the Wisdom of God, "ordereth all things sweetly" and in a fitting manner, according to Wis. 8:1.

I answer that, Christ manifested His Resurrection in two ways: namely, by testimony; and by proof or sign: and each manifestation was sufficient in its own class. For in order to manifest His Resurrection He made use of a double testimony, neither of which can be rebutted. The first of these was the angels' testimony, who announced the Resurrection to the women, as is seen in all the Evangelists: the other was the testimony of the Scriptures, which He set before them to show the truth of the Resurrection, as is narrated in the last chapter of Luke.

Again, the proofs were sufficient for showing that the Resurrection was both true and glorious. That it was a true Resurrection He shows first on the part of the body; and this He shows in three respects; first of all, that it was a true and solid body, and not phantastic or rarefied, like the air. And He establishes this by offering His body to be handled; hence He says in the last chapter of Luke (39): "Handle and see; for a spirit hath not flesh and bones, as you see Me to have." Secondly, He shows that it was a human body, by presenting His true features for them to behold. Thirdly, He shows that it was identically the same body which He had before, by showing them the scars of the wounds; hence, as we read in the last chapter of Luke (39) he said to them: "See My hands and feet, that it is I Myself."

Secondly, He showed them the truth of His Resurrection on the part of His soul reunited with His body: and He showed this by the works of the threefold life. First of all, in the operations of the nutritive life, by eating and drinking with His disciples, as we read in the last chapter of Luke. Secondly, in the works of the sensitive life, by replying to His disciples' questions, and by greeting them when they were in His presence, showing thereby that He both saw and heard; thirdly, in the works of the intellective life by their conversing with Him, and discoursing on the Scriptures. And, in order that nothing might be wanting to make the manifestation complete, He also showed that He had the Divine Nature, by working the miracle of the draught of fishes, and further by ascending into heaven while they were beholding Him: because, according to Jn. 3:13: "No man hath ascended into heaven, but He that descended from heaven, the Son of Man who is in heaven."

He also showed His disciples the glory of His Resurrection by entering in among them when the doors were closed: as Gregory says (Hom. xxvi in Evang.): "Our Lord allowed them to handle His flesh which He had brought through closed doors, to show that His body was of the same nature but of different glory." It likewise was part of the property of glory that "He vanished suddenly from their eyes," as related in the last chapter of Luke; because thereby it was shown that it lay in His power to be seen or not seen; and this belongs to a glorified body, as stated above ([4308]Q[54], A[1], ad 2, A[2], ad 1).

Reply to Objection 1: Each separate argument would not suffice of itself for showing perfectly Christ's Resurrection, yet all taken collectively establish it completely, especially owing to the testimonies of the Scriptures, the sayings of the angels, and even Christ's own assertion supported by miracles. As to the angels who appeared, they did not say they were men, as Christ asserted that He was truly a man. Moreover, the manner of eating was different in Christ and the angels: for since the bodies assumed by the angels were neither living nor animated, there was no true eating, although the food was really masticated and passed into the interior of the assumed body: hence the angels said to Tobias (12:18,19): "When I was with you . . . I seemed indeed to eat and drink with you; but I use an invisible meat." But since Christ's body was truly animated, His eating was genuine. For, as Augustine observes (De Civ. Dei xiii), "it is not the power but the need of eating that shall be taken away from the bodies of them who rise again." Hence Bede says on Lk. 24:41: "Christ ate because He could, not because He needed."

Reply to Objection 2: As was observed above, some proofs were employed by Christ to prove the truth of His human nature, and others to show forth His glory in rising again. But the condition of human nature, as considered in itself, namely, as to its present state, is opposite to the condition of glory, as is said in 1 Cor. 15:43: "It is sown in weakness, it shall rise in power." Consequently, the proofs brought forward for showing the condition of glory, seem to be in opposition to nature, not absolutely, but according to the present state, and conversely. Hence Gregory says (Hom. xxvi in Evang.): "The Lord manifested two wonders, which are mutually contrary according to human reason, when after the Resurrection He showed His body as incorruptible and at the same time palpable."

Reply to Objection 3: As Augustine says (Tract. cxxi super Joan.), "these words of our Lord, 'Do not touch Me, for I am not yet ascended to My Father,'" show "that in that woman there is a figure of the Church of the Gentiles, which did not believe in Christ until He was ascended to the Father. Or Jesus would have men to believe in Him, i.e. to touch Him spiritually, as being Himself one with the Father. For to that man's innermost perceptions He is, in some sort, ascended unto the Father, who has become so far proficient in Him, as to recognize in Him the equal with the Father . . . whereas she as yet believed in Him but carnally, since she wept for Him as for a man." But when one reads elsewhere of Mary having touched Him, when with the other women, she "'came up and took hold of His feet,' that matters little," as Severianus says [*Chrysologus, Serm. lxxvi], "for, the first act relates to figure, the other to sex; the former is of Divine grace, the latter of human nature." Or as Chrysostom says (Hom. lxxxvi in Joan.): "This woman wanted to converse with Christ just as before the Passion, and out of joy was thinking of nothing great, although Christ's flesh had become much nobler by rising again." And therefore He said: "I have not yet ascended to My Father"; as if to say: "Do not suppose I am leading an earthly life; for if you see Me upon earth, it is because I have not yet ascended to My Father, but I am going to ascend shortly." Hence He goes on to say: "I ascend to My Father, and to your Father."

Reply to Objection 4: As Augustine says ad Orosium (Dial. lxv, Qq.): "Our Lord rose in clarified flesh; yet He did not wish to appear before the disciples in that condition of clarity, because their eyes could not gaze upon that brilliancy. For if before He died for us and rose again the disciples could not look upon Him when He was transfigured upon the mountain, how much less were they able to gaze upon Him when our Lord's flesh was glorified." It must also be borne in mind that after His Resurrection our Lord wished especially to show that He was the same as had died; which the manifestation of His brightness would have hindered considerably: because change of features shows more than anything else the difference in the person seen: and this is because sight specially judges of the common sensibles, among which is one and many, or the same and different. But before the Passion, lest His disciples might despise its weakness, Christ meant to show them the glory of His majesty; and this the brightness of the body specially indicates. Consequently, before the Passion He showed the disciples His glory by brightness, but after the Resurrection by other tokens.

Reply to Objection 5: As Augustine says (De Consens. Evang. iii): "We can understand one angel to have been seen by the women, according to both Matthew and Mark, if we take them as having entered the sepulchre, that is, into some sort of walled enclosure, and that there they saw an angel sitting upon the stone which was rolled back from the monument, as Matthew says; and that this is Mark's expression---'sitting on the right side'; afterwards when they scanned the spot where the Lord's body had lain, they beheld two angels, who were at first seated, as John says, and who afterwards rose so as to be seen standing, as Luke relates."

Day 286

OF THE CAUSALITY OF CHRIST'S RESURRECTION (TWO ARTICLES)
We have now to consider the causality of Christ's Resurrection, concerning which there are two points of inquiry:
(1) Whether Christ's Resurrection is the cause of our resurrection?
(2) Whether it is the cause of our justification?

Whether Christ's Resurrection is the cause of the resurrection of our bodies?
Objection 1: It would seem that Christ's Resurrection is not the cause of the resurrection of our bodies, because, given a sufficient cause, the effect must follow of necessity. If, then, Christ's Resurrection be the sufficient cause of the resurrection of our bodies, then all the dead should have risen again as soon as He rose.

Objection 2: Further, Divine justice is the cause of the resurrection of the dead, so that the body may be rewarded or punished together with the soul, since they shared in merit or sin, as Dionysius says (Eccles. Hier. vii) and Damascene (De Fide Orth. iv). But God's justice must necessarily be accomplished, even if Christ had not risen. Therefore the dead would rise again even though Christ did not. Consequently Christ's Resurrection is not the cause of the resurrection of our bodies.

Objection 3: Further, if Christ's Resurrection be the cause of the resurrection of our bodies, it would be either the exemplar, or the efficient, or the meritorious cause. Now it is not the exemplar cause; because it is God who will bring about the resurrection of our bodies, according to Jn. 5:21: "The Father raiseth up the dead": and God has no need to look at any exemplar cause outside Himself. In like manner it is not the efficient cause; because an efficient cause acts only through contact, whether spiritual or corporeal. Now it is evident that Christ's Resurrection has no corporeal contact with the dead who shall rise again, owing to distance of time and place; and similarly it has no spiritual contact, which is through faith and charity, because even unbelievers and sinners shall rise again. Nor again is it the meritorious cause, because when Christ rose He was no longer a wayfarer, and consequently not in a state of merit. Therefore, Christ's Resurrection does not appear to be in any way the cause of ours.

Objection 4: Further, since death is the privation of life, then to destroy death seems to be nothing else than to bring life back again; and this is resurrection. But "by dying, Christ destroyed our death" [*Preface of Mass in Paschal Time]. Consequently, Christ's death, not His Resurrection, is the cause of our resurrection.

On the contrary, on 1 Cor. 15:12: "Now if Christ be preached, that He rose again from the dead," the gloss says: "Who is the efficient cause of our resurrection."

I answer that, As stated in 2 Metaphysics, text 4: "Whatever is first in any order, is the cause of all that come after it." But Christ's Resurrection was the first in the order of our resurrection, as is evident from what was said above ([4309]Q[53], A[3]). Hence Christ's Resurrection must be the cause of ours: and this is what the Apostle says (1 Cor. 15:20,21): "Christ is risen from the dead, the first-fruits of them that sleep; for by a man came death, and by a man the resurrection of the dead."

And this is reasonable. Because the principle of human life-giving is the Word of God, of whom it is said (Ps. 35:10): "With Thee is the fountain of life": hence He Himself says (Jn. 5:21): "As the Father raiseth up the dead, and giveth life; so the Son also giveth life to whom He will." Now the divinely established natural order is that every cause operates first upon what is nearest to it, and through it upon others which are more remote; just as fire first heats the nearest air, and through it it heats bodies that are further off: and God Himself first enlightens those substances which are closer to Him, and through them others that are more remote, as Dionysius says (Coel. Hier. xiii). Consequently, the Word of God first bestows immortal life upon that body which is naturally united with Himself, and through it works the resurrection in all other bodies.

Reply to Objection 1: As was stated above, Christ's Resurrection is the cause of ours through the power of the united Word, who operates according to His will. And consequently, it is not necessary for the effect to follow at once, but according as the Word of God disposes, namely, that first of all we be conformed to the suffering and dying Christ in this suffering and mortal life; and afterwards may come to share in the likeness of His Resurrection.

Reply to Objection 2: God's justice is the first cause of our resurrection, whereas Christ's Resurrection is the secondary, and as it were the instrumental cause. But although the power of the principal cause is not restricted to one instrument determinately, nevertheless since it works through this instrument, such instrument causes the effect. So, then, the Divine justice in itself is not tied down to Christ's Resurrection as a means of bringing about our resurrection: because God could deliver us in some other way than through Christ's Passion and Resurrection, as already stated ([4310]Q[46], A[2]). But having once decreed to deliver us in this way, it is evident that Christ's Resurrection is the cause of ours.

Reply to Objection 3: Properly speaking, Christ's Resurrection is not the meritorious cause, but the efficient and exemplar cause of our resurrection. It is the efficient cause, inasmuch as Christ's humanity, according to which He rose again, is as it were the instrument of His Godhead, and works by Its power, as stated above ([4311]Q[13], AA[2],3). And therefore, just as all other things which Christ did and endured in His humanity are profitable to our salvation through the power of the Godhead, as already stated ([4312]Q[48], A[6]), so also is Christ's Resurrection the efficient cause of ours, through the Divine power whose office it is to quicken the dead; and this power by its presence is in touch with all places and times; and such virtual contact suffices for its efficiency. And since, as was stated above (ad 2), the primary cause of human resurrection is the Divine justice, from which Christ has "the power of passing judgment, because He is the Son of Man" (Jn. 5:27); the efficient power of His Resurrection extends to the good and wicked alike, who are subject to His judgment.

But just as the Resurrection of Christ's body, through its personal union with the Word, is first in point of time, so also is it first in dignity and perfection; as the gloss says on 1 Cor. 15:20,23. But whatever is most perfect is always the exemplar, which the less perfect copies according to its mode; consequently Christ's Resurrection is the exemplar of ours. And this is necessary, not on the part of Him who rose again, who needs no exemplar, but on the part of them who are raised up, who must be likened to that Resurrection, according to Phil. 3:21: "He will reform the body of our lowness, made like to the body of His glory." Now although the efficiency of Christ's Resurrection extends to the resurrection of the good and wicked alike, still its exemplarity extends properly only to the just, who are made conformable with His Sonship, according to Rom. 8:29.

Reply to Objection 4: Considered on the part of their efficiency, which is dependent on the Divine power, both Christ's death and His Resurrection are the cause both of the destruction of death and of the renewal of life: but considered as exemplar causes, Christ's death---by which He withdrew from mortal life---is the cause of the destruction of our death; while His Resurrection, whereby He inaugurated immortal life, is the cause of the repairing of our life. But Christ's Passion is furthermore a meritorious cause, as stated above ([4313]Q[48], A[1]).

Whether Christ's Resurrection is the cause of the resurrection of souls?

Objection 1: It would seem that Christ's Resurrection is not the cause of the resurrection of souls, because Augustine says (Tract. xxiii super Joan.) that "bodies rise by His human dispensation, but souls rise by the Substance of God." But Christ's Resurrection does not belong to God's Substance, but to the dispensation of His humanity. Therefore, although Christ's Resurrection is the cause of bodies rising, nevertheless it does not seem to be the cause of the resurrection of souls.

Objection 2: Further, a body does not act upon a spirit. But the Resurrection belongs to His body, which death laid low. Therefore His Resurrection is not the cause of the resurrection of souls.

Objection 3: Further, since Christ's Resurrection is the cause why bodies rise again, the bodies of all men shall rise again, according to 1 Cor. 15:51: "We shall all indeed rise again." But the souls of all will not rise again, because according to Mat. 25:46: "some shall go into everlasting punishment." Therefore Christ's Resurrection is not the cause of the resurrection of souls.

Objection 4: Further, the resurrection of souls comes of the forgiveness of sins. But this was effected by Christ's Passion, according to Apoc. 1:5: "He washed us from our sins in His own blood." Consequently, Christ's Passion even more than His Resurrection is the cause of the resurrection of souls.

On the contrary, The Apostle says (Rom. 4:25): "He rose again for our justification," which is nothing else than the resurrection of souls: and on Ps. 29:6: "In the evening weeping shall have place," the gloss says, "Christ's Resurrection is the cause of ours, both of the soul at present, and of the body in the future."

I answer that, As stated above, Christ's Resurrection works in virtue of the Godhead; now this virtue extends not only to the resurrection of bodies, but also to that of souls: for it comes of God that the soul lives by grace, and that the body lives by the soul. Consequently, Christ's Resurrection has instrumentally an effective power not only with regard to the resurrection of bodies, but also with respect to the resurrection of souls. In like fashion it is an exemplar cause with regard to the resurrection of souls, because even in our souls we must be conformed with the rising Christ: as the Apostle says (Rom. 6:4-11) "Christ is risen from the dead by the glory of the Father, so we also may walk in newness of life": and as He, "rising again from the dead, dieth now no more, so let us reckon that we (Vulg.: 'you')" are dead to sin, that we may "live together with Him."

Reply to Objection 1: Augustine says that the resurrection of souls is wrought by God's Substance, as to participation, because souls become good and just by sharing in the Divine goodness, but not by sharing in anything created. Accordingly, after saying that souls rise by the Divine Substance, he adds: the soul is beatified by a participation with God, and not by a participation with a holy soul. But our bodies are made glorious by sharing in the glory of Christ's body.

Reply to Objection 2: The efficacy of Christ's Resurrection reaches souls not from any special virtue of His risen body, but from the virtue of the Godhead personally united with it.

Reply to Objection 3: The resurrection of souls pertains to merit, which is the effect of justification; but the resurrection of bodies is ordained for punishment or reward, which are the effects of Him who judges. Now it belongs to Christ, not to justify all men, but to judge them: and therefore He raises up all as to their bodies, but not as to their souls.

Reply to Objection 4: Two things concur in the justification of souls, namely, forgiveness of sin and newness of life through grace. Consequently, as to efficacy, which comes of the Divine power, the Passion as well as the Resurrection of Christ is the cause of justification as to both the above. But as to exemplarity, properly speaking Christ's Passion and death are the cause of the forgiveness of guilt, by which forgiveness we die unto sin: whereas Christ's Resurrection is the cause of newness of life, which comes through grace or justice: consequently, the Apostle says (Rom. 4:25) that "He was delivered up," i.e. to death, "for our sins," i.e. to take them away, "and rose again for our justification." But Christ's Passion was also a meritorious cause, as stated above (A[1], ad 4;[4314] Q[48], A[1]).

OF THE ASCENSION OF CHRIST (SIX ARTICLES)
We have now to consider Christ's Ascension: concerning which there are six points of inquiry:
(1) Whether it belonged for Christ to ascend into heaven?
(2) According to which nature did it become Him to ascend?
(3) Whether He ascended by His own power?
(4) Whether He ascended above all the corporeal heavens?
(5) Whether He ascended above all spiritual creatures?
(6) Of the effect of the Ascension.

Whether it was fitting for Christ to ascend into heaven?
Objection 1: It would seem that it was not fitting for Christ to ascend into heaven. For the Philosopher says (De Coelo ii) that "things which are in a state of perfection possess their good without movement." But Christ was in a state of perfection, since He is the Sovereign Good in respect of His Divine Nature, and sovereignly glorified in respect of His human nature. Consequently, He has His good without movement. But ascension is movement. Therefore it was not fitting for Christ to ascend.

Objection 2: Further, whatever is moved, is moved on account of something better. But it was no better thing for Christ to be in heaven than upon earth, because He gained nothing either in soul or in body by being in heaven. Therefore it seems that Christ should not have ascended into heaven.

Objection 3: Further, the Son of God took human flesh for our salvation. But it would have been more beneficial for men if He had tarried always with us upon earth; thus He said to His disciples (Lk. 17:22): "The days will come when you shall desire to see one day of the Son of man; and you shall not see it." Therefore it seems unfitting for Christ to have ascended into heaven.

Objection 4: Further, as Gregory says (Moral. xiv), Christ's body was in no way changed after the Resurrection. But He did not ascend into heaven immediately after rising again, for He said after the Resurrection (Jn. 20:17): "I am not yet ascended to My Father." Therefore it seems that neither should He have ascended after forty days.

On the contrary, Are the words of our Lord (Jn. 20:17): "I ascend to My Father and to your Father."

I answer that, The place ought to be in keeping with what is contained therein. Now by His Resurrection Christ entered upon an immortal and incorruptible life. But whereas our dwelling-place is one of generation and corruption, the heavenly place is one of incorruption. And consequently it was not fitting that Christ should remain upon earth after the Resurrection; but it was fitting that He should ascend to heaven.

Reply to Objection 1: That which is best and possesses its good without movement is God Himself, because He is utterly unchangeable, according to Malachi 3:6: "I am the Lord, and I change not." But every creature is changeable in some respect, as is evident from Augustine (Gen. ad lit. viii). And since the nature assumed by the Son of God remained a creature, as is clear from what was said above ([4315]Q[2], A[7];[4316] Q[16], AA[8],10;[4317] Q[20], A[1]), it is not unbecoming if some movement be attributed to it.

Reply to Objection 2: By ascending into heaven Christ acquired no addition to His essential glory either in body or in soul: nevertheless He did acquire something as to the fittingness of place, which pertains to the well-being of glory: not that His body acquired anything from a heavenly body by way of perfection or preservation; but merely out of a certain fittingness. Now this in a measure belonged to His glory; and He had a certain kind of joy from such fittingness, not indeed that He then began to derive joy from it when He ascended into heaven, but that He rejoiced thereat in a new way, as at a thing completed. Hence, on Ps. 15:11: "At Thy right hand are delights even unto the end," the gloss says: "I shall delight in sitting nigh to Thee, when I shall be taken away from the sight of men."

Reply to Objection 3: Although Christ's bodily presence was withdrawn from the faithful by the Ascension, still the presence of His Godhead is ever with the faithful, as He Himself says (Mat. 28:20): "Behold, I am with you all days, even to the consummation of the world." For, "by ascending into heaven He did not abandon those whom He adopted," as Pope Leo says (De Resurrec., Serm. ii). But Christ's Ascension into heaven, whereby He withdrew His bodily presence from us, was more profitable for us than His bodily presence would have been.

First of all, in order to increase our faith, which is of things unseen. Hence our Lord said (Jn. 26) that the Holy Ghost shall come and "convince the world . . . of justice," that is, of the justice "of those that believe," as Augustine says (Tract. xcv super Joan.): "For even to put the faithful beside the unbeliever is to put the unbeliever to shame"; wherefore he goes on to say (10): "'Because I go to the Father; and you shall see Me no longer'"---"For 'blessed are they that see not, yet believe.' Hence it is of our justice that the world is reproved: because 'you will believe in Me whom you shall not see.'"

Secondly, to uplift our hope: hence He says (Jn. 14:3): "If I shall go, and prepare a place for you, I will come again, and will take you to Myself; that where I am, you also may be." For by placing in heaven the human nature which He assumed, Christ gave us the hope of going thither; since "wheresoever the body shall be, there shall the eagles also be gathered together," as is written in Mat. 24:28. Hence it is written likewise (Mic. 2:13): "He shall go up that shall open the way before them."

Thirdly, in order to direct the fervor of our charity to heavenly things. Hence the Apostle says (Col. 3:1,2): "Seek the things that are above, where Christ is sitting at the right hand of God. Mind the things that are above, not the things that are upon the earth": for as is said (Mat. 6:21): "Where thy treasure is, there is thy heart also." And since the Holy Ghost is love drawing us up to heavenly things, therefore our Lord said to His disciples (Jn. 16:7): "It is expedient to you that I go; for if I go not, the Paraclete will not come to you; but if I go, I will send Him to you." On which words Augustine says (Tract. xciv super Joan.): "Ye cannot receive the Spirit, so long as ye persist in knowing Christ according to the flesh. But when Christ withdrew in body, not only the Holy Ghost, but both Father and Son were present with them spiritually."

Reply to Objection 4: Although a heavenly place befitted Christ when He rose to immortal life, nevertheless He delayed the Ascension in order to confirm the truth of His Resurrection. Hence it is written (Acts 1:3), that "He showed Himself alive after His Passion, by many proofs, for forty days appearing to them": upon which the gloss says that "because He was dead for forty hours, during forty days He established the fact of His being alive again. Or the forty days may be understood as a figure of this world, wherein Christ dwells in His Church: inasmuch as man is made out of the four elements, and is cautioned not to transgress the Decalogue."

Whether Christ's Ascension into heaven belonged to Him according to His Divine Nature?

Objection 1: It would seem that Christ's Ascension into heaven belonged to Him according to His Divine Nature. For, it is written (Ps. 46:6): "God is ascended with jubilee": and (Dt. 33:26): "He that is mounted upon the heaven is thy helper." But these words were spoken of God even before Christ's Incarnation. Therefore it belongs to Christ to ascend into heaven as God.

Objection 2: Further, it belongs to the same person to ascend into heaven as to descend from heaven, according to Jn. 3:13: "No man hath ascended into heaven, but He that descended from heaven": and Eph. 4:10: "He that descended is the same also that ascended." But Christ came down from heaven not as man, but as God: because previously His Nature in heaven was not human, but Divine. Therefore it seems that Christ ascended into heaven as God.

Objection 3: Further, by His Ascension Christ ascended to the Father. But it was not as man that He rose to equality with the Father; for in this respect He says: "He is greater than I," as is said in Jn. 14:28. Therefore it seems that Christ ascended as God.

On the contrary, on Eph. 4:10: "That He ascended, what is it, but because He also descended," a gloss says: "It is clear that He descended and ascended according to His humanity."

I answer that, The expression "according to" can denote two things; the condition of the one who ascends, and the cause of his ascension. When taken to express the condition of the one ascending, the Ascension in no wise belongs to Christ according to the condition of His Divine Nature; both because there is nothing higher than the Divine Nature to which He can ascend; and because ascension is local motion, a thing not in keeping with the Divine Nature, which is immovable and outside all place. Yet the Ascension is in keeping with Christ according to His human nature, which is limited by place, and can be the subject of motion. In this sense, then, we can say that Christ ascended into heaven as man, but not as God.

But if the phrase "according to" denote the cause of the Ascension, since Christ ascended into heaven in virtue of His Godhead, and not in virtue of His human nature, then it must be said that Christ ascended into heaven not as man, but as God. Hence Augustine says in a sermon on the Ascension: "It was our doing that the Son of man hung upon the cross; but it was His own doing that He ascended."

Reply to Objection 1: These utterances were spoken prophetically of God who was one day to become incarnate. Still it can be said that although to ascend does not belong to the Divine Nature properly, yet it can metaphorically; as, for instance, it is said "to ascend in the heart of man" (cf. Ps. 83:6), when his heart submits and humbles itself before God: and in the same way God is said to ascend metaphorically with regard to every creature, since He subjects it to Himself.

Reply to Objection 2: He who ascended is the same as He who descended. For Augustine says (De Symb. iv): "Who is it that descends? The God-Man. Who is it that ascends? The self-same God-Man." Nevertheless a twofold descent is attributed to Christ; one, whereby He is said to have descended from heaven, which is attributed to the God-Man according as He is God: for He is not to be understood as having descended by any local movement, but as having "emptied Himself," since "when He was in the form of God He took the form of a servant." For just as He is said to be emptied, not by losing His fulness, but because He took our littleness upon Himself, so likewise He is said to have descended from heaven, not that He deserted heaven, but because He assumed human nature in unity of person.

And there is another descent whereby He descended "into the lower regions of the earth," as is written Eph. 4:9; and this is local descent: hence this belongs to Christ according to the condition of human nature.

Reply to Objection 3: Christ is said to ascend to the Father, inasmuch as He ascends to sit on the right hand of the Father; and this is befitting Christ in a measure according to His Divine Nature, and in a measure according to His human nature, as will be said later ([4318]Q[58], A[3])

Whether Christ ascended by His own power?

Objection 1: It would seem that Christ did not ascend by His own power, because it is written (Mk. 16:19) that "the Lord Jesus, after He had spoken to them, was taken up to heaven"; and (Acts 1:9) that, "while they looked on, He was raised up, and a cloud received Him out of their sight." But what is taken up, and lifted up, appears to be moved by another. Consequently, it was not by His own power, but by another's that Christ was taken up into heaven.

Objection 2: Further, Christ's was an earthly body, like to ours. But it is contrary to the nature of an earthly body to be borne upwards. Moreover, what is moved contrary to its nature is nowise moved by its own power. Therefore Christ did not ascend to heaven by His own power.

Objection 3: Further, Christ's own power is Divine. But this motion does not seem to have been Divine, because, whereas the Divine power is infinite, such motion would be instantaneous; consequently, He would not have been uplifted to heaven "while" the disciples "looked on," as is stated in Acts 1:9. Therefore, it seems that Christ did not ascend to heaven by His own power.

On the contrary, It is written (Is. 63:1): "This beautiful one in his robe, walking in the greatness of his strength." Also Gregory says in a Homily on the Ascension (xxix): "It is to be noted that we read of Elias having ascended in a chariot, that it might be shown that one who was mere man needed another's help. But we do not read of our Saviour being lifted up either in a chariot or by angels, because He who had made all things was taken up above all things by His own power."

I answer that, There is a twofold nature in Christ, to wit, the Divine and the human. Hence His own power can be accepted according to both. Likewise a twofold power can be accepted regarding His human nature: one is natural, flowing from the principles of nature; and it is quite evident that Christ did not ascend into heaven by such power as this. The other is the power of glory, which is in Christ's human nature; and it was according to this that He ascended to heaven.

Now there are some who endeavor to assign the cause of this power to the nature of the fifth essence. This, as they say, is light, which they make out to be of the composition of the human body, and by which they contend that contrary elements are reconciled; so that in the state of this mortality, elemental nature is predominant in human bodies: so that, according to the nature of this predominating element the human body is borne downwards by its own power: but in the condition of glory the heavenly nature will predominate, by whose tendency and power Christ's body and the bodies of the saints are lifted up to heaven. But we have already treated of this opinion in the [4319]FP, Q[76], A[7], and shall deal with it more fully in treating of the general resurrection ([4320]XP, Q[84], A[1]).

Setting this opinion aside, others assign as the cause of this power the glorified soul itself, from whose overflow the body will be glorified, as Augustine writes to Dioscorus (Ep. cxviii). For the glorified body will be so submissive to the glorified soul, that, as Augustine says (De Civ. Dei xxii), "wheresoever the spirit listeth, thither the body will be on the instant; nor will the spirit desire anything unbecoming to the soul or the body." Now it is befitting the glorified and immortal body for it to be in a heavenly place, as stated above [4321](A[1]). Consequently, Christ's body ascended into heaven by the power of His soul willing it. But as the body is made glorious by participation with the soul, even so, as Augustine says (Tract. xxiii in Joan.), "the soul is beatified by participating in God." Consequently, the Divine power is the first source of the ascent into heaven. Therefore Christ ascended into heaven by His own power, first of all by His Divine power, and secondly by the power of His glorified soul moving His body at will.

Reply to Objection 1: As Christ is said to have risen by His own power, though He was raised to life by the power of the Father, since the Father's power is the same as the Son's; so also Christ ascended into heaven by His own power, and yet was raised up and taken up to heaven by the Father.

Reply to Objection 2: This argument proves that Christ did not ascend into heaven by His own power, i.e. that which is natural to human nature: yet He did ascend by His own power, i.e. His Divine power, as well as by His own power, i.e. the power of His beatified soul. And although to mount upwards is contrary to the nature of a human body in its present condition, in which the body is not entirely dominated by the soul, still it will not be unnatural or forced in a glorified body, whose entire nature is utterly under the control of the spirit.

Reply to Objection 3: Although the Divine power be infinite, and operate infinitely, so far as the worker is concerned, still the effect thereof is received in things according to their capacity, and as God disposes. Now a body is incapable of being moved locally in an instant, because it must be commensurate with space, according to the division of which time is reckoned, as is proved in Physics vi. Consequently, it is not necessary for a body moved by God to be moved instantaneously, but with such speed as God disposes.

Whether Christ ascended above all the heavens?

Objection 1: It would seem that Christ did not ascend above all the heavens, for it is written (Ps. 10:5): "The Lord is in His holy temple, the Lord's throne is in heaven." But what is in heaven is not above heaven. Therefore Christ did not ascend above all the heavens.

Objection 2: [*This objection with its solution is omitted in the Leonine edition as not being in the original manuscript.]

Further, there is no place above the heavens, as is proved in De Coelo i. But every body must occupy a place. Therefore Christ's body did not ascend above all the heavens.

Objection 3: Further, two bodies cannot occupy the same place. Since, then, there is no passing from place to place except through the middle space, it seems that Christ could not have ascended above all the heavens unless heaven were divided; which is impossible.

Objection 4: Further, it is narrated (Acts 1:9) that "a cloud received Him out of their sight." But clouds cannot be uplifted beyond heaven. Consequently, Christ did not ascend above all the heavens.

Objection 5: Further, we believe that Christ will dwell for ever in the place whither He has ascended. But what is against nature cannot last for ever, because what is according to nature is more prevalent and of more frequent occurrence. Therefore, since it is contrary to nature for an earthly body to be above heaven, it seems that Christ's body did not ascend above heaven.

On the contrary, It is written (Eph. 4:10): "He ascended above all the heavens that He might fill all things."

I answer that, The more fully anything corporeal shares in the Divine goodness, the higher its place in the corporeal order, which is order of place. Hence we see that the more formal bodies are naturally the higher, as is clear from the Philosopher (Phys. iv; De Coelo ii), since it is by its form that every body partakes of the Divine Essence, as is shown in Physics i. But through glory the body derives a greater share in the Divine goodness than any other natural body does through its natural form; while among other glorious bodies it is manifest that Christ's body shines with greater glory. Hence it was most fitting for it to be set above all bodies. Thus it is that on Eph. 4:8: "Ascending on high," the gloss says: "in place and dignity."

Reply to Objection 1: God's seat is said to be in heaven, not as though heaven contained Him, but rather because it is contained by Him. Hence it is not necessary for any part of heaven to be higher, but for Him to be above all the heavens; according to Ps. 8:2: "For Thy magnificence is elevated above the heavens, O God!"

Reply to Objection 2: [*Omitted in Leonine edition; see OBJ[2]]

A place implies the notion of containing; hence the first container has the formality of first place, and such is the first heaven. Therefore bodies need in themselves to be in a place, in so far as they are contained by a heavenly body. But glorified bodies, Christ's especially, do not stand in need of being so contained, because they draw nothing from the heavenly bodies, but from God through the soul. So there is nothing to prevent Christ's body from being beyond the containing radius of the heavenly bodies, and not in a containing place. Nor is there need for a vacuum to exist outside heaven, since there is no place there, nor is there any potentiality susceptive of a body, but the potentiality of reaching thither lies in Christ. So when Aristotle proves (De Coelo ii) that there is no body beyond heaven, this must be understood of bodies which are in a state of pure nature, as is seen from the proofs.

Reply to Objection 3: Although it is not of the nature of a body for it to be in the same place with another body, yet God can bring it about miraculously that a body be with another in the same place, as Christ did when He went forth from the Virgin's sealed womb, also when He entered among the disciples through closed doors, as Gregory says (Hom. xxvi). Therefore Christ's body can be in the same place with another body, not through some inherent property in the body, but through the assistance and operation of the Divine power.

Reply to Objection 4: That cloud afforded no support as a vehicle to the ascending Christ: but it appeared as a sign of the Godhead, just as God's glory appeared to Israel in a cloud over the Tabernacle (Ex. 40:32; Num. 9:15).

Reply to Objection 5: A glorified body has the power to be in heaven or above heaven. not from its natural principles, but from the beatified soul, from which it derives its glory: and just as the upward motion of a glorified body is not violent, so neither is its rest violent: consequently, there is nothing to prevent it from being everlasting.

Whether Christ's body ascended above every spiritual creature?

Objection 1: It would seem that Christ's body did not ascend above every spiritual creature. For no fitting comparison can be made between things which have no common ratio. But place is not predicated in the same ratio of bodies and of spiritual creatures, as is evident from what was said in the [4322]FP, Q[8], A[2], ad 1,2; [4323]FP, Q[52], A[1]. Therefore it seems that Christ's body cannot be said to have ascended above every spiritual creature.

Objection 2: Further, Augustine says (De Vera Relig. lv) that a spirit always takes precedence over a body. But the higher place is due to the higher things. Therefore it does not seem that Christ ascended above every spiritual creature.

Objection 3: Further, in every place a body exists, since there is no such thing as a vacuum in nature. Therefore if no body obtains a higher place than a spirit in the order of natural bodies, then there will be no place above every spiritual creature. Consequently, Christ's body could not ascend above every spiritual creature.

On the contrary, It is written (Eph. 1:21): "God set Him above all principality, and Power, and every name that is named, not only in this world, but also in that which is to come."

I answer that, The more exalted place is due to the nobler subject, whether it be a place according to bodily contact, as regards bodies, or whether it be by way of spiritual contact, as regards spiritual substances; thus a heavenly place which is the highest of places is becomingly due to spiritual substances, since they are highest in the order of substances. But although Christ's body is beneath spiritual substances, if we weigh the conditions of its corporeal nature, nevertheless it surpasses all spiritual substances in dignity, when we call to mind its dignity of union whereby it is united personally with God. Consequently, owing to this very fittingness, a higher place is due to it above every spiritual creature. Hence Gregory says in a Homily on the Ascension (xxix in Evang.) that "He who had made all things, was by His own power raised up above all things."

447

Reply to Objection 1: Although a place is differently attributed to corporeal and spiritual substances, still in either case this remains in common, that the higher place is assigned to the worthier.

Reply to Objection 2: This argument holds good of Christ's body according to the conditions of its corporeal nature, but not according to its formality of union.

Reply to Objection 3: This comparison may be considered either on the part of the places; and thus there is no place so high as to exceed the dignity of a spiritual substance: in this sense the objection runs. Or it may be considered on the part of the dignity of the things to which a place is attributed: and in this way it is due to the body of Christ to be above spiritual creatures.

Whether Christ's Ascension is the cause of our salvation?

Objection 1: It would seem that Christ's Ascension is not the cause of our salvation. For, Christ was the cause of our salvation in so far as He merited it. But He merited nothing for us by His Ascension, because His Ascension belongs to the reward of His exaltation: and the same thing is not both merit and reward, just as neither are a road and its terminus the same. Therefore it seems that Christ's Ascension is not the cause of our salvation.

Objection 2: Further, if Christ's Ascension be the cause of our salvation, it seems that this is principally due to the fact that His Ascension is the cause of ours. But this was bestowed upon us by His Passion, for it is written (Heb. 10:19): "We have [Vulg.: 'Having'] confidence in the entering into the holies by" His "blood." Therefore it seems that Christ's Ascension was not the cause of our salvation.

Objection 3: Further, the salvation which Christ bestows is an everlasting one, according to Is. 51:6: "My salvation shall be for ever." But Christ did not ascend into heaven to remain there eternally; for it is written (Acts 1:11): "He shall so come as you have seen Him going, into heaven." Besides, we read of Him showing Himself to many holy people on earth after He went up to heaven. to Paul, for instance (Acts 9). Consequently, it seems that Christ's Ascension is not the cause of our salvation.

On the contrary, He Himself said (Jn. 16:7): "It is expedient to you that I go"; i.e. that I should leave you and ascend into heaven.

I answer that, Christ's Ascension is the cause of our salvation in two ways: first of all, on our part; secondly, on His.

On our part, in so far as by the Ascension our souls are uplifted to Him; because, as stated above (A[1], ad 3), His Ascension fosters, first, faith; secondly, hope; thirdly, charity. Fourthly, our reverence for Him is thereby increased, since we no longer deem Him an earthly man, but the God of heaven; thus the Apostle says (2 Cor. 5:16): "If we have known Christ according to the flesh---'that is, as mortal, whereby we reputed Him as a mere man,'" as the gloss interprets the words---"but now we know Him so no longer."

On His part, in regard to those things which, in ascending, He did for our salvation. First, He prepared the way for our ascent into heaven, according to His own saying (Jn. 14:2): "I go to prepare a place for you," and the words of Micheas (2:13), "He shall go up that shall open the way before them." For since He is our Head the members must follow whither the Head has gone: hence He said (Jn. 14:3): "That where I am, you also may be." In sign whereof He took to heaven the souls of the saints delivered from hell, according to Ps. 67:19 (Cf. Eph. 4:8): "Ascending on high, He led captivity captive," because He took with Him to heaven those who had been held captives by the devil---to heaven, as to a place strange to human nature. captives in deed of a happy taking, since they were acquired by His victory.

Secondly, because as the high-priest under the Old Testament entered the holy place to stand before God for the people, so also Christ entered heaven "to make intercession for us," as is said in Heb. 7:25. Because the very showing of Himself in the human nature which He took with Him to heaven is a pleading for us. so that for the very reason that God so exalted human nature in Christ, He may take pity on them for whom the Son of God took human nature. Thirdly, that being established in His heavenly seat as God and Lord, He might send down gifts upon men, according to Eph. 4:10: "He ascended above all the heavens, that He might fill all things," that is, "with His gifts," according to the gloss.

Reply to Objection 1: Christ's Ascension is the cause of our salvation by way not of merit, but of efficiency, as was stated above regarding His Resurrection ([4324]Q[56], A[1], ad 3,4).

Reply to Objection 2: Christ's Passion is the cause of our ascending to heaven, properly speaking, by removing the hindrance which is sin, and also by way of merit: whereas Christ's Ascension is the direct cause of our ascension, as by beginning it in Him who is our Head, with whom the members must be united.

Reply to Objection 3: Christ by once ascending into heaven acquired for Himself and for us in perpetuity the right and worthiness of a heavenly dwelling-place; which worthiness suffers in no way, if, from some special dispensation, He sometimes comes down in body to earth; either in order to show Himself to the whole world, as at the judgment; or else to show Himself particularly to some individual, e.g. in Paul's case, as we read in Acts 9. And lest any man may think that Christ was not bodily present when this occurred, the contrary is shown from what the Apostle says in 1 Cor. 14:8, to confirm faith in the Resurrection: "Last of all He was seen also by me, as by one born out of due time": which vision would not confirm the truth of the Resurrection except he had beheld Christ's very body.

Day 287

OF CHRIST'S SITTING AT THE RIGHT HAND OF THE FATHER (FOUR ARTICLES)
WE have now to consider Christ's sitting at the right hand of the Father, concerning which there are four points of inquiry:
(1) Whether Christ is seated at the right hand of the Father?
(2) Whether this belongs to Him according to the Divine Nature?
(3) Whether it belongs to Him according to His human nature?
(4) Whether it is something proper to Christ?

Whether it is fitting that Christ should sit at the right hand of God the Father?

Objection 1: It would seem unfitting that Christ should sit at the right hand of God the Father. For right and left are differences of bodily position. But nothing corporeal can be applied to God, since "God is a spirit," as we read in Jn. 4:24. Therefore it seems that Christ does not sit at the right hand of the Father.

Objection 2: Further, if anyone sits at another's right hand, then the latter is seated on his left. Consequently, if Christ sits at the right hand of the Father, it follows that the Father is seated on the left of the Son; which is unseemly.

Objection 3: Further, sitting and standing savor of opposition. But Stephen (Acts 7:55) said: "Behold, I see the heavens opened, and the Son of man standing on the right hand of God." Therefore it seems that Christ does not sit at the right hand of the Father.

On the contrary, It is written in the last chapter of Mark (16:19): "The Lord Jesus, after He had spoken to them, was taken up to heaven, and sitteth on the right hand of God."

I answer that, The word "sitting" may have a twofold meaning; namely, "abiding" as in Lk. 24:49: "Sit [Douay: 'Stay'] you in the city": and royal or judiciary "power," as in Prov. 20:8: "The king, that sitteth on the throne of judgment, scattereth away all evil with his look." Now in either sense it belongs to Christ to sit at the Father's right hand. First of all inasmuch as He abides eternally unchangeable in the Father's bliss, which is termed His right hand, according to Ps. 15:11: "At Thy right hand are delights even to the end." Hence Augustine says (De Symb. i): "'Sitteth at the right hand of the Father': To sit means to dwell, just as we say of any man: 'He sat in that country for three years': Believe, then, that Christ dwells so at the right hand of the Father: for He is happy, and the Father's right hand is the name for His bliss." Secondly, Christ is said to sit at the right hand of the Father inasmuch as He reigns together with the Father, and has judiciary power from Him; just as he who sits at the king's right hand helps him in ruling and judging. Hence Augustine says (De Symb. ii): "By the expression 'right hand,' understand the power which this Man, chosen of God, received, that He might come to judge, who before had come to be judged."

Reply to Objection 1: As Damascene says (De Fide Orth. iv): "We do not speak of the Father's right hand as of a place, for how can a place be designated by His right hand, who Himself is beyond all place? Right and left belong to things definable by limit. But we style, as the Father's right hand, the glory and honor of the Godhead."

Reply to Objection 2: The argument holds good if sitting at the right hand be taken corporeally. Hence Augustine says (De Symb. i): "If we accept it in a carnal sense that Christ sits at the Father's right hand, then the Father will be on the left. But there"---that is, in eternal bliss, "it is all right hand, since no misery is there."

Reply to Objection 3: As Gregory says in a Homily on the Ascension (Hom. xxix in Evang.), "it is the judge's place to sit, while to stand is the place of the combatant or helper. Consequently, Stephen in his toil of combat saw Him standing whom He had as his helper. But Mark describes Him as seated after the Ascension, because after the glory of His Ascension He will at the end be seen as judge."

Whether it belongs to Christ as God to sit at the right hand of the Father?

Objection 1: It would seem that it does not belong to Christ as God to sit at the right hand of the Father. For, as God, Christ is the Father's right hand. But it does not appear to be the same thing to be the right hand of anyone and to sit on his right hand. Therefore, as God, Christ does not sit at the right hand of the Father.

Objection 2: Further, in the last chapter of Mark (16:19) it is said that "the Lord Jesus was taken up into heaven, and sitteth on the right hand of God." But it was not as God that Christ was taken up to heaven. Therefore neither does He, as God, sit at the right hand of God.

Objection 3: Further, Christ as God is the equal of the Father and of the Holy Ghost. Consequently, if Christ sits as God at the right hand of the Father, with equal reason the Holy Ghost sits at the right hand of the Father and of the Son, and the Father Himself on the right hand of the Son; which no one is found to say.

On the contrary, Damascene says (De Fide Orth. iv): that "what we style as the Father's right hand, is the glory and honor of the Godhead, wherein the Son of God existed before ages as God and as consubstantial with the Father."

I answer that, As may be gathered from what has been said [4325](A[1]) three things can be understood under the expression "right hand." First of all, as Damascene takes it, "the glory of the Godhead": secondly, according to Augustine "the beatitude of the Father": thirdly, according to the same authority, "judiciary power." Now as we observed [4326](A[1]) "sitting denotes" either abiding, or royal or judiciary dignity. Hence, to sit on the right hand of the Father is nothing else than to share in the glory of the Godhead with the Father, and to possess beatitude and judiciary power, and that unchangeably and royally. But this belongs to the Son as God. Hence it is manifest that Christ as God sits at the right hand of the Father; yet so that this preposition "at," which is a transitive one, implies merely personal distinction and order of origin, but not degree of nature or dignity, for there is no such thing in the Divine Persons, as was shown in the [4327]FP, Q[42], AA[3],4.

Reply to Objection 1: The Son of God is called the Father's "right hand" by appropriation, just as He is called the "Power" of the Father (1 Cor. 1:24). But "right hand of the Father," in its three meanings given above, is something common to the three Persons.

Reply to Objection 2: Christ as man is exalted to Divine honor; and this is signified in the aforesaid sitting; nevertheless such honor belongs to Him as God, not through any assumption, but through His origin from eternity.

Reply to Objection 3: In no way can it be said that the Father is seated at the right hand of the Son or of the Holy Ghost; because the Son and the Holy Ghost derive their origin from the Father, and not conversely. The Holy Ghost, however, can be said properly to sit at the right hand of the Father or of the Son, in the aforesaid sense, although by a kind of appropriation it is attributed to the Son, to whom equality is appropriated; thus Augustine says (De Doctr. Christ. i) that "in the Father there is unity, in the Son equality, in the Holy Ghost the connection of unity with equality."

Whether it belongs to Christ as man to sit at the right hand of the Father?

Objection 1: It would seem that it does not belong to Christ as man to sit at the right hand of the Father, because, as Damascene says (De Fide Orth. iv): "What we call the Father's right hand is the glory and honor of the Godhead." But the glory and honor of the Godhead do not belong to Christ as man. Consequently, it seems that Christ as man does not sit at the right hand of the Father.

Objection 2: Further, to sit on the ruler's right hand seems to exclude subjection, because one so sitting seems in a measure to be reigning with him. But Christ as man is "subject unto" the Father, as is said in 1 Cor. 15:28. Therefore it seems that Christ as man does not sit at the Father's right hand.

Objection 3: Further, on Rom. 8:34: "Who is at the right hand of God," the gloss adds: "that is, equal to the Father in that honor, whereby God is the Father: or, on the right hand of the Father, that is, in the mightier gifts of God." And on Heb. 1:3: "sitteth on the right hand of the majesty on high," the gloss adds, "that is, in equality with the Father over all things, both in place and dignity." But equality with God does not belong to Christ as man; for in this respect Christ Himself says (Jn. 14:28): "The Father is greater than I." Consequently, it appears unseemly for Christ as man to sit on the Father's right hand.

On the contrary, Augustine says (De Symb. ii): "By the expression 'right hand' understand the power which this Man, chosen of God, received, that He might come as judge, who before had come to be judged."

I answer that, As stated above [4328](A[2]), by the expression "right hand" is understood either the glory of His Godhead, or His eternal beatitude, or His judicial and royal power. Now this preposition "at" signifies a kind of approach to the right hand; thus denoting something in common, and yet with a distinction, as already observed (De Symb. ii). And this can be in three ways: first of all, by something common in nature, and a distinction in person; and thus Christ as the Son of God, sits at the right hand of the Father, because He has the same Nature as the Father: hence these things belong to the Son essentially, just as to the Father; and this is to be in equality with the Father. Secondly, according to the grace of union, which, on the contrary, implies distinction of nature, and unity of person. According to this, Christ as man is the Son of God, and consequently sits at the Father's right hand; yet so that the expression "as" does not denote condition of nature, but unity of suppositum, as explained above (Q[16], AA[10],11). Thirdly, the said approach can be understood according to habitual grace, which is more fully in Christ than in all other creatures, so much so that human nature in Christ is more blessed than all other creatures, and possesses over all other creatures royal and judiciary power.

So, then, if "as" denote condition of nature, then Christ, as God, sits "at the Father's right hand," that is, "in equality with the Father"; but as man, He sits "at the right hand of the Father," that is, "in the Father's mightier gifts beyond all other creatures," that is to say, "in greater beatitude," and "exercising judiciary power." But if "as" denote unity of person, thus again as man, He sits at the Father's right hand "as to equality of honor," inasmuch as with the same honor we venerate the Son of God with His assumed nature, as was said above ([4329]Q[25], A[1]).

Reply to Objection 1: Christ's humanity according to the conditions of His nature has not the glory or honor of the Godhead, which it has nevertheless by reason of the Person with whom it is united. Hence Damascene adds in the passage quoted: "In which," that is, in the glory of the Godhead, "the Son of God existing before ages, as God and consubstantial with the Father, sits in His conglorified flesh; for, under one adoration the one hypostasis, together with His flesh, is adored by every creature."

Reply to Objection 2: Christ as man is subject to the Father, if "as" denote the condition of nature: in which respect it does not belong to Him as man to sit at the Father's right hand, by reason of their mutual equality. But it does thus belong to Him to sit at the right hand of the Father, according as is thereby denoted the excellence of beatitude and His judiciary power over every creature.

Reply to Objection 3: It does not belong to Christ's human nature to be in equality with the Father, but only to the Person who assumed it; but it does belong even to the assumed human nature to share in God's mightier gifts, in so far as it implies exaltation above other creatures.

Whether it is proper to Christ to sit at the right hand of the Father?

Objection 1: It would seem that it is not proper to Christ to sit at the right hand of the Father, because the Apostle says (Eph. 2:4, 6): "God . . . hath raised us up together, and hath made us sit together in the heavenly places through Christ Jesus." But to be raised up is not proper to Christ. Therefore for like reason neither is it proper to Him to sit "on the right hand" of God "on high" (Heb. 1:3).

Objection 2: Further, as Augustine says (De Symb. i): "For Christ to sit at the right hand of the Father, is to dwell in His beatitude." But many more share in this. Therefore it does not appear to be proper to Christ to sit at the right hand of the Father.

Objection 3: Further, Christ Himself says (Apoc. 3:21): "To him that shall overcome, I will give to sit with Me in My throne: as I also have overcome, and am set down with My Father in His throne." But it is by sitting on His Father's throne that Christ is seated at His right hand. Therefore others who overcome likewise, sit at the Father's right hand.

Objection 4: Further, the Lord says (Mat. 20:23): "To sit on My right or left hand, is not Mine to give to you, but to them for whom it is prepared by My Father." But no purpose would be served by saying this, unless it was prepared for some. Consequently, to sit at the right hand is not proper to Christ.

On the contrary, It is written (Heb. 1:13): "To which of the angels said He at any time: Sit thou on My right hand, i.e. 'in My mightier gifts,'" or "'as my equal in the Godhead'"? [*The comment is from the gloss of Peter Lombard] as if to answer: "To none." But angels are higher than other creatures. Therefore, much less does it belong to anyone save Christ to sit at the Father's right hand.

I answer that, As stated above [4330](A[3]), Christ is said to sit at the Father's right hand inasmuch as He is on equality with the Father in respect of His Divine Nature, while in respect of His humanity, He excels all creatures in the possession of Divine gifts. But each of these belongs exclusively to Christ. Consequently, it belongs to no one else, angel or man, but to Christ alone, to sit at the right hand of the Father.

Reply to Objection 1: Since Christ is our Head, then what was bestowed on Christ is bestowed on us through Him. And on this account, since He is already raised up, the Apostle says that God has, so to speak, "raised us up together with Him," still we ourselves are not raised up yet, but are to be raised up, according to Rom. 8:11: "He who raised up Jesus from the dead, shall quicken also your mortal bodies": and after the same manner of speech the Apostle adds that "He has made us to sit together with Him, in the heavenly places"; namely, for the very reason that Christ our Head sits there.

Reply to Objection 2: Since the right hand is the Divine beatitude, then "to sit on the right hand" does not mean simply to be in beatitude, but to possess beatitude with a kind of dominative power, as a property and part of one's nature. This belongs to Christ alone, and to no other creature. Yet it can be said that every saint in bliss is placed on God's right hand; hence it is written (Mat. 25:33): "He shall set the sheep on His right hand."

Reply to Objection 3: By the "throne" is meant the judiciary power which Christ has from the Father: and in this sense He is said "to sit in the Father's throne." But other saints have it from Christ; and in this respect they are said "to sit on Christ's throne"; according to Mat. 19:28: "You also shall sit upon twelve seats, judging the twelve tribes of Israel."

Reply to Objection 4: As Chrysostom says (Hom. lxv in Matth.), "that place," to wit, sitting at the right hand, "is closed not only to all men, but likewise to angels: for, Paul declares it to be the prerogative of Christ, saying: 'To which of the angels said He at any time: Sit on My right hand?'" Our Lord therefore "replied not as though some were going to sit there one day, but condescending to the supplication of the questioners; since more than others they sought this one thing alone, to stand nigh to Him." Still it can be said that the sons of Zebedee sought for higher excellence in sharing His judiciary power; hence they did not ask to sit on the Father's right hand or left, but on Christ's.

OF CHRIST'S JUDICIARY POWER (SIX ARTICLES)
We have now to consider Christ's judiciary power. Under this head there are six points of inquiry:
(1) Whether judiciary power is to be attributed to Christ?
(2) Whether it belongs to Him as man?
(3) Whether He acquired it by merits?
(4) Whether His judiciary power is universal with regard to all men?
(5) Whether besides the judgment that takes place now in time, we are to expect Him in the future general judgment?
(6) Whether His judiciary power extends likewise to the angels?
It will be more suitable to consider the execution of the Last Judgment when we treat of things pertaining to the end of the world [*See XP, QQ[88], seqq.]. For the present it will be enough to touch on those points that concern Christ's dignity.

Whether judiciary power is to be specially attributed to Christ?
Objection 1: It would seem that judiciary power is not to be specially attributed to Christ. For judgment of others seems to belong to their lord; hence it is written (Rom. 14:4): "Who art thou that judgest another man's servant?" But, it belongs to the entire Trinity to be Lord over creatures. Therefore judiciary power ought not to be attributed specially to Christ.

Objection 2: Further, it is written (Dan. 7:9): "The Ancient of days sat"; and further on (Dan. 7:10), "the judgment sat, and the books were opened." But the Ancient of days is understood to be the Father, because as Hilary says (De Trin. ii): "Eternity is in the Father." Consequently, judiciary power ought rather to be attributed to the Father than to Christ.

Objection 3: Further, it seems to belong to the same person to judge as it does to convince. But it belongs to the Holy Ghost to convince: for our Lord says (Jn. 16:8): "And when He is come," i.e. the Holy Ghost, "He will convince the world of sin, and of justice, and of judgment." Therefore judiciary power ought to be attributed to the Holy Ghost rather than to Christ.

On the contrary, It is said of Christ (Acts 10:42): "It is He who was appointed by God, to be judge of the living end of the dead."

I answer that, Three things are required for passing judgment: first, the power of coercing subjects; hence it is written (Ecclus. 7:6): "Seek not to be made a judge unless thou have strength enough to extirpate iniquities." The second thing required is upright zeal, so as to pass judgment not out of hatred or malice, but from love of justice, according to Prov. 3:12: "For whom the Lord loveth, He chasteneth: and as a father in the son He pleaseth Himself." Thirdly, wisdom is needed, upon which judgment is based, according to Ecclus. 10:1: "A wise judge shall judge his people." The first two are conditions for judging; but on the third the very rule of judgment is based, because the standard of judgment is the law of wisdom or truth, according to which the judgment is passed.

Now because the Son is Wisdom begotten, and Truth proceeding from the Father, and His perfect Image, consequently, judiciary power is properly attributed to the Son of God. Accordingly Augustine says (De Vera Relig. xxxi): "This is that unchangeable Truth, which is rightly styled the law of all arts, and the art of the Almighty Craftsman. But even as we and all rational souls judge aright of the things beneath us, so does He who alone is Truth itself pass judgment on us, when we cling to Him. But the Father judges Him not, for He is the Truth no less than Himself. Consequently, whatever the Father judges, He judges through It." Further on he concludes by saying: "Therefore the Father judges no man, but has given all judgment to the Son."

Reply to Objection 1: This argument proves that judiciary power is common to the entire Trinity, which is quite true: still by special appropriation such power is attributed to the Son, as stated above.

Reply to Objection 2: As Augustine says (De Trin. vi), eternity is attributed to the Father, because He is the Principle, which is implied in the idea of eternity. And in the same place Augustine says that the Son is the art of the Father. So, then, judiciary authority is attributed to the Father, inasmuch as He is the Principle of the Son, but the very rule of judgment is attributed to the Son who is the art and wisdom of the Father, so that as the Father does all things through the Son, inasmuch as the Son is His art, so He judges all things through the Son, inasmuch as the Son is His wisdom and truth. And this is implied by Daniel, when he says in the first passage that "the Ancient of days sat," and when he subsequently adds that the Son of Man "came even to the Ancient of days, who gave Him power, and glory, and a kingdom": and thereby we are given to understand that the authority for judging lies with the Father, from whom the Son received the power to judge.

Reply to Objection 3: As Augustine says (Tract. xcv in Joan.): "Christ said that the Holy Ghost shall convince the world of sin, as if to say 'He shall pour out charity upon your hearts.' For thus, when fear is driven away, you shall have freedom for convincing." Consequently, then, judgment is attributed to the Holy Ghost, not as regards the rule of judgment, but as regards man's desire to judge others aright.

Whether judiciary power belongs to Christ as man?

Objection 1: It would seem that judiciary power does not belong to Christ as man. For Augustine says (De Vera Relig. xxxi) that judgment is attributed to the Son inasmuch as He is the law of the first truth. But this is Christ's attribute as God. Consequently, judiciary power does not belong to Christ as man but as God.

Objection 2: Further, it belongs to judiciary power to reward the good, just as to punish the wicked. But eternal beatitude, which is the reward of good works, is bestowed by God alone: thus Augustine says (Tract. xxiii super Joan.) that "the soul is made blessed by participation of God, and not by participation of a holy soul." Therefore it seems that judiciary power does not belong to Christ as man, but as God.

Objection 3: Further, it belongs to Christ's judiciary power to judge secrets of hearts, according to 1 Cor. 4:5: "Judge not before the time; until the Lord come, who both will bring to light the hidden things of darkness, and will make manifest the counsels of the hearts." But this belongs exclusively to the Divine power, according to Jer. 17:9,10: "The heart of man is perverse and unsearchable, who can know it? I am the Lord who search the heart, and prove the reins: who give to every one according to his way." Therefore judiciary power does not belong to Christ as man but as God.

On the contrary, It is said (Jn. 5:27): "He hath given Him power to do judgment, because He is the Son of man."

I answer that, Chrysostom (Hom. xxxix in Joan.) seems to think that judiciary power belongs to Christ not as man, but only as God. Accordingly he thus explains the passage just quoted from John: "'He gave Him power to do judgment, because He is the Son of man: wonder not at this.' For He received judiciary power, not because He is man; but because He is the Son of the ineffable God, therefore is He judge. But since the expressions used were greater than those appertaining to man, He said in explanation: 'Wonder not at this, because He is the Son of man, for He is likewise the Son of God.'" And he proves this by the effect of the Resurrection: wherefore He adds: "Because the hour cometh when the dead in their graves shall hear the voice of the Son of God."

But it must be observed that although the primary authority of judging rests with God, nevertheless the power to judge is committed to men with regard to those subject to their jurisdiction. Hence it is written (Dt. 1:16): "Judge that which is just"; and further on (Dt. 1:17): "Because it is the judgment of God," that is to say, it is by His authority that you judge. Now it was said before ([4331]Q[8], AA[1],4) that Christ even in His human nature is Head of the entire Church, and that God has "put all things under His feet." Consequently, it belongs to Him, even according to His human nature, to exercise judiciary power. on this account. it seems that the authority of Scripture quoted above must be interpreted thus: "He gave Him power to do judgment, because He is the Son of Man"; not on account of the condition of His nature, for thus all men would have this kind of power, as Chrysostom objects (Hom. xxxix in Joan.); but because this belongs to the grace of the Head, which Christ received in His human nature.

Now judiciary power belongs to Christ in this way according to His human nature on three accounts. First, because of His likeness and kinship with men; for, as God works through intermediary causes, as being closer to the effects, so He judges men through the Man Christ, that His judgment may be sweeter to men. Hence (Heb. 4:15) the Apostle says: "For we have not a high-priest, who cannot have compassion on our infirmities; but one tempted in all things like as we are, without sin. Let us go therefore with confidence to the throne of His grace." Secondly, because at the last judgment, as Augustine says (Tract. xix in Joan.), "there will be a resurrection of dead bodies, which God will raise up through the Son of Man"; just as by "the same Christ He raises souls," inasmuch as "He is the Son of God." Thirdly, because, as Augustine observes (De Verb. Dom., Serm. cxxvii): "It was but right that those who were to be judged should see their judge. But those to be judged were the good and the bad. It follows that the form of a servant should be shown in the judgment to both good and wicked, while the form of God should be kept for the good alone."

Reply to Objection 1: Judgment belongs to truth as its standard, while it belongs to the man imbued with truth, according as he is as it were one with truth, as a kind of law and "living justice" [*Aristotle, Ethic. v]. Hence Augustine quotes (De Verb. Dom., Serm. cxxvii) the saying of 1 Cor. 2:15: "The spiritual man judgeth all things." But beyond all creatures Christ's soul was more closely united with truth, and more full of truth; according to Jn. 1:14: "We saw Him . . . full of grace and truth." And according to this it belongs principally to the soul of Christ to judge all things.

Reply to Objection 2: It belongs to God alone to bestow beatitude upon souls by a participation with Himself; but it is Christ's prerogative to bring them to such beatitude, inasmuch as He is their Head and the author of their salvation, according to Heb. 2:10: "Who had brought many children into glory, to perfect the author of their salvation by His Passion."

Reply to Objection 3: To know and judge the secrets of hearts, of itself belongs to God alone; but from the overflow of the Godhead into Christ's soul it belongs to Him also to know and to judge the secrets of hearts, as we stated above ([4332]Q[10], A[2]), when dealing with the knowledge of Christ. Hence it is written (Rom. 2:16): "In the day when God shall judge the secrets of men by Jesus Christ."

Whether Christ acquired His judiciary power by His merits?

Objection 1: It would seem that Christ did not acquire His judiciary power by His merits. For judiciary power flows from the royal dignity: according to Prov. 20:8: "The king that sitteth on the throne of judgment, scattereth away all evil with his look." But it was without merits that Christ acquired royal power, for it is His due as God's Only-begotten Son: thus it is written (Lk. 1:32): "The Lord God shall give unto Him the throne of David His father, and He shall reign in the house of Jacob for ever." Therefore Christ did not obtain judiciary power by His merits.

Objection 2: Further, as stated above [4333](A[2]), judiciary power is Christ's due inasmuch as He is our Head. But the grace of headship does not belong to Christ by reason of merit, but follows the personal union of the Divine and human natures: according to Jn. 1:14, 16: "We saw His glory . . . as of the Only-Begotten of the Father, full of grace and truth . . . and of His fulness we all have received": and this pertains to the notion of headship. Consequently, it seems that Christ did not have judiciary power from merits.

Objection 3: Further, the Apostle says (1 Cor. 2:15): "The spiritual man judgeth all things." But a man becomes spiritual through grace, which is not from merits; otherwise it is "no more grace," as is said in Rom. 11:6. Therefore it seems that judiciary power belongs neither to Christ nor to others from any merits, but from grace alone.

On the contrary, It is written (Job 36:17): "Thy cause hath been judged as that of the wicked, cause and judgment thou shalt recover." And Augustine says (Serm. cxxvii): "The Judge shall sit, who stood before a judge; He shall condemn the truly wicked, who Himself was falsely reputed wicked."

I answer that, There is nothing to hinder one and the same thing from being due to some one from various causes: as the glory of the body in rising was due to Christ not only as befitting His Godhead and His soul's glory, but likewise "from the merit of the lowliness of His Passion" [*Cf. Augustine, Tract. civ in Joan.]. And in the same way it must be said that judiciary power belongs to the Man Christ on account of both His Divine personality, and the dignity of His headship, and the fulness of His habitual grace: and yet He obtained it from merit, so that, in accordance with the Divine justice, He should be judge who fought for God's justice, and conquered, and was unjustly condemned. Hence He Himself says (Apoc. 3:21): "I have overcome and am set down in My Father's throne [Vulg.: 'with My Father in His throne']." Now judiciary power is understood by "throne," according to Ps. 9:5: "Thou hast sat on the throne, who judgest justice."

Reply to Objection 1: This argument holds good of judiciary power according as it is due to Christ by reason of the union with the Word of God.

Reply to Objection 2: This argument is based on the ground of His grace as Head.

Reply to Objection 3: This argument holds good in regard to habitual grace, which perfects Christ's soul. But although judiciary power be Christ's due in these ways, it is not hindered from being His due from merit.

Whether judiciary power belongs to Christ with respect to all human affairs?

Objection 1: It would seem that judiciary power concerning all human affairs does not belong to Christ. For as we read in Lk. 12:13,14, when one of the crowd said to Christ: "Speak to my brother that he divide the inheritance with me; He said to him: Man, who hath appointed Me judge, or divider over you?" Consequently, He does not exercise judgment over all human affairs.

Objection 2: Further, no one exercises judgment except over his own subjects. But, according to Heb. 2:8, "we see not as yet all things subject to" Christ. Therefore it seems that Christ has not judgment over all human affairs.

Objection 3: Further, Augustine says (De Civ. Dei xx) that it is part of Divine judgment for the good to be afflicted sometimes in this world, and sometimes to prosper, and in like manner the wicked. But the same was the case also before the Incarnation. Consequently, not all God's judgments regarding human affairs are included in Christ's judiciary power.

On the contrary, It is said (Jn. 5:22): "The Father hath given all judgment to the Son."

I answer that, If we speak of Christ according to His Divine Nature, it is evident that every judgment of the Father belongs to the Son; for, as the Father does all things through His Word, so He judges all things through His Word.

But if we speak of Christ in His human nature, thus again is it evident that all things are subject to His judgment. This is made clear if we consider first of all the relationship subsisting between Christ's soul and the Word of God; for, if "the spiritual man judgeth all things," as is said in 1 Cor. 2:15, inasmuch as his soul clings to the Word of God, how much more Christ's soul, which is filled with the truth of the Word of God, passes judgment upon all things.

Secondly, the same appears from the merit of His death; because, according to Rom. 14:9: "To this end Christ died and rose again; that He might be Lord both of the dead and of the living." And therefore He has judgment over all men; and on this account the Apostle adds (Rom. 14:10): "We shall all stand before the judgment seat of Christ": and (Dan. 7:14) it is written that "He gave Him power, and glory, and a kingdom; and all peoples, tribes, and tongues shall serve Him."

Thirdly, the same thing is evident from comparison of human affairs with the end of human salvation. For, to whomsoever the substance is entrusted, the accessory is likewise committed. Now all human affairs are ordered for the end of beatitude, which is everlasting salvation, to which men are admitted, or from which they are excluded by Christ's judgment, as is evident from Mat. 25:31,40. Consequently, it is manifest that all human affairs are included in Christ's judiciary power.

Reply to Objection 1: As was said above (A[3], OBJ[1]), judiciary power goes with royal dignity. Now Christ, although established king by God, did not wish while living on earth to govern temporally an earthly kingdom; consequently He said (Jn. 18:36): "My kingdom is not of this world." In like fashion He did not wish to exercise judiciary power over temporal concerns, since He came to raise men to Divine things. Hence Ambrose observes on this passage in Luke: "It is well that He who came down with a Divine purpose should hold Himself aloof from temporal concerns; nor does He deign to be a judge of quarrels and an arbiter of property, since He is judge of the quick and the dead, and the arbitrator of merits."

Reply to Objection 2: All things are subject to Christ in respect of that power, which He received from the Father, over all things, according to Mat. 28:18: "All power is given to Me in heaven and in earth." But as to the exercise of this power, all things are not yet subject to Him: this will come to pass in the future, when He shall fulfil His will regarding all things, by saving some and punishing others.

Reply to Objection 3: Judgments of this kind were exercised by Christ before His Incarnation, inasmuch as He is the Word of God: and the soul united with Him personally became a partaker of this power by the Incarnation.

Whether after the Judgment that takes place in the present time, there remains yet another General Judgment?

Objection 1: It would seem that after the Judgment that takes place in the present time, there does not remain another General Judgment. For a judgment serves no purpose after the final allotment of rewards and punishments. But rewards and punishments are allotted in this present time: for our Lord said to the thief on the cross (Lk. 23:43): "This day thou shalt be with Me in paradise": and (Lk. 16:22) it is said that "the rich man died and was buried in hell." Therefore it is useless to look forward to a final Judgment.

Objection 2: Further, according to another (the Septuagint) version of Nahum 1:9, "God shall not judge the same thing a second time." But in the present time God judges both temporal and spiritual matters. Therefore, it does not seem that another final judgment is to be expected.

Objection 3: Further, reward and punishment correspond with merit and demerit. But merit and demerit bear relation to the body only in so far as it is the instrument of the soul. Therefore reward or punishment is not due to the body save as the soul's instrument. Therefore no other Judgment is called for at the end (of the world) to requite man with reward or punishment in the body, besides that Judgment in which souls are now punished or rewarded.

On the contrary, It is said in Jn. 12:48: "The word that I have spoken, the same shall judge you [Vulg.: 'him'] in the last day." Therefore there will be a Judgment at the last day besides that which takes place in the present time.

I answer that, Judgment cannot be passed perfectly upon any changeable subject before its consummation: just as judgment cannot be given perfectly regarding the quality of any action before its completion in itself and in its results: because many actions appear to be profitable, which in their effects prove to be hurtful. And in the same way perfect judgment cannot be passed upon any man before the close of his life, since he can be changed in many respects from good to evil, or conversely, or from good to better, or from evil to worse. Hence the Apostle says (Heb. 9:27): "It is appointed unto men once to die, and after this the Judgment."

But it must be observed that although man's temporal life in itself ends with death, still it continues dependent in a measure on what comes after it in the future. In one way, as it still lives on in men's memories, in which sometimes, contrary to the truth, good or evil reputations linger on. In another way in a man's children, who are so to speak something of their parent, according to Ecclus. 30:4: "His father is dead, and he is as if he were not dead, for he hath left one behind him that is like himself." And yet many good men have wicked sons, and conversely. Thirdly, as to the result of his actions: just as from the deceit of Arius and other false leaders unbelief continues to flourish down to the close of the world; and even until then faith will continue to derive its progress from the preaching of the apostles. In a fourth way, as to the body, which is sometimes buried with honor and sometimes left unburied, and finally falls to dust utterly. In a fifth way, as to the things upon which a man's heart is set, such as temporal concerns, for example, some of which quickly lapse, while others endure longer.

Now all these things are submitted to the verdict of the Divine Judgment; and consequently, a perfect and public Judgment cannot be made of all these things during the course of this present time. Wherefore, there must be a final Judgment at the last day, in which everything concerning every man in every respect shall be perfectly and publicly judged.

Reply to Objection 1: Some men have held the opinion that the souls of the saints shall not be rewarded in heaven, nor the souls of the lost punished in hell, until the Judgment-day. That this is false appears from the testimony of the Apostle (2 Cor. 5:8), where he says: "We are confident and have a good will to be absent rather from the body, and to be present with the Lord": that is, not to "walk by faith" but "by sight," as appears from the context. But this is to see God in His Essence, wherein consists "eternal life," as is clear from Jn. 17:3. Hence it is manifest that the souls separated from bodies are in eternal life.

Consequently, it must be maintained that after death man enters into an unchangeable state as to all that concerns the soul: and therefore there is no need for postponing judgment as to the reward of the soul. But since there are some other things pertaining to a man which go on through the whole course of time, and which are not foreign to the Divine judgment, all these things must be brought to judgment at the end of time. For although in regard to such things a man neither merits nor demerits, still in a measure they accompany his reward or punishment. Consequently all these things must be weighed in the final judgment.

Reply to Objection 2: "God shall not judge twice the same thing," i.e. in the same respect; but it is not unseemly for God to judge twice according to different respects.

Reply to Objection 3: Although the reward or punishment of the body depends upon the reward or punishment of the soul, nevertheless, since the soul is changeable only accidentally, on account of the body, once it is separated from the body it enters into an unchangeable condition, and receives its judgment. But the body remains subject to change down to the close of time: and therefore it must receive its reward or punishment then, in the last Judgment.

Whether Christ's judiciary power extends to the angels?

Objection 1: It would seem that Christ's judiciary power does not extend to the angels, because the good and wicked angels alike were judged in the beginning of the world, when some fell through sin while others were confirmed in bliss. But those already judged have no need of being judged again. Therefore Christ's judiciary power does not extend to the angels.

Objection 2: Further, the same person cannot be both judge and judged. But the angels will come to judge with Christ, according to Mat. 25:31: "When the Son of Man shall come in His majesty, and all the angels with Him." Therefore it seems that the angels will not be judged by Christ.

Objection 3: Further, the angels are higher than other creatures. If Christ, then, be judge not only of men but likewise of angels, then for the same reason He will be judge of all creatures; which seems to be false, since this belongs to God's providence: hence it is written (Job 34:13): "What other hath He appointed over the earth? or whom hath He set over the world which He made?" Therefore Christ is not the judge of the angels.

On the contrary, The Apostle says (1 Cor. 6:3): "Know you not that we shall judge angels?" But the saints judge only by Christ's authority. Therefore, much more does Christ possess judiciary power over the angels.

I answer that, The angels are subjects of Christ's judiciary power, not only with regard to His Divine Nature, as He is the Word of God, but also with regard to His human nature. And this is evident from three considerations. First of all, from the closeness of His assumed nature to God; because, according to Heb. 2:16: "For nowhere doth He take hold of the angels, but of the seed of Abraham He taketh hold." Consequently, Christ's soul is more filled with the truth of the Word of God than any angel: for which reason He also enlightens the angels, as Dionysius says (Coel. Hier. vii), and so He has power to judge them. Secondly, because by the lowliness of His Passion, human nature in Christ merited to be exalted above the angels; so that, as is said in Phil. 2:10: "In the name of Jesus every knee should bow, of those that are in heaven, on earth, and under the earth." And therefore Christ has judiciary power even over the good and wicked angels: in token whereof it is said in the Apocalypse (7:11) that "all the angels stood round about the throne." Thirdly, on account of what they do for men, of whom Christ is the Head in a special manner. Hence it is written (Heb. 1:14): "They are [Vulg.: 'Are they not'] all ministering spirits, sent to minister for them, who shall receive the inheritance of salvation (?)." But they are submitted to Christ's judgment, first, as regards the dispensing of those things which are done through them; which dispensing is likewise done by the Man Christ, to whom the angels ministered, as related (Mat. 4:11), and from whom the devils besought that they might be sent into the swine, according to Mat. 8:31. Secondly, as to other accidental rewards of the good angels, such as the joy which they have at the salvation of men, according to Lk. 15:10: "There shall be joy before the angels of God upon one sinner doing penance": and furthermore as to the accidental punishments of the devils wherewith they are either tormented here, or are shut up in hell; and this also belongs to the Man Christ: hence it is written (Mk. 1:24) that the devil cried out: "What have we to do with thee, Jesus of Nazareth? art Thou come to destroy us?" Thirdly, as to the essential reward of the good angels, which is everlasting bliss; and as to the essential punishment of the wicked angels, which is everlasting damnation. But this was done by Christ from the beginning of the world, inasmuch as He is the Word of God.

Reply to Objection 1: This argument considers judgment as to the essential reward and chief punishment.

Reply to Objection 2: As Augustine says (De Vera Relig. xxxi): "Although the spiritual man judgeth all things, still he is judged by Truth Itself." Consequently, although the angels judge, as being spiritual creatures, still they are judged by Christ, inasmuch as He is the Truth.

Reply to Objection 3: Christ judges not only the angels, but also the administration of all creatures. For if, as Augustine says (De Trin. iii) the lower things are ruled by God through the higher, in a certain order, it must be said that all things are ruled by Christ's soul, which is above every creature. Hence the Apostle says (Heb. 2:5): "For God hath not subjected unto angels the world to come"---subject namely to Christ---"of whom we speak" [Douay: 'whereof we speak'] [*The words "subject namely to Christ" are from a gloss]. Nor does it follow that God set another over the earth; since one and the same Person is God and Man, our Lord Jesus Christ.

Let what has been said of the Mystery of His Incarnation suffice for the present.

TREATISE ON THE SACRAMENTS (QQ[60]-90)

WHAT IS A SACRAMENT? (EIGHT ARTICLES)

After considering those things that concern the mystery of the incarnate Word, we must consider the sacraments of the Church which derive their efficacy from the Word incarnate Himself. First we shall consider the sacraments in general; secondly, we shall consider specially each sacrament.

Concerning the first our consideration will be fivefold: (1) What is a sacrament? (2) Of the necessity of the sacraments; (3) of the effects of the sacraments; (4) Of their cause; (5) Of their number.

Under the first heading there are eight points of inquiry:

(1) Whether a sacrament is a kind of sign?
(2) Whether every sign of a sacred thing is a sacrament?
(3) Whether a sacrament is a sign of one thing only, or of several?
(4) Whether a sacrament is a sign that is something sensible?
(5) Whether some determinate sensible thing is required for a sacrament?
(6) Whether signification expressed by words is necessary for a sacrament?
(7) Whether determinate words are required?
(8) Whether anything may be added to or subtracted from these words?

Whether a sacrament is a kind of sign?

Objection 1: It seems that a sacrament is not a kind of sign. For sacrament appears to be derived from "sacring" [sacrando]; just as medicament, from "medicando" [healing]. But this seems to be of the nature of a cause rather than of a sign. Therefore a sacrament is a kind of cause rather than a kind of sign.

Objection 2: Further, sacrament seems to signify something hidden, according to Tob. 12:7: "It is good to hide the secret [sacramentum] of a king"; and Eph. 3:9: "What is the dispensation of the mystery [sacramenti] which hath been hidden from eternity in God." But that which is hidden, seems foreign to the nature of a sign; for "a sign is that which conveys something else to the mind, besides the species which it impresses on the senses," as Augustine explains (De Doctr. Christ. ii). Therefore it seems that a sacrament is not a kind of sign.

Objection 3: Further, an oath is sometimes called a sacrament: for it is written in the Decretals (Caus. xxii, qu. 5): "Children who have not attained the use of reason must not be obliged to swear: and whoever has foresworn himself once, must no more be a witness, nor be allowed to take a sacrament," i.e. an oath. But an oath is not a kind of sign, therefore it seems that a sacrament is not a kind of sign.

On the contrary, Augustine says (De Civ. Dei x): "The visible sacrifice is the sacrament, i.e. the sacred sign, of the invisible sacrifice."

I answer that, All things that are ordained to one, even in different ways, can be denominated from it: thus, from health which is in an animal, not only is the animal said to be healthy through being the subject of health: but medicine also is said to be healthy through producing health; diet through preserving it; and urine, through being a sign of health. Consequently, a thing may be called a "sacrament," either from having a certain hidden sanctity, and in this sense a sacrament is a "sacred secret"; or from having some relationship to this sanctity, which relationship may be that of a cause, or of a sign or of any other relation. But now we are speaking of sacraments in a special sense, as implying the habitude of sign: and in this way a sacrament is a kind of sign.

Reply to Objection 1: Because medicine is an efficient cause of health, consequently whatever things are denominated from medicine are to be referred to some first active cause: so that a medicament implies a certain causality. But sanctity from which a sacrament is denominated, is not there taken as an efficient cause, but rather as a formal or a final cause. Therefore it does not follow that a sacrament need always imply causality.

Reply to Objection 2: This argument considers sacrament in the sense of a "sacred secret." Now not only God's but also the king's, secret, is said to be sacred and to be a sacrament: because according to the ancients, whatever it was unlawful to lay violent hands on was said to be holy or sacrosanct, such as the city walls, and persons of high rank. Consequently those secrets, whether Divine or human, which it is unlawful to violate by making them known to anybody whatever, are called "sacred secrets or sacraments."

Reply to Objection 3: Even an oath has a certain relation to sacred things, in so far as it consists in calling a sacred thing to witness. And in this sense it is called a sacrament: not in the sense in which we speak of sacraments now; the word "sacrament" being thus used not equivocally but analogically, i.e. by reason of a different relation to the one thing, viz. something sacred.

Whether every sign of a holy thing is a sacrament?

Objection 1: It seems that not every sign of a sacred thing is a sacrament. For all sensible creatures are signs of sacred things; according to Rom. 1:20: "The invisible things of God are clearly seen being understood by the things that are made." And yet all sensible things cannot be called sacraments. Therefore not every sign of a sacred thing is a sacrament.

Objection 2: Further, whatever was done under the Old Law was a figure of Christ Who is the "Holy of Holies" (Dan. 9:24), according to 1 Cor. 10:11: "All (these) things happened to them in figure"; and Col. 2:17: "Which are a shadow of things to come, but the body is Christ's." And yet not all that was done by the Fathers of the Old Testament, not even all the ceremonies of the Law, were sacraments, but only in certain special cases, as stated in the [4334]FS, Q[101], A[4]. Therefore it seems that not every sign of a sacred thing is a sacrament.

Objection 3: Further, even in the New Testament many things are done in sign of some sacred thing; yet they are not called sacraments; such as sprinkling with holy water, the consecration of an altar, and such like. Therefore not every sign of a sacred thing is a sacrament.

On the contrary, A definition is convertible with the thing defined. Now some define a sacrament as being "the sign of a sacred thing"; moreover, this is clear from the passage quoted above [4335](A[1]) from Augustine. Therefore it seems that every sign of a sacred thing is a sacrament.

I answer that, Signs are given to men, to whom it is proper to discover the unknown by means of the known. Consequently a sacrament properly so called is that which is the sign of some sacred thing pertaining to man; so that properly speaking a sacrament, as considered by us now, is defined as being the "sign of a holy thing so far as it makes men holy."

Reply to Objection 1: Sensible creatures signify something holy, viz. Divine wisdom and goodness inasmuch as these are holy in themselves; but not inasmuch as we are made holy by them. Therefore they cannot be called sacraments as we understand sacraments now.

Reply to Objection 2: Some things pertaining to the Old Testament signified the holiness of Christ considered as holy in Himself. Others signified His holiness considered as the cause of our holiness; thus the sacrifice of the Paschal Lamb signified Christ's Sacrifice whereby we are made holy: and such like are properly styled sacraments of the Old Law.

Reply to Objection 3: Names are given to things considered in reference to their end and state of completeness. Now a disposition is not an end, whereas perfection is. Consequently things that signify disposition to holiness are not called sacraments, and with regard to these the objection is verified: only those are called sacraments which signify the perfection of holiness in man.

Whether a sacrament is a sign of one thing only?

Objection 1: It seems that a sacrament is a sign of one thing only. For that which signifies many things is an ambiguous sign, and consequently occasions deception: this is clearly seen in equivocal words. But all deception should be removed from the Christian religion, according to Col. 2:8: "Beware lest any man cheat you by philosophy and vain deceit." Therefore it seems that a sacrament is not a sign of several things.

Objection 2: Further, as stated above [4336](A[2]), a sacrament signifies a holy thing in so far as it makes man holy. But there is only one cause of man's holiness, viz. the blood of Christ; according to Heb. 13:12: "Jesus, that He might sanctify the people by His own blood, suffered without the gate." Therefore it seems that a sacrament does not signify several things.

Objection 3: Further, it has been said above (A[2], ad 3) that a sacrament signifies properly the very end of sanctification. Now the end of sanctification is eternal life, according to Rom. 6:22: "You have your fruit unto sanctification, and the end life everlasting." Therefore it seems that the sacraments signify one thing only, viz. eternal life.

On the contrary, In the Sacrament of the Altar, two things are signified, viz. Christ's true body, and Christ's mystical body; as Augustine says (Liber Sent. Prosper.).

I answer that, As stated above [4337](A[2]) a sacrament properly speaking is that which is ordained to signify our sanctification. In which three things may be considered; viz. the very cause of our sanctification, which is Christ's passion; the form of our sanctification, which is grace and the virtues; and the ultimate end of our sanctification, which is eternal life. And all these are signified by the sacraments. Consequently a sacrament is a sign that is both a reminder of the past, i.e. the passion of Christ; and an indication of that which is effected in us by Christ's passion, i.e. grace; and a prognostic, that is, a foretelling of future glory.

Reply to Objection 1: Then is a sign ambiguous and the occasion of deception, when it signifies many things not ordained to one another. But when it signifies many things inasmuch as, through being mutually ordained, they form one thing, then the sign is not ambiguous but certain: thus this word "man" signifies the soul and body inasmuch as together they form the human nature. In this way a sacrament signifies the three things aforesaid, inasmuch as by being in a certain order they are one thing.

Reply to Objection 2: Since a sacrament signifies that which sanctifies, it must needs signify the effect, which is implied in the sanctifying cause as such.

Reply to Objection 3: It is enough for a sacrament that it signify that perfection which consists in the form, nor is it necessary that it should signify only that perfection which is the end.

Whether a sacrament is always something sensible?

Objection 1: It seems that a sacrament is not always something sensible. Because, according to the Philosopher (Prior. Anal. ii), every effect is a sign of its cause. But just as there are some sensible effects, so are there some intelligible effects; thus science is the effect of a demonstration. Therefore not every sign is sensible. Now all that is required for a sacrament is something that is a sign of some sacred thing, inasmuch as thereby man is sanctified, as stated above [4338](A[2]). Therefore something sensible is not required for a sacrament.

Objection 2: Further, sacraments belong to the kingdom of God and the Divine worship. But sensible things do not seem to belong to the Divine worship: for we are told (Jn. 4:24) that "God is a spirit; and they that adore Him, must adore Him in spirit and in truth"; and (Rom. 14:17) that "the kingdom of God is not meat and drink." Therefore sensible things are not required for the sacraments.

Objection 3: Further. Augustine says (De Lib. Arb. ii) that "sensible things are goods of least account, since without them man can live aright." But the sacraments are necessary for man's salvation, as we shall show farther on ([4339]Q[61], A[1]): so that man cannot live aright without them. Therefore sensible things are not required for the sacraments.

On the contrary, Augustine says (Tract. lxxx super Joan.): "The word is added to the element and this becomes a sacrament"; and he is speaking there of water which is a sensible element. Therefore sensible things are required for the sacraments.

I answer that, Divine wisdom provides for each thing according to its mode; hence it is written (Wis. 8:1) that "she . . . ordereth all things sweetly": wherefore also we are told (Mat. 25:15) that she "gave to everyone according to his proper ability." Now it is part of man's nature to acquire knowledge of the intelligible from the sensible. But a sign is that by means of which one attains to the knowledge of something else. Consequently, since the sacred things which are signified by the sacraments, are the spiritual and intelligible goods by means of which man is sanctified, it follows that the sacramental signs consist in sensible things: just as in the Divine Scriptures spiritual things are set before us under the guise of things sensible. And hence it is that sensible things are required for the sacraments; as Dionysius also proves in his book on the heavenly hierarchy (Coel. Hier. i).

Reply to Objection 1: The name and definition of a thing is taken principally from that which belongs to a thing primarily and essentially: and not from that which belongs to it through something else. Now a sensible effect being the primary and direct object of man's knowledge (since all our knowledge springs from the senses) by its very nature leads to the knowledge of something else: whereas intelligible effects are not such as to be able to lead us to the knowledge of something else, except in so far as they are manifested by some other thing, i.e. by certain sensibles. It is for this reason that the name sign is given primarily and principally to things which are offered to the senses; hence Augustine says (De Doctr. Christ. ii) that a sign "is that which conveys something else to the mind, besides the species which it impresses on the senses." But intelligible effects do not partake of the nature of a sign except in so far as they are pointed out by certain signs. And in this way, too, certain things which are not sensible are termed sacraments as it were, in so far as they are signified by certain sensible things, of which we shall treat further on ([4340]Q[63], A[1], ad 2; A[3], ad 2; [4341] Q[73], A[6];[4342] Q[74], A[1], ad 3).

Reply to Objection 2: Sensible things considered in their own nature do not belong to the worship or kingdom of God: but considered only as signs of spiritual things in which the kingdom of God consists.

Reply to Objection 3: Augustine speaks there of sensible things, considered in their nature; but not as employed to signify spiritual things, which are the highest goods.

Whether determinate things are required for a sacrament?

Objection 1: It seems that determinate things are not required for a sacrament. For sensible things are required in sacraments for the purpose of signification, as stated above [4343](A[4]). But nothing hinders the same thing being signified by divers sensible things: thus in Holy Scripture God is signified metaphorically, sometimes by a stone (2 Kings 22:2; Zech. 3:9; 1 Cor. 10:4; Apoc. 4:3); sometimes by a lion (Is. 31:4; Apoc. 5:5); sometimes by the sun (Is. 60:19,20; Mal. 4:2), or by something similar. Therefore it seems that divers things can be suitable to the same sacrament. Therefore determinate things are not required for the sacraments.

Objection 2: Further, the health of the soul is more necessary than that of the body. But in bodily medicines, which are ordained to the health of the body, one thing can be substituted for another which happens to be wanting. Therefore much more in the sacraments, which are spiritual remedies ordained to the health of the soul, can one thing be substituted for another when this happens to be lacking.

Objection 3: Further, it is not fitting that the salvation of men be restricted by the Divine Law: still less by the Law of Christ, Who came to save all. But in the state of the Law of nature determinate things were not required in the sacraments, but were put to that use through a vow, as appears from Gn. 28, where Jacob vowed that he would offer to God tithes and peace-offerings. Therefore it seems that man should not have been restricted, especially under the New Law, to the use of any determinate thing in the sacraments.

On the contrary, our Lord said (Jn. 3:5): "Unless a man be born again of water and the Holy Ghost, he cannot enter into the kingdom of God."

I answer that, In the use of the sacraments two things may be considered, namely, the worship of God, and the sanctification of man: the former of which pertains to man as referred to God, and the latter pertains to God in reference to man. Now it is not for anyone to determine that which is in the power of another, but only that which is in his own power. Since, therefore, the sanctification of man is in the power of God Who sanctifies, it is not for man to decide what things should be used for his sanctification, but this should be determined by Divine institution. Therefore in the sacraments of the New Law, by which man is sanctified according to 1 Cor. 6:11, "You are washed, you are sanctified," we must use those things which are determined by Divine institution.

Reply to Objection 1: Though the same thing can be signified by divers signs, yet to determine which sign must be used belongs to the signifier. Now it is God Who signifies spiritual things to us by means of the sensible things in the sacraments, and of similitudes in the Scriptures. And consequently, just as the Holy Ghost decides by what similitudes spiritual things are to be signified in certain passages of Scripture, so also must it be determined by Divine institution what things are to be employed for the purpose of signification in this or that sacrament.

Reply to Objection 2: Sensible things are endowed with natural powers conducive to the health of the body: and therefore if two of them have the same virtue, it matters not which we use. Yet they are ordained unto sanctification not through any power that they possess naturally, but only in virtue of the Divine institution. And therefore it was necessary that God should determine the sensible things to be employed in the sacraments.

Reply to Objection 3: As Augustine says (Contra Faust. xix), diverse sacraments suit different times; just as different times are signified by different parts of the verb, viz. present, past, and future. Consequently, just as under the state of the Law of nature man was moved by inward instinct and without any outward law, to worship God, so also the sensible things to be employed in the worship of God were determined by inward instinct. But later on it became necessary for a law to be given (to man) from without: both because the Law of nature had become obscured by man's sins; and in order to signify more expressly the grace of Christ, by which the human race is sanctified. And hence the need for those things to be determinate, of which men have to make use in the sacraments. Nor is the way of salvation narrowed thereby: because the things which need to be used in the sacraments, are either in everyone's possession or can be had with little trouble.

Whether words are required for the signification of the sacraments?

Objection 1: It seems that words are not required for the signification of the sacraments. For Augustine says (Contra Faust. xix): "What else is a corporeal sacrament but a kind of visible word?" Wherefore to add words to the sensible things in the sacraments seems to be the same as to add words to words. But this is superfluous. Therefore words are not required besides the sensible things in the sacraments .

Objection 2: Further, a sacrament is some one thing, but it does not seem possible to make one thing of those that belong to different genera. Since, therefore, sensible things and words are of different genera, for sensible things are the product of nature, but words, of reason; it seems that in the sacraments, words are not required besides sensible things.

Objection 3: Further, the sacraments of the New Law succeed those of the Old Law: since "the former were instituted when the latter were abolished," as Augustine says (Contra Faust. xix). But no form of words was required in the sacraments of the Old Law. Therefore neither is it required in those of the New Law.

On the contrary, The Apostle says (Eph. 5:25,26): "Christ loved the Church, and delivered Himself up for it; that He might sanctify it, cleansing it by the laver of water in the word of life." And Augustine says (Tract. xxx in Joan.): "The word is added to the element, and this becomes a sacrament."

I answer that, The sacraments, as stated above ([4344]AA[2],3), are employed as signs for man's sanctification. Consequently they can be considered in three ways: and in each way it is fitting for words to be added to the sensible signs. For in the first place they can be considered in regard to the cause of sanctification, which is the Word incarnate: to Whom the sacraments have a certain conformity, in that the word is joined to the sensible sign, just as in the mystery of the Incarnation the Word of God is united to sensible flesh.

Secondly, sacraments may be considered on the part of man who is sanctified, and who is composed of soul and body: to whom the sacramental remedy is adjusted, since it touches the body through the sensible element, and the soul through faith in the words. Hence Augustine says (Tract. lxxx in Joan.) on Jn. 15:3, "Now you are clean by reason of the word," etc.: "Whence hath water this so great virtue, to touch the body and wash the heart, but by the word doing it, not because it is spoken, but because it is believed?"

Thirdly, a sacrament may be considered on the part of the sacramental signification. Now Augustine says (De Doctr. Christ. ii) that "words are the principal signs used by men"; because words can be formed in various ways for the purpose of signifying various mental concepts, so that we are able to express our thoughts with greater distinctness by means of words. And therefore in order to insure the perfection of sacramental signification it was necessary to determine the signification of the sensible things by means of certain words. For water may signify both a cleansing by reason of its humidity, and refreshment by reason of its being cool: but when we say, "I baptize thee," it is clear that we use water in baptism in order to signify a spiritual cleansing.

458

Reply to Objection 1: The sensible elements of the sacraments are called words by way of a certain likeness, in so far as they partake of a certain significative power, which resides principally in the very words, as stated above. Consequently it is not a superfluous repetition to add words to the visible element in the sacraments; because one determines the other, as stated above.

Reply to Objection 2: Although words and other sensible things are not in the same genus, considered in their natures, yet have they something in common as to the thing signified by them: which is more perfectly done in words than in other things. Wherefore in the sacraments, words and things, like form and matter, combine in the formation of one thing, in so far as the signification of things is completed by means of words, as above stated. And under words are comprised also sensible actions, such as cleansing and anointing and such like: because they have a like signification with the things.

Reply to Objection 3: As Augustine says (Contra Faust. xix), the sacraments of things present should be different from sacraments of things to come. Now the sacraments of the Old Law foretold the coming of Christ. Consequently they did not signify Christ so clearly as the sacraments of the New Law, which flow from Christ Himself, and have a certain likeness to Him, as stated above. Nevertheless in the Old Law, certain words were used in things pertaining to the worship of God, both by the priests, who were the ministers of those sacraments, according to Num. 6:23,24: "Thus shall you bless the children of Israel, and you shall say to them: The Lord bless thee," etc.; and by those who made use of those sacraments, according to Dt. 26:3: "I profess this day before the Lord thy God," etc.

Day 289

Whether determinate words are required in the sacraments?

Objection 1: It seems that determinate words are not required in the sacraments. For as the Philosopher says (Peri Herm. i), "words are not the same for all." But salvation, which is sought through the sacraments, is the same for all. Therefore determinate words are not required in the sacraments.

Objection 2: Further, words are required in the sacraments forasmuch as they are the principal means of signification, as stated above [4345](A[6]). But it happens that various words mean the same. Therefore determinate words are not required in the sacraments.

Objection 3: Further, corruption of anything changes its species. But some corrupt the pronunciation of words, and yet it is not credible that the sacramental effect is hindered thereby; else unlettered men and stammerers, in conferring sacraments, would frequently do so invalidly. Therefore it seems that determinate words are not required in the sacraments.

On the contrary, our Lord used determinate words in consecrating the sacrament of the Eucharist, when He said (Mat. 26:26): "This is My Body." Likewise He commanded His disciples to baptize under a form of determinate words, saying (Mat. 28:19): "Go ye and teach all nations, baptizing them in the name of the Father, and of the Son, and of the Holy Ghost."

I answer that, As stated above (A[6], ad 2), in the sacraments the words are as the form, and sensible things are as the matter. Now in all things composed of matter and form, the determining principle is on the part of the form, which is as it were the end and terminus of the matter. Consequently for the being of a thing the need of a determinate form is prior to the need of determinate matter: for determinate matter is needed that it may be adapted to the determinate form. Since, therefore, in the sacraments determinate sensible things are required, which are as the sacramental matter, much more is there need in them of a determinate form of words.

Reply to Objection 1: As Augustine says (Tract. lxxx super Joan.), the word operates in the sacraments "not because it is spoken," i.e. not by the outward sound of the voice, "but because it is believed" in accordance with the sense of the words which is held by faith. And this sense is indeed the same for all, though the same words as to their sound be not used by all. Consequently no matter in what language this sense is expressed, the sacrament is complete.

Reply to Objection 2: Although it happens in every language that various words signify the same thing, yet one of those words is that which those who speak that language use principally and more commonly to signify that particular thing: and this is the word which should be used for the sacramental signification. So also among sensible things, that one is used for the sacramental signification which is most commonly employed for the action by which the sacramental effect is signified: thus water is most commonly used by men for bodily cleansing, by which the spiritual cleansing is signified: and therefore water is employed as the matter of baptism.

Reply to Objection 3: If he who corrupts the pronunciation of the sacramental words---does so on purpose, he does not seem to intend to do what the Church intends: and thus the sacrament seems to be defective. But if he do this through error or a slip of the tongue, and if he so far mispronounce the words as to deprive them of sense, the sacrament seems to be defective. This would be the case especially if the mispronunciation be in the beginning of a word, for instance, if one were to say "in nomine matris" instead of "in nomine Patris." If, however, the sense of the words be not entirely lost by this mispronunciation, the sacrament is complete. This would be the case principally if the end of a word be mispronounced; for instance, if one were to say "patrias et filias." For although the words thus mispronounced have no appointed meaning, yet we allow them an accommodated meaning corresponding to the usual forms of speech. And so, although the sensible sound is changed, yet the sense remains the same.

What has been said about the various mispronunciations of words, either at the beginning or at the end, holds forasmuch as with us a change at the beginning of a word changes the meaning, whereas a change at the end generally speaking does not effect such a change: whereas with the Greeks the sense is changed also in the beginning of words in the conjugation of verbs.

Nevertheless the principle point to observe is the extent of the corruption entailed by mispronunciation: for in either case it may be so little that it does not alter the sense of the words; or so great that it destroys it. But it is easier for the one to happen on the part of the beginning of the words, and the other at the end.

Whether it is lawful to add anything to the words in which the sacramental form consists?

459

Objection 1: It seems that it is not lawful to add anything to the words in which the sacramental form consists. For these sacramental words are not of less importance than are the words of Holy Scripture. But it is not lawful to add anything to, or to take anything from, the words of Holy Scripture: for it is written (Dt. 4:2): "You shall not add to the word that I speak to you, neither shall you take away from it"; and (Apoc. 22:18,19): "I testify to everyone that heareth the words of the prophecy of this book: if any man shall add to these things, God shall add to him the plagues written in this book. And if any man shall take away . . . God shall take away his part out of the book of life." Therefore it seems that neither is it lawful to add anything to, or to take anything from, the sacramental forms.

Objection 2: Further, in the sacraments words are by way of form, as stated above (A[6], ad 2; A[7]). But any addition or subtraction in forms changes the species, as also in numbers (Metaph. viii). Therefore it seems that if anything be added to or subtracted from a sacramental form, it will not be the same sacrament.

Objection 3: Further, just as the sacramental form demands a certain number of words, so does it require that these words should be pronounced in a certain order and without interruption. If therefore, the sacrament is not rendered invalid by addition or subtraction of words, in like manner it seems that neither is it, if the words be pronounced in a different order or with interruptions.

On the contrary, Certain words are inserted by some in the sacramental forms, which are not inserted by others: thus the Latins baptize under this form: "I baptize thee in the name of the Father, and of the Son, and of the Holy Ghost"; whereas the Greeks use the following form: "The servant of God, N . . . is baptized in the name of the Father," etc. Yet both confer the sacrament validly. Therefore it is lawful to add something to, or to take something from, the sacramental forms.

I answer that, With regard to all the variations that may occur in the sacramental forms, two points seem to call for our attention. one is on the part of the person who says the words, and whose intention is essential to the sacrament, as will be explained further on ([4346]Q[64], A[8]). Wherefore if he intends by such addition or suppression to perform a rite other from that which is recognized by the Church, it seems that the sacrament is invalid: because he seems not to intend to do what the Church does.

The other point to be considered is the meaning of the words. For since in the sacraments, the words produce an effect according to the sense which they convey, as stated above (A[7], ad 1), we must see whether the change of words destroys the essential sense of the words: because then the sacrament is clearly rendered invalid. Now it is clear, if any substantial part of the sacramental form be suppressed, that the essential sense of the words is destroyed; and consequently the sacrament is invalid. Wherefore Didymus says (De Spir. Sanct. ii): "If anyone attempt to baptize in such a way as to omit one of the aforesaid names," i.e. of the Father, Son, and Holy Ghost, "his baptism will be invalid." But if that which is omitted be not a substantial part of the form, such an omission does not destroy the essential sense of the words, nor consequently the validity of the sacrament. Thus in the form of the Eucharist---"For this is My Body," the omission of the word "for" does not destroy the essential sense of the words, nor consequently cause the sacrament to be invalid; although perhaps he who makes the omission may sin from negligence or contempt.

Again, it is possible to add something that destroys the essential sense of the words: for instance, if one were to say: "I baptize thee in the name of the Father Who is greater, and of the Son Who is less," with which form the Arians baptized: and consequently such an addition makes the sacrament invalid. But if the addition be such as not to destroy the essential sense, the sacrament is not rendered invalid. Nor does it matter whether this addition be made at the beginning, in the middle, or at the end: For instance, if one were to say, "I baptize thee in the name of the Father Almighty, and of the only Begotten Son, and of the Holy Ghost, the Paraclete," the baptism would be valid; and in like manner if one were to say, "I baptize thee in the name of the Father, and of the Son, and of the Holy Ghost"; and may the Blessed Virgin succour thee, the baptism would be valid.

Perhaps, however, if one were to say, "I baptize thee in the name of the Father, and of the Son, and of the Holy Ghost, and of the Blessed Virgin Mary," the baptism would be void; because it is written (1 Cor. 1:13): "Was Paul crucified for you or were you baptized in the name of Paul?" But this is true if the intention be to baptize in the name of the Blessed Virgin as in the name of the Trinity, by which baptism is consecrated: for such a sense would be contrary to faith, and would therefore render the sacrament invalid: whereas if the addition, "and in the name of the Blessed Virgin" be understood, not as if the name of the Blessed Virgin effected anything in baptism, but as intimating that her intercession may help the person baptized to preserve the baptismal grace, then the sacrament is not rendered void.

Reply to Objection 1: It is not lawful to add anything to the words of Holy Scripture as regards the sense; but many words are added by Doctors by way of explanation of the Holy Scriptures. Nevertheless, it is not lawful to add even words to Holy Scripture as though such words were a part thereof, for this would amount to forgery. It would amount to the same if anyone were to pretend that something is essential to a sacramental form, which is not so.

Reply to Objection 2: Words belong to a sacramental form by reason of the sense signified by them. Consequently any addition or suppression of words which does not add to or take from the essential sense, does not destroy the essence of the sacrament.

Reply to Objection 3: If the words are interrupted to such an extent that the intention of the speaker is interrupted, the sacramental sense is destroyed, and consequently, the validity of the sacrament. But this is not the case if the interruption of the speaker is so slight, that his intention and the sense of the words is not interrupted.

The same is to be said of a change in the order of the words. Because if this destroys the sense of the words, the sacrament is invalidated: as happens when a negation is made to precede or follow a word. But if the order is so changed that the sense of the words does not vary, the sacrament is not invalidated, according to the Philosopher's dictum: "Nouns and verbs mean the same though they be transposed" (Peri Herm. x).

OF THE NECESSITY OF THE SACRAMENTS (FOUR ARTICLES)
We must now consider the necessity of the sacraments; concerning which there are four points of inquiry:
(1) Whether sacraments are necessary for man's salvation?

(2) Whether they were necessary in the state that preceded sin?

(3) Whether they were necessary in the state after sin and before Christ?

(4) Whether they were necessary after Christ's coming?

Whether sacraments are necessary for man's salvation?

Objection 1: It seems that sacraments are not necessary for man's salvation. For the Apostle says (1 Tim. 4:8): "Bodily exercise is profitable to little." But the use of sacraments pertains to bodily exercise; because sacraments are perfected in the signification of sensible things and words, as stated above ([4347]Q[60], A[6]). Therefore sacraments are not necessary for the salvation of man.

Objection 2: Further, the Apostle was told (2 Cor. 12:9): "My grace is sufficient for thee." But it would not suffice if sacraments were necessary for salvation. Therefore sacraments are not necessary for man's salvation.

Objection 3: Further, given a sufficient cause, nothing more seems to be required for the effect. But Christ's Passion is the sufficient cause of our salvation; for the Apostle says (Rom. 5:10): "If, when we were enemies, we were reconciled to God by the death of His Son: much more, being reconciled, shall we be saved by His life." Therefore sacraments are not necessary for man's salvation.

On the contrary, Augustine says (Contra Faust. xix): "It is impossible to keep men together in one religious denomination, whether true or false, except they be united by means of visible signs or sacraments." But it is necessary for salvation that men be united together in the name of the one true religion. Therefore sacraments are necessary for man's salvation.

I answer that, Sacraments are necessary unto man's salvation for three reasons. The first is taken from the condition of human nature which is such that it has to be led by things corporeal and sensible to things spiritual and intelligible. Now it belongs to Divine providence to provide for each one according as its condition requires. Divine wisdom, therefore, fittingly provides man with means of salvation, in the shape of corporeal and sensible signs that are called sacraments.

The second reason is taken from the state of man who in sinning subjected himself by his affections to corporeal things. Now the healing remedy should be given to a man so as to reach the part affected by disease. Consequently it was fitting that God should provide man with a spiritual medicine by means of certain corporeal signs; for if man were offered spiritual things without a veil, his mind being taken up with the material world would be unable to apply itself to them.

The third reason is taken from the fact that man is prone to direct his activity chiefly towards material things. Lest, therefore, it should be too hard for man to be drawn away entirely from bodily actions, bodily exercise was offered to him in the sacraments, by which he might be trained to avoid superstitious practices, consisting in the worship of demons, and all manner of harmful action, consisting in sinful deeds.

It follows, therefore, that through the institution of the sacraments man, consistently with his nature, is instructed through sensible things; he is humbled, through confessing that he is subject to corporeal things, seeing that he receives assistance through them: and he is even preserved from bodily hurt, by the healthy exercise of the sacraments.

Reply to Objection 1: Bodily exercise, as such, is not very profitable: but exercise taken in the use of the sacraments is not merely bodily, but to a certain extent spiritual, viz. in its signification and in its causality.

Reply to Objection 2: God's grace is a sufficient cause of man's salvation. But God gives grace to man in a way which is suitable to him. Hence it is that man needs the sacraments that he may obtain grace.

Reply to Objection 3: Christ's Passion is a sufficient cause of man's salvation. But it does not follow that the sacraments are not also necessary for that purpose: because they obtain their effect through the power of Christ's Passion; and Christ's Passion is, so to say, applied to man through the sacraments according to the Apostle (Rom. 6:3): "All we who are baptized in Christ Jesus, are baptized in His death."

Whether before sin sacraments were necessary to man?

Objection 1: It seems that before sin sacraments were necessary to man. For, as stated above (A[1], ad 2) man needs sacraments that he may obtain grace. But man needed grace even in the state of innocence, as we stated in the [4348]FP, Q[95], A[4] (cf. [4349]FS, Q[109], A[2]; [4350]FS, Q[114], A[2]). Therefore sacraments were necessary in that state also.

Objection 2: Further, sacraments are suitable to man by reason of the conditions of human nature, as stated above [4351](A[1]). But man's nature is the same before and after sin. Therefore it seems that before sin, man needed the sacraments.

Objection 3: Further, matrimony is a sacrament, according to Eph. 5:32: "This is a great sacrament; but I speak in Christ and in the Church." But matrimony was instituted before sin, as may be seen in Gn. 2. Therefore sacraments were necessary to man before sin.

On the contrary, None but the sick need remedies, according to Mat. 9:12: "They that are in health need not a physician." Now the sacraments are spiritual remedies for the healing of wounds inflicted by sin. Therefore they were not necessary before sin.

I answer that, Sacraments were not necessary in the state of innocence. This can be proved from the rectitude of that state, in which the higher (parts of man) ruled the lower, and nowise depended on them: for just as the mind was subject to God, so were the lower powers of the soul subject to the mind, and the body to the soul. And it would be contrary to this order if the soul were perfected either in knowledge or in grace, by anything corporeal; which happens in the sacraments. Therefore in the state of innocence man needed no sacraments, whether as remedies against sin or as means of perfecting the soul.

Reply to Objection 1: In the state of innocence man needed grace: not so that he needed to obtain grace by means of sensible signs, but in a spiritual and invisible manner.

Reply to Objection 2: Man's nature is the same before and after sin, but the state of his nature is not the same. Because after sin, the soul, even in its higher part, needs to receive something from corporeal things in order that it may be perfected: whereas man had no need of this in that state.

Reply to Objection 3: Matrimony was instituted in the state of innocence, not as a sacrament, but as a function of nature. Consequently, however, it foreshadowed something in relation to Christ and the Church: just as everything else foreshadowed Christ.

461

Whether there should have been sacraments after sin, before Christ?

Objection 1: It seems that there should have been no sacraments after sin, before Christ. For it has been stated that the Passion of Christ is applied to men through the sacraments: so that Christ's Passion is compared to the sacraments as cause to effect. But effect does not precede cause. Therefore there should have been no sacraments before Christ's coming.

Objection 2: Further, sacraments should be suitable to the state of the human race, as Augustine declares (Contra Faust. xix). But the state of the human race underwent no change after sin until it was repaired by Christ. Neither, therefore, should the sacraments have been changed, so that besides the sacraments of the natural law, others should be instituted in the law of Moses.

Objection 3: Further, the nearer a thing approaches to that which is perfect, the more like it should it be. Now the perfection of human salvation was accomplished by Christ; to Whom the sacraments of the Old Law were nearer than those that preceded the Law. Therefore they should have borne a greater likeness to the sacraments of Christ. And yet the contrary is the case, since it was foretold that the priesthood of Christ would be "according to the order of Melchisedech, and not . . . according to the order of Aaron" (Heb. 7:11). Therefore sacraments were unsuitably instituted before Christ.

On the contrary, Augustine says (Contra Faust. xix) that "the first sacraments which the Law commanded to be solemnized and observed were announcements of Christ's future coming." But it was necessary for man's salvation that Christ's coming should be announced beforehand. Therefore it was necessary that some sacraments should be instituted before Christ.

I answer that, Sacraments are necessary for man's salvation, in so far as they are sensible signs of invisible things whereby man is made holy. Now after sin no man can be made holy save through Christ, "Whom God hath proposed to be a propitiation, through faith in His blood, to the showing of His justice . . . that He Himself may be just, and the justifier of him who is of the faith of Jesus Christ" (Rom. 3:25,26). Therefore before Christ's coming there was need for some visible signs whereby man might testify to his faith in the future coming of a Saviour. And these signs are called sacraments. It is therefore clear that some sacraments were necessary before Christ's coming.

Reply to Objection 1: Christ's Passion is the final cause of the old sacraments: for they were instituted in order to foreshadow it. Now the final cause precedes not in time, but in the intention of the agent. Consequently, there is no reason against the existence of sacraments before Christ's Passion.

Reply to Objection 2: The state of the human race after sin and before Christ can be considered from two points of view. First, from that of faith: and thus it was always one and the same: since men were made righteous, through faith in the future coming of Christ. Secondly, according as sin was more or less intense, and knowledge concerning Christ more or less explicit. For as time went on sin gained a greater hold on man, so much so that it clouded man's reason, the consequence being that the precepts of the natural law were insufficient to make man live aright, and it became necessary to have a written code of fixed laws, and together with these certain sacraments of faith. For it was necessary, as time went on, that the knowledge of faith should be more and more unfolded, since, as Gregory says (Hom. vi in Ezech.): "With the advance of time there was an advance in the knowledge of Divine things." Consequently in the old Law there was also a need for certain fixed sacraments significative of man's faith in the future coming of Christ: which sacraments are compared to those that preceded the Law, as something determinate to that which is indeterminate: inasmuch as before the Law it was not laid down precisely of what sacraments men were to make use: whereas this was prescribed by the Law; and this was necessary both on account of the overclouding of the natural law, and for the clearer signification of faith.

Reply to Objection 3: The sacrament of Melchisedech which preceded the Law is more like the Sacrament of the New Law in its matter: in so far as "he offered bread and wine" (Gn. 14:18), just as bread and wine are offered in the sacrifice of the New Testament. Nevertheless the sacraments of the Mosaic Law are more like the thing signified by the sacrament, i.e. the Passion of Christ: as clearly appears in the Paschal Lamb and such like. The reason of this was lest, if the sacraments retained the same appearance, it might seem to be the continuation of one and the same sacrament, where there was no interruption of time.

Whether there was need for any sacraments after Christ came?

Objection 1: It seems that there was no need for any sacraments after Christ came. For the figure should cease with the advent of the truth. But "grace and truth came by Jesus Christ" (Jn. 1:17). Since, therefore, the sacraments are signs or figures of the truth, it seems that there was no need for any sacraments after Christ's Passion.

Objection 2: Further, the sacraments consist in certain elements, as stated above ([4352]Q[60], A[4]). But the Apostle says (Gal. 4:3,4) that "when we were children we were serving under the elements of the world": but that now "when the fulness of time" has "come," we are no longer children. Therefore it seems that we should not serve God under the elements of this world, by making use of corporeal sacraments.

Objection 3: Further, according to James 1:17 with God "there is no change, nor shadow of alteration." But it seems to argue some change in the Divine will that God should give man certain sacraments for his sanctification now during the time of grace, and other sacraments before Christ's coming. Therefore it seems that other sacraments should not have been instituted after Christ.

On the contrary, Augustine says (Contra Faust. xix) that the sacraments of the Old Law "were abolished because they were fulfilled; and others were instituted, fewer in number, but more efficacious, more profitable, and of easier accomplishment."

I answer that, As the ancient Fathers were saved through faith in Christ's future coming, so are we saved through faith in Christ's past birth and Passion. Now the sacraments are signs in protestation of the faith whereby man is justified; and signs should vary according as they signify the future, the past, or the present; for as Augustine says (Contra Faust. xix), "the same thing is variously pronounced as to be done and as having been done: for instance the word 'passurus' [going to suffer] differs from 'passus' [having suffered]." Therefore the sacraments of the New Law, that signify Christ in relation to the past, must needs differ from those of the Old Law, that foreshadowed the future.

Reply to Objection 1: As Dionysius says (Eccl. Hier. v), the state of the New Law. is between the state of the Old Law, whose figures are fulfilled in the New, and the state of glory, in which all truth will be openly and perfectly revealed. Wherefore then there will be no sacraments. But now, so long as we know "through a glass in a dark manner," (1 Cor. 13:12) we need sensible signs in order to reach spiritual things: and this is the province of the sacraments.

Reply to Objection 2: The Apostle calls the sacraments of the Old Law "weak and needy elements" (Gal. 4:9) because they neither contained nor caused grace. Hence the Apostle says that those who used these sacraments served God "under the elements of this world": for the very reason that these sacraments were nothing else than the elements of this world. But our sacraments both contain and cause grace: consequently the comparison does not hold.

Reply to Objection 3: Just as the head of the house is not proved to have a changeable mind, through issuing various commands to his household at various seasons, ordering things differently in winter and summer; so it does not follow that there is any change in God, because He instituted sacraments of one kind after Christ's coming, and of another kind at the time of the Law. because the latter were suitable as foreshadowing grace; the former as signifying the presence of grace,

OF THE SACRAMENTS' PRINCIPAL EFFECT, WHICH IS GRACE (SIX ARTICLES)

We have now to consider the effect of the sacraments. First of their principal effect, which is grace; secondly, of their secondary effect, which is a character. Concerning the first there are six points of inquiry:
(1) Whether the sacraments of the New Law are the cause of grace?
(2) Whether sacramental grace confers anything in addition to the grace of the virtues and gifts?
(3) Whether the sacraments contain grace?
(4) Whether there is any power in them for the causing of grace?
(5) Whether the sacraments derive this power from Christ's Passion?
(6) Whether the sacraments of the Old Law caused grace?

Whether the sacraments are the cause of grace?

Objection 1: It seems that the sacraments are not the cause of grace. For it seems that the same thing is not both sign and cause: since the nature of sign appears to be more in keeping with an effect. But a sacrament is a sign of grace. Therefore it is not its cause.

Objection 2: Further, nothing corporeal can act on a spiritual thing: since "the agent is more excellent than the patient," as Augustine says (Gen. ad lit. xii). But the subject of grace is the human mind, which is something spiritual. Therefore the sacraments cannot cause grace.

Objection 3: Further, what is proper to God should not be ascribed to a creature. But it is proper to God to cause grace, according to Ps. 83:12: "The Lord will give grace and glory." Since, therefore, the sacraments consist in certain words and created things, it seems that they cannot cause grace.

On the contrary, Augustine says (Tract. lxxx in Joan.) that the baptismal water "touches the body and cleanses the heart." But the heart is not cleansed save through grace. Therefore it causes grace: and for like reason so do the other sacraments of the Church.

I answer that, We must needs say that in some way the sacraments of the New Law cause grace. For it is evident that through the sacraments of the New Law man is incorporated with Christ: thus the Apostle says of Baptism (Gal. 3:27): "As many of you as have been baptized in Christ have put on Christ." And man is made a member of Christ through grace alone.

Some, however, say that they are the cause of grace not by their own operation, but in so far as God causes grace in the soul when the sacraments are employed. And they give as an example a man who on presenting a leaden coin, receives, by the king's command, a hundred pounds: not as though the leaden coin, by any operation of its own, caused him to be given that sum of money; this being the effect of the mere will of the king. Hence Bernard says in a sermon on the Lord's Supper: "Just as a canon is invested by means of a book, an abbot by means of a crozier, a bishop by means of a ring, so by the various sacraments various kinds of grace are conferred." But if we examine the question properly, we shall see that according to the above mode the sacraments are mere signs. For the leaden coin is nothing but a sign of the king's command that this man should receive money. In like manner the book is a sign of the conferring of a canonry. Hence, according to this opinion the sacraments of the New Law would be mere signs of grace; whereas we have it on the authority of many saints that the sacraments of the New Law not only signify, but also cause grace.

We must therefore say otherwise, that an efficient cause is twofold, principal and instrumental. The principal cause works by the power of its form, to which form the effect is likened; just as fire by its own heat makes something hot. In this way none but God can cause grace: since grace is nothing else than a participated likeness of the Divine Nature, according to 2 Pet. 1:4: "He hath given us most great and precious promises; that we may be [Vulg.: 'you may be made'] partakers of the Divine Nature." But the instrumental cause works not by the power of its form, but only by the motion whereby it is moved by the principal agent: so that the effect is not likened to the instrument but to the principal agent: for instance, the couch is not like the axe, but like the art which is in the craftsman's mind. And it is thus that the sacraments of the New Law cause grace: for they are instituted by God to be employed for the purpose of conferring grace. Hence Augustine says (Contra Faust. xix): "All these things," viz. pertaining to the sacraments, "are done and pass away, but the power," viz. of God, "which works by them, remains ever." Now that is, properly speaking, an instrument by which someone works: wherefore it is written (Titus 3:5): "He saved us by the laver of regeneration."

Reply to Objection 1: The principal cause cannot properly be called a sign of its effect, even though the latter be hidden and the cause itself sensible and manifest. But an instrumental cause, if manifest, can be called a sign of a hidden effect, for this reason, that it is not merely a cause but also in a measure an effect in so far as it is moved by the principal agent. And in this sense the sacraments of the New Law are both cause and signs. Hence, too, is it that, to use the common expression, "they effect what they signify." From this it is clear that they perfectly fulfil the conditions of a sacrament; being ordained to something sacred, not only as a sign, but also as a cause.

Reply to Objection 2: An instrument has a twofold action; one is instrumental, in respect of which it works not by its own power but by the power of the principal agent: the other is its proper action, which belongs to it in respect of its proper form: thus it belongs to an axe to cut asunder by reason of its sharpness, but to make a couch, in so far as it is the instrument of an art. But it does not accomplish the instrumental action save by exercising its proper action: for it is by cutting that it makes a couch. In like manner the corporeal sacraments by their operation, which they exercise on the body that they touch, accomplish through the Divine institution an instrumental operation on the soul; for example, the water of baptism, in respect of its proper power, cleanses the body, and thereby, inasmuch as it is the instrument of the Divine power, cleanses the soul: since from soul and body one thing is made. And thus it is that Augustine says (Gen. ad lit. xii) that it "touches the body and cleanses the heart."

Reply to Objection 3: This argument considers that which causes grace as principal agent; for this belongs to God alone, as stated above.

Whether sacramental grace confers anything in addition to the grace of the virtues and gifts?

Objection 1: It seems that sacramental grace confers nothing in addition to the grace of the virtues and gifts. For the grace of the virtues and gifts perfects the soul sufficiently, both in its essence and in its powers; as is clear from what was said in the [4353]FS, Q[110], AA[3],4. But grace is ordained to the perfecting of the soul. Therefore sacramental grace cannot confer anything in addition to the grace of the virtues and gifts.

Objection 2: Further, the soul's defects are caused by sin. But all sins are sufficiently removed by the grace of the virtues and gifts: because there is no sin that is not contrary to some virtue. Since, therefore, sacramental grace is ordained to the removal of the soul's defects, it cannot confer anything in addition to the grace of the virtues and gifts.

Objection 3: Further, every addition or subtraction of form varies the species (Metaph. viii). If, therefore, sacramental grace confers anything in addition to the grace of the virtues and gifts, it follows that it is called grace equivocally: and so we are none the wiser when it is said that the sacraments cause grace.

On the contrary, If sacramental grace confers nothing in addition to the grace of the virtues and gifts, it is useless to confer the sacraments on those who have the virtues and gifts. But there is nothing useless in God's works. Therefore it seems that sacramental grace confers something in addition to the grace of the virtues and gifts.

I answer that, As stated in the [4354]FS, Q[110], AA[3],4, grace, considered in itself, perfects the essence of the soul, in so far as it is a certain participated likeness of the Divine Nature. And just as the soul's powers flow from its essence, so from grace there flow certain perfections into the powers of the soul, which are called virtues and gifts, whereby the powers are perfected in reference to their actions. Now the sacraments are ordained unto certain special effects which are necessary in the Christian life: thus Baptism is ordained unto a certain spiritual regeneration, by which man dies to vice and becomes a member of Christ: which effect is something special in addition to the actions of the soul's powers: and the same holds true of the other sacraments. Consequently just as the virtues and gifts confer, in addition to grace commonly so called, a certain special perfection ordained to the powers' proper actions, so does sacramental grace confer, over and above grace commonly so called, and in addition to the virtues and gifts, a certain Divine assistance in obtaining the end of the sacrament. It is thus that sacramental grace confers something in addition to the grace of the virtues and gifts.

Reply to Objection 1: The grace of the virtues and gifts perfects the essence and powers of the soul sufficiently as regards ordinary conduct: but as regards certain special effects which are necessary in a Christian life, sacramental grace is needed.

Reply to Objection 2: Vices and sins are sufficiently removed by virtues and gifts, as to present and future time. in so far as they prevent man from sinning. But in regard to past sins, the acts of which are transitory whereas their guilt remains, man is provided with a special remedy in the sacraments.

Reply to Objection 3: Sacramental grace is compared to grace commonly so called, as species to genus. Wherefore just as it is not equivocal to use the term "animal" in its generic sense, and as applied to a man, so neither is it equivocal to speak of grace commonly so called and of sacramental grace.

Day 290

Whether the sacraments of the New Law contain grace?

Objection 1: It seems that the sacraments of the New Law do not contain grace. For it seems that what is contained is in the container. But grace is not in the sacraments; neither as in a subject, because the subject of grace is not a body but a spirit; nor as in a vessel, for according to Phys. iv, "a vessel is a movable place," and an accident cannot be in a place. Therefore it seems that the sacraments of the New Law do not contain grace.

Objection 2: Further, sacraments are instituted as means whereby men may obtain grace. But since grace is an accident it cannot pass from one subject to another. Therefore it would be of no account if grace were in the sacraments.

Objection 3: Further, a spiritual thing is not contained by a corporeal, even if it be therein; for the soul is not contained by the body; rather does it contain the body. Since, therefore, grace is something spiritual, it seems that it cannot be contained in a corporeal sacrament.

On the contrary, Hugh of S. Victor says (De Sacram. i) that "a sacrament, through its being sanctified, contains an invisible grace."

I answer that, A thing is said to be in another in various ways; in two of which grace is said to be in the sacraments. First, as in its sign; for a sacrament is a sign of grace. Secondly, as in its cause; for, as stated above [4355](A[1]) a sacrament of the New Law is an instrumental cause of grace. Wherefore grace is in a sacrament of the New Law, not as to its specific likeness, as an effect in its univocal cause; nor as to some proper and permanent form proportioned to such an effect, as effects in non-univocal causes, for instance, as things generated are in the sun; but as to a certain instrumental power transient and incomplete in its natural being, as will be explained later on [4356](A[4]).

Reply to Objection 1: Grace is said to be in a sacrament not as in its subject; nor as in a vessel considered as a place, but understood as the instrument of some work to be done, according to Ezech. 9:1: "Everyone hath a destroying vessel [Douay: 'weapon'] in his hand."

Reply to Objection 2: Although an accident does not pass from one subject to another, nevertheless in a fashion it does pass from its cause into its subject through the instrument; not so that it be in each of these in the same way, but in each according to its respective nature.

Reply to Objection 3: If a spiritual thing exist perfectly in something, it contains it and is not contained by it. But, in a sacrament, grace has a passing and incomplete mode of being: and consequently it is not unfitting to say that the sacraments contain grace.

Whether there be in the sacraments a power of causing grace?

Objection 1: It seems that there is not in the sacraments a power of causing grace. For the power of causing grace is a spiritual power. But a spiritual power cannot be in a body; neither as proper to it, because power flows from a thing's essence and consequently cannot transcend it; nor as derived from something else, because that which is received into anything follows the mode of the recipient. Therefore in the sacraments there is no power of causing grace.

Objection 2: Further, whatever exists is reducible to some kind of being and some degree of good. But there is no assignable kind of being to which such a power can belong; as anyone may see by running. through them all. Nor is it reducible to some degree of good; for neither is it one of the goods of least account, since sacraments are necessary for salvation: nor is it an intermediate good, such as are the powers of the soul, which are natural powers; nor is it one of the greater goods, for it is neither grace nor a virtue of the mind. Therefore it seems that in the sacraments there is no power of causing grace.

Objection 3: Further, if there be such a power in the sacraments, its presence there must be due to nothing less than a creative act of God. But it seems unbecoming that so excellent a being created by God should cease to exist as soon as the sacrament is complete. Therefore it seems that in the sacraments there is no power for causing grace.

Objection 4: Further, the same thing cannot be in several. But several things concur in the completion of a sacrament, namely, words and things: while in one sacrament there can be but one power. Therefore it seems that there is no power of causing grace in the sacraments.

On the contrary, Augustine says (Tract. lxxx in Joan.): "Whence hath water so great power, that it touches the body and cleanses the heart?" And Bede says that "Our Lord conferred a power of regeneration on the waters by the contact of His most pure body."

I answer that, Those who hold that the sacraments do not cause grace save by a certain coincidence, deny the sacraments any power that is itself productive of the sacramental effect, and hold that the Divine power assists the sacraments and produces their effect. But if we hold that a sacrament is an instrumental cause of grace, we must needs allow that there is in the sacraments a certain instrumental power of bringing about the sacramental effects. Now such power is proportionate to the instrument: and consequently it stands in comparison to the complete and perfect power of anything, as the instrument to the principal agent. For an instrument, as stated above [4357](A[1]), does not work save as moved by the principal agent, which works of itself. And therefore the power of the principal agent exists in nature completely and perfectly: whereas the instrumental power has a being that passes from one thing into another, and is incomplete; just as motion is an imperfect act passing from agent to patient.

Reply to Objection 1: A spiritual power cannot be in a corporeal subject, after the manner of a permanent and complete power, as the argument proves. But there is nothing to hinder an instrumental spiritual power from being in a body; in so far as a body can be moved by a particular spiritual substance so as to produce a particular spiritual effect; thus in the very voice which is perceived by the senses there is a certain spiritual power, inasmuch as it proceeds from a mental concept, of arousing the mind of the hearer. It is in this way that a spiritual power is in the sacraments, inasmuch as they are ordained by God unto the production of a spiritual effect.

Reply to Objection 2: Just as motion, through being an imperfect act, is not properly in a genus, but is reducible to a genus of perfect act, for instance, alteration to the genus of quality: so, instrumental power, properly speaking, is not in any genus, but is reducible to a genus and species of perfect act.

Reply to Objection 3: Just as an instrumental power accrues to an instrument through its being moved by the principal agent, so does a sacrament receive spiritual power from Christ's blessing and from the action of the minister in applying it to a sacramental use. Hence Augustine says in a sermon on the Epiphany (St. Maximus of Turin, Serm. xii): "Nor should you marvel, if we say that water, a corporeal substance, achieves the cleansing of the soul. It does indeed, and penetrates every secret hiding-place of the conscience. For subtle and clear as it is, the blessing of Christ makes it yet more subtle, so that it permeates into the very principles of life and searches the inner-most recesses of the heart."

Reply to Objection 4: Just as the one same power of the principal agent is instrumentally in all the instruments that are ordained unto the production of an effect, forasmuch as they are one as being so ordained: so also the one same sacramental power is in both words and things, forasmuch as words and things combine to form one sacrament.

Whether the sacraments of the New Law derive their power from Christ's Passion?

Objection 1: It seems that the sacraments of the New Law do not derive their power from Christ's Passion. For the power of the sacraments is in the causing of grace which is the principle of spiritual life in the soul. But as Augustine says (Tract. xix in Joan.): "The Word, as He was in the beginning with God, quickens souls; as He was made flesh, quickens bodies." Since, therefore, Christ's Passion pertains to the Word as made flesh, it seems that it cannot cause the power of the sacraments.

Objection 2: Further, the power of the sacraments seems to depend on faith. for as Augustine says (Tract. lxxx in Joan.), the Divine Word perfects the sacrament "not because it is spoken, but because it is believed." But our faith regards not only Christ's Passion, but also the other mysteries of His humanity, and in a yet higher measure, His Godhead. Therefore it seems that the power of the sacraments is not due specially to Christ's Passion.

Objection 3: Further, the sacraments are ordained unto man's justification, according to 1 Cor. 6:11: "You are washed . . . you are justified." Now justification is ascribed to the Resurrection, according to Rom. 4:25: "(Who) rose again for our justification." Therefore it seems that the sacraments derive their power from Christ's Resurrection rather than from His Passion.

On the contrary, on Rom. 5:14: "After the similitude of the transgression of Adam," etc., the gloss says: "From the side of Christ asleep on the Cross flowed the sacraments which brought salvation to the Church." Consequently, it seems that the sacraments derive their power from Christ's Passion.

I answer that, As stated above [4358](A[1]) a sacrament in causing grace works after the manner of an instrument. Now an instrument is twofold. the one, separate, as a stick, for instance; the other, united, as a hand. Moreover, the separate instrument is moved by means of the united instrument, as a stick by the hand. Now the principal efficient cause of grace is God Himself, in comparison with Whom Christ's humanity is as a united instrument, whereas the sacrament is as a separate instrument. Consequently, the saving power must needs be derived by the sacraments from Christ's Godhead through His humanity.

Now sacramental grace seems to be ordained principally to two things: namely, to take away the defects consequent on past sins, in so far as they are transitory in act, but endure in guilt; and, further, to perfect the soul in things pertaining to Divine Worship in regard to the Christian Religion. But it is manifest from what has been stated above ([4359]Q[48], AA[1],2,6;[4360] Q[49], AA[1],3) that Christ delivered us from our sins principally through His Passion, not only by way of efficiency and merit, but also by way of satisfaction. Likewise by His Passion He inaugurated the Rites of the Christian Religion by offering "Himself---an oblation and a sacrifice to God" (Eph. 5:2). Wherefore it is manifest that the sacraments of the Church derive their power specially from Christ's Passion, the virtue of which is in a manner united to us by our receiving the sacraments. It was in sign of this that from the side of Christ hanging on the Cross there flowed water and blood, the former of which belongs to Baptism, the latter to the Eucharist, which are the principal sacraments.

Reply to Objection 1: The Word, forasmuch as He was in the beginning with God, quickens souls as principal agent; but His flesh, and the mysteries accomplished therein, are as instrumental causes in the process of giving life to the soul: while in giving life to the body they act not only as instrumental causes, but also to a certain extent as exemplars, as we stated above ([4361]Q[56], A[1], ad 3).

Reply to Objection 2: Christ dwells in us "by faith" (Eph. 3:17). Consequently, by faith Christ's power is united to us. Now the power of blotting out sin belongs in a special way to His Passion. And therefore men are delivered from sin especially by faith in His Passion, according to Rom. 3:25: "Whom God hath proposed to be a propitiation through faith in His Blood." Therefore the power of the sacraments which is ordained unto the remission of sins is derived principally from faith in Christ's Passion.

Reply to Objection 3: Justification is ascribed to the Resurrection by reason of the term "whither," which is newness of life through grace. But it is ascribed to the Passion by reason of the term "whence," i.e. in regard to the forgiveness of sin.

Whether the sacraments of the Old Law caused grace?

Objection 1: It seems that the sacraments of the Old Law caused grace. For, as stated above (A[5], ad 2) the sacraments of the New Law derive their efficacy from faith in Christ's Passion. But there was faith in Christ's Passion under the Old Law, as well as under the New, since we have "the same spirit of faith" (2 Cor. 4:13). Therefore just as the sacraments of the New Law confer grace, so did the sacraments of the Old Law.

Objection 2: Further, there is no sanctification save by grace. But men were sanctified by the sacraments of the Old Law: for it is written (Lev. 8:31): "And when he," i.e. Moses, "had sanctified them," i.e. Aaron and his sons, "in their vestments," etc. Therefore it seems that the sacraments of the Old Law conferred grace.

Objection 3: Further, Bede says in a homily on the Circumcision: "Under the Law circumcision provided the same health-giving balm against the wound of original sin, as baptism in the time of revealed grace." But Baptism confers grace now. Therefore circumcision conferred grace; and in like manner, the other sacraments of the Law; for just as Baptism is the door of the sacraments of the New Law, so was circumcision the door of the sacraments of the Old Law: hence the Apostle says (Gal. 5:3): "I testify to every man circumcising himself, that he is a debtor to the whole law."

On the contrary, It is written (Gal. 4:9): "Turn you again to the weak and needy elements?" i.e. "to the Law," says the gloss, "which is called weak, because it does not justify perfectly." But grace justifies perfectly. Therefore the sacraments of the old Law did not confer grace.

I answer that, It cannot be said that the sacraments of the Old Law conferred sanctifying grace of themselves, i.e. by their own power: since thus Christ's Passion would not have been necessary, according to Gal. 2:21: "If justice be by the Law, then Christ died in vain."

But neither can it be said that they derived the power of conferring sanctifying grace from Christ's Passion. For as it was stated above (A[5]), the power of Christ's Passion is united to us by faith and the sacraments, but in different ways; because the link that comes from faith is produced by an act of the soul; whereas the link that comes from the sacraments, is produced by making use of exterior things. Now nothing hinders that which is subsequent in point of time, from causing movement, even before it exists in reality, in so far as it pre-exists in an act of the soul: thus the end, which is subsequent in point of time, moves the agent in so far as it is apprehended and desired by him. On the other hand, what does not yet actually exist, does not cause movement if we consider the use of exterior things. Consequently, the efficient cause cannot in point of time come into existence after causing movement, as does the final cause. It is therefore clear that the sacraments of the New Law do reasonably derive the power of justification from Christ's Passion, which is the cause of man's righteousness; whereas the sacraments of the Old Law did not.

Nevertheless the Fathers of old were justified by faith in Christ's Passion, just as we are. And the sacraments of the old Law were a kind of protestation of that faith, inasmuch as they signified Christ's Passion and its effects. It is therefore manifest that the sacraments of the Old Law were not endowed with any power by which they conduced to the bestowal of justifying grace: and they merely signified faith by which men were justified.

Reply to Objection 1: The Fathers of old had faith in the future Passion of Christ, which, inasmuch as it was apprehended by the mind, was able to justify them. But we have faith in the past Passion of Christ, which is able to justify, also by the real use of sacramental things as stated above.

Reply to Objection 2: That sanctification was but a figure: for they were said to be sanctified forasmuch as they gave themselves up to the Divine worship according to the rite of the Old Law, which was wholly ordained to the foreshadowing of Christ's Passion.

Reply to Objection 3: There have been many opinions about Circumcision. For, according to some, Circumcision conferred no grace, but only remitted sin. But this is impossible; because man is not justified from sin save by grace, according to Rom. 3:24: "Being justified freely by His grace."

Wherefore others said that by Circumcision grace is conferred, as to the privative effects of sin, but not as to its positive effects. But this also appears to be false, because by Circumcision, children received the faculty of obtaining glory, which is the ultimate positive effect of grace. Moreover, as regards the order of the formal cause, positive effects are naturally prior to privative effects, though according to the order of the material cause, the reverse is the case: for a form does not exclude privation save by informing the subject.

Hence others say that Circumcision conferred grace also as regards a certain positive effect, i.e. by making man worthy of eternal life, but not so as to repress concupiscence which makes man prone to sin. And so at one time it seemed to me. But if the matter be considered carefully, this too appears to be untrue; because the very least grace is sufficient to resist any degree of concupiscence, and to merit eternal life.

And therefore it seems better to say that Circumcision was a sign of justifying faith: wherefore the Apostle says (Rom. 4:11) that Abraham "received the sign of Circumcision, a seal of the justice of faith." Consequently grace was conferred in Circumcision in so far as it was a sign of Christ's future Passion, as will be made clear further on ([4362]Q[70], A[4]).

OF THE OTHER EFFECT OF THE SACRAMENTS, WHICH IS A CHARACTER (SIX ARTICLES)

We have now to consider the other effect of the sacraments, which is a character: and concerning this there are six points of inquiry:

(1) Whether by the sacraments a character is produced in the soul?
(2) What is this character?
(3) Of whom is this character?
(4) What is its subject?
(5) Is it indelible?
(6) Whether every sacrament imprints a character?

Whether a sacrament imprints a character on the soul?

Objection 1: It seems that a sacrament does not imprint a character on the soul. For the word "character" seems to signify some kind of distinctive sign. But Christ's members are distinguished from others by eternal predestination, which does not imply anything in the predestined, but only in God predestinating, as we have stated in the [4363]FP, Q[23], A[2]. For it is written (2 Tim. 2:19): "The sure foundation of God standeth firm, having this seal: The Lord knoweth who are His." Therefore the sacraments do not imprint a character on the soul.

Objection 2: Further, a character is a distinctive sign. Now a sign, as Augustine says (De Doctr. Christ. ii) "is that which conveys something else to the mind, besides the species which it impresses on the senses." But nothing in the soul can impress a species on the senses. Therefore it seems that no character is imprinted on the soul by the sacraments.

Objection 3: Further, just as the believer is distinguished from the unbeliever by the sacraments of the New Law, so was it under the Old Law. But the sacraments of the Old Law did not imprint a character; whence they are called "justices of the flesh" (Heb. 9:10) by the Apostle. Therefore neither seemingly do the sacraments of the New Law.

On the contrary, The Apostle says (2 Cor. 1:21,22): "He . . . that hath anointed us is God; Who also hath sealed us, and given the pledge of the spirit in our hearts." But a character means nothing else than a kind of sealing. Therefore it seems that by the sacraments God imprints His character on us.

I answer that, As is clear from what has been already stated ([4364]Q[62], A[5]) the sacraments of the New Law are ordained for a twofold purpose; namely, for a remedy against sins; and for the perfecting of the soul in things pertaining to the Divine worship according to the rite of the Christian life. Now whenever anyone is deputed to some definite purpose he is wont to receive some outward sign thereof; thus in olden times soldiers who enlisted in the ranks used to be marked with certain characters on the body, through being deputed to a bodily service. Since, therefore, by the sacraments men are deputed to a spiritual service pertaining to the worship of God, it follows that by their means the faithful receive a certain spiritual character. Wherefore Augustine says (Contra Parmen. ii): "If a deserter from the battle, through dread of the mark of enlistment on his body, throws himself on the emperor's clemency, and having besought and received mercy, return to the fight; is that character renewed, when the man has been set free and reprimanded? is it not rather acknowledged and approved? Are the Christian sacraments, by any chance, of a nature less lasting than this bodily mark?"

Reply to Objection 1: The faithful of Christ are destined to the reward of the glory that is to come, by the seal of Divine Predestination. But they are deputed to acts becoming the Church that is now, by a certain spiritual seal that is set on them, and is called a character.

Reply to Objection 2: The character imprinted on the soul is a kind of sign in so far as it is imprinted by a sensible sacrament: since we know that a certain one has received the baptismal character, through his being cleansed by the sensible water. Nevertheless from a kind of likeness, anything that assimilates one thing to another, or discriminates one thing from another, even though it be not sensible, can be called a character or a seal; thus the Apostle calls Christ "the figure" or {charakter} "of the substance of the Father" (Heb. 1:3).

Reply to Objection 3: As stated above ([4365]Q[62], A[6]) the sacraments of the Old Law had not in themselves any spiritual power of producing a spiritual effect. Consequently in those sacraments there was no need of a spiritual character, and bodily circumcision sufficed, which the Apostle calls "a seal" (Rom. 4:11).

Whether a character is a spiritual power?

Objection 1: It seems that a character is not a spiritual power. For "character" seems to be the same thing as "figure"; hence (Heb. 1:3), where we read "figure of His substance, "for "figure" the Greek has {charakter}. Now "figure" is in the fourth species of quality, and thus differs from power which is in the second species. Therefore character is not a spiritual power.

Objection 2: Further, Dionysius says (Eccl. Hier. ii): "The Divine Beatitude admits him that seeks happiness to a share in Itself, and grants this share to him by conferring on him Its light as a kind of seal." Consequently, it seems that a character is a kind of light. Now light belongs rather to the third species of quality. Therefore a character is not a power, since this seems to belong to the second species.

Objection 3: Further, character is defined by some thus: "A character is a holy sign of the communion of faith and of the holy ordination conferred by a hierarch." Now a sign is in the genus of "relation," not of "power." Therefore a character is not a spiritual power.

Objection 4: Further, a power is in the nature of a cause and principle (Metaph. v). But a "sign" which is set down in the definition of a character is rather in the nature of an effect. Therefore a character is not a spiritual power.

On the contrary, The Philosopher says (Ethic. ii): "There are three things in the soul, power, habit, and passion." Now a character is not a passion: since a passion passes quickly, whereas a character is indelible, as will be made clear further on [4366](A[5]). In like manner it is not a habit: because no habit is indifferent to acting well or ill: whereas a character is indifferent to either, since some use it well, some ill. Now this cannot occur with a habit: because no one abuses a habit of virtue, or uses well an evil habit. It remains, therefore, that a character is a power.

I answer that, As stated above [4367](A[1]), the sacraments of the New Law produce a character, in so far as by them we are deputed to the worship of God according to the rite of the Christian religion. Wherefore Dionysius (Eccl. Hier. ii), after saying that God "by a kind of sign grants a share of Himself to those that approach Him," adds "by making them Godlike and communicators of Divine gifts." Now the worship of God consists either in receiving Divine gifts, or in bestowing them on others. And for both these purposes some power is needed; for to bestow something on others, active power is necessary; and in order to receive, we need a passive power. Consequently, a character signifies a certain spiritual power ordained unto things pertaining to the Divine worship.

But it must be observed that this spiritual power is instrumental: as we have stated above ([4368]Q[62], A[4]) of the virtue which is in the sacraments. For to have a sacramental character belongs to God's ministers: and a minister is a kind of instrument, as the Philosopher says (Polit. i). Consequently, just as the virtue which is in the sacraments is not of itself in a genus, but is reducible to a genus, for the reason that it is of a transitory and incomplete nature: so also a character is not properly in a genus or species, but is reducible to the second species of quality.

Reply to Objection 1: Configuration is a certain boundary of quantity. Wherefore, properly speaking, it is only in corporeal things; and of spiritual things is said metaphorically. Now that which decides the genus or species of a thing must needs be predicated of it properly. Consequently, a character cannot be in the fourth species of quality, although some have held this to be the case.

Reply to Objection 2: The third species of quality contains only sensible passions or sensible qualities. Now a character is not a sensible light. Consequently, it is not in the third species of quality as some have maintained.

Reply to Objection 3: The relation signified by the word "sign" must needs have some foundation. Now the relation signified by this sign which is a character, cannot be founded immediately on the essence of the soul: because then it would belong to every soul naturally. Consequently, there must be something in the soul on which such a relation is founded. And it is in this that a character essentially consists. Therefore it need not be in the genus "relation" as some have held.

Reply to Objection 4: A character is in the nature of a sign in comparison to the sensible sacrament by which it is imprinted. But considered in itself, it is in the nature of a principle, in the way already explained.

Whether the sacramental character is the character of Christ?

Objection 1: It seems that the sacramental character is not the character of Christ. For it is written (Eph. 4:30): "Grieve not the Holy Spirit of God, whereby you are sealed." But a character consists essentially in some. thing that seals. Therefore the sacramental character should be attributed to the Holy Ghost rather than to Christ.

Objection 2: Further, a character has the nature of a sign. And it is a sign of the grace that is conferred by the sacrament. Now grace is poured forth into the soul by the whole Trinity; wherefore it is written (Ps. 83:12): "The Lord will give grace and glory." Therefore it seems that the sacramental character should not be attributed specially to Christ.

Objection 3: Further, a man is marked with a character that he may be distinguishable from others. But the saints are distinguishable from others by charity, which, as Augustine says (De Trin. xv), "alone separates the children of the Kingdom from the children of perdition": wherefore also the children of perdition are said to have "the character of the beast" (Apoc. 13:16,17). But charity is not attributed to Christ, but rather to the Holy Ghost according to Rom. 5:5: "The charity of God is poured forth in our hearts, by the Holy Ghost, Who is given to us"; or even to the Father, according to 2 Cor. 13:13: "The grace of our Lord Jesus Christ and the charity of God." Therefore it seems that the sacramental character should not be attributed to Christ.

On the contrary, Some define character thus: "A character is a distinctive mark printed in a man's rational soul by the eternal Character, whereby the created trinity is sealed with the likeness of the creating and re-creating Trinity, and distinguishing him from those who are not so enlikened, according to the state of faith." But the eternal Character is Christ Himself, according to Heb. 1:3: "Who being the brightness of His glory and the figure," or character, "of His substance." It seems, therefore, that the character should properly be attributed to Christ.

I answer that, As has been made clear above [4369](A[1]), a character is properly a kind of seal, whereby something is marked, as being ordained to some particular end: thus a coin is marked for use in exchange of goods, and soldiers are marked with a character as being deputed to military service. Now the faithful are deputed to a twofold end. First and principally to the enjoyment of glory. And for this purpose they are marked with the seal of grace according to Ezech. 9:4: "Mark Thou upon the foreheads of the men that sigh and mourn"; and Apoc. 7:3: "Hurt not the earth, nor the sea, nor the trees, till we sign the servants of our God in their foreheads."

Secondly, each of the faithful is deputed to receive, or to bestow on others, things pertaining to the worship of God. And this, properly speaking, is the purpose of the sacramental character. Now the whole rite of the Christian religion is derived from Christ's priesthood. Consequently, it is clear that the sacramental character is specially the character of Christ, to Whose character the faithful are likened by reason of the sacramental characters, which are nothing else than certain participations of Christ's Priesthood, flowing from Christ Himself.

Reply to Objection 1: The Apostle speaks there of that sealing by which a man is assigned to future glory, and which is effected by grace. Now grace is attributed to the Holy Ghost, inasmuch as it is through love that God gives us something gratis, which is the very nature of grace: while the Holy Ghost is love. Wherefore it is written (1 Cor. 12:4): "There are diversities of graces, but the same Spirit."

Reply to Objection 2: The sacramental character is a thing as regards the exterior sacrament, and a sacrament in regard to the ultimate effect. Consequently, something can be attributed to a character in two ways. First, if the character be considered as a sacrament: and thus it is a sign of the invisible grace which is conferred in the sacrament. Secondly, if it be considered as a character. And thus it is a sign conferring on a man a likeness to some principal person in whom is vested the authority over that to which he is assigned: thus soldiers who are assigned to military service, are marked with their leader's sign, by which they are, in a fashion, likened to him. And in this way those who are deputed to the Christian worship, of which Christ is the author, receive a character by which they are likened to Christ. Consequently, properly speaking, this is Christ's character.

Reply to Objection 3: A character distinguishes one from another, in relation to some particular end, to which he, who receives the character is ordained: as has been stated concerning the military character [4370](A[1]) by which a soldier of the king is distinguished from the enemy's soldier in relation to the battle. In like manner the character of the faithful is that by which the faithful of Christ are distinguished from the servants of the devil, either in relation to eternal life, or in relation to the worship of the Church that now is. Of these the former is the result of charity and grace, as the objection runs; while the latter results from the sacramental character. Wherefore the "character of the beast" may be understood by opposition, to mean either the obstinate malice for which some are assigned to eternal punishment, or the profession of an unlawful form of worship.

Whether the character be subjected in the powers of the soul?

Objection 1: It seems that the character is not subjected in the powers of the soul. For a character is said to be a disposition to grace. But grace is subjected in the essence of the soul as we have stated in the [4371]FS, Q[110], A[4]. Therefore it seems that the character is in the essence of the soul and not in the powers.

Objection 2: Further, a power of the soul does not seem to be the subject of anything save habit and disposition. But a character, as stated above [4372](A[2]), is neither habit nor disposition, but rather a power: the subject of which is nothing else than the essence of the soul. Therefore it seems that the character is not subjected in a power of the soul, but rather in its essence.

Objection 3: Further, the powers of the soul are divided into those of knowledge and those of appetite. But it cannot be said that a character is only in a cognitive power, nor, again, only in an appetitive power: since it is neither ordained to knowledge only, nor to desire only. Likewise, neither can it be said to be in both, because the same accident cannot be in several subjects. Therefore it seems that a character is not subjected in a power of the soul, but rather in the essence.

On the contrary, A character, according to its definition given above [4373](A[3]), is imprinted in the rational soul "by way of an image." But the image of the Trinity in the soul is seen in the powers. Therefore a character is in the powers of the soul.

I answer that, As stated above [4374](A[3]), a character is a kind of seal by which the soul is marked, so that it may receive, or bestow on others, things pertaining to Divine worship. Now the Divine worship consists in certain actions: and the powers of the soul are properly ordained to actions, just as the essence is ordained to existence. Therefore a character is subjected not in the essence of the soul, but in its power.

Reply to Objection 1: The subject is ascribed to an. accident in respect of that to which the accident disposes it proximately, but not in respect of that to which it disposes it remotely or indirectly. Now a character disposes the soul directly and proximately to the fulfilling of things pertaining to Divine worship: and because such cannot be accomplished suitably without the help of grace, since, according to Jn. 4:24, "they that adore" God "must adore Him in spirit and in truth," consequently, the Divine bounty bestows grace on those who receive the character, so that they may accomplish worthily the service to which they are deputed. Therefore the subject should be ascribed to a character in respect of those actions that pertain to the Divine worship, rather than in respect of grace.

Reply to Objection 2: The subject of the natural power, which flows from the principles of the essence. Now a character is not a power of this kind. but a spiritual power coming from without. Wherefore, just as the essence of the soul, from which man has his natural life, is perfected by grace from which the soul derives spiritual life; so the natural power of the soul is perfected by a spiritual power, which is a character. For habit and disposition belong to a power of the soul, since they are ordained to actions of which the powers are the principles. And in like manner whatever is ordained to action, should be attributed to a power.

Reply to Objection 3: As stated above, a character is ordained unto things pertaining to the Divine worship; which is a protestation of faith expressed by exterior signs. Consequently, a character needs to be in the soul's cognitive power, where also is faith.

Day 291

Whether a character can be blotted out from the soul?

Objection 1: It seems that a character can be blotted out from the soul. Because the more perfect an accident is, the more firmly does it adhere to its subject. But grace is more perfect than a character; because a character is ordained unto grace as to a further end. Now grace is lost through sin. Much more, therefore, is a character so lost.

Objection 2: Further, by a character a man is deputed to the Divine worship, as stated above ([4375]AA[3],4). But some pass from the worship of God to a contrary worship by apostasy from the faith. It seems, therefore, that such lose the sacramental character.

Objection 3: Further, when the end ceases, the means to the end should cease also: thus after the resurrection there will be no marriage, because begetting will cease, which is the purpose of marriage. Now the exterior worship to which a character is ordained, will not endure in heaven, where there will be no shadows, but all will be truth without a veil. Therefore the sacramental character does not last in the soul for ever: and consequently it can be blotted out.

On the contrary, Augustine says (Contra Parmen. ii): "The Christian sacraments are not less lasting than the bodily mark" of military service. But the character of military service is not repeated, but is "recognized and approved" in the man who obtains the emperor's forgiveness after offending him. Therefore neither can the sacramental character be blotted out.

I answer that, As stated above [4376](A[3]), in a sacramental character Christ's faithful have a share in His Priesthood; in the sense that as Christ has the full power of a spiritual priesthood, so His faithful are likened to Him by sharing a certain spiritual power with regard to the sacraments and to things pertaining to the Divine worship. For this reason it is unbecoming that Christ should have a character: but His Priesthood is compared to a character, as that which is complete and perfect is compared to some participation of itself. Now Christ's Priesthood is eternal, according to Ps. 109:4: "Thou art a priest for ever, according to the order of Melchisedech." Consequently, every sanctification wrought by His Priesthood, is perpetual, enduring as long as the thing sanctified endures. This is clear even in inanimate things; for the consecration of a church or an altar lasts for ever unless they be destroyed. Since, therefore, the subject of a character is the soul as to its intellective part, where faith resides, as stated above (A[4], ad 3); it is clear that, the intellect being perpetual and incorruptible, a character cannot be blotted out from the soul.

Reply to Objection 1: Both grace and character are in the soul, but in different ways. For grace is in the soul, as a form having complete existence therein: whereas a character is in the soul, as an instrumental power, as stated above [4377](A[2]). Now a complete form is in its subject according to the condition of the subject. And since the soul as long as it is a wayfarer is changeable in respect of the free-will, it results that grace is in the soul in a changeable manner. But an instrumental power follows rather the condition of the principal agent: and consequently a character exists in the soul in an indelible manner, not from any perfection of its own, but from the perfection of Christ's Priesthood, from which the character flows like an instrumental power.

Reply to Objection 2: As Augustine says (Contra Parmen. ii), "even apostates are not deprived of their baptism, for when they repent and return to the fold they do not receive it again; whence we conclude that it cannot be lost." The reason of this is that a character is an instrumental power, as stated above (ad 1), and the nature of an instrument as such is to be moved by another, but not to move itself; this belongs to the will. Consequently, however much the will be moved in the contrary direction, the character is not removed, by reason of the immobility of the principal mover.

Reply to Objection 3: Although external worship does not last after this life, yet its end remains. Consequently, after this life the character remains, both in the good as adding to their glory, and in the wicked as increasing their shame: just as the character of the military service remains in the soldiers after the victory, as the boast of the conquerors, and the disgrace of the conquered.

Whether a character is imprinted by each sacrament of the New Law?

Objection 1: It seems that a character is imprinted by all the sacraments of the New Law: because each sacrament of the New Law makes man a participator in Christ's Priesthood. But the sacramental character is nothing but a participation in Christ's Priesthood, as already stated ([4378]AA[3],5). Therefore it seems that a character is imprinted by each sacrament of the New Law.

Objection 2: Further, a character may be compared to the soul in which it is, as a consecration to that which is consecrated. But by each sacrament of the New Law man becomes the recipient of sanctifying grace, as stated above ([4379]Q[62], A[1]). Therefore it seems that a character is imprinted by each sacrament of the New Law.

Objection 3: Further, a character is both a reality and a sacrament. But in each sacrament of the New Law, there is something which is only a reality, and something which is only a sacrament, and something which is both reality and sacrament. Therefore a character is imprinted by each sacrament of the New Law.

On the contrary, Those sacraments in which a character is imprinted, are not reiterated, because a character is indelible, as stated above [4380](A[5]): whereas some sacraments are reiterated, for instance, penance and matrimony. Therefore not all the sacraments imprint a character.

I answer that, As stated above ([4381]Q[62], AA[1],5), the sacraments of the New Law are ordained for a twofold purpose, namely, as a remedy for sin, and for the Divine worship. Now all the sacraments, from the fact that they confer grace, have this in common, that they afford a remedy against sin: whereas not all the sacraments are directly ordained to the Divine worship. Thus it is clear that penance, whereby man is delivered from sin, does not afford man any advance in the Divine worship, but restores him to his former state.

Now a sacrament may belong to the Divine worship in three ways: first in regard to the thing done; secondly, in regard to the agent; thirdly, in regard to the recipient. In regard to the thing done, the Eucharist belongs to the Divine worship, for the Divine worship consists principally therein, so far as it is the sacrifice of the Church. And by this same sacrament a character is not imprinted on man; because it does not ordain man to any further sacramental action or benefit received, since rather is it "the end and consummation of all the sacraments," as Dionysius says (Eccl. Hier. iii). But it contains within itself Christ, in Whom there is not the character, but the very plenitude of the Priesthood.

But it is the sacrament of order that pertains to the sacramental agents: for it is by this sacrament that men are deputed to confer sacraments on others: while the sacrament of Baptism pertains to the recipients, since it confers on man the power to receive the other sacraments of the Church; whence it is called the "door of the sacraments." In a way Confirmation also is ordained for the same purpose, as we shall explain in its proper place ([4382]Q[65], A[3]). Consequently, these three sacraments imprint a character, namely, Baptism, Confirmation, and order.

Reply to Objection 1: Every sacrament makes man of the a participator in Christ's Priesthood, from the fact that it confers on him some effect thereof. But every sacrament does not depute a man to do or receive something pertaining to the worship of the priesthood of Christ: while it is just this that is required for a sacrament to imprint a character.

Reply to Objection 2: Man is sanctified by each of the sacraments, since sanctity means immunity from sin, which is the effect of grace. But in a special way some sacraments, which imprint a character, bestow on man a certain consecration, thus deputing him to the Divine worship: just as inanimate things are said to be consecrated forasmuch as they are deputed to Divine worship.

Reply to Objection 3: Although a character is a reality and a sacrament, it does not follow that whatever is a reality and a sacrament, is also a character. With regard to the other sacraments we shall explain further on what is the reality and what is the sacrament.

OF THE CAUSES OF THE SACRAMENTS (TEN ARTICLES)

In the next place we have to consider the causes of the sacraments, both as to authorship and as to ministration. Concerning which there are ten points of inquiry:

(1) Whether God alone works inwardly in the sacraments?
(2) Whether the institution of the sacraments is from God alone?
(3) Of the power which Christ exercised over the sacraments;
(4) Whether He could transmit that power to others?
(5) Whether the wicked can have the power of administering the sacraments?
(6) Whether the wicked sin in administering the sacraments?
(7) Whether the angels can be ministers of the sacraments?
(8) Whether the minister's intention is necessary in the sacraments?
(9) Whether right faith is required therein; so that it be impossible for an unbeliever to confer a sacrament?
(10) Whether a right intention is required therein?

Whether God alone, or the minister also, works inwardly unto the sacramental effect?

Objection 1: It seems that not God alone, but also the minister, works inwardly unto the sacramental effect. For the inward sacramental effect is to cleanse man from sin and enlighten him by grace. But it belongs to the ministers of the Church "to cleanse, enlighten and perfect," as Dionysius explains (Coel. Hier. v). Therefore it seems that the sacramental effect is the work not only of God, but also of the ministers of the Church.

Objection 2: Further, certain prayers are offered up in conferring the sacraments. But the prayers of the righteous are more acceptable to God than those of any other, according to Jn. 9:31: "If a man be a server of God, and doth His will, him He heareth." Therefore it stems that a man obtains a greater sacramental effect if he receive it from a good minister. Consequently, the interior effect is partly the work of the minister and not of God alone.

Objection 3: Further, man is of greater account than an inanimate thing. But an inanimate thing contributes something to the interior effect: since "water touches the body and cleanses the soul," as Augustine says (Tract. lxxx in Joan.). Therefore the interior sacramental effect is partly the work of man and not of God alone.

On the contrary, It is written (Rom. 8:33): "God that justifieth." Since, then, the inward effect of all the sacraments is justification, it seems that God alone works the interior sacramental effect.

I answer that, There are two ways of producing an effect; first, as a principal agent; secondly, as an instrument. In the former way the interior sacramental effect is the work of God alone: first, because God alone can enter the soul wherein the sacramental effect takes place; and no agent can operate immediately where it is not: secondly, because grace which is an interior sacramental effect is from God alone, as we have established in the [4383]FS, Q[112], A[1]; while the character which is the interior effect of certain sacraments, is an instrumental power which flows from the principal agent, which is God. In the second way, however, the interior sacramental effect can be the work of man, in so far as he works as a minister. For a minister is of the nature of an instrument, since the action of both is applied to something extrinsic, while the interior effect is produced through the power of the principal agent, which is God.

Reply to Objection 1: Cleansing in so far as it is attributed to the ministers of the Church is not a washing from sin: deacons are said to "cleanse," inasmuch as they remove the unclean from the body of the faithful, or prepare them by their pious admonitions for the reception of the sacraments. In like manner also priests are said to "enlighten" God's people, not indeed by giving them grace, but by conferring on them the sacraments of grace; as Dionysius explains (Coel. Hier. v).

Reply to Objection 2: The prayers which are said in giving the sacraments, are offered to God, not on the part of the individual, but on the part of the whole Church, whose prayers are acceptable to God, according to Mat. 18:19: "If two of you shall consent upon earth, concerning anything whatsoever they shall ask, it shall be done to them by My Father." Nor is there any reason why the devotion of a just man should not contribute to this effect. But that which is the sacramental effect is not impetrated by the prayer of the Church or of the minister, but through the merit of Christ's Passion, the power of which operates in the sacraments, as stated above ([4384]Q[62], A[5]). Wherefore the sacramental effect is made no better by a better minister. And yet something in addition may be impetrated for the receiver of the sacrament through the devotion of the minister: but this is not the work of the minister, but the work of God Who hears the minister's prayer.

Reply to Objection 3: Inanimate things do not produce the sacramental effect, except instrumentally, as stated above. In like manner neither do men produce the sacramental effect, except ministerially, as also stated above.

Whether the sacraments are instituted by God alone?

Objection 1: It seems that the sacraments are not instituted by God alone. For those things which God has instituted are delivered to us in Holy Scripture. But in the sacraments certain things are done which are nowhere mentioned in Holy Scripture; for instance, the chrism with which men are confirmed, the oil with which priests are anointed, and many others, both words and actions, which we employ in the sacraments. Therefore the sacraments were not instituted by God alone.

Objection 2: Further, a sacrament is a kind of sign. Now sensible things have their own natural signification. Nor can it be said that God takes pleasure in certain significations and not in others; because He approves of all that He made. Moreover, it seems to be peculiar to the demons to be enticed to something by means of signs; for Augustine says (De Civ. Dei xxi): "The demons are enticed . . . by means of creatures, which were created not by them but by God, by various means of attraction according to their various natures, not as an animal is enticed by food, but as a spirit is drawn by a sign." It seems, therefore, that there is no need for the sacraments to be instituted by God.

Objection 3: Further, the apostles were God's vicegerents on earth: hence the Apostle says (2 Cor. 2:10): "For what I have pardoned, if I have pardoned anything, for your sakes have I done it in the person of Christ," i.e. as though Christ Himself had pardoned. Therefore it seems that the apostles and their successors can institute new sacraments.

On the contrary, The institutor of anything is he who gives it strength and power: as in the case of those who institute laws. But the power of a sacrament is from God alone, as we have shown above [4385](A[1]; Q[62], A[1]). Therefore God alone can institute a sacrament.

I answer that, As appears from what has been said above [4386](A[1]; Q[62], A[1]), the sacraments are instrumental causes of spiritual effects. Now an instrument has its power from the principal agent. But an agent in respect of a sacrament is twofold; viz. he who institutes the sacraments, and he who makes use of the sacrament instituted, by applying it for the production of the effect. Now the power of a sacrament cannot be from him who makes use of the sacrament: because he works but as a minister. Consequently, it follows that the power of the sacrament is from the institutor of the sacrament. Since, therefore, the power of the sacrament is from God alone, it follows that God alone can institute the sacraments.

Reply to Objection 1: Human institutions observed in the sacraments are not essential to the sacrament; but belong to the solemnity which is added to the sacraments in order to arouse devotion and reverence in the recipients. But those things that are essential to the sacrament, are instituted by Christ Himself, Who is God and man. And though they are not all handed down by the Scriptures, yet the Church holds them from the intimate tradition of the apostles, according to the saying of the Apostle (1 Cor. 11:34): "The rest I will set in order when I come."

Reply to Objection 2: From their very nature sensible things have a certain aptitude for the signifying of spiritual effects: but this aptitude is fixed by the Divine institution to some special signification. This is what Hugh of St. Victor means by saying (De Sacram. i) that "a sacrament owes its signification to its institution." Yet God chooses certain things rather than others for sacramental signification, not as though His choice were restricted to them, but in order that their signification be more suitable to them.

Reply to Objection 3: The apostles and their successors are God's vicars in governing the Church which is built on faith and the sacraments of faith. Wherefore, just as they may not institute another Church, so neither may they deliver another faith, nor institute other sacraments: on the contrary, the Church is said to be built up with the sacraments "which flowed from the side of Christ while hanging on the Cross."

Whether Christ as man had the power of producing the inward sacramental effect?

Objection 1: It seems that Christ as man had the power of producing the interior sacramental effect. For John the Baptist said (Jn. 1:33): "He, Who sent me to baptize in water, said to me: He upon Whom thou shalt see the Spirit descending and remaining upon Him, He it is that baptizeth with the Holy Ghost." But to baptize with the Holy Ghost is to confer inwardly the grace of the Holy Ghost. And the Holy Ghost descended upon Christ as man, not as God: for thus He Himself gives the Holy Ghost. Therefore it seems that Christ, as man, had the power of producing the inward sacramental effect.

Objection 2: Further, our Lord said (Mat. 9:6): "That you may know that the Son of Man hath power on earth to forgive sins." But forgiveness of sins is an inward sacramental effect. Therefore it seems that Christ as man produces the inward sacramental effect.

Objection 3: Further, the institution of the sacraments belongs to him who acts as principal agent in producing the inward sacramental effect. Now it is clear that Christ instituted the sacraments. Therefore it is He that produces the inward sacramental effect.

Objection 4: Further, no one can confer the sacramental effect without conferring the sacrament, except he produce the sacramental effect by his own power. But Christ conferred the sacramental effect without conferring the sacrament; as in the case of Magdalen to whom He said: "Thy sins are forgiven Thee" (Lk. 7:48). Therefore it seems that Christ, as man, produces the inward sacramental effect.

Objection 5: Further, the principal agent in causing the inward effect is that in virtue of which the sacrament operates. But the sacraments derive their power from Christ's Passion and through the invocation of His Name; according to 1 Cor. 1:13: "Was Paul then crucified for you? or were you baptized in the name of Paul?" Therefore Christ, as man, produces the inward sacramental effect.

On the contrary, Augustine (Isidore, Etym. vi) says: "The Divine power in the sacraments works inwardly in producing their salutary effect." Now the Divine power is Christ's as God, not as man. Therefore Christ produces the inward sacramental effect, not as man but as God.

I answer that, Christ produces the inward sacramental effect, both as God and as man, but not in the same way. For, as God, He works in the sacraments by authority: but, as man, His operation conduces to the inward sacramental effects meritoriously and efficiently, but instrumentally. For it has been stated ([4387]Q[48], AA[1],6;[4388] Q[49], A[1]) that Christ's Passion which belongs to Him in respect of His human nature, is the cause of justification, both meritoriously and efficiently, not as the principal cause thereof, or by His own authority, but as an instrument, in so far as His humanity is the instrument of His Godhead, as stated above ([4389]Q[13], AA[2],3;[4390] Q[19], A[1]).

Nevertheless, since it is an instrument united to the Godhead in unity of Person, it has a certain headship and efficiency in regard to extrinsic instruments, which are the ministers of the Church and the sacraments themselves, as has been explained above [4391] (A[1]). Consequently, just as Christ, as God, has power of "authority" over the sacraments, so, as man, He has the power of ministry in chief, or power of "excellence." And this consists in four things. First in this, that the merit and power of His Passion operates in the sacraments, as stated above (Q[62], A[5]). And because the power of the Passion is communicated to us by faith, according to Rom. 3:25: "Whom God hath proposed to be a propitiation through faith in His blood," which faith we proclaim by calling on the name of Christ: therefore, secondly, Christ's power of excellence over the sacraments consists in this, that they are sanctified by the invocation of His name. And because the sacraments derive their power from their institution, hence, thirdly, the excellence of Christ's power consists in this, that He, Who gave them their power, could institute the sacraments. And since cause does not depend on effect, but rather conversely, it belongs to the excellence of Christ's power, that He could bestow the sacramental effect without conferring the exterior sacrament. Thus it is clear how to solve the objections; for the arguments on either side are true to a certain extent, as explained above.

Whether Christ could communicate to ministers the power which He had in the sacraments?

Objection 1: It seems that Christ could not communicate to ministers the power which He had in the sacraments. For as Augustine argues against Maximin, "if He could, but would not, He was jealous of His power." But jealousy was far from Christ Who had the fulness of charity. Since, therefore, Christ did not communicate His power to ministers, it seems that He could not.

Objection 2: Further, on Jn. 14:12: "Greater than these shall he do," Augustine says (Tract. lxxii): "I affirm this to be altogether greater," namely, for a man from being ungodly to be made righteous, "than to create heaven and earth." But Christ could not communicate to His disciples the power of creating heaven and earth: neither, therefore, could He give them the power of making the ungodly to be righteous. Since, therefore, the justification of the ungodly is effected by the power that Christ has in the sacraments, it seems that He could not communicate that power to ministers.

Objection 3: Further, it belongs to Christ as Head of the Church that grace should flow from Him to others, according to Jn. 1:16: "Of His fulness we all have received." But this could not be communicated to others; since then the Church would be deformed, having many heads. Therefore it seems that Christ could not communicate His power to ministers.

On the contrary, on Jn. 1:31: "I knew Him not," Augustine says (Tract. v) that "he did not know that our Lord having the authority of baptizing . . . would keep it to Himself." But John would not have been in ignorance of this, if such a power were incommunicable. Therefore Christ could communicate His power to ministers.

I answer that, As stated above [4392](A[3]), Christ had a twofold power in the sacraments. one was the power of "authority," which belongs to Him as God: and this power He could not communicate to any creature; just as neither could He communicate the Divine Essence. The other was the power of "excellence," which belongs to Him as man. This power He could communicate to ministers; namely, by giving them such a fulness of grace---that their merits would conduce to the sacramental effect---that by the invocation of their names, the sacraments would be sanctified---and that they themselves might institute sacraments, and by their mere will confer the sacramental effect without observing the sacramental rite. For a united instrument, the more powerful it is, is all the more able to lend its power to the separated instrument; as the hand can to a stick.

Reply to Objection 1: It was not through jealousy that Christ refrained from communicating to ministers His power of excellence, but for the good of the faithful; lest they should put their trust in men, and lest there should be various kinds of sacraments, giving rise to division in the Church; as may be seen in those who said: "I am of Paul, I am of Apollo, and I of Cephas" (1 Cor. 1:12).

Reply to Objection 2: This objection is true of the power of authority, which belongs to Christ as God. At the same time the power of excellence can be called authority in comparison to other ministers. Whence on 1 Cor. 1:13: "Is Christ divided?" the gloss says that "He could give power of authority in baptizing, to those to whom He gave the power of administering it."

Reply to Objection 3: It was in order to avoid the incongruity of many heads in the Church, that Christ was unwilling to communicate to ministers His power of excellence. If, however, He had done so, He would have been Head in chief; the others in subjection to Him.

Whether the sacraments can be conferred by evil ministers?

Objection 1: It seems that the sacraments cannot be conferred by evil ministers. For the sacraments of the New Law are ordained for the purpose of cleansing from sin and for the bestowal of grace. Now evil men, being themselves unclean, cannot cleanse others from sin, according to Ecclus. 34:4: "Who [Vulg.: 'What'] can be made clean by the unclean?" Moreover, since they have not grace, it seems that they cannot give grace, for "no one gives what he has not." It seems, therefore, that the sacraments cannot be conferred by wicked men.

Objection 2: Further, all the power of the sacraments is derived from Christ, as stated above [4393](A[3]; Q[62], A[5]). But evil men are cut off from Christ: because they have not charity, by which the members are united to their Head, according to 1 Jn. 4:16: "He that abideth in charity, abideth in God, and God in him." Therefore it seems that the sacraments cannot be conferred by evil men.

Objection 3: Further, if anything is wanting that is required for the sacraments, the sacrament is invalid; for instance, if the required matter or form be wanting. But the minister required for a sacrament is one who is without the stain of sin, according to Lev. 21:17,18: "Whosoever of thy seed throughout their families, hath a blemish, he shall not offer bread to his God, neither shall he approach to minister to Him." Therefore it seems that if the minister be wicked, the sacrament has no effect.

On the contrary, Augustine says on Jn. 1:33: "He upon Whom thou shalt see the Spirit," etc. (Tract. v in Joan.), that "John did not know that our Lord, having the authority of baptizing, would keep it to Himself, but that the ministry would certainly pass to both good and evil men . . . What is a bad minister to thee, where the Lord is good?"

I answer that, As stated above [4394](A[1]), the ministers of the Church work instrumentally in the sacraments, because, in a way, a minister is of the nature of an instrument. But, as stated above (Q[62], AA[1],4), an instrument acts not by reason of its own form, but by the power of the one who moves it. Consequently, whatever form or power an instrument has in addition to that which it has as an instrument, is accidental to it: for instance, that a physician's body, which is the instrument of his soul, wherein is his medical art, be healthy or sickly; or that a pipe, through which water passes, be of silver or lead. Therefore the ministers of the Church can confer the sacraments, though they be wicked.

Reply to Objection 1: The ministers of the Church do not by their own power cleanse from sin those who approach the sacraments, nor do they confer grace on them: it is Christ Who does this by His own power while He employs them as instruments. Consequently, those who approach the sacraments receive an effect whereby they are enlikened not to the ministers but to Christ.

Reply to Objection 2: Christ's members are united to their Head by charity, so that they may receive life from Him; for as it is written (1 Jn. 3:14): "He that loveth not abideth in death." Now it is possible for a man to work with a lifeless instrument, and separated from him as to bodily union, provided it be united to him by some sort of motion: for a workman works in one way with his hand, in another with his axe. Consequently, it is thus that Christ works in the sacraments, both by wicked men as lifeless instruments, and by good men as living instruments.

Reply to Objection 3: A thing is required in a sacrament in two ways. First, as being essential to it: and if this be wanting, the sacrament is invalid; for instance, if the due form or matter be wanting. Secondly, a thing is required for a sacrament, by reason of a certain fitness. And in this way good ministers are required for a sacrament.

Whether wicked men sin in administering the sacraments?

Objection 1: It seems that wicked men do not sin in administering the sacraments. For just as men serve God in the sacraments, so do they serve Him in works of charity; whence it is written (Heb. 13:16): "Do not forget to do good and to impart, for by such sacrifices God's favor is obtained." But the wicked do not sin in serving God by works of charity: indeed, they should be persuaded to do so, according to Dan. 4:24: "Let my counsel be acceptable" to the king; "Redeem thou thy sins with alms." Therefore it seems that wicked men do not sin in administering the sacraments.

Objection 2: Further, whoever co-operates with another in his sin, is also guilty of sin, according to Rom. 1:32: "He is [Vulg.: 'They are'] worthy of death; not only he that commits the sin, but also he who consents to them that do them." But if wicked ministers sin in administering sacraments, those who receive sacraments from them, co-operate in their sin. Therefore they would sin also; which seems unreasonable.

Objection 3: Further, it seems that no one should act when in doubt, for thus man would be driven to despair, as being unable to avoid sin. But if the wicked were to sin in administering sacraments, they would be in a state of perplexity: since sometimes they would sin also if they did not administer sacraments; for instance, when by reason of their office it is their bounden duty to do so; for it is written (1 Cor. 9:16): "For a necessity lieth upon me: Woe is unto me if I preach not the gospel." Sometimes also on account of some danger; for instance, if a child in danger of death be brought to a sinner for baptism. Therefore it seems that the wicked do not sin in administering the sacraments.

On the contrary, Dionysius says (Eccl. Hier. i) that "it is wrong for the wicked even to touch the symbols," i.e. the sacramental signs. And he says in the epistle to Demophilus: "It seems presumptuous for such a man," i.e. a sinner, "to lay hands on priestly things; he is neither afraid nor ashamed, all unworthy that he is, to take part in Divine things, with the thought that God does not see what he sees in himself: he thinks, by false pretenses, to cheat Him Whom he calls his Father; he dares to utter, in the person of Christ, words polluted by his infamy, I will not call them prayers, over the Divine symbols."

I answer that, A sinful action consists in this, that a man "fails to act as he ought to," as the Philosopher explains (Ethic. ii). Now it has been said (A[5], ad 3) that it is fitting for the ministers of sacraments to be righteous; because ministers should be like unto their Lord, according to Lev. 19:2: "Be ye holy, because I . . . am holy"; and Ecclus. 10:2: "As the judge of the people is himself, so also are his ministers." Consequently, there can be no doubt that the wicked sin by exercising the ministry of God and the Church, by conferring the sacraments. And since this sin pertains to irreverence towards God and the contamination of holy things, as far as the man who sins is concerned, although holy things in themselves cannot be contaminated; it follows that such a sin is mortal in its genus.

Reply to Objection 1: Works of charity are not made holy by some process of consecration, but they belong to the holiness of righteousness, as being in a way parts of righteousness. Consequently, when a man shows himself as a minister of God, by doing works of charity, if he be righteous, he will be made yet holier; but if he be a sinner, he is thereby disposed to holiness. On the other hand, the sacraments are holy in themselves owing to their mystical consecration. Wherefore the holiness of righteousness is required in the minister, that he may be suitable for his ministry: for which reason he acts unbecomingly and sins, if while in a state of sin he attempts to fulfil that ministry.

Reply to Objection 2: He who approaches a sacrament, receives it from a minister of the Church, not because he is such and such a man, but because he is a minister of the Church. Consequently, as long as the latter is tolerated in the ministry, he that receives a sacrament from him, does not communicate in his sin, but communicates with the Church from. whom he has his ministry. But if the Church, by degrading, excommunicating, or suspending him, does not tolerate him in the ministry, he that receives a sacrament from him sins, because he communicates in his sin.

Reply to Objection 3: A man who is in mortal sin is not perplexed simply, if by reason of his office it be his bounden duty to minister sacraments; because he can repent of his sin and so minister lawfully. But there is nothing unreasonable in his being perplexed, if we suppose that he wishes to remain in sin.

However, in a case of necessity when even a lay person might baptize, he would not sin in baptizing. For it is clear that then he does not exercise the ministry of the Church, but comes to the aid of one who is in need of his services. It is not so with the other sacraments, which are not so necessary as baptism, as we shall show further on ([4395]Q[65], AA[3],4;[4396] Q[62], A[3]).

Day 292

Whether angels can administer sacraments?

Objection 1: It seems that angels can administer sacraments. Because a higher minister can do whatever the lower can; thus a priest can do whatever a deacon can: but not conversely. But angels are higher ministers in the hierarchical order than any men whatsoever, as Dionysius says (Coel. Hier. ix). Therefore, since men can be ministers of sacraments, it seems that much more can angels be.

Objection 2: Further, in heaven holy men are likened to the angels (Mat. 22:30). But some holy men, when in heaven, can be ministers of the sacraments; since the sacramental character is indelible, as stated above ([4397]Q[63], A[5]). Therefore it seems that angels too can be ministers of sacraments.

Objection 3: Further, as stated above ([4398]Q[8], A[7]), the devil is head of the wicked, and the wicked are his members. But sacraments can be administered by the wicked. Therefore it seems that they can be administered even by demons.

On the contrary, It is written (Heb. 5:1): "Every high priest taken from among men, is ordained for men in the things that appertain to God." But angels whether good or bad are not taken from among men. Therefore they are not ordained ministers in the things that appertain to God, i.e. in the sacraments.

I answer that, As stated above [4399](A[3]; Q[62], A[5]), the whole power of the sacraments flows from Christ's Passion, which belongs to Him as man. And Him in their very nature men, not angels, resemble; indeed, in respect of His Passion, He is described as being "a little lower than the angels" (Heb. 2:9). Consequently, it belongs to men, but not to angels, to dispense the sacraments and to take part in their administration.

But it must be observed that as God did not bind His power to the sacraments, so as to be unable to bestow the sacramental effect without conferring the sacrament; so neither did He bind His power to the ministers of the Church so as to be unable to give angels power to administer the sacraments. And since good angels are messengers of truth; if any sacramental rite were performed by good angels, it should be considered valid, because it ought to be evident that this is being done by the will of God: for instance, certain churches are said to have been consecrated by the ministry of the angels [*See Acta S.S., September 29]. But if demons, who are "lying spirits," were to perform a sacramental rite, it should be pronounced as invalid.

Reply to Objection 1: What men do in a less perfect manner, i.e. by sensible sacraments, which are proportionate to their nature, angels also do, as ministers of a higher degree, in a more perfect manner, i.e. invisibly---by cleansing, enlightening, and perfecting.

Reply to Objection 2: The saints in heaven resemble the angels as to their share of glory, but not as to the conditions of their nature: and consequently not in regard to the sacraments.

Reply to Objection 3: Wicked men do not owe their power of conferring sacraments to their being members of the devil. Consequently, it does not follow that "a fortiori" the devil, their head, can do so.

Whether the minister's intention is required for the validity of a sacrament?

Objection 1: It seems that the minister's intention is not required for the validity of a sacrament. For the minister of a sacrament works instrumentally. But the perfection of an action does not depend on the intention of the instrument, but on that of the principal agent. Therefore the minister's intention is not necessary for the perfecting of a sacrament.

Objection 2: Further, one man's intention cannot be known to another. Therefore if the minister's intention were required for the validity of a sacrament, he who approaches a sacrament could not know whether he has received the sacrament. Consequently he could have no certainty in regard to salvation; the more that some sacraments are necessary for salvation, as we shall state further on ([4400]Q[65], A[4]).

Objection 3: Further, a man's intention cannot bear on that to which he does not attend. But sometimes ministers of sacraments do not attend to what they say or do, through thinking of something else. Therefore in this respect the sacrament would be invalid through want of intention.

On the contrary, What is unintentional happens by chance. But this cannot be said of the sacramental operation. Therefore the sacraments require the intention of the minister.

I answer that, When a thing is indifferent to many uses, it must needs be determined to one, if that one has to be effected. Now those things which are done in the sacraments, can be done with various intent; for instance, washing with water, which is done in baptism, may be ordained to bodily cleanliness, to the health of the body, to amusement, and many other similar things. Consequently, it needs to be determined to one purpose, i.e. the sacramental effect, by the intention of him who washes. And this intention is expressed by the words which are pronounced in the sacraments; for instance the words, "I baptize thee in the name of the Father," etc.

Reply to Objection 1: An inanimate instrument has no intention regarding the effect; but instead of the intention there is the motion whereby it is moved by the principal agent. But an animate instrument, such as a minister, is not only moved, but in a sense moves itself, in so far as by his will he moves his bodily members to act. Consequently, his intention is required, whereby he subjects himself to the principal agent; that is, it is necessary that he intend to do that which Christ and the Church do.

Reply to Objection 2: On this point there are two opinions. For some hold that the mental intention of the minister is necessary; in the absence of which the sacrament is invalid: and that this defect in the case of children who have not the intention of approaching the sacrament, is made good by Christ, Who baptizes inwardly: whereas in adults, who have that intention, this defect is made good by their faith and devotion.

This might be true enough of the ultimate effect, i.e. justification from sins; but as to that effect which is both real and sacramental, viz. the character, it does not appear possible for it to be made good by the devotion of the recipient, since a character is never imprinted save by a sacrament.

Consequently, others with better reason hold that the minister of a sacrament acts in the person of the whole Church, whose minister he is; while in the words uttered by him, the intention of the Church is expressed; and that this suffices for the validity of the sacrament, except the contrary be expressed on the part either of the minister or of the recipient of the sacrament.

Reply to Objection 3: Although he who thinks of something else, has no actual intention, yet he has habitual intention, which suffices for the validity of the sacrament; for instance if, when a priest goes to baptize someone, he intends to do to him what the Church does. Wherefore if subsequently during the exercise of the act his mind be distracted by other matters, the sacrament is valid in virtue of his original intention. Nevertheless, the minister of a sacrament should take great care to have actual intention. But this is not entirely in man's power, because when a man wishes to be very intent on something, he begins unintentionally to think of other things, according to Ps. 39:18: "My heart hath forsaken me."

Whether faith is required of necessity in the minister of a sacrament?

Objection 1: It seems that faith is required of necessity in the minister of a sacrament. For, as stated above [4401](A[8]), the intention of the minister is necessary for the validity of a sacrament. But "faith directs in intention" as Augustine says against Julian (In Psalm xxxi, cf. Contra Julian iv). Therefore, if the minister is without the true faith, the sacrament is invalid.

Objection 2: Further, if a minister of the Church has not the true faith, it seems that he is a heretic. But heretics, seemingly, cannot confer sacraments. For Cyprian says in an epistle against heretics (lxxiii): "Everything whatsoever heretics do, is carnal, void and counterfeit, so that nothing that they do should receive our approval." And Pope Leo says in his epistle to Leo Augustus (clvi): "It is a matter of notoriety that the light of all the heavenly sacraments is extinguished in the see of Alexandria, by an act of dire and senseless cruelty. The sacrifice is no longer offered, the chrism is no longer consecrated, all the mysteries of religion have fled at the touch of the parricide hands of ungodly men." Therefore a sacrament requires of necessity that the minister should have the true faith.

Objection 3: Further, those who have not the true faith seem to be separated from the Church by excommunication: for it is written in the second canonical epistle of John (10): "If any man come to you, and bring not this doctrine, receive him not into the house, nor say to him; God speed you": and (Titus 3:10): "A man that is a heretic, after the first and second admonition avoid." But it seems that an excommunicate cannot confer a sacrament of the Church: since he is separated from the Church, to whose ministry the dispensation of the sacraments belongs. Therefore a sacrament requires of necessity that the minister should have the true faith.

On the contrary, Augustine says against the Donatist Petilian: "Remember that the evil lives of wicked men are not prejudicial to God's sacraments, by rendering them either invalid or less holy."

I answer that, As stated above [4402](A[5]), since the minister works instrumentally in the sacraments, he acts not by his own but by Christ's power. Now just as charity belongs to a man's own power so also does faith. Wherefore, just as the validity of a sacrament does not require that the minister should have charity, and even sinners can confer sacraments, as stated above [4403](A[5]); so neither is it necessary that he should have faith, and even an unbeliever can confer a true sacrament, provided that the other essentials be there.

Reply to Objection 1: It may happen that a man's faith is defective in regard to something else, and not in regard to the reality of the sacrament which he confers: for instance, he may believe that it is unlawful to swear in any case whatever, and yet he may believe that baptism is an efficient cause of salvation. And thus such unbelief does not hinder the intention of conferring the sacrament. But if his faith be defective in regard to the very sacrament that he confers, although he believe that no inward effect is caused by the thing done outwardly, yet he does know that the Catholic Church intends to confer a sacrament by that which is outwardly done. Wherefore, his unbelief notwithstanding, he can intend to do what the Church does, albeit he esteem it to be nothing. And such an intention suffices for a sacrament: because as stated above (A[8], ad 2) the minister of a sacrament acts in the person of the Church by whose faith any defect in the minister's faith is made good.

Reply to Objection 2: Some heretics in conferring sacraments do not observe the form prescribed by the Church: and these confer neither the sacrament nor the reality of the sacrament. But some do observe the form prescribed by the Church: and these confer indeed the sacrament but not the reality. I say this in the supposition that they are outwardly cut off from the Church; because from the very fact that anyone receives the sacraments from them, he sins; and consequently is hindered from receiving the effect of the sacrament. Wherefore Augustine (Fulgentius, De Fide ad Pet.) says: "Be well assured and have no doubt whatever that those who are baptized outside the Church, unless they come back to the Church, will reap disaster from their Baptism." In this sense Pope Leo says that "the light of the sacraments was extinguished in the Church of Alexandria"; viz. in regard to the reality of the sacrament, not as to the sacrament itself.

Cyprian, however, thought that heretics do not confer even the sacrament: but in this respect we do not follow his opinion. Hence Augustine says (De unico Baptismo xiii): "Though the martyr Cyprian refused to recognize Baptism conferred by heretics or schismatics, yet so great are his merits, culminating in the crown of martyrdom, that the light of his charity dispels the darkness of his fault, and if anything needed pruning, the sickle of his passion cut it off."

Reply to Objection 3: The power of administering the sacraments belongs to the spiritual character which is indelible, as explained above ([4404]Q[63], A[3]). Consequently, if a man be suspended by the Church, or excommunicated or degraded, he does not lose the power of conferring sacraments, but the permission to use this power. Wherefore he does indeed confer the sacrament, but he sins in so doing. He also sins that receives a sacrament from such a man: so that he does not receive the reality of the sacrament, unless ignorance excuses him.

Whether the validity of a sacrament requires a good intention in the minister?

Objection 1: It seems that the validity of a sacrament requires a good intention in the minister. For the minister's intention should be in conformity with the Church's intention, as explained above (A[8], ad 1). But the intention of the Church is always good. Therefore the validity of a sacrament requires of necessity a good intention in the minister.

Objection 2: Further, a perverse intention seems worse than a playful one. But a playful intention destroys a sacrament: for instance, if someone were to baptize anybody not seriously but in fun. Much more, therefore, does a perverse intention destroy a sacrament: for instance, if somebody were to baptize a man in order to kill him afterwards.

Objection 3: Further, a perverse intention vitiates the whole work, according to Lk. 11:34: "If thy eye be evil, thy" whole "body will be darksome." But the sacraments of Christ cannot be contaminated by evil men; as Augustine says against Petilian (Cont. Litt. Petil ii). Therefore it seems that, if the minister's intention is perverse, the sacrament is invalid.

On the contrary, A perverse intention belongs to the wickedness of the minister. But the wickedness of the minister does not annul the sacrament: neither, therefore, does his perverse intention.

I answer that, The minister's intention may be perverted in two ways. First in regard to the sacrament: for instance, when a man does not intend to confer a sacrament, but to make a mockery of it. Such a perverse intention takes away the truth of the sacrament, especially if it be manifested outwardly.

Secondly, the minister's intention may be perverted as to something that follows the sacrament: for instance, a priest may intend to baptize a woman so as to be able to abuse her; or to consecrate the Body of Christ, so as to use it for sorcery. And because that which comes first does not depend on that which follows, consequently such a perverse intention does not annul the sacrament; but the minister himself sins grievously in having such an intention.

Reply to Objection 1: The Church has a good intention both as to the validity of the sacrament and as to the use thereof: but it is the former intention that perfects the sacrament, while the latter conduces to the meritorious effect. Consequently, the minister who conforms his intention to the Church as to the former rectitude, but not as to the latter, perfects the sacrament indeed, but gains no merit for himself.

Reply to Objection 2: The intention of mimicry or fun excludes the first kind of right intention, necessary for the validity of a sacrament. Consequently, there is no comparison.

Reply to Objection 3: A perverse intention perverts the action of the one who has such an intention, not the action of another. Consequently, the perverse intention of the minister perverts the sacrament in so far as it is his action: not in so far as it is the action of Christ, Whose minister he is. It is just as if the servant [minister] of some man were to carry alms to the poor with a wicked intention, whereas his master had commanded him with a good intention to do so.

OF THE NUMBER OF THE SACRAMENTS (FOUR ARTICLES)

We have now to consider the number of the sacraments: and concerning this there are four points of inquiry:

(1) Whether there are seven sacraments?

(2) The order of the sacraments among themselves;

(3) Their mutual comparison;

(4) Whether all the sacraments are necessary for salvation?

Whether there should be seven sacraments?

Objection 1: It seems that there ought not to be seven sacraments. For the sacraments derive their efficacy from the Divine power, and the power of Christ's Passion. But the Divine power is one, and Christ's Passion is one; since "by one oblation He hath perfected for ever them that are sanctified" (Heb. 10:14). Therefore there should be but one sacrament.

Objection 2: Further, a sacrament is intended as a remedy for the defect caused by sin. Now this is twofold, punishment and guilt. Therefore two sacraments would be enough.

Objection 3: Further, sacraments belong to the actions of the ecclesiastical hierarchy, as Dionysius explains (Eccl. Hier. v). But, as he says, there are three actions of the ecclesiastical hierarchy, namely, "to cleanse, to enlighten, to perfect." Therefore there should be no more than three sacraments.

Objection 4: Further, Augustine says (Contra Faust. xix) that the "sacraments" of the New Law are "less numerous" than those of the Old Law. But in the Old Law there was no sacrament corresponding to Confirmation and Extreme Unction. Therefore these should not be counted among the sacraments of the New Law.

Objection 5: Further, lust is not more grievous than other sins, as we have made clear in the [4405]FS, Q[74], A[5]; [4406]SS, Q[154], A[3]. But there is no sacrament instituted as a remedy for other sins. Therefore neither should matrimony be instituted as a remedy for lust.

Objection 6: On the other hand, It seems that there should be more than seven sacraments. For sacraments are a kind of sacred sign. But in the Church there are many sanctifications by sensible signs, such as Holy Water the Consecration of Altars, and such like. Therefore there are more than seven sacraments.

Objection 7: Further, Hugh of St. Victor (De Sacram. i) says that the sacraments of the Old Law were oblations, tithes and sacrifices. But the Sacrifice of the Church is one sacrament, called the Eucharist. Therefore oblations also and tithes should be called sacraments.

Objection 8: Further, there are three kinds of sin, original, mortal and venial. Now Baptism is intended as a remedy against original sin, and Penance against mortal sin. Therefore besides the seven sacraments, there should be another against venial sin.

I answer that, As stated above ([4407]Q[62], A[5];[4408] Q[63], A[1]), the sacraments of the Church were instituted for a twofold purpose: namely, in order to perfect man in things pertaining to the worship of God according to the religion of Christian life, and to be a remedy against the defects caused by sin. And in either way it is becoming that there should be seven sacraments.

For spiritual life has a certain conformity with the life of the body: just as other corporeal things have a certain likeness to things spiritual. Now a man attains perfection in the corporeal life in two ways: first, in regard to his own person; secondly, in regard to the whole community of the society in which he lives, for man is by nature a social animal. With regard to himself man is perfected in the life of the body, in two ways; first, directly [per se], i.e. by acquiring some vital perfection; secondly, indirectly [per accidens], i.e. by the removal of hindrances to life, such as ailments, or the like. Now the life of the body is perfected "directly," in three ways. First, by generation whereby a man begins to be and to live: and corresponding to this in the spiritual life there is Baptism, which is a spiritual regeneration, according to Titus 3:5: "By the laver of regeneration," etc. Secondly, by growth whereby a man is brought to perfect size and strength: and corresponding to this in the spiritual life there is Confirmation, in which the Holy Ghost is given to strengthen us. Wherefore the disciples who were already baptized were bidden thus: "Stay you in the city till you be endued with power from on high" (Lk. 24:49). Thirdly, by nourishment, whereby life and strength are preserved to man; and corresponding to this in the spiritual life there is the Eucharist. Wherefore it is said (Jn. 6:54): "Except you eat of the flesh of the Son of Man, and drink His blood, you shall not have life in you."

And this would be enough for man if he had an impassible life, both corporally and spiritually; but since man is liable at times to both corporal and spiritual infirmity, i.e. sin, hence man needs a cure from his infirmity; which cure is twofold. one is the healing, that restores health: and corresponding to this in the spiritual life there is Penance, according to Ps. 40:5: "Heal my soul, for I have sinned against Thee." The other is the restoration of former vigor by means of suitable diet and exercise: and corresponding to this in the spiritual life there is Extreme Unction, which removes the remainder of sin, and prepares man for final glory. Wherefore it is written (James 5:15): "And if he be in sins they shall be forgiven him."

In regard to the whole community, man is perfected in two ways. First, by receiving power to rule the community and to exercise public acts: and corresponding to this in the spiritual life there is the sacrament of order, according to the saying of Heb. 7:27, that priests offer sacrifices not for themselves only, but also for the people. Secondly in regard to natural propagation. This is accomplished by Matrimony both in the corporal and in the spiritual life: since it is not only a sacrament but also a function of nature.

We may likewise gather the number of the sacraments from their being instituted as a remedy against the defect caused by sin. For Baptism is intended as a remedy against the absence of spiritual life; Confirmation, against the infirmity of soul found in those of recent birth; the Eucharist, against the soul's proneness to sin; Penance, against actual sin committed after baptism; Extreme Unction, against the remainders of sins---of those sins, namely, which are not sufficiently removed by Penance, whether through negligence or through ignorance; order, against divisions in the community; Matrimony, as a remedy against concupiscence in the individual, and against the decrease in numbers that results from death.

Some, again, gather the number of sacraments from a certain adaptation to the virtues and to the defects and penal effects resulting from sin. They say that Baptism corresponds to Faith, and is ordained as a remedy against original sin; Extreme Unction, to Hope, being ordained against venial sin; the Eucharist, to Charity, being ordained against the penal effect which is malice. order, to Prudence, being ordained against ignorance; Penance to Justice, being ordained against mortal sin; Matrimony, to Temperance, being ordained against concupiscence; Confirmation, to Fortitude, being ordained against infirmity.

Reply to Objection 1: The same principal agent uses various instruments unto various effects, in accordance with the thing to be done. In the same way the Divine power and the Passion of Christ work in us through the various sacraments as through various instruments.

Reply to Objection 2: Guilt and punishment are diversified both according to species, inasmuch as there are various species of guilt and punishment, and according to men's various states and habitudes. And in this respect it was necessary to have a number of sacraments, as explained above.

Reply to Objection 3: In hierarchical actions we must consider the agents, the recipients and the actions. The agents are the ministers of the Church; and to these the sacrament of order belongs. The recipients are those who approach the sacraments: and these are brought into being by Matrimony. The actions are "cleansing," "enlightening," and "perfecting." Mere cleansing, however, cannot be a sacrament of the New Law, which confers grace: yet it belongs to certain sacramentals, i.e. catechism and exorcism. But cleansing coupled with enlightening, according to Dionysius, belongs to Baptism; and, for him who falls back into sin, they belong secondarily to Penance and Extreme Unction. And perfecting, as regards power, which is, as it were, a formal perfection, belongs to Confirmation: while, as regards the attainment of the end, it belongs to the Eucharist.

Reply to Objection 4: In the sacrament of Confirmation we receive the fulness of the Holy Ghost in order to be strengthened; while in Extreme Unction man is prepared for the immediate attainment of glory; and neither of these two purposes was becoming to the Old

Testament. Consequently, nothing in the old Law could correspond to these sacraments. Nevertheless, the sacraments of the old Law were more numerous, on account of the various kinds of sacrifices and ceremonies.

Reply to Objection 5: There was need for a special sacrament to be applied as a remedy against venereal concupiscence: first because by this concupiscence, not only the person but also the nature is defiled: secondly, by reason of its vehemence whereby it clouds the reason.

Reply to Objection 6: Holy Water and other consecrated things are not called sacraments, because they do not produce the sacramental effect, which is the receiving of grace. They are, however, a kind of disposition to the sacraments: either by removing obstacles. thus holy water is ordained against the snares of the demons, and against venial sins: or by making things suitable for the conferring of a sacrament; thus the altar and vessels are consecrated through reverence for the Eucharist.

Reply to Objection 7: Oblations and tithes, both the Law of nature and in the Law of Moses, ere ordained not only for the sustenance of the ministers and the poor, but also figuratively; and consequently they were sacraments. But now they remain no longer as figures, and therefore they are not sacraments.

Reply to Objection 8: The infusion of grace is not necessary for the blotting out of venial sin. Wherefore, since grace is infused in each of the sacraments of the New Law, none of them was instituted directly against venial sin. This is taken away by certain sacramentals, for instance, Holy Water and such like. Some, however, hold that Extreme Unction is ordained against venial sin. But of this we shall speak in its proper place ([4409]XP, Q[30], A[1]).

Whether the order of the sacraments, as given above, is becoming?

Objection 1: It seems that the order of the sacraments as given above is unbecoming. For according to the Apostle (1 Cor. 15:46), "that was . . . first . . . which is natural, afterwards that which is spiritual." But man is begotten through Matrimony by a first and natural generation; while in Baptism he is regenerated as by a second and spiritual generation. Therefore Matrimony should precede Baptism.

Objection 2: Further, through the sacrament of order man receives the power of agent in sacramental actions. But the agent precedes his action. Therefore order should precede Baptism and the other sacraments.

Objection 3: Further, the Eucharist is a spiritual food; while Confirmation is compared to growth. But food causes, and consequently precedes, growth. Therefore the Eucharist precedes Confirmation.

Objection 4: Further, Penance prepares man for the Eucharist. But a disposition precedes perfection. Therefore Penance should precede the Eucharist.

Objection 5: Further, that which is nearer the last end comes after other things. But, of all the sacraments, Extreme Unction is nearest to the last end which is Happiness. Therefore it should be placed last among the sacraments.

On the contrary, The order of the sacraments, as given above, is commonly adopted by all.

I answer that, The reason of the order among the sacraments appears from what has been said above [4410](A[1]). For just as unity precedes multitude, so those sacraments which are intended for the perfection of the individual, naturally precede those which are intended for the perfection of the multitude; and consequently the last place among the sacraments is given to order and Matrimony, which are intended for the perfection of the multitude: while Matrimony is placed after order, because it has less participation in the nature of the spiritual life, to which the sacraments are ordained. Moreover, among things ordained to the perfection of the individual, those naturally come first which are ordained directly to the perfection of the spiritual life, and afterwards, those which are ordained thereto indirectly, viz. by removing some supervening accidental cause of harm; such are Penance and Extreme Unction: while, of these, Extreme Unction is naturally placed last, for it preserves the healing which was begun by Penance.

Of the remaining three, it is clear that Baptism which is a spiritual regeneration, comes first; then Confirmation, which is ordained to the formal perfection of power; and after these the Eucharist which is ordained to final perfection.

Reply to Objection 1: Matrimony as ordained to natural life is a function of nature. But in so far as it has something spiritual it is a sacrament. And because it has the least amount of spirituality it is placed last.

Reply to Objection 2: For a thing to be an agent it must first of all be perfect in itself. Wherefore those sacraments by which a man is perfected in himself, are placed before the sacrament of order, in which a man is made a perfecter of others.

Reply to Objection 3: Nourishment both precedes growth, as its cause; and follows it, as maintaining the perfection of size and power in man. Consequently, the Eucharist can be placed before Confirmation, as Dionysius places it (Eccl. Hier. iii, iv), and can be placed after it, as the Master does (iv, 2,8).

Reply to Objection 4: This argument would hold if Penance were required of necessity as a preparation to the Eucharist. But this is not true: for if anyone be without mortal sin, he does not need Penance in order to receive the Eucharist. Thus it is clear that Penance is an accidental preparation to the Eucharist, that is to say, sin being supposed. Wherefore it is written in the last chapter of the second Book of Paralipomenon (cf. 2 Paral 33:18): "Thou, O Lord of the righteous, didst not impose penance on righteous men." [*The words quoted are from the apocryphal Prayer of Manasses, which, before the Council of Trent, was to be found inserted in some Latin copies of the Bible.]

Reply to Objection 5: Extreme Unction, for this very reason, is given the last place among those sacraments which are ordained to the perfection of the individual.

Whether the Eucharist is the greatest of the sacraments?

Objection 1: It seems that the Eucharist is not the principal of the sacraments. For the common good is of more account than the good of the individual (1 Ethic. ii). But Matrimony is ordained to the common good of the human race by means of generation: whereas the sacrament of the Eucharist is ordained to the private good of the recipient. Therefore it is not the greatest of the sacraments.

Objection 2: Further, those sacraments, seemingly, are greater, which are conferred by a greater minister. But the sacraments of Confirmation and order are conferred by a bishop only, who is a greater minister than a mere minister such as a priest, by whom the sacraments of the Eucharist is conferred. Therefore those sacraments are greater.

Objection 3: Further, those sacraments are greater that have the greater power. But some of the sacraments imprint a character, viz. Baptism, Confirmation and order; whereas the Eucharist does not. Therefore those sacraments are greater.

Objection 4: Further, that seems to be greater, on which others depend without its depending on them. But the Eucharist depends on Baptism: since no one can receive the Eucharist except he has been baptized. Therefore Baptism is greater than the Eucharist.

On the contrary, Dionysius says (Eccl. Hier. iii) that "No one receives hierarchical perfection save by the most God-like Eucharist." Therefore this sacrament is greater than all the others and perfects them.

I answer that, Absolutely speaking, the sacrament of the Eucharist is the greatest of all the sacraments: and this may be shown in three ways. First of all because it contains Christ Himself substantially: whereas the other sacraments contain a certain instrumental power which is a share of Christ's power, as we have shown above ([4411]Q[62], A[4], ad 3, A[5]). Now that which is essentially such is always of more account than that which is such by participation.

Secondly, this is made clear by considering the relation of the sacraments to one another. For all the other sacraments seem to be ordained to this one as to their end. For it is manifest that the sacrament of order is ordained to the consecration of the Eucharist: and the sacrament of Baptism to the reception of the Eucharist: while a man is perfected by Confirmation, so as not to fear to abstain from this sacrament. By Penance and Extreme Unction man is prepared to receive the Body of Christ worthily. And Matrimony at least in its signification, touches this sacrament; in so far as it signifies the union of Christ with the Church, of which union the Eucharist is a figure: hence the Apostle says (Eph. 5:32): "This is a great sacrament: but I speak in Christ and in the Church."

Thirdly, this is made clear by considering the rites of the sacraments. For nearly all the sacraments terminate in the Eucharist, as Dionysius says (Eccl. Hier. iii): thus those who have been ordained receive Holy Communion, as also do those who have been baptized, if they be adults.

The remaining sacraments may be compared to one another in several ways. For on the ground of necessity, Baptism is the greatest of the sacraments; while from the point of view of perfection, order comes first; while Confirmation holds a middle place. The sacraments of Penance and Extreme Unction are on a degree inferior to those mentioned above; because, as stated above [4412](A[2]), they are ordained to the Christian life, not directly, but accidentally, as it were, that is to say, as remedies against supervening defects. And among these, Extreme Unction is compared to Penance, as Confirmation to Baptism; in such a way, that Penance is more necessary, whereas Extreme Unction is more perfect.

Reply to Objection 1: Matrimony is ordained to the common good as regards the body. But the common spiritual good of the whole Church is contained substantially in the sacrament itself of the Eucharist.

Reply to Objection 2: By order and Confirmation the faithful of Christ are deputed to certain special duties; and this can be done by the prince alone. Consequently the conferring of these sacraments belongs exclusively to a bishop, who is, as it were, a prince in the Church. But a man is not deputed to any duty by the sacrament of the Eucharist, rather is this sacrament the end of all duties, as stated above.

Reply to Objection 3: The sacramental character, as stated above ([4413]Q[63], A[3]), is a kind of participation in Christ's priesthood. Wherefore the sacrament that unites man to Christ Himself, is greater than a sacrament that imprints Christ's character.

Reply to Objection 4: This argument proceeds on the ground of necessity. For thus Baptism, being of the greatest necessity, is the greatest of the sacraments, just as order and Confirmation have a certain excellence considered in their administration; and Matrimony by reason of its signification. For there is no reason why a thing should not be greater from a certain point of view which is not greater absolutely speaking.

Whether all the sacraments are necessary for salvation?

Objection 1: It seems that all the sacraments are necessary for salvation. For what is not necessary seems to be superfluous. But no sacrament is superfluous, because "God does nothing without a purpose" (De Coelo et Mundo i). Therefore all the sacraments are necessary for salvation.

Objection 2: Further, just as it is said of Baptism (Jn. 3:5): "Unless a man be born again of water and the Holy Ghost, he cannot enter in to the kingdom of God," so of the Eucharist is it said (Jn. 6:54): "Except you eat of the flesh of the Son of Man, and drink of His blood, you shall not have life in you." Therefore, just as Baptism is a necessary sacrament, so is the Eucharist.

Objection 3: Further, a man can be saved without the sacrament of Baptism, provided that some unavoidable obstacle, and not his contempt for religion, debar him from the sacrament, as we shall state further on ([4414]Q[68], A[2]). But contempt of religion in any sacrament is a hindrance to salvation. Therefore, in like manner, all the sacraments are necessary for salvation.

On the contrary, Children are saved by Baptism alone without the other sacraments.

I answer that, Necessity of end, of which we speak now, is twofold. First, a thing may be necessary so that without it the end cannot be attained; thus food is necessary for human life. And this is simple necessity of end. Secondly, a thing is said to be necessary, if, without it, the end cannot be attained so becomingly: thus a horse is necessary for a journey. But this is not simple necessity of end.

In the first way, three sacraments are necessary for salvation. Two of them are necessary to the individual; Baptism, simply and absolutely; Penance, in the case of mortal sin committed after Baptism; while the sacrament of order is necessary to the Church, since "where there is no governor the people shall fall" (Prov. 11:14).

But in the second way the other sacraments are necessary. For in a sense Confirmation perfects Baptism; Extreme Unction perfects Penance; while Matrimony, by multiplying them, preserves the numbers in the Church.

Reply to Objection 1: For a thing not to be superfluous it is enough if it be necessary either in the first or the second way. It is thus that the sacraments are necessary, as stated above.

Reply to Objection 2: These words of our Lord are to be understood of spiritual, and not of merely sacramental, eating, as Augustine explains (Tract. xxvi super Joan.).

Reply to Objection 3: Although contempt of any of the sacraments is a hindrance to salvation, yet it does not amount to contempt of the sacrament, if anyone does not trouble to receive a sacrament that is not necessary for salvation. Else those who do not receive orders, and those who do not contract Matrimony, would be guilty of contempt of those sacraments.

Day 293

OF THE SACRAMENT OF BAPTISM (TWELVE ARTICLES)

We have now to consider each sacrament specially: (1) Baptism; (2) Confirmation; (3) the Eucharist; (4) Penance; (5) Extreme Unction; (6) Order; (7) Matrimony.

Concerning the first, our consideration will be twofold: (1) of Baptism itself; (2) of things preparatory to Baptism.

Concerning the first, four points arise for our consideration: (1) Things pertaining to the sacrament of Baptism; (2) The minister of this sacrament; (3) The recipients of this sacrament; (4) The effect of this sacrament.

Concerning the first there are twelve points of inquiry:

(1) What is Baptism? Is it a washing?

(2) Of the institution of this sacrament;

(3) Whether water be the proper matter of this sacrament?

(4) Whether plain water be required?

(5) Whether this be a suitable form of this sacrament: "I baptize thee in the name of the Father, and of the Son, and of the Holy Ghost"?

(6) Whether one could baptize with this form: "I baptize thee in the name of Christ?"

(7) Whether immersion is necessary for Baptism?

(8) Whether trine immersion is necessary?

(9) Whether Baptism can be reiterated?

(10) Of the Baptismal rite;

(11) Of the various kinds of Baptism;

(12) Of the comparison between various Baptisms.

Whether Baptism is the mere washing?

Objection 1: It seems that Baptism is not the mere washing. For the washing of the body is something transitory: but Baptism is something permanent. Therefore Baptism is not the mere washing; but rather is it "the regeneration, the seal, the safeguarding, the enlightenment," as Damascene says (De Fide Orth. iv).

Objection 2: Further, Hugh of St. Victor says (De Sacram. ii) that "Baptism is water sanctified by God's word for the blotting out of sins." But the washing itself is not water, but a certain use of water.

Objection 3: Further, Augustine says (Tract. lxxx super Joan.): "The word is added to the element, and this becomes a sacrament." Now, the element is the water. Therefore Baptism is the water and not the washing.

On the contrary, It is written (Ecclus. 34:30): "He that washeth himself [baptizatur] after touching the dead, if he touch him again, what does his washing avail?" It seems, therefore, that Baptism is the washing or bathing.

I answer that, In the sacrament of Baptism, three things may be considered: namely, that which is "sacrament only"; that which is "reality and sacrament"; and that which is "reality only." That which is sacrament only, is something visible and outward; the sign, namely, of the inward effect: for such is the very nature of a sacrament. And this outward something that can be perceived by the sense is both the water itself and its use, which is the washing. Hence some have thought that the water itself is the sacrament: which seems to be the meaning of the passage quoted from Hugh of St. Victor. For in the general definition of a sacrament he says that it is "a material element": and in defining Baptism he says it is "water."

But this is not true. For since the sacraments of the New Law effect a certain sanctification, there the sacrament is completed where the sanctification is completed. Now, the sanctification is not completed in water; but a certain sanctifying instrumental virtue, not permanent but transient, passes from the water, in which it is, into man who is the subject of true sanctification. Consequently the sacrament is not completed in the very water, but in applying the water to man, i.e. in the washing. Hence the Master (iv, 3) says that "Baptism is the outward washing of the body done together with the prescribed form of words."

The Baptismal character is both reality and sacrament: because it is something real signified by the outward washing; and a sacramental sign of the inward justification: and this last is the reality only, in this sacrament---namely, the reality signified and not signifying.

Reply to Objection 1: That which is both sacrament and reality---i.e. the character---and that which is reality only---i.e. the inward justification---remain: the character remains and is indelible, as stated above ([4415]Q[63], A[5]); the justification remains, but can be lost. Consequently Damascene defined Baptism, not as to that which is done outwardly, and is the sacrament only; but as to that which is inward. Hence he sets down two things as pertaining to the character---namely, "seal" and "safeguarding"; inasmuch as the character which is called a seal, so far as itself is concerned, safeguards the soul in good. He also sets down two things as pertaining to the ultimate reality of the sacrament---namely, "regeneration" which refers to the fact that man by being baptized begins the new life of righteousness; and "enlightenment," which refers especially to faith, by which man receives spiritual life, according to Habac 2 (Heb. 10:38; cf. Habac 2:4): "But (My) just man liveth by faith"; and Baptism is a sort of protestation of faith; whence it is called the "Sacrament of Faith." Likewise Dionysius defined Baptism by its relation to the other sacraments, saying (Eccl. Hier. ii) that it is "the principle that forms the habits of the soul for the reception of those most holy words and sacraments"; and again by its relation to heavenly glory, which is the universal end of all the sacraments, when he adds, "preparing the way for us, whereby we mount to the repose of the heavenly kingdom"; and again as to the beginning of spiritual life, when he adds, "the conferring of our most sacred and Godlike regeneration."

Reply to Objection 2: As already stated, the opinion of Hugh of St. Victor on this question is not to be followed. Nevertheless the saying that "Baptism is water" may be verified in so far as water is the material principle of Baptism: and thus there would be "causal predication."

Reply to Objection 3: When the words are added, the element becomes a sacrament, not in the element itself, but in man, to whom the element is applied, by being used in washing him. Indeed, this is signified by those very words which are added to the element, when we say: "I baptize thee," etc.

Whether Baptism was instituted after Christ's Passion?

Objection 1: It seems that Baptism was instituted after Christ's Passion. For the cause precedes the effect. Now Christ's Passion operates in the sacraments of the New Law. Therefore Christ's Passion precedes the institution of the sacraments of the New Law: especially the sacrament of Baptism since the Apostle says (Rom. 6:3): "All we, who are baptized in Christ Jesus, are baptized in His death," etc.

Objection 2: Further, the sacraments of the New Law derive their efficacy from the mandate of Christ. But Christ gave the disciples the mandate of Baptism after His Passion and Resurrection, when He said: "Going, teach ye all nations, baptizing them in the name of the Father," etc. (Mat. 28:19). Therefore it seems that Baptism was instituted after Christ's Passion.

Objection 3: Further, Baptism is a necessary sacrament, as stated above ([4416]Q[65] , A[4]): wherefore, seemingly, it must have been binding on man as soon as it was instituted. But before Christ's Passion men were not bound to be baptized: for Circumcision was still in force, which was supplanted by Baptism. Therefore it seems that Baptism was not instituted before Christ's Passion.

On the contrary, Augustine says in a sermon on the Epiphany (Append. Serm., clxxxv): "As soon as Christ was plunged into the waters, the waters washed away the sins of all." But this was before Christ's Passion. Therefore Baptism was instituted before Christ's Passion.

I answer that, As stated above ([4417]Q[62], A[1]), sacraments derive from their institution the power of conferring grace. Wherefore it seems that a sacrament is then instituted, when it receives the power of producing its effect. Now Baptism received this power when Christ was baptized. Consequently Baptism was truly instituted then, if we consider it as a sacrament. But the obligation of receiving this sacrament was proclaimed to mankind after the Passion and Resurrection. First, because Christ's Passion put an end to the figurative sacraments, which were supplanted by Baptism and the other sacraments of the New Law. Secondly, because by Baptism man is "made conformable" to Christ's Passion and Resurrection, in so far as he dies to sin and begins to live anew unto righteousness. Consequently it behooved Christ to suffer and to rise again, before proclaiming to man his obligation of conforming himself to Christ's Death and Resurrection.

Reply to Objection 1: Even before Christ's Passion, Baptism, inasmuch as it foreshadowed it, derived its efficacy therefrom; but not in the same way as the sacraments of the Old Law. For these were mere figures: whereas Baptism derived the power of justifying from Christ Himself, to Whose power the Passion itself owed its saving virtue.

Reply to Objection 2: It was not meet that men should be restricted to a number of figures by Christ, Who came to fulfil and replace the figure by His reality. Therefore before His Passion He did not make Baptism obligatory as soon as it was instituted; but wished men to become accustomed to its use; especially in regard to the Jews, to whom all things were figurative, as Augustine says (Contra Faust. iv). But after His Passion and Resurrection He made Baptism obligatory, not only on the Jews, but also on the Gentiles, when He gave the commandment: "Going, teach ye all nations."

Reply to Objection 3: Sacraments are not obligatory except when we are commanded to receive them. And this was not before the Passion, as stated above. For our Lord's words to Nicodemus (Jn. 3:5), "Unless a man be born again of water and the Holy Ghost, he cannot enter into the kingdom of God, seem to refer to the future rather than to the present."

Whether water is the proper matter of Baptism?

Objection 1: It seems that water is not the proper matter of Baptism. For Baptism, according to Dionysius (Eccl. Hier. v) and Damascene (De Fide Orth. iv), has a power of enlightening. But enlightenment is a special characteristic of fire. Therefore Baptism should be conferred with fire rather than with water: and all the more since John the Baptist said when foretelling Christ's Baptism (Mat. 3:11): "He shall baptize you in the Holy Ghost and fire."

Objection 2: Further, the washing away of sins is signified in Baptism. But many other things besides water are employed in washing, such as wine, oil, and such like. Therefore Baptism can be conferred with these also; and consequently water is not the proper matter of Baptism.

Objection 3: Further, the sacraments of the Church flowed from the side of Christ hanging on the cross, as stated above ([4418]Q[62], A[5]). But not only water flowed therefrom, but also blood. Therefore it seems that Baptism can also be conferred with blood. And this seems to be more in keeping with the effect of Baptism, because it is written (Apoc. 1:5): "(Who) washed us from our sins in His own blood."

Objection 4: Further, as Augustine (cf. Master of the Sentences, iv, 3) and Bede (Exposit. in Luc. iii, 21) say, Christ, by "the touch of His most pure flesh, endowed the waters with a regenerating and cleansing virtue." But all waters are not connected with the waters of the Jordan which Christ touched with His flesh. Consequently it seems that Baptism cannot be conferred with any water; and therefore water, as such, is not the proper matter of Baptism.

Objection 5: Further, if water, as such, were the proper matter of Baptism, there would be no need to do anything to the water before using it for Baptism. But in solemn Baptism the water which is used for baptizing, is exorcized and blessed. Therefore it seems that water, as such, is not the proper matter of Baptism.

On the contrary, our Lord said (Jn. 3:5): "Unless a man be born again of water and the Holy Ghost, he cannot enter into the kingdom of God."

I answer that, By Divine institution water is the proper matter of Baptism; and with reason. First, by reason of the very nature of Baptism, which is a regeneration unto spiritual life. And this answers to the nature of water in a special degree; wherefore seeds, from which all living things, viz. plants and animals are generated, are moist and akin to water. For this reason certain philosophers held that water is the first principle of all things.

Secondly, in regard to the effects of Baptism, to which the properties of water correspond. For by reason of its moistness it cleanses; and hence it fittingly signifies and causes the cleansing from sins. By reason of its coolness it tempers superfluous heat: wherefore it fittingly mitigates the concupiscence of the fomes. By reason of its transparency, it is susceptive of light; hence its adaptability to Baptism as the "sacrament of Faith."

Thirdly, because it is suitable for the signification of the mysteries of Christ, by which we are justified. For, as Chrysostom says (Hom. xxv in Joan.) on Jn. 3:5, "Unless a man be born again," etc., "When we dip our heads under the water as in a kind of tomb our old man is buried, and being submerged is hidden below, and thence he rises again renewed."

Fourthly, because by being so universal and abundant, it is a matter suitable to our need of this sacrament: for it can easily be obtained everywhere.

Reply to Objection 1: Fire enlightens actively. But he who is baptized does not become an enlightener, but is enlightened by faith, which "cometh by hearing" (Rom. 10:17). Consequently water is more suitable, than fire, for Baptism.

But when we find it said: "He shall baptize you in the Holy Ghost and fire," we may understand fire, as Jerome says (In Matth. ii), to mean the Holy Ghost, Who appeared above the disciples under the form of fiery tongues (Acts 2:3). Or we may understand it to mean tribulation, as Chrysostom says (Hom. iii in Matth.): because tribulation washes away sin, and tempers concupiscence. Or again, as Hilary says (Super Matth. ii) that "when we have been baptized in the Holy Ghost," we still have to be "perfected by the fire of the judgment."

Reply to Objection 2: Wine and oil are not so commonly used for washing, as water. Neither do they wash so efficiently: for whatever is washed with them, contracts a certain smell therefrom; which is not the case if water be used. Moreover, they are not so universal or so abundant as water.

Reply to Objection 3: Water flowed from Christ's side to wash us; blood, to redeem us. Wherefore blood belongs to the sacrament of the Eucharist, while water belongs to the sacrament of Baptism. Yet this latter sacrament derives its cleansing virtue from the power of Christ's blood.

Reply to Objection 4: Christ's power flowed into all waters, by reason of, not connection of place, but likeness of species, as Augustine says in a sermon on the Epiphany (Append. Serm. cxxxv): "The blessing that flowed from the Saviour's Baptism, like a mystic river, swelled the course of every stream, and filled the channels of every spring."

Reply to Objection 5: The blessing of the water is not essential to Baptism, but belongs to a certain solemnity, whereby the devotion of the faithful is aroused, and the cunning of the devil hindered from impeding the baptismal effect.

Whether plain water is necessary for Baptism?

Objection 1: It seems that plain water is not necessary for Baptism. For the water which we have is not plain water; as appears especially in sea-water, in which there is a considerable proportion of the earthly element, as the Philosopher shows (Meteor. ii). Yet this water may be used for Baptism. Therefore plain and pure water is not necessary for Baptism.

Objection 2: Further, in the solemn celebration of Baptism, chrism is poured into the water. But this seems to take away the purity and plainness of the water. Therefore pure and plain water is not necessary for Baptism.

Objection 3: Further, the water that flowed from the side of Christ hanging on the cross was a figure of Baptism, as stated above (A[3], ad 3). But that water, seemingly, was not pure, because the elements do not exist actually in a mixed body, such as Christ's. Therefore it seems that pure or plain water is not necessary for Baptism.

Objection 4: Further, lye does not seem to be pure water, for it has the properties of heating and drying, which are contrary to those of water. Nevertheless it seems that lye can be used for Baptism; for the water of the Baths can be so used, which has filtered through a sulphurous vein, just as lye percolates through ashes. Therefore it seems that plain water is not necessary for Baptism.

Objection 5: Further, rose-water is distilled from roses, just as chemical waters are distilled from certain bodies. But seemingly, such like waters may be used in Baptism; just as rain-water, which is distilled from vapors. Since, therefore, such waters are not pure and plain water, it seems that pure and plain water is not necessary for Baptism.

On the contrary, The proper matter of Baptism is water, as stated above [4419](A[3]). But plain water alone has the nature of water. Therefore pure plain water is necessary for Baptism.

I answer that, Water may cease to be pure or plain water in two ways: first, by being mixed with another body; secondly, by alteration. And each of these may happen in a twofold manner; artificially and naturally. Now art fails in the operation of nature: because nature gives the substantial form, which art cannot give; for whatever form is given by art is accidental; except perchance when art applies a proper agent to its proper matter, as fire to a combustible; in which manner animals are produced from certain things by way of putrefaction.

Whatever artificial change, then, takes place in the water, whether by mixture or by alteration, the water's nature is not changed. Consequently such water can be used for Baptism: unless perhaps such a small quantity of water be mixed artificially with a body that the compound is something other than water; thus mud is earth rather than water, and diluted wine is wine rather than water.

But if the change be natural, sometimes it destroys the nature of the water; and this is when by a natural process water enters into the substance of a mixed body: thus water changed into the juice of the grape is wine, wherefore it has not the nature of water. Sometimes, however, there may be a natural change of the water, without destruction of species: and this, both by alteration, as we may see in the case of water heated by the sun; and by mixture, as when the water of a river has become muddy by being mixed with particles of earth.

We must therefore say that any water may be used for Baptism, no matter how much it may be changed, as long as the species of water is not destroyed; but if the species of water be destroyed, it cannot be used for Baptism.

Reply to Objection 1: The change in sea-water and in other waters which we have to hand, is not so great as to destroy the species of water. And therefore such waters may be used for Baptism.

Reply to Objection 2: Chrism does not destroy the nature of the water by being mixed with it: just as neither is water changed wherein meat and the like are boiled: except the substance boiled be so dissolved that the liquor be of a nature foreign to water; in this we may be guided by the specific gravity [spissitudine]. If, however, from the liquor thus thickened plain water be strained, it can be used for Baptism: just as water strained from mud, although mud cannot be used for baptizing.

Reply to Objection 3: The water which flowed from the side of Christ hanging on the cross, was not the phlegmatic humor, as some have supposed. For a liquid of this kind cannot be used for Baptism, as neither can the blood of an animal, or wine, or any liquid extracted from plants. It was pure water gushing forth miraculously like the blood from a dead body, to prove the reality of our Lord's body, and confute the error of the Manichees: water, which is one of the four elements, showing Christ's body to be composed of the four elements; blood, proving that it was composed of the four humors.

Reply to Objection 4: Baptism may be conferred with lye and the waters of Sulphur Baths: because such like waters are not incorporated, artificially or naturally, with certain mixed bodies, and suffer only a certain alteration by passing through certain bodies.

Reply to Objection 5: Rose-water is a liquid distilled from roses: consequently it cannot be used for Baptism. For the same reason chemical waters cannot be used, as neither can wine. Nor does the comparison hold with rain-water, which for the most part is formed by the condensing of vapors, themselves formed from water, and contains a minimum of the liquid matter from mixed bodies; which liquid matter by the force of nature, which is stronger than art, is transformed in this process of condensation into real water, a result which cannot be produced artificially. Consequently rain-water retains no properties of any mixed body; which cannot be said of rose-water or chemical waters.

Whether this be a suitable form of Baptism: "I baptize thee in the name of the Father, and of the Son, and of the Holy Ghost"?

Objection 1: It seems that this is not a suitable form of Baptism: "I baptize thee in the name of the Father, and of the Son, and of the Holy Ghost." For action should be ascribed to the principal agent rather than to the minister. Now the minister of a sacrament acts as an instrument, as stated above ([4420]Q[64], A[1]); while the principal agent in Baptism is Christ, according to Jn. 1:33, "He upon Whom thou shalt see the Spirit descending and remaining upon Him, He it is that baptizeth." It is therefore unbecoming for the minister to say, "I baptize thee": the more so that "Ego" [I] is understood in the word "baptizo" [I baptize], so that it seems redundant.

Objection 2: Further, there is no need for a man who does an action, to make mention of the action done; thus he who teaches, need not say, "I teach you." Now our Lord gave at the same time the precepts both of baptizing and of teaching, when He said (Mat. 28:19): "Going, teach ye all nations," etc. Therefore there is no need in the form of Baptism to mention the action of baptizing.

Objection 3: Further, the person baptized sometimes does not understand the words; for instance, if he be deaf, or a child. But it is useless to address such a one; according to Ecclus. 32:6: "Where there is no hearing, pour not out words." Therefore it is unfitting to address the person baptized with these words: "I baptize thee."

Objection 4: Further, it may happen that several are baptized by several at the same time; thus the apostles on one day baptized three thousand, and on another, five thousand (Acts 2, 4). Therefore the form of Baptism should not be limited to the singular number in the words, "I baptize thee": but one should be able to say, "We baptize you."

Objection 5: Further, Baptism derives its power from Christ's Passion. But Baptism is sanctified by the form. Therefore it seems that Christ's Passion should be mentioned in the form of Baptism.

Objection 6: Further, a name signifies a thing's property. But there are three Personal Properties of the Divine Persons, as stated in the [4421]FP, Q[32], A[3]. Therefore we should not say, "in the name," but "in the names of the Father, and of the Son, and of the Holy Ghost."

Objection 7: Further, the Person of the Father is designated not only by the name Father, but also by that of "Unbegotten and Begetter"; and the Son by those of "Word," "Image," and "Begotten"; and the Holy Ghost by those of "Gift," "Love," and the "Proceeding One." Therefore it seems that Baptism is valid if conferred in these names.

On the contrary, our Lord said (Mat. 28:19): "Going . . . teach ye all nations, baptizing them in the name of the Father, and of the Son, and of the Holy Ghost."

I answer that, Baptism receives its consecration from its form, according to Eph. 5:26: "Cleansing it by the laver of water in the word of life." And Augustine says (De Unico Baptismo iv) that "Baptism is consecrated by the words of the Gospel." Consequently the cause of Baptism needs to be expressed in the baptismal form. Now this cause is twofold; the principal cause from which it derives its virtue, and this is the Blessed Trinity; and the instrumental cause, viz. the minister who confers the sacrament outwardly. Wherefore both causes should be expressed in the form of Baptism. Now the minister is designated by the words, "I baptize thee"; and the principal cause in the words, "in the name of the Father, and of the Son, and of the Holy Ghost." Therefore this is the suitable form of Baptism: "I baptize thee in the name of the Father, and of the Son, and of the Holy Ghost."

Reply to Objection 1: Action is attributed to an instrument as to the immediate agent; but to the principal agent inasmuch as the instrument acts in virtue thereof. Consequently it is fitting that in the baptismal form the minister should be mentioned as performing the act of baptizing, in the words, "I baptize thee"; indeed, our Lord attributed to the ministers the act of baptizing, when He said:

"Baptizing them," etc. But the principal cause is indicated as conferring the sacrament by His own power, in the words, "in the name of the Father, and of the Son, and of the Holy Ghost": for Christ does not baptize without the Father and the Holy Ghost.

The Greeks, however, do not attribute the act of baptizing to the minister, in order to avoid the error of those who in the past ascribed the baptismal power to the baptizers, saying (1 Cor. 1:12): "I am of Paul . . . and I of Cephas." Wherefore they use the form: "May the servant of Christ, N . . ., be baptized, in the name of the Father," etc. And since the action performed by the minister is expressed with the invocation of the Trinity, the sacrament is validly conferred. As to the addition of "Ego" in our form, it is not essential; but it is added in order to lay greater stress on the intention.

Reply to Objection 2: Since a man may be washed with water for several reasons, the purpose for which it is done must be expressed by the words of the form. And this is not done by saying: "In the name of the Father, and of the Son, and of the Holy Ghost"; because we are bound to do all things in that Name (Col. 3:17). Wherefore unless the act of baptizing be expressed, either as we do, or as the Greeks do, the sacrament is not valid; according to the decretal of Alexander III: "If anyone dip a child thrice in the water in the name of the Father, and of the Son, and of the Holy Ghost, Amen, without saying, I baptize thee in the name of the Father, and of the Son, and of the Holy Ghost, Amen, the child is not baptized."

Reply to Objection 3: The words which are uttered in the sacramental forms, are said not merely for the purpose of signification, but also for the purpose of efficiency, inasmuch as they derive efficacy from that Word, by Whom "all things were made." Consequently they are becomingly addressed not only to men, but also to insensible creatures; for instance, when we say: "I exorcize thee, creature salt" (Roman Ritual).

Reply to Objection 4: Several cannot baptize one at the same time: because an action is multiplied according to the number of the agents, if it be done perfectly by each. So that if two were to combine, of whom one were mute, and unable to utter the words, and the other were without hands, and unable to perform the action, they could not both baptize at the same time, one saying the words and the other performing the action.

On the other hand, in a case of necessity, several could be baptized at the same time; for no single one of them would receive more than one baptism. But it would be necessary, in that case, to say: "I baptize ye." Nor would this be a change of form, because "ye" is the same as "thee and thee." Whereas "we" does not mean "I and I," but "I and thou"; so that this would be a change of form.

Likewise it would be a change of form to say, "I baptize myself": consequently no one can baptize himself. For this reason did Christ choose to be baptized by John (Extra, De Baptismo et ejus effectu, cap. Debitum).

Reply to Objection 5: Although Christ's Passion is the principal cause as compared to the minister, yet it is an instrumental cause as compared to the Blessed Trinity. For this reason the Trinity is mentioned rather than Christ's Passion.

Reply to Objection 6: Although there are three personal names of the three Persons, there is but one essential name. Now the Divine power which works in Baptism, pertains to the Essence; and therefore we say, "in the name," and not, "in the names."

Reply to Objection 7: Just as water is used in Baptism, because it is more commonly employed in washing, so for the purpose of designating the three Persons, in the form of Baptism, those names are chosen, which are generally used, in a particular language, to signify the Persons. Nor is the sacrament valid if conferred in any other names.

Whether Baptism can be conferred in the name of Christ?

Objection 1: It seems that Baptism can be conferred in the name of Christ. For just as there is "one Faith," so is there "one Baptism" (Eph. 4:5). But it is related (Acts 8:12) that "in the name of Jesus Christ they were baptized, both men and women." Therefore now also can Baptism be conferred in the name of Christ.

Objection 2: Further, Ambrose says (De Spir. Sanct. i): "If you mention Christ, you designate both the Father by Whom He was anointed, and the Son Himself, Who was anointed, and the Holy Ghost with Whom He was anointed." But Baptism can be conferred in the name of the Trinity: therefore also in the name of Christ.

Objection 3: Further, Pope Nicholas I, answering questions put to him by the Bulgars, said: "Those who have been baptized in the name of the Trinity, or only in the name of Christ, as we read in the Acts of the Apostles (it is all the same, as Blessed Ambrose saith), must not be rebaptized." But they would be baptized again if they had not been validly baptized with that form. Therefore Baptism can be celebrated in the name of Christ by using this form: "I baptize thee in the name of Christ."

On the contrary, Pope Pelagius II wrote to the Bishop Gaudentius: "If any people living in your Worship's neighborhood, avow that they have been baptized in the name of the Lord only, without any hesitation baptize them again in the name of the Blessed Trinity, when they come in quest of the Catholic Faith." Didymus, too, says (De Spir. Sanct.): "If indeed there be such a one with a mind so foreign to faith as to baptize while omitting one of the aforesaid names," viz. of the three Persons, "he baptizes invalidly."

I answer that, As stated above ([4422]Q[64], A[3]), the sacraments derive their efficacy from Christ's institution. Consequently, if any of those things be omitted which Christ instituted in regard to a sacrament, it is invalid; save by special dispensation of Him Who did not bind His power to the sacraments. Now Christ commanded the sacrament of Baptism to be given with the invocation of the Trinity. And consequently whatever is lacking to the full invocation of the Trinity, destroys the integrity of Baptism.

Nor does it matter that in the name of one Person another is implied, as the name of the Son is implied in that of the Father, or that he who mentions the name of only one Person may believe aright in the Three; because just as a sacrament requires sensible matter, so does it require a sensible form. Hence, for the validity of the sacrament it is not enough to imply or to believe in the Trinity, unless the Trinity be expressed in sensible words. For this reason at Christ's Baptism, wherein was the source of the sanctification of our Baptism, the Trinity was present in sensible signs: viz. the Father in the voice, the Son in the human nature, the Holy Ghost in the dove.

Reply to Objection 1: It was by a special revelation from Christ that in the primitive Church the apostles baptized in the name of Christ; in order that the name of Christ, which was hateful to Jews and Gentiles, might become an object of veneration, in that the Holy Ghost was given in Baptism at the invocation of that Name.

Reply to Objection 2: Ambrose here gives this reason why exception could, without inconsistency, be allowed in the primitive Church; namely, because the whole Trinity is implied in the name of Christ, and therefore the form prescribed by Christ in the Gospel was observed in its integrity, at least implicitly.

Reply to Objection 3: Pope Nicolas confirms his words by quoting the two authorities given in the preceding objections: wherefore the answer to this is clear from the two solutions given above.

Whether immersion in water is necessary for Baptism?

Objection 1: It seems that immersion in water is necessary for Baptism. Because it is written (Eph. 4:5): "One faith, one baptism." But in many parts of the world the ordinary way of baptizing is by immersion. Therefore it seems that there can be no Baptism without immersion.

Objection 2: Further, the Apostle says (Rom. 6:3,4): "All we who are baptized in Christ Jesus, are baptized in His death: for we are buried together with Him, by Baptism into death." But this is done by immersion: for Chrysostom says on Jn. 3:5: "Unless a man be born again of water and the Holy Ghost," etc.: "When we dip our heads under the water as in a kind of tomb, our old man is buried, and being submerged, is hidden below, and thence he rises again renewed." Therefore it seems that immersion is essential to Baptism.

Objection 3: Further, if Baptism is valid without total immersion of the body, it would follow that it would be equally sufficient to pour water over any part of the body. But this seems unreasonable; since original sin, to remedy which is the principal purpose of Baptism, is not in only one part of the body. Therefore it seems that immersion is necessary for Baptism, and that mere sprinkling is not enough.

On the contrary, It is written (Heb. 10:22): "Let us draw near with a true heart in fulness of faith, having our hearts sprinkled from an evil conscience, and our bodies washed with clean water."

I answer that, In the sacrament of Baptism water is put to the use of a washing of the body, whereby to signify the inward washing away of sins. Now washing may be done with water not only by immersion, but also by sprinkling or pouring. And, therefore, although it is safer to baptize by immersion, because this is the more ordinary fashion, yet Baptism can be conferred by sprinkling or also by pouring, according to Ezech. 36:25: "I will pour upon you clean water," as also the Blessed Lawrence is related to have baptized. And this especially in cases of urgency: either because there is a great number to be baptized, as was clearly the case in Acts 2 and 4, where we read that on one day three thousand believed, and on another five thousand: or through there being but a small supply of water, or through feebleness of the minister, who cannot hold up the candidate for Baptism; or through feebleness of the candidate, whose life might be endangered by immersion. We must therefore conclude that immersion is not necessary for Baptism.

Reply to Objection 1: What is accidental to a thing does not diversify its essence. Now bodily washing with water is essential to Baptism: wherefore Baptism is called a "laver," according to Eph. 5:26: "Cleansing it by the laver of water in the word of life." But that the washing be done this or that way, is accidental to Baptism. And consequently such diversity does not destroy the oneness of Baptism.

Reply to Objection 2: Christ's burial is more clearly represented by immersion: wherefore this manner of baptizing is more frequently in use and more commendable. Yet in the other ways of baptizing it is represented after a fashion, albeit not so clearly; for no matter how the washing is done, the body of a man, or some part thereof, is put under water, just as Christ's body was put under the earth.

Reply to Objection 3: The principal part of the body, especially in relation to the exterior members, is the head, wherein all the senses, both interior and exterior, flourish. And therefore, if the whole body cannot be covered with water, because of the scarcity of water, or because of some other reason, it is necessary to pour water over the head, in which the principle of animal life is made manifest.

And although original sin is transmitted through the members that serve for procreation, yet those members are not to be sprinkled in preference to the head, because by Baptism the transmission of original sin to the offspring by the act of procreation is not deleted, but the soul is freed from the stain and debt of sin which it has contracted. Consequently that part of the body should be washed in preference, in which the works of the soul are made manifest.

Nevertheless in the Old Law the remedy against original sin was affixed to the member of procreation; because He through Whom original sin was to be removed, was yet to be born of the seed of Abraham, whose faith was signified by circumcision according to Rom. 4:11.

Whether trine immersion is essential to Baptism?

Objection 1: It seems that trine immersion is essential to Baptism. For Augustine says in a sermon on the Symbol, addressed to the Neophytes: "Rightly were you dipped three times, since you were baptized in the name of the Trinity. Rightly were you dipped three times, because you were baptized in the name of Jesus Christ, Who on the third day rose again from the dead. For that thrice repeated immersion reproduces the burial of the Lord by which you were buried with Christ in Baptism." Now both seem to be essential to Baptism, namely, that in Baptism the Trinity of Persons should be signified, and that we should be conformed to Christ's burial. Therefore it seems that trine immersion is essential to Baptism.

Objection 2: Further, the sacraments derive their efficacy from Christ's mandate. But trine immersion was commanded by Christ: for Pope Pelagius II wrote to Bishop Gaudentius: "The Gospel precept given by our Lord God Himself, our Saviour Jesus Christ, admonishes us to confer the sacrament of Baptism to each one in the name of the Trinity and also with trine immersion." Therefore, just as it is essential to Baptism to call on the name of the Trinity, so is it essential to baptize by trine immersion.

Objection 3: Further, if trine immersion be not essential to Baptism, it follows that the sacrament of Baptism is conferred at the first immersion; so that if a second or third immersion be added, it seems that Baptism is conferred a second or third time. which is absurd. Therefore one immersion does not suffice for the sacrament of Baptism, and trine immersion is essential thereto.

On the contrary, Gregory wrote to the Bishop Leander: "It cannot be in any way reprehensible to baptize an infant with either a trine or a single immersion: since the Trinity can be represented in the three immersions, and the unity of the Godhead in one immersion."

I answer that As stated above (A[7], ad 1), washing with water is of itself required for Baptism, being essential to the sacrament: whereas the mode of washing is accidental to the sacrament. Consequently, as Gregory in the words above quoted explains, both single and trine immersion are lawful considered in themselves; since one immersion signifies the oneness of Christ's death and of the Godhead; while trine immersion signifies the three days of Christ's burial, and also the Trinity of Persons.

But for various reasons, according as the Church has ordained, one mode has been in practice, at one time, the other at another time. For since from the very earliest days of the Church some have had false notions concerning the Trinity, holding that Christ is a mere man, and that He is not called the "Son of God" or "God" except by reason of His merit, which was chiefly in His death; for this reason they did not baptize in the name of the Trinity, but in memory of Christ's death, and with one immersion. And this was condemned in the early Church. Wherefore in the Apostolic Canons (xlix) we read: "If any priest or bishop confer baptism not with the trine immersion in the one administration, but with one immersion, which baptism is said to be conferred by some in the death of the Lord, let him be deposed": for our Lord did not say, "Baptize ye in My death," but "In the name of the Father and of the Son, and of the Holy Ghost."

Later on, however, there arose the error of certain schismatics and heretics who rebaptized: as Augustine (Super. Joan., cf. De Haeres. lxix) relates of the Donatists. Wherefore, in detestation of their error, only one immersion was ordered to be made, by the (fourth) council of Toledo, in the acts of which we read: "In order to avoid the scandal of schism or the practice of heretical teaching let us hold to the single baptismal immersion."

But now that this motive has ceased, trine immersion is universally observed in Baptism: and consequently anyone baptizing otherwise would sin gravely, through not following the ritual of the Church. It would, however, be valid Baptism.

Reply to Objection 1: The Trinity acts as principal agent in Baptism. Now the likeness of the agent enters into the effect, in regard to the form and not in regard to the matter. Wherefore the Trinity is signified in Baptism by the words of the form. Nor is it essential for the Trinity to be signified by the manner in which the matter is used; although this is done to make the signification clearer.

In like manner Christ's death is sufficiently represented in the one immersion. And the three days of His burial were not necessary for our salvation, because even if He had been buried or dead for one day, this would have been enough to consummate our redemption: yet those three days were ordained unto the manifestation of the reality of His death, as stated above ([4423]Q[53], A[2]). It is therefore clear that neither on the part of the Trinity, nor on the part of Christ's Passion, is the trine immersion essential to the sacrament.

Reply to Objection 2: Pope Pelagius understood the trine immersion to be ordained by Christ in its equivalent; in the sense that Christ commanded Baptism to be conferred "in the name of the Father, and of the Son, and of the Holy Ghost." Nor can we argue from the form to the use of the matter, as stated above (ad 1).

Reply to Objection 3: As stated above ([4424]Q[64], A[8]), the intention is essential to Baptism. Consequently, one Baptism results from the intention of the Church's minister, who intends to confer one Baptism by a trine immersion. Wherefore Jerome says on Eph. 4:5,6: "Though the Baptism," i.e. the immersion, "be thrice repeated, on account of the mystery of the Trinity, yet it is reputed as one Baptism."

If, however, the intention were to confer one Baptism at each immersion together with the repetition of the words of the form, it would be a sin, in itself, because it would be a repetition of Baptism.

Day 294

Whether Baptism may be reiterated?

Objection 1: It seems that Baptism may be reiterated. For Baptism was instituted, seemingly, in order to wash away sins. But sins are reiterated. Therefore much more should Baptism be reiterated: because Christ's mercy surpasses man's guilt.

Objection 2: Further, John the Baptist received special commendation from Christ, Who said of him (Mat. 11:11): "There hath not risen among them that are born of women, a greater than John the Baptist." But those whom John had baptized were baptized again, according to Acts 19:1-7, where it is stated that Paul rebaptized those who had received the Baptism of John. Much more, therefore, should those be rebaptized, who have been baptized by heretics or sinners.

Objection 3: Further, it was decreed in the Council of Nicaea (Can. xix) that if "any of the Paulianists or Cataphrygians should be converted to the Catholic Church, they were to be baptized": and this seemingly should be said in regard to other heretics. Therefore those whom the heretics have baptized, should be baptized again.

Objection 4: Further, Baptism is necessary for salvation. But sometimes there is a doubt about the baptism of those who really have been baptized. Therefore it seems that they should be baptized again.

Objection 5: Further, the Eucharist is a more perfect sacrament than Baptism, as stated above ([4425]Q[65], A[3]). But the sacrament of the Eucharist is reiterated. Much more reason, therefore, is there for Baptism to be reiterated.

On the contrary, It is written, (Eph. 4:5): "One faith, one Baptism."

I answer that, Baptism cannot be reiterated.

First, because Baptism is a spiritual regeneration; inasmuch as a man dies to the old life, and begins to lead the new life. Whence it is written (Jn. 3:5): "Unless a man be born again of water and the Holy Ghost, He cannot see [Vulg.: 'enter into'] the kingdom of God." Now one man can be begotten but once. Wherefore Baptism cannot be reiterated, just as neither can carnal generation. Hence Augustine says on Jn. 3:4: "'Can he enter a second time into his mother's womb and be born again': So thou," says he, "must understand the birth of the Spirit, as Nicodemus understood the birth of the flesh . . . . As there is no return to the womb, so neither is there to Baptism."

Secondly, because "we are baptized in Christ's death," by which we die unto sin and rise again unto "newness of life" (cf. Rom. 6:3,4). Now "Christ died" but "once" (Rom. 6:10). Wherefore neither should Baptism be reiterated. For this reason (Heb. 6:6) is it said against some who wished to be baptized again: "Crucifying again to themselves the Son of God"; on which the gloss observes: "Christ's one death hallowed the one Baptism."

Thirdly, because Baptism imprints a character, which is indelible, and is conferred with a certain consecration. Wherefore, just as other consecrations are not reiterated in the Church, so neither is Baptism. This is the view expressed by Augustine, who says (Contra Epist. Parmen. ii) that "the military character is not renewed": and that "the sacrament of Christ is not less enduring than this bodily mark, since we see that not even apostates are deprived of Baptism, since when they repent and return they are not baptized anew."

Fourthly, because Baptism is conferred principally as a remedy against original sin. Wherefore, just as original sin is not renewed, so neither is Baptism reiterated, for as it is written (Rom. 5:18), "as by the offense of one, unto all men to condemnation, so also by the justice of one, unto all men to justification of life."

Reply to Objection 1: Baptism derives its efficacy from Christ's Passion, as stated above (A[2], ad 1). Wherefore, just as subsequent sins do not cancel the virtue of Christ's Passion, so neither do they cancel Baptism, so as to call for its repetition. on the other hand the sin which hindered the effect of Baptism is blotted out on being submitted to Penance.

Reply to Objection 2: As Augustine says on Jn. 1:33: "'And I knew Him not': Behold; after John had baptized, Baptism was administered; after a murderer has baptized, it is not administered: because John gave his own Baptism; the murderer, Christ's; for that sacrament is so sacred, that not even a murderer's administration contaminates it."

Reply to Objection 3: The Paulianists and Cataphrygians used not to baptize in the name of the Trinity. Wherefore Gregory, writing to the Bishop Quiricus, says: "Those heretics who are not baptized in the name of the Trinity, such as the Bonosians and Cataphrygians" (who were of the same mind as the Paulianists), "since the former believe not that Christ is God" (holding Him to be a mere man), "while the latter," i.e. the Cataphrygians, "are so perverse as to deem a mere man," viz. Montanus, "to be the Holy Ghost: all these are baptized when they come to holy Church, for the baptism which they received while in that state of error was no Baptism at all, not being conferred in the name of the Trinity." On the other hand, as set down in De Eccles. Dogm. xxii: "Those heretics who have been baptized in the confession of the name of the Trinity are to be received as already baptized when they come to the Catholic Faith."

Reply to Objection 4: According to the Decretal of Alexander III: "Those about whose Baptism there is a doubt are to be baptized with these words prefixed to the form: 'If thou art baptized, I do not rebaptize thee; but if thou art not baptized, I baptize thee,' etc.: for that does not appear to be repeated, which is not known to have been done."

Reply to Objection 5: Both sacraments, viz. Baptism and the Eucharist, are a representation of our Lord's death and Passion, but not in the same way. For Baptism is a commemoration of Christ's death in so far as man dies with Christ, that he may be born again into a new life. But the Eucharist is a commemoration of Christ's death, in so far as the suffering Christ Himself is offered to us as the Paschal banquet, according to 1 Cor. 5:7,8: "Christ our pasch is sacrificed; therefore let us feast." And forasmuch as man is born once, whereas he eats many times, so is Baptism given once, but the Eucharist frequently.

Whether the Church observes a suitable rite in baptizing?

Objection 1: It seems that the Church observes an unsuitable rite in baptizing. For as Chrysostom (Chromatius, in Matth. 3:15) says: "The waters of Baptism would never avail to purge the sins of them that believe, had they not been hallowed by the touch of our Lord's body." Now this took place at Christ's Baptism, which is commemorated in the Feast of the Epiphany. Therefore solemn Baptism should be celebrated at the Feast of the Epiphany rather than on the eves of Easter and Whitsunday.

Objection 2: Further, it seems that several matters should not be used in the same sacrament. But water is used for washing in Baptism. Therefore it is unfitting that the person baptized should be anointed thrice with holy oil first on the breast, and then between the shoulders, and a third time with chrism on the top of the head.

Objection 3: Further, "in Christ Jesus . . . there is neither male nor female" (Gal. 3:23) . . . "neither Barbarian nor Scythian" (Col. 3:11), nor, in like manner, any other such like distinctions. Much less, therefore can a difference of clothing have any efficacy in the Faith of Christ. It is consequently unfitting to bestow a white garment on those who have been baptized.

Objection 4: Further, Baptism can be celebrated without such like ceremonies. Therefore it seems that those mentioned above are superfluous; and consequently that they are unsuitably inserted by the Church in the baptismal rite.

On the contrary, The Church is ruled by the Holy Ghost, Who does nothing inordinate.

I answer that, In the sacrament of Baptism something is done which is essential to the sacrament, and something which belongs to a certain solemnity of the sacrament. Essential indeed, to the sacrament are both the form which designates the principal cause of the sacrament; and the minister who is the instrumental cause; and the use of the matter, namely, washing with water, which designates the principal sacramental effect. But all the other things which the Church observes in the baptismal rite, belong rather to a certain solemnity of the sacrament.

And these, indeed, are used in conjunction with the sacrament for three reasons. First, in order to arouse the devotion of the faithful, and their reverence for the sacrament. For if there were nothing done but a mere washing with water, without any solemnity, some might easily think it to be an ordinary washing.

Secondly, for the instruction of the faithful. Because simple and unlettered folk need to be taught by some sensible signs, for instance, pictures and the like. And in this way by means of the sacramental ceremonies they are either instructed, or urged to seek the signification of such like sensible signs. And consequently, since, besides the principal sacramental effect, other things should be known about Baptism, it was fitting that these also should be represented by some outward signs.

Thirdly, because the power of the devil is restrained, by prayers, blessings, and the like, from hindering the sacramental effect.

Reply to Objection 1: Christ was baptized on the Epiphany with the Baptism of John, as stated above ([4426]Q[39], A[2]), with which baptism, indeed, the faithful are not baptized, rather are they baptized with Christ's Baptism. This has its efficacy from the Passion of Christ, according to Rom. 6:3: "We who are baptized in Christ Jesus, are baptized in His death"; and in the Holy Ghost, according to Jn. 3:5: "Unless a man be born again of water and the Holy Ghost." Therefore it is that solemn Baptism is held in the Church, both on Easter Eve, when we commemorate our Lord's burial and resurrection; for which reason our Lord gave His disciples the commandment concerning Baptism as related by Matthew (28:19): and on Whitsun-eve, when the celebration of the Feast of the Holy Ghost begins; for which reason the apostles are said to have baptized three thousand on the very day of Pentecost when they had received the Holy Ghost.

Reply to Objection 2: The use of water in Baptism is part of the substance of the sacrament; but the use of oil or chrism is part of the solemnity. For the candidate is first of all anointed with Holy oil on the breast and between the shoulders, as "one who wrestles for God," to use Ambrose's expression (De Sacram. i): thus are prize-fighters wont to besmear themselves with oil. Or, as Innocent III says in a decretal on the Holy Unction: "The candidate is anointed on the breast, in order to receive the gift of the Holy Ghost, to cast off error and ignorance, and to acknowledge the true faith, since 'the just man liveth by faith'; while he is anointed between the shoulders, that he may be clothed with the grace of the Holy Ghost, lay aside indifference and sloth, and become active in good works; so that the sacrament of faith may purify the thoughts of his heart, and strengthen his shoulders for the burden of labor." But after Baptism, as Rabanus says (De Sacram. iii), "he is forthwith anointed on the head by the priest with Holy Chrism, who proceeds at once to offer up a prayer that the neophyte may have a share in Christ's kingdom, and be called a Christian after Christ." Or, as Ambrose says (De Sacram. iii), his head is anointed, because "the senses of a wise man are in his head" (Eccl 2:14): to wit, that he may "be ready to satisfy everyone that asketh" him to give "a reason of his faith" (cf. 1 Pet. 3:15; Innocent III, Decretal on Holy Unction).

Reply to Objection 3: This white garment is given, not as though it were unlawful for the neophyte to use others: but as a sign of the glorious resurrection, unto which men are born again by Baptism; and in order to designate the purity of life, to which he will be bound after being baptized, according to Rom. 6:4: "That we may walk in newness of life."

Reply to Objection 4: Although those things that belong to the solemnity of a sacrament are not essential to it, yet are they not superfluous, since they pertain to the sacrament's wellbeing, as stated above.

Whether three kinds of Baptism are fittingly described---viz. Baptism of Water, of Blood, and of the Spirit?

Objection 1: It seems that the three kinds of Baptism are not fittingly described as Baptism of Water, of Blood, and of the Spirit, i.e. of the Holy Ghost. Because the Apostle says (Eph. 4:5): "One Faith, one Baptism." Now there is but one Faith. Therefore there should not be three Baptisms.

Objection 2: Further, Baptism is a sacrament, as we have made clear above ([4427]Q[65], A[1]). Now none but Baptism of Water is a sacrament. Therefore we should not reckon two other Baptisms.

Objection 3: Further, Damascene (De Fide Orth. iv) distinguishes several other kinds of Baptism. Therefore we should admit more than three Baptisms.

On the contrary, on Heb. 6:2, "Of the doctrine of Baptisms," the gloss says: "He uses the plural, because there is Baptism of Water, of Repentance, and of Blood."

I answer that, As stated above ([4428]Q[62], A[5]), Baptism of Water has its efficacy from Christ's Passion, to which a man is conformed by Baptism, and also from the Holy Ghost, as first cause. Now although the effect depends on the first cause, the cause far surpasses the effect, nor does it depend on it. Consequently, a man may, without Baptism of Water, receive the sacramental effect from Christ's Passion, in so far as he is conformed to Christ by suffering for Him. Hence it is written (Apoc. 7:14): "These are they who are come out of great tribulation, and have washed their robes and have made them white in the blood of the Lamb." In like manner a man receives the effect of Baptism by the power of the Holy Ghost, not only without Baptism of Water, but also without Baptism of Blood: forasmuch as his heart is moved by the Holy Ghost to believe in and love God and to repent of his sins: wherefore this is also called Baptism of Repentance. Of this it is written (Is. 4:4): "If the Lord shall wash away the filth of the daughters of Zion, and shall wash away the blood of Jerusalem out of the midst thereof, by the spirit of judgment, and by the spirit of burning." Thus, therefore, each of these other Baptisms is called Baptism, forasmuch as it takes the place of Baptism. Wherefore Augustine says (De Unico Baptismo Parvulorum iv): "The Blessed Cyprian argues with considerable reason from the thief to whom, though not baptized, it was said: 'Today shalt thou be with Me in Paradise' that suffering can take the place of Baptism. Having weighed this in my mind again and again, I perceive that not only can suffering for the name of Christ supply for what was lacking in Baptism, but even faith and conversion of heart, if perchance on account of the stress of the times the celebration of the mystery of Baptism is not practicable."

Reply to Objection 1: The other two Baptisms are included in the Baptism of Water, which derives its efficacy, both from Christ's Passion and from the Holy Ghost. Consequently for this reason the unity of Baptism is not destroyed.

Reply to Objection 2: As stated above ([4429]Q[60], A[1]), a sacrament is a kind of sign. The other two, however, are like the Baptism of Water, not, indeed, in the nature of sign, but in the baptismal effect. Consequently they are not sacraments.

Reply to Objection 3: Damascene enumerates certain figurative Baptisms. For instance, "the Deluge" was a figure of our Baptism, in respect of the salvation of the faithful in the Church; since then "a few . . . souls were saved in the ark [Vulg.: 'by water']," according to 1 Pet. 3:20. He also mentions "the crossing of the Red Sea": which was a figure of our Baptism, in respect of our delivery from the bondage of sin; hence the Apostle says (1 Cor. 10:2) that "all . . . were baptized in the cloud and in the sea." And again he mentions "the various washings which were customary under the Old Law," which were figures of our Baptism, as to the cleansing from sins: also "the Baptism of John," which prepared the way for our Baptism.

Whether the Baptism of Blood is the most excellent of these?

Objection 1: It seems that the Baptism of Blood is not the most excellent of these three. For the Baptism of Water impresses a character; which the Baptism of Blood cannot do. Therefore the Baptism of Blood is not more excellent than the Baptism of Water.

Objection 2: Further, the Baptism of Blood is of no avail without the Baptism of the Spirit, which is by charity; for it is written (1 Cor. 13:3): "If I should deliver my body to be burned, and have not charity, it profiteth me nothing." But the Baptism of the Spirit avails without the Baptism of Blood; for not only the martyrs are saved. Therefore the Baptism of Blood is not the most excellent.

Objection 3: Further, just as the Baptism of Water derives its efficacy from Christ's Passion, to which, as stated above [4430] (A[11]), the Baptism of Blood corresponds, so Christ's Passion derives its efficacy from the Holy Ghost, according to Heb. 9:14: "The Blood of Christ, Who by the Holy Ghost offered Himself unspotted unto God, shall cleanse our conscience from dead works," etc. Therefore the Baptism of the Spirit is more excellent than the Baptism of Blood. Therefore the Baptism of Blood is not the most excellent.

On the contrary, Augustine (Ad Fortunatum) speaking of the comparison between Baptisms says: "The newly baptized confesses his faith in the presence of the priest: the martyr in the presence of the persecutor. The former is sprinkled with water, after he has confessed; the latter with his blood. The former receives the Holy Ghost by the imposition of the bishop's hands; the latter is made the temple of the Holy Ghost."

I answer that, As stated above [4431](A[11]), the shedding of blood for Christ's sake, and the inward operation of the Holy Ghost, are called baptisms, in so far as they produce the effect of the Baptism of Water. Now the Baptism of Water derives its efficacy from Christ's Passion and from the Holy Ghost, as already stated [4432](A[11]). These two causes act in each of these three Baptisms; most excellently, however, in the Baptism of Blood. For Christ's Passion acts in the Baptism of Water by way of a figurative representation; in the Baptism of the Spirit or of Repentance, by way of desire. but in the Baptism of Blood, by way of imitating the (Divine) act. In like manner, too, the power of the Holy Ghost acts in the Baptism of Water through a certain hidden power. in the Baptism of Repentance by moving the heart; but in the Baptism of Blood by the highest degree of fervor of dilection and love, according to Jn. 15:13: "Greater love than this no man hath that a man lay down his life for his friends."

Reply to Objection 1: A character is both reality and a sacrament. And we do not say that the Baptism of Blood is more excellent, considering the nature of a sacrament; but considering the sacramental effect.

Reply to Objection 2: The shedding of blood is not in the nature of a Baptism if it be without charity. Hence it is clear that the Baptism of Blood includes the Baptism of the Spirit, but not conversely. And from this it is proved to be more perfect.

Reply to Objection 3: The Baptism owes its pre-eminence not only to Christ's Passion, but also to the Holy Ghost, as stated above.

OF THE MINISTERS BY WHOM THE SACRAMENT OF BAPTISM IS CONFERRED (EIGHT ARTICLES)

We have now to consider the ministers by whom the sacrament of Baptism is conferred. And concerning this there are eight points of inquiry:

(1) Whether it belongs to a deacon to baptize?
(2) Whether this belongs to a priest, or to a bishop only?
(3) Whether a layman can confer the sacrament of Baptism?
(4) Whether a woman can do this?
(5) Whether an unbaptized person can baptize?
(6) Whether several can at the same time baptize one and the same person?
(7) Whether it is essential that someone should raise the person baptized from the sacred font?
(8) Whether he who raises someone from the sacred font is bound to instruct him?

Whether it is part of a deacon's duty to baptize?

Objection 1: It seems that it is part of a deacon's duty to baptize. Because the duties of preaching and of baptizing were enjoined by our Lord at the same time, according to Mat. 28:19: "Going . . . teach ye all nations, baptizing them," etc. But it is part of a deacon's duty to preach the gospel. Therefore it seems that it is also part of a deacon's duty to baptize.

Objection 2: Further, according to Dionysius (Eccl. Hier. v) to "cleanse" is part of the deacon's duty. But cleansing from sins is effected specially by Baptism, according to Eph. 5:26: "Cleansing it by the laver of water in the word of life." Therefore it seems that it belongs to a deacon to baptize.

Objection 3: Further, it is told of Blessed Laurence, who was a deacon, that he baptized many. Therefore it seems that it belongs to deacons to baptize.

On the contrary, Pope Gelasius I says (the passage is to be found in the Decrees, dist. 93): "We order the deacons to keep within their own province"; and further on: "Without bishop or priest they must not dare to baptize, except in cases of extreme urgency, when the aforesaid are a long way off."

I answer that, Just as the properties and duties of the heavenly orders are gathered from their names, as Dionysius says (Coel. Hier. vi), so can we gather, from the names of the ecclesiastical orders, what belongs to each order. Now "deacons" are so called from being "ministers"; because, to wit, it is not in the deacon's province to be the chief and official celebrant in conferring a sacrament, but to minister to others, his elders, in the sacramental dispensations. And so it does not belong to a deacon to confer the sacrament of Baptism officially as it were; but to assist and serve his elders in the bestowal of this and other sacraments. Hence Isidore says (Epist. ad Ludifred.): "It is a deacon's duty to assist and serve the priests, in all the rites of Christ's sacraments, viz. those of Baptism, of the Chrism, of the Paten and Chalice."

Reply to Objection 1: It is the deacon's duty to read the Gospel in church, and to preach it as one catechizing; hence Dionysius says (Eccl. Hier. v) that a deacon's office involves power over the unclean among whom he includes the catechumens. But to teach, i.e. to expound the Gospel, is the proper office of a bishop, whose action is "to perfect," as Dionysius teaches (Eccl. Hier. v); and "to perfect" is the same as "to teach." Consequently, it does not follow that the office of baptizing belongs to deacons.

Reply to Objection 2: As Dionysius says (Eccl. Hier. ii), Baptism has a power not only of "cleansing" but also of "enlightening." Consequently, it is outside the province of the deacon whose duty it is to cleanse only: viz. either by driving away the unclean, or by preparing them for the reception of a sacrament.

Reply to Objection 3: Because Baptism is a necessary sacrament, deacons are allowed to baptize in cases of urgency when their elders are not at hand; as appears from the authority of Gelasius quoted above. And it was thus that Blessed Laurence, being but a deacon, baptized.

Whether to baptize is part of the priestly office, or proper to that of bishops?

Objection 1: It seems that to baptize is not part of the priestly office, but proper to that of bishops. Because, as stated above (A[1], OBJ[1]), the duties of teaching and baptizing are enjoined in the same precept (Mat. 28:19). But to teach, which is "to perfect," belongs to the office of bishop, as Dionysius declares (Eccl. Hier. v, vi). Therefore to baptize also belongs to the episcopal office.

Objection 2: Further, by Baptism a man is admitted to the body of the Christian people: and to do this seems consistent with no other than the princely office. Now the bishops hold the position of princes in the Church, as the gloss observes on Lk. 10:1: indeed, they even take the place of the apostles, of whom it is written (Ps. 44:17): "Thou shalt make them princes over all the earth." Therefore it seems that to baptize belongs exclusively to the office of bishops.

Objection 3: Further, Isidore says (Epist. ad Ludifred.) that "it belongs to the bishop to consecrate churches, to anoint altars, to consecrate [conficere] the chrism; he it is that confers the ecclesiastical orders, and blesses the consecrated virgins." But the sacrament of Baptism is greater than all these. Therefore much more reason is there why to baptize should belong exclusively to the episcopal office.

On the contrary, Isidore says (De Officiis. ii): "It is certain that Baptism was entrusted to priests alone."

I answer that, Priests are consecrated for the purpose of celebrating the sacrament of Christ's Body, as stated above ([4433]Q[65], A[3]). Now that is the sacrament of ecclesiastical unity, according to the Apostle (1 Cor. 10:17): "We, being many, are one bread, one body, all that partake of one bread and one chalice." Moreover, by Baptism a man becomes a participator in ecclesiastical unity, wherefore also he receives the right to approach our Lord's Table. Consequently, just as it belongs to a priest to consecrate the Eucharist, which is the principal purpose of the priesthood, so it is the proper office of a priest to baptize: since it seems to belong to one and the same, to produce the whole and to dispose the part in the whole.

Reply to Objection 1: Our Lord enjoined on the apostles, whose place is taken by the bishops, both duties, namely, of teaching and of baptizing, but in different ways. Because Christ committed to them the duty of teaching, that they might exercise it themselves as being the most important duty of all: wherefore the apostles themselves said (Acts 6:2): "It is not reason that we should leave the word of God and serve tables." On the other hand, He entrusted the apostles with the office of baptizing, to be exercised vicariously; wherefore the Apostle says (1 Cor. 1:17): "Christ sent me not to baptize, but to preach the Gospel." And the reason for this was that the merit and wisdom of the minister have no bearing on the baptismal effect, as they have in teaching, as may be seen from what we have stated above (Q[64], A[1], ad 2; [4434]AA[5],9). A proof of this is found also in the fact that our Lord Himself did not baptize, but His disciples, as John relates (4:2). Nor does it follow from this that bishops cannot baptize; since what a lower power can do, that can also a higher power. Wherefore also the Apostle says (1 Cor. 1:14, 16) that he had baptized some.

Reply to Objection 2: In every commonwealth minor affairs are entrusted to lower officials, while greater affairs are restricted to higher officials; according to Ex. 18:22: "When any great matter soever shall fall out, let them refer it to thee, and let them judge the lesser matters only." Consequently it belongs to the lower officials of the state to decide matters concerning the lower orders; while to the highest it belongs to set in order those matters that regard the higher orders of the state. Now by Baptism a man attains only to the lowest rank among the Christian people: and consequently it belongs to the lesser officials of the Church
to baptize, namely, the priests, who hold the place of the seventy-two disciples of Christ, as the gloss says in the passage quoted from Luke 10.

Reply to Objection 3: As stated above ([4435]Q[65], A[3]), the sacrament of Baptism holds the first place in the order of necessity; but in the order of perfection there are other greater sacraments which are reserved to bishops.

Whether a layman can baptize?

Objection 1: It seems that a layman cannot baptize. Because, as stated above [4436](A[2]), to baptize belongs properly to the priestly order. But those things which belong to an order cannot be entrusted to one that is not ordained. Therefore it seems that a layman, who has no orders, cannot baptize.

Objection 2: Further, it is a greater thing to baptize, than to perform the other sacramental rites of Baptism, such as to catechize, to exorcize, and to bless the baptismal water. But these things cannot be done by laymen, but only by priests. Therefore it seems that much less can laymen baptize.

Objection 3: Further, just as Baptism is a necessary sacrament, so is Penance. But a layman cannot absolve in the tribunal of Penance. Neither, therefore, can he baptize.

On the contrary, Pope Gelasius I and Isidore say that "it is often permissible for Christian laymen to baptize, in cases of urgent necessity."

I answer that, It is due to the mercy of Him "Who will have all men to be saved" (1 Tim. 2:4) that in those things which are necessary for salvation, man can easily find the remedy. Now the most necessary among all the sacraments is Baptism, which is man's regeneration unto spiritual life: since for children there is no substitute, while adults cannot otherwise than by Baptism receive a full remission both of guilt and of its punishment. Consequently, lest man should have to go without so necessary a remedy, it was ordained, both that the matter of Baptism should be something common that is easily obtainable by all, i.e. water; and that the minister of Baptism should be anyone, even not in orders, lest from lack of being baptized, man should suffer loss of his salvation.

Reply to Objection 1: To baptize belongs to the priestly order by reason of a certain appropriateness and solemnity; but this is not essential to the sacrament. Consequently, if a layman were to baptize even outside a case of urgency; he would sin, yet he would confer the sacrament; nor would the person thus baptized have to be baptized again.

Reply to Objection 2: These sacramental rites of Baptism belong to the solemnity of, and are not essential to, Baptism. And therefore they neither should nor can be done by a layman, but only by a priest, whose office it is to baptize solemnly.

Reply to Objection 3: As stated above ([4437]Q[65], AA[3],4), Penance is not so necessary as Baptism; since contrition can supply the defect of the priestly absolution which does not free from the whole punishment, nor again is it given to children. Therefore the comparison with Baptism does not stand, because its effect cannot be supplied by anything else.

Whether a woman can baptize?

Objection 1: It seems that a woman cannot baptize. For we read in the acts of the Council of Carthage (iv): "However learned and holy a woman may be, she must not presume to teach men in the church, or to baptize." But in no case is a woman allowed to teach in church, according to 1 Cor. 14:35: "It is a shame for a woman to speak in the church." Therefore it seems that neither is a woman in any circumstances permitted to baptize.

Objection 2: Further, to baptize belongs to those having authority. wherefore baptism should be conferred by priests having charge of souls. But women are not qualified for this; according to 1 Tim. 2:12: "I suffer not a woman to teach, nor to use authority over man, but to be subject to him [Vulg.: 'but to be in silence']." Therefore a woman cannot baptize.

Objection 3: Further, in the spiritual regeneration water seems to hold the place of the mother's womb, as Augustine says on Jn. 3:4, "Can" a man "enter a second time into his mother's womb, and be born again?" While he who baptizes seems to hold rather the position of father. But this is unfitting for a woman. Therefore a woman cannot baptize.

On the contrary, Pope Urban II says (Decreta xxx): "In reply to the questions asked by your beatitude, we consider that the following answer should be given: that the baptism is valid when, in cases of necessity, a woman baptizes a child in the name of the Trinity."

I answer that, Christ is the chief Baptizer, according to Jn. 1:33: "He upon Whom thou shalt see the Spirit descending and remaining upon Him, He it is that baptizeth." For it is written in Col. 3 (cf. Gal. 3:28), that in Christ there is neither male nor female. Consequently, just as a layman can baptize, as Christ's minister, so can a woman.

But since "the head of the woman is the man," and "the head of . . . man, is Christ" (1 Cor. 11:3), a woman should not baptize if a man be available for the purpose; just as neither should a layman in the presence of a cleric, nor a cleric in the presence of a priest. The last, however, can baptize in the presence of a bishop, because it is part of the priestly office.

Reply to Objection 1: Just as a woman is not suffered to teach in public, but is allowed to instruct and admonish privately; so she is not permitted to baptize publicly and solemnly, and yet she can baptize in a case of urgency.

Reply to Objection 2: When Baptism is celebrated solemnly and with due form, it should be conferred by a priest having charge of souls, or by one representing him. But this is not required in cases of urgency, when a woman may baptize.

Reply to Objection 3: In carnal generation male and female co-operate according to the power of their proper nature; wherefore the female cannot be the active, but only the passive, principle of generation. But in spiritual generation they do not act, either of them, by their proper power, but only instrumentally by the power of Christ. Consequently, on the same grounds either man or woman can baptize in a case of urgency.

If, however, a woman were to baptize without any urgency for so doing. there would be no need of rebaptism: as we have said in regard to laymen (A[3], ad 1). But the baptizer herself would sin, as also those who took part with her therein, either by receiving Baptism from her, or by bringing someone to her to be baptized.

Day 295

Whether one that is not baptized can confer the sacrament of Baptism?

Objection 1: It seems that one that is not baptized cannot confer the sacrament of Baptism. For "none gives what he has not." But a non-baptized person has not the sacrament of Baptism. Therefore he cannot give it.

Objection 2: Further, a man confers the sacrament of Baptism inasmuch as he is a minister of the Church. But one that is not baptized, belongs nowise to the Church, i.e. neither really nor sacramentally. Therefore he cannot confer the sacrament of Baptism.

Objection 3: Further, it is more to confer a sacrament than to receive it. But one that is not baptized, cannot receive the other sacraments. Much less, therefore, can he confer any sacrament.

On the contrary, Isidore says: "The Roman Pontiff does not consider it to be the man who baptizes, but that the Holy Ghost confers the grace of Baptism, though he that baptizes be a pagan." But he who is baptized, is not called a pagan. Therefore he who is not baptized can confer the sacrament of Baptism.

I answer that, Augustine left this question without deciding it. For he says (Contra Ep. Parmen. ii): "This is indeed another question, whether even those can baptize who were never Christians; nor should anything be rashly asserted hereupon, without the authority of a sacred council such as suffices for so great a matter." But afterwards it was decided by the Church that the unbaptized, whether Jews or pagans, can confer the sacrament of Baptism, provided they baptize in the form of the Church. Wherefore Pope Nicolas I replies to the questions propounded by the Bulgars: "You say that many in your country have been baptized by someone, whether Christian or pagan you know not. If these were baptized in the name of the Trinity, they must not be rebaptized." But if the form of the Church be not observed, the sacrament of Baptism is not conferred. And thus is to be explained what Gregory II [*Gregory III] writes to Bishop Boniface: "Those whom you assert to have been baptized by pagans," namely, with a form not recognized by the Church, "we command you to rebaptize in the name of the Trinity." And the reason of this is that, just as on the part of the matter, as far as the essentials of the sacrament are concerned, any water will suffice, so, on the part of the minister, any man is competent. Consequently, an unbaptized person can baptize in a case of urgency. So that two unbaptized persons may baptize one another, one baptizing the other and being afterwards baptized by him: and each would receive not only the sacrament but also the reality of the sacrament. But if this were done outside a case of urgency, each would sin grievously, both the baptizer and the baptized, and thus the baptismal effect would be frustrated, although the sacrament itself would not be invalidated.

Reply to Objection 1: The man who baptizes offers but his outward ministration; whereas Christ it is Who baptizes inwardly, Who can use all men to whatever purpose He wills. Consequently, the unbaptized can baptize: because, as Pope Nicolas I says, "the Baptism is not theirs," i.e. the baptizers', "but His," i.e. Christ's.

Reply to Objection 2: He who is not baptized, though he belongs not to the Church either in reality or sacramentally, can nevertheless belong to her in intention and by similarity of action, namely, in so far as he intends to do what the Church does, and in baptizing observes the Church's form, and thus acts as the minister of Christ, Who did not confine His power to those that are baptized, as neither did He to the sacraments.

Reply to Objection 3: The other sacraments are not so necessary as Baptism. And therefore it is allowable that an unbaptized person should baptize rather than that he should receive other sacraments.

Whether several can baptize at the same time?

Objection 1: It seems that several can baptize at the same time. For unity is contained in multitude, but not "vice versa." Wherefore it seems that many can do whatever one can but not "vice versa": thus many draw a ship which one could draw. But one man can baptize. Therefore several, too, can baptize one at the same time.

Objection 2: Further, it is more difficult for one agent to act on many things, than for many to act at the same time on one. But one man can baptize several at the same time. Much more, therefore, can many baptize one at the same time.

Objection 3: Further, Baptism is a sacrament of the greatest necessity. Now in certain cases it seems necessary for several to baptize one at the same time; for instance, suppose a child to be in danger of death, and two persons present, one of whom is dumb, and the other without hands or arms; for then the mutilated person would have to pronounce the words, and the dumb person would have to perform the act of baptizing. Therefore it seems that several can baptize one at the same time.

On the contrary, Where there is one agent there is one action. If, therefore, several were to baptize one, it seems to follow that there would be several baptisms: and this is contrary to Eph. 4:5: "one Faith, one Baptism."

I answer that, The Sacrament of Baptism derives its power principally from its form, which the Apostle calls "the word of life" (Eph. 5:26). Consequently, if several were to baptize one at the same time, we must consider what form they would use. For were they to say: "We baptize thee in the name of the Father and of the Son and of the Holy Ghost," some maintain that the sacrament of Baptism would not be conferred, because the form of the Church would not be observed, i.e. "I baptize thee in the name of the Father and of the Son and of the Holy Ghost." But this reasoning is disproved by the form observed in the Greek Church. For they might say: "The servant of God, N . . ., is baptized in the name of the Father and of the Son and of the Holy Ghost," under which form the Greeks receive the sacrament of Baptism: and yet this form differs far more from the form that we use, than does this: "We baptize thee."

The point to be observed, however, is this, that by this form, "We baptize thee," the intention expressed is that several concur in conferring one Baptism: and this seems contrary to the notion of a minister; for a man does not baptize save as a minister of Christ, and as standing in His place; wherefore just as there is one Christ, so should there be one minister to represent Christ. Hence the Apostle says pointedly (Eph. 4:5): "one Lord, one Faith, one Baptism." Consequently, an intention which is in opposition to this seems to annul the sacrament of Baptism.

On the other hand, if each were to say: "I baptize thee in the name of the Father and of the Son and of the Holy Ghost," each would signify his intention as though he were conferring Baptism independently of the other. This might occur in the case where both were striving to baptize someone; and then it is clear that whichever pronounced the words first would confer the sacrament of Baptism; while the other, however great his right to baptize, if he presume to utter the words, would be liable to be punished as a rebaptizer. If, however, they were to pronounce the words absolutely at the same time, and dipped or sprinkled the man together, they should be punished for baptizing in an improper manner, but not for rebaptizing: because each would intend to baptize an unbaptized person, and each, so far as he is concerned, would baptize. Nor would they confer several sacraments: but the one Christ baptizing inwardly would confer one sacrament by means of both together.

Reply to Objection 1: This argument avails in those agents that act by their own power. But men do not baptize by their own, but by Christ's power, Who, since He is one, perfects His work by means of one minister.

Reply to Objection 2: In a case of necessity one could baptize several at the same time under this form: "I baptize ye": for instance, if they were threatened by a falling house, or by the sword or something of the kind, so as not to allow of the delay involved by baptizing them singly. Nor would this cause a change in the Church's form, since the plural is nothing but the singular doubled: especially as we find the plural expressed in Mat. 28:19: "Baptizing them," etc. Nor is there parity between the baptizer and the baptized; since Christ, the baptizer in chief, is one: while many are made one in Christ by Baptism.

Reply to Objection 3: As stated above ([4438]Q[66], A[1]), the integrity of Baptism consists in the form of words and the use of the matter. Consequently, neither he who only pronounces the words, baptizes, nor he who dips. Where fore if one pronounces the words and the other dips, no form of words can be fitting. For neither could he say: "I baptize thee": since he dips not, and therefore baptizes not. Nor could they say: "We baptize thee": since neither baptizes. For if of two men, one write one part of a book, and the other write the other, it would not be a proper form of speech to say: "We wrote this book," but the figure of synecdoche in which the whole is put for the part.

Whether in Baptism it is necessary for someone to raise the baptized from the sacred font?

Objection 1: It seems that in Baptism it is not necessary for someone to raise the baptized from the sacred font. For our Baptism is consecrated by Christ's Baptism and is conformed thereto. But Christ when baptized was not raised by anyone from the font, but according to Mat. 3:16, "Jesus being baptized, forthwith came out of the water." Therefore it seems that neither when others are baptized should anyone raise the baptized from the sacred font.

Objection 2: Further, Baptism is a spiritual regeneration, as stated above [4439](A[3]). But in carnal generation nothing else is required but the active principle, i.e. the father, and the passive principle, i.e. the mother. Since, then, in Baptism he that baptizes takes the place of the father, while the very water of Baptism takes the place of the mother, as Augustine says in a sermon on the Epiphany (cxxxv); it seems that there is no further need for someone to raise the baptized from the sacred font.

Objection 3: Further, nothing ridiculous should be observed in the sacraments of the Church. But it seems ridiculous that after being baptized, adults who can stand up of themselves and leave the sacred font, should be held up by another. Therefore there seems no need for anyone, especially in the Baptism of adults, to raise the baptized from the sacred font.

On the contrary, Dionysius says (Eccl. Hier. ii) that "the priests taking the baptized hand him over to his sponsor and guide."

I answer that, The spiritual regeneration, which takes place in Baptism, is in a certain manner likened to carnal generation: wherefore it is written (1 Pet. 2:2): "As new-born babes, endowed with reason desire milk [Vulg.: 'desire reasonable milk'] without guile." Now, in carnal generation the new-born child needs nourishment and guidance: wherefore, in spiritual generation also, someone is needed to undertake the office of nurse and tutor by forming and instructing one who is yet a novice in the Faith, concerning things pertaining to Christian faith and mode of life, which the clergy have not the leisure to do through being busy with watching over the people generally: because little children and novices need more than ordinary care. Consequently someone is needed to receive the baptized from the sacred font as though for the purpose of instructing and guiding them. It is to this that Dionysius refers (Eccl. Hier. xi) saying: "It occurred to our heavenly guides," i.e. the Apostles, "and they decided, that infants should be taken charge of thus: that the parents of the child should hand it over to some instructor versed in holy things, who would thenceforth take charge of the child, and be to it a spiritual father and a guide in the road of salvation."

Reply to Objection 1: Christ was baptized not that He might be regenerated, but that He might regenerate others: wherefore after His Baptism He needed no tutor like other children.

Reply to Objection 2: In carnal generation nothing is essential besides a father and a mother: yet to ease the latter in her travail, there is need for a midwife; and for the child to be suitably brought up there is need for a nurse and a tutor: while their place is taken in Baptism by him who raises the child from the sacred font. Consequently this is not essential to the sacrament, and in a case of necessity one alone can baptize with water.

Reply to Objection 3: It is not on account of bodily weakness that the baptized is raised from the sacred font by the godparent, but on account of spiritual weakness, as stated above.

Whether he who raises anyone from the sacred font is bound to instruct him?

Objection 1: It seems that he who raises anyone from the sacred font is not bound to instruct him. For none but those who are themselves instructed can give instruction. But even the uneducated and ill-instructed are allowed to raise people from the sacred font. Therefore he who raises a baptized person from the font is not bound to instruct him.

Objection 2: Further, a son is instructed by his father better than by a stranger: for, as the Philosopher says (Ethic. viii), a son receives from his father, "being, food, and education." If, therefore, godparents are bound to instruct their godchildren, it would be fitting for the carnal father, rather than another, to be the godparent of his own child. And yet this seems to be forbidden, as may be seen in the Decretals (xxx, qu. 1, Cap. Pervenit and Dictum est).

Objection 3: Further, it is better for several to instruct than for one only. If, therefore, godparents are bound to instruct their godchildren, it would be better to have several godparents than only one. Yet this is forbidden in a decree of Pope Leo, who says: "A child should not have more than one godparent, be this a man or a woman."

On the contrary, Augustine says in a sermon for Easter (clxviii): "In the first place I admonish you, both men and women, who have raised children in Baptism, that ye stand before God as sureties for those whom you have been seen to raise from the sacred font."

I answer that, Every man is bound to fulfil those duties which he has undertaken to perform. Now it has been stated above [4440] (A[7]) that godparents take upon themselves the duties of a tutor. Consequently they are bound to watch over their godchildren when there is need for them to do so: for instance when and where children are brought up among unbelievers. But if they are brought up among Catholic Christians, the godparents may well be excused from this responsibility, since it may be presumed that the children will be carefully instructed by their parents. If, however, they perceive in any way that the contrary is the case, they would be bound, as far as they are able, to see to the spiritual welfare of their godchildren.

Reply to Objection 1: Where the danger is imminent, the godparent, as Dionysius says (Eccl. Hier. vii), should be someone "versed in holy things." But where the danger is not imminent, by reason of the children being brought up among Catholics, anyone is admitted to this position, because the things pertaining to the Christian rule of life and faith are known openly by all. Nevertheless an unbaptized person cannot be a godparent, as was decreed in the Council of Mainz, although an unbaptized person: because the person baptizing is essential to the sacrament, wherefore as the godparent is not, as stated above (A[7], ad 2).

Reply to Objection 2: Just as spiritual generation is distinct from carnal generation, so is spiritual education distinct from that of the body; according to Heb. 12:9: "Moreover we have had fathers of our flesh for instructors, and we reverenced them: shall we not much more obey the Father of Spirits, and live?" Therefore the spiritual father should be distinct from the carnal father, unless necessity demanded otherwise.

Reply to Objection 3: Education would be full of confusion if there were more than one head instructor. Wherefore there should be one principal sponsor in Baptism: but others can be allowed as assistants.

OF THOSE WHO RECEIVE BAPTISM (TWELVE ARTICLES)

We have now to consider those who receive Baptism; concerning which there are twelve points of inquiry:

(1) Whether all are bound to receive Baptism?
(2) Whether a man can be saved without Baptism?
(3) Whether Baptism should be deferred?
(4) Whether sinners should be baptized?
(5) Whether works of satisfaction should be enjoined on sinners that have been baptized?
(6) Whether Confession of sins is necessary?
(7) Whether an intention is required on the part of the one baptized?
(8) Whether faith is necessary?
(9) Whether infants should be baptized?
(10) Whether the children of Jews should be baptized against the will of their parents?
(11) Whether anyone should be baptized in the mother's womb?
(12) Whether madmen and imbeciles should be baptized?

Whether all are bound to receive Baptism?

Objection 1: It seems that not all are bound to receive Baptism. For Christ did not narrow man's road to salvation. But before Christ's coming men could be saved without Baptism: therefore also after Christ's coming.

Objection 2: Further, Baptism seems to have been instituted principally as a remedy for original sin. Now, since a man who is baptized is without original sin, it seems that he cannot transmit it to his children. Therefore it seems that the children of those who have been baptized, should not themselves be baptized.

Objection 3: Further, Baptism is given in order that a man may, through grace, be cleansed from sin. But those who are sanctified in the womb, obtain this without Baptism. Therefore they are not bound to receive Baptism.

On the contrary, It is written (Jn. 3:5): "Unless a man be born again of water and the Holy Ghost, he cannot enter into the kingdom of God." Again it is stated in De Eccl. Dogm. xli, that "we believe the way of salvation to be open to those only who are baptized."

I answer that, Men are bound to that without which they cannot obtain salvation. Now it is manifest that no one can obtain salvation but through Christ; wherefore the Apostle says (Rom. 5:18): "As by the offense of one unto all men unto condemnation; so also by the justice of one, unto all men unto justification of life." But for this end is Baptism conferred on a man, that being regenerated thereby, he may be incorporated in Christ, by becoming His member: wherefore it is written (Gal. 3:27): "As many of you as have been baptized in Christ, have put on Christ." Consequently it is manifest that all are bound to be baptized: and that without Baptism there is no salvation for men.

Reply to Objection 1: At no time, not even before the coming of Christ, could men be saved unless they became members of Christ: because, as it is written (Acts 4:12), "there is no other name under heaven given to men, whereby we must be saved." But before Christ's coming, men were incorporated in Christ by faith in His future coming: of which faith circumcision was the "seal," as the Apostle calls it (Rom. 4:11): whereas before circumcision was instituted, men were incorporated in Christ by "faith alone," as Gregory says (Moral. iv), together with the offering of sacrifices, by means of which the Fathers of old made profession of their faith. Again, since Christ's coming, men are incorporated in Christ by faith; according to Eph. 3:17: "That Christ may dwell by faith in your hearts." But faith in a thing already present is manifested by a sign different from that by which it was manifested when that thing was yet in the future: just as we use other parts of the verb, to signify the present, the past, and the future. Consequently although the sacrament itself of Baptism was not always necessary for salvation, yet faith, of which Baptism is the sacrament, was always necessary.

Reply to Objection 2: As we have stated in the [4441]FS, Q[81], A[3], ad 2, those who are baptized are renewed in spirit by Baptism, while their body remains subject to the oldness of sin, according to Rom. 8:10: "The body, indeed, is dead because of sin, but the spirit liveth because of justification." Wherefore Augustine (Contra Julian. vi) proves that "not everything that is in man is baptized." Now it is manifest that in carnal generation man does not beget in respect of his soul, but in respect of his body. Consequently the children of those who are baptized are born with original sin; wherefore they need to be baptized.

Reply to Objection 3: Those who are sanctified in the womb, receive indeed grace which cleanses them from original sin, but they do not therefore receive the character, by which they are conformed to Christ. Consequently, if any were to be sanctified in the womb now, they would need to be baptized, in order to be conformed to Christ's other members by receiving the character.

Whether a man can be saved without Baptism?

Objection 1: It seems that no man can be saved without Baptism. For our Lord said (Jn. 3:5): "Unless a man be born again of water and the Holy Ghost, he cannot enter the kingdom of God." But those alone are saved who enter God's kingdom. Therefore none can be saved without Baptism, by which a man is born again of water and the Holy Ghost.

Objection 2: Further, in the book De Eccl. Dogm. xli, it is written: "We believe that no catechumen, though he die in his good works, will have eternal life, except he suffer martyrdom, which contains all the sacramental virtue of Baptism." But if it were possible for anyone to be saved without Baptism, this would be the case specially with catechumens who are credited with good works, for they seem to have the "faith that worketh by charity" (Gal. 5:6). Therefore it seems that none can be saved without Baptism.

Objection 3: Further, as stated above [4442](A[1]; Q[65], A[4]), the sacrament of Baptism is necessary for salvation. Now that is necessary "without which something cannot be" (Metaph. v). Therefore it seems that none can obtain salvation without Baptism.

On the contrary, Augustine says (Super Levit. lxxxiv) that "some have received the invisible sanctification without visible sacraments, and to their profit; but though it is possible to have the visible sanctification, consisting in a visible sacrament, without the invisible sanctification, it will be to no profit." Since, therefore, the sacrament of Baptism pertains to the visible sanctification, it seems that a man can obtain salvation without the sacrament of Baptism, by means of the invisible sanctification.

I answer that, The sacrament or Baptism may be wanting to someone in two ways. First, both in reality and in desire; as is the case with those who neither are baptized, nor wished to be baptized: which clearly indicates contempt of the sacrament, in regard to those who have the use of the free-will. Consequently those to whom Baptism is wanting thus, cannot obtain salvation: since neither sacramentally nor mentally are they incorporated in Christ, through Whom alone can salvation be obtained.

Secondly, the sacrament of Baptism may be wanting to anyone in reality but not in desire: for instance, when a man wishes to be baptized, but by some ill-chance he is forestalled by death before receiving Baptism. And such a man can obtain salvation without being actually baptized, on account of his desire for Baptism, which desire is the outcome of "faith that worketh by charity," whereby God, Whose power is not tied to visible sacraments, sanctifies man inwardly. Hence Ambrose says of Valentinian, who died while yet a catechumen: "I lost him whom I was to regenerate: but he did not lose the grace he prayed for."

Reply to Objection 1: As it is written (1 Kings 16:7), "man seeth those things that appear, but the Lord beholdeth the heart." Now a man who desires to be "born again of water and the Holy Ghost" by Baptism, is regenerated in heart though not in body. thus the Apostle says (Rom. 2:29) that "the circumcision is that of the heart, in the spirit, not in the letter; whose praise is not of men but of God."

Reply to Objection 2: No man obtains eternal life unless he be free from all guilt and debt of punishment. Now this plenary absolution is given when a man receives Baptism, or suffers martyrdom: for which reason is it stated that martyrdom "contains all the sacramental virtue of Baptism," i.e. as to the full deliverance from guilt and punishment. Suppose, therefore, a catechumen to have the desire for Baptism (else he could not be said to die in his good works, which cannot be without "faith that worketh by charity"), such a one, were he to die, would not forthwith come to eternal life, but would suffer punishment for his past sins, "but he himself shall be saved, yet so as by fire" as is stated 1 Cor. 3:15.

Reply to Objection 3: The sacrament of Baptism is said to be necessary for salvation in so far as man cannot be saved without, at least, Baptism of desire; "which, with God, counts for the deed" (Augustine, Enarr. in Ps. 57).

Whether Baptism should be deferred?

Objection 1: It seems that Baptism should be deferred. For Pope Leo says (Epist. xvi): "Two seasons," i.e. Easter and Whitsuntide, "are fixed by the Roman Pontiff for the celebration of Baptism. Wherefore we admonish your Beatitude not to add any other days to this custom." Therefore it seems that Baptism should be conferred not at once, but delayed until the aforesaid seasons.

Objection 2: Further, we read in the decrees of the Council of Agde (Can. xxxiv): "If Jews whose bad faith often "returns to the vomit," wish to submit to the Law of the Catholic Church, let them for eight months enter the porch of the church with the catechumens; and if they are found to come in good faith then at last they may deserve the grace of Baptism." Therefore men should not be baptized at once, and Baptism should be deferred for a certain fixed time.

Objection 3: Further, as we read in Is. 27:9, "this is all the fruit, that the sin . . . should be taken away." Now sin seems to be taken away, or at any rate lessened, if Baptism be deferred. First, because those who sin after Baptism, sin more grievously, according to Heb. 10:29: "How much more, do you think, he deserveth worse punishments, who hath . . . esteemed the blood of the testament," i.e. Baptism, "unclean, by which he was sanctified?" Secondly, because Baptism takes away past, but not future, sins: wherefore the more it is deferred, the more sins it takes away. Therefore it seems that Baptism should be deferred for a long time.

On the contrary, It is written (Ecclus. 5:8): "Delay not to be converted to the Lord, and defer it not from day to day." But the perfect conversion to God is of those who are regenerated in Christ by Baptism. Therefore Baptism should not be deferred from day to day.

I answer that, In this matter we must make a distinction and see whether those who are to be baptized are children or adults. For if they be children, Baptism should not be deferred. First, because in them we do not look for better instruction or fuller conversion. Secondly, because of the danger of death, for no other remedy is available for them besides the sacrament of Baptism.

On the other hand, adults have a remedy in the mere desire for Baptism, as stated above [4443](A[2]). And therefore Baptism should not be conferred on adults as soon as they are converted, but it should be deferred until some fixed time. First, as a safeguard to the Church, lest she be deceived through baptizing those who come to her under false pretenses, according to 1 Jn. 4:1: "Believe not every spirit, but try the spirits, if they be of God." And those who approach Baptism are put to this test, when their faith and morals are subjected to proof for a space of time. Secondly, this is needful as being useful for those who are baptized; for they require a certain space of time in order to be fully instructed in the faith, and to be drilled in those things that pertain to the Christian mode of life. Thirdly, a certain reverence for the sacrament demands a delay whereby men are admitted to Baptism at the principal festivities, viz. of Easter and Pentecost, the result being that they receive the sacrament with greater devotion.

There are, however, two reasons for forgoing this delay. First, when those who are to be baptized appear to be perfectly instructed in the faith and ready for Baptism; thus, Philip baptized the Eunuch at once (Acts 8); and Peter, Cornelius and those who were with him (Acts 10). Secondly, by reason of sickness or some kind of danger of death. Wherefore Pope Leo says (Epist. xvi): "Those who are threatened by death, sickness, siege, persecution, or shipwreck, should be baptized at any time." Yet if a man is forestalled by death, so as to have no time to receive the sacrament, while he awaits the season appointed by the Church, he is saved, yet "so as by fire," as stated above (A[2], ad 2). Nevertheless he sins if he defer being baptized beyond the time appointed by the Church, except this be for an unavoidable cause and with the permission of the authorities of the Church. But even this sin, with his other sins, can be washed away by his subsequent contrition, which takes the place of Baptism, as stated above ([4444]Q[66], A[11]).

Reply to Objection 1: This decree of Pope Leo, concerning the celebration of Baptism at two seasons, is to be understood "with the exception of the danger of death" (which is always to be feared in children) as stated above.

Reply to Objection 2: This decree concerning the Jews was for a safeguard to the Church, lest they corrupt the faith of simple people, if they be not fully converted. Nevertheless, as the same passage reads further on, "if within the appointed time they are threatened with danger of sickness, they should be baptized."

Reply to Objection 3: Baptism, by the grace which it bestows, removes not only past sins, but hinders the commission of future sins. Now this is the point to be considered---that men may not sin: it is a secondary consideration that their sins be less grievous, or that their sins be washed away, according to 1 Jn. 2:1,2: "My little children, these things I write to you, that you may not sin. But if any man sin, we have an advocate with the Father, Jesus Christ the just; and He is the propitiation for our sins."

Whether sinners should be baptized?
Objection 1: It seems that sinners should be baptized. For it is written (Zech. 13:1): "In that day there shall be a fountain open to the House of David, and to the inhabitants of Jerusalem: for the washing of the sinner and of the unclean woman": and this is to be understood of the fountain of Baptism. Therefore it seems that the sacrament of Baptism should be offered even to sinners.

Objection 2: Further, our Lord said (Mat. 9:12): "They that are in health need not a physician, but they that are ill." But they that are ill are sinners. Therefore since Baptism is the remedy of Christ the physician of our souls, it seems that this sacrament should be offered to sinners.

Objection 3: Further, no assistance should be withdrawn from sinners. But sinners who have been baptized derive spiritual assistance from the very character of Baptism, since it is a disposition to grace. Therefore it seems that the sacrament of Baptism should be offered to sinners.

On the contrary, Augustine says (Serm. clxix): "He Who created thee without thee, will not justify thee without thee." But since a sinner's will is ill-disposed, he does not co-operate with God. Therefore it is useless to employ Baptism as a means of justification.

I answer that, A man may be said to be a sinner in two ways. First, on account of the stain and the debt of punishment incurred in the past: and on sinners in this sense the sacrament of Baptism should be conferred, since it is instituted specially for this purpose, that by it the uncleanness of sin may be washed away, according to Eph. 5:26: "Cleansing it by the laver of water in the word of life."

Secondly, a man may be called a sinner because he wills to sin and purposes to remain in sin: and on sinners in this sense the sacrament of Baptism should not be conferred. First, indeed, because by Baptism men are incorporated in Christ, according to Gal. 3:27: "As many of you as have been baptized in Christ, have put on Christ." Now so long as a man wills to sin, he cannot be united to Christ, according to 2 Cor. 6:14: "What participation hath justice with injustice?" Wherefore Augustine says in his book on Penance (Serm. cccli) that "no man who has the use of free-will can begin the new life, except he repent of his former life." Secondly, because there should be nothing useless in the works of Christ and of the Church. Now that is useless which does not reach the end to which it is ordained; and, on the other hand, no one having the will to sin can, at the same time, be cleansed from sin, which is the purpose of Baptism; for this would be to combine two contradictory things. Thirdly, because there should be no falsehood in the sacramental signs. Now a sign is false if it does not correspond with the thing signified. But the very fact that a man presents himself to be cleansed by Baptism, signifies that he prepares himself for the inward cleansing: while this cannot be the case with one who purposes to remain in sin. Therefore it is manifest that on such a man the sacrament of Baptism is not to be conferred.

Reply to Objection 1: The words quoted are to be understood of those sinners whose will is set on renouncing sin.

Reply to Objection 2: The physician of souls, i.e. Christ, works in two ways. First, inwardly, by Himself: and thus He prepares man's will so that it wills good and hates evil. Secondly, He works through ministers, by the outward application of the sacraments: and in this way His work consists in perfecting what was begun outwardly. Therefore the sacrament of Baptism is not to be conferred save on those in whom there appears some sign of their interior conversion: just as neither is bodily medicine given to a sick man, unless he show some sign of life.

Reply to Objection 3: Baptism is the sacrament of faith. Now dead faith does not suffice for salvation; nor is it the foundation, but living faith alone, "that worketh by charity" (Gal. 5:6), as Augustine says (De Fide et oper.). Neither, therefore, can the sacrament of Baptism give salvation to a man whose will is set on sinning, and hence expels the form of faith. Moreover, the impression of the baptismal character cannot dispose a man for grace as long as he retains the will to sin; for "God compels no man to be virtuous," as Damascene says (De Fide Orth. ii).

Day 296

Whether works of satisfaction should be enjoined on sinners that have been baptized?
Objection 1: It seems that works of satisfaction should be enjoined on sinners that have been baptized. For God's justice seems to demand that a man should be punished for every sin of his, according to Eccles. 12:14: "All things that are done, God will bring into judgment." But works of satisfaction are enjoined on sinners in punishment of past sins. Therefore it seems that works of satisfaction should be enjoined on sinners that have been baptized.

Objection 2: Further, by means of works of satisfaction sinners recently converted are drilled into righteousness, and are made to avoid the occasions of sin: "for satisfaction consists in extirpating the causes of vice, and closing the doors to sin" (De Eccl. Dogm. iv). But this is most necessary in the case of those who have been baptized recently. Therefore it seems that works of satisfaction should be enjoined on sinners.

Objection 3: Further, man owes satisfaction to God not less than to his neighbor. But if those who were recently baptized have injured their neighbor, they should be told to make reparation to God by works of penance.

On the contrary, Ambrose commenting on Rom. 11:29: "The gifts and the calling of God are without repentance," says: "The grace of God requires neither sighs nor groans in Baptism, nor indeed any work at all, but faith alone; and remits all, gratis."

I answer that, As the Apostle says (Rom. 6:3,4), "all we who are baptized in Christ Jesus, are baptized in His death: for we are buried together with Him, by Baptism unto death"; which is to say that by Baptism man is incorporated in the very death of Christ. Now it is manifest from what has been said above ([4445]Q[48], AA[2],4;[4446] Q[49], A[3]) that Christ's death satisfied sufficiently for sins, "not for ours only, but also for those of the whole world," according to 1 Jn. 2:2. Consequently no kind of satisfaction should be enjoined on one who is being baptized, for any sins whatever: and this would be to dishonor the Passion and death of Christ, as being insufficient for the plenary satisfaction for the sins of those who were to be baptized.

Reply to Objection 1: As Augustine says in his book on Infant Baptism (De Pecc. Merit. et Remiss. i), "the effect of Baptism is to make those, who are baptized, to be incorporated in Christ as His members." Wherefore the very pains of Christ were satisfactory for the sins of those who were to be baptized; just as the pain of one member can be satisfactory for the sin of another member. Hence it is written (Is. 53:4): "Surely He hath borne our infirmities and carried our sorrows."

Reply to Objection 2: Those who have been lately baptized should be drilled into righteousness, not by penal, but by "easy works, so as to advance to perfection by taking exercise, as infants by taking milk," as a gloss says on Ps. 130:2: "As a child that is weaned is towards his mother." For this reason did our Lord excuse His disciples from fasting when they were recently converted, as we read in Mat. 9:14,15: and the same is written 1 Pet. 2:2: "As new-born babes desire . . . milk . . . that thereby you may grow unto salvation."

Reply to Objection 3: To restore what has been ill taken from one's neighbor, and to make satisfaction for wrong done to him, is to cease from sin: for the very fact of retaining what belongs to another and of not being reconciled to one's neighbor, is a sin. Wherefore those who are baptized should be enjoined to make satisfaction to their neighbor, as also to desist from sin. But they are not to be enjoined to suffer any punishment for past sins.

Whether sinners who are going to be baptized are bound to confess their sins?

Objection 1: It seems that sinners who are going to be baptized are bound to confess their sins. For it is written (Mat. 3:6) that many "were baptized" by John "in the Jordan confessing their sins." But Christ's Baptism is more perfect than John's. Therefore it seems that there is yet greater reason why they who are about to receive Christ's Baptism should confess their sins.

Objection 2: Further, it is written (Prov. 28:13): "He that hideth his sins, shall not prosper; but he that shall confess and forsake them, shall obtain mercy." Now for this is a man baptized, that he may obtain mercy for his sins. Therefore those who are going to be baptized should confess their sins.

Objection 3: Further, Penance is required before Baptism, according to Acts 2:38: "Do penance and be baptized every one of you." But confession is a part of Penance. Therefore it seems that confession of sins should take place before Baptism.

On the contrary, Confession of sins should be sorrowful: thus Augustine says (De Vera et Falsa Poenit. xiv): "All these circumstances should be taken into account and deplored." Now, as Ambrose says on Rom. 11:29, "the grace of God requires neither sighs nor groans in Baptism." Therefore confession of sins should not be required of those who are going to be baptized.

I answer that, Confession of sins is twofold. One is made inwardly to God: and such confession of sins is required before Baptism: in other words, man should call his sins to mind and sorrow for them; since "he cannot begin the new life, except he repent of his former life," as Augustine says in his book on Penance (Serm. cccli). The other is the outward confession of sins, which is made to a priest; and such confession is not required before Baptism. First, because this confession, since it is directed to the person of the minister, belongs to the sacrament of Penance, which is not required before Baptism, which is the door of all the sacraments. Secondly, because the reason why a man makes outward confession to a priest, is that the priest may absolve him from his sins, and bind him to works of satisfaction, which should not be enjoined on the baptized, as stated above [4447](A[5]). Moreover those who are being baptized do not need to be released from their sins by the keys of the Church, since all are forgiven them in Baptism. Thirdly, because the very act of confession made to a man is penal, by reason of the shame it inflicts on the one confessing: whereas no exterior punishment is enjoined on a man who is being baptized.

Therefore no special confession of sins is required of those who are being baptized; but that general confession suffices which they make when in accordance with the Church's ritual they "renounce Satan and all his works." And in this sense a gloss explains Mat. 3:6, saying that in John's Baptism "those who are going to be baptized learn that they should confess their sins and promise to amend their life."

If, however, any persons about to be baptized, wish, out of devotion, to confess their sins, their confession should be heard; not for the purpose of enjoining them to do satisfaction, but in order to instruct them in the spiritual life as a remedy against their vicious habits.

Reply to Objection 1: Sins were not forgiven in John's Baptism, which, however, was the Baptism of Penance. Consequently it was fitting that those who went to receive that Baptism, should confess their sins, so that they should receive a penance in proportion to their sins. But Christ's Baptism is without outward penance, as Ambrose says (on Rom. 11:29); and therefore there is no comparison.

Reply to Objection 2: It is enough that the baptized make inward confession to God, and also an outward general confession, for them to "prosper and obtain mercy": and they need no special outward confession, as stated above.

Reply to Objection 3: Confession is a part of sacramental Penance, which is not required before Baptism, as stated above: but the inward virtue of Penance is required.

Whether the intention of receiving the sacrament of Baptism is required on the part of the one baptized?

Objection 1: It seems that the intention of receiving the sacrament of Baptism is not required on the part of the one baptized. For the one baptized is, as it were, "patient" in the sacrament. But an intention is required not on the part of the patient but on the part of the agent. Therefore it seems that the intention of receiving Baptism is not required on the part of the one baptized.

Objection 2: Further, if what is necessary for Baptism be omitted, the Baptism must be repeated; for instance, if the invocation of the Trinity be omitted, as stated above ([4448]Q[66], A[9], ad 3). But it does not seem that a man should be rebaptized through not having had the intention of receiving Baptism: else, since his intention cannot be proved, anyone might ask to be baptized again on account of his lack of intention. Therefore it seems that no intention is required on the part of the one baptized, in order that he receive the sacrament.

Objection 3: Further, Baptism is given as a remedy for original sin. But original sin is contracted without the intention of the person born. Therefore, seemingly, Baptism requires no intention on the part of the person baptized.

On the contrary, According to the Church's ritual, those who are to be baptized ask of the Church that they may receive Baptism: and thus they express their intention of receiving the sacrament.

I answer that, By Baptism a man dies to the old life of sin, and begins a certain newness of life, according to Rom. 6:4: "We are buried together with" Christ "by Baptism into death; that, as Christ is risen from the dead . . . so we also may walk in newness of life." Consequently, just as, according to Augustine (Serm. cccli), he who has the use of free-will, must, in order to die to the old life, "will to repent of his former life"; so must he, of his own will, intend to lead a new life, the beginning of which is precisely the receiving of the sacrament. Therefore on the part of the one baptized, it is necessary for him to have the will or intention of receiving the sacrament.

Reply to Objection 1: When a man is justified by Baptism, his passiveness is not violent but voluntary: wherefore it is necessary for him to intend to receive that which is given him.

Reply to Objection 2: If an adult lack the intention of receiving the sacrament, he must be rebaptized. But if there be doubt about this, the form to be used should be: "If thou art not baptized, I baptize thee."

Reply to Objection 3: Baptism is a remedy not only against original, but also against actual sins, which are caused by our will and intention.

Whether faith is required on the part of the one baptized?

Objection 1: It seems that faith is required on the part of the one baptized. For the sacrament of Baptism was instituted by Christ. But Christ, in giving the form of Baptism, makes faith to precede Baptism (Mk. 16:16): "He that believeth and is baptized, shall be saved." Therefore it seems that without faith there can be no sacrament of Baptism.

Objection 2: Further, nothing useless is done in the sacraments of the Church. But according to the Church's ritual, the man who comes to be baptized is asked concerning his faith: "Dost thou believe in God the Father Almighty?" Therefore it seems that faith is required for Baptism.

Objection 3: Further, the intention of receiving the sacrament is required for Baptism. But this cannot be without right faith, since Baptism is the sacrament of right faith: for thereby men "are incorporated in Christ," as Augustine says in his book on Infant Baptism (De Pecc. Merit. et Remiss. i); and this cannot be without right faith, according to Eph. 3:17: "That Christ may dwell by faith in your hearts." Therefore it seems that a man who has not right faith cannot receive the sacrament of Baptism.

Objection 4: Further, unbelief is a most grievous sin, as we have shown in the [4449]SS, Q[10], A[3]. But those who remain in sin should not be baptized: therefore neither should those who remain in unbelief.

On the contrary, Gregory writing to the bishop Quiricus says: "We have learned from the ancient tradition of the Fathers that when heretics, baptized in the name of the Trinity, come back to Holy Church, they are to be welcomed to her bosom, either with the anointing of chrism, or the imposition of hands, or the mere profession of faith." But such would not be the case if faith were necessary for a man to receive Baptism.

I answer that, As appears from what has been said above ([4450]Q[63], A[6];[4451] Q[66], A[9]) Baptism produces a twofold effect in the soul, viz. the character and grace. Therefore in two ways may a thing be necessary for Baptism. First, as something without which grace, which is the ultimate effect of the sacrament, cannot be had. And thus right faith is necessary for Baptism, because, as it appears from Rom. 3:22, the justice of God is by faith of Jesus Christ.

Secondly, something is required of necessity for Baptism, because without it the baptismal character cannot be imprinted And thus right faith is not necessary in the one baptized any more than in the one who baptizes: provided the other conditions are fulfilled which are essential to the sacrament. For the sacrament is not perfected by the righteousness of the minister or of the recipient of Baptism, but by the power of God.

Reply to Objection 1: Our Lord is speaking there of Baptism as bringing us to salvation by giving us sanctifying grace: which of course cannot be without right faith: wherefore He says pointedly: "He that believeth and is baptized, shall be saved."

Reply to Objection 2: The Church's intention in Baptizing men is that they may be cleansed from sin, according to Is. 27:9: "This is all the fruit, that the sin . . . should be taken away." And therefore, as far as she is concerned, she does not intend to give Baptism save to those who have right faith, without which there is no remission of sins. And for this reason she asks those who come to be baptized whether they believe. If, on the contrary, anyone, without right faith, receive Baptism outside the Church, he does not receive it unto salvation. Hence Augustine says (De Baptism. contr. Donat. iv): "From the Church being compared to Paradise we learn that men can receive her Baptism even outside her fold, but that elsewhere none can receive or keep the salvation of the blessed."

Reply to Objection 3: Even he who has not right faith on other points, can have right faith about the sacrament of Baptism: and so he is not hindered from having the intention of receiving that sacrament. Yet even if he think not aright concerning this sacrament, it is enough, for the receiving of the sacrament, that he should have a general intention of receiving Baptism, according as Christ instituted, and as the Church bestows it.

Reply to Objection 4: Just as the sacrament of Baptism is not to be conferred on a man who is unwilling to give up his other sins, so neither should it be given to one who is unwilling to renounce his unbelief. Yet each receives the sacrament if it be conferred on him, though not unto salvation.

Whether children should be baptized?

Objection 1: It seems that children should not be baptized. For the intention to receive the sacrament is required in one who is being baptized, as stated above [4452](A[7]). But children cannot have such an intention, since they have not the use of free-will. Therefore it seems that they cannot receive the sacrament of Baptism.

Objection 2: Further, Baptism is the sacrament of faith, as stated above ([4453]Q[39], A[5];[4454] Q[66], A[1], ad 1). But children have not faith, which demands an act of the will on the part of the believer, as Augustine says (Super Joan. xxvi). Nor can it be said that their salvation is implied in the faith of their parents; since the latter are sometimes unbelievers, and their unbelief would conduce rather to the damnation of their children. Therefore it seems that children cannot be baptized.

Objection 3: Further, it is written (1 Pet. 3:21) that "Baptism saveth" men; "not the putting away of the filth of the flesh, but the examination of a good conscience towards God." But children have no conscience, either good or bad, since they have not the use of reason: nor can they be fittingly examined, since they understand not. Therefore children should not be baptized.

On the contrary, Dionysius says (Eccl. Hier. iii): "Our heavenly guides," i.e. the Apostles, "approved of infants being admitted to Baptism."

I answer that, As the Apostle says (Rom. 5:17), "if by one man's offense death reigned through one," namely Adam, "much more they who receive abundance of grace, and of the gift, and of justice, shall reign in life through one, Jesus Christ." Now children contract original sin from the sin of Adam; which is made clear by the fact that they are under the ban of death, which "passed upon all" on account of the sin of the first man, as the Apostle says in the same passage (Rom. 5:12). Much more, therefore, can children receive grace through Christ, so as to reign in eternal life. But our Lord Himself said (Jn. 3:5): "Unless a man be born again of water and the Holy Ghost, he cannot enter into the kingdom of God." Consequently it became necessary to baptize children, that, as in birth they incurred damnation through Adam so in a second birth they might obtain salvation through Christ. Moreover it was fitting that children should receive Baptism, in order that being reared from childhood in things pertaining to the Christian mode of life, they may the more easily persevere therein; according to Prov. 22:5: "A young man according to his way, even when he is old, he will not depart from it." This reason is also given by Dionysius (Eccl. Hier. iii).

Reply to Objection 1: The spiritual regeneration effected by Baptism is somewhat like carnal birth, in this respect, that as the child while in the mother's womb receives nourishment not independently, but through the nourishment of its mother, so also children before the use of reason, being as it were in the womb of their mother the Church, receive salvation not by their own act, but by the act of the Church. Hence Augustine says (De Pecc. Merit. et Remiss. i): "The Church, our mother, offers her maternal mouth for her children, that they may imbibe the sacred mysteries: for they cannot as yet with their own hearts believe unto justice, nor with their own mouths confess unto salvation . . . And if they are rightly said to believe, because in a certain fashion they make profession of faith by the words of their sponsors, why should they not also be said to repent, since by the words of those same sponsors they evidence their renunciation of the devil and this world?" For the same reason they can be said to intend, not by their own act of intention, since at times they struggle and cry; but by the act of those who bring them to be baptized.

Reply to Objection 2: As Augustine says, writing to Boniface (Cont. duas Ep. Pelag. i), "in the Church of our Saviour little children believe through others, just as they contracted from others those sins which are remitted in Baptism." Nor is it a hindrance to their salvation if their parents be unbelievers, because, as Augustine says, writing to the same Boniface (Ep. xcviii), "little children are offered that they may receive grace in their souls, not so much from the hands of those that carry them (yet from these too, if they be good and faithful) as from the whole company of the saints and the faithful. For they are rightly considered to be offered by those who are pleased at their being offered, and by whose charity they are united in communion with the Holy Ghost." And the unbelief of their own parents, even if after Baptism these strive to infect them with the worship of demons, hurts not the children. For as Augustine says (Cont. duas Ep. Pelag. i) "when once the child has been begotten by the will of others, he cannot subsequently be held by the bonds of another's sin so long as he consent not with his will, according to" Ezech. 18:4: "'As the soul of the Father, so also the soul of the son is mine; the soul that sinneth, the same shall die.' Yet he contracted from Adam that which was loosed by the grace of this sacrament, because as yet he was not endowed with a separate existence." But the faith of one, indeed of the whole Church, profits the child through the operation of the Holy Ghost, Who unites the Church together, and communicates the goods of one member to another.

Reply to Objection 3: Just as a child, when he is being baptized, believes not by himself but by others, so is he examined not by himself but through others, and these in answer confess the Church's faith in the child's stead, who is aggregated to this faith by the sacrament of faith. And the child acquires a good conscience in himself, not indeed as to the act, but as to the habit, by sanctifying grace.

Whether children of Jews or other unbelievers be baptized against the will of their parents?

Objection 1: It seems that children of Jews or other unbelievers should be baptized against the will of their parents. For it is a matter of greater urgency to rescue a man from the danger of eternal death than from the danger of temporal death. But one ought to rescue a child that is threatened by the danger of temporal death, even if its parents through malice try to prevent its being rescued. Therefore much more reason is there for rescuing the children of unbelievers from the danger of eternal death, even against their parents' will.

Objection 2: The children of slaves are themselves slaves, and in the power of their masters. But Jews and all other unbelievers are the slaves of kings and rulers. Therefore without any injustice rulers can have the children of Jews baptized, as well as those of other slaves who are unbelievers.

Objection 3: Further, every man belongs more to God, from Whom he has his soul, than to his carnal father, from whom he has his body. Therefore it is not unjust if the children of unbelievers are taken away from their carnal parents, and consecrated to God by Baptism.

On the contrary, It is written in the Decretals (Dist. xlv), quoting the council of Toledo: "In regard to the Jews the holy synod commands that henceforward none of them be forced to believe: for such are not to be saved against their will, but willingly, that their righteousness may be without flaw."

I answer that, The children of unbelievers either have the use of reason or they have not. If they have, then they already begin to control their own actions, in things that are of Divine or natural law. And therefore of their own accord, and against the will of their parents, they can receive Baptism, just as they can contract marriage. Consequently such can lawfully be advised and persuaded to be baptized.

If, however, they have not yet the use of free-will, according to the natural law they are under the care of their parents as long as they cannot look after themselves. For which reason we say that even the children of the ancients "were saved through the faith of their parents." Wherefore it would be contrary to natural justice if such children were baptized against their parents' will; just as it would be if one having the use of reason were baptized against his will. Moreover under the circumstances it would be dangerous to baptize the children of unbelievers; for they would be liable to lapse into unbelief, by reason of their natural affection for their parents. Therefore it is not the custom of the Church to baptize the children of unbelievers against their parents' will.

Reply to Objection 1: It is not right to rescue a man from death of the body against the order of civil law: for instance, if a man be condemned to death by the judge who has tried him, none should use force in order to rescue him from death. Consequently, neither should anyone infringe the order of the natural law, in virtue of which a child is under the care of its father, in order to rescue it from the danger of eternal death.

Reply to Objection 2: Jews are slaves of rulers by civil slavery, which does not exclude the order of the natural and Divine law.

Reply to Objection 3: Man is ordained unto God through his reason, by which he can know God. Wherefore a child, before it has the use of reason, is ordained to God, by a natural order, through the reason of its parents, under whose care it naturally lies, and it is according to their ordering that things pertaining to God are to be done in respect of the child.

Whether a child can be baptized while yet in its mother's womb?

Objection 1: It seems that a child can be baptized while yet in its mother's womb. For the gift of Christ is more efficacious unto salvation than Adam's sin unto condemnation, as the Apostle says (Rom. 5:15). But a child while yet in its mother's womb is under sentence of condemnation on account of Adam's sin. For much more reason, therefore, can it be saved through the gift of Christ, which is bestowed by means of Baptism. Therefore a child can be baptized while yet in its mother's womb.

Objection 2: Further, a child, while yet in its mother's womb, seems to be part of its mother. Now, when the mother is baptized, whatever is in her and part of her, is baptized. Therefore it seems that when the mother is baptized, the child in her womb is baptized.

Objection 3: Further, eternal death is a greater evil than death of the body. But of two evils the less should be chosen. If, therefore, the child in the mother's womb cannot be baptized, it would be better for the mother to be opened, and the child to be taken out by force and baptized, than that the child should be eternally damned through dying without Baptism.

Objection 4: Further, it happens at times that some part of the child comes forth first, as we read in Gn. 38:27: "In the very delivery of the infants, one put forth a hand, whereon the midwife tied a scarlet thread, saying: This shall come forth the first. But he drawing back his hand, the other came forth." Now sometimes in such cases there is danger of death. Therefore it seems that that part should be baptized, while the child is yet in its mother's womb.

On the contrary, Augustine says (Ep. ad Dardan.): "No one can be born a second time unless he be born first." But Baptism is a spiritual regeneration. Therefore no one should be baptized before he is born from the womb.

I answer that, It is essential to Baptism that some part of the body of the person baptized be in some way washed with water, since Baptism is a kind of washing, as stated above ([4455]Q[66], A[1]). But an infant's body, before being born from the womb, can nowise be washed with water; unless perchance it be said that the baptismal water, with which the mother's body is washed, reaches the child while yet in its mother's womb. But this is impossible: both because the child's soul, to the sanctification of which Baptism is ordained, is distinct from the soul of the mother; and because the body of the animated infant is already formed, and consequently distinct from the body of the mother. Therefore the Baptism which the mother receives does not overflow on to the child which is in her womb. Hence Augustine says (Cont. Julian. vi): "If what is conceived within a mother belonged to her body, so as to be considered a part thereof, we should not baptize an infant whose mother, through danger of death, was baptized while she bore it in her womb. Since, then, it," i.e. the infant, "is baptized, it certainly did not belong to the mother's body while it was in the womb." It follows, therefore, that a child can nowise be baptized while in its mother's womb.

Reply to Objection 1: Children while in the mother's womb have not yet come forth into the world to live among other men. Consequently they cannot be subject to the action of man, so as to receive the sacrament, at the hands of man, unto salvation. They can, however, be subject to the action of God, in Whose sight they live, so as, by a kind of privilege, to receive the grace of sanctification; as was the case with those who were sanctified in the womb.

Reply to Objection 2: An internal member of the mother is something of hers by continuity and material union of the part with the whole: whereas a child while in its mother's womb is something of hers through being joined with, and yet distinct from her. Wherefore there is no comparison.

Reply to Objection 3: We should "not do evil that there may come good" (Rom. 3:8). Therefore it is wrong to kill a mother that her child may be baptized. If, however, the mother die while the child lives yet in her womb, she should be opened that the child may be baptized.

Reply to Objection 4: Unless death be imminent, we should wait until the child has entirely come forth from the womb before baptizing it. If, however, the head, wherein the senses are rooted, appear first, it should be baptized, in cases of danger: nor should it be baptized again, if perfect birth should ensue. And seemingly the same should be done in cases of danger no matter what part of the body appear first. But as none of the exterior parts of the body belong to its integrity in the same degree as the head, some hold that since the matter is doubtful, whenever any other part of the body has been baptized, the child, when perfect birth has taken place, should be baptized with the form: "If thou art not baptized, I baptize thee," etc.

Whether madmen and imbeciles should be baptized?
Objection 1: It seems that madmen and imbeciles should not be baptized. For in order to receive Baptism, the person baptized must have the intention, as stated above [4456](A[7]). But since madmen and imbeciles lack the use of reason, they can have but a disorderly intention. Therefore they should not be baptized.

Objection 2: Further, man excels irrational animals in that he has reason. But madmen and imbeciles lack the use of reason, indeed in some cases we do not expect them ever to have it, as we do in the case of children. It seems, therefore, that just as irrational animals are not baptized, so neither should madmen and imbeciles in those cases be baptized.

Objection 3: Further, the use of reason is suspended in madmen and imbeciles more than it is in one who sleeps. But it is not customary to baptize people while they sleep. Therefore it should not be given to madmen and imbeciles.

On the contrary, Augustine says (Confess. iv) of his friend that "he was baptized when his recovery was despaired of": and yet Baptism was efficacious with him. Therefore Baptism should sometimes be given to those who lack the use of reason.

I answer that, In the matter of madmen and imbeciles a distinction is to be made. For some are so from birth, and have no lucid intervals, and show no signs of the use of reason. And with regard to these it seems that we should come to the same decision as with regard to children who are baptized in the Faith of the Church, as stated above (A[9], ad 2).

But there are others who have fallen from a state of sanity into a state of insanity. And with regard to these we must be guided by their wishes as expressed by them when sane: so that, if then they manifested a desire to receive Baptism, it should be given to them when in a state of madness or imbecility, even though then they refuse. If, on the other hand, while sane they showed no desire to receive Baptism, they must not be baptized.

Again, there are some who, though mad or imbecile from birth, have, nevertheless, lucid intervals, in which they can make right use of reason. Wherefore, if then they express a desire for Baptism, they can be baptized though they be actually in a state of madness. And in this case the sacrament should be bestowed on them if there be fear of danger otherwise it is better to wait until the time when they are sane, so that they may receive the sacrament more devoutly. But if during the interval of lucidity they manifest no desire to receive Baptism, they should not be baptized while in a state of insanity.

Lastly there are others who, though not altogether sane, yet can use their reason so far as to think about their salvation, and understand the power of the sacrament. And these are to be treated the same as those who are sane, and who are baptized if they be willing, but not against their will.

Reply to Objection 1: Imbeciles who never had, and have not now, the use of reason, are baptized, according to the Church's intention, just as according to the Church's ritual, they believe and repent; as we have stated above of children (A[9], ad OBJ). But those who have had the use of reason at some time, or have now, are baptized according to their own intention, which they have now, or had when they were sane.

Reply to Objection 2: Madmen and imbeciles lack the use of reason accidentally, i.e. through some impediment in a bodily organ; but not like irrational animals through want of a rational soul. Consequently the comparison does not hold.

Reply to Objection 3: A person should not be baptized while asleep, except he be threatened with the danger of death. In which case he should be baptized, if previously he has manifested a desire to receive Baptism, as we have stated in reference to imbeciles: thus Augustine relates of his friend that "he was baptized while unconscious," because he was in danger of death (Confess. iv).

Day 297

OF THE EFFECTS OF BAPTISM (TEN ARTICLES)
We must now consider the effects of Baptism, concerning which there are ten points of inquiry:
(1) Whether all sins are taken away by Baptism?
(2) Whether man is freed from all punishment by Baptism?
(3) Whether Baptism takes away the penalties of sin that belong to this life?
(4) Whether grace and virtues are bestowed on man by Baptism?
(5) Of the effects of virtue which are conferred by Baptism?
(6) Whether even children receive grace and virtues in Baptism?
(7) Whether Baptism opens the gates of the heavenly kingdom to those who are baptized?
(8) Whether Baptism produces an equal effect in all who are baptized?
(9) Whether insincerity hinders the effect of Baptism?
(10) Whether Baptism takes effect when the insincerity ceases?

Whether all sins are taken away by Baptism?

Objection 1: It seems that not all sins are taken away by Baptism. For Baptism is a spiritual regeneration, which corresponds to carnal generation. But by carnal generation man contracts none but original sin. Therefore none but original sin is taken away by Baptism.

Objection 2: Further, Penance is a sufficient cause of the remission of actual sins. But penance is required in adults before Baptism, according to Acts 2:38: "Do penance and be baptized every one of you." Therefore Baptism has nothing to do with the remission of actual sins.

Objection 3: Further, various diseases demand various remedies: because as Jerome says on Mk. 9:27,28: "What is a cure for the heel is no cure for the eye." But original sin, which is taken away by Baptism, is generically distinct from actual sin. Therefore not all sins are taken away by Baptism.

On the contrary, It is written (Ezech. 36:25): "I will pour upon you clean water, and you shall be cleansed from all your filthiness."

I answer that, As the Apostle says (Rom. 6:3), "all we, who are baptized in Christ Jesus, are baptized in His death." And further on he concludes (Rom. 6:11): "So do you also reckon that you are dead to sin, but alive unto God in Christ Jesus our Lord." Hence it is clear that by Baptism man dies unto the oldness of sin, and begins to live unto the newness of grace. But every sin belongs to the primitive oldness. Consequently every sin is taken away by Baptism.

Reply to Objection 1: As the Apostle says (Rom. 5:15,16), the sin of Adam was not so far-reaching as the gift of Christ, which is bestowed in Baptism: "for judgment was by one unto condemnation; but grace is of many offenses, unto justification." Wherefore Augustine says in his book on Infant Baptism (De Pecc. Merit. et Remiss. i), that "in carnal generation, original sin alone is contracted; but when we are born again of the Spirit, not only original sin but also wilful sin is forgiven."

Reply to Objection 2: No sin can be forgiven save by the power of Christ's Passion: hence the Apostle says (Heb. 9:22) that "without shedding of blood there is no remission." Consequently no movement of the human will suffices for the remission of sin, unless there be faith in Christ's Passion, and the purpose of participating in it, either by receiving Baptism, or by submitting to the keys of the Church. Therefore when an adult approaches Baptism, he does indeed receive the forgiveness of all his sins through his purpose of being baptized, but more perfectly through the actual reception of Baptism.

Reply to Objection 3: This argument is true of special remedies. But Baptism operates by the power of Christ's Passion, which is the universal remedy for all sins; and so by Baptism all sins are loosed.

Whether man is freed by Baptism from all debt of punishment due to sin?

Objection 1: It seems that man is not freed by Baptism from all debt of punishment due to sin. For the Apostle says (Rom. 13:1): "Those things that are of God are well ordered [Vulg.: 'Those that are, are ordained of God']." But guilt is not set in order save by punishment, as Augustine says (Ep. cxl). Therefore Baptism does not take away the debt of punishment due to sins already committed.

Objection 2: Further, the effect of a sacrament has a certain likeness to the sacrament itself; since the sacraments of the New Law "effect what they signify," as stated above ([4457]Q[62], A[1], ad 1). But the washing of Baptism has indeed a certain likeness with the cleansing from the stain of sin, but none, seemingly, with the remission of the debt of punishment. Therefore the debt of punishment is not taken away by Baptism.

Objection 3: Further, when the debt of punishment has been remitted, a man no longer deserves to be punished, and so it would be unjust to punish him. If, therefore, the debt of punishment be remitted by Baptism, it would be unjust, after Baptism, to hang a thief who had committed murder before. Consequently the severity of human legislation would be relaxed on account of Baptism; which is undesirable. Therefore Baptism does not remit the debt of punishment.

On the contrary, Ambrose, commenting on Rom. 11:29, "The gifts and the calling of God ate without repentance," says: "The grace of God in Baptism remits all, gratis."

I answer that, As stated above ([4458]Q[49], A[3], ad 2;[4459] Q[68], AA[1],4,5) by Baptism a man is incorporated in the Passion and death of Christ, according to Rom. 6:8: "If we be dead with Christ, we believe that we shall live also together with Christ." Hence it is clear that the Passion of Christ is communicated to every baptized person, so that he is healed just as if he himself had suffered and died. Now Christ's Passion, as stated above ([4460]Q[68], A[5]), is a sufficient satisfaction for all the sins of all men. Consequently he who is baptized, is freed from the debt of all punishment due to him for his sins, just as if he himself had offered sufficient satisfaction for all his sins.

Reply to Objection 1: Since the pains of Christ's Passion are communicated to the person baptized, inasmuch as he is made a member of Christ, just as if he himself had borne those pains, his sins are set in order by the pains of Christ's Passion.

Reply to Objection 2: Water not only cleanses but also refreshes. And thus by refreshing it signifies the remission of the debt of punishment, just as by cleansing it signifies the washing away of guilt.

Reply to Objection 3: In punishments inflicted by a human tribunal, we have to consider not only what punishment a man deserves in respect of God, but also to what extent he is indebted to men who are hurt and scandalized by another's sin. Consequently, although a murderer is freed by Baptism from his debt of punishment in respect of God, he remains, nevertheless, in debt to men; and it is right that they should be edified at his punishment, since they were scandalized at his sin. But the sovereign may remit the penalty to such like out of kindness.

Whether Baptism should take away the penalties of sin that belong to this life?

Objection 1: It seems that Baptism should take away the penalties of sin that belong to this life. For as the Apostle says (Rom. 5:15), the gift of Christ is farther-reaching than the sin of Adam. But through Adam's sin, as the Apostle says (Rom. 5:12), "death entered into this world," and, consequently, all the other penalties of the present life. Much more, therefore, should man be freed from the penalties of the present life, by the gift of Christ which is received in Baptism.

Objection 2: Further, Baptism takes away the guilt of both original and actual sin. Now it takes away the guilt of actual sin in such a way as to free man from all debt of punishment resulting therefrom. Therefore it also frees man from the penalties of the present life, which are a punishment of original sin.

Objection 3: Further, if the cause be removed, the effect is removed. But the cause of these penalties is original sin, which is taken away by Baptism. Therefore such like penalties should not remain.

On the contrary, on Rom. 6:6, "that the body of sin may be destroyed," a gloss says: "The effect of Baptism is that the old man is crucified, and the body of sin destroyed, not as though the living flesh of man were delivered by the destruction of that concupiscence with which it has been bespattered from its birth; but that it may not hurt him, when dead, though it was in him when he was born." Therefore for the same reason neither are the other penalties taken away by Baptism.

I answer that, Baptism has the power to take away the penalties of the present life yet it does not take them away during the present life, but by its power they will be taken away from the just in the resurrection when "this mortal hath put on immortality" (1 Cor. 15:54). And this is reasonable. First, because, by Baptism, man is incorporated in Christ, and is made His member, as stated above [4461](A[3]; Q[68], A[5]). Consequently it is fitting that what takes place in the Head should take place also in the member incorporated. Now, from the very beginning of His conception Christ was "full of grace and truth," yet He had a passible body, which through His Passion and death was raised up to a life of glory. Wherefore a Christian receives grace in Baptism, as to his soul; but he retains a passible body, so that he may suffer for Christ therein: yet at length he will be raised up to a life of impassibility. Hence the Apostle says (Rom. 8:11): "He that raised up Jesus Christ from the dead, shall quicken also our [Vulg.: 'your'] mortal bodies, because of His Spirit that dwelleth in us [Vulg.: 'you']": and further on in the same chapter (Rom. 8:17): "Heirs indeed of God, and joint heirs with Christ: yet so, if we suffer with Him, that we may be also glorified with Him."

Secondly, this is suitable for our spiritual training: namely, in order that, by fighting against concupiscence and other defects to which he is subject, man may receive the crown of victory. Wherefore on Rom. 6:6, "that the body of sin may be destroyed," a gloss says: "If a man after Baptism live in the flesh, he has concupiscence to fight against, and to conquer by God's help." In sign of which it is written (Judges 3:1,2): "These are the nations which the Lord left, that by them He might instruct Israel . . . that afterwards their children might learn to fight with their enemies, and to be trained up to war."

Thirdly, this was suitable, lest men might seek to be baptized for the sake of impassibility in the present life, and not for the sake of the glory of life eternal. Wherefore the Apostle says (1 Cor. 15:19): "If in this life only we have hope in Christ, we are of all men most miserable."

Reply to Objection 1: As a gloss says on Rom. 6:6, "that we may serve sin no longer---Like a man who, having captured a redoubtable enemy, slays him not forthwith, but suffers him to live for a little time in shame and suffering; so did Christ first of all fetter our punishment, but at a future time He will destroy it."

Reply to Objection 2: As the gloss says on the same passage (cf. ad 1), "the punishment of sin is twofold, the punishment of hell, and temporal punishment. Christ entirely abolished the punishment of hell, so that those who are baptized and truly repent, should not be subject to it. He did not, however, altogether abolish temporal punishment yet awhile; for hunger, thirst, and death still remain. But He overthrew its kingdom and power" in the sense that man should no longer be in fear of them: "and at length He will altogether exterminate it at the last day."

Reply to Objection 3: As we stated in the [4462]FS, Q[81], A[1]; [4463]FS, Q[82], A[1], ad 2 original sin spread in this way, that at first the person infected the nature, and afterwards the nature infected the person. Whereas Christ in reverse order at first repairs what regards the person, and afterwards will simultaneously repair what pertains to the nature in all men. Consequently by Baptism He takes away from man forthwith the guilt of original sin and the punishment of being deprived of the heavenly vision. But the penalties of the present life, such as death, hunger, thirst, and the like, pertain to the nature, from the principles of which they arise, inasmuch as it is deprived of original justice. Therefore these defects will not be taken away until the ultimate restoration of nature through the glorious resurrection.

Whether grace and virtues are bestowed on man by Baptism?

Objection 1: It seems that grace and virtues are not bestowed on man by Baptism. Because, as stated above ([4464]Q[62], A[1], ad 1), the sacraments of the New Law "effect what they signify." But the baptismal cleansing signifies the cleansing of the soul from guilt, and not the fashioning of the soul with grace and virtues. Therefore it seems that grace and virtues are not bestowed on man by Baptism.

Objection 2: Further, one does not need to receive what one has already acquired. But some approach Baptism who have already grace and virtues: thus we read (Acts 10:1,2): "There was a certain man in Cesarea, named Cornelius, a centurion of that which is called the Italian band, a religious man and fearing God"; who, nevertheless, was afterwards baptized by Peter. Therefore grace and virtues are not bestowed by Baptism.

Objection 3: Further, virtue is a habit: which is defined as a "quality not easily removed, by which one may act easily and pleasurably." But after Baptism man retains proneness to evil which removes virtue; and experiences difficulty in doing good, in which the act of virtue consists. Therefore man does not acquire grace and virtue in Baptism.

On the contrary, The Apostle says (Titus 3:5,6): "He saved us by the laver of regeneration," i.e. by Baptism, "and renovation of the Holy Ghost, Whom He hath poured forth upon us abundantly," i.e. "unto the remission of sins and the fulness of virtues," as a gloss expounds. Therefore the grace of the Holy Ghost and the fulness of virtues are given in Baptism.

I answer that, As Augustine says in the book on Infant Baptism (De Pecc. Merit. et Remiss. i) "the effect of Baptism is that the baptized are incorporated in Christ as His members." Now the fulness of grace and virtues flows from Christ the Head to all His members, according to Jn. 1:16: "Of His fulness we all have received." Hence it is clear that man receives grace and virtues in Baptism.

Reply to Objection 1: As the baptismal water by its cleansing signifies the washing away of guilt, and by its refreshment the remission of punishment, so by its natural clearness it signifies the splendor of grace and virtues.

Reply to Objection 2: As stated above (A[1], ad 2;[4465] Q[68], A[2]) man receives the forgiveness of sins before Baptism in so far as he has Baptism of desire, explicitly or implicitly; and yet when he actually receives Baptism, he receives a fuller remission, as to the remission of the entire punishment. So also before Baptism Cornelius and others like him receive grace and virtues through their faith in Christ and their desire for Baptism, implicit or explicit: but afterwards when baptized, they receive a yet greater fulness of grace and virtues. Hence in Ps. 22:2, "He hath brought me up on the water of refreshment," a gloss says: "He has brought us up by an increase of virtue and good deeds in Baptism."

Reply to Objection 3: Difficulty in doing good and proneness to evil are in the baptized, not through their lacking the habits of the virtues, but through concupiscence which is not taken away in Baptism. But just as concupiscence is diminished by Baptism, so as not to enslave us, so also are both the aforesaid defects diminished, so that man be not overcome by them.

Whether certain acts of the virtues are fittingly set down as effects of Baptism, to wit---incorporation in Christ, enlightenment, and fruitfulness?

Objection 1: It seems that certain acts of the virtues are unfittingly set down as effects of Baptism, to wit---"incorporation in Christ, enlightenment, and fruitfulness." For Baptism is not given to an adult, except he believe; according to Mk. 16:16: "He that believeth and is baptized, shall be saved." But it is by faith that man is incorporated in Christ, according to Eph. 3:17: "That Christ may dwell by faith in your hearts." Therefore no one is baptized except he be already incorporated in Christ. Therefore incorporation with Christ is not the effect of Baptism.

Objection 2: Further, enlightenment is caused by teaching, according to Eph. 3:8,9: "To me the least of all the saints, is given this grace . . . to enlighten all men," etc. But teaching by the catechism precedes Baptism. Therefore it is not the effect of Baptism.

Objection 3: Further, fruitfulness pertains to active generation. But a man is regenerated spiritually by Baptism. Therefore fruitfulness is not an effect of Baptism.

On the contrary, Augustine says in the book on Infant Baptism (De Pecc. Merit. et Remiss. i) that "the effect of Baptism is that the baptized are incorporated in Christ." And Dionysius (Eccl. Hier. ii) ascribes enlightenment to Baptism. And on Ps. 22:2, "He hath brought me up on the water of refreshment," a gloss says that "the sinner's soul, sterilized by drought, is made fruitful by Baptism."

I answer that, By Baptism man is born again unto the spiritual life, which is proper to the faithful of Christ, as the Apostle says (Gal. 2:20): "And that I live now in the flesh; I live in the faith of the Son of God." Now life is only in those members that are united to the head, from which they derive sense and movement. And therefore it follows of necessity that by Baptism man is incorporated in Christ, as one of His members. Again, just as the members derive sense and movement from the material head, so from their spiritual Head, i.e. Christ, do His members derive spiritual sense consisting in the knowledge Of truth, and spiritual movement which results from the instinct of grace. Hence it is written (Jn. 1:14, 16): "We have seen Him . . . full of grace and truth; and of His fulness we all have received." And it follows from this that the baptized are enlightened by Christ as to the knowledge of truth, and made fruitful by Him with the fruitfulness of good works by the infusion of grace.

Reply to Objection 1: Adults who already believe in Christ are incorporated in Him mentally. But afterwards, when they are baptized, they are incorporated in Him, corporally, as it were, i.e. by the visible sacrament; without the desire of which they could not have been incorporated in Him even mentally.

Reply to Objection 2: The teacher enlightens outwardly and ministerially by catechizing: but God enlightens the baptized inwardly, by preparing their hearts for the reception of the doctrines of truth, according to Jn. 6:45: "It is written in the prophets . . . They shall all be taught of God."

Reply to Objection 3: The fruitfulness which i ascribed as an effect of Baptism is that by which man brings forth good works; not that by which he begets others in Christ, as the Apostle says (1 Cor. 4:15): "In Christ Jesus by the Gospel I have begotten you."

Whether children receive grace and virtue in Baptism?

Objection 1: It seems that children do not receive grace and virtues in Baptism. For grace and virtues are not possessed without faith and charity. But faith, as Augustine says (Ep. xcviii), "depends on the will of the believer": and in like manner charity depends on the will of the lover. Now children have not the use of the will, and consequently they have neither faith nor charity. Therefore children do not receive grace and virtues in Baptism.

Objection 2: Further, on Jn. 14:12, "Greater than these shall he do," Augustine says that in order for the ungodly to be made righteous "Christ worketh in him, but not without him." But a child, through not having the use of free-will, does not co-operate with Christ unto its justification: indeed at times it does its best to resist. Therefore it is not justified by grace and virtues.

Objection 3: Further, it is written (Rom. 4:5): "To him that worketh not, yet believing in Him that justifieth the ungodly, his faith is reputed to justice according to the purpose of the grace of God." But a child believeth not "in Him that justifieth the ungodly." Therefore a child receives neither sanctifying grace nor virtues.

Objection 4: Further, what is done with a carnal intention does not seem to have a spiritual effect. But sometimes children are taken to Baptism with a carnal intention, to wit, that their bodies may be healed. Therefore they do not receive the spiritual effect consisting in grace and virtue.

On the contrary, Augustine says (Enchiridion lii): "When little children are baptized, they die to that sin which they contracted in birth: so that to them also may be applied the words: 'We are buried together with Him by Baptism unto death'": (and he continues thus) "'that as Christ is risen from the dead by the glory of the Father, so we also may walk in newness of life.'" Now newness of life is through grace and virtues. Therefore children receive grace and virtues in Baptism.

I answer that, Some of the early writers held that children do not receive grace and virtues in Baptism, but that they receive the imprint of the character of Christ, by the power of which they receive grace and virtue when they arrive at the perfect age. But this is evidently false, for two reasons. First, because children, like adults, are made members of Christ in Baptism; hence they must, of necessity, receive an influx of grace and virtues from the Head. Secondly, because, if this were true, children that die after Baptism, would not come to eternal life; since according to Rom. 6:23, "the grace of God is life everlasting." And consequently Baptism would not have profited them unto salvation.

Now the source of their error was that they did not recognize the distinction between habit and act. And so, seeing children to be incapable of acts of virtue, they thought that they had no virtues at all after Baptism. But this inability of children to act is not due to the absence of habits, but to an impediment on the part of the body: thus also when a man is asleep, though he may have the habits of virtue, yet is he hindered from virtuous acts through being asleep.

Reply to Objection 1: Faith and charity depend on man's will, yet so that the habits of these and other virtues require the power of the will which is in children; whereas acts of virtue require an act of the will, which is not in children. In this sense Augustine says in the book on Infant Baptism (Ep. xcviii): "The little child is made a believer, not as yet by that faith which depends on the will of the believer, but by the sacrament of faith itself," which causes the habit of faith.

Reply to Objection 2: As Augustine says in his book on Charity (Ep. Joan. ad Parth. iii), "no man is born of water and the Holy Ghost unwillingly which is to be understood not of little children but of adults." In like manner we are to understand as applying to adults, that man "without himself is not justified by Christ." Moreover, if little children who are about to be baptized resist as much as they can, "this is not imputed to them, since so little do they know what they do, that they seem not to do it at all": as Augustine says in a book on the Presence of God, addressed to Dardanus (Ep. clxxxvii).

Reply to Objection 3: As Augustine says (Serm. clxxvi): "Mother Church lends other feet to the little children that they may come; another heart that they may believe; another tongue that they may confess." So that children believe, not by their own act, but by the faith of the Church, which is applied to them: by the power of which faith, grace and virtues are bestowed on them.

Reply to Objection 4: The carnal intention of those who take children to be baptized does not hurt the latter, as neither does one's sin hurt another, unless he consent. Hence Augustine says in his letter to Boniface (Ep. xcviii): "Be not disturbed because some bring children to be baptized, not in the hope that they may be born again to eternal life by the spiritual grace, but because they think it to be a remedy whereby they may preserve or recover health. For they are not deprived of regeneration, through not being brought for this intention."

Whether the effect of Baptism is to open the gates of the heavenly kingdom?

Objection 1: It seems that it is not the effect of Baptism, to open the gates of the heavenly kingdom. For what is already opened needs no opening. But the gates of the heavenly kingdom were opened by Christ's Passion: hence it is written (Apoc. 4:1): "After these things I looked and behold (a great) door was opened in heaven." Therefore it is not the effect of Baptism, to open the gates of the heavenly kingdom.

Objection 2: Further, Baptism has had its effects ever since it was instituted. But some were baptized with Christ's Baptism, before His Passion, according to Jn. 3:22, 26: and if they had died then, the gates of the heavenly kingdom would not have been opened to them, since none entered therein before Christ, according to Mic. 2:13: "He went up [Vulg.: 'shall go up'] that shall open the way before them." Therefore it is not the effect of Baptism, to open the gates of the heavenly kingdom.

Objection 3: Further, the baptized are still subject to death and the other penalties of the present life, as stated above [4466](A[3]). But entrance to the heavenly kingdom is opened to none that are subject to punishment: as is clear in regard to those who are in purgatory. Therefore it is not the effect of Baptism, to open the gates of the heavenly kingdom.

On the contrary, on Lk. 3:21, "Heaven was opened," the gloss of Bede says: "We see here the power of Baptism; from which when a man comes forth, the gates of the heavenly kingdom are opened unto him."

I answer that, To open the gates of the heavenly kingdom is to remove the obstacle that prevents one from entering therein. Now this obstacle is guilt and the debt of punishment. But it has been shown above ([4467]AA[1] ,2) that all guilt and also all debt of punishment are taken away by Baptism. It follows, therefore, that the effect of Baptism is to open the gates of the heavenly kingdom.

Reply to Objection 1: Baptism opens the gates of the heavenly kingdom to the baptized in so far as it incorporates them in the Passion of Christ, by applying its power to man.

Reply to Objection 2: When Christ's Passion was not as yet consummated actually but only in the faith of believers, Baptism proportionately caused the gates to be opened, not in fact but in hope. For the baptized who died then looked forward, with a sure hope, to enter the heavenly kingdom.

Reply to Objection 3: The baptized are subject to death and the penalties of the present life, not by reason of a personal debt of punishment but by reason of the state of their nature. And therefore this is no bar to their entrance to the heavenly kingdom, when death severs the soul from the body; since they have paid, as it were, the debt of nature.

Whether Baptism has an equal effect in all?

Objection 1: It seems that Baptism has not an equal effect in all. For the effect of Baptism is to remove guilt. But in some it takes away more sins than in others; for in children it takes away only original sins, whereas in adults it takes away actual sins, in some many, in others few. Therefore Baptism has not an equal effect in all.

Objection 2: Further, grace and virtues are bestowed on man by Baptism. But some, after Baptism, seem to have more grace and more perfect virtue than others who have been baptized. Therefore Baptism has not an equal effect in all.

Objection 3: Further, nature is perfected by grace, as matter by form. But a form is received into matter according to its capacity. Therefore, since some of the baptized, even children, have greater capacity for natural gifts than others have, it seems that some receive greater grace than others.

Objection 4: Further, in Baptism some receive not only spiritual, but also bodily health; thus Constantine was cleansed in Baptism from leprosy. But all the infirm do not receive bodily health in Baptism. Therefore it has not an equal effect in all.

On the contrary, It is written (Eph. 4:5): "One Faith, one Baptism." But a uniform cause has a uniform effect. Therefore Baptism has an equal effect in all.

I answer that, The effect of Baptism is twofold, the essential effect, and the accidental. The essential effect of Baptism is that for which Baptism was instituted, namely, the begetting of men unto spiritual life. Therefore, since all children are equally disposed to Baptism, because they are baptized not in their own faith, but in that of the Church, they all receive an equal effect in Baptism. Whereas adults, who approach Baptism in their own faith, are not equally disposed to Baptism; for some approach thereto with greater, some with less, devotion. And therefore some receive a greater, some a smaller share of the grace of newness; just as from the same fire, he receives more heat who approaches nearest to it, although the fire, as far as it is concerned, sends forth its heat equally to all.

But the accidental effect of Baptism, is that to which Baptism is not ordained, but which the Divine power produces miraculously in Baptism: thus on Rom. 6:6, "that we may serve sin no longer," a gloss says: "this is not bestowed in Baptism, save by an ineffable miracle of the Creator, so that the law of sin, which is in our members, be absolutely destroyed." And such like effects are not equally received by all the baptized, even if they approach with equal devotion: but they are bestowed according to the ordering of Divine providence.

Reply to Objection 1: The least baptismal grace suffices to blot out all sins. Wherefore that in some more sins are loosed than in others is not due to the greater efficacy of Baptism, but to the condition of the recipient: for in each one it looses whatever it finds.

Reply to Objection 2: That greater or lesser grace appears in the baptized, may occur in two ways. First, because one receives greater grace in Baptism than another, on account of his greater devotion, as stated above. Secondly, because, though they receive equal grace, they do not make an equal use of it, but one applies himself more to advance therein, while another by his negligence baffles grace.

Reply to Objection 3: The various degrees of capacity in men arise, not from a variety in the mind which is renewed by Baptism (since all men, being of one species, are of one form), but from the diversity of bodies. But it is otherwise with the angels, who differ in species. And therefore gratuitous gifts are bestowed on the angels according to their diverse capacity for natural gifts, but not on men.

Reply to Objection 4: Bodily health is not the essential effect of Baptism, but a miraculous work of Divine providence.

Day 298

Whether insincerity hinders the effect of Baptism?

Objection 1: It seems that insincerity does not hinder the effect of Baptism. For the Apostle says (Gal. 3:27): "As many of you as have been baptized in Christ Jesus, have put on Christ." But all that receive the Baptism of Christ, are baptized in Christ. Therefore they all put on Christ: and this is to receive the effect of Baptism. Consequently insincerity does not hinder the effect of Baptism.

Objection 2: Further, the Divine power which can change man's will to that which is better, works in Baptism. But the effect of the efficient cause cannot be hindered by that which can be removed by that cause. Therefore insincerity cannot hinder the effect of Baptism.

Objection 3: Further, the effect of Baptism is grace, to which sin is in opposition. But many other sins are more grievous than insincerity, which are not said to hinder the effect of Baptism. Therefore neither does insincerity.

On the contrary, It is written (Wis. 1:5): "The Holy Spirit of discipline will flee from the deceitful." But the effect of Baptism is from the Holy Ghost. Therefore insincerity hinders the effect of Baptism.

I answer that, As Damascene says (De Fide Orth. ii), "God does not compel man to be righteous." Consequently in order that a man be justified by Baptism, his will must needs embrace both Baptism and the baptismal effect. Now, a man is said to be insincere by reason of his will being in contradiction with either Baptism or its effect. For, according to Augustine (De Bapt. cont. Donat. vii), a man is said to be insincere, in four ways: first, because he does not believe, whereas Baptism is the sacrament of Faith; secondly, through scorning the sacrament itself; thirdly, through observing a rite which differs from that prescribed by the Church in conferring the sacrament; fourthly, through approaching the sacrament without devotion. Wherefore it is manifest that insincerity hinders the effect of Baptism.

Reply to Objection 1: "To be baptized in Christ," may be taken in two ways. First, "in Christ," i.e. "in conformity with Christ." And thus whoever is baptized in Christ so as to be conformed to Him by Faith and Charity, puts on Christ by grace. Secondly, a man is said to be baptized in Christ, in so far as he receives Christ's sacrament. And thus all put on Christ, through being configured to Him by the character, but not through being conformed to Him by grace.

Reply to Objection 2: When God changes man's will from evil to good, man does not approach with insincerity. But God does not always do this. Nor is this the purpose of the sacrament, that an insincere man be made sincere; but that he who comes in sincerity, be justified.

Reply to Objection 3: A man is said to be insincere who makes a show of willing what he wills not. Now whoever approaches Baptism, by that very fact makes a show of having right faith in Christ, of veneration for this sacrament, and of wishing to conform to the Church, and to renounce sin. Consequently, to whatever sin a man wishes to cleave, if he approach Baptism, he approaches insincerely, which is the same as to approach without devotion. But this must be understood of mortal sin, which is in opposition to grace: but not of venial sin. Consequently, here insincerity includes, in a way, every sin.

Whether Baptism produces its effect when the insincerity ceases?

Objection 1: It seems that Baptism does not produce its effect, when the insincerity ceases. For a dead work, which is void of charity, can never come to life. But he who approaches Baptism insincerely, receives the sacrament without charity. Therefore it can never come to life so as to bestow grace.

Objection 2: Further, insincerity seems to be stronger than Baptism, because it hinders its effect. But the stronger is not removed by the weaker. Therefore the sin of insincerity cannot be taken away by Baptism which has been hindered by insincerity. And thus Baptism will not receive its full effect, which is the remission of all sins.

Objection 3: Further, it may happen that a man approach Baptism insincerely, and afterwards commit a number of sins. And yet these sins will not be taken away by Baptism; because Baptism washes away past, not future, sins. Such a Baptism, therefore, will never have its effect, which is the remission of all sins.

On the contrary, Augustine says (De Bapt. cont. Donat. i): "Then does Baptism begin to have its salutary effect, when truthful confession takes the place of that insincerity which hindered sins from being washed away, so long as the heart persisted in malice and sacrilege."

I answer that, As stated above ([4468]Q[66], A[9]), Baptism is a spiritual regeneration. Now when a thing is generated, it receives together with the form, the form's effect, unless there be an obstacle; and when this is removed, the form of the thing generated produces its effect: thus at the same time as a weighty body is generated, it has a downward movement, unless something prevent this; and when the obstacle is removed, it begins forthwith to move downwards. In like manner when a man is baptized, he receives the character, which is like a form; and he receives in consequence its proper effect, which is grace whereby all his sins are remitted. But this effect is sometimes hindered by insincerity. Wherefore, when this obstacle is removed by Penance, Baptism forthwith produces its effect.

Reply to Objection 1: The sacrament of Baptism is the work of God, not of man. Consequently, it is not dead in the man, who being insincere, is baptized without charity.

Reply to Objection 2: Insincerity is not removed by Baptism but by Penance: and when it is removed, Baptism takes away all guilt, and all debt of punishment due to sins, whether committed before Baptism, or even co-existent with Baptism. Hence Augustine says (De Bapt. cont. Donat. i): "Yesterday is blotted out, and whatever remains over and above, even the very last hour and moment preceding Baptism, the very moment of Baptism. But from that moment forward he is bound by his obligations." And so both Baptism and Penance concur in producing the effect of Baptism, but Baptism as the direct efficient cause, Penance as the indirect cause, i.e. as removing the obstacle.

Reply to Objection 3: The effect of Baptism is to take away not future, but present and past sins. And consequently, when the insincerity passes away, subsequent sins are indeed remitted, but by Penance, not by Baptism. Wherefore they are not remitted, like the sins which preceded Baptism, as to the whole debt of punishment.

OF CIRCUMCISION (FOUR ARTICLES)

We have now to consider things that are preparatory to Baptism: and (1) that which preceded Baptism, viz. Circumcision, (2) those which accompany Baptism, viz. Catechism and Exorcism.

Concerning the first there are four points of inquiry:

(1) Whether circumcision was a preparation for, and a figure of, Baptism?
(2) Its institution;
(3) Its rite;
(4) Its effect.

Whether circumcision was a preparation for, and a figure of Baptism?

Objection 1: It seems that circumcision was not a preparation for, and a figure of Baptism. For every figure has some likeness to that which it foreshadows. But circumcision has no likeness to Baptism. Therefore it seems that it was not a preparation for, and a figure of Baptism.

Objection 2: Further, the Apostle, speaking of the Fathers of old, says (1 Cor. 10:2), that "all were baptized in the cloud, and in the sea": but not that they were baptized in circumcision. Therefore the protecting pillar of a cloud, and the crossing of the Red Sea, rather than circumcision, were a preparation for, and a figure of Baptism.

Objection 3: Further, it was stated above ([4469]Q[38], AA[1],3) that the baptism of John was a preparation for Christ's. Consequently, if circumcision was a preparation for, and a figure of Christ's Baptism, it seems that John's baptism was superfluous: which is unseemly. Therefore circumcision was not a preparation for, and a figure of Baptism.

On the contrary, The Apostle says (Col. 2:11,12): "You are circumcised with circumcision, not made by hand in despoiling the body of the flesh, but in the circumcision of Christ, buried with Him in Baptism."

I answer that, Baptism is called the Sacrament of Faith; in so far, to wit, as in Baptism man makes a profession of faith, and by Baptism is aggregated to the congregation of the faithful. Now our faith is the same as that of the Fathers of old, according to the Apostle (2 Cor. 4:13): "Having the same spirit of faith . . . we . . . believe." But circumcision was a protestation of faith; wherefore by circumcision also men of old were aggregated to the body of the faithful. Consequently, it is manifest that circumcision was a preparation for Baptism and a figure thereof, forasmuch as "all things happened" to the Fathers of old "in figure" (1 Cor. 10:11); just as their faith regarded things to come.

Reply to Objection 1: Circumcision was like Baptism as to the spiritual effect of the latter. For just as circumcision removed a carnal pellicule, so Baptism despoils man of carnal behavior.

Reply to Objection 2: The protecting pillar of cloud and the crossing of the Red Sea were indeed figures of our Baptism, whereby we are born again of water, signified by the Red Sea; and of the Holy Ghost, signified by the pillar of cloud: yet man did not make, by means of these, a profession of faith, as by circumcision; so that these two things were figures but not sacraments. But circumcision was a sacrament, and a preparation for Baptism; although less clearly figurative of Baptism, as to externals, than the aforesaid. And for this reason the Apostle mentions them rather than circumcision.

Reply to Objection 3: John's baptism was a preparation for Christ's as to the act done: but circumcision, as to the profession of faith, which is required in Baptism, as stated above.

Whether circumcision was instituted in a fitting manner?

Objection 1: It seems that circumcision was instituted in an unfitting manner. For as stated above [4470](A[1]) a profession of faith was made in circumcision. But none could ever be delivered from the first man's sin, except by faith in Christ's Passion, according to Rom. 3:25: "Whom God hath proposed to be a propitiation, through faith in His blood." Therefore circumcision should have been instituted forthwith after the first man's sin, and not at the time of Abraham.

Objection 2: Further, in circumcision man made profession of keeping the Old Law, just as in Baptism he makes profession of keeping the New Law; wherefore the Apostle says (Gal. 5:3): "I testify . . . to every man circumcising himself, that he is a debtor to do the whole Law." But the observance of the Law was not promulgated at the time of Abraham, but rather at the time of Moses. Therefore it was unfitting for circumcision to be instituted at the time of Abraham

Objection 3: Further, circumcision was a figure of, and a preparation for, Baptism. But Baptism is offered to all nations, according to Mat. 28:19: "Going . . . teach ye all nations, baptizing them." Therefore circumcision should have been instituted as binding, not the Jews only, but also all nations.

Objection 4: Further, carnal circumcision should correspond to spiritual circumcision, as the shadow to the reality. But spiritual circumcision which is of Christ, regards indifferently both sexes, since "in Christ Jesus there is neither male nor female," as is written Col. 3 [*Gal. 3:28]. Therefore the institution of circumcision which concerns only males, was unfitting.

On the contrary, We read (Gn. 17) that circumcision was instituted by God, Whose "works are perfect" (Dt. 32:4).

I answer that, As stated above [4471](A[1]) circumcision was a preparation for Baptism, inasmuch as it was a profession of faith in Christ, which we also profess in Baptism. Now among the Fathers of old, Abraham was the first to receive the promise of the future birth of Christ, when it was said to him: "In thy seed shall all the nations of the earth be blessed" (Gn. 22:18). Moreover, he was the first to cut himself off from the society of unbelievers, in accordance with the commandment of the Lord, Who said to him (Gn. 13:1): "Go forth out of thy country and from thy kindred." Therefore circumcision was fittingly instituted in the person of Abraham.

Reply to Objection 1: Immediately after the sin of our first parent, on account of the knowledge possessed by Adam, who was fully instructed about Divine things, both faith and natural reason flourished in man to such an extent, that there was no need for any signs of faith and salvation to be prescribed to him, but each one was wont to make protestation of his faith, by outward signs of his profession, according as he thought best. But about the time of Abraham faith was on the wane, many being given over to idolatry. Moreover, by the growth of carnal concupiscence natural reason was clouded even in regard to sins against nature. And therefore it was fitting that then, and not before, circumcision should be instituted, as a profession of faith and a remedy against carnal concupiscence.

Reply to Objection 2: The observance of the Law was not to be promulgated until the people were already gathered together: because the law is ordained to the public good, as we have stated in the [4472]FS, Q[90], A[2]. Now it behooved the body of the faithful to be gathered together by a sensible sign, which is necessary in order that men be united together in any religion, as Augustine says (Contra Faust. xix). Consequently, it was necessary for circumcision to be instituted before the giving of the Law. Those Fathers, however, who lived before the Law, taught their families concerning Divine things by way of paternal admonition. Hence the Lord said of Abraham (Gn. 18:19): "I know that he will command his children, and his household after him to keep the way of the Lord."

Reply to Objection 3: Baptism contains in itself the perfection of salvation, to which God calls all men, according to 1 Tim. 2:4: "Who will have all men to be saved." Wherefore Baptism is offered to all nations. On the other hand circumcision did not contain the perfection of salvation, but signified it as to be achieved by Christ, Who was to be born of the Jewish nation. For this reason circumcision was given to that nation alone.

Reply to Objection 4: The institution of circumcision is as a sign of Abraham's faith, who believed that himself would be the father of Christ Who was promised to him: and for this reason it was suitable that it should be for males only. Again, original sin, against which circumcision was specially ordained, is contracted from the father, not from the mother, as was stated in the [4473]FS, Q[81], A[5]. But Baptism contains the power of Christ, Who is the universal cause of salvation for all, and is "The Remission of all sins" (Post-Communion, Tuesday in Whitweek).

Whether the rite of circumcision was fitting?

Objection 1: It seems that the rite of circumcision was unfitting. For circumcision, as stated above ([4474]AA[1],2), was a profession of faith. But faith is in the apprehensive power, whose operations appear mostly in the head. Therefore the sign of circumcision should have been conferred on the head rather than on the virile member.

Objection 2: Further, in the sacraments we make use of such things as are in more frequent use; for instance, water, which is used for washing, and bread, which we use for nourishment. But, in cutting, we use an iron knife more commonly than a stone knife. Therefore circumcision should not have been performed with a stone knife.

Objection 3: Further, just as Baptism was instituted as a remedy against original sin, so also was circumcision, as Bede says (Hom. in Circum.). But now Baptism is not put off until the eighth day, lest children should be in danger of loss on account of original sin, if they should die before being baptized. On the other hand, sometimes Baptism is put off until after the eighth day. Therefore the eighth day should not have been fixed for circumcision, but this day should have been anticipated, just as sometimes it was deferred.

On the contrary, The aforesaid rite of circumcision is fixed by a gloss on Rom. 4:11: "And he received the sign of circumcision."

I answer that, As stated above [4475](A[2]), circumcision was established, as a sign of faith, by God "of" Whose "wisdom there is no number" (Ps. 146:5). Now to determine suitable signs is a work of wisdom. Consequently, it must be allowed that the rite of circumcision was fitting.

Reply to Objection 1: It was fitting for circumcision to be performed on the virile member. First, because it was a sign of that faith whereby Abraham believed that Christ would be born of his seed. Secondly, because it was to be a remedy against original sin, which is contracted through the act of generation. Thirdly, because it was ordained as a remedy for carnal concupiscence, which thrives principally in those members, by reason of the abundance of venereal pleasure.

Reply to Objection 2: A stone knife was not essential to circumcision. Wherefore we do not find that an instrument of this description is required by any divine precept; nor did the Jews, as a rule, make use of such a knife for circumcision; indeed, neither do they now. Nevertheless, certain well-known circumcisions are related as having been performed with a stone knife, thus (Ex. 4:25) we read that "Sephora took a very sharp stone and circumcised the foreskin of her son," and (Joshua 5:2): "Make thee knives of stone, and circumcise the second time the children of Israel." Which signified that spiritual circumcision would be done by Christ, of Whom it is written (1 Cor. 10:4): "Now the rock was Christ."

Reply to Objection 3: The eighth day was fixed for circumcision: first, because of the mystery; since, Christ, by taking away from the elect, not only guilt but also all penalties, will perfect the spiritual circumcision, in the eighth age (which is the age of those that rise again), as it were, on the eighth day. Secondly, on account of the tenderness of the infant before the eighth day. Wherefore even in regard to other animals it is prescribed (Lev. 22:27): "When a bullock, or a sheep, or a goat, is brought forth, they shall be seven days under the udder of their dam: but the eighth day and thenceforth, they may be offered to the Lord."

Moreover, the eighth day was necessary for the fulfilment of the precept; so that, to wit, those who delayed beyond the eighth day, sinned, even though it were the sabbath, according to Jn. 7:23: "(If) a man receives circumcision on the sabbath-day, that the Law of Moses may not be broken." But it was not necessary for the validity of the sacrament: because if anyone delayed beyond the eighth day, they could be circumcised afterwards.

Some also say that in imminent danger of death, it was allowable to anticipate the eighth day. But this cannot be proved either from the authority of Scripture or from the custom of the Jews. Wherefore it is better to say with Hugh of St. Victor (De Sacram. i) that the eighth day was never anticipated for any motive, however urgent. Hence on Prov. 4:3: "I was . . . an only son in the sight of my mother," a gloss says, that Bersabee's other baby boy did not count because through dying before the eighth day it received no name; and consequently neither was it circumcised.

Whether circumcision bestowed sanctifying grace?

Objection 1: It seems that circumcision did not bestow sanctifying grace. For the Apostle says (Gal. 2:21): "If justice be by the Law, then Christ died in vain," i.e. without cause. But circumcision was an obligation imposed by the Law, according to Gal. 5:3: "I testify . . . to every man circumcising himself, that ne is a debtor to do the whole law." Therefore, if justice be by circumcision, "Christ died in vain," i.e. without cause. But this cannot be allowed. Therefore circumcision did not confer grace whereby the sinner is made righteous.

Objection 2: Further, before the institution of circumcision faith alone sufficed for justification; hence Gregory says (Moral. iv): "Faith alone did of old in behalf of infants that for which the water of Baptism avails with us." But faith has lost nothing of its strength through the commandment of circumcision. Therefore faith alone justified little ones, and not circumcision.

Objection 3: Further, we read (Joshua 5:5,6) that "the people that were born in the desert, during the forty years . . . were uncircumcised." If, therefore, original sin was taken away by circumcision, it seems that all who died in the desert, both little children and adults, were lost. And the same argument avails in regard to those who died before the eighth day, which was that of circumcision, which day could nol be anticipated, as stated above (A[3], ad 3).

Objection 4: Further, nothing but sin closes the entrance to the heavenly kingdom. But before the Passion the entrance to the heavenly kingdom was closed to the circumcised. Therefore men were not justified from sin by circumcision.

Objection 5: Further, original sin is not remitted without actual sin being remitted also: because "it is wicked to hope for half forgiveness from God," as Augustine says (De Vera et Falsa Poenit. ix). But we read nowhere of circumcision as remitting actual sin. Therefore neither did it remit original sin.

On the contrary, Augustine says, writing to Valerius in answer to Julian (De Nup. et Concup. ii): "From the time that circumcision was instituted among God's people, as 'a seal of the justice of the faith,' it availed little children unto sanctification by cleansing them from the original and bygone sin; just as Baptism also from the time of its institution began to avail unto the renewal of man."

I answer that, All are agreed in saying that original sin was remitted in circumcision. But some said that no grace was conferred, and that the only effect was to remit sin. The Master holds this opinion (Sent. iv, D, 1), and in a gloss on Rom. 4:11. But this is impossible, since guilt is not remitted except by grace, according to Rom. 3:2: "Being justified freely by His grace," etc.

Wherefore others said that grace was bestowed by circumcision, as to that effect which is the remission of guilt, but not as to its positive effects; lest they should be compelled to say that the grace bestowed in circumcision sufficed for the fulfiling of the precepts of the Law, and that, consequently, the coming of Christ was unnecessary. But neither can this opinion stand. First, because by circumcision children. received the power of obtaining glory at the allotted time, which is the last positive effect of grace. Secondly, because, in the order of the formal cause, positive effects naturally precede those that denote privation, although it is the reverse in the order of the material cause: since a form does not remove a privation save by informing the subject.

Consequently, others said that grace was conferred in circumcision, also as a particular positive effect consisting in being made worthy of eternal life; but not as to all its effects, for it did not suffice for the repression of the concupiscence of the fomes, nor again for the fulfilment of the precepts of the Law. And this was my opinion at one time (Sent. iv, D, 1;[4476] Q[2], A[4]). But if one consider the matter carefully, it is clear that this is not true. Because the least grace can resist any degree of concupiscence, and avoid every mortal sin, that is committed in transgressing the precepts of the Law; for the smallest degree of charity loves God more than cupidity loves "thousands of gold and silver" (Ps. 118:72).

We must say, therefore, that grace was bestowed in circumcision as to all the effects of grace, but not as in Baptism. Because in Baptism grace is bestowed by the very power of Baptism itself, which power Baptism has as the instrument of Christ's Passion already consummated. Whereas circumcision bestowed grace, inasmuch as it was a sign of faith in Christ's future Passion: so that the man who was circumcised, professed to embrace that faith; whether, being an adult, he made profession for himself, or, being a child, someone else made profession for him. Hence, too, the Apostle says (Rom. 4:11), that Abraham "received the sign of circumcision, a seal of the justice of the faith": because, to wit, justice was of faith signified: not of circumcision signifying. And since Baptism operates instrumentally by the power of Christ's Passion, whereas circumcision does not, therefore Baptism imprints a character that incorporates man in Christ, and bestows grace more copiously than does circumcision; since greater is the effect of a thing already present, than of the hope thereof.

Reply to Objection 1: This argument would prove if justice were of circumcision otherwise than through faith in Christ's Passion.

Reply to Objection 2: Just as before the institution of circumcision, faith in Christ to come justified both children and adults, so, too, after its institution. But before, there was no need of a sign expressive of this faith; because as yet believers had not begun to be united together apart from unbelievers for the worship of one God. It is probable, however, that parents who were believers offered up some prayers to God for their children, especially if these were in any danger. Or bestowed some blessing on them, as a "seal of faith"; just as the adults offered prayers and sacrifices for themselves.

Reply to Objection 3: There was an excuse for the people in the desert failing to fulfil the precept of circumcision, both because they knew not when the camp was removed, and because, as Damascene says (De Fide Orth. iv) they needed no distinctive sign while they dwelt apart from other nations. Nevertheless, as Augustine says (QQ. in Josue vi), those were guilty of disobedience who failed to obey through contempt.

It seems, however, that none of the uncircumcised died in the desert, for it is written (Ps. 104:37): "There was not among their tribes one that was feeble": and that those alone died in the desert, who had been circumcised in Egypt. If, however, some of the uncircumcised did die there, the same applies to them as to those who died before the institution of circumcision. And this applies also to those children who, at the time of the Law, died before the eighth day.

Reply to Objection 4: Original sin was taken away in circumcision, in regard to the person; but on the part of the entire nature, there remained the obstacle to the entrance of the kingdom of heaven, which obstacle was removed by Christ's Passion. Consequently, before Christ's Passion not even Baptism gave entrance to the kingdom. But were circumcision to avail after Christ's Passion, it would give entrance to the kingdom.

Reply to Objection 5: When adults were circumcised, they received remission not only of original, but also of actual sin: yet not so as to be delivered from all debt of punishment, as in Baptism, in which grace is conferred more copiously.

OF THE PREPARATIONS THAT ACCOMPANY BAPTISM (FOUR ARTICLES)
We have now to consider the preparations that accompany Baptism: concerning which there are four points of inquiry:
(1) Whether catechism should precede Baptism?
(2) Whether exorcism should precede Baptism?
(3) Whether what is done in catechizing and exorcizing, effects anything, or is a mere sign?
(4) Whether those who are to be baptized should be catechized or exorcized by priests?

Whether catechism should precede Baptism?
Objection 1: It seems that catechism should not precede Baptism. For by Baptism men are regenerated unto the spiritual life. But man begins to live before being taught. Therefore man should not be catechized, i.e. taught, before being baptized.

Objection 2: Further, Baptism is given not only to adults, but also to children, who are not capable of being taught, since they have not the use of reason. Therefore it is absurd to catechize them.

Objection 3: Further, a man, when catechized, confesses his faith. Now a child cannot confess its faith by itself, nor can anyone else in its stead; both because no one can bind another to do anything; and because one cannot know whether the child, having come to the right age, will give its assent to faith. Therefore catechism should not precede Baptism.

On the contrary, Rabanus says (De Instit. Cleric. i): "Before Baptism man should be prepared by catechism, in order that the catechumen may receive the rudiments of faith."

I answer that, As stated above ([4477]Q[70], A[1]), Baptism is the Sacrament of Faith: since it is a profession of the Christian faith. Now in order that a man receive the faith, he must be instructed therein, according to Rom. 10:14: "How shall they believe Him, of Whom they have not heard? And how shall they hear without a preacher?" And therefore it is fitting that catechism should precede

Baptism. Hence when our Lord bade His disciples to baptize, He made teaching to precede Baptism, saying: "Go ye . . . and teach all nations, baptizing them," etc.

Reply to Objection 1: The life of grace unto which a man is regenerated, presupposes the life of the rational nature, in which man is capable of receiving instruction.

Reply to Objection 2: Just as Mother Church, as stated above ([4478]Q[69], A[6], ad 3), lends children another's feet that they may come, and another's heart that they may believe, so, too, she lends them another's ears, that they may hear, and another's mind, that through others they may be taught. And therefore, as they are to be baptized, on the same grounds they are to be instructed.

Reply to Objection 3: He who answers in the child's stead: "I do believe," does not foretell that the child will believe when it comes to the right age, else he would say: "He will believe"; but in the child's stead he professes the Church's faith which is communicated to that child, the sacrament of which faith is bestowed on it, and to which faith he is bound by another. For there is nothing unfitting in a person being bound by another in things necessary for salvation. In like manner the sponsor, in answering for the child, promises to use his endeavors that the child may believe. This, however, would not be sufficient in the case of adults having the use of reason.

Whether exorcism should precede Baptism?

Objection 1: It seems that exorcism should not precede Baptism. For exorcism is ordained against energumens or those who are possessed. But not all are such like. Therefore exorcism should not precede Baptism.

Objection 2: Further, so long as man is a subject of sin, the devil has power over him, according to Jn. 8:34: "Whosoever committeth sin is the servant of sin." But sin is taken away by Baptism. Therefore men should not be exorcized before Baptism.

Objection 3: Further, Holy water was introduced in order to ward off the power of the demons. Therefore exorcism was not needed as a further remedy.

On the contrary, Pope Celestine says (Epist. ad Episcop. Galliae): "Whether children or young people approach the sacrament of regeneration, they should not come to the fount of life before the unclean spirit has been expelled from them by the exorcisms and breathings of the clerics."

I answer that, Whoever purposes to do a work wisely, first removes the obstacles to his work; hence it is written (Jer. 4:3): "Break up anew your fallow ground and sow not upon thorns." Now the devil is the enemy of man's salvation, which man acquires by Baptism; and he has a certain power over man from the very fact that the latter is subject to original, or even actual, sin. Consequently it is fitting that before Baptism the demons should be cast out by exorcisms, lest they impede man's salvation. Which expulsion is signified by the (priest) breathing (upon the person to be baptized); while the blessing, with the imposition of hands, bars the way against the return of him who was cast out. Then the salt which is put in the mouth, and the anointing of the nose and ears with spittle, signify the receiving of doctrine, as to the ears; consent thereto as to the nose; and confession thereof, as to the mouth. And the anointing with oil signifies man's ability to fight against the demons.

Reply to Objection 1: The energumens are so-called from "laboring inwardly" under the outward operation of the devil. And though not all that approach Baptism are troubled by him in their bodies, yet all who are not baptized are subject to the power of the demons, at least on account of the guilt of original sin.

Reply to Objection 2: The power of the devil in so far as he hinders man from obtaining glory, is expelled from man by the baptismal ablution; but in so far as he hinders man from receiving the sacrament, his power is cast out by the exorcisms.

Reply to Objection 3: Holy water is used against the assaults of demons from without. But exorcisms are directed against those assaults of the demons which are from within. hence those who are exorcized are called energumens, as it were "laboring inwardly."

Or we may say that just as Penance is given as a further remedy against sin, because Baptism is not repeated; so Holy Water is given as a further remedy against the assaults of demons, because the baptismal exorcisms are not given a second time.

Day 299

Whether what is done in the exorcism effects anything, or is a mere sign?

Objection 1: It seems that what is done in the exorcism does not effect anything, but is a mere sign. For if a child die after the exorcisms, before being baptized, it is not saved. But the effects of what is done in the sacraments are ordained to the salvation of man; hence it is written (Mk. 16:16): "He that believeth and is baptized shall be saved." Therefore what is done in the exorcism effects nothing, but is a mere sign.

Objection 2: Further, nothing is required for a sacrament of the New Law, but that it should be a sign and a cause, as stated above ([4479]Q[62], A[1]). If, therefore, the things done in the exorcism effect anything, it seems that each of them is a sacrament.

Objection 3: Further, just as the exorcism is ordained to Baptism, so if anything be effected in the exorcism, it is ordained to the effect of Baptism. But disposition must needs precede the perfect form: because form is not received save into matter already disposed. It would follow, therefore, that none could obtain the effect of Baptism unless he were previously exorcized; which is clearly false. Therefore what is done in the exorcisms has no effect.

Objection 4: Further, just as some things are done in the exorcism before Baptism, so are some things done after Baptism; for instance, the priest anoints the baptized on the top of the head. But what is done after Baptism seems to have no effect; for, if it had, the effect of Baptism would be imperfect. Therefore neither have those things an effect, which are done in exorcism before Baptism.

On the contrary, Augustine says (De Symbolo I): "Little children are breathed upon and exorcized, in order to expel from them the devil's hostile power, which deceived man." But the Church does nothing in vain. Therefore the effect of these breathings is that the power of the devils is expelled.

I answer that, Some say that the things done in the exorcism have no effect, but are mere signs. But this is clearly false; since in exorcizing, the Church uses words of command to cast out the devil's power, for instance, when she says: "Therefore, accursed devil, go out from him," etc.

Therefore we must say that they have some effect, but, other than that of Baptism. For Baptism gives man grace unto the full remission of sins. But those things that are done in the exorcism remove the twofold impediment against the reception of saving grace. Of these, one is the outward impediment, so far as the demons strive to hinder man's salvation. And this impediment is removed by the breathings, whereby the demon's power is cast out, as appears from the passage quoted from Augustine, i.e. as to the devil not placing obstacles against the reception of the sacrament. Nevertheless, the demon's power over man remains as to the stain of sin, and the debt of punishment, until sin be washed away by Baptism. And in this sense Cyprian says (Epist. lxxvi): "Know that the devil's evil power remains until the pouring of the saving water: but in Baptism he loses it all."

The other impediment is within, forasmuch as, from having contracted original sin, man's sense is closed to the perception of the mysteries of salvation. Hence Rabanus says (De Instit. Cleric. i) that "by means of the typifying spittle and the touch of the priest, the Divine wisdom and power brings salvation to the catechumen, that his nostrils being opened he may perceive the odor of the knowledge of God, that his ears be opened to hear the commandments of God, that his senses be opened in his inmost heart to respond."

Reply to Objection 1: What is done in the exorcism does not take away the sin for which man is punished after death; but only the impediments against his receiving the remission of sin through the sacrament. Wherefore exorcism avails a man nothing after death if he has not been baptized.

Praepositivus, however, says that children who die after being exorcized but before being baptized are subjected to lesser darkness. But this does not seem to be true: because that darkness consists in privation of the vision of God, which cannot be greater or lesser.

Reply to Objection 2: It is essential to a sacrament to produce its principal effect, which is grace that remits sin, or supplies some defect in man. But those things that are done in the exorcism do not effect this; they merely remove these impediments. Consequently, they are not sacraments but sacramentals.

Reply to Objection 3: The disposition that suffices for receiving the baptismal grace is the faith and intention, either of the one baptized, if it be an adult, or of the Church, if it be a child. But these things that are done in the exorcism, are directed to the removal of the impediments. And therefore one may receive the effect of Baptism without them.

Yet they are not to be omitted save in a case of necessity. And then, if the danger pass, they should be supplied, that uniformity in Baptism may be observed. Nor are they supplied to no purpose after Baptism: because, just as the effect of Baptism may be hindered before it is received, so can it be hindered after it has been received.

Reply to Objection 4: Of those things that are done after Baptism in respect of the person baptized, something is done which is not a mere sign, but produces an effect, for instance, the anointing on the top of the head, the effect of which is the preservation of baptismal grace. And there is something which has no effect, but is a mere sign, for instance, the baptized are given a white garment to signify the newness of life.

Whether it belongs to a priest to catechize and exorcize the person to be baptized?

Objection 1: It seems that it does not belong to a priest to catechize and exorcize the person to be baptized. For it belongs to the office of ministers to operate on the unclean, as Dionysius says (Eccl. Hier. v). But catechumens who are instructed by catechism, and "energumens" who are cleansed by exorcism, are counted among the unclean, as Dionysius says in the same place. Therefore to catechize and to exorcize do not belong to the office of the priests, but rather to that of the ministers.

Objection 2: Further, catechumens are instructed in the Faith by the Holy Scripture which is read in the church by ministers: for just as the Old Testament is recited by the Readers, so the New Testament is read by the Deacons and Subdeacons. And thus it belongs to the ministers to catechize. In like manner it belongs, seemingly, to the ministers to exorcize. For Isidore says (Epist. ad Ludifred.): "The exorcist should know the exorcisms by heart, and impose his hands on the energumens and catechumens during the exorcism." Therefore it belongs not to the priestly office to catechize and exorcize.

Objection 3: Further, "to catechize" is the same as "to teach," and this is the same as "to perfect." Now this belongs to the office of a bishop, as Dionysius says (Eccl. Hier. v). Therefore it does not belong to the priestly office.

On the contrary, Pope Nicolas I says: "The catechizing of those who are to be baptized can be undertaken by the priests attached to each church." And Gregory says (Hom. xxix super Ezech.): "When priests place their hands on believers for the grace of exorcism, what else do they but cast out the devils?"

I answer that, The minister compared to the priest, is as a secondary and instrumental agent to the principal agent: as is implied in the very word "minister." Now the secondary agent does nothing without the principal agent in operating. And the more mighty the operation, so much the mightier instruments does the principal agent require. But the operation of the priest in conferring the sacrament itself is mightier than in those things that are preparatory to the sacrament. And so the highest ministers who are called deacons co-operate with the priest in bestowing the sacraments themselves: for Isidore says (Epist. ad Ludifred.) that "it belongs to the deacons to assist the priests in all things that are done in Christ's sacraments, in Baptism, to wit, in the Chrism, in the Paten and Chalice"; while the inferior ministers assist the priest in those things which are preparatory to the sacraments: the readers, for instance, in catechizing; the exorcists in exorcizing.

Reply to Objection 1: The minister's operation in regard to the unclean is ministerial and, as it were, instrumental, but the priest's is principal.

Reply to Objection 2: To readers and exorcists belongs the duty of catechizing and exorcizing, not, indeed, principally, but as ministers of the priest in these things.

Reply to Objection 3: Instruction is manifold. one leads to the embracing of the Faith; and is ascribed by Dionysius to bishops (Eccl. Hier. ii) and can be undertaken by any preacher, or even by any believer. Another is that by which a man is taught the rudiments of faith, and how to comport himself in receiving the sacraments: this belongs secondarily to the ministers, primarily to the priests. A third is instruction in the mode of Christian life: and this belongs to the sponsors. A fourth is the instruction in the profound mysteries of faith, and on the perfection of Christian life: this belongs to bishops "ex officio," in virtue of their office.

CONFIRMATION (Q[72])
OF THE SACRAMENT OF CONFIRMATION (TWELVE ARTICLES)
We have now to consider the Sacrament of Confirmation. Concerning this there are twelve points of inquiry:
(1) Whether Confirmation is a sacrament?
(2) Its matter;
(3) Whether it is essential to the sacrament that the chrism should have been previously consecrated by a bishop?
(4) Its form;
(5) Whether it imprints a character?
(6) Whether the character of Confirmation presupposes the character of Baptism?
(7) Whether it bestows grace?
(8) Who is competent to receive this sacrament?
(9) In what part of the body?
(10) Whether someone is required to stand for the person to be confirmed?
(11) Whether this sacrament is given by bishops only?
(12) Of its rite.

Whether confirmation is a sacrament?
Objection 1: It seems that Confirmation is not a sacrament. For sacraments derive their efficacy from the Divine institution, as stated above ([4480]Q[64] , A[2]). But we read nowhere of Confirmation being instituted by Christ. Therefore it is not a sacrament.
Objection 2: Further, the sacraments of the New Law were foreshadowed in the Old Law; thus the Apostle says (1 Cor. 10:2-4), that "all in Moses were baptized, in the cloud and in the sea; and did all eat the same spiritual food, and all drank the same spiritual drink." But Confirmation was not foreshadowed in the old Testament. Therefore it is not a sacrament.
Objection 3: Further, the sacraments are ordained unto man's salvation. But man can be saved without Confirmation: since children that are baptized, who die before being confirmed, are saved. Therefore Confirmation is not a sacrament.
Objection 4: Further, by all the sacraments of the Church, man is conformed to Christ, Who is the Author of the sacraments. But man cannot be conformed to Christ by Confirmation, since we read nowhere of Christ being confirmed.
On the contrary, Pope Melchiades wrote to the bishops of Spain: "Concerning the point on which you sought to be informed, i.e. whether the imposition of the bishop's hand were a greater sacrament than Baptism, know that each is a great sacrament."
I answer that, The sacraments of the New Law are ordained unto special effects of grace: and therefore where there is a special effect of grace, there we find a special sacrament ordained for the purpose. But since sensible and material things bear a likeness to things spiritual and intelligible, from what occurs in the life of the body, we can perceive that which is special to the spiritual life. Now it is evident that in the life of the body a certain special perfection consists in man's attaining to the perfect age, and being able to perform the perfect actions of a man: hence the Apostle says (1 Cor. 13:11): "When I became a man, I put away the things of a child." And thence it is that besides the movement of generation whereby man receives life of the body, there is the movement of growth, whereby man is brought to the perfect age. So therefore does man receive spiritual life in Baptism, which is a spiritual regeneration: while in Confirmation man arrives at the perfect age, as it were, of the spiritual life. Hence Pope Melchiades says: "The Holy Ghost, Who comes down on the waters of Baptism bearing salvation in His flight, bestows at the font, the fulness of innocence; but in Confirmation He confers an increase of grace. In Baptism we are born again unto life; after Baptism we are strengthened." And therefore it is evident that Confirmation is a special sacrament.
Reply to Objection 1: Concerning the institution of this sacrament there are three opinions. Some (Alexander of Hales, Summa Theol. P. IV, Q. IX; St. Bonaventure, Sent. iv, D, 7) have maintained that this sacrament was instituted neither by Christ, nor by the apostles; but later in the course of time by one of the councils. Others (Pierre de Tarentaise, Sent. iv, D, 7) held that it was instituted by the apostles. But this cannot be admitted; since the institution of a new sacrament belongs to the power of excellence, which belongs to Christ alone.
And therefore we must say that Christ instituted this sacrament not by bestowing, but by promising it, according to Jn. 16:7: "If I go not, the Paraclete will not come to you, but if I go, I will send Him to you." And this was because in this sacrament the fulness of the Holy Ghost is bestowed, which was not to be given before Christ's Resurrection and Ascension; according to Jn. 7:39: "As yet the Spirit was not given, because Jesus was not yet glorified."
Reply to Objection 2: Confirmation is the sacrament of the fulness of grace: wherefore there could be nothing corresponding to it in the Old Law, since "the Law brought nothing to perfection" (Heb. 7:19).
Reply to Objection 3: As stated above ([4481]Q[65], A[4]), all the sacraments are in some way necessary for salvation: but some, so that there is no salvation without them; some as conducing to the perfection of salvation; and thus it is that Confirmation is necessary for salvation: although salvation is possible without it, provided it be not omitted out of contempt.
Reply to Objection 4: Those who receive Confirmation, which is the sacrament of the fulness of grace, are conformed to Christ, inasmuch as from the very first instant of His conception He was "full of grace and truth" (Jn. 1:14). This fulness was made known at

His Baptism, when "the Holy Ghost descended in a bodily shape . . . upon Him" (Lk. 3:22). Hence (Lk. 4:1) it is written that "Jesus being full of the Holy Ghost, returned from the Jordan." Nor was it fitting to Christ's dignity, that He, Who is the Author of the sacraments, should receive the fulness of grace from a sacrament.

Whether chrism is a fitting matter for this sacrament?

Objection 1: It seems that chrism is not a fitting matter for this sacrament. For this sacrament, as stated above (A[1], ad 1), was instituted by Christ when He promised His disciples the Holy Ghost. But He sent them the Holy Ghost without their being anointed with chrism. Moreover, the apostles themselves bestowed this sacrament without chrism, by the mere imposition of hands: for it is written (Acts 8:17) that the apostles "laid their hands upon" those who were baptized, "and they received the Holy Ghost." Therefore chrism is not the matter of this sacrament: since the matter is essential to the sacrament.

Objection 2: Further, Confirmation perfects, in a way, the sacrament of Baptism, as stated above ([4482]Q[65], AA[3],4): and so it ought to be conformed to it as perfection to the thing perfected. But the matter, in Baptism, is a simple element, viz. water. Therefore chrism, which is made of oil and balm, is not a fitting matter for this sacrament.

Objection 3: Further, oil is used as the matter of this sacrament for the purpose of anointing. But any oil will do for anointing: for instance, oil made from nuts, and from anything else. Therefore not only olive oil should be used for this sacrament.

Objection 4: Further, it has been stated above ([4483]Q[66], A[3]) that water is used as the matter of Baptism, because it is easily procured everywhere. But olive oil is not to be procured everywhere; and much less is balm. Therefore chrism, which is made of these, is not a fitting matter for this sacrament.

On the contrary, Gregory says (Registr. iv): "Let no priest dare to sign the baptized infants on the brow with the sacred chrism." Therefore chrism is the matter of this sacrament.

I answer that, Chrism is the fitting matter of this sacrament. For, as stated above [4484](A[1]), in this sacrament the fulness of the Holy Ghost is given for the spiritual strength which belongs to the perfect age. Now when man comes to perfect age he begins at once to have intercourse with others; whereas until then he lives an individual life, as it were, confined to himself. Now the grace of the Holy Ghost is signified by oil; hence Christ is said to be "anointed with the oil of gladness" (Ps. 44:8), by reason of His being gifted with the fulness of the Holy Ghost. Consequently oil is a suitable matter of this sacrament. And balm is mixed with the oil, by reason of its fragrant odor, which spreads about: hence the Apostle says (2 Cor. 2:15): "We are the good odor of Christ," etc. And though many other things be fragrant, yet preference is given to balm, because it has a special odor of its own, and because it confers incorruptibility: hence it is written (Ecclus. 24:21): "My odor is as the purest balm."

Reply to Objection 1: Christ, by the power which He exercises in the sacraments, bestowed on the apostles the reality of this sacrament, i.e. the fulness of the Holy Ghost, without the sacrament itself, because they had received "the first fruits of the Spirit" (Rom. 8:23). Nevertheless, something of keeping with the matter of this sacrament was displayed to the apostles in a sensible manner when they received the Holy Ghost. For that the Holy Ghost came down upon them in a sensible manner under the form of fire, refers to the same signification as oil: except in so far as fire has an active power, while oil has a passive power, as being the matter and incentive of fire. And this was quite fitting: for it was through the apostles that the grace of the Holy Ghost was to flow forth to others. Again, the Holy Ghost came down on the apostles in the shape of a tongue. Which refers to the same signification as balm: except in so far as the tongue communicates with others by speech, but balm, by its odor. because, to wit, the apostles were filled with the Holy Ghost, as teachers of the Faith; but the rest of the believers, as doing that which gives edification to the faithful.

In like manner, too, when the apostles imposed their hands, and when they preached, the fulness of the Holy Ghost came down under visible signs on the faithful, just as, at the beginning, He came down on the apostles: hence Peter said (Acts 11:15): "When I had begun to speak, the Holy Ghost fell upon them, as upon us also in the beginning." Consequently there was no need for sacramental sensible matter, where God sent sensible signs miraculously.

However, the apostles commonly made use of chrism in bestowing the sacrament, when such like visible signs were lacking. For Dionysius says (Eccl. Hier. iv): "There is a certain perfecting operation which our guides," i.e. the apostles, "call the sacrifice of Chrism."

Reply to Objection 2: Baptism is bestowed that spiritual life may be received simply; wherefore simple matter is fitting to it. But this sacrament is given that we may receive the fulness of the Holy Ghost, Whose operations are manifold, according to Wis. 7:22, "In her is the" Holy "Spirit . . . one, manifold"; and 1 Cor. 12:4, "There are diversities of graces, but the same Spirit." Consequently a compound matter is appropriate to this sacrament.

Reply to Objection 3: These properties of oil, by reason of which it symbolizes the Holy Ghost, are to be found in olive oil rather than in any other oil. In fact, the olive-tree itself, through being an evergreen, signifies the refreshing and merciful operation of the Holy Ghost.

Moreover, this oil is called oil properly, and is very much in use, wherever it is to be had. And whatever other liquid is so called, derives its name from its likeness to this oil: nor are the latter commonly used, unless it be to supply the want of olive oil. Therefore it is that this oil alone is used for this and certain other sacraments.

Reply to Objection 4: Baptism is the sacrament of absolute necessity; and so its matter should be at hand everywhere. But it is enough that the matter of this sacrament, which is not of such great necessity, be easily sent to all parts of the world.

Whether it is essential to this sacrament that the chrism which is its matter be previously consecrated by a bishop?

Objection 1: It seems that it is not essential to this sacrament, that the chrism, which is its matter, be previously consecrated by a bishop. For Baptism which bestows full remission of sins is not less efficacious than this sacrament. But, though the baptismal water receives a kind of blessing before being used for Baptism; yet this is not essential to the sacrament: since in a case of necessity it can be dispensed with. Therefore neither is it essential to this sacrament that the chrism should be previously consecrated by a bishop.

Objection 2: Further, the same should not be consecrated twice. But the sacramental matter is sanctified, in the very conferring of the sacrament, by the form of words wherein the sacrament is bestowed; hence Augustine says (Tract. lxxx in Joan.): "The word is added to the element, and this becomes a sacrament." Therefore the chrism should not be consecrated before this sacrament is given.

Objection 3: Further, every consecration employed in the sacraments is ordained to the bestowal of grace. But the sensible matter composed of oil and balm is not receptive of grace. Therefore it should not be consecrated.

On the contrary, Pope Innocent I says (Ep. ad Decent.): "Priests, when baptizing, may anoint the baptized with chrism, previously consecrated by a bishop: but they must not sign the brow with the same oil; this belongs to the bishop alone, when he gives the Paraclete." Now this is done in this sacrament. Therefore it is necessary for this sacrament that its matter be previously consecrated by a bishop.

I answer that, The entire sanctification of the sacraments is derived from Christ, as stated above ([4485]Q[64], A[3]). But it must be observed that Christ did use certain sacraments having a corporeal matter, viz. Baptism, and also the Eucharist. And consequently, from Christ's very act in using them, the matter of these sacraments received a certain aptitude to the perfection of the sacrament. Hence Chrysostom (Chromatius, In Matth. 3:15) says that "the waters of Baptism could never wash away the sins of believers, had they not been sanctified by contact with our Lord's body." And again, our Lord Himself "taking bread . . . blessed . . . and in like manner the chalice" (Mat. 26:26,27; Lk. 22:19, 20). For this reason there is no need for the matter of these sacraments to be blessed previously, since Christ's blessing is enough. And if any blessing be used, it belongs to the solemnity of the sacrament, not to its essence. But Christ did not make use of visible anointings, so as not to slight the invisible unction whereby He was "anointed above" His "fellows" (Ps. 44:8). And hence both chrism, and the holy oil, and the oil of the sick are blessed before being put to sacramental use. This suffices for the reply to the First Objection.

Reply to Objection 2: Each consecration of the chrism has not the same object. For just as an instrument derives instrumental power in two ways, viz. when it receives the form of an instrument, and when it is moved by the principal agent; so too the sacramental matter needs a twofold sanctification, by one of which it becomes fit matter for the sacrament, while by the other it is applied to the production of the effect.

Reply to Objection 3: Corporeal matter is receptive of grace, not so as to be the subject of grace, but only as the instrument of grace, as explained above ([4486]Q[62], A[3]). And this sacramental matter is consecrated, either by Christ, or by a bishop, who, in the Church, impersonates Christ.

Whether the proper form of this sacrament is: "I sign thee with the sign of the cross," etc.?

Objection 1: It seems that the proper form of this sacrament is not: "I sign thee with the sign of the cross, I confirm thee with the chrism of salvation, in the name of the Father and of the Son and of the Holy Ghost. Amen." For the use of the sacraments is derived from Christ and the apostles. But neither did Christ institute this form, nor do we read of the apostles making use of it. Therefore it is not the proper form of this sacrament.

Objection 2: Further, just as the sacrament is the same everywhere, so should the form be the same: because everything has unity, just as it has being, from its form. But this form is not used by all: for some say: "I confirm thee with the chrism of sanctification." Therefore the above is not the proper form of this sacrament.

Objection 3: Further, this sacrament should be conformed to Baptism, as the perfect to the thing perfected, as stated above (A[2], OBJ[2]). But in the form of Baptism no mention is made of signing the character; nor again of the cross of Christ, though in Baptism man dies with Christ, as the Apostle says (Rom. 6:3-8); nor of the effect which is salvation, though Baptism is necessary for salvation. Again, in the baptismal form, only one action is included; and the person of the baptizer is expressed in the words: "I baptize thee, whereas the contrary is to be observed in the above form." Therefore this is not the proper form of this sacrament.

On the contrary, Is the authority of the Church, who always uses this form.

I answer that, The above form is appropriate to this sacrament. For just as the form of a natural thing gives it its species, so a sacramental form should contain whatever belongs to the species of the sacrament. Now as is evident from what has been already said ([4487]AA[1],2), in this sacrament the Holy Ghost is given for strength in the spiritual combat. Wherefore in this sacrament three things are necessary; and they are contained in the above form. The first of these is the cause conferring fulness of spiritual strength which cause is the Blessed Trinity: and this is expressed in the words, "In the name of the Father," etc. The second is the spiritual strength itself bestowed on man unto salvation by the sacrament of visible matter; and this is referred to in the words, "I confirm thee with the chrism of salvation." The third is the sign which is given to the combatant, as in a bodily combat: thus are soldiers marked with the sign of their leaders. And to this refer the words, "I sign thee with the sign of the cross," in which sign, to wit, our King triumphed (cf. Col. 2:15).

Reply to Objection 1: As stated above (A[2], ad 1), sometimes the effect of this sacrament, i.e. the fulness of the Holy Ghost, was given through the ministry of the apostles, under certain visible signs, wrought miraculously by God, Who can bestow the sacramental effect, independently of the sacrament. In these cases there was no need for either the matter or the form of this sacrament. On the other hand, sometimes they bestowed this sacrament as ministers of the sacraments. And then, they used both matter and form according to Christ's command. For the apostles, in conferring the sacraments, observed many things which are not handed down in those Scriptures that are in general use. Hence Dionysius says at the end of his treatise on the Ecclesiastical Hierarchy (chap. vii): "It is not allowed to explain in writing the prayers which are used in the sacraments, and to publish their mystical meaning, or the power which, coming from God, gives them their efficacy; we learn these things by holy tradition without any display,"* i.e. secretly. [*The passage quoted in the text of the Summa differs slightly from the above, which is translated directly from the works of Dionysius.] Hence the Apostle, speaking of the celebration of the Eucharist, writes (1 Cor. 11:34): "The rest I will set in order, when I come."

Reply to Objection 2: Holiness is the cause of salvation. Therefore it comes to the same whether we say "chrism of salvation" or "of sanctification."

Reply to Objection 3: Baptism is the regeneration unto the spiritual life, whereby man lives in himself. And therefore in the baptismal form that action alone is expressed which refers to the man to be sanctified. But this sacrament is ordained not only to the sanctification of man in himself, but also to strengthen him in his outward combat. Consequently not only is mention made of interior sanctification, in the words, "I confirm thee with the chrism of salvation": but furthermore man is signed outwardly, as it were with the standard of the cross, unto the outward spiritual combat; and this is signified by the words, "I sign thee with the sign of the cross."

But in the very word "baptize," which signifies "to cleanse," we can understand both the matter, which is the cleansing water, and the effect, which is salvation. Whereas these are not understood by the word "confirm"; and consequently they had to be expressed.

Again, it has been said above (Q[66], A[5], ad 1) that the pronoun "I" is not necessary to the Baptismal form, because it is included in the first person of the verb. It is, however, included in order to express the intention. But this does not seem so necessary in Confirmation, which is conferred only by a minister of excellence, as we shall state later on [4488](A[11]).

Whether the sacrament of Confirmation imprints a character?

Objection 1: It seems that the sacrament of Confirmation does not imprint a character. For a character means a distinctive sign. But a man is not distinguished from unbelievers by the sacrament of Confirmation, for this is the effect of Baptism; nor from the rest of the faithful, because this sacrament is ordained to the spiritual combat, which is enjoined to all the faithful. Therefore a character is not imprinted in this sacrament.

Objection 2: Further, it was stated above ([4489]Q[63], A[2]) that a character is a spiritual power. Now a power must be either active or passive. But the active power in the sacraments is conferred by the sacrament of order: while the passive or receptive power is conferred by the sacrament of Baptism. Therefore no character is imprinted by the sacrament of Confirmation.

Objection 3: Further, in circumcision, which is a character of the body, no spiritual character is imprinted. But in this sacrament a character is imprinted on the body, when the sign of the cross is signed with chrism on man's brow. Therefore a spiritual character is not imprinted by this sacrament.

On the contrary, A character is imprinted in every sacrament that is not repeated. But this sacrament is not repeated: for Gregory II says (Ep. iv ad Bonifac.): "As to the man who was confirmed a second time by a bishop, such a repetition must be forbidden." Therefore a character is imprinted in Confirmation.

I answer that, As stated above (Q[63], A[2]), a character is a spiritual power ordained to certain sacred actions. Now it has been said above [4490](A[1]; Q[65], A[1]) that, just as Baptism is a spiritual regeneration unto Christian life, so also is Confirmation a certain spiritual growth bringing man to perfect spiritual age. But it is evident, from a comparison with the life of the body, that the action which is proper to man immediately after birth, is different from the action which is proper to him when he has come to perfect age. And therefore by the sacrament of Confirmation man is given a spiritual power in respect of sacred actions other than those in respect of which he receives power in Baptism. For in Baptism he receives power to do those things which pertain to his own salvation, forasmuch as he lives to himself: whereas in Confirmation he receives power to do those things which pertain to the spiritual combat with the enemies of the Faith. This is evident from the example of the apostles, who, before they received the fulness of the Holy Ghost, were in the "upper room . . . persevering . . . in prayer" (Acts 1:13,14); whereas afterwards they went out and feared not to confess their faith in public, even in the face of the enemies of the Christian Faith. And therefore it is evident that a character is imprinted in the sacrament of Confirmation.

Reply to Objection 1: All have to wage the spiritual combat with our invisible enemies. But to fight against visible foes, viz. against the persecutors of the Faith, by confessing Christ's name, belongs to the confirmed, who have already come spiritually to the age of virility, according to 1 Jn. 2:14: "I write unto you, young men, because you are strong, and the word of God abideth in you, and you have overcome the wicked one." And therefore the character of Confirmation is a distinctive sign, not between unbelievers and believers, but between those who are grown up spiritually and those of whom it is written: "As new-born babes" (1 Pet. 2:2).

Reply to Objection 2: All the sacraments are protestations of faith. Therefore just as he who is baptized receives the power of testifying to his faith by receiving the other sacraments; so he who is confirmed receives the power of publicly confessing his faith by words, as it were "ex officio."

Reply to Objection 3: The sacraments of the Old Law are called "justice of the flesh" (Heb. 9:10) because, to wit, they wrought nothing inwardly. Consequently in circumcision a character was imprinted in the body only, but not in the soul. But in Confirmation, since it is a sacrament of the New Law, a spiritual character is imprinted at the same time, together with the bodily character.

Whether the character of Confirmation presupposes of necessity, the baptismal character?

Objection 1: It seems that the character of Confirmation does not presuppose, of necessity, the baptismal character. For the sacrament of Confirmation is ordained to the public confession of the Faith of Christ. But many, even before Baptism, have publicly confessed the Faith of Christ by shedding their blood for the Faith. Therefore the character of Confirmation does not presuppose the baptismal character.

Objection 2: Further, it is not related of the apostles that they were baptized; especially, since it is written (Jn. 4:2) that Christ "Himself did not baptize, but His disciples." Yet afterwards they were confirmed by the coming of the Holy Ghost. Therefore, in like manner, others can be confirmed before being baptized.

Objection 3: Further, it is written (Acts 10:44-48) that "while Peter was yet speaking . . . the Holy Ghost fell on all them that heard the word . . . and [Vulg.: 'for'] they heard them speaking with tongues": and afterwards "he commanded them to be baptized." Therefore others with equal reason can be confirmed before being baptized.

On the contrary, Rabanus says (De Instit. Cleric. i): "Lastly the Paraclete is given to the baptized by the imposition of the high priest's hands, in order that the baptized may be strengthened by the Holy Ghost so as to publish his faith."

I answer that, The character of Confirmation, of necessity supposes the baptismal character: so that, in effect, if one who is not baptized were to be confirmed, he would receive nothing, but would have to be confirmed again after receiving Baptism. The reason of this is that, Confirmation is to Baptism as growth to birth, as is evident from what has been said above [4491](A[1]; Q[65], A[1]). Now it is clear that no one can be brought to perfect age unless he be first born: and in like manner, unless a man be first baptized, he cannot receive the sacrament of Confirmation.

Reply to Objection 1: The Divine power is not confined to the sacraments. Hence man can receive spiritual strength to confess the Faith of Christ publicly, without receiving the sacrament of Confirmation: just as he can also receive remission of sins without Baptism. Yet, just as none receive the effect of Baptism without the desire of Baptism; so none receive the effect of Confirmation, without the desire of Confirmation. And man can have this even before receiving Baptism.

Reply to Objection 2: As Augustine says (Ep. cclxv), from our Lord's words, "'He that is washed, needeth not but to wash his feet' (Jn. 13:10), we gather that Peter and Christ's other disciples had been baptized, either with John's Baptism, as some think; or with Christ's, which is more credible. For He did not refuse to administer Baptism, so as to have servants by whom to baptize others."

Reply to Objection 3: Those who heard the preaching of Peter received the effect of Confirmation miraculously: but not the sacrament of Confirmation. Now it has been stated (ad 1) that the effect of Confirmation can be bestowed on man before Baptism, whereas the sacrament cannot. For just as the effect of Confirmation, which is spiritual strength, presupposes the effect of Baptism, which is justification, so the sacrament of Confirmation presupposes the sacrament of Baptism.

Day 300

Whether sanctifying grace is bestowed in this sacrament?

Objection 1: It seems that sanctifying grace is not bestowed in this sacrament. For sanctifying grace is ordained against sin. But this sacrament, as stated above [4492](A[6]) is given only to the baptized, who are cleansed from sin. Therefore sanctifying grace is not bestowed in this sacrament.

Objection 2: Further, sinners especially need sanctifying grace, by which alone can they be justified. If, therefore, sanctifying grace is bestowed in this sacrament, it seems that it should be given to those who are in sin. And yet this is not true.

Objection 3: Further, there can only be one species of sanctifying grace, since it is ordained to one effect. But two forms of the same species cannot be in the same subject. Since, therefore, man receives sanctifying grace in Baptism, it seems that sanctifying grace is not bestowed in Confirmation, which is given to none but the baptized.

On the contrary, Pope Melchiades says (Ep. ad Episc. Hispan.): "The Holy Ghost bestows at the font the fulness of innocence; but in Confirmation He confers an increase of grace."

I answer that, In this sacrament, as stated above ([4493]AA[1],4), the Holy Ghost is given to the baptized for strength: just as He was given to the apostles on the day of Pentecost, as we read in Acts 2; and just as He was given to the baptized by the imposition of the apostles' hands, as related in Acts 8:17. Now it has been proved in the [4494]FP, Q[43], A[3] that the Holy Ghost is not sent or given except with sanctifying grace. Consequently it is evident that sanctifying grace is bestowed in this sacrament.

Reply to Objection 1: Sanctifying grace does indeed take away sin; but it has other effects also, because it suffices to carry man through every step as far as eternal life. Hence to Paul was it said (2 Cor. 12:9): "My grace is sufficient for thee": and he says of himself (1 Cor. 15:10): "By the grace of God I am what I am." Therefore sanctifying grace is given not only for the remission of sin, but also for growth and stability in righteousness. And thus is it bestowed in this sacrament.

Reply to Objection 2: Further, as appears from its very name, this sacrament is given in order "to confirm" what it finds already there. And consequently it should not be given to those who are not in a state of grace. For this reason, just as it is not given to the unbaptized, so neither should it be given to the adult sinners, except they be restored by Penance. Wherefore was it decreed in the Council of Orleans (Can. iii) that "men should come to Confirmation fasting; and should be admonished to confess their sins first, so that being cleansed they may be able to receive the gift of the Holy Ghost." And then this sacrament perfects the effects of Penance, as of Baptism: because by the grace which he has received in this sacrament, the penitent will obtain fuller remission of his sin. And if any adult approach, being in a state of sin of which he is not conscious or for which he is not perfectly contrite, he will receive the remission of his sins through the grace bestowed in this sacrament.

Reply to Objection 3: As stated above ([4495]Q[62], A[2]), the sacramental grace adds to the sanctifying grace taken in its wide sense, something that produces a special effect, and to which the sacrament is ordained. If, then, we consider, in its wide sense, the grace bestowed in this sacrament, it does not differ from that bestowed in Baptism, but increases what was already there. On the other hand, if we consider it as to that which is added over and above, then one differs in species from the other.

Whether this sacrament should be given to all?

Objection 1: It seems that this sacrament should not be given to all. For this sacrament is given in order to confer a certain excellence, as stated above (A[11], ad 2). But all are not suited for that which belongs to excellence. Therefore this sacrament should not be given to all.

Objection 2: Further, by this sacrament man advances spiritually to perfect age. But perfect age is inconsistent with childhood. Therefore at least it should not be given to children.

Objection 3: Further, as Pope Melchiades says (Ep. ad Episc. Hispan.) "after Baptism we are strengthened for the combat." But women are incompetent to combat, by reason of the frailty of their sex. Therefore neither should women receive this sacrament.

Objection 4: Further, Pope Melchiades says (Ep. ad Episc. Hispan.): "Although the benefit of Regeneration suffices for those who are on the point of death, yet the graces of Confirmation are necessary for those who are to conquer. Confirmation arms and strengthens those to whom the struggles and combats of this world are reserved. And he who comes to die, having kept unsullied the innocence he acquired in Baptism, is confirmed by death; for after death he can sin no more." Therefore this sacrament should not be given to those who are on the point of death: and so it should not be given to all.

On the contrary, It is written (Acts 2:2) that the Holy Ghost in coming, "filled the whole house," whereby the Church is signified; and afterwards it is added that "they were all filled with the Holy Ghost." But this sacrament is given that we may receive that fulness. Therefore it should be given to all who belong to the Church.

I answer that, As stated above [4496](A[1]), man is spiritually advanced by this sacrament to perfect age. Now the intention of nature is that everyone born corporally, should come to perfect age: yet this is sometimes hindered by reason of the corruptibility of the body, which is forestalled by death. But much more is it God's intention to bring all things to perfection, since nature shares in this intention inasmuch as it reflects Him: hence it is written (Dt. 32:4): "The works of God are perfect." Now the soul, to which spiritual birth and perfect spiritual age belong, is immortal; and just as it can in old age attain to spiritual birth, so can it attain to perfect (spiritual) age in youth or childhood; because the various ages of the body do not affect the soul. Therefore this sacrament should be given to all.

Reply to Objection 1: This sacrament is given in order to confer a certain excellence, not indeed, like the sacrament of order, of one man over another, but of man in regard to himself: thus the same man, when arrived at maturity, excels himself as he was when a boy.

Reply to Objection 2: As stated above, the age of the body does not affect the soul. Consequently even in childhood man can attain to the perfection of spiritual age, of which it is written (Wis. 4:8): "Venerable old age is not that of long time, nor counted by the number of years." And hence it is that many children, by reason of the strength of the Holy Ghost which they had received, fought bravely for Christ even to the shedding of their blood.

Reply to Objection 3: As Chrysostom says (Hom. i De Machab.), "in earthly contests fitness of age, physique and rank are required; and consequently slaves, women, old men, and boys are debarred from taking part therein. But in the heavenly combats, the Stadium is open equally to all, to every age, and to either sex." Again, he says (Hom. de Militia Spirit.): "In God's eyes even women fight, for many a woman has waged the spiritual warfare with the courage of a man. For some have rivaled men in the courage with which they have suffered martyrdom; and some indeed have shown themselves stronger than men." Therefore this sacrament should be given to women.

Reply to Objection 4: As we have already observed, the soul, to which spiritual age belongs, is immortal. Wherefore this sacrament should be given to those on the point of death, that they may be seen to be perfect at the resurrection, according to Eph. 4:13: "Until we all meet into the unity of faith . . . unto the measure of the age of the fulness of Christ." And hence Hugh of St. Victor says (De Sacram. ii), "It would be altogether hazardous, if anyone happened to go forth from this life without being confirmed": not that such a one would be lost, except perhaps through contempt; but that this would be detrimental to his perfection. And therefore even children dying after Confirmation obtain greater glory, just as here below they receive more grace. The passage quoted is to be taken in the sense that, with regard to the dangers of the present combat, those who are on the point of death do not need this sacrament.

Whether this sacrament should be given to man on the forehead?

Objection 1: It seems that this sacrament should not be given to man on the forehead. For this sacrament perfects Baptism, as stated above ([4497]Q[65], AA[3],4). But the sacrament of Baptism is given to man over his whole body. Therefore this sacrament should not be given on the forehead only.

Objection 2: Further, this sacrament is given for spiritual strength, as stated above ([4498]AA[1],2,4). But spiritual strength is situated principally in the heart. Therefore this sacrament should be given over the heart rather than on the forehead.

Objection 3: Further, this sacrament is given to man that he may freely confess the faith of Christ. But "with the mouth, confession is made unto salvation," according to Rom. 10:10. Therefore this sacrament should be given about the mouth rather than on the forehead.

On the contrary, Rabanus says (De Instit. Cleric. i): "The baptized is signed by the priest with chrism on the top of the head, but by the bishop on the forehead."

I answer that, As stated above ([4499]AA[1],4), in this sacrament man receives the Holy Ghost for strength in the spiritual combat, that he may bravely confess the Faith of Christ even in face of the enemies of that Faith. Wherefore he is fittingly signed with the sign of the cross on the forehead, with chrism, for two reasons. First, because he is signed with the sign of the cross, as a soldier with the sign of his leader, which should be evident and manifest. Now, the forehead, which is hardly ever covered, is the most conspicuous part of the human body. Wherefore the confirmed is anointed with chrism on the forehead, that he may show publicly that he is a Christian: thus too the apostles after receiving the Holy Ghost showed themselves in public, whereas before they remained hidden in the upper room.

Secondly, because man is hindered from freely confessing Christ's name, by two things---by fear and by shame. Now both these things betray themselves principally on the forehead on account of the proximity of the imagination, and because the (vital) spirits mount directly from the heart to the forehead: hence "those who are ashamed, blush, and those who are afraid, pale" (Ethic. iv). And therefore man is signed with chrism, that neither fear nor shame may hinder him from confessing the name of Christ.

Reply to Objection 1: By baptism we are regenerated unto spiritual life, which belongs to the whole man. But in Confirmation we are strengthened for the combat; the sign of which should be borne on the forehead, as in a conspicuous place.

Reply to Objection 2: The principle of fortitude is in the heart, but its sign appears on the forehead: wherefore it is written (Ezech. 3:8): "Behold I have made . . . thy forehead harder than their foreheads." Hence the sacrament of the Eucharist, whereby man is confirmed in himself, belongs to the heart, according to Ps. 103:15: "That bread may strengthen man's heart." But the sacrament of Confirmation is required as a sign of fortitude against others; and for this reason it is given on the forehead.

Reply to Objection 3: This sacrament is given that we may confess freely: but not that we may confess simply, for this is also the effect of Baptism. And therefore it should not be given on the mouth, but on the forehead, where appear the signs of those passions which hinder free confession.

Whether he who is confirmed needs one to stand* for him? [*Literally, "to hold him"]

Objection 1: It seems that he who is confirmed needs no one to stand for him. For this sacrament is given not only to children but also to adults. But adults can stand for themselves. Therefore it is absurd that someone else should stand for them.

Objection 2: Further, he that belongs already to the Church, has free access to the prince of the Church, i.e. the bishop. But this sacrament, as stated above [4500](A[6]), is given only to one that is baptized, who is already a member of the Church. Therefore it seems that he should not be brought by another to the bishop in order to receive this sacrament.

Objection 3: Further, this sacrament is given for spiritual strength, which has more vigor in men than in women, according to Prov. 31:10: "Who shall find a valiant woman?" Therefore at least a woman should not stand for a man in confirmation.

On the contrary, Are the following words of Pope Innocent, which are to be found in the Decretals (XXX, Q[4]): "If anyone raise the children of another's marriage from the sacred font, or stand for them in Confirmation," etc. Therefore, just as someone is required as sponsor of one who is baptized, so is someone required to stand for him who is to be confirmed .

I answer that, As stated above ([4501]AA[1],4,9), this sacrament is given to man for strength in the spiritual combat. Now, just as one newly born requires someone to teach him things pertaining to ordinary conduct, according to Heb. 12:9: "We have had fathers of our flesh, for instructors, and we obeyed [Vulg.: 'reverenced']" them; so they who are chosen for the fight need instructors by whom they are informed of things concerning the conduct of the battle, and hence in earthly wars, generals and captains are appointed to the command of the others. For this reason he also who receives this sacrament, has someone to stand for him, who, as it were, has to instruct him concerning the fight.

Likewise, since this sacrament bestows on man the perfection of spiritual age, as stated above ([4502]AA[2],5), therefore he who approaches this sacrament is upheld by another, as being spiritually a weakling and a child.

Reply to Objection 1: Although he who is confirmed, be adult in body, nevertheless he is not yet spiritually adult.

Reply to Objection 2: Though he who is baptized is made a member of the Church, nevertheless he is not yet enrolled as a Christian soldier. And therefore he is brought to the bishop, as to the commander of the army, by one who is already enrolled as a Christian soldier. For one who is not yet confirmed should not stand for another in Confirmation.

Reply to Objection 3: According to Col. 3 *(Gal. 3:28), "in Christ Jesus there is neither male nor female." Consequently it matters not whether a man or a woman stand for one who is to be confirmed.

Whether only a bishop can confer this sacrament?

Objection 1: It seems that not only a bishop can confer this sacrament. For Gregory (Regist. iv), writing to Bishop Januarius, says: "We hear that some were scandalized because we forbade priests to anoint with chrism those who have been baptized. Yet in doing this we followed the ancient custom of our Church: but if this trouble some so very much we permit priests, where no bishop is to be had, to anoint the baptized on the forehead with chrism." But that which is essential to the sacraments should not be changed for the purpose of avoiding scandal. Therefore it seems that it is not essential to this sacrament that it be conferred by a bishop.

Objection 2: Further, the sacrament of Baptism seems to be more efficacious than the sacrament of Confirmation: since it bestows full remission of sins, both as to guilt and as to punishment, whereas this sacrament does not. But a simple priest, in virtue of his office, can give the sacrament of Baptism: and in a case of necessity anyone, even without orders, can baptize. Therefore it is not essential to this sacrament that it be conferred by a bishop.

Objection 3: Further, the top of the head, where according to medical men the reason is situated (i.e. the "particular reason," which is called the "cogitative faculty"), is more noble than the forehead, which is the site of the imagination. But a simple priest can anoint the baptized with chrism on the top of the head. Therefore much more can he anoint them with chrism on the forehead, which belongs to this sacrament.

On the contrary, Pope Eusebius (Ep. iii ad Ep. Tusc.) says: "The sacrament of the imposition of the hand should be held in great veneration, and can be given by none but the high priests. Nor is it related or known to have been conferred in apostolic times by others than the apostles themselves; nor can it ever be either licitly or validly performed by others than those who stand in their place. And if anyone presume to do otherwise, it must be considered null and void; nor will such a thing ever be counted among the sacraments of the Church." Therefore it is essential to this sacrament, which is called "the sacrament of the imposition of the hand," that it be given by a bishop.

I answer that, In every work the final completion is reserved to the supreme act or power; thus the preparation of the matter belongs to the lower craftsmen, the higher gives the form, but the highest of all is he to whom pertains the use, which is the end of things made by art; thus also the letter which is written by the clerk, is signed by his employer. Now the faithful of Christ are a Divine work, according to 1 Cor. 3:9: "You are God's building"; and they are also "an epistle," as it were, "written with the Spirit of God," according to 2 Cor. 3:2,3. And this sacrament of Confirmation is, as it were, the final completion of the sacrament of Baptism; in the sense that by Baptism man is built up into a spiritual dwelling, and is written like a spiritual letter; whereas by the sacrament of Confirmation, like a house already built, he is consecrated as a temple of the Holy Ghost, and as a letter already written, is signed with the sign of the cross. Therefore the conferring of this sacrament is reserved to bishops, who possess supreme power in the Church: just as in the primitive Church, the fulness of the Holy Ghost was given by the apostles, in whose place the bishops stand (Acts 8). Hence Pope Urban I says: "All the faithful should. after Baptism, receive the Holy Ghost by the imposition of the bishop's hand, that they may become perfect Christians."

Reply to Objection 1: The Pope has the plenitude of power in the Church, in virtue of which he can commit to certain lower orders things that belong to the higher orders: thus he allows priests to confer minor orders, which belong to the episcopal power. And in virtue of this fulness of power the Pope, Blessed Gregory, allowed simple priests to confer this sacrament, so long as the scandal was ended.

Reply to Objection 2: The sacrament of Baptism is more efficacious than this sacrament as to the removal of evil, since it is a spiritual birth, that consists in change from non-being to being. But this sacrament is more efficacious for progress in good; since it is a spiritual growth from imperfect being to perfect being. And hence this sacrament is committed to a more worthy minister.

Reply to Objection 3: As Rabanus says (De Instit. Cleric. i), "the baptized is signed by the priest with chrism on the top of the head, but by the bishop on the forehead; that the former unction may symbolize the descent of the Holy Ghost on hint, in order to consecrate a dwelling to God: and that the second also may teach us that the sevenfold grace of the same Holy Ghost descends on man with all fulness of sanctity, knowledge and virtue." Hence this unction is reserved to bishops, not on account of its being applied to a more worthy part of the body, but by reason of its having a more powerful effect.

Whether the rite of this sacrament is appropriate?

Objection 1: It seems that the rite of this sacrament is not appropriate. For the sacrament of Baptism is of greater necessity than this, as stated above (A[2], ad 4;[4503] Q[65], AA[3],4). But certain seasons are fixed for Baptism, viz. Easter and Pentecost. Therefore some fixed time of the year should be chosen for this sacrament.

Objection 2: Further, just as this sacrament requires devotion both in the giver and in the receiver, so also does the sacrament of Baptism. But in the sacrament of Baptism it is not necessary that it should be received or given fasting. Therefore it seems unfitting for the Council of Orleans to declare that "those who come to Confirmation should be fasting"; and the Council of Meaux, "that bishops should not give the Holy Ghost with imposition of the hand except they be fasting."

Objection 3: Further, chrism is a sign of the fulness of the Holy Ghost, as stated above [4504](A[2]). But the fulness of the Holy Ghost was given to Christ's faithful on the day of Pentecost, as related in Acts 2:1. Therefore the chrism should be mixed and blessed on the day of Pentecost rather than on Maundy Thursday.

On the contrary, Is the use of the Church, who is governed by the Holy Ghost.

I answer that, Our Lord promised His faithful (Mat. 18:20) saying: "Where there are two or three gathered together in My name, there am I in the midst of them." And therefore we must hold firmly that the Church's ordinations are directed by the wisdom of Christ. And for this reason we must look upon it as certain that the rite observed by the Church, in this and the other sacraments, is appropriate.

Reply to Objection 1: As Pope Melchiades says (Ep. ad Epis. Hispan.), "these two sacraments," viz. Baptism and Confirmation, "are so closely connected that they can nowise be separated save by death intervening, nor can one be duly celebrated without the other." Consequently the same seasons are fixed for the solemn celebration of Baptism and of this sacrament. But since this sacrament is given only by bishops, who are not always present where priests are baptizing, it was necessary, as regards the common use, to defer the sacrament of Confirmation to other seasons also.

Reply to Objection 2: The sick and those in danger of death are exempt from this prohibition, as we read in the decree of the Council of Meaux. And therefore, on account of the multitude of the faithful, and on account of imminent dangers, it is allowed for this sacrament, which can be given by none but a bishop, to be given or received even by those who are not fasting: since one bishop, especially in a large diocese, would not suffice to confirm all, if he were confined to certain times. But where it can be done conveniently, it is more becoming that both giver and receiver should be fasting.

Reply to Objection 3: According to the acts of the Council of Pope Martin, "it was lawful at all times to prepare the chrism." But since solemn Baptism, for which chrism has to be used, is celebrated on Easter Eve, it was rightly decreed, that chrism should be consecrated by the bishop two days beforehand, that it may be sent to the various parts of the diocese. Moreover, this day is sufficiently appropriate to the blessing of sacramental matter, since thereon was the Eucharist instituted, to which, in a certain way, all the other sacraments are ordained, as stated above ([4505]Q[65], A[3]).

OF THE SACRAMENT OF THE EUCHARIST (SIX ARTICLES)

We have now to consider the sacrament of the Eucharist; and first of all we treat of the sacrament itself; secondly, of its matter; thirdly, of its form; fourthly, of its effects; fifthly, of the recipients of this sacrament; sixthly, of the minister; seventhly, of the rite.

Under the first heading there are six points of inquiry:

(1) Whether the Eucharist is a sacrament?

(2) Whether it is one or several sacraments?

(3) Whether it is necessary for salvation?

(4) Its names;

(5) Its institution;

(6) Its figures.

Whether the Eucharist is a sacrament?

Objection 1: It seems that the Eucharist is not a sacrament. For two sacraments ought not to be ordained for the same end, because every sacrament is efficacious in producing its effect. Therefore, since both Confirmation and the Eucharist are ordained for perfection, as Dionysius says (Eccl. Hier. iv), it seems that the Eucharist is not a sacrament, since Confirmation is one, as stated above ([4506]Q[65], A[1];[4507] Q[72], A[1]).

Objection 2: Further, in every sacrament of the New Law, that which comes visibly under our senses causes the invisible effect of the sacrament, just as cleansing with water causes the baptismal character and spiritual cleansing, as stated above ([4508]Q[63], A[6]; [4509] Q[66], AA[1],3,7). But the species of bread and wine, which are the objects of our senses in this sacrament, neither produce Christ's true body, which is both reality and sacrament, nor His mystical body, which is the reality only in the Eucharist. Therefore, it seems that the Eucharist is not a sacrament of the New Law.

Objection 3: Further, sacraments of the New Law, as having matter, are perfected by the use of the matter, as Baptism is by ablution, and Confirmation by signing with chrism. If, then, the Eucharist be a sacrament, it would be perfected by the use of the matter, and not by its consecration. But this is manifestly false, because the words spoken in the consecration of the matter are the form of this sacrament, as will be shown later on ([4510]Q[78], A[1]). Therefore the Eucharist is not a sacrament.

On the contrary, It is said in the Collect [*Postcommunion "pro vivis et defunctis"]: "May this Thy Sacrament not make us deserving of punishment."

I answer that, The Church's sacraments are ordained for helping man in the spiritual life. But the spiritual life is analogous to the corporeal, since corporeal things bear a resemblance to spiritual. Now it is clear that just as generation is required for corporeal life, since thereby man receives life; and growth, whereby man is brought to maturity: so likewise food is required for the preservation of life. Consequently, just as for the spiritual life there had to be Baptism, which is spiritual generation; and Confirmation, which is spiritual growth: so there needed to be the sacrament of the Eucharist, which is spiritual food.

Reply to Objection 1: Perfection is twofold. The first lies within man himself; and he attains it by growth: such perfection belongs to Confirmation. The other is the perfection which comes to man from the addition of food, or clothing, or something of the kind; and such is the perfection befitting the Eucharist, which is the spiritual refreshment.

Reply to Objection 2: The water of Baptism does not cause any spiritual effect by reason of the water, but by reason of the power of the Holy Ghost, which power is in the water. Hence on Jn. 5:4, "An angel of the Lord at certain times," etc., Chrysostom observes: "The water does not act simply as such upon the baptized, but when it receives the grace of the Holy Ghost, then it looses all sins." But the true body of Christ. bears the same relation to the species of the bread and wine, as the power of the Holy Ghost does to the water of Baptism: hence the species of the bread and wine produce no effect except from the virtue of Christ's true body.

Reply to Objection 3: A sacrament is so termed because it contains something sacred. Now a thing can be styled sacred from two causes; either absolutely, or in relation to something else. The difference between the Eucharist and other sacraments having sensible matter is that whereas the Eucharist contains something which is sacred absolutely, namely, Christ's own body; the baptismal water contains something which is sacred in relation to something else, namely, the sanctifying power: and the same holds good of chrism and such like. Consequently, the sacrament of the Eucharist is completed in the very consecration of the matter, whereas the other sacraments are completed in the application of the matter for the sanctifying of the individual. And from this follows another difference. For, in the sacrament of the Eucharist, what is both reality and sacrament is in the matter itself. but what is reality only, namely, the grace bestowed, is in the recipient; whereas in Baptism both are in the recipient, namely, the character, which is both reality and sacrament, and the grace of pardon of sins, which is reality only. And the same holds good of the other sacraments.

Whether the Eucharist is one sacrament or several?

Objection 1: It seems that the Eucharist is not one sacrament but several, because it is said in the Collect [*Postcommunion "pro vivis et defunctis"]: "May the sacraments which we have received purify us, O Lord": and this is said on account of our receiving the Eucharist. Consequently the Eucharist is not one sacrament but several.

Objection 2: Further, it is impossible for genera to be multiplied without the species being multiplied: thus it is impossible for one man to be many animals. But, as stated above ([4511]Q[60], A[1]), sign is the genus of sacrament. Since, then, there are more signs than one, to wit, bread and wine, it seems to follow that here must be more sacraments than one.

Objection 3: Further, this sacrament is perfected in the consecration of the matter, as stated above (A[1], ad 3). But in this sacrament there is a double consecration of the matter. Therefore, it is a twofold sacrament.

On the contrary, The Apostle says (1 Cor. 10:17): "For we, being many, are one bread, one body, all that partake of one bread": from which it is clear that the Eucharist is the sacrament of the Church's unity. But a sacrament bears the likeness of the reality whereof it is the sacrament. Therefore the Eucharist is one sacrament.

I answer that, As stated in Metaph. v, a thing is said to be one, not only from being indivisible, or continuous, but also when it is complete; thus we speak of one house, and one man. A thing is one in perfection, when it is complete through the presence of all that is needed for its end; as a man is complete by having all the members required for the operation of his soul, and a house by having all the parts needful for dwelling therein. And so this sacrament is said to be one. Because it is ordained for spiritual refreshment, which is conformed to corporeal refreshment. Now there are two things required for corporeal refreshment, namely, food, which is dry sustenance, and drink, which is wet sustenance. Consequently, two things concur for the integrity of this sacrament, to wit, spiritual food and spiritual drink, according to John: "My flesh is meat indeed, and My blood is drink indeed." Therefore, this sacrament is materially many, but formally and perfectively one.

Reply to Objection 1: The same Collect at first employs the plural: "May the sacraments which we have received purify us"; and afterwards the singular number: "May this sacrament of Thine not make us worthy of punishment": so as to show that this sacrament is in a measure several, yet simply one.

Reply to Objection 2: The bread and wine are materially several signs, yet formally and perfectively one, inasmuch as one refreshment is prepared therefrom.

Reply to Objection 3: From the double consecration of the matter no more can be gathered than that the sacrament is several materially, as stated above.

Whether the Eucharist is necessary for salvation?

Objection 1: It seems that this sacrament is necessary for salvation. For our Lord said (Jn. 6:54): "Except you eat the flesh of the Son of Man, and drink His blood, you shall not have life in you." But Christ's flesh is eaten and His blood drunk in this sacrament. Therefore, without this sacrament man cannot have the health of spiritual life.

Objection 2: Further, this sacrament is a kind of spiritual food. But bodily food is requisite for bodily health. Therefore, also is this sacrament, for spiritual health.

Objection 3: Further, as Baptism is the sacrament of our Lord's Passion, without which there is no salvation, so also is the Eucharist. For the Apostle says (1 Cor. 11:26): "For as often as you shall eat this bread, and drink the chalice, you shall show the death of the Lord, until He come." Consequently, as Baptism is necessary for salvation, so also is this sacrament.

On the contrary, Augustine writes (Ad Bonifac. contra Pelag. I): "Nor are you to suppose that children cannot possess life, who are deprived of the body and blood of Christ."

I answer that, Two things have to be considered in this sacrament, namely, the sacrament itself, and what is contained in it. Now it was stated above (A[1], OBJ[2]) that the reality of the sacrament is the unity of the mystical body, without which there can be no salvation; for there is no entering into salvation outside the Church, just as in the time of the deluge there was none outside the Ark, which denotes the Church, according to 1 Pet. 3:20,21. And it has been said above ([4512]Q[68], A[2]), that before receiving a sacrament, the reality of the sacrament can be had through the very desire of receiving the sacrament. Accordingly, before actual reception of this sacrament, a man can obtain salvation through the desire of receiving it, just as he can before Baptism through the desire of Baptism, as stated above ([4513]Q[68], A[2]). Yet there is a difference in two respects. First of all, because Baptism is the beginning of the spiritual life, and the door of the sacraments; whereas the Eucharist is, as it were, the consummation of the spiritual life, and the end of all the sacraments, as was observed above ([4514]Q[63], A[6]): for by the hallowings of all the sacraments preparation is made for receiving or consecrating the Eucharist. Consequently, the reception of Baptism is necessary for starting the spiritual life, while the receiving of the Eucharist is requisite for its consummation; by partaking not indeed actually, but in desire, as an end is possessed in desire and intention. Another difference is because by Baptism a man is ordained to the Eucharist, and therefore from the fact of children being baptized, they are destined by the Church to the Eucharist; and just as they believe through the Church's faith, so they desire the Eucharist through the Church's intention, and, as a result, receive its reality. But they are not disposed for Baptism by any previous sacrament, and consequently before receiving Baptism, in no way have they Baptism in desire; but adults alone have: consequently, they cannot have the reality of the sacrament without receiving the sacrament itself. Therefore this sacrament is not necessary for salvation in the same way as Baptism is.

Reply to Objection 1: As Augustine says, explaining Jn. 6:54, "This food and this drink," namely, of His flesh and blood: "He would have us understand the fellowship of His body and members, which is the Church in His predestinated, and called, and justified, and glorified, His holy and believing ones." Hence, as he says in his Epistle to Boniface (Pseudo-Beda, in 1 Cor. 10:17): "No one should entertain the slightest doubt, that then every one of the faithful becomes a partaker of the body and blood of Christ, when in Baptism he is made a member of Christ's body; nor is he deprived of his share in that body and chalice even though he depart from this world in the unity of Christ's body, before he eats that bread and drinks of that chalice."

Reply to Objection 2: The difference between corporeal and spiritual food lies in this, that the former is changed into the substance of the person nourished, and consequently it cannot avail for supporting life except it be partaken of; but spiritual food changes man into itself, according to that saying of Augustine (Confess. vii), that he heard the voice of Christ as it were saying to him: "Nor shalt thou change Me into thyself, as food of thy flesh, but thou shalt be changed into Me." But one can be changed into Christ, and be incorporated in Him by mental desire, even without receiving this sacrament. And consequently the comparison does not hold.

Reply to Objection 3: Baptism is the sacrament of Christ's death and Passion, according as a man is born anew in Christ in virtue of His Passion; but the Eucharist is the sacrament of Christ's Passion according as a man is made perfect in union with Christ Who suffered. Hence, as Baptism is called the sacrament of Faith, which is the foundation of the spiritual life, so the Eucharist is termed the sacrament of Charity, which is "the bond of perfection" (Col. 3:14).

Whether this sacrament is suitably called by various names?

Objection 1: It seems that this sacrament is not suitably called by various names. For names should correspond with things. But this sacrament is one, as stated above [4515](A[2]). Therefore, it ought not to be called by various names.

Objection 2: Further, a species is not properly denominated by what is common to the whole genus. But the Eucharist is a sacrament of the New Law; and it is common to all the sacraments for grace to be conferred by them, which the name "Eucharist" denotes, for it is the same thing as "good grace." Furthermore, all the sacraments bring us help on our journey through this present life, which is the notion conveyed by "Viaticum." Again something sacred is done in all the sacraments, which belongs to the notion of "Sacrifice"; and the faithful intercommunicate through all the sacraments, which this Greek word {Synaxis} and the Latin "Communio" express. Therefore, these names are not suitably adapted to this sacrament.

Objection 3: Further, a host [*From Latin "hostia," a victim] seems to be the same as a sacrifice. Therefore, as it is not properly called a sacrifice, so neither is it properly termed a "Host."

On the contrary, is the use of these expressions by the faithful.

I answer that, This sacrament has a threefold significance. one with regard to the past, inasmuch as it is commemorative of our Lord's Passion, which was a true sacrifice, as stated above ([4516]Q[48], A[3]), and in this respect it is called a "Sacrifice."

With regard to the present it has another meaning, namely, that of Ecclesiastical unity, in which men are aggregated through this Sacrament; and in this respect it is called "Communion" or {Synaxis}. For Damascene says (De Fide Orth. iv) that "it is called

Communion because we communicate with Christ through it, both because we partake of His flesh and Godhead, and because we communicate with and are united to one another through it."

With regard to the future it has a third meaning, inasmuch as this sacrament foreshadows the Divine fruition, which shall come to pass in heaven; and according to this it is called "Viaticum," because it supplies the way of winning thither. And in this respect it is also called the "Eucharist," that is, "good grace," because "the grace of God is life everlasting" (Rom. 6:23); or because it really contains Christ, Who is "full of grace."

In Greek, moreover, it is called {Metalepsis}, i.e. "Assumption," because, as Damascene says (De Fide Orth. iv), "we thereby assume the Godhead of the Son."

Reply to Objection 1: There is nothing to hinder the same thing from being called by several names, according to its various properties or effects.

Reply to Objection 2: What is common to all the sacraments is attributed antonomastically to this one on account of its excellence.

Reply to Objection 3: This sacrament is called a "Sacrifice" inasmuch as it represents the Passion of Christ; but it is termed a "Host" inasmuch as it contains Christ, Who is "a host (Douay: 'sacrifice') . . . of sweetness" (Eph. 5:2).

Whether the institution of this sacrament was appropriate?

Objection 1: It seems that the institution of this sacrament was not appropriate, because as the Philosopher says (De Gener. ii): "We are nourished by the things from whence we spring." But by Baptism, which is spiritual regeneration, we receive our spiritual being, as Dionysius says (Eccl. Hier. ii). Therefore we are also nourished by Baptism. Consequently there was no need to institute this sacrament as spiritual nourishment.

Objection 2: Further, men are united with Christ through this sacrament as the members with the head. But Christ is the Head of all men, even of those who have existed from the beginning of the world, as stated above ([4517]Q[8], AA[3],6). Therefore the institution of this sacrament should not have been postponed till the Lord's supper.

Objection 3: Further, this sacrament is called the memorial of our Lord's Passion, according to Mat. 26 (Lk. 22:19): "Do this for a commemoration of Me." But a commemoration is of things past. Therefore, this sacrament should not have been instituted before Christ's Passion.

Objection 4: Further, a man is prepared by Baptism for the Eucharist, which ought to be given only to the baptized. But Baptism was instituted by Christ after His Passion and Resurrection, as is evident from Mat. 28:19. Therefore, this sacrament was not suitably instituted before Christ's Passion.

On the contrary, This sacrament was instituted by Christ, of Whom it is said (Mk. 7:37) that "He did all things well."

I answer that, This sacrament was appropriately instituted at the supper, when Christ conversed with His disciples for the last time. First of all, because of what is contained in the sacrament: for Christ is Himself contained in the Eucharist sacramentally. Consequently, when Christ was going to leave His disciples in His proper species, He left Himself with them under the sacramental species; as the Emperor's image is set up to be reverenced in his absence. Hence Eusebius says: "Since He was going to withdraw His assumed body from their eyes, and bear it away to the stars, it was needful that on the day of the supper He should consecrate the sacrament of His body and blood for our sakes, in order that what was once offered up for our ransom should be fittingly worshiped in a mystery."

Secondly, because without faith in the Passion there could never be any salvation, according to Rom. 3:25: "Whom God hath proposed to be a propitiation, through faith in His blood." It was necessary accordingly that there should be at all times among men something to show forth our Lord's Passion; the chief sacrament of which in the old Law was the Paschal Lamb. Hence the Apostle says (1 Cor. 5:7): "Christ our Pasch is sacrificed." But its successor under the New Testament is the sacrament of the Eucharist, which is a remembrance of the Passion now past, just as the other was figurative of the Passion to come. And so it was fitting that when the hour of the Passion was come, Christ should institute a new Sacrament after celebrating the old, as Pope Leo I says (Serm. lviii).

Thirdly, because last words, chiefly such as are spoken by departing friends, are committed most deeply to memory; since then especially affection for friends is more enkindled, and the things which affect us most are impressed the deepest in the soul. Consequently, since, as Pope Alexander I says, "among sacrifices there can be none greater than the body and blood of Christ, nor any more powerful oblation"; our Lord instituted this sacrament at His last parting with His disciples, in order that it might be held in the greater veneration. And this is what Augustine says (Respons. ad Januar. i): "In order to commend more earnestly the death of this mystery, our Saviour willed this last act to be fixed in the hearts and memories of the disciples whom He was about to quit for the Passion."

Reply to Objection 1: We are nourished from the same things of which we are made, but they do not come to us in the same way; for those out of which we are made come to us through generation, while the same, as nourishing us, come to us through being eaten. Hence, as we are new-born in Christ through Baptism, so through the Eucharist we eat Christ.

Reply to Objection 2: The Eucharist is the perfect sacrament of our Lord's Passion, as containing Christ crucified; consequently it could not be instituted before the Incarnation; but then there was room for only such sacraments as were prefigurative of the Lord's Passion.

Reply to Objection 3: This sacrament was instituted during the supper, so as in the future to be a memorial of our Lord's Passion as accomplished. Hence He said expressively: "As often as ye shall do these things" [*Cf. Canon of the Mass], speaking of the future.

Reply to Objection 4: The institution responds to the order of intention. But the sacrament of the Eucharist, although after Baptism in the receiving, is yet previous to it in intention; and therefore it behooved to be instituted first. or else it can be said that Baptism was already instituted in Christ's Baptism; hence some were already baptized with Christ's Baptism, as we read in Jn. 3:22.

Whether the Paschal Lamb was the chief figure of this sacrament?

Objection 1: It seems that the Paschal Lamb was not the chief figure of this sacrament, because (Ps. 109:4) Christ is called "a priest according to the order of Melchisedech," since Melchisedech bore the figure of Christ's sacrifice, in offering bread and wine. But the expression of likeness causes one thing to be named from another. Therefore, it seems that Melchisedech's offering was the "principal" figure of this sacrament.

Objection 2: Further, the passage of the Red Sea was a figure of Baptism, according to 1 Cor. 10:2: "All . . . were baptized in the cloud and in the sea." But the immolation of the Paschal Lamb was previous to the passage of the Red Sea, and the Manna came after it, just as the Eucharist follows Baptism. Therefore the Manna is a more expressive figure of this sacrament than the Paschal Lamb.

Objection 3: Further, the principal power of this sacrament is that it brings us into the kingdom of heaven, being a kind of "viaticum." But this was chiefly prefigured in the sacrament of expiation when the "high-priest entered once a year into the Holy of Holies with blood," as the Apostle proves in Heb. 9. Consequently, it seems that that sacrifice was a more significant figure of this sacrament than was the Paschal Lamb.

On the contrary, The Apostle says (1 Cor. 5:7,8): "Christ our Pasch is sacrificed; therefore let us feast . . . with the unleavened bread of sincerity and truth."

I answer that, We can consider three things in this sacrament: namely, that which is sacrament only, and this is the bread and wine; that which is both reality and sacrament, to wit, Christ's true body; and lastly that which is reality only, namely, the effect of this sacrament. Consequently, in relation to what is sacrament only, the chief figure of this sacrament was the oblation of Melchisedech, who offered up bread and wine. In relation to Christ crucified, Who is contained in this sacrament, its figures were all the sacrifices of the Old Testament, especially the sacrifice of expiation, which was the most solemn of all. While with regard to its effect, the chief figure was the Manna, "having in it the sweetness of every taste" (Wis. 16:20), just as the grace of this sacrament refreshes the soul in all respects.

The Paschal Lamb foreshadowed this sacrament in these three ways. First of all, because it was eaten with unleavened loaves, according to Ex. 12:8: "They shall eat flesh . . . and unleavened bread." As to the second because it was immolated by the entire multitude of the children of Israel on the fourteenth day of the moon; and this was a figure of the Passion of Christ, Who is called the Lamb on account of His innocence. As to the effect, because by the blood of the Paschal Lamb the children of Israel were preserved from the destroying Angel, and brought from the Egyptian captivity; and in this respect the Paschal Lamb is the chief figure of this sacrament, because it represents it in every respect.

From this the answer to the Objections is manifest.

OF THE MATTER OF THIS SACRAMENT (EIGHT ARTICLES)

We have now to consider the matter of this sacrament: and first of all as to its species; secondly, the change of the bread and wine into the body of Christ; thirdly, the manner in which Christ's body exists in this sacrament; fourthly, the accidents of bread and wine which continue in this sacrament.

Under the first heading there are eight points for inquiry:
(1) Whether bread and wine are the matter of this sacrament?
(2) Whether a determinate quantity of the same is required for the matter of this sacrament?
(3) Whether the matter of this sacrament is wheaten bread?
(4) Whether it is unleavened or fermented bread?
(5) Whether the matter of this sacrament is wine from the grape?
(6) Whether water should be mixed with it?
(7) Whether water is of necessity for this sacrament?
(8) Of the quantity of the water added.

Whether the matter of this sacrament is bread and wine?

Objection 1: It seems that the matter of this sacrament is not bread and wine. Because this sacrament ought to represent Christ's Passion more fully than did the sacraments of the Old Law. But the flesh of animals, which was the matter of the sacraments under the Old Law, shows forth Christ's Passion more fully than bread and wine. Therefore the matter of this sacrament ought rather to be the flesh of animals than bread and wine.

Objection 2: Further, this sacrament is to be celebrated in every place. But in many lands bread is not to be found, and in many places wine is not to be found. Therefore bread and wine are not a suitable matter for this sacrament.

Objection 3: Further, this sacrament is for both hale and weak. But to some weak persons wine is hurtful. Therefore it seems that wine ought not to be the matter of this sacrament.

On the contrary, Pope Alexander I says (Ep. ad omnes orth. i): "In oblations of the sacraments only bread and wine mixed with water are to be offered."

I answer that, Some have fallen into various errors about the matter of this sacrament. Some, known as the Artotyrytae, as Augustine says (De Haeres. xxviii), "offer bread and cheese in this sacrament, contending that oblations were celebrated by men in the first ages, from fruits of the earth and sheep." Others, called Cataphrygae and Pepuziani, "are reputed to have made their Eucharistic bread with infants' blood drawn from tiny punctures over the entire body, and mixed with flour." Others, styled Aquarii, under guise of sobriety, offer nothing but water in this sacrament.

Now all these and similar errors are excluded by the fact that Christ instituted this sacrament under the species of bread and wine, as is evident from Mat. 26. Consequently, bread and wine are the proper matter of this sacrament. And the reasonableness of this is seen first, in the use of this sacrament, which is eating: for, as water is used in the sacrament of Baptism for the purpose of spiritual cleansing, since bodily cleansing is commonly done with water; so bread and wine, wherewith men are commonly fed, are employed in this sacrament for the use of spiritual eating.

Secondly, in relation to Christ's Passion, in which the blood was separated from the body. And therefore in this sacrament, which is the memorial of our Lord's Passion, the bread is received apart as the sacrament of the body, and the wine as the sacrament of the blood.

Thirdly, as to the effect, considered in each of the partakers. For, as Ambrose (Mag. Sent. iv, D, xi) says on 1 Cor. 11:20, this sacrament "avails for the defense of soul and body"; and therefore "Christ's body is offered" under the species of bread "for the health of the body, and the blood" under the species of wine "for the health of the soul," according to Lev. 17:14: "The life of the animal [Vulg.: 'of all flesh'] is in the blood."

Fourthly, as to the effect with regard to the whole Church, which is made up of many believers, just "as bread is composed of many grains, and wine flows from many grapes," as the gloss observes on 1 Cor. 10:17: "We being many are . . . one body," etc.

Reply to Objection 1: Although the flesh of slaughtered animals represents the Passion more forcibly, nevertheless it is less suitable for the common use of this sacrament, and for denoting the unity of the Church.

Reply to Objection 2: Although wheat and wine are not produced in every country, yet they can easily be conveyed to every land, that is, as much as is needful for the use of this sacrament: at the same time one is not to be consecrated when the other is lacking, because it would not be a complete sacrament.

Reply to Objection 3: Wine taken in small quantity cannot do the sick much harm: yet if there be fear of harm, it is not necessary for all who take Christ's body to partake also of His blood, as will be stated later ([4518]Q[80], A[12]).

Whether a determinate quantity of bread and wine is required for the matter of this sacrament?

Objection 1: It seems that a determinate quantity of bread and wine is required for the matter of this sacrament. Because the effects of grace are no less set in order than those of nature. But, "there is a limit set by nature upon all existing things, and a reckoning of size and development" (De Anima ii). Consequently, in this sacrament, which is called "Eucharist," that is, "a good grace," a determinate quantity of the bread and wine is required.

Objection 2: Further, Christ gave no power to the ministers of the Church regarding matters which involve derision of the faith and of His sacraments, according to 2 Cor. 10:8: "Of our power which the Lord hath given us unto edification, and not for your destruction." But it would lead to mockery of this sacrament if the priest were to wish to consecrate all the bread which is sold in the market and all the wine in the cellar. Therefore he cannot do this.

Objection 3: Further, if anyone be baptized in the sea, the entire sea-water is not sanctified by the form of baptism, but only the water wherewith the body of the baptized is cleansed. Therefore, neither in this sacrament can a superfluous quantity of bread be consecrated.

On the contrary, Much is opposed to little, and great to small. But there is no quantity, however small, of the bread and wine which cannot be consecrated. Therefore, neither is there any quantity, however great, which cannot be consecrated.

I answer that, Some have maintained that the priest could not consecrate an immense quantity of bread and wine, for instance, all the bread in the market or all the wine in a cask. But this does not appear to be true, because in all things containing matter, the reason for the determination of the matter is drawn from its disposition to an end, just as the matter of a saw is iron, so as to adapt it for cutting. But the end of this sacrament is the use of the faithful. Consequently, the quantity of the matter of this sacrament must be determined by comparison with the use of the faithful. But this cannot be determined by comparison with the use of the faithful who are actually present; otherwise the parish priest having few parishioners could not consecrate many hosts. It remains, then, for the matter of this sacrament to be determined in reference to the number of the faithful absolutely. But the number of the faithful is not a determinate one. Hence it cannot be said that the quantity of the matter of this sacrament is restricted.

Reply to Objection 1: The matter of every natural object has its determinate quantity by comparison with its determinate form. But the number of the faithful, for whose use this sacrament is ordained, is not a determinate one. Consequently there is no comparison.

Reply to Objection 2: The power of the Church's ministers is ordained for two purposes: first for the proper effect, and secondly for the end of the effect. But the second does not take away the first. Hence, if the priest intends to consecrate the body of Christ for an evil purpose, for instance, to make mockery of it, or to administer poison through it, he commits sin by his evil intention, nevertheless, on account of the power committed to him, he accomplishes the sacrament.

Reply to Objection 3: The sacrament of Baptism is perfected in the use of the matter: and therefore no more of the water is hallowed than what is used. But this sacrament is wrought in the consecration of the matter. Consequently there is no parallel.

Whether wheaten bread is required for the matter of this sacrament?

Objection 1: It seems that wheaten bread is not requisite for the matter of this sacrament, because this sacrament is a reminder of our Lord's Passion. But barley bread seems to be more in keeping with the Passion than wheaten bread, as being more bitter, and because Christ used it to feed the multitudes upon the mountain, as narrated in Jn. 6. Therefore wheaten bread is not the proper matter of this sacrament.

Objection 2: Further, in natural things the shape is a sign of species. But some cereals resemble wheat, such as spelt and maize, from which in some localities bread is made for the use of this sacrament. Therefore wheaten bread is not the proper matter of this sacrament.

Objection 3: Further, mixing dissolves species. But wheaten flour is hardly to be found unmixed with some other species of grain, except in the instance of specially selected grain. Therefore it does not seem that wheaten bread is the proper matter for this sacrament.

Objection 4: Further, what is corrupted appears to be of another species. But some make the sacrament from bread which is corrupted, and which no longer seems to be wheaten bread. Therefore, it seems that such bread is not the proper matter of this sacrament.

On the contrary, Christ is contained in this sacrament, and He compares Himself to a grain of wheat, saying (Jn. 12:24): "Unless the grain of wheat falling into the ground die, itself remaineth alone." Therefore bread from corn, i.e. wheaten bread, is the matter of this sacrament.

I answer that, As stated above [4519](A[1]), for the use of the sacraments such matter is adopted as is commonly made use of among men. Now among other breads wheaten bread is more commonly used by men; since other breads seem to be employed when this fails. And consequently Christ is believed to have instituted this sacrament under this species of bread. Moreover this bread strengthens man, and so it denotes more suitably the effect of this sacrament. Consequently, the proper matter for this sacrament is wheaten bread.

Reply to Objection 1: Barley bread serves to denote the hardness of the Old Law; both on account of the hardness of the bread, and because, as Augustine says ([4520]Q[83]): "The flour within the barley, wrapped up as it is within a most tenacious fibre, denotes either the Law itself, which was given in such manner as to be vested in bodily sacraments; or else it denotes the people themselves, who were not yet despoiled of carnal desires, which clung to their hearts like fibre." But this sacrament belongs to Christ's "sweet yoke," and to the truth already manifested, and to a spiritual people. Consequently barley bread would not be a suitable matter for this sacrament.

Reply to Objection 2: A begetter begets a thing like to itself in species. yet there is some unlikeness as to the accidents, owing either to the matter, or to weakness within the generative power. And therefore, if there be any cereals which can be grown from the seed of the wheat (as wild wheat from wheat seed grown in bad ground), the bread made from such grain can be the matter of this sacrament: and this does not obtain either in barley, or in spelt, or even in maize, which is of all grains the one most resembling the wheat grain. But the resemblance as to shape in such seems to denote closeness of species rather than identity; just as the resemblance in shape between the dog and the wolf goes to show that they are allied but not of the same species. Hence from such grains, which cannot in any way be generated from wheat grain, bread cannot be made such as to be the proper matter of this sacrament.

Reply to Objection 3: A moderate mixing does not alter the species, because that little is as it were absorbed by the greater. Consequently, then, if a small quantity of another grain be mixed with a much greater quantity of wheat, bread may be made therefrom so as to be the proper matter of this sacrament; but if the mixing be notable, for instance, half and half; or nearly so, then such mixing alters the species; consequently, bread made therefrom will not be the proper matter of this sacrament.

Reply to Objection 4: Sometimes there is such corruption of the bread that the species of bread is lost, as when the continuity of its parts is destroyed, and the taste, color, and other accidents are changed; hence the body of Christ may not be made from such matter. But sometimes there is not such corruption as to alter the species, but merely disposition towards corruption, which a slight change in the savor betrays, and from such bread the body of Christ may be made: but he who does so, sins from irreverence towards the sacrament. And because starch comes of corrupted wheat, it does not seem as if the body of Christ could be made of the bread made therefrom, although some hold the contrary.

Whether this sacrament ought to be made of unleavened bread?

Objection 1: It seems that this sacrament ought not to be made of unleavened bread. because in this sacrament we ought to imitate Christ's institution. But Christ appears to have instituted this sacrament in fermented bread, because, as we have read in Ex. 12, the Jews, according to the Law, began to use unleavened bread on the day of the Passover which is celebrated on the fourteenth day of the moon; and Christ instituted this sacrament at the supper which He celebrated "before the festival day of the Pasch" (Jn. 13:1, 4). Therefore we ought likewise to celebrate this sacrament with fermented bread.

Objection 2: Further, legal observances ought not to be continued in the time of grace. But the use of unleavened bread was a ceremony of the Law, as is clear from Ex. 12. Therefore we ought not to use unfermented bread in this sacrament of grace.

Objection 3: Further, as stated above ([4521]Q[65], A[1];[4522] Q[73], A[3]), the Eucharist is the sacrament of charity just as Baptism is the sacrament of faith. But the fervor of charity is signified by fermented bread, as is declared by the gloss on Mat. 13:33: "The kingdom of heaven is like unto leaven," etc. Therefore this sacrament ought to be made of leavened bread.

Objection 4: Further, leavened or unleavened are mere accidents of bread, which do not vary the species. But in the matter for the sacrament of Baptism no difference is observed regarding the variation of the accidents, as to whether it be salt or fresh, warm or cold water. Therefore neither ought any distinction to be observed, as to whether the bread be unleavened or leavened.

On the contrary, According to the Decretals (Extra, De Celebr. Miss.), a priest is punished "for presuming to celebrate, using fermented bread and a wooden cup."

I answer that, Two things may be considered touching the matter of this sacrament namely, what is necessary, and what is suitable. It is necessary that the bread be wheaten, without which the sacrament is not valid, as stated above [4523](A[3]). It is not, however, necessary for the sacrament that the bread be unleavened or leavened, since it can be celebrated in either.

But it is suitable that every priest observe the rite of his Church in the celebration of the sacrament. Now in this matter there are various customs of the Churches: for, Gregory says: "The Roman Church offers unleavened bread, because our Lord took flesh without union of sexes: but the Greek Churches offer leavened bread, because the Word of the Father was clothed with flesh; as leaven is mixed with the flour." Hence, as a priest sins by celebrating with fermented bread in the Latin Church, so a Greek priest celebrating with unfermented bread in a church of the Greeks would also sin, as perverting the rite of his Church. Nevertheless the custom of celebrating with unleavened bread is more reasonable. First, on account of Christ's institution: for He instituted this sacrament "on the first day of the Azymes" (Mat. 26:17; Mk. 14:12; Lk. 22:7), on which day there ought to be nothing fermented in the houses of the Jews, as is stated in Ex. 12:15,19. Secondly, because bread is properly the sacrament of Christ's body, which was conceived without

527

corruption, rather than of His Godhead, as will be seen later ([4524]Q[76], A[1], ad 1). Thirdly, because this is more in keeping with the sincerity of the faithful, which is required in the use of this sacrament, according to 1 Cor. 5:7: "Christ our Pasch is sacrificed: therefore let us feast . . . with the unleavened bread of sincerity and truth."

However, this custom of the Greeks is not unreasonable both on account of its signification, to which Gregory refers, and in detestation of the heresy of the Nazarenes, who mixed up legal observances with the Gospel.

Reply to Objection 1: As we read in Ex. 12, the paschal solemnity began on the evening of the fourteenth day of the moon. So, then, after immolating the Paschal Lamb, Christ instituted this sacrament: hence this day is said by John to precede the day of the Pasch, while the other three Evangelists call it "the first day of the Azymes," when fermented bread was not found in the houses of the Jews, as stated above. Fuller mention was made of this in the treatise on our Lord's Passion ([4525]Q[46], A[9], ad 1).

Reply to Objection 2: Those who celebrate the sacrament with unleavened bread do not intend to follow the ceremonial of the Law, but to conform to Christ's institution; so they are not Judaizing; otherwise those celebrating in fermented bread would be Judaizing, because the Jews offered up fermented bread for the first-fruits.

Reply to Objection 3: Leaven denotes charity on account of one single effect, because it makes the bread more savory and larger; but it also signifies corruption from its very nature.

Reply to Objection 4: Since whatever is fermented partakes of corruption, this sacrament may not be made from corrupt bread, as stated above (A[3], ad 4); consequently, there is a wider difference between unleavened and leavened bread than between warm and cold baptismal water: because there might be such corruption of fermented bread that it could not be validly used for the sacrament.

Day 302

Whether wine of the grape is the proper matter of this sacrament?

Objection 1: It seems that wine of the grape is not the proper matter of this sacrament. Because, as water is the matter of Baptism, so is wine the matter of this sacrament. But Baptism can be conferred with any kind of water. Therefore this sacrament can be celebrated in any kind of wine, such as of pomegranates, or of mulberries; since vines do not grow in some countries.

Objection 2: Further, vinegar is a kind of wine drawn from the grape, as Isidore says (Etym. xx). But this sacrament cannot be celebrated with vinegar. Therefore, it seems that wine from the grape is not the proper matter of this sacrament.

Objection 3: Further, just as the clarified wine is drawn from grapes, so also are the juice of unripe grapes and must. But it does not appear that this sacrament may be made from such, according to what we read in the Sixth Council (Trull., Can. 28): "We have learned that in some churches the priests add grapes to the sacrifice of the oblation; and so they dispense both together to the people. Consequently we give order that no priest shall do this in future." And Pope Julius I rebukes some priests "who offer wine pressed from the grape in the sacrament of the Lord's chalice." Consequently, it seems that wine from the grape is not the proper matter of this sacrament.

On the contrary, As our Lord compared Himself to the grain of wheat, so also He compared Himself to the vine, saying (Jn. 15:1): "I am the true vine." But only bread from wheat is the matter of this sacrament, as stated above [4526](A[3]). Therefore, only wine from the grape is the proper matter of this sacrament.

I answer that, This sacrament can only be performed with wine from the grape. First of all on account of Christ's institution, since He instituted this sacrament in wine from the grape, as is evident from His own words, in instituting this sacrament (Mat. 26:29): "I will not drink from henceforth of this fruit of the vine." Secondly, because, as stated above [4527](A[3]), that is adopted as the matter of the sacraments which is properly and universally considered as such. Now that is properly called wine, which is drawn from the grape, whereas other liquors are called wine from resemblance to the wine of the grape. Thirdly, because the wine from the grape is more in keeping with the effect of this sacrament, which is spiritual; because it is written (Ps. 103:15): "That wine may cheer the heart of man."

Reply to Objection 1: Such liquors are called wine, not properly but only from their resemblance thereto. But genuine wine can be conveyed to such countries wherein the grape-vine does not flourish, in a quantity sufficient for this sacrament.

Reply to Objection 2: Wine becomes vinegar by corruption; hence there is no returning from vinegar to wine, as is said in Metaph. viii. And consequently, just as this sacrament may not be made from bread which is utterly corrupt, so neither can it be made from vinegar. It can, however, be made from wine which is turning sour, just as from bread turning corrupt, although he who does so sins, as stated above [4528](A[3]).

Reply to Objection 3: The juice of unripe grapes is at the stage of incomplete generation, and therefore it has not yet the species of wine: on which account it may not be used for this sacrament. Must, however, has already the species of wine, for its sweetness [*"Aut dulcis musti Vulcano decoquit humorem"; Virgil, Georg. i, 295] indicates fermentation which is "the result of its natural heat" (Meteor. iv); consequently this sacrament can be made from must. Nevertheless entire grapes ought not to be mixed with this sacrament, because then there would be something else besides wine. It is furthermore forbidden to offer must in the chalice, as soon as it has been squeezed from the grape, since this is unbecoming owing to the impurity of the must. But in case of necessity it may be done: for it is said by the same Pope Julius, in the passage quoted in the argument: "If necessary, let the grape be pressed into the chalice."

Whether water should be mixed with the wine?

Objection 1: It seems that water ought not to be mixed with the wine, since Christ's sacrifice was foreshadowed by that of Melchisedech, who (Gn. 14:18) is related to have offered up bread and wine only. Consequently it seems that water should not be added in this sacrament.

Objection 2: Further, the various sacraments have their respective matters. But water is the matter of Baptism. Therefore it should not be employed as the matter of this sacrament.

Objection 3: Further, bread and wine are the matter of this sacrament. But nothing is added to the bread. Therefore neither should anything be added to the wine.

On the contrary, Pope Alexander I writes (Ep. 1 ad omnes orth.): "In the sacramental oblations which in mass are offered to the Lord, only bread and wine mixed with water are to be offered in sacrifice."

I answer that, Water ought to be mingled with the wine which is offered in this sacrament. First of all on account of its institution: for it is believed with probability that our Lord instituted this sacrament in wine tempered with water according to the custom of that country: hence it is written (Prov. 9:5): "Drink the wine which I have mixed for you." Secondly, because it harmonizes with the representation of our Lord's Passion: hence Pope Alexander I says (Ep. 1 ad omnes orth.): "In the Lord's chalice neither wine only nor water only ought to be offered, but both mixed because we read that both flowed from His side in the Passion." Thirdly, because this is adapted for signifying the effect of this sacrament, since as Pope Julius says (Concil. Bracarens iii, Can. 1): "We see that the people are signified by the water, but Christ's blood by the wine. Therefore when water is mixed with the wine in the chalice, the people is made one with Christ." Fourthly, because this is appropriate to the fourth effect of this sacrament, which is the entering into everlasting life: hence Ambrose says (De Sacram. v): "The water flows into the chalice, and springs forth unto everlasting life."

Reply to Objection 1: As Ambrose says (De Sacram. v), just as Christ's sacrifice is denoted by the offering of Melchisedech, so likewise it is signified by the water which flowed from the rock in the desert, according to 1 Cor. 10:4: "But they drank of the spiritual rock which came after them."

Reply to Objection 2: In Baptism water is used for the purpose of ablution: but in this sacrament it is used by way of refreshment, according to Ps. 22:3: "He hath brought me up on the water of refreshment."

Reply to Objection 3: Bread is made of water and flour; and therefore, since water is mixed with the wine, neither is without water.

Whether the mixing with water is essential to this sacrament?

Objection 1: It seems that the mixing with water is essential to this sacrament. Because Cyprian says to Cecilius (Ep. lxiii): "Thus the Lord's chalice is not water only and wine only, but both must be mixed together: in the same way as neither the Lord's body be of flour only, except both," i.e. the flour and the water "be united as one." But the admixture of water with the flour is necessary for this sacrament. Consequently, for the like reason, so is the mixing of water with the wine.

Objection 2: Further, at our Lord's Passion, of which this is the memorial, water as well as blood flowed from His side. But wine, which is the sacrament of the blood, is necessary for this sacrament. For the same reason, therefore, so is water.

Objection 3: Further, if water were not essential to this sacrament, it would not matter in the least what kind of water was used; and so water distilled from roses, or any other kind might be employed; which is contrary to the usage of the Church. Consequently water is essential to this sacrament.

On the contrary, Cyprian says (Ep. lxiii): "If any of our predecessors, out of ignorance or simplicity, has not kept this usage," i.e. of mixing water with the wine, "one may pardon his simplicity"; which would not be the case if water were essential to the sacrament, as the wine or the bread. Therefore the mingling of water with the wine is not essential to the sacrament.

I answer that, Judgment concerning a sign is to be drawn from the thing signified. Now the adding of water to the wine is for the purpose of signifying the sharing of this sacrament by the faithful, in this respect that by the mixing of the water with the wine is signified the union of the people with Christ, as stated [4529](A[6]). Moreover, the flowing of water from the side of Christ hanging on the cross refers to the same, because by the water is denoted the cleansing from sins, which was the effect of Christ's Passion. Now it was observed above (Q[73], A[1], ad 3), that this sacrament is completed in the consecration of the matter: while the usage of the faithful is not essential to the sacrament, but only a consequence thereof. Consequently, then, the adding of water is not essential to the sacrament.

Reply to Objection 1: Cyprian's expression is to be taken in the same sense in which we say that a thing cannot be, which cannot be suitably. And so the comparison refers to what ought to be done, not to what is essential to be done; since water is of the essence of bread, but not of the essence of wine.

Reply to Objection 2: The shedding of the blood belonged directly to Christ's Passion: for it is natural for blood to flow from a wounded human body. But the flowing of the water was not necessary for the Passion; but merely to show its effect, which is to wash away sins, and to refresh us from the heat of concupiscence. And therefore the water is not offered apart from the wine in this sacrament, as the wine is offered apart from the bread; but the water is offered mixed with the wine to show that the wine belongs of itself to this sacrament, as of its very essence; but the water as something added to the wine.

Reply to Objection 3: Since the mixing of water with the wine is not necessary for the sacrament, it does not matter, as to the essence of the sacrament, what kind of water is added to the wine, whether natural water, or artificial, as rose-water, although, as to the propriety of the sacrament, he would sin who mixes any other than natural and true water, because true water flowed from the side of Christ hanging on the cross, and not phlegm, as some have said, in order to show that Christ's body was truly composed of the four elements; as by the flowing blood, it was shown to be composed of the four humors, as Pope Innocent III says in a certain Decree. But because the mixing of water with flour is essential to this sacrament, as making the composition of bread, if rose-water, or any other liquor besides true water, be mixed with the flour, the sacrament would not be valid, because it would not be true bread.

Whether water should be added in great quantity?

Objection 1: It seems that water ought to be added in great quantity, because as blood flowed sensibly from Christ's side, so did water: hence it is written (Jn. 19:35): "He that saw it, hath given testimony." But water could not be sensibly present in this sacrament except it were used in great quantity. Consequently it seems that water ought to be added in great quantity.

529

Objection 2: Further, a little water mixed with much wine is corrupted. But what is corrupted no longer exists. Therefore, it is the same thing to add a little water in this sacrament as to add none. But it is not lawful to add none. Therefore, neither is it lawful to add a little.

Objection 3: Further, if it sufficed to add a little, then as a consequence it would suffice to throw one drop of water into an entire cask. But this seems ridiculous. Therefore it does not suffice for a small quantity to be added.

On the contrary, It is said in the Decretals (Extra, De Celeb. Miss.): "The pernicious abuse has prevailed in your country of adding water in greater quantity than the wine, in the sacrifice, where according to the reasonable custom of the entire Church more wine than water ought to be employed."

I answer that, There is a threefold opinion regarding the water added to the wine, as Pope Innocent III says in a certain Decretal. For some say that the water remains by itself when the wine is changed into blood: but such an opinion cannot stand, because in the sacrament of the altar after the consecration there is nothing else save the body and the blood of Christ. Because, as Ambrose says in De Officiis (De Mysteriis ix): "Before the blessing it is another species that is named, after the blessing the Body is signified; otherwise it would not be adored with adoration of latria." And therefore others have said that as the wine is changed into blood, so the water is changed into the water which flowed from Christ's side. But this cannot be maintained reasonably, because according to this the water would be consecrated apart from the wine, as the wine is from the bread.

And therefore as he (Innocent III, Decretals, Extra, De Celeb. Miss.) says, the more probable opinion is that which holds that the water is changed into wine, and the wine into blood. Now, this could not be done unless so little water was used that it would be changed into wine. Consequently, it is always safer to add little water, especially if the wine be weak, because the sacrament could not be celebrated if there were such addition of water as to destroy the species of the wine. Hence Pope Julius I reprehends some who "keep throughout the year a linen cloth steeped in must, and at the time of sacrifice wash a part of it with water, and so make the offering."

Reply to Objection 1: For the signification of this sacrament it suffices for the water to be appreciable by sense when it is mixed with the wine: but it is not necessary for it to be sensible after the mingling.

Reply to Objection 2: If no water were added, the signification would be utterly excluded: but when the water is changed into wine, it is signified that the people is incorporated with Christ.

Reply to Objection 3: If water were added to a cask, it would not suffice for the signification of this sacrament, but the water must be added to the wine at the actual celebration of the sacrament.

OF THE CHANGE OF BREAD AND WINE INTO THE BODY AND BLOOD OF CHRIST (EIGHT ARTICLES)

We have to consider the change of the bread and wine into the body and blood of Christ; under which head there are eight points of inquiry:

(1) Whether the substance of bread and wine remain in this sacrament after the consecration?*
(2) Whether it is annihilated?
(3) Whether it is changed into the body and blood of Christ?
(4) Whether the accidents remain after the change?
(5) Whether the substantial form remains there?
(6) Whether this change is instantaneous?
(7) Whether it is more miraculous than any other change?
(8) By what words it may be suitably expressed?

[*The titles of the Articles here given were taken by St. Thomas from his Commentary on the Sentences (Sent. iv, D, 90). However, in writing the Articles he introduced a new point of inquiry, that of the First Article; and substituted another division of the matter under discussion, as may be seen by referring to the titles of the various Articles. Most editions have ignored St. Thomas's original division, and give the one to which he subsequently adhered.]

Whether the body of Christ be in this sacrament in very truth, or merely as in a figure or sign?

Objection 1: It seems that the body of Christ is not in this sacrament in very truth, but only as in a figure, or sign. For it is written (Jn. 6:54) that when our Lord had uttered these words: "Except you eat the flesh of the Son of Man, and drink His blood," etc., "Many of His disciples on hearing it said: 'this is a hard saying'": to whom He rejoined: "It is the spirit that quickeneth; the flesh profiteth nothing": as if He were to say, according to Augustine's exposition on Ps. 4 [*On Ps. 98:9]: "Give a spiritual meaning to what I have said. You are not to eat this body which you see, nor to drink the blood which they who crucify Me are to spill. It is a mystery that I put before you: in its spiritual sense it will quicken you; but the flesh profiteth nothing."

Objection 2: Further, our Lord said (Mat. 28:20): "Behold I am with you all days even to the consummation of the world." Now in explaining this, Augustine makes this observation (Tract. xxx in Joan.): "The Lord is on high until the world be ended; nevertheless the truth of the Lord is here with us; for the body, in which He rose again, must be in one place; but His truth is spread abroad everywhere." Therefore, the body of Christ is not in this sacrament in very truth, but only as in a sign.

Objection 3: Further, no body can be in several places at the one time. For this does not even belong to an angel; since for the same reason it could be everywhere. But Christ's is a true body, and it is in heaven. Consequently, it seems that it is not in very truth in the sacrament of the altar, but only as in a sign.

Objection 4: Further, the Church's sacraments are ordained for the profit of the faithful. But according to Gregory in a certain Homily (xxviii in Evang.), the ruler is rebuked "for demanding Christ's bodily presence." Moreover the apostles were prevented from receiving the Holy Ghost because they were attached to His bodily presence, as Augustine says on Jn. 16:7: "Except I go, the Paraclete will not come to you" (Tract. xciv in Joan.). Therefore Christ is not in the sacrament of the altar according to His bodily presence.

On the contrary, Hilary says (De Trin. viii): "There is no room for doubt regarding the truth of Christ's body and blood; for now by our Lord's own declaring and by our faith His flesh is truly food, and His blood is truly drink." And Ambrose says (De Sacram. vi): "As the Lord Jesus Christ is God's true Son so is it Christ's true flesh which we take, and His true blood which we drink."

I answer that, The presence of Christ's true body and blood in this sacrament cannot be detected by sense, nor understanding, but by faith alone, which rests upon Divine authority. Hence, on Lk. 22:19: "This is My body which shall be delivered up for you," Cyril says: "Doubt not whether this be true; but take rather the Saviour's words with faith; for since He is the Truth, He lieth not."

Now this is suitable, first for the perfection of the New Law. For, the sacrifices of the Old Law contained only in figure that true sacrifice of Christ's Passion, according to Heb. 10:1: "For the law having a shadow of the good things to come, not the very image of the things." And therefore it was necessary that the sacrifice of the New Law instituted by Christ should have something more, namely, that it should contain Christ Himself crucified, not merely in signification or figure, but also in very truth. And therefore this sacrament which contains Christ Himself, as Dionysius says (Eccl. Hier. iii), is perfective of all the other sacraments, in which Christ's virtue is participated.

Secondly, this belongs to Christ's love, out of which for our salvation He assumed a true body of our nature. And because it is the special feature of friendship to live together with friends, as the Philosopher says (Ethic. ix), He promises us His bodily presence as a reward, saying (Mat. 24:28): "Where the body is, there shall the eagles be gathered together." Yet meanwhile in our pilgrimage He does not deprive us of His bodily presence; but unites us with Himself in this sacrament through the truth of His body and blood. Hence (Jn. 6:57) he says: "He that eateth My flesh, and drinketh My blood, abideth in Me, and I in him." Hence this sacrament is the sign of supreme charity, and the uplifter of our hope, from such familiar union of Christ with us.

Thirdly, it belongs to the perfection of faith, which concerns His humanity just as it does His Godhead, according to Jn. 14:1: "You believe in God, believe also in Me." And since faith is of things unseen, as Christ shows us His Godhead invisibly, so also in this sacrament He shows us His flesh in an invisible manner.

Some men accordingly, not paying heed to these things, have contended that Christ's body and blood are not in this sacrament except as in a sign, a thing to be rejected as heretical, since it is contrary to Christ's words. Hence Berengarius, who had been the first deviser of this heresy, was afterwards forced to withdraw his error, and to acknowledge the truth of the faith.

Reply to Objection 1: From this authority the aforesaid heretics have taken occasion to err from evilly understanding Augustine's words. For when Augustine says: "You are not to eat this body which you see," he means not to exclude the truth of Christ's body, but that it was not to be eaten in this species in which it was seen by them. And by the words: "It is a mystery that I put before you; in its spiritual sense it will quicken you," he intends not that the body of Christ is in this sacrament merely according to mystical signification, but "spiritually," that is, invisibly, and by the power of the spirit. Hence (Tract. xxvii), expounding Jn. 6:64: "the flesh profiteth nothing," he says: "Yea, but as they understood it, for they understood that the flesh was to be eaten as it is divided piecemeal in a dead body, or as sold in the shambles, not as it is quickened by the spirit . . . Let the spirit draw nigh to the flesh . . . then the flesh profiteth very much: for if the flesh profiteth nothing, the Word had not been made flesh, that It might dwell among us."

Reply to Objection 2: That saying of Augustine and all others like it are to be understood of Christ's body as it is beheld in its proper species; according as our Lord Himself says (Mat. 26:11): "But Me you have not always." Nevertheless He is invisibly under the species of this sacrament, wherever this sacrament is performed.

Reply to Objection 3: Christ's body is not in this sacrament in the same way as a body is in a place, which by its dimensions is commensurate with the place; but in a special manner which is proper to this sacrament. Hence we say that Christ's body is upon many altars, not as in different places, but "sacramentally": and thereby we do not understand that Christ is there only as in a sign, although a sacrament is a kind of sign; but that Christ's body is here after a fashion proper to this sacrament, as stated above.

Reply to Objection 4: This argument holds good of Christ's bodily presence, as He is present after the manner of a body, that is, as it is in its visible appearance, but not as it is spiritually, that is, invisibly, after the manner and by the virtue of the spirit. Hence Augustine (Tract. xxvii in Joan.) says: "If thou hast understood" Christ's words spiritually concerning His flesh, "they are spirit and life to thee; if thou hast understood them carnally, they are also spirit and life, but not to thee."

Whether in this sacrament the substance of the bread and wine remains after the consecration?

Objection 1: It seems that the substance of the bread and wine does remain in this sacrament after the consecration: because Damascene says (De Fide Orth. iv): "Since it is customary for men to eat bread and drink wine, God has wedded his Godhead to them, and made them His body and blood": and further on: "The bread of communication is not simple bread, but is united to the Godhead." But wedding together belongs to things actually existing. Therefore the bread and wine are at the same time, in this sacrament, with the body and the blood of Christ.

Objection 2: Further, there ought to be conformity between the sacraments. But in the other sacraments the substance of the matter remains, like the substance of water in Baptism, and the substance of chrism in Confirmation. Therefore the substance of the bread and wine remains also in this sacrament.

Objection 3: Further, bread and wine are made use of in this sacrament, inasmuch as they denote ecclesiastical unity, as "one bread is made from many grains and wine from many grapes," as Augustine says in his book on the Creed (Tract. xxvi in Joan.). But this belongs to the substance of bread and wine. Therefore, the substance of the bread and wine remains in this sacrament.

On the contrary, Ambrose says (De Sacram. iv): "Although the figure of the bread and wine be seen, still, after the Consecration, they are to be believed to be nothing else than the body end blood of Christ."

I answer that, Some have held that the substance of the bread and wine remains in this sacrament after the consecration. But this opinion cannot stand: first of all, because by such an opinion the truth of this sacrament is destroyed, to which it belongs that Christ's true body exists in this sacrament; which indeed was not there before the consecration. Now a thing cannot be in any place, where it was not previously, except by change of place, or by the conversion of another thing into itself; just as fire begins anew to be in some house, either because it is carried thither, or because it is generated there. Now it is evident that Christ's body does not begin to be present in this sacrament by local motion. First of all, because it would follow that it would cease to be in heaven: for what is moved locally does not come anew to some place unless it quit the former one. Secondly, because every body moved locally passes through all intermediary spaces, which cannot be said here. Thirdly, because it is not possible for one movement of the same body moved locally to be terminated in different places at the one time, whereas the body of Christ under this sacrament begins at the one time to be in several places. And consequently it remains that Christ's body cannot begin to be anew in this sacrament except by change of the substance of bread into itself. But what is changed into another thing, no longer remains after such change. Hence the conclusion is that, saving the truth of this sacrament, the substance of the bread cannot remain after the consecration.

Secondly, because this position is contrary to the form of this sacrament, in which it is said: "This is My body," which would not be true if the substance of the bread were to remain there; for the substance of bread never is the body of Christ. Rather should one say in that case: "Here is My body."

Thirdly, because it would be opposed to the veneration of this sacrament, if any substance were there, which could not be adored with adoration of latria.

Fourthly, because it is contrary to the rite of the Church, according to which it is not lawful to take the body of Christ after bodily food, while it is nevertheless lawful to take one consecrated host after another. Hence this opinion is to be avoided as heretical.

Reply to Objection 1: God "wedded His Godhead," i.e. His Divine power, to the bread and wine, not that these may remain in this sacrament, but in order that He may make from them His body and blood.

Reply to Objection 2: Christ is not really present in the other sacraments, as in this; and therefore the substance of the matter remains in the other sacraments, but not in this.

Reply to Objection 3: The species which remain in this sacrament, as shall be said later [4530](A[5]), suffice for its signification; because the nature of the substance is known by its accidents.

Whether the substance of the bread or wine is annihilated after the consecration of this sacrament, or dissolved into their original matter?

Objection 1: It seems that the substance of the bread is annihilated after the consecration of this sacrament, or dissolved into its original matter. For whatever is corporeal must be somewhere. But the substance of bread, which is something corporeal, does not remain, in this sacrament, as stated above [4531](A[2]); nor can we assign any place where it may be. Consequently it is nothing after the consecration. Therefore, it is either annihilated, or dissolved into its original matter.

Objection 2: Further, what is the term "wherefrom" in every change exists no longer, except in the potentiality of matter; e.g. when air is changed into fire, the form of the air remains only in the potentiality of matter; and in like fashion when what is white becomes black. But in this sacrament the substance of the bread or of the wine is the term "wherefrom," while the body or the blood of Christ is the term "whereunto": for Ambrose says in De Officiis (De Myster. ix): "Before the blessing it is called another species, after the blessing the body of Christ is signified." Therefore, when the consecration takes place, the substance of the bread or wine no longer remains, unless perchance dissolved into its (original) matter.

Objection 3: Further, one of two contradictories must be true. But this proposition is false: "After the consecration the substance of the bread or wine is something." Consequently, this is true: "The substance of the bread or wine is nothing."

On the contrary, Augustine says ([4532]Q[83]): "God is not the cause of tending to nothing." But this sacrament is wrought by Divine power. Therefore, in this sacrament the substance of the bread or wine is not annihilated.

I answer that, Because the substance of the bread and wine does not remain in this sacrament, some, deeming that it is impossible for the substance of the bread and wine to be changed into Christ's flesh and blood, have maintained that by the consecration, the substance of the bread and wine is either dissolved into the original matter, or that it is annihilated.

Now the original matter into which mixed bodies can be dissolved is the four elements. For dissolution cannot be made into primary matter, so that a subject can exist without a form, since matter cannot exist without a form. But since after the consecration nothing remains under the sacramental species except the body and the blood of Christ, it will be necessary to say that the elements into which the substance of the bread and wine is dissolved, depart from thence by local motion, which would be perceived by the senses. In like manner also the substance of the bread or wine remains until the last instant of the consecration; but in the last instant of the consecration there is already present there the substance of the body or blood of Christ, just as the form is already present in the last instant of generation. Hence no instant can be assigned in which the original matter can be there. For it cannot be said that the substance of the bread or wine is dissolved gradually into the original matter, or that it successively quits the species, for if this began to be done in the last instant of its consecration, then at the one time under part of the host there would be the body of Christ together with the substance of bread, which is contrary to what has been said above [4533](A[2]). But if this begin to come to pass before the consecration, there will then be a time in which under one part of the host there will be neither the substance of bread nor the body of Christ, which is not fitting. They seem indeed to have taken this into careful consideration, wherefore they formulated their proposition with an alternative viz. that (the substance) may be annihilated. But even this cannot stand, because no way can be assigned whereby Christ's true body can begin to be in this sacrament, except by the change of the substance of bread into it, which change is excluded the moment we admit either annihilation of the substance of the bread, or dissolution into the original matter. Likewise no cause can be assigned for such dissolution or annihilation, since the effect of the sacrament is signified by the form: "This is My body." Hence it is clear that the aforesaid opinion is false.

Reply to Objection 1: The substance of the bread or wine, after the consecration, remains neither under the sacramental species, nor elsewhere; yet it does not follow that it is annihilated; for it is changed into the body of Christ; just as if the air, from which fire is generated, be not there or elsewhere, it does not follow that it is annihilated.

Reply to Objection 2: The form, which is the term "wherefrom," is not changed into another form; but one form succeeds another in the subject; and therefore the first form remains only in the potentiality of matter. But here the substance of the bread is changed into the body of Christ, as stated above. Hence the conclusion does not follow.

Reply to Objection 3: Although after the consecration this proposition is false: "The substance of the breed is something," still that into which the substance of the bread is changed, is something, and consequently the substance of the bread is not annihilated.

Whether bread can be converted into the body of Christ?

Objection 1: It seems that bread cannot be converted into the body of Christ. For conversion is a kind of change. But in every change there must be some subject, which from being previously in potentiality is now in act. because as is said in Phys. iii: "motion is the act of a thing existing in potentiality." But no subject can be assigned for the substance of the bread and of the body of Christ, because it is of the very nature of substance for it "not to be in a subject," as it is said in Praedic. iii. Therefore it is not possible for the whole substance of the bread to be converted into the body of Christ.

Objection 2: Further, the form of the thing into which another is converted, begins anew to inhere in the matter of the thing converted into it: as when air is changed into fire not already existing, the form of fire begins anew to be in the matter of the air; and in like manner when food is converted into non-pre-existing man, the form of the man begins to be anew in the matter of the food. Therefore, if bread be changed into the body of Christ, the form of Christ's body must necessarily begin to be in the matter of the bread, which is false. Consequently, the bread is not changed into the substance of Christ's body.

Objection 3: Further, when two things are diverse, one never becomes the other, as whiteness never becomes blackness, as is stated in Phys. i. But since two contrary forms are of themselves diverse, as being the principles of formal difference, so two signate matters are of themselves diverse, as being the principles of material distinction. Consequently, it is not possible for this matter of bread to become this matter whereby Christ's body is individuated, and so it is not possible for this substance of bread to be changed into the substance of Christ's body.

On the contrary, Eusebius Emesenus says: "To thee it ought neither to be a novelty nor an impossibility that earthly and mortal things be changed into the substance of Christ."

I answer that, As stated above [4534](A[2]), since Christ's true body is in this sacrament, and since it does not begin to be there by local motion, nor is it contained therein as in a place, as is evident from what was stated above (A[1], ad 2), it must be said then that it begins to be there by conversion of the substance of bread into itself.

Yet this change is not like natural changes, but is entirely supernatural, and effected by God's power alone. Hence Ambrose says [(De Sacram. iv): "See how Christ's word changes nature's laws, as He wills: a man is not wont to be born save of man and woman: see therefore that against the established law and order a man is born of a Virgin": and] [*The passage in the brackets is not in the Leonine edition] (De Myster. iv): "It is clear that a Virgin begot beyond the order of nature: and what we make is the body from the Virgin. Why, then, do you look for nature's order in Christ's body, since the Lord Jesus was Himself brought forth of a Virgin beyond nature?" Chrysostom likewise (Hom. xlvii), commenting on Jn. 6:64: "The words which I have spoken to you," namely, of this sacrament, "are spirit and life," says: i.e. "spiritual, having nothing carnal, nor natural consequence; but they are rent from all such necessity which exists upon earth, and from the laws here established."

For it is evident that every agent acts according as it is in act. But every created agent is limited in its act, as being of a determinate genus and species: and consequently the action of every created agent bears upon some determinate act. Now the determination of every thing in actual existence comes from its form. Consequently, no natural or created agent can act except by changing the form in something; and on this account every change made according to nature's laws is a formal change. But God is infinite act, as stated in the [4535]FP, Q[7], A[1]; Q[26], A[2]; hence His action extends to the whole nature of being. Therefore He can work not only formal conversion, so that diverse forms succeed each other in the same subject; but also the change of all being, so that, to wit, the whole substance of one thing be changed into the whole substance of another. And this is done by Divine power in this sacrament; for the whole substance of the bread is changed into the whole substance of Christ's body, and the whole substance of the wine into the whole substance of Christ's blood. Hence this is not a formal, but a substantial conversion; nor is it a kind of natural movement: but, with a name of its own, it can be called "transubstantiation."

Reply to Objection 1: This objection holds good in respect of formal change, because it belongs to a form to be in matter or in a subject; but it does not hold good in respect of the change of the entire substance. Hence, since this substantial change implies a certain order of substances, one of which is changed into the other, it is in both substances as in a subject, just as order and number.

Reply to Objection 2: This argument also is true of formal conversion or change, because, as stated above (ad 1), a form must be in some matter or subject. But this is not so in a change of the entire substance; for in this case no subject is possible.

Reply to Objection 3: Form cannot be changed into form, nor matter into matter by the power of any finite agent. Such a change, however, can be made by the power of an infinite agent, which has control over all being, because the nature of being is common to both forms and to both matters; and whatever there is of being in the one, the author of being can change into whatever there is of being in the other, withdrawing that whereby it was distinguished from the other.

Day 303

Whether the accidents of the bread and wine remain in this sacrament after the change?

Objection 1: It seems that the accidents of the bread and wine do not remain in this sacrament. For when that which comes first is removed, that which follows is also taken away. But substance is naturally before accident, as is proved in Metaph. vii. Since, then, after consecration, the substance of the bread does not remain in this sacrament, it seems that its accidents cannot remain.

Objection 2: Further, there ought not to be any deception in a sacrament of truth. But we judge of substance by accidents. It seems, then, that human judgment is deceived, if, while the accidents remain, the substance of the bread does not. Consequently this is unbecoming to this sacrament.

Objection 3: Further, although our faith is not subject to reason, still it is not contrary to reason, but above it, as was said in the beginning of this work ([4536]FP, Q[1], A[6], ad 2; A[8]). But our reason has its origin in the senses. Therefore our faith ought not to be contrary to the senses, as it is when sense judges that to be bread which faith believes to be the substance of Christ's body. Therefore it is not befitting this sacrament for the accidents of bread to remain subject to the senses, and for the substance of bread not to remain.

Objection 4: Further, what remains after the change has taken place seems to be the subject of change. If therefore the accidents of the bread remain after the change has been effected, it seems that the accidents are the subject of the change. But this is impossible; for "an accident cannot have an accident" (Metaph. iii). Therefore the accidents of the bread and wine ought not to remain in this sacrament.

On the contrary, Augustine says in his book on the Sentences of Prosper (Lanfranc, De Corp. et Sang. Dom. xiii): "Under the species which we behold, of bread and wine, we honor invisible things, i.e. flesh and blood."

I answer that, It is evident to sense that all the accidents of the bread and wine remain after the consecration. And this is reasonably done by Divine providence. First of all, because it is not customary, but horrible, for men to eat human flesh, and to drink blood. And therefore Christ's flesh and blood are set before us to be partaken of under the species of those things which are the more commonly used by men, namely, bread and wine. Secondly, lest this sacrament might be derided by unbelievers, if we were to eat our Lord under His own species. Thirdly, that while we receive our Lord's body and blood invisibly, this may redound to the merit of faith.

Reply to Objection 1: As is said in the book De Causis, an effect depends more on the first cause than on the second. And therefore by God's power, which is the first cause of all things, it is possible for that which follows to remain, while that which is first is taken away.

Reply to Objection 2: There is no deception in this sacrament; for the accidents which are discerned by the senses are truly present. But the intellect, whose proper object is substance as is said in De Anima iii, is preserved by faith from deception.

And this serves as answer to the third argument; because faith is not contrary to the senses, but concerns things to which sense does not reach.

Reply to Objection 4: This change has not properly a subject, as was stated above (A[4], ad 1); nevertheless the accidents which remain have some resemblance of a subject.

Whether the substantial form of the bread remains in this sacrament after the consecration?

Objection 1: It seems that the substantial form of the bread remains in this sacrament after the consecration. For it has been said [4537](A[5]) that the accidents remain after the consecration. But since bread is an artificial thing, its form is an accident. Therefore it remains after the consecration.

Objection 2: Further, the form of Christ's body is His soul: for it is said in De Anima ii, that the soul "is the act of a physical body which has life in potentiality". But it cannot be said that the substantial form of the bread is changed into the soul. Therefore it appears that it remains after the consecration.

Objection 3: Further, the proper operation of a things follows its substantial form. But what remains in this sacrament, nourishes, and performs every operation which bread would do were it present. Therefore the substantial form of the bread remains in this sacrament after the consecration.

On the contrary, The substantial form of bread is of the substance of bread. But the substance of the bread is changed into the body of Christ, as stated above ([4538]AA[2],3,4). Therefore the substantial form of the bread does not remain.

I answer that, Some have contended that after the consecration not only do the accidents of the bread remain, but also its substantial form. But this cannot be. First of all, because if the substantial form of the bread were to remain, nothing of the bread would be changed into the body of Christ, excepting the matter; and so it would follow that it would be changed, not into the whole body of Christ, but into its matter, which is repugnant to the form of the sacrament, wherein it is said: "This is My body."

Secondly, because if the substantial form of the bread were to remain, it would remain either in matter, or separated from matter. The first cannot be, for if it were to remain in the matter of the bread, then the whole substance of the bread would remain, which is against what was said above [4539](A[2]). Nor could it remain in any other matter, because the proper form exists only in its proper matter. But if it were to remain separate from matter, it would then be an actually intelligible form, and also an intelligence; for all forms separated from matter are such.

Thirdly, it would be unbefitting this sacrament: because the accidents of the bread remain in this sacrament, in order that the body of Christ may be seen under them, and not under its proper species, as stated above [4540](A[5]).

And therefore it must be said that the substantial form of the bread does not remain.

Reply to Objection 1: There is nothing to prevent art from making a thing whose form is not an accident, but a substantial form; as frogs and serpents can be produced by art: for art produces such forms not by its own power, but by the power of natural energies. And in this way it produces the substantial forms of bread, by the power of fire baking the matter made up of flour and water.

Reply to Objection 2: The soul is the form of the body, giving it the whole order of perfect being, i.e. being, corporeal being, and animated being, and so on. Therefore the form of the bread is changed into the form of Christ's body, according as the latter gives corporeal being, but not according as it bestows animated being.

Reply to Objection 3: Some of the operations of bread follow it by reason of the accidents, such as to affect the senses, and such operations are found in the species of the bread after the consecration on account of the accidents which remain. But some other operations follow the bread either by reason of the matter, such as that it is changed into something else, or else by reason of the substantial form, such as an operation consequent upon its species, for instance, that it "strengthens man's heart" (Ps. 103:15); and such operations are found in this sacrament, not on account of the form or matter remaining, but because they are bestowed miraculously upon the accidents themselves, as will be said later (Q[77], A[3], ad 2,3; [4541]AA[5],6).

Whether this change is wrought instantaneously?

Objection 1: It seems that this change is not wrought instantaneously, but successively. For in this change there is first the substance of bread, and afterwards the substance of Christ's body. Neither, then, is in the same instant, but in two instants. But there is a mid-time between every two instants. Therefore this change must take place according to the succession of time, which is between the last instant in which the bread is there, and the first instant in which the body of Christ is present.

Objection 2: Further, in every change something is "in becoming" and something is "in being." But these two things do not exist at the one time for, what is "in becoming," is not yet, whereas what is "in being," already is. Consequently, there is a before and an after in such change: and so necessarily the change cannot be instantaneous, but successive.

Objection 3: Further, Ambrose says (De Sacram. iv) that this sacrament "is made by the words of Christ." But Christ's words are pronounced successively. Therefore the change takes place successively.

On the contrary, This change is effected by a power which is infinite, to which it belongs to operate in an instant.

I answer that, A change may be instantaneous from a threefold reason. First on the part of the form, which is the terminus of the change. For, if it be a form that receives more and less, it is acquired by its subject successively, such as health; and therefore because a substantial form does not receive more and less, it follows that its introduction into matter is instantaneous.

Secondly on the part of the subject, which sometimes is prepared successively for receiving the form; thus water is heated successively. When, however, the subject itself is in the ultimate disposition for receiving the form, it receives it suddenly, as a transparent body is illuminated suddenly. Thirdly on the part of the agent, which possesses infinite power: wherefore it can instantly dispose the matter for the form. Thus it is written (Mk. 7:34) that when Christ had said, "'Ephpheta,' which is 'Be thou opened,' immediately his ears were opened, and the string of his tongue was loosed."

For these three reasons this conversion is instantaneous. First, because the substance of Christ's body which is the term of this conversion, does not receive more or less. Secondly, because in this conversion there is no subject to be disposed successively. Thirdly, because it is effected by God's infinite power.

Reply to Objection 1: Some [*Cf. Albert the Great, Sent. iv, D, 11; St. Bonaventure, Sent., iv, D, 11] do not grant simply that there is a mid-time between every two instants. For they say that this is true of two instants referring to the same movement, but not if they refer to different things. Hence between the instant that marks the close of rest, and another which marks the beginning of movement, there is no mid-time. But in this they are mistaken, because the unity of time and of instant, or even their plurality, is not taken according to movements of any sort, but according to the first movement of the heavens, which is the measure of all movement and rest.

Accordingly others grant this of the time which measures movement depending on the movement of the heavens. But there are some movements which are not dependent on the movement of the heavens, nor measured by it, as was said in the [4542]FP, Q[53], A[3] concerning the movements of the angels. Hence between two instants responding to those movements there is no mid-time. But this is not to the point, because although the change in question has no relation of itself to the movement of the heavens, still it follows the pronouncing of the words, which (pronouncing) must necessarily be measured by the movement of the heavens. And therefore there must of necessity be a mid-time between every two signate instants in connection with that change.

Some say therefore that the instant in which the bread was last, and the instant in which the body of Christ is first, are indeed two in comparison with the things measured, but are one comparatively to the time measuring; as when two lines touch, there are two points on the part of the two lines, but one point on the part of the place containing them. But here there is no likeness, because instant and time is not the intrinsic measure of particular movements, as a line and point are of a body, but only the extrinsic measure, as place is to bodies.

Hence others say that it is the same instant in fact, but another according to reason. But according to this it would follow that things really opposite would exist together; for diversity of reason does not change a thing objectively.

And therefore it must be said that this change, as stated above, is wrought by Christ's words which are spoken by the priest, so that the last instant of pronouncing the words is the first instant in which Christ's body is in the sacrament; and that the substance of the bread is there during the whole preceding time. Of this time no instant is to be taken as proximately preceding the last one, because time is not made up of successive instants, as is proved in Phys. vi. And therefore a first instant can be assigned in which Christ's body is present; but a last instant cannot be assigned in which the substance of bread is there, but a last time can be assigned. And the same holds good in natural changes, as is evident from the Philosopher (Phys. viii).

Reply to Objection 2: In instantaneous changes a thing is "in becoming," and is "in being" simultaneously; just as becoming illuminated and to be actually illuminated are simultaneous: for in such, a thing is said to be "in being" according as it now is; but to be "in becoming," according as it was not before.

Reply to Objection 3: As stated above (ad 1), this change comes about in the last instant of the pronouncing of the words, for then the meaning of the words is finished, which meaning is efficacious in the forms of the sacraments. And therefore it does not follow that this change is successive.

Whether this proposition is false: "The body of Christ is made out of bread"?

Objection 1: It seems that this proposition is false: "The body of Christ is made out of bread." For everything out of which another is made, is that which is made the other; but not conversely: for we say that a black thing is made out of a white thing, and that a white thing is made black: and although we may say that a man becomes black still we do not say that a black thing is made out of a man, as is shown in Phys. i. If it be true, then, that Christ's body is made out of bread, it will be true to say that bread is made the body of Christ. But this seems to be false, because the bread is not the subject of the making, but rather its term. Therefore, it is not said truly that Christ's body is made out of bread.

Objection 2: Further, the term of "becoming" is something that is, or something that is "made." But this proposition is never true: "The bread is the body of Christ"; or "The bread is made the body of Christ"; or again, "The bread will be the body of Christ." Therefore it seems that not even this is true: "The body of Christ is made out of bread."

Objection 3: Further, everything out of which another is made is converted into that which is made from it. But this proposition seems to be false: "The bread is converted into the body of Christ," because such conversion seems to be more miraculous than the creation of the world, in which it is not said that non-being is converted into being. Therefore it seems that this proposition likewise is false: "The body of Christ is made out of bread."

Objection 4: Further, that out of which something is made, can be that thing. But this proposition is false: "Bread can be the body of Christ." Therefore this is likewise false: "The body of Christ is made out of bread."

On the contrary, Ambrose says (De Sacram. iv): "When the consecration takes place, the body of Christ is made out of the bread."

I answer that, This conversion of bread into the body of Christ has something in common with creation, and with natural transmutation, and in some respect differs from both. For the order of the terms is common to these three; that is, that after one thing there is another (for, in creation there is being after non-being; in this sacrament, Christ's body after the substance of bread; in natural transmutation white after black, or fire after air); and that the aforesaid terms are not coexistent.

Now the conversion, of which we are speaking, has this in common with creation, that in neither of them is there any common subject belonging to either of the extremes; the contrary of which appears in every natural transmutation.

Again, this conversion has something in common with natural transmutation in two respects, although not in the same fashion. First of all because in both, one of the extremes passes into the other, as bread into Christ's body, and air into fire; whereas non-being is not converted into being. But this comes to pass differently on the one side and on the other; for in this sacrament the whole substance of the bread passes into the whole body of Christ; whereas in natural transmutation the matter of the one receives the form of the other, the previous form being laid aside. Secondly, they have this in common, that on both sides something remains the same; whereas this does not happen in creation: yet differently; for the same matter or subject remains in natural transmutation; whereas in this sacrament the same accidents remain.

From these observations we can gather the various ways of speaking in such matters. For, because in no one of the aforesaid three things are the extremes coexistent, therefore in none of them can one extreme be predicated of the other by the substantive verb of the present tense: for we do not say, "Non-being is being" or, "Bread is the body of Christ," or, "Air is fire," or, "White is black." Yet because of the relationship of the extremes in all of them we can use the preposition "ex" [out of], which denotes order; for we can truly and properly say that "being is made out of non-being," and "out of bread, the body of Christ," and "out of air, fire," and "out of white, black." But because in creation one of the extremes does not pass into the other, we cannot use the word "conversion" in creation, so as to say that "non-being is converted into being": we can, however, use the word in this sacrament, just as in natural transmutation. But since in this sacrament the whole substance is converted into the whole substance, on that account this conversion is properly termed transubstantiation.

Again, since there is no subject of this conversion, the things which are true in natural conversion by reason of the subject, are not to be granted in this conversion. And in the first place indeed it is evident that potentiality to the opposite follows a subject, by reason whereof we say that "a white thing can be black," or that "air can be fire"; although the latter is not so proper as the former: for the subject of whiteness, in which there is potentiality to blackness, is the whole substance of the white thing; since whiteness is not a part thereof; whereas the subject of the form of air is part thereof: hence when it is said, "Air can be fire," it is verified by synecdoche by reason of the part. But in this conversion, and similarly in creation, because there is no subject, it is not said that one extreme can be the other, as that "non-being can be being," or that "bread can be the body of Christ": and for the same reason it cannot be properly said that "being is made of [de] non-being," or that "the body of Christ is made of bread," because this preposition "of" [de] denotes a consubstantial cause, which consubstantiality of the extremes in natural transmutations is considered according to something common in the subject. And for the same reason it is not granted that "bread will be the body of Christ," or that it "may become the body of Christ," just as it is not granted in creation that "non-being will be being," or that "non-being may become being," because this manner of speaking is verified in natural transmutations by reason of the subject: for instance, when we say that "a white thing becomes black," or "a white thing will be black."

Nevertheless, since in this sacrament, after the change, something remains the same, namely, the accidents of the bread, as stated above [4543](A[5]), some of these expressions may be admitted by way of similitude, namely, that "bread is the body of Christ," or, "bread will be the body of Christ," or "the body of Christ is made of bread"; provided that by the word "bread" is not understood the substance of bread, but in general "that which is contained under the species of bread," under which species there is first contained the substance of bread, and afterwards the body of Christ.

Reply to Objection 1: That out of which something else is made, sometimes implies together with the subject, one of the extremes of the transmutation, as when it is said "a black thing is made out of a white one"; but sometimes it implies only the opposite or the extreme, as when it is said---"out of morning comes the day." And so it is not granted that the latter becomes the former, that is, "that morning becomes the day." So likewise in the matter in hand, although it may be said properly that "the body of Christ is made out of bread," yet it is not said properly that "bread becomes the body of Christ," except by similitude, as was said above.

Reply to Objection 2: That out of which another is made, will sometimes be that other because of the subject which is implied. And therefore, since there is no subject of this change, the comparison does not hold.

Reply to Objection 3: In this change there are many more difficulties than in creation, in which there is but this one difficulty, that something is made out of nothing; yet this belongs to the proper mode of production of the first cause, which presupposes nothing else. But in this conversion not only is it difficult for this whole to be changed into that whole, so that nothing of the former may remain (which does not belong to the common mode of production of a cause), but furthermore it has this difficulty that the accidents remain while the substance is destroyed, and many other difficulties of which we shall treat hereafter ([4544]Q[77]). Nevertheless the word "conversion" is admitted in this sacrament, but not in creation, as stated above.

Reply to Objection 4: As was observed above, potentiality belongs to the subject, whereas there is no subject in this conversion. And therefore it is not granted that bread can be the body of Christ: for this conversion does not come about by the passive potentiality of the creature, but solely by the active power of the Creator.

OF THE WAY IN WHICH CHRIST IS IN THIS SACRAMENT (EIGHT ARTICLES)
We have now to consider the manner in which Christ exists in this sacrament; and under this head there are eight points of inquiry:
(1) Whether the whole Christ is under this sacrament?
(2) Whether the entire Christ is under each species of the sacrament?
(3) Whether the entire Christ is under every part of the species?
(4) Whether all the dimensions of Christ's body are in this sacrament?
(5) Whether the body of Christ is in this sacrament locally?
(6) Whether after the consecration, the body of Christ is moved when the host or chalice is moved?
(7) Whether Christ's body, as it is in this sacrament, can be seen by the eye?
(8) Whether the true body of Christ remains in this sacrament when He is seen under the appearance of a child or of flesh?

Whether the whole Christ is contained under this sacrament?
Objection 1: It seems that the whole Christ is not contained under this sacrament, because Christ begins to be in this sacrament by conversion of the bread and wine. But it is evident that the bread and wine cannot be changed either into the Godhead or into the soul of Christ. Since therefore Christ exists in three substances, namely, the Godhead, soul and body, as shown above ([4545]Q[2], A[5]; [4546] Q[5], AA[1],3), it seems that the entire Christ is not under this sacrament.

Objection 2: Further, Christ is in this sacrament, forasmuch as it is ordained to the refection of the faithful, which consists in food and drink, as stated above ([4547]Q[74], A[1]). But our Lord said (Jn. 6:56): "My flesh is meat indeed, and My blood is drink indeed." Therefore, only the flesh and blood of Christ are contained in this sacrament. But there are many other parts of Christ's body, for instance, the nerves, bones, and such like. Therefore the entire Christ is not contained under this sacrament.

Objection 3: Further, a body of greater quantity cannot be contained under the measure of a lesser. But the measure of the bread and wine is much smaller than the measure of Christ's body. Therefore it is impossible that the entire Christ be contained under this sacrament.

On the contrary, Ambrose says (De Officiis): "Christ is in this sacrament."

I answer that, It is absolutely necessary to confess according to Catholic faith that the entire Christ is in this sacrament. Yet we must know that there is something of Christ in this sacrament in a twofold manner: first, as it were, by the power of the sacrament; secondly, from natural concomitance. By the power of the sacrament, there is under the species of this sacrament that into which the pre-existing substance of the bread and wine is changed, as expressed by the words of the form, which are effective in this as in the other sacraments; for instance, by the words: "This is My body," or, "This is My blood." But from natural concomitance there is also in this sacrament that which is really united with that thing wherein the aforesaid conversion is terminated. For if any two things be really united, then wherever the one is really, there must the other also be: since things really united together are only distinguished by an operation of the mind.

Reply to Objection 1: Because the change of the bread and wine is not terminated at the Godhead or the soul of Christ, it follows as a consequence that the Godhead or the soul of Christ is in this sacrament not by the power of the sacrament, but from real concomitance. For since the Godhead never set aside the assumed body, wherever the body of Christ is, there, of necessity, must the Godhead be; and therefore it is necessary for the Godhead to be in this sacrament concomitantly with His body. Hence we read in the profession of faith at Ephesus (P. I., chap. xxvi): "We are made partakers of the body and blood of Christ, not as taking common flesh, nor as of a holy man united to the Word in dignity, but the truly life-giving flesh of the Word Himself."

On the other hand, His soul was truly separated from His body, as stated above ([4548]Q[50], A[5]). And therefore had this sacrament been celebrated during those three days when He was dead, the soul of Christ would not have been there, neither by the power of the sacrament, nor from real concomitance. But since "Christ rising from the dead dieth now no more" (Rom. 6:9), His soul is always really united with His body. And therefore in this sacrament the body indeed of Christ is present by the power of the sacrament, but His soul from real concomitance.

Reply to Objection 2: By the power of the sacrament there is contained under it, as to the species of the bread, not only the flesh, but the entire body of Christ, that is, the bones the nerves, and the like. And this is apparent from the form of this sacrament, wherein it is not said: "This is My flesh," but "This is My body." Accordingly, when our Lord said (Jn. 6:56): "My flesh is meat indeed," there the word flesh is put for the entire body, because according to human custom it seems to be more adapted for eating, as men commonly are fed on the flesh of animals, but not on the bones or the like.

Reply to Objection 3: As has been already stated ([4549]Q[75], A[5]), after the consecration of the bread into the body of Christ, or of the wine into His blood, the accidents of both remain. From which it is evident that the dimensions of the bread or wine are not changed into the dimensions of the body of Christ, but substance into substance. And so the substance of Christ's body or blood is under this sacrament by the power of the sacrament, but not the dimensions of Christ's body or blood. Hence it is clear that the body of Christ is in this sacrament "by way of substance," and not by way of quantity. But the proper totality of substance is contained indifferently in a small or large quantity; as the whole nature of air in a great or small amount of air, and the whole nature of a man in a big or small individual. Wherefore, after the consecration, the whole substance of Christ's body and blood is contained in this sacrament, just as the whole substance of the bread and wine was contained there before the consecration.

Whether the whole Christ is contained under each species of this sacrament?

Objection 1: It seems that the whole Christ is not contained under both species of this sacrament. For this sacrament is ordained for the salvation of the faithful, not by virtue of the species, but by virtue of what is contained under the species, because the species were there even before the consecration, from which comes the power of this sacrament. If nothing, then, be contained under one species, but what is contained under the other, and if the whole Christ be contained under both, it seems that one of them is superfluous in this sacrament.

Objection 2: Further, it was stated above (A[1], ad 1) that all the other parts of the body, such as the bones, nerves, and the like, are comprised under the name of flesh. But the blood is one of the parts of the human body, as Aristotle proves (De Anima Histor. i). If, then, Christ's blood be contained under the species of bread, just as the other parts of the body are contained there, the blood ought not to be consecrated apart, just as no other part of the body is consecrated separately.

Objection 3: Further, what is once "in being" cannot be again "in becoming." But Christ's body has already begun to be in this sacrament by the consecration of the bread. Therefore, it cannot begin again to be there by the consecration of the wine; and so Christ's body will not be contained under the species of the wine, and accordingly neither the entire Christ. Therefore the whole Christ is not contained under each species.

On the contrary, The gloss on 1 Cor. 11:25, commenting on the word "Chalice," says that "under each species," namely, of the bread and wine, "the same is received"; and thus it seems that Christ is entire under each species.

I answer that, After what we have said above [4550](A[1]), it must be held most certainly that the whole Christ is under each sacramental species yet not alike in each. For the body of Christ is indeed present under the species of bread by the power of the sacrament, while the blood is there from real concomitance, as stated above (A[1], ad 1) in regard to the soul and Godhead of Christ; and under the species of wine the blood is present by the power of the sacrament, and His body by real concomitance, as is also His soul and Godhead: because now Christ's blood is not separated from His body, as it was at the time of His Passion and death. Hence if this sacrament had been celebrated then, the body of Christ would have been under the species of the bread, but without the blood; and, under the species of the wine, the blood would have been present without the body, as it was then, in fact.

Reply to Objection 1: Although the whole Christ is under each species, yet it is so not without purpose. For in the first place this serves to represent Christ's Passion, in which the blood was separated from the body; hence in the form for the consecration of the blood mention is made of its shedding. Secondly, it is in keeping with the use of this sacrament, that Christ's body be shown apart to the faithful as food, and the blood as drink. Thirdly, it is in keeping with its effect, in which sense it was stated above ([4551]Q[74], A[1]) that "the body is offered for the salvation of the body, and the blood for the salvation of the soul."

Reply to Objection 2: In Christ's Passion, of which this is the memorial, the other parts of the body were not separated from one another, as the blood was, but the body remained entire, according to Ex. 12:46: "You shall not break a bone thereof." And therefore in this sacrament the blood is consecrated apart from the body, but no other part is consecrated separately from the rest.

Reply to Objection 3: As stated above, the body of Christ is not under the species of wine by the power of the sacrament, but by real concomitance: and therefore by the consecration of the wine the body of Christ is not there of itself, but concomitantly.

Whether Christ is entire under every part of the species of the bread and wine?

Objection 1: It seems that Christ is not entire under every part of the species of bread and wine. Because those species can be divided infinitely. If therefore Christ be entirely under every part of the said species, it would follow that He is in this sacrament an infinite number of times: which is unreasonable; because the infinite is repugnant not only to nature, but likewise to grace.

Objection 2: Further, since Christ's is an organic body, it has parts determinately distant. for a determinate distance of the individual parts from each other is of the very nature of an organic body, as that of eye from eye, and eye from ear. But this could not be so, if Christ were entire under every part of the species; for every part would have to be under every other part, and so where one part would be, there another part would be. It cannot be then that the entire Christ is under every part of the host or of the wine contained in the chalice.

Objection 3: Further, Christ's body always retains the true nature of a body, nor is it ever changed into a spirit. Now it is the nature of a body for it to be "quantity having position" (Predic. iv). But it belongs to the nature of this quantity that the various parts exist in various parts of place. Therefore, apparently it is impossible for the entire Christ to be under every part of the species.

On the contrary, Augustine says in a sermon (Gregory, Sacramentarium): "Each receives Christ the Lord, Who is entire under every morsel, nor is He less in each portion, but bestows Himself entire under each."

I answer that, As was observed above (A[1], ad 3), because the substance of Christ's body is in this sacrament by the power of the sacrament, while dimensive quantity is there by reason of real concomitance, consequently Christ's body is in this sacrament substantively, that is, in the way in which substance is under dimensions, but not after the manner of dimensions, which means, not in the way in which the dimensive quantity of a body is under the dimensive quantity of place.

Now it is evident that the whole nature of a substance is under every part of the dimensions under which it is contained; just as the entire nature of air is under every part of air, and the entire nature of bread under every part of bread; and this indifferently, whether the dimensions be actually divided (as when the air is divided or the bread cut), or whether they be actually undivided, but potentially divisible. And therefore it is manifest that the entire Christ is under every part of the species of the bread, even while the host remains entire, and not merely when it is broken, as some say, giving the example of an image which appears in a mirror, which appears as one in the unbroken mirror, whereas when the mirror is broken, there is an image in each part of the broken mirror: for the comparison is not perfect, because the multiplying of such images results in the broken mirror on account of the various reflections in the various parts of the mirror; but here there is only one consecration, whereby Christ's body is in this sacrament.

Reply to Objection 1: Number follows division, and therefore so long as quantity remains actually undivided, neither is the substance of any thing several times under its proper dimensions, nor is Christ's body several times under the dimensions of the bread; and consequently not an infinite number of times, but just as many times as it is divided into parts.

Reply to Objection 2: The determinate distance of parts in an organic body is based upon its dimensive quantity; but the nature of substance precedes even dimensive quantity. And since the conversion of the substance of the bread is terminated at the substance of the body of Christ, and since according to the manner of substance the body of Christ is properly and directly in this sacrament; such distance of parts is indeed in Christ's true body, which, however, is not compared to this sacrament according to such distance, but according to the manner of its substance, as stated above (A[1], ad 3).

Reply to Objection 3: This argument is based on the nature of a body, arising from dimensive quantity. But it was said above (ad 2) that Christ's body is compared with this sacrament not by reason of dimensive quantity, but by reason of its substance, as already stated.

Whether the whole dimensive quantity of Christ's body is in this sacrament?

Objection 1: It seems that the whole dimensive quantity of Christ's body is not in this sacrament. For it was said [4552](A[3]) that Christ's entire body is contained under every part of the consecrated host. But no dimensive quantity is contained entirely in any whole, and in its every part. Therefore it is impossible for the entire dimensive quantity of Christ's body to be there.

Objection 2: Further, it is impossible for two dimensive quantities to be together, even though one be separate from its subject, and the other in a natural body, as is clear from the Philosopher (Metaph. iii). But the dimensive quantity of the bread remains in this sacrament, as is evident to our senses. Consequently, the dimensive quantity of Christ's body is not there.

Objection 3: Further, if two unequal dimensive quantities be set side by side, the greater will overlap the lesser. But the dimensive quantity of Christ's body is considerably larger than the dimensive quantity of the consecrated host according to every dimension. Therefore, if the dimensive quantity of Christ's body be in this sacrament together with the dimensive quantity of the host, the dimensive quantity of Christ's body is extended beyond the quantity of the host, which nevertheless is not without the substance of Christ's body. Therefore, the substance of Christ's body will be in this sacrament even outside the species of the bread, which is unreasonable, since the substance of Christ's body is in this sacrament, only by the consecration of the bread, as stated above [4553] (A[2]). Consequently, it is impossible for the whole dimensive quantity of Christ's body to be in this sacrament.

On the contrary, The existence of the dimensive quantity of any body cannot be separated from the existence of its substance. But in this sacrament the entire substance of Christ's body is present, as stated above ([4554]AA[1],3). Therefore the entire dimensive quantity of Christ's body is in this sacrament.

I answer that, As stated above [4555](A[1]), any part of Christ is in this sacrament in two ways: in one way, by the power of the sacrament; in another, from real concomitance. By the power of the sacrament the dimensive quantity of Christ's body is not in this sacrament; for, by the power of the sacrament that is present in this sacrament, whereat the conversion is terminated. But the conversion which takes place in this sacrament is terminated directly at the substance of Christ's body, and not at its dimensions; which is evident from the fact that the dimensive quantity of the bread remains after the consecration, while only the substance of the bread passes away.

Nevertheless, since the substance of Christ's body is not really deprived of its dimensive quantity and its other accidents, hence it comes that by reason of real concomitance the whole dimensive quantity of Christ's body and all its other accidents are in this sacrament.

Reply to Objection 1: The manner of being of every thing is determined by what belongs to it of itself, and not according to what is coupled accidentally with it: thus an object is present to the sight, according as it is white, and not according as it is sweet, although the same object may be both white and sweet; hence sweetness is in the sight after the manner of whiteness, and not after that of sweetness. Since, then, the substance of Christ's body is present on the altar by the power of this sacrament, while its dimensive quantity is there concomitantly and as it were accidentally, therefore the dimensive quantity of Christ's body is in this sacrament, not according to its proper manner (namely, that the whole is in the whole, and the individual parts in individual parts), but after the manner of substance, whose nature is for the whole to be in the whole, and the whole in every part.

Reply to Objection 2: Two dimensive quantities cannot naturally be in the same subject at the same time, so that each be there according to the proper manner of dimensive quantity. But in this sacrament the dimensive quantity of the bread is there after its proper manner, that is, according to commensuration: not so the dimensive quantity of Christ's body, for that is there after the manner of substance, as stated above (ad 1).

Reply to Objection 3: The dimensive quantity of Christ's body is in this sacrament not by way of commensuration, which is proper to quantity, and to which it belongs for the greater to be extended beyond the lesser; but in the way mentioned above (ad 1,2).

Day 304

Whether Christ's body is in this sacrament as in a place?

Objection 1: It seems that Christ's body is in this sacrament as in a place. Because, to be in a place definitively or circumscriptively belongs to being in a place. But Christ's body seems to be definitively in this sacrament, because it is so present where the species of the bread and wine are, that it is nowhere else upon the altar: likewise it seems to be there circumscriptively, because it is so contained under the species of the consecrated host, that it neither exceeds it nor is exceeded by it. Therefore Christ's body is in this sacrament as in a place.

Objection 2: Further, the place of the bread and wine is not empty, because nature abhors a vacuum; nor is the substance of the bread there, as stated above ([4556]Q[75], A[2]); but only the body of Christ is there. Consequently the body of Christ fills that place. But whatever fills a place is there locally. Therefore the body of Christ is in this sacrament locally.

Objection 3: Further, as stated above [4557](A[4]), the body of Christ is in this sacrament with its dimensive quantity, and with all its accidents. But to be in a place is an accident of a body; hence "where" is numbered among the nine kinds of accidents. Therefore Christ's body is in this sacrament locally.

On the contrary, The place and the object placed must be equal, as is clear from the Philosopher (Phys. iv). But the place, where this sacrament is, is much less than the body of Christ. Therefore Christ's body is not in this sacrament as in a place.

I answer that, As stated above (A[1], ad 3; A[3]), Christ's body is in this sacrament not after the proper manner of dimensive quantity, but rather after the manner of substance. But every body occupying a place is in the place according to the manner of dimensive quantity, namely, inasmuch as it is commensurate with the place according to its dimensive quantity. Hence it remains that Christ's body is not in this sacrament as in a place, but after the manner of substance, that is to say, in that way in which substance is contained by dimensions; because the substance of Christ's body succeeds the substance of bread in this sacrament: hence as the substance of bread was not locally under its dimensions, but after the manner of substance, so neither is the substance of Christ's body. Nevertheless the substance of Christ's body is not the subject of those dimensions, as was the substance of the bread: and therefore the substance of the bread was there locally by reason of its dimensions, because it was compared with that place through the medium of its own dimensions; but the substance of Christ's body is compared with that place through the medium of foreign dimensions, so that, on the contrary, the proper dimensions of Christ's body are compared with that place through the medium of substance; which is contrary to the notion of a located body.

Hence in no way is Christ's body locally in this sacrament.

Reply to Objection 1: Christ's body is not in this sacrament definitively, because then it would be only on the particular altar where this sacrament is performed: whereas it is in heaven under its own species, and on many other altars under the sacramental species. Likewise it is evident that it is not in this sacrament circumscriptively, because it is not there according to the commensuration of its own quantity, as stated above. But that it is not outside the superficies of the sacrament, nor on any other part of the altar, is due not to its being there definitively or circumscriptively, but to its being there by consecration and conversion of the bread and wine, as stated above [4558](A[1]; Q[15], A[2], sqq.).

Reply to Objection 2: The place in which Christ's body is, is not empty; nor yet is it properly filled with the substance of Christ's body, which is not there locally, as stated above; but it is filled with the sacramental species, which have to fill the place either because of the nature of dimensions, or at least miraculously, as they also subsist miraculously after the fashion of substance.

Reply to Objection 3: As stated above [4559](A[4]), the accidents of Christ's body are in this sacrament by real concomitance. And therefore those accidents of Christ's body which are intrinsic to it are in this sacrament. But to be in a place is an accident when compared with the extrinsic container. And therefore it is not necessary for Christ to be in this sacrament as in a place.

Whether Christ's body is in this sacrament movably?

Objection 1: It seems that Christ's body is movably in this sacrament, because the Philosopher says (Topic. ii) that "when we are moved, the things within us are moved": and this is true even of the soul's spiritual substance. "But Christ is in this sacrament," as shown above ([4560]Q[74], A[1]). Therefore He is moved when it is moved.

Objection 2: Further, the truth ought to correspond with the figure. But, according to the commandment (Ex. 12:10), concerning the Paschal Lamb, a figure of this sacrament, "there remained nothing until the morning." Neither, therefore, if this sacrament be reserved until morning, will Christ's body be there; and so it is not immovably in this sacrament.

Objection 3: Further, if Christ's body were to remain under this sacrament even until the morrow, for the same reason it will remain there during all coming time; for it cannot be said that it ceases to be there when the species pass, because the existence of Christ's body is not dependent on those species. Yet Christ does not remain in this sacrament for all coming time. It seems, then, that straightway on the morrow, or after a short time, He ceases to be under this sacrament. And so it seems that Christ is in this sacrament movably.

On the contrary, it is impossible for the same thing to be in motion and at rest, else contradictories would be verified of the same subject. But Christ's body is at rest in heaven. Therefore it is not movably in this sacrament.

I answer that, When any thing is one, as to subject, and manifold in being, there is nothing to hinder it from being moved in one respect, and yet to remain at rest in another just as it is one thing for a body to be white, and another thing, to be large; hence it can be moved as to its whiteness, and yet continue unmoved as to its magnitude. But in Christ, being in Himself and being under the sacrament are not the same thing, because when we say that He is under this sacrament, we express a kind of relationship to this sacrament. According to this being, then, Christ is not moved locally of Himself, but only accidentally, because Christ is not in this sacrament as in a place, as stated above [4561](A[5]). But what is not in a place, is not moved of itself locally, but only according to the motion of the subject in which it is.

In the same way neither is it moved of itself according to the being which it has in this sacrament, by any other change whatever, as for instance, that it ceases to be under this sacrament: because whatever possesses unfailing existence of itself, cannot be the principle of failing; but when something else fails, then it ceases to be in it; just as God, Whose existence is unfailing and immortal, ceases to be in some corruptible creature because such corruptible creature ceases to exist. And in this way, since Christ has unfailing and incorruptible being, He ceases to be under this sacrament, not because He ceases to be, nor yet by local movement of His own, as is clear from what has been said, but only by the fact that the sacramental species cease to exist.

Hence it is clear that Christ, strictly speaking is immovably in this sacrament.

Reply to Objection 1: This argument deals with accidental movement, whereby things within us are moved together with us. But with things which can of themselves be in a place, like bodies, it is otherwise than with things which cannot of themselves be in a place, such as forms and spiritual substances. And to this mode can be reduced what we say of Christ, being moved accidentally, according to the existence which He has in this sacrament, in which He is not present as in a place.

Reply to Objection 2: It was this argument which seems to have convinced those who held that Christ's body does not remain under this sacrament if it be reserved until the morrow. It is against these that Cyril says (Ep. lxxxiii): "Some are so foolish as to say that the mystical blessing departs from the sacrament, if any of its fragments remain until the next day: for Christ's consecrated body is not changed, and the power of the blessing, and the life-giving grace is perpetually in it." Thus are all other consecrations irremovable so long as the consecrated things endure; on which account they are not repeated. And although the truth corresponds with the figure, still the figure cannot equal it.

Reply to Objection 3: The body of Christ remains in this sacrament not only until the morrow, but also in the future, so long as the sacramental species remain: and when they cease, Christ's body ceases to be under them, not because it depends on them, but because the relationship of Christ's body to those species is taken away, in the same way as God ceases to be the Lord of a creature which ceases to exist.

Whether the body of Christ, as it is in this sacrament, can be seen by any eye, at least by a glorified one?

Objection 1: It seems that the body of Christ, as it is in this sacrament, can be seen by the eye, at least by a glorified one. For our eyes are hindered from beholding Christ's body in this sacrament, on account of the sacramental species veiling it. But the glorified eye cannot be hindered by anything from seeing bodies as they are. Therefore, the glorified eye can see Christ's body as it is in this sacrament.

Objection 2: Further, the glorified bodies of the saints will be "made like to the body" of Christ's "glory," according to Phil. 3:21. But Christ's eye beholds Himself as He is in this sacrament. Therefore, for the same reason, every other glorified eye can see Him.

Objection 3: Further, in the resurrection the saints will be equal to the angels, according to Lk. 20:36. But the angels see the body of Christ as it is in this sacrament, for even the devils are found to pay reverence thereto, and to fear it. Therefore, for like reason, the glorified eye can see Christ as He is in this sacrament.

On the contrary, As long as a thing remains the same, it cannot at the same time be seen by the same eye under diverse species. But the glorified eye sees Christ always, as He is in His own species, according to Is. 33:17: "(His eyes) shall see the king in his beauty." It seems, then, that it does not see Christ, as He is under the species of this sacrament.

I answer that, The eye is of two kinds, namely, the bodily eye properly so-called, and the intellectual eye, so-called by similitude. But Christ's body as it is in this sacrament cannot be seen by any bodily eye. First of all, because a body which is visible brings about an alteration in the medium, through its accidents. Now the accidents of Christ's body are in this sacrament by means of the substance; so that the accidents of Christ's body have no immediate relationship either to this sacrament or to adjacent bodies; consequently they do not act on the medium so as to be seen by any corporeal eye. Secondly, because, as stated above (A[1], ad 3; A[3]), Christ's body is substantially present in this sacrament. But substance, as such, is not visible to the bodily eye, nor does it come under any one of the senses, nor under the imagination, but solely under the intellect, whose object is "what a thing is" (De Anima iii). And therefore, properly speaking, Christ's body, according to the mode of being which it has in this sacrament, is perceptible neither by the sense nor by the imagination, but only by the intellect, which is called the spiritual eye.

Moreover it is perceived differently by different intellects. For since the way in which Christ is in this sacrament is entirely supernatural, it is visible in itself to a supernatural, i.e. the Divine, intellect, and consequently to a beatified intellect, of angel or of man, which, through the participated glory of the Divine intellect, sees all supernatural things in the vision of the Divine Essence. But it can be seen by a wayfarer through faith alone, like other supernatural things. And not even the angelic intellect of its own natural power is capable of beholding it; consequently the devils cannot by their intellect perceive Christ in this sacrament, except through faith, to which they do not pay willing assent; yet they are convinced of it from the evidence of signs, according to James 2:19: "The devils believe, and tremble."

Reply to Objection 1: Our bodily eye, on account of the sacramental species, is hindered from beholding the body of Christ underlying them, not merely as by way of veil (just as we are hindered from seeing what is covered with any corporeal veil), but also because Christ's body bears a relation to the medium surrounding this sacrament, not through its own accidents, but through the sacramental species.

Reply to Objection 2: Christ's own bodily eye sees Himself existing under the sacrament, yet it cannot see the way in which it exists under the sacrament, because that belongs to the intellect. But it is not the same with any other glorified eye, because Christ's eye is under this sacrament, in which no other glorified eye is conformed to it.

Reply to Objection 3: No angel, good or bad, can see anything with a bodily eye, but only with the mental eye. Hence there is no parallel reason, as is evident from what was said above.

Whether Christ's body is truly there when flesh or a child appears miraculously in this sacrament?

Objection 1: It seems that Christ's body is not truly there when flesh or a child appears miraculously in this sacrament. Because His body ceases to be under this sacrament when the sacramental species cease to be present, as stated above [4562](A[6]). But when flesh or a child appears, the sacramental species cease to be present. Therefore Christ's body is not truly there.

Objection 2: Further, wherever Christ's body is, it is there either under its own species, or under those of the sacrament. But when such apparitions occur, it is evident that Christ is not present under His own species, because the entire Christ is contained in this sacrament, and He remains entire under the form in which He ascended to heaven: yet what appears miraculously in this sacrament is sometimes seen as a small particle of flesh, or at times as a small child. Now it is evident that He is not there under the sacramental species, which is that of bread or wine. Consequently, it seems that Christ's body is not there in any way.

Objection 3: Further, Christ's body begins to be in this sacrament by consecration and conversion, as was said above ([4563]Q[75], AA[2],3,4). But the flesh and blood which appear by miracle are not consecrated, nor are they converted into Christ's true body and blood. Therefore the body or the blood of Christ is not under those species.

On the contrary, When such apparition takes place, the same reverence is shown to it as was shown at first, which would not be done if Christ were not truly there, to Whom we show reverence of "latria." Therefore, when such apparition occurs, Christ is under the sacrament.

I answer that, Such apparition comes about in two ways, when occasionally in this sacrament flesh, or blood, or a child, is seen. Sometimes it happens on the part of the beholders, whose eyes are so affected as if they outwardly saw flesh, or blood, or a child, while no change takes place in the sacrament. And this seems to happen when to one person it is seen under the species of flesh or of a child, while to others it is seen as before under the species of bread; or when to the same individual it appears for an hour under the appearance of flesh or a child, and afterwards under the appearance of bread. Nor is there any deception there, as occurs in the feats of magicians, because such species is divinely formed in the eye in order to represent some truth, namely, for the purpose of showing that Christ's body is truly under this sacrament; just as Christ without deception appeared to the disciples who were going to Emmaus. For Augustine says (De Qq. Evang. ii) that "when our pretense is referred to some significance, it is not a lie, but a figure of the truth." And since in this way no change is made in the sacrament, it is manifest that, when such apparition occurs, Christ does not cease to be under this sacrament.

But it sometimes happens that such apparition comes about not merely by a change wrought in the beholders, but by an appearance which really exists outwardly. And this indeed is seen to happen when it is beheld by everyone under such an appearance, and it remains so not for an hour, but for a considerable time; and, in this case some think that it is the proper species of Christ's body. Nor does it matter that sometimes Christ's entire body is not seen there, but part of His flesh, or else that it is not seen in youthful guise. but in the semblance of a child, because it lies within the power of a glorified body for it to be seen by a non-glorified eye either entirely or in part, and under its own semblance or in strange guise, as will be said later ([4564]XP, Q[85], AA[2],3).

But this seems unlikely. First of all, because Christ's body under its proper species can be seen only in one place, wherein it is definitively contained. Hence since it is seen in its proper species, and is adored in heaven, it is not seen under its proper species in this sacrament. Secondly, because a glorified body, which appears at will, disappears when it wills after the apparition; thus it is related (Lk. 24:31) that our Lord "vanished out of sight" of the disciples. But that which appears under the likeness of flesh in this sacrament, continues for a long time; indeed, one reads of its being sometimes enclosed, and, by order of many bishops, preserved in a pyx, which it would be wicked to think of Christ under His proper semblance.

Consequently, it remains to be said, that, while the dimensions remain the same as before, there is a miraculous change wrought in the other accidents, such as shape, color, and the rest, so that flesh, or blood, or a child, is seen. And, as was said already, this is not deception, because it is done "to represent the truth," namely, to show by this miraculous apparition that Christ's body and blood are truly in this sacrament. And thus it is clear that as the dimensions remain, which are the foundation of the other accidents, as we shall see later on ([4565]Q[77], A[2]), the body of Christ truly remains in this sacrament.

Reply to Objection 1: When such apparition takes place, the sacramental species sometimes continue entire in themselves; and sometimes only as to that which is principal, as was said above.

Reply to Objection 2: As stated above, during such apparitions Christ's proper semblance is not seen, but a species miraculously formed either in the eyes of the beholders, or in the sacramental dimensions themselves, as was said above.

Reply to Objection 3: The dimensions of the consecrated bread and wine continue, while a miraculous change is wrought in the other accidents, as stated above.

OF THE ACCIDENTS WHICH REMAIN IN THIS SACRAMENT (EIGHT ARTICLES)

We must now consider the accidents which remain in this sacrament; under which head there are eight points of inquiry:

(1) Whether the accidents which remain are without a subject?

(2) Whether dimensive quantity is the subject of the other accidents?

(3) Whether such accidents can affect an extrinsic body?

(4) Whether they can be corrupted?

(5) Whether anything can be generated from them?

(6) Whether they can nourish?

(7) Of the breaking of the consecrated bread?

(8) Whether anything can be mixed with the consecrated wine?

Whether the accidents remain in this sacrament without a subject?

Objection 1: It seems that the accidents do not remain in this sacrament without a subject, because there ought not to be anything disorderly or deceitful in this sacrament of truth. But for accidents to be without a subject is contrary to the order which God established in nature; and furthermore it seems to savor of deceit, since accidents are naturally the signs of the nature of the subject. Therefore the accidents are not without a subject in this sacrament.

Objection 2: Further, not even by miracle can the definition of a thing be severed from it, or the definition of another thing be applied to it; for instance, that, while man remains a man, he can be an irrational animal. For it would follow that contradictories can exist at the one time: for the "definition of a thing is what its name expresses," as is said in Metaph. iv. But it belongs to the definition of an accident for it to be in a subject, while the definition of substance is that it must subsist of itself, and not in another. Therefore it cannot come to pass, even by miracle, that the accidents exist without a subject in this sacrament.

Objection 3: Further, an accident is individuated by its subject. If therefore the accidents remain in this sacrament without a subject, they will not be individual, but general, which is clearly false, because thus they would not be sensible, but merely intelligible.

Objection 4: Further, the accidents after the consecration of this sacrament do not obtain any composition. But before the consecration they were not composed either of matter and form, nor of existence [quo est] and essence [quod est]. Therefore, even after consecration they are not composite in either of these ways. But this is unreasonable, for thus they would be simpler than angels, whereas at the same time these accidents are perceptible to the senses. Therefore, in this sacrament the accidents do not remain without a subject.

On the contrary, Gregory says in an Easter Homily (Lanfranc, De Corp. et Sang. Dom. xx) that "the sacramental species are the names of those things which were there before, namely, of the bread and wine." Therefore since the substance of the bread and the wine does not remain, it seems that these species remain without a subject.

I answer that, The species of the bread and wine, which are perceived by our senses to remain in this sacrament after consecration, are not subjected in the substance of the bread and wine, for that does not remain, as stated above ([4566]Q[75], A[2]); nor in the substantial form, for that does not remain ([4567]Q[75], A[6]), and if it did remain, "it could not be a subject," as Boethius declares (De Trin. i). Furthermore it is manifest that these accidents are not subjected in the substance of Christ's body and blood, because the substance of the human body cannot in any way be affected by such accidents; nor is it possible for Christ's glorious and impassible body to be altered so as to receive these qualities.

Now there are some who say that they are in the surrounding atmosphere as in a subject. But even this cannot be: in the first place, because atmosphere is not susceptive of such accidents. Secondly, because these accidents are not where the atmosphere is, nay more, the atmosphere is displaced by the motion of these species. Thirdly, because accidents do not pass from subject to subject, so that the same identical accident which was first in one subject be afterwards in another; because an accident is individuated by the subject; hence it cannot come to pass for an accident remaining identically the same to be at one time in one subject, and at another time in another. Fourthly, since the atmosphere is not deprived of its own accidents, it would have at the one time its own accidents and others foreign to it. Nor can it be maintained that this is done miraculously in virtue of the consecration, because the words of consecration do not signify this, and they effect only what they signify.

Therefore it follows that the accidents continue in this sacrament without a subject. This can be done by Divine power: for since an effect depends more upon the first cause than on the second, God Who is the first cause both of substance and accident, can by His unlimited power preserve an accident in existence when the substance is withdrawn whereby it was preserved in existence as by its proper cause, just as without natural causes He can produce other effects of natural causes, even as He formed a human body in the Virgin's womb, "without the seed of man" (Hymn for Christmas, First Vespers).

Reply to Objection 1: There is nothing to hinder the common law of nature from ordaining a thing, the contrary of which is nevertheless ordained by a special privilege of grace, as is evident in the raising of the dead, and in the restoring of sight to the blind: even thus in human affairs, to some individuals some things are granted by special privilege which are outside the common law. And so, even though it be according to the common law of nature for an accident to be in a subject, still for a special reason, according to the order of grace, the accidents exist in this sacrament without a subject, on account of the reasons given above ([4568]Q[75] , A[5]).

Reply to Objection 2: Since being is not a genus, then being cannot be of itself the essence of either substance or accident. Consequently, the definition of substance is not---"a being of itself without a subject," nor is the definition of accident---"a being in a subject"; but it belongs to the quiddity or essence of substance "to have existence not in a subject"; while it belongs to the quiddity or essence of accident "to have existence in a subject." But in this sacrament it is not in virtue of their essence that accidents are not in a subject, but through the Divine power sustaining them; and consequently they do not cease to be accidents, because neither is the definition of accident withdrawn from them, nor does the definition of substance apply to them.

Reply to Objection 3: These accidents acquired individual being in the substance of the bread and wine; and when this substance is changed into the body and blood of Christ, they remain in that individuated being which they possessed before, hence they are individual and sensible.

Reply to Objection 4: These accidents had no being of their own nor other accidents, so long as the substance of the bread and wine remained; but their subjects had "such" being through them, just as snow is "white" through whiteness. But after the consecration the accidents which remain have being; hence they are compounded of existence and essence, as was said of the angels, in the [4569]FP, Q[50], A[2], ad 3; and besides they have composition of quantitative parts.

Whether in this sacrament the dimensive quantity of the bread or wine is the subject of the other accidents?

Objection 1: It seems that in this sacrament the dimensive quantity of the bread or wine is not the subject of the other accidents. For accident is not the subject of accident; because no form can be a subject, since to be a subject is a property of matter. But dimensive quantity is an accident. Therefore dimensive quantity cannot be the subject of the other accidents.

Objection 2: Further, just as quantity is individuated by substance, so also are the other accidents. If, then, the dimensive quantity of the bread or wine remains individuated according to the being it had before, in which it is preserved, for like reason the other accidents remain individuated according to the existence which they had before in the substance. Therefore they are not in dimensive quantity as in a subject, since every accident is individuated by its own subject.

Objection 3: Further, among the other accidents that remain, of the bread and wine, the senses perceive also rarity and density, which cannot be in dimensive quantity existing outside matter; because a thing is rare which has little matter under great dimensions, while a thing is dense which has much matter under small dimensions, as is said in Phys. iv. It does not seem, then, that dimensive quantity can be the subject of the accidents which remain in this sacrament.

Objection 4: Further, quantity abstract from matter seems to be mathematical quantity, which is not the subject of sensible qualities. Since, then, the remaining accidents in this sacrament are sensible, it seems that in this sacrament they cannot be subjected in the dimensive quantity of the bread and wine that remains after consecration.

On the contrary, Qualities are divisible only accidentally, that is, by reason of the subject. But the qualities remaining in this sacrament are divided by the division of dimensive quantity, as is evident through our senses. Therefore, dimensive quantity is the subject of the accidents which remain in this sacrament.

I answer that, It is necessary to say that the other accidents which remain in this sacrament are subjected in the dimensive quantity of the bread and wine that remains: first of all, because something having quantity and color and affected by other accidents is perceived by the senses; nor is sense deceived in such. Secondly, because the first disposition of matter is dimensive quantity, hence Plato also assigned "great" and "small" as the first differences of matter (Aristotle, Metaph. iv). And because the first subject is matter, the consequence is that all other accidents are related to their subject through the medium of dimensive quantity; just as the first subject of color is said to be the surface, on which account some have maintained that dimensions are the substances of bodies, as is said in Metaph. iii. And since, when the subject is withdrawn, the accidents remain according to the being which they had before, it follows that all accidents remain founded upon dimensive quantity.

Thirdly, because, since the subject is the principle of individuation of the accidents, it is necessary for what is admitted as the subject of some accidents to be somehow the principle of individuation: for it is of the very notion of an individual that it cannot be in several; and this happens in two ways. First, because it is not natural to it to be in any one; and in this way immaterial separated forms, subsisting of themselves, are also individuals of themselves. Secondly, because a form, be it substantial or accidental, is naturally in someone indeed, not in several, as this whiteness, which is in this body. As to the first, matter is the principle of individuation of all inherent forms, because, since these forms, considered in themselves, are naturally in something as in a subject, from the very fact that one of them is received in matter, which is not in another, it follows that neither can the form itself thus existing be in another. As to the second, it must be maintained that the principle of individuation is dimensive quantity. For that something is naturally in another one solely, is due to the fact that that other is undivided in itself, and distinct from all others. But it is on account of quantity that substance can be divided, as is said in Phys. i. And therefore dimensive quantity itself is a particular principle of individuation in forms of this kind, namely, inasmuch as forms numerically distinct are in different parts of the matter. Hence also dimensive quantity has of itself a kind of individuation, so that we can imagine several lines of the same species, differing in position, which is included in the notion of this quantity; for it belongs to dimension for it to be "quantity having position" (Aristotle, Categor. iv), and therefore dimensive quantity can be the subject of the other accidents, rather than the other way about.

Reply to Objection 1: One accident cannot of itself be the subject of another, because it does not exist of itself. But inasmuch as an accident is received in another thing, one is said to be the subject of the other, inasmuch as one is received in a subject through another, as the surface is said to be the subject of color. Hence when God makes an accident to exist of itself, it can also be of itself the subject of another.

Reply to Objection 2: The other accidents, even as they were in the substance of the bread, were individuated by means of dimensive quantity, as stated above. And therefore dimensive quantity is the subject of the other accidents remaining in this sacrament, rather than conversely.

Reply to Objection 3: Rarity and density are particular qualities accompanying bodies, by reason of their having much or little matter under dimensions; just as all other accidents likewise follow from the principles of substance. And consequently, as the accidents are preserved by Divine power when the substance is withdrawn, so, when matter is withdrawn, the qualities which go with matter, such as rarity and density, are preserved by Divine power.

Reply to Objection 4: Mathematical quantity abstracts not from intelligible matter, but from sensible matter, as is said in Metaph. vii. But matter is termed sensible because it underlies sensible qualities. And therefore it is manifest that the dimensive quantity, which remains in this sacrament without a subject, is not mathematical quantity.

Whether the species remaining in this sacrament can change external objects?

Objection 1: It seems that the species which remain in this sacrament cannot affect external objects. For it is proved in Phys. vii, that forms which are in matter are produced by forms that are in matter, but not from forms which are without matter, because like makes like. But the sacramental species are species without matter, since they remain without a subject, as is evident from what was said above [4570](A[1]). Therefore they cannot affect other matter by producing any form in it.

Objection 2: Further, when the action of the principal agent ceases, then the action of the instrument must cease, as when the carpenter rests, the hammer is moved no longer. But all accidental forms act instrumentally in virtue of the substantial form as the principal agent. Therefore, since the substantial form of the bread and wine does not remain in this sacrament, as was shown above ([4571]Q[75], A[6]), it seems that the accidental forms which remain cannot act so as to change external matter.

Objection 3: Further, nothing acts outside its species, because an effect cannot surpass its cause. But all the sacramental species are accidents. Therefore they cannot change external matter, at least as to a substantial form.

On the contrary, If they could not change external bodies, they could not be felt; for a thing is felt from the senses being changed by a sensible thing, as is said in De Anima ii.

I answer that, Because everything acts in so far as it is an actual being, the consequence is that everything stands in the same relation to action as it does to being. Therefore, because, according to what was said above [4572](A[1]), it is an effect of the Divine power that the sacramental species continue in the being which they had when the substance of the bread and wine was present, it follows that they continue in their action. Consequently they retain every action which they had while the substance of the bread and wine remained, now that the substance of the bread and wine has passed into the body and blood of Christ. Hence there is no doubt but that they can change external bodies.

Reply to Objection 1: The sacramental species, although they are forms existing without matter, still retain the same being which they had before in matter, and therefore as to their being they are like forms which are in matter.

Reply to Objection 2: The action of an accidental form depends upon the action of a substantial form in the same way as the being of accident depends upon the being of substance; and therefore, as it is an effect of Divine power that the sacramental species exist without substance, so is it an effect of Divine power that they can act without a substantial form, because every action of a substantial or accidental form depends upon God as the first agent.

Reply to Objection 3: The change which terminates in a substantial form is not effected by a substantial form directly, but by means of the active and passive qualities, which act in virtue of the substantial form. But by Divine power this instrumental energy is retained in the sacramental species, just as it was before: and consequently their action can be directed to a substantial form instrumentally, just in the same way as anything can act outside its species, not as by its own power, but by the power of the chief agent.

Whether the sacramental species can be corrupted?

Objection 1: It seems that the sacramental species cannot be corrupted, because corruption comes of the separation of the form from the matter. But the matter of the bread does not remain in this sacrament, as is clear from what was said above ([4573]Q[75], A[2]). Therefore these species cannot be corrupted.

Objection 2: Further, no form is corrupted except accidentally, that is, when its subject is corrupted; hence self-subsisting forms are incorruptible, as is seen in spiritual substances. But the sacramental species are forms without a subject. Therefore they cannot be corrupted.

Objection 3: Further, if they be corrupted, it will either be naturally or miraculously. But they cannot be corrupted naturally, because no subject of corruption can be assigned as remaining after the corruption has taken place. Neither can they be corrupted miraculously, because the miracles which occur in this sacrament take place in virtue of the consecration, whereby the sacramental species are preserved: and the same thing is not the cause of preservation and of corruption. Therefore, in no way can the sacramental species be corrupted.

On the contrary, We perceive by our senses that the consecrated hosts become putrefied and corrupted.

I answer that, Corruption is "movement from being into non-being" (Aristotle, Phys. v). Now it has been stated [4574](A[3]) that the sacramental species retain the same being as they had before when the substance of the bread was present. Consequently, as the being of those accidents could be corrupted while the substance of the bread and wine was present, so likewise they can be corrupted now that the substance has passed away.

But such accidents could have been previously corrupted in two ways: in one way, of themselves; in another way, accidentally. They could be corrupted of themselves, as by alteration of the qualities, and increase or decrease of the quantity, not in the way in which increase or decrease is found only in animated bodies, such as the substances of the bread and wine are not, but by addition or division; for, as is said in Metaph. iii, one dimension is dissolved by division, and two dimensions result; while on the contrary, by addition, two dimensions become one. And in this way such accidents can be corrupted manifestly after consecration, because the dimensive quantity which remains can receive division and addition; and since it is the subject of sensible qualities, as stated above [4575](A[1]), it can likewise be the subject of their alteration, for instance, if the color or the savor of the bread or wine be altered.

An accident can be corrupted in another way, through the corruption of its subject, and in this way also they can be corrupted after consecration; for although the subject does not remain, still the being which they had in the subject does remain, which being is proper, and suited to the subject. And therefore such being can be corrupted by a contrary agent, as the substance of the bread or wine was subject to corruption, and, moreover, was not corrupted except by a preceding alteration regarding the accidents.

Nevertheless, a distinction must be made between each of the aforesaid corruptions; because, when the body and the blood of Christ succeed in this sacrament to the substance of the bread and wine, if there be such change on the part of the accidents as would not have sufficed for the corruption of the bread and wine, then the body and blood of Christ do not cease to be under this sacrament on account of such change, whether the change be on the part of the quality, as for instance, when the color or the savor of the bread or wine is slightly modified; or on the part of the quantity, as when the bread or the wine is divided into such parts as to keep in them the nature of bread or of wine. But if the change be so great that the substance of the bread or wine would have been corrupted, then Christ's body and blood do not remain under this sacrament; and this either on the part of the qualities, as when the color, savor, and other qualities of the bread and wine are so altered as to be incompatible with the nature of bread or of wine; or else on the part of the quantity, as, for instance, if the bread be reduced to fine particles, or the wine divided into such tiny drops that the species of bread or wine no longer remain.

Reply to Objection 1: Since it belongs essentially to corruption to take away the being of a thing, in so far as the being of some form is in matter, it results that by corruption the form is separated from the matter. But if such being were not in matter, yet like such being as is in matter, it could be taken away by corruption, even where there is no matter; as takes place in this sacrament, as is evident from what was said above.

Reply to Objection 2: Although the sacramental species are forms not in matter, yet they have the being which they had in matter.

Reply to Objection 3: This corruption of species is not miraculous, but natural; nevertheless, it presupposes the miracle which is wrought in the consecration, namely, that those sacramental species retain without a subject, the same being as they had in a subject; just as a blind man, to whom sight is given miraculously, sees naturally.

Day 305

Whether anything can be generated from the sacramental species?

Objection 1: It seems that nothing can be generated from the sacramental species: because, whatever is generated, is generated out of some matter: for nothing is generated out of nothing, although by creation something is made out of nothing. But there is no matter underlying the sacramental species except that of Christ's body, and that body is incorruptible. Therefore it seems that nothing can be generated from the sacramental species.

Objection 2: Further, things which are not of the same genus cannot spring from one another: thus a line is not made of whiteness. But accident and substance differ generically. Therefore, since the sacramental species are accidents, it seems that no substance can be generated from them.

Objection 3: Further, if any corporeal substance be generated from them, such substance will not be without accident. Therefore, if any corporeal substance be generated from the sacramental species, then substance and accident would be generated from accident, namely, two things from one, which is impossible. Consequently, it is impossible for any corporeal substance to be generated out of the sacramental species.

On the contrary, The senses are witness that something is generated out of the sacramental species, either ashes, if they be burned, worms if they putrefy, or dust if they be crushed.

I answer that, Since "the corruption of one thing is the generation of another" (De Gener. i), something must be generated necessarily from the sacramental species if they be corrupted, as stated above [4576](A[4]); for they are not corrupted in such a way that they disappear altogether, as if reduced to nothing; on the contrary, something sensible manifestly succeeds to them.

Nevertheless, it is difficult to see how anything can be generated from them. For it is quite evident that nothing is generated out of the body and blood of Christ which are truly there, because these are incorruptible. But if the substance, or even the matter, of the bread and wine were to remain in this sacrament, then, as some have maintained, it would be easy to account for this sensible object which succeeds to them. But that supposition is false, as was stated above ([4577]Q[75], AA[2],4,8).

Hence it is that others have said that the things generated have not sprung from the sacramental species, but from the surrounding atmosphere. But this can be shown in many ways to be impossible. In the first place, because when a thing is generated from another, the latter at first appears changed and corrupted; whereas no alteration or corruption appeared previously in the adjacent atmosphere; hence the worms or ashes are not generated therefrom. Secondly, because the nature of the atmosphere is not such as to permit of such things being generated by such alterations. Thirdly, because it is possible for many consecrated hosts to be burned or putrefied; nor would it be possible for an earthen body, large enough to be generated from the atmosphere, unless a great and, in fact, exceedingly sensible condensation of the atmosphere took place. Fourthly, because the same thing can happen to the solid bodies surrounding them, such as iron or stone, which remain entire after the generation of the aforesaid things. Hence this opinion cannot stand, because it is opposed to what is manifest to our senses.

And therefore others have said that the substance of the bread and wine returns during the corruption of the species, and so from the returning substance of the bread and wine, ashes or worms or something of the kind are generated. But this explanation seems an impossible one. First of all, because if the substance of the bread and wine be converted into the body and blood of Christ, as was shown above (Q[75], AA[2],4), the substance of the bread and wine cannot return, except the body and blood of Christ be again changed back into the substance of bread and wine, which is impossible: thus if air be turned into fire, the air cannot return without the fire being again changed into air. But if the substance of bread or wine be annihilated, it cannot return again, because what lapses into nothing does not return numerically the same. Unless perchance it be said that the said substance returns, because God creates anew another new substance to replace the first. Secondly, this seems to be impossible, because no time can be assigned when the substance of the bread returns. For, from what was said above [4578](A[4]; Q[76], A[6], ad 3), it is evident that while the species of the bread and wine remain, there remain also the body and blood of Christ, which are not present together with the substance of the bread and wine in this sacrament, according to what was stated above (Q[75], A[2]). Hence the substance of the bread and wine cannot return while the sacramental species remain; nor, again, when these species pass away; because then the substance of the bread and wine would be without their proper accidents, which is impossible. Unless perchance it be said that in the last instant of the corruption of the species there returns (not, indeed, the substance of bread and wine, because it is in that very instant that they have the being of the substance generated from the species, but) the matter of the bread and wine; which, matter, properly speaking, would be more correctly described as created anew, than as returning. And in this sense the aforesaid position might be held.

However, since it does not seem reasonable to say that anything takes place miraculously in this sacrament, except in virtue of the consecration itself, which does not imply either creation or return of matter, it seems better to say that in the actual consecration it is miraculously bestowed on the dimensive quantity of the bread and wine to be the subject of subsequent forms. Now this is proper to matter; and therefore as a consequence everything which goes with matter is bestowed on dimensive quantity; and therefore everything which could be generated from the matter of bread or wine, if it were present, can be generated from the aforesaid dimensive quantity of the bread or wine, not, indeed, by a new miracle, but by virtue of the miracle which has already taken place.

Reply to Objection 1: Although no matter is there out of which a thing may be generated, nevertheless dimensive quantity supplies the place of matter, as stated above.

Reply to Objection 2: Those sacramental species are indeed accidents, yet they have the act and power of substance, as stated above [4579](A[3]).

Reply to Objection 3: The dimensive quantity of the bread and wine retains its own nature, and receives miraculously the power and property of substance; and therefore it can pass to both, that is, into substance and dimension.

Whether the sacramental species can nourish?

Objection 1: It seems that the sacramental species cannot nourish, because, as Ambrose says (De Sacram. v), "it is not this bread that enters into our body, but the bread of everlasting life, which supports the substance of our soul." But whatever nourishes enters into the body. Therefore this bread does not nourish: and the same reason holds good of the wine.

Objection 2: Further, as is said in De Gener. ii, "We are nourished by the very things of which we are made." But the sacramental species are accidents, whereas man is not made of accidents, because accident is not a part of substance. Therefore it seems that the sacramental species cannot nourish.

Objection 3: Further, the Philosopher says (De Anima ii) that "food nourishes according as it is a substance, but it gives increase by reason of its quantity." But the sacramental species are not a substance. Consequently they cannot nourish.

On the contrary, The Apostle speaking of this sacrament says (1 Cor. 11:21): "One, indeed, is hungry, and another is drunk": upon which the gloss observes that "he alludes to those who after the celebration of the sacred mystery, and after the consecration of the bread and wine, claimed their oblations, and not sharing them with others, took the whole, so as even to become intoxicated thereby." But this could not happen if the sacramental species did not nourish. Therefore the sacramental species do nourish.

I answer that, This question presents no difficulty, now that we have solved the preceding question. Because, as stated in De Anima ii, food nourishes by being converted into the substance of the individual nourished. Now it has been stated [4580](A[5]) that the sacramental species can be converted into a substance generated from them. And they can be converted into the human body for the same reason as they can into ashes or worms. Consequently, it is evident that they nourish.

But the senses witness to the untruth of what some maintain; viz. that the species do not nourish as though they were changed into the human body, but merely refresh and hearten by acting upon the senses (as a man is heartened by the odor of meat, and intoxicated by the fumes of wine). Because such refreshment does not suffice long for a man, whose body needs repair owing to constant waste: and yet a man could be supported for long if he were to take hosts and consecrated wine in great quantity.

In like manner the statement advanced by others cannot stand, who hold that the sacramental species nourish owing to the remaining substantial form of the bread and wine: both because the form does not remain, as stated above ([4581]Q[75], A[6]): and because to nourish is the act not of a form but rather of matter, which takes the form of the one nourished, while the form of the nourishment passes away: hence it is said in De Anima ii that nourishment is at first unlike, but at the end is like.

Reply to Objection 1: After the consecration bread can be said to be in this sacrament in two ways. First, as to the species, which retain the name of the previous substance, as Gregory says in an Easter Homily (Lanfranc, De Corp. et Sang. Dom. xx). Secondly, Christ's very body can be called bread, since it is the mystical bread "coming down from heaven." Consequently, Ambrose uses the word "bread" in this second meaning, when he says that "this bread does not pass into the body," because, to wit, Christ's body is not changed into man's body, but nourishes his soul. But he is not speaking of bread taken in the first acceptation.

Reply to Objection 2: Although the sacramental species are not those things out of which the human body is made, yet they are changed into those things stated above.

Reply to Objection 3: Although the sacramental species are not a substance, still they have the virtue of a substance, as stated above.

Whether the sacramental species are broken in this sacrament?

Objection 1: It seems that the sacramental species are not broken in this sacrament, because the Philosopher says in Meteor. iv that bodies are breakable owing to a certain disposition of the pores; a thing which cannot be attributed to the sacramental species. Therefore the sacramental species cannot be broken.

Objection 2: Further, breaking is followed by sound. But the sacramental species emit no sound: because the Philosopher says (De Anima ii), that what emits sound is a hard body, having a smooth surface. Therefore the sacramental species are not broken.

Objection 3: Further, breaking and mastication are seemingly of the same object. But it is Christ's true body that is eaten, according to Jn. 6:57: "He that eateth My flesh, and drinketh My blood." Therefore it is Christ's body that is broken and masticated: and hence it is said in the confession of Berengarius: "I agree with the Holy Catholic Church, and with heart and lips I profess, that the bread and wine which are placed on the altar, are the true body and blood of Christ after consecration, and are truly handled and broken by the priest's hands, broken and crushed by the teeth of believers." Consequently, the breaking ought not to be ascribed to the sacramental species.

On the contrary, Breaking arises from the division of that which has quantity. But nothing having quantity except the sacramental species is broken here, because neither Christ's body is broken, as being incorruptible, nor is the substance of the bread, because it no longer remains. Therefore the sacramental species are broken.

I answer that, Many opinions prevailed of old on this matter. Some held that in this sacrament there was no breaking at all in reality, but merely in the eyes of the beholders. But this contention cannot stand, because in this sacrament of truth the sense is not deceived with regard to its proper object of judgment, and one of these objects is breaking, whereby from one thing arise many: and these are common sensibles, as is stated in De Anima ii.

Others accordingly have said that there was indeed a genuine breaking, but without any subject. But this again contradicts our senses; because a quantitative body is seen in this sacrament, which formerly was one, and is now divided into many, and this must be the subject of the breaking.

But it cannot be said that Christ's true body is broken. First of all, because it is incorruptible and impassible: secondly, because it is entire under every part, as was shown above ([4582]Q[76], A[3]), which is contrary to the nature of a thing broken.

It remains, then, that the breaking is in the dimensive quantity of the bread, as in a subject, just as the other accidents. And as the sacramental species are the sacrament of Christ's true body, so is the breaking of these species the sacrament of our Lord's Passion, which was in Christ's true body.

Reply to Objection 1: As rarity and density remain under the sacramental species, as stated above (A[2], ad 3), so likewise porousness remains, and in consequence breakableness.

Reply to Objection 2: Hardness results from density; therefore, as density remains under the sacramental species, hardness remains there too, and the capability of sound as a consequence.

Reply to Objection 3: What is eaten under its own species, is also broken and masticated under its own species; but Christ's body is eaten not under its proper, but under the sacramental species. Hence in explaining Jn. 6:64, "The flesh profiteth nothing," Augustine (Tract. xxvii in Joan.) says that this is to be taken as referring to those who understood carnally: "for they understood the flesh, thus, as it is divided piecemeal, in a dead body, or as sold in the shambles." Consequently, Christ's very body is not broken, except according to its sacramental species. And the confession made by Berengarius is to be understood in this sense, that the breaking and the crushing with the teeth is to be referred to the sacramental species, under which the body of Christ truly is.

Whether any liquid can be mingled with the consecrated wine?

Objection 1: It seems that no liquid can be mingled with the consecrated wine, because everything mingled with another partakes of its quality. But no liquid can share in the quality of the sacramental species, because those accidents are without a subject, as stated above [4583](A[1]). Therefore it seems that no liquid can be mingled with the sacramental species of the wine.

Objection 2: Further, if any kind of liquid be mixed with those species, then some one thing must be the result. But no one thing can result from the liquid, which is a substance, and the sacramental species, which are accidents; nor from the liquid and Christ's blood, which owing to its incorruptibility suffers neither increase nor decrease. Therefore no liquid can be mixed with the consecrated wine.

Objection 3: Further, if any liquid be mixed with the consecrated wine, then that also would appear to be consecrated; just as water added to holy-water becomes holy. But the consecrated wine is truly Christ's blood. Therefore the liquid added would likewise be Christ's blood otherwise than by consecration, which is unbecoming. Therefore no liquid can be mingled with the consecrated wine.

Objection 4: Further, if one of two things be entirely corrupted, there is no mixture (De Gener. i). But if we mix any liquid, it seems that the entire species of the sacramental wine is corrupted, so that the blood of Christ ceases to be beneath it; both because great and little are difference of quantity, and alter it, as white and black cause a difference of color; and because the liquid mixed, as having no obstacle, seems to permeate the whole, and so Christ's blood ceases to be there, since it is not there with any other substance. Consequently, no liquid can be mixed with the consecrated wine.

On the contrary, It is evident to our senses that another liquid can be mixed with the wine after it is consecrated, just as before.

I answer that, The truth of this question is evident from what has been said already. For it was said above [4584](A[3]; A[5], ad 2) that the species remaining in this sacrament, as they acquire the manner of being of substance in virtue of the consecration, so likewise do they obtain the mode of acting and of being acted upon, so that they can do or receive whatever their substance could do or receive, were it there present. But it is evident that if the substance of wine were there present, then some other liquid could be mingled with it.

Nevertheless there would be a different effect of such mixing both according to the form and according to the quantity of the liquid. For if sufficient liquid were mixed so as to spread itself all through the wine, then the whole would be a mixed substance. Now what is made up of things mixed is neither of them, but each passes into a third resulting from both: hence it would result that the former wine would remain no longer. But if the liquid added were of another species, for instance, if water were mixed, the species of the wine would be dissolved, and there would be a liquid of another species. But if liquid of the same species were added, of instance, wine with wine, the same species would remain, but the wine would not be the same numerically, as the diversity of the accidents shows: for instance, if one wine were white and the other red.

But if the liquid added were of such minute quantity that it could not permeate the whole, the entire wine would not be mixed, but only part of it, which would not remain the same numerically owing to the blending of extraneous matter: still it would remain the same specifically, not only if a little liquid of the same species were mixed with it, but even if it were of another species, since a drop of water blended with much wine passes into the species of wine (De Gener. i).

Now it is evident that the body and blood of Christ abide in this sacrament so long as the species remain numerically the same, as stated above [4585](A[4]; Q[76], A[6], ad 3); because it is this bread and this wine which is consecrated. Hence, if the liquid of any kind whatsoever added be so much in quantity as to permeate the whole of the consecrated wine, and be mixed with it throughout, the result would be something numerically distinct, and the blood of Christ will remain there no longer. But if the quantity of the liquid added be so slight as not to permeate throughout, but to reach only a part of the species, Christ's blood will cease to be under that part of the consecrated wine, yet will remain under the rest.

Reply to Objection 1: Pope Innocent III in a Decretal writes thus: "The very accidents appear to affect the wine that is added, because, if water is added, it takes the savor of the wine. The result is, then, that the accidents change the subject, just as subject changes accidents; for nature yields to miracle, and power works beyond custom." But this must not be understood as if the same identical accident, which was in the wine previous to consecration, is afterwards in the wine that is added; but such change is the result of action; because the remaining accidents of the wine retain the action of substance, as stated above, and so they act upon the liquid added, by changing it.

Reply to Objection 2: The liquid added to the consecrated wine is in no way mixed with the substance of Christ's blood. Nevertheless it is mixed with the sacramental species, yet so that after such mixing the aforesaid species are corrupted entirely or in part, after the way mentioned above [4586](A[5]), whereby something can be generated from those species. And if they be entirely corrupted, there remains no further question, because the whole will be uniform. But if they be corrupted in part, there will be one dimension according to the continuity of quantity, but not one according to the mode of being, because one part thereof will be without a subject while the other is in a subject; as in a body that is made up of two metals, there will be one body quantitatively, but not one as to the species of the matter.

Reply to Objection 3: As Pope Innocent says in the aforesaid Decretal, "if after the consecration other wine be put in the chalice, it is not changed into the blood, nor is it mingled with the blood, but, mixed with the accidents of the previous wine, it is diffused throughout the body which underlies them, yet without wetting what surrounds it." Now this is to be understood when there is not sufficient mixing of extraneous liquid to cause the blood of Christ to cease to be under the whole; because a thing is said to be "diffused throughout," not because it touches the body of Christ according to its proper dimensions, but according to the sacramental dimensions, under which it is contained. Now it is not the same with holy water, because the blessing works no change in the substance of the water, as the consecration of the wine does.

Reply to Objection 4: Some have held that however slight be the mixing of extraneous liquid, the substance of Christ's blood ceases to be under the whole, and for the reason given above (OBJ[4]); which, however, is not a cogent one; because "more" or "less" diversify dimensive quantity, not as to its essence, but as to the determination of its measure. In like manner the liquid added can be so small as on that account to be hindered from permeating the whole, and not simply by the dimensions; which, although they are present without a subject, still they are opposed to another liquid, just as substance would be if it were present, according to what was said at the beginning of the article.

OF THE FORM OF THIS SACRAMENT (SIX ARTICLES)

We must now consider the form of this sacrament; concerning which there are six points of inquiry:
(1) What is the form of this sacrament?
(2) Whether the form for the consecration of the bread is appropriate?
(3) Whether the form for the consecration of the blood is appropriate?
(4) Of the power of each form?
(5) Of the truth of the expression?
(6) Of the comparison of the one form with the other?

Whether this is the form of this sacrament: "This is My body," and "This is the chalice of My blood"?

Objection 1: It seems that this is not the form of this sacrament: "This is My body," and, "This is the chalice of My blood." Because those words seem to belong to the form of this sacrament, wherewith Christ consecrated His body and blood. But Christ first blessed the bread which He took, and said afterwards: "Take ye and eat; this is My body" (Mat. 26:26). Therefore the whole of this seems to belong to the form of this sacrament: and the same reason holds good of the words which go with the consecration of the blood.

Objection 2: Further, Eusebius Emissenus (Pseudo-Hieron: Ep. xxix; Pseudo-Isid.: Hom. iv) says: "The invisible Priest changes visible creatures into His own body, saying: 'Take ye and eat; this is My body.'" Therefore, the whole of this seems to belong to the form of this sacrament: and the same hold good of the works appertaining to the blood.

Objection 3: Further, in the form of Baptism both the minister and his act are expressed, when it is said, "I baptize thee." But in the words set forth above there is no mention made either of the minister or of his act. Therefore the form of the sacrament is not a suitable one.

Objection 4: Further, the form of the sacrament suffices for its perfection; hence the sacrament of Baptism can be performed sometimes by pronouncing the words of the form only, omitting all the others. Therefore, if the aforesaid words be the form of this sacrament, it would seem as if this sacrament could be performed sometimes by uttering those words alone, while leaving out all the others which are said in the mass; yet this seems to be false, because, were the other words to be passed over, the said words would be taken as spoken in the person of the priest saying them, whereas the bread and wine are not changed into his body and blood. Consequently, the aforesaid words are not the form of this sacrament.

On the contrary, Ambrose says (De Sacram. iv): "The consecration is accomplished by the words and expressions of the Lord Jesus. Because, by all the other words spoken, praise is rendered to God, prayer is put up for the people, for kings, and others; but when the time comes for perfecting the sacrament, the priest uses no longer his own words, but the words of Christ. Therefore, it is Christ's words that perfect this sacrament."

I answer that, This sacrament differs from the other sacraments in two respects. First of all, in this, that this sacrament is accomplished by the consecration of the matter, while the rest are perfected in the use of the consecrated matter. Secondly, because in the other sacraments the consecration of the matter consists only in a blessing, from which the matter consecrated derives instrumentally a spiritual power, which through the priest who is an animated instrument, can pass on to inanimate instruments. But in this sacrament the consecration of the matter consists in the miraculous change of the substance, which can only be done by God; hence the minister in performing this sacrament has no other act save the pronouncing of the words. And because the form should suit the thing, therefore the form of this sacrament differs from the forms of the other sacraments in two respects. First, because the form of the other sacraments implies the use of the matter, as for instance, baptizing, or signing; but the form of this sacrament implies merely the consecration of the matter, which consists in transubstantiation, as when it is said, "This is My body," or, "This is the chalice of My blood." Secondly, because the forms of the other sacraments are pronounced in the person of the minister, whether by way of exercising an act, as when it is said, "I baptize thee," or "I confirm thee," etc.; or by way of command, as when it is said in the sacrament of order, "Take the power," etc.; or by way of entreaty, as when in the sacrament of Extreme Unction it is said, "By this anointing and our intercession," etc. But the form of this sacrament is pronounced as if Christ were speaking in person, so that it is given to be understood that the minister does nothing in perfecting this sacrament, except to pronounce the words of Christ.

Reply to Objection 1: There are many opinions on this matter. Some have said that Christ, Who had power of excellence in the sacraments, performed this sacrament without using any form of words, and that afterwards He pronounced the words under which others were to consecrate thereafter. And the words of Pope Innocent III seem to convey the same sense (De Sacr. Alt. Myst. iv), where he says: "In good sooth it can be said that Christ accomplished this sacrament by His Divine power, and subsequently expressed the form under which those who came after were to consecrate." But in opposition to this view are the words of the Gospel in which it is said that Christ "blessed," and this blessing was effected by certain words. Accordingly those words of Innocent are to be considered as expressing an opinion, rather than determining the point.

Others, again, have said that the blessing was effected by other words not known to us. But this statement cannot stand, because the blessing of the consecration is now performed by reciting the things which were then accomplished; hence, if the consecration was not performed then by these words, neither would it be now.

Accordingly, others have maintained that this blessing was effected by the same words as are used now; but that Christ spoke them twice, at first secretly, in order to consecrate, and afterwards openly, to instruct others. But even this will not hold good, because the priest in consecrating uses these words, not as spoken in secret, but as openly pronounced. Accordingly, since these words have no power except from Christ pronouncing them, it seems that Christ also consecrated by pronouncing them openly.

And therefore others said that the Evangelists did not always follow the precise order in their narrative as that in which things actually happened, as is seen from Augustine (De Consens. Evang. ii). Hence it is to be understood that the order of what took place can be expressed thus: "Taking the bread He blessed it, saying: This is My body, and then He broke it, and gave it to His disciples." But the same sense can be had even without changing the words of the Gospel; because the participle "saying" implies sequence of the words uttered with what goes before. And it is not necessary for the sequence to be understood only with respect to the last word spoken, as if Christ had just then pronounced those words, when He gave it to His disciples; but the sequence can be understood with regard to all that had gone before; so that the sense is: "While He was blessing, and breaking, and giving it to His disciples, He spoke the words, 'Take ye,'" etc.

Reply to Objection 2: In these words, "Take ye and eat," the use of the consecrated, matter is indicated, which is not of the necessity of this sacrament, as stated above ([4587]Q[74], A[7]). And therefore not even these words belong to the substance of the form. Nevertheless, because the use of the consecrated matter belongs to a certain perfection of the sacrament, in the same way as operation is not the first but the second perfection of a thing, consequently, the whole perfection of this sacrament is expressed by all those words: and it was in this way that Eusebius understood that the sacrament was accomplished by those words, as to its first and second perfection.

Reply to Objection 3: In the sacrament of Baptism the minister exercises an act regarding the use of the matter, which is of the essence of the sacrament: such is not the case in this sacrament; hence there is no parallel.

Reply to Objection 4: Some have contended that this sacrament cannot be accomplished by uttering the aforesaid words, while leaving out the rest, especially the words in the Canon of the Mass. But that this is false can be seen both from Ambrose's words quoted above, as well as from the fact that the Canon of the Mass is not the same in all places or times, but various portions have been introduced by various people.

Accordingly it must be held that if the priest were to pronounce only the aforesaid words with the intention of consecrating this sacrament, this sacrament would be valid because the intention would cause these words to be understood as spoken in the person of Christ, even though the words were pronounced without those that precede. The priest, however, would sin gravely in consecrating the sacrament thus, as he would not be observing the rite of the Church. Nor does the comparison with Baptism prove anything; for it is a sacrament of necessity: whereas the lack of this sacrament can be supplied by the spiritual partaking thereof, as Augustine says (cf. [4588] Q[73], A[3], ad 1).

Whether this is the proper form for the consecration of the bread: "This is My body"?

Objection 1: It seems that this is not the proper form of this sacrament: "This is My body." For the effect of a sacrament ought to be expressed in its form. But the effect of the consecration of the bread is the change of the substance of the bread into the body of Christ, and this is better expressed by the word "becomes" than by "is." Therefore, in the form of the consecration we ought to say: "This becomes My body."

Objection 2: Further, Ambrose says (De Sacram. iv), "Christ's words consecrate this sacrament. What word of Christ? This word, whereby all things are made. The Lord commanded, and the heavens and earth were made. " Therefore, it would be a more proper form of this sacrament if the imperative mood were employed, so as to say: "Be this My body."

Objection 3: Further, that which is changed is implied in the subject of this phrase, just as the term of the change is implied in the predicate. But just as that into which the change is made is something determinate, for the change is into nothing else but the body of Christ, so also that which is converted is determinate, since only bread is converted into the body of Christ. Therefore, as a noun is inserted on the part of the predicate, so also should a noun be inserted in the subject, so that it be said: "This bread is My body."

Objection 4: Further, just as the term of the change is determinate in nature, because it is a body, so also is it determinate in person. Consequently, in order to determine the person, it ought to be said: "This is the body of Christ."

Objection 5: Further, nothing ought to be inserted in the form except what is substantial to it. Consequently, the conjunction "for" is improperly added in some books, since it does not belong to the substance of the form.

On the contrary, our Lord used this form in consecrating, as is evident from Mat. 26:26.

I answer that, This is the proper form for the consecration of the bread. For it was said [4589](A[1]) that this consecration consists in changing the substance of bread into the body of Christ. Now the form of a sacrament ought to denote what is done in the sacrament. Consequently the form for the consecration of the bread ought to signify the actual conversion of the bread into the body of Christ. And herein are three things to be considered: namely, the actual conversion, the term "whence," and the term "whereunto."

Now the conversion can be considered in two ways: first, in "becoming," secondly, in "being." But the conversion ought not to be signified in this form as in "becoming," but as in "being." First, because such conversion is not successive, as was said above ([4590]Q[75], A[7]), but instantaneous; and in such changes the "becoming" is nothing else than the "being." Secondly, because the sacramental forms bear the same relation to the signification of the sacramental effect as artificial forms to the representation of the effect of art. Now an artificial form is the likeness of the ultimate effect, on which the artist's intention is fixed ;. just as the art-form in the builder's mind is principally the form of the house constructed, and secondarily of the constructing. Accordingly, in this form also the conversion ought to be expressed as in "being," to which the intention is referred.

And since the conversion is expressed in this form as in "being," it is necessary for the extremes of the conversion to be signified as they exist in the fact of conversion. But then the term "whereunto" has the proper nature of its own substance; whereas the term "whence" does not remain in its own substance, but only as to the accidents whereby it comes under the senses, and can be determined in relation to the senses. Hence the term "whence" of the conversion is conveniently expressed by the demonstrative pronoun, relative to the sensible accidents which continue; but the term "whereunto" is expressed by the noun signifying the nature of the thing which terminates the conversion, and this is Christ's entire body, and not merely His flesh; as was said above ([4591]Q[76], A[1], ad 2). Hence this form is most appropriate: "This is My body."

Reply to Objection 1: The ultimate effect of this conversion is not a "becoming" but a "being," as stated above, and consequently prominence should be given to this in the form.

Reply to Objection 2: God's word operated in the creation of things, and it is the same which operates in this consecration, yet each in different fashion: because here it operates effectively and sacramentally, that is, in virtue of its signification. And consequently the last effect of the consecration must needs be signified in this sentence by a substantive verb of the indicative mood and present time. But in the creation of things it worked merely effectively, and such efficiency is due to the command of His wisdom; and therefore in the creation of things the Lord's word is expressed by a verb in the imperative mood, as in Gn. 1:3: "Let there be light, and light was made."

Reply to Objection 3: The term "whence" does not retain the nature of its substance in the "being" of the conversion, as the term "whereunto" does. Therefore there is no parallel.

Reply to Objection 4: The pronoun "My," which implicitly points to the chief person, i.e. the person of the speaker, sufficiently indicates Christ's person, in Whose person these words are uttered, as stated above [4592](A[1]).

Reply to Objection 5: The conjunction "for" is set in this form according to the custom of the Roman Church, who derived it from Peter the Apostle; and this on account of the sequence with the words preceding: and therefore it is not part of the form, just as the words preceding the form are not.

Whether this is the proper form for the consecration of the wine: "This is the chalice of My blood," etc.?

Objection 1: It seems that this is not the proper form for the consecration of the wine. "This is the chalice of My blood, of the New and Eternal Testament, the Mystery of Faith, which shall be shed for you and for many unto the forgiveness of sins." For as the bread is changed by the power of consecration into Christ's body, so is the wine changed into Christ's blood, as is clear from what was said above ([4593]Q[76], AA[1],2,3). But in the form of the consecration of the bread, the body of Christ is expressly mentioned, without any addition. Therefore in this form the blood of Christ is improperly expressed in the oblique case, and the chalice in the nominative, when it is said: "This is the chalice of My blood."

Objection 2: Further, the words spoken in the consecration of the bread are not more efficacious than those spoken in the consecration of the wine, since both are Christ's words. But directly the words are spoken---"This is My body," there is perfect consecration of the bread. Therefore, directly these other words are uttered---"This is the chalice of My blood," there is perfect consecration of the blood; and so the words which follow do not appeal to be of the substance of the form, especially since they refer to the properties of this sacrament.

Objection 3: Further, the New Testament seems to be an internal inspiration, as is evident from the Apostle quoting the words of Jeremias (31:31): "I will perfect unto the house of Israel a New Testament . . . I will give My laws into their mind" (Heb. 8:8). But a sacrament is an outward visible act. Therefore, in the form of the sacrament the words "of the New Testament" are improperly added.

Objection 4: Further, a thing is said to be new which is near the beginning of its existence. But what is eternal has no beginning of its existence. Therefore it is incorrect to say "of the New and Eternal," because it seems to savor of a contradiction.

Objection 5: Further, occasions of error ought to be withheld from men, according to Is. 57:14: "Take away the stumbling blocks out of the way of My people." But some have fallen into error in thinking that Christ's body and blood are only mystically present in this sacrament. Therefore it is out of place to add "the mystery of faith."

Objection 6: Further, it was said above ([4594]Q[73], A[3], ad 3), that as Baptism is the sacrament of faith, so is the Eucharist the sacrament of charity. Consequently, in this form the word "charity" ought rather to be used than "faith."

Objection 7: Further, the whole of this sacrament, both as to body and blood, is a memorial of our Lord's Passion, according to 1 Cor. 11:26: "As often as you shall eat this bread and drink the chalice, you shall show the death of the Lord." Consequently, mention ought to be made of Christ's Passion and its fruit rather in the form of the consecration of the blood, than in the form of the consecration of the body, especially since our Lord said: "This is My body, which shall be delivered up for you" (Lk. 22:19).

Objection 8: Further, as was already observed ([4595]Q[48], A[2];[4596] Q[49], A[3]), Christ's Passion sufficed for all; while as to its efficacy it was profitable for many. Therefore it ought to be said: "Which shall be shed for all," or else "for many," without adding, "for you."

Objection 9: Further, the words whereby this sacrament is consecrated draw their efficacy from Christ's institution. But no Evangelist narrates that Christ spoke all these words. Therefore this is not an appropriate form for the consecration of the wine.

On the contrary, The Church, instructed by the apostles, uses this form.

I answer that, There is a twofold opinion regarding this form. Some have maintained that the words "This is the chalice of My blood" alone belong to the substance of this form, but not those words which follow. Now this seems incorrect, because the words which follow them are determinations of the predicate, that is, of Christ's blood. consequently they belong to the integrity of the expression.

And on this account others say more accurately that all the words which follow are of the substance of the form down to the words, "As often as ye shall do this," which belong to the use of this sacrament, and consequently do not belong to the substance of the form. Hence it is that the priest pronounces all these words, under the same rite and manner, namely, holding the chalice in his hands. Moreover, in Lk. 22:20, the words that follow are interposed with the preceding words: "This is the chalice, the new testament in My blood."

Consequently it must be said that all the aforesaid words belong to the substance of the form; but that by the first words, "This is the chalice of My blood," the change of the wine into blood is denoted, as explained above [4597](A[2]) in the form for the consecration of the bread; but by the words which come after is shown the power of the blood shed in the Passion, which power works in this sacrament, and is ordained for three purposes. First and principally for securing our eternal heritage, according to Heb. 10:19: "Having confidence in the entering into the holies by the blood of Christ"; and in order to denote this, we say, "of the New and Eternal Testament." Secondly, for justifying by grace, which is by faith according to Rom. 3:25,26: "Whom God hath proposed to be a propitiation, through faith in His blood . . . that He Himself may be just, and the justifier of him who is of the faith of Jesus Christ": and on this account we add, "The Mystery of Faith." Thirdly, for removing sins which are the impediments to both of these things, according to Heb. 9:14: "The blood of Christ . . . shall cleanse our conscience from dead works," that is, from sins; and on this account, we say, "which shall be shed for you and for many unto the forgiveness of sins."

Reply to Objection 1: The expression "This is the chalice of My blood" is a figure of speech, which can be understood in two ways. First, as a figure of metonymy; because the container is put for the contained, so that the meaning is: "This is My blood contained in the chalice"; of which mention is now made, because Christ's blood is consecrated in this sacrament, inasmuch as it is the drink of the faithful, which is not implied under the notion of blood; consequently this had to be denoted by the vessel adapted for such usage.

Secondly, it can be taken by way of metaphor, so that Christ's Passion is understood by the chalice by way of comparison, because, like a cup, it inebriates, according to Lam. 3:15: "He hath filled me with bitterness, he hath inebriated me with wormwood": hence our Lord Himself spoke of His Passion as a chalice, when He said (Mat. 26:39): "Let this chalice pass away from Me": so that the meaning is: "This is the chalice of My Passion." This is denoted by the blood being consecrated apart from the body; because it was by the Passion that the blood was separated from the body.

Reply to Objection 2: As was said above (ad 1;[4598] Q[76], A[2], ad 1), the blood consecrated apart expressly represents Christ's Passion, and therefore mention is made of the fruits of the Passion in the consecration of the blood rather than in that of the body, since the body is the subject of the Passion. This is also pointed out in our Lord's saying, "which shall be delivered up for you," as if to say, "which shall undergo the Passion for you."

Reply to Objection 3: A testament is the disposal of a heritage. But God disposed of a heavenly heritage to men, to be bestowed through the virtue of the blood of Jesus Christ; because, according to Heb. 9:16: "Where there is a testament the death of the testator must of necessity come in." Now Christ's blood was exhibited to men in two ways. First of all in figure, and this belongs to the Old Testament; consequently the Apostle concludes (Heb. 9:16): "Whereupon neither was the first indeed dedicated without blood," which is evident from this, that as related in Ex. 24:7,8, "when every" commandment of the law "had been read" by Moses, "he sprinkled all the people" saying: "This is the blood of the testament which the Lord hath enjoined unto you."

Secondly, it was shown in very truth; and this belongs to the New Testament. This is what the Apostle premises when he says (Rom. 9:15): "Therefore He is the Mediator of the New Testament, that by means of His death . . . they that are called may receive the promise of eternal inheritance." Consequently, we say here, "The blood of the New Testament," because it is shown now not in figure but in truth; and therefore we add, "which shall be shed for you." But the internal inspiration has its origin in the power of this blood, according as we are justified by Christ's Passion.

Reply to Objection 4: This Testament is a "new one" by reason of its showing forth: yet it is called "eternal" both on account of God's eternal pre-ordination, as well as on account of the eternal heritage which is prepared by this testament. Moreover, Christ's Person is eternal, in Whose blood this testament is appointed.

Reply to Objection 5: The word "mystery" is inserted, not in order to exclude reality, but to show that the reality is hidden, because Christ's blood is in this sacrament in a hidden manner, and His Passion was dimly foreshadowed in the Old Testament.

Reply to Objection 6: It is called the "Sacrament of Faith," as being an object of faith: because by faith alone do we hold the presence of Christ's blood in this sacrament. Moreover Christ's Passion justifies by faith. Baptism is called the "Sacrament of Faith" because it is a profession of faith. This is called the "Sacrament of Charity," as being figurative and effective thereof.

Reply to Objection 7: As stated above (ad 2), the blood consecrated apart represents Christ's blood more expressively; and therefore mention is made of Christ's Passion and its fruits, in the consecration of the blood rather than in that of the body.

Reply to Objection 8: The blood of Christ's Passion has its efficacy not merely in the elect among the Jews, to whom the blood of the Old Testament was exhibited, but also in the Gentiles; nor only in priests who consecrate this sacrament, and in those others who partake of it; but likewise in those for whom it is offered. And therefore He says expressly, "for you," the Jews, "and for many," namely the Gentiles; or, "for you" who eat of it, and "for many," for whom it is offered.

Reply to Objection 9: The Evangelists did not intend to hand down the forms of the sacraments, which in the primitive Church had to be kept concealed, as Dionysius observes at the close of his book on the ecclesiastical hierarchy; their object was to write the story of Christ. Nevertheless nearly all these words can be culled from various passages of the Scriptures. Because the words, "This is the chalice," are found in Lk. 22:20, and 1 Cor. 11:25, while Matthew says in chapter 26:28: "This is My blood of the New Testament, which shall be shed for many unto the remission of sins." The words added, namely, "eternal" and "mystery of faith," were handed down to the Church by the apostles, who received them from our Lord, according to 1 Cor. 11:23: "I have received of the Lord that which also I delivered unto you."

Whether in the aforesaid words of the forms there be any created power which causes the consecration?

Objection 1: It seems that in the aforesaid words of the forms there is no created power which causes the consecration. Because Damascene says (De Fide Orth. iv): "The change of the bread into Christ's body is caused solely by the power of the Holy Ghost." But the power of the Holy Ghost is uncreated. Therefore this sacrament is not caused by any created power of those words.

Objection 2: Further, miraculous works are wrought not by any created power, but solely by Divine power, as was stated in the [4599]FP, Q[110], A[4]. But the change of the bread and wine into Christ's body and blood is a work not less miraculous than the creation of things, or than the formation of Christ's body in the womb of a virgin: which things could not be done by any created power. Therefore, neither is this sacrament consecrated by any created power of the aforesaid words.

Objection 3: Further, the aforesaid words are not simple, but composed of many; nor are they uttered simultaneously, but successively. But, as stated above ([4600]Q[75], A[7]), this change is wrought instantaneously. hence it must be done by a simple power. Therefore it is not effected by the power of those words.

On the contrary, Ambrose says (De Sacram. iv): "If there be such might in the word of the Lord Jesus that things non-existent came into being, how much more efficacious is it to make things existing to continue, and to be changed into something else? And so, what was bread before consecration is now the body of Christ after consecration, because Christ's word changes a creature into something different."

I answer that, Some have maintained that neither in the above words is there any created power for causing the transubstantiation, nor in the other forms of the sacraments, or even in the sacraments themselves, for producing the sacramental effects. This, as was shown above ([4601]Q[62], A[1]), is both contrary to the teachings of the saints, and detracts from the dignity of the sacraments of the New Law. Hence, since this sacrament is of greater worth than the others, as stated above ([4602]Q[65], A[3]), the result is that there is in the words of the form of this sacrament a created power which causes the change to be wrought in it: instrumental, however, as in the other sacraments, as stated above ([4603]Q[62], AA[3],4). For since these words are uttered in the person of Christ, it is from His command that they receive their instrumental power from Him, just as His other deeds and sayings derive their salutary power instrumentally, as was observed above ([4604]Q[48], A[6];[4605] Q[56], A[1], ad 3).

Reply to Objection 1: When the bread is said to be changed into Christ's body solely by the power of the Holy Ghost, the instrumental power which lies in the form of this sacrament is not excluded: just as when we say that the smith alone makes a knife we do not deny the power of the hammer.

Reply to Objection 2: No creature can work miracles as the chief agent. yet it can do so instrumentally, just as the touch of Christ's hand healed the leper. And in this fashion Christ's words change the bread into His body. But in Christ's conception, whereby His body was fashioned, it was impossible for anything derived from His body to have the instrumental power of forming that very body. Likewise in creation there was no term wherein the instrumental action of a creature could be received. Consequently there is no comparison.

Reply to Objection 3: The aforesaid words, which work the consecration, operate sacramentally. Consequently, the converting power latent under the forms of these sacraments follows the meaning, which is terminated in the uttering of the last word. And therefore the aforesaid words have this power in the last instant of their being uttered, taken in conjunction with those uttered before. And this power is simple by reason of the thing signified, although there be composition in the words uttered outwardly.

Day 306

Whether the aforesaid expressions are true?

Objection 1: It seems that the aforesaid expressions are not true. Because when we say: "This is My body," the word "this" designates a substance. But according to what was said above ([4606]AA[1],4, ad 3;[4607] Q[75], AA[2],7), when the pronoun "this" is spoken, the substance of the bread is still there, because the transubstantiation takes place in the last instant of pronouncing the words. But it is false to say: "Bread is Christ's body." Consequently this expression, "This is My body," is false.

Objection 2: Further, the pronoun "this" appeals to the senses. But the sensible species in this sacrament are neither Christ's body nor even its accidents. Therefore this expression, "This is My body," cannot be true.

Objection 3: Further, as was observed above (A[4], ad 3), these words, by their signification, effect the change of the bread into the body of Christ. But an effective cause is understood as preceding its effect. Therefore the meaning of these words is understood as preceding the change of the bread into the body of Christ. But previous to the change this expression, "This is My body," is false. Therefore the expression is to be judged as false simply; and the same reason holds good of the other phrase: "This is the chalice of My blood," etc.

On the contrary, These words are pronounced in the person of Christ, Who says of Himself (Jn. 14:6): "I am the truth."

I answer that, There have been many opinions on this point. Some have said that in this expression, "This is My body," the word "this" implies demonstration as conceived, and not as exercised, because the whole phrase is taken materially, since it is uttered by a way of narration: for the priest relates that Christ said: "This is My body."

But such a view cannot hold good, because then these words would not be applied to the corporeal matter present, and consequently the sacrament would not be valid: for Augustine says (Tract. lxxx in Joan.): "The word is added to the element, and this becomes a sacrament." Moreover this solution ignores entirely the difficulty which this question presents: for there is still the objection in regard to the first uttering of these words by Christ; since it is evident that then they were employed, not materially, but significatively. And therefore it must be said that even when spoken by the priest they are taken significatively, and not merely materially. Nor does it matter that the priest pronounces them by way of recital, as though they were spoken by Christ, because owing to Christ's infinite power, just as through contact with His flesh the regenerative power entered not only into the waters which came into contact with Christ, but into all waters throughout the whole world and during all future ages, so likewise from Christ's uttering these words they derived their consecrating power, by whatever priest they be uttered, as if Christ present were saying them.

And therefore others have said that in this phrase the word "this" appeals, not to the senses, but to the intellect; so that the meaning is, "This is My body"---i.e. "The thing signified by 'this' is My body." But neither can this stand, because, since in the sacraments the effect is that which is signified, from such a form it would not result that Christ's body was in very truth in this sacrament, but merely as in a sign, which is heretical, as stated above ([4608]Q[85], A[1]).

Consequently, others have said that the word "this" appeals to the senses; not at the precise instant of its being uttered, but merely at the last instant thereof; as when a man says, "Now I am silent," this adverb "now" points to the instant immediately following the speech: because the sense is: "Directly these words are spoken I am silent." But neither can this hold good, because in that case the meaning of the sentence would be: "My body is My body," which the above phrase does not effect, because this was so even before the utterance of the words: hence neither does the aforesaid sentence mean this.

Consequently, then, it remains to be said, as stated above [4609](A[4]), that this sentence possesses the power of effecting the conversion of the bread into the body of Christ. And therefore it is compared to other sentences, which have power only of signifying and not of producing, as the concept of the practical intellect, which is productive of the thing, is compared to the concept of our speculative intellect which is drawn from things. because "words are signs of concepts," as the Philosopher says (Peri Herm. i). And therefore as the concept of the practical intellect does not presuppose the thing understood, but makes it, so the truth of this expression does not presuppose the thing signified, but makes it; for such is the relation of God's word to the things made by the Word. Now this change takes place not successively, but in an instant, as stated above (Q[77], A[7]). Consequently one must understand the aforesaid expression with reference to the last instant of the words being spoken, yet not so that the subject may be understood to have stood for that which is the term of the conversion; viz. that the body of Christ is the body of Christ; nor again that the subject be understood to stand for that which it was before the conversion, namely, the bread. but for that which is commonly related to both, i.e. that which is contained in general under those species. For these words do not make the body of Christ to be the body of Christ, nor do they make the bread to be the body of Christ; but what was contained under those species, and was formerly bread, they make to be the body of Christ. And therefore expressly our Lord did not say: "This bread is My body," which would be the meaning of the second opinion; nor "This My body is My body," which would be the meaning of the third opinion: but in general: "This is My body," assigning no noun on the part of the subject, but only a pronoun, which signifies substance in common, without quality, that is, without a determinate form.

Reply to Objection 1: The term "this" points to a substance, yet without determining its proper nature, as stated above.

Reply to Objection 2: The pronoun "this" does not indicate the accidents, but the substance underlying the accidents, which at first was bread, and is afterwards the body of Christ, which body, although not informed by those accidents, is yet contained under them.

Reply to Objection 3: The meaning of this expression is, in the order of nature, understood before the thing signified, just as a cause is naturally prior to the effect; but not in order of time, because this cause has its effect with it at the same time, and this suffices for the truth of the expression.

Whether the form of the consecration of the bread accomplishes its effect before the form of the consecration of the wine be completed?

Objection 1: It seems that the form of the consecration of the bread does not accomplish its effect until the form for the consecration of the wine be completed. For, as Christ's body begins to be in this sacrament by the consecration of the bread, so does His blood come to be there by the consecration of the wine. If, then, the words for consecrating the bread were to produce their effect before the consecration of the wine, it would follow that Christ's body would be present in this sacrament without the blood, which is improper.

Objection 2: Further, one sacrament has one completion: hence although there be three immersions in Baptism, yet the first immersion does not produce its effect until the third be completed. But all this sacrament is one, as stated above ([4610]Q[73], A[2]). Therefore the words whereby the bread is consecrated do not bring about their effect without the sacramental words whereby the wine is consecrated.

Objection 3: Further, there are several words in the form for consecrating the bread, the first of which do not secure their effect until the last be uttered, as stated above (A[4], ad 3). Therefore, for the same reason, neither do the words for the consecration of Christ's body produce their effect, until the words for consecrating Christ's blood are spoken.

On the contrary, Directly the words are uttered for consecrating the bread, the consecrated host is shown to the people to be adored, which would not be done if Christ's body were not there, for that would be an act of idolatry. Therefore the consecrating words of the bread produce their effect before. the words are spoken for consecrating the wine.

I answer that, Some of the earlier doctors said that these two forms, namely, for consecrating the bread and the wine, await each other's action, so that the first does not produce its effect until the second be uttered.

But this cannot stand, because, as stated above (A[5], ad 3), for the truth of this phrase, "This is My body," wherein the verb is in the present tense, it is required for the thing signified to be present simultaneously in time with the signification of the expression used; otherwise, if the thing signified had to be awaited for afterwards, a verb of the future tense would be employed, and not one of the present tense, so that we should not say, "This is My body," but "This will be My body." But the signification of this speech is complete directly those words are spoken. And therefore the thing signified must be present instantaneously, and such is the effect of this sacrament; otherwise it would not be a true speech. Moreover, this opinion is against the rite of the Church, which forthwith adores the body of Christ after the words are uttered.

Hence it must be said that the first form does not await the second in its action, but has its effect on the instant.

Reply to Objection 1: It is on this account that they who maintained the above opinion seem to have erred. Hence it must be understood that directly the consecration of the bread is complete, the body of Christ is indeed present by the power of the sacrament, and the blood by real concomitance; but afterwards by the consecration of the wine, conversely, the blood of Christ is there by the power of the sacrament, and the body by real concomitance, so that the entire Christ is under either species, as stated above ([4611]Q[76], A[2]).

Reply to Objection 2: This sacrament is one in perfection, as stated above ([4612]Q[73] , A[2]), namely, inasmuch as it is made up of two things, that is, of food and drink, each of which of itself has its own perfection; but the three immersions of Baptism are ordained to one simple effect, and therefore there is no resemblance.

Reply to Objection 3: The various words in the form for consecrating the bread constitute the truth of one speech, but the words of the different forms do not, and consequently there is no parallel.

OF THE EFFECTS OF THIS SACRAMENT (EIGHT ARTICLES)
We must now consider the effects of this sacrament, and under this head there are eight points of inquiry:
(1) Whether this sacrament bestows grace?
(2) Whether the attaining of glory is an effect of this sacrament?
(3) Whether the forgiveness of mortal sin is an effect of this sacrament?
(4) Whether venial sin is forgiven by this sacrament?
(5) Whether the entire punishment due for sin is forgiven by this sacrament?
(6) Whether this sacrament preserves man from future sins?
(7) Whether this sacrament benefits others besides the recipients?
(8) Of the obstacles to the effect of this sacrament.

Whether grace is bestowed through this sacrament?
Objection 1: It seems that grace is not bestowed through this sacrament. For this sacrament is spiritual nourishment. But nourishment is only given to the living. Therefore since the spiritual life is the effect of grace, this sacrament belongs only to one in the state of grace. Therefore grace is not bestowed through this sacrament for it to be had in the first instance. In like manner neither is it given so as grace may be increased, because spiritual growth belongs to the sacrament of Confirmation, as stated above ([4613]Q[72], A[1]). Consequently, grace is not bestowed through this sacrament.

Objection 2: Further, this sacrament is given as a spiritual refreshment. But spiritual refreshment seems to belong to the use of grace rather than to its bestowal. Therefore it seems that grace is not given through this sacrament.

Objection 3: Further, as was said above (Q[74], A[1]), "Christ's body is offered up in this sacrament for the salvation of the body, and His blood for that of the soul." Now it is not the body which is the subject of grace, but the soul, as was shown in the [4614]FS, Q[110], A[4]. Therefore grace is not bestowed through this sacrament, at least so far as the body is concerned.

On the contrary, Our Lord says (Jn. 6:52): "The bread which I will give, is My flesh for the life of the world." But the spiritual life is the effect of grace. Therefore grace is bestowed through this sacrament.

I answer that, The effect of this sacrament ought to be considered, first of all and principally, from what is contained in this sacrament, which is Christ; Who, just as by coming into the world, He visibly bestowed the life of grace upon the world, according to Jn. 1:17: "Grace and truth came by Jesus Christ," so also, by coming sacramentally into man causes the life of grace, according to Jn. 6:58: "He that eateth Me, the same also shall live by Me." Hence Cyril says on Lk. 22:19: "God's life-giving Word by uniting Himself with His own flesh, made it to be productive of life. For it was becoming that He should be united somehow with bodies through His sacred flesh and precious blood, which we receive in a life-giving blessing in the bread and wine."

Secondly, it is considered on the part of what is represented by this sacrament, which is Christ's Passion, as stated above ([4615]Q[74], A[1];[4616] Q[76] , A[2], ad 1). And therefore this sacrament works in man the effect which Christ's Passion wrought in the world. Hence, Chrysostom says on the words, "Immediately there came out blood and water" (Jn. 19:34): "Since the sacred mysteries derive their origin from thence, when you draw nigh to the awe-inspiring chalice, so approach as if you were going to drink from Christ's own side." Hence our Lord Himself says (Mat. 26:28): "This is My blood . . . which shall be shed for many unto the remission of sins."

Thirdly, the effect of this sacrament is considered from the way in which this sacrament is given; for it is given by way of food and drink. And therefore this sacrament does for the spiritual life all that material food does for the bodily life, namely, by sustaining, giving increase, restoring, and giving delight. Accordingly, Ambrose says (De Sacram. v): "This is the bread of everlasting life, which supports the substance of our soul." And Chrysostom says (Hom. xlvi in Joan.): "When we desire it, He lets us feel Him, and eat Him, and embrace Him." And hence our Lord says (Jn. 6:56): "My flesh is meat indeed, and My blood is drink indeed."

Fourthly, the effect of this sacrament is considered from the species under which it is given. Hence Augustine says (Tract. xxvi in Joan.): "Our Lord betokened His body and blood in things which out of many units are made into some one whole: for out of many grains is one thing made," viz. bread; "and many grapes flow into one thing," viz. wine. And therefore he observes elsewhere (Tract. xxvi in Joan.): "O sacrament of piety, O sign of unity, O bond of charity!"

And since Christ and His Passion are the cause of grace. and since spiritual refreshment, and charity cannot be without grace, it is clear from all that has been set forth that this sacrament bestows grace.

Reply to Objection 1: This sacrament has of itself the power of bestowing grace; nor does anyone possess grace before receiving this sacrament except from some desire thereof; from his own desire, as in the case of the adult. or from the Church's desire in the case of children, as stated above ([4617]Q[73], A[3]). Hence it is due to the efficacy of its power, that even from desire thereof a man procures grace whereby he is enabled to lead the spiritual life. It remains, then, that when the sacrament itself is really received, grace is increased, and the spiritual life perfected: yet in different fashion from the sacrament of Confirmation, in which grace is increased and perfected for resisting the outward assaults of Christ's enemies. But by this sacrament grace receives increase, and the spiritual life is perfected, so that man may stand perfect in himself by union with God.

Reply to Objection 2: This sacrament confers grace spiritually together with the virtue of charity. Hence Damascene (De Fide Orth. iv) compares this sacrament to the burning coal which Isaias saw (Is. 6:6): "For a live ember is not simply wood, but wood united to fire; so also the bread of communion is not simple bread but bread united with the Godhead." But as Gregory observes in a Homily for Pentecost, "God's love is never idle; for, wherever it is it does great works." And consequently through this sacrament, as far as its power is concerned, not only is the habit of grace and of virtue bestowed, but it is furthermore aroused to act, according to 2 Cor. 5:14: "The charity of Christ presseth us." Hence it is that the soul is spiritually nourished through the power of this sacrament, by being spiritually gladdened, and as it were inebriated with the sweetness of the Divine goodness, according to Cant 5:1: "Eat, O friends, and drink, and be inebriated, my dearly beloved."

Reply to Objection 3: Because the sacraments operate according to the similitude by which they signify, therefore by way of assimilation it is said that in this sacrament "the body is offered for the salvation of the body, and the blood for the salvation of the soul," although each works for the salvation of both, since the entire Christ is under each, as stated above ([4618]Q[76], A[2]). And although the body is not the immediate subject of grace, still the effect of grace flows into the body while in the present life we present "our [Vulg.: 'your'] members" as "instruments of justice unto God" (Rom. 6:13), and in the life to come our body will share in the incorruption and the glory of the soul.

Whether the attaining of glory is an effect of this sacrament?

Objection 1: It seems that the attaining of glory is not an effect of this sacrament. For an effect is proportioned to its cause. But this sacrament belongs to "wayfarers" [viatoribus], and hence it is termed "Viaticum." Since, then, wayfarers are not yet capable of glory, it seems that this sacrament does not cause the attaining of glory.

Objection 2: Further, given sufficient cause, the effect follows. But many take this sacrament who will never come to glory, as Augustine declares (De Civ. Dei xxi). Consequently, this sacrament is not the cause of attaining unto glory.

Objection 3: Further, the greater is not brought about by the lesser, for nothing acts outside its species. But it is the lesser thing to receive Christ under a strange species, which happens in this sacrament, than to enjoy Him in His own species, which belongs to glory. Therefore this sacrament does not cause the attaining of glory.

On the contrary, It is written (Jn. 6:52): "If any man eat of this bread, he shall live for ever." But eternal life is the life of glory. Therefore the attaining of glory is an effect of this sacrament.

I answer that, In this sacrament we may consider both that from which it derives its effect, namely, Christ contained in it, as also His Passion represented by it; and that through which it works its effect, namely, the use of the sacrament, and its species.

Now as to both of these it belongs to this sacrament to cause the attaining of eternal life. Because it was by His Passion that Christ opened to us the approach to eternal life, according to Heb. 9:15: "He is the Mediator of the New Testament; that by means of His death . . . they that are called may receive the promise of eternal inheritance." Accordingly in the form of this sacrament it is said: "This is the chalice of My blood, of the New and Eternal Testament."

In like manner the refreshment of spiritual food and the unity denoted by the species of the bread and wine are to be had in the present life, although imperfectly. but perfectly in the state of glory. Hence Augustine says on the words, "My flesh is meat indeed" (Jn. 6:56): "Seeing that in meat and drink, men aim at this, that they hunger not nor thirst, this verily nought doth afford save only this meat and drink which maketh them who partake thereof to be immortal and incorruptible, in the fellowship of the saints, where shall be peace, and unity, full and perfect."

Reply to Objection 1: As Christ's Passion, in virtue whereof this sacrament is accomplished, is indeed the sufficient cause of glory, yet not so that we are thereby forthwith admitted to glory, but we must first "suffer with Him in order that we may also be glorified" afterwards "with Him" (Rom. 8:17), so this sacrament does not at once admit us to glory, but bestows on us the power of coming unto glory. And therefore it is called "Viaticum," a figure whereof we read in 3 Kings 19:8: "Elias ate and drank, and walked in the strength of that food forty days and forty nights unto the mount of God, Horeb."

Reply to Objection 2: Just as Christ's Passion has not its effect in them who are not disposed towards it as they should be, so also they do not come to glory through this sacrament who receive it unworthily. Hence Augustine (Tract. xxvi in Joan.), expounding the same passage, observes: "The sacrament is one thing, the power of the sacrament another. Many receive it from the altar . . . and by receiving" . . . die . . . Eat, then, spiritually the heavenly "bread, bring innocence to the altar." It is no wonder, then, if those who do not keep innocence, do not secure the effect of this sacrament.

Reply to Objection 3: That Christ is received under another species belongs to the nature of a sacrament, which acts instrumentally. But there is nothing to prevent an instrumental cause from producing a more mighty effect, as is evident from what was said above ([4619]Q[77], A[3], ad 3).

Whether the forgiveness of mortal sin is an effect of this sacrament?

Objection 1: It seems that the forgiveness of mortal sin is an effect of this sacrament. For it is said in one of the Collects (Postcommunion, Pro vivis et defunctis): "May this sacrament be a cleansing from crimes." But mortal sins are called crimes. Therefore mortal sins are blotted out by this sacrament.

Objection 2: Further, this sacrament, like Baptism, works by the power of Christ's Passion. But mortal sins are forgiven by Baptism, as stated above ([4620]Q[69], A[1]). Therefore they are forgiven likewise by this sacrament, especially since in the form of this sacrament it is said: "Which shall be shed for many unto the forgiveness of sins."

Objection 3: Further, grace is bestowed through this sacrament, as stated above [4621](A[1]). But by grace a man is justified from mortal sins, according to Rom. 3:24: "Being justified freely by His grace." Therefore mortal sins are forgiven by this sacrament.

On the contrary, It is written (1 Cor. 11:29): "He that eateth and drinketh unworthily, eateth and drinketh judgment to himself": and a gloss of the same passage makes the following commentary: "He eats and drinks unworthily who is in the state of sin, or who handles (the sacrament) irreverently; and such a one eats and drinks judgment, i.e. damnation, unto himself." Therefore, he that is in mortal sin, by taking the sacrament heaps sin upon sin, rather than obtains forgiveness of his sin.

I answer that, The power of this sacrament can be considered in two ways. First of all, in itself: and thus this sacrament has from Christ's Passion the power of forgiving all sins, since the Passion is the fount and cause of the forgiveness of sins.

Secondly, it can be considered in comparison with the recipient of the sacrament, in so far as there is, or is not, found in him an obstacle to receiving the fruit of this sacrament. Now whoever is conscious of mortal sin, has within him an obstacle to receiving the effect of this sacrament; since he is not a proper recipient of this sacrament, both because he is not alive spiritually, and so he ought not to eat the spiritual nourishment, since nourishment is confined to the living; and because he cannot be united with Christ, which is the effect of this sacrament, as long as he retains an attachment towards mortal sin. Consequently, as is said in the book De Eccles. Dogm.: "If the soul leans towards sin, it is burdened rather than purified from partaking of the Eucharist." Hence, in him who is conscious of mortal sin, this sacrament does not cause the forgiveness of sin.

Nevertheless this sacrament can effect the forgiveness of sin in two ways. First of all, by being received, not actually, but in desire; as when a man is first justified from sin. Secondly, when received by one in mortal sin of which he is not conscious, and for which he has no attachment; since possibly he was not sufficiently contrite at first, but by approaching this sacrament devoutly and reverently he obtains the grace of charity, which will perfect his contrition and bring forgiveness of sin.

Reply to Objection 1: We ask that this sacrament may be the "cleansing of crimes," or of those sins of which we are unconscious, according to Ps. 18:13: "Lord, cleanse me from my hidden sins"; or that our contrition may be perfected for the forgiveness of our sins; or that strength be bestowed on us to avoid sin.

Reply to Objection 2: Baptism is spiritual generation, which is a transition from spiritual non-being into spiritual being, and is given by way of ablution. Consequently, in both respects he who is conscious of mortal sin does not improperly approach Baptism. But in this sacrament man receives Christ within himself by way of spiritual nourishment, which is unbecoming to one that lies dead in his sins. Therefore the comparison does not hold good.

Reply to Objection 3: Grace is the sufficient cause of the forgiveness of mortal sin; yet it does not forgive sin except when it is first bestowed on the sinner. But it is not given so in this sacrament. Hence the argument does not prove.

Whether venial sins are forgiven through this sacrament?

Objection 1: It seems that venial sins are not forgiven by this sacrament, because this is the "sacrament of charity," as Augustine says (Tract. xxvi in Joan.). But venial sins are not contrary to charity, as was shown in the [4622]FS, Q[88], AA[1],2; [4623]SS, Q[24], A[10]. Therefore, since contrary is taken away by its contrary, it seems that venial sins are not forgiven by this sacrament.

Objection 2: Further, if venial sins be forgiven by this sacrament, then all of them are forgiven for the same reason as one is. But it does not appear that all are forgiven, because thus one might frequently be without any venial sin, against what is said in 1 Jn. 1:8: "If we say that we have no sin, we deceive ourselves." Therefore no venial sin is forgiven by this sacrament.

Objection 3: Further, contraries mutually exclude each other. But venial sins do not forbid the receiving of this sacrament: because Augustine says on the words, "If any man eat of it he shall [Vulg.: 'may'] not die for ever" (Jn. 6:50): "Bring innocence to the altar: your sins, though they be daily . . . let them not be deadly." Therefore neither are venial sins taken away by this sacrament.

On the contrary, Innocent III says (De S. Alt. Myst. iv) that this sacrament "blots out venial sins, and wards off mortal sins."

I answer that, Two things may be considered in this sacrament, to wit, the sacrament itself, and the reality of the sacrament: and it appears from both that this sacrament has the power of forgiving venial sins. For this sacrament is received under the form of nourishing food. Now nourishment from food is requisite for the body to make good the daily waste caused by the action of natural heat. But something is also lost daily of our spirituality from the heat of concupiscence through venial sins, which lessen the fervor of charity, as was shown in the [4624]SS, Q[24], A[10]. And therefore it belongs to this sacrament to forgive venial sins. Hence Ambrose says (De Sacram. v) that this daily bread is taken "as a remedy against daily infirmity."

The reality of this sacrament is charity, not only as to its habit, but also as to its act, which is kindled in this sacrament; and by this means venial sins are forgiven. Consequently, it is manifest that venial sins are forgiven by the power of this sacrament.

Reply to Objection 1: Venial sins, although not opposed to the habit of charity, are nevertheless opposed to the fervor of its act, which act is kindled by this sacrament; by reason of which act venial sins are blotted out.

Reply to Objection 1: The passage quoted is not to be understood as if a man could not at some time be without all guilt of venial sin: but that the just do not pass through this life without committing venial sins.

Reply to Objection 3: The power of charity, to which this sacrament belongs, is greater than that of venial sins: because charity by its act takes away venial sins, which nevertheless cannot entirely hinder the act of charity. And the same holds good of this sacrament.

Whether the entire punishment due to sin is forgiven through this sacrament?

Objection 1: It seems that the entire punishment due to sin is forgiven through this sacrament. For through this sacrament man receives the effect of Christ's Passion within himself as stated above ([4625]AA[1],2), just as he does through Baptism. But through Baptism man receives forgiveness of all punishment, through the virtue of Christ's Passion, which satisfied sufficiently for all sins, as was explained above (Q[69], A[2]). Therefore it seems the whole debt of punishment is forgiven through this sacrament.

Objection 2: Further, Pope Alexander I says (Ep. ad omnes orth.): "No sacrifice can be greater than the body and the blood of Christ." But man satisfied for his sins by the sacrifices of the old Law: for it is written (Lev. 4, 5): "If a man shall sin, let him offer" (so and so) "for his sin, and it shall be forgiven him." Therefore this sacrament avails much more for the forgiveness of all punishment.

Objection 3: Further, it is certain that some part of the debt of punishment is forgiven by this sacrament; for which reason it is sometimes enjoined upon a man, by way of satisfaction, to have masses said for himself. But if one part of the punishment is forgiven, for the same reason is the other forgiven: owing to Christ's infinite power contained in this sacrament. Consequently, it seems that the whole punishment can be taken away by this sacrament.

On the contrary, In that case no other punishment would have to be enjoined; just as none is imposed upon the newly baptized.

I answer that, This sacrament is both a sacrifice and a sacrament. it has the nature of a sacrifice inasmuch as it is offered up; and it has the nature of a sacrament inasmuch as it is received. And therefore it has the effect of a sacrament in the recipient, and the effect of a sacrifice in the offerer, or in them for whom it is offered.

If, then, it be considered as a sacrament, it produces its effect in two ways: first of all directly through the power of the sacrament; secondly as by a kind of concomitance, as was said above regarding what is contained in the sacrament ([4626]Q[76], AA[1],2). Through the power of the sacrament it produces directly that effect for which it was instituted. Now it was instituted not for satisfaction, but for nourishing spiritually through union between Christ and His members, as nourishment is united with the person nourished. But because this union is the effect of charity, from the fervor of which man obtains forgiveness, not only of guilt but also of punishment, hence it is that as a consequence, and by concomitance with the chief effect, man obtains forgiveness of the punishment, not indeed of the entire punishment, but according to the measure of his devotion and fervor.

But in so far as it is a sacrifice, it has a satisfactory power. Yet in satisfaction, the affection of the offerer is weighed rather than the quantity of the offering. Hence our Lord says (Mk. 12:43: cf. Lk. 21:4) of the widow who offered "two mites" that she "cast in more than all." Therefore, although this offering suffices of its own quantity to satisfy for all punishment, yet it becomes satisfactory for them for whom it is offered, or even for the offerers, according to the measure of their devotion, and not for the whole punishment.

Reply to Objection 1: The sacrament of Baptism is directly ordained for the remission of punishment and guilt: not so the Eucharist, because Baptism is given to man as dying with Christ, whereas the Eucharist is given as by way of nourishing and perfecting him through Christ. Consequently there is no parallel.

Reply to Objection 2: Those other sacrifices and oblations did not effect the forgiveness of the whole punishment, neither as to the quantity of the thing offered, as this sacrament does, nor as to personal devotion; from which it comes to pass that even here the whole punishment is not taken away.

Reply to Objection 3: If part of the punishment and not the whole be taken away by this sacrament, it is due to a defect not on the part of Christ's power, but on the part of man's devotion.

Whether man is preserved by this sacrament from future sins?

Objection 1: It seems that man is not preserved by this sacrament from future sins. For there are many that receive this sacrament worthily, who afterwards fall into sin. Now this would not happen if this sacrament were to preserve them from future sins. Consequently, it is not an effect of this sacrament to preserve from future sins.

Objection 2: Further, the Eucharist is the sacrament of charity, as stated above [4627](A[4]). But charity does not seem to preserve from future sins, because it can be lost through sin after one has possessed it, as was stated in the [4628]SS, Q[24], A[11]. Therefore it seems that this sacrament does not preserve man from sin.

Objection 3: Further, the origin of sin within us is "the law of sin, which is in our members," as declared by the Apostle (Rom. 7:23). But the lessening of the fomes, which is the law of sin, is set down as an effect not of this sacrament, but rather of Baptism. Therefore preservation from sin is not an effect of this sacrament.

On the contrary, our Lord said (Jn. 6:50): "This is the bread which cometh down from heaven; that if any man eat of it, he may not die": which manifestly is not to be understood of the death of the body. Therefore it is to be understood that this sacrament preserves from spiritual death, which is through sin.

I answer that, Sin is the spiritual death of the soul. Hence man is preserved from future sin in the same way as the body is preserved from future death of the body: and this happens in two ways. First of all, in so far as man's nature is strengthened inwardly against inner decay, and so by means of food and medicine he is preserved from death. Secondly, by being guarded against outward assaults; and thus he is protected by means of arms by which he defends his body.

Now this sacrament preserves man from sin in both of these ways. For, first of all, by uniting man with Christ through grace, it strengthens his spiritual life, as spiritual food and spiritual medicine, according to Ps. 103:5: "(That) bread strengthens [Vulg.: 'may strengthen'] man's heart." Augustine likewise says (Tract. xxvi in Joan.): "Approach without fear; it is bread, not poison." Secondly, inasmuch as it is a sign of Christ's Passion, whereby the devils are conquered, it repels all the assaults of demons. Hence Chrysostom says (Hom. xlvi in Joan.): "Like lions breathing forth fire, thus do we depart from that table, being made terrible to the devil."

Reply to Objection 1: The effect of this sacrament is received according to man's condition: such is the case with every active cause in that its effect is received in matter according to the condition of the matter. But such is the condition of man on earth that his free-will can be bent to good or evil. Hence, although this sacrament of itself has the power of preserving from sin, yet it does not take away from man the possibility of sinning.

Reply to Objection 2: Even charity of itself keeps man from sin, according to Rom. 13:10: "The love of our neighbor worketh no evil": but it is due to the mutability of free-will that a man sins after possessing charity, just as after receiving this sacrament.

Reply to Objection 3: Although this sacrament is not ordained directly to lessen the fomes, yet it does lessen it as a consequence, inasmuch as it increases charity, because, as Augustine says ([4629]Q[83]), "the increase of charity is the lessening of concupiscence." But it directly strengthens man's heart in good; whereby he is also preserved from sin.

Day 307

Whether this sacrament benefit others besides the recipients?

Objection 1: It seems that this sacrament benefits only the recipients. For this sacrament is of the same genus as the other sacraments, being one of those into which that genus is divided. But the other sacraments only benefit the recipients; thus the baptized person alone receives effect of Baptism. Therefore, neither does this sacrament benefit others than the recipients.

Objection 2: Further, the effects of this sacrament are the attainment of grace and glory, and the forgiveness of sin, at least of venial sin. If therefore this sacrament were to produce its effects in others besides the recipients, a man might happen to acquire grace and glory and forgiveness of sin without doing or receiving anything himself, through another receiving or offering this sacrament.

Objection 3: Further, when the cause is multiplied, the effect is likewise multiplied. If therefore this sacrament benefit others besides the recipients, it would follow that it benefits a man more if he receive this sacrament through many hosts being consecrated in one mass, whereas this is not the Church's custom: for instance, that many receive communion for the salvation of one individual. Consequently, it does not seem that this sacrament benefits anyone but the recipient.

On the contrary, Prayer is made for many others during the celebration of this sacrament; which would serve no purpose were the sacrament not beneficial to others. Therefore, this sacrament is beneficial not merely to them who receive it.

I answer that, As stated above [4630](A[3]), this sacrament is not only a sacrament, but also a sacrifice. For, it has the nature of a sacrifice inasmuch as in this sacrament Christ's Passion is represented, whereby Christ "offered Himself a Victim to God" (Eph. 5:2), and it has the nature of a sacrament inasmuch as invisible grace is bestowed in this sacrament under a visible species. So, then, this sacrament benefits recipients by way both of sacrament and of sacrifice, because it is offered for all who partake of it. For it is said in the Canon of the Mass: "May as many of us as, by participation at this Altar, shall receive the most sacred body and blood of Thy Son, be filled with all heavenly benediction and grace."

But to others who do not receive it, it is beneficial by way of sacrifice, inasmuch as it is offered for their salvation. Hence it is said in the Canon of the Mass: "Be mindful, O Lord, of Thy servants, men and women . . . for whom we offer, or who offer up to Thee, this sacrifice of praise for themselves and for all their own, for the redemption of their souls, for the hope of their safety and salvation." And our Lord expressed both ways, saying (Mat. 26:28, with Lk. 22:20): "Which for you," i.e. who receive it, "and for many," i.e. others, "shall be shed unto remission of sins."

Reply to Objection 1: This sacrament has this in addition to the others, that it is a sacrifice: and therefore the comparison fails.

Reply to Objection 2: As Christ's Passion benefits all, for the forgiveness of sin and the attaining of grace and glory, whereas it produces no effect except in those who are united with Christ's Passion through faith and charity, so likewise this sacrifice, which is the memorial of our Lord's Passion, has no effect except in those who are united with this sacrament through faith and charity. Hence Augustine says to Renatus (De Anima et ejus origine i): "Who may offer Christ's body except for them who are Christ's members?" Hence in the Canon of the Mass no prayer is made for them who are outside the pale of the Church. But it benefits them who are members, more or less, according to the measure of their devotion.

Reply to Objection 3: Receiving is of the very nature of the sacrament, but offering belongs to the nature of sacrifice: consequently, when one or even several receive the body of Christ, no help accrues to others. In like fashion even when the priest consecrates several hosts in one mass, the effect of this sacrament is not increased, since there is only one sacrifice; because there is no more power in several hosts than in one, since there is only one Christ present under all the hosts and under one. Hence, neither will any one receive greater effect from the sacrament by taking many consecrated hosts in one mass. But the oblation of the sacrifice is multiplied in several masses, and therefore the effect of the sacrifice and of the sacrament is multiplied.

Whether the effect of this sacrament is hindered by venial sin?

Objection 1: It seems that the effect of this sacrament is not hindered by venial sin. For Augustine (Tract. xxvi in Joan.), commenting on Jn. 6:52, "If any man eat of this bread," etc., says: "Eat the heavenly bread spiritually; bring innocence to the altar; your sins, though they be daily, let them not be deadly." From this it is evident that venial sins, which are called daily sins, do not prevent spiritual eating. But they who eat spiritually, receive the effect of this sacrament. Therefore, venial sins do not hinder the effect of this sacrament.

Objection 2: Further, this sacrament is not less powerful than Baptism. But, as stated above ([4631]Q[69], AA[9],10), only pretense checks the effect of Baptism, and venial sins do not belong to pretense; because according to Wis. 1:5: "the Holy Spirit of discipline will flee from the deceitful," yet He is not put to flight by venial sins. Therefore neither do venial sins hinder the effect of this sacrament.

Objection 3: Further, nothing which is removed by the action of any cause, can hinder the effect of such cause. But venial sins are taken away by this sacrament. Therefore, they do not hinder its effect.

On the contrary, Damascene says (De Fide Orth. iv): "The fire of that desire which is within us, being kindled by the burning coal," i.e. this sacrament, "will consume our sins, and enlighten our hearts, so that we shall be inflamed and made godlike." But the fire of our desire or love is hindered by venial sins, which hinder the fervor of charity, as was shown in the [4632]FS, Q[81], A[4]; [4633]SS, Q[24], A[10]. Therefore venial sins hinder the effect of this sacrament.

I answer that, Venial sins can be taken in two ways: first of all as past, secondly as in the act of being committed. Venial sins taken in the first way do not in any way hinder the effect of this sacrament. For it can come to pass that after many venial sins a man may approach devoutly to this sacrament and fully secure its effect. Considered in the second way venial sins do not utterly hinder the effect of this sacrament, but merely in part. For, it has been stated above [4634](A[1]), that the effect of this sacrament is not only the obtaining of habitual grace or charity, but also a certain actual refreshment of spiritual sweetness: which is indeed hindered if anyone approach to this sacrament with mind distracted through venial sins; but the increase of habitual grace or of charity is not taken away.

Reply to Objection 1: He that approaches this sacrament with actual venial sin, eats spiritually indeed, in habit but not in act: and therefore he shares in the habitual effect of the sacrament, but not in its actual effect.

Reply to Objection 2: Baptism is not ordained, as this sacrament is, for the fervor of charity as its actual effect. Because Baptism is spiritual regeneration, through which the first perfection is acquired, which is a habit or form; but this sacrament is spiritual eating, which has actual delight.

Reply to Objection 3: This argument deals with past venial sins, which are taken away by this sacrament.

OF THE USE OR RECEIVING OF THIS SACRAMENT IN GENERAL (TWELVE ARTICLES)

We have now to consider the use or receiving of this sacrament, first of all in general; secondly, how Christ used this sacrament.

Under the first heading there are twelve points of inquiry:

(1) Whether there are two ways of eating this sacrament, namely, sacramentally and spiritually?
(2) Whether it belongs to man alone to eat this sacrament spiritually?
(3) Whether it belongs to the just man only to eat it sacramentally?
(4) Whether the sinner sins in eating it sacramentally?
(5) Of the degree of this sin;
(6) Whether this sacrament should be refused to the sinner that approaches it?
(7) Whether nocturnal pollution prevents man from receiving this sacrament?
(8) Whether it is to be received only when one is fasting?
(9) Whether it is to be given to them who lack the use of reason?
(10) Whether it is to be received daily?
(11) Whether it is lawful to refrain from it altogether?
(12) Whether it is lawful to receive the body without the blood?

Whether there are two ways to be distinguished of eating Christ's body?

Objection 1: It seems that two ways ought not to be distinguished of eating Christ's body, namely, sacramentally and spiritually. For, as Baptism is spiritual regeneration, according to Jn. 3:5: "Unless a man be born again of water and the Holy Ghost," etc., so also this sacrament is spiritual food: hence our Lord, speaking of this sacrament, says (Jn. 6:64): "The words that I have spoken to you are spirit and life." But there are no two distinct ways of receiving Baptism, namely, sacramentally and spiritually. Therefore neither ought this distinction to be made regarding this sacrament.

Objection 2: Further, when two things are so related that one is on account of the other, they should not be put in contra-distinction to one another, because the one derives its species from the other. But sacramental eating is ordained for spiritual eating as its end. Therefore sacramental eating ought not to be divided in contrast with spiritual eating.

Objection 3: Further, things which cannot exist without one another ought not to be divided in contrast with each other. But it seems that no one can eat spiritually without eating sacramentally; otherwise the fathers of old would have eaten this sacrament spiritually. Moreover, sacramental eating would be to no purpose, if the spiritual eating could be had without it. Therefore it is not right to distinguish a twofold eating, namely, sacramental and spiritual.

On the contrary, The gloss says on 1 Cor. 11:29: "He that eateth and drinketh unworthily," etc.: "We hold that there are two ways of eating, the one sacramental, and the other spiritual."

I answer that, There are two things to be considered in the receiving of this sacrament, namely, the sacrament itself, and its fruits, and we have already spoken of both (QQ[73],79). The perfect way, then, of receiving this sacrament is when one takes it so as to partake of its effect. Now, as was stated above ([4635]Q[79], AA[3],8), it sometimes happens that a man is hindered from receiving the effect of this sacrament; and such receiving of this sacrament is an imperfect one. Therefore, as the perfect is divided against the imperfect, so sacramental eating, whereby the sacrament only is received without its effect, is divided against spiritual eating, by which one receives the effect of this sacrament, whereby a man is spiritually united with Christ through faith and charity.

Reply to Objection 1: The same distinction is made regarding Baptism and the other sacraments: for, some receive the sacrament only, while others receive the sacrament and the reality of the sacrament. However, there is a difference, because, since the other sacraments are accomplished in the use of the matter, the receiving of the sacrament is the actual perfection of the sacrament; whereas this sacrament is accomplished in the consecration of the matter: and consequently both uses follow the sacrament. On the other hand, in Baptism and in the other sacraments that imprint a character, they who receive the sacrament receive some spiritual effect, that is, the character. which is not the case in this sacrament. And therefore, in this sacrament, rather than in Baptism, the sacramental use is distinguished from the spiritual use.

Reply to Objection 2: That sacramental eating which is also a spiritual eating is not divided in contrast with spiritual eating, but is included under it; but that sacramental eating which does not secure the effect, is divided in contrast with spiritual eating; just as the imperfect, which does not attain the perfection of its species, is divided in contrast with the perfect.

Reply to Objection 3: As stated above ([4636]Q[73], A[3]), the effect of the sacrament can be secured by every man if he receive it in desire, though not in reality. Consequently, just as some are baptized with the Baptism of desire, through their desire of baptism, before being baptized in the Baptism of water; so likewise some eat this sacrament spiritually ere they receive it sacramentally. Now this happens in two ways. First of all, from desire of receiving the sacrament itself, and thus are said to be baptized, and to eat spiritually, and not sacramentally, they who desire to receive these sacraments since they have been instituted. Secondly, by a figure: thus the Apostle says (1 Cor. 10:2), that the fathers of old were "baptized in the cloud and in the sea," and that "they did eat . . . spiritual food, and . . . drank . . . spiritual drink." Nevertheless sacramental eating is not without avail, because the actual receiving of the sacrament produces more fully the effect of the sacrament than does the desire thereof, as stated above of Baptism ([4637]Q[69] , A[4], ad 2).

Whether it belongs to man alone to eat this sacrament spiritually?

Objection 1: It seems that it does not belong to man alone to eat this sacrament spiritually, but likewise to angels. Because on Ps. 77:25: "Man ate the bread of angels," the gloss says: "that is, the body of Christ, Who i's truly the food of angels." But it would not be so unless the angels were to eat Christ spiritually. Therefore the angels eat Christ spiritually.

Objection 2: Further, Augustine (Tract. xxvi in Joan.) says: By "this meat and drink, He would have us to understand the fellowship of His body and members, which is the Church in His predestinated ones." But not only men, but also the holy angels belong to that fellowship. Therefore the holy angels eat of it spiritually.

Objection 3: Further, Augustine in his book De Verbis Domini (Serm. cxlii) says: "Christ is to be eaten spiritually, as He Himself declares: 'He that eateth My flesh and drinketh My blood, abideth in Me, and I in him.'" But this belongs not only to men, but also to the holy angels, in whom Christ dwells by charity, and they in Him. Consequently, it seems that to eat Christ spiritually is not for men only, but also for the angels.

On the contrary, Augustine (Tract. xxvi in Joan.) says: "Eat the bread" of the altar "spiritually; take innocence to the altar." But angels do not approach the altar as for the purpose of taking something therefrom. Therefore the angels do not eat spiritually.

I answer that, Christ Himself is contained in this sacrament, not under His proper species, but under the sacramental species. Consequently there are two ways of eating spiritually. First, as Christ Himself exists under His proper species, and in this way the angels eat Christ spiritually inasmuch as they are united with Him in the enjoyment of perfect charity, and in clear vision (and this is the bread we hope for in heaven), and not by faith, as we are united with Him here.

In another way one may eat Christ spiritually, as He is under the sacramental species, inasmuch as a man believes in Christ, while desiring to receive this sacrament; and this is not merely to eat Christ spiritually, but likewise to eat this sacrament; which does not fall to the lot of the angels. And therefore although the angels feed on Christ spiritually, yet it does not belong to them to eat this sacrament spiritually.

Reply to Objection 1: The receiving of Christ under this sacrament is ordained to the enjoyment of heaven, as to its end, in the same way as the angels enjoy it; and since the means are gauged by the end, hence it is that such eating of Christ whereby we receive Him under this sacrament, is, as it were, derived from that eating whereby the angels enjoy Christ in heaven. Consequently, man is said to eat the "bread of angels," because it belongs to the angels to do so firstly and principally, since they enjoy Him in his proper species; and secondly it belongs to men, who receive Christ under this sacrament.

Reply to Objection 2: Both men and angels belong to the fellowship of His mystical body; men by faith, and angels by manifest vision. But the sacraments are proportioned to faith, through which the truth is seen "through a glass" and "in a dark manner." And therefore, properly speaking, it does not belong to angels, but to men, to eat this sacrament spiritually.

Reply to Objection 3: Christ dwells in men through faith, according to their present state, but He is in the blessed angels by manifest vision. Consequently the comparison does not hold, as stated above (ad 2).

Whether the just man alone may eat Christ sacramentally?

Objection 1: It seems that none but the just man may eat Christ sacramentally. For Augustine says in his book De Remedio Penitentiae (cf. Tract. in Joan. xxv, n. 12; xxvi, n. 1): "Why make ready tooth and belly? Believe, and thou hast eaten . . . For to believe in Him, this it is, to eat the living bread." But the sinner does not believe in Him; because he has not living faith, to which it belongs to believe "in God," as stated above in the [4638]SS, Q[2], A[2]; [4639]SS, Q[4], A[5]. Therefore the sinner cannot eat this sacrament, which is the living bread.

Objection 2: Further, this sacrament is specially called "the sacrament of charity," as stated above ([4640]Q[78], A[3], ad 6). But as unbelievers lack faith, so all sinners lack charity. Now unbelievers do not seem to be capable of eating this sacrament, since in the sacramental form it is called the "Mystery of Faith." Therefore, for like reason, the sinner cannot eat Christ's body sacramentally.

Objection 3: Further, the sinner is more abominable before God than the irrational creature: for it is said of the sinner (Ps. 48:21): "Man when he was in honor did not understand; he hath been compared to senseless beasts, and made like to them." But an irrational animal, such as a mouse or a dog, cannot receive this sacrament, just as it cannot receive the sacrament of Baptism. Therefore it seems that for the like reason neither may sinners eat this sacrament.

On the contrary, Augustine (Tract. xxvi in Joan.), commenting on the words, "that if any man eat of it he may not die," says: "Many receive from the altar, and by receiving die: whence the Apostle saith, 'eateth and drinketh judgment to himself.'" But only sinners die by receiving. Therefore sinners eat the body of Christ sacramentally, and not the just only.

I answer that, In the past, some have erred upon this point, saying that Christ's body is not received sacramentally by sinners; but that directly the body is touched by the lips of sinners, it ceases to be under the sacramental species.

But this is erroneous; because it detracts from the truth of this sacrament, to which truth it belongs that so long as the species last, Christ's body does not cease to be under them, as stated above ([4641]Q[76], A[6], ad 3;[4642] Q[77], A[8]). But the species last so long as the substance of the bread would remain, if it were there, as was stated above ([4643]Q[77], A[4]). Now it is clear that the substance of bread taken by a sinner does not at once cease to be, but it continues until digested by natural heat: hence Christ's body remains just as long under the sacramental species when taken by sinners. Hence it must be said that the sinner, and not merely the just, can eat Christ's body.

Reply to Objection 1: Such words and similar expressions are to be understood of spiritual eating, which does not belong to sinners. Consequently, it is from such expressions being misunderstood that the above error seems to have arisen, through ignorance of the distinction between corporeal and spiritual eating.

Reply to Objection 2: Should even an unbeliever receive the sacramental species, he would receive Christ's body under the sacrament: hence he would eat Christ sacramentally, if the word "sacramentally" qualify the verb on the part of the thing eaten. But if it qualify the verb on the part of the one eating, then, properly speaking, he does not eat sacramentally, because he uses what he takes, not as a sacrament, but as simple food. Unless perchance the unbeliever were to intend to receive what the Church bestows; without having proper faith regarding the other articles, or regarding this sacrament.

Reply to Objection 3: Even though a mouse or a dog were to eat the consecrated host, the substance of Christ's body would not cease to be under the species, so long as those species remain, and that is, so long as the substance of bread would have remained; just as if it were to be cast into the mire. Nor does this turn to any indignity regarding Christ's body, since He willed to be crucified by sinners without detracting from His dignity; especially since the mouse or dog does not touch Christ's body in its proper species, but only as to its sacramental species. Some, however, have said that Christ's body would cease to be there, directly it were touched by a mouse or a dog; but this again detracts from the truth of the sacrament, as stated above. None the less it must not be said that the irrational animal eats the body of Christ sacramentally; since it is incapable of using it as a sacrament. Hence it eats Christ's body "accidentally," and not sacramentally, just as if anyone not knowing a host to be consecrated were to consume it. And since no genus is divided by an accidental difference, therefore this manner of eating Christ's body is not set down as a third way besides sacramental and spiritual eating.

Whether the sinner sins in receiving Christ's body sacramentally?

Objection 1: It seems that the sinner does not sin in receiving Christ's body sacramentally, because Christ has no greater dignity under the sacramental species than under His own. But sinners did not sin when they touched Christ's body under its proper species; nay, rather they obtained forgiveness of their sins, as we read in Lk. 7 of the woman who was a sinner; while it is written (Mat. 14:36) that "as many as touched the hem of His garment were healed." Therefore, they do not sin, but rather obtain salvation, by receiving the body of Christ.

Objection 2: Further, this sacrament, like the others, is a spiritual medicine. But medicine is given to the sick for their recovery, according to Mat. 9:12: "They that are in health need not a physician." Now they that are spiritually sick or infirm are sinners. Therefore this sacrament can be received by them without sin.

Objection 3: Further, this sacrament is one of our greatest gifts, since it contains Christ. But according to Augustine (De Lib. Arb. ii), the greatest gifts are those "which no one can abuse." Now no one sins except by abusing something. Therefore no sinner sins by receiving this sacrament.

Objection 4: Further, as this sacrament is perceived by taste and touch, so also is it by sight. Consequently, if the sinner sins by receiving the sacrament, it seems that he would sin by beholding it, which is manifestly untrue, since the Church exposes this sacrament to be seen and adored by all. Therefore the sinner does not sin by eating this sacrament.

Objection 5: Further, it happens sometimes that the sinner is unconscious of his sin. Yet such a one does not seem to sin by receiving the body of Christ, for according to this all who receive it would sin, as exposing themselves to danger, since the Apostle says (1 Cor. 4:4): "I am not conscious to myself of anything, yet I am not hereby justified." Therefore, the sinner, if he receive this sacrament, does not appear to be guilty of sin.

On the contrary, The Apostle says (1 Cor. 11:29): "He that eateth and drinketh unworthily, eateth and drinketh judgment to himself." Now the gloss says on this passage: "He eats and drinks unworthily who is in sin, or who handles it irreverently." Therefore, if anyone, while in mortal sin, receives this sacrament, he purchases damnation, by sinning mortally.

I answer that, In this sacrament, as in the others, that which is a sacrament is a sign of the reality of the sacrament. Now there is a twofold reality of this sacrament, as stated above ([4644]Q[73], A[6]): one which is signified and contained, namely, Christ Himself; while the other is signified but not contained, namely, Christ's mystical body, which is the fellowship of the saints. Therefore, whoever receives this sacrament, expresses thereby that he is made one with Christ, and incorporated in His members; and this is done by living faith, which no one has who is in mortal sin. And therefore it is manifest that whoever receives this sacrament while in mortal sin, is guilty of lying to this sacrament, and consequently of sacrilege, because he profanes the sacrament: and therefore he sins mortally.

Reply to Objection 1: When Christ appeared under His proper species, He did not give Himself to be touched by men as a sign of spiritual union with Himself, as He gives Himself to be received in this sacrament. And therefore sinners in touching Him under His proper species did not incur the sin of lying to Godlike things, as sinners do in receiving this sacrament.

Furthermore, Christ still bore the likeness of the body of sin; consequently He fittingly allowed Himself to be touched by sinners. But as soon as the body of sin was taken away by the glory of the Resurrection, he forbade the woman to touch Him, for her faith in Him was defective, according to Jn. 20:17: "Do not touch Me, for I am not yet ascended to My Father," i.e. "in your heart," as Augustine explains (Tract. cxxi in Joan.). And therefore sinners, who lack living faith regarding Christ are not allowed to touch this sacrament.

Reply to Objection 2: Every medicine does not suit every stage of sickness; because the tonic given to those who are recovering from fever would be hurtful to them if given while yet in their feverish condition. So likewise Baptism and Penance are as purgative medicines, given to take away the fever of sin; whereas this sacrament is a medicine given to strengthen, and it ought not to be given except to them who are quit of sin.

Reply to Objection 3: By the greatest gifts Augustine understands the soul's virtues, "which no one uses to evil purpose," as though they were principles of evil. Nevertheless sometimes a man makes a bad use of them, as objects of an evil use, as is seen in those who are proud of their virtues. So likewise this sacrament, so far as the sacrament is concerned, is not the principle of an evil use, but the object thereof. Hence Augustine says (Tract. lxii in Joan.): "Many receive Christ's body unworthily; whence we are taught what need there is to beware of receiving a good thing evilly . . . For behold, of a good thing, received evilly, evil is wrought": just as on the other hand, in the Apostle's case, "good was wrought through evil well received," namely, by bearing patiently the sting of Satan.

Reply to Objection 4: Christ's body is not received by being seen, but only its sacrament, because sight does not penetrate to the substance of Christ's body, but only to the sacramental species, as stated above ([4645]Q[76], A[7]). But he who eats, receives not only the sacramental species, but likewise Christ Himself Who is under them. Consequently, no one is forbidden to behold Christ's body, when once he has received Christ's sacrament, namely, Baptism: whereas the non-baptized are not to be allowed even to see this sacrament, as is clear from Dionysius (Eccl. Hier. vii). But only those are to be allowed to share in the eating who are united with Christ not merely sacramentally, but likewise really.

Reply to Objection 5: The fact of a man being unconscious of his sin can come about in two ways. First of all through his own fault, either because through ignorance of the law (which ignorance does not excuse him), he thinks something not to be sinful which is a sin, as for example if one guilty of fornication were to deem simple fornication not to be a mortal sin; or because he neglects to examine his conscience, which is opposed to what the Apostle says (1 Cor. 11:28): "Let a man prove himself, and so let him eat of that bread, and drink of the chalice." And in this way nevertheless the sinner who receives Christ's body commits sin, although unconscious thereof, because the very ignorance is a sin on his part.

Secondly, it may happen without fault on his part, as, for instance, when he has sorrowed over his sin, but is not sufficiently contrite: and in such a case he does not sin in receiving the body of Christ, because a man cannot know for certain whether he is truly contrite. It suffices, however, if he find in himself the marks of contrition, for instance, if he "grieve over past sins," and "propose to avoid them in the future" [*Cf. Rule of Augustine]. But if he be ignorant that what he did was a sinful act, through ignorance of the fact, which excuses, for instance, if a man approach a woman whom he believed to be his wife whereas she was not, he is not to be called a sinner on that account; in the same way if he has utterly forgotten his sin, general contrition suffices for blotting it out, as will be said hereafter ([4646]XP, Q[2], A[3], ad 2); hence he is no longer to be called a sinner.

Whether to approach this sacrament with consciousness of sin is the gravest of all sins?

Objection 1: It seems that to approach this sacrament with consciousness of sin is the gravest of all sins; because the Apostle says (1 Cor. 11:27): "Whosoever shall eat this bread, or drink the chalice of the Lord unworthily, shall be guilty of the body and of the blood of the Lord": upon which the gloss observes: "He shall be punished as though he slew Christ." But the sin of them who slew Christ seems to have been most grave. Therefore this sin, whereby a man approaches Christ's table with consciousness of sin, appears to be the gravest.

Objection 2: Further, Jerome says in an Epistle (xlix): "What hast thou to do with women, thou that speakest familiarly with God at the altar?" [*The remaining part of the quotation is not from St. Jerome]. Say, priest, say, cleric, how dost thou kiss the Son of God with the same lips wherewith thou hast kissed the daughter of a harlot? "Judas, thou betrayest the Son of Man with a kiss!" And thus it appears that the fornicator approaching Christ's table sins as Judas did, whose sin was most grave. But there are many other sins which are graver than fornication, especially the sin of unbelief. Therefore the sin of every sinner approaching Christ's table is the gravest of all.

Objection 3: Further, spiritual uncleanness is more abominable to God than corporeal. But if anyone was to cast Christ's body into mud or a cess-pool, his sin would be reputed a most grave one. Therefore, he sins more deeply by receiving it with sin, which is spiritual uncleanness, upon his soul.

On the contrary, Augustine says on the words, "If I had not come, and had not spoken to them, they would be without sin" (Tract. lxxxix in Joan.), that this is to be understood of the sin of unbelief, "in which all sins are comprised," and so the greatest of all sins appears to be, not this, but rather the sin of unbelief.

I answer that, As stated in the [4647]FS, Q[73], AA[3],6; [4648]SS, Q[73], A[3], one sin can be said to be graver than another in two ways: first of all essentially, secondly accidentally. Essentially, in regard to its species, which is taken from its object: and so a sin is greater according as that against which it is committed is greater. And since Christ's Godhead is greater than His humanity, and His humanity greater than the sacraments of His humanity, hence it is that those are the gravest sins which are committed against the Godhead, such as unbelief and blasphemy. The second degree of gravity is held by those sins which are committed against His humanity: hence it is written (Mat. 12:32): "Whosoever shall speak a word against the Son of Man, it shall be forgiven him; but he that shall speak against the Holy Ghost, it shall not be forgiven him, neither in this world nor in the world to come." In the third place come sins committed against the sacraments, which belong to Christ's humanity; and after these are the other sins committed against mere creatures.

Accidentally, one sin can be graver than another on the sinner's part. for example, the sin which is the result of ignorance or of weakness is lighter than one arising from contempt, or from sure knowledge; and the same reason holds good of other circumstances. And according to this, the above sin can be graver in some, as happens in them who from actual contempt and with consciousness of sin approach this sacrament: but in others it is less grave; for instance, in those who from fear of their sin being discovered, approach this sacrament with consciousness of sin.

So, then, it is evident that this sin is specifically graver than many others, yet it is not the greatest of all.

Reply to Objection 1: The sin of the unworthy recipient is compared to the sin of them who slew Christ, by way of similitude, because each is committed against Christ's body; but not according to the degree of the crime. Because the sin of Christ's slayers was much graver, first of all, because their sin was against Christ's body in its own species, while this sin is against it under sacramental species; secondly, because their sin came of the intent of injuring Christ, while this does not.

Reply to Objection 2: The sin of the fornicator receiving Christ's body is likened to Judas kissing Christ, as to the resemblance of the sin, because each outrages Christ with the sign of friendship. but not as to the extent of the sin, as was observed above (ad 1). And this resemblance in crime applies no less to other sinners than to fornicators: because by other mortal sins, sinners act against the charity of Christ, of which this sacrament is the sign, and all the more according as their sins are graver. But in a measure the sin of fornication makes one more unfit for receiving this sacrament, because thereby especially the spirit becomes enslaved by the flesh, which is a hindrance to the fervor of love required for this sacrament.

However, the hindrance to charity itself weighs more than the hindrance to its fervor. Hence the sin of unbelief, which fundamentally severs a man from the unity of the Church, simply speaking, makes him to be utterly unfit for receiving this sacrament; because it is the sacrament of the Church's unity, as stated above ([4649]Q[61], A[2]). Hence the unbeliever who receives this sacrament sins more grievously than the believer who is in sin; and shows greater contempt towards Christ Who is in the sacrament, especially if he does not believe Christ to be truly in this sacrament; because, so far as lies in him, he lessens the holiness of the sacrament, and the power of Christ acting in it, and this is to despise the sacrament in itself. But the believer who receives the sacrament with consciousness of sin, by receiving it unworthily despises the sacrament, not in itself, but in its use. Hence the Apostle (1 Cor. 11:29) in assigning the cause of this sin, says, "not discerning the body of the Lord," that is, not distinguishing it from other food: and this is what he does who disbelieves Christ's presence in this sacrament.

Reply to Objection 3: The man who would throw this sacrament into the mire would be guilty of more heinous sin than another approaching the sacrament fully conscious of mortal sin. First of all, because he would intend to outrage the sacrament, whereas the sinner receiving Christ's body unworthily has no such intent; secondly, because the sinner is capable of grace; hence he is more capable of receiving this sacrament than any irrational creature. Hence he would make a most revolting use of this sacrament who would throw it to dogs to eat, or fling it in the mire to be trodden upon.

Whether the priest ought to deny the body of Christ to the sinner seeking it?

Objection 1: It seems that the priest should deny the body of Christ to the sinner seeking it. For Christ's precept is not to be set aside for the sake of avoiding scandal or on account of infamy to anyone. But (Mat. 7:6) our Lord gave this command: "Give not that which is holy to dogs." Now it is especially casting holy things to dogs to give this sacrament to sinners. Therefore, neither on account of avoiding scandal or infamy should this sacrament be administered to the sinner who asks for it.

Objection 2: Further, one must choose the lesser of two evils. But it seems to be the lesser evil if the sinner incur infamy; or if an unconsecrated host be given to him; than for him to sin mortally by receiving the body of Christ. Consequently, it seems that the course to be adopted is either that the sinner seeking the body of Christ be exposed to infamy, or that an unconsecrated host be given to him.

Objection 3: Further, the body of Christ is sometimes given to those suspected of crime in order to put them to proof. Because we read in the Decretals: "It often happens that thefts are perpetrated in monasteries of monks; wherefore we command that when the brethren have to exonerate themselves of such acts, that the abbot shall celebrate Mass, or someone else deputed by him, in the presence of the community; and so, when the Mass is over, all shall communicate under these words: 'May the body of Christ prove thee today.'" And further on: "If any evil deed be imputed to a bishop or priest, for each charge he must say Mass and communicate, and show that he is innocent of each act imputed." But secret sinners must not be disclosed, for, once the blush of shame is set aside, they will indulge the more in sin, as Augustine says (De Verbis. Dom.; cf. Serm. lxxxii). Consequently, Christ's body is not to be given to occult sinners, even if they ask for it.

On the contrary, on Ps. 21:30: "All the fat ones of the earth have eaten and have adored," Augustine says: "Let not the dispenser hinder the fat ones of the earth," i.e. sinners, "from eating at the table of the Lord."

I answer that, A distinction must be made among sinners: some are secret; others are notorious, either from evidence of the fact, as public usurers, or public robbers, or from being denounced as evil men by some ecclesiastical or civil tribunal. Therefore Holy Communion ought not to be given to open sinners when they ask for it. Hence Cyprian writes to someone (Ep. lxi): "You were so kind as to consider that I ought to be consulted regarding actors, end that magician who continues to practice his disgraceful arts among you; as to whether I thought that Holy Communion ought to be given to such with the other Christians. I think that it is beseeming neither the Divine majesty, nor Christian discipline, for the Church's modesty and honor to be defiled by such shameful and infamous contagion."

But if they be not open sinners, but occult, the Holy Communion should not be denied them if they ask for it. For since every Christian, from the fact that he is baptized, is admitted to the Lord's table, he may not be robbed of his right, except from some open cause. Hence on 1 Cor. 5:11, "If he who is called a brother among you," etc., Augustine's gloss remarks: "We cannot inhibit any person from Communion, except he has openly confessed, or has been named and convicted by some ecclesiastical or lay tribunal." Nevertheless a priest who has knowledge of the crime can privately warn the secret sinner, or warn all openly in public, from approaching the Lord's table, until they have repented of their sins and have been reconciled to the Church; because after repentance and reconciliation, Communion must not be refused even to public sinners, especially in the hour of death. Hence in the (3rd) Council of Carthage (Can. xxxv) we read: "Reconciliation is not to be denied to stage-players or actors, or others of the sort, or to apostates, after their conversion to God."

Reply to Objection 1: Holy things are forbidden to be given to dogs, that is, to notorious sinners: whereas hidden deeds may not be published, but are to be left to the Divine judgment.

Reply to Objection 2: Although it is worse for the secret sinner to sin mortally in taking the body of Christ, rather than be defamed, nevertheless for the priest administering the body of Christ it is worse to commit mortal sin by unjustly defaming the hidden sinner than that the sinner should sin mortally; because no one ought to commit mortal sin in order to keep another out of mortal sin. Hence Augustine says (Quaest. super Gen. 42): "It is a most dangerous exchange, for us to do evil lest another perpetrate a greater evil." But the secret sinner ought rather to prefer infamy than approach the Lord's table unworthily.

Yet by no means should an unconsecrated host be given in place of a consecrated one; because the priest by so doing, so far as he is concerned, makes others, either the bystanders or the communicant, commit idolatry by believing that it is a consecrated host; because, as Augustine says on Ps. 98:5: "Let no one eat Christ's flesh, except he first adore it." Hence in the Decretals (Extra, De Celeb. Miss., Ch. De Homine) it is said: "Although he who reputes himself unworthy of the Sacrament, through consciousness of his sin, sins gravely, if he receive; still he seems to offend more deeply who deceitfully has presumed to simulate it."

Reply to Objection 3: Those decrees were abolished by contrary enactments of Roman Pontiffs: because Pope Stephen V writes as follows: "The Sacred Canons do not allow of a confession being extorted from any person by trial made by burning iron or boiling water; it belongs to our government to judge of public crimes committed, and that by means of confession made spontaneously, or by proof of witnesses: but private and unknown crimes are to be left to Him Who alone knows the hearts of the sons of men." And the same is found in the Decretals (Extra, De Purgationibus, Ch. Ex tuarum). Because in all such practices there seems to be a tempting of God; hence such things cannot be done without sin. And it would seem graver still if anyone were to incur judgment of death through this sacrament, which was instituted as a means of salvation. Consequently, the body of Christ should never be given to anyone suspected of crime, as by way of examination.

Whether the seminal loss that occurs during sleep hinders anyone from receiving this sacrament?

Objection 1: It seems that seminal loss does not hinder anyone from receiving the body of Christ: because no one is prevented from receiving the body of Christ except on account of sin. But seminal loss happens without sin: for Augustine says (Gen. ad lit. xii) that "the same image that comes into the mind of a speaker may present itself to the mind of the sleeper, so that the latter be unable to distinguish the image from the reality, and is moved carnally and with the result that usually follows such motions; and there is as little sin in this as there is in speaking and therefore thinking about such things." Consequently these motions do not prevent one from receiving this sacrament.

Objection 2: Further, Gregory says in a Letter to Augustine, Bishop of the English (Regist. xi): "Those who pay the debt of marriage not from lust, but from desire to have children, should be left to their own judgment, as to whether they should enter the church and receive the mystery of our Lord's body, after such intercourse: because they ought not to be forbidden from receiving it, since they have passed through the fire unscorched."

From this it is evident that seminal loss even of one awake, if it be without sin, is no hindrance to receiving the body of Christ. Consequently, much less is it in the case of one asleep.

Objection 3: Further, these movements of the flesh seem to bring with them only bodily uncleanness. But there are other bodily defilements which according to the Law forbade entrance into the holy places, yet which under the New Law do not prevent receiving this sacrament: as, for instance, in the case of a woman after child-birth, or in her periods, or suffering from issue of blood, as Gregory writes to Augustine, Bishop of the English (Regist. xi). Therefore it seems that neither do these movements of the flesh hinder a man from receiving this sacrament.

Objection 4: Further, venial sin is no hindrance to receiving the sacrament, nor is mortal sin after repentance. But even supposing that seminal loss arises from some foregoing sin, whether of intemperance, or of bad thoughts, for the most part such sin is venial; and if occasionally it be mortal, a man may repent of it by morning and confess it. Consequently, it seems that he ought not to be prevented from receiving this sacrament.

Objection 5: Further, a sin against the Fifth Commandment is greater than a sin against the Sixth. But if a man dream that he has broken the Fifth or Seventh or any other Commandment, he is not on that account debarred from receiving this sacrament. Therefore it seems that much less should he be debarred through defilement resulting from a dream against the Sixth Commandment.

On the contrary, It is written (Lev. 15:16): "The man from whom the seed of copulation goeth out . . . shall be unclean until evening." But for the unclean there is no approaching to the sacraments. Therefore, it seems that owing to such defilement of the flesh a man is debarred from taking this which is the greatest of the sacraments.

I answer that, There are two things to be weighed regarding the aforesaid movements: one on account of which they necessarily prevent a man from receiving this sacrament; the other, on account of which they do so, not of necessity, but from a sense of propriety.

Mortal sin alone necessarily prevents anyone from partaking of this sacrament: and although these movements during sleep, considered in themselves, cannot be a mortal sin, nevertheless, owing to their cause, they have mortal sin connected with them; which cause, therefore, must be investigated. Sometimes they are due to an external spiritual cause, viz. the deception of the demons, who can stir up phantasms, as was stated in the [4650]FP, Q[111], A[3], through the apparition of which, these movements occasionally follow. Sometimes they are due to an internal spiritual cause, such as previous thoughts. At other times they arise from some internal corporeal cause, as from abundance or weakness of nature, or even from surfeit of meat or drink. Now every one of these three causes can be without sin at all, or else with venial sin, or with mortal sin. If it be without sin, or with venial sin, it does not necessarily prevent the receiving of this sacrament, so as to make a man guilty of the body and blood of the Lord: but should it be with mortal sin, it prevents it of necessity.

For such illusions on the part of demons sometimes come from one's not striving to receive fervently; and this can be either a mortal or a venial sin. At other times it is due to malice alone on the part of the demons who wish to keep men from receiving this sacrament. So we read in the Conferences of the Fathers (Cassian, Collat. xxii) that when a certain one always suffered thus on those feast-days on which he had to receive Communion, his superiors, discovering that there was no fault on his part, ruled that he was not to refrain from communicating on that account, and the demoniacal illusion ceased.

In like fashion previous evil thoughts can sometimes be without any sin whatever, as when one has to think of such things on account of lecturing or debating; and if it be done without concupiscence and delectation, the thoughts will not be unclean but honest; and yet defilement can come of such thoughts, as is clear from the authority of Augustine (OBJ[1]). At other times such thoughts come of concupiscence and delectation, and should there be consent, it will be a mortal sin: otherwise it will be a venial sin.

In the same way too the corporeal cause can be without sin, as when it arises from bodily debility, and hence some individuals suffer seminal loss without sin even in their wakeful hours; or it can come from the abundance of nature: for, just as blood can flow without sin, so also can the semen which is superfluity of the blood, according to the Philosopher (De Gener. Animal. i). But occasionally it is with sin, as when it is due to excess of food or drink. And this also can be either venial or mortal sin; although more frequently the sin is mortal in the case of evil thoughts on account of the proneness to consent, rather than in the case of consumption of food and drink. Hence Gregory, writing to Augustine, Bishop of the English (Regist. xi), says that one ought to refrain from Communion when this arises from evil thoughts, but not when it arises from excess of food or drink, especially if necessity call for Communion. So, then, one must judge from its cause whether such bodily defilement of necessity hinders the receiving of this sacrament.

At the same time a sense of decency forbids Communion on two accounts. The first of these is always verified, viz. the bodily defilement, with which, out of reverence for the sacrament, it is unbecoming to approach the altar (and hence those who wish to touch any sacred object, wash their hands): except perchance such uncleanness be perpetual or of long standing, such as leprosy or issue of blood, or anything else of the kind. The other reason is the mental distraction which follows after the aforesaid movements, especially when they take place with unclean imaginings. Now this obstacle, which arises from a sense of decency, can be set aside owing to any necessity, as Gregory says (Regist. xi): "As when perchance either a festival day calls for it, or necessity compels one to exercise the ministry because there is no other priest at hand."

Reply to Objection 1: A person is hindered necessarily, only by mortal sin, from receiving this sacrament: but from a sense of decency one may be hindered through other causes, as stated above.

Reply to Objection 2: Conjugal intercourse, if it be without sin, (for instance, if it be done for the sake of begetting offspring, or of paying the marriage debt), does not prevent the receiving of this sacrament for any other reason than do those movements in question which happen without sin, as stated above; namely, on account of the defilement to the body and distraction to the mind. On this account Jerome expresses himself in the following terms in his commentary on Matthew (Epist. xxviii, among St. Jerome's works): "If the loaves of Proposition might not be eaten by them who had known their wives carnally, how much less may this bread which has come down from heaven be defiled and touched by them who shortly before have been in conjugal embraces? It is not that we condemn marriages, but that at the time when we are going to eat the flesh of the Lamb, we ought not to indulge in carnal acts." But since this is to be understood in the sense of decency, and not of necessity, Gregory says that such a person "is to be left to his own judgment." "But if," as Gregory says (Regist. xi), "it be not desire of begetting offspring, but lust that prevails," then such a one should be forbidden to approach this sacrament.

Reply to Objection 3: As Gregory says in his Letter quoted above to Augustine, Bishop of the English, in the Old Testament some persons were termed polluted figuratively, which the people of the New Law understand spiritually. Hence such bodily uncleannesses, if perpetual or of long standing, do not hinder the receiving of this saving sacrament, as they prevented approaching those figurative sacraments; but if they pass speedily, like the uncleanness of the aforesaid movements, then from a sense of fittingness they hinder the receiving of this sacrament during the day on which it happens. Hence it is written (Dt. 23:10): "If there be among you any man, that is defiled in a dream by night, he shall go forth out of the camp; and he shall not return before he be washed with water in the evening."

Reply to Objection 4: Although the stain of guilt be taken away by contrition and confession nevertheless the bodily defilement is not taken away, nor the mental distraction which follows therefrom.

Reply to Objection 5: To dream of homicide brings no bodily uncleanness, nor such distraction of mind as fornication, on account of its intense delectation; still if the dream of homicide comes of a cause sinful in itself, especially if it be mortal sin, then owing to its cause it hinders the receiving of this sacrament.

Day 308

Whether food or drink taken beforehand hinders the receiving of this sacrament?

Objection 1: It seems that food or drink taken beforehand does not hinder the receiving of this sacrament. For this sacrament was instituted by our Lord at the supper. But when the supper was ended our Lord gave the sacrament to His disciples, as is evident from Lk. 22:20, and from 1 Cor. 11:25. Therefore it seems that we ought to take this sacrament after receiving other food.

Objection 2: Further, it is written (1 Cor. 11:33): "When you come together to eat," namely, the Lord's body, "wait for one another; if any man be hungry, let him eat at home": and thus it seems that after eating at home a man may eat Christ's body in the Church.

Objection 3: Further, we read in the (3rd) Council of Carthage (Can. xxix): "Let the sacraments of the altar be celebrated only by men who are fasting, with the exception of the anniversary day on which the Lord's Supper is celebrated." Therefore, at least on that day, one may receive the body of Christ after partaking of other food.

Objection 4: Further, the taking of water or medicine, or of any other food or drink in very slight quantity, or of the remains of food continuing in the mouth, neither breaks the Church's fast, nor takes away the sobriety required for reverently receiving this sacrament. Consequently, one is not prevented by the above things from receiving this sacrament.

Objection 5: Further, some eat and drink late at night, and possibly after passing a sleepless night receive the sacred mysteries in the morning when the food it not digested. But it would savor more of moderation if a man were to eat a little in the morning and afterwards receive this sacrament about the ninth hour, since also there is occasionally a longer interval of time. Consequently, it seems that such taking of food beforehand does not keep one from this sacrament.

Objection 6: Further, there is no less reverence due to this sacrament after receiving it, than before. But one may take food and drink after receiving the sacrament. Therefore one may do so before receiving it.

On the contrary, Augustine says (Resp. ad Januar., Ep. liv): "It has pleased the Holy Ghost that, out of honor for this great sacrament, the Lord's body should enter the mouth of a Christian before other foods."

I answer that, A thing may prevent the receiving of this sacrament in two ways: first of all in itself, like mortal sin, which is repugnant to what is signified by this sacrament, as stated above [4651](A[4]): secondly, on account of the Church's prohibition; and thus a man is prevented from taking this sacrament after receiving food or drink, for three reasons. First, as Augustine says (Resp. ad Januar., Ep. liv), "out of respect for this sacrament," so that it may enter into a mouth not yet contaminated by any food or drink. Secondly, because of its signification. i.e. to give us to understand that Christ, Who is the reality of this sacrament, and His charity, ought to be first of all established in our hearts, according to Mat. 6:33: "Seek first the kingdom of God." Thirdly, on account of the danger of vomiting and intemperance, which sometimes arise from over-indulging in food, as the Apostle says (1 Cor. 11:21): "One, indeed, is hungry, and another is drunk."

Nevertheless the sick are exempted from this general rule, for they should be given Communion at once, even after food, should there be any doubt as to their danger, lest they die without Communion, because necessity has no law. Hence it is said in the Canon de Consecratione: "Let the priest at once take Communion to the sick person, lest he die without Communion."

Reply to Objection 1: As Augustine says in the same book, "the fact that our Lord gave this sacrament after taking food is no reason why the brethren should assemble after dinner or supper in order to partake of it, or receive it at meal-time, as did those whom the Apostle reproves and corrects. For our Saviour, in order the more strongly to commend the depth of this mystery, wished to fix it closely in the hearts and memories of the disciples. and on that account He gave no command for it to be received in that order, leaving this to the apostles, to whom He was about to entrust the government of the churches."

Reply to Objection 2: The text quoted is thus paraphrased by the gloss: "If any man be hungry and loath to await the rest, let him partake of his food at home, that is, let him fill himself with earthly bread, without partaking of the Eucharist afterwards."

Reply to Objection 3: The wording of this decree is in accordance with the former custom observed by some of receiving the body of Christ on that day after breaking their fast, so as to represent the Lord's supper. But this is now abrogated, because as Augustine says (Resp. ad Januar., Ep. liv), it is customary throughout the whole world for Christ's body to be received before breaking the fast.

Reply to Objection 4: As stated in the [4652]SS, Q[147], A[6], ad 2, there are two kinds of fast. First, there is the natural fast, which implies privation of everything taken before-hand by way of food or drink: and such fast is required for this sacrament for the reasons given above. And therefore it is never lawful to take this sacrament after taking water, or other food or drink, or even medicine, no matter how small the quantity be. Nor does it matter whether it nourishes or not, whether it be taken by itself or with other things, provided it be taken by way of food or drink. But the remains of food left in the mouth, if swallowed accidentally, do not hinder receiving this sacrament, because they are swallowed not by way of food but by way of saliva. The same holds good of the unavoidable remains of the water or wine wherewith the mouth is rinsed, provided they be not swallowed in great quantity, but mixed with saliva.

Secondly, there is the fast of the Church, instituted for afflicting the body: and this fast is not hindered by the things mentioned (in the objection), because they do not give much nourishment, but are taken rather as an alterative.

Reply to Objection 5: That this sacrament ought to enter into the mouth of a Christian before any other food must not be understood absolutely of all time, otherwise he who had once eaten or drunk could never afterwards take this sacrament: but it must be understood of the same day; and although the beginning of the day varies according to different systems of reckoning (for some begin their day at noon, some at sunset, others at midnight, and others at sunrise), the Roman Church begins it at midnight. Consequently, if any person takes anything by way of food or drink after midnight, he may not receive this sacrament on that day; but he can do so if the food was taken before midnight. Nor does it matter, so far as the precept is concerned, whether he has slept after taking food or drink, or whether he has digested it; but it does matter as to the mental disturbance which one suffers from want of sleep or from indigestion, for, if the mind be much disturbed, one becomes unfit for receiving this sacrament.

Reply to Objection 6: The greatest devotion is called for at the moment of receiving this sacrament, because it is then that the effect of the sacrament is bestowed, and such devotion is hindered more by what goes before it than by what comes after it. And therefore it was ordained that men should fast before receiving the sacrament rather than after. Nevertheless there ought to be some interval between receiving this sacrament and taking other food. Consequently, both the Postcommunion prayer of thanksgiving is said in the Mass, and the communicants say their own private prayers.

However, according to the ancient Canons, the following ordination was made by Pope Clement I, (Ep. ii), "If the Lord's portion be eaten in the morning, the ministers who have taken it shall fast until the sixth hour, and if they take it at the third or fourth hour, they shall fast until evening." For in olden times, the priest celebrated Mass less frequently, and with greater preparation: but now, because the sacred mysteries have to be celebrated oftener, the same could not be easily observed, and so it has been abrogated by contrary custom.

Whether those who have not the use of reason ought to receive this sacrament?

Objection 1: It seems that those who have not the use of reason ought not to receive this sacrament. For it is required that man should approach this sacrament with devotion and previous self-examination, according to 1 Cor. 11:28: "Let a man prove himself, and so let him eat of that bread, and drink of the chalice." But this is not possible for those who are devoid of reason. Therefore this sacrament should not be given to them.

Objection 2: Further, among those who have not the use of reason are the possessed, who are called energumens. But such persons are kept from even beholding this sacrament, according to Dionysius (Eccl. Hier. iii). Therefore this sacrament ought not to be given to those who have not the use of reason.

Objection 3: Further, among those that lack the use of reason are children, the most innocent of all. But this sacrament is not given to children. Therefore much less should it be given to others deprived of the use of reason.

On the contrary, We read in the First Council of Orange, (Canon 13); and the same is to be found in the Decretals (xxvi, 6): "All things that pertain to piety are to be given to the insane": and consequently, since this is the "sacrament of piety," it must be given to them.

I answer that, Men are said to be devoid of reason in two ways. First, when they are feeble-minded, as a man who sees dimly is said not to see: and since such persons can conceive some devotion towards this sacrament, it is not to be denied them.

In another way men are said not to possess fully the use of reason. Either, then, they never had the use of reason, and have remained so from birth; and in that case this sacrament is not to be given to them, because in no way has there been any preceding devotion towards the sacrament: or else, they were not always devoid of reason, and then, if when they formerly had their wits they showed devotion towards this sacrament, it ought to be given to them in the hour of death; unless danger be feared of vomiting or spitting it out. Hence we read in the acts of the Fourth Council of Carthage (Canon 76). and the same is to be found in the Decretals (xxvi, 6): "If a sick man ask to receive the sacrament of Penance; and if, when the priest who has been sent for comes to him, he be so weak as to be unable to speak, or becomes delirious, let them, who heard him ask, bear witness, and let him receive the sacrament of Penance. then if it be thought that he is going to die shortly, let him be reconciled by imposition of hands, and let the Eucharist be placed in his mouth."

Reply to Objection 1: Those lacking the use of reason can have devotion towards the sacrament; actual devotion in some cases, and past in others.

Reply to Objection 2: Dionysius is speaking there of energumens who are not yet baptized, in whom the devil's power is not yet extinct, since it thrives in them through the presence of original sin. But as to baptized persons who are vexed in body by unclean spirits, the same reason holds good of them as of others who are demented. Hence Cassian says (Collat. vii): "We do not remember the most Holy Communion to have ever been denied by our elders to them who are vexed by unclean spirits."

Reply to Objection 3: The same reason holds good of newly born children as of the insane who never have had the use of reason: consequently, the sacred mysteries are not to be given to them. Although certain Greeks do the contrary, because Dionysius says (Eccl. Hier. ii) that Holy Communion is to be given to them who are baptized; not understanding that Dionysius is speaking there of the Baptism of adults. Nor do they suffer any loss of life from the fact of our Lord saying (Jn. 6:54), "Except you eat the flesh of the Son of Man, and drink His blood, you shall not have life in you"; because, as Augustine writes to Boniface (Pseudo-Beda, Comment. in 1 Cor. 10:17), "then every one of the faithful becomes a partaker," i.e. spiritually, "of the body and blood of the Lord, when he is made a member of Christ's body in Baptism." But when children once begin to have some use of reason so as to be able to conceive some devotion for the sacrament, then it can be given to them.

Whether it is lawful to receive this sacrament daily?

Objection 1: It does not appear to be lawful to receive this sacrament daily, because, as Baptism shows forth our Lord's Passion, so also does this sacrament. Now one may not be baptized several times, but only once, because "Christ died once" only "for our sins," according to 1 Pet. 3:18. Therefore, it seems unlawful to receive this sacrament daily.

Objection 2: Further, the reality ought to answer to the figure. But the Paschal Lamb, which was the chief figure of this sacrament, as was said above (Q[73], A[9]) was eaten only once in the year; while the Church once a year commemorates Christ's Passion, of which this sacrament is the memorial. It seems, then, that it is lawful to receive this sacrament not daily, but only once in the year.

Objection 3: Further, the greatest reverence is due to this sacrament as containing Christ. But it is a token of reverence to refrain from receiving this sacrament; hence the Centurion is praised for saying (Mat. 8:8), "Lord, I am not worthy that Thou shouldst enter under my roof"; also Peter, for saying (Lk. 5:8), "Depart from me, for I am a sinful man, O Lord." Therefore, it is not praiseworthy for a man to receive this sacrament daily.

Objection 4: Further, if it were a praiseworthy custom to receive this sacrament frequently, then the oftener it were taken the more praise-worthy it would be. But there would be greater frequency if one were to receive it several. times daily; and yet this is not the custom of the Church. Consequently, it does not seem praiseworthy to receive it daily.

Objection 5: Further, the Church by her statutes intends to promote the welfare of the faithful. But the Church's statute only requires Communion once a year; hence it is enacted (Extra, De Poenit. et Remiss. xii): "Let every person of either sex devoutly receive the sacrament of the Eucharist at least at Easter; unless by the advice of his parish priest, and for some reasonable cause, he considers he ought to refrain from receiving for a time." Consequently, it is not praiseworthy to receive this sacrament daily.

On the contrary, Augustine says (De Verb. Dom., Serm. xxviii): "This is our daily bread; take it daily, that it may profit thee daily."

I answer that, There are two things to be considered regarding the use of this sacrament. The first is on the part of the sacrament itself, the virtue of which gives health to men; and consequently it is profitable to receive it daily so as to receive its fruits daily. Hence Ambrose says (De Sacram. iv): "If, whenever Christ's blood is shed, it is shed for the forgiveness of sins, I who sin often, should receive it often: I need a frequent remedy." The second thing to be considered is on the part of the recipient, who is required to approach this sacrament with great reverence and devotion. Consequently, if anyone finds that he has these dispositions every day, he will do well to receive it daily. Hence, Augustine after saying, "Receive daily, that it may profit thee daily," adds: "So live, as to deserve to receive it daily." But because many persons are lacking in this devotion, on account of the many drawbacks both spiritual and corporal from which they suffer, it is not expedient for all to approach this sacrament every day; but they should do so as often as they find themselves properly disposed. Hence it is said in De Eccles. Dogmat. liii: "I neither praise nor blame daily reception of the Eucharist."

Reply to Objection 1: In the sacrament of Baptism a man is conformed to Christ's death, by receiving His character within him. And therefore, as Christ died but once, so a man ought to be baptized but once. But a man does not receive Christ's character in this sacrament; He receives Christ Himself, Whose virtue endures for ever. Hence it is written (Heb. 10:14): "By one oblation He hath perfected for ever them that are sanctified." Consequently, since man has daily need of Christ's health-giving virtue, he may commendably receive this sacrament every day.

And since Baptism is above all a spiritual regeneration, therefore, as a man is born naturally but once, so ought he by Baptism to be reborn spiritually but once, as Augustine says (Tract. xi in Joan.), commenting on Jn. 3:4, "How can a man be born again, when he is grown old?" But this sacrament is spiritual food; hence, just as bodily food is taken every day, so is it a good thing to receive this sacrament every day. Hence it is that our Lord (Lk. 11:3), teaches us to pray, "Give us this day our daily bread": in explaining which words Augustine observes (De Verb. Dom., Serm. xxviii): "If you receive it," i.e. this sacrament, every day, "every day is today for thee, and Christ rises again every day in thee, for when Christ riseth it is today."

Reply to Objection 2: The Paschal Lamb was the figure of this sacrament chiefly as to Christ's Passion represented therein; and therefore it was partaken of once a year only, since Christ died but once. And on this account the Church celebrates once a year the remembrance of Christ's Passion. But in this sacrament the memorial of His Passion is given by way of food which is partaken of daily; and therefore in this respect it is represented by the manna which was given daily to the people in the desert.

Reply to Objection 3: Reverence for this sacrament consists in fear associated with love; consequently reverential fear of God is called filial fear, as was said in the [4653]FS, Q[67], A[4], ad 2; [4654]SS, Q[19], AA[9],11,12; because the desire of receiving arises from love, while the humility of reverence springs from fear. Consequently, each of these belongs to the reverence due to this sacrament; both as to receiving it daily, and as to refraining from it sometimes. Hence Augustine says (Ep. liv): "If one says that the Eucharist should not be received daily, while another maintains the contrary, let each one do as according to his devotion he thinketh right; for Zaccheus and the Centurion did not contradict one another while the one received the Lord with joy, whereas the other said: 'Lord I am not worthy that Thou shouldst enter under my roof'; since both honored our Saviour, though not in the same way." But love and hope, whereunto the Scriptures constantly urge us, are preferable to fear. Hence, too, when Peter had said, "Depart from me, for I am a sinful man, O Lord," Jesus answered: "Fear not."

Reply to Objection 4: Because our Lord said (Lk. 11:3), "Give us this day our daily bread," we are not on that account to communicate several times daily, for, by one daily communion the unity of Christ's Passion is set forth.

Reply to Objection 5: Various statutes have emanated according to the various ages of the Church. In the primitive Church, when the devotion of the Christian faith was more flourishing, it was enacted that the faithful should communicate daily: hence Pope Anaclete says (Ep. i): "When the consecration is finished, let all communicate who do not wish to cut themselves off from the Church; for so the apostles have ordained, and the holy Roman Church holds." Later on, when the fervor of faith relaxed, Pope Fabian (Third Council of Tours, Canon 1) gave permission "that all should communicate, if not more frequently, at least three times in the year, namely, at Easter, Pentecost, and Christmas." Pope Soter likewise (Second Council of Chalon, Canon xlvii) declares that Communion should be received "on Holy Thursday," as is set forth in the Decretals (De Consecratione, dist. 2). Later on, when "iniquity abounded and charity grew cold" (Mat. 24:12), Pope Innocent III commanded that the faithful should communicate "at least once a year," namely, "at Easter." However, in De Eccles. Dogmat. xxiii, the faithful are counseled "to communicate on all Sundays."

Whether it is lawful to abstain altogether from communion?

Objection 1: It seems to be lawful to abstain altogether from Communion. Because the Centurion is praised for saying (Mat. 8:8): "Lord, I am not worthy that Thou shouldst enter under my roof"; and he who deems that he ought to refrain entirely from Communion can be compared to the Centurion, as stated above (A[10], ad 3). Therefore, since we do not read of Christ entering his house, it seems to be lawful for any individual to abstain from Communion his whole life long.

Objection 2: Further, it is lawful for anyone to refrain from what is not of necessity for salvation. But this sacrament is not of necessity for salvation, as was stated above ([4655]Q[73], A[3]). Therefore it is permissible to abstain from Communion altogether.

Objection 3: Further, sinners are not bound to go to Communion: hence Pope Fabian (Third Council of Tours, Canon 1) after saying, "Let all communicate thrice each year," adds: "Except those who are hindered by grievous crimes." Consequently, if those who are not in the state of sin are bound to go to Communion, it seems that sinners are better off than good people, which is unfitting. Therefore, it seems lawful even for the godly to refrain from Communion.

On the contrary, Our Lord said (Jn. 6:54): "Except ye eat the flesh of the Son of Man, and drink His blood, you shall not have life in you."

I answer that, As stated above [4656](A[1]), there are two ways of receiving this sacrament namely, spiritually and sacramentally. Now it is clear that all are bound to eat it at least spiritually, because this is to be incorporated in Christ, as was said above (Q[73], A[3], ad 1). Now spiritual eating comprises the desire or yearning for receiving this sacrament, as was said above (A[1], ad 3, A[2]). Therefore, a man cannot be saved without desiring to receive this sacrament.

Now a desire would be vain except it were fulfilled when opportunity presented itself. Consequently, it is evident that a man is bound to receive this sacrament, not only by virtue of the Church's precept, but also by virtue of the Lord's command (Lk. 22:19): "Do this in memory of Me." But by the precept of the Church there are fixed times for fulfilling Christ's command.

Reply to Objection 1: As Gregory says: "He is truly humble, who is not obstinate in rejecting what is commanded for his good." Consequently, humility is not praiseworthy if anyone abstains altogether from Communion against the precept of Christ and the Church. Again the Centurion was not commanded to receive Christ into his house.

Reply to Objection 2: This sacrament is said not to be as necessary as Baptism, with regard to children, who can be saved without the Eucharist, but not without the sacrament of Baptism: both, however, are of necessity with regard to adults.

Reply to Objection 3: Sinners suffer great loss in being kept back from receiving this sacrament, so that they are not better off on that account; and although while continuing in their sins they are not on that account excused from transgressing the precept, nevertheless, as Pope Innocent III says, penitents, "who refrain on the advice of their priest," are excused.

Whether it is lawful to receive the body of Christ without the blood?

Objection 1: It seems unlawful to receive the body of Christ without the blood. For Pope Gelasius says (cf. De Consecr. ii): "We have learned that some persons after taking only a portion of the sacred body, abstain from the chalice of the sacred blood. I know not for what superstitious motive they do this: therefore let them either receive the entire sacrament, or let them be withheld from the sacrament altogether." Therefore it is not lawful to receive the body of Christ without His blood.

Objection 2: Further, the eating of the body and the drinking of the blood are required for the perfection of this sacrament, as stated above ([4657]Q[73], A[2];[4658] Q[76], A[2], ad 1). Consequently, if the body be taken without the blood, it will be an imperfect sacrament, which seems to savor of sacrilege; hence Pope Gelasius adds (cf. De Consecr. ii), "because the dividing of one and the same mystery cannot happen without a great sacrilege."

Objection 3: Further, this sacrament is celebrated in memory of our Lord's Passion, as stated above ([4659]Q[73], AA[4],5;[4660] Q[74], A[1]), and is received for the health of soul. But the Passion is expressed in the blood rather than in the body; moreover, as stated above ([4661]Q[74], A[1]), the blood is offered for the health of the soul. Consequently, one ought to refrain from receiving the body rather than the blood. Therefore, such as approach this sacrament ought not to take Christ's body without His blood.

On the contrary, It is the custom of many churches for the body of Christ to be given to the communicant without His blood.

I answer that, Two points should be observed regarding the use of this sacrament, one on the part of the sacrament, the other on the part of the recipients; on the part of the sacrament it is proper for both the body and the blood to be received, since the perfection of the sacrament lies in both, and consequently, since it is the priest's duty both to consecrate and finish the sacrament, he ought on no account to receive Christ's body without the blood.

But on the part of the recipient the greatest reverence and caution are called for, lest anything happen which is unworthy of so great a mystery. Now this could especially happen in receiving the blood, for, if incautiously handled, it might easily be spilt. And because the multitude of the Christian people increased, in which there are old, young, and children, some of whom have not enough discretion to observe due caution in using this sacrament, on that account it is a prudent custom in some churches for the blood not to be offered to the reception of the people, but to be received by the priest alone.

Reply to Objection 1: Pope Gelasius is speaking of priests, who, as they consecrate the entire sacrament, ought to communicate in the entire sacrament. For, as we read in the (Twelfth) Council of Toledo, "What kind of a sacrifice is that, wherein not even the sacrificer is known to have a share?"

Reply to Objection 2: The perfection of this sacrament does not lie in the use of the faithful, but in the consecration of the matter. And hence there is nothing derogatory to the perfection of this sacrament; if the people receive the body without the blood, provided that the priest who consecrates receive both.

Reply to Objection 3: Our Lord's Passion is represented in the very consecration of this sacrament, in which the body ought not to be consecrated without the blood. But the body can be received by the people without the blood: nor is this detrimental to the sacrament. Because the priest both offers and consumes the blood on behalf of all; and Christ is fully contained under either species, as was shown above ([4662]Q[76], A[2]).

OF THE USE WHICH CHRIST MADE OF THIS SACRAMENT AT ITS INSTITUTION (FOUR ARTICLES)

We have now to consider the use which Christ made of this sacrament at its institution; under which heading there are four points of inquiry:

(1) Whether Christ received His own body and blood?

(2) Whether He gave it to Judas?

(3) What kind of body did He receive or give, namely, was it passible or impassible?

(4) What would have been the condition of Christ's body under this sacrament, if it had been reserved or consecrated during the three days He lay dead?

Whether Christ received His own body and blood?

Objection 1: It seems that Christ did not receive His own body and blood, because nothing ought to be asserted of either Christ's doings or sayings, which is not handed down by the authority of Sacred Scripture. But it is not narrated in the gospels that He ate His own body or drank His own blood. Therefore we must not assert this as a fact.

Objection 2: Further, nothing can be within itself except perchance by reason of its parts, for instance. as one part is in another, as is stated in Phys. iv. But what is eaten and drunk is in the eater and drinker. Therefore, since the entire Christ is under each species of the sacrament, it seems impossible for Him to have received this sacrament.

Objection 3: Further, the receiving of this sacrament is twofold, namely, spiritual and sacramental. But the spiritual was unsuitable for Christ, as He derived no benefit from the sacrament. and in consequence so was the sacramental, since it is imperfect without the spiritual, as was observed above ([4663]Q[80], A[1]). Consequently, in no way did Christ partake of this sacrament.

On the contrary, Jerome says (Ad Hedib., Ep. xxx), "The Lord Jesus Christ, Himself the guest and banquet, is both the partaker and what is eaten."

I answer that, Some have said that Christ during the supper gave His body and blood to His disciples, but did not partake of it Himself. But this seems improbable. Because Christ Himself was the first to fulfill what He required others to observe: hence He willed first to be baptized when imposing Baptism upon others: as we read in Acts 1:1: "Jesus began to do and to teach." Hence He first of all took His own body and blood, and afterwards gave it to be taken by the disciples. And hence the gloss upon Ruth 3:7, "When he had eaten and drunk, says: Christ ate and drank at the supper, when He gave to the disciples the sacrament of His body and blood. Hence, 'because the children partook [*Vulg.: 'are partakers' (Heb. 2:14)] of His flesh and blood, He also hath been partaker in the same.'"

Reply to Objection 1: We read in the Gospels how Christ "took the bread . . . and the chalice"; but it is not to be understood that He took them merely into His hands, as some say. but that He took them in the same way as He gave them to others to take. Hence when He said to the disciples, "Take ye and eat," and again, "Take ye and drink," it is to be understood that He Himself, in taking it, both ate and drank. Hence some have composed this rhyme:

"The King at supper sits,
The twelve as guests He greets,
Clasping Himself in His hands,
The food Himself now eats."

Reply to Objection 2: As was said above ([4664]Q[76], A[5]), Christ as contained under this sacrament stands in relation to place, not according to His own dimensions, but according to the dimensions of the sacramental species; so that Christ is Himself in every place where those species are. And because the species were able to be both in the hands and the mouth of Christ, the entire Christ could be in both His hands and mouth. Now this could not come to pass were His relation to place to be according to His proper dimensions.

Reply to Objection 3: As was stated above ([4665]Q[79], A[1], ad 2), the effect of this sacrament is not merely an increase of habitual grace, but furthermore a certain actual delectation of spiritual sweetness. But although grace was not increased in Christ through His receiving this sacrament, yet He had a certain spiritual delectation from the new institution of this sacrament. Hence He Himself said (Lk. 22:15): "With desire I have desired to eat this Pasch with you," which words Eusebius explains of the new mystery of the New Testament, which He gave to the disciples. And therefore He ate it both spiritually and sacramentally, inasmuch as He received His own body under the sacrament which sacrament of His own body He both understood and prepared; yet differently from others who partake of it both sacramentally and spiritually, for these receive an increase of grace, and they have need of the sacramental signs for perceiving its truth.

Whether Christ gave His body to Judas?

Objection 1: It seems that Christ did not give His body to Judas. Because, as we read (Mat. 26:29), our Lord, after giving His body and blood to the disciples, said to them: "I will not drink from henceforth of this fruit of the vine, until that day when I shall drink it with you new in the kingdom of My Father." From this it appears that those to whom He had given His body and blood were to drink of it again with Him. But Judas did not drink of it afterwards with Him. Therefore he did not receive Christ's body and blood with the other disciples.

Objection 2: Further, what the Lord commanded, He Himself fulfilled, as is said in Acts 1:1: "Jesus began to do and to teach." But He gave the command (Mat. 7:6): "Give not that which is holy to dogs." Therefore, knowing Judas to be a sinner, seemingly He did not give him His body and blood.

Objection 3: Further, it is distinctly related (Jn. 13:26) that Christ gave dipped bread to Judas. Consequently, if He gave His body to him, it appears that He gave it him in the morsel, especially since we read (Jn. 13:26) that "after the morsel, Satan entered into him." And on this passage Augustine says (Tract. lxii in Joan.): "From this we learn how we should beware of receiving a good thing in an evil way . . . For if he be 'chastised' who does 'not discern,' i.e. distinguish, the body of the Lord from other meats, how must he be 'condemned' who, feigning himself a friend, comes to His table a foe?" But (Judas) did not receive our Lord's body with the dipped morsel; thus Augustine commenting on Jn. 13:26, "When He had dipped the bread, He gave it to Judas, the son of Simon the Iscariot [Vulg.: 'to Judas Iscariot, the son of Simon],'" says (Tract. lxii in Joan.): "Judas did not receive Christ's body then, as some think who read carelessly." Therefore it seems that Judas did not receive the body of Christ.

On the contrary, Chrysostom says (Hom. lxxxii in Matth.): "Judas was not converted while partaking of the sacred mysteries: hence on both sides his crime becomes the more heinous, both because imbued with such a purpose he approached the mysteries, and because he became none the better for approaching, neither from fear, nor from the benefit received, nor from the honor conferred on him."

I answer that, Hilary, in commenting on Mat. 26:17, held that Christ did not give His body and blood to Judas. And this would have been quite proper, if the malice of Judas be considered. But since Christ was to serve us as a pattern of justice, it was not in keeping with His teaching authority to sever Judas, a hidden sinner, from Communion with the others without an accuser and evident proof. lest the Church's prelates might have an example for doing the like, and lest Judas himself being exasperated might take occasion of sinning. Therefore, it remains to be said that Judas received our Lord's body and blood with the other disciples, as Dionysius says (Eccl. Hier. iii), and Augustine (Tract. lxii in Joan.).

Reply to Objection 1: This is Hilary's argument, to show that Judas did not receive Christ's body. But it is not cogent; because Christ is speaking to the disciples, from whose company Judas separated himself: and it was not Christ that excluded him. Therefore Christ for His part drinks the wine even with Judas in the kingdom of God; but Judas himself repudiated this banquet.

Reply to Objection 2: The wickedness of Judas was known to Christ as God; but it was unknown to Him, after the manner in which men know it. Consequently, Christ did not repel Judas from Communion; so as to furnish an example that such secret sinners are not to be repelled by other priests.

Reply to Objection 3: Without any doubt Judas did not receive Christ's body in the dipped bread; he received mere bread. Yet as Augustine observes (Tract. lxii in Joan.), "perchance the feigning of Judas is denoted by the dipping of the bread; just as some things are dipped to be dyed. If, however, the dipping signifies here anything good" (for instance, the sweetness of the Divine goodness, since bread is rendered more savory by being dipped), "then, not undeservedly, did condemnation follow his ingratitude for that same good." And owing to that ingratitude, "what is good became evil to him, as happens to them who receive Christ's body unworthily."

And as Augustine says (Tract. lxii in Joan.), "it must be understood that our Lord had already distributed the sacrament of His body and blood to all His disciples, among whom was Judas also, as Luke narrates: and after that, we came to this, where, according to the relation of John, our Lord, by dipping and handing the morsel, does most openly declare His betrayer."

Whether Christ received and gave to the disciples His impassible body?

Objection 1: It seems that Christ both received and gave to the disciples His impassible body. Because on Mat. 17:2, "He was transfigured before them," the gloss says: "He gave to the disciples at the supper that body which He had through nature, but neither mortal nor passible." And again, on Lev. 2:5, "if thy oblation be from the frying-pan," the gloss says: "The Cross mightier than all things made Christ's flesh fit for being eaten, which before the Passion did not seem so suited." But Christ gave His body as suited for eating. Therefore He gave it just as it was after the Passion, that is, impassible and immortal.

Objection 2: Further, every passible body suffers by contact and by being eaten. Consequently, if Christ's body was passible, it would have suffered both from contact and from being eaten by the disciples.

Objection 3: Further, the sacramental words now spoken by the priest in the person of Christ are not more powerful than when uttered by Christ Himself. But now by virtue of the sacramental words it is Christ's impassible and immortal body which is consecrated upon the altar. Therefore, much more so was it then.

On the contrary, As Innocent III says (De Sacr. Alt. Myst. iv), "He bestowed on the disciples His body such as it was." But then He had a passible and a mortal body. Therefore, He gave a passible and mortal body to the disciples.

I answer that, Hugh of Saint Victor (Innocent III, De Sacr. Alt. Myst. iv), maintained, that before the Passion, Christ assumed at various times the four properties of a glorified body ---namely, subtlety in His birth, when He came forth from the closed womb of the Virgin; agility, when He walked dryshod upon the sea; clarity, in the Transfiguration; and impassibility at the Last Supper, when He gave His body to the disciples to be eaten. And according to this He gave His body in an impassible and immortal condition to His disciples.

But whatever may be the case touching the other qualities, concerning which we have already stated what should be held ([4666]Q[28], A[2], ad 3;[4667] Q[45], A[2]), nevertheless the above opinion regarding impassibility is inadmissible. For it is manifest that the same body of Christ which was then seen by the disciples in its own species, was received by them under the sacramental species. But as seen in its own species it was not impassible; nay more, it was ready for the Passion. Therefore, neither was Christ's body impassible when given under the sacramental species.

Yet there was present in the sacrament, in an impassible manner, that which was passible of itself; just as that was there invisibly which of itself was visible. For as sight requires that the body seen be in contact with the adjacent medium of sight, so does passion require contact of the suffering body with the active agents. But Christ's body, according as it is under the sacrament, as stated above (A[1], ad 2;[4668] Q[76], A[5]), is not compared with its surroundings through the intermediary of its own dimensions, whereby bodies touch each other, but through the dimensions of the bread and wine; consequently, it is those species which are acted upon and are seen, but not Christ's own body.

Reply to Objection 1: Christ is said not to have given His mortal and passible body at the supper, because He did not give it in mortal and passible fashion. But the Cross made His flesh adapted for eating, inasmuch as this sacrament represents Christ's Passion.

Reply to Objection 2: This argument would hold, if Christ's body, as it was passible, were also present in a passible manner in this sacrament.

Reply to Objection 3: As stated above ([4669]Q[76], A[4]), the accidents of Christ's body are in this sacrament by real concomitance, but not by the power of the sacrament, whereby the substance of Christ's body comes to be there. And therefore the power of the sacramental words extends to this, that the body, i.e. Christ's, is under this sacrament, whatever accidents really exist in it.

Whether, if this sacrament had been reserved in a pyx, or consecrated at the moment of Christ's death by one of the apostles, Christ Himself would have died there?

Objection 1: It seems that if this sacrament had been reserved in a pyx at the moment of Christ's death, or had then been consecrated by one of the apostles, that Christ would not have died there. For Christ's death happened through His Passion. But even then He was in this sacrament in an impassible manner. Therefore, He could not die in this sacrament.

Objection 2: Further, on the death of Christ, His blood was separated from the body. But His flesh and blood are together in this sacrament. Therefore He could not die in this sacrament.

Objection 3: Further, death ensues from the separation of the soul from the body. But both the body and the soul of Christ are contained in this sacrament. Therefore Christ could not die in this sacrament.

On the contrary, The same Christ Who was upon the cross would have been in this sacrament. But He died upon the cross. Therefore, if this sacrament had been reserved, He would have died therein.

I answer that, Christ's body is substantially the same in this sacrament, as in its proper species, but not after the same fashion; because in its proper species it comes in contact with surrounding bodies by its own dimensions: but it does not do so as it is in this sacrament, as stated above [4670](A[3]). And therefore, all that belongs to Christ, as He is in Himself, can be attributed to Him both in His proper species, and as He exists in the sacrament; such as to live, to die, to grieve, to be animate or inanimate, and the like; while all that belongs to Him in relation to outward bodies, can be attributed to Him as He exists in His proper species, but not as He is in this sacrament; such as to be mocked, to be spat upon, to be crucified, to be scourged, and the rest. Hence some have composed this verse:

"Our Lord can grieve beneath the sacramental veils But cannot feel the piercing of the thorns and nails."

Reply to Objection 1: As was stated above, suffering belongs to a body that suffers in respect of some extrinsic body. And therefore Christ, as in this sacrament, cannot suffer; yet He can die.

Reply to Objection 2: As was said above ([4671]Q[76], A[2]), in virtue of the consecration, the body of Christ is under the species of bread, while His blood is under the species of wine. But now that His blood is not really separated from His body; by real concomitance, both His blood is present with the body under the species of the bread, and His body together with the blood under the species of the wine. But at the time when Christ suffered, when His blood was really separated from His body, if this sacrament had been consecrated, then the body only would have been present under the species of the bread, and the blood only under the species of the wine.

Reply to Objection 3: As was observed above ([4672]Q[76], A[1], ad 1), Christ's soul is in this sacrament by real concomitance; because it is not without the body: but it is not there in virtue of the consecration. And therefore, if this sacrament had been consecrated then, or reserved, when His soul was really separated from His body, Christ's soul would not have been under this sacrament, not from any defect in the form of the words, but owing to the different dispositions of the thing contained.

Day 309

OF THE MINISTER OF THIS SACRAMENT (TEN ARTICLES)
We now proceed to consider the minister of this sacrament: under which head there are ten points for our inquiry:
(1) Whether it belongs to a priest alone to consecrate this sacrament?
(2) Whether several priests can at the same time consecrate the same host?
(3) Whether it belongs to the priest alone to dispense this sacrament?
(4) Whether it is lawful for the priest consecrating to refrain from communicating?
(5) Whether a priest in sin can perform this sacrament?
(6) Whether the Mass of a wicked priest is of less value than that of a good one?
(7) Whether those who are heretics, schismatics, or excommunicated, can perform this sacrament?
(8) Whether degraded priests can do so?
(9) Whether communicants receiving at their hands are guilty of sinning?
(10) Whether a priest may lawfully refrain altogether from celebrating?
[*This is the order observed by St. Thomas in writing the Articles; but in writing this prologue, he placed Article 10 immediately after Article 4 (Cf. Leonine edition).]

Whether the consecration of this sacrament belongs to a priest alone?
Objection 1: It seems that the consecration of this sacrament does not belong exclusively to a priest. Because it was said above ([4673]Q[78], A[4]) that this sacrament is consecrated in virtue of the words, which are the form of this sacrament. But those words are not changed, whether spoken by a priest or by anyone else. Therefore, it seems that not only a priest, but anyone else, can consecrate this sacrament.

Objection 2: Further, the priest performs this sacrament in the person of Christ. But a devout layman is united with Christ through charity. Therefore, it seems that even a layman can perform this sacrament. Hence Chrysostom (Opus imperfectum in Matth., Hom. xliii) says that "every holy man is a priest."

Objection 3: Further, as Baptism is ordained for the salvation of mankind, so also is this sacrament, as is clear from what was said above ([4674]Q[74], A[1] ;[4675] Q[79], A[2]). But a layman can also baptize, as was stated above ([4676]Q[67] , A[3]). Consequently, the consecration of this sacrament is not proper to a priest.

Objection 4: Further, this sacrament is completed in the consecration of the matter. But the consecration of other matters such as the chrism, the holy oil, and blessed oil, belongs exclusively to a bishop; yet their consecration does not equal the dignity of the consecration of the Eucharist, in which the entire Christ is contained. Therefore it belongs, not to a priest, but only to a bishop, to perform this sacrament.

On the contrary, Isidore says in an Epistle to Ludifred (Decretals, dist. 25): "It belongs to a priest to consecrate this sacrament of the Lord's body and blood upon God's altar."

I answer that, As stated above ([4677]Q[78], AA[1],4), such is the dignity of this sacrament that it is performed only as in the person of Christ. Now whoever performs any act in another's stead, must do so by the power bestowed by such a one. But as the power of receiving this sacrament is conceded by Christ to the baptized person, so likewise the power of consecrating this sacrament on Christ's behalf is bestowed upon the priest at his ordination: for thereby he is put upon a level with them to whom the Lord said (Lk. 22:19): "Do this for a commemoration of Me." Therefore, it must be said that it belongs to priests to accomplish this sacrament.

Reply to Objection 1: The sacramental power is in several things, and not merely in one: thus the power of Baptism lies both in the words and in the water. Accordingly the consecrating power is not merely in the words, but likewise in the power delivered to the priest in his consecration and ordination, when the bishop says to him: "Receive the power of offering up the Sacrifice in the Church for the living as well as for the dead." For instrumental power lies in several instruments through which the chief agent acts.

Reply to Objection 2: A devout layman is united with Christ by spiritual union through faith and charity, but not by sacramental power: consequently he has a spiritual priesthood for offering spiritual sacrifices, of which it is said (Ps. 1:19): "A sacrifice to God is an afflicted spirit"; and (Rom. 12:1): "Present your bodies a living sacrifice." Hence, too, it is written (1 Pet. 2:5): "A holy priesthood, to offer up spiritual sacrifices."

Reply to Objection 3: The receiving of this sacrament is not of such necessity as the receiving of Baptism, as is evident from what was said above ([4678]Q[65], AA[3],4;[4679] Q[80], A[11], ad 2). And therefore, although a layman can baptize in case of necessity, he cannot perform this sacrament.

Reply to Objection 4: The bishop receives power to act on Christ's behalf upon His mystical body, that is, upon the Church; but the priest receives no such power in his consecration, although he may have it by commission from the bishop. Consequently all such things as do not belong to the mystical body are not reserved to the bishop, such as the consecration of this sacrament. But it belongs to the bishop to deliver, not only to the people, but likewise to priests, such things as serve them in the fulfillment of their respective duties. And because the blessing of the chrism, and of the holy oil, and of the oil of the sick, and other consecrated things, such as altars, churches, vestments, and sacred vessels, makes such things fit for use in performing the sacraments which belong to the priestly duty, therefore such consecrations are reserved to the bishop as the head of the whole ecclesiastical order.

Whether several priests can consecrate one and the same host?

Objection 1: It seems that several priests cannot consecrate one and the same host. For it was said above ([4680]Q[67], A[6]), that several cannot at the same time baptize one individual. But the power of a priest consecrating is not less than that of a man baptizing. Therefore, several priests cannot consecrate one host at the same time.

Objection 2: Further, what can be done by one, is superfluously done by several. But there ought to be nothing superfluous in the sacraments. Since, then, one is sufficient for consecrating, it seems that several cannot consecrate one host.

Objection 3: Further, as Augustine says (Tract. xxvi in Joan.), this is "the sacrament of unity." But multitude seems to be opposed to unity. Therefore it seems inconsistent with the sacrament for several priests to consecrate the same host.

On the contrary, It is the custom of some Churches for priests newly ordained to co-celebrate with the bishop ordaining them.

I answer that, As stated above [4681](A[1]), when a priest is ordained he is placed on a level with those who received consecrating power from our Lord at the Supper. And therefore, according to the custom of some Churches, as the apostles supped when Christ supped, so the newly ordained co-celebrate with the ordaining bishop. Nor is the consecration, on that account, repeated over the same host, because as Innocent III says (De Sacr. Alt. Myst. iv), the intention of all should be directed to the same instant of the consecration.

Reply to Objection 1: We do not read of Christ baptizing with the apostles when He committed to them the duty of baptizing; consequently there is no parallel.

Reply to Objection 2: If each individual priest were acting in his own power, then other celebrants would be superfluous, since one would be sufficient. But whereas the priest does not consecrate except as in Christ's stead; and since many are "one in Christ" (Gal. 3:28); consequently it does not matter whether this sacrament be consecrated by one or by many, except that the rite of the Church must be observed.

Reply to Objection 3: The Eucharist is the sacrament of ecclesiastical unity, which is brought about by many being "one in Christ."

Whether dispensing of this sacrament belongs to a priest alone?

Objection 1: It seems that the dispensing of this sacrament does not belong to a priest alone. For Christ's blood belongs to this sacrament no less than His body. But Christ's blood is dispensed by deacons: hence the blessed Lawrence said to the blessed Sixtus (Office of St. Lawrence, Resp. at Matins): "Try whether you have chosen a fit minister, to whom you have entrusted the dispensing of the Lord's blood." Therefore, with equal reason the dispensing of Christ's body does not belong to priests only.

Objection 2: Further, priests are the appointed ministers of the sacraments. But this sacrament is completed in the consecration of the matter, and not in the use, to which the dispensing belongs. Therefore it seems that it does not belong to a priest to dispense the Lord's body.

Objection 3: Further, Dionysius says (Eccl. Hier. iii, iv) that this sacrament, like chrism, has the power of perfecting. But it belongs, not to priests, but to bishops, to sign with the chrism. Therefore likewise, to dispense this sacrament belongs to the bishop and not to the priest.

On the contrary, It is written (De Consecr., dist. 12): "It has come to our knowledge that some priests deliver the Lord's body to a layman or to a woman to carry it to the sick: The synod therefore forbids such presumption to continue; and let the priest himself communicate the sick."

I answer that, The dispensing of Christ's body belongs to the priest for three reasons. First, because, as was said above [4682] (A[1]), he consecrates as in the person of Christ. But as Christ consecrated His body at the supper, so also He gave it to others to be partaken of by them. Accordingly, as the consecration of Christ's body belongs to the priest, so likewise does the dispensing belong to him. Secondly, because the priest is the appointed intermediary between God and the people; hence as it belongs to him to offer the people's gifts to God, so it belongs to him to deliver consecrated gifts to the people. Thirdly, because out of reverence towards this sacrament, nothing touches it, but what is consecrated; hence the corporal and the chalice are consecrated, and likewise the priest's hands, for touching this sacrament. Hence it is not lawful for anyone else to touch it except from necessity, for instance, if it were to fall upon the ground, or else in some other case of urgency.

Reply to Objection 1: The deacon, as being nigh to the priestly order, has a certain share in the latter's duties, so that he may dispense the blood; but not the body, except in case of necessity, at the bidding of a bishop or of a priest. First of all, because Christ's blood is contained in a vessel, hence there is no need for it to be touched by the dispenser, as Christ's body is touched. Secondly, because the blood denotes the redemption derived by the people from Christ; hence it is that water is mixed with the blood, which water denotes the people. And because deacons are between priest and people, the dispensing of the blood is in the competency of deacons, rather than the dispensing of the body.

Reply to Objection 2: For the reason given above, it belongs to the same person to dispense and to consecrate this sacrament.

Reply to Objection 3: As the deacon, in a measure, shares in the priest's "power of enlightening" (Eccl. Hier. v), inasmuch as he dispenses the blood. so the priest shares in the "perfective dispensing" (Eccl. Hier. v) of the bishop, inasmuch as he dispenses this sacrament whereby man is perfected in himself by union with Christ. But other perfections whereby a man is perfected in relation to others, are reserved to the bishop.

Whether the priest who consecrates is bound to receive this sacrament?

Objection 1: It seems that the priest who consecrates is not bound to receive this sacrament. Because, in the other consecrations, he who consecrates the matter does not use it, just as the bishop consecrating the chrism is not anointed therewith. But this sacrament consists in the consecration of the matter. Therefore, the priest performing this sacrament need not use the same, but may lawfully refrain from receiving it.

Objection 2: Further, in the other sacraments the minister does not give the sacrament to himself: for no one can baptize himself, as stated above ([4683]Q[66], A[5], ad 4). But as Baptism is dispensed in due order, so also is this sacrament. Therefore the priest who consecrates this sacrament ought not to receive it at his own hands.

Objection 3: Further, it sometimes happens that Christ's body appears upon the altar under the guise of flesh, and the blood under the guise of blood; which are unsuited for food and drink: hence, as was said above ([4684]Q[75], A[5]), it is on that account that they are given under another species, lest they beget revulsion in the communicants. Therefore the priest who consecrates is not always bound to receive this sacrament.

On the contrary, We read in the acts of the (Twelfth) Council of Toledo (Can. v), and again (De Consecr., dist. 2): "It must be strictly observed that as often as the priest sacrifices the body and blood of our Lord Jesus Christ upon the altar, he must himself be a partaker of Christ's body and blood."

I answer that, As stated above ([4685]Q[79], AA[5],7), the Eucharist is not only a sacrament, but also a sacrifice. Now whoever offers sacrifice must be a sharer in the sacrifice, because the outward sacrifice he offers is a sign of the inner sacrifice whereby he offers himself to God, as Augustine says (De Civ. Dei x). Hence by partaking of the sacrifice he shows that the inner one is likewise his. In the same way also, by dispensing the sacrifice to the people he shows that he is the dispenser of Divine gifts, of which he ought himself to be the first to partake, as Dionysius says (Eccl. Hier. iii). Consequently, he ought to receive before dispensing it to the people. Accordingly we read in the chapter mentioned above (Twelfth Council of Toledo, Can. v): "What kind of sacrifice is that wherein not even the sacrificer is known to have a share?" But it is by partaking of the sacrifice that he has a share in it, as the Apostle says (1 Cor. 10:18): "Are not they that eat of the sacrifices, partakers of the altar?" Therefore it is necessary for the priest, as often as he consecrates, to receive this sacrament in its integrity.

Reply to Objection 1: The consecration of chrism or of anything else is not a sacrifice, as the consecration of the Eucharist is: consequently there is no parallel.

Reply to Objection 2: The sacrament of Baptism is accomplished in the use of the matter, and consequently no one can baptize himself, because the same person cannot be active and passive in a sacrament. Hence neither in this sacrament does the priest consecrate himself, but he consecrates the bread and wine, in which consecration the sacrament is completed. But the use thereof follows the sacrament, and therefore there is no parallel.

Reply to Objection 3: If Christ's body appears miraculously upon the altar under the guise of flesh, or the blood under the guise of blood, it is not to be received. For Jerome says upon Leviticus (cf. De Consecr., dist. 2): "It is lawful to eat of this sacrifice which is wonderfully performed in memory of Christ: but it is not lawful for anyone to eat of that one which Christ offered on the altar of the cross." Nor does the priest transgress on that account, because miraculous events are not subject to human laws. Nevertheless the priest would be well advised to consecrate again and receive the Lord's body and blood.

Whether a wicked priest can consecrate the Eucharist?

Objection 1: It seems that a wicked priest cannot consecrate the Eucharist. For Jerome, commenting on Sophon. iii, 4, says: "The priests who perform the Eucharist, and who distribute our Lord's blood to the people, act wickedly against Christ's law, in deeming that the Eucharist is consecrated by a prayer rather than by a good life; and that only the solemn prayer is requisite, and not the priest's merits: of whom it is said: 'Let not the priest, in whatever defilement he may be, approach to offer oblations to the Lord'" (Lev. 21:21, Septuagint). But the sinful priest, being defiled, has neither the life nor the merits befitting this sacrament. Therefore a sinful priest cannot consecrate the Eucharist.

Objection 2: Further, Damascene says (De Fide Orth. iv) that "the bread and wine are changed supernaturally into the body and blood of our Lord, by the coming of the Holy Ghost." But Pope Gelasius I says (Ep. ad Elphid., cf. Decret. i, q. 1): "How shall the Holy Spirit, when invoked, come for the consecration of the Divine Mystery, if the priest invoking him be proved full of guilty deeds?" Consequently, the Eucharist cannot be consecrated by a wicked priest.

Objection 3: Further, this sacrament is consecrated by the priest's blessing. But a sinful priest's blessing is not efficacious for consecrating this sacrament, since it is written (Malachi 2:2): "I will curse your blessings." Again, Dionysius says in his Epistle (viii) to the monk Demophilus: "He who is not enlightened has completely fallen away from the priestly order; and I wonder that such a man dare to employ his hands in priestly actions, and in the person of Christ to utter, over the Divine symbols, his unclean infamies, for I will not call them prayers."

On the contrary, Augustine (Paschasius) says (De Corp. Dom. xii): "Within the Catholic Church, in the mystery of the Lord's body and blood, nothing greater is done by a good priest, nothing less by an evil priest, because it is not by the merits of the consecrator that the sacrament is accomplished, but by the Creator's word, and by the power of the Holy Spirit."

I answer that, As was said above ([4686]AA[1],3), the priest consecrates this sacrament not by his own power, but as the minister of Christ, in Whose person he consecrates this sacrament. But from the fact of being wicked he does not cease to be Christ's minister; because our Lord has good and wicked ministers or servants. Hence (Mat. 24:45) our Lord says: "Who, thinkest thou, is a faithful and wise servant?" and afterwards He adds: "But if that evil servant shall say in his heart," etc. And the Apostle (1 Cor. 4:1) says: "Let a man so account of us as of the ministers of Christ"; and afterwards he adds: "I am not conscious to myself of anything; yet am I not hereby justified." He was therefore certain that he was Christ's minister; yet he was not certain that he was a just man. Consequently, a man can be Christ's minister even though he be not one of the just. And this belongs to Christ's excellence, Whom, as the true God, things both good and evil serve, since they are ordained by His providence for His glory. Hence it is evident that priests, even though they be not godly, but sinners, can consecrate the Eucharist.

Reply to Objection 1: In those words Jerome is condemning the error of priests who believed they could consecrate the Eucharist worthily, from the mere fact of being priests, even though they were sinners; and Jerome condemns this from the fact that persons defiled are forbidden to approach the altar; but this does not prevent the sacrifice, which they offer, from being a true sacrifice, if they do approach.

Reply to Objection 2: Previous to the words quoted, Pope Gelasius expresses himself as follows: "That most holy rite, which contains the Catholic discipline, claims for itself such reverence that no one may dare to approach it except with clean conscience." From this it is evident that his meaning is that the priest who is a sinner ought not to approach this sacrament. Hence when he resumes, "How shall the Holy Spirit come when summoned," it must be understood that He comes, not through the priest's merits, but through the power of Christ, Whose words the priest utters.

Reply to Objection 3: As the same action can be evil, inasmuch as it is done with a bad intention of the servant; and good from the good intention of the master; so the blessing of a sinful priest, inasmuch as he acts unworthily is deserving of a curse, and is reputed an infamy and a blasphemy, and not a prayer; whereas, inasmuch as it is pronounced in the person of Christ, it is holy and efficacious. Hence it is said with significance: "I will curse your blessings."

Whether the mass of a sinful priest is of less worth than the mass of a good priest?

Objection 1: It seems that the mass of a sinful priest is not of less worth than that of a good priest. For Pope Gregory says in the Register: "Alas, into what a great snare they fall who believe that the Divine and hidden mysteries can be sanctified more by some than by others; since it is the one and the same Holy Ghost Who hallows those mysteries in a hidden and invisible manner." But these hidden mysteries are celebrated in the mass. Therefore the mass of a sinful priest is not of less value than the mass of a good priest.

Objection 2: Further, as Baptism is conferred by a minister through the power of Christ Who baptizes, so likewise this sacrament is consecrated in the person of Christ. But Baptism is no better when conferred by a better priest, as was said above ([4687]Q[64], A[1], ad 2). Therefore neither is a mass the better, which is celebrated by a better priest.

Objection 3: Further, as the merits of priests differ in the point of being good and better, so they likewise differ in the point of being good and bad. Consequently, if the mass of a better priest be itself better, it follows that the mass of a bad priest must be bad. Now this is unreasonable, because the malice of the ministers cannot affect Christ's mysteries, as Augustine says in his work on Baptism (Contra Donat. xii). Therefore neither is the mass of a better priest the better.

On the contrary, It is stated in Decretal i, q. 1: "The worthier the priest, the sooner is he heard in the needs for which he prays."

I answer that, There are two things to be considered in the mass. namely, the sacrament itself, which is the chief thing; and the prayers which are offered up in the mass for the quick and the dead. So far as the mass itself is concerned, the mass of a wicked priest is not of less value than that of a good priest, because the same sacrifice is offered by both.

Again, the prayer put up in the mass can be considered in two respects: first of all, in so far as it has its efficacy from the devotion of the priest interceding, and in this respect there is no doubt but that the mass of the better priest is the more fruitful. In another respect, inasmuch as the prayer is said by the priest in the mass in the place of the entire Church, of which the priest is the minister; and this ministry remains even in sinful men, as was said above [4688](A[5]) in regard to Christ's ministry. Hence, in this respect the prayer even of the sinful priest is fruitful, not only that which he utters in the mass, but likewise all those he recites in the ecclesiastical offices, wherein he takes the place of the Church. on the other hand, his private prayers are not fruitful, according to Prov. 28:9: "He that turneth away his ears from hearing the law, his prayer shall be an abomination."

Reply to Objection 1: Gregory is speaking there of the holiness of the Divine sacrament.

Reply to Objection 2: In the sacrament of Baptism solemn prayers are not made for all the faithful, as in the mass; therefore there is no parallel in this respect. There is, however, a resemblance as to the effect of the sacrament.

Reply to Objection 3: By reason of the power of the Holy Ghost, Who communicates to each one the blessings of Christ's members on account of their being united in charity, the private blessing in the mass of a good priest is fruitful to others. But the private evil of one man cannot hurt another, except the latter, in some way, consent, as Augustine says (Contra Parmen. ii).

Whether heretics, schismatics, and excommunicated persons can consecrate?

Objection 1: It seems that heretics, schismatics, and excommunicated persons are not able to consecrate the Eucharist. For Augustine says (Liber sentent. Prosperi xv) that "there is no such thing as a true sacrifice outside the Catholic Church": and Pope Leo I says (Ep. lxxx; cf. Decretal i, q. 1): Elsewhere "(i.e. than in the Church which is Christ's body) there is neither valid priesthood nor true sacrifice." But heretics, schismatics, and excommunicated persons are severed from the Church. Therefore they are unable to offer a true sacrifice.

Objection 2: Further (Decretal, caus. i, q. 1), Innocent I is quoted as saying: "Because we receive the laity of the Arians and other pestilential persons, if they seem to repent, it does not follow that their clergy have the dignity of the priesthood or of any other ministerial office, for we allow them to confer nothing save Baptism." But none can consecrate the Eucharist, unless he have the dignity of the priesthood. Therefore heretics and the like cannot consecrate the Eucharist.

Objection 3: Further, it does not seem feasible for one outside the Church to act on behalf of the Church. But when the priest consecrates the Eucharist, he does so in the person of the entire Church, as is evident from the fact of his putting up all prayers in the person of the Church. Therefore, it seems that those who are outside the Church, such as those who are heretics, schismatics, and excommunicate, are not able to consecrate the Eucharist.

On the contrary, Augustine says (Contra Parmen. ii): "Just as Baptism remains in them," i.e. in heretics, schismatics, and those who are excommunicate, "so do their orders remain intact." Now, by the power of his ordination, a priest can consecrate the Eucharist. Therefore, it seems that heretics, schismatics, and those who are excommunicate, can consecrate the Eucharist, since their orders remain entire.

I answer that, Some have contended that heretics, schismatics, and the excommunicate, who are outside the pale of the Church, cannot perform this sacrament. But herein they are deceived, because, as Augustine says (Contra Parmen. ii), "it is one thing to lack something utterly, and another to have it improperly"; and in like fashion, "it is one thing not to bestow, and quite another to bestow, but not rightly." Accordingly, such as, being within the Church, received the power of consecrating the Eucharist through being ordained to the priesthood, have such power rightly indeed; but they use it improperly if afterwards they be separated from the Church by heresy, schism, or excommunication. But such as are ordained while separated from the Church, have neither the power rightly, nor do they use it rightly. But that in both cases they have the power, is clear from what Augustine says (Contra Parmen. ii), that when they return to the unity of the Church, they are not re-ordained, but are received in their orders. And since the consecration of the Eucharist is an act which follows the power of order, such persons as are separated from the Church by heresy, schism, or excommunication, can indeed consecrate the Eucharist, which on being consecrated by them contains Christ's true body and blood; but they act wrongly, and sin by doing so; and in consequence they do not receive the fruit of the sacrifice, which is a spiritual sacrifice.

Reply to Objection 1: Such and similar authorities are to be understood in this sense, that the sacrifice is offered wrongly outside the Church. Hence outside the Church there can be no spiritual sacrifice that is a true sacrifice with the truth of its fruit, although it be a true sacrifice with the truth of the sacrament; thus it was stated above ([4689]Q[80], A[3]), that the sinner receives Christ's body sacramentally, but not spiritually.

Reply to Objection 2: Baptism alone is allowed to be conferred by heretics, and schismatics, because they can lawfully baptize in case of necessity; but in no case can they lawfully consecrate the Eucharist, or confer the other sacraments.

Reply to Objection 3: The priest, in reciting the prayers of the mass, speaks instead of the Church, in whose unity he remains; but in consecrating the sacrament he speaks as in the person of Christ, Whose place he holds by the power of his orders. Consequently, if a priest severed from the unity of the Church celebrates mass, not having lost the power of order, he consecrates Christ's true body and blood; but because he is severed from the unity of the Church, his prayers have no efficacy.

Whether a degraded priest can consecrate this sacrament?

Objection 1: It seems that a degraded priest cannot consecrate this sacrament. For no one can perform this sacrament except he have the power of consecrating. But the priest "who has been degraded has no power of consecrating, although he has the power of baptizing" (App. Gratiani). Therefore it seems that a degraded priest cannot consecrate the Eucharist.

Objection 2: Further, he who gives can take away. But the bishop in ordaining gives to the priest the power of consecrating. Therefore he can take it away by degrading him.

Objection 3: Further, the priest, by degradation, loses either the power of consecrating, or the use of such power. But he does not lose merely the use, for thus the degraded one would lose no more than one excommunicated, who also lacks the use. Therefore it seems that he loses the power to consecrate, and in consequence that he cannot perform this sacrament.

On the contrary, Augustine (Contra Parmen. ii) proves that "apostates" from the faith "are not deprived of their Baptism," from the fact that "it is not restored to them when they return repentant; and therefore it is deemed that it cannot be lost." But in like fashion, if the degraded man be restored, he has not to be ordained over again. Consequently, he has not lost the power of consecrating, and so the degraded priest can perform this sacrament.

I answer that, The power of consecrating the Eucharist belongs to the character of the priestly order. But every character is indelible, because it is given with a kind of consecration, as was said above ([4690]Q[63], A[5]), just as the consecrations of all other things are perpetual, and cannot be lost or repeated. Hence it is clear that the power of consecrating is not lost by degradation. For, again, Augustine says (Contra Parmen. ii): "Both are sacraments," namely Baptism and order, "and both are given to a man with a kind of consecration; the former, when he is baptized; the latter when he is ordained; and therefore it is not lawful for Catholics to repeat either of them." And thus it is evident that the degraded priest can perform this sacrament.

Reply to Objection 1: That Canon is speaking, not as by way of assertion, but by way of inquiry, as can be gleaned from the context.

Reply to Objection 2: The bishop gives the priestly power of order, not as though coming from himself, but instrumentally, as God's minister, and its effect cannot be taken away by man, according to Mat. 19:6: "What God hath joined together, let no man put asunder." And therefore the bishop cannot take this power away, just as neither can he who baptizes take away the baptismal character.

Reply to Objection 3: Excommunication is medicinal. And therefore the ministry of the priestly power is not taken away from the excommunicate, as it were, perpetually, but only for a time, that they may mend; but the exercise is withdrawn from the degraded, as though condemned perpetually.

Day 310

Whether it is permissible to receive communion from heretical, excommunicate, or sinful priests, and to hear mass said by them?

Objection 1: It seems that one may lawfully receive Communion from heretical, excommunicate, or even sinful priests, and to hear mass said by them. Because, as Augustine says (Contra Petilian. iii), "we should not avoid God's sacraments, whether they be given by a good man or by a wicked one." But priests, even if they be sinful, or heretics, or excommunicate, perform a valid sacrament. Therefore it seems that one ought not to refrain from receiving Communion at their hands, or from hearing their mass.

Objection 2: Further, Christ's true body is figurative of His mystical body, as was said above ([4691]Q[67], A[2]). But Christ's true body is consecrated by the priests mentioned above. Therefore it seems that whoever belongs to His mystical body can communicate in their sacrifices.

Objection 3: Further, there are many sins graver than fornication. But it is not forbidden to hear the masses of priests who sin otherwise. Therefore, it ought not to be forbidden to hear the masses of priests guilty of this sin.

On the contrary, The Canon says (Dist. 32): "Let no one hear the mass of a priest whom he knows without doubt to have a concubine." Moreover, Gregory says (Dial. iii) that "the faithless father sent an Arian bishop to his son, for him to receive sacrilegiously the consecrated Communion at his hands. But, when the Arian bishop arrived, God's devoted servant rebuked him, as was right for him to do."

I answer that, As was said above ([4692]AA[5],7), heretical, schismatical, excommunicate, or even sinful priests, although they have the power to consecrate the Eucharist, yet they do not make a proper use of it; on the contrary, they sin by using it. But whoever communicates with another who is in sin, becomes a sharer in his sin. Hence we read in John's Second Canonical Epistle (11) that "He that saith unto him, God speed you, communicateth with his wicked works." Consequently, it is not lawful to receive Communion from them, or to assist at their mass.

Still there is a difference among the above, because heretics, schismatics, and excommunicates, have been forbidden, by the Church's sentence, to perform the Eucharistic rite. And therefore whoever hears their mass or receives the sacraments from them, commits sin. But not all who are sinners are debarred by the Church's sentence from using this power: and so, although suspended by the Divine sentence, yet they are not suspended in regard to others by any ecclesiastical sentence: consequently, until the Church's sentence is pronounced, it is lawful to receive Communion at their hands, and to hear their mass. Hence on 1 Cor. 5:11, "with such a one not so much as to eat," Augustine's gloss runs thus: "In saying this he was unwilling for a man to be judged by his fellow man on arbitrary suspicion, or even by usurped extraordinary judgment, but rather by God's law, according to the Church's ordering, whether he confess of his own accord, or whether he be accused and convicted."

Reply to Objection 1: By refusing to hear the masses of such priests, or to receive Communion from them, we are not shunning God's sacraments; on the contrary, by so doing we are giving them honor (hence a host consecrated by such priests is to be adored, and if it be reserved, it can be consumed by a lawful priest): but what we shun is the sin of the unworthy ministers.

Reply to Objection 2: The unity of the mystical body is the fruit of the true body received. But those who receive or minister unworthily, are deprived of the fruit, as was said above [4693](A[7]; Q[80], A[4]). And therefore, those who belong to the unity of the Faith are not to receive the sacrament from their dispensing.

Reply to Objection 3: Although fornication is not graver than other sins, yet men are more prone to it, owing to fleshly concupiscence. Consequently, this sin is specially inhibited to priests by the Church, lest anyone hear the mass of one living in concubinage. However, this is to be understood of one who is notorious, either from being convicted and sentenced, or from having acknowledged his guilt in legal form, or from it being impossible to conceal his guilt by any subterfuge.

Whether it is lawful for a priest to refrain entirely from consecrating the Eucharist?

Objection 1: It seems to be lawful for a priest to refrain entirely from consecrating the Eucharist. Because, as it is the priest's office to consecrate the Eucharist, so it is likewise to baptize and administer the other sacraments. But the priest is not bound to act as a minister of the other sacraments, unless he has undertaken the care of souls. Therefore, it seems that likewise he is not bound to consecrate the Eucharist except he be charged with the care of souls.

Objection 2: Further, no one is bound to do what is unlawful for him to do; otherwise he would be in two minds. But it is not lawful for the priest who is in a state of sin, or excommunicate, to consecrate the Eucharist, as was said above [4694](A[7]). Therefore it seems that such men are not bound to celebrate, and so neither are the others; otherwise they would be gainers by their fault.

Objection 3: Further, the priestly dignity is not lost by subsequent weakness: because Pope Gelasius I says (cf. Decretal, Dist. 55): "As the canonical precepts do not permit them who are feeble in body to approach the priesthood, so if anyone be disabled when once in that state, he cannot lose that he received at the time he was well." But it sometimes happens that those who are already ordained as priests incur defects whereby they are hindered from celebrating, such as leprosy or epilepsy, or the like. Consequently, it does not appear that priests are bound to celebrate.

On the contrary, Ambrose says in one of his Orations (xxxiii): "It is a grave matter if we do not approach Thy altar with clean heart and pure hands; but it is graver still if while shunning sins we also fail to offer our sacrifice."

I answer that, Some have said that a priest may lawfully refrain altogether from consecrating, except he be bound to do so, and to give the sacraments to the people, by reason of his being entrusted with the care of souls.

But this is said quite unreasonably, because everyone is bound to use the grace entrusted to him, when opportunity serves, according to 2 Cor. 6:1: "We exhort you that you receive not the grace of God in vain." But the opportunity of offering sacrifice is considered not merely in relation to the faithful of Christ to whom the sacraments must be administered, but chiefly with regard to God to Whom the sacrifice of this sacrament is offered by consecrating. Hence, it is not lawful for the priest, even though he has not the care of souls, to refrain altogether from celebrating; and he seems to be bound to celebrate at least on the chief festivals, and especially on those days on which the faithful usually communicate. And hence it is that (2 Macc. 4:14) it is said against some priests that they "were not now occupied about the offices of the altar . . . despising the temple and neglecting the sacrifices."

Reply to Objection 1: The other sacraments are accomplished in being used by the faithful, and therefore he alone is bound to administer them who has undertaken the care of souls. But this sacrament is performed in the consecration of the Eucharist, whereby a sacrifice is offered to God, to which the priest is bound from the order he has received.

Reply to Objection 2: The sinful priest, if deprived by the Church's sentence from exercising his order, simply or for a time, is rendered incapable of offering sacrifice; consequently, the obligation lapses. But if not deprived of the power of celebrating, the obligation is not removed; nor is he in two minds, because he can repent of his sin and then celebrate.

Reply to Objection 3: Weakness or sickness contracted by a priest after his ordination does not deprive him of his orders; but hinders him from exercising them, as to the consecration of the Eucharist: sometimes by making it impossible to exercise them, as, for example, if he lose his sight, or his fingers, or the use of speech; and sometimes on account of danger, as in the case of one suffering from epilepsy, or indeed any disease of the mind; and sometimes, on account of loathsomeness, as is evident in the case of a leper, who ought not to celebrate in public: he can, however, say mass privately, unless the leprosy has gone so far that it has rendered him incapable owing to the wasting away of his limbs.

OF THE RITE OF THIS SACRAMENT (SIX ARTICLES)

We have now to consider the Rite of this sacrament, under which head there are six points of inquiry:

(1) Whether Christ is sacrificed in the celebration of this mystery?
(2) Of the time of celebrating;
(3) Of the place and other matters relating to the equipment for this celebration;
(4) Of the words uttered in celebrating this mystery;
(5) Of the actions performed in celebrating this mystery.
(6) Of the defects which occur in the celebration of this sacrament.

Whether Christ is sacrificed in this sacrament?

Objection 1: It seems that Christ is not sacrificed in the celebration of this sacrament. For it is written (Heb. 10:14) that "Christ by one oblation hath perfected for ever them that are sanctified." But that oblation was His oblation. Therefore Christ is not sacrificed in the celebration of this sacrament.

Objection 2: Further, Christ's sacrifice was made upon the cross, whereon "He delivered Himself for us, an oblation and a sacrifice to God for an odor of sweetness," as is said in Eph. 5:2. But Christ is not crucified in the celebration of this mystery. Therefore, neither is He sacrificed.

Objection 3: Further, as Augustine says (De Trin. iv), in Christ's sacrifice the priest and the victim are one and the same. But in the celebration of this sacrament the priest and the victim are not the same. Therefore, the celebration of this sacrament is not a sacrifice of Christ.

On the contrary, Augustine says in the Liber Sentent. Prosp. (cf. Ep. xcviii): "Christ was sacrificed once in Himself, and yet He is sacrificed daily in the Sacrament."

I answer that, The celebration of this sacrament is called a sacrifice for two reasons. First, because, as Augustine says (Ad Simplician. ii), "the images of things are called by the names of the things whereof they are the images; as when we look upon a picture or a fresco, we say, 'This is Cicero and that is Sallust.'" But, as was said above ([4695]Q[79], A[1]), the celebration of this sacrament is an image representing Christ's Passion, which is His true sacrifice. Accordingly the celebration of this sacrament is called Christ's sacrifice. Hence it is that Ambrose, in commenting on Heb. 10:1, says: "In Christ was offered up a sacrifice capable of giving eternal salvation; what then do we do? Do we not offer it up every day in memory of His death?" Secondly it is called a sacrifice, in respect of the effect of His Passion: because, to wit, by this sacrament, we are made partakers of the fruit of our Lord's Passion. Hence in one of the Sunday Secrets (Ninth Sunday after Pentecost) we say: "Whenever the commemoration of this sacrifice is celebrated, the work of our redemption is enacted." Consequently, according to the first reason, it is true to say that Christ was sacrificed, even in the figures of the Old Testament: hence it is stated in the Apocalypse (13:8): "Whose names are not written in the Book of Life of the Lamb, which was slain from the beginning of the world." But according to the second reason, it is proper to this sacrament for Christ to be sacrificed in its celebration.

Reply to Objection 1: As Ambrose says (commenting on Heb. 10:1), "there is but one victim," namely that which Christ offered, and which we offer, "and not many victims, because Christ was offered but once: and this latter sacrifice is the pattern of the former. For, just as what is offered everywhere is one body, and not many bodies, so also is it but one sacrifice."

Reply to Objection 2: As the celebration of this sacrament is an image representing Christ's Passion, so the altar is representative of the cross itself, upon which Christ was sacrificed in His proper species.

Reply to Objection 3: For the same reason (cf. Reply OBJ[2]) the priest also bears Christ's image, in Whose person and by Whose power he pronounces the words of consecration, as is evident from what was said above ([4696]Q[82], AA[1],3). And so, in a measure, the priest and victim are one and the same.

Whether the time for celebrating this mystery has been properly determined?

Objection 1: It seems that the time for celebrating this mystery has not been properly determined. For as was observed above [4697](A[1]), this sacrament is representative of our Lord's Passion. But the commemoration of our Lord's Passion takes place in the Church once in the year: because Augustine says (Enarr. ii in Ps. 21): "Is not Christ slain as often as the Pasch is celebrated? Nevertheless, the anniversary remembrance represents what took place in by-gone days; and so it does not cause us to be stirred as if we saw our Lord hanging upon the cross." Therefore this sacrament ought to be celebrated but once a year.

Objection 2: Further, Christ's Passion is commemorated in the Church on the Friday before Easter, and not on Christmas Day. Consequently, since this sacrament is commemorative of our Lord's Passion, it seems unsuitable for this sacrament to be celebrated thrice on Christmas Day, and to be entirely omitted on Good Friday.

Objection 3: Further, in the celebration of this sacrament the Church ought to imitate Christ's institution. But it was in the evening that Christ consecrated this sacrament. Therefore it seems that this sacrament ought to be celebrated at that time of day.

Objection 4: Further, as is set down in the Decretals (De Consecr., dist. i), Pope Leo I wrote to Dioscorus, Bishop of Alexandria, that "it is permissible to celebrate mass in the first part of the day." But the day begins at midnight, as was said above ([4698]Q[80], A[8], ad 5). Therefore it seems that after midnight it is lawful to celebrate.

Objection 5: Further, in one of the Sunday Secrets (Ninth Sunday after Pentecost) we say: "Grant us, Lord, we beseech Thee, to frequent these mysteries." But there will be greater frequency if the priest celebrates several times a day. Therefore it seems that the priest ought not to be hindered from celebrating several times daily.

On the contrary is the custom which the Church observes according to the statutes of the Canons.

I answer that, As stated above [4699](A[1]), in the celebration of this mystery, we must take into consideration the representation of our Lord's Passion, and the participation of its fruits; and the time suitable for the celebration of this mystery ought to be determined by each of these considerations. Now since, owing to our daily defects, we stand in daily need of the fruits of our Lord's Passion, this sacrament is offered regularly every day in the Church. Hence our Lord teaches us to pray (Lk. 11:3): "Give us this day our daily bread": in explanation of which words Augustine says (De Verb. Dom. xxviii): "If it be a daily bread, why do you take it once a year, as the Greeks have the custom in the east? Receive it daily that it may benefit you every day."

But since our Lord's Passion was celebrated from the third to the ninth hour, therefore this sacrament is solemnly celebrated by the Church in that part of the day.

Reply to Objection 1: Christ's Passion is recalled in this sacrament, inasmuch as its effect flows out to the faithful; but at Passion-tide Christ's Passion is recalled inasmuch as it was wrought in Him Who is our Head. This took place but once; whereas the faithful receive daily the fruits of His Passion: consequently, the former is commemorated but once in the year, whereas the latter takes place every day, both that we may partake of its fruit and in order that we may have a perpetual memorial.

Reply to Objection 2: The figure ceases on the advent of the reality. But this sacrament is a figure and a representation of our Lord's Passion, as stated above. And therefore on the day on which our Lord's Passion is recalled as it was really accomplished, this sacrament is not consecrated. Nevertheless, lest the Church be deprived on that day of the fruit of the Passion offered to us by this sacrament, the body of Christ consecrated the day before is reserved to be consumed on that day; but the blood is not reserved, on account of danger, and because the blood is more specially the image of our Lord's Passion, as stated above ([4700]Q[78], A[3], ad 2). Nor is it true, as some affirm, that the wine is changed into blood when the particle of Christ's body is dropped into it. Because this cannot be done otherwise than by consecration under the due form of words.

On Christmas Day, however, several masses are said on account of Christ's threefold nativity. Of these the first is His eternal birth, which is hidden in our regard. and therefore one mass is sung in the night, in the "Introit" of which we say: "The Lord said unto Me: Thou art My Son, this day have I begotten Thee." The second is His nativity in time, and the spiritual birth, whereby Christ rises "as the day-star in our [Vulg.: 'your'] hearts" (2 Pet. 1:19), and on this account the mass is sung at dawn, and in the "Introit" we say: "The light will shine on us today." The third is Christ's temporal and bodily birth, according as He went forth from the virginal womb, becoming visible to us through being clothed with flesh: and on that account the third mass is sung in broad daylight, in the "Introit" of which we say: "A child is born to us." Nevertheless, on the other hand, it can be said that His eternal generation, of itself, is in the full light, and on this account in the gospel of the third mass mention is made of His eternal birth. But regarding His birth in the body, He was literally born during the night, as a sign that He came to the darknesses of our infirmity; hence also in the midnight mass we say the gospel of Christ's nativity in the flesh.

Likewise on other days upon which many of God's benefits have to be recalled or besought, several masses are celebrated on one day, as for instance, one for the feast, and another for a fast or for the dead.

Reply to Objection 3: As already observed ([4701]Q[73], A[5]), Christ wished to give this sacrament last of all, in order that it might make a deeper impression on the hearts of the disciples; and therefore it was after supper, at the close of day, that He consecrated this sacrament and gave it to His disciples. But we celebrate at the hour when our Lord suffered, i.e. either, as on feast-days, at the hour of Terce, when He was crucified by the tongues of the Jews (Mk. 15:25), and when the Holy Ghost descended upon the disciples (Acts 2:15); or, as when no feast is kept, at the hour of Sext, when He was crucified at the hands of the soldiers (Jn. 19:14), or, as on fasting days, at None, when crying out with a loud voice He gave up the ghost (Mat. 27:46, 50).

Nevertheless the mass can be postponed, especially when Holy orders have to be conferred, and still more on Holy Saturday; both on account of the length of the office, and also because orders belong to the Sunday, as is set forth in the Decretals (dist. 75).

Masses, however, can be celebrated "in the first part of the day," owing to any necessity; as is stated De Consecr., dist. 1.

Reply to Objection 4: As a rule mass ought to be said in the day and not in the night, because Christ is present in this sacrament, Who says (Jn. 9:4,5): "I must work the works of Him that sent Me, whilst it is day: because the night cometh when no man can work; as long as I am in the world, I am the light of the world." Yet this should be done in such a manner that the beginning of the day is not to be taken from midnight; nor from sunrise, that is, when the substance of the sun appears above the earth; but when the dawn begins to show: because then the sun is said to be risen when the brightness of his beams appears. Accordingly it is written (Mk. 16:1) that "the women came to the tomb, the sun being now risen"; though, as John relates (Jn. 20:1), "while it was yet dark they came to the tomb." It is in this way that Augustine explains this difference (De Consens. Evang. iii).

Exception is made on the night of Christmas eve, when mass is celebrated, because our Lord was born in the night (De Consecr., dist. 1). And in like manner it is celebrated on Holy Saturday towards the beginning of the night, since our Lord rose in the night, that is, "when it was yet dark, before the sun's rising was manifest."

Reply to Objection 5: As is set down in the decree (De Consecr., dist. 1), in virtue of a decree of Pope Alexander II, "it is enough for a priest to celebrate one mass each day, because Christ suffered once and redeemed the whole world; and very happy is he who can worthily celebrate one mass. But there are some who say one mass for the dead, and another of the day, if need be. But I do not deem that those escape condemnation who presume to celebrate several masses daily, either for the sake of money, or to gain flattery from the laity." And Pope Innocent III says (Extra, De Celebr. Miss., chap. Consuluisti) that "except on the day of our Lord's birth, unless necessity urges, it suffices for a priest to celebrate only one mass each day."

Whether this sacrament ought to be celebrated in a house and with sacred vessels?

Objection 1: It seems that this sacrament ought not to be celebrated in a house and with sacred vessels. For this sacrament is a representation of our Lord's Passion. But Christ did not suffer in a house, but outside the city gate, according to Heb. 1:12: "Jesus, that He might sanctify the people by His own blood, suffered without the gate." Therefore, it seems that this sacrament ought not to be celebrated in a house, but rather in the open air.

Objection 2: Further, in the celebration of this sacrament the Church ought to imitate the custom of Christ and the apostles. But the house wherein Christ first wrought this sacrament was not consecrated, but merely an ordinary supper-room prepared by the master of the house, as related in Lk. 22:11,12. Moreover, we read (Acts 2:46) that "the apostles were continuing daily with one accord in the temple; and, breaking bread from house to house, they took their meat with gladness." Consequently, there is no need for houses, in which this sacrament is celebrated, to be consecrated.

Objection 3: Further, nothing that is to no purpose ought to be done in the Church, which is governed by the Holy Ghost. But it seems useless to consecrate a church, or an altar, or such like inanimate things, since they are not capable of receiving grace or spiritual virtue. Therefore it is unbecoming for such consecrations to be performed in the Church.

Objection 4: Further, only Divine works ought to be recalled with solemnity, according to Ps. 91:5: "I shall rejoice in the works of Thy hands." Now the consecration of a church or altar, is the work of a man; as is also the consecration of the chalice, and of the ministers, and of other such things. But these latter consecrations are not commemorated in the Church. Therefore neither ought the consecration of a church or of an altar to be commemorated with solemnity.

Objection 5: Further, the truth ought to correspond with the figure. But in the Old Testament, which was a figure of the New, the altar was not made of hewn stones: for, it is written (Ex. 20:24): "You shall make an altar of earth unto Me . . . and if thou make an altar of stone unto Me, thou shalt not build it of hewn stones." Again, the altar is commanded to be made of "setim-wood," covered "with brass" (Ex. 27:1,2), or "with gold" (Ex. 25). Consequently, it seems unfitting for the Church to make exclusive use of altars made of stone.

Objection 6: Further, the chalice with the paten represents Christ's tomb, which was "hewn in a rock," as is narrated in the Gospels. Consequently, the chalice ought to be of stone, and not of gold or of silver or tin.

Objection 7: Further, just as gold is the most precious among the materials of the altar vessels, so are cloths of silk the most precious among other cloths. Consequently, since the chalice is of gold, the altar cloths ought to be made of silk and not of linen.

Objection 8: Further, the dispensing and ordering of the sacraments belong to the Church's ministers, just as the ordering of temporal affairs is subject to the ruling of secular princes; hence the Apostle says (1 Cor. 4:1): "Let a man so esteem us as the ministers of Christ end the dispensers of the mysteries of God." But if anything be done against the ordinances of princes it is deemed void. Therefore, if the various items mentioned above are suitably commanded by the Church's prelates, it seems that the body of Christ could not be consecrated unless they be observed; and so it appears to follow that Christ's words are not sufficient of themselves for consecrating this sacrament: which is contrary to the fact. Consequently, it does not seem fitting for such ordinances to be made touching the celebration of this sacrament.

On the contrary, The Church's ordinances are Christ's own ordinances; since He said (Mat. 18:20): "Wherever two or three are gathered together in My name, there am I in the midst of them."

I answer that, There are two things to be considered regarding the equipment of this sacrament: one of these belongs to the representation of the events connected with our Lord's Passion; while the other is connected with the reverence due to the sacrament, in which Christ is contained verily, and not in figure only.

Hence we consecrate those things which we make use of in this sacrament; both that we may show our reverence for the sacrament, and in order to represent the holiness which is the effect of the Passion of Christ, according to Heb. 13:12: "Jesus, that He might sanctify the people by His own blood," etc.

Reply to Objection 1: This sacrament ought as a rule to be celebrated in a house, whereby the Church is signified, according to 1 Tim. 3:15: "That thou mayest know how thou oughtest to behave thyself in the house of God, which is the Church of the living God." Because "outside the Church there is no place for the true sacrifice," as Augustine says (Liber Sentent. Prosp. xv). And because the Church was not to be confined within the territories of the Jewish people, but was to be established throughout the whole world, therefore Christ's Passion was not celebrated within the city of the Jews, but in the open country, that so the whole world might serve as a house for Christ's Passion. Nevertheless, as is said in De Consecr., dist. 1, "if a church be not to hand, we permit travelers to celebrate mass in the open air, or in a tent, if there be a consecrated altar-table to hand, and the other requisites belonging to the sacred function."

Reply to Objection 2: The house in which this sacrament is celebrated denotes the Church, and is termed a church; and so it is fittingly consecrated, both to represent the holiness which the Church acquired from the Passion, as well as to denote the holiness required of them who have to receive this sacrament. By the altar Christ Himself is signified, of Whom the Apostle says (Heb. 13:15): "Through Him we offer a sacrifice of praise to God." Hence the consecration of the altar signifies Christ's holiness, of which it was said (Lk. 1:35): "The Holy one born of thee shall be called the Son of God." Hence we read in De Consecr., dist. 1: "It has seemed pleasing for the altars to be consecrated not merely with the anointing of chrism, but likewise with the priestly blessing."

And therefore, as a rule, it is not lawful to celebrate this sacrament except in a consecrated house. Hence it is enacted (De Consecr., dist. 1): "Let no priest presume to say mass except in places consecrated by the bishop." And furthermore because pagans and other unbelievers are not members of the Church, therefore we read (De Consecr., dist. 1): "It is not lawful to bless a church in which the bodies of unbelievers are buried, but if it seem suitable for consecration, then, after removing the corpses and tearing down the walls or beams, let it be rebuilt. If, however, it has been already consecrated, and the faithful lie in it, it is lawful to celebrate mass therein." Nevertheless in a case of necessity this sacrament can be performed in houses which have not been consecrated, or which have been profaned; but with the bishop's consent. Hence we read in the same distinction: "We deem that masses are not to be celebrated everywhere, but in places consecrated by the bishop, or where he gives permission." But not without a portable altar consecrated by the bishop: hence in the same distinction we read: "We permit that, if the churches be devastated or burned, masses may be celebrated in chapels, with a consecrated altar." For because Christ's holiness is the fount of all the Church's holiness, therefore in necessity a consecrated altar suffices for performing this sacrament. And on this account a church is never consecrated without consecrating the altar. Yet sometimes an altar is consecrated apart from the church, with the relics of the saints, "whose lives are hidden with Christ in God" (Col. 3:3). Accordingly under the same distinction we read: "It is our pleasure that altars, in which no relics of saints are found enclosed, be thrown down, if possible, by the bishops presiding over such places."

Reply to Objection 3: The church, altar, and other like inanimate things are consecrated, not because they are capable of receiving grace, but because they acquire special spiritual virtue from the consecration, whereby they are rendered fit for the Divine worship, so that man derives devotion therefrom, making him more fitted for Divine functions, unless this be hindered by want of reverence. Hence it is written (2 Macc. 3:38): "There is undoubtedly in that place a certain power of God; for He that hath His dwelling in the heavens is the visitor, and the protector of that place."

Hence it is that such places are cleansed and exorcised before being consecrated, that the enemy's power may be driven forth. And for the same reason churches defiled by shedding of blood or seed are reconciled: because some machination of the enemy is apparent on account of the sin committed there. And for this reason we read in the same distinction: "Wherever you find churches of the Arians, consecrate them as Catholic churches without delay by means of devout prayers and rites." Hence, too, it is that some say with probability, that by entering a consecrated church one obtains forgiveness of venial sins, just as one does by the sprinkling of holy water; alleging the words of Ps. 84:2,3: "Lord, Thou hast blessed Thy land . . . Thou hast forgiven the iniquity of Thy people." And therefore, in consequence of the virtue acquired by a church's consecration, the consecration is never repeated. Accordingly we find in the same distinction the following words quoted from the Council of Nicaea: "Churches which have once been consecrated, must not be consecrated again, except they be devastated by fire, or defiled by shedding of blood or of anyone's seed; because, just as a child once baptized in the name of the Father, and of the Son, and of the Holy Ghost, ought not to be baptized again, so neither ought a place, once dedicated to God, to be consecrated again, except owing to the causes mentioned above; provided that the consecrators held faith in the Holy Trinity": in fact, those outside the Church cannot consecrate. But, as we read in the same distinction: "Churches or altars of doubtful consecration are to be consecrated anew."

And since they acquire special spiritual virtue from their consecration, we find it laid down in the same distinction that "the beams of a dedicated church ought not to be used for any other purpose, except it be for some other church, or else they are to be burned, or put to the use of brethren in some monastery: but on no account are they to be discarded for works of the laity." We read there, too, that "the altar covering, chair, candlesticks, and veil, are to be burned when warn out; and their ashes are to be placed in the baptistery, or in the walls, or else cast into the trenches beneath the flag-stones, so as not to be defiled by the feet of those that enter."

Reply to Objection 4: Since the consecration of the altar signifies Christ's holiness, and the consecration of a house the holiness of the entire Church, therefore the consecration of a church or of an altar is more fittingly commemorated. And on this account the solemnity of a church dedication is observed for eight days, in order to signify the happy resurrection of Christ and of the Church's members. Nor is the consecration of a church or altar man's doing only, since it has a spiritual virtue. Hence in the same distinction (De Consecr.) it is said: "The solemnities of the dedication of churches are to be solemnly celebrated each year: and that dedications are to be kept up for eight days, you will find in the third book of Kings" (8:66).

Reply to Objection 5: As we read in De Consecr., dist. 1, "altars, if not of stone, are not to be consecrated with the anointing of chrism." And this is in keeping with the signification of this sacrament; both because the altar signifies Christ, for in 1 Cor. 10:3, it is written, "But the rock was Christ": and because Christ's body was laid in a stone sepulchre. This is also in keeping with the use of the sacrament. Because stone is solid, and may be found everywhere. which was not necessary in the old Law, when the altar was made in one place. As to the commandment to make the altar of earth, or of unhewn stones, this was given in order to remove idolatry.

Reply to Objection 6: As is laid down in the same distinction, "formerly the priests did not use golden but wooden chalices; but Pope Zephyrinus ordered the mass to be said with glass patens; and subsequently Pope Urban had everything made of silver." Afterwards it was decided that "the Lord's chalice with the paten should be made entirely of gold, or of silver or at least of tin. But it is not to be made of brass, or copper, because the action of the wine thereon produces verdigris, and provokes vomiting. But no one is to presume to sing mass with a chalice of wood or of glass," because as the wood is porous, the consecrated blood would remain in it;

while glass is brittle and there might arise danger of breakage; and the same applies to stone. Consequently, out of reverence for the sacrament, it was enacted that the chalice should be made of the aforesaid materials.

Reply to Objection 7: Where it could be done without danger, the Church gave order for that thing to be used which more expressively represents Christ's Passion. But there was not so much danger regarding the body which is placed on the corporal, as there is with the blood contained in the chalice. And consequently, although the chalice is not made of stone, yet the corporal is made of linen, since Christ's body was wrapped therein. Hence we read in an Epistle of Pope Silvester, quoted in the same distinction: "By a unanimous decree we command that no one shall presume to celebrate the sacrifice of the altar upon a cloth of silk, or dyed material, but upon linen consecrated by the bishop; as Christ's body was buried in a clean linen winding-sheet." Moreover, linen material is becoming, owing to its cleanness, to denote purity of conscience, and, owing to the manifold labor with which it is prepared, to denote Christ's Passion.

Reply to Objection 8: The dispensing of the sacraments belongs to the Church's ministers; but their consecration is from God Himself. Consequently, the Church's ministers can make no ordinances regarding the form of the consecration, and the manner of celebrating. And therefore, if the priest pronounces the words of consecration over the proper matter with the intention of consecrating, then, without every one of the things mentioned above---namely, without house, and altar, consecrated chalice and corporal, and the other things instituted by the Church---he consecrates Christ's body in very truth; yet he is guilty of grave sin, in not following the rite of the Church.

Whether the words spoken in this sacrament are properly framed?

Objection 1: It seems that the words spoken in this sacrament are not properly framed. For, as Ambrose says (De Sacram. iv), this sacrament is consecrated with Christ's own words. Therefore no other words besides Christ's should be spoken in this sacrament.

Objection 2: Further, Christ's words and deeds are made known to us through the Gospel. But in consecrating this sacrament words are used which are not set down in the Gospels: for we do not read in the Gospel, of Christ lifting up His eyes to heaven while consecrating this sacrament: and similarly it is said in the Gospel: "Take ye and eat" [comedite] without the addition of the word "all," whereas in celebrating this sacrament we say: "Lifting up His eyes to heaven," and again, "Take ye and eat [manducate] of this." Therefore such words as these are out of place when spoken in the celebration of this sacrament.

Objection 3: Further, all the other sacraments are ordained for the salvation of all the faithful. But in the celebration of the other sacraments there is no common prayer put up for the salvation of all the faithful and of the departed. Consequently it is unbecoming in this sacrament.

Objection 4: Further, Baptism especially is called the sacrament of faith. Consequently, the truths which belong to instruction in the faith ought rather to be given regarding Baptism than regarding this sacrament, such as the doctrine of the apostles and of the Gospels.

Objection 5: Further, devotion on the part of the faithful is required in every sacrament. Consequently, the devotion of the faithful ought not to be stirred up in this sacrament more than in the others by Divine praises and by admonitions, such as, "Lift up your hearts."

Objection 6: Further, the minister of this sacrament is the priest, as stated above ([4702]Q[82], A[1]). Consequently, all the words spoken in this sacrament ought to be uttered by the priest, and not some by the ministers, and some by the choir.

Objection 7: Further, the Divine power works this sacrament unfailingly. Therefore it is to no purpose that the priest asks for the perfecting of this sacrament, saying: "Which oblation do thou, O God, in all," etc.

Objection 8: Further, the sacrifice of the New Law is much more excellent than the sacrifice of the fathers of old. Therefore, it is unfitting for the priest to pray that this sacrifice may be as acceptable as the sacrifice of Abel, Abraham, and Melchisedech.

Objection 9: Further, just as Christ's body does not begin to be in this sacrament by change of place, as stated above ([4703]Q[75], A[2]), so likewise neither does it cease to be there. Consequently, it is improper for the priest to ask: "Bid these things be borne by the hands of thy holy angel unto Thine altar on high."

On the contrary, We find it stated in De Consecr., dist. 1, that "James, the brother of the Lord according to the flesh, and Basil, bishop of Caesarea, edited the rite of celebrating the mass": and from their authority it is manifest that whatever words are employed in this matter, are chosen becomingly.

I answer that, Since the whole mystery of our salvation is comprised in this sacrament, therefore is it performed with greater solemnity than the other sacraments. And since it is written (Eccles. 4:17): "Keep thy foot when thou goest into the house of God"; and (Ecclus. 18:23): "Before prayer prepare thy soul," therefore the celebration of this mystery is preceded by a certain preparation in order that we may perform worthily that which follows after. The first part of this preparation is Divine praise, and consists in the "Introit": according to Ps. 49:23: "The sacrifice of praise shall glorify me; and there is the way by which I will show him the salvation of God": and this is taken for the most part from the Psalms, or, at least, is sung with a Psalm, because, as Dionysius says (Eccl. Hier. iii): "The Psalms comprise by way of praise whatever is contained in Sacred Scripture."

The second part contains a reference to our present misery, by reason of which we pray for mercy, saying: "Lord, have mercy on us," thrice for the Person of the Father, and "Christ, have mercy on us," thrice for the Person of the Son, and "Lord, have mercy on us," thrice for the Person of the Holy Ghost; against the threefold misery of ignorance, sin, and punishment; or else to express the "circuminsession" of all the Divine Persons.

The third part commemorates the heavenly glory, to the possession of which, after this life of misery, we are tending, in the words, "Glory be to God on high," which are sung on festival days, on which the heavenly glory is commemorated, but are omitted in those sorrowful offices which commemorate our unhappy state.

The fourth part contains the prayer which the priest makes for the people, that they may be made worthy of such great mysteries.

There precedes, in the second place, the instruction of the faithful, because this sacrament is "a mystery of faith," as stated above ([4704]Q[78], A[3], ad 5). Now this instruction is given "dispositively," when the Lectors and Sub-deacons read aloud in the church the teachings of the prophets and apostles: after this "lesson," the choir sing the "Gradual," which signifies progress in life; then the "Alleluia" is intoned, and this denotes spiritual joy; or in mournful offices the "Tract", expressive of spiritual sighing; for all these things ought to result from the aforesaid teaching. But the people are instructed "perfectly" by Christ's teaching contained in the Gospel, which is read by the higher ministers, that is, by the Deacons. And because we believe Christ as the Divine truth, according to Jn. 8:46, "If I tell you the truth, why do you not believe Me?" after the Gospel has been read, the "Creed" is sung in which the people show that they assent by faith to Christ's doctrine. And it is sung on those festivals of which mention is made therein, as on the festivals of Christ, of the Blessed Virgin, and of the apostles, who laid the foundations of this faith, and on other such days.

So then, after the people have been prepared and instructed, the next step is to proceed to the celebration of the mystery, which is both offered as a sacrifice, and consecrated and received as a sacrament: since first we have the oblation; then the consecration of the matter offered; and thirdly, its reception.

In regard to the oblation, two things are done, namely, the people's praise in singing the "offertory," expressing the joy of the offerers, and the priest's prayer asking for the people's oblation to be made acceptable to God. Hence David said (1 Para 29:17): "In the simplicity of my heart, I have . . . offered all these things: and I have seen with great joy Thy people which are here present, offer Thee their offerings": and then he makes the following prayer: "O Lord God . . . keep . . . this will."

Then, regarding the consecration, performed by supernatural power, the people are first of all excited to devotion in the "Preface," hence they are admonished "to lift up their hearts to the Lord," and therefore when the "Preface" is ended the people devoutly praise Christ's Godhead, saying with the angels: "Holy, Holy, Holy"; and His humanity, saying with the children: "Blessed is he that cometh." In the next place the priest makes a "commemoration," first of those for whom this sacrifice is offered, namely, for the whole Church, and "for those set in high places" (1 Tim. 2:2), and, in a special manner, of them "who offer, or for whom the mass is offered." Secondly, he commemorates the saints, invoking their patronage for those mentioned above, when he says: "Communicating with, and honoring the memory," etc. Thirdly, he concludes the petition when he says: "Wherefore that this oblation," etc., in order that the oblation may be salutary to them for whom it is offered.

Then he comes to the consecration itself. Here he asks first of all for the effect of the consecration, when he says: "Which oblation do Thou, O God," etc. Secondly, he performs the consecration using our Saviour's words, when he says: "Who the day before," etc. Thirdly, he makes excuse for his presumption in obeying Christ's command, saying: "Wherefore, calling to mind," etc. Fourthly, he asks that the sacrifice accomplished may find favor with God, when he says: "Look down upon them with a propitious," etc. Fifthly, he begs for the effect of this sacrifice and sacrament, first for the partakers, saying: "We humbly beseech Thee"; then for the dead, who can no longer receive it, saying: "Be mindful also, O Lord," etc.; thirdly, for the priests themselves who offer, saying: "And to us sinners," etc.

Then follows the act of receiving the sacrament. First of all, the people are prepared for Communion; first, by the common prayer of the congregation, which is the Lord's Prayer, in which we ask for our daily bread to be given us; and also by private prayer, which the priest puts up specially for the people, when he says: "Deliver us, we beseech Thee, O Lord," etc. Secondly, the people are prepared by the "Pax" which is given with the words, "Lamb of God," etc., because this is the sacrament of unity and peace, as stated above ([4705]Q[73], A[4];[4706] Q[79], A[1]). But in masses for the dead, in which the sacrifice is offered not for present peace, but for the repose of the dead, the "Pax" is omitted.

Then follows the reception of the sacrament, the priest receiving first, and afterwards giving it to others, because, as Dionysius says (Eccl. Hier. iii), he who gives Divine things to others, ought first to partake thereof himself.

Finally, the whole celebration of mass ends with the thanksgiving, the people rejoicing for having received the mystery (and this is the meaning of the singing after the Communion); and the priest returning thanks by prayer, as Christ, at the close of the supper with His disciples, "said a hymn" (Mat. 26:30).

Reply to Objection 1: The consecration is accomplished by Christ's words only; but the other words must be added to dispose the people for receiving it, as stated above.

Reply to Objection 2: As is stated in the last chapter of John (verse 25), our Lord said and did many things which are not written down by the Evangelists; and among them is the uplifting of His eyes to heaven at the supper; nevertheless the Roman Church had it by tradition from the apostles. For it seems reasonable that He Who lifted up His eyes to the Father in raising Lazarus to life, as related in Jn. 11:41, and in the prayer which He made for the disciples (Jn. 17:1), had more reason to do so in instituting this sacrament, as being of greater import.

The use of the word "manducate" instead of "comedite" makes no difference in the meaning, nor does the expression signify, especially since those words are no part of the form, as stated above ([4707]Q[78], A[1], ad 2,4).

The additional word "all" is understood in the Gospels, although not expressed, because He had said (Jn. 6:54): "Except you eat the flesh of the Son of Man . . . you shall not have life in you."

Reply to Objection 3: The Eucharist is the sacrament of the unity of the whole Church: and therefore in this sacrament, more than in the others, mention ought to be made of all that belongs to the salvation of the entire Church.

Reply to Objection 4: There is a twofold instruction in the Faith: the first is for those receiving it for the first time, that is to say, for catechumens, and such instruction is given in connection with Baptism. The other is the instruction of the faithful who take part in this sacrament; and such instruction is given in connection with this sacrament. Nevertheless catechumens and unbelievers are not excluded therefrom. Hence in De Consecr., dist. 1, it is laid down: "Let the bishop hinder no one from entering the church, and hearing the word of God, be they Gentiles, heretics, or Jews, until the mass of the Catechumens begins," in which the instruction regarding the Faith is contained.

Reply to Objection 5: Greater devotion is required in this sacrament than in the others, for the reason that the entire Christ is contained therein. Moreover, this sacrament requires a more general devotion, i.e. on the part of the whole people, since for them it is offered; and not merely on the part of the recipients, as in the other sacraments. Hence Cyprian observes (De Orat. Domin. 31), "The priest, in saying the Preface, disposes the souls of the brethren by saying, 'Lift up your hearts,' and when the people answer---'We have lifted them up to the Lord,' let them remember that they are to think of nothing else but God."

Reply to Objection 6: As was said above (ad 3), those things are mentioned in this sacrament which belong to the entire Church; and consequently some things which refer to the people are sung by the choir, and same of these words are all sung by the choir, as though inspiring the entire people with them; and there are other words which the priest begins and the people take up, the priest then acting as in the person of God; to show that the things they denote have come to the people through Divine revelation, such as faith and heavenly glory; and therefore the priest intones the "Creed" and the "Gloria in excelsis Deo." Other words are uttered by the ministers, such as the doctrine of the Old and New Testament, as a sign that this doctrine was announced to the peoples through ministers sent by God. And there are other words which the priest alone recites, namely, such as belong to his personal office, "that he may offer up gifts and prayers for the people" (Heb. 5:1). Some of these, however, he says aloud, namely, such as are common to priest and people alike, such as the "common prayers"; other words, however, belong to the priest alone, such as the oblation and the consecration; consequently, the prayers that are said in connection with these have to be said by the priest in secret. Nevertheless, in both he calls the people to attention by saying: "The Lord be with you," and he waits for them to assent by saying "Amen." And therefore before the secret prayers he says aloud, "The Lord be with you," and he concludes, "For ever and ever." Or the priest secretly pronounces some of the words as a token that regarding Christ's Passion the disciples acknowledged Him only in secret.

Reply to Objection 7: The efficacy of the sacramental words can be hindered by the priest's intention. Nor is there anything unbecoming in our asking of God for what we know He will do, just as Christ (Jn. 17:1, 5) asked for His glorification.

But the priest does not seem to pray there for the consecration to be fulfilled, but that it may be fruitful in our regard, hence he says expressively: "That it may become 'to us' the body and the blood." Again, the words preceding these have that meaning, when he says: "Vouchsafe to make this oblation blessed," i.e. according to Augustine (Paschasius, De Corp. et Sang. Dom. xii), "that we may receive a blessing," namely, through grace; "'enrolled,' i.e. that we may be enrolled in heaven; 'ratified,' i.e. that we may be incorporated in Christ; 'reasonable,' i.e. that we may be stripped of our animal sense; 'acceptable,' i.e. that we who in ourselves are displeasing, may, by its means, be made acceptable to His only Son."

Reply to Objection 8: Although this sacrament is of itself preferable to all ancient sacrifices, yet the sacrifices of the men of old were most acceptable to God on account of their devotion. Consequently the priest asks that this sacrifice may be accepted by God through the devotion of the offerers, just as the former sacrifices were accepted by Him.

Reply to Objection 9: The priest does not pray that the sacramental species may be borne up to heaven; nor that Christ's true body may be borne thither, for it does not cease to be there; but he offers this prayer for Christ's mystical body, which is signified in this sacrament, that the angel standing by at the Divine mysteries may present to God the prayers of both priest and people, according to Apoc. 8:4: "And the smoke of the incense of the prayers of the saints ascended up before God, from the hand of the angel." But God's "altar on high" means either the Church triumphant, unto which we pray to be translated, or else God Himself, in Whom we ask to share; because it is said of this altar (Ex. 20:26): "Thou shalt not go up by steps unto My altar, i.e. thou shalt make no steps towards the Trinity." Or else by the angel we are to understand Christ Himself, Who is the "Angel of great counsel" (Is. 9:6: Septuagint), Who unites His mystical body with God the Father and the Church triumphant.

And from this the mass derives its name [missa]; because the priest sends [mittit] his prayers up to God through the angel, as the people do through the priest. or else because Christ is the victim sent [missa] to us: accordingly the deacon on festival days "dismisses" the people at the end of the mass, by saying: "Ite, missa est," that is, the victim has been sent [missa est] to God through the angel, so that it may be accepted by God.

Whether the actions performed in celebrating this sacrament are becoming?

Objection 1: It seems that the actions performed in celebrating this mystery are not becoming. For, as is evident from its form, this sacrament belongs to the New Testament. But under the New Testament the ceremonies of the old are not to be observed, such as that the priests and ministers were purified with water when they drew nigh to offer up the sacrifice: for we read (Ex. 30:19,20): "Aaron and his sons shall wash their hands and feet . . . when they are going into the tabernacle of the testimony . . . and when they are to come to the altar." Therefore it is not fitting that the priest should wash his hands when celebrating mass.

Objection 2: Further, (Ex. 30:7), the Lord commanded Aaron to "burn sweet-smelling incense" upon the altar which was "before the propitiatory": and the same action was part of the ceremonies of the Old Law. Therefore it is not fitting for the priest to use incense during mass.

Objection 3: Further, the ceremonies performed in the sacraments of the Church ought not to be repeated. Consequently it is not proper for the priest to repeat the sign of the cross many times over this sacrament.

Objection 4: Further, the Apostle says (Heb. 7:7): "And without all contradiction, that which is less, is blessed by the better." But Christ, Who is in this sacrament after the consecration, is much greater than the priest. Therefore quite unseemingly the priest, after the consecration, blesses this sacrament, by signing it with the cross.

Objection 5: Further, nothing which appears ridiculous ought to be done in one of the Church's sacraments. But it seems ridiculous to perform gestures, e.g. for the priest to stretch out his arms at times, to join his hands, to join together his fingers, and to bow down. Consequently, such things ought not to be done in this sacrament.

Objection 6: Further, it seems ridiculous for the priest to turn round frequently towards the people, and often to greet the people. Consequently, such things ought not to be done in the celebration of this sacrament.

Objection 7: Further, the Apostle (1 Cor. 13) deems it improper for Christ to be divided. But Christ is in this sacrament after the consecration. Therefore it is not proper for the priest to divide the host.

Objection 8: Further, the ceremonies performed in this sacrament represent Christ's Passion. But during the Passion Christ's body was divided in the places of the five wounds. Therefore Christ's body ought to be broken into five parts rather than into three.

Objection 9: Further, Christ's entire body is consecrated in this sacrament apart from the blood. Consequently, it is not proper for a particle of the body to be mixed with the blood.

Objection 10: Further, just as, in this sacrament, Christ's body is set before us as food, so is His blood, as drink. But in receiving Christ's body no other bodily food is added in the celebration of the mass. Therefore, it is out of place for the priest, after taking Christ's blood, to receive other wine which is not consecrated.

Objection 11: Further, the truth ought to be conformable with the figure. But regarding the Paschal Lamb, which was a figure of this sacrament, it was commanded that nothing of it should "remain until the morning." It is improper therefore for consecrated hosts to be reserved, and not consumed at once.

Objection 12: Further, the priest addresses in the plural number those who are hearing mass, when he says, "The Lord be with you": and, "Let us return thanks." But it is out of keeping to address one individual in the plural number, especially an inferior. Consequently it seems unfitting for a priest to say mass with only a single server present. Therefore in the celebration of this sacrament it seems that some of the things done are out of place.

On the contrary, The custom of the Church stands for these things: and the Church cannot err, since she is taught by the Holy Ghost.

I answer that, As was said above ([4708]Q[60], A[6]), there is a twofold manner of signification in the sacraments, by words, and by actions, in order that the signification may thus be more perfect. Now, in the celebration of this sacrament words are used to signify things pertaining to Christ's Passion, which is represented in this sacrament; or again, pertaining to Christ's mystical body, which is signified therein; and again, things pertaining to the use of this sacrament, which use ought to be devout and reverent. Consequently, in the celebration of this mystery some things are done in order to represent Christ's Passion, or the disposing of His mystical body, and some others are done which pertain to the devotion and reverence due to this sacrament.

Reply to Objection 1: The washing of the hands is done in the celebration of mass out of reverence for this sacrament; and this for two reasons: first, because we are not wont to handle precious objects except the hands be washed; hence it seems indecent for anyone to approach so great a sacrament with hands that are, even literally, unclean. Secondly, on account of its signification, because, as Dionysius says (Eccl. Hier. iii), the washing of the extremities of the limbs denotes cleansing from even the smallest sins, according to Jn. 13:10: "He that is washed needeth not but to wash his feet." And such cleansing is required of him who approaches this sacrament; and this is denoted by the confession which is made before the "Introit" of the mass. Moreover, this was signified by the washing of the priests under the Old Law, as Dionysius says (Eccl. Hier. iii). However, the Church observes this ceremony, not because it was prescribed under the Old Law, but because it is becoming in itself, and therefore instituted by the Church. Hence it is not observed in the same way as it was then: because the washing of the feet is omitted, and the washing of the hands is observed; for this can be done more readily, and suffices far denoting perfect cleansing. For, since the hand is the "organ of organs" (De Anima iii), all works are attributed to the hands: hence it is said in Ps. 25:6: "I will wash my hands among the innocent."

Reply to Objection 2: We use incense, not as commanded by a ceremonial precept of the Law, but as prescribed by the Church; accordingly we do not use it in the same fashion as it was ordered under the Old Law. It has reference to two things: first, to the reverence due to this sacrament, i.e. in order by its good odor, to remove any disagreeable smell that may be about the place; secondly, it serves to show the effect of grace, wherewith Christ was filled as with a good odor, according to Gn. 27:27: "Behold, the odor of my son is like the odor of a ripe field"; and from Christ it spreads to the faithful by the work of His ministers, according to 2 Cor. 2:14: "He manifesteth the odor of his knowledge by us in every place"; and therefore when the altar which represents Christ, has been incensed on every side, then all are incensed in their proper order.

Reply to Objection 3: The priest, in celebrating the mass, makes use of the sign of the cross to signify Christ's Passion which was ended upon the cross. Now, Christ's Passion was accomplished in certain stages. First of all there was Christ's betrayal, which was the work of God, of Judas, and of the Jews; and this is signified by the triple sign of the cross at the words, "These gifts, these presents, these holy unspotted sacrifices."

Secondly, there was the selling of Christ. Now he was sold to the Priests, to the Scribes, and to the Pharisees: and to signify this the threefold sign of the cross is repeated, at the words, "blessed, enrolled, ratified." Or again, to signify the price for which He was sold, viz. thirty pence. And a double cross is added at the words---"that it may become to us the Body and the Blood," etc., to signify the person of Judas the seller, and of Christ Who was sold.

Thirdly, there was the foreshadowing of the Passion at the last supper. To denote this, in the third place, two crosses are made, one in consecrating the body, the other in consecrating the blood; each time while saying, "He blessed."

Fourthly, there was Christ's Passion itself. And so in order to represent His five wounds, in the fourth place, there is a fivefold signing of the cross at the words, "a pure Victim, a holy Victim, a spotless Victim, the holy bread of eternal life, and the cup of everlasting salvation."

Fifthly, the outstretching of Christ's body, and the shedding of the blood, and the fruits of the Passion, are signified by the triple signing of the cross at the words, "as many as shall receive the body and blood, may be filled with every blessing," etc.

Sixthly, Christ's threefold prayer upon the cross is represented; one for His persecutors when He said, "Father, forgive them"; the second for deliverance from death, when He cried, "My God, My God, why hast Thou forsaken Me?" the third referring to His entrance into glory, when He said, "Father, into Thy hands I commend My spirit"; and in order to denote these there is a triple signing with the cross made at the words, "Thou dost sanctify, quicken, bless."

Seventhly, the three hours during which He hung upon the cross, that is, from the sixth to the ninth hour, are represented; in signification of which we make once more a triple sign of the cross at the words, "Through Him, and with Him, and in Him."

Eighthly, the separation of His soul from the body is signified by the two subsequent crosses made over the chalice.

Ninthly, the resurrection on the third day is represented by the three crosses made at the words---"May the peace of the Lord be ever with you."

In short, we may say that the consecration of this sacrament, and the acceptance of this sacrifice, and its fruits, proceed from the virtue of the cross of Christ, and therefore wherever mention is made of these, the priest makes use of the sign of the cross.

Reply to Objection 4: After the consecration, the priest makes the sign of the cross, not for the purpose of blessing and consecrating, but only for calling to mind the virtue of the cross, and the manner of Christ's suffering, as is evident from what has been said (ad 3).

Reply to Objection 5: The actions performed by the priest in mass are not ridiculous gestures, since they are done so as to represent something else. The priest in extending his arms signifies the outstretching of Christ's arms upon the cross. He also lifts up his hands as he prays, to point out that his prayer is directed to God for the people, according to Lam. 3:41: "Let us lift up our hearts with our hands to the Lord in the heavens": and Ex. 17:11: "And when Moses lifted up his hands Israel overcame." That at times he joins his hands, and bows down, praying earnestly and humbly, denotes the humility and obedience of Christ, out of which He suffered. He closes his fingers, i.e. the thumb and first finger, after the consecration, because, with them, he had touched the consecrated body of Christ; so that if any particle cling to the fingers, it may not be scattered: and this belongs to the reverence for this sacrament.

Reply to Objection 6: Five times does the priest turn round towards the people, to denote that our Lord manifested Himself five times on the day of His Resurrection, as stated above in the treatise on Christ's Resurrection ([4709]Q[55], A[3], OBJ[3]). But the priest greets the people seven times, namely, five times, by turning round to the people, and twice without turning round, namely, when he says, "The Lord be with you" before the "Preface," and again when he says, "May the peace of the Lord be ever with you": and this is to denote the sevenfold grace of the Holy Ghost. But a bishop, when he celebrates on festival days, in his first greeting says, "Peace be to you," which was our Lord's greeting after Resurrection, Whose person the bishop chiefly represents.

Reply to Objection 7: The breaking of the host denotes three things: first, the rending of Christ's body, which took place in the Passion; secondly, the distinction of His mystical body according to its various states; and thirdly, the distribution of the graces which flow from Christ's Passion, as Dionysius observes (Eccl. Hier. iii). Hence this breaking does not imply severance in Christ.

Reply to Objection 8: As Pope Sergius says, and it is to be found in the Decretals (De Consecr., dist. ii), "the Lord's body is threefold; the part offered and put into the chalice signifies Christ's risen body," namely, Christ Himself, and the Blessed Virgin, and the other saints, if there be any, who are already in glory with their bodies. "The part consumed denotes those still walking upon earth," because while living upon earth they are united together by this sacrament; and are bruised by the passions, just as the bread eaten is bruised by the teeth. "The part reserved on the altar till the close of the mass, is His body hidden in the sepulchre, because the bodies of the saints will be in their graves until the end of the world": though their souls are either in purgatory, or in heaven. However, this rite of reserving one part on the altar till the close of the mass is no longer observed, on account of the danger; nevertheless, the same meaning of the parts continues, which some persons have expressed in verse, thus:

"The host being rent---
What is dipped, means the blest;
What is dry, means the living;
What is kept, those at rest."

Others, however, say that the part put into the chalice denotes those still living in this world. while the part kept outside the chalice denotes those fully blessed both in soul and body; while the part consumed means the others.

Reply to Objection 9: Two things can be signified by the chalice: first, the Passion itself, which is represented in this sacrament, and according to this, by the part put into the chalice are denoted those who are still sharers of Christ's sufferings; secondly, the enjoyment of the Blessed can be signified, which is likewise foreshadowed in this sacrament; and therefore those whose bodies are already in full beatitude, are denoted by the part put into the chalice. And it is to be observed that the part put into the chalice ought not to be given to the people to supplement the communion, because Christ gave dipped bread only to Judas the betrayer.

Reply to Objection 10: Wine, by reason of its humidity, is capable of washing, consequently it is received in order to rinse the mouth after receiving this sacrament, lest any particles remain: and this belongs to reverence for the sacrament. Hence (Extra, De Celebratione missae, chap. Ex parte), it is said: "The priest should always cleanse his mouth with wine after receiving the entire sacrament of Eucharist: except when he has to celebrate another mass on the same day, lest from taking the ablution-wine he be prevented from celebrating again"; and it is for the same reason that wine is poured over the fingers with which he had touched the body of Christ.

Reply to Objection 11: The truth ought to be conformable with the figure, in some respect: namely, because a part of the host consecrated, of which the priest and ministers or even the people communicate, ought not to be reserved until the day following. Hence, as is laid down (De Consecr., dist. ii), Pope Clement I ordered that "as many hosts are to be offered on the altar as shall suffice for the people; should any be left over, they are not to be reserved until the morrow, but let the clergy carefully consume them with fear and trembling." Nevertheless, since this sacrament is to be received daily, whereas the Paschal Lamb was not, it is therefore necessary for other hosts to be reserved for the sick. Hence we read in the same distinction: "Let the priest always have the Eucharist ready, so that, when anyone fall sick, he may take Communion to him at once, lest he die without it."

Reply to Objection 12: Several persons ought to be present at the solemn celebration of the mass. Hence Pope Soter says (De Consecr., dist. 1): "It has also been ordained, that no priest is to presume to celebrate solemn mass, unless two others be present answering him, while he himself makes the third; because when he says in the plural, 'The Lord be with you,' and again in the Secrets, 'Pray ye for me,' it is most becoming that they should answer his greeting." Hence it is for the sake of greater solemnity that we find it decreed (De Consecr. dist. 1) that a bishop is to solemnize mass with several assistants. Nevertheless, in private masses it suffices to have one server, who takes the place of the whole Catholic people, on whose behalf he makes answer in the plural to the priest.

Whether the defects occurring during the celebration of this sacrament can be sufficiently met by observing the Church's statutes?

Objection 1: It seems that the defects occurring during the celebration of this sacrament cannot be sufficiently met by observing the statutes of the Church. For it sometimes happens that before or after the consecration the priest dies or goes mad, or is hindered by some other infirmity from receiving the sacrament and completing the mass. Consequently it seems impossible to observe the Church's statute, whereby the priest consecrating must communicate of his own sacrifice.

Objection 2: Further, it sometimes happens that, before the consecration, the priest remembers that he has eaten or drunk something, or that he is in mortal sin, or under excommunication, which he did not remember previously. Therefore, in such a dilemma a man must necessarily commit mortal sin by acting against the Church's statute, whether he receives or not.

Objection 3: Further, it sometimes happens that a fly or a spider, or some other poisonous creature falls into the chalice after the consecration. Or even that the priest comes to know that poison has been put in by some evilly disposed person in order to kill him. Now in this instance, if he takes it, he appears to sin by killing himself, or by tempting God: also in like manner if he does not take it, he sins by acting against the Church's statute. Consequently, he seems to be perplexed, and under necessity of sinning, which is not becoming.

Objection 4: Further, it sometimes happens from the server's want of heed that water is not added to the chalice, or even the wine overlooked, and that the priest discovers this. Therefore he seems to be perplexed likewise in this case, whether he receives the body without the blood, thus making the sacrifice to be incomplete, or whether he receives neither the body nor the blood.

Objection 5: Further, it sometimes happens that the priest cannot remember having said the words of consecration, or other words which are uttered in the celebration of this sacrament. In this case he seems to sin, whether he repeats the words over the same matter, which words possibly he has said before, or whether he uses bread and wine which are not consecrated, as if they were consecrated.

Objection 6: Further, it sometimes comes to pass owing to the cold that the host will slip from the priest's hands into the chalice, either before or after the breaking. In this case then the priest will not be able to comply with the Church's rite, either as to the breaking, or else as to this, that only a third part is put into the chalice.

Objection 7: Further, sometimes, too, it happens, owing to the priest's want of care, that Christ's blood is spilled, or that he vomits the sacrament received, or that the consecrated hosts are kept so long that they become corrupt, or that they are nibbled by mice, or lost in any manner whatsoever; in which cases it does not seem possible for due reverence to be shown towards this sacrament, as the Church's ordinances require. It does not seem then that such defects or dangers can be met by keeping to the Church's statutes.

On the contrary, Just as God does not command an impossibility, so neither does the Church.

I answer that, Dangers or defects happening to this sacrament can be met in two ways: first, by preventing any such mishaps from occurring: secondly, by dealing with them in such a way, that what may have happened amiss is put right, either by employing a remedy, or at least by repentance on his part who has acted negligently regarding this sacrament.

Reply to Objection 1: If the priest be stricken by death or grave sickness before the consecration of our Lord's body and blood, there is no need for it to be completed by another. But if this happens after the consecration is begun, for instance, when the body has been consecrated and before the consecration of the blood, or even after both have been consecrated, then the celebration of the mass ought to be finished by someone else. Hence, as is laid down (Decretal vii, q. 1), we read the following decree of the (Seventh) Council of Toledo: "We consider it to be fitting that when the sacred mysteries are consecrated by priests during the time of mass, if any sickness supervenes, in consequence of which they cannot finish the mystery begun, let it be free for the bishop or another priest to finish the consecration of the office thus begun. For nothing else is suitable for completing the mysteries commenced, unless the consecration be completed either by the priest who began it, or by the one who follows him: because they cannot be completed except they be performed in perfect order. For since we are all one in Christ, the change of persons makes no difference, since unity of faith insures the happy issue of the mystery. Yet let not the course we propose for cases of natural debility, be presumptuously abused: and let no minister or priest presume ever to leave the Divine offices unfinished, unless he be absolutely prevented from continuing. If anyone shall have rashly presumed to do so, he will incur sentence of excommunication."

Reply to Objection 2: Where difficulty arises, the less dangerous course should always be followed. But the greatest danger regarding this sacrament lies in whatever may prevent its completion, because this is a heinous sacrilege; while that danger is of less account which regards the condition of the receiver. Consequently, if after the consecration has been begun the priest remembers that he has eaten or drunk anything, he ought nevertheless to complete the sacrifice and receive the sacrament. Likewise, if he recalls a sin committed, he ought to make an act of contrition, with the firm purpose of confessing and making satisfaction for it: and thus he will not receive the sacrament unworthily, but with profit. The same applies if he calls to mind that he is under some excommunication; for he ought to make the resolution of humbly seeking absolution; and so he will receive absolution from the invisible High Priest Jesus Christ for his act of completing the Divine mysteries.

But if he calls to mind any of the above facts previous to the consecration, I should deem it safer for him to interrupt the mass begun, especially if he has broken his fast, or is under excommunication, unless grave scandal were to be feared.

Reply to Objection 3: If a fly or a spider falls into the chalice before consecration, or if it be discovered that the wine is poisoned, it ought to be poured out, and after purifying the chalice, fresh wine should be served for consecration. But if anything of the sort happen after the consecration, the insect should be caught carefully and washed thoroughly, then burned, and the "ablution," together with the ashes, thrown into the sacrarium. If it be discovered that the wine has been poisoned, the priest should neither receive it nor administer it to others on any account, lest the life-giving chalice become one of death, but it ought to be kept in a suitable vessel with the relics: and in order that the sacrament may not remain incomplete, he ought to put other wine into the chalice, resume the mass from the consecration of the blood, and complete the sacrifice.

Reply to Objection 4: If before the consecration of the blood, and after the consecration of the body the priest detect that either the wine or the water is absent, then he ought at once to add them and consecrate. But if after the words of consecration he discover that the water is absent, he ought notwithstanding to proceed straight on, because the addition of the water is not necessary for the sacrament, as stated above ([4710]Q[74], A[7]): nevertheless the person responsible for the neglect ought to be punished. And on no account should water be mixed with the consecrated wine, because corruption of the sacrament would ensue in part, as was said above ([4711]Q[77], A[8]). But if after the words of consecration the priest perceive that no wine has been put in the chalice, and if he detect it before receiving the body, then rejecting the water, he ought to pour in wine with water, and begin over again the consecrating words of the blood. But if he notice it after receiving the body, he ought to procure another host which must be consecrated together with the blood; and I say so for this reason, because if he were to say only the words of consecration of the blood, the proper order of consecrating would not be observed; and, as is laid down by the Council of Toledo, quoted above (ad 1), sacrifices cannot be perfect, except they be performed in perfect order. But if he were to begin from the consecration of the blood, and were to repeat all the words which follow, it would not suffice, unless there was a consecrated host present, since in those words there are things to be said and done not only regarding the blood, but also regarding the body; and at the close he ought once more to receive the consecrated host and blood, even if he had already taken the water which was in the chalice, because the precept of the completing this sacrament is of greater weight than the precept of receiving the sacrament while fasting, as stated above ([4712]Q[80], A[8]).

Reply to Objection 5: Although the priest may not recollect having said some of the words he ought to say, he ought not to be disturbed mentally on that account; for a man who utters many words cannot recall to mind all that he has said; unless perchance in uttering them he adverts to something connected with the consecration; for so it is impressed on the memory. Hence, if a man pays attention to what he is saying, but without adverting to the fact that he is saying these particular words, he remembers soon after that he has said them; for, a thing is presented to the memory under the formality of the past (De Mem. et Remin. i).

But if it seem to the priest that he has probably omitted some of the words that are not necessary for the sacrament, I think that he ought not to repeat them on that account, changing the order of the sacrifice, but that he ought to proceed: but if he is certain that he has left out any of those that are necessary for the sacrament, namely, the form of the consecration, since the form of the consecration is necessary for the sacrament, just as the matter is, it seems that the same thing ought to be done as was stated above (ad 4) with regard to defect in the matter, namely, that he should begin again with the form of the consecration, and repeat the other things in order, lest the order of the sacrifice be altered.

Reply to Objection 6: The breaking of the consecrated host, and the putting of only one part into the chalice, regards the mystical body, just as the mixing with water signifies the people, and therefore the omission of either of them causes no such imperfection in the sacrifice, as calls for repetition regarding the celebration of this sacrament.

Reply to Objection 7: According to the decree, De Consecr., dist. ii, quoting a decree of Pope Pius I, "If from neglect any of the blood falls upon a board which is fixed to the ground, let it be taken up with the tongue, and let the board be scraped. But if it be not a board, let the ground be scraped, and the scrapings burned, and the ashes buried inside the altar and let the priest do penance for forty days. But if a drop fall from the chalice on to the altar, let the minister suck up the drop, and do penance during three days; if it falls upon the altar cloth and penetrates to the second altar cloth, let him do four days' penance; if it penetrates to the third, let him do nine days' penance; if to the fourth, let him do twenty days' penance; and let the altar linens which the drop touched be washed three times by the priest, holding the chalice below, then let the water be taken and put away nigh to the altar." It might even be drunk by the minister, unless it might be rejected from nausea. Some persons go further, and cut out that part of the linen, which they burn, putting the ashes in the altar or down the sacrarium. And the Decretal continues with a quotation from the Penitential of Bede the Priest: "If, owing to drunkenness or gluttony, anyone vomits up the Eucharist, let him do forty days' penance, if he be a layman; but let clerics or monks, deacons and priests, do seventy days' penance; and let a bishop do ninety days'. But if they vomit from sickness, let them do penance for seven days." And in the same distinction, we read a decree of the (Fourth) Council of Arles: "They who do not keep proper custody over the sacrament, if a mouse or other animal consume it, must do forty days' penance: he who loses it in a church, or if a part fall and be not found, shall do thirty days' penance." And the priest seems to deserve the same penance, who from neglect allows the hosts to putrefy. And on those days the one doing penance ought to fast, and abstain from Communion. However, after weighing the circumstances of the fact and of the person, the said penances may be lessened or increased. But it must be observed that wherever the species are found to be entire, they must be preserved reverently, or consumed; because Christ's body is there so long as the species last, as stated above ([4713]Q[77], AA[4],5). But if it can be done conveniently, the things in which they are found are to be burned, and the ashes put in the sacrarium, as was said of the scrapings of the altar-table, here above.